LET'S GO

EASTERN EUROPE

2003

JENNIFER ANNE O'BRIEN EDITOR
SUSAN E. BELL ASSOCIATE EDITOR
ROCHELLE LUNDY ASSOCIATE EDITOR
MAHMOUD YOUSSEF ASSOCIATE EDITOR

RESEARCHER-WRITERS

CHARLES L. BLACK
DUNIA DICKEY
A. NICHOLAS GOSSEN
CLAY KAMINSKY
SANDRA NAGY
WERNER SCHÄFER

STEPHANIE VIDEKA SHERMAN
DALIBOR ERIC SNYDER
BARBARA URBAŃCZYK
VIK VAZ
MATEJ SAPAK
GRAEME WOOD

ANDY C. POON MAP EDITOR
MICHELLE R. BOWMAN MANAGING EDITOR
NATHANIEL BROOKS TYPESETTER

ST. MARTIN'S PRESS ❧ NEW YORK

Maps by David Lindroth copyright © 2003 by St. Martin's Press.

Distributed outside the USA and Canada by Macmillan.

ISBN: 0-312-30571-0

First edition
10 9 8 7 6 5 4 3 2 1

Let's Go: Eastern Europe is written by Let's Go Publications, 67 Mount Auburn Street, Cambridge, MA 02138, USA.

LET'S GO

■ THE RESOURCE FOR THE INDEPENDENT TRAVELER

"The guides are aimed not only at young budget travelers but at the indepedent traveler; a sort of streetwise cookbook for traveling alone."

—*The New York Times*

"Unbeatable; good sight-seeing advice; up-to-date info on restaurants, hotels, and inns; a commitment to money-saving travel; and a wry style that brightens nearly every page."

—*The Washington Post*

"Lighthearted and sophisticated, informative and fun to read. [Let's Go] helps the novice traveler navigate like a knowledgeable old hand."

—*Atlanta Journal-Constitution*

"A world-wise traveling companion—always ready with friendly advice and helpful hints, all sprinkled with a bit of wit."

—*The Philadelphia Inquirer*

■ THE BEST TRAVEL BARGAINS IN YOUR PRICE RANGE

"All the dirt, dirt cheap."

—*People*

"Anything you need to know about budget traveling is detailed in this book."

—*The Chicago Sun-Times*

"Let's Go follows the creed that you don't have to toss your life's savings to the wind to travel—unless you want to."

—*The Salt Lake Tribune*

■ REAL ADVICE FOR REAL EXPERIENCES

"The writers seem to have experienced every rooster-packed bus and lunar-surfaced mattress about which they write."

—*The New York Times*

"A guide should tell you what to expect from a destination. Here Let's Go shines."

—*The Chicago Tribune*

LET'S GO PUBLICATIONS

TRAVEL GUIDES

Alaska & the Pacific Northwest 2003
Australia 2003
Austria & Switzerland 2003
Britain & Ireland 2003
California 2003
Central America 8th edition
Chile 1st edition **NEW TITLE**
China 4th edition
Costa Rica 1st edition **NEW TITLE**
Eastern Europe 2003
Egypt 2nd edition
Europe 2003
France 2003
Germany 2003
Greece 2003
Hawaii 2003 **NEW TITLE**
India & Nepal 7th edition
Ireland 2003
Israel 4th edition
Italy 2003
Mexico 19th edition
Middle East 4th edition
New Zealand 6th edition
Peru, Ecuador & Bolivia 3rd edition
South Africa 5th edition
Southeast Asia 8th edition
Southwest USA 2003
Spain & Portugal 2003
Thailand 1st edition **NEW TITLE**
Turkey 5th edition
USA 2003
Western Europe 2003

CITY GUIDES

Amsterdam 2003
Barcelona 2003
Boston 2003
London 2003
New York City 2003
Paris 2003
Rome 2003
San Francisco 2003
Washington, D.C. 2003

MAP GUIDES

Amsterdam
Berlin
Boston
Chicago
Dublin
Florence
Hong Kong
London
Los Angeles
Madrid
New Orleans
New York City
Paris
Prague
Rome
San Francisco
Seattle
Sydney
Venice
Washington, D.C.

WHO WE ARE

A NEW LET'S GO FOR 2003

With a sleeker look and innovative new content, we have revamped the entire series to reflect more than ever the needs and interests of the independent traveler. Here are just some of the improvements you will notice when traveling with the new *Let's Go*.

MORE PRICE OPTIONS

Still the best resource for budget travelers, *Let's Go* recognizes that everyone needs the occassional indulgence. Our "Big Splurges" indicate establishments that are actually worth those extra pennies (pulas, pesos, or pounds), and price-level symbols (❶ ❷ ❸ ❹ ❺) allow you to quickly determine whether an accommodation or restaurant will break the bank. We may have diversified, but we'll never lose our budget focus—"Hidden Deals" reveal the best-kept travel secrets.

BEYOND THE TOURIST EXPERIENCE

Our Alternatives to Tourism chapter offers ideas on immersing yourself in a new community through study, work, or volunteering.

AN INSIDER'S PERSPECTIVE

As always, every item is written and researched by our on-site writers. This year we have highlighted more viewpoints to help you gain an even more thorough understanding of the places you are visiting.

IN RECENT NEWS. *Let's Go* correspondents around the globe report back on current regional issues that may affect you as a traveler.

CONTRIBUTING WRITERS. Respected scholars and former *Let's Go* writers discuss topics on society and culture, going into greater depth than the usual guidebook summary.

THE LOCAL STORY. From the Parisian monk toting a cell phone to the Russian *babushka* confronting capitalism, *Let's Go* shares its revealing conversations with local personalities—a unique glimpse of what matters to real people.

FROM THE ROAD. Always helpful and sometimes downright hilarious, our researchers share useful insights on the typical (and atypical) travel experience.

SLIMMER SIZE

Don't be fooled by our new, smaller size. *Let's Go* is still packed with invaluable travel advice, but now it's easier to carry with a more compact design.

FORTY-THREE YEARS OF WISDOM

For over four decades *Let's Go* has provided the most up-to-date information on the hippest cafes, the most pristine beaches, and the best routes from border to border. It all started in 1960 when a few well-traveled students at Harvard University handed out a 20-page mimeographed pamphlet of their tips on budget travel to passengers on student charter flights to Europe. From humble beginnings, *Let's Go* has grown to cover six continents and *Let's Go: Europe* still reigns as the world's best-selling travel guide. This year we've beefed up our coverage of Latin America with *Let's Go: Costa Rica* and *Let's Go: Chile;* on the other side of the globe, we've added *Let's Go: Thailand* and *Let's Go: Hawaii.* Our new guides bring the total number of titles to 61, each infused with the spirit of adventure that travelers around the world have come to count on.

CONTENTS

HOW TO USE THIS BOOK

Welcome, comrades, to *Let's Go: Eastern Europe 2003*. We are a good fraternal socialist publication, but we have to change with the times and this year is no exception. First off, the book is no longer free. We found that some comrades, having received the book without paying, were no longer completing their duties at the tractor factory. Also, Misha was selling copies on the black market. Second, it is smaller and lighter, as we are no longer evaluated on tonnage sold. Although we continue to maintain that last year's lead-bound book built socialist character, after Vasily's back injury we decided to scale things back a bit. That was a joke. Laugh, comrades, laugh! You—Boris—not too enthusiastically, now. The Western imperialist dogs may tell you that you can't take a true proletarian vacation in Europe these days, but we know the truth and we've put it in this book! Read, comrades, about beds so cheap the Americans don't want you to know about them! About trans-continental train rides for the price of one night in a bourgeois hotel! Take the wisdom of the Party to heart, comrades, and your vacation will be one long stretch of fraternal proletarian socialist ecstasy.

INTRODUCTORY MATERIAL. The first chapter of this book, **Discover Eastern Europe,** provides an overview of travel in the region, including the our KGB officer's **"Suggested" Itineraries** to give you an idea of what you shouldn't miss in the region. **Life and Times** provides a brief synopsis of the culture and history of the region, while the **Essentials** section outlines practical information you need to prepare and execute your trip.

THE BODY. No, not the one in the trunk. Each chapter covers one country, except **Gateway Cities,** which covers several major entry-points into the region. When you are waiting hours at the border, beating your head against this portion may help to relieve stress. Also in each chapter is country-specific travel advice.

PRICE RANGES AND RANKINGS. Our researchers list establishments in order of value from best to worst. Our absolute favorites are denoted by the *Let's Go* thumbs-up (🖾). Despite what the propaganda of the Western capitalist swine might say, best value does not always mean the cheapest price, and so Natasha has incorporated a system of price ranges into the guide. The price bracket is based on a scale from ❶ to ❺, where each icon corresponds to a specific range. There are tables at the beginning of each chapter that list price ranges for each country.

PHONE CODES AND TELEPHONE NUMBERS. The **phone code** for each area appears opposite the name of that city or town, and is denoted by the ☎ icon. Like Ivan says, dial the number in parenthesis only when calling within the country.

GLOSSARIES. For key words and useful phrases in a variety of Eastern European languages, see the **Language** section of each chapter and the **Glossary.**

A NOTE TO OUR READERS The information for this book was gathered by *Let's Go* researchers from May through August of 2002. Each listing is based on one researcher's opinion, formed during his or her visit at a particular time. Those traveling at other times may have different experiences since prices, dates, hours, and conditions are always subject to change. You are urged to check the facts presented in this book beforehand to avoid inconvenience and surprises.

RESEARCHER-WRITERS

Charles L. Black *European Russia*

Self-described as intrepid, tall, dark, handsome, and eligible, Charlie conquered the raucous nightlife of Moscow and St. Petersburg. A student of Russian language and literature, Charlie sought to introduce culture and history to all of his research. Even after being involved in a Moscow riot in search of a story and facing off a surly leather-wearing mugger, Charlie never ceased to add humor, imagination, and romance to his coverage.

Dunia Dickey *Estonia, Latvia, Lithuania, Kaliningrad Region*

A native Russian who immigrated to the United States at the age of seven, Dunia's language skills and knowledge of the culture paved her way. A woman who knows how to travel in style, Dunia diversified the coverage in her four countries with fabulous new listings, and the adventurer in her enjoyed biking through the rugged Estonian islands. Page after page of Dunia's beautiful copy described the beauty of these four nations with professional thoroughness.

A. Nicholas Gossen *Bosnia and Herzegovina, Croatia*

With extensive travel experience in many different countries including Thailand, Spain, and Turkey, Nick also spent over a year in Bosnia working for the International Rescue Committee. He brought proficient Serbian/Croatian language skills and the knowledge of a local to his impeccable coverage of the former Yugoslavia. His adventurous nature and charm even got him into a tour of a deserted island with the lovely contestants of Miss Eurosport 2002.

Clay Kaminsky *Moldova, Romania*

With his "cocked noggin," sweet smile, and an uncanny ability to pick up foreign languages, Clay cruised through Dracula's homeland with proficient Romanian language skills. His enthusiasm led him hundreds of miles out of his way just to write up Săpânta, a small town featuring the "Merry Graveyard," and his friendliness garnered him fascinating stories. Clay's love for people, languages, and new places has clearly shone through in his coverage.

Sandra Nagy *Eastern Slovak Republic, Hungary*

A consummate adventurer, Sandra has traveled as a student, businesswoman, and tourist to Israel, Europe, Thailand, Portugal, the Caribbean, and more. In her latest venture, she used her native Hungarian language skills to befriend locals and learn fascinating stories about her family history. This master of the Hidden Deal probed past the tourist traps on her route and penned her knowledge of the real Hungary with style and maturity.

Matej Sapak *Bratislava*

After a full route in Frankfurt for *Let's Go: Germany 2003*, Matej returned to his hometown of Bratislava to get back to his Eastern European roots. With indispensable local knowledge of the Slovak Republic's shining capital city, Matej breezed through the tourist traps and pulled to the surface the tidbits that only a native could discover. As Jesse Andrews once said, "multi-talent, thy name is Matej." We couldn't agree more.

Werner Schäfer   *Belarus, Ukraine*

A German native and Social Studies scholar, Werner's sensitivity to the political histories and current situations of his countries was reflected in his coverage. His previous traveling experiences from Europe to Southeast Asia helped this trooper dig deeply under Belarus's veneer and discover the untouched attractions of Minsk and beyond. Despite waiting in countless lines and staving off Ukranian street-walkers, Werner still retained his sense of fun.

Stephanie Videka Sherman   *Bulgaria, Romanian Black Sea Coast*

An experienced hiker, Steph has ambled all over Europe, including a six-month stay in Bulgaria when she was 13. Years later and with Bulgarian language proficiency, Steph returned to the Black Sea Coast. Cruising through Bulgaria and introducing new coverage of Ruse, Steph treated the country with thoroughness and care. And when times got her down, she just hopped on the oversized rubber banana and sped away in the Black Sea.

Dalibor Eric Snyder   *Czech Republic*

Named after a Czech folk story, stoic and knowledgeable Dali traveled to the land of his ancestors to experience Czech culture and politics first-hand. Proficient in both French and Czech, Dali also has a citation in the International Language of Love, as some ladies in the Republic found out. His coverage of the tourist hot-spot Prague and the small, picturesque towns that dot the Czech landscape was thorough, inquisitive, and above all, off the beaten track.

Barbara Urbańczyk   *Poland*

Armed with only a laptop, Barb set off to conquer the country of her parents. Fluent in French and Polish, she had previously traveled across Europe, including a one-month stint in Poland at age 16. Despite adding extensive new coverage on the Baltic coast and sliding down a mountain, Barb's hardest challenge was balancing work with the smothering hospitality of a 70-year-old. If the parrot lady was right, however, Barb has years of adventure ahead of her.

Vik Vaz   *Slovenia, Western Slovak Republic*

Passionate about history, with a penchant for trivia (he has already been a lifeline on TV's *Who Wants to be a Millionaire?* four times), Vik yearned to discover the spirit of Eastern Europe. His periods of residence in Chile, India, Algeria, and Aruba prove that Vik is at ease in strange places. From exploring Ljubliana to hiking through the Carpathian Mountains, he sent picturesque postcards and news stories back to us at the office, making us very jealous.

Graeme Wood   *Trans-Siberian Railroad*

With shifting ethnicity and blending features, Graeme seems made for solo travel to isolated and dangerous places. A two-time *Let's Go* Researcher-Writer and Editor of *Let's Go: Southeast Asia 2001*, he has ticked off over 60 countries to date. In addition to his language experience in Persian, Russian, and Uzbek, Graeme's love of adventure made him jump at the chance to travel deep into Russia. Marvelously handling new coverage of the Trans-Mongolian and Vladivostok, Graeme seems almost superhuman. His advice to you? "Always bring food. Food brings people together."

Jane Caflisch   *Helsinki, Finland*

A demure but thorough researcher, Jane finished her Finland route in capital city Helsinki with a flourish, single-handedly conquering the cafe culture.

Cassim Shepard   *İstanbul, Turkey*

Perceptive Cassim employed his keen powers of observation to penetrate the touristy veneer of İstanbul and discover the city's diamonds in the Rough.

Lora Sweeney   *Vienna, Austria*

Trading her labcoat for Lederhosen, biochem major Lora took Vienna's Inner and Outer Rings by storm to find the perfect place to get your groove on.

Tanna Tanlamai   *Beijing, China*

In Beijing, Tanna hit the pubs and clubs and sampled the city's cuisine, all the while turning in upbeat, amazingly thorough copy.

Ben Davis, Allison Melia	*Editors*, Let's Go: Turkey
Jeffrey Dubner	*Editor*, Let's Go: Europe
Elizabeth Little, Jing Lin, Angie Sun	*Editors*, Let's Go: China
Joanna Shawn Brigid O'Leary, Deborah Harrison	*Editors*, Let's Go: Austria & Switzerland

CONTRIBUTING WRITERS

Alicia DeSantis was a Researcher-Writer for *Let's Go: Eastern Europe 2000*.

David Egan was a Researcher-Writer for *Let's Go: Eastern Europe 2001* and *India & Nepal 2002*. He now works for Shakespeare & Company.

Jeremy Faro was a Researcher-Writer for *Let's Go: Britain & Ireland 1995*. He worked in London as a Senior Consultant for Interbrand, and is now a Master's student in European Studies at the University of Cambridge in England.

Susan Legro was a Researcher-Writer for *Let's Go: Europe 1990* in the former Soviet Union and an editor for *California & Hawaii 1989*. She now covers energy and environmental projects for the UN Development Program in 28 countries around the world.

Benjamin Paloff was a Researcher-Writer for *Let's Go: Eastern Europe 1998*, the editor of *Eastern Europe 1999*, and a Managing Editor for the 2000 series. He has a B.A. and an M.A. from Harvard in Slavic Languages and Literatures, and is currently working on his Ph.D. in Slavic Literature at Harvard.

Bede Sheppard was an Associate Editor for *Let's Go: Eastern Europe 1998*, a Researcher-Writer for *Europe 1999* and *Eastern Europe 1999*, an Editor for *Australia 2000*, and a Managing Editor for the 2001 series. He lived in Zagreb, Croatia working for the UN High Commission for Refugees and is currently pursuing a law degree.

ACKNOWLEDGMENTS

LET'S GO

WE AWARD RADIOACTIVE FLOWERS TO: all our incredible tireless and dedicated RWs, for entertaining anecdotes and European candy; Michelle, for being our friend and our ME; Andy, the tsar of cartography; Jen, our sister-in-arms, for tackling 15 countries; Team WEUR/EUR, our capitalist co-conspirators in world domination; Noah, for putting the cold in Cold War ("what? 78 degrees?"); Prod, for enduring dia-critical hell; Chairmen Matt and Brian; Vlad the purple dragon; the pod fish who died during our reign; the tank; 11th hour caffeine; and Belarus, for sticking it out.

JENN THANKS: Sue, for devotion and wontons; Rochelle, for brilliance and too much info about Africa; Moudy, for ceaseless energy and new vocab; Michelle, the über-ME; and Andy, for the sea monsters—you five have made this book and this year unforgettable. Jen, for the late, *late* shift; Brieff for 7 months of madness; Audrey, for infamous office calls; Steph for Harry Potter in Bulgarian; Annie, CJ, Jess, Christina, Holly, Eddie, Sonya, and the usual suspects; Mom and Dad, for saying yes back when this all began.

SUE THANKS: Moudy, for being hilarious; Rochelle, for countless chats; Jenn, for being the awesomest editor ever; Michelle, for being the only ME for me; the Frostitutes and Lampy for constant fun and craziness; Brian and Jorge, for always wanting to do the same things as me; Heather, Dani, and Joe, for chill nights; the "weirdos" in the office; Dad, Mad, Mamie, Mike, Chris, Sari, Sean, and Dev for being a wonderful family; and Mikey, for being my panda.

ROCHELLE THANKS: Jenn, for aquarium adventures and tolerance of my early-morning ways; Sue, for appreciation of good tea and *American Idol;* Moudy, for humor and enthusiasm—lay off those find/changes!; Michelle, for being my friend first; Jen for Mole 2 and life at SFP; Nora for bubble tea and a temporary home; the ex-roomies for email—see you on 12/18/02!; and my family for Sundays at 8am and something to look forward to in September.

MOUDY THANKS: Rochelle, for laughing at my stupid jokes; Sue, for your fun and easygoing nature; Jenn, for being phe and nomenal; Michelle, for being so capable and rad. The entire bookteam, for not committing me to any centers. Debra, for still hanging on after all these years. Erin, Paul, Alex, and Eli, for making this summer a classic. Sue and Annalise, for good conversation. Mom and Dad, for love and faith. Mona, Susan, and Ahmad, for always looking out.

ANDY THANKS: Jenn, Sue, Rochelle and Moudy for having capitalist diligence under the guise of communism; you all are the best! Steven and Jake for pickup b-ball and N64. Adam for poker and a place to crash. Becky for always being there. Mom and Dad for ending love and support.

Editor
Jennifer Anne O'Brien
Associate Editors
Susan E. Bell, Rochelle Lundy, Mahmoud Youssef
Managing Editor
Michelle R. Bowman
Map Editor
Andy C. Poon

Publishing Director
Matthew Gibson
Editor-in-Chief
Brian R. Walsh
Production Manager
C. Winslow Clayton
Cartography Manager
Julie Stephens
Design Manager
Amy Cain
Editorial Managers
Christopher Blazejewski,
Abigail Burger, D. Cody Dydek,
Harriett Green, Angela Mi Young Hur,
Marla Kaplan, Celeste Ng
Financial Manager
Noah Askin
Marketing & Publicity Managers
Michelle Bowman, Adam M. Grant
New Media Managers
Jesse Tov, Kevin Yip
Online Manager
Amélie Cherlin
Personnel Managers
Alex Leichtman, Owen Robinson
Production Associates
Caleb Epps, David Muehlke
Network Administrators
Steven Aponte, Eduardo Montoya
Design Associate
Juice Fong
Financial Assistant
Suzanne Siu
Office Coordinators
Alex Ewing, Adam Kline,
Efrat Kussell

Director of Advertising Sales
Erik Patton
Senior Advertising Associates
Patrick Donovan, Barbara Eghan,
Fernanda Winthrop
Advertising Artwork Editor
Leif Holtzman
Cover Photo Research
Laura Wyss

President
Bradley J. Olson
General Manager
Robert B. Rombauer
Assistant General Manager
Anne E. Chisholm

Railways of Eastern Europe

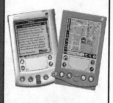

DISCOVER EASTERN EUROPE

Not much holds the amorphous region known as Eastern Europe together anymore. Countries that once lived on the same Bloc now have little in common and, in some cases, little to do with each other. The Baltics have lost touch with their Balkan cousins; Central Europe has shed her Soviet skin more quickly than her step-sisters Belarus and Ukraine; while Russia has kept herself audacious, unpredictable, and isolated from most of her neighbors. Regional unity—if it ever really existed in the first place—was forsaken at the hands of reborn nationalism and cultural pride as well as increased integration into the global community. States such as Latvia, which has only been independent for a total of 34 years throughout history, at last have the opportunity to truly define themselves as nations and come into their own.

Perhaps all that *can* be said of the countries in the region is that after over a decade of transformation, they're still changing—and, of course, that they're still a haven for budget travelers. Undiscovered cities, pristine national parks, empty hostel beds, and ridiculously cheap beer lure seekers of adventure, culture, and bargains to this vast and varied expanse. Prague, St. Petersburg, Budapest, and Kraków will charm even the most jaded backpacker, while the jagged peaks of the Tatras, the dazzling beaches of the Dalmatian Coast, and the isolated marvels of Siberia will stagger even the most experienced outdoor adventurers.

The distances are great, and the bureaucracies often infuriating, but hitting the road here is always rewarding. Your senses will be bombarded and, more likely than not, your conceptions of rationality challenged: you can't use a bottle of vodka as a Visa just anywhere, let alone take the same train across seven time zones, riding the whole way with family pets. Should the absurdity of the post-Soviet world ever get you down, take comfort in knowing that for every stony border guard and badgering *babushka* (grandmotherly old women common in the region), there are countless locals willing to give you a bed, a shot of homemade liquor, and a ride to the next town. If you bring along your flexibility, patience, and resilience, you'll have an incredible journey through one of the most geographically varied, historically rich, and culturally dynamic areas of the world.

WHEN TO GO

Summer is Eastern Europe's high season. What high season means, however, varies for each country and region. Prague, Kraków, and Budapest are swarmed with backpackers. In the countryside, high season simply means that hotels might actually have guests staying in them. In Croatia and along the Baltic and Black Sea Coasts, things fill up as soon as it is warm enough to lounge on the beach, usually from June to September. In the Tatras, Julian Alps, and Transylvanian Alps, there is both a summer high season for hiking (usually July to August) and a winter season for skiing (November to March). In the low season, you'll often be the only tourist in town. Although securing accommodations and strolling down the street will be easier in low season, high season brings with it an entire subculture of young backpackers. You decide whether that's a good thing. For a temperature chart, please see p. 18. Major national holidays are listed in the introduction to each country, while festivals are detailed in city listings where appropriate; major festivals in each country are summarized on p. 16.

WHAT TO DO

Like a tracksuit-clad mafioso on a Moscow street corner, Eastern Europe has got what you need. Its vastness encompasses both heavily-backpacked cities and sleepy hamlets. Perhaps the only constant is the generally good, though rather strong, alcohol. For more specific regional attractions—from absinthe to *żubrówka*—see the **Let's Go Picks** ■ throughout each chapter.

THE GREAT OUTDOORS

Leave the urban bustle behind to explore the wonders of the Eastern European wilderness. From the rolling hills of Poland and the Czech Republic to stark Siberia, the untamed corners are a thrill-seeker's Eden. The **High Tatras, SLK** (p. 763) can compete with any mountain range in the world; head here for jagged peaks, Olympic-quality skiing, and heart-stopping hang-gliding. Isolated adventure awaits along the **Trans-Siberian Railroad, RUS** (p. 706), especially in the environs of **Lake Baikal** (p. 725), the deepest, oldest, and largest freshwater lake on Earth. Acres of giant, windswept dunes rise above the sparkling waters of the Baltic in **Nida, LIT**, the darling of the **Curionian Spit** (p. 461). The seven-day **Trail of Eagles' Nests** (p. 531) runs through the heart of Poland's green uplands past limestone eruptions and castle ruins. Other outdoor wonderlands include: the lakes of **Mazury, POL** (p. 572); the spas of the **Julian Alps, SLN** (p. 794); the winding rivers of **Southern Bohemia, CZR** (p. 268); the deserted bison-land of **Białowieski Park Narodowy, POL** (p. 574); Dracula's mountains in **Transylvania, ROM** (p. 595); the rocky coastline of **Lahemaa National Reserve, EST** (p. 310); the waterfalls of **Plitvice Lakes National Park, CRO** (p. 168); and the untouched island of **Mljet National Park, CRO** (p. 215).

BEACH BUMMING

Most travelers don't come to Eastern Europe for its beaches, but they should: the region boasts enough surf and sand to accommodate months of lounging and sunning from June to August. The indisputable star of the Mediterranean is Croatia's **Dalmatian Coast** (p. 183). From the karst-lined cliffs near **Dubrovnik** (p. 208) to the isolated beaches of **Hvar** (p. 204) and **Vis** (p. 202), the azure waters of the Adriatic lap at the feet of this coastal god. Spear-fishing and rock-climbing are only a few of the diversions in **Crimea, UKR** (p. 824), the starlet of the Black Sea. For more relaxed Crimean days, lounge with wealthy Russians on the pebbled beaches around **Yalta, UKR** (p. 836). Chillier waters await to the north in the Baltics, where you can bike for days along the deserted roads of the untouched **Estonian Islands** (p. 317) past wind-swept beaches and gently spinning windmills, or lounge on the white sands of **Jūrmala, LAT** (p. 424). Or try the Baltic sands near the **Tri-City Area, POL** (p. 558) or the Curonian Spit near **Kaliningrad, RUS** (p. 706) and **Klaipėda, LIT** (p. 456). If you can't make it to the coast, Hungary has the answer: **Lake Balaton** (p. 373) is like a slice of sea in the middle of the Hungarian plain, complete with tanned masses, endless water sports, and tacky discos. It's fun, we swear. You can also play Beach Blanket Bingo on the Black Sea coast of **Bulgaria** (p. 130), **Neptun, ROM** (p. 620), or **Sochi, RUS** (p. 701).

THE LEGACY OF THE 20TH CENTURY

While most of the region is successfully rebuilding after the fall of Communism, it can't quite shake off the devastating legacy of the past century. Though not the most uplifting of the region's highlights, the towns' memorializing events of the past 100 years provide some of the most powerful experiences to be had in Eastern Europe. The Resistance movement of Nazi-occupied **Odessa, UKR** (p. 836) hid itself underground during World War II; its headquarters is now one of Europe's most stirring war memorials. More sobering, however, are the numerous concentration camps. **Auschwitz-Birkenau, POL** (p. 512), the largest and most infamous of the Nazi death camps, today houses a large museum on the Holocaust; the remains of smaller camps are in **Majdanek, POL** (p. 518), **Terezín, CZR** (p. 257), **Salaspils, LAT** (p. 425), and **Paneriai, LIT** (p. 445). Almost entirely destroyed by German bombers in World War II, reconstructed **Warsaw, POL** (p. 481) is a testament to the region's admirable ability to regroup and rebuild, even in the face of utter ruin. Meanwhile, **Sarajevo, BOS** (p. 88), still ravaged by the land mines and violence from the recent war with Serbia, emphasizes how long regrouping and rebuilding take. The shadows of Joseph Stalin, Nicolae Ceauşescu, and Josip Brož Tito fall all over Eastern Europe, but **Moscow, RUS** (p. 634), **Minsk, BLR** (p. 72), **Bucharest, ROM** (p. 584), and the **Brijuni Archipelago, CRO** (p. 174) aren't bad places to start looking for them. You can see where World War II kicked off in **Gdańsk, POL** (p. 558) and then where the Big Yalta Three wound it down in **Livadia, UKR** (p. 832). Battles for independence were waged in **Cesis, LAT** (p. 428), **Vis, CRO** (p. 202), and **Kaunas, LIT** (p. 448).

AH, THE LITERARY LIFE

Eastern Europeans love their poets. And their novelists. And, for that matter, their playwrights, song writers, and essayists. So much that they frequently elect them as presidents and prime ministers. The strongest doses of literary adoration are dispensed in Russia (p. 621). Sample it first-hand at the **Moscow** (p. 653) museums devoted to (among others): **Anton Chekhov, Fyodor Dostoevsky, Nikolai Gogol, Alexandr Pushkin,** and **Leo Tolstoy.** Or, pay your respects to the graves of Gogol, Chekhov, and Mikhail Bulgakov by stopping by **Novodevichy Cemetery** (p. 648). If that doesn't wear you out, venture on to **St. Petersburg** and stop by Dostoevsky's grave (p. 682) and the statue that inspired Pushkin's poem "The Bronze Horseman" (p. 679). Pay homage to poetess **Anna Akhmatova** (p. 685) while you're there. Although it might not be *quite* as vocal about its local talent as Russian cities are, **Prague, CZR** won't let you visit without appreciating **Milan Kundera** and **Franz Kafka,** two Czech sons. If you're a devout member of the literati, make a pilgrimage to Kafka's grave in the **New Jewish Cemetery** (p. 251). Or, stop by the wine-cottage "Bar Apertif Winifera" in **Gdańsk, POL** (p. 558) to see a haunt that Nobel prize-winner **Günter Grass** wrote about. While in Poland, it's difficult to miss statues and references to Romantic poet extraordinaire **Adam Mickiewicz;** swing by the museum devoted to him in **Warsaw, POL** (p. 484) or venture up to **Vilnius, LIT** to see his old apartment (p. 439). For a little philosophy, visit **Immanuel Kant's** grave in **Kaliningrad, RUS** (p. 706).

SUGGESTED ITINERARIES

BEST OF CENTRAL EUROPE

Pécs, HUN (p. 384; 2 days), the most vivacious Hungarian town outside of inexhaustible **Budapest, HUN** (p. 339; 5 days). Descend into the wine cellars of **Eger, HUN** (p. 400; 1 day) before heading on to hike the **Tatras** (3 days). The best base to explore these Alpine rivals is **Zakopane, POL** (p. 519; 1 day). The true gem of Poland is UNESCO-protected **Kraków, POL** (p. 514; 3 days); explore the dreamy city and take the time to visit the sobering **Auschwitz** death camp (p. 512; 1 day). **Warsaw, POL** (p. 481; 2 days) is sprawling, hectic, and still struggling to recover from World War II. Tiny **Toruń, POL** (p. 547; 1 day), birthplace of Copernicus, is a peaceful stop on the way back to Prague.

THE BEST OF CENTRAL EUROPE (50 DAYS)

Lively **Prague, CZR** (p. 226; 5 days), home to beer, absinthe, ghosts and *golems*, is an ideal beginning point. Backpackers' heaven **Český Krumlov, CZR** (p. 273; 3 days) is a twisting maze of medieval streets and a perfect stop on the way to **Vienna, AUS** (p. 849; 3 days). **Bratislava, SLK** is replete with old-world charm (p. 751; 2 days). **Ljubljana, SLN** (p. 787; 2 days) is a lively capital overflowing with students and Josip Plečnik's creations, while the spas of **Bled, SLN** (p. 794; 2 days) are among the best in the world. **Pula, CRO** (p. 168; 2 days) boasts more Roman ruins than many a town in Italy; it comes as no surprise that Diocletian summered in **Split, CRO** (p. 195; 2 days). Stop in at **Hvar**, ranked one of the most beautiful islands in the world (p. 204; 3 days) en route to **Dubrovnik, CRO** (p. 208; 3 days), a startlingly beautiful Adriatic outpost. To witness the rebirth of a city, visit **Sarajevo, BOS** (p. 88; 2 days). Going north, stop at enchanting **Zagreb, CRO** (p. 159; 2 days). A lively modern art scene thrives in

VIA BALTICA

VIA BALTICA (36 DAYS)

Although not officially Baltic, **St. Petersburg, RUS** (p. 666; 6 days) is the alter-ego of the former Soviet Union: more cultured, friendlier, and much less overwhelming. Multicultural **Helsinki, FIN** (p. 857; 3 days) is the epitome of chill. **Tallinn, EST** (p. 303; 3 days) is surprisingly cosmopolitan. **Tartu, EST** (p. 324; 1 day) is the oldest city in the Baltics. Get muddy in **Pärnu, EST** (p. 312; 1 day) at one of the town's famous spas. The island of **Saaremaa, EST** (p. 317; 3 days) is more Estonian than Estonia itself, complete with windmills, meteor craters, and unspoiled beaches. **Rīga, LAT** (p. 417; 3 days) is decidedly more Soviet than its neighbors, while the red-tile roofs of **Kuldīga, LAT** (p. 429; 1 day) were unscathed by the rule of the USSR. Lithuania's third-largest city, **Klaipėda, LIT** (p. 456; 3 days) is the gateway to the Curonian Spit; climb 90m sand dunes in **Nida, LIT** (p. 461; 1 day). On your way to Vilnius, stop by serene, trendy **Kaunas, LIT** (p. 448; 2 days), Lithuania's second-largest city. **Vilnius, LIT** (p. 439; 3 days), long considered the "Jerusalem of Europe," is now touted the "New Prague." Missing Mother Russia? Make your way to **Kaliningrad, RUS** (p. 706; 2 days), the birthplace of Immanuel Kant. The port of **Gdańsk, POL** (p. 558; 2 days), will take you back to the 19th century, while the popular beaches of **Sopot, POL** (p. 565; 1 day) make a good stop on the way to your final destination: **Hel** (p. 571; 1 day).

ing spot in **Transylvania.** Marvel at the exquisite painted monasteries of **Bukovina, ROM** (p. 611; 3 days), which are among the great wonders of the world. Head up to Moldova's capital, **Chişinau** (p. 469; 2 days), which still considers itself Soviet, despite its long Romanian history. **Odessa, UKR** (p. 836; 3 days) is the splendid—if corrupt—boom-town of the Black Sea. Check out Ukraine's **Crimea** (p. 824; 3 days) on the way to **Sochi, RUS** (p. 701; 3 days)— with boardwalks and palm trees, you won't believe you're in Russia.

BLACK SEA SWING

BACK IN THE USSR

BLACK SEA SWING (38 DAYS).

Start your adventure in **İstanbul, TUR** (p. 861; 4 days), the gateway to the Black Sea. Head north to **Sinemorets, BUL** (p. 139) and **Sozopol, BUL** (p. 138) for Bulgaria's warmest water (2 days). Continue on to the country's beautiful cultural capital, **Plovdiv, BUL** (p. 119; 3 days). The official capital, **Sofia, BUL** (p. 110; 4 days), is colored by Soviet, Orthodox, and Turkish influence. Don't leave without taking a daytrip to the magnificent **Rila Monastery** (p. 118; 1 day). Museum-hop and beach-bum in **Varna, BUL** (p. 130; 2 days) before traveling north to the Black Sea resorts of **Constanţa, ROM** (p. 617) and **Neptun, ROM** (p. 620), the country's most pristine coastal towns (2 days). Head west to **Bucharest, ROM** (p. 584; 4 days), once dubbed "Little Paris" but now a reminder of Soviet days past. **Sigişoara, ROM** (p. 595; 2 days) is the most enchant-

BACK IN THE USSR (32 DAYS).

Start in spectacular **Vilnius, LIT** (p. 439; 4 days), one of the most attractive capitals in Europe. Prepare for a shock when you reach totalitarian but beautiful **Minsk, BEL** (p. 72; 2 days). Play soldier at the "hero-fortress" that valiantly defended the Soviets during WWII in **Brest, BEL** (p. 78; 1 day). Wander the steeple-filled streets of **Lviv, UKR** (p. 842; 3 days), the urban sophisticate of the region, and then head on to less European **Kyiv, UKR** (p. 811; 4 days), a capital still stepping out of its Soviet skin. From there, jump to **Yalta, UKR** (p. 836; 3 days), the playground of the Russian literati and one of the Black Sea's least-spoiled resorts. Then, head north to the source of it all, **Moscow, RUS** (p. 634; 6 days), and then glimpse Europe from **St. Petersburg, RUS** (p. 666; 6 days), the country's window to the West. The final stop is **Rīga, LAT** (p. 417; 3 days), a city redefining itself between the acronyms USSR and EU.

THE RUSSIAN OBSESSION

RUSSIA

St. Petersburg
Novgorod
Sergiev Posad
Yaroslavl
Moscow
Novosibirsk
Irkutsk
Ulan Ude
Lake Baikal
TO KHABAROVSK & VLADIVOSTOK
TO ULAANBAATAR & BEIJING

RUSSIAN OBSESSION (40 DAYS).

Start your monumental journey in **St. Petersburg** (p. 666; 7 days) and then hit **Moscow** (p. 634; 7 days) to stock up on supplies and civilization, stopping in ancient **Novgorod** (p. 693; 2 days) on the way south. From Moscow, you can jaunt to the pilgrimage point of **Sergiev Posad** (p. 658; 1 day). The first stop on the Trans-Siberian is **Yaroslavl** (p. 659; 4½hr.; 2 days), a flourishing city offering the comforts of a capital. **Novosibirsk** (p. 718; 46hr.; 2 days) brings you to the heart of central Asia. Continue on to **Irkutsk** (p. 722; 33hr.; 2 days), a former Siberian trading-post where you can rest up before trekking to **Lake Baikal** (p. 725; 3 days), the world's deepest freshwater lake. **Ulan Ude** (p. 727; 8hr.; 2 days), the center of Russian Buddhism, is quite possibly Russia's most surreal city. If your enthusiasm for all things Russian is waning, head to **Ulaanbaatar, MON** (p. 729; 22hr.; 3 days) and end in **Beijing, CHI** (p. 868; 31hr.; 3 days). If you're ready to jump back on the Trans-Siberian, however, roll on to **Khabarovsk** (p. 732; 50hr.; 2 days), Russia's summer paradise. Then, explore **Vladivostok** (p. 733; 14hr.; 4 days), Russia's eastern terminus and a city only open to foreigners since 1990.

WITH OR WITHOUT EU

European Union Enlargement in Eastern Europe

By your next visit to Europe, the continent's political geography may have completely changed. Ten Eastern European countries have applied to join the EU, and eight of them may do so early as January 1, 2004, uniting almost the entire continent in one big, happy, free-market economy. Despite enthusiasm and a widespread sense of the moral importance of the project, enlargement does have its opponents. The countries that joined the original six-member EU were relatively wealthy and developed and they came into the fold slowly and one-by-one. It's proving difficult for the EU's current members to contemplate the necessity of dividing the spoils of the Union—agricultural subsidies, regional-development funds, and chairs at the EU's tables of power—with their neighbors to the east. And, of course, designers and financiers across the continent have already begun to despair at the implications for the current flag and currency designs.

The enlargement process began philosophically after the fall of the Berlin Wall, but took a decade to pick up any real steam. The hot favorites from the beginning were the large countries closest to the EU—Poland, Hungary, and the Czech and Slovak Republics—but a little-known contender has taken the lead in the race to the finish line: Slovenia. Having closed all but the three most difficult chapters of the *acquis communautaire* (the body of EU legislation that every applicant country is required to adopt before acceding), Slovenia looks like it may be 100% EU-compliant before the end of 2002. Indeed, the plucky little nation is already looking and acting like the newest member of the club, with shiny new superhighways connecting it with Italy, Austria and Hungary, and a GDP per capita that's higher than all of the other applicant countries.

The Czech Republic and Hungary have made great strides in the race, and both nations' recent election of Europhilic governments—in stark contrast to the general swing toward the Euroskeptic right in the current member-states—is likely to keep them on track for an early accession. The Slovak Republic was initially overtaken by its ex due to some messy domestic politics—including allegations of undemocratic practices and corruption—but has been catching up fast after a bit of chastising from the EU and some dramatic reforms. Poland has proven to be a stubborn contender. As the most-populous country and largest market, Poland has been holding out in some negotiations in hopes that it can get a better accession package. Analysts say it may be 2010 before Romania and Bulgaria make it to the finish line. As of yet, both have dozens of chapters of the *acquis* to close, and a lot of progress to make in terms of economic stabilization. On the geographic fringe, and yet critical in providing a corridor between member-state Greece and the rest of the EU, the Union is taking a keen interest in helping them along.

After a slow start, Lithuania and Latvia have made good progress in closing in on their Baltic sister-state, Estonia—who was fast out of the starting blocks due to a total political-economic overhaul and some solid coaching from Finland. Yet, despite booming growth, being one of the world's freest economies, and receiving positive signals from the EU, Estonia's own public opinion regarding accession has cooled quickly. The most recent survey showed public support for EU membership at a mere 38%—compared to 85% in Romania and 70% in Hungary, for instance. Some of this is due to popular exhaustion in the wake of the EU's much-delayed plans for their accession—common, indeed, in most of the applicant nations—but scepticism plays a role here as well. As one Estonian-on-the-street put it, "We just left a Union, and look where that one got us." Estonian opinion polls, for one, show that referenda may prove to be EU enlargement's Achilles' heel. Indeed, this entire project hangs on the consent of, well…the Irish. Having rejected the enlargement-focused Treaty of Nice at the polls in June 2001, the good people of Ireland now seem to hold the future of Europe in their hands.

Jeremy Faro wrote for Let's Go: Britain & Ireland 1995. He worked in London as a Senior Consultant for Interbrand, and is now a Master's student in European Studies at the University of Cambridge in England.

EASTERN EUROPE: AN INTRODUCTION

During the Cold War, Westerners imposed the name "Eastern Europe" on the Soviet satellites east of the Berlin Wall. The title has always been somewhat of a misnomer, capturing a political rather than geographical reality: Vienna lies farther east than Prague, Croatia sprawls along the Mediterranean, the geometric center of the European continent is in Lithuania, and most of Russia is, in fact, in Asia. To understand the remarkable complexity of Eastern Europe is to imagine a map of the region a little over a decade ago: in 1989, there were a total of seven countries behind the Iron Curtain; today, that same area is comprised of 19 independent states. In that time, the region has undergone an astounding political and cultural transformation. While Communism has fallen from power throughout most of Europe and the Soviet Union no longer exists, Eastern Europe continues to be defined by its historical legacy. The region is united by what it longs to leave behind—a history of political upheaval and foreign domination—and by what it now confronts—a more optimistic but similarly uncertain future. In the process of breaking from the Communist mold and redefining themselves, these newly sovereign states have created another Europe, a Europe which some might consider backward, others more authentic, and still others simply distinct. As it looks to shed its troubled past, Eastern Europe stands on the brink of its own dissolution. Exactly what shall emerge is unclear, but it's certain to be a diverse set of nations.

HISTORY OF HALF THE WORLD IN FIVE PAGES

SLAVS (BEFORE 800 AD)

With the exception of Hungary, Romania, and the Baltic countries, Eastern Europe is populated primarily by **Slavic** peoples, who constitute the largest ethnic and linguistic group in Europe. Originally believed to come from the Caucasus, the Slavs migrated to the Dnieper region in today's Ukraine during the 2nd or 3rd millennium BC. The movement of ancient tribes westward in the 5th and 6th centuries AD sparked the **Great Migration,** during which Slavs penetrated deeply into Europe, displacing Celts in the Czech and Slovak lands, Illyrians in the Balkans, Turks and Avars in Bulgaria, Vikings in Russia and western Ukraine, and Germanic tribes in Hungary. Poland, which was conquered in the 9th century AD, was the last to be settled by Slavs. Unlike other migrating tribes at this time, the Slavs were cultivators and settlers rather than pillagers. In the mid-9th century, Slavs in modern Ukraine established the first major civilization in Eastern Europe, **Kyivan Rus.**

Despite their shared roots, there has never been any natural unity between all the Slavic peoples that settled in these lands. The division of Christendom in 395 into the Roman Empire and the Byzantine Empire had split the Slavs into two culturally distinct groups. The fault line between the two cultures ran directly through the Balkans: the Slovenes and Croats were yoked to Rome, while the Bulgarians, Romanians, and Serbs were loyal to Constantinople. Since the split, the political and social history of the western Slavs has been inextricably linked to

Western Europe, while the history of the southern and eastern Slavs has been influenced far more by their eastern neighbors, especially the **Ottoman Turks.**

The non-Slavic lands in Eastern Europe were inhabited by a vast array of settlers and invaders. Estonia was invaded by **Vikings** and **Finns** in the 9th and 11th centuries respectively. Latvians and Lithuanians are of **Balt** descent. All of the original non-Slavic areas, including Romania, Hungary, and Bulgaria, intermingled and were strongly influenced by their Slavic neighbors and settlers. Romanians, who belong to indigenous **Dacian** tribes, assimilated the Slavic migrants of the 6th century while the **Magyars,** who hailed from the area between the Baltics and the Ural Mountains, began invading Hungary in the 9th century. The originally **Turkic** Bulgarians adopted a Slavic language and are now considered Slavs.

OTTOMANS AND HABSBURGS (800-1914)

Beginning in the 8th century, several short-lasting kingdoms emerged in Eastern Europe, such as the **Empire of Great Moravia** in Bohemia, Moravia, Hungary and Slovakia in 830. The **Hungarian Kingdom,** one of the few Eastern European empires to actually achieve longevity and greatness, first came to power in the late 9th century and kept growing for 700 years to include Polish Silesia, Croatian Pannonia, and as far east as Romanian Wallachia and Bessarabia. The Kingdom came to an end at the **Battle of Mohács** in 1526, when Louis II, king of Hungary and Bohemia, lost to the Ottomans. The **Ottoman Empire** firmly established itself in southeastern Europe when it crushed the **Serbs** on June 28, 1389 at the **Battle of Kosovo.** This victory confirmed Constantinople's dominion over what are now Bosnia, Bulgaria, inland Croatia, Hungary, Macedonia, Montenegro, Romania, and Serbia. The Ottoman infiltration of Europe was forever halted by defeat at the **Siege of Vienna** in 1683. The loss marked the beginning of Ottoman decline, which was sped along by a series of losses to Russia from the 17th to the 19th century.

As the Ottoman Empire was declining, the **Russian Empire** was rapidly expanding east to the Pacific and west into Poland and Ukraine. At the **first partition of Poland** in 1772, the Russians wrested the control of Estonia and Lithuania from Sweden and eventually dissolved the **Polish-Lithuanian Commonwealth** (1569-1792), which had been one of the largest realms in Europe and the earliest democratic state of the modern period. Two years later, the **Treaty of Kuchuk Kainardji** between Russia and Turkey placed the Orthodox subjects of the Ottoman Empire under the control of the Russian tsar. Under the landmark treaty, Russia was granted the right to intervene in the Balkans in the name of protecting Christians under Muslim rule. By 1801, the Russians controlled Belarus, Estonia, Latvia, Lithuania, eastern Poland, and Ukraine, but further expansion was halted in the 19th century. The **1878 Congress of Berlin** marked the end of the **Russo-Turkish Wars;** in Eastern Europe, only Bulgaria and Macedonia remained in the Ottoman sphere of influence. All other nations were either granted independence or ceded to the Russian and Austro-Hungarian Empires.

The colossal **Austrian Empire** ultimately swallowed most of Central and Eastern Europe. Although the Habsburgs' rule in Austria dates back to the early 13th century, they did not come to dominate Central Europe until after the Battle of Mohács in 1526, when the Hungarian kingdom was split between Turkish and Austrian control. The Austrians acquired Bohemia, Moravia, Slovakia, and parts of Croatia, including Zagreb and Rijeka. After a series of Hungarian uprisings in 1699, the Turks relinquished the rest of Hungary to the Habsburgs. The Hungarians remained restive subjects, however, and in 1867 the Austrians entered into a **dual monarchy** with the Hungarians creating the **Austro-Hungarian Empire,** in which Hungary was granted internal independence while sharing certain ministries with the Austrian government. From 1867 to 1918, Austria-Hungary controlled what is now the Czech and Slovak Republics, Bosnia, Croatia, Slovenia, and parts of Belarus, Poland, Romania, and Ukraine. Following **Napoleon's** brief dominion over Europe at the beginning of the 19th century and **Industrial Revolution,** a wave of **Pan-Slavism,** or a belief in the unity of Slavic people, swept across the subordinated nations. Although it was confined to intellectual circles, it contributed to Europe's emerging **nationalism.** By the 19th century, nearly all of Eastern Europe was controlled by either the Ottoman, Russian, or Austro-Hungarian Empires.

DEATH OF THE GREAT EMPIRES (1914-1938)

World War I started with an attempt by the Serbs to free the South Slavs from the clutches of the Austro-Hungarian Empire. Serb nationalists of the illegal **Black Hand** movement believed that their cause would best be served by the death of **Archduke Franz Ferdinand d'Este,** heir to the Austro-Hungarian throne. On June 28, 1914, Bosnian Serb nationalist **Gavrilo Princip** assassinated Ferdinand and his wife Sophia in Sarajevo. Exactly one month later, Austria-Hungary declared war on the Serbs. What started as an attempt to overthrow the Empire snowballed during the ensuing months into a series of war declarations by France, Germany, Russia, Belgium, Great Britain, Montenegro, Serbia, and the Ottoman Empire. Because they were controlled by the Austro-Hungarian and Ottoman Empires, most Eastern European nations fought alongside the **Central Powers.** The Baltic nations were controlled by both Germans and Russians and remained divided in their alliances between the Allied and Central Powers. The only nations to wholeheartedly support the Allies were Russia, Bosnia, Montenegro, and Serbia. Belarus and Ukraine became hotly contested battlegrounds between the Germans and the Russians and eventually fell to German wartime occupation.

As the war dragged on, Russia's participation became more tenuous. The Russians had entered the war because of their dual interests in the demise of the Ottoman and Austro-Hungarian Empires and the growth of strong, Russia-friendly Slavic nations throughout Eastern Europe. As catastrophic losses caused the death toll to skyrocket, the Russian people became increasingly frustrated with an inefficient government. Coupled with a crippled wartime economy, the tension finally erupted into the **Russian Revolution.** Riots began over food shortages in March 1917, leading to the Tsar's abdication. In November, the **Bolsheviks,** led by **Vladimir Ilyich Lenin,** took power, establishing Russia's first communist government. Russia witnessed the crumbling of her empire as nationalist independence movements emerged on the heels of the March 1917 revolution. American president Woodrow Wilson's **Fourteen Points,** which followed the 1919 **Treaty of Versailles** that ended World War I, argued for the self-determination of all nations under the yoke of the great empires. With support from the West, Latvia, Estonia, and Ukraine declared independence from Russia, and Lithuania declared independence from Germany. Poland, which had been partitioned by Prussia, Austria, and Russia, became one state for the first time since 1792.

While the Russian Empire disintegrated, the defeated Austria-Hungary was mercilessly dismantled by the victorious powers. The Czechs and Slovaks united to create **Czechoslovakia.** Romania's size doubled with the addition of Transylvania, Wallachia, and Bukovina. Finally, in keeping with the vision of South Slav nationalism which had sparked the war, 1918 saw the creation of the **Kingdom of Serbs, Croats and Slovenes,** later known as **Yugoslavia.** In 1922 the **Union of Soviet Socialist Republics (USSR)** was declared. The **interwar period** was a turbulent time in Eastern Europe, as many states, independent for the first time in centuries (or, in the case of Latvia, ever), struggled to establish their own governments, economies, and societies in a period made even more unstable by the global 1930s **Depression.**

"PEACE IN OUR TIME" (1938-1945)

World War II was essentially sparked by the continuation of many unresolved conflicts from World War I. Adolf Hitler was determined to reclaim the "Germanic" parts of Poland, Bohemia, and Moravia that Germany had lost in the Treaty of Versailles. He claimed that the three million Germans living in the Czechoslovak **Sudetenland** were being discriminated against by the government. Hoping to avoid another war, France and Britain ignored Hitler's glaringly aggressive moves against a sovereign country and adopted their infamous policy of **appeasement.** France and Britain sealed Czechoslovakia's fate by signing the **Munich Agreement** with Germany on September 30, 1938, ordering all non-German inhabitants of the Sudetenland to vacate their homes within 24 hours and allowing the German army to invade. Upon his return from Munich, Britain's Prime Minister Neville Chamberlain mistakenly believed he had secured "peace in our time." Hitler, however, ignored the stipulations of the agreement and proceeded to annex the remainder of Czechoslovakia, which he turned into the **Bohemian-Moravian Protectorate** in March 1939. Hitler and Stalin shocked the world by signing the **Molotov-Ribbentrop Non-Aggression Pact,** forging an uneasy alliance between the two historical enemies. Secret clauses detailed a dual invasion of Poland, in which Germany would control the western third while the USSR would keep the eastern two-thirds. In September 1939, Hitler annexed Poland, sparking World War II.

Hitler had no intention of upholding the Pact, and in June 1941 he launched an offensive against the Soviet Union. An unsuccessful attempt to capture Moscow marked the beginning of the end for the German army, as it prompted the Soviets to join the Allied forces, led by Great Britain and the United States. The **Anglo-Soviet Agreement** of 1941 was a turning point in the war, as were the Allies' decisive wins in 1942. Total war casualties for both civilians and military personnel are estimated at 50-60 million. Of these, Eastern Europe suffered the most losses. The USSR lost 20 million of its citizens (10% of its population), more than any other nation involved in the war. Yugoslavia also lost over 10% of its population. Poland lost nearly 6 million people, a staggering 20% of its prewar population, only about 200,000 of which were military casualties. More than half of the 6 million estimated Jews murdered in **Nazi concentration camps** were Polish. Before World War II, Eastern Europe had been the geographical center of the world's Jewish population but Hitler's **"final solution"** succeeded in almost entirely eliminating the Jewish communities of the Czech and Slovak Republics, Hungary, Lithuania, Moldova, Poland, and Ukraine through both genocide and forced emigration.

THE RUSSIANS ARE COMING! (1945-1989)

The wartime alliance between the Soviet Union and the West had been an uneasy one. The West was opposed to the ideological expansion of Communism, but Russia claimed it necessary in order to prevent another German threat to the Slavic nations. Plans for post-war division of power in Europe were sketched out as early as 1944, but sealed at the **Yalta Conference** in February 1945. Wary of Winston Churchill's colonial nostalgia as much as Soviet Communism, the United States reluctantly agreed to recognize Eastern Europe as the Soviet sphere of influence. The institution of Communist governments in Czechoslovakia, Poland, Hungary, Yugoslavia, Romania, and Bulgaria from 1946 to 1949 established a ring of satellite People's Democracies in Eastern Europe. With the division of Germany between Capitalist West and Communist East, the **Cold War** had begun.

The Iron Curtain first descended with the founding of the **Council for Mutual Economic Assistance (COMECON)** in January 1949, an organization meant to facilitate and coordinate the economic growth of the Soviet Bloc and created in rejection of the 1948 **Marshall Plan,** which poured US dollars into the reconstruction of Western Europe. The West reacted to this new, formal alliance in April with the creation of the **North Atlantic Treaty Organization (NATO),** a military alliance meant to "keep the Americans in, the Russians out, and the Germans down." In typical Cold War fashion, the Eastern Bloc retaliated in 1955 with a similar alliance, the **Warsaw Pact.** The pact allowed for the maintenance of Soviet military bases throughout Eastern Europe, and tightened Russia's grip on its satellite countries. The only Communist European country never to join the Warsaw Pact was **Yugoslavia** as former partisan **Josip Broz Tito** broke away from Moscow as early as 1948 and followed his own path, combining Communism with a market economy.

After Stalin's death in 1953, and his denunciation by **Nikita Khrushchev** in his so-called **Secret Speech** of 1956, the Soviet bloc was plagued by chaos. The 1950s saw the emergence of **National Communism,** or the belief that the attainment of ultimate communist goals should be dictated internally rather than by orders from Moscow. The presence of Russian troops in Eastern Europe, however, enabled Moscow to respond to rising nationalist movements with military force. Such was the case in 1956, when the Soviets violently suppressed the Hungarian Revolution and workers' strikes in Poland. The **Berlin Wall** was erected in 1961, creating a physical symbol of the economic, political, and ideological divide between East and West. The **Prague Spring** of 1968 witnessed another wave of violent suppression as the emerging Czechoslovak dissidence movement demanded increased freedom and attention to human rights. Russia consistently used the Warsaw Pact to justify military occupation and the institution of martial law. Political repression coupled with the economic stagnancy of the Leonid Brezhnev years (1964-1982) increased unrest and disapproval for Moscow and its policies among the satellites.

BRAVE NEW WORLD (1989 ONWARD)

When **Mikhail Gorbachev** became Secretary General of the Communist Party in 1985, he began to dismantle the totalitarian aspects of the Communist regime through his policies of **glasnost** (openness) and **perestroika** (restructuring). The new freedom of political expression led to a snowballing of dissidence, which finally erupted in 1989 with a series of revolutions throughout Eastern Europe. The first occurred in June when the Poles voted the Communists out of office. In their place, they elected **Lech Wałęsa** and the **Solidarity** party to create a new government. This Polish victory was swiftly followed by a new democratic constitution in **Hungary** in October, the crumbling of the **Berlin Wall** on November 9, the resignation of the **Bulgarian** Communists on November 10, the **Velvet Revolution** in Czechoslovakia on November 17 and the televised execution of Romania's communist dictator, **Nicolae Ceauşescu,** on December 25. Almost all of the Warsaw Pact nations had successfully—and almost bloodlessly—broken away from the Soviet Union and begun the move toward democracy.

The **USSR** crumbled shortly after its empire. Within the first five months of 1990, **Lithuania, Estonia, Latvia,** and **Ukraine** all declared independence from Moscow. In an attempt to keep the Soviet Union together, Gorbachev condoned military force against the rebellious Baltic republics. A bloody conflict erupted in Vilnius in January, 1991. By September, the Soviet Union had dissolved and all of its constituent republics and satellite nations were fully independent. Belarus, Moldova, Russia, Ukraine, and the former Soviet republics of Central Asia formed the **Commonwealth of Independent States (CIS)** on December 8, 1991.

Meanwhile, following Tito's death in 1980, Yugoslavia was slowly disintegrating. Economic inequality between its different republics led to the resurfacing of suppressed nationalist sentiments. Inspired by the developments in the rest of Eastern Europe, both **Slovenia** and **Croatia** declared independence on June 25, 1991, to which the Serbian-controlled government responded with military force. The conflict in Slovenia lasted only ten days, but Croatia's attempts to secede resulted in a war that involved Bosnia and Herzegovina, Croatia, Montenegro, and Serbia and continued until the signing of the US-negotiated **Dayton Peace Agreement** in November 1995. The only republics remaining in Yugoslavia were Serbia and Montenegro. Four years later, Serbia's ultra-nationalist leader **Slobodan Milosevic** dragged the region into another military conflict in the Serbian province of **Kosovo**. In an attempt to stop the ethnic cleansing of Kosovo's Albanian majority by the Serbian army, **NATO** launched an intensive air campaign, which ruined the country's economy and led to Serbia's withdrawal.

With the exception of the tumultuous Balkans, the former Soviet satellites are progressing, with varying degrees of success, toward democracy and a market economy. In March 1999, the Czech Republic, Poland, and Hungary joined NATO. May 2002 saw the ironic formation of the **NATO-Russia Council,** a strategic alliance between Russia and the organization originally established as a military alliance against Russia. Today, Bulgaria, Croatia, the Czech Republic, Estonia, Hungary, Latvia, Lithuania, Poland, Romania, Slovenia, and the Slovak Republic are all vying to join the **European Union (EU).** The EU's next round of member selection will draw these countries even farther westward, perhaps as early as 2004.

CULTURE

THE PEOPLES OF EASTERN EUROPE

Although the region is becoming increasingly diversified in light of its recent opening up to the world, Eastern Europe's population still remains fairly homogeneous. Most Eastern European countries are inhabited by **Slavic people.** After the Great Migration (see p. 8), the Slavs split into the **West Slavs** (Czechs, Poles, and Slovaks), **South Slavs** (Croats, Macedonians, Serbs, and Slovenes) and **East Slavs** (Belarussians, Russians and Ukrainians). **Bulgarians,** originally of Turkic origin, became completely Slavified when the Slavs swept across Europe.

The non-Slavic nations inhabiting Central and Eastern Europe include Hungarians, Latvians, Lithuanians, and Estonians. **Latvians** (a.k.a. Letts) and **Lithuanians** belong to the Baltic branch of the Indo-European family. The Balts originally included more ethnic groups that are now extinct, such as the Prussians, the Curonians, and the Selonians. **Estonians,** who also occupy the Baltic Coast, form a branch of the Baltic Finns, descendants of the Finno-Ugric family who have been strongly Germanized. **Hungarians** constitute the "Ugric" part of the Finno-Ugric family. They separated from other Ugric tribes in the Urals and migrated southwest to the Carpathian Basin, which they inhabit today, at the end of the 9th century. Large Hungarian minorities still live in Romanian Transylvania, the southern region of the Slovak Republic. **Romanians** are descendants of Dacians, the earliest known inhabitants of the Balkan Peninsula, together with Thracians and Illyrians.

There are significant **Jewish** communities living in Poland, the Czech Republic, Hungary, and Russia, although their numbers decreased dramatically after World War II as a result of Hitler's "final solution." Well integrated into the society in most countries, Jewish people still face severe anti-Semitism in Russia and Belarus. Nomadic **Roma,** or gypsies (see **Gypsy Kings,** below), live in small communities (or rather ghettos) across Eastern Europe, particularly in the Czech and Slovak Republics, Hungary, Bulgaria, and Romania. Finally, American and British **expats** flooded Eastern Europe after the fall of the Berlin Wall, creating distinct cultures in Prague, Budapest, St. Petersburg, and other parts of Eastern Europe. Today, around 10,000 native English speakers call Prague home.

GYPSY KINGS. The Roma migrated to Europe from their homeland in northern India sometime around the 14th and 15th century. Also known throughout Europe as gypsies, they refer to themselves as Roma, meaning *man* or *husband* in their native tongue, Romany. Most Roma speak their native language, as well as the language of the country in which they settled. Their nomadic nature and darker skin color prevented any integration with white Europeans and in the early years of their immigration, Roma were regarded as exotic. When they first came to France in the 15th century, the French referred to them as "Bohemians," meaning "coming from Bohemia." Later, the word Bohemian acquired the meaning as we know it today, describing anyone who leads an unconventional lifestyle like the Roma. Despite (and perhaps due to) their exotic image, the Roma have always found themselves on the edge of society. Today, Roma in Eastern Europe are treated quite poorly. In June 1998, the local government of Ústí nad Labem, in Northern Bohemia, built a wall through the center of town to separate the "good" Czech citizens from the "bad" Roma. Although the wall was later torn down in response to pressure from the international community, the situation of the Roma remains dismal. Faced with extreme discrimination and violent attacks by skinheads, thousands of Roma left the Czech Republic in 1998 and 1999 to seek refuge, first in Great Britain, then in Canada. Nearly all of them were sent back.

RELIGION

The majority of Eastern Europe converted to **Christianity** by the 10th century, and it remains the principal religion on the continent to this day. The monks **Cyril and Methodius** brought Christianity to the Slavs (see **Languages** and **It's All Greek to Me,** p. 15); most Belarussians, Bulgarians, Macedonians, Romanians, Russians, Serbs, and Ukrainians subscribe to the **Eastern Orthodox** faith. With the exception of the Baltic states, which have been influenced by German **Protestantism,** all other nations of Eastern Europe are predominantly **Roman Catholic.** Birthplace of the present Pope, John Paul II, Poland is one of the world's most strongly Catholic countries. In the Czech Republic, which lies geographically on the boundary between Protestant and Catholic Europe, both Catholicism and Protestantism are common. Religious dissent against Catholicism originated in the Czech lands in the 14th century, when **Jan Hus** (see p. 218) preached church reform, preceding Luther's **Protestant Reformation** by a full century. The doctrine of Communism and the sense of hopelessness that followed the World Wars spread **atheism** across Eastern Europe. **Islam** came to Europe with the Ottoman Empire. Although they were referred to as Muslims during the recent wars, Bosnians are Islamicized Serbo-Croats. There are significant Muslim Albanian minorities in Macedonia and Bulgaria. **Judaism** constitutes another important minority religion, practiced mainly in the Czech Republic, Poland, Russia and Hungary.

LANGUAGES

With the exception of Estonian and Hungarian, which are **Finno-Ugric** (though not mutually intelligible), all nations in Eastern Europe speak languages of **Indo-European** origin. Romanian belongs to the **Romance** branch (similar to Italian), and **Latvian** and **Lithuanian** to the Baltic branch. Belarussian, Bulgarian, Czech, Macedonian, Polish, Serbo-Croatian, Slovak, Slovene, Russian and Ukrainian are all **Slavic** languages. The **Cyrillic alphabet** is a script used in Belarus, Bulgaria, Macedonia, Moldova, Serbia, Russia, and Ukraine. For many centuries, Cyrillic was a source of unity for the Slavic nations who wrote in it, and its use (or non-use) still makes a political statement in some parts of the world (such as Moldova, where it is currently a major political issue; see **What's in a Name,** p. 472). One of the major differences between the otherwise very similar Serb and Croat languages is that Croatian is written in the Latin alphabet, while Serbian is written in Cyrillic. Other

IT'S ALL GREEK TO ME. When the Greek priest Constantine and his brother Methodius set off on a Christian mission to convert the Slavs in 863, they brought with them more than their religion. To succeed where others had failed, Constantine translated liturgical text into the language of the people, using an alphabet he invented based on Greek script. The new script, **Old Church Slavonic,** was a smashing success among the people, facilitating unions in the name of religion and language that made the great empires of the Bulgarians and the Kyivan Rus possible. Rome, however, was less than thrilled to hear that the Word of God was being spread in any language less dignified than Greek or Latin. The brothers were summoned to explain themselves before Pope Nicholas I, who died before they arrived in 868. While his successor Adrian II gave their mission his full blessing, Constantine fell ill and died before he could return to preach. Before he passed away, he adopted the name Cyril, which has been immortalized as the name of the alphabet that evolved from his work.

republics of the former Soviet Union are also replacing Cyrillic with their own scripts, a political gesture to emphasize their break with Moscow. For phrasebooks and glossaries of key Eastern European languages, see the **Glossary,** p. 873.

The Russian Cyrillic transliteration index is given below. Other languages include some additional letters and pronounce certain letters differently. Each country's **Language** section outlines these distinctions.

CYRILLIC	ENGLISH	PRONOUNCE	CYRILLIC	ENGLISH	PRONOUNCE
А а	a	Garden	Р р	r	Random
Б б	b	Mr. Burns	С с	s	Saucy
В в	v	Village People	Т т	t	Tantalize
Г г	g	Galina	У у	oo	Doodle
Д д	d	David	Ф ф	f	Absolutely Fab
Е е	ye or e	Yellow	Х х	kh	Chutzpah (hkh)
Ё ё	yo	Your	Ц ц	ts	Let's Go
Ж ж	zh	Persia	Ч ч	ch	Chinese
З з	z	Zany	Ш ш	sh	Champagne
И и	ee	Kathleen	Щ щ	shch	Khrushchev
Й й	y	(see * below)	Ъ ъ	(hard)	(no sound)
К к	k	Killjoy	Ы ы	y	lit
Л л	l	Louis	Ь ь	(soft)	(no sound)
М м	m	Meteor	Э э	eh	Alexander
Н н	n	Nikki	Ю ю	yoo	You
О о	o	Hole	Я я	yah	yacht
П п	p	Peter the Great			

* Й creates dipthongs, altering the sounds of the vowels it follows: ОЙ is pronounced "oy" (boy), АЙ is pronounced "aye" (bye), ИЙ is pronounced "ee" (baby), and ЕЙ is pronounced "ehy" (bay).

FOOD

Although food specialities vary from region to region, Eastern Europe stands united in its love of **sausage.** Packed meat products come in an endless number of varieties, the spiciest ones being from Hungary. Central European cuisine is characterized by lots of meat floating in a sauce accompanied by cabbage and potatoes, whereas on the coasts, a lighter, sea-based cuisine predominates. **Vegetarian** restaurants are still few and far between, but they are becoming more common, especially in Central Europe. Delicious **breads** are baked throughout the region, and always provide a welcome substitute for the region's heavy dishes. **Dairy products** are extremely popular throughout Eastern Europe.

ALCOHOLIC DELIGHTS

Mmm...beer. And vodka. Absinthe. Plum brandy. Kvas. Even wine. Eastern Europe is perhaps most loved for its endless shelves of locally produced, throat-burning liquors. Don't limit yourself to imported, far-away versions; drink these magic liquids straight from the source. The word's best hops are in the Czech Republic: the world famous **Pilsner Urquell** is produced in Plzeň (p. 220) while České Budějovice (p. 268) brews the delectable **Budvar** (*not* to be confused with American Budweiser). The best beer in the Czech Republic, **Krušovice,** is produced right in Prague (p. 226);

FESTIVALS IN EASTERN EUROPE

The following list is by no means exhaustive; it is meant to suggest highlights of Eastern European revelries in 2003.

COUNTRY	APR. – JUNE	JULY – AUG.	SEPT. – MAR.
BOSNIA		**Futura 2003** July, Sarajevo (p. 95) **Turkish Nights** July, Sarajevo (p. 95) **Int'l Youth Festival** Aug., Međugorje (p. 100)	**Sarajevan Winter** Dec. (p. 95)
BULGARIA	**Rose Festival** June, Kazanluk (p. 128) **Madara Music Days** June-July(p. 149)	**Varna Summer** July (p. 134) **Love is Folly Film Fest.** Aug.-Sept., Varna (p. 134)	**Arts Festival Apolonia** Sept., Sozopol (p. 138) **Int'l Jazz Festival** Oct., Bansko (p. 124)
CROATIA	**Animated Film Fest.** May, Zagreb (p. 166) **Eurokaz Theater Fest.** June, Zagreb (p. 166) **Cest d'Best** June, Zagreb (p. 166)	**Dubrovnik Summer Fest.** July-Aug. (p. 214) **Summer Festival** July-Aug., Split (p. 200) **Festival of Sword Dances** July, Korčula (p. 206)	**Int'l Puppet Festival** Sept., Zagreb (p. 166) **Marco Polo Festival** Sept., Korčula (p. 206) **Int'l Jazz Festival** Oct., Zagreb (p. 166)
CZECH REPUBLIC	**Prague Spring** May (p. 253) **Five-Petal Rose Festival** June, Č. Krumlov (p. 278) **European Theater Fest.** June, H. Králové (p. 283)	**Int'l Film Festival** July, Karlovy Vary (p. 268) **Early Music Festival** July, Č. Krumlov (p. 278) **Int'l Music Festival** Aug.,Č. Krumlov (p. 278)	**Int'l Organ Festival** Sept., Olomouc (p. 294) **Jazz Goes To Town** Oct., H. Králové (p. 283)
ESTONIA	**Rock Box Festival** May, Tartu (p. 327) **Old Town Days** June, Tallinn (p. 310) **Hello Pärnu Summer!** June (p. 314)	**Beersummer** July, Tallinn (p. 310) **Int'l Bagpipe Festival** July, Lahemma (p. 310) **White Lady Days** Aug., Haapsalu (p. 316)	**Dark Nights Film Festival** Dec., Tallinn (p. 310) **Student Jazz Festival** February, Tallinn (**p. 310**) **Dionysia Arts Festival** Mar.-Apr., Tartu (p. 327)
HUNGARY	**Jazz Days** May, Debrecen (p. 391) **Sopron Festival Weeks** June, Sopron (p. 370) **Szentivánéji Festivities** June, Szombath. (p. 373) **Golden Shell Folklore** June, Siófok (p. 377)	**Béla Bartók Choir Fest.** July, Debrecen (p. 391) **Baroque Festival** July, Eger (p. 404) **Visegrád Palace Games** July, Visegrád (p. 362) **Szeged Open Air Festival** Aug. (p. 396) **Sziget (Rock) Festival** Aug., Budapest (p. 356)	**Haydn Festival** Sept., Fertőd (p. 370) **Hírős Food Festival** Sept., Kecskem. (p. 400) **Eger Vintage Days** Sept. (p. 404) **Festival of Wine Songs** Sept., Pécs (p. 387)
LATVIA	**Eurovision 2003** May, Rīga (p. 424) **Int'l Ballooning Festival** May, Sigulda (p. 427)	**Fest. of Song and Dance** June-July, Rīga (p. 424) **Int'l Organ Music Fest.** July, Riga (**p. 424**) **Kuldīga Town Festival** July (p. 430)	**Cēsis Music Festival** Aug. (p. 429)

enjoy it along with a fiery glass of **absinthe.** While it pales next to the Czechs' brews, the Polish **Żywiec** is concocted just south of Bielsko-Biała (p. 524). The Ukrainian version of beer, **kvas,** is sold from barrels on the streets of Kyiv (p. 811), even in the pouring rain. In Karlovy Vary, CZR (p. 265), you can imbibe **Becherovka,** an herb liquor purported to have "curative powers." For good **vodka,** head anywhere in Russia (p. 621). Better yet, head to the Latvian/Estonian or Belarussian/Polish borders, where vodka smuggling makes for very cheap inebriation. Hungary currently holds the crown for Eastern Europe's finest **wines**—don't miss **Bull's Blood** in Eger (p. 400), **Aszú vintages** in Tokaj (p. 407), and the **Balaton-flavored wines** of Badascony (p. 383)—but Croatia (p. 150) has recently begun to seriously challenge Hungary for top spot. The wines of twin cities Mélník, CZR (p. 259) and Melnik, BUL (p. 126) are so good, Churchill had them shipped to England, even during World War II.

°COUNTRY	APR. – JUNE	JULY – AUG.	SEPT. – MAR.
LITHUANIA	Vilniaus Festivalis May (p. 447) Jazz Festival June, Klaipėda (p. 460)	Lithuanian Song Festival July, Vilnius (p. 447) Thomas Mann Festival July, Nida (p. 462) Night Serenades, June-Aug., Palanga (p. 456)	
POLAND	International Short Film May, Kraków (p. 514) Probaltica May, Toruń (p. 547) Music and Architecture May, Toruń (p. 547) Jazz nad Odrą May, Wrocław (p. 536) Fest. of Jewish Culture June, Kraków (p. 514)	Street Theater July, Kraków (p. 514) Country Picnic Fest. July-Aug., Mrąg. (p. 574) Highlander Folklore Aug., Zakopane (p. 524) Rock and Pop Music Aug., Sopot (p. 565)	Kraków Jazz Festival Oct. (p. 514) National Blues Music Nov., Toruń (p. 547)
ROMANIA	Sibiu Jazz Festival May-June (p. 600) Int'l Folk Music Fest. June, Timişoara (p. 607)	Int'l Chamber Music July, Braşov (p. 599) Medieval Festival Aug., Sibiu (p. 601)	Golden Stag Festival Sept., Braşov (p. 599)
RUSSIA	White Nights Festival June, St. Petersburg (p. 687)	St. Petersburg 300th Anniversary Year-round (p. 688)	Sochi Art Festival Sept. (p. 705) Russian Winter Festival Dec.-Jan., Irkutsk (p. 725)
SLOVAK REPUBLIC	Ghosts and Spirits May, Bojnice (p. 753) Den Mesta June, Bardejov (p. 778)	Fest. of Marian Devotion July, Levoča (p. 760)	Bratislava Music Fest Sept.-Oct. (p. 750) Festival of Knights Sept., Bojnice (p. 753)
SLOVENIA	Slovene Music Days Apr., Ljubljana (p. 792) Int'l Jazz Festival June, Ljubljana (p. 792) Primorska Summer Fest. June-Aug., Piran (p. 801)	Int'l Summer Festival July, Ljubljana (p. 792) Bled Days July (p. 795) No Borders Folk Festival July, L. Bohinj (p. 797)	Cow Ball Sept., L. Bohinj (p. 797) Int'l Film Festival Nov., Ljubljana (p. 792)
UKRAINE	Kyiv Days May (p. 823)	Int'l Film Festival July, Kyiv (p. 823)	Kyiv Theater Festival Mar. (p. 823)

GEOGRAPHY

CLIMATE

Avg Temp (hi/lo)	January		April		July		October	
	°C	°F	°C	°F	°C	°F	°C	°F
Bratislava, SLK	02/-03	36/26	15/04	60/40	26/14	79/58	15/7	05/42
Bucharest, ROM	02/-05	36/23	16/05	62/42	27/15	82/60	17/06	63/43
Budapest, HUN	02/-03	36/25	15/05	60/41	26/15	79/59	15/06	59/43
Chişinău, MOL	00/-05	32/23	14/06	58/43	25/16	77/61	14/06	58/43
Kyiv, UKR	-02/-09	27/15	12/02	55/37	23/13	75/56	11/02	53/37
Ljubljana, SLN	02/-05	36/23	13/02	57/37	22/11	73/52	14/05	58/41
Minsk, BEL	-03/-07	26/18	10/01	51/35	21/12	70/55	08/03	48/38
Moscow, RUS	-06/-11	21/11	09/01	49/34	21/12	71/55	07/00	45/33
Prague, CZR	01/-04	34/24	12/02	54/36	22/12	72/54	12/03	54/39
Rīga, LAT	-01/-05	29/22	08/01	48/35	20/13	69/56	10/05	50/41
Sarajevo, BOS	02/-05	36/23	14/03	58/39	25/13	78/56	16/05	61/42
Sofia, BUL	02/-03	38/25	17/06	64/43	30/15	86/60	19/07	67/45
Tallinn, EST	-02/-06	28/21	07/00	45/33	20/12	68/55	08/03	47/38
Vilnius, LIT	-04/-09	26/16	11/02	51/35	22/12	72/54	10/03	50/38
Warsaw, POL	00/-04	33/24	12/02	54/37	22/12	73/55	12/04	54/40
Zagreb, CRO	03/-02	37/28	11/03	52/37	27/17	81/63	15/08	59/46

The sun shines on the Eastern Bloc, despite what Western propaganda against communism—television images of rainy Moscow and ice-cold Siberia—used to suggest. But don't get us wrong, it can get darn cold up in northern Siberia. Eastern Europe, however, is so vast that its climate is extremely varied. The **central regions,** such as Poland and the Czech and Slovak Republics, get warm summers (May-Sept.) and bitingly cold winters (Dec.-Feb.). **South** of these countries, however, toward the Mediterranean Sea, in Slovenia, and Croatia, summers become extremely hot and winters pleasantly mild. It gets just as hot along the Bulgarian, Romanian, Russian, and Ukrainian **Black Sea Coast.**

LAND AND WATER

The vast majority of Eastern Europe consists of several low-altitude plains. The North and East European Plains span from Poland to the Baltic states, Belarus, Ukraine and European Russia. The Hungarian Plain covers the southern Slovak Republic and most of Hungary, whereas the Romanian Plain dominates southern Romania. Most of the Czech Republic sits on a plateau, the Bohemian Massif. The largest mountains in Central Europe are the **Carpathians** (which include the **Tatras**), running along the Polish-Slovak border. South of the lowlands lie Europe's highest mountain ranges, the **Alps** in Austria and Slovenia, and the **Balkan Mountains** in Croatia, Bosnia, Macedonia and Bulgaria.

Europe's longest river is the **Volga** in Russia. The **Danube,** which creates a natural border between Hungary and the Slovak Republic and between Bulgaria and Romania, is the region's most economically and historically important river. Other rivers include the **Dnieper** in Ukraine, the **Elbe** in the Czech Republic, and the **Oder** and **Vistula** in Poland. Eastern European rivers dump their water (and waste) into three seas: the **Baltic,** the **Adriatic,** and the **Black Sea.** Whereas the Baltic coast is entirely composed of lowlands, the Adriatic is characterized by dramatic mountains, jagged peninsulas and miniature islands. **Lake Balaton,** in Hungary, is the largest (and most popular) lake in Europe west of Russia; **Lake Ladoga,** in northwestern Russia, is the largest in Europe (though not the largest *in* Russia—Lake Baikal, in Asia, is bigger), but definitely not the most popular.

GEOGRAPHICAL FEATURES

The following table is by no means complete. It is meant solely to give a taste of what Eastern Europe has to offer.

COUNTRY	MAJOR NATIONAL PARKS	NOTABLE NATURAL FEATURES
Belarus	Belavezhskaya, Narochanski, Blaslau Lakes, Pripyatsky	Berezina Plains, Dnieper Lowlands, Neman Lowlands, Paliesse Plains and Swamps
Bosnia	Jahorina, Kozara, Perucica, Sutjeska, Trebevic	Kozara Mountains, Lake Buško, Lake Bilećko, Majevica Mountains
Bulgaria	Pirin, Rila, Strandzha, Vitosha, Vratchansky	Black Sea Coast; Pirin, Rila, and Rodopi Mountains; Thracian Plain
Croatia	Mijet, Plitvice Lakes, Risnjak	Mediterranean Coast and 1100 Islands
Czech Republic	Český Kras, Český Ráj, Sumava, Palava	Bohemian Forest, Karlovy Vary Natural Spas, Moravský Krav Caves, Sudety Mountains
Estonia	Endla, Lahemaa, Matsalu, Nigula, Saaremaa	Baltic Coastline, 1521 Islands, Haapsalu and Pärnu Mud Baths, Pandivere Upland
Hungary	Bükk, Duna-Dráva, Hortobágy, Kiskunság	Baradlá Caves, Danube Bend, Great and Little Alföld Mountains, Lake Balaton, Őrség Hills, Nagyaföld Plain
Latvia	Gauja, Kemeri, Slitere, Taicija	Baltic Coast, Kurzeme Uplands, Sigulda Caves
Lithuania	Aukstaitija, Dzukija, Kuršių Nerija, Trakai, Zemaitija	Baltic Coast, Baltic Highlands, Curonian Spit, Druskininkai Lakes
Moldova	Codri, Iagorlic	Bulgeac Plain, Codri Hills, Lake Stânca-Costeşti
Poland	Białowieski, Karkonosze, Tatra, Woliński	Baltic Coast, Carpathian Mountains, Pomeranian Lakeland, Tatras Mountains
Romania	Danube Delta, Ceahlau, Pietrosul Mare, Retezat	Black Sea Coast, Bucegi Mountains, Cibin Mountains, Danube Delta, Eastern and Western Carpathians, Făgăraş Mountains, Oas-Harghita Volcanic Range, Transylvanian Alps
Russia	Barguzinsky, Kutsa, Laplandski, Vodlozero, Yugud-Va	Bering, Black, and Caspian Sea Coasts; Curonian Spit; Lake Baikal; Russian Plain; Siberian Plateau; Ural Mountains
Slovak Republic	Pieniny, Slovenský Raj, Tatras, Velka Fatra	Bardejov Baths, Dobšinská Ice Caves, High and Low Tatras Mountains, Malá Fatra Mountains,
Slovenia	Strunjan, Triglav	Biejski Vintgar Gorge, Julian Alps, Lake Bled, Lake Bohinj, Mediterranean Coast, Postojna Caves, Škocjanske Caves
Ukraine	Askania Nova, Hortytsya, Medobory, Roztochchya, Shatsk, Sinevir	Black Sea Coast, Carpathian Mountains, Crimean Peninsula, Dnieper Uplands and Lowlands

CULTURAL GODS, EARTHLY PRACTICES
Literary Hero-Worship in Eastern Europe

First-time visitors to Eastern Europe are likely to find themselves either charmed or bewildered by the extraordinary esteem in which the local residents hold their cultural heroes. In the English-speaking world, we have little to compare with the countless monuments and museum-apartments dedicated to the exceptional writers the eastern corner of Europe has produced. In this regard, Whitman, Dickinson, and even Shakespeare have nothing on Aleksandr Pushkin (1799-1837), Russia's most powerful literary personality, or Adam Mickiewicz (1798-1855), the great Polish poet.

Aficionados of nineteenth-century Russian poetry can choose among any number of apartments or estates wholly dedicated to the life and work of a favorite artist. If you miss the huge statues of Mickiewicz in Warsaw or Kraków, there's still the museum in Vilnius created from the rooms where he spent a few weeks in 1822 (see p. 447). In St. Petersburg, marvel as schoolchildren dutifully recite verse over the couch where Pushkin, fatally wounded in a duel with the French diplomat Dantes, took his last breath (see p. 685). Even Goethe deserves some mention here: an engraved cornerstone in a building on Kraków's main square marks the place where he once lived—for three days.

Many cities are actually more concerned with the luminaries' connection to the region—however tenuous it may be—than their work. Thus the uninspiring museum-apartment in Moscow dedicated to Pushkin, principally a Petersburg poet, favors his most minute connections to the capital over his great works (see p. 651). Likewise, the Fryderyc Chopin estate in Żelazowa Wola remains a point of pilgrimage, even though he only lived here for the first few months of his life (see p. 500).

As most of these shrines were established long after the death of their subjects, the few personal possessions museum curators have managed to recover—a comb, an inkwell, or a desk, often sealed behind protective glass—draw all the fascination and reverence of saintly relics. There might well be a vital link between the practices of cultural hero-worship and Eastern Europe's prevalent spiritual traditions, mainly Russian Orthodoxy and Catholicism, both of which emphasize the sanctity of objects associated with holy figures. As with a religious martyr, artifacts and locales connected to the artist's death—deathbeds, death masks, burial places, and even replicas of dueling pistols—serve as the *piece de resistance* of many exhibits and tours.

In much of Eastern Europe, the Soviet Era represented the heyday of cultural hero-worship, at least for those personalities whose work was approved by the fickle regime. In a society where the flow of information was centrally controlled, the celebration of a particular author or composer could be coordinated with the publishing schedule, the state pedagogical program, and the process whereby certain figures were selected to have statues and monuments erected in their honor. Thus Maxim Gorky (1868-1936), now of scant interest in the West, is like a demi-god in European Russia.

But the real origins of this practice are in the Romantic period of the 19th century, when writers like Pushkin and Mickiewicz developed the rhetoric of the "poet-prophet" so effectively, and with such profound originality, that their readers were quite convinced of their prophetic powers. This effect had special momentum in Russia, which in the 19th century suddenly found itself overwhelmed by the innovative genius of such writers as Pushkin, Nikolai Gogol (1809-1852), and Mikhail Lermontov (1814-1841). In Poland, the works of Romantic writers were closely linked to the struggle for national self-determination, and Mickiewicz gets much better publicity than his Renaissance and Baroque predecessors. And in Bohemia, the slightest connection to the life of Antonín Dvořák (1841-1904), whose fondness for traditional folk music had a profound influence on his music, warrants a sculpture or plaque. Thus celebrating the artist became tantamount to honoring the nation itself.

Benjamin Paloff was a Researcher-Writer for Let's Go: Eastern Europe 1998, *the editor of* Eastern Europe 1999, *and a Managing Editor of the 2000 series. He has a B.A. and an M.A. from Harvard in Slavic Languages and Literatures, and is currently working on his Ph.D. in Slavic Literature at Harvard.*

PDAs & Travel

LET'S GO

(it's not what you're thinking)

Let's Go City Guides are now available for Palm OS™ PDAs. Download a free trial at http://**mobile.letsgo.com**

ESSENTIALS

ESSENTIALS

At times frustratingly bureaucratic, at times politically unstable, Eastern Europe is never predictable. Exchange rates, phone numbers, and even borders can change rapidly in this part of the world. It's wise to obtain the appropriate visas from local consulates the moment you decide to take a trip here, but it's not worth plotting much else too carefully, as you'll likely have to scrap your original plans while on the road. Hands down, the most important things to bring are flexibility and a sense of adventure.

EMBASSIES AND CONSULATES

Eastern European embassies and consulates abroad are listed in the **Documents and Formalities: Embassies and Consulates** section at the beginning of each country chapter. American, Australian, British, Canadian, Irish, New Zealand, and South African embassies and consulates in Eastern European countries are listed in the **Practical Information** sections for the capitals of each country.

DOCUMENTS AND FORMALITIES

PASSPORTS

REQUIREMENTS. Citizens of Australia, Canada, Ireland, New Zealand, South Africa, the UK, and the US need valid passports to enter any country in Eastern Europe and to re-enter their own. Many European countries will not allow you to enter if your passport expires within six months of your trip. Returning home with an expired passport is illegal and may result in a fine. Citizens of Australia, Canada, Ireland, New Zealand, the United Kingdom, and the United States can apply for a passport at the nearest post office, passport office, or court of law. Citizens of South Africa can apply for a passport at the nearest office of Foreign Affairs. Those living abroad who need a passport or renewal services should contact the nearest consular service of their home country.

PASSPORT MAINTENANCE. Photocopy the page of your passport that contains your photograph and passport number, along with other important documents such as visas, travel insurance policies, airplane tickets, and traveler's check serial numbers in case of loss or theft. Carry one set of copies in a safe place apart from the originals and leave another set at home. Also, pack an expired passport or an official copy of your birth certificate separate from other documents.

If you lose your passport, immediately notify the local police and the nearest embassy or consulate of your home government. As of 2002, American and Canadian passports are no longer processed abroad. You can still request a new passport while abroad, but you'll have to wait longer to receive it, as the processing is done in the United States or Canada and then sent overseas. Emergency travel documents will still be available from American and Canadian embassies. To expedite replacement you'll need to show identification and proof of citizenship. Any visas stamped in your old passport will be irretrievably lost. Your passport is a public document belonging to your nation's government—you may have to surrender it to a foreign government official, but if you don't get it back in a reasonable amount of time, inform the nearest consulate of your home country.

VISAS, INVITATIONS, AND PERMITS

VISAS. Visas can be purchased from your destination country's consulate or embassy. In most cases, you will have to send a completed visa application (also obtained from the consulate), the required fee, and your passport. You may also want to check for organizations within your own country that offer visa services. For more information on each country's visa requirements, see the **Documents and Formalities** section at the beginning of each country chapter. US citizens can take advantage of the **Center for International Business and Travel** (**CIBT;** ☎ 800-925-2428), which secures visas for travel to almost all countries for a variable service charge.

VISA REQUIREMENTS		A U S	C A N	I R E	N Z	S A	U K	U S
	BELARUS	Y*	Y*	Y*	Y*	Y*	Y*	Y*
	BOSNIA	Y	N	Y	Y	N	N	N
	BULGARIA	N¹	N¹	N¹	N¹	Y	N¹	N¹
	CROATIA	N	N	N	N	Y°	N	N
	CZECH REP.	Y	Y	N	N	Y	N	N
	ESTONIA	N	Y*	N	N	Y*	N	N
	HUNGARY	Y	N	N	N	Y	N	N
	LATVIA	Y‡	Y	N	Y	Y	N	N
	LITHUANIA	N	N	N	N	Y	N	N
	MOLDOVA	Y*	Y*	Y*	Y*	Y*	Y	Y*
	POLAND	Y	Y	N	Y	Y	N	N
	ROMANIA	Y	N	N¹	Y	Y	N¹	N¹
	RUSSIA	Y*	Y*	Y*	Y*	Y*	Y*	Y*
	SLOVAK REP.	N	N	N	N	N¹	N	N¹
	SLOVENIA	N	N	N	Y	Y	N	N
	UKRAINE	Y*	Y°	Y°	Y*	Y*	Y°	Y°

KEY			
Y	visa required	N	no visa required
°	proof of travel required	*	invitation required
‡	tourists can stay without a visa for up to 10 days	₁	tourists can stay without a visa for up to 30 days

INVITATIONS. To obtain a visa, visitors to some countries must also acquire an invitation from a sponsoring individual or organization (for applicable countries, see the table above). Specialized travel agencies can often arrange an invitation for those without private sponsors; for agencies that specialize in countries of the former USSR, see **Russia Essentials: Visa and Entry Information,** p. 630. Requirements change rapidly, so always double-check with the relevant embassy.

WORK AND STUDY PERMITS. Admission as a visitor does not include the right to work, which is authorized only by a work permit. Entering to study also requires a special visa. Many countries require both a work permit and a special "visa with work permit." The former is issued by the country's Labor Office, and the latter by the consulate. For more information, see **Alternatives to Tourism,** p. 60, and the **Essentials** section of the country to which you're traveling.

IDENTIFICATION

When you travel, always carry two or more forms of identification with you, including at least one photo ID. A passport combined with a driver's license or birth certificate usually serves as adequate proof of your identity and citizenship. Many establishments, especially banks, require several IDs before cashing traveler's checks. Never carry all your forms of ID together. For more information on all the forms of identification listed below, contact the **International Student Travel Confederation (ISTC),** Herengracht 479, 1017 BS Amsterdam, Netherlands (☎31 20 421 28 00; fax 421 28 10; www.istc.org).

STUDENT, TEACHER, AND YOUTH IDENTIFICATION. The **International Student Identity Card (ISIC),** the most widely accepted form of student identification in Eastern Europe, provides discounts on sights, accommodations, food, and transport. Check out the ISIC discount database for local specials (www.istc-net.org/DiscountDatabase). The ISIC is preferable to an institution-specific card (such as a university ID) because it is more likely to be recognized (and honored) abroad. All cardholders have access to a 24hr. emergency helpline for medical, legal, and financial emergencies (call US collect ☎715-345-0505, UK collect 44 20 8762 8110, or France collect 33 155 633 144), and holders of US-issued cards are also eligible for insurance benefits (see **Insurance,** p. 35). Many student travel agencies—including Campus Travel, Council Travel, SASTS, STA Travel, and usit NOW—issue ISICs. The card is valid from September to December of the following year and costs US$22, AUS$13, or UK£5. Applicants must be degree-seeking students of a secondary or post-secondary school and must be of at least 12 years of age. Because of the proliferation of fake ISICs, some services (particularly airlines) require additional proof of student identity, such as a school ID or a letter attesting to your student status, signed by your registrar and stamped with your school seal. The **International Teacher Identity Card (ITIC)** offers the same insurance coverage as well as similar discounts (US$22, AUS$13, or UK£5). The ITIC also issues a discount card to travelers who are 26 years old or under, but are not students. This one-year **International Youth Travel Card (IYTC;** formerly the **GO 25 Card)** offers many of the same benefits as the ISIC. Most organizations that sell the ISIC also sell the IYTC (US$22, AUS$13, or UK£5).

CUSTOMS

Upon entering any country, you must declare certain items and pay a duty on all articles that exceed the allowance established by that country's customs service. Keeping receipts for purchases made abroad will help establish values when you return. It is wise to make a list, including serial numbers, of any valuables that you carry with you from home; if you register this list with customs before your departure and have an official stamp it, you will avoid import duty charges and ensure an easy passage upon your return. Be especially careful to document items manufactured abroad. Upon returning home, you must similarly declare all articles acquired abroad and pay a **duty**. For more specific information on customs requirements, contact the customs information center in your home country.

MONEY

The biggest single expense on your trip will probably be your round-trip airfare to Eastern Europe, which can be much more expensive than a ticket to Western Europe (see **Getting There,** p. 45). Before you go, spend some time calculating a reasonable per-day budget that will meet your needs. A threadbare day in Eastern Europe (camping or sleeping in hostels, buying food at supermarkets) runs US$10-20; a slightly more comfortable day (sleeping in hostels and the occasional budget hotel, eating one meal a day at a restaurant, going out at night) runs US$20-30. If you spend more than that you'll be living like royalty. But even these ranges vary throughout the region: expect to spend US$5-10 more per day in Slovenia and Croatia and US$5 less in Romania and Bulgaria. Don't forget to factor reserve funds into your budget in case of emergency (at least US$200). Carrying cash with you is risky but necessary; personal checks from home are never accepted and even traveler's checks may not be accepted in some locations, particularly Russia. Your safest bet for carrying money, checks, and your passport is a flat money pouch worn around your waist and underneath your clothing.

CURRENCY AND EXCHANGE

A chart at the beginning of each country chapter lists the September 2002 exchange rates between local currency and Australian dollars (AUS$), British pounds (UK£), Canadian dollars (CDN$), EU euros (EUR€), New Zealand dollars (NZ$), South African rand (ZAR), and US dollars (US$). Check the currency converter on the Let's Go website (www.letsgo.com/thumb) or a local newspaper for the latest exchange rates. As a general rule, it is cheaper to convert money abroad than at home. Bring enough foreign currency to last the first 24-72hr. of a trip to avoid being penniless after banking hours or on a holiday. ATM (cash) cards or credit cards (see **Credit, Debit, and ATM Cards,** p. 26) offer the best exchange rates.

If an ATM isn't available, go to banks or exchange offices that have at most a 5% margin between their buy and sell prices. Since you lose money with every transaction, convert large sums but no more than you'll need within that one country, since it may be difficult or impossible to change it back. Some countries, such as the Czech Republic, the Slovak Republic, and Russia, may require transaction receipts to reconvert local currency. Of foreign currencies, US$ or EUR€ are the most widely—and at times the only—foreign currencies accepted for exchange in Eastern Europe. Carry your money in a variety of forms like cash, traveler's checks, an ATM card, and credit cards. Always carry some small denominations should you have to exchanging money in an emergency at a disadvantageous rate.

In some countries of Eastern Europe it is illegal to pay with foreign currency. In other parts, however, US$ or EUR€ will be preferred to local currency. Some establishments post prices in US$ or EUR€ due to high inflation and will insist that they don't accept anything else, but avoid using Western money when you can. Not only are prices quoted in US$ or EUR€ generally more expensive than those in the local currency, but Western currency may also attract thieves.

ESSENTIALS

TRAVELER'S CHECKS

Traveler's checks are one of the safest and least troublesome means of carrying funds, since they can be refunded if stolen. Unfortunately, it is difficult—if not impossible—to cash these checks in Bosnia, Belarus, and Russia. Several agencies and banks sell them, usually for face value plus a small percentage commission. **American Express, MasterCard,** and **Visa** are the most widely recognized. It is best to get checks in either US$ or EUR€. While traveling, keep check receipts and a record of which checks you've cashed separate from the checks themselves. Also leave a list of check numbers with someone at home. Never countersign or date checks until you're ready to cash them, and always bring your passport with you to cash them. If your checks are lost or stolen, immediately contact a refund center (of the company that issued your checks) to be reimbursed; they may require a police report verifying the loss or theft. Less-touristed countries may not have refund centers at all, in which case you might have to wait to be reimbursed. Ask about toll-free refund hotlines and the location of refund centers when purchasing checks, and always carry emergency cash.

American Express: In Australia call ☎ 1800 251 902, New Zealand 0800 441 068, the UK 0800 521 313, and the US and Canada 800-221-7282; elsewhere call the US collect ☎ 801-964-6665 or see www.aexp.com. Purchase checks for 1-4% commission at AmEx Travel Offices, banks, and American Automobile Association (AAA) offices. AAA members can buy checks commission-free. AmEx offices cash checks commission-free (unless prohibited by national governments), but often at worse rates than banks.

Thomas Cook MasterCard: In Canada and the US call ☎ 800-223-7373, the UK call 0800 62 101; elsewhere call the UK collect ☎ 44 1733 31 89 50. Checks available in 13 currencies at 1-2% commission. Thomas Cook offices cash checks commission-free but are much less common in Eastern Europe than American Express.

Visa: In the UK call ☎ 0800 89 50 78, the US call 800-227-6811; elsewhere call the UK collect ☎ 44 20 7937 8091. Ask for the location of the nearest office.

CREDIT CARDS

Where they are accepted, credit cards not only offer superior exchange rates, but their companies may also offer services like insurance or emergency help. In addition, they are sometimes required to reserve hotel rooms or rental cars. Although credit cards are becoming more commonly accepted throughout the region, few budget accommodations currently accept them. Credit cards are also useful for **cash advances,** which allow you to extract local currency from associated banks and teller machines instantly. High fees for all credit-card advances (up to US$10 per advance, plus 2-3% extra for foreign conversions) typically make credit cards a more costly means of withdrawing cash than ATMs or traveler's checks. **MasterCard (MC)** and **Visa (V)** are the most welcomed; **American Express (AmEx)** cards work at some ATMs, as well as at AmEx offices and major airports.

ATM AND DEBIT CARDS

Depending on the system that your home bank uses, you can probably access your personal bank account from abroad. **ATMs** get the same exchange rate as credit cards, but there is often a limit on the amount of money you can withdraw per day (around US$500), and the computer networks sometimes fail. There is typically a surcharge of US$1-5 per withdrawal. **Debit cards** are a relatively new form of purchasing power that are as convenient as credit cards but have a more immediate impact on your funds. A debit card can be used wherever its associated credit card company (usually Mastercard or Visa) is accepted, but the money is withdrawn directly from the holder's checking account. Debit cards often also function as ATM cards and can be used to withdraw cash from associated banks and ATMs throughout Eastern Europe. To locate ATMs around the world, consult the two major international money networks: **Cirrus** (US ☎ 800-424-7787; www.mastercard.com/atm) and **PLUS** (US ☎ 800-843-7587; www.visa.com/pd/atm). Cirrus is linked to Mastercard, while PLUS is linked to Visa. In this book, any ATM labeled "MC" takes cards linked to Cirrus, while any ATM labeled "V" takes PLUS cards.

PIN NUMBERS AND ATMS. To use a cash or credit card to withdraw money from an ATM in Eastern Europe, you must have a four-digit **Personal Identification Number (PIN).** If your PIN is longer than four digits, ask your bank whether you can just use the first four, or whether you'll need a new one. **Credit cards** don't usually come with PINs, so if you intend to hit up ATMs in Eastern Europe with a credit card to get cash advances, call your company before leaving to request one. People with alphabetic, rather than numeric, PINs may also be thrown off by the lack of letters on European cash machines. Use these corresponding numbers: 1=QZ; 2=ABC; 3=DEF; 4=GHI; 5=JKL; 6=MNO; 7=PRS; 8=TUV; and 9=WXY. Note that if you mistakenly punch the wrong code into the machine three times, it will swallow your card for good.

GETTING MONEY FROM HOME

If you run out of money while traveling, the easiest and cheapest solution is to have someone back home make a deposit to your credit or ATM card. Failing that, consider one of the following options:

WIRING MONEY. It is possible to arrange a **bank money transfer,** which means asking a bank back home to wire money to a bank abroad. This is the cheapest way to transfer cash, but it's also the slowest, usually taking several days or more, and especially difficult with a language barrier. Note that some banks may only release your funds in local currency, potentially sticking you with a poor exchange rate; inquire about this in advance. Money transfer services like **Western Union** are faster and more convenient than bank transfers—but also much pricier. Western Union has many locations worldwide. For more info, visit www.westernunion.com or call ☎ 800 501 500 in Australia, 800-235-0000 in Canada, 800 27 0000 in New Zealand, 0860 100031 in South Africa, 0800 83 38 33 in the UK, or 800-325-6000 in the US. **American Express** and **Thomas Cook** offices also handle money transfers.

US STATE DEPARTMENT (US CITIZENS ONLY). In emergencies, US citizens can have money sent via the State Department. For US$15, they will forward money within hours to the nearest consular office, which will disburse it according to instructions. The office serves only Americans in dire circumstances abroad; non-American travelers should contact their embassies for information on wiring cash. Contact the Overseas Citizens Service, American Citizens Services, Consular Affairs, Room 4811, US Department of State, Washington, D.C. 20520 (☎ 202-647-5225; nights, Sundays, and holidays 647-4000; fax (on demand only) 647-3000; http://travel.state.gov).

THE ART OF THE DEAL Bargaining in Eastern Europe is common: prices are often not set in stone, and vendors and drivers will automatically quote you a price that is several times too high; it's up to you to get them down to a reasonable rate. With the following tips and some finesse, you might be able to impress even the most hardened hawkers and get yourself a better deal:

1. Know when to bargain. In most cases, it's quite clear when it's appropriate to bargain. Things for sale in outdoor markets are all fair game. Don't bargain with street food vendors or in restaurants. When in doubt, ask tactfully, "Is that your lowest price?" or whether discounts are given.

2. Start low. Never feel guilty offering what seems to be a ridiculously low price. Your starting price should be no more than one-third to one-half the asking price.

3. Bargaining needn't be a fierce struggle laced with barbs. Quite the opposite: good-natured wrangling with a cheerful smiling face may prove your biggest weapon.

4. Use your poker face. The less your face betrays your interest in the item, the better. Never get too enthusiastic about the object in question; point out flaws in workmanship and design while remaining respectful of the vendor's work. Be cool.

5. Know when to turn away. Feel free to refuse any vendor or driver who bargains rudely, and don't hesitate to move on to another vendor if one will not be reasonable about the final price he offers. However, to start bargaining without an intention to buy is a major *faux pas*. Turn away slowly with a smile and "thank you" upon hearing a ridiculous price—the price may plummet.

TIPS FOR SAVING MONEY

Eastern Europe is the budget traveler's paradise. The price of a hostel in London equals that of a quality hotel in most of Eastern Europe, while local restaurants and transportation services charge a fraction of their western counterparts. Often the difference of a couple US$ or EUR€ in price means an improvement by leaps and bounds in quality. Nonetheless, some simple ways to cut down costs include searching out opportunities for free entertainment, splitting accommodation and food costs with other trustworthy fellow travelers, and buying food in **supermarkets** rather than eating out. Bring a **sleepsack** (see p. 36) to save on linen charges in hostels and some hotels, and do your **laundry** in the sink (unless you're explicitly prohibited from doing so). Though staying within your budget is important, don't do so at the expense of your health or a fantastic travel experience.

SAFETY AND SECURITY

Eastern Europe is generally regarded as a safe region for travel. The Czech Republic and Poland, for example, are as safe as—if not safer than—Western Europe and are far removed from the situations in the Balkans and Russia. In most countries, crime is restricted primarily to pickpocketing on crowded streets and public transportation. For concerns specific to individual regions, see the **Essentials: Health and Safety** section of each country chapter.

BLENDING IN. Consider dressing like an Eastern European. For women, that means skirts rather than shorts, and for both men and women, avoiding baggy jeans, sneakers, and sandals, as well as flashy, brightly colored clothing. Bring a head covering for church and monastery visits. Backpacks also stand out as particularly touristy; courier or shoulder bags are less likely to draw attention. Familiarize yourself with your surroundings before setting out; if you must check

LET'S (NOT) GO: TRAVEL WARNINGS. The US State Department issues **Travel Warnings** against unnecessary travel to politically unstable or dangerous regions. In 2002, Travel Warnings were updated for **Macedonia**, for **Kosovo** and its environs, for the Yugoslav provinces of **Serbia** and **Montenegro**, and for **Albania.** As a result of incidents of violence targeted at both Americans and other foreigners, a June 2002 warning (see p. 80) cautions persons traveling in certain regions of **Bosnia and Herzegovina**, including Mostar, Medjugorje, Grude, Posusje, Livno, Tomislavgrad, Republika Srpska, and Siroki Brijeg. Other regional warnings have been issued as well: the State Department cautions travelers to the **Transdniester** region of Moldova and **Eastern Slavonia** in Croatia, and warns against travel to the **Chechnya** province and bordering areas in Russia. Due to the regional unrest and at the advice of the State Department, *Let's Go* was unable to send researchers for the 2003 guide to Serbia and Montenegro, Macedonia, Kosovo, and Albania. The following government offices provide travel information and advisories by telephone, by fax, or via the web:

Australian Department of Foreign Affairs and Trade: ☎ 300 555 135; fax 02 6261 1299; www.dfat.gov.au.

Canadian Department of Foreign Affairs and International Trade (DFAIT): In Canada and the US call ☎ 800-267-6788, elsewhere call +1-613-944-6788; www.dfait-maeci.gc.ca. Call for their free booklet, *Bon Voyage...But.*

New Zealand Ministry of Foreign Affairs: ☎ 04 494 8500; fax 494 8506; www.mft.govt.nz/trav.html.

United Kingdom Foreign and Commonwealth Office: ☎ 020 7008 0232; fax 7008 0155; www.fco.gov.uk.

US Department of State: ☎ 202-647-5225; fax 647-3000; www.travel.state.gov. For *A Safe Trip Abroad,* call ☎ 512-1800.

a map on the street, duck into a cafe or shop. Most importantly, carry yourself with confidence. If you are traveling solo, be sure that someone at home knows your itinerary and **never admit that you're traveling alone.**

AVOIDING HAZARDS. As much as you may be tempted, do not "explore" in Bosnia and Croatia; the countryside is littered with landmines and unexploded ordnance (UXO). While de-mining is underway, it will be years before all the mines are removed. UXOs are not a danger on paved roads or in major cities. Road shoulders and abandoned buildings are particularly likely to harbor UXOs.

TERRORISM. As a result of September 11, airports throughout the world have heightened security measures. Terrorist acts are rare in Eastern Europe, and potentially violent situations are confined to Russia and the Balkan states of Bosnia and Herzegovina, the former Yugoslavia, Macedonia, and Albania. Russian terrorism has been blamed on the Chechen separatists, a largely Muslim ethnic group in the Russian Caucasus region. Their drawn-out fight for independence from Moscow has attracted Muslim militants from around the world, and they reportedly have connections with the terrorist group al-Qaeda. The US Department of State strongly warns against travel to Chechnya and surrounding areas.

SELF DEFENSE. There is no sure-fire way to avoid all the threatening situations you might encounter while you travel, but a good self-defense course will give you concrete ways to react in a dangerous situation. **Impact, Prepare, and Model Mug-**

ging lists local self-defense courses in the US (☎ 800-345-5425). Visit the website at www.impactsafety.org/chapters.htm for chapters around the world. Workshops for both men and women (2-3hr.) start at US$50; full courses run US$350-500.

PROTECTING YOUR VALUABLES. There are a few steps you can take to minimize the financial risk associated with traveling. First, **bring as little with you as possible.** Second, buy a few combination **padlocks** to secure your belongings either in your pack, a hostel, or a locker. Never leave your belongings unattended or unsecured; crime occurs in even the most friendly-looking hostel or hotel. Third, **carry as little cash as possible.** Keep your traveler's checks and ATM/credit cards in a **money belt**—not a fanny pack, but rather a pouch worn under clothing—along with your passport and ID cards. Fourth, **keep a small cash reserve separate from your primary stash.** This should be about US$50-100 secured in the depths of your pack, along with your traveler's check numbers and photocopies of important documents.

CON ARTISTS AND PICKPOCKETS. Con artists are most prevalent in large cities. They often work in groups, and children are among the most effective. Beware of certain classics: sob stories that require money, rolls of bills "found" on the street, mustard spilled (or saliva spit) on your shoulder to distract you while they snatch your bag. Don't ever hand over your passport to someone whose authority you question (ask to accompany them to a police station if they insist), and **never let your passport or your bags out of your sight.** In city crowds and especially on public transportation, pickpockets are amazingly swift. Stay alert in public telephone booths. If you must say your calling card number, do so very quietly; if you punch it in, make sure no one can look over your shoulder.

PUBLIC TRANSPORTATION. On **buses** carry your backpack in front of you where you can see it and lock each compartment. Similarly, don't check baggage on **trains,** and don't trust anyone to "watch your bag for a second." Thieves thrive on trains; professionals wait for tourists to fall asleep and then carry off everything they can. When traveling in a group, sleep in alternating shifts; when alone, use good judgment in selecting a compartment and never stay in an empty one. Keep important documents and other valuables on your body and try to sleep on top bunks with the luggage locked and stored in a nearby overhead compartment (if not in bed with you). In **Russia,** try to sleep on bottom bunks where luggage is stored in a lower compartment; the only way to lift it is by moving you. Theft occurs most frequently on trains between major cities (e.g. Moscow-St. Petersburg or Prague-Warsaw) than on local trains.

DRUGS

Remember that you are subject to the laws of the country in which you travel, not to those of your home country. Throughout Eastern Europe, all recreational drugs—including marijuana—are illegal, and often carry a much heavier jail sentence than in the West. For more specific information on the drug laws of Eastern European countries, consult the website at the US State Department's Bureau for International Narcotics and Law Enforcement Affairs (www.state.gov/g/inl/). If you carry **prescription drugs** while you travel, bring a copy of the prescriptions themselves and a note from a doctor.

HEALTH

Common sense is the simplest prescription for good health while you travel. Travelers complain most often about their feet and their stomach, so take precautionary measures: drink lots of fluids to prevent dehydration and constipation; wear sturdy, broken-in shoes and clean socks; and use talcum powder to keep your feet dry. Since tap water quality in Eastern Europe is highly variable depending on region, it is a good idea to buy bottled water or to boil your own.

BEFORE YOU GO

In your **passport**, write the names of any people you wish to be contacted in case of a medical emergency, and also list any allergies or medical conditions of which you would want doctors to be aware. Matching a **prescription** to a foreign equivalent is not always easy, safe, or possible. Carry up-to-date, legible prescriptions or a statement from your doctor stating the medication's trade name, manufacturer, chemical name, and dosage. While traveling, be sure to keep all medication with you in your carry-on luggage.

IMMUNIZATIONS AND PRECAUTIONS

Take a look at your immunization records before you go. Travelers should be sure that the following vaccines are up to date: **MMR** (for measles, mumps, and rubella), **DTaP** or **Td** (for diphtheria, tetanus, and pertussis), **OPV** (for polio), **HbCV** (for haemophilus influenza B), and **HBV** (for hepatitis B). Adults traveling to the CIS should consider getting an additional dose of **polio** vaccine if they have not already had one during their adult years. **Hepatitis A** vaccine and/or immune globulin (IG) is recommended for all travelers to Eastern Europe. A **certificate of yellow fever vaccination** may be required for entry if you are coming from a tropical South American or sub-Saharan African country. If you will be spending more than four weeks in Eastern Europe, you should be vaccinated for **typhoid.** Belarus, Moldova, Russia, and Ukraine all require documentation verifying that you are **HIV negative** in order to issue visas for periods longer than three months; the Slovak Republic and Hungary require documentation for persons staying longer than one year. In addition, a **rabies** vaccine is recommended due to the many wild dogs in Eastern Europe, especially in Romania. For recommendations on immunizations and prophylaxes, consult the CDC (see below) in the US or the equivalent in your home country.

USEFUL ORGANIZATIONS AND PUBLICATIONS

The US **Centers for Disease Control and Prevention** (**CDC; ☎**877-FYI-TRIP (394-8747); toll-free fax 888-232-3299; www.cdc.gov/travel) maintains an international travelers' hotline and an informative website. The CDC's comprehensive booklet *Health Information for International Travel*, an annual rundown of disease, immunization, and general health advice, is free online or US$25 via the Public Health Foundation (☎877-252-1200). For quick information on health and other travel warnings, call the **Overseas Citizens Services** (☎202-647-5225, after-hours 647-400), or contact a passport agency, embassy, or consulate abroad. US citizens can send a self-addressed, stamped envelope to the Overseas Citizens Services, Bureau of Consular Affairs, #4811, US Department of State, Washington, D.C. 20520. For information on medical evacuation services and travel insurance firms, see the US government's website at http://travel.state.gov/medical.html or the **British Foreign and Commonwealth Office** (www.fco.gov.uk). For a country-by-country overview of diseases and a list of travel clinics in the US, try the **International Travel Health Guide,** by Stuart Rose, (www.travmed.com).

MEDICAL ASSISTANCE WHILE TRAVELING

The quality and availability of medical assistance varies greatly throughout Eastern Europe. In major cities such as Prague or Budapest, there are generally English-speaking medical centers or hospitals for foreigners; the care there tends to be better than elsewhere in the region. In the countryside and in relatively untouristed countries such as Belarus, English-speaking facilities are virtually impossible to find. First go to your embassy for emergency aid and recommendations. Tourist offices may sometimes have names of local doctors who speak English. In general, the medical service in these regions is uncertain at best, as very few hospitals are maintained at Western standards. In these countries, private hospitals will generally have better facilities than the state-operated hospitals.

ESSENTIALS

If you are concerned about being able to access medical support while traveling, there are special support services you may employ. The *MedPass* from **GlobalCare, Inc.,** 6875 Shiloh Rd. E., Alpharetta, GA 30005-8732, USA (☎800-860-1111; fax 678-341-1800; www.globalems.com), provides 24hr. international medical assistance, support, and medical evacuation resources. The **International Association for Medical Assistance to Travelers (IAMAT;** US ☎716-754-4883, Canada 416-652-0137; www.iamat.org) has free membership and lists English-speaking doctors worldwide. If your **insurance** policy does not cover travel abroad, you may wish to purchase additional coverage. Those with medical conditions (diabetes, allergies to antibiotics, epilepsy, heart conditions) may want to obtain a stainless-steel **Medic Alert ID Tag** (first year US$35, annually thereafter US$20), which identifies the condition and gives a 24hr. collect-call number. Contact the Medic Alert Foundation, 2323 Colorado Ave; Turlock, CA 95382, USA (☎888-633-4298, outside US 209-668-3333; www.medicalert.org).

ONCE IN EASTERN EUROPE

ENVIRONMENTAL HAZARDS

Heat Exhaustion and Dehydration: Heat exhaustion can lead to fatigue, headaches, and wooziness. Drink plenty of fluids and avoid consuming salty foods (e.g. crackers) and dehydrating beverages, such as those containing alcohol and caffeine. Continuous heat stress can eventually lead to heatstroke, a far more serious condition which is indicated by a rising body temperature, severe headache, and cessation of sweating. Cool off victims with wet towels and seek immediate medical assistance.

Hypothermia and Frostbite: Winter in Eastern Europe can be extremely cold, and mountainous regions are often freezing even in summer. A rapid drop in body temperature is the clearest sign of overexposure to cold. Victims may also shiver, feel exhausted, have poor coordination or slurred speech, hallucinate, or suffer amnesia. *Do not let hypothermia victims fall asleep,* or their body temperature will continue to drop and they may die. Synthetic and wool fabric help retain heat in wet weather, while most other fabrics—particularly cotton—will make you colder. If skin turns white, waxy, and cold, do not rub the area. Instead, drink warm beverages, get dry, and slowly warm the area with dry fabric or steady body contact until a doctor can be found.

High Altitude: At high altitudes, such as in the Tatras, allow your body a couple of days to adjust to less oxygen before exerting yourself. Note that alcohol is more potent and UV rays are stronger at high elevations.

INSECT-BORNE DISEASES

Many diseases are transmitted by insects—mainly mosquitoes, fleas, ticks, and lice. Be aware of insects in wet or forested areas, especially while hiking and camping; wear long pants and long sleeves, tuck your pants into your socks, and buy a mosquito net. Use insect repellents such as DEET and soak or spray your gear with permethrin (licensed in the US for use on clothing).

Tick-Bourne Encephalitis: A viral infection of the central nervous system transmitted by tick bites or by the consumption of unpasteurized dairy products. Occurs in wooded areas of Bosnia and Herzegovina, Bulgaria, the Czech Republic, Hungary, Poland, Romania, the Slovak Republic, the former Soviet Union, and former Yugoslavia. The risk of contracting the disease is low when precautions are taken against ticks.

Lyme Disease: A bacterial infection carried by ticks and marked by a circular bull's-eye rash of 2cm or more. Later symptoms include fever, headache, fatigue, and aches and pains. Antibiotics are effective if administered early. Left untreated, Lyme can cause problems in the joints, the heart, and the nervous system. If you find a tick, grasp the head with tweezers as close to your skin as possible and apply slow, steady traction. Removing a tick within 24 hours greatly reduces the risk of infection. Do not remove ticks by burning them or by coating them with nail polish remover or petroleum jelly.

Other Insect-Borne Diseases: Filariasis is a roundworm infestation transmitted by mosquitoes. Infection causes enlargement of extremities and has no vaccine. **Leishmaniasis,** a parasite transmitted by sand flies, can occur in most parts of Eastern Europe. Common symptoms are fever, weakness, and swelling of the spleen. There is a treatment, but no vaccine.

FOOD- AND WATER-BORNE DISEASES

If you do get sick while visiting Eastern Europe, it will probably be a result of something you ate or drank. A diet high in meat and proteins and low in vegetables and fibers will sometimes induce cases of severe constipation. Prevention is the best cure: be sure that your food is properly cooked and the water you drink is clean. Peel fruits and veggies and avoid tap water (including ice cubes and anything washed in tap water, like salad). Watch out for food from markets or street vendors that may have been cooked in unhygienic conditions. Other common causes of illness include raw shellfish, unpasteurized dairy products, and sauces containing raw eggs. Buy imported bottled water, or purify your own water by bringing it to a rolling boil or treating it with **iodine tablets;** note however that some parasites such as *giardia* resist iodine treatment, so boiling is more reliable.

Cholera: An intestinal disease caused by a bacteria found in contaminated food. Symptoms include diarrhea, dehydration, vomiting, and muscle cramps. See a doctor immediately; if left untreated, cholera may be deadly. Antibiotics are available, but the most important treatment is rehydration. Travelers are at risk for cholera in Moldova, Russia, and Ukraine. Consider getting a vaccine (50% effective) if you have stomach problems (e.g. ulcers) or will be in an area where water is unreliable. The CDC maintains an active website monitoring regional outbreaks of cholera (www.cdc.gov/travel/diseases.html).

Dysentery: Results from a serious intestinal infection caused by certain bacteria. The most common type is bacillary dysentery, also called shigellosis. Symptoms include bloody diarrhea (sometimes mixed with mucus), fever, and abdominal pain and tenderness. Bacillary dysentery generally only lasts a week, but it is highly contagious. Amoebic dysentery, which develops more slowly, is a more serious disease and may cause long-term damage if left untreated. Dysentery can be treated with the drugs norfloxacin or ciprofloxacin (commonly known as Cipro). A stool test can determine which kind you have; seek medical help immediately.

Hepatitis A: A viral infection of the liver acquired primarily through contaminated water. Symptoms include fatigue, fever, loss of appetite, nausea, dark urine, jaundice, vomiting, aches and pains, and light stools. Visitors to Eastern Europe are at risk of contracting the infection; the risk is highest in rural areas and the countryside, but it may also be present in urban areas. Ask your doctor about the vaccine (Havrix or Vaqta) or an injection of immune globulin (IG; formerly called gamma globulin).

Parasites: Microbes, tapeworms, etc. that hide in unsafe water and food. **Giardiasis,** for example, is acquired by drinking untreated water from streams or lakes. Symptoms include swollen glands or lymph nodes, fever, rashes or itchiness, digestive problems, eye problems, and anemia. Boil water, wear shoes, avoid bugs, and eat only cooked food.

Traveler's Diarrhea: There is a high occurrence of traveler's diarrhea among visitors to Eastern Europe, resulting from drinking untreated water or eating uncooked foods. It also indicates a temporary (and fairly common) reaction of the body to the bacteria in new food ingredients. Symptoms include nausea, bloating, urgency, and malaise. Try non-sugary foods with protein and carbohydrates to keep your strength up. Over-the-counter anti-diarrheals (e.g. Imodium) may counteract diarrhea, but can complicate serious infections. The most dangerous side effect is dehydration; drink 8 oz. of water with ½ tsp. of sugar or honey and a pinch of salt or uncaffeinated soft drinks, or eat salted crackers. If you develop a fever or your symptoms don't go away after 4-5 days, consult a doctor. Consult a doctor immediately for treatment of diarrhea in children.

Typhoid Fever: Caused by the salmonella bacteria; common in villages and rural areas in the developing countries of Eastern Europe. A vaccine is required for a stay longer than four weeks. While mostly transmitted through contaminated food and water, it may also be acquired by direct contact with another person. Early symptoms include fever, headaches, fatigue, loss of appetite, constipation, and sometimes a rash on the abdomen or chest. Antibiotics can treat typhoid, but a vaccination is recommended.

OTHER INFECTIOUS DISEASES

Diphtheria: The 1990s saw a massive diphtheria outbreak in the former Soviet Union, and travelers to this area are still at risk for this highly infectious disease. Early symptoms, including severe sore throat, swollen lymph nodes, and slight fever, can lead to heart failure, difficulty breathing, paralysis, and death. Be up-to-date on diphtheria vaccinations before traveling to the former USSR.

Hepatitis B: A viral infection of the liver, transmitted via bodily fluids or needle sharing. Symptoms may not surface until years after infection. A 3-shot vaccination sequence is recommended for health-care workers, sexually active travelers, and anyone planning to seek medical treatment abroad; it must begin 6 months before traveling.

Hepatitis C: Like Hepatitis B, but the mode of transmission differs. IV drug users, those with occupational exposure to blood, hemodialysis patients, and recipients of blood transfusions are at the highest risk, but the disease can also be spread through sexual contact or sharing items like razors and toothbrushes that may have traces of blood on them. No vaccine is available.

Rabies: Transmitted through the saliva of infected animals; fatal if untreated. By the time symptoms appear (thirst and muscle spasms), the disease is in its terminal stage. If you are bitten, wash the wound thoroughly, seek immediate medical care, and try to have the animal located. A rabies vaccine, which consists of 3 shots given over a 21-day period, is available, but is only semi-effective. Those who will be exposed to or handling wild animals should consider getting the vaccine.

Tuberculosis: After a long period of decline, tuberculosis (TB) is currently on the rise throughout Eastern Europe. Symptoms include fever, a persistent cough, and bloody phlegm. TB is transmitted via coughing; infectious droplets can hang in the air for hours. If untreated, the disease is fatal; usually, however, it will respond to antibiotics. If you think you are infected, tell your doctor you have been to Eastern Europe recently, as the recent return of TB indicates a drug-resistant strain that requires special treatment.

AIDS, HIV, AND STDS

The Council on International Educational Exchange's pamphlet, **Travel Safe: AIDS and International Travel,** is posted on their website (www.ciee.org/travel-safe.cfm), along with links to other online and phone resources. Several countries in Eastern Europe (including Belarus, Bulgaria, Moldova, Russia, and Ukraine) screen incoming travelers for AIDS, primarily those planning extended visits for work or study; some of these countries will deny entrance to those who test HIV-positive. The US State Department maintains a relatively current listing of HIV testing requirements in foreign countries (http://

travel.state.gov/HIVtestingreqs.html). **Sexually transmitted diseases (STDs)** such as gonorrhea, chlamydia, genital warts, syphilis, and herpes are easier to catch than HIV and can be just as deadly. **Hepatitis** B and C can also be transmitted sexually (see above). Though condoms may protect you from some STDs, oral or even tactile contact can lead to transmission. If you think you may have contracted an STD, see a doctor immediately.

WOMEN'S HEALTH

Women traveling in unsanitary conditions are vulnerable to **urinary tract** and **bladder infections,** common and very uncomfortable bacterial conditions that cause a burning sensation and painful (sometimes frequent) urination. If symptoms persist, see a doctor. **Vaginal yeast infections** may flare up in hot and humid climates. Wearing loosely fitting trousers or a skirt and cotton underwear will help, as will over-the-counter remedies like Monistat or Gynelotrimin. Bring supplies from home if you are prone to infection, as they are difficult to find in much of Eastern Europe. **Tampons** and **pads** are sometimes hard to find in areas of Eastern Europe; often, only non-applicator tampons are available. It's advisable to take supplies along. **Reliable contraceptive devices** may also be difficult to find. Women on birth control pills should bring enough to allow for possible loss or extended stays. Bring a prescription, since forms of the pill vary a good deal. Though condoms are increasingly available throughout the region, you might want to stock up on your favorite brand before you go, as they are usually expensive and variable in quality.

INSURANCE

Travel insurance generally covers four basic areas: medical/health problems, property loss, trip cancellation/interruption, and emergency evacuation. Although your regular insurance policies may well extend to travel-related accidents, you might consider purchasing travel insurance if the cost of potential trip cancellation/interruption or emergency medical evacuation is greater than you can absorb. Full travel insurance purchased separately generally runs about US$50 per week for full coverage, while trip cancellation/interruption may be purchased separately at a rate of about US$5.50 per US$100 of coverage. **Medical insurance** (especially university policies) often covers costs incurred abroad; check with your provider. **US Medicare** does not cover foreign travel. **Canadians** are protected by their home province's health insurance plan for up to 90 days after leaving the country; check with the provincial Ministry of Health or Health Plan Headquarters for details. **Homeowners' insurance** (or your family's coverage) often covers theft during travel and loss of travel documents (passport, plane ticket, railpass, etc.) up to US$500.

ISIC INSURANCE. ISIC and **ITIC** (see p. 24) provide basic insurance benefits, including US$100 per day of in-hospital care for up to 60 days, US$3000 of accident-related medical reimbursement, and US$25,000 for emergency medical transport. Cardholders have access to a toll-free 24hr. helpline (run by the insurance provider **TravelGuard**) for medical, legal, and financial emergencies overseas (US and Canada ☎ 877-370-4742, elsewhere US collect ☎ 715-345-0505). **American Express** (US ☎ 800-528-4800) grants most cardholders automatic car rental insurance (collision and theft, but not liability) and ground travel accident coverage of US$100,000 on flight purchases made with the card.

INSURANCE PROVIDERS. Council and **STA** (see p. 49) offer a range of plans that can supplement your basic coverage. Other private providers in the US and Canada include: **Access America** (☎800-284-8300; www.accessamerica.com), **Berkely Group/Carefree Travel Insurance** (☎800-323-3149; www.berkely.com), **Globalcare Travel Insurance** (☎800-821-2488; www.globalcare-cocco.com), and **Travel Assistance International** (☎800-821-2828; www.travelassistance.com). In the **UK**, try **Columbus Direct** (☎020 7375 0011; www.columbusdirect.net). In **Australia**, contact **AFTA** (☎02 9375 4955).

PACKING

Pack lightly. Lay out only what you absolutely need, then take half the clothes and twice the money. If you plan on doing a lot of travel in the outdoors, see **Camping and the Outdoors,** p. 40.

LUGGAGE. If you plan to cover most of your itinerary by foot, a sturdy **frame backpack** is unbeatable. Toting a **suitcase** or **trunk** is fine if you plan to live in one or two cities and explore from there, but a very bad idea if you're going to be moving around a lot. In addition to your main piece of luggage, a **daypack** (a small backpack or courier bag, and never a fanny pack) is a must.

CLOTHING. Eastern European climate is highly variable from region to region, so be prepared for all kinds of weather. No matter when you're traveling, it's always a good idea to bring a **warm jacket** or wool sweater, a **rain jacket** (Gore-Tex® is both waterproof and breathable), sturdy shoes or **hiking boots**, and **thick socks**. **Flip-flops** or waterproof sandals are must-haves for grubby hostel showers. Bring a head covering for monastery visits. Black boots are acceptable everywhere; sneakers are rare, as are sandals, except for along the Dalmatian Coast in Croatia.

CONTACT LENSES. Contact lenses will prove expensive and difficult to find, so bring enough extra pairs and solution for your entire trip. Also bring your glasses and a copy of your prescription in case you need emergency replacements.

SLEEPSACK. Some hostels in Eastern Europe require that you either provide your own linen or rent sheets from them. Save cash by making your own sleepsack: fold a full-size sheet in half the long way, then sew it closed along the long side and one of the short sides.

CONVERTERS AND ADAPTERS. Throughout Eastern Europe, electricity is 220 volts, enough to fry any 110V North American appliance. **Americans** and **Canadians** should buy an **adapter** (which changes the shape of the plug) and a **converter** (which changes the voltage; US$20). Don't make the mistake of using only an adapter (unless appliance instructions explicitly state otherwise). **New Zealanders** and **South Africans** (who both use 220V at home) as well as **Australians** (who use 240/250V) won't need a converter, but they will need a set of adapters to use anything electrical. Check out http://kropla.com/electric.htm for more information.

FIRST-AID KIT. For a basic first-aid kit, pack: bandages, pain reliever, antibiotic cream, a thermometer, a Swiss Army knife, tweezers, moleskin, decongestant, motion-sickness remedy, diarrhea or upset-stomach medication (Pepto Bismol or Imodium), an antihistamine, sunscreen, insect repellent, and burn ointment.

OTHER USEFUL ITEMS. For safety purposes, you should bring a **money belt** and small **padlock**. Basic **outdoors equipment** (plastic water bottle, compass, waterproof matches, pocketknife, sunglasses, sunscreen, hat) may also prove useful. **Other things** you're liable to forget: an umbrella; sealable **plastic bags** (for damp clothes, soap, food, shampoo, and other spillables); an **alarm clock;** safety pins; rubber bands; a flashlight; earplugs; garbage bags; and a small **calculator**.

ACCOMMODATIONS

HOSTELS

Hostels generally have the layout of a dormitory and are equipped with large single-sex rooms and bunk beds, although a small number do offer private rooms for families and couples. They sometimes have kitchens and utensils for your use, bike rentals, storage areas, and laundry facilities. There can be drawbacks to the hostel stay, however: some hostels close during certain daytime "lockout" hours, have a curfew, don't accept reservations, impose a maximum stay, require a minimum stay, or less frequently, require that you do chores. In Eastern Europe, a bed in any sort of hostel will usually cost you US$5-15.

HOSTELLING INTERNATIONAL

Joining the youth hostel association in your own country (listed below) automatically grants you membership privileges in **Hostelling International (HI)**, a federation of national hosteling associations. HI hostels are scattered irregularly throughout Eastern Europe, but if you will be spending time in the more Westernized countries of Poland and the Czech Republic, getting an HI card is a worthwhile investment. Hostels in Croatia, the Czech Republic, Estonia, Hungary, and Lithuania accept reservations via the **International Booking Network** (☎ 202-783-6161; www.hostelbooking.com). HI's web page (www.iyhf.org), which lists the web addresses and phone numbers of all national associations, is a great place to begin researching hostels in a specific region. Other comprehensive hosteling websites include www.hostels.com and www.hostelplanet.com. **Guest memberships** are not valid in much of Eastern Europe, but it is a good idea to ask anyway. Most student travel agencies (see p. 49) sell HI cards, as do all of the national hosteling organizations listed below. All prices listed below are valid for **one-year memberships,** unless otherwise noted.

An Óige (Irish Youth Hostel Association), 61 Mountjoy St., Dublin 7 (☎ 01 830 4555; www.irelandyha.org). EUR€12.70, under 18 EUR€5.

Australian Youth Hostels Association (AYHA), Level 3, 10 Mallett St., Camperdown NSW 2050 (☎ 02 9565 1699; www.yha.org.au). AUS$52, under 18 AUS$16.

Hostelling International-American Youth Hostels (HI-AYH), 733 15th St. NW, #840, Washington, D.C. 20005 (☎ 202-783-6161; www.hiayh.org). US$25, under 18 free.

Hostelling International-Canada (HI-C), 400-205 Catherine St., Ottawa, ON K2P 1C3 (☎ 800-663-5777; www.hihostels.ca). CDN$35, under 18 free.

Hostelling International Northern Ireland (HINI), 22-32 Donegall Rd., Belfast BT12 5JN, Northern Ireland (☎ 02890 31 54 35; www.hini.org.uk). UK£10, under 18 UK£6.

Hostels Association of South Africa, 73 St. George's House, 3rd fl., P.O. Box 4402, Cape Town 8000 (☎ 021 424 2511; www.hisa.org.za). ZAR55, under 18 ZAR30.

Scottish Youth Hostels Association (SYHA), 7 Glebe Crescent, Stirling FK8 2JA (☎ 01786 89 14 00; www.syha.org.uk). UK£6.

Youth Hostels Association of New Zealand (YHANZ), P.O. Box 436, 193 Cashel St., Union House, Christchurch (☎ 03 379 9970; www.yha.org.nz). NZ$40, under 17 free.

Youth Hostels Association (England and Wales) Ltd., Trevelyan House, Dimple Road, Matlock, Devonshire, DE4 3YH (☎ 01 629 59 26 00; www.yha.org.uk). UK£13, under 18 UK£6.50, families UK£26.

HOTELS AND GUESTHOUSES

Hotel singles in Eastern Europe cost about US$15-30 per night, doubles US$20-60. You'll typically share a hall bathroom; a private bathroom will cost extra, as may hot showers. Smaller **guest houses** and **pensions** are often cheaper than hotels. Not all hotels take reservations, and few accept checks in foreign currency. After hostels, pensions are the most common budget accommodation in Eastern Europe. A cross between a hostel and a hotel, a pension is generally intimate and run by a family, similar to a bed and breakfast. They usually rent by the room, although they occasionally offer dorm-style accommodations. Pensions are often the cleanest, safest, and friendliest budget accommodations available, with the owners going out of their way to arrange private excursions and help with such daily chores as doing laundry, checking e-mail, and communicating with locals. In Eastern Europe, a single room in a pension runs US$10-20.

UNIVERSITY DORMS

Many colleges and universities open their residence halls to travelers when school is not in session; some do so even during term-time. Usually situated amid student centers, these dorms often prove to be invaluable sources on things to do in and around the city. Getting a room may take a couple of phone calls and require advanced planning, but the hassle can be worth it. Rates tend to be low, and many offer free local calls. *Let's Go* lists colleges that rent rooms among the accommodations for appropriate cities; local tourist offices can often provide more information about this option.

PRIVATE ROOMS AND HOMESTAYS

PRIVATE ROOMS

An increasingly popular option in out-of-the-way locations is to rent a room in a private home. Families throughout Eastern Europe rent out spare bedrooms to weary backpackers. Although it may seem dangerous at first, going home with an old woman *(babushka)* from the train station or knocking on doors with *Zimmer Frei* signs is absolutely legitimate, generally reliable, and often preferable to staying in a hostel. In small towns, private homes may well be the only option and offer added perks such as immaculate rooms, laundry, home-cooked meals, and a native tour guide. Prices vary but tend to hover between hostel and pension prices.

HOME EXCHANGES AND HOME RENTALS

Home exchanges offer the traveler various types of homes (houses, apartments, condominiums, villas, and even castles in some cases), plus the opportunity to live like a native and to cut down on accommodation fees. For more information, contact the following numbers.

HomeExchange.Com, P.O. Box 30085, Santa Barbara, CA 93130, USA (☎800-877-8723; fax 310-798-3865; www.homeexchange.com). Includes listings from the Czech Republic, Estonia, Hungary, Latvia, Poland, Russia, and the former Yugoslavia.

Intervac International Home Exchange (www.intervac.com). Has 2 offices in Eastern Europe. **Intervac Czech Republic,** Antonin and Lenka Machackovi, Pod Stanici 25/603, 10200 Prague 10/CSFR, CZR (☎0271 96 16 47; fax 786 00 61); **Intervac Poland,** Ewa and Stanisław Krupscy, ul. Mackiewicza 12, 31-213 Krakow, POL (☎012 415 18 18; fax 415 14 14; york@kraknet.pl).

The Invented City: International Home Exchange, 41 Sutter St., Suite 1090, San Francisco, CA 94104, USA (in the US ☎800-788-2489, elsewhere call the US collect 415-252-1141; www.invented-city.com). For US$40, you get your offer listed for one year and unlimited access to a database of thousands of homes.

CAMPING AND THE OUTDOORS

Eastern Europe offers many opportunities for hiking, biking, mountain climbing, camping, trekking, and spelunking. **Camping** is one of the most authentic ways to experience the vacation culture of the region: Eastern Europeans tend to spend their vacations exploring the outdoors. There is, unfortunately, very little English-language literature on outdoor opportunities and adventures in the region. Undiscovered as the Eastern European wilderness is, it's surprisingly difficult to truly rough it. In most countries, camping within the boundaries of national parks is either illegal or heavily restricted; many areas require a camping permit. Check with the local tourist office or locals before setting up camp in an area that's not explicitly designated for camping. Alternately, one can often stay in a **chaty** located within the park interiors; these huts offer dorm-style rooms for US$5-10, running water (not always hot), and some sort of mess hall. **Organized campgrounds** that offer tent space and bungalows are often situated around the borders of parks. All campgrounds have running water; some offer restaurants and other facilities. Tent sites range from US$1-10 per person with a flat tent fee of US$5-10. Bungalow fees hover around US$5-10.

USEFUL PUBLICATIONS AND RESOURCES

For information about camping, hiking, and biking, write or call the publishers listed below to receive a catalog. Travelers planning to camp extensively in Eastern Europe might consider buying an International Camping Carnet. Similar to a hostel membership card, it's required at some campgrounds and provides discounts at many others. It's available in North America from the Family Campers and RVers Association (www.fcrv.org); in the UK, from The Caravan Club (see below). An excellent general resource for travelers planning on camping or spending time in the outdoors is the **Great Outdoor Recreation Pages** (www.gorp.com).

Automobile Association, AA Publishing. Orders and inquiries to TBS Frating Distribution Centre, Colchester, Essex, CO7 7DW, UK (☎01 206 25 56 78; www.theaa.co.uk). Publishes *Caravan and Camping: Europe* (UK£9). They also offer *Road Atlases for Europe*.

The Caravan Club, East Grinstead House, East Grinstead, West Sussex, RH19 1UA, UK (☎01 342 32 69 44; www.caravanclub.co.uk). For UK£27.50, members receive equipment discounts, a 700-page directory and handbook, and a monthly magazine.

The Mountaineers Books, 1001 SW Klickitat Way, #201, Seattle, WA 98134, USA (☎800-553-4453 or 206-223-6303; www.mountaineersbooks.org). Over 400 titles on hiking, biking, mountaineering, natural history, and conservation. Publishes *Trekking in Russia and Central Asia: A Traveler's Guide,* by Frith Maier (US$17).

WILDERNESS SAFETY

Stay warm, stay dry, and stay hydrated. The vast majority of life-threatening wilderness situations can be avoided by following this simple advice. On any hike, however brief, you should pack enough equipment to keep you alive should disaster strike. This includes rain gear, a hat and mittens, a first-aid kit, a reflector, a whistle, high energy food, and extra water. Be sure to check all equipment before setting out. Dress in wool or warm layers of synthetic materials designed for the outdoors. Whenever possible, let someone know when and where you are going hiking: either a friend, your hostel owner, a park ranger, or a local hiking organization. See **Health,** p. 30, for information about outdoor ailments such as heatstroke, dehydration, hypothermia, rabies, and insects, as well as basic medical concerns and first-aid. To read up on wilderness safety, check out *How to Stay Alive in the Woods*, by Bradford Angier (Macmillan Press, US$8).

CAMPING AND HIKING EQUIPMENT
WHAT TO BUY...

Sleeping Bag: Most good sleeping bags are rated by "season," or the lowest outdoor temperature at which they will keep you warm ("summer" means 30-40°F/-1-5°C at night and "four-season" or "winter" usually means below 0°F/-18°C). Sleeping bags are made either of down (warmer and lighter but miserable when wet; US$250-600) or of synthetic material (heavier, more durable, and warmer when wet; US$60-200).

Tent: The best tents are free-standing, containing their own frames and suspension systems; they can be set up quickly and only require staking in high winds. Low-profile dome tents are the best all-around, providing ample internal space and little unnecessary bulk. Good 2-person tents start at US$100, 4-person tents at US$300. Seal the seams with a waterproofing treatment (US$6-15), and make sure it has a rain fly.

Backpack: Internal-frame packs mold better to your back, keep a lower center of gravity, and can flex adequately on difficult hikes that require a lot of bending and maneuvering. Look for a pack with a strong, padded hip belt to transfer weight from your shoulders to your hips. Good packs cost anywhere from US$150 to US$500. Before purchasing a pack, try on a number of styles and add weight to them to test their comfort. Any serious backpacking requires a pack of at least 4000 cubic inches (65L). Allow an additional 500 cubic inches (8L) for your sleeping bag in internal-frame packs. A **waterproof backpack cover** will prove invaluable.

Boots: Be sure to wear hiking boots with good **ankle support.** They should fit snugly and comfortably over one or two pairs of wool socks and a pair of thin liner socks. Break in boots several weeks before setting out in order to spare yourself debilitating blisters.

Other Necessities: Raingear in two pieces, a top and pants, provides better protection than a poncho. **Synthetics,** like polypropylene tops, socks, and long underwear, will keep you warm even when wet. It's a good idea to bring along a **"space blanket,"** which helps you to retain your body heat and doubles as a groundcloth (US$5-15). Plastic **canteens** or water bottles keep water cool and are virtually shatter- and leakproof. Large, collapsible **water sacks** take up less space than bottles and weigh very little when empty. Bring **water-purification tablets** for when you can't boil water. A **first-aid kit, swiss army knife, insect repellent, calamine lotion,** and **waterproof matches** or a **lighter** are also outdoor essentials.

...AND WHERE TO BUY IT

The mail-order and online companies listed below offer lower prices than many retail stores, but a visit to a local camping or outdoors store will give you a good sense of the look and weight of certain items and allow you to check the fit of backpacks or boots.

Campmor, 28 Parkway, P.O. Box 700, Upper Saddle River, NJ 07458, USA (in the US ☎800-525-4784, elsewhere 201-825-8300; www.campmor.com).

Eastern Mountain Sports (EMS), 327 Jaffrey Rd., Peterborough, NH 03458, USA (☎888-463-6367 or 603-924-7231; www.shopems.com).

L.L. Bean, Freeport, ME 04033, USA (in the US and Canada ☎800-441-5713, the UK 0800 891 297, elsewhere call 207-552-3028; www.llbean.com).

Mountain Designs, 51 Bishop Street, Kelvin Grove, Queensland 4089, Australia (☎07 3856 2344; www.mountaindesign.com).

Mountain Equipment Co-op, 130 West Broadway, Vancouver, BC V5Y 1P3, Canada (☎888-847-0770 or 604-709-6241; www.mec.ca).

Recreational Equipment, Inc. (REI), Sumner, WA 98352, USA (☎800-426-4840 or 253-891-2500; www.rei.com).

YHA Adventure Shop, 152-160 Wardour St., London, W1F 8YA, UK (☎020 7025 1900).

KEEPING IN TOUCH

The ease of communication varies widely from country to country. In Central European countries, such as Hungary, Poland, and the Czech Republic, postal and telephone systems are as reliable and efficient as in the US and Western Europe. Even the Russian mail system now offers relatively speedy delivery to the West. However, in Belarus, Bulgaria, and Ukraine—particularly outside the capital cities—postal services are less predictable and should not be depended upon. Phone cards can also be problematic throughout the region: double-check with your phone card carrier before departure in order to ensure that their service will allow you to call home. Like doing many things in Eastern Europe, keeping in touch can be problematic, inefficient, and downright mind boggling. For country-specific information, read **Essentials: Keeping in Touch** in each country chapter.

BY MAIL

SENDING MAIL TO EASTERN EUROPE

Mark envelopes "air mail," "par avion," or air mail in the language of the country in which you are staying, otherwise your letter or postcard will never arrive. If regular airmail is too slow, **Federal Express** (US ☎800-247-4747; www.fedex.com) offers three-day service to the majority of Eastern Europe, though international rates are expensive. **Surface mail** is by far the cheapest way to send mail, though it is also the slowest. It takes one to three months to cross the Atlantic and two to four to cross the Pacific. **General delivery** averages 6-7 days to Eastern Europe. From: **Australia** (5-7 days; postcards AUS$1; letters AUS$1.50 up to 50g; packages AUS$13 up to 0.5kg); **Canada** (6-8 days; postcards/letters CDN$1.25 up to 30g; packages CDN$10 up to 0.5kg); **Ireland** (3-7 days; postcards/letters EUR€0.57 up to 25g; packages EUR€8 up to 0.5kg); **New Zealand** (4-10 days; postcards NZ$1.50; letters NZ$2-5 up to 200g; packages NZ$14.70-16.40 up to 0.5kg); **UK** (3-7 days; postcards/letters UK£0.37 up to 20g; packages UK£3.99 up to 0.5kg); **US** (4-7 days; postcards US$0.70; letters US$0.80 up to 1 oz.; packages US$14 up to 1 lb.).

ESSENTIALS

RECEIVING MAIL IN EASTERN EUROPE

There are several ways to arrange pick-up of letters sent to you by friends and relatives while you are in Eastern Europe.

GENERAL DELIVERY. Mail can be sent to Eastern Europe through **Poste Restante** (the international phrase for General Delivery) to almost any city or town with a post office. While Poste Restante is reliable in most countries, it is unlikely to reach its intended recipient in Belarus, Russia, or Ukraine. Addressing conventions for Poste Restante vary by country; *Let's Go* gives instructions in the **Essentials: Keeping in Touch** section at the beginning of each country's chapter. Be sure to include the street address of the post office on the third line or mail may never reach the recipient. As a rule, it is best to use the largest post office in the area, as mail may be sent there regardless of what is written on the envelope. When possible, it is usually safer and quicker to send mail express or registered—this also ensures that mail will arrive in postally problematic countries. When picking up your mail, bring a passport for identification. There is often no surcharge; if there is a charge, it usually does not exceed the cost of domestic postage. If the clerks insist that there is nothing for you, have them check under your first name as well.

AMERICAN EXPRESS. AmEx's travel offices will act as a mail service for cardholders if contacted in advance. Under this free **Client Letter Service,** they will hold mail for up to 30 days and forward upon request. Some offices will offer these services to non-cardholders (especially those who have purchased AmEx Travelers Cheques), but you must call ahead. *Let's Go* lists AmEx office locations in the **Practical Information** section of most large cities.

TELEPHONES

CALLING TO OR FROM EASTERN EUROPE

 PLACING INTERNATIONAL CALLS. For the international dialing prefixes and country codes of countries in Eastern Europe, see the inside back cover.

1. The **international dialing prefix.** To dial out of **Australia,** dial 0011; **Canada** or the **US,** 011; the **Republic of Ireland, New Zealand,** or the **UK,** 00; **South Africa,** 09.

2. The **country code** of the country you want to call. To call **Australia,** dial 61; **Canada** or the **US,** 1; the **Republic of Ireland,** 353; **New Zealand,** 64; **South Africa,** 27; the **UK,** 44.

3. The **city/area code.** *Let's Go* lists the city/area codes for cities and towns in Eastern Europe opposite the city or town name, next to a ☎. If the first digit is a zero, omit the zero when calling from abroad.

4. The **local number.**

A **calling card** is probably your best and cheapest bet. Calls are billed either collect or to your account. Many companies provide card holders with services that provide legal and medical advice, exchange rate information, and translation services. To obtain a calling card from your national telecommunications service before you leave home, contact the appropriate company below. Be warned, however, that not all calling card companies offer service in every

Eastern European country. It can be particularly difficult to successfully use a calling card in Belarus, Bosnia, Russia, Slovenia, and Ukraine. Before purchasing any calling card, always be sure to compare rates with other cards, and to make sure it serves your needs. *Let's Go* has recently partnered with **ekit.com** to provide a calling card that offers a number of services, including email and voice messaging. For more information, visit **www.letsgo.ekit.com.**

Australia: Telstra **Australia Direct** (☎0213 2200).

Canada: Canada Direct (☎800-561-8868).

Ireland: Telecom Éireann **Ireland Direct** (☎800 40 00 00).

New Zealand: Telecom New Zealand (☎0800 00 00 00).

South Africa: Telkom South Africa (☎0800 012 255).

UK: British Telecom **BT Direct** (☎0800 34 51 44).

US: AT&T (☎800-222-0300); **Sprint** (☎800-877-4646); or **MCI** (☎800-444-3333).

To call home with a calling card, contact the local operator for your service provider by dialing the access numbers listed in the **Essentials: Keeping in Touch** section at the beginning of each country chapter. Not all of these numbers are toll-free; in many countries, phones will require a coin or card deposit to call the operator. Wherever possible, use a calling card for international calls—the long-distance rates for national phone services are often exorbitant. Where available, locally purchased **prepaid phone cards** can be used for direct international calls, but they are still less cost-efficient than calling cards purchased through the service providers listed above. **In-room hotel calls** invariably include an arbitrary and sky-high surcharge, and will sometimes charge you for the call even if you use a calling card.

You can usually make **direct** international calls from pay phones, but if you aren't using a calling card you may need to drop coins at a frenetic pace. If you do dial direct, dial the international access code for the country you're in, then dial the country code of the country you are trying to reach, followed by the local number. **Country codes** include: Australia 61; Ireland 353; New Zealand 64; South Africa 27; UK 44; US and Canada 1. The alternative to dialing direct or using a calling card is to place a **collect call.** To reach an English-speaking operator, you must dial the phone company access number for the country you're in.

CALLING WITHIN EASTERN EUROPE
The simplest way to call within the country is to use a coin-operated phone or to use **prepaid phone cards,** which are slowly phasing out coins in most Eastern European countries. Phone cards carry a certain amount of phone time depending on the card's denomination; the time is measured in minutes or impulses. Phone cards can usually be purchased at tobacco stands, post offices, train stations, and magazine stands. Phone rates tend to be highest in the morning, lower in the evening, and lowest on Sunday and late at night.

TIME DIFFERENCES
A map with Eastern European time zones is on the inside back cover of this book.

GMT + 1			GMT +2			GMT + 3
Bosnia	Croatia	Czech Rep.	Belarus	Bulgaria	Estonia	European Russia, including Moscow and St. Petersburg
Hungary	Poland	Slovak Rep.	Latvia	Lithuania	Romania	
Slovenia	Serbia and Montenegro		Ukraine	W. Russia		

BY EMAIL AND INTERNET

The World Wide Web is quickly making its way into Eastern Europe. Every major city now has some sort of Internet access, usually cyber cafes. Access is more difficult to find in smaller towns but is often available in public libraries, hostels, and tourist offices. Rates are very reasonable; one hour costs US$3 on average, although rates fluctuate from country to country. Free web-based email providers, such as Hotmail (www.hotmail.com) and Yahoo! Mail (www.yahoo.com), allow travelers to access their email account through any Internet-connected computer. Many free email providers are funded by advertising and some require subscribers to fill out a questionnaire.

GETTING TO EASTERN EUROPE

BY PLANE

When it comes to airfare, a little effort can save you a bundle. If your plans are flexible enough to deal with the restrictions, courier fares are the cheapest. Tickets bought from consolidators and standby seating are also good deals, but last-minute specials, airfare wars, and charter flights often beat these fares. Students, seniors, and those under 26 should never pay full price for a ticket.

AIRFARES

Airfares to Eastern Europe peak between mid-June and early September (the high season); holidays are also expensive. The cheapest times to travel are November through mid-December and mid-January through March. Midweek (M-Th morning) round-trip flights run US$40-100 cheaper than weekend flights, but they are generally more crowded and less likely to permit frequent-flier upgrades. Not fixing a return date ("open return") or arriving in and departing from different cities ("open-jaw") can be pricier than round-trip flights. Patching one-way flights together is the most expensive way to travel. For those willing to make the extra effort, the least expensive route is often to fly into London, Paris, Munich, or Milan and reach your destination by train or bus; it will often be necessary to connect from one of these cities regardless.

If your destination is only one stop on a more extensive globe-hop, consider a round-the-world (RTW) ticket. Tickets usually include at least five stops and are valid for about a year; prices range US$1200-5000. Try **Northwest Airlines/ KLM** (US ☎ 800-447-4747; www.nwa.com) or **Star Alliance,** a consortium of 22 airlines including United Airlines (US ☎ 800-241-6522; www.star-alliance.com). Round-trip commercial **fares** to the larger, more touristed cities (Budapest, Prague, Warsaw) from the US or Canadian east coast can usually be found, with some work, for US$500-600 in high season; from the UK, UK£140-180; from Australia, AUS$2000-2500; from New Zealand, NZ$2500-3000. Tickets to mid-range cities—including Bucharest, Moscow, Sofia, and Zagreb—generally cost about US$100 more, while Bratislava, Kyiv, Minsk, and the Baltic capitals can cost US$750-900/UK£180-250/AUS$2200-2600/NZ$2700-3100. Prices drop US$200-500 the rest of the year.

GET CARD.

TRAVEL HARD.

There's only one way to max out your travel experience and make the most of your time on the road: The International Student Identity Card.

 Packed with travel discounts, benefits and services, this card will keep your travel days and your wallet full. Get it before you hit it!

Visit **ISICUS.com** to get the full story on the benefits of carrying the ISIC.

BUDGET AND STUDENT TRAVEL AGENCIES

While knowledgeable agents specializing in flights to Eastern Europe can make your life easy and help you save some money, they may not spend the time to find the lowest possible fare as they get paid on commission. Travelers holding **ISIC** or **IYTC cards** (see p. 24) qualify for big discounts from student travel agencies. Most flights from budget agencies are on major airlines, but in peak season some may sell seats on less-reliable chartered aircraft.

Council Travel (www.counciltravel.com). Countless US offices, including branches in Atlanta, Boston, Chicago, L.A., New York, San Francisco, Seattle, and Washington, D.C. Check the website or call 800-2-COUNCIL (226-8624) for the office nearest you. Another office is at 28A Poland St. (Oxford Circus), London, W1V 3DB, **UK** (☎0207 437 77 67). *As of May 2002, Council had declared bankruptcy and was subsumed under STA. However, their offices are still in existence and transacting business.*

CTS Travel (www.ctstravelusa.com). Offices in Italy, Paris, London, and New York (toll free ☎877-287-6665). In the UK, 44 Goodge St., London W1T 2AD (☎0207 636 0031; fax 637 5328; ctsinfo@ctstravel.co.uk).

STA Travel, 7890 S. Hardy Dr. suite 110, Tempe, AZ 85284, USA (24hr. reservations and info US ☎800-777-0112; fax 480-592-0876; www.statravel.com). A student travel agency with over 250 offices worldwide. In the **US,** there are offices in Boston, Chicago, L.A., New York, San Francisco, Seattle, and Washington, D.C. **Australia,** 366 Lygon St., Melbourne Vic 3053 (☎03 9349 4344); **New Zealand,** 10 High St., Auckland (☎09 309 0458); **UK,** 11 Goodge St., London W1T 2PF (☎0870 160 6070).

Travel CUTS (Canadian Universities Travel Services Limited), 187 College St., Toronto, ON M5T 1P7, **Canada** (☎416-979-2406; fax 979-8167; www.travelcuts.com). In the **UK,** 295-A Regent St., London W1R 7YA (☎0207 255 1944).

usit world (www.usitworld.com). Over 50 **usit campus** branches in the **UK** (www.usitcampus.co.uk), including 52 Grosvenor Gardens, London SW1W 0AG (☎0870 240 1010); Manchester (☎0161 273 1880); Edinburgh (☎0131 668 3303). Nearly 20 **usit NOW** offices in **Ireland,** including 19-21 Aston Quay, O'Connell Bridge, Dublin 2 (☎01 602 1600; www.usitnow.ie), and Belfast (☎02 890 327 111; www.usitnow.com). Additional offices in Athens, Auckland, Brussels, Frankfurt, Johannesburg, Lisbon, Luxembourg, Madrid, Paris, Sofia, and Warsaw.

Wasteels, Skoubogade 6, 1158 Copenhagen K, **Denmark.** (☎3314 4633; fax 7630 0865; www.wasteels.dk/uk). A huge chain with 165 locations across Europe, including many Eastern European capitals.

FLIGHT PLANNING ON THE INTERNET. Many airline sites offer last-minute deals on the Web—check out the carriers listed below. Other sites do the legwork and compile deals for you—try www.bestfares.com, www.flights.com, www.hotdeals.com, www.onetravel.com, and www.travelzoo.com.

StudentUniverse *(www.studentuniverse.com)* and **STA** *(www.statravel.com)* provide quotes on student tickets, while **Expedia** (www.expedia.com), **Orbitz.com,** and **Travelocity** (www.travelocity.com) offer full travel services. **Priceline** (www.priceline.com) allows you to specify a price, and obligates you to buy any ticket that meets or beats it; be prepared for antisocial hours and odd routes. **Skyauction** (www.skyauction.com) allows you to bid on both last-minute and advance-purchase tickets.

COMMERCIAL AIRLINES

The commercial airlines' lowest regular offer is the **APEX** (Advance Purchase Excursion) fare, which provides confirmed reservations and allows "open-jaw" tickets. Generally, reservations must be made 1-3 weeks ahead of departure, with 1-2 week minimum-stay and up to 90-day maximum-stay restrictions. These fares carry hefty cancellation and change penalties. Book peak-season APEX fares early; by May you will have a hard time getting your desired departure date. Use **Microsoft Expedia** (http://msn.expedia.com) or **Travelocity** (www.travelocity.com) to get an idea of the lowest published fares, then use the resources outlined here to beat those fares. Popular carriers to Eastern Europe include:

FROM NORTH AMERICA AND WESTERN EUROPE

Air France (☎0820 820 820 in France, 800-237-2747 in the US and Canada; www.airfrance.com) covers much of Eastern Europe via Western Europe.

Austrian Airways (☎020 7434 7350; www.aua.com) connects to many Eastern European cities via Vienna.

British Airways (☎0845 77 33 77 in the UK, 800-545-7644 in the US and Canada; www.british-airways.com) flies into most large cities in Eastern Europe.

Delta Air Lines (☎0800 41 47 67 in the UK, 800-241-4141 in the US and Canada; www.delta.com) is one of the more reliable US carriers serving Eastern Europe.

KLM (☎0870 507 40 74; www.klmuk.com) connects to a number of cities in Eastern Europe via Amsterdam.

Lufthansa (☎800-563-5954 in Canada, 800-645-3880 in the US; www.lufthansa.com) has a wide variety of routes covering most of Eastern Europe.

SAS (☎0845 607 27 27 in the UK, 800-221-2350 in the US and Canada; www.scandanavian.net) reliably connects to Baltic cities.

FROM AUSTRALIA, NEW ZEALAND, AND SOUTH AFRICA

Air New Zealand (☎0800 737 000; www.airnewzealand.com) has reasonable fares from Auckland to London and often offers special sales at much lower prices.

Lufthansa (☎0861 842 538; www.lufthansa.com) offers reliable flights which connect to a number of cities throughout Eastern Europe. ·

Qantas (☎13 13 13; www.qantas.com) flies from a variety of cities in Australia and New Zealand to London, where connecting flights are easy to find.

South African Airways (SAA) (☎08 6135 9722; www.flysaa.com) flies directly into major Western European cities, where connections to Eastern Europe are easy to find.

AIR COURIER FLIGHTS

Those who travel light should consider courier flights. Couriers help transport cargo on international flights by using their checked luggage space for freight. Generally, couriers must travel with carry-ons only and deal with complex flight restrictions. Most flights are round-trip only, with short fixed-length stays (usually one week) and a limit of a one ticket per issue. Most of these flights also operate only out of major gateway cities in North America, such as New York, Los Angeles, San Francisco, or Miami in the US; and from Montreal, Toronto, or Vancouver in Canada. Generally, you must be over 21 (in some cases 18). Super-discounted fares are common for "last-minute" flights (three to 14 days ahead).

Air Courier Association, 350 Indiana St. #300, Golden, CO 80401, USA (☎800-282-1202; www.aircourier.org). Connects to select cities in Eastern Europe (high-season round-trip US$200-450). One-year membership US$49.

International Association of Air Travel Couriers (IAATC), PO Box 980, Keystone Heights, FL 32656, USA (☎352-475-1584; fax 475-5326; www.courier.org). Frequently flies from London to Budapest. One-year membership US$45.

STANDBY FLIGHTS

Traveling standby requires considerable flexibility in arrival and departure dates and cities. Companies dealing in standby flights sell vouchers rather than tickets, along with the promise to get you to your destination (or near your destination) within a limited window of time (typically 1-5 days). You call in before your specific window of time to hear flight options and the probability that you will be able to board each flight. You can then decide which flights you want to try to make, show up at the appropriate airport at the appropriate time, present your voucher, and board if space is available. Vouchers can usually be bought for both one-way and round-trip travel. You may receive a monetary refund only if every available flight within your date range is full; if you opt not to take an available (but perhaps less convenient) flight, you can only receive credit toward future travel. Carefully read agreements with any company offering standby flights as tricky fine print can leave you in the lurch. To check on a company's service record in the US, consult the Better Business Bureau (☎ 703-276-0100; www.bbb.org).

TICKET CONSOLIDATORS

Ticket consolidators, or "bucket shops," buy unsold tickets in bulk from commercial airlines and sell them at discounted rates. Look is in the Sunday travel section of any major newspaper (such as the *New York Times*), where many bucket shops place tiny ads. Call quickly, as availability is typically extremely limited. Not all bucket shops are reliable, so insist on a receipt that gives full details of restrictions, refunds, and tickets, and pay by credit card (in spite of the 2-5% fee) so you can stop payment if you never receive your tickets. For more info, see www.travel-library.com/air-travel/consolidators.html.

TRAVELING FROM THE US AND CANADA

Travel Avenue (☎ 800-333-3335; www.travelavenue.com) searches for best available published fares and then uses several consolidators to attempt to beat that fare. **NOW Voyager,** 74 Varick St., Ste. 307, New York, NY 10013, USA (☎ 212-431-1616; fax 219-1793; www.nowvoyagertravel.com), arranges discounted flights, mostly from New York, to Barcelona, London, Madrid, Milan, Paris, and Rome, all of which connect to Eastern Europe. Other consolidators worth trying are **Interworld** (☎ 305-443-4929; fax 443-0351), **Pennsylvania Travel** (☎ 800-331-0947), **Rebel** (☎ 800-227-3235; www.rebeltours.com), **Cheap Tickets** (☎ 800-377-1000; www.cheaptickets.com), and **Travac** (☎ 800-872-8800; fax 212-714-9063; www.travac.com). Yet more consolidators on the web include the **Internet Travel Network** (www.itn.com), **Travel Information Services** (www.tiss.com), **TravelHUB** (www.travelhub.com), and **The Travel Site** (www.thetravelsite.com). Keep in mind that these are just suggestions to get you started; *Let's Go* does not endorse any of these agencies. As always, be cautious, and research companies before you hand over your credit card number.

TRAVELING FROM THE UK, AUSTRALIA, AND NEW ZEALAND

In London, the Air Travel Advisory Bureau (☎ 0207-636-5000; www.atab.co.uk) can provide names of reliable consolidators and discount flight specialists. From Australia and New Zealand, look for consolidator ads in the travel section of the *Sydney Morning Herald* and other papers.

CHARTER FLIGHTS

Charters are flights a tour operator contracts with an airline to fly extra loads of passengers during peak season. Charter flights fly less frequently than major airlines (making refunds particularly difficult), and are almost always fully booked. Schedules and itineraries may also change or be cancelled at the last moment (as late as 48 hours before the trip, and without a full refund), and check-in, boarding, and baggage claim are often much slower. However, charter flights can be cheaper. **Discount clubs** and **fare brokers** offer members savings on last-minute charter and tour deals. Study contracts closely; you don't want to end up with an unwanted overnight layover.

BY TRAIN

Flying into a Western European city and then taking a train to Eastern Europe often proves to be the cheapest option. Many travelers fly into Milan to connect by train to the Balkans; Munich or Berlin to reach Poland, the Baltics, and Ukraine; and Vienna for the short train ride to the Czech and Slovak Republics and Hungary. Check out **transit visa** requirements if you plan on passing through other Eastern European countries en route to your final destination. Those touring the EU on their way to or from Eastern Europe might consider a **Eurailpass**—keep in mind that it is **not valid in Eastern Europe,** with the exception of Hungary.

ESSENTIALS

GETTING AROUND

Trains and buses are the primary mode of transportation in Eastern Europe. All transportation fares are either "single" (one-way) or "return" (round-trip). Unless stated otherwise, *Let's Go* always lists single fares. Round-trip fares on trains and buses in most of Eastern Europe are double the one-way fare.

BY PLANE

 AIRCRAFT SAFETY. The airlines of the former Soviet Republics often do not meet safety standards, especially for internal flights. When flying within Eastern Europe, it's often safest to spend the few extra rubles and book a seat on a Western airline rather than a domestic carrier. When a foreign carrier is not an option, the *Official Airline Guide* (www.oag.com) and many travel agencies can tell you the type and age of aircraft on a particular route. The **International Airline Passengers Association** (US ☎800-821-4272, UK ☎020 8681 6555) provides region-specific safety information. The American **Federal Aviation Administration** (www.faa.gov) reviews the airline authorities for countries whose airlines enter the US.

Flying across Eastern Europe on regularly scheduled flights can devour your budget, but if you are short on time (or flush with cash) you might consider it. Student travel agencies sell cheap tickets, and budget fares are frequently available in the spring and summer on high-volume routes. Consult budget travel agents and local newspapers for more info. In addition, a number of European airlines offer discount coupon packets. Most are only available as tack-ons for transatlantic passengers, but some are stand-alone offers. Most must be purchased before departure, so research in advance.

Europe by Air: ☎888-321-4737; www.europebyair.com. *FlightPass* allows you to country-hop between over 150 European cities. US$99 per flight.

SAS: ☎800-221-2350; www.scandinavian.net. One-way coupons for travel within the Baltics and greater Europe. Most are available only to transatlantic SAS passengers, but some United and Lufthansa passengers also qualify. US$65-225 each.

BY TRAIN

ESSENTIALS

> **READING AND RESOURCES ON TRAIN TRAVEL.**
> **Info on rail travel and railpasses:** www.raileurope.com.
> **Point-to-point fares and schedules:** www.raileurope.com/us/rail/
> fares_schedules/index.htm. Allows you to calculate whether buying a railpass
> would save you money.
> **European Railway Server:** http://mercurio.iet.unipi.it/home.html. Links to rail
> servers throughout Europe.
> ***Thomas Cook European Timetable,*** updated monthly, covers all major and
> most minor train routes in Europe. In the US, order it from Forsyth Travel
> Library (US$28; ☎800-367-7984; www.forsyth.com). In Europe, find it at any
> Thomas Cook Money Exchange Center. Alternatively, buy directly from Thomas
> Cook (www.thomascook.com).
> ***On the Rails Around Europe: A Comprehensive Guide to Travel by Train,*** Mel-
> issa Shales. Thomas Cook Ltd.

Trains are often the fastest and easiest way to travel within Eastern Europe.
Second-class seating is pleasant, and compartments, which fit two to six, are
great places to meet fellow travelers. Trains, however, are not always safe in
terms of personal safety, especially at night. For safety tips, see **Safety and Security: Public Transportation,** p. 30. For long trips make sure you are on the correct
car, as trains sometimes split at crossroads. Destinations listed in parentheses
on Eastern European train schedules require a train switch, usually at the town
listed immediately before the parenthesis. When traveling through Eastern
Europe by train, you can either buy a **railpass,** which allows you unlimited travel

within a particular region for a given period of time, or rely on buying individual **point-to-point** tickets as you go. Almost all countries give students or youths (under 26) discounts on domestic rail tickets, and many sell a student or youth card that provides 20-50% off all fares.

VISAS AND RESERVATIONS

TRANSIT VISAS. Plan ahead: some Eastern European countries require **transit visas** for all travelers just passing through the country by train. All trains from Central Europe, for instance, must pass through Belarus to reach the Baltics or Russia. To avoid getting detained in Minsk, or elsewhere, make sure your paperwork is in order, or that your route works around countries with transit visas. For more information, consult the **Visa and Entry Info** section of each country.

RESERVATIONS. Many train stations have different counters for domestic and international tickets, seat reservations, and information—check before lining up. While seat reservations (usually US$3-10) are only required on select trains (usually major international lines), you are not guaranteed a seat without one. Reservations are available on major trains as much as two months in advance, and Europeans often reserve far ahead of time (the Moscow-St. Petersburg train is famous for selling out weeks in advance during the summer). You should strongly consider reserving a seat during peak holiday and tourist seasons.

RAILPASSES

It may be tough to make your railpass pay for itself in Eastern Europe, where train fares are ridiculously cheap and buses are sometimes preferable. In general, it's better to buy point-to-point tickets, which are almost always a better deal. If you must purchase a pass, do so before you arrive in Europe, as most passes are available only to non-Europeans and are consequently difficult to find in Europe. Try **Rail Europe,** 500 Mamaroneck Ave., Harrison, NY 10528, USA (☎888-382-7245, fax 800-432-1329; Canada ☎800-361-7245, fax 905-602-4198; UK ☎0990 84 88 48; www.raileurope.com); or **DER Travel Services,** 9501 W. Devon Ave. #301, Rosemont, IL 60018, USA (☎888-337-7350; fax 800-282-7474; www.dertravel.com).

MULTINATIONAL RAILPASSES. For those dead set on purchasing a multinational railpass, there are a few options. A **Eurailpass,** however, is not one of them: it covers only Hungary in Eastern Europe. The **European East Pass** covers Austria, the Czech Republic, Hungary, Poland, and the Slovak Republic (5 days in 1 month 1st class US$220, 2nd class US$154). The **Balkan Flexipass** is valid for travel in Bulgaria, Greece, the Former Yugoslav Republic of Macedonia, Romania, Serbia-Montenegro, and Turkey (5 days in 1 month US$152, under 26 US$90; 10 and 15 day passes also available). The **Freedom Pass,** offered only in the UK, allows unlimited rail travel in a single country. Passes are available for Bulgaria, Croatia, Czech Republic, Hungary, Poland, Romania, the Slovak Republic, Slovenia, and the former Yugoslavia for three (UK£28-51, under 26 UK£22-34) to eight (UK£46-95/£42-61) days. Contact **Council Travel,** 52 Grosvenor Gardens, London SW1W 0AG (☎087 024 01 010), or **Railchoice** (www.railchoice.co.uk).

NATIONAL PASSES. **Bulgarian Flexipass, Czech Flexipass, Hungarian Pass, Polrail Pass,** and **Romanian Flexipass** are the only national passes available. These tend not to be as economical as point-to-point travel, but if you're spending a significant amount of time in one country, they can be a worthwhile investment. Another type of regional pass covers a specific area within a country or a round-trip from any border to a particular destination and back. Examples include the **Prague Excursion Pass,** which covers travel from any Czech border to Prague and back out of the country (round-trip must be completed within 7 days; 1st class US$55, 2nd US$35; under 26 US$45/30). For more information, contact Rail Europe (see above).

INTERRAIL PASSES. InterRail passes can only be purchased in Europe, by people who have lived in Europe for at least six months. Valid in Russia, Belarus, Ukraine, Moldova, Estonia, Latvia, and Lithuania, they prove an economical option. There are eight InterRail zones. The Under 26 InterRail Card allows either 21 consecutive days or one month of unlimited travel within one, two, three or all of the eight zones; the cost is determined by the number of zones the pass covers (UK£119-249). A card can also be purchased for 12 days of travel in one zone (UK£119). The Over 26 InterRail Card provides the same services as the Under 26 InterRail Card, but at higher prices (UK£169-355). The new Child Pass (ages 4-11) offers the same services (UK£85-178). For info and ticket sales, contact **Student Travel Centre,** 24 Rupert St., 1st fl., London W1V 7FN, UK (☎020 74 37 81 01; fax 77 34 38 36; www.student-travel-centre.com). Tickets are also available from travel agents, at major train stations throughout Europe, or online (www.railpassdirect.co.uk).

EURO DOMINO. Like the InterRail Pass, the Euro Domino pass is available to anyone who has lived in Europe for at least six months; however, it is only valid in one country (which you designate when buying the pass). It is available for 29 European countries, including Bulgaria, Croatia, the Czech Republic, Poland, Romania, the Slovak Republic, Slovenia, and the former Yugoslavia. Reservations must still be paid for separately. **Supplements** are included for many high-speed trains. The pass must be bought within your country of residence; each country has its own price for the pass. Inquire with your national rail company for more info.

BY BUS

All over Eastern Europe, buses reach rural areas inaccessible by train. In addition, long-distance bus networks may be more extensive, efficient, and occasionally even more comfortable than train services. In the Balkans, air-conditioned buses run by private companies are a godsend. **Contiki Holidays** (888-CONTIKI; www.contiki.com) offers a variety of European vacation packages designed exclusively for 18- to 35-year-olds. For an average cost of $60 per day, tours include accommodations, transportation, guided sightseeing and some meals. **Eurolines,** 4 Cardiff Rd., Luton, Bedfordshire, L41 1PP, UK (☎0990 14 32 19; fax 01582 400 694; www.eurolines.uk.com), is Europe's largest coach operator, offering passes (UK£99-267) for unlimited 15-, 30-, or 60-day travel between 500 destinations in 30 countries, including many spots in Eastern Europe and Russia. It has offices in most countries in Eastern Europe; see the website for details.

BY BOAT

Sometimes, yes, boats go to Yalta...but not today.
　　—Ferry ticket clerk in Odessa

Ferries in the **North** and **Baltic Seas** are reliable, comfortable, and comprehensive. Those in the **Black Sea,** however, are much less predictable, and traveling between the coasts of Romania, Bulgaria, Ukraine, and Russia is no easy task. Those content with deck passage rarely need to book ahead, but you should check in a few hours early for a good seat and allow extra time to get to the port.

Polferries: Sweden ☎46 40 97 61 80; www.polferries.se. Goes from Ystad, Sweden to Świnoujście, Poland (7hr.) and Oxelösund-Stockholm to Gdańsk (17hr.).

Silja Line: US sales ☎800-323-7436, Finland ☎358 09 18041; www.silja.com. Helsinki to Stockholm (16hr., June-Dec.); Tallinn, Estonia (3hr., June to mid-Sept.); and Rostock, Germany (23-25hr., June to mid-Sept.). Also Turku to Stockholm (12hr.).

BY CAR

Public transportation is the best way to get around Eastern Europe, and travelers unfamiliar with the region and its roads should follow the local flow and catch a bus or train. Car rental prices in Eastern Europe can be among the highest on the continent and petrol is not always readily available (particularly unleaded), making travel by bus, train, and sometimes even by plane, cheaper alternatives. Eastern European roads are often poorly maintained and roadside assistance rarely exists, contributing to some of the highest driving fatality rates in the world. On the whole, conditions worsen the farther east you travel. However, as driving gains popularity in Central Europe, support services for drivers have been on the rise in countries such as the Czech Republic, Hungary, and Poland. If you do choose to strike off on your own, know the laws of the countries in which you'll be driving and read up on local road conditions. For an informal primer on European road signs and conventions, check out www.travlang.com/signs. The **Association for Safe International Road Travel (ASIRT)**, 11769 Gainsborough Rd., Potomac, MD 20854, USA (☎ 301-983-5252; fax 983-3663; www.asirt.org), can provide more specific information about road conditions.

DRIVING PERMITS AND CAR INSURANCE

INTERNATIONAL DRIVING PERMIT (IDP). If you plan to drive a car while in Eastern Europe, you should have an International Driving Permit (IDP), though certain countries allow travelers to drive with a valid American or Canadian license for a limited number of months. It may be a good idea to get one anyway, in case you're in a situation (e.g. an accident or stranded in a small town) where the police do not speak English; information on the IDP is printed in ten languages, including German and Russian. An IDP, valid for one year, must be issued in your own country before you depart. An application for an IDP usually needs to include one or two photos, a current local license, an additional form of identification, and a fee. To apply, contact your home country's Automobile Association.

CAR INSURANCE. Most credit cards cover standard insurance. If you rent, lease, or borrow a car, you will need a green card, or International Insurance Certificate, to certify that you have liability insurance and that it applies abroad. Green cards can be obtained at car rental agencies, car dealers (for those leasing cars), some travel agents, and some border crossings. Rental agencies in some countries may require you to purchase theft insurance.

BY BICYCLE

Many places in Eastern Europe lack the infrastructure to support much mountain and road biking. Generally, the farther east you go, the less likely it becomes that there will be any well-maintained trails, safety networks should you run into trouble, or stores that stock biking supplies. In most of Eastern Europe, it is unlikely that bringing your own bike will be worthwhile. However, in many countries, especially Estonia, Poland, and Slovenia, **renting** a bike will allow you to see much more of the natural scenery. For more information, consult the **Practical Information** section of the city or town in which you will be traveling.

BY THUMB

Hitchhiking involves serious risks. It means entrusting your life to a complete stranger who just happens to stop next to you on the road. You risk theft, assault, sexual harassment, and unsafe driving. In spite of this, there are advantages to hitching when it is safe: it allows you to meet local people and get where you're going, especially in places where public transportation is unreliable. The choice, however, remains yours. If you decide to hitch, consider where you are. Hitching remains common in Eastern Europe, though Westerners are a definite target for theft. In Russia, the Baltics, and some other Eastern European countries, hitchhiking can be as ordinary as hailing a taxi, and drivers will likely expect to be paid a sum at least equivalent to a bus ticket to your destination.

 Let's Go strongly urges you to seriously consider the risks before you choose to hitchhike. We do not recommend hitching as a safe means of transportation.

ADDITIONAL INFORMATION

SPECIFIC CONCERNS

WOMEN TRAVELERS

Solo female travelers are still a relatively novel phenomenon in Eastern Europe, particularly in public places like bars and restaurants, and women traveling alone may encounter quizzical stares. The attitudes that contribute to these surprised looks, when coupled with crime in urban areas, can make for dangerous situations. Hostels which offer single rooms that lock from the inside or religious organizations that provide rooms for women only offer female travelers the most security. Communal showers in some hostels are safer than others; check before settling in. Stick to centrally located accommodations and avoid solitary late-night walks or metro rides. Always carry extra money for a phone call, bus, or taxi. Hitchhiking is never safe for lone women, or even for two women traveling together. Choose train compartments occupied by women or couples; ask the conductor to put together a women-only compartment if there isn't one. Look as if you know where you're going and approach older women or couples for directions if you're lost or uncomfortable.

Generally, the less you look like a tourist, the better off you'll be. Dress conservatively, especially in rural areas. Wearing the shirts and long skirts that are fashionable among local women will cut down on stares, and a *babushka*-style kerchief discourages even the most tenacious of cat callers. Some travelers report that wearing a wedding band or carrying pictures of a "husband" or "children" is extremely useful to help document marital status. Even mention of a husband waiting back at the hotel may be enough to discount your potentially vulnerable, unattached appearance. In cities, you may be harassed no matter how you're dressed. Your best answer to verbal harassment is no answer at all; feigned deafness, sitting motionless, and staring straight ahead will do a world of good that reactions usually don't achieve. The extremely persistent can sometimes be dissuaded by a firm, loud, and very public "Go away!" in the appropriate language. If need be, turn to an older woman for help; her stern rebukes should usually embarrass the most persistent harassers into silence.

Let's Go lists emergency numbers (including rape crisis lines) in the **Practical Information** of most major cities. Memorize the emergency numbers in places you visit, and consider carrying a whistle on your keychain. A self-defense course will not only prepare you for a potential attack but also heighten your awareness and boost your confidence (see **Self Defense**, p. 29). To further prepare yourself, make sure you are aware of the health concerns that women face when traveling (see **Women's Health**, p. 35, and the **Health and Safety** section at the beginning of each country's chapter).

OLDER TRAVELERS

Discounts for senior citizens are not common in Eastern Europe. That said, it never hurts to ask, especially on public transportation. Agencies catering to senior group travel are growing in enrollment and popularity. These are only a few:

ElderTreks, 597 Markham St., Toronto, ON M6G 2L7, Canada (☎800-741-7956; www.eldertreks.com). Adventure travel programs for the 50+ traveler in Eastern Europe.

Elderhostel, 11 Ave. de Lafayette, Boston, MA 02111, USA (☎877-426-8056; www.elderhostel.org). Organizes 1- to 4-week "educational adventures" in various regions of Eastern Europe. Recent programs have taken place in the Baltics, Bulgaria, Croatia, the Czech Republic, Hungary, Poland, and Western Russia. Participants must be 50+ (spouse can be of any age).

The Mature Traveler, P.O. Box 50400, Reno, NV 89513, USA (☎800-460-6676). Deals, discounts, and travel packages for the 50+ traveler. Subscription US$30.

Walking the World, P.O. Box 1186, Fort Collins, CO 80522, USA (☎800-340-9255; www.walkingtheworld.com). Active trips for 50+ travelers to the Czech and Slovak Republics, and Slovenia.

BISEXUAL, GAY, AND LESBIAN TRAVELERS

Homosexuality is legal in every Eastern European country. However, it is strongly stigmatized in Romania, much of the former Soviet Union (especially in Belarus, where homosexuality was only legalized in 1994), and rural areas. Whatever the law says, homophobic views persist throughout much of Eastern Europe and public displays of homosexuality can give local authorities an excuse to be troublesome in many countries. Even within major cities, gay nightclubs and social centers are often clandestine and frequently change location. For coverage of the current legal and social climate in each country, consult the website of the **International Lesbian and Gay Association** (www.ilga.org). While *Let's Go* lists local gay and lesbian bars and clubs, word of mouth is often the best method for finding the latest hotspots. Listed below are contact organizations, mail-order bookstores, and publishers that offer materials addressing some specific concerns. **Out and About** (www.outandabout.com) offers a bi-weekly newsletter and a comprehensive site addressing gay travel concerns.

Gay's the Word, 66 Marchmont St., London WC1N 1AB, UK (☎020 7278 7654; www.gaystheword.co.uk). The largest gay and lesbian bookshop in the UK, with both fiction and nonfiction titles. Mail-order service available.

International Lesbian and Gay Association (ILGA), 81 rue Marché-au-Charbon, B-1000 Brussels, Belgium (☎02 502 2471; www.ilga.org). Provides political information, including homosexuality laws of individual countries.

 FOR FURTHER READING: BISEXUAL, GAY, AND LESBIAN.

Spartacus International Gay Guide 2002-2003. Bruno Gmunder Verlag.

Damron Men's Guide, Damron's Accommodations, and The Women's Traveller. Damron Travel Guides. For more info, call ☎800-462-6654 or visit www.damron.com.

Odysseus: The International Gay Travel Planner. Odysseus Enterprises Ltd.

Gay Travel A to Z: The World of Gay and Lesbian Travel Options at Your Fingertips. SCB Distributors.

TRAVELERS WITH DISABILITIES

Unfortunately, compared to other travel destinations, Eastern Europe is largely inaccessible to disabled travelers. Ramps and other such amenities are all but non-existent in most countries. As a result, some extra planning before your trip will be necessary to ensure everything goes smoothly: contact your destination's consulate or tourist office for information, arrange transportation early, and inform airlines and hotels of any special accommodations required ahead of time. Guide-dog owners should inquire as to the specific quarantine policies of each destination. At the very least, you will need to provide a certificate of immunization against rabies. Support organizations in your home country can often provide assistance in planning successful trips abroad. **Rail** is probably the most convenient form of travel for disabled travelers in Eastern Europe: many stations have ramps, and some trains have wheelchair lifts, special seating areas, and specially equipped toilets. Poland, Bulgaria, the Czech Republic, Hungary, and the Slovak Republic's rail systems all offer limited resources for wheelchair accessibility. For those who wish to rent cars, some major **car rental** agencies (Hertz, Avis, and National) offer hand-controlled vehicles.

USEFUL ORGANIZATIONS AND AGENCIES

Mobility International USA (MIUSA), P.O. Box 10767, Eugene, OR 97440, USA (☎541-343-1284; www.miusa.org). Sells *A World of Options: A Guide to International Educational Exchange, Community Service, and Travel for Persons with Disabilities.*

Society for the Accessible Travel and Hospitality (SATH), 347 Fifth Ave. #610, New York, NY 10016 USA (☎212-447-7284; www.sath.org). An advocacy group that publishes free online travel information and the travel magazine *OPEN WORLD* (US$18, free for members). Annual membership US$45, students and seniors US$30.

MINORITY TRAVELERS

Roma (Gypsies) encounter substantial hostility in Eastern Europe. Travelers with darker skin of any nationality might be mistaken for Roma and therefore face some of the same prejudice. Other minority travelers, especially those of African or Asian descent, will usually meet with more curiosity than hostility, especially outside big cities. The ranks of skinheads are on the rise in Eastern Europe, and minority travelers, especially Jews and blacks, should regard them with caution. Anti-Semitism is still a problem in many countries, including Poland and the former Soviet Union; it is generally best to be discreet about your religion.

DIETARY CONCERNS

Vegetarian and **kosher** dining is often a challenge in Eastern Europe. Most of the national cuisines tend to be meat- (and especially pork-) heavy. **Markets** are often a good bet for fresh vegetables, fruit, cheese, and bread. The North American Vegetarian Society, P.O. Box 72, Dolgeville, NY 13329, USA (☎518-568-7970; www.navs-online.org), offers information and publications for vegetarian travelers. Travelers who keep kosher should contact synagogues in larger cities for information on kosher restaurants. Your own synagogue or college Hillel should have access to lists of Jewish institutions across Eastern Europe. If you are strict in your observance, you may have to prepare your own food on the road. A good resource is the *Jewish Travel Guide,* by Michael Zaidner (Vallentine Mitchell; US$17). It lists synagogues, kosher restaurants, and Jewish institutions in over 80 countries. Available from Vallentine Mitchell Publishers; in the UK, Crown House, 47 Chase Side, Southgate, London N14 5BP (☎020 8920 2100); in the US, 5824 NE Hassallo St., Portland, OR 97213-3644 (☎800-944-6190).

THE WORLD WIDE WEB

Many countries' embassies now maintain websites where you can check visa requirements and news related to your destination (see **Embassies and Consulates**, p. 22). There are also a number of sites that provide good general information about the region. Among them are:

CIA World Factbook: www.odci.gov/cia/publications/factbook/index.html. Tons of vital statistics on Eastern Europe's geography, government, economy, and people.

Foreign Language for Travelers: www.travlang.com. Provides free online translating dictionaries and lists of phrases in various Eastern European languages.

In Your Pocket: www.inyourpocket.com. The online version of an excellent series of city and regional guides. The coverage of the Baltic states is particularly thorough.

MyTravelGuide: www.mytravelguide.com. Country overviews, with everything from history to transportation to live web cam coverage of Eastern Europe.

PlanetRider: www.planetrider.com. A subjective list of links to the "best" websites covering the culture and tourist attractions of several countries.

TravelPage: www.travelpage.com. Links to official tourist offices across the region.

World Travel Guide: www.travel-guides.com/navigate/world.asp. Helpful practical info.

THE ART OF BUDGET TRAVEL

Atevo Travel: www.atevo.com/guides/destinations. Detailed introductions, travel tips, and suggested itineraries.

Backpacker's Ultimate Guide: www.bugeurope.com. Tips on packing, transportation, and where to go. Includes country-specific travel information.

How to See the World: www.artoftravel.com. A compendium of great travel tips, from cheap flights to self defense to local culture.

Lycos: http://travel.lycos.com. General introductions to cities and regions throughout Eastern Europe, accompanied by links to history, news, and local tourism sites.

Travel Library: www.travel-library.com. A fantastic set of links for general information and personal travelogues.

OUR PERSONAL FAVORITE...

WWW.LETSGO.COM Our newly designed website now features the full online content of all of our guides. In addition, trial versions of all nine City Guides are available for download on Palm OS™ PDAs. Our website also contains our newsletter, links to photos and streaming video, online ordering of our titles, info about our books, and a travel forum buzzing with stories and tips.

ALTERNATIVES TO TOURISM

While traversing the globe jumping from hostel to hotel is undoubtedly a memorable and worthwhile way to experience a foreign country, it is possible to experience a foreign culture without becoming a perennial tourist. By working, volunteering, or studying for an extended period of time in Eastern Europe, visitors can gain a deeper understanding of life in the region and participate in its post-Soviet transformation. While the expat populations of Prague and Budapest continue to blossom, other travelers find themselves drawn to reconstruction efforts in war-torn Sarajevo or Russian language programs at Moscow's finest universities. Volunteers and workers help the region tackle the economic, environmental, and linguistic challenges involved in reintegrating into the modern market economy. It's an exciting time for Eastern Europe, and by choosing one of the alternatives to tourism detailed in this chapter, you're bound to have an experience that is more meaningful than the routine excursion.

STUDYING

Study abroad programs range from basic language lessons to university-level courses. In order to choose a program that best fits your needs, is important to find out who participates in the program and what sort of accommodations are provided. Programs in which many students speak your language may allow you to feel comfortable in the community, but will limit your opportunities to practice or to befriend other international students. Foreign study programs have multiplied rapidly in Eastern Europe. Most American undergraduates enroll in programs sponsored by US universities and many college study abroad offices can provide advice and information. Libraries and bookstores are also helpful sources of current information on study abroad programs, as are www.language-learning.net, www.studyabroad.com, and www.worldwide.edu. If you are fluent in an Eastern European language, you may want to consider enrolling directly in a foreign university. This route is usually less expensive and more immersive than programs run through American universities, though it may be harder to get university credit for your adventures abroad. Contact the nearest consulate for a list of educational institutions in your country of choice. There are also several international and national fellowships available (e.g. Fulbright or Rotary) to fund stays abroad. In most Eastern European countries, studying requires a special **student visa.** Applying for such a visa usually requires proof of admission to a university or program in your home country. Below are several organizations that run programs to Eastern European countries.

American Field Service (AFS), 71 W. 23rd St., 17th fl., New York, NY 10010, USA (☎212-807-8686; fax 807-1001; www.afs.org), has branches in over 50 countries. Summer-, semester-, and year-long homestay exchange programs for high school students and graduating seniors in the Czech Republic, Hungary, Latvia, Russia, and the Slovak Republic. Community service programs also offered. Financial aid available.

American Institute for Foreign Study, River Plaza, 9 West Broad St., Stamford, CT 06902, USA (☎800-727-2437; www.aifsabroad.com). Organizes programs for high school and college study in universities in the Czech Republic, Poland, and Russia.

Council on International Educational Exchange (CIEE), 633 3rd Ave., 20th fl., New York, NY 10017-6706, USA (☎ 800-407-8839; www.ciee.org). Sponsors work, volunteer, and academic programs in the Czech Republic, Hungary, Poland, and Russia.

International Association for the Exchange of Students for Technical Experience (IAESTE), 10400 Little Patuxent Pkwy., Suite 250, Columbia, MD 21044-3519, USA (☎ 410-997-2200; www.aipt.org). 8- to 12-week programs in Eastern Europe for college students who have completed 2 years of technical study. US$25 application fee.

School for International Training, College Semester Abroad, Admissions, Kipling Rd., P.O. Box 676, Brattleboro, VT 05302, USA (☎ 800-257-7751 or 802-257-7751; www.sit.edu). Semester- and year-long programs in the Czech Republic and Russia US$12,000-13,000. Also runs the **Experiment in International Living** (☎ 800-345-2929; fax 802-258-3428; www.usexperiment.org), 3- to 5-week summer programs that offer high-school students cross-cultural homestays, community service, ecological adventure, and language training in Poland (US$5000).

Youth for Understanding International Exchange (YFU), 3501 Newark St. NW, Washington, D.C. 20016, USA (☎ 800-833-6243; fax 895-1104; www.yfu.org). Places US high school students for a year, semester, or summer in the Czech and Slovak Republics, Estonia, Latvia, Hungary, Poland, Russia, and Ukraine. US$75 application fee.

LANGUAGE SCHOOLS

Language schools are frequently independently-run organizations or divisions of foreign universities that rarely offer college credit. Unlike other study abroad programs, they focus exclusively on learning the language. Language schools are a good alternative to university study if you desire a deeper focus on the language or a slightly less rigorous courseload. Some good programs that offer opportunities in Eastern Europe include:

American Council for International Education, 1776 Massachusetts Ave., NW, Suite 700, Washington, D.C., 20036, USA (202-833-7522; fax 202-833-7523; www.actr.org). Offers summer, semester, and year-long college-level language study programs throughout Eastern Europe. Programs in Russia range from US$6000-15,000. Prices for programs in Central Europe vary depending on location and specifics, but are generally lower. US$35 application fee.

Eurocentres, 101 N. Union St., Suite 300, Alexandria, VA 22314, USA (☎ 703-684-1494; www.eurocentres.com). Head Office, Seestr. 247, 8038 Zurich, Switzerland (☎ 485 50 40; fax 481 61 24). Language programs for beginning to advanced students with homestays in Russia.

Russian and East European Partnerships, REEP Inc., PO Box 227, Fineview, NY 13640, USA (☎ 888-USE-REEP; fax 800-910-1777; www.usereep.com). Offers 4-week language and cultural immersion programs in Belarus, Bulgaria, Croatia, the Czech Republic, Estonia, Hungary, Latvia, Lithuania, Poland, Romania, Russia, Slovenia, and Ukraine. Programs can be customized and start at US$2900.

WORKING

Not all travelers are in search of the same type of employment. Some want long-term jobs that allow them to get to know another part of the world in depth. Others seek out short-term jobs to finance their travel, working until they are able to afford the next leg of their journey. This section discusses both short-term and long-term opportunities for employment in Eastern Europe. While working in Eastern Europe is rewarding, it does entail jumping through a whole new set of bureaucratic hoops. Most countries require a work permit as well as a visa or a permit for temporary residency. In some countries, to make it all the more confusing, a particular type of visa, often called a "visa with work permit", is required in addition to (not as a replacement for) a work permit. These visas are issued from the nearest consulate or embassy (see the **Embassies and Consulates** section of each country). Applying for it, however, will require that you present your work permit, which must be issued directly from the Labor Bureau in the country in question. Given these complications, making contact with prospective employers within the country can prove extremely useful in expediting permits or arranging work-for-accommodations swaps. For US college students and young adults, the simplest way to get legal permission to work abroad is through **Council Exchanges Work Abroad Programs,** which can help you obtain a three- to six-month work permit/visa and provide assistance finding jobs and housing (US$300-425).

LOCAL CLASSIFIEDS

Eastern European capitals produce a weekly English-language publication in which local organizations recruit foreign workers:

Czech Republic: The Prague Post (www.praguepost.com). Published weekly.

Hungary: The Budapest Sun (www.budapestsun.com). Published weekly.

Poland: The Warsaw Voice (www.warsawvoice.pl). Published weekly.

Russia: The Russia Journal (www.russiajournal.com). Published weekly.

Slovak Republic: The Slovak Spectator (www.slovakspectator.sk). Published weekly.

Ukraine: The Kyiv Post (www.kpnews.com). Published weekly.

LONG-TERM WORK

If you're planning to spend a substantial amount of time (more than three months) working in Eastern Europe, search for a job well in advance. International placement agencies are often the easiest way to find employment abroad, especially for teaching English. **Internships,** usually for college students, are a good transition to working abroad, although they are often unpaid. Be wary of advertisements or companies that claim they will get you a job abroad for a fee—often the same listings they provide are available online or in newspapers, or are out of date. Always check an organization's reputation in advance. Some good ones include:

American Chamber of Commerce in Russia, Dolgorukovskaya ul. 7, 14th fl., 103006 Moscow, Russia (☎7 095 961 2141; www.amcham.ru). Assists American citizens and businesses attempting to work in Russia.

Irex (International Research and Exchanges Board), 2121 K Street NW, Suite 700, Washington, D.C. 20037, USA (☎202-628-8188; www.irex.org/careers). Promoting civil society; and recruits for positions in the Balkans, Russia, and Ukraine.

Jobs in Russia and the New Independent States (www.departments.bucknell.edu/russian/jobs.html). Website offers general advice for job-hunting in the former Soviet Union, as well as links to employment opportunities.

Organization for Security and Cooperation in Europe, Recruitment, Kartner Ring 5-7, 4th fl., 1010 Vienna, Austria (☎431 514 360; www.osce.org/employment). Recruits for positions requiring a range of skill levels and qualifications. The majority of positions relate to the monitoring of elections throughout the Balkans.

Russian and East European Institute (www.indiana.edu/~reeiweb/indemp.html). Extensive website detailing resources for those seeking jobs in Eastern Europe.

TEACHING ENGLISH

Teaching jobs abroad are rarely well-paid, although elite American or international schools usually offer competitive salaries. Volunteering as a teacher is a popular option, and volunteering teachers often get some sort of a daily stipend to help cover living expenses. In almost all cases, you must have at least a bachelor's degree to be a full-fledged teacher, although college undergraduates can sometimes obtain summer positions as tutors. There remains a high demand for English instructors in Eastern Europe, though the market has been saturated in highly touristed countries, such as Hungary and the Czech Republic. Many schools require teachers to have a **Teaching English as a Foreign Language (TEFL)** certificate. Those without the certificate are not necessarily excluded from teaching, but certified teachers often find higher-paying jobs. Placement agencies or university fellowship programs are the best resources for finding teaching jobs in Eastern Europe. The alternative is to make contact with schools or to try your luck once you get there. If you are going to try the latter, the best time of the year is several weeks before the start of the school year (August). Taking on individual students as a private English tutor is a popular alternative to traditional teaching positions in Eastern Europe; contact schools about potential pupils to help you get started. The following organizations are extremely helpful in placing teachers:

Central Bureau for Educational Visits and Exchanges, 10 Spring Gardens, London SW1A 2BN, UK (020 7389 4383; fax 7389 4292; www.britishcouncil.org/education/assistants/index.htm). Places qualified British undergraduates and teachers in teaching positions in Bulgaria, Hungary, Russia, and Slovenia.

Central European Teaching Program, Beloit College, 700 College Street, Beloit, WI 53511, USA (☎ 608-363-2619; www.beloit.edu/~cetp). Arranges 10-month teaching positions in Hungary, Poland, and Romania. US$3400 placement fee includes airfare, housing, and paid teaching contract.

International Schools Services (ISS), 15 Roszel Rd., P.O. Box 5910, Princeton, NJ 08543, USA (☎ 609-452-0990; fax 452-2690; www.iss.edu). Hires teachers for more than 200 overseas schools, including many in Eastern European countries. Candidates should have experience with teaching or international affairs; 2-year committment.

Office of Overseas Schools, US Department of State, Room H328, SA-1, Washington, D.C. 20522, USA (☎ 202-261-8200; fax 261-8224; www.state.gov/m/a/os/). Keeps comprehensive lists of schools abroad and agencies that arrange placement for Americans to teach abroad.

Petro-Teach, Westpost, P.O. Box 109, Lappeenranta 53101, Finland (gannon@online.ru; www.petroteach.com). Places teachers from abroad in St. Petersburg schools for a semester or the full academic year.

AU PAIR WORK

Au pairs are typically women, aged 18-27, who work as live-in nannies, caring for children and doing light housework in exchange for room, board, and a small spending allowance or stipend. While the au pair experience allows foreigners to get to know a country without the high expenses of traveling, the job often involves long hours and somewhat mediocre pay. Payment for au pairs varies with placement, and much of the au pair experience really does depend on the family for which you'll be working. The agencies below can help you find employment as an au pair.

Accord Cultural Exchange, 750 La Playa, San Francisco, CA 94121, USA (☎ 415-386-6203; www.cognitext.com/accord).

Childcare International, Ltd., Trafalgar House, Grenville Pl., London NW7 3SA, UK (☎020 8906 3116; fax 8906-3461; www.childint.co.uk).

InterExchange, 161 Sixth Ave., New York, NY 10013, USA (☎212-924-0446; fax 924-0575; www.interexchange.org).

SHORT-TERM WORK

Traveling for long periods of time can get expensive; therefore, many travelers try their hand at odd jobs for a few weeks at a time to make some extra cash to carry them through another month or two of touring around. Obtaining a short-term paid position can prove problematic as unemployment continues to plague much of Eastern Europe. With a good number of qualified locals unable to find jobs, many local establishments are unlikely to hire foreigners, particularly those who are not fluent in the native tongue. But with the necessary language skills and extra effort, work can still be found. Working in a hostel or restaurant and teaching English are the most common forms of employment among travelers to Eastern Europe. Opportunities tend to be more abundant in larger cities, but so do prospective workers, resulting in increased competition. Word-of-mouth is often the best resource when seeking a job, especially if foreign employees are being hired without the appropriate visa or work permit arrangements; ask other backpackers and friendly hostel-owners for tips on locating an appropriate opportunity. Another popular option is to work several hours a day at a hostel in exchange for free or discounted room or board.

VOLUNTEERING

Volunteering can be an extremely fulfilling experience and is very common in Eastern Europe, particularly in Bosnia and the rest of the Balkans. Many volunteer services charge you a fee to participate. These fees can be surprisingly hefty (although they frequently cover airfare and most, if not all, living expenses). Try to research a program before committing—talk to people who have previously participated and find out exactly what you're getting into, as living and working conditions can vary greatly. Different programs are geared toward different ages and levels of experience, so make sure that you are not taking on too much or too little. The more informed you are and the more realistic expectations you have, the more enjoyable the program will be. Most people choose to go through a parent organization that takes care of logistical details, and frequently provides a group environment and support system. Many of these organizations are religious, although there are rarely restrictions on who is eligible to participate.

Archaeological Institute of America, 656 Beacon St., Boston, MA 02215, USA (☎617-353-9361; www.archaeological.org). The *Archaeological Fieldwork Opportunities Bulletin,* available on the organization's website, lists field sites throughout Europe.

Business Enterprises for Sustainable Travel (BEST) (www.sustainabletravel.org). Supports travel that helps communities preserve natural and cultural resources and to create sustainable livelihoods. Their website has listings of local programs, innovative travel opportunities, and internships.

Earthwatch, 3 Clocktower Pl., Suite 100, P.O. Box 75, Maynard, MA 01754, USA (☎800-776-0188 or 978-461-0081; www.earthwatch.org). Arranges 1- to 3-week programs in the Czech Republic (forests of Bohemia) and Russia (Lake Baikal) to promote conservation of natural resources. Programs average US$1700.

Elderhostel, Inc., 11 Avenue de Lafayette, Boston, MA 02111-1746, USA (☎877-426-8056; fax 877-426-2166; www.elderhostel.org). Sends volunteers age 55 and over to Poland, Russia, and other destinations to work in construction, research, teaching, and many other projects. Costs average US$100 per day plus airfare.

Habitat for Humanity International, 121 Habitat St., Americus, GA 31709, USA (☎229-924-6935 ext. 2551; www.habitat.org). Volunteers build houses in over 83 countries, including Hungary, Poland, and the Slovak Republic, for anywhere from 2 weeks to 3 years. Short-term European program costs range from US$1800-2600.

Oxfam International, 266 Banbury Road, Suite 20, Oxford, OX2 7DL, UK (☎18 65 31 39 39; fax 31 37 70; www.oxfam.org). Runs poverty relief campaigns, including one centered in Sarajevo at Hiseta 2 (☎66 81 33).

Peace Corps, Office of Volunteer Recruitment and Selection, 1111 20th St. NW, Washington, D.C. 20526, USA (☎800-424-8580; www.peacecorps.gov). Sends volunteers to developing nations, including Bulgaria, Estonia, Latvia, Lithuania, Moldova, Poland, Romania, Russia, the Slovak Republic, and Ukraine. Typical assignments in Eastern Europe focus on business, education, or environmental issues. Must be a US citizen age 18 or over willing to make a 2-year commitment. Bachelor's degree is usually required.

Service Civil International Voluntary Service (SCI-IVS), SCI USA, 3213 W. Wheeler St., #384, Seattle, WA 98199, USA (☎/fax 206-350-6585; www.sci-ivs.org). Arranges placement in work camps in Eastern Europe for those 18+. Application fee US$65-125.

UNICEF, 333 E. 38th St., 6th fl., New York, NY 10016, USA (☎800-367-5437; www.unicef.org). Offices in Belarus, Bosnia, Croatia, Macedonia, Moldova, Montenegro, Romania, Russia, Ukraine, and Serbia.

UNHCR (United Nations High Commission for Refugees), Case Postale 2500, CH-1211 Genève 2 Dépôt, Switzerland (☎22 739 8111; www.unhcr.org), will gladly provide advice on how and where to help. Sarajevo office ☎66 61 60.

Volunteers for Peace, 1034 Tiffany Rd., Belmont., VT 05730, USA (☎802-259-2759; www.vfp.org). Arranges placement in work camps in Eastern Europe. Membership required for registration. Annual *International Workcamp Directory* US$20. Programs average US$200-500 for 2-3 weeks.

FOR FURTHER READING ON ALTERNATIVES TO TOURISM

Alternatives to the Peace Corps: A Directory of Third World and U.S. Volunteer Opportunities, by Joan Powell. Food First Books, 2000 (US$10).

How to Live Your Dream of Volunteering Oversees, by Collins, DeZerega, and Heckscher. Penguin Books, 2002 (US$17).

International Directory of Voluntary Work, by Whetter and Pybus. Peterson's Guides and Vacation Work, 2000 (US$16).

International Jobs, by Kocher and Segal. Perseus Books, 1999 (US$18).

Overseas Summer Jobs 2002, by Collier and Woodworth. Peterson's Guides and Vacation Work, 2002 (US$18).

Peterson's Study Abroad Guide. Peterson's (US$30).

Work Abroad: The Complete Guide to Finding a Job Overseas, by Hubbs, Griffith, and Nolting. Transitions Abroad Publishing, 2000 ($16).

Work Your Way Around the World, by Susan Griffith. Worldview Publishing Services, 2001 (US$18).

BELARUS
(БЕЛАРУСЬ)

BELARUSSIAN RUBLE

AUS$1 = 1014.93BR	1000BR = AUS$0.99
CDN$1 = 1184.13BR	1000BR = CDN$0.84
EUR€1 = 1813.72BR	1000BR = EUR€0.55
NZ$1 = 864.94BR	1000BR = NZ$1.16
UK£1 = 2856.43BR	1000BR = UK£0.35
US$1 = 1842.00BR	1000BR = US$0.54
ZAR1 = 173.69BR	1000BR = ZAR5.76

A country of sprawling urban landscapes surrounded by unspoiled villages, Belarus has become the unwanted stepchild of Mother Russia. While Minsk evokes the glorious days of the Soviet Union, the countryside calls back to an earlier period of agricultural beauty and tranquility. For those willing to endure the difficulties of travel, Belarus presents a unique look at a people in transition.

BELARUS AT A GLANCE

OFFICIAL NAME: Republic of Belarus

CAPITAL: Minsk (pop. 1.67 million)

POPULATION: 10.4 million (81% Belarussian, 11% Russian, 4% Polish and Ukrainian, 4% other)

LANGUAGES: Belarussian, Russian

CURRENCY: Belarussian ruble (BR)

RELIGION: 80% Eastern Orthodox, 20% other

LAND AREA: 207,600km²

CLIMATE: Continental and maritime

GEOGRAPHY: Plains, marshes

BORDERS: Latvia, Lithuania, Poland, Russia, Ukraine

ECONOMY: 13% Agriculture, 46% Industry, 41% Services

GDP: US$7500 per capita

COUNTRY CODE: 375

INTERNATIONAL DIALING PREFIX: 810

HISTORY

DIVIDE AND CONQUER. Belarus was one of the first areas settled by the **Slavs,** and by the mid-1000s it was taken under the wing of **Kyivan Rus,** the precursor of Russia and Ukraine. When the Mongols sacked Kyiv in 1240, they destroyed nascent Belarussian settlements and cleared the way for the **Duchy of Lithuania,** which ruled alone until the 1386 creation of the **Polish-Lithuanian Commonwealth.** Under the new empire, Belarus began to develop its own language and culture; this growing national identity stirred unrest among the people and eventually led to a 1648 Cossack rebellion. In the late 18th century, the **First and Second Partitions of Poland** (see **Poland: History,** p. 476) handed the territory over to Russia. Despite new industry under Russian rule, the failing economy forced some 600,000 people to abandon Belarus for, of all places, Siberia.

MORE OF THE SAME. World War I brought heavy fighting to the region, so it was fitting that **Brest-Litovsk** (see p. 78) hosted the 1918 treaty that got Russia out of the war—and ceded Belarus to **Germany** in a stunning demonstration of loyalty on Rus-

sia's part. The treaty lasted only a few months, but it was long enough for Belarus to declare **independence.** As soon as the Germans departed, the Poles and Bolsheviks divided the region, and Belarus became a charter member of the **USSR.** The Russian portion of Belarus got the full Stalinist package: more industry and fewer dissidents and intellectuals after the purges of the 1930s.

THE GOOD OL' DAYS. With **World War II** came another wave of German soldiers; the confrontation between Germany and Russia destroyed most of Minsk in the process. Belarus was unified upon Stalin's victory and the nation bounced back quickly after the war. **Minsk,** intended to become the model Soviet city, was rebuilt in grand Stalinist style. Industry boomed and rural Belarussians migrated to the growing cities for better job prospects.

WHAT NUCLEAR EXPLOSION? On the day of the 1986 explosion at **Chernobyl,** just across the border in modern Ukraine, the wind happened to be blowing northwest, spewing radioactive material across southern Belarus. Chernobyl's tragic legacy still haunts Belarus; the long-term effects of the country's contamination with radioactive cesium are beginning to surface in the form of childhood thyroid cancer. Content with the Communist system, Belarus reluctantly declared sovereignty on July 27, 1990 and **independence** on August 25, 1991, as Moscow fell into political turmoil. The fledgling republic quickly found a security blanket in the **Commonwealth of Independent States** (**CIS,** see **Russia: History,** p. 624) and has not strayed far from Mother Russia since.

TODAY

Of all the former Soviet republics, Belarus has the weakest national identity, is the most Russified, and has clamored the least for independence. Indeed, President **Aleksandr Lukashenka** publicly decreed that Belarus was to be "Slavic, Russian, and Orthodox." In 1995 he also embarked the country on the road to what he called **"market socialism,"** clinging to the communist structure from the Soviet Era and isolating Belarus from the open-market economies of the West. Lukashenka has garnered much **criticism** from the West as he has resorted to **suppressing the media, arresting dissenters,** and even **dissolving Parliament** to maintain power. The US government reports that since April 1999 at least three prominent members of Lukashenka's opposition and one journalist have **vanished** without a trace. Much to the chagrin of opposition in Belarus and abroad, however, Lukashenka's following among the people is solid and almost cultish. The **Union Treaty of 1996** was supposed to move toward reunification with Russia, but in the face of Belarus's struggling economy, Russia has gotten a case of **cold feet.** On December 8, 1999 Belarus and Russia signed an accord promising future economic integration and possibly political union. In June 2002, however, President Putin of Russia again brought the process to a halt, accusing Lukashenka of trying to resurrect the Soviet Union.

PEOPLE AND CULTURE

LANGUAGE

Most Belarussians speak **Russian** and very rarely Belarussian (see **The Cyrillic Alphabet,** p. 15, and **Glossary: Russian,** p. 889), although Belarussian does still appear in print. If you can handle substituting the Belarussian "i" for the Russian "и" and other minor spelling changes, you'll be fine. The only major difference is that the Cyrillic letter "г," which is pronounced "g" in Russian, is transliterated as "h" in Belarussian. *Let's Go* lists place names in Belarussian in deference to the official line, but in order to be understood, you'll have to replace "h" with "g" ("Hrodna" is more commonly pronounced "Grodno").

FOOD AND DRINK

BELARUS	❶	❷	❸	❹	❺
FOOD	under US$2	US$2-5	US$6-10	US$11-20	over US$20

Belarussian cuisine consists of what farmers can either grow or fatten: potatoes, bread, chicken, and pork. If you guess at a menu, you'll probably receive bread, sausage, and a vegetable. Locals eat *morozhenoye* (мороженое; ice cream) at all hours of the day. The favorite Belarussian drink is the bread-based *kvas* (квас), which is sold at stores or from huge kegs on the street—look for the long line.

THE ARTS

Domination by myriad rulers put off Belarus's cultural growth until the 15th century, when Polatsk-born **Frantsishek Skaryna** translated the Bible into Old Church Slavonic (with original prefaces and postscripts in Belarussian). Resurgence came with the 1906 egalitarian journal *Our Cornfield (Nasha Niva)*, which drew contributions from 500 villages and launched the careers of **Yakub Kolas** and **Yanka**

Kupala, known for their portrayal of Belarus's revolutionary struggles. After the death of Stalin, prose and poetry were finally able to flourish. Today's major figures include poets **Pimen Pachanka** and **Arkady Kalyashov** and novelists **Yanka Bryl** and **Ivan Shamyakin.** Despite a long tradition of folk and church music, **classical composition** has only developed since World War II. Notable composers include exile **Kulikovich Shchahlow** and **Yawhen Hlyebaw.**

HOLIDAYS AND FESTIVALS

NATIONAL HOLIDAYS IN 2003

January 1 New Year's Day

January 7 Orthodox Christmas

March 8 International Women's Day

March 15 Constitution Day

April 20-21 Catholic Easter

April 27 Orthodox Easter

May 1 Labor Day

May 9 Victory Day and Mother's Day

June 15 Radunitsa (Holy Trinity)

July 3 Independence Day

November 2 Remembrance Day

November 7 October Revolution Day

December 25 Christmas

BELARUS ESSENTIALS

ENTRANCE REQUIREMENTS

Passport: Required of all travelers.

Visa: Required of all travelers.

Letter of Invitation: Required of all travelers.

Inoculations: None required. Recommended up-to-date on MMR (measles, mumps, and rubella), DTaP (diphtheria), Polio booster, Typhoid, Tetanus, Hepatitis A, and Hepatitis B.

Work Permit: Required of all foreigners planning to work in Belarus.

International Driving Permit: Required of all those planning to drive.

DOCUMENTS AND FORMALITIES

EMBASSIES AND CONSULATES

Embassies and consulates of other countries in Belarus are all in Minsk (see p. 73). Belarus's embassies and consulates abroad include:

Canada: 130 Albert St. Suite 600, Ottawa, Ontario K1P 5G4 (☎613-233-9994; fax 233-8500).

UK: 6 Kensington Ct., London, W8 5DL (☎020 7937 3288; fax 7361 0005).

US: 1619 New Hampshire Ave. NW, Washington D.C. 20009 (☎202-986-1606; fax 986-1805; www.belarusembassy.org).

VISA AND ENTRY INFORMATION

To visit Belarus, you must secure an invitation, a visa, and medical insurance—an expensive and head-spinning process. If you have an acquaintance in Belarus who can provide you with an official invitation, you may obtain a 90-day single-

STICKY FINGERS AND GREASY PALMS. One of Belarus's anything-goes bargaining practices is the *vzyat* (bribe). Do your best to avoid this: cross borders in the daytime, travel in train compartments with locals, and make sure your documents are in line before departing. Given enough time, though, even the most cautious will end up in a situation where cash is the only method of payment and receipts are not available. The uninitiated wonder how to price in such situations, but the answer is simple supply and demand. The man with the semi-automatic weapon demands money and you supply all you have. The key is to limit the supply— as a rule, do not carry wads of cash. US$20 is usually plenty, since that's more than enough to buy a night's supply of beer.

entry (5-day service US$50, next-day US$100) or multiple-entry (5-day processing US$170, next day US$305) visa at an embassy or consulate by submitting your passport, the application, a check or money order, and a photograph. For mail orders include a self-addressed stamped envelope. Those without Belarussian friends can turn to **Russia House** (see **Russia: Visa and Invitation Information,** p. 630), which will get you an invitation and visa in 5 business days (US$225, 3-day processing US$275, next-day US$325). Transit visas (US$40), valid for 48 hours, are issued at a consulate and at the border. As of October 1, 2000, Belarus requires all foreign nationals to purchase **medical insurance** at the port of entry (US$1 for a one-day stay, US$15 for 60 days, and up to US$85 for a year).

TRANSPORTATION

BY PLANE. The hard-core traveler can fly into Minsk on **Belavia,** Belarus's national airline from many European capitals. **Lufthansa** has daily direct flights from Frankfurt. Be aware that Minsk's airport, **Minsk-II,** often fails to meet Western safety standards. Stick to the extensive train and bus lines.

BY TRAIN OR BUS. Trains and **buses** are both reliable means of transportation within Belarus. Some international **train** tickets must be paid partly in US dollars and partly in Belarussian rubles. All immigration and customs are done on the trains. For city **buses,** buy tickets at a kiosk and punch them on board.

TOURIST SERVICES AND MONEY

 INFLATION. Inflation is rampant in Belarus; *Let's Go* lists many prices in US$. Posted prices in Belarus drop the final three zeros and prices in this chapter follow that convention. Bills printed in 2000 and later also omit the zeros, but the old bills remain in circulation and are difficult to distinguish from the new ones. Take the time to organize and acquaint yourself with Belarus's currency, lest you accidentally pay 5,000,000BR for something that costs 5000BR.

Belintourist (Белінтурíст) is helpful and often the only resource. Hotel Belarus and Hotel Yubilyenaya in Minsk have **private travel agencies.** US dollars and Russian rubles are preferred; you'll have trouble exchanging other currencies, even British pounds. **Traveler's checks** are rarely accepted. There are no **ATMs** aside from one or two that have recently popped up in Minsk. Some hotels accept **credit cards.**

HEALTH AND SAFETY

 EMERGENCY NUMBERS: Police: ☎0 Fire: ☎02 Emergency: ☎03

HEALTH AND SAFETY. Belarus was more affected by the 1986 **Chernobyl** accident than any other region. The faulty reactor was situated in Ukraine, just 12km south of the Belarussian border, and an area of approximately 1200 sq. km just north of Chernobyl has been evacuated because of high concentrations of strontium-90, plutonium-239/240, and cesium-137. Today, experts say that a week's stay there is no worse than receiving an X-ray. *Let's Go* does not cover the affected regions. Avoid cheap **dairy products,** which may come from contaminated areas—opt instead for something German or Dutch—and stay away from **mushrooms** and **berries,** which collect radioactivity. Drink bottled water; **tap water** may be contaminated. **Toilet paper** is available in most supermarkets, making its absence from public toilets befuddling. **Condoms** and **feminine hygiene** supplies from the West are becoming available. Your embassy is a better bet than the police in an emergency. For children under 18 unaccompanied by an adult, there is a **mandatory 11pm curfew.** It's a good idea to stay clear of dodgy nightclubs, which are mostly run by the mafia.

MINORITY AND BGLT TRAVELERS. Discrimination exists in Belarus, especially against people with dark skin. Also, if you want to fit in, don't smile too much. **Homosexuality** is definitely frowned upon, but no one will you assume you are gay unless you announce it.

ACCOMMODATIONS

BELARUS	❶	❷	❸	❹	❺
ACCOM.	under US$10	US$10-15	US$16-25	US$26-55	over US$55

HOTELS AND PRIVATE ROOMS. Keep receipts from hotels; you might have to show them to the authorities to avoid fines when leaving Belarus. Hotels have three rates—very cheap for Belarussians, outrageous for foreigners, and in-between for CIS citizens. The desk clerks request passports, making it impossible to pass as a native. To find a private room, look around for postings at train stations or ask taxi drivers, who may know of a lead. The *babushki* (older women) at train stations are willing to feed and house you for US$10 or less.

KEEPING IN TOUCH

MAIL. Avoid the **mail** system; almost everything is opened by the authorities and often discarded.

TELEPHONES AND INTERNET ACCESS. Local calls require tokens sold at kiosks or magnetic cards, available at the post office and some hotels (200-500BR). **International calls** must be placed at the telephone office and paid for in advance, in cash. Calls to the US and Western Europe cost US$1-3 per minute. **Email** is the easiest and cheapest way to communicate with the outside world. Internet cafes have yet to make a noticeable appearance in Belarus, so you'll have to check the local post office for Internet access.

MINSK (MIHCK) (8)017

If you're looking for a true Soviet city, skip Moscow and head to Minsk (pop. 1,700,000), where the fall of Communism has led to a reluctant shuffle, rather than an enthusiastic gallop west. A handful of streets have been renamed, but Lenin's statue still presides over Independence Square. With imaginary political reforms and concrete everywhere, not to mention the omnipresent police, everyone is asking if the government is really giving Minsk a new face or just a new facade.

▐▘ TRANSPORTATION

Flights: Minsk-II (☎279 17 30) is the main airport. Buses run to the central bus station (40min., every hr., 590BR). From the bus station, walk next door to the train station and cross the street to catch the Metro (M-red: pl. Nezalezhnasti). If you don't speak Russian, a taxi will cost US$25-40. If arriving from **Minsk-I** (info ☎006), located south of downtown, take trolleybus #2 or 18 to the city's main square, pl. Nezalezhnasti.

Trains: Chigunachni Vokzal (Чыгуначны Вокзал; ☎225 54 10, domestic info 005, international info 225-67 05), pl. Privakzalnaya. M-blue: pl. Nezalezhnasti. Tickets are sold on the 1st floor of the new train station building. Purchase advance tickets at **Belintourist**. To: **Brest** (4½hr.; 12 per day; 14,000BR); **Kyiv, UKR** (14hr.; 1 per day; 29,000BR); **Moscow, RUS** (14hr.; 7 per day; 59,000BR); **St. Petersburg, RUS** (2 per day; 63,000BR); **Vilnius, LIT** (4½hr., 1 per day, 9000BR). Other trains run to **Berlin, Prague,** and **Warsaw**.

Buses: Avtovakzal Tsentralni (Автовакзал Цэнтральны), vul. Babruyskaya 6 (Бабруйская; ☎227 41 89, info 004). M-blue: pl. Nezalezhnasti. Next to the train station. Buses run to: **Hrodna** (10 per day; 10,500BR); **Bialystok, POL** (2 per day; 22,000BR); **Prague, CZR** (1 per day; 90,500BR); **Vilnius, LIT** (3 per day, 7895BR). Buy tickets to non-CIS countries on the 3rd floor. Open M-F 8am-9pm, Sa-Su 8am-noon and 1-5pm.

Public Transportation: The **Metro, buses, trolleys,** and **trains** run 5:30am-1am (120BR). While the new stop names are announced and used on maps, many platforms still bear the old signs. The 10-day pass is good on all local transport (3000BR). The Metro is sufficiently simple: there are two lines, red and blue, which meet at the center, Kastrytchinskaya.

Taxis: Toll-free ☎081. At kiosks throughout the city. Do not pay more than US$2 for a 10min. ride. All city cabs are equipped with meters. Make sure the meter is running. The initial fare is 500BR, but rates change after midnight.

▐▌ ORIENTATION

The center of town lies in the 3km between northeastern **pl. Peramohi** (Перамогі) and southwestern **pl. Nezalezhnastsi** (Незалежнасці; Independence Square), with the city's main street, **pr. Frantsishka Skoriny** (Францішка Скорины), connecting the two. **Pr. Masherava** (Машэрава), which turns into **vul. Lenina** (Леніна) after pl. Svabody, runs perpendicular to pr. F. Skoriny. The **Svislac River** divides the city, with most of the attractions located on the southwest bank. The **train station** sits behind **pl. Privakzalnaya** (Прівакзальная). To get to the center of town, walk up vul. Leningradskaya and go left on Sverdlova (Свердлова) to reach pl. Nezalezhnastsi; from there, pr. Skoriny will take you through the center.

◪ PRACTICAL INFORMATION

Tourist Office: Belintourist (Белінтурíст), pr. Masherava 19 (☎226 90 56; fax 223 11 43; www.belintourist.by). Next to Gastsinitsa Yubileyny. M-red: Nyamiha. Plane and train tickets are sold on the 1st floor. Open M-F 8am-1pm and 2-8pm, Sa-Su 9am-5pm. Information about the city, accommodations, visa extensions, and tours available in room #29 on the 2nd floor. Tours of Minsk (3hr.) and outlying areas US$25-60, depending on demand. Call ahead to arrange a tour. Open M-F 10am-6pm.

Travel Agencies: Carlson WagonLit, pr. Masherova 5 (☎206 54 40; fax 223 51 25). **Vneshlutourist,** vul. Storozhevskaya 15 (Сторожевская; ☎234 97 82; fax 239 17 09; www.vneshintourist.com), on the 2nd fl. of the Belarus Hotel. Belarus's first private travel company arranges tours and books hotel rooms for groups and individuals.

Passport Office: All foreigners visiting Minsk must **register** their passports at **OVIR** (ОВИР), pr. Skoriny 48b (☎231 91 74 or 231 32 02), near the concert hall, 2 courtyards behind Skoriny 48. M-blue: Yakuba Kolasa. If you are staying at a hotel, your visa will be automatically registered. Open M-F 9am-1pm and 2-6pm. Visiting hours for foreigners Tu and F 2:30-5pm.

Embassies: Russia, vul. Staravilenskaya 48 (Старавіленская; ☎222 49 85). Open M-F 9am-1pm. **UK,** vul. Karla Магха 37 (Карла Маркса; ☎210 59 20; fax 229 23 11). Open M-F 9am-6pm. **Ukraine,** vul. Staravilenskaya 51 (☎283 19 58; fax 283 19 80). Open M-F 9-1pm. **US,** vul. Staravilenskaya 46 (☎210 12 83; fax 234 71 60). Open M-F 8:30am-5:30pm.

Currency Exchange: Look for the "Абмен Валюты" signs. Cash AmEx **Traveler's Cheques** at the local **AmEx** representative in Victory Square, 40 pr. Skoriny. Open M-F 9am-6pm, Sa-Su 10am-4pm. **ATMs** are at Lenina 10 and pr. Masherova 17.

Luggage Storage: Downstairs in the new train station (400BR per day). You can also store luggage downstairs in the bus station. 400BR per bag. Open daily 6-10pm.

English-Language Bookstore: Podpicniye Izdanly (Подписные здание), pr. Skoriny 14 (☎227 63 61). Open Su-F 10am-7pm, Sa 10am-6pm. Small selection of English, German, French, and Spanish fiction and classics (3000-12,000BR).

Bi-Gay-Lesbian Organizations: Check out www.belgays.gay.ru.

Pharmacy: Apteka #13, pr. Skoriny 16. Open M-F 8am-8pm, Sa-Su 11am-6pm.

Hospital: City Hospital #2 (Бальніца), vul. Maksima Bogdanovicha 2 (☎234 01 40). M-red: Nyamiha. Located next to the opera and ballet theater; entrance on Yanki Kupaly (Янки Купалы).

Telephones: Central Telegraph Office, to the left upon entering the post office. Make all international calls here. Open daily 8am-10pm.

Internet Access: Internet Klass (Интернет Класс), vul. Karla Marksa 10 (☎206 63 37), on the 1st floor of the Palace of Chess and Checkers (Дворец шахмат и шашек; Dvorets Shakhmat i shashek). M-blue: pl. Nezalazhnasti. 1400BR per hr. Open daily 10am-10pm.

Post Office: Pr. Skoriny 10 (☎227 77 71). Open M-Sa 8am-8pm, Su 10am-5pm. **Poste Restante** available.

Postal Code: 220 050.

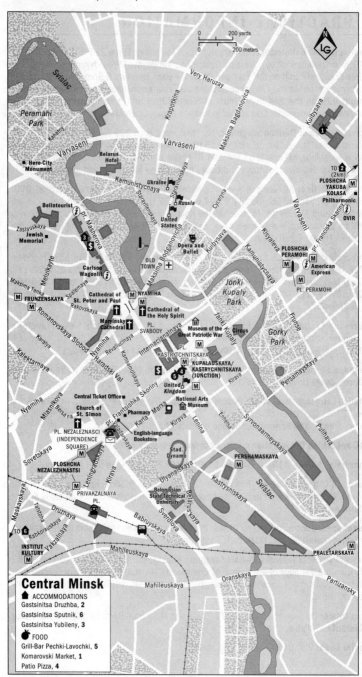

Central Minsk

▲ ACCOMMODATIONS
Gastsinitsa Druzhba, **2**
Gastsinitsa Sputnik, **6**
Gastsinitsa Yubileny, **3**

🍗 FOOD
Grill-Bar Pechki-Lavochki, **5**
Komarovski Market, **1**
Patio Pizza, **4**

ACCOMMODATIONS

Private rooms are the best option around. **Travel agencies** can often get you cheaper rates at hotels.

Gastsinitsa Sputnik (Спутник), vul. Brilevskaya 2 (Брилевская; ☎229 36 19). From both the train and bus stations, walk to pl. Nezalezhnasti, cross the street, and take trolleybus #2 from the stop in front of the red cathedral. The hotel is just past the second bridge, on the same side of the street as the bus stop (5min.). Rooms all have bath, fridge, and TV. Singles 45,000BR; doubles 64,000BR. ❸

Gastsinitsa Druzhba (Дружба), vul. Tolbukhina 3 (☎266 24 81). M-blue: Park Chelyuskintsev (Парк Челюскинцев). Exit the Metro station at the front of your train, go down the left staircase, then right on the road in front of you. Singles and doubles with renovated bathrooms. Breakfast included. Singles 59,000BR; doubles 86,000BR. ❸

Gastsinitsa Yubileny, pr. Masherova 19 (☎226 90 24; fax 226 91 71). More expensive, but centrally located. Singles US$47; doubles US$58. ❹

FOOD

Patio Pizza (Патио-Пицца), pr. Skoriny 22 (☎227 17 91). M-red/blue: pl. Kastrytchitskaya. A generic American pizza parlor in this oh-so-Soviet city. Friendly service, waiters in polos, plastic red-and-white plaid table cloths, a TV, and an all-you-can-eat-salad bar. Pizza 4000-14,000BR, pasta 5000-15,000BR. MC/V. ❸

Grill-Bar Pechki-Lavochki (Печки-Лавочки), F. Skoriny 22 (☎227 78 79; ☎/fax 227 61 02). M-red/blue: pl. Kastrytchitskaya. Next to Patio Pizza (see above). Watch the cook prepare your food in a brick oven. Order the smooth, 42-proof "honey drink" (медовый напой; myodoviy napoi). Entrees 8000-25,000BR. Open daily noon-midnight. ❸

Komarovski Market (Комаровский Рынк; Komarovskii Rink). M-blue: pl. Yakuba Kolasa. Take a left on ver. Haruzay and walk down 1 block. All the meat you could ever imagine. Open daily 7am-7pm.

SIGHTS

More than 80% of Minsk's buildings were obliterated and 60% of its population was killed between 1941 and 1944. The postwar city was rebuilt in grand Stalinist style, with gargantuan buildings and wide boulevards. Today the Soviet influence in both the architecture and the people draws backpackers to Minsk, eager to catch a glimpse of the former USSR.

INDEPENDENCE SQUARE. (пл. Незалежнасци; pl. Nezalezhnastsi.) This square was once pl. Lenina but now stands as the symbol of Belarussian independence. It is currently a giant construction site as, after much controversy, a department store is being built on part of the area, while the rest will be repaved. The statue of **St. Simon** slaying a dragon stands before the crimson church dedicated to his name. *(Savetskaya 15. M-blue: Nezalezhnastsi. Just north of the train station.)*

WORLD WAR II MEMORIALS. Victory Square is "the holiest place in Minsk" according to the state tourism literature. A 40m obelisk crowns the grand pr. Skoriny, celebrating the defeat of the German army in World War II. *(M-red: pl. Peramohi (пл. Перамогі.) North of Svisloch island, the flatness of Minsk is broken by the* **Minsk Hero-City Monument.** The **Jewish memorial** remembers the 5000 Jews shot and buried by the Nazis here in 1942. *(M-blue: Frunzenskaya (Фрунзенская). Exit the Metro onto vul. Melnikaite (Мельникайте); the memorial will be to your left. Continue walking down Melnikaite and turn left on Masherova to find the Hero-City Monument.)*

FROM THE ROAD

THE BELARUSSIAN EURO

In 2001, a poster appeared all over Europe displaying banknotes and coins of different sizes and colors against a blue background. Soon after, these notes and coins became legal tender in eleven countries, collectively known as the Eurozone. In Belarus, I came across this poster again. At first I was a bit puzzled, as I didn't think Belarus was part of the EU, but I soon learned the riddle's simple solution.

For a country with a miniscule tourism industry, Belarus has an excessive number of currency exchange booths. Yet, when I first tried to participate, I stood about three feet behind the person at the counter, discreetly awaiting a turn that never came. People just passed me, went straight up, inspected each other's transactions, and jumped in to do theirs.

A strong, slightly drunk man peeking over my shoulder made me a bit uncomfortable, but I soon realized that Belarussians weren't out to rob me. They merely wanted to get rid of their rubles. In the 1990s, the country experienced hyperinflation; the cost of everyday goods were in the millions of rubles. In 2000, the government ordered the last three zeros from all prices and banknotes to be dropped. The situation has stabilized a bit recently, but Belarussians still prefer hard currency. Taxi drivers, hotel clients, and police officers asked me for dollars; even the country's few toll roads demand them. Until recently, the Deutsche Mark was as popular as the greenback, but Belarussians are slowly getting used to the Euro.

—Werner Schäfer

■ NATIONAL ARTS MUSEUM. (Нацыянальны Мастацкі Музей Распублікі Беларусь; Natsyanalny Mastatski Muzey Raspubliki Belarus.) The museum exhibits closely hung Russian and Belarussian paintings, sculptures, and furniture from the 18th to 20th centuries. *(Pr. Lenina 20. ☎ 227 56 72 or 227 71 63. M-red/blue: Kastrytchnitskaya. Open W-M 11am-7pm. 5000BR.)*

MUSEUM OF THE GREAT PATRIOTIC WAR. (Музей Великой Отечественной Войны; Muzey Velikoy Otechestvennoy Voyny.) Paints a suitably grim picture of the war in which Belarus lost 25% of its population, and glorifies in the heroism of the Soviet Union. *(Pr. Skoriny 25a. ☎ 227 56 11 or 227 76 35. M-red/blue: Kastrytchnitskaya. Open Tu-Su 10am-5pm. 3000BR.)*

🎵 ENTERTAINMENT

Small bars line pl. Skoriny and ul. Karla Marksa. For a complete list of Minsk nightlife, consult *What and Where in Minsk*, available at major hotels, tourist centers, and at www.wwminsk.com.

Opera and Ballet Theater, vul. Paryzhskai Kamuny 1 (Парыжскай Камуны; ☎ 234 06 66, ballet ticket office 234 06 66). M-red: Nyamiha. Exit the Metro on Maksima Bagdanovica; the theater is in the park on your right. The best seats in the house go for under US$5. Purchase advance tickets from the Central Ticket Office, pr. Skoriny 13 (open M-F 9:30am-8pm, Sa 10am-7pm, Su noon-5pm) or at the theater. The opera and ballet seasons run late Sept.-May.

Minsk Circus, pr. Skoriny 32 (☎ 227 22 45 or 227 78 42). M-blue: pl. Peramohi (Перамогі). Tickets 3000-8000BR. Children under 5 free. Box office open M-F 9am-2pm and 3-8pm, Sa-Su 9am-3pm and 4-8pm. Performances Sept.-July. Sa 3pm, Su 11:30am and 3pm, Tu-Su 7pm.

🔁 DAYTRIP FROM MINSK

MIR CASTLE

Take a bus from Minsk to Mir (3394BR), and ask the bus driver to drop you off at Mirski Zamak (Мирски Замак). Museum 5000BR.

Far out in the Belarussian countryside, Mir (Мир) Castle is a prime example of Gothic architecture. In 2000, the castle became the first Belarussian monument to appear on UNESCO's World Cultural Heritage list. Duke Ilich built the Gothic castle in the early 16th century. The Radzivil family, taking over in 1568, preferred the ways of the Renaissance and finished the job accordingly. Despite thick earth walls and a water moat surrounding it, the castle was severely damaged several times, once by Napoleon's soldiers of the 1812 war. Today, artisans and construction workers are again restoring the castle and its environs to its former grandeur. A small museum, located in one of the five towers, displays relics of the castle's past, including weapons, clay pots, coins, and traditionally embroidered garments. To get to the exhibits, you have to climb tall, irregular, spiralling stairs, a climb your legs will remember for days. A museum *babushka* carrying large old keys will unlock the doors for you. The top of the tower affords a great view of the countryside through the shootingholes-turned-windows. The less adventurous can book organized tours from Belintourist or Vueshintourist (see **Practical Information: Travel Agencies**, p. 73). Such tours are rather expensive for individuals (US$50-100), but quite affordable for groups.

HRODNA (ГРОДНА) ☎(8)152

Hrodna (pop. 310,000) has seen many different sovereigns. Long a part of the Duchy of Lithuania (which later became the Lithuanian-Polish Commonwealth), Hrodna was taken over by the Russian Empire in 1795. Since the Poles were able to maintain influence over the town even after partition, Hrodna retains the feel of a Polish town. While Soviet planners had their way with the city's endless industrial outskirts, the center dates to an earlier and prettier age. Several townhouses and churches have been restored, leaving hope for a more attractive future.

▛ TRANSPORTATION. The train station, **Chigunachni Vakzal** (Чыгуначный Вакзал; ☎44 85 56), is on vul. Budyenovo (Буденного), northwest of the city. Buy international tickets at windows #13 and 14. Trains run to: **Minsk** (6-8 hr., 2 per day, 8000BR); **Bialystok, POL** (5hr.; 3 per day; 16,747BR) via **Kusniza; Moscow, RUS** (12hr.; 1 per day; 28,000BR); **Warsaw, POL** (6hr.; 3 per day, 28,000BR). The bus station, **Autovakzal** (Аўтовакзал), vul. Krasnoarmeyskaya 7a (Красноармейская; ☎72 37 24), is 1km from the center, down vul. Karla Marksce from pl. Stefana Batorya. Bus #15 runs along vul. Budonova between the bus and train stations. Buses run to: **Brest** (6hr.; 4 per day; 14,000BR); **Minsk** (5½hr.; every hr.; 10,300BR); **Bialystok, POL** (3 hr., 1 per day M-Sa, 9500BR); **Druskininkai, LIT** (1½hr., 3 per day, 2885BR); **St. Petersburg, RUS** (Tu, Th, Sa-Su 1 per day; 40,000BR); **Vilnius, LIT** (5hr., F-Su 1 per day, 7000BR); **Warsaw, POL** (6hr.; 2 per day Su-F, 16,000BR). You may need to buy a baggage ticket to store luggage under the bus. Purchase local bus/trolleybus tickets in sets of 6 from the driver. Validate tickets on board.

▛▟ ORIENTATION AND PRACTICAL INFORMATION. Pl. Stefana Batorya (Стефана Баторя) is the city's main square. In front of the gray building with pseudo-greek columns (the House of Culture), **vul. Savetskaya** (Савецкая), the main pedestrian thoroughfare, begins on your right. At the end of vul. Savetskaya, **Belarus Bank** (Бепарус Ванк) offers an **ATM, currency exchange, cash advances** and a **Western Union** counter. (Open M-F 9am-2pm, 3pm-7pm, Sa 9am-3pm.) Walking the opposite direction from Stefana atorya, past a monument and a bank, you'll reach **Prior Bank** (Пріор Ванк), vul. Mostovaya 37. It offers the same services and also cashes **traveler's checks**, albeit at outrageous commission. (Open M-F 9am-1pm and 1:30pm-3pm.) Just left of the House of Culture, there is a **pharmacy**, Apteka Belfarm (Белфарм), vul. Mactavaya. (Open M-F 8am-9pm, Sa 9am-4pm.) **Internet access** is available inside. (☎72 01 79. 1134BR per hr. Open M-F 8am-2pm and 3-8pm, Sa-Su 10am-2pm and 3-4pm). The 24hr. **telephone office** is next door. The **post office** is at Vul. Karla Marksa 29 (Карла Маркса), the road starting to the right of the large white church on Stefana Batorya. (Open M-F 8am-8pm, Sa-Su 10am-4pm.) **Postal Code:** 230 025.

BELARUS

⛏🛏 ACCOMMODATIONS AND FOOD. Take a taxi (US$2-3) to **Gastsinitsa Turist ❷** (Гасцініца Туріст), J. Kupala 63 (Купала), as it is far from the train and bus stations. From the hotel, take trolleybus #9 or bus #1 to pl. Stefan Batorya. (☎269 948 or 26 55 20; fax 26 98 73. Singles 40,000BR; doubles 55,000BR.) Advance reservations are recommended. Other accommodations are available, but save yourself the hassle by reserving with Gastinitsa Turista. There are plenty of **cafes** and **supermarkets** along vul. Savetskaya. Located in a cabin just off vul. Savetskaya, **Cafe Kronon ❶** (Кронон) is one of the few restaurants in the city. To reach the restaurant from pl. Stefan Batorya, walk half of a block down Savetskaya, turn right and pass the concrete building labelled "Grodno" (Гродно). The restaurant is hidden behind a house on the left. (☎44 12 52. Entrees 1000-4000BR. Open noon-midnight.)

◪ SIGHTS. The city's best sights are its castles, which overlook the Neman river. From pl. Stefana Batorya (пл. Стефана Баторья), take vul. Zamkavaya (Замковая), and go straight to the House of Culture. On your right, you will pass a small **monument** in memory of the 29,000 Hrodna Jews who perished in the Holocaust. At the intersection, with a tower on the right, go straight on the higher road. **Old Castle** (Стары Замак; Stary Zamak), on the right, was built in the 1570s. Its 20 rooms cover Hrodna's history. Exhibits include excavations from Pompeii, Mammoth bones, dinosaur models, and uniforms from the "Great Patriotic War." (Open Tu-Su 10am-6pm; *kassa* closes at 5pm. 2225BR.) On the opposite side of the hill, **New Castle** (Новы Замак; Novy Zamak) houses another exhibit on the city's history, along with stuffed animals and paintings of Soviet luminaries. (☎44 40 68. Open Tu-Su 10am-6pm; *kassa* closes at 5pm. 1200BR.) An English language brochure about both museums is available for 634BR. Hrodna also has a number of beautiful churches that are worth seeing, such as **Farce Cathedral** on pl. Stefana Batorya, which was recently renovated. Walk down vul. Savetskaya and turn right at its end to reach Hrodna's **park,** a favorite local hangout.

BREST (БРЕСТ) ☎(8)016

From the windows of a train, Brest looks like a city comprised entirely of vast railroad yards. A stroll through the generic Soviet center won't do much to change that impression. Yet the trees along its avenues, the ubiquitous street vendors, and the occasional restored facade make for a pleasant atmosphere. In 1965, the Brest-Litovsk Fortress was designated a Soviet hero-city, in honor of those who valiantly defended the fortress against the Nazi invaders during WWII.

⛏ TRANSPORTATION. The palatial **train station** (☎27 32 77), just north of vul. Ardzhanikidze, is the main border crossing for trains running between Moscow and Warsaw. Trains run to: **Minsk** (4½hr.; 11 per day; 10,605BR); **Kyiv, UKR** (16½hr.; 1 per day; 29,000BR); **Moscow, RUS** (16hr.; 8 per day; 46,000BR); **Prague, CZR** (18hr.; 1 per day; 110,000BR); **Warsaw, POL** (2 per day; 36,000BR). The **bus station** is on the corner of vul. Kuybyshava (Куйбышава) and vul. Mitskevicha (Міцкевіча; ☎23 81 42). From vul. Pushkiuskaya, take a left on Sovietskaya and turn right after the yellow church. Buses run to **Hrodna** (8hr.; 2 per day; 10,800BR) and **Warsaw, POL** (6hr.; 1-3 per day; 12,000BR).

⛏⛏ ORIENTATION AND PRACTICAL INFORMATION. The **Mukhavets River** marks the southern boundary of the city, while the **Bug River** is both the western boundary and the border with Poland. The **Brest-Litovsk Fortress** lies at the confluence of these two rivers. At the train station, head toward the pedestrian overpass on your left and take a right over the tracks. The first right leads to **vul. Ardzhoni-**

kidze (Арджонікідзе). After two blocks, you'll reach **vul. Lenina** (Леніна). Head left to reach **pl. Lenina,** the main square; **vul. Pushkinskaya** (Пушкінская) runs to the left. Three blocks down vul. Pushkinskaya, take a right on vul. Sovietskaya (Савецкая), a pedestrian area that is almost picturesque. Farther down vul. Lenina is **vul. Gogalya** (Гогаля), the main east-west thoroughfare; the next major intersection is **vul. Masherova** (Машерова).

The staff at **Gastsinitsa Intourist** (see **Accommodations and Food,** below) speaks English and will arrange English **tours** of the fortress if you call a week in advance. (☎20 55 71; fax 22 19 00. US$40 for groups; cheaper for small groups.) **Belarus Bank** (Беларусъ Ванк) on pl. Lenina gives **MC cash advances** and provides **Western Union** services. (Open M-F 8:30am-2pm and 3-7:30pm, Sa 8:30am-2pm and 3-6:30pm, Su 8:30am-2pm and 3-5:30pm.) Exchange windows abound, and there is an **ATM** at the train station. **Store luggage** in the train or bus stations (320BR). A **pharmacy** (аптека) lies on the intersection of vul. Pushkinskaya and vul. Sovietskaya (open 8am-midnight). **Belpak** (Белпак), Masherova 21, in the phone office, through the door on your right, offers **Internet access.** (☎22 13 15. 19BR per min. Open Tu-F 8:30-11:45am, 1-4:30pm, and 5:30-10pm; Sa and M 10am-1:45pm and 3-7pm.) The **post office** is at Masherova 32. (☎20 12 48. **Poste Restante** available. Open M-F 8am-8pm, Sa 8am-5pm, Su 9am-2pm.) **Postal Code:** 224 000.

▌▐ ACCOMMODATIONS AND FOOD. ▌**Gastsinitsa Vesta ❸** (Веста), vul. Krupskoi 16 (Крупской), is very clean and has a decent restaurant. Walk about 200m through the park behind the Lenin statue and take the a left on the first road. (☎23 71 69; fax 23 78 39. Singles 46,665BR; doubles 93,330BR.) Slightly more upscale is **Gastsinitsa Intourist ❹,** vul. Masherova 15. (☎20 09 50; fax 22 19 00. Singles 53,060BR; doubles 91,880. MC/V.) If you're really looking to spend money, rent one of their suites (277,000BR) or try your luck in the hotel's casino. (Open daily 4pm-8am.) There are plenty of bars, cafes, and restaurants on vul. Sovietskaya. **Traktir "U Osera" ❷** (Трактир "У Озеро") is harder to find but located under beautiful ancient trees by a small pond. The waiters don folk outfits and speak very little English. (☎23 57 63. Entrees 5000-15,000BR. Open daily noon-11:30pm.) From pl. Lenina, walk toward the bridge over the railroad but don't cross it. Take a left into the park and go straight until you see the pond on the right.

◗ SIGHTS. ▌**Brest-Litovsk Fortress** (Крэпасць Брэст-Літовск; Krepasts Brest-Litovsk) is between the Bug and Mukhavets rivers. From pl. Lenina, turn right on vul. Masherova and walk 15min. Or take bus #17 or a taxi (US$1-2). This fortress was the site of the 1918 signing of the Brest-Litovsk peace treaty in which Russia pledged an end hostilities against Germany. During WWII, Brest's citizens held onto the fortress for 10 days, until they were unable to withstand the Nazi onslaught. Today, the area is covered by a park, frequented by the people of Brest for Sunday strolls and wedding processions. The main **monument,** a landmark of Soviet grandeur, consists of an obelisk next to a giant rock with carved sculptures, with an eternal flame that burns on the grave of the unknown soldier. The names of the dead are carved into marble walls. To the right of the monument, the **Museum of the Defense of the Brest Hero-Fortress** (Музей Абароны Брэсцкой Крэпасці-Героя; Muzey Abarony Brestskoi Krepastsi-Geroya), in the reconstructed barracks, describes the history of the fortress and recounts the siege. (☎20 03 65. Open Mar.-Oct. Tu-Su 9:30am-6pm; Nov.-Feb. Tu-Su 9:30am-5pm. *Kassa* open until 4:30pm. Closed last Tu of each month. 3000BR.) On your way back from the fortress, check out the steam engines at the **railway museum** on your left. (Open daily 10am-6pm.)

B E L A R U S

BOSNIA AND HERZEGOVINA
(BOSNA I HERCEGOVINA)

CONVERTIBLE MARK

AUS$1 = 1.09KM	1 KM = AUS$0.92
CDN$1 = 1.28KM	1 KM = CDN$0.78
EUR€1 = 1.96KM	1 KM = EUR€0.51
NZ$1 = 0.93KM	1 KM = NZ$1.07
UK£1 = 3.08KM	1 KM = UK£0.32
US$1 = 1.99KM	1 KM = US$0.50
ZAR1 = 0.19KM	1 KM = ZAR5.34

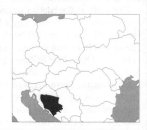

TRAVEL WARNING. In June 2002, the US State Department issued a Travel Warning against unnecessary travel to certain regions in Bosnia, particularly the Republika Srpska. The warning notes that there "are still risks from occasional localized political violence, land mines and unexploded ordnance," stating that despite demining efforts there are still over 500,000 live landmines around Sarajevo and throughout the country. In 2001 there were occasional outbreaks of mob violence targeting foreign visitors in Mostar, Medjugorje, Grunde, Posusje, Livno, Tomislavgrad, Banja Luka, and Siroki Brijeg. Travelers are advised to check the State Department web page (www.travel.state.gov/travel_warnings.html) for more complete information and further updates.

The mountainous centerpiece of the former Yugoslavia, Bosnia and Herzegovina defied all odds throughout the centuries to stand as an independent nation today. Bosnia's distinctiveness—and its troubles—spring from its role as a mixing ground for Muslim Bosniaks, Catholic Croats, and Orthodox Serbs. In Sarajevo, the country's cosmopolitan capital, that ideal is at least verbally maintained, but ethnic tensions contnue in the countryside. Though marked by rolling hills and sparkling rivers, Bosnia's lush valleys are now punctuated by abandoned houses and gaping rooftops. The past decade has not been kind to Bosnia, and its future is uncertain. However, its resilient people are optimistic and in this period of peace, reconstruction has begun.

BOSNIA AND HERZEGOVINA AT A GLANCE

OFFICIAL NAME: Bosnia and Herzegovina

CAPITAL: Sarajevo (pop. 387,900)

POPULATION: 4.4 million (44% Bosniak, 31% Serb, 17% Croat, 6% Yugoslav)

LANGUAGES: Bosnian, Croatian, Serbian

CURRENCY: 1 convertible mark (KM) = 100 convertible pfennigs

RELIGION: 40% Muslim, 31% Orthodox, 15% Catholic, 4% Protestant, 10% other

LAND AREA: 51,129km²

GEOGRAPHY: Mountainous, plains in the north, 20km of coast

CLIMATE: Mild continental

BORDERS: Croatia, Serbia and Montenegro

ECONOMY: 58% Services, 23% Industry, 19% Agriculture

GDP: US$1720 per capita

COUNTRY CODE: 387

INTERNATIONAL DIALING PREFIX: 00

BOSNIA

CROATIA

Novi Sad

Glina

Una River

Slavonski Brod

Bosanska Gradiška

Velika Kladuša · Bosanski Novi

Bosanski Dubica

Srbac

Sava River

Bosanski Krupa

Vrbas River

Bosna River

Brčko

Bihać

Sanski Most

Banja Luka

Doboj

Gračanica

Bijeljina

Drina River

Bosanski Petrovac · Ključ

Teslić

Lukavac

Lopare

Tuzla

Drvar

REPUBLIKA SRPSKA

Jajce

Travnik

Zenica

Zavidovići

Kladanj

Zvornik

Šipovo

Bugojno

Vareš

Olovo

Bratunac

Srebrenica

CROATIA

Bosansko Grahovo

Kupres

Glamoc

MUSLIM-CROAT FEDERATION

Visoko

Pale

Višegrad

Livno

Prozor

Sarajevo

Jahorina

Buška jezero

Jablanica

Konjic

Gorazde

Split

Neretva River

Foča

Adriatic Sea

Brač

Hvar

Vis

Međugorje

Mostar

SERBIA AND MONTENEGRO

Korčula

Ploče

Gacko

0   50 miles

Peljesac

Neum

Bileća

0   50 kilometers

Bosnia and Herzegovina

Trebinje

Dubrovnik

Podgorica

N LG

HISTORY

THE BEGINNINGS... Bosnia was part of the sprawling **Roman Empire;** after it fell, the region became a battleground between the Empire's Frankish and Byzantine successors. When the Byzantines lost control of the region in 1180, and neither the Croatian nor the Serbian kingdoms could establish rule over the territory, Bosnia emerged as an independent nation. It remained free for more than 260 years, populated almost entirely by Christians.

...AND THE ENDS. In the late 14th century, the flourishing **Ottoman Empire** invaded the Balkans, and by 1463 it had swallowed Bosnia. Due in part to the organizational weaknesses of the established Churches (both Catholic and Orthodox), **Islam** gained more converts in Bosnia than in neighboring countries. Despite this religious diversity, Christians and Muslims lived in relative harmony and referred to themselves simply as Bosnians. During 400 years of Turkish rule, the region developed into a prosperous and autonomous province of the empire.

YOU TOO WILL BE OURS. In 1878 the Western European powers took advantage of the Ottoman Empire's increasing weakness, and, at the **Congress of Berlin,** transferred Bosnia to **Austria-Hungary.** Resentment toward Austrian rule sparked nationalistic sentiments throughout Bosnia and led to the establishment of a Bosnian Serb terrorist organization, the **Black Hand.** Austria-Hungary tightened its grip on Bosnia and annexed the country in 1908. As was the case in other Balkan countries, increased repression and imported Russian ideology contributed to a desire for **South Slav** unity and sovereignty. On June 28, 1914, **Gavrilo Princip,** a zealous member of the Black Hand, assassinated the Austrian heir to the throne, **Archduke Franz Ferdinand,** in Sarajevo, triggering the events that led to **World War I.**

THE LAND OF SOUTH SLAVS. After the war Pan-Slavism took on a concrete shape in the **Kingdom of Serbs, Croats, and Slovenes.** When Hitler put an end to the kingdom by invading Yugoslavia in 1941, Bosnia was handed over to Croatia, an obedient satellite of Hitler's regime. The majority of Bosnians joined the pro-Allies Partisans led by **Josip Broz Tito** during **World War II.** In 1945, Bosnia joined its Slavic neighbors as one of the six constituent republics of **Yugoslavia.**

TROUBLED TIMES. Nationalist sentiment was suppressed under Tito, but his death in 1980 triggered a revival. Tensions increased in 1986 with the rise of the Serb nationalist **Slobodan Milosević,** who sought to abolish the federation and create a unitary state under Serbian control, and the collapse of the republic began in 1990. Following the 1991 secession of Slovenia and Croatia from the federation, Bosnia held a referendum on independence. Much to the outrage of Milosević, 70% of Bosnians, including much of the Serbian population, voted in favor of independence. Violence broke out as the federal army and Serb militias quickly took control of 70% of Bosnian territory. Sarajevo suffered a brutal **siege** that lasted from May 2, 1992 to February 26, 1996. A United Nations force sent to deliver humanitarian assistance had little success in stopping the "ethnic cleansing" undertaken by both Serb and Croat forces.

PEACE AT LAST. The international community remained largely unaware of the conflict until footage of the "ethnic cleansing" of **Srebrenica,** documenting the first genocide in Europe since World War II, was broadcast on international television. The atrocities continued until 1995, when American Richard Holbrooke negotiated the **Dayton Peace Accords.** Dayton brought a fragile peace to the region, which UN peacekeeping forces have helped to sustain until this day.

TODAY

Present-day Bosnia and Herzegovina consists of two governing bodies, the Muslim/Croat **Federation of Bosnia and Herzegovina** and the Serbian **Republika Srpska (RS).** A central government and a three-person rotating presidency connect the two entities. According to the constitution drafted in Dayton, the presidents must be a Croat, a Serb, and a Bosniak (Muslim), elected by a popular vote for four-year terms. The offices are presently held by Serb **Zivko Radisić,** Croat **Jozo Krizanović,** and Bosniak **Beriz Belkić.** Today's Bosnia, however, resembles more of an international protectorate than an independent nation. A diplomat appointed by the UN Security Council to implement the Dayton Peace Accords has the power to issue legal decrees and dismiss any member of the government. It is expected that Bosnia and Herzegovina will remain under direct international supervision for at least another eight years. However, the international community is cautiously optimistic about Bosnia's prospects for permanent stability and peace. Though economic issues remain a substantial problem as **unemployment** continues to grow and **international aid** is being reduced, funds from tourism and investors are beginning to flow through the country once more, bringing hopes of a more prosperous future.

PEOPLE AND CULTURE

DEMOGRAPHICS AND RELIGION

Bosnia and Herzegovina's population is as diverse as they come. Making matters even more confusing is the fact that although they have different traditions and label themselves differently, all Bosnians share a **South Slavic** origin and speak mutually intelligible languages. The largest group, 44% of the population, is predominantly Muslim and call themselves **"Bosniaks."** **Serbs,** almost all of whom live in the Republika Srpska (RS), make up 31% of the population, while **Croats** comprise 17%. Bosnia's religious composition is the most complex in Eastern Europe. There are three large religious minorities, none of which is small enough to be subjugated or large enough to completely assert itself. Bosnia's Croats and Serbs are Christians; the Croats are strongly **Catholic,** and Serbs subscribe to **Eastern Orthodoxy. Muslim** Bosniaks form the largest religious group in Bosnia and Herzegovina. While devout, most Muslims do not keep to the strict cultural standards that are the norm in many Islamic nations; women only wear head coverings on religious occasions and alcohol is regularly consumed.

LANGUAGE

When in Bosnia, speak **Bosnian,** unless in the RS, where **Serbian** prevails. When in Croatia, speak Croatian; in Serbia, Serbian. For a phrasebook and glossary, see **Glossary: Croatian,** p. 875. The difference is political rather than substantive, but never underestimate its importance; languages in the former Yugoslavia have become tools of nationalism. The languages do have certain distinctions. For example, coffee is *kava* in Croatian term, and *kafa* in Bosnian. will still get you by in Bosnia. Foreigners who attempt to speak a little Bosnian are the exception, not the rule; an effort to pronounce even a few sentences will endear you to locals. **English** and **German** are widely spoken, especially in Sarajevo.

FOOD AND DRINK

BOSNIA	❶	❷	❸	❹	❺
FOOD	under 4KM	4-6KM	7-10KM	11-14KM	over 14KM

Bosnian cuisine has a mixed heritage, and proudly shows its Central European, Mediterranean, and Middle Eastern influences. Sausages and patties are common fare, and are usually made from a mixture of beef, pork, and lamb. *Bosanki lonac,* a layered stew of meat and vegetables, is the national dish and is served in the ceramic pot in which it is cooked. *Burek,* a stuffed pastry, is also popular; vegetarians should try cheese or spinach fillings. The popularity of sweets like baklava and *lokum* (Turkish Delight) betray Bosnia's Eastern origin. Strong, Turkish-style coffee is drunk throughout the day. Festive occasions, however, call for *slivovitz,* a homemade plum brandy.

CUSTOMS AND ETIQUETTE

Tipping is not expected, though feel free to add a gratuity for excellent service. At restaurants and cafes, the bill is never split; instead, one person pays, and it is assumed that the other will pay next time. It is customary for the waiter, or a man, to open and pour a woman's drink. In **Muslim homes** and **mosques,** always remove your shoes at the door. **Smoking** is very common; most Sarajevans smoke the local *Drina* or *Aura.* **Bargaining** is a must, particularly in clothing markets. Ask a Bosnian to accompany you; prices will be miraculously lower. **Fashion** is important, so be sure to dress neatly in public.

THE ARTS

HISTORY

The Balkans have shared literary and artistic traditions dating back to the Middle Ages, but it is only in the recent past that Bosnia has come into its own in the artistic world. **Mak Dizdar** is celebrated as the nation's greatest poet. He revolutionized post-World War I poetry with his stark modernist style and refusal to pander to Socialist Realism. Bosnian Serb **Ivo Andrić,** who won the Nobel Prize for Literature in 1961, is one of the few Bosnian writers to receive international acclaim. The sober compassion and beauty of his works are exemplified by *The Bridge on the Drina* and *The Travnik Chronicles*, which focus on delicate political issues.

CURRENT SCENE

The post-war period has brought new energy to the arts. Theatrical productions are common in Sarajevo, as entertainers follow in the footsteps of the Sarajevo War Theatre, a group of playwrights and actors who performed almost 2000 productions during the four-year siege of Sarajevo. In the wake of the war, Bosnian authors have turned their energies to war memoirs and diaries. *Zlata's Diary*, by **Zlata Filipović,** a teenager during the siege of Sarajevo, is a poignant personal account of growing up during the conflict. **Semezdin Mehmedinović** presents a darker, more mature picture of wartime in the internationally acclaimed *Sarajevo Blues*, a 1998 collection of prose and poetry. In 1993 several Bosnian artists organized the **Witnesses of Existence** exhibit in which language and national context were interpreted using shrapnel and bullets as media. The exhibit toured Italy and the US, but its creators were trapped in Sarajevo and unable to travel with it. Film has also become a popular medium with the recent picture *No Man's Land* (2001), directed by **Danis Tanovic,** which won an Oscar for Best Foreign Film—Bosnia's first and only Academy Award.

HOLIDAYS AND FESTIVALS

NATIONAL HOLIDAYS IN 2003	
January 1 New Year's Day (Catholic)	**May 1** Labor Day
January 7 Orthodox Christmas	**April 25-27** Orthodox Easter
January 14 New Year's Day (Orthodox)	**November 1** All Saints Day (Catholic)
March 1 Independence Day	**November 25** National Day
April 20-21 Catholic Easter	**December 25** Catholic Christmas

Thanks to its diversity, Bosnia and Herzegovina probably celebrates more religious holidays than any other European nation. Festivals, however, are less common, which is understandable given the country's economic situation.

SARAJEVSKA ZIMA. (Sarajevan Winter.) This festival has been held annually from December to January since the Sarajevo Winter Olympics in 1984. This celebration of art and culture is beloved by locals, as it persisted throughout the war.

BAŠČARŠIJA NOCI. (Turkish Nights.) An outdoor celebration of music, theater, and film, this festival is held every July in Sarajevo's Turkish Quarter.

ADDITIONAL RESOURCES

GENERAL HISTORY

Bosnia: A Short History, by Noel Malcolm (1996). A concise yet comprehensive account of the nation's troubled past.

The Balkans, by Misha Glenny (2000). Engaging survey of the history of the Balkans over the past century, with a special emphasis on the recent fall of Yugoslavia.

FICTION, NONFICTION, AND FILM

Balkan Ghosts: A Journey Through History, by Robert Kaplan (1994). A travel journal dealing with the political complexities of Bosnia and Herzegovina and its neighbors.

Death and the Dervish, by Mesa Selimović (1996). A philosophical piece that explores the difference between good and evil while examining Bosnian Muslim culture.

No Man's Land, directed by Danis Tanović (2002). This film about two soldiers, a Bosniak and a Serb, who find themselves trapped together in a mined trench between enemy lines recently won Bosnia's first Academy Award.

Zlata's Diary, by Zlata Filipović (1995). A memoir of one teenager's struggle to live a normal life during the disintegration of Yugoslavia.

BOSNIA ESSENTIALS

ENTRANCE REQUIREMENTS

Passport: Required of all travelers.

Visa: Required of citizens of Australia, Ireland, and New Zealand; required for citizens of Ireland after 30 days and of Canada, South Africa, the UK, and the US after 90 days.

Letter of Invitation: Not required.

Inoculations: None required. Recommended up-to-date on MMR (measles, mumps, and rubella), DTaP (diptheria), Polio booster, Hepatitis A, Hepatitis B.

Work Permit: Required of all foreigners planning to work in Bosnia.

International Driving Permit: Required of all those planning to drive.

DOCUMENTS AND FORMALITIES

EMBASSIES AND CONSULATES

Embassies and consulates of other countries in Bosnia and Herzegovina are all in Sarajevo (see p. 90). Bosnia's embassies and consulates abroad include:

Australia: 5 Beale Crescent, Deakin, ACT 2600 (☎61 6232 4646; fax 6232 5554).

Canada: 130 Albert St. Suite 805, Ottawa, Ontario K1P 5G4 (☎613-236-0028).

South Africa: 25 Stella St., Brooklyn 0181, Pretoria (☎012 346 5546; fax 346 2295).

UK: Morley House, 320 Regent St. 4th fl., London W1R 3BF (☎020 7255 3758; fax 7255 3760; bosnia@embassy_london.ision.co.uk).

US: 2109 E St. NW, Washington, D.C. 20037 (☎202-337-1500; fax 337-1502; www.bosnianembassy.org). **Consulate:** 866 UN Plaza Suite 580, New York, NY 10017 (☎212-593-0264; fax 593-0843).

BOSNIA

VISA AND ENTRY INFORMATION

Citizens of Canada, South Africa, the UK, and the US may visit Bosnia visa-free for up to three months; visas are required for citizens of Australia, Ireland, and New Zealand. A valid passport is required to enter and leave the country. Applications take approximately two weeks to process: send your passport; one passport-sized photo; a copy of your round-trip ticket; a copy of your last bank statement as proof of sufficient funds to cover expenses during your stay; a voucher from your travel agency or hotel reservations if available; a completed visa application; a self-addressed, stamped envelope; and a money order for the proper fee (single-entry valid for 30 days and transit US$35, multiple-entry valid for 90 days US$65, multiple-entry valid for more than 90 days US$85). There are occasional police checkpoints within Bosnia; register with your embassy within 48hr. of arrival, and keep your papers with you at all times. You must also **register** with the police upon arrival—accommodations will usually do it for you. Crossing the **border,** with its congregation of trucks and army vehicles, can be somewhat intimidating, but entering is usually a smooth procedure. Bosnian visas are not available at the border and there is no fee for crossing.

TRANSPORTATION

BY PLANE. Commercial plane service into Sarajevo is limited and expensive, but is the main recourse for the troops, journalists, and relief workers entering the country. **Croatia Airlines** has regular service from Zagreb. Travel agencies in Sarajevo can arrange and change flights, but you must purchase tickets with cash.

BY TRAIN. Railways are barely functional and not a viable option.

BY BUS. Buses run daily between Sarajevo and Dubrovnik, CRO (the most popular route into the country); Split, CRO; and Zagreb, CRO. Buses are reliable, clean, and not very crowded, but brace yourself for Balkan driving.

TOURIST SERVICES AND MONEY

Tourist offices only really exist in Sarajevo and Medugorje. The **US Embassy** also has useful information. Several independent tourist agencies have sprung up, but most focus on arranging vacations for locals. The new Bosnian currency, the **convertible mark (KM),** was introduced in summer 1998. It is currently fixed firmly to the Euro at a 1KM=EUR€0.51 exchange rate. Beware store clerks trying to pass unsuspecting foreigners old Bosnian dinars: the dinar is no longer a valid currency. In addition, the **Croatian kuna** was named an official Bosnian currency in summer 1997. The kuna is not legal tender in Sarajevo, but it is accepted in the western (Croatian) area of divided Mostar. Change your money back to Euros when you leave, as convertible marks are inconvertible outside Bosnia. Inflation in Bosnia is 3.5%, so prices should remain relatively stable over the next year. **Banks** are the best places to exchange money. **Traveler's checks** can be cashed at some Sarajevo banks. **ATMs** are available in Banja Luka, Medugorje, and Sarajevo. **Western Union** in the capital has an extremely competent English-speaking staff. Most post offices give MC **cash advances.** If your itinerary lies outside of Sarajevo, bring Euros with you.

HEALTH AND SAFETY

 EMERGENCY NUMBERS: Police: ☎92 **Fire:** ☎93 **Ambulance:** ☎94

HEALTH. In Sarajevo, finding **medical help** and supplies is not a problem; your embassy is your best resource. Peacekeeping operations have brought English-speaking doctors, but not insurance; cash is the only method of payment. All drugs are sold at **pharmacies**, and basic hygiene products are sold at many drugstores. Condoms are available, but expensive. Bandages are even harder to find.

SAFETY. Outside Sarajevo, **do not set foot off the pavement** under any circumstances. Even in Sarajevo, de-mining experts recommend staying on paved roads and hard-covered surfaces. Do not pick up any objects off the ground. Hundreds of thousands of **landmines** and **unexploded ordnance** (UXOs) cover the country. Mine injuries occur daily. About 15% of landmine injuries occur on road shoulders partly because farmers who find unexploded ordnance in their fields bring it to the roadsides for the troops to pick up. Should your car veer off the road, carefully retrace your tracks back to the pavement; if you want to take pictures, do so from your car while the car remains firmly on pavement. If you must go to the bathroom during a road trip, stop at a gas station. Abandoned houses are unsafe as well; many have been rigged with booby traps. Absolute caution is essential at all times. It is estimated that 30 years of intensive, full-time effort would be necessary to declare Bosnia "mine-free"—and even de-mining is not 100% fool-proof. For details on the **Mine Action Center**, see **Sarajevo: Local Services**, p. 91.

WOMEN, MINORITY, AND BGLT TRAVELERS. **Women** should take the usual precautions, but most likely will not encounter difficulties traveling in Bosnia. **Minority** travelers will probably get stares but generally are not hassled. **Homosexuality** is still treated with hostility, particularly outside Sarajevo.

ACCOMMODATIONS AND CAMPING

BOSNIA	❶	❷	❸	❹	❺
ACCOM.	under 35KM	35-40KM	41-50KM	51-60KM	over 61KM

Accommodations options are still very limited in Bosnia and the only choice is usually a **hotel. Private rooms** only exist in Sarajevo, and usually cost the same as cheaper hotels (30-40KM). **Camping** should be avoided due to the threat of landmines and UXOs; the only safe way to camp is through a specialized organization, such as **Green Visions** (see p. 88).

KEEPING IN TOUCH

MAIL. Bosnia's **postal** system, operative since 1996, is increasingly efficient. Yellow-and-white "PTT" signs indicate post offices. Mail takes 3-5 days to Europe, and 7-10 days to North America. **Poste Restante** just arrived in Sarajevo. Address envelope as follows: Nick (First name) GOSSEN (LAST NAME), POSTE RESTANTE, Zmaja od Bosne 88 (post office address), Sarajevo (city) 71000 (postal code), BOSNIA AND HERZEGOVINA.

TELEPHONES AND INTERNET ACCESS. Telephone connections are troublesome and expensive; the best option is to call collect from the main Sarajevo post office. Calling the UK is roughly 3.50KM per minute, to the US 5KM; however, prices vary significantly depending on where you are. **Faxes** can be sent from the post office; it's 3KM per page to Australia or the UK and 5KM to the US. **Internet access** is becoming increasingly available in Bosnia.

THE HIDDEN DEAL

GREEN VISIONS

Foreign visitors to Bosnia are often amazed by the beauty of the countryside. The towering mountains and blue-green rivers are a far cry from the gray, dreary images of Bosnia's civil war. With miles of untouched wilderness, Bosnia should be an outdoorsman's paradise. There's just one enormous problem—during the war fighting covered the country, and wherever there was a front line, there are now landmines.

Green Visions, an eco-tourism company founded in 2000, is dedicated to determining safe locations in the country for outdoor exploration. It provides trips throughout Bosnia, ranging from three-hour walks in the mountains around Sarajevo (65KM) to week-long treks to some of the most inaccessible parts of the country (700KM, including equipment and food). Before planning trips, the Green Visions staff consults the Mine Action Center (see **Local Services and Communication,** p. 91) as well as the armies of both the Muslim-Croat Federation and the Serb Republic to determine if there are any mines. If there is any possibility of danger, they simply don't go, and any trip they do run is thoroughly scouted beforehand. Green Visions also organizes rafting expeditions in Bosnia and Montenegro, rock-climbing trips for climbers of all levels, homestays in remote mountain villages, and paragliding courses. (☎/fax 33 20 71 69; www.greenvisions.ba.)

—A. Nicholas Gossen

SARAJEVO ☎(0)33

Once the proud host of the 1984 Olympic games, Sarajevo (pop. 360,000) now evokes the memory of its brutal siege by Bosnian Serbs from 1992 to 1995. Although reconstruction projects have helped hide the massive destruction, the emotional and physical scars are slow to fade. Many of the old tourist draws of Sarajevo were destroyed or are non-functional, but the lively marketplace of the old Turkish Quarter, a burgeoning arts scene, and a revived nightlife are inspiring signs for the future. Upon arrival, newcomers find themselves welcomed by a warm international company of uniformed Stabilization Force (SFOR) officers, camera-wielding journalists, and foreign aid workers. Wary of Western media stereotypes, the city remains aloof from the short-term visitor. It is just that elusiveness, though, that makes finding the real Sarajevo all the more rewarding.

⊠ INTERCITY TRANSPORTATION

Flights: The airport is along the southwestern edge of the city. **Taxi** service from the airport 18KM. To: **Berlin, GER; Istanbul, TUR; Ljubljana, SLN; Paris, FRA; Rome, ITA; Zagreb, CRO.** Buy tickets at **Centrotrans,** Ferhadija 16 (☎21 12 82 or 21 12 83; fax 20 54 81). Open M-F 8am-8pm, Sa 8am-3pm. For other ticket providers, see **Tourist and Financial Services,** p. 90.

Trains: (☎65 53 30). Next to the bus station. Open daily 5am-9pm. To **Mostar** (3hr.; 1 per day; 11.80KM, 18.80KM round-trip) and **Zagreb, CRO** (9hr., 1 per day, 44.40KM). There are no other international connections, though schedules claim otherwise.

Buses: Station, Kranjčevića 9 (☎53 28 74; fax 53 28 81), behind the Holiday Inn at the corner with Halida Kajtaza. Ticket window (☎21 31 00) open daily 7am-7pm. Centrotrans (see **Flights,** above) sells tickets at the Ferhadija office or at the bus station. To: **Banja Luka** (5hr., 3 per day, 23KM); **Mostar** (3hr., 13 per day, 13KM); **Dubrovnik, CRO** (7hr., 2 per day, 40KM); **Frankfurt, GER** (15hr., 1 per day, 196KM); **Split, CRO** (8hr., 4 per day, 36KM); **Vienna, AUS** (12hr., 1 per day, 81KM); **Zagreb, CRO** (9hr., 3 per day, 51KM). 2KM extra per bag. For **Serbia-Montenegro,** use the Lukavica bus station in **Srpsko Sarajevo** (Serb Sarajevo). To get there, take trolley #103 to **Dobrinja** from Austrijski Trg to the end of the line (about 30min.). To **Belgrade, SER** (7hr., 1 per hr., 28KM) and **Podgorica, MON** (4½hr., 5 per day, 21KM).

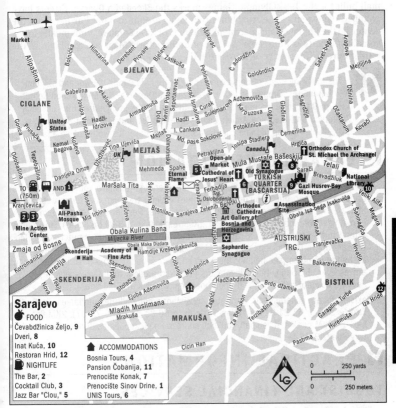

Sarajevo

FOOD
Čevabdžinica Željo, **9**
Dveri, **8**
Inat Kuća, **10**
Restoran Hrid, **12**

NIGHTLIFE
The Bar, **2**
Cocktail Club, **3**
Jazz Bar "Clou," **5**

ACCOMMODATIONS
Bosnia Tours, **4**
Pansion Čobanija, **11**
Prenočište Konak, **7**
Prenočište Sinov Drine, **1**
UNIS Tours, **6**

⚡ ORIENTATION

The bus station is far enough away from the center that catching a cab (7-8KM) is reasonable. To reach the center on foot, turn left from the station, walk past the taxi stands and the train station, and continue through the first intersection. Walk on **Kranjćevića** until the mosque at the large intersection (20min.). Go straight on **Maršala Tita,** which branches at the Eternal Flame into Sarajevo's two walkways. Sarajevo's center is a series of easily navigable streets running parallel to the **Mili-jacka** river that can be traversed end-to-end in less than 30min. Maršala Tita is the main street, running from the yellow Holiday Inn to the **Eternal Flame,** a 1945 war memorial. Address numbers increase toward the Flame. At the Flame, Maršala Tita branches into **Ferhadija,** the city's main pedestrian thoroughfare, and **Mula Mustafe Baseskije,** a heavily-trafficked street with narrow sidewalks. Follow Fer-hadija for about 10min. to reach the cobblestoned streets of **Bašćaršija** (Turkish Quarter). A walk in the opposite direction of the Flame down Maršala Tita leads to the stark **Zmaja od Bosne** (Dragon of Bosnia), called **"Sniper's Alley"** during the war—a nickname not used casually. Between the Holiday Inn and the eternal flame, **Alipašina** bisects Maršala Tita. Look toward the river—the sprawling strip mall built for the 1984 Olympic Games marks the **Skenderija Quarter.** Streets have changed names since the war, but street signs are up-to-date. Farther from the center lie the innumerable apartment buildings of **Novo Sarajevo,** built mostly in the socialist "beauty is bourgeois" school of architecture. **Maps** are available at the tourist bureau (free) or bookstores (10KM).

The following areas of Sarajevo were battlegrounds during the war and still contain **landmines:** Grbavica, Lukavica, Illidža, and Dobrinja. The Mine Action Center (see p. 91), however, emphasizes that the entire city is high-risk. The Turistička Zajednica and the Mine Action Center (see **Tourist and Financial Services,** p. 90), display a map of mine contamination in Sarajevo; it's worth taking a look.

◰ LOCAL TRANSPORTATION

Public Transportation: Central Sarajevo is small enough to allow you to avoid public transit altogether, but if you're in a rush, an excellent **tram** network loops west along Maršala Tita and back east along Obala Kulina Bana. Regular service runs 6am-10pm or midnight, depending on the route (1.2KM from kiosks; 1.5KM on board). **Bus** routes extend farther from the town center, but operate mainly during commuter hours (M-F 6:45am-6pm). Monthly bus pass 12KM. A listing of the tram and bus lines is available at the tourist office (see below). There are no exact schedules, but most transportation arrives every 5-15min. Ticket inspectors are often present and always vigilant; if you have no ticket or fail to punch it upon boarding, you risk a 20KM fine.

Taxis: Taxis are generally fair, with rates consistent among all the companies. Try **Radio Taxi** (☎970 or 65 21 31) or **Yellow Taxicab** (☎66 35 55 or 65 73 07). 2KM flat rate plus 1.30KM per km. If you call, you'll be charged for pickup. Fares 30% higher at night. Large bags 2KM per piece.

◱ PRACTICAL INFORMATION

TOURIST AND FINANCIAL SERVICES

Tourist Office: Turistička Zajednica, Zelenih Beretki 22a (☎22 07 24; fax 53 22 81). From Maršala Tita, bear right at the Eternal Flame, turn right down Strossmajerova, then left on Zelenih Beretki; the tourist office is 1 block down. Staffed by friendly folks who provide extensive advice on accommodation. Free **maps** and **city guides.** Open M-Sa 9am-8pm, Su 10am-6pm. The **Consular Department** (☎44 57 00; fax 65 97 22; www.usis.com) of the US Embassy (see below) is also helpful. Ask for its weekly newsletter, *The Sarajevo Chronicle,* complete with consular news, film listings, special events schedules, and classified ads. Open Tu and Th 8am-noon, 2pm-4pm.

Budget Travel: Air Bosna, Ferhadija 15 (☎20 31 67 or 21 48 72; fax 66 79 54), arranges flights on all airlines. Open M-F 9am-5pm, Sa 9am-1pm. **Kompas Tours,** Maršala Tita 8 (☎20 80 14; fax 20 80 15), past the intersection with Alipašina toward the Holiday Inn. Open M-F 8:30am-5:30pm and Sa 9am-2pm.

Embassies: Australia: Contact the embassy in Austria, Mattiellistr. 2, 1040 Vienna. **Canada:** Logavina 7 (š44 79 00; fax 44 79 01). Open M-F 8:30am-noon and 1-5pm. **New Zealand:** Contact the embassy in Italy, Via Zara 28, 00 198 Rome (☎6 440 29 28; fax 440 29 84). **UK:** Tina Ujevica 8 (š44 44 29; fax 66 61 31). Open M-F 8:30am-5pm. **US:** Alipašina 43 (š44 57 00; fax 65 97 22). Open M-F 9am-1pm.

Currency Exchange: Central Profit Banka, Zelenih Beretki 24 (☎53 36 88; fax 53 24 06), cashes **traveler's checks** for 1.5% commission and **exchanges currency** for 1-4% commission. Open M-F 8am-7pm, Sa 8am-1pm.

ATMs: There are several along Maršala Tita 48, a few blocks before the flame; a MC/V ATM stands at Ferhadija 17 on the corner with Jelica Ulica. There are also **24hr. ATMs** at the Central Profit Banka.

LOCAL SERVICES AND COMMUNICATIONS

Mine Action Center (MAC), Zmaja od Bosne 8 (☎66 73 10 or 20 12 99; fax 66 73 11). Follow signs through the barracks on the right side of the street. Provides maps detailing the location of landmines. Open M-F 8am-4pm.

English-Language Bookstores: Šahinpašić, Mula Mustafe Bašeskije 1 (☎22 01 12), near the Eternal Flame, sells English classics, dictionaries, guidebooks, maps, international magazines, and newspapers. Open M-Sa 9am-8pm, Su 10am-2pm. **Buybook,** Radićeva 3, towards Skenderija, offers an excellent selection of English books, as well as a wide selection of music. Open M-Sa 9am-10pm, Su 10am-6pm.

Ambulance: ☎94 and 61 11 11.

Hospital: Koševo University Medical Center, Bolnicka 25 (☎66 66 20 or 44 48 00). **State Hospital,** Kranjčevića 12 (☎66 47 24; fax 47 24 98). Both speak English.

24-Hour Pharmacy: Baščaršija Apoteka, Obala Kulina Bana 40 (☎23 67 00).

Internet: There are a number of Internet cafes in town, including several along Ferhadija (2-3KM per hr.). **Internet Club,** upstairs at Ferhadija 21 (☎53 41 16). 2KM per hr. Open daily 8.30am-10:30pm. **Internet Club Click,** Kundurdziluk 1, in Baščaršija (☎23 69 14). 3KM per hr. Open daily 9am-11pm.

Telephones: Inside and outside any post office. The most central is behind the Eternal Flame on Ferhadija. Open M-Sa 7am-8pm. Phone cards sold at any post office, 50 local calls 5KM. The main branch (see below) and the post office between the bus and train stations are the only places with phones that don't require a card. The main branch is the only place where you can call collect or use AT&T or MCI numbers. **Directory info:** ☎988. **International operator:** ☎900.

Post Office: PTT Saobracaj Sarajevo, Zmaja od Bosne 88 (☎65 43 65; fax 47 31 03), well past the Holiday Inn in New Sarajevo. Take tram #3 west to the 3rd stop after the Holiday Inn, and follow the tram 100m. **Fax service** available. Open M-Sa 7am-8pm.

Postal Code: 71000.

BOSNIA

♌ ACCOMMODATIONS

Until recently, housing in Sarajevo was absurdly expensive, but prices are dropping as competition works its capitalist magic. You can get a room in a **pension** for as little as 30KM or find relatively cheap **private rooms ❶** (30-50KM) all over town. Discounts are usually available for longer stays. If you arrive late at night without prior arrangements, ask a taxi driver at the station for help—they often make deals with local families offering private rooms. The drivers might not speak English, but they'll understand "room" and "center" and will write down a price. The room price will be competitive, but the fare to get you there will be increased.

PRIVATE ROOM AGENCIES

Bosnia Tours, Maršala Tita 54 (☎20 20 59; ☎/fax 20 22 06). Before the Eternal Flame. Books rooms in family apartments along Maršala Tita and across the river. Call at least 1 day ahead. Doubles as a Croatian Airlines ticket agent. Breakfast 5-10KM. Singles 40KM; doubles 70KM. Open M-F 9am-5pm, Sa 9am-2pm. ❷

UNIS Tours, Ferhadija 16 (☎/fax 20 90 89). Walk down Ferhadija to the right of the Eternal Flame; the office is behind the Swiss Air desk, opposite the Cathedral. The staff finds centrally located rooms with all the amenities. Call 1-2 days ahead. Open M-F 8am-8pm, Sa 9am-5pm. Singles 42KM; doubles 74KM. ❷

PENSIONS

■ **Pansion Čobanija,** Čobanija 29 (☎44 17 49; fax 20 39 37). With your back to the Eternal Flame, take the 1st left onto Kulovica, which crosses the river and becomes Čobanija. The *pansion* is at the end of the street, 5min. from the center. Don't let the old exterior fool you; the place is so modern that every bathroom has a telephone and every room has a satellite TV. If that doesn't spoil you, the sleek furniture, leather chairs, and chandeliers surely will. Breakfast included. Reception 24hr. Must reserve by fax or in person 5-7 days in advance. Singles 80KM; doubles 120KM. ❺

Prenoćište Konak, Mula Mustafe Bašeskije 48 (☎53 35 06). From Maršala Tita, bear left past the Eternal Flame and pass the market. Clean, no-frills rooms in the center of town. A house across the street provides additional space. Reception 7am-midnight. Check-out noon. Singles 40KM, 30KM for stays over 4 nights; doubles 60KM. ❷

Prenoćište Sinovi Drine, Put Života bb (☎44 56 51). Opposite the bus and train stations. If you arrive in Sarajevo and need to crash immediately, this place has clean sheets on hospital beds in doubles, triples, and quads. Breakfast included. Reception 24hr. Dorms 32KM. ❶

🖸 FOOD

Sarajevan cuisine is quintessentially Balkan—meaty, cheesy, and greasy—but also has distinctive Middle Eastern influences. For an authentic Bosnian meal, scour the Turkish Quarter for **čevabdžinica** (kebab) shops. The depressed economy puts many restaurants beyond the reach of most Bosnians; if you choose to eat out, SFOR troops, journalists, and businesspeople may be the only other patrons. There are no large grocery stores in the center of town, but the small **Max Market** at Mula Mustafe Bašeskije 3, past the Eternal flame, is well-stocked and open 24hr. Two main **markets** provide fresh vegetables and baked goods. The more convenient one lies on Mula Mustafe Bašeskija, a few blocks from the Eternal Flame. (Open M-Sa 8am-5pm, Su 8am-noon.) The larger one, under the Ciglane bridge on Alipašina, is 5min. from the US Embassy. (Open in summer M-Sa 8am-5pm, Su 8am-noon; off-season M-F 8am-dusk.) You'll find a spotless **meat** and **cheese market** at Ferhadija 7. (Open M-Sa 7am-5pm.)

■ **Dveri,** Prote Bakovice 12 (☎53 70 20). Walking up Ferhadija from the Baščaršija end, turn right at the first side street, then left into the small alley. For authentic, delicious Bosnian food, look no further. This small restaurant feels like a country kitchen and serves great homemade wine. The menu rotates every few days, but it's always superb and has vegetarian options. Entrees 7-15KM. Open M-Sa 11am-4pm, 5pm-11pm. ❸

■ **Restoran Hrid,** Iza Hrida 7 (☎061 22 27 08). The best way to get to the restaurant is simply to hail a cab and pay the 5KM to get up the hill. If you want a workout before dinner, walk up ul. Bistrik from Austrijski Trg, follow it to the left when it reaches the transit road, and bear left up the hill; the restaurant is on the left. However you get there, the trip is worth it. A panoramic view of the city and live music on weekends accompany your meal—at dusk the city lights are spectacular. The food is good Bosnian grill fare, but the real reason to go is the vibrant, romantic atmosphere. Entrees 7-16KM. Open daily 10am-midnight. ❸

Inat Kuća (Despite House), Veliki Alifakovac 1 (☎44 78 67). Walk past the Turkish Quarter along the river; at the National Library, cross the bridge onto Veliki Alifakovac and head left. The restaurant dishes up some of the best Bosnian food in town. Try *dolmes* (stuffed onions; 5KM) or the *Bosnian Pot* (thick lamb and vegetable stew; 6KM). Entrees 5-18KM. Open daily 9am-11pm. ❷

Čevabdžinica Željo, Kundurdžiluk 19 (☎ 44 70 00), in the Turkish Quarter. Named after a local team, this restaurant brims with sporty patriotism and crowds of hungry locals. Željo is always full, so if need be, walk 15m down the street to Željo 2. Both serve only one entree–*čevap* (4KM)–but its really good *čevap*. Open daily 8am-10pm. ❷

◉ SIGHTS

ETERNAL FLAME. The Eternal Flame, where Maršala Tita splits into Ferhadija and Mula Mustafe Bašeskije, was lit in 1945 as a memorial to all Sarajevans who died in World War II. Its dedication to South Slav unity now seems painfully ironic.

NATIONAL LIBRARY. The National Library, at the tip of the Turkish Quarter on Obala Kulina Bana, exemplifies Sarajevo's recent tragedy. The 1896 Moorish-style building, once the most beautiful in the city, served as town hall until 1945, when it was converted into the university library. The besieging Serbs, attempting to demoralize the city, targeted civilian institutions early in the war; the library was firebombed on August 25, 1992, exactly 100 years after construction began. As it burned, citizens risked their lives to rescue the library's treasures, but almost the entire collection burned. Shortly after the war, the Austrian government paid for a new roof to prevent further damage. An EU effort to restore the structure to its former dignity was supposed to have begun, but nothing has been accomplished to date. *(From Maršala Tita, walk toward the river to Obala Kulina Bana and turn left.)*

REMNANTS OF THE SIEGE. All along Sarajevo's main thoroughfare, **Maršala Tita,** the pavement is littered with splash-shaped indentations. These distinctive marks were created by exploding shells during the siege of the city. After the war, some of the marks were filled in with red concrete and dubbed **Sarajevo Roses,** in memory of those killed on the spots. Even in the most normalized of Sarajevo's neighborhoods, they are a constant reminder of the war and the thousands of Bosnians lost. The glaring **treeline** in the hills above the city clearly marks the war's front lines. Bosnians trapped in Sarajevo cut down all the safely available wood for winter heat. Across the street from the Holiday Inn and next to the National Museum (see below), the shattered tower of the **Parliament Building** is a stunning reminder of what most of the city looked like immediately following the war. A walk past the Parliament on ul. Vrbanja brings you to the **bridge** where Sarajevo suffered its first casualties. In 1992, a peace rally began to march across the bridge when Serb snipers in the apartments beside the river opened fire, killing three protesters. A small **monument** to their memory can be found covered in flowers by the bridge. During the siege, the city's defenders built a **tunnel** under the runway of Butmir airport to a nearby suburb. It became the city's lifeline, the only route by which food, arms, and medicine were smuggled in to and the wounded evacuated out of the city. Ask at the tourist office about hiring a guide to explore the accessible section of the tunnel.

CHURCHES, MOSQUES, AND SYNAGOGUES. The structures of various religions huddle together in Central Sarajevo, representing the mixing that once inspired Sarajevo's nickname, "The Jerusalem of Europe." That coexistence may not be as easy now—Jerusalem isn't doing so well either—but Sarajevo remains a unique religious melting pot. The 16th-century **Gazi Husrev-Bey Mosque,** perhaps Sarajevo's most famous building, dominates the Turkish Quarter. The interior is closed for renovations, but it's possible to visit the courtyard and its birdcage fountain. Prayer takes place on the outdoor terrace. *(12 Sarači.*

BOSNIA

THE BIG SPLURGE

THESE SHOES ARE MADE FOR WALKING

If you find your wallet getting unbearably heavy, Sarajevo has a couple of very pleasant ways of lightening it. Both take advantage of the tradition of hand-craftsmanship that is alive and well in Bosnia, despite modern mass production.

Bosnian carpets are a unique and beautiful souvenir. The tradition of carpet-making extends back to the Ottoman occupation, when Bosnians adopted the Turkish weaving techniques used to produce carpets but developed their own patterns and color schemes. The best place in town to buy Bosnian carpets is **SZR Ketar,** Trgovke 41, in Baščaršija. Owner Nijaz Sabljica's excellent English and encyclopedic knowledge of the symbolism of traditional patterns makes looking for a carpet a very pleasant experience. Older carpets are rarer, so a large, antique carpet can easily cost over US$1000. If that's the amount you plan to live off for the next month, a high-quality new carpet will cost about US$150 for a 1½ x2m carpet.

Sarajevo's other specialty is its **custom-made shoes.** Any of the *obućars* (cobblers) in Baščaršija will measure your feet and whip up a pair of shoes to your exact specifications, right down to the color of the leather you want on the lining. You can get a good pair for 70-100KM. If they seem unbearably tight, don't panic—it takes a few days for the leather to stretch to fit your feet, at which point you'll have the best-fitting shoes you've ever owned.

—A. Nicholas Gossen

Facing the flame, walk right onto Ferhadija, which becomes Sarači *after several blocks.)* The **Orthodox Cathedral,** built in 1871, is a beautiful but now mostly empty space, as much of the city's Serb community fled during the war. *(Trg Oslobođenje, off Ferhadija. Open to visitors, but hours are irregular.)* The ancient Orthodox **Church of St. Michael the Archangel** is a dollhouse-sized church that guards a trove of medieval iconography on its interior balcony. *(Mula Mustafe Baš eskije 59, 10min. from the Flame.* ☎*53 47 83. Open daily 7am-6pm.)* The 1889 Catholic **Cathedral of Jesus' Heart** (Katedrala Srce Isusovo), on Ferhadija, is a mundane mix of Gothic and Romanesque styles. Its steps serve as a popular meeting place for the city's youth and a venue for occasional concerts during the summer. *(Trg Grge Martica 2.* ☎*53 69 17. Mass daily 8am and 6pm. Mass in English Su noon.)* The **old synagogue** preserved an art collection among sand bags during the war. Now it houses the **Galerija Novi Hvam.** *(On Mula Mustafe Baš eskije, between the Eternal Flame and St. Michael's.)* The 1892 **Sephardic Synagogue** serves as the base for *La Benevolencija*, the Jewish Community Center's service organization. *(Hamdije Kreš evljakovica 59. From the Cathedral, walk to the river and cross over to the building directly opposite on the far bank. Enter around the block on Hamdije Kresevljakovica.* ☎*66 34 72. Service F 7:30pm. Open M-F 9am-3:30pm. Tour on request.)*

TURKISH QUARTER. (Baščaršija.) The centerpiece of the mosque-flanked Turkish Quarter is a traditional Turkish-style bazaar: squares interlaced with tiny streets packed with shops that offer a spectacular array of war kitsch and other souvenirs, ranging from engraved artillery shells to Bosnian coffee sets. Always bargain aggressively and have someone who speaks Bosnian at your side if possible. The **Sebilj,** a wooden fountain in Baščaršija's main square, is notable more for its dynamic surroundings than for its beauty. Legend has it that once you sip the fountain water, you'll never leave the city. *(At the end of Ferhadija from the Eternal Flame.)*

ASSASSINATION SITE. On this spot Gavrilo Princip shot Austrian Archduke Franz Ferdinand and his wife Sofia on June 28, 1914, leading to Austria's declaration of war on Serbia and the subsequent maelstrom that spawned World War I. Princip was a Serb from Belgrade and part of the *Black Hand* terrorist group that fought Austrian rule (see **History,** p. 81). He was actually the third in a string of assassins who attacked within a matter of minutes. The first, carrying a rifle, lost his nerve and didn't shoot. The second threw a grenade that overshot the royal carriage and blew up the first assassin. Princip took no such chances and shot at near point-blank range. During the recent war, the plaque that formerly marked the historic spot with Princip's footprints was ripped out of the ground. *(The comer that made Sarajevo (in)famous is at the intersection of Obala Kulina Bana and the second bridge when walking from the National Library toward the center.)*

🏛 MUSEUMS

Many museums in Sarajevo found themselves homeless after the war. Some, such as the Olympic Museum and the Jewish Museum, still have collections in storage until a new space can be found. Contact the **Turistička Zajednica** (see **Tourist and Financial Services,** p. 90) to find out if any other museums have recently reopened.

◼ NATIONAL MUSEUM. (Zemaljski Muzej.) Among the Balkans' best and most famous museums, the National Museum brims with botanical gardens, Roman stonework from the 1st to 3rd centuries, and a superb ethnographic collection. The museum will be under construction for much of 2003, but will remain open the entire time. *(Zmaja od Bosne 3. From the Eternal Flame, walk toward the bus station on Mašala Tita until it runs into Zmaja od Bosne; the museum is the large yellow building on the left. ☎ 66 80 27. Open Tu, Th-F, and Su 10am-2pm; W 11am-7pm. 5KM, students 1KM.)*

HISTORY MUSEUM. (Historijski Muzej.) Exhibits contemporary art donated by major European museums, as well as work by local artists. Much of the collection reflects on Bosnia's most recent war. *(Zmaja od Bosne 5. Next to the National Museum. ☎ 21 04 16. Open M-F 9am-2pm, Sa-Su 9am-1pm. Free.)*

ART GALLERY OF BOSNIA AND HERZEGOVINA. (Umjetnička Galerija Bosne i Hercegovine.) The museum houses a small but impressive permanent collection of 20th-century painting and sculpture from throughout the former Yugoslavia. *(Zelenih Beretki 8. Take the 1st right onto Ferhadija after the Flame and follow Zelenih Beretki 2 blocks to the left. ☎ 26 65 50 or 26 65 51. Open M-Sa noon-8pm. Free.)*

ACADEMY OF FINE ARTS. If you're interested in Sarajevo's current art scene, this is the place to go. Rotating exhibits and a pleasant cafe full of art students are on the ground floor. *(Obala Maka Dizdara 3, on the river near the Skenderija complex. ☎ 21 03 69. Open M-F 10am-9pm. Free.)*

🏮 FESTIVALS

Sarajevo has year-round artistic events. Every summer in July, the Turkish Quarter hosts the **Baščaršija Noci** (Turkish Nights), featuring open-air music, theater, and film. The festival is coordinated by the Sarajevo Art Center, Dalmatinska 2/1. (☎ 20 79 21; fax 20 79 72.) Ask for a schedule at the tourist office. In late August, the **Sarajevo Film Festival** gets rolling in theaters throughout the city: locals turn up for eight days of American blockbusters, contemporary European productions, and domestic films. In the recent past, the festival has selected the likes of Ingmar Bergman, Susan Sontag, Susan Sarandon, and Bono for its "Honorary Board." (☎/fax 66 45 47; www.sff.ba. Box office open in summer M-F 9am-6pm. 4-5KM per film.) Since 1984, Sarajevo has also held an annual **Sarajevska Zima** (Sarajevan Winter) from late December to early January, a celebration of culture and art that persisted even through the siege and continues to attract international performers. For more details, call the festival office at Maršala Tita 9. (☎ 20 79 48; fax 66 36 26.) **Futura 2003** will be the 6th annual techno and rave festival, featuring DJs from around the world. The Bosnian answer to Berlin's Love Parade, it takes place for a weekend in mid-July. A DJ and ravers cruise around town on a slow-moving flatbed truck a week before the event. There are always underground events going on; the best way to find out about them is to befriend young Sarajevans.

▣ NIGHTLIFE

In the warmer months, the entire city is on the streets with a beer. Popular music fans will revel in the cafes along **Ferhadija** and **Maršala Tita.** The best nightlife, however, is in basement bars and side-street cafes.

■ **Jazz Bar "Clou,"** Mula Mustafe Bašeskije 5 (mobile ☎066 18 24 45), through the marked doorway near the Flame. By far the best music selection in town: rock, jazz, funk, drum 'n bass, and blues. Lounge on the open-air patio or descend to the moody basement, where local bands play live F-Sa. Wet your lips with pints of beer (5KM). Open daily 8:30pm-5am.

The Bar, Maršala Tita 5 (☎23 34 95), draws an international crowd. Basement doubles as a disco. During the summer, you can recline outside on platforms covered with enormous cushions while sipping your drink. Cover F-Su 10KM. Open M-Th and Su 11am-midnight, F-Sa 11am-2am.

Cocktail Club, Kranjčevića 1 (☎22 06 05), behind The Bar (see above). Sit on the high terrace while you toss back a bottle of Heineken (0.33L 4KM) or the tasty Balkan liquor *Stock* (3KM). If you come in a group of more than 10, the drink prices are cut by 30%. A DJ inside spins disco and rave F-Su. Open M-Th and Su 8am-1am, F-Sa 8am-4am.

▣ DAYTRIP FROM SARAJEVO

TRAVNIK

Buses run to Tranvik from the main bus station in Sarajevo (1½hr., 1 per hr., 10KM). The Travnik bus station is at the far end of town; to return to the center, turn around and walk until you reach a pedestrian underpass; turn left and walk up the hill (5min.). The Old Town is over the bridge to your right. To get to modern Travnik, turn right at the pedestrian walkway.

It's hard to imagine when you first see Travnik, but this humble town was the capital of Bosnia for almost 150 years under Ottoman rule. Legend has it that after conquering Bosnia, the Ottoman emperor decided to make Sarajevo his provincial capital. This injured the pride of local leaders, however, and even though they had been defeated militarily, they kicked up enough of a fuss that the emperor eventually agreed, making Travnik his official capital instead. A total of 77 viziers served in Travnik before the collapse of the empire, and in 1660 it had 17 mosques. After the Ottoman empire disintegrated, Travnik became an important battleground in the tug-of-war between the various Great Powers with interests in the Balkans. These power struggles are the focus of **Ivo Andrić**'s famed *Chronicles of Travnik*. The Nobel Prize-winning author was born here, and his house still stands in the center of town, although it's now occupied by a restaurant. The town's main attraction is the **Stari Grad** (Old Town). Originally built as a fortress to hold back Turkish attacks in the 15th century, it was occupied by the Turks in 1463 and greatly expanded. After becoming the capital of Bosnia, the town grew steadily and spread out around the fortress. Unfortunately, most of these structures, including the palatial vizier's residence, were destroyed in 1950 as part of the communist government's attempts to erase the history (particularly the Muslim history) of Bosnia. Now all that remains are the fortress walls. Even so, they represent some of the best-preserved late medieval architecture in Bosnia. (Stari Grad's gates open daily 10am-6pm. 1KM.) Along the main street of the new part of town, the **Multi-Colored Mosque** (Sulejmania) is the other unique feature of Travnik. Built in 1851, after an older mosque on the same site burned to the ground, it is known for the intricate and colorful designs painted on the outside. Unlike most mosques, the minaret rises on the east side, rather than the west.

MOSTAR ☎ (0)36

As Bosnia and Herzegovina's second-largest city, Mostar spreads out on either side of the blue-green Neretva River, which winds through the surrounding mountains. The 16th-century Turkish city takes its name from the *Mostari*, the keepers of the famous *Stari Most* (Old Bridge). After the fall of the Ottoman Empire at the end of the 19th century, Mostar became increasingly defined by its capacity to harbor Catholic, Muslim, and Orthodox citizens together in a peaceful, tolerant environment. Recent civil war shattered that balance, as well as the Old Bridge and much of the city—the devastation remains shocking and unsettling. Reconstruction on the bridge has begun with international assistance, but far more challenging is the task of helping the citizens of this starkly divided city rebuild their lives.

📠 **TRANSPORTATION.** The **bus station** (☎ 55 20 25) lies 50m from the river on the east bank in the northern part of the city. To reach the east side of Kujundžiluk, face away from the bus station and turn left down Maršala Tita (15min.). To get to the west side, walk straight across the bridge on Deset Hercegivaške Brigade. At the Hotel Ero, just past the bridge, turn left on Aleske Šantica, walk for 15min., and turn left when it runs into Rade Bitange. To: **Sarajevo** (3hr., 6 per day, 11KM); **Dubrovnik, CRO** (3hr., 2 per day, 21KM); **Split, CRO** (4hr., 3 per day, 16KM); **Zagreb, CRO** (9hr., 1 per day, 41KM). **Trains,** behind the bus station, go *only* to **Sarajevo** (3hr.; 2 per day; 11.80KM, 18.80KM round-trip).

🗓️🄴 **ORIENTATION AND PRACTICAL INFORMATION.** Mostar is a large, sprawling city with no compact downtown. The **Neretva River** divides the city from north to south, paralleled on the east by **Maršala Tita**, the main street, and on the west by **Aleske Šantića. Kujundžiluk,** the Old Town, straddles both sides of the river toward the southern end of the two main streets. You can cross the river at three spots: the street near the bus station, **Deset Hercegivaške Brigade;** the pedestrian crossing farther south, **Mostarskog Bataljona;** and the new pedestrian crossing opposite the ruins of Stari Most in Kujundžiluk. In general, Muslims live on the east side and Croats on the west side, though some Muslims also inhabit the west bank. If you don't know which side you're on, just look up—the side with the enormous cross on top of the mountain is (surprise) the Croat side.

Tourist Office: Atlas, Ante Starčevica bb (☎/fax 31 87 71 or 32 66 31), on the right side of the Hotel Ero complex, provides the best tourist information services in town. The friendly staff speaks English, checks bus schedules, and sells detailed maps (7KM) and guidebooks. Open M-F 8am-4pm, Sa 8am-noon.

Currency Exchange: Zagrebačka Banka, Kardinala Stepinca bb (☎ 31 21 20), next to Atlas (see above). The bank will **exchange currency** for 1% commission and **traveler's checks** for 1.5% commission. Open M-F 8am-2:30pm, Sa 8am-noon. There is a 24hr. MC/V **ATM** in front of the bank.

Pharmacy: Kardinala Stepinca 17 (☎ 32 82 68), opposite the traffic bridge. Open M-F 8am-9pm, Sa 8am-7pm.

Telephone Office: (☎ 32 83 62), next to the post office (see below). Open in summer M-F 7am-9pm, Sa 7am-8pm; off-season M-F 7am-8pm, Sa 7am-7pm.

Post Office: Ante Starčevića bb, a block from Atlas (see above). **Exchanges currency** for no commission and holds **Poste Restante.** (☎ 32 83 62. Open in summer M-F 7am-8pm, Sa 7am-7pm; off-season M-F 7am-7pm, Sa 7am-6pm.)

Postal Code: 88000.

⌂ ACCOMMODATIONS. Unless you plan to spend a pretty penny in one of Mostar's modern hotels, lodging is limited. Pansions are your best bet. A 5min. walk from Kujundžiluk, **Villa Ossa ❶**, Vukovića 40b, offers five spotless rooms with double beds, showers, A/C, and new furniture. With your back to the bus station, walk across the bridge and turn left just after Hotel Ero, at the Zagrebačka Banka. Walk down Ante Starčevica and continue along Bolevar Hrvatskih (20min.); turn left at the third traffic light and then bear right over the bridge at Restoran Oscar on Vokovića. (☎57 83 22 or mobile 090 17 53 51. Reserve 2-3 days in advance. Check-out 10am. Singles 30KM; doubles 40KM.) Another option on the west side of the Old Town is the **pansion ❶** at Maršala Tita 189, run by Erna Puzić. The rooms are simple but clean and are a short walk from Kujundžiluk. (☎55 04 16. Singles 20KM; doubles 40KM.) If you need to be near the bus station or just want to feel like a diplomat on an expense account, the **Hotel Ero ❺**, Ante Starčevića bb, is good for both. With attractive rooms and a great cocktail bar below, it's worth the hefty price. (☎38 67 77; fax 38 67 00. Singles 79KM; doubles 136KM. AmEx/MC/V.)

◻ FOOD. The best places to dine are in Kujundžiluk. On the west side, try **Konoba Taurus ❺**, Kriva Cuprija bb, a local favorite tucked in a stone hut above a stream. From Oneščukova take the small stone steps down to your left. Enjoy the house specialty *snicla "Stari Most"* (shnITZ-la; 15KM), breaded veal cutlet rolled and filled with egg, ham, cheese, mushrooms, and onions. (☎21 26 17. Open daily 11am-11pm). At **Caffe Restaurant Šadrvan ❷**, Jusovina 11, right before the ruins of Stari Most and the pedestrian bridge, sit in the quiet, shady courtyard by a bubbling Turkish fountain with beers chilling in it. The offerings on the Bosnian menu include *Đulbastija* (beef steak smothered in *ajvar* and onions with french fries; 10KM) and *Kajmak* (soft goat cheese reminiscent of feta; 3KM). Live music on Friday nights. (☎57 90 57. Open M-Sa 8am-11pm.) On the east side, **Terasa Labirint ❷** offers views of the river and of the remains of Stari Most. (☎19 47 02. Grilled dishes 4-10KM. Open daily 8am-midnight.)

◧ ◪ SIGHTS AND NIGHTLIFE. The famous **Old Bridge** (Stari Most), though no longer extant, remains the symbol of Mostar and one of the most potent metaphors for the war in Bosnia. Built by the Turks in the 16th century, it survived the fall of the Ottoman Empire and two World Wars, connecting the Muslim and Croat halves of the city. On November 9, 1993, Bosnian Croat gunmen defied UNESCO protection and senselessly brought it down, inspiring an official Bosnian day of mourning. Today, reconstruction has begun with international funding, and is projected to end by 2005. The enchanting cobblestone **Kujundžiluk** (Old Town) lies on both sides of the bridge's ruins. Locals sell Turkish-style souvenirs out of low medieval buildings; bargain hard. The most famous mosque in Mostar is the **Karadžozbeg Mosque,** built in 1557. From Kujundžiluk, walk north along the river on Ulica Brače Fejića for 5min. It's open to visitors most of the day, but remember to take your shoes off. For a glimpse of how things used to be, head to the **Turkish House,** Bišćevića 13. This beautiful house has a spectacular view of the river and features works of traditional Turkish arts and crafts. Watch for marauding turtles in the courtyard. (Open M-Sa 8am-8pm. 5KM.) Although much of Mostar has been rebuilt since the 1992-1995 civil war, the old **front line** on the west side remains virtually untouched. Three kilometers of shocking post-apocalyptic destruction start at the Hotel Ero, run down Aleske Santića for a block, then move away from the river to Bulevar Hrvatskih Branitelja, and continue south. The line now divides the living areas of Muslims and Croats in Mostar.

MEÐUGORJE

☎ (0)66

On June 24, 1981, six teenagers from Meðugorje were playing on a nearby hill when a vision of the Virgin Mary appeared and spoke to them. This apparition, which has visited them daily ever since, has made this small mountain town one of the most popular destinations for Catholic pilgrims from around the world. The town estimates that 20 million visitors have passed through since 1981, and a large church complex has been built to accommodate the ever-increasing numbers.

▛ TRANSPORTATION. Buses run to: **Mostar** 45min., 4 per day, 2KM); **Sarajevo** (3½hr., 1 per day, 13KM); **Split, CRO** (2½hr., 3 per day, 19KM). For the bus schedule, look on the door of the post office next door.

▟▛ ORIENTATION AND PRACTICAL INFORMATION. A single main street, **Meðugorje,** runs through the center of town, and nearly every business is clustered around it. The **bus stop** is at the far end of town; to get into Meðugorje, follow the road to the left and around the corner. At the other end of Meðugorje is **St. James's Church,** the focal point of visiting worshippers. There are no street numbers, but everything is easy to find. The **tourist office,** just to left of the church, has information on the history of the visions and the schedule of services. (☎ 65 11 00; fax 65 13 00; www.medugorje.com. Open M-F 7am-8pm.) Directly opposite St. James's is **Zagrebačka Banka,** which **exchanges currency** for no commission, cashes **traveler's checks** for 1.5% commission, and has the town's only **24hr. ATM.** (Open M-Sa 8am-6pm.) Farther down the street on the same side is the **pharmacy.** (Open M-F 8am-8pm, Sa 8am-7.30pm. MC/V.). Continuing to where Meðugorje curves brings you to the **post office,** next to the bus stop. The post office has **phones** outside and offers MC **cash advances.** It also offers the best **Internet access** in town. (4KM per hr. Open M-Sa 7am-8pm.) **Postal Code:** 88266.

▛▟ ACCOMMODATIONS AND FOOD. Meðugorje is small, but it's easy to find a good, fairly cheap room. Dozens of nondescript **private pansions** line Meðugorje. For sheer convenience, you can't beat the **pansion ❶** of Ivan and Ivanka Čilić, opposite the bus station. The large rooms have private bathrooms and the location makes it easy to catch the morning bus. Inquire at the cafe below. (☎/fax 65 18 55. Singles 25KM; doubles 35KM.) Restaurants in Meðugorje are as indistinguishable as the *pansions.* Most of the restaurants scattered between the religious souvenir shops offer cheap but mediocre pizza and pasta dishes. **Restaurant Galija ❸,** toward the post office end of Meðugorje, stands a step above the rest. The well-made pizza (7-8KM), pasta (7-10KM), and grill standards (7-14KM) are served in a comfortable, air-conditioned dining room. (Open daily 10am-11pm.)

◙ SIGHTS. At the heart of Meðugorje is **St. James's Church.** Built in 1969, long before the visions of Mary, the church has been expanded to accommodate the thousands of pilgrims who pass through. One of the additions is the bank of 25 confessionals to the left of the church, which offer confession in a stunning 19 different languages, including Arabic and Korean. Behind the church is an open-air theater, where multilingual **prayer services** take place daily 6pm-9pm. The full schedule of services is posted around the church. The hamlet of **Podbrdo** is a pleasant 1.5km walk from the church. It was here on the **Hill of Apparitions** that the children first saw the Virgin Mary appear. A rocky path up the hill is marked by reliefs depicting mysteries of the rosary by Italian sculptor Carmelo Puzzolo. A more strenuous 2.5km walk from the church brings you up **Križevac,** the mountain above Meðugorje topped by the enormous (8.5m) **cross.** This path is also marked with bronze reliefs of the Way of the Cross. The view from the top is spectacular.

BOSNIA

⚫⚫ ENTERTAINMENT AND NIGHTLIFE. The two most important festivals in Međugorje are the **Anniversary of the Apparitions,** on June 25, and the massive **International Youth Festival,** from July 31 to August 6. It's worth booking rooms in advance . For information on other festivals, check out the tourist office's web site.

BANJA LUKA ☎(0)36

Banja Luka, the capital of the Republika Srpska (RS), is not a tourist town. Most of its old town was leveled by a massive earthquake in 1969. Outpourings from throughout the former Yugoslavia helped rebuild the city in a remarkably short period of time and turn it into an industrial center. Today, it is a pleasant modern city with tree-lined boulevards and the lovely Vrbas River, and a great place to stop for a taste of the RS.

⚫ TRANSPORTATION. Trains run to **Sarajevo** (6hr., 1 per day, 27KM) and **Zagreb, CRO** (3hr., 1 per day, 19KM). **Buses** run to: **Mostar** (8hr., 2 per day, 30KM); **Sarajevo** (5½hr., 8 per day, 23KM); **Belgrade, SER** (4hr., 20 per day, 20KM); **Zadar, CRO** (8hr., 1 per day, 46KM); **Zagreb, CRO** (3hr., 6 per day, 20KM).

⚫⚫ ORIENTATION AND PRACTICAL INFORMATION. Banja Luka is a sprawling city that can be difficult to navigate. The **Vrbas River** divides Banja Luka in two, with the commercial center on the north side. The bus and train stations are a 30min. walk from the center of town; since the walk takes you along major highways, your best bet is to take a taxi into the center (7KM). The main street, **Kralja Petra I Karađorđevića,** leads through the center of town and is paralleled by the pedestrian streets **Veselina Masleše** and **Milosavljevića.** The area around these streets makes up the main commercial and social center of town. **Trg Srpskih Vladara,** between Karađorđevića and Masleše, is the site of the reconstruction of **Church of Christ Savior.** There is no official tourist office in Banja Luka. The unnamed **knjižara** (bookstore), Masleše 15, sells helpful city **maps** (2.5KM). At the end of Masleše, **Cristal Banka,** on the ground floor of the **Boska** department store, **exchanges currency** for no commission and offers **Western Union** services. (Open W-F 8am-3pm, Sa 8am-1pm). There are no functional **ATMs** in Banja Luka. A **pharmacy** is opposite the bookstore. (Open M-Sa 7:30am-9pm, Su 7:30am-2:30pm). There are a number of **Internet** centers. **Softline Internet Klub,** Jevrejska 1, off Masleše, up the stairs offers Internet access for 2KM per hr. (Open daily 9am-10pm). The **post office,** Karađorđevića 93, has pay phones and an exchange office that does not charge commission and offers MC **cash advances.** (Open 24hr.) **Postal Code:** 78000.

⚫⚫ ACCOMMODATIONS AND FOOD. There is no such thing as a budget accommodation in Banja Luka. Options are very limited, and the only places to stay within walking distance of the center are large hotels. The best deal available is the **Hotel Palace ❺,** Karađorđevića 60. Rooms are spacious, pleasant, and modern, with TV and phone. (☎21 87 23. Breakfast included. Singles 100KM; doubles 160KM.) The enormous **Hotel Bosna ❺,** Karađorđevića 97, costs about the same as the Hotel Palace, but is less charming. Bosna is right in the middle of town—its cafe and restaurant attract people throughout the day and night. The comfortable rooms come with TV and telephone. (☎21 57 75; fax 21 69 42. Singles 100KM; doubles 170KM.) Dining options are far better and more affordable than lodging choices. At the top of the list is **Kod Muje ❷,** a Banja Luka tradition hidden through the passageway by Milosavljevića 34. This grill serves up the best *ćevapi* (seasoned Bosnian sausage) in town, and locals would argue the best in the world. A combination plate with both Banja Luka *ćevapi* and *šiš ćevapi* (shish-kebab) costs only 5KM. (☎35 84 92. Open daily 9am-9pm.) For a culinary change of pace, try **Grill Pizzeria Master ❸,** Sime Šolaje 7, off Milosavljevića. This friendly restaurant covers everything from pizzas (6-10KM) to burritos (9-12KM) and good margaritas (6KM), attracting a mixture of locals and expats. (☎31 74 44. Open Su-Th 7:30am-midnight, F-Sa 7:30am-1am.)

◙ SIGHTS. While Banja Luka is a fairly old town, a brutal series of fires, floods, earthquakes, and wars over the centuries have erased much of that history, leaving few historical buildings. Banja Luka's central square, Trg Srpskih Vladara, is currently occupied by the reconstruction site of the **Church of Christ Savior.** The original church was dedicated in 1939, just in time for the outbreak of World War II. In 1941, invading Nazis bombed the church. Reconstruction began in 1993, but it still has a long way to go. Perhaps Banja Luka's most distinctive building is the enormous **Kastel,** by the Vrbas River. Originally built by Romans to protect an important trade route, it was added to and rebuilt countless times by various forces that occupied Banja Luka. It has now been converted into a park and several cafes. During late July, the annual Banja Luka **Summer Festival** takes place inside, featuring an eclectic mix of classical, rock, and techno music. To get there, walk down Karađorđevića and turn left on Dušana. Sadly, one of the city's most beautiful buildings, the **Ferhat-Pasha Mosque,** was destroyed during the recent war when Muslims were expelled from Banja Luka. In 2001, the ground-breaking ceremony for a new mosque on the sight was disrupted by violent riots opposing Muslim return.

◪◙ ENTERTAINMENT AND NIGHTLIFE. Social life in Banja Luka revolves around the dozens of cafe-bars that line every street. At night, the pedestrian area along Masleše and Milosavljevića fills with people of all ages wandering up and down the street and stopping at cafes. But the best place for talking and drinking, day or night, is at the strip of cafes that line the Vrbas River, a short walk from the center of town. **Klub Castra,** Save Kovačevića 48, is the best of the bunch. Its multiple terraces look out over the river and are filled with comfortable chairs. The crowds keep coming and the music keeps going into the wee hours of the morning. To get there, follow Dušana past the Kastel until it ends, then turn left and quickly right onto Rakića. Follow the street until it becomes Save Kovačevića; Castra will be on your right. (☎31 84 11. Open Su-Th 8am-2am, F-Sa 8am-3am.)

B O S N I A

BULGARIA
(БЪЛГАРИЯ)

LEVA

AUS$1 = 1.09LV	1LV = AUS$0.92
CDN$1 = 1.27LV	1LV = CDN$0.78
EUR€1 = 1.95LV	1LV = EUR€0.51
NZ$1 = 0.93LV	1LV = NZ$1.07
UK£1 = 3.07LV	1LV = UK£0.33
US$1 = 1.98LV	1LV = US$0.50
ZAR1 = 0.19LV	1LV = ZAR5.34

From the pine-covered slopes of the Rila, Pirin, and Rodopi mountains in the southwest to the beaches of the Black Sea, Bulgaria is blessed with a countryside rich in natural resources and steeped in ancient traditions. The history of the Bulgarian people, however, is not as serene as the landscape: crumbling Greco-Thracian ruins and Soviet-style high-rises attest to centuries of turmoil and political struggle. Today, Bulgaria's flagging economy and unlikely EU accession are problems heightened by the recent Balkan wars. However, many travelers still find rewarding vacations on the beautiful Bulgarian Black Sea Coast, in cosmopolitan Sofia and Plovdiv, and picturesque surrounding villages.

BULGARIA AT A GLANCE

OFFICIAL NAME: Republic of Bulgaria

CAPITAL: Sofia (pop. 1.2 million)

POPULATION: 7.7 million

LANGUAGE: Bulgarian

CURRENCY: 1 leva (lv) = 100 stotinki

RELIGION: 85% Orthodox Christian, 13% Muslim, 2% other

CLIMATE: Temperate

GEOGRAPHY: Mountains and plains

LAND AREA: 110,910km²

BORDERS: Greece, Macedonia, Romania, Serbia and Montenegro, Turkey

ECONOMY: 46% Services, 29% Industry, 26% Agriculture

GDP: US$6200 per capita

COUNTRY CODE: 359

INTERNATIONAL DIALING PREFIX: 00

HISTORY

BULGARIA IS BORN. The ancient **Thracian tribes,** who occupied Bulgaria during the Bronze Age (circa 3500 BC), were gradually assimilated or expelled by Greek and Roman settlers. The Western Roman Empire crumbled in 476, and by the 7th century the Slavs had invaded the Balkan Peninsula. The late 7th century also brought the **Bulgars,** nomads from central Asia. The year 681 marks the birth of the Bulgarian state (the third oldest in Europe), when Byzantium recognized Bulgar control between the Balkans and the Danube.

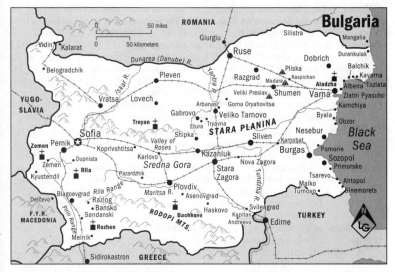

FIRST AND SECOND BULGARIAN EMPIRES. Under **Boris I** and his son **Simeon I,** the Bulgars and Slavs integrated under a common language (Old Church Slavonic) and religion (Christianity). This **First Bulgarian Empire** saw vast artistic development and the construction of many sumptuous palaces. After Simeon I's death, however, the empire became weak from internal divisions and fell prey to Byzantine invasion. A revolt in 1185, led by the brothers **Ivan** and **Peter Asen** of Tarnovo, forced Constantinople to recognize the independence of the **Second Bulgarian Empire,** which came to extend from the Black Sea to the Aegean (and, after 1204, to the Adriatic) and was the leading power in the Balkans.

REVOLUTIONARY RUMBLINGS. Internal upheaval, wars with the Serbian and Hungarian kingdoms, and attacks by Mongols from the north soon weakened the new empire, and by 1396 what remained of Bulgarian independence was lost to the Turks. For the next 500 years, Bulgaria suffered under the **"Turkish yoke,"** during which the local nobility was obliterated and the peasantry enserfed. During this period of repression, bandits known as **haiduti** kept the spirit of resistance alive. The **National Revival,** a period of Bulgarian cultural and educational awakening, was led by **Lyuben Karavelov** and **Vasil Levsky,** who created the Bulgarian Secret Central Committee in Bucharest as a base for national uprising preparations. Levsky, captured and hanged trying to, is considered the greatest hero of the revolutionary movement. The revolutionaries planned an uprising in 1876, but it erupted too soon and was put down brutally by the Turks. The suppression of the **April Uprising** was so violent that it outraged the rest of Europe, and became known as the **Bulgarian Horrors.** A conference of European statesmen convened after the uprising and proposed reforms, which Turkey rejected. Russia declared war in response.

BOUNDARIES CHALLENGED. The **Russo-Turkish War** (1877-78) ended with the **Treaty of San Stefano,** which fulfilled Bulgaria's territorial ambitions by granting it boundaries stretching from the Danube to the Aegean and from the Vardar and Morava valleys to the Black Sea. Austria-Hungary and Britain, however, were not pleased with such a large Slavic state in the Russian sphere of influence; at the 1878 **Congress of Berlin** they redrew the boundaries to create a much smaller state that included less of Macedonia. Simmering tensions over the new borders erupted in the **First** and **Second Balkan Wars** in the 1910s. These resulted in a further loss of territory for frustrated Bulgaria, which surrendered its neutrality in **World War I** and sided with the Central Powers in the hope of recovering its losses. Unsuccessful, Bulgaria lost land in the 1919 **Treaty of Neuilly** at the end of the war. Though neutral at the start of **World War II**, a lust for Greek and Yugoslav territories caused **Boris III** (1918-1943) to join the Axis Powers in 1941, and in 1944 the Soviet Union declared war on Bulgaria. The **Fatherland Front,** an anti-German resistance group, led a successful *coup d'état* four days later, and the new prime minister sought an immediate armistice with the USSR. Elections in 1945 left Bulgaria a communist republic.

A NEW BULGARIA. Bulgaria saw nationalization under communist leader **Georgi Dimitrov** in the late 1940s, isolationism under **Vulko Chervenkov** in the 1950s, and rapid industrialization and alignment with the Soviet Union under **Todor Zhivkov** from 1962-89. Unpopular and much-ridiculed, Zhivkov was retired by the Bulgarian Communist Party on November 10, 1989. The party was renamed the **Bulgarian Socialist Party (BSP)** to symbolize a break from the past, and the Union of Democratic Forces became the leading dissident party. The state adopted a new constitution in 1991 and held its first open presidential elections in 1992. With sociologist **Zhelyu Zhelev** as president and poet **Blaga Dimitrova** as vice-president, the new government embraced openness and pluralism and ended repression of ethnic Turks.

The 1990s were not kind to Bulgaria. The country's first elections were won by reform Communists of the BSP. President Zhelev experienced political opposition that rendered Prime Minister **Andrei Lukanov**'s cabinet impotent. A "government of national unity" took over to produce a new constitution. Currency troubles led to the resurgence of the BSP in 1994, but they only managed to drive the economy farther into the ground. The leva fell from 71lv to the US dollar in April 1996 to 3000lv in February 1997. The **United Democratic Forces,** a coalition led by Prime Minister **Ivan Kostov,** managed to stabilize the economy. Under public scrutiny for instituting reforms that have incurred record unemployment, Kostov continued with his plans in the hopes that they improve Bulgaria's chances of joining the EU.

TODAY

In 2001, however, the Bulgarian electorate brought the **Simeon II National Movement (SNM)** and the Bulgarian monarch to power. Despite promises of economic revival, Bulgaria is still one of Europe's poorest countries. In September 2002, Bulgaria is scheduled to sell one of its largest banks, Biohim, to Austria Creditanstalt as part of a plan to revive its economy. To qualify for loans from the **World Bank,** the country must also sell three other state-owned companies. Bulgaria hopes to join **NATO** after the organization's upcoming summit, when membership invitations will be decided.

PEOPLE AND CULTURE

LANGUAGE

Bulgarian is a South Slavic language. A few words are borrowed from Turkish and Greek, but most vocabulary is similar to Russian and other Slavic languages. **English** is spoken by young people and in tourist areas. **German** and **Russian** are often understood. It's advisable to learn the Cyrillic alphabet to sound out cognates. Street names are in the process of changing; you may need both old and new names. Bulgarian transliteration is much the same as Russian (see **The Cyrillic Alphabet,** p. 15) except that "х" is *h*, "щ" is *sht*, and "ъ" is either *a* or *u* (pronounced like the "u" in bug). *Let's Go* transliterates this letter with a *u*. For a phrasebook and glossary, see **Glossary: Bulgarian,** p. 873.

RELIGION

The state continued to encourage **atheism** after 1989, but religion is gradually more tolerated. Today most Bulgarians are **Eastern Orthodox,** with Muslim, Jewish, Catholic, Protestant, and Gregorian Armenian minorities.

FOOD AND DRINK

BULGARIA	❶	❷	❸	❹	❺
FOOD	under 4lv	4-10lv	11-14lv	15-18lv	over 18lv

Food from **kiosks** is cheap (0.60-2lv); **restaurants** average 6lv per meal. Kiosks sell *kebabcheta* (кебабчета; sausage burgers), sandwiches, pizzas, and *banitsa sus sirene* (баница със сирене; feta cheese filled pastries). Try *shopska salata* (шопска салата), a mix of tomatoes, peppers, and cucumbers with feta cheese. *Tarator* (таратор), a cold soup made with yogurt, cucumber, garlic, and sometimes walnuts, is also tasty. Bulgaria enjoys meat. *Kavarma* (кавърма), meat with onions, spices, and egg is slightly more expensive than *skara* (скара; grills). **Vegetarians** should request *iastia bez meso* (iahs-tea-ah bez meh-so) for meals without meat. Bulgarians are known for cheese and yogurt—the bacteria that makes yogurt from milk bears the scientific name *bacilicus bulgaricus. Ayran* (айран; yogurt with water and ice cubes) and *boza* (боза; similar to beer, but sweet and thicker) are popular drinks that complement breakfast. Bulgaria exports mineral water and locals swear by its healing qualities. **Tap water** is safe to drink. Melnik (see p. 126) produces famous red **wine** and the northeast is known for excellent white wines. On the Black Sea Coast, Albenu is a good sparkling wine. Bulgarians begin meals with *rakia* (ракия; grape brandy). Good Bulgarian **beers** include Kamenitza and Zagorka. The drinking age is 18; carding is rare but increasing due to the tragic death of seven children outside a club in December 2001 (see **Disco Tragedy,** p. 135).

CUSTOMS AND ETIQUETTE.

YES AND NO. Bulgarians shake their heads from side to side to indicate "yes" and up and down to indicate "no," the exact opposite of Brits and Yanks. For the uncoordinated, it's easier to just hold your head still and say *da* or *neh*.

Businesses usually open at 8 or 9am and take a one-hour lunch break sometime between 11am and 2pm. Banks are usually open 8:30am to 4pm, but some close at 2pm. Tourist offices, post offices, and shops stay open until 6 or 8pm; in tourist areas and big cities, shops may close as late as 10pm. Seat yourself at **restaurants** and ask for the *smetka* (сметка; bill) when you're done. It is customary to share tables in restaurants and taverns. *Nazdrave!* (Наздраве!) means **"Cheers!"**—you're sure to hear this in bars. When clinking glasses (or beer mugs), make sure to look the person in the eye and call *Nazdrave!* loudly. **Tipping** is not obligatory, as most people just round up to the nearest leva, but 10% doesn't hurt, especially in Sofia where waitstaff expect it. A 7-10% service charge will occasionally be added for you; always check the bill or the menu to see if it's listed. Restaurants and *mehani* (механи; taverns) usually charge a small fee to use the restrooms. Tipping **taxi drivers** usually means rounding up to the nearest leva or half-leva. Bargaining for fares is rare, but be sure to agree on a price before getting in. For fair deals, bargain with street vendors down to 60% of the original price, especially in touristy areas.

BULGARIA

THE ARTS

HISTORY

LITERATURE AND ART. With Tsar Boris's conversion to Christianity came the first major epoch of Bulgarian literature, the **Old Bulgarian** period (AD 900-1200). Under the guidance of the first Slavic language school in Preslav, the translation of religious texts flourished. Bulgarian culture during this **Golden Age** was on pace to compete with that of the Byzantine capital of **Constantinople,** when conquest by the Byzantines stalled progress until the **Middle Bulgarian** period (13th-17th centuries).

Art and literature went into hibernation during the 500 years of Ottoman rule, but monasteries managed to preserve manuscript writing and iconography until the coming of the **National Revival** *(Vuzrazhdane)* in 1762. The Revival coincided with **Paisy of Hilendar's** romanticized *Istoria slavyanobulgarska* (Slavo-Bulgarian History), which helped sow the first seeds of nationalism. Using their works as a tool toward liberation, realists **L. Karavelov** and **V. Drumev** depicted small-town life, **Hristo Botev** wrote impassioned revolutionary poetry, and **Petko Slaveykov** and **Georgi Rakovski** drew on folklore to whip the populace into a revolutionary fervor. Meanwhile, brothers **Dimitar** and **Zahari Zograf** painted church walls and secular portraits (see **Plovdiv: Sights,** p. 123; **Bachkovo Monastery,** p. 123; **Rila Monastery,** p. 118; **Bansko: Sights,** p. 125; and **Troyan Monastery,** p. 147). The works of poet **Ivan Vazov** span the gap from subjugation to liberation, recounting the struggle against the Turks.

Several female poets have emerged in recent decades. **Petya Dubarova's** promising career was cut short by her early death in 1979; her collection *Here I Am, in Perfect Leaf Today* was recently published in English. Bulgaria's most important 20th-century poet, **Elisaveta Bagryana,** skillfully fused the experimental and the traditional in her love poems.

CURRENT SCENE

Young Bulgarian contemporary artists broke through the wall of Communist-mandated art in the late 1980s and have jumped onto the postmodern bandwagon. These individual, self-conscious works are edgy and surprising, from **Nikolai Alexiev's** surreal canvases to **George Kalenderov's** conceptual installations.

HOLIDAYS AND FESTIVALS

NATIONAL HOLIDAYS IN 2003	
January 1 New Year's Day	**May 24** Education and Culture Day; Day of Slavic Heritage
March 1 Baba Marta (Spring Festival)	
March 3 Liberation Day (1878)	**June 1** Festival of the Roses (Kazaluk)
April 18 Good Friday	**September 6** Day of Union
April 20-21 Easter	**September 22** Independence Day
May 1 International Labor Day	**December 24-26** Christmas

Colorful Bulgarian folk costumes, music, and dance augment and meld with traditional Christian and ancient Thracian holidays to create a unique festive atmosphere. Plan your vacation around these exciting celebrations, but make reservations far in advance.

CHRISTMAS AND NEW YEAR'S. These holidays are characterized by the two related Bulgarian customs of *sourvakari* and *koledouvane.* On Christmas, groups of people go from house to house and perform *koledouvane,* or caroling, while holding beautifully carved oak sticks called *koledarkas.* On New Year's, a group of *sourvakari*, usually male, wish their neighbors well while holding decorated cornel rods called *sourvachka*. Both rites have to do with the anticipation of fertility.

BABA MARTA. (Spring Festival.) Baba Marta (March 1st) celebrates the beginning of Spring. Bulgarians traditionally give each other *martenitzas*, small red and white tassels formed to look like a boy and a girl. These fertility charms are meant to be worn around the neck or pinned on until a stork is seen.

FESTIVAL OF THE ROSES. This festival is celebrated in Kazanluk and Karlovo on the first Sunday in June (June 1st in 2003), and revels in the beauty of one of Bulgaria's most famous exports. Carnivals, feasts, and folk dances abound.

ADDITIONAL RESOURCES

GENERAL HISTORY

A Concise History of Bulgaria, by R.J. Crampton (1997). An easy and quick introduction to Bulgaria's history.

Beyond Hitler's Grasp: The Heroic Rescue of Bulgaria's Jews, by Michael Bar Zohar (2001). An in-depth study of one of Bulgaria's proudest moments.

FICTION AND NONFICTION

Penelope of the 20th Century: Selected Poems of Elisiveta Bagryana. Features an introduction by Blaga Dimitrova.

Balkan Ghosts: A Journey Through History, by Robert Kaplan (1994). Both an engaging travelogue and an accessible regional history.

BULGARIA ESSENTIALS

ENTRANCE REQUIREMENTS
Passport: Required of all travelers.
Visa: Not required.
Letter of Invitation: Required if not a US citizen.
Inoculations: Recommended up-to-date on MMR (measles, mumps, and rubella), DTaP (diphtheria), Polio booster, Hepatitis A, and Hepatitis B.
Work Permit: Required of all foreigners planning to work in Bulgaria.
International Driving Permit: Required of all those planning to drive.

DOCUMENTS AND FORMALITIES

EMBASSIES AND CONSULATES

Embassies of other countries in Bulgaria are all in Sofia (see p. 110). Bulgaria's embassies and consulates abroad include:

Australia: Consulate: 14 Carlotta Rd., Double Bay, Sydney, NSW 2028; P.O. Box 1000, Double Bay, NSW 1360 (☎02 9327 7592; fax 9327 8067; bgconsul@ihug.com.au).

Canada: 325 Stewart St., Ottawa, ON K1N 6K5 (☎613-789-3215; fax 789-3524).

Ireland: 22 Bulington Rd. Dublin 4 (☎01 660 3293; fax 01 660 3915).

South Africa: 1071 Church St., Hatfield, Pretoria 0083; P.O. Box 32569, Arcadia (☎012 342 37 20; fax 342 37 21; embulgsa@iafrica.com).

UK: 186-188 Queensgate, London SW7 5HL (☎020 7584 9400; fax 7584 4948).

US: 1621 22nd St. NW, Washington, D.C. 20008 (☎202-387-0174 or 387-7969; fax 234-7973; consulate@bulgaria-embassy.org; www.bulgaria-embassy.org).

VISA AND ENTRY INFORMATION

Citizens of Australia, Canada, the EU, New Zealand, and the US may visit Bulgaria visa-free for up to 30 days. Citizens of South Africa and anyone planning to stay more than 30 days must obtain a 90-day visa from their local embassy or consulate (see above). Single-entry visas are US$50 for ten business days processing, US$65 for five business days, and US$85 for overnight service (only available to US citizens). Multiple-entry visas cost US$120, transit (valid 24hr.) US$40, and double transit (valid 24hr.) US$60. Prices include a border tax of approximately US$20; those not needing visas are required to pay the tax upon entering the country. The application requires a passport valid more than six months after return from Bulgaria, a passport photograph, an invitation (if not a US citizen), a copy of your green card (if applicable), payment by cash or money order, and a self-addressed, stamped envelope. There is no express service for multiple-entry visas. Visas may be extended at police stations in major cities before the date of expiration, but at a high cost. A Bulgarian **border crossing** can take several hours, as there are three different checkpoints: passport control, customs, and police. Visas cannot be purchased at the border. Walking across the border is not permitted. The border crossing into Turkey is particularly difficult. It is easiest to cross on an officially chartered bus, specifically a direct bus or train from Sofia to a neighboring capital. Enter from Romania at Ruse.

Upon crossing the border, citizens of South Africa may receive a **statistical card** to document where they sleep. If you don't get a card, don't worry. **Foreigner registration** is required as of March 2002 in response to September 11. If you are staying in Bulgaria for more than 48 hours, you must be registered with the police. The hotel/hostel you are staying in will do this for you, and may ask for your passport, but should return it immediately. Keep the registration with your passport, and make sure you are re-registered every time you change accommodations. If you are staying with friends, register yourself with the **Bulgarian Registration Office;** see the consular section of your embassy for details.

TRANSPORTATION

BY PLANE. All flights to Sofia connect through England or Western Europe. Tickets into the capital may run up to US$1400 during the summer months. Budget travelers might want to fly into a nearby capital—Athens, İstanbul, or Bucharest—and take a bus to Sofia.

BY TRAIN. Bulgarian trains run to **Hungary, Romania,** and **Turkey** and are better for transportation in the north; **Rila** is the main international train company. The train system is comprehensive but slow, crowded, and old. Buy tickets at the Ticket Center (Билетен Център; Bileti Tsentur) stations. There are three types of trains express (експрес; *ekspres*), fast (бърз; *burz*), and slow (пътнически; *putnicheski*). Avoid *putnicheski* like the plague—they stop at anything that looks inhabited, even if only by goats. Arrive at the station well in advance if you want a seat. Stations are poorly marked and often only in Cyrillic; know when you're reaching your destination, bring a map, and ask for help. First class (първа класа; *purva klasa*) is very similar to second class (втора класа; *vtora klasa*), and probably not worth the extra money. Store luggage at the "гардероб" (garderob).

BY BUS. Buses are better for travel in eastern and western Bulgaria and are often faster than trains—they are also less frequent and less comfortable. Buses head north from Ruse, to İstanbul from anywhere on the Black Sea Coast, and to Greece from Blagoevgrad. For long distances, **Group Travel** and **Etap** offer modern buses with air-conditioning, bathrooms, and VCRs at prices 50% higher than trains. Some buses have set departure times; others leave when full. Grueling local buses stop everywhere for a bumpy (and in the summer, sweaty) ride. Due to the current political situation in Serbia and Montenegro, *Let's Go* does not recommend that travelers take direct buses from Bulgaria to Central and Western Europe. Instead, go to Bucharest and begin your journey westward from there.

BY FERRY. Ferries from Varna and Burgas go to **İstanbul, TUR** and **Odessa, UKR.**

BY TAXI. Yellow taxis are everywhere in cities. Refuse to pay in dollars and insist on a ride *sus apparata* (with meter); ask the distance and price per kilometer. Some Black Sea towns can only be reached by taxi.

BY THUMB. Hitching is rare because drivers hardly ever stop, but it is generally safe if precautions are taken. *Let's Go* does not recommend hitchhiking.

TOURIST SERVICES AND MONEY

Tourist offices and local travel agencies are fairly common and are good at reserving private rooms; otherwise, they mostly plan itineraries. Staffs are helpful and usually speak English and German. A good resource is a big hotel, where you can often find an English-speaking receptionist and **maps.** The **lev** (lv; plural leva) is the standard monetary unit, and is fully convertible (1 lev=100 stotinki), though sometimes US dollars or Euros are accepted. **Inflation** is around 7.4%, so expect prices to change over the next year. Both private banks and exchange bureaus exchange money, but bank rates are more reliable. The four largest **banks** are Bulbank, Biohim, Hebros, and OBB. **Traveler's checks** can only be cashed at banks (with the exception of a few change bureaus). Many banks also give **Visa cash advances. Credit cards** are rarely accepted. **ATMs** are common, usually accept MC/V, and give the best rates. It is illegal to exchange currency on the street.

HEALTH AND SAFETY

 EMERGENCY NUMBERS: Police: ☎ 166 **Fire:** ☎ 160 **Emergency:** ☎ 150

Emergency care is far better in Sofia than in the rest of the country; services at the Pirogov State Hospital are free, some doctors speak English or German, and the tourist office will send someone along to interpret for you. The sign "Аптека" (apteka) denotes a **pharmacy.** There is always a night-duty pharmacy in larger towns. *Analgin* is headache medicine; *analgin chinin* is for colds and flu; bandages are *sitoplast.* Foreign brands of *prezervatifs* (condoms) are safer. Public **bathrooms** (Ж for women, M for men) are often holes in the ground; pack toilet paper and expect to pay 0.05-0.20lv. **Tampons** are widely available. Don't buy bottles of **alcohol** from street vendors, and be careful with homemade liquor—there have been cases of poisoning and contamination.

WOMEN, DISABLED, AND MINORITY TRAVELERS. It is fine for **women** to travel alone, though the usual precautions should be exercised. Wear skirts and blouses to avoid unwanted attention; only young girls wear sneakers, tank tops, or shorts outside of big cities. Although access is slowly improving, visitors with physical **disabilities** will confront many challenges in Bulgaria. **Discrimination** is focused on the **Roma** (gypsies), who are considered a nuisance at best and thieves at worst. While hate crimes are rare, persons of a foreign ethnicity might receive stares. The Bulgarian government has recently recognized **homosexuality,** but acceptance is slow in coming: discretion is wise.

ACCOMMODATIONS AND CAMPING

BULGARIA	❶	❷	❸	❹	❺
ACCOM.	under 20lv	20-40lv	41-60lv	61-80lv	over 80lv

HOTELS AND HOSTELS. Bulgarian **hotels** are classed on a star system and licensed by the Government Committee on Tourism; rooms in one-star hotels are almost identical to those in two- and three-star hotels, but have no private bathrooms. All accommodations provide sheets and towels. Expect to pay US$8-40 per night, although foreigners are sometimes charged higher prices. Private rooms are cheap and usually have all the amenities of a good hotel (US$6-15). Only Sofia has **hostels,** and they are generally excellent.

CAMPING. Outside major towns, most **campgrounds** provide spartan bungalows and tent space. Call ahead in the summer to reserve bungalows. Some facilities are poorly maintained or unpredictable, so check before it is too late to stay elsewhere.

KEEPING IN TOUCH

MAIL. "Свъздушна поща" on letters indicates **airmail.** It is far more reliable than ground transport mail, but sometimes it is difficult to convince the postal workers to let you pay extra to have it sent by air. Sending a letter abroad costs 0.60lv to Europe, 0.80lv to the US, and 0.80-1.00lv to Australia, New Zealand, or South Africa; note that a Bulgarian return address is required. Packages must be unwrapped for inspection. Register important packages, and allow 2 weeks for it to arrive. Mail can be received general delivery through Poste Restante, though it is unreliable. Address envelope as follows: Stephanie (first name), SHERMAN (last name), POSTE RESTANTE, писма до поискване централна поща, Гурко 6 (post office address), София (city) 1000 (postal code), България (Bulgaria).

TELEPHONES. Making international **telephone** calls from Bulgaria can be a challenge. Pay phones are ludicrously expensive; opt for the phone offices. If you must make an **international call** from a pay phone with a card, purchase the 400 unit, 20lv card. Units run out quickly on international calls, so talk fast or have multiple cards ready. There are two brands: **BulFon** (orange) and **Mobika** (blue), which work only at telephones of the same brand. One minute costs 2.40lv to Australia, Canada, or the US; 1.80lv to the UK 1.80lv; and 3.60lv to New Zealand. To **call collect,** dial ☎ 01 23 for an international operator The Bulgarian phrase for collect call is *za tyahna smetka* (за тяхна сметка). For **local calls,** pay phones will accept coins, but it's best to buy a phone card (see above). You can also call from the post office, where a clerk assigns you a booth, a meter records your bill, and you pay when finished.

INTERNET ACCESS. Internet cafes can be found throughout urban centers, cost about 1 lv per hr., and are often open 24hr.

SOFIA (СОФИЯ) ☎(0)2

A history of national submission has left Bulgaria a little unsure of itself, but Sofia resolves the identity crisis by adopting multiple personalities. Spray-painted skateboarding ramps front the iron Soviet Army monument, while *babushkas* tote their bread loaves home in Harry Potter shopping bags. Though a high unemployment rate is still evident, a noticeable reduction in street litter shows some municipal improvement. More McDonalds exist than ever before, but the dome of St. Alexander Nevsky Cathedral is still the most dominant golden landmark. Indeed, national culture has proven so resilient that a trip to Bulgaria turns out to be just that—a trip to Bulgaria.

🎞 **INTERCITY TRANSPORTATION**

Flights: Airport Sofia (international info ☎ 79 80 35 or 72 06 72). Bus #84 is to the right as you exit international arrivals. Buy tickets at kiosks with a "Билети" (bileti; tickets) sign. Runs from the airport to Eagle Bridge (Орлов Мост) near Sofia University, a 10min. walk from the city center. Minibus #30 (in front of the international arrivals exit, 1lv) runs between the airport and pl. Sv. Nedelya along bul. Tsar Osvoboditel; since the minibus has no specific stops, those who wish to board the vehicle must flag it down and request their stop. Taxis in front of the airport charge expensive fares (up to 25lv), but taxis ordered by phone from the airport should charge more reasonably (5lv). Airlines include: **Air France,** Suborna 5 (Суборна; ☎ 981 78 30; open M-F 9am-6pm); **British Airways,** Alibin 56 (Алибин; ☎ 981 70 00; open M-F 9am-5pm); **Lufthansa,** Suborna 9 (☎ 980 41 41; open M-F 9am-5pm).

Trains: Tsentralna Gara (Централна Гара; Central Train Station), Knyaginya Maria Luiza St. (Мария Луиза), a 20min. walk (1.6km) from pl. Sv. Nedelya past the department store Tsum (Цум) and the mosque. Trams #1 and 7 run between pl. Sveta Nedelya and the station; #9 and 12 head down Hristo Botev (Христо Ботев) and Vitosha (Витоша). Info booth and tickets for north Bulgaria are on the first floor. To: **Burgas** (7 per day; 8.20-12lv, round-trip 12.30-16.50lv); **Plovdiv** (13 per day; 3.80-5.40lv, round-trip 5.70-7.30lv); **Ruse** (4 per day; 8.20-11.20lv, round-trip 12.30-15.30lv); **Varna** (6 per day; 10.20-14lv, round-trip 15.30-19.50lv). Trip lengths depend on type of train (Пътнически, slow; Бърз, fast; Експрес, express). Train schedules change with the season, so call ahead. International tickets available at the **ticket office** (☎ 931 11 11). Open M-F 7am-7pm. International trips must be approved by border officers. To the left of the main entrance, **Rila Travel Bureau** (Рила; ☎ 932 33 46) sells international tickets to: **Athens, GRE** via **Thessaloniki, GRE** (1 per day, 65-90lv) and **Budapest, HUN** via **Bucharest, ROM** (1 per day, 110-135lv). Open daily 7am-11pm.

Buses: Private buses, which leave from the parking lot across from the train station, are reasonably priced and usually fast. The length of the trip varies depending on the road taken. **Group Travel** (☎ 320 122) sends buses to: **Burgas** (2 per day, 16lv); **Veliko Tarnovo** (4 per day, 9lv); **Varna** (3 per day, 16lv). Buy tickets at kiosks labeled "Биллетн Център" (Billeten Tsentur; Ticket Center). Pay in lv or US$. Arrive 30-45min. early to be guaranteed a seat. Open daily 6:30am-9pm.

❖ ORIENTATION

The city center, **pl. Sveta Nedelya** (Света Неделя), is a triangle formed by the Tsurkva (church) Sv. Nedelya, the wide Sheraton Hotel, and the department store Tsentralen Universalen Magazin (TSUM). **Bul. Knyaginya Maria Luiza** (Княгиня Мария Луиза) connects pl. Sveta Nedelya to the train station. Trams #1 and 7 run from the train station through pl. Sveta Nedelya to **bul. Vitosha** (Витоша), one of the main shopping and nightlife thoroughfares. Bul. Vitosha links pl. Sveta Nedelya to **pl. Bulgaria** and the huge, concrete **Natsionalen Dvorets Kultura** (Национален Дворец Култура; **NDK, National Palace of Culture**). Historic **bul. Tsar Osvoboditel** (Цар Освободител; Tsar the Liberator) is on your right as you go down bul. Maria Luiza, and heads to both **Sofia University** and the hottest spots for dancing and drinking. The monthly **Sofia City Guide** (2.40lv, available at the Sheraton Hotel and at tourist centers) is a great English publication with loads of tourist information. **Maps** are also available in the lobby of the Sheraton Hotel (open 24hr.) and the outdoor book market at Slaveikov Sq. (Славейков) on Graf Ignatiev (Граф Игнатиев).

❒ LOCAL TRANSPORTATION

Public Transportation: Trams, trolleybuses, and buses cost 0.40lv per ride, 0.70lv for two rides, day pass 2lv, 5-day pass 9lv. Buy tickets at kiosks with a "билети" (bileti; tickets) sign stuck to the store window or from the driver. Punch the tickets in the machines on board to avoid a 10lv fine. If you put your backpack on a seat, you may be required to buy a second ticket, or pay a 4lv fine for an "unticketed passenger." All transportation runs daily 5am-11:30pm, but after 9pm service becomes less frequent.

Taxis: While some travelers have terrible taxi tales, **Taxi-S-Express** (☎912 80), **OK Taxi** (☎973 21 21), and **INEX** (☎919 19) are reliable options. Always make sure that the name of the company and its phone number are listed on the side of the car. Instead of bargaining, simply insist that the driver turn on the meter. Drivers don't speak English, so it's wise to learn how to pronounce the Bulgarian names for destinations. Fares are 0.30-0.40lv per km, slightly more expensive from 10pm-8am.

❼ PRACTICAL INFORMATION

TOURIST AND FINANCIAL SERVICES

Tourist Office: Odysseia-In/Zig Zag Holidays, bul. Stamboliskii 20-B (Стамболийски; ☎980 5102; fax 980 32 00; zigzag@omega.bg; http://zigzag.dir.bg). From pl. Sv. Nedelya, head down Stamboliskii and take the 2nd right on Lavele; Odysseia is halfway down on the left, 2 floors up. The staff offers homestays in Bulgarian villages and a variety of outdoor activities: rock climbing, spelunking, biking, skiing, and snowshoeing. Consultation 5lv per session. Open M-Sa 9am-6:30pm.

Embassies: Citizens of **Australia, Canada,** and **New Zealand** should contact the British Embassy. **South Africa,** ul. Gendov, bl. 1 (☎971 21 38). Open M and Th 10am-noon. **UK,** ul. Moskovska 9 (Московска; ☎933 92 22). Register either by phone or in person upon arrival in Bulgaria. Open M-F 8am-12:30pm and 1:30-5pm. **US,** ul. Suborna 1a (Суборна; ☎937 51 004), 3 blocks from pl. Sv. Nedelya behind the Sheraton. Open M-F 8:30am-1pm and 2-5pm. Consular section at Kapitan Andreev 1 (Капитан Андреев; ☎963 20 22), behind the NDK. Open M-F 9am-5pm.

Currency Exchange: Bulbank (Булбанк; ☎923 21 11), pl. Sv. Nedelya 7, cashes **traveler's checks** (1.4% commission, minimum US$3 fee) and gives Visa **cash advances** (4% commission). Open M-F 8:30am-6:30pm.

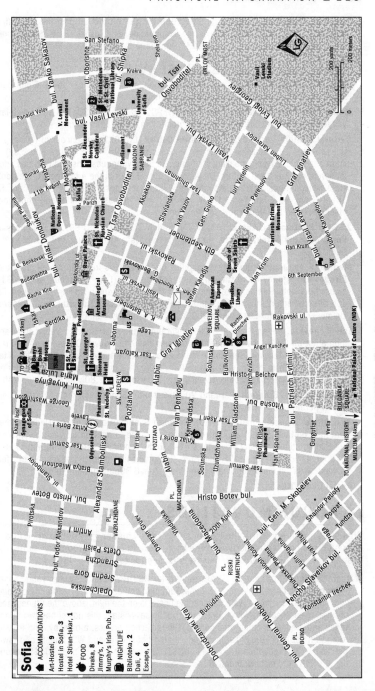

Sofia

ACCOMMODATIONS
Art-Hostel, 9
Hostel in Sofia, 3
Hotel Stivan-Iskar, 1

FOOD
Divaka, 8
Jimmy's, 7
Murphy's Irish Pub, 5

NIGHTLIFE
Biblioteka, 2
Dali, 4
Escape, 6

American Express: Ul. Vasil Levski 21 (☎988 49 43), on the left past the post office heading toward Slaveikov Sq. Issues (1% commission) and cashes (3.5% commission) AmEx Traveler's Cheques. Open daily M-F 9am-6pm, Sa 9am-noon.

LOCAL AND EMERGENCY SERVICES

Luggage Storage: Downstairs at the central train station. 0.80lv per piece. Claim bags 30min. before departure. Open daily 5:30am-midnight.

Library: Biblioteka Slaveikov, Slaveikov 4 (☎980 66 88, ext. 530) has an English-language library. Library cards 4lv. Open W noon-6pm, Th-Tu 10am-6pm.

Cultural Center: Euro-Bulgarian Cultural Centre (**EBCC;** Евро-Български Кулстурен Център), bul. Stamboliskii 17 (Стамболийски; ☎/fax 988 00 84; www.eubcc.bg). A knowledgeable, English-speaking staff answers all of your questions and provides information about Bulgarian culture. On your way out, check out the Arts Cinema, the bookstore Helikan (Хеликон), and the art gallery. **Internet access** (open M-F 9am-10pm, Sa 10am-10pm, Su 10am-7pm) 1.80lv per hr. The office has a scanner and photocopy machine. Open M-F 9am-7pm, Sa 10am-6pm.

24-Hour Pharmacies: Apteka #7, pl. Sv. Nedelya 5 (☎987 50 89), at Stamboliskii. **Purva Chastna Apteka** (Първа Частна Аптека), Tsar Asen 42 (☎952 26 22), near Neofit Rilski.

Medical Assistance: State-owned hospitals offer foreigners free 24hr. emergency aid. **Pirogov Emergency Hospital,** bul. Gen. Totleben 21 (Ген. Тотлебен; ☎515 31), across from Hotel Rodina. Take trolley #5 or 19 from the center. No English spoken. For dog bites or emergency tetanus shots, go to the **First City Hospital,** bul. Patriarch Evtimii 37 (Патриарх Евтимий; ☎988 36 31). Open daily 8am-6pm.

Telephones: Ul. Stefan Gurko 4. Take a right out of the post office on Vasil Levski and then a left on Gurko; it's a large white building one block down. Offers telephone, fax, photocopy, and telegram service. To make a call, go to windows 2 or 3; the staff will tell you which booth to call from. Local call or phone card charge 0.09lv. Pay at window when finished. **Internet access** 1lv for 1hr., 1.90lv for 2hr., 2.80lv for 3hr. Open 24hr.

Internet Access: Stargate, Pozitano 20 (Позитано), 30m on left facing Hostel Sofia. 0.80lv per hr. Open 24hr.

Post Office: General Gurko 6 (Гурко). Go down Suborna behind pl. Sv. Nedelya, then turn right on Lege (Леге) and left on Gurko; entrance to right on ul. Vasil Levsky (*not* bul.). International mailing at windows #6-8, in the first hall. **Poste Restante** at window #12, in the first hall (open M-F 8am-8pm, Sa 8am-noon). International money transfers at window #7, in the second hall. Open M-Sa 7am-8:30pm, Su 8am-1pm.

Postal Code: 1000.

⋔ ACCOMMODATIONS

Big hotels are rarely worth the exorbitant prices—smaller, privately owned hotels or hostels are better alternatives. If the hostels are full, private rooms are often the best options (available through Odysseia-In, see **Tourist Office,** p. 112).

▨ **Hostel in Sofia,** Pozitano 16 (Позитано; ☎/fax 989 85 82; hostelsofia@yahoo.com). From pl. Sv. Nedelya, walk down Vitosha. Turn right on Pozitano, just before the building with lion statues in front. Walk 1 block; the hostel is on the right, above the Chinese restaurant. Great location. With a boisterous, Sofia-savvy staff, this hostel has two dormitories and a summer-camp atmosphere. Offers kitchen access, a balcony, and a living room with cable TV. Breakfast included. Shared hot shower and WC. Sheets and towel provided. 24hr. reception. No curfew. US$10 per person for first night, US$9 second night, US$8 third night or more. ❶

Art-Hostel, ul. Angel Kunchev 21A (Ангел Кънуев; ☎987 05 45 or 980 91 30; art-hostel@art-hostel.com; www.art-hostel.com). From pl. Sv. Nedelya, walk down Vitosha and turn left on William Gladstone. Walk 2 blocks and turn right on Angel Kunchev. The hostel will be on the left. Part gallery, part hostel, this new, spacious facility will surely allow you to rediscover the "art of travel." Two new dormitories, kitchen, bar, Internet access (1lv per hr.), tea room, and popular garden. Two shared showers and WCs. Sheets provided. Laundry 4lv. 24hr. reception. US$9 per person. ❶

Hotel Stivan-Iskar, ul. Iskar 11b (☎986 67 50; fax 980 43 45; www.hoteliskar.com). Walk up bul. Maria Luiza to ul. Ekzarh Iosif. Go right for two blocks, then another right on Bacho Kiro, and then left on Iskar. Comfortable new rooms. Breakfast US$2. Check-out noon. Doubles US$25, with bath US$37; apartments with refrigerator and bath US$50 for 2 people, US$55 for 3 people. ❸

🍴 FOOD

From fast food to Bulgarian specialties, low-priced meals are easy to find. You won't have any trouble finding small cafes offering assorted snacks and drinks. Large markets called **Hali** (Хали) and **Women's Bazaar** (Жени Пазар) are across bul. Maria Luiza from the department store TSUM (Цум).

🔲 **Divaka,** ul. William Gladstone 54 (Уилям Гладстон; ☎989 95 43). Facing the McDonalds in Slaveikov Sq., go down the sidestreet to the left. Stay to the right when the street forks around. Divaka is on the left. So popular you might have to share a table with other patrons in the greenhouse dining area. Try the seemingly bottomless bowls of salad (1.50-3.50lv) and *sacheta*, sizzling heaps of veggies and meat cooked and served on an iron plate (4.50lv). Open 24hr. ❶

Murphy's Irish Pub, Karnigradska 6 (Кърниградска; ☎980 28 70). An international crowd bonds at this chain Irish pub which feels quite un-Bulgarian–probably because both the food and the ambience are imported. Large portions of flavorful meals include steak (10.50lv), a Leprechaun burger (6.50lv), or a Shamrock sandwich (6.50lv). Special "Irish breakfast" (2 meals in itself) comes with a drink. Open daily noon-1am. ❷

Jimmy's, Angel Kunchev 11 (Ангел Кънчев; www.jimmys.bg). Jimmy's serves 29 flavors of gourmet ice cream (0.50lv per scoop) on crowded outdoor tables. Try Jimmy's alcoholic ice cream cocktails (1.85lv) like "bitter almond," a blend of ice cream, milk, and almond liqueur. ❶

🔘 SIGHTS

ST. ALEXANDER NEVSKY CATHEDRAL. (Св. Александър Невски; Sv. Aleksandr Nevsky.) The gold-domed Byzantine-style cathedral, erected from 1904 to 1912 in memory of the 200,000 Russians who died in the 1877-78 Russo-Turkish War, was named after the patron saint of the tsar-liberator. It is the largest Christian Orthodox Church on the Balkan Peninsula and one of the most ornate, housing over 400 frescoes by Russian and Bulgarian artists. In a separate entrance to the left of the church, the **crypt** contains a spectacular array of painted icons and religious artifacts from the past 1500 years. The adjacent square has become a marketplace for religious souvenirs. *(In the center of pl. Alexander Nevsky. Cathedral open daily 7:30am-7pm; crypt open W-M 10:30am-6:30pm. Cathedral free; crypt 3lv, students 1.50lv. Guided tours of the crypt 15lv for more than 10 people, 10lv for fewer than 10 people. Free M.)*

CATHEDRAL OF ST. NEDELYA. (Катедрален Храм Св. Неделя; Katedralen Hram Sv. Nedelya.) The focal point of pl. Sveta Nedelya and all of Sofia, the cathedral is a reconstruction of the 14th-century original, which was destroyed by a bomb in an attempted assassination on the life of Boris III in 1925. The current frescoes date from 1975, but are already blackened with the soot of candles (0.10-2lv), lit daily by visitors and worshipers. The church has great acoustics and an imposing altar. *(At the center of pl. Sveta Nedelya. Open daily 7am-6pm.)*

ST. NICHOLAS RUSSIAN CHURCH. (Св. Николай; Sv. Nikolai.) Named for the patron saint of marriage, fish, and sailors, this 1913 church has five traditional Russian Orthodox-style onion domes. Richly hued patterns, icons fashioned by painters from the Novgorod school, and exquisite ornamentation make this building a site to behold. *(Down bul. Tsar Osvoboditel from pl. Sv. Nedelya. Open daily 9am-10:30pm. Services W and Sa 5-7pm.)*

SYNAGOGUE OF SOFIA. (Софийска Синагога; Sofiiska Sinagoga.) Built upon a foundation of Jewish gravestones, Sofia's only synagogue opened for services in 1909. The interior is currently undergoing renovation to repair damage done by a stray Allied bomb from World War II, which miraculously did not explode. A museum upstairs outlines the history of Jews in Bulgaria. *(On the corner of Ekzarh Iosif and George Washington. Walk to the gate on Ekzarh Iosif and ring the bell. Open M-F 9:30am-2pm. Weekly services F 7pm, Sa 10am. Donation requested for restoration project.)*

ST. GEORGE'S ROTUNDA. (Св. Георги; Sv. Georgi.) The 4th-century St. George's stands near a former Roman bath and the ruins of the ancient town of Serdica. St. George's itself is covered in 11th- to 14th-century murals. After it was converted from a bath to a church in the 5th century, it served as a house of worship under Bulgarians, Byzantines, and Turks. The beautiful original murals, which were covered up by the Ottomans in an attempt to obscure the building's Christian past, have been restored and now adorn a museum and a functioning church. *(In the courtyard enclosed by the Sheraton Hotel and the Presidency. Enter from bul. Tsar Osvoboditel or ul. Suborna. Open in summer daily 8am-6pm; in winter 8am-5pm. Daily services 9am.)*

ST. SOFIA CHURCH. (Св. София; Sv. Sofia.) The city adopted the saint's name in the 14th century. During the 19th century, while the church was used as Sofia's main mosque, a series of earthquakes repeatedly destroyed the minarets. Amazingly, the 5th-century floor mosaic survived. This church is unique in Sofia because of its sparsely-ornamented white-walled interior. *(On pl. Alexander Nevsky. Open daily 8am-7pm. Donation requested.)*

BUL. TSAR OSVOBODITEL. (Тсар Освободител.) As you stroll down bul. Tsar Osvoboditel, keep in mind that your boots are stepping on the first paved street in Sofia, weighted down on either end by the **House of Parliament** and the **Royal Palace.** The 1884 **National Assembly** provides a backdrop for a dramatic equestrian statue of the tsar *osvoboditel* (liberator) himself, Russian Tsar Alexander II.

THEATERS. Rakovski (Раковски) is Bulgaria's theater hub, with half a dozen theaters on a 1km stretch. A left on Rakovski leads to the columns of the **National Opera House,** built in 1950. *(Rakovski 59, main entrance at Vrabcha 1 (Врабча). ☎ 987 13 66 or 981 15 49, for group visits 981 15 67. Shows Tu-Sa 6pm. Box office open M-Tu 9:30am-2pm and 2:30-6:30pm, W-F 8:30am-7:30pm, Sa 10:30am-6:30pm, Su 10am-6pm. 5-20lv.)*

NATIONAL PALACE OF CULTURE. (Национален Дворец Култура; NDK, Natsionalen Dvorets Kultura.) This monolith was erected by the Communist government in 1981. It houses a number of restaurants, cinemas (screening both local and American movies), and theaters (tickets 3-15lv). The square is full of people and cafes. *(In Yuzhen Park. From pl. Sv. Nedelya, take bul. Vitosha to bul. Patriarch Evtimii and enter the park. The Palace is at its far end. Open daily 10am-7pm; box office open daily 9am-7pm.)*

🏛 MUSEUMS

NATIONAL HISTORY MUSEUM. (Национален Исторически Музей; Natsionalen Istoricheski Muzey.) This museum traces the evolution of Bulgarian culture since prehistoric times, and is well worth the trip. It also houses some of Bulgaria's most precious archaeological finds. Look for the silver Thracian treasures. *(Residence Boyana, Palace 1. Take trolley #2, or bus #63 or 111 to Boyana. ☎ 955 42 80. Open daily 9:30am-6pm. 10lv, students 5lv, guided tour 10lv.)*

NATIONAL MUSEUM OF ETHNOGRAPHY. (Национален Етнографически Музей; Natsionalen Etnograficheski Muzey.) Founded after the 1878 liberation (see **History,** p. 102), the museum covers the past 400 years of Bulgarian folk history. The upper floor exhibits a detailed photographic history, while the ground floor has the most extensive folk art and crafts shop in Bulgaria. *(In the Royal Palace on bul. Tsar Osvoboditel. Open Tu-Su 10am-5:30pm. 3lv, students 1.50lv. Guided tour for groups of more than five 15lv, individual tour 15lv.)*

NATIONAL ART GALLERY. (Национална Художествена Галериа; Natsionalna Hudozhestvena Galeriya.) This gallery displays Bulgaria's best contemporary art, but don't expect to see artists of other nationalities represented here. *(In the Royal Palace on bul. Tsar Osvoboditel. Open Tu-Su 10:30am-6:30pm. 3lv, students 1.50lv. Guided tours in English 10lv for up to 5 people, 15lv for more than 5 people.)*

🎵 NIGHTLIFE

Most nightlife centers around **bul. Vitosha** or the University of Sofia at the intersection of **Vasil Levsky** and **Tsar Osvoboditel.** Young people often meet at **Popa,** the irreverent nickname for Patriarch Evtimii's monument, where bul. Patriarch Evtimii intersects with Vasil Levsky and **Graf Ignatiev.** The city is more dangerous at night, so try not to attract undue attention.

Biblioteka (Библиотека; ☎ 943 39 78), in St. Cyril and Methodius Library. Enter from Oborishte. Grab a drink (beer 1.85-8lv; shots 2-2.8lv) and chuckle at karaoke or jive to bands in the next room. Cover Sa 4lv, Su-F 3lv. Open daily 8pm-6am.

Dali (☎ 946 51 29), behind the university on Krakra. The best Latin club in Sofia. Plenty of room to spin and swivel to the orchestra's and DJ's selections or lean back in a comfortable booth and enjoy the sights. Call ahead to reserve a table. Men pay 3lv. Reservations 10lv per person. Open daily 8pm-5am.

Escape, Angel Kunchev 1 (Ангел Кънуев; ☎ 988 59 22). Gyrate with Sofia's beautiful people at this bi-level dance club. Women 3lv, men 4lv. Open W-Sa 10:30pm-4am.

🏞 DAYTRIP FROM SOFIA

VITOSHA NATIONAL PARK (ПРИРОДЕН ПАРК ВИТОША)

Take tram #9 from the intersection of Hriste Botev and Makedanya to Hladilnika Station, the last stop. Walk between kiosks to the bus station behind the tram stop to the far set of steps. Take bus #93 to stop with chairlift and Vitosha Park signs (last bus 7pm).

Although it lies right next to Sofia, Vitosha National Park successfully mutes the din of the neighboring metropolis. The park shelters a monastery, a stone river, a waterfall, and a peat reserve, but Mount Vitosha dominates this natural sanctuary, rising 2290m at the peak, Cherni Vruh (Черни Връх). Established in 1934 by the

Ministry of Environment and Water, this verdant haven is traversed by Bulgarians and tourists alike. Conquering the mountain is the most popular activity at the park. Pick up English maps and brochures from the Prirodashtiten Information Center (Природащтитен), a five-minute walk uphill between Restaurant Vodenitsata and Vodenicharski Mehani. For those who want a work-out, paths at the top of the mountain are marked on the map, but there are few trail markers. The most direct, difficult path starts at the lift station by the bus station. Ride the rickety yet functional **chairlift** to either the Bai Krustjo station or the higher Goli Vruh station (one-way 0.80lv, 1.20lv). Other exploration opportunities include **hikes** to the **peak**, the **Dragalevtsi Monastery, Boyanna Waterfall,** and **Peat Branishte Reserve.** The paths are dotted with well-marked **campsites** and shelters, but be sure to bring bug spray. For a taste of Bulgarian folk culture and a classy dining experience, try a house salad (9.90lv) and salmon (17.90lv) at **Restaurant Vodenitsata,** set next to its picturesque namesake waterwheel by the chair lift. (☎467 10 58. Entrees 9-18lv. Open daily noon-midnight. ❸)

RILA MONASTERY (РИЛСКИ МАНАСТИР) ☎(0)7054

Holy Ivan of Rila built Rila Monastery (Rilski Manastir) in the 10th century as a refuge from the lascivious outside world. It sheltered the arts of icon-painting and manuscript-copying during the Byzantine and Ottoman occupations, remaining an oasis of Bulgarian culture during five centuries of foreign rule. Rila Monastery is a pleasant hideaway from the noise and heat of the city.

▐ ▐ TRANSPORTATION AND PRACTICAL INFORMATION. Take **tram** #5 from in front of Hostel Sofia to Ovcha Kupel Station (Овча Къпел) to make the bus to Rila Town (2hr., 2 per day, 4.50lv). From there, you can hop on a **bus** to the monastery (30min., 3 per day, 1.10lv). Staying the night is recommended, as there are few buses back to Sofia. There are no **currency exchanges** nearby, but there is an **ATM** on the storefront opposite the bus station in Rila town. Blue Mobika **telephones** are by the shops behind the monastery; phone cards are available in Hotel Tsarev Vruh.

▐ ▐ ACCOMMODATIONS AND FOOD. Hotel Tsarev Vruh ❷ (Царев Врьх) features private baths, telephones, a restaurant, and a wine cellar. The reception also organizes sightseeing trips in the area and gives fishing advice. From behind the monastery, the hotel is 100m down the path that passes through the outdoor dining area of Restaurant Rila. (☎/fax 22 80. Hot water 6pm-midnight and 6-9am. US$15, plus US$2 for breakfast.) Inquire at room #170 in the monastery about staying in a heated **monastic cell ❷,** but be prepared for bare rooms, cold water, and no shower. (☎22 08. Curfew midnight. 3- to 4-bed cells US$10, 2- to 3-bed cells US$15. **Camping Bor ❶** is tucked away at the base of the mountains with clean but bare campsites and bungalows. Walk down the left-most road behind the monastery and take a right across the bridge at the triangular intersection. Then take a left and follow the signs. (3lv per person, 2lv per tent; 2-bed bungalows 20lv. 3lv per car. Student groups 10% off.) Behind the monastery are several cafes and a mini-market. Try the monks' homemade bread (0.50lv) or eat at **Restaurant Rila ❶,** a *mehani* (механи; Bulgarian folk restaurant) in which the waiters wear traditional dress. (Behind the monastery. ☎045 890 418. Entrees 2.50-12lv. 4% service fee. Open daily 8am-11pm.)

◪ SIGHTS. The original 10th-century monastery was destroyed. Today's monastery was built between 1834 and 1837; only a brick tower remains from the 14th-century structure. The monastery's vibrant murals were painted by brothers Dimitar and Zahari Zograf—"Zograf" actually means "mural painter"—who were famous for their work at the Troyan and Bachkovo monasteries (see **Daytrip from Plovdiv,** p. 123). The 1200 frescoes on the central chapel form a brilliantly-colored outdoor art display. The iconostasis is also one of the largest and most ornate in Bulgaria. Inside lies the grave of Bulgaria's last tsar, Boris III. (Open daily 7am-9pm. Backpacks, cameras, shorts, and sleeveless shirts not permitted. Free.) The **museum** in the far right corner of the monastery displays weapons, embroidery, illuminated texts, and icons. The exhibit includes a wooden cross that took 12 years to carve and left its creator, the monk Rafail, blind. The cross is carved with miniature figures that depict scenes from the Bible and the lives of the saints. (Open daily 8:30am-4:30pm. 5lv, students 3lv. Sporadic English tours 15lv.)

🖪 **HIKING.** Maps and hiking routes through **Rila National Park** are on signs outside the monastery. Alternatively, look in the **Manastirski Padarutsi** (Манастирски Падаръци) alcove, just outside the monastery's back entry, for a Cyrillic map of the paths (8lv). Incredible views—particularly at **Seventh Lake** (Седемە Езера; Sedemte Ezera) and **Malyovitsa** (Мальовица)—and welcoming huts *(hizhi)* await within the park. Expect to pay around US$2 for a spot (not necessarily a bed) to sleep. Follow the **yellow markings** to the **Hizha Sedemte Ezera** (Хижа Седемте Езера; Seventh Lake Hut; 6hr.). The **blue** trail leads to **Hizha Malyovitsa** (Мальовица; 7hr.). **Red** leads to the highest hut in the Balkans (6hr.).

Don't miss the short hike (1hr.) to the **cave** where Holy Ivan lived and prayed for years. To reach it, walk down the road behind the monastery. After the triangular intersection, head left up the path through the field. Follow the signs for the grave (гроб; grob), which point the way to the church where Ivan was originally buried. Behind the church is the entrance to the cave. It's believed that passing through will purify your soul. Enter at the bottom and crawl through the dark winding passages. **The cave's upper exit is very narrow. Large or claustrophobic travelers should think twice about attempting the trip through the cave.** A flashlight or lighter is helpful. According to legend, this part of the journey represents the journey out of the womb. Emerge at the top for a symbolic rebirth—unless you have sinned too much, in which case, legend holds that rocks will fall on you. Next, continue uphill 40m to the spring and cleanse yourself near the shrine to St. Ivan. You're now ready to enter the chapel guilt-free.

SOUTHERN MOUNTAINS

The Rila, Pirin, and Rodopi mountain ranges sheltered Bulgaria's cultural and political dissidents during 500 years of Turkish rule. During this era, local monks chose to perpetuate their culture in secret by copying manuscripts in remote monasteries. Others, such as the *haiduti* bandits, took a more activist approach, using mountain hideouts to launch attacks against unwanted visitors. Today, however, folk culture is celebrated and the region welcomes newcomers wholeheartedly. The strongly rooted traditions and natural lushness now provide tourist attractions such as wine tasting in Melnik and hiking near Bansko.

PLOVDIV (ПЛОВДИВ)   ☎ (0)32

Although it's slightly smaller than Sofia, Plovdiv (pop. 376,000) is widely regarded as the cultural capital of Bulgaria. Founded around 600 BC as Philipopolis (in honor of Philip II of Macedonia), the city's long history includes centuries of trade fairs and arts festivals that continue to enthrall visitors.

🚆 TRANSPORTATION

Trains: The main **train station** is on corner of bul. Ruski (Руски) and bul. Hristo Botev (Христо Ботев). To: **Burgas** (5hr., 7 per day, 6-8.20lv); **Sofia** (2½hr., 14 per day, 3.80-5.40lv); **Varna** (5½hr., 3 per day, 7.80-10.80lv). Most trains from Sofia to **Istanbul,**

BULGARIA

TUR or **Burgas** stop in Plovdiv. Only the station **Rila,** bul. Hristo Botev 31a (☎44 61 20), sells international train tickets. Open M-F 8am-6:30pm, Sa 8am-2pm.

Buses: Matpu (Матпу; ☎63 19 48 or 63 26 33). Walk down the block to the right of Hotel Trimontium (Тримонциум); Matpu is on your left. To: **Ohrid, MAC** (daily 7pm, 35lv) and **Thessaloniki, GRE** (1 per day 11am; 52.50lv, students 42.50lv). Open daily 8am-6pm. In addition, 3 separate stations serve the towns indicated:

Sever (Север; North; ☎95 37 05), at the intersection of Dimitur Stambolov (Димитър Стамболов) and Pobeda (Победа), north of bul. Bulgaria. Ruski becomes Pobeda when it crosses the river. Take bus #12 from the intersection of Ruski and Gladston (Гладстон). Buses to: **Koprivshtitsa** (2hr., 4:30pm, 4.50lv); **Ruse** (5hr., 8am, 10lv); **Pleven** (4hr., 3pm, 8lv).

Yug (Юг; South; ☎62 69 37), bul. Hristo Botev 47, on the other side of the street from the train station. Open 5:30am-9pm. Buses service South Bulgaria and go to: **Asenovgrad** (30min., every 30min., 0.70lv); **Blagoevgrad** (4hr., 7:30am and 1:40pm, 7-9lv); **Sofia** (2hr., 15 per day, 7lv); **Istanbul, TUR** (5 per day, 30-35lv, 10% student discount). **Viktari 13** (Виктари 13; ☎63 20 95), in Yug's main ticket center. To **Burgas** (3:30pm, 10lv).

Rodopi (Родопи; ☎77 76 07), for the **Rodopi Mountains,** behind the train station through the underpass beneath the trains. To **Smolyan** (1hr., 5 per day, 5.50lv). Open 5am-7pm.

■ ORIENTATION

With no clearly defined center and poorly-marked streets, Plovdiv is difficult to navigate; an up-to-date **map** is essential. Street vendors sell good Cyrillic maps for 3lv. Running past the train station, the east-west thoroughfare **bul. Hristo Botev** (Христо Ботев) marks the southern end of town. With your back to the train station, turn left on Hristo Botev to **bul. Ruski** (Руски); a right turn on Ruski will take you to across the river and to bus station Sever. Hristo Botev also intersects with **bul. Tsar Boris III Obedinitel** (Цар Борис III Обединител) which runs to the **Maritsa River** (Марица), at the northern end of **Stari Grad** (Стари Град; Old Town). In the middle of town, bul. Tsar Boris III Obedinitel runs along the east side of **pl. Tsentralen** (Централен). To get to pl. Tsentralen from the train station, take bus #20 or 26 (0.40lv) or cross bul. Hristo Botev via the underpass and take Ivan Vazov (Иван Вазов) to the square.

■ PRACTICAL INFORMATION

Tourist Office: The tourist office in Plovdiv recently closed.

Currency Exchange: Bulbank (Булбанк; ☎60 16 01), ul. Ivan Vazov 4, a right when facing Hotel Trimontium. Cashes **traveler's checks** for 0.2% commission and minimum US$1 fee. Open M-F 8:30am-4:30pm.

ATM: MC/V ATM in front of Bulbank. MC ATM outside the post office on pl. Tsentralen.

Luggage Storage: In the train station. Open 24hr. with breaks. 0.80lv per bag.

24-hour Pharmacy: Apteka 47 Tunela (Аптека Тунела), bul. Tsar Boris III Obedinitel 62 (☎27 07 93). From pl. Tsentralen, follow bul. Tsar Boris III through the tunnel.

Internet Access: Speed, Kryaz Aleksander 12, on the left before the mosque. A new and very modern wired joint. 1.20lv per hr. Open 24hr.

Telephones: In the post office. Open daily 6am-11pm. **Faxes** (fax 27 02 70) sent and received daily 8am-8pm.

Post Office: Pl. Tsentralen. **Poste Restante** in the room to the left of the entrance across from the park. Open M-Sa 7am-7pm, Su 7-11am.

Postal Code: 4000.

BULGARIA

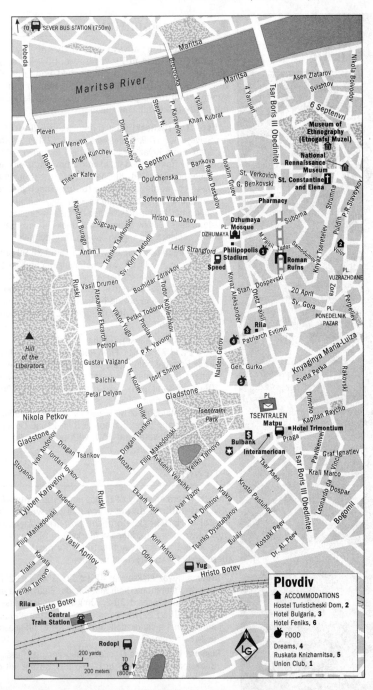

TO SEVER BUS STATION (750m)

Pobeda

Maritsa

Brezovska

Maritsa

Maritsa River

Pleven

Yuri Venelin

Angel Kunchev

Eliezer Kalev

Ruski

Stepka N.

P. Karavelov

Vsila

Khan Kubrat

4 Yanuari

Dim. Tsonchev

6 Septenvri

Bankova

Raiko Daskalov

Ioakim Gruev

St. Verkovich

G. Benkovski

Tsar Boris III Obedinitel

Asen Zlatarov

Svishtov

Nikola Bowodov

6 Septenvri

Museum of
Ethnography
(Etnogafsi Muzei)

National
Rennaissance
Museum

St. Constantine
and Elena

Strumma

Puldin P. R. Slaveykov

Opulchenska

Sofronii Vrachanski

Hristo G. Danov

Sugcasit

Antim I

Kapitan Burago

Tsanko Tsarkovici

Sv. Kiril I Metodii

Leidi Strangford

Bozhidar Zdravkov

Todor Kobleshkov

Petko Todorov

Viktor Yugo

Preslav

Dzhumaya
PL. Mosque

DZHUMAYA

Philippolis
Stadium

Speed

M Paisii

Suborna

Tudor Samodumov

Roman
Ruins

PL.
VUZRAZHDANE

Knyaz Tseretelev

Zora

Yolov

2

PL.

Stan. Dospevski

Otez Paisii

Knyaz Aleksander

20 April

Sv. Gora

PL.
PONEDELNIK
PAZAR

Perpeliev

Vasil Drumen

Ruski

Alexander Ekzarch

Petropi

Gustav Vaigand

Balchik

Petar Delyan

P.K. Yavorov

N. Kozlev

Iosif Shniter

Rila

3

Patriarch Evtimii

Naiden Gerov

Gen. Gurko

5

Knyaginya Maria-Luiza

Sveta Petka

Rakovski

Hill
of the
Liberators

Nikola Petkov

Gladstone

Stoyanov

Ivan Andonov

Dragan Tsankov

Iordan Iovkov

Lyuben Karavelov

Radetski

Filip Makedonski

Gladstone

Shiller

Dragan Tsankov

Mozart

Ruski

Ekzarh Iosif

Filip Makedonski

Avkseni Veleshki

Veliko Tarnovo

Ivan Vazov

Krakra

G.M. Dimitrov

Tsanko Dyustabanov

Tsentralni
Park

PL.

TSENTRALEN
Matpu

Bulbank

Interamerican

Hotel Trimontium

Praga

Tsar Asen

Krysto Pasuhov

Bulair

Kostaki Peev

Dimcho

Kapitan Raycho

Pavlikenne

Praga

Graf Ignatiev

Krali Marco

Leonardo da Dospar

da Vinci

Tsar Boris III Obedinitel

Bogomil

Kiril Hristov

Odrin

Yug

Hristo Botev

Trakia

Kavala

Veliko Tarnovo

Rila

Hristo Botev

Central
Train Station

Rodopi

Vasil Aprilov

TO
6
(800m)

0   200 yards
0   200 meters

N

LG

Plovdiv

▲ ACCOMMODATIONS
Hostel Turisticheski Dom, 2
Hotel Bulgaria, 3
Hotel Feniks, 6

🍴 FOOD
Dreams, 4
Ruskata Knizharnitsa, 5
Union Club, 1

Pharmacy

IN RECENT NEWS

EDUCATIONAL FAMINE

Bulgaria's education system was under stress in 2002 as conflicts arose between the Bulgarian Teachers' Union (Синдикат Набългарските Ууители) and the Ministry of Education and Science. In the past few years, primary and secondary public school teachers have suffered lay-offs, low salaries, and no pay for months at a time. Current Ministry measures under Minister Vladimir Atanascu call for a 10% education budget cut and a reduction in the number of public schools, while the teachers' union demands a 20% pay raise and amendments to education laws and regulations. From May 20-30, 2002, the teachers' union, under syndicate leader Yanka Takieva, held events to raise awareness about the plight of 12 specific instructors in Bulgaria. This included a one-hour protest involving 90,000 teachers representing 90% of Bulgaria's schools, a day-long strike, and a rally in Nevski Plaza in Sofia.

Education problems in Bulgaria, however, extend beyond the issues of salary and unemployment. With no unified curriculum across the nation, students are not adequately prepared for their *matura* (матчра; final high school exams). In reaction to strikingly low marks on preliminary exams, secondary school students have spoken to Minister Atanascu about conformity in curriculum.

—*Stephanie Videka Sherman*

ACCOMMODATIONS

Higher prices don't always mean higher quality, as is certainly the case in Plovdiv. Avoid eye-catching high-rise hotels. Prices triple during trade fairs (the first weeks of May and the end of September). In the summer months, especially July and August, budget hotels are often full; call ahead.

Hotel Turisticheski Dom (Туристически Дом), P.R. Slaveykov 5 (П.Р. Славейков; ☎63 32 11), in Stari Grad. From Kryaz Aleksander, take Patriarch Evtimii (across from McDonald's) into Stari Grad, passing under bul. Tsar Boris III Obedinitel. Turn left uphill on Slaveykov at pl. Vuzrazhdane (Възраждане), past the fruit market. Spacious rooms with high ceilings and sinks in a National Revival health. Cafe and restaurant downstairs. Curfew 11pm. Call 3 weeks in advance for Aug. bookings. No English spoken. 22lv per person. ❷

Hotel Bulgaria, Patriarch Evtimii 13 (☎63 35 99 or 63 36 62; fax 63 34 03; www.hotelbulgaria.net), at the major intersection with Kryaz Aleksander. Great location at Plovdiv's pedestrian center. Immaculate rooms with TV, A/C, and private bath. Sauna, fitness center, and 24hr. casino. 24hr. reception. Check-out noon. Singles US$50. ❺

Hotel Feniks (Феникс), Silivria 18A (Силиврия; ☎77 48 51 and 77 49 51). From Rodopi bus station, head away from the train tracks on Dimitur Talev (Димитър Талев) for 15min. After crossing Nikola Vaptsarov (Никола Вапцаров), take the 2nd right; it's 200m down on the right. Offers a choice of small rooms with shared bathrooms or with large glass stalls containing a shower and toilet. Reception 8am-11pm. Doubles 35lv, with private bath 45lv, with private toilet and shared shower 40lv. ❷

FOOD

Plovdiv offers an array of Bulgarian restaurants with pleasant outdoor dining areas. On the way to the Hostel Turisticheski Dom, the *ponedelnik pazar* (понеделник пазар; **Monday Market**) in pl. Vuzrazhdane sells fruit and veggies for 2-3lv per kilo. Get there early for the freshest produce.

Dreams, Kryaz Aleksander 42 (☎62 71 42 or 62 71 43), two storefronts from McDonalds. Enjoy a simple meal (sandwiches 1.30-2.30lv) and ornate dessert (0.80-2.20lv) as you people-watch on the shaded patio. Open summer daily 8am-midnight.; off-season daily 8am-2pm. ❶

Ruskata Knizharnitsa (Руската Книжарница; Russian Bookstore; ☎62 76 33 or 62 76 38), on the left of

Knyaz Aleksander where it hits pl. Tsentralen. A tastefully tiled restaurant that serves classic Bulgarian fare as the crowds amble by. Entrees 1.60-8lv. 8% service fee. Open daily 8am-midnight. ❷

Union Club (Юнинъ Клуб), Mitropolit Paisii 6 (☎ 27 05 51). Take Suborna from pl. Dzhu-maya, then make a sharp right on Mitropolit Paisii; go through a wooden gate on the right. Enjoy your meal in the restaurant's high-walled garden. Choose from a variety of dishes from pancakes (1.40-1.60lv) to *tatarsko kufte*, a big meatball stuffed with cheese (3.30lv). Entrees 2.20-8.90lv. Open daily 9:30am-11:30pm. ❷

◎ SIGHTS

Most of Plovdiv's historical and cultural treasures are concentrated among Stari Grad's **Trimondium,** or three hills.

ROMAN RUINS. The 2nd-century Roman ⊠**Amphitheater** (Античен Театр; Anti-chen Teatr) looks out over the city on high. It serves as a popular venue for con-certs and shows, hosting the **Festival of the Arts** in the summer and early fall and the annual **Opera Festival** in June. Most festival tickets are available in the Opera box office on the ground floor of the Interamerican building on pl. Tsentralen, next to Hotel Trimantium. Movies are often screened here; keep an eye out for schedules. *(Take a right off Kryaz Aleksander on Suborna, and right again up the steps along Mitropolit Paisii. Continue uphill until you reach another small set of steps next to the music academy building. At the top, walk past the cafes to the theater. Open daily 9am-9pm. 3lv.)* **Philipopolis Stadium,** which once seated 30,000 spectators, now consists of just the poorly-preserved bottom 10-15 rows still accessible to the public. The gladiator's entrance is still intact—some locals claim that lion bones were found inside. *(Follow Knyaz Aleksandr to the end; the stadium is underneath pl. Dzhumaya. Free.)*

MUSEUMS. The **Museum of Ethnography** (Етнографски Музей; Etnografski Muzey) displays artifacts from Bulgaria's past, including clothes, musical instru-ments, and tools in a quintessential National Revival building. Check out the *kuk-erski maksi*, masks used to ward off evil spirits during the Christmas season. *(At the end of Suborna. ☎ 62 56 54. Open Tu-Th and Sa-Su 9am-noon and 2-5pm. 3lv, students 0.50lv.)* Each room in the **National Renaissance Museum** details a different stage in Bulgarian history through the 1800s. *(Tsanko Lavrenov 1* (Цанко Лавренов)*. Turn right at the end of Suborna and head through the Turkish Gate. ☎ 62 33 78. Open M-F 9:30am-noon and 1-6pm, Sa 10am-5pm. 2lv, students 0.40lv.)*

CHURCH OF ST. CONSTANTINE AND ELENA. Built in the 4th century, this is the oldest Orthodox church in Plovdiv. The church was renovated in 1832, complete with murals and icons by Bulgarian artist Zahari Zograf. *(On Suborna, before the Museum of Ethnography. Open daily 9am-7pm. Free.)*

OTHER SIGHTS. Enjoy the beautifully patterned mosaic walls of pl. Dzhumaya's namesake, **Dzhumaya Mosque** (Джумая Джамия; Dzhumaya Dzhamiya), as well as the throne of the sultan. *(Go past pl. Dzhumaya and turn right to reach the main entrance. Free.)* On a cool evening, head to the picturesque fountainside cafe in **Tsentralni Park** (Централни Парк), by pl. Tsentralen.

◪ DAYTRIP FROM PLOVDIV

BACHKOVO MONASTERY (БАЧКОВСКИ МАНАСТИР)
Buses run from Plovdiv's Yug station to Asenovgrad (25min., every 30min., 0.70lv), as do trains (25min., 17 per day, 0.80lv). From the Asenovgrad bus station, catch a bus headed to Luki (Лъки) for the monastery (20min., 4 per day, 0.60lv). Get off at the 3rd

*stop (after the 2 tunnels) and follow the cobblestones up the incline. **Monastery** open daily 7am-8pm. Free. You can sleep in **monastery cells ❶**, but they have no shower and a shared toilet. (2- to 20-bed rooms 10lv; furnished double 20lv.) **Vodapada Restaurant ❷** serves Bulgarian food. Entrees 2-15.20lv. (☎03 32 73 89 Open daily 10am-2am.)*

Twenty-eight kilometers south of Plovdiv, in the Rodopi mountains, stands Bulgaria's second-largest monastery. Bachkovo Monastery (Bachkovski Manastir) was built in 1083 by Georgian brothers Grigory and Abazy Bakuriani, and is known for its original architecture and fine murals. An oasis of Bulgarian culture, history, and literature during the 500 years of Turkish rule, Bachkovo today draws crowds to its phenomenal art exhibits. The main church is home to the **icon of the Virgin Mary and Child** (икона Света Богородица; ikona Sveta Bogoroditsa), which is said to have miraculous healing power. When the Turks plundered the monastery, the icon was hidden in the mountains by monks until it was rediscovered by an unsuspecting shepherd centuries later.

Next door, the brightly colored paintings of famed National Revival artist Zahari Zograf (see **The Arts**, p. 105) decorate the 12th-century **Church of Archangels.** Ask to be let into the **Trapezaria** (old dining room; 2lv) across the courtyard. Along either of the roads leading uphill from the monastery, there are other small shrines and paths labeled with yellow and white markings that make for great day-hiking, with picnic areas and some of the most breathtaking mountain vistas in Bulgaria. Below, shops and cafes flank the road leading to the monastery. The **Vodapada Restaurant** (Водапада; Waterfall), is named for the cascade alongside its patio.

BANSKO (БАНСКО) ☎(0)7443

An appropriate destination for lovers of the outdoors, Bansko (pop. 91,700) is surrounded by countless lakes and the Pirin Mountains, whose highest peak is the 2914m Mount Vihren. While the mountain range around Bansko offers hiking, skiing, and breathtaking views, the cobblestone streets and taverns below come alive during the town's annual **International Jazz Festival,** Aug. 8-13 in 2003.

✦ ⁊ ORIENTATION AND PRACTICAL INFORMATION

Take a **bus** from **Blagoevgrad** (2hr., 4 per day, 2.40lv) or **Sofia**'s Ovcha Kupel station (3hr., 5 per day, 6lv). For a **taxi,** call ☎47 43. **Luggage storage** is available in the station (0.50lv per piece). From Bansko's bus station, exit the parking lot and turn left on Patriarch Evtimy (Патриарх Евтимий). Take a right at the tiny pl. Makedonia (Македония), marked by the stairways leading under the street and the "Bansko Skiing Centre" sign, and then veer left on **Todor Aleksandrov** (Тодор Александров), which leads to the fountain-filled **pl. Vaptsarov** (Вапцаров). Continue on **ul. Pirin** (Пирин), in the upper right corner of pl. Vaptsarov as you enter the square from Todor Aleksandrov, to the second square, **pl. Vuzrazhdane** (Възраждане).

⁊ PRACTICAL INFORMATION

You can get a **map** from a newsstand on pl. Vaptsarov (3lv) or from the **Tourist Information Center** (Туристически Информационен Центр; Turisticheski Informatsionen Tsentr), to the right as you enter pl. Vaptsarov. (☎22 85 or 087 23 17 90. Open Dec.-Aug.; closed Sa.) **Bulgarian Post Bank,** Hristo Botev 1 (Христо Ботев), **exchanges currency** and gives Visa cash advances for 4% commission. (☎21 86. Open M-F 8am-noon and 1-4:30pm.) A **pharmacy** is at Tsar Simeon 57, near Todor Aleksandrov. (☎23 43. Open M-Sa 7:30am-8pm, Su 9am-6pm.) The **post office,** Tsar Simeon 69 (open M-F 7:30am-noon and 1-5pm), has **telephones** (open daily 7am-10pm). **Postal Code:** 2770.

ACCOMMODATIONS AND FOOD

Private rooms ❶ can be arranged informally with locals (8-10lv per person), but finding cheap accommodations is not a problem. ■ **Hotel Mir ❷** (Мир), Neofit Rilski 28 (Неофит Рилски), offers spacious rooms, spotless bathrooms, hot water, cable TV, and a shared sauna. From pl. Vaptsarov with your back to ul. Todor Aleksandrov, take a left on Tsar Simeon and turn right on ul. Bulgaria. Continue straight and turn left on Rilski just after the playground. (☎25 00; fax 21 60; www.mir.domino.bg. Breakfast US$2. Singles US$18; doubles US$24.)

If you want to live lavishly, **Hotel Glazne ❹** (Глазне), provides its guests with luxurious facilities, including a pool, fitness room, and sauna. Feel pampered in rooms with a phone, satellite television, refrigerator, and balcony at a reasonable price. (☎41 51; http://glazne.search.bg. Breakfast included. Doubles from Apr. 14-June 1 and Sept. 21-Dec. 14 58lv during week, 68lv on weekend; June 2-Sept. 20 68lv/78lv; Dec. 15-Apr. 13 82lv/98lv.)

With a *mehana* (механа; tavern) in almost every house or courtyard, you'll never be at a loss for a meal in Bansko. **Dudo Pene ❷** (Дъдо Пене), Aleksander Buynov 1 (Александър Буйнов), is a rugged restaurant that greets you at the door with a line of shepherd bells. It grows many of its own vegetables and maintains its own slaughterhouse. Try the house specialty, *file Diadke* (fillet Diadke; 6.50lv). Live folk music after 7:30pm on weekends and sometimes on Mondays. (☎50 71 or 50 73; dudopene@mbox.cit.bg. Entrees 2.20-7lv. Open daily 9am-late.)

SIGHTS

■ **NIKOLA VAPTSAROV HOUSE-MUSEUM.** (Къща-Музей Никола Вапцаров; Kushta-Muzey Nikola Vaptsarov.) The permanent exhibit recounts the life and work of the 20th-century poet who gave his life in the struggle against Fascism. Ticket includes admission to the House of Poetry and Art (Дом Поези и Искуство; Dom Poezi i Iskustvo), which exhibits images of the National Revival movement and photographs of the region. *(On the corner of pl. Demokratsia and Vaptsarov. ☎30 38. Open M-F 8am-noon and 2-4pm. 2lv, students 1lv. Taped tours in English 1lv.)*

HOLY TRINITY CHURCH. (Църква Света Троица; Tsurkva Sveta Troitsa.) The 1835 Holy Trinity is actually a product of Turkish rule, when Bulgarian Orthodox Churches were restricted to small buildings on the outskirts of town. According to legend, the local Turkish governor dreamt of an icon several of Bansko's resilient faithful had carefully hidden beneath pl. Vuzrazhdane. He was convinced by the townspeople that it was a sign from God to build an Orthodox church where the icon was hidden. An Islamic crescent was added next to the cross on the church door, making the building a symbol of both faiths. *(On pl. Vuzrazhdane, at the corner of Neofit Rilski. Open M-Th and Sa-Su 9am-noon and 2-6pm. Free; large groups 1lv per person.)*

NEOFIT RILSKI HOUSE-MUSEUM. (Къща-Музей Неофит Рилски; Kushta-Muzey Neofit Rilski.) This house was home to one of the National Revival movement's forefathers, who later became Father Superior at Rila Monastery (see p. 118). The founder of the Rila School of church singing, Rilski also taught painter Zahari Zograf. *(At the corner of Pirin and Rilski, next to Holy Trinity Church. ☎25 40. Open daily 9am-noon and 2-5pm. 2lv, students 1lv. Taped English tour 1lv.)*

ICON EXHIBIT. (Експозиция на икони; Ekspozitsiya na ikoni.) A nunnery when it was built in 1749, the house now shelters icons, including one once considered sacrilegious. Why? The angels portrayed are female. *(Down Yanel Sandanski from pl. Vuzrazhdane on the left. Open M-Sa 9am-noon and 2-5pm. 1lv.)*

🏃 HIKING

Hiking routes are marked with different-colored signs. Ask at the tourist office for info on mountain guides, accommodations and transportation. Maps of the town sold at newspaper kiosks in Bansko include detailed maps of the mountain routes as well as suggested itineraries. Many trails start at **hizha Vihren** (хижа Вихрен; Vihren Hut). From town, take any street leading to the Glazne (Глазне) River. At the river, follow the Glazne road upstream and out of town to the entrance of **Pirin National Park** (Народен Парк Пирин). Hike to the hut (5hr. each way) or drive. The route, marked with a yellow line on white background, runs past **hizhen Bunderitsa** (Бъндерица; Bunderitsa Hut) and **baikushevata mura** (байкушевата мура), a 1300 year old fir tree that has lived as long as the Bulgarian state.

Four trails begin at the hut and lead over a rocky peak. After 10min., the red and green trails branch off and cross the river. The **red** leads up Vihren peak (2914m) to **hizha Yavorov** (Яворов; Javor's Hut; 1740m). The **green** trail scales Todorin peak (Тодорин) to **hizha Demyanitsa** (Демяница; 6hr.). **Hizha Bezbog** (Безбог), which is becoming increasingly popular as a ski resort, is another 8hr. away. A **lift** connects it to **hizha Gotse Delchev** (Гоце Делчев), which is 2hr. by foot from the village of Dobrinishte (Добринище). You can a catch **bus** to **Bansko** or **Razlog** there, which makes this an excellent three-day hike. The **blue trail** goes in the other direction and is much shorter, reaching **Sini vraha** in only 4hr. You'll have plenty of time to turn back or to continue on the **yellow trail** to chalet **Yanel Sandanski** (5hr.). Mountain huts scattered throughout the park provide the barest of accommodations for the barest of prices (US$4-5). Bring your own food.

MELNIK (МЕЛНИК)   ☎ (0)7437

Bulgaria's smallest town, Melnik (pop. 300), and its exquisite National Revival houses, sit in a sandstone gorge where life goes on as it has for centuries. While the whitewashed walls of the town's houses are enough to charm any visitor, Melnik is best known for what it keeps concealed below: barrels of delicious wine.

Even Winston Churchill had his favorite wine shipped all the way from Melnik during World War II. Travelers can see the famous wine in its original storage place at ⬛ **Kordopulova Kushta** (Кордопулова Къща), the biggest National Revival house in Bulgaria. Built in 1754, the house also contains the largest wine cellar in Melnik—the caves inside the sandstone hill took a full 12 years to carve and can store up to 300 tons of wine. Stop by for a relaxing afternoon and a free glass of wine. To get to the house, follow the main road uphill, take the right fork, and go left up the steep stone path. (☎265. Open daily 8am-9pm. 2lv. Wine bottles 3-4lv.) Next door, Mitko Manolev's **wine-tasting cellar** (Изба за Дегустация на Вино; Izba za Degustatsiya na Vino) is a 200-year-old establishment that boasts naturally cool caverns and serves some of the best Melnik wine straight from the barrel. (☎234 or 087 54 57 95. Open daily 9am-9pm. Glass 0.50lv, bottle 3lv.)

Melnik is an ideal base for several good day **hikes**. All paths are poorly marked by an orange-and-white line painted on trees and rocks. A plateau with a beautiful vista of Melnik and of the surrounding hills awaits 15min. up the path to the left of Sv. Nikola church (the trail begins opposite Hotel Vinarna). A 7km hike takes you to the 13th-century **Rozhen Monastery** (Роженски Манастир; Rozhenski Manastir). The monastery houses impressive 16th-century murals and 17th-century stained glass, and allows its visitors magnificent views of the countryside.

Buses leave from Melnik's main street daily for Sandanski (40min., 5 per day, 1.7lv) and Sofia (3½hr., 1 per day via earliest bus to Sandanski, 12lv). The **post office** is up main street on the left. (Open M-F 7:30am-noon and 1-4:30pm.) For **private rooms** ❶ look for "rooms to sleep" (Стаи зи Нощувка) signs all over town (6-15lv).

Uzunova Kushta ❶ (Узунова Къща) rooms have fridges and private bath. (☎371. 8lv per person). **Mencheva Kusta ❷** (Мечева Куста), past the river, on the left side of the main street's right fork, is a traditional restaurant with tasty food. (☎048 86 24 01. Entrees 3.50-10lv. Open May-Aug. daily 8am-11:30pm; Sept.-Apr. 8am-10pm. A **mini-market** (мини маркет) is on the left side of the main street as you head uphill. (Open daily 7am-10pm.)

VALLEY OF ROSES (РОЗОВА ДОЛИНА)

Between the Stara Planina and Sredna Gora mountain ranges await opportunities to retrace the paths of Bulgarian revolutionaries, sniff 250 varieties of roses, and slurp water-buffalo yogurt. While Shipka Town lies in the shadow of the Freedom Monument and the pivotal battle it commemorates, Kazanluk blooms yearly with its Rose Festival, where visitors can celebrate with a shot or two of rose brandy.

KOPRIVSHTITSA (КОПРИВЩИЦА) ☎(0)7184

Todor Kableshkov's 1876 "letter of blood," urging rebellion against Ottoman rule, incited the War of Liberation in this little town, tucked away in the Sredna Gora mountains along the Topolka River. Today, Koprivshtitsa is home to Bulgaria's most popular folk festival and over 250 National Revival structures.

⛊ TRANSPORTATION. A bus runs from the train station into town (15min., 9 per day timed to meet trains, 1lv). **Trains** go to **Plovdiv** (3½hr., 4 per day, 2.60-3.20lv) via **Karlovo** and **Sofia** (2hr., 3 per day, 2.40-2.80lv). **Private buses** also go to **Plovdiv** (2½hr., 1 per day, 4.50lv) and **Sofia** (2hr., 2 per day, 4.50lv). The Koprivshtitsa **bus station** posts bus and train schedules in Bulgarian. (Open daily 6am-10:30pm.)

⛊⛊ ORIENTATION AND PRACTICAL INFORMATION. To reach the **main square** from the bus station, walk left 200m on the road that runs next to the river. The staff at the **tourist office**, on 20 April (Април), in the main square, speaks English and offers an invaluable **map** (2lv) of the town. (☎21 91. Open daily 10am-6pm.) There is **no currency exchange** in town. **Pharmacy Apteka Lyusi** (Аптека Люси), Lyuben Karavelov 2 (Любен Каравелов) is on your left after the park ends on the road directly in front of the tourist office. (☎20 06. Open M-Sa 9am-noon and 3-6pm.) Across the street is the town's **medical clinic** (Амбулатория), Lyuben Karavelov 3, 2nd floor. (☎21 21. Open M-F 8am-noon and 3-5pm.) The **post office**, Lyuben Karavelov 14, is on the square farther down the same street, and has **telephones.** (Open M-F 7:30am-noon and 1:30-4:30pm.) **Postal Code:** 2077.

⛊⛊ ACCOMMODATIONS AND FOOD. There are many hotels and **private rooms ❶** in Koprivshtitsa. (Info available at the bus station and the tourist office, see above. US$7-10 for a room in the center. Call ahead during festivals.) A great budget option is ◪**Hotel Troyanova Kushta ❷** (Троянова Къща), ul. Gerenilogo 5 (Геренилого). Turn right from the tourist office and continue past Restaurant Byaloto Konche (Бялото Конче); the house is on the first left. The hotel has homey rooms with private baths. (☎22 50 or 30 57. BulFon telephones available. Breakfast included. Reception 24hr. Check-out noon. US$10 per person.) **Bonchova Kushta ❷** (Бончова Къща), ul. Tumangelova Cheta 1 (Тумангелова Чета), has newly renovated rooms. With your back to the tourist office, follow the road past the park and pharmacy until you reach an arched stone bridge, then turn left. (☎26 14. Breakfast 3lv. Reception 24hr. Check-out noon. Singles 19lv; doubles 24lv.) It's easy to find great Bulgarian food in any one of the town's *mehana* (механа; taverns). The attentive staff of **National Restaurant "20 April"** ❶ (20 Април), in the main square, serves a wide variety of Bulgarian dishes. Try the scrumptious *sirene pod pohlupak*. (Сирене под похлупак; fried and stewed cheese) for 3.30lv. (☎21 02. Entrees 3-5lv. Open 8am-10pm.)

◙ SIGHTS. Every street says something about Koprivshtitsa's heroic past. The wonderfully preserved **National Revival houses,** the homes of the town's first settlers, are an important part of Bulgaria's heritage. Many homes have enclosed verandas and delicate woodwork, and six (see **History,** p. 102) have been turned into **museums.** Tickets are available at any of the houses or at the shop (купчийница) next to the tourist office. (Open daily 9am-noon and 1:30-5:30pm. 5lv, students 3lv. English guided tours 15lv.) The 1831 **Georgi Benkovski Museum-House** (Георги Бенковски) immortalizes the life of the leader of the "Flying Troop," a calvary unit that fought in the revolution. From in front of the post office, walk across the bridge and up the cobblestone road; take a right at the top on ul. Petko Kulev (Петко Кълев) and go straight for 5min. The museum will be on your right downstairs. (☎28 11. Open W-M 9:30am-5:30pm.)

The **Dimcho Debelyanov Museum-House** (Димчо Дебелянов) is the birthplace of Debelyanov, one of Bulgaria's best lyric poets (see **The Arts,** p. 105), who was killed in World War I. There are originals of his works on the first floor and a photographic history on the second. (☎20 77. Open Tu-Su 9:30am-5:30pm.) The house of the merchant **Lyutovata** (Лютовата) stands as a unique monument to the Bulgarian National Revival with spectacular wall decoration and a collection of fine carpets. (☎21 38. Open W-M 9:30am-5:30pm.)

KAZANLUK (КАЗАНЛЪК)　　　　☎(0)431

In the first week of June, Kazanluk (pop. 61,000) hosts the annual **Rose Festival,** celebrated with traditional song-and-dance troupes and comedians. Arrive after the festivities and you'll only see a few struggling rose bushes against a quintessential Bulgarian metropolitan background.

▟ TRANSPORTATION. Trains go to: **Burgas** (3½hr., 5 per day, 5-6lv); **Plovdiv** (3hr., 6 per day, 3-4lv) via **Karlovo** (1hr., 1.90-2.40lv); **Ruse** (3hr., 5 per day, 5-6.50lv); **Sofia** (3½hr., 3 per day, 4.80-5.90lv); and **Varna** (3½hr., 4 per day, 6.40-7.50lv). The bus station is across from the train station. **Buses** go to: **Burgas** (4hr., 1 per day, 8lv); **Pleven** (3½hr., 3 per day, 11lv); **Plovdiv** (2hr., 4 per day, 6lv); **Sofia** (3½hr., 4 per day, 4.50-7lv); and **Veliko Tarnovo** (3½hr., 3 per day, 6lv).

▋▟ ORIENTATION AND PRACTICAL INFORMATION. To reach the city center from the train station, go left 100m and turn right on ul. Rozova Dolina (Розова Долина) as it extends off an overpass. The road leads to the main square, **pl. Sevtopolis** (Севтополис). The main street, **23ti Pehoten Shipchenski Polk** (23ти Пехотен Шипченски Полк), runs perpendicular to ul. Rozova Dolina. **Bulbank** (Булбанк) Sevtopolis II, to the right down 23ti Pehoten Shipchenski when your back is to the main square, **exchanges currency** and cashes **traveler's checks** for 1% commission. (☎6 47 77 or 6 43 89. Open M-F 8:30-noon and 1-4pm.) MC/V **ATMs** stand on 23ti Pehoten Shipchenski near the post office and in front of Bulbank. **Store luggage** at the train station. (0.80lv. Open within 15min. of train arrivals or departures.) A **pharmacy** is located on 23ti Pehoten Shipchenski across from Bulbank. (☎2 69 40. Open daily 8am-8:30pm.) The **post office,** also on 23ti Pehoten Shipchenski, sells Bulfon and Mobika phone cards, offers **Poste Restante** in the room to the left after the stairs by the row of yellow mailboxes, and provides telephone and fax services. (Fax 6 24 25. Telephones open daily 9:30am-1pm and 2-6pm; faxes available

M-F 8am-7:30pm, Sa-Su 8am-noon and 2-6pm. Open M-F 8:30am-6:30pm, Sa 8:30am-12:30pm.) **Postal Code:** 6100.

▐▏▐▘ ACCOMMODATIONS AND FOOD. For a bed during the Rose Festival, call at least one month in advance. ▨**Hotel Palas ❸**, ul. Petko Stainov 9 (Петко Стайнов), truly deserves its name. Facing away from pl. Sevtopolis (the main square), go right on 23ti Pehoten Shipchenski. Turn left at ul. Petko Stainov. Palas offers a pool, a sauna, a solarium (2lv for 10min.), and massages. (Upper body 10lv; full body 15lv. ☎6 21 61 or 6 23 11; palas@infotour.org. Breakfast included. Singles US$35; doubles US$40.) While in an inconvenient location, ▨**Hotel Arsenal ❷** (Арсенал) is the best deal in Kazanluk. Head away from pl. Sevtopolis on the small road behind Hotel Kazanluk, take the first left onto Iskra (Искра), continue past the museum on the right, and take Oreshaka (Орешака) to the right when the road splits. Arsenal is 10min. past Hotel Vesta, inside the yellow-and-white sports complex on the left. Take a taxi after dark (2lv from the train station). Arsenal has spacious doubles with comfortable beds. Have a basketball game (1-2lv) or a table tennis match (1lv. ☎6 37 63. TVs in common lounges. Check-out noon. 25.50lv per person; during festivals US$35.) Find some of Bulgaria's best Italian food at **Pizzeria Ezh Besh ❶**, located off the main square across from Hotel Kazanluk. Order traditional pizza or a more exotic pie like "Tutti Frutti"—everything is delicious. (☎2 12 37. Entrees 2.50-6.50lv. Open daily 7am-11pm.) The **restaurant ❶** at Hotel Palas offers a superb lunch menu. (Entrees 1.20-13lv. Open daily 7:30am-11pm.)

◪ SIGHTS. While best known for its roses, Kazanluk harbors sights that maintain the town's spirit during the off-season. Kazanluk's foremost museum, the **Iskra Art Gallery and Historical Museum** (Художествена Галерия и Исторически Музей Искра; Hudozhestvena Galeriya i Istoricheski Muzey Iskra), St. Kiril i Metodii 9, features pieces by Bulgaria's most famous artists as well as tools, pottery, and other items from Thracian and Roman times. Stand across pl. Svetopolis from Hotel Kazanluk with your back to the hotel. Proceed one block to the right and the museum will be on the right at the next intersection. (☎6 37 62. Open daily 8:30am-noon and 1-5:30pm. 2lv, students 1lv.) With your back to the steps of the museum, walk right one block and take another right on Stara Reka (Стара Река) when you get to the large, concrete building that says "Ресторант Капитал" on the front. Head down the street, cross the small bridge, and up the stone steps to reach the Thracian Tomb (Тракийска Грбника; Trakiiska Grobnitsa), located inside a city park. While the original 3rd century BC tomb and the early Hellenistic frescoes inside are sealed off, a replica of the tomb's interior, complete with frescoes from the Soviet era, lies 20m away. (☎2 47 50. Open daily 9am-5:30pm. 2lv, students 1lv.) If you are just passing through Kazanluk and don't have the time to visit the Rose Museum (see below), check out the **Ethnographic Complex of Kulata** (Етнографски Комплекс Кулата; Etnografski Komplex Kulata) to see a village house and a city dwelling from the Revival years. At the end of your visit you'll be treated to a shot of genuine **rose brandy.** The museum's highlight is a wonderfully sculpted garden courtyard in which a distillery demonstrates the traditional method for making rose oil and liquor. Facing the base of the steps to the tomb, head right on Tyulbenska (Тюлбенска), then take the first right on the narrow cobblestone path, Knyaz Mirski (Княз Мирски). The Ethnographic Complex will be on your right just before Knyaz Mirski becomes a square. (☎2 37 62. Open daily 9am-noon and 1-5pm. 2lv, students 1lv.) To understand what this town is all about, visit the **Rose Museum and Gardens** (Музей на Розата; Muzey na Rozata), a 30min. walk from pl. Sevtopolis to bul. Osvobozhdenie (Освобождение). Head out of the center on General Skobelev (Генерал Скобелев), opposite Hotel Kazanluk, bearing right when Skobelev forks, and proceed on Osvobozhdenie. Alternatively, catch bus #5 or 6 across from Hotel Kazanluk (15min., every 30min., 0.40lv) and ask to get off at the *muzey*. The museum teaches visitors everything they ever wanted to know about producing rose oil. The souvenir shop sells such indispensable rose products as liquor, jam, and oil. To glimpse the flowers from which all this rosiness springs, head next door to the **Scientific Research Institute for Roses, Aromatic, and Medicinal Plants** (Інститчт по Розата и Егеричномасленіг Кчлгури), home to experimental gardens that grow 250 varieties of roses. (☎2 50 70. Open daily 9am-5pm. No English. 2lv, students 1lv.)

■ DAYTRIP FROM KAZANLUK

SHIPKA (ШИПКА) ☎(0)4324

To get to Shipka Town from Kazanluk, take city bus #6 from the train station or the stop opposite Hotel Kazanluk to the end of the line (25min., every hr., 0.80lv). To reach Shipka Pass and the monument, take an intercity bus from Kazanluk to Gabrovo, Pleven, or Veliko Tarnovo and get off at the pass (30min., 6 per day, 1.50lv), or hike up the trail behind St. Nicholas church in Shipka Town (1hr.).

At the Rose Valley's northern edge lies the small town of Shipka, shaded by the legendary **Shipchenski Prohod** (Шипченски Проход; ship-CHEN-skee pra-HOHD; Shipka Pass), site of the bloody and pivotal battle that lasted an entire winter and ultimately liberated Bulgaria from the Turks in 1878 (see **History,** p. 102). The traditional golden domes of **St. Nicholas Memorial Church** are visible from almost every point in town. This Russian Orthodox church was built in honor of the Russian and Bulgarian soldiers who lost their lives here. With your back to the bus stop, turn left at the end of the adjacent building, then left out of the little square on Hristo Patrev (Христо Патрев). Continue for 10min. to the concrete steps leading up to the church on the right. (Open daily June-Aug. 8am-7pm; Sept.-May 8:30am-5pm. 2lv, students 1lv.) From the center of Shipka Pass, follow the road toward the looming **Monument to Freedom** (Паметник на Свободата; Pametnik na Svobodata), and climb the 912 stone steps to the ridge above the pass. A lion looking to the east guards the entrance, demonstrating Bulgaria's gratitude to Russia. Many of the manuscript fragments inside the monument are taken from Ivan Vazov's legendary poem "Shipka" (see **The Arts,** p. 105), which most Bulgarian students learn by heart. Climb to the top of the monument for a breathtaking view of the valley and the Planina Mountains. (Open daily June-Aug. 9am-5pm; Sept.-May 9am-4:30pm. 2lv. English tour 3lv.) Be sure to try the water-buffalo yogurt (1.30lv per 0.35kg; 1.90lv per 0.5kg), a treat found only at the pass.

BLACK SEA COAST (ЧЕРНО МОРЕ)

Bulgaria's most popular destination for foreigners and natives alike, the Black Sea Coast *(Cherno More)* is covered with centuries-old fishing villages, secluded bays, energetic seaside towns, and plastic resorts. In Varna the folk traditions of the past often clash with luxury resorts and bronzed German tourists, but more secluded beaches and tiny villages lie only slightly off the beaten track.

VARNA (ВАРНА) ☎(0)52

In the 6th century BC, Varna (pop. 329,000), then called Odessos, was already crawling with sunburned Greek sailors. By the time the Romans arrived, the city had evolved into a cosmopolitan destination, and it has remained the seaside commercial and cultural center of Bulgaria ever since. Thanks to a history of conquest and reconquest, the city's rich museums house some of the country's best exhibits. Today, Varna attracts many tourists to its beaches and Mediterranean climate.

ORIENTATION

Despite Varna's sprawl, its sights are within a 30-minute walk of one another. To get to the central **pl. Nezavisimost** (пл. Независимост) from the train station, take **Tsar Simeon I** (Цар Симеон I). Varna's main pedestrian artery, **bul. Kryaz Boris I** (Княз Борис I), starts at pl. Nezavisimost, and **Slivnitsa** connects it to the sea garden's main entrance. Preslav (Преслав) heads from pl. Nezavisimost to the **Sv. Bogoroditsa Cathedral.** To reach the beach and seaside gardens from the station, go right on Primorski (Приморски).

TRANSPORTATION

Trains: Near the commercial harbor. To: **Gorna Oryahovitza** (4hr., 5 per day, 5.40-7.60lv); **Plovdiv** (7hr., 3 per day, 7.80-10.80lv); **Ruse** (4hr., 2 per day, 5.10-7.30lv); **Shumen** (11 per day, 2.80-4.40lv); **Sofia** (8hr., 6 per day, 10.20-13.20lv). **Rila,** ul. Preslav 13 (☎63 23 47), goes to **Budapest, HUN** (27hr.; Tu, F, Su at 5:30 pm; 121lv) and **Istanbul, TUR** via **Staru Zagora** (12hr.; 1 per day; 38lv, 58lv with bed). Open M-F 8am-6:30pm, Sa 8am-3pm.

Buses: Ul. Vladislav Varenchik (Владислав Варенчик). To reach the bus station, take city bus #1, 22, 40, or 41 from either the train station or the north side of the cathedral, opposite the post office. Alternatively, walk 30min. on Preslav from pl. Nezavisimost to Varnenchik. Buses are the best way to and from **Burgas** (2½hr., 5 per day, 6lv). Ticket office open daily 6am-7pm. Private buses leave for **Sofia** from the bus station (6hr., 16 per day, 18lv). **Group Travel** (☎50 49 59 or 25 67 34), behind the public bus station, sends buses to: **Sofia** (6½hr., 3 per day, 16lv); **Budapest, HUN** (13-16hr., Tu-W and F-Sa 4:30 pm, US$40) via **Sofia;** and **Prague, CZR** (24hr., 10am, 80lv) via **Sofia.** Buy tickets in advance. Open daily 6am-1am.

Minibuses: They leave from the private station **Mladost** (Младост). To catch one, cross the busy street in front of the station. Continue past the concrete apartment buildings. The private bus station is a block down on the left; the minibuses are parked in front. To: **Balchik** (40min., 1 per hr. 6:30am-7pm, 2.50lv) and **Burgas** (2hr.; 1 per hr. 7:30am, 9am-5pm, 5:30pm; 6lv).

Public Transportation: Buses cost 0.40lv; pay on board. Bus stops are clearly marked with small black signs displaying the bus number.

Map labels: ROMANIA, Kardam, General Toshevo, Durankulak, Krapets, Dobrich, Shabla, Tyulenovo, Kavarna, Kamen Bryag, Tuzlata, Balchik, Bulgarevo, Rusalka, Albena, Sveti Nikola, Aladzha, Kranevo, Golden Sands, Varna, Sveti Konstantin, Galata, Kamchiya, Kamchiya, Novo Oryahovo, Shkorpilovtsi, Byala, Obzor, Emona, Ravda, Sunny Beach, Nesebur, Saratovo, Pomorie, Burgas, Chernomorets, Sozopol, Kraimotie, Primorsko, Kiten, Lozenets, Tsarevo, Veleka, Varvara, Ahtopol, Sinemorets, Malko Tarnovo, Rezovo, TURKEY, **Black Sea Coast of Bulgaria**, 0 20 miles, 0 20 kilometers

BULGARIA

🛈 PRACTICAL INFORMATION

Tourist Office: There is no official tourist office in Varna. Try **Megatours,** Slivnitsa 33 (☎61 27 61 or 61 27 62; fax 61 27 63; www.megatours.dolphins-3.bg), in the Hotel Cherno More, sells a **map** of Varna (4lv). Open June-Sept. M-F 9am-7pm, Sa 9am-3pm; Oct.-May M-F 9am-7pm, Sa 9am-2pm. English spoken.

Currency Exchange: Bulgarian Post Bank, Zamenhoff 1 (☎60 33 16 or 60 33 17), in the main square. Cashes **traveler's checks** (US$5 commission) and gives Visa **cash advances** (4% commission and a US$5 min.). Open M-F 8:30am-4:30pm.

ATMs: Outside the Valentina shopping complex next to Bulgarian Post Bank (see above). There are more MC/V ATMs on ul. Slivnitsa, on the stretch from Hotel Cherno More to the port, and in front of banks on Maria Luiza between Varenchik and Dragoman.

American Express: In Megatours (see **Tourist Office,** above).

Luggage Storage: At the train station, by the end of track #8. 1lv. Open daily 6am-10:50pm.

Laundromat: Byalata Pantera (Бялата Пантера), zh. Kyuri 28 (Ж. Кюри) and Dospat 2 (Доспат). Washer 1.90lv, dryer 1.20lv, detergent 0.30-0.50lv. Open daily 9am-9pm.

Hospital: Polyclinic Sv. Klementina (Клементина), Suborni 40 (Съборни; ☎22 31 14 or 60 38 02), next to the post office.

Pharmacy: Apteka Haneman (Ханеман), bul. Kryaz Boris I 29 (☎60 71 97). Open M-Sa 8am-midnight, Su 8am-10pm.

Internet Access: Doom, 27ti Yuli 13 (27ти Юли; ☎61 09 21; www.doom.bg), off Kryaz Boris. 9am-4pm 1.40lv per hr.; 9pm-9am 11lv per hr. Open 24hr.

Telephones: Enter to the right of the post office's main entrance. Open daily 7am-11pm. **Fax** services (fax 60 00 81 or 61 04 50) open daily 7am-9pm.

Post Office: Bul. Suborni 49 (Съборни), behind the cathedral. **Poste Restante** in the central room at window #12 (0.25lv per item). Open M-Sa 7am-7pm, Su 8am-noon.

Postal Code: 9000.

🏠 ACCOMMODATIONS

Tourist Agency CM'92 ❶, ul. Tsar Simeon I 36 near the train station, offers **private rooms.** (Apr.-May US$5 per person; May-Sept. singles US$9; doubles US$12.) The office also has helpful information about the nearby resorts. (☎63 07 76; fax 60 23 51. Open June and Sept. M-Sa 9am-6pm; July-Aug. M-Sa 9am-8pm, Su 8am-2pm.) **Astra Tour ❶,** near track #6 at the train station, also finds private rooms for US$6-10 per person. (☎60 58 61; fax 61 00 70; atratur@mail.vega.bg. Open in summer daily 6am-10pm.) Locals approach backpackers at the train station and offer lodging for 8-10lv per person.

Hotel Trite Delfina (Трите Делфина; Three Dolphins), ul. Gabrovo 27 (☎60 09 11 or 60 09 17). Close to the train station. Go up Simeon from the train station and take a right on Gabrovo. Well-kept, spacious rooms with large windows, cable TV, private baths and well-lit desks. Breakfast included. 24hr. reception. Check-out noon. Call 3-4 days ahead. Singles US$15-20; doubles US$20-25. ❷

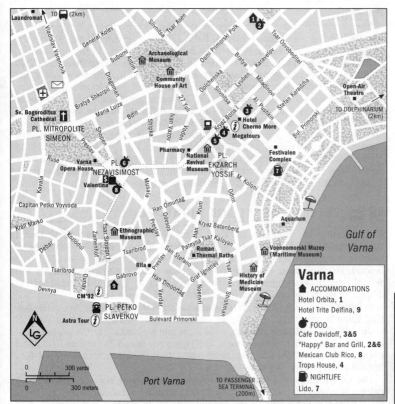

Hotel Orbita (Орбита), bul. Tsar Osvoboditel 25 (☎61 23 50; fax 60 26 17; orbita@abv.bg). Despite its drab exterior and lobby, the hotel provides recently renovated rooms with unique modern bathrooms. Singles US$21, with TV and minibar US$26; doubles US$30/US$38. 10% student discount. ❸

⬛ FOOD

Bul. Kryaz Boris I and **Slivnitsa** swarm with cafes, kiosks, and vendors. Many restaurants along the beach serve fresh seafood. Two chains, **"Happy" Bar and Grill ❶** and **Cafe Davidoff ❶,** are everywhere. Happy serves quasi-American food in a hip sports bar atmosphere. (Entrees 2-5lv. Open daily 8am-2am.) Davidoff specializes in desserts and fresh fruit concoctions. (Entrees 2-10lv. Open daily 7am-1am.)

▧ **Trops House** (Тропс Къща), bul. Kryaz Boris I 42, before Hotel Cherno More. Perfect for those still struggling with Cyrillic menus. Trops House serves filling portions of Bulgarian dishes in a cafeteria-style setting. Entrees 0.90-3.20lv. For dessert, try the *krem karamel* (0.90lv). Open daily 8am-10:30pm. ❶

Mexican Club Rico, at the intersection of Tsar Simeon I and pl. Nezavisimost, serves scrumptious Mexican food to spice up your Bulgarian diet. Look for the fluorescent tables and the flashing cactus at night. Entrees 5.50-9lv. Open daily 11am-midnight. ❷

BULGARIA

◉ SIGHTS

The well-preserved ▨ **Roman Thermal Baths** (Римски Терми; Rimski Termi), the largest ancient complex in Bulgaria, stand on San Stefano in the old quarter, **Grutska Makhala.** (Гръцка Махала. Open Tu-Su 10am-5pm. 3lv, students 2lv.) Two buildings display 19th-century folk crafts from Bulgaria's historic National Revival period. The **Ethnographic Museum** (Етнографски Музей; Etnografski Muzey) is at Panagyishte 22 (Панагюище; ☎63 05 88. Open summer Tu-Su 10am-5pm; winter Tu-F 10am-5pm. 4lv, students 2lv.) The **National Revival Museum** sits just off pl. Ekzarkh Yossif (Екзарх Йосиф). The museum houses the first Bulgarian school and Orthodox church in Varna. (Open Tu-Su 10am-5pm. 1.50lv.) The **Archaeological Museum** (Археологически Музей; Arheologicheski Muzey), in the park behind Maria Luiza, traces the country's history from the Stone Age, with objects from the past 100,000 years and the world's oldest golden artifacts. (Open in summer Tu-Su 10am-5pm; winter Tu-Sa 10am-5pm. English booklet 6lv. 4lv, students 2lv.)

♫ ▣ ENTERTAINMENT AND NIGHTLIFE

Hidden among the fountains and trees in the seaside gardens is a vine-covered **open-air theater** (☎22 83 85; open M-F 10am-8pm), home of bi-annual **international ballet festivals** (May-Oct.). Buy tickets at the gate or at the festival ticket office (see below). The pink **Opera House** on the main square has weekly performances and sells theater tickets. (Opera ☎22 33 88, theater 22 25 44. Open M-F 10am-1pm and 2-6pm, Sa 10am-1pm and 4-6pm. Theater approx. 6lv, opera 10-20lv.)

In late August, Varna holds an **International Jazz Festival.** The chamber music festival **Varna Summer** (Варненско Лято; Varnensko Lyato) runs from around June 23 to July 10. The **Festivalen Complex,** with cafes and a cinema (4lv, 6lv for two tickets), is popular with younger crowds and is another source for tickets to cultural events. From late August to early September, the international **"Love is Folly"** film festival takes place at the complex.

The family-dominated **beaches** are cramped in summer, but still make for an enjoyable afternoon. The sands stretch north from the train station and are separated from bul. Primorsky by the seaside gardens. In summer, a good number of discos and bars rock the beach. Crowds pack the island-paradise-themed **Lido** on Saturday night. Watch out; you might get caught dancing by the roaming video camera and projected on screen. To get there, take Slivnitsa to its end at the sea garden, proceed down the steps and head right. The club will be on your left. (Drinks 1-7lv. Cover 21lv. Open daily 10pm-5am.)

▣ DAYTRIPS FROM VARNA

BALCHIK (БАЛЧИК)

Minibuses (40min., every hr. 6:30am-7:30pm, 2.50lv) run from Varna's private bus station, Mladost. From Balchik's bus station, walk downhill on the main street, Cherno More (Черно Море), *to pl. Nezavisimost; from there continue downhill on Cherno More to reach Pl. Ribarski. Ul. Primorska is on the other side of the plaza and runs along the shore.*

For a break from Varna's crowded streets and boardwalks, visit Balchik (BAHL-chik). Life in this fishing village, with houses carved into the chalky cliffs, moves at a pleasant pace. Picturesque Balchik acquired the conveniences of a resort, while avoiding resort prices and crowds. The **public beach** is very small—arrive early to secure a spot. The best sands lie sheltered by Romanian Queen Marie's ▨**Summer**

BULGARIA

Palace. To reach the palace from pl. Ribarski (Рибарски), turn right and walk along Primorska (Приморска) or along the beach boardwalk (20min.). You can sit on a marble throne and explore the garden and the largest cactus collection in the Balkans. (Open daily 8am-8pm. 4lv. English booklet 3lv.)

For an epidermal treat, visit the mud baths of **Tuzlata,** 7km north of Balchik. Take a **taxi** from pl. Ribarski (4lv) and ask for the sanatorium. Although the spa has seen better, muddier days, you can still get a great *grazni banya* (грязни баня; grand bath). Women should enter on the right, men on the left; get naked and take a preparatory dip in the water, then rub mud all over yourself and sit in the sun while it dries. It's supposedly good for skin problems and rheumatism—or just for fun. (Open daily in summer 8:30am-7pm. 2lv.)

Tourist Agency Chaika (Чайка) on pl. Ribarski 2, sells maps of Balchik (2lv) and arranges **private rooms ❶**. (☎7 20 53 or 7 37 75; www.bgtur.hit.bg. Singles US$8; doubles US$6 per person. Open in summer daily 8am-8pm.) Restaurant **Morsko Oko ❷** (Морско Око; Eye of the Sea) is off ul. Cherno More, between pl. Nezavisimost and pl. Ribarski. Sit in the shade and sample some tasty fish dishes. (☎7 57 05. Entrees 4-8lv. Open daily 7:30am-midnight.)

ALADZHA MONASTERY (АЛАДЖА МАНАСТИР)

Bus #29 travels to the monastery from the train station, but only in late afternoon (20min., 2 per day, 0.70lv). Alternatively, ask a minibus headed to Balchik (see p. 134) to stop at Golden Sands Resort. From there take a taxi to the monastery (4lv). Monastery ☎35 54 60. Open daily 9am-6pm. In the effort to preserve its treasures, the chapel is open only by appointment with the curator.

Known as the rock *(skalen)* monastery, Aladzha, 14km from Varna, was carved from the side of a mountain during the 13th and 14th centuries. No written records of the monastery exist, and its original name remains a mystery (*"aladzha"* is Turkish for "patterned"). Now devoted entirely to life as a tourist attraction, the monastery rises two levels in the 40m white limestone cliff. The **chapel** preserves frescoes of biblical scenes. Church music, which can be heard everywhere in the vicinity, transports visitors to the time when monks held regular services at the chapel. The view of the sea from the open cells is fantastic. A **museum,** to the left as you enter the premises, exhibits medieval paintings and gives historical information about the monastery and **Golden Sands National Park** (Народен Парк "Златни Пясъци;" Naroden Park Zlatni Pyastsi), which surrounds the

IN RECENT NEWS

DISCO TRAGEDY

Recently, some Bulgarian nightlife venues have begun carding to ensure that patrons are over the legal drinking age of 18. Bar and disco proprietors have not always been concerned with customers' ages, but a recent tragedy initiated this change in policy. On December 21, 2001, 21 youths aged 10-14 were killed or injured outside Indigo, a popular nightclub. In an effort to enter the club, a crowd trampled the children on the icy steps leading inside the building. Among the seven who perished, one died on the spot and six died in the hospital from suffocation. A national outcry ensued, and Prime Minister Simeon Saxe-Coburg declared a day of mourning for the victims and their families.

In an effort to curb the negligence, the police inspected over 2000 pubs and discos within three days of the incident. Over 160 police orders were written, over 1500 warnings were issued, and 15 venues were closed. In the months following the horrifying event, a national task force chaired by Education Minister Vladimir Atanasov was formed to address the religious and cultural education of children and the institution of anti-drug and violence education. In addition, the head of the Child Protection Agency declared that the serving of alcohol to minors should be punishable beyond the current fine, and that a preventative program for teenagers 12-18 should be created. Despite these efforts, the public wants more to be done to ensure that safety takes precedence over profit in the nightlife business.

—Stephanie Videka Sherman

THE LOCAL STORY

PETKO PETKOV, AGE 9

Petko was interviewed by Let's Go *Researcher Stephanie Videka Sherman on a June afternoon at his mother's English-language school in Burgas, Bulgaria. He graciously took a break from his Star Wars computer game to give* Let's Go *his thoughts on his native country.*

Q: What's your favorite town in Bulgaria?
A: My favorite town is Varna because Varna is a very beautiful town and the sea is very clear, not like in Burgas because in Burgas the sea is dirty.
Q: Favorite Bulgarian TV show?
A: Uh, Slavi Trifonor. This is a comedy, and when you watch it you're laughing at the jokes of Slavi, jokes with the president and government.
Q: What do you think is the best thing about Bulgaria?
A: Because I live in Bulgaria, this is the best thing.
Q: And the worst thing?
A: The poor people.
Q: Do you think people should help the poor people?
A: Yes, there are many rich people in Bulgaria who don't care about the civilization of Bulgaria—that the people are poor—and they have to help the poorest people to live like normal people.
Q: Do you think Bulgaria is getting better as a country?
A: Yes, we are getting better and I hope we become a good country, like New York, Hollywood, and others.
Q: And what is the one thing you would never change about Bulgaria?
A: Bulgaria.

monastery. Northeast along the forest trail (800m), past the museum, the **catacombs,** a group of caves once inhabited by hermits, offers a look into the life of 14th-century monks.

BURGAS (БУРГАС)　　　　☎(0)56

Bulgaria's main industrial port, Burgas (BOOR-gas; pop. 21,000) is characterized by the hulking freight ships that dominate almost pristine bays. The city is an ideal base from which to explore the coast. Although less popular among tourists than Varna, Burgas maintains a vibrant night scene. The city is best enjoyed, however, by a stroll along the beach or by a sunset visit to the seaside gardens.

Trains run to: **Plovdiv** (5hr., 6 per day, 6-8lv); **Sofia** (6-8hr., 6 per day, 8-11lv) via **Plovdiv** or **Karlovo;** and **Varna** (5hr., 6 per day, 4.80-7lv) via **Karnobat.** To the left when you face the train station, **minibuses** go to the resorts including **Ahtopol** (2hr., 3 per day, 4lv); **Nesebur** (40min.; every 20min. 6am-8:20pm plus 9:10 and 10:30pm; 2lv); **Primorsko** (50min., 11 per day, 3.10lv); **Sozopol** (40min., every 30min. 6am-10:30pm, 1.90lv); and **Varna** (2hr., 15 per day, 6lv).

The Burgas **train** and **bus stations** are located near the port at **pl. Garov** (пл. Гаров). **Aleksandrovska** (Александровска), the main pedestrian drag, begins across the street and extends through **Troykata Square** (Тройката) to **ul. San Stefano** (Сан Стефано). **Bulbank,** across the street from Hotel Bulgaria on Aleksandrovska, cashes **traveler's checks** for 1.5% commission and has a MC/V **ATM.** (Open M-F 8:30am-4pm.) Other **ATMs** stand outside the two banks across from McDonald's, farther up Aleksandrovska. Find **Internet** access at **The Gate,** Alexsandrovska 24, past Hotel Bulgaria on the right. (1lv per hr. noon-8am, 0.70lv per hr. 8am-noon. Open 24hr.) To get to the new **post office,** walk through Troykata Square to the end of Alexsandrovska and turn right on San Stefano. It's one block down on the left, with **telephones** inside. (Open M-F 7am-6:30pm. Phones open daily 7am-10pm.) **Poste Restante** is to the left of the main entrance of the old post office. Walk down Aleksandrovska, turn right at the train station, and then right on Tsar Retur. The old post office will be on your left. (Open M-F 7am-8pm, Sa 8am-noon and 1-5pm, Su 8am-1pm.) **Postal Code:** 8000.

For overnight stays, **private rooms** are most convenient. You can secure private rooms at **Febtours Bourgas ❶** (Фебтурс), 20 Lermnotov. (Лермонтов. ☎84 20 30; febtours@abv.bg. Open M-F 10am-5pm. Singles 12lv; doubles 20lv.) Otherwise, check in to the **Hotel Mirage ❶** (Мираж), Lermontov 18. From the station, go up Alexsandrovska, take a right on Bogoridi (Богориди), pass Hotel Bulgaria, and take the second left on Lermontov. (☎ 84 56 57. Breakfast included. Reception 24hr. Check-out noon. TV US$2. Doubles US$20; triples US$28.)

There are plenty of seaside vendors hawking cheap food. For sit-down dining, there's **Grand Italia** ❷ (Грано Италия). Take the last possible right on Republikanska (Републиканска) as you head toward the sea garden. At the end of the block, cross the busy street and the restaurant will be in front of you. This classy place serves up flavorful pizzas. (3.60-12.10lv, pastas 4-6.50lv. Open daily 8:30am-midnight.) Dance the night away at **Egoist.** To reach the club, head down Aleksandrovska away from the train station. Before you reach Troykata Square, take the last possible left on Aleksander Velina. The club will be on your right. (Open Th-Sa 10pm-5am.)

SOUTH OF BURGAS

Heading south from Burgas, you'll come across a surprising array of seaside beauties, from the pristine hamlets of Kiten and Sinemorets to the thriving artistic and cultural centers of Sozopol and Nesebur. Primorsko, Bulgaria's biggest youth center, lies only a short bus ride away. All of these make good daytrips from Burgas, though many locals rent private rooms in the small resorts.

NESEBUR (НЕСЕБЪР)   ☎ (0)554

Buses from Burgas (40min., every 40min. 6am-9pm, 2lv) stop at the Old Nesebur port and at the gate leading to town. Minibuses heading for Sunny Beach also make the trip from Burgas (30min., every 30-40min., 2lv) but only stop in New Nesebur. Take a city bus (10min., every 10min., 0.50lv) from there, or head left with your back to the bus station (15min.) to get to Stari Grad.

Nesebur (neh-SEH-bur; pop. 10,000) is a museum town atop the peninsula at the south end of Sunny Beach. Don't expect a respite from the summer crowds, however; this might be the most popular town in Bulgaria. A walk through the ancient **Stari Grad** (Old Town) begins with the 3rd-century stone **fortress walls.** The Byzantine **gate** and **port** date from the 5th century. The **Archaeological Museum** (Археологически Музей; Arheologicheski Muzey), to the right of the town gate, exhibits ancient ceramics. Check out the stone anchors from the 12th century BC. The museum also sells a **map** (0.50lv) of Old Nesebur's sights in Bulgarian and German. (☎ 4 60 18 or 4 60 19. Open May-Oct. M-F 9am-12:30pm and 1-7pm, Sa-Su 9am-1pm and 2-5pm; Nov.-Apr. M-F 9am-5pm. 2.50lv, children 1.5lv; English tour 5lv per group.) The 13th-century **Church of Christ the Almighty** (Христос Пантократор; Hristos Pantokrator) in the main square doubles as an art gallery in summer. You'll have to use your imagination to reconstruct the original interior of the church, which is now covered by the paintings of contemporary Bulgarian artists. (☎ 4 50 00. Open daily 9am-9pm.) The UNESCO-protected **Temple of John the Baptist** (Йоан Кръстител; Yoan Krustitel), now an art gallery, has been around since the 10th century. To reach the church, walk on Mitropolitska from the center; the church is on the left. (Open daily 10am-10pm. Free.)

If you choose to stay overnight, **private rooms** are the best option. Ask the locals or look for signs that say "Стая за Нощуыа" (room for rent). **Hotel Rony** ❹ (Хотел Рони), just past the Archaeological Museum, is fully equipped with A/C, cable TV, minibars, and very modern private bathrooms, but is consequently expensive. (Breakfast included. In June doubles 65lv; triples 85lv. July-Aug. doubles 85lv; triples 105lv.) Along the harbor, street kiosks sell fruit, nuts, and small meals (fish with fries and *shopska* salad 4lv). Dine on fresh seafood at a table overlooking the sea at **Restaurant Vega** ❷ (Вега), ul. Ivan Aleksander 3. After entering the gate to Stari Grad, turn right on Mena. When the street ends at the ruins of sv. Ivan Neosveteni (Iван Неосветени), take the steps behind the ruins down to ul. Ivan Aleksander beside the sea. (☎ 4 25 04. Entrees 4-19lv Open 24hr.)

SOZOPOL (СОЗОПОЛ)   ☎(0)5514

Minibuses arrive from Burgas (45min., every 30min. 5am-10pm, 1.90lv). Turn left on Apo-lonia (Аполония) to reach the Old Town. To get to the New Town, turn right from the bus station and bear left when the road forks; this street is Republikanska (Републиканска).

Thirty-four kilometers south of Burgas, Sozopol (soh-ZO-pohl), settled in 610 BC, is Bulgaria's oldest Black Sea town. Once the resort of choice for Bulgaria's artistic community, it still serves as a haven for the creative set. Take a **boat cruise** around Sozopol (5lv per person) from the seaport (behind the bus station) to get a closer look at the two adjacent islands, **St. Peter** and **St. Ivan.** The boats leave twice per day (7 and 8:15pm). The entrance to the public beach is in the park across from the bus station. To explore some of Sozopol's less popular **beaches,** rent a **motorbike** near the bus station and cruise along the shoreline (10lv per hr.). Awaken your inner child on the **trampoline** (1lv per 10 min.) or take a ride on a **oversized rubber banana** pulled by a motorboat (6lv per person; minimum 6 riders). The newest club in town, **Disco Club Teodora,** is located past the food market to the right of the bus station. (Open nightly 10pm-sunrise. Cover 2lv.) During the first 10 days of September, Bulgarian artists take over the town for the **Arts Festival Apolonia. Excursion Travel Agency,** Republikan-ska 31 (Републиканска), arranges **private rooms ❶** and trips to Istanbul. After taking the left fork into New Town on Republikanska, the office will be 1km down on the left. In July and August, call two weeks in advance. (☎43 30; fax 40 38. Open daily 8am-8pm. June and Sept. US$7 per person; July-Aug. US$9 per person.) At Apolonia 23, you'll find the **Internet Club.** (☎20 82. 1.50lv per hr. Open daily 9:30am-1am.) A few buildings before it is **Biohim Bank,** which cashes **traveler's checks** for 2% commission and US$2 minimum. (☎24 85. Open M-F 8:30am-noon and 12:30am-4:30pm.) For a Sozopol experience, visit a locally popular restaurant, ▧**Vyaturna Melnitsa ❶** (Вятърна Мелница; Windmill), Morski Skali 27a (Морски Скали), on the street run-ning along the tip of the Old Town peninsula; look for a little windmill. (Entrees 3-8lv. ☎28 44. Open daily 10am-11:30pm. Summer folk shows nightly 9pm.)

PRIMORSKO (ПРИМОРСКО)   ☎(0)5561

Minibuses from Burgas are the best way to get to Primorsko (1hr., every 40-50min. 6am-8pm, 3.10lv). All lines stop at Primorsko's main street, ul. Cherno More (Черно Море). To reach the main complex of the ММЦ (International Youth Center) from the Primorsko bus station, take a right facing away from the station and head out of town. Turn left at the open intersection. Cross the bridge over Dyavolka Reka (Дяволка Река; Devil's River) and continue for 15min. (30min. in all). A cab to the complex costs 4-5lv.

Young Bulgarians know Primorsko (pree-MOR-sko) as the site of the **International Youth Center** (ММЦ, or Международни Младежки Център; Mezhdunarodni Mla-dezhki Tsentur), where the best Communist Pioneers were sent to strengthen global camaraderie. The complex and its five hotels have numerous sport facilities, restau-rants, and conference halls. (July-Aug. 30lv per person; June and Sept. 16-18lv.) Slightly cheaper hotels can be found near **ul. Cherno More** (Черно Море), a 30min. walk from the complex. At the manicured **beach,** you can lie under an umbrella (2lv) or rent a paddleboat (*vodna kolelo*; 15lv per hr.). In the oak forest between the beach and the complex you can play tennis, basketball, handball, or table tennis. (2lv per hr. Open daily 8am-8pm.) If you're feeling more adventurous, rent a **bike** (3lv per hr.) and explore the area. To the right when facing the beach there is an open-air **theater** and a **cinema.** The theater hosts concerts by popular Bulgarian bands and folk groups, while the cinema shows subtitled American films nightly at 9 and 11pm (3-5lv). There are six **discos** in town, but the most popular venue is **Stop** (open daily 10pm to sun-rise), which is adjacent to a **medical center, post office,** and **grocery store.** For a free **map,** head to the **information office** in room #1 of the building to the right of Hotel Druzhba, labeled "ММЦ Direction." (☎21 01. Open Apr.-Oct. daily 8am-5:30pm.)

SINEMORETS (СИНЕМОРЕЦ)   ☎(0)55

Minibuses run from Ahtopol (10min., 7am and 12:10pm, 0.40lv). From Sinemorets you can catch one to: Burgas (2hr., 6:50am and 12:30am, 5.50lv); Rezovo (10min., 6am and 3:30pm, 0.50lv); and Tsarevo (45min., 3 per day, 1lv). To get to the beach from the center where the minibuses stop, turn right at the 1st street after a trio of cafes, then take the 1st left. After Complex Domingo (К-С Доминго) take a right on the road going downhill; this street leads to the beach (10min.).

Sinemorets, a tiny village of 400 inhabitants only 10km north of Turkey, maintains Bulgaria's most beautiful beach, nestled below a high grassy bluff. This tiny town has no post office, no pharmacy, no bank, and no street names. The best hotel and restaurant are at ■ **Complex Domingo's ❶** (К-С Доминго), on the road to the beach; signs point the way from the town center. The bright rooms have balconies with distant seaside views, tiled floors, and private baths. (☎21 93; fax 29 95. July-Aug. 18lv per person; June and Sept. 12-15lv per person.) Domingo's patio **restaurant ❶** specializes in fresh seafood served under a ceiling of cascading grapevines. (Entrees 1.4-13lv. Open daily 8am-midnight.)

NORTHERN BULGARIA

From the ancient ruins of Bulgaria's first capitals at Pliska and Veliki Preslav to the war memorial in Pleven, the region between the Danube and the Balkan Mountains is most notable for its historic relics. Veliko Tarnovo preserves evidence of the last 5000 years in Bulgaria, while Ruse is subject to the prosperous trade and warring invaders the Danube brings.

VELIKO TARNOVO (ВЕЛИКО ТЪРНОВО) ☎(0)62

Perched on steep hills above the twisting Yantra River, Veliko Tarnovo (Veh-LEEK-oh-TURN-oh-voh) has peered over Bulgaria for 5000 years. For centuries this picturesque city has been the center of Bulgarian politics. As the capital from 1185 to 1393, it was home to Bulgaria's greatest kings—Petur, Asen I, Kaloyan, and Asen II. In an attempt to tap into its glorious legacy, Bulgarian revolutionaries wrote their country's first constitution here in 1879. Veliko Tarnovo's cozy balconies provide an amazing view of the fortress ruins and the sparkling river, lifting even the most jaded traveler's spirits.

▐ TRANSPORTATION

Trains: All trains north head to nearby **Gorna Oryahovitsa** (Горна Оряховица; 20min., 10 per day, 0.80lv), where connecting trains are scheduled to meet them. You can also take a **bus** to the Gorna train station (see **Buses,** below). Trains run to **Gabrovo** (1½hr., 6 per day, 1.70lv). From Gorna Oryahovitsa to: **Burgas** (6hr., 1 per day, 7lv); **Pleven** (1½hr., 16 per day, 3lv); **Ruse** (2½hr., 10 per day, 3.50lv); **Sofia** (5hr., 11 per day, 7.50lv); **Varna** (4hr., 5 per day, 6.80lv).

Buses: Station on Nikola Gabrovsky (Никола Габровски), 5 stops from the center on bus #7 or 10 (0.40lv), heading to the right when facing the post office. Sends buses to **Gabrovo** (40min., 13 per day, 2.50lv) and **Stara Zagora** (3hr., 7 per day, 5-6.50lv). Minibuses and buses connect V. Tarnovo with Gorna: **minibuses** run between the intersection of Nikola Gabrovsky and ul. Bulgaria in V. Tarnovo to Gorna's train station (20min., every 30min., 1lv). Bus #10 goes from V. Tarnovo's bus station through the center to Gorna's train station (30min., every 30min. before noon and every hour after that, 1.20lv). **Etap** (☎63 05 64) runs buses to **Sofia** (3hr.; 10 per day; 9lv, students 8lv) and **Varna** (3hr.; 9 per day; 9lv, students 8lv). The company is located in Hotel Etur; walk down Hristo Botev and turn left on Alexander Stamboliyski; Etap is a tall tower about 40m down. Open 24hr.

ORIENTATION

Veliko Tarnovo is spread along a loop of the Yantra River with its center, **pl. Maika Bulgaria** (Майка България), located on the outside bank. Through the center, the main drag follows the river east, changing its name as it goes: it begins as **bul. Vasil Levski**, becomes **Nezavisimost** (Независимост), turns into **Stefan Stambolov** (Стефан Стамболов), **V. Dzhandzhiyata** (В. Джанджията), **Nikola Pikolo** (Никола Пиколо), and **Mitropolska** (Митрополска) as it reaches the ruins of **Tsarevets Krepost** (Царевец Крепост). The other key street, **Hristo Botev** (Христо Ботев), intersects Nezavisimost at pl. Maika Bulgaria. With your back to the **train station,** go uphill along the river to the left for 10min. and then cross the bridge, which leads to **Aleksandur Stamboliyski** (Александър Стамболийски). Turn right on Hristo Botev (Христо Ботев) to reach the center. You can also take almost any of the buses (0.40lv, timed to meet trains) from the station; ask the driver *"za tsentura?"* ("to the center?").

PRACTICAL INFORMATION

Tourist Office: Hristo Botev 5, on the left just after pl. Maika Bulgaria. English spoken. Maps 2.50lv. Open M-F 9am-6pm.

Currency Exchange: Biohim Bank (Биохим; ☎ 62 39 55), Rafael Mihailov 4 (Рафаел Михайлов). Facing away from the post office, walk right on Nezavisimost; the bank is on the 1st street to your left. Cashes **traveler's checks** for 1% commission and US$2 minimum. Open M-F 8:30am-4:30pm.

ATM: On Hristo Botev, opposite La Scalla Pizzeria.

Luggage Storage: At the train station. 0.80lv per day. Luggage must be claimed at least 30min. prior to departure of train.

24-Hour Pharmacy: Ul. Vasil Levski 29 (Васил Левски; ☎ 60 04 33).

Hospital: St. Cherkezov Regional Hospital (Св. Черкезов; ☎ 26 842), Nish 1 (Ниш), off Nikola Gabrovsky.

Telephones: (fax 62 98 77) At the post office. BulFon and Betkom cards sold. Open daily 7am-10pm. **Faxes** sent abroad 1.68lv per min., received 0.24lv per min. Open M-F 7:30am-9pm, Sa 8am-noon and 1-7pm.

Internet Access: Bezanata (Безаната; ☎ 60 21 18), Otets Paisii 10. On the street behind Bar Poltava off pl. Maika Bulgaria. Look for the submarine decor (0.90lv per hr.). Open 24hr.

Post Office: Pl. Maika Bulgaria. **Poste Restante** in the building down the stairs 30m to the left of the main entrance. Open M-F 7am-7pm, Sa 8am-noon and 1-4:30pm.

Postal Code: 5000.

ACCOMMODATIONS

Rooms in Veliko Tarnovo are plentiful, and if you wear a backpack for over 5 seconds in public, you'll be approached by locals offering **private rooms ❷** (US$12-22).

■ **Hotel Comfort,** Panayot Tipografov 5 (Панайот Типографов; ☎ 287 28). With your back to the post office, head right up Nezavisimost through its name change to Stambolov. Veer left on Rakovski (Раковски), the cobblestone street that splits off the main road.

After all the souvenir shops, turn left at the small square and continue straight; the hotel is on the left. Clean rooms, beautiful bathrooms, and amazing views of Tsarevets. The top-floor apartment (US$40) sleeps 4 and has spectacular views of the evening light shows. Reception 24hr. Check-out 11am. US$10 per person. ❶

Hotel Trapezitsa (HI; Трапезица), Stefan Stambolov 79 (☎2 20 61). From the center, walk on Nezavisimost to the post office and follow the street to the right (5min.). Clean sheets and private bathrooms. Request a room with a view. Reception 24hr. Check-out 11am. Singles 28lv; doubles 38lv; triples 48lv. ISIC discounts available. ❷

Hotel Etur (Етър; ☎62 18 90 or 62 18 38). Walk down Hristo Botev, away from pl. Maika Bulgaria; turn left on Stambolysky. Rooms with terraces to enjoy the fantastic view. Clean private bathrooms. Breakfast included. Reception 24hr. Check-out noon. Singles US$15; doubles US$30. ❷

◗ FOOD

A large **outdoor market** sells fresh fruit and veggies (0.60-2.50lv per kg) daily from dawn to dusk at the corner of Bulgaria and Nikola Gabrovsky, while multiple *mehana* (механа; taverns) make use of the balconies overlooking the river.

Pizzeria Gustoso (Густозо; ☎3 38 48), at pl. Velocha Zavera (Велоча Завера). From the small square next to Samovodska Sreshta, continue down Stamboliyski and go down the stairs; Gustoso is on your right. The best of the town's disproportionate number of pizza joints. Pizzas 1.50-5.50lv. Open daily 11am-11pm. ❶

Samovodska Sreshta (Самоводска Среща; ☎62 39 10), Rakovski 33, on the way to Hotel Comfort. Extensive menu of traditional Bulgarian food. Break free of the *shopska salat* dependency by trying their fried pumpkin slices (тиквички; *tikvichki;* 1.70lv). Kebab with wine 4.20lv. Entrees 3-10lv. Open daily 11am-11pm. ❶

Cafe Aqua, Nezavisimost 3, next to Hotel Trapezitsa. Cool off with a shake (1.40-1.90lv) or an iced tea (0.60lv). Scrumptious desserts start at 1lv. Open daily 8am-midnight. ❶

◉ SIGHTS

The ruins of ◪**Tsarevets** (Царевец), a fortress that once housed the royal palace and a cathedral, stretch across a hilltop outside the city. Nikola Pikolo leads to the gates, where the *kasa* (каса; ticket counter) stands. (4lv. Open 8am-7pm.) Climb uphill to the beautiful **Church of the Ascension** (Църква Възнесениегосподне; Tsurkva Vuzneseniegospodne), restored in 1981 for the 1300th anniversary of Bulgaria. (Open 8am-6pm.) There's a free **puppet show** (15min.) shown inside the gates in Bulgarian, English, French, German, and Russian throughout the day. **The National Revival Museum** (Музей на Възраждането; Muzey na Vuzrazhdaneto) exhibits relics from the National Revival movement, including the first Bulgarian Parliament chamber (see **History**, p. 102) and the first Bulgarian constitution. From the center, follow Nezavisimost until it becomes Nikola Pikolo, then veer right on ul. Ivan Vazov (Иван Вазов). It's a light blue building, set off the street. (☎2 98 21. Open M and W-Su from 8am-noon and 1-6pm. 4lv. English tours 8lv.) Go left, down the stairs, and around to the back to reach the **Museum of the Second Bulgarian Kingdom** (Музей Второто Българско Царство; Muzey Vtoroto Bulgarsko Tsarstvo). Ring the bell if the door is locked. Medieval crafts from Tarnovo and religious frescoes trace the region's history from the Stone Age to the Middle Ages. (Open Tu-Su 8am-noon and 1-6pm. 4lv, English tours 8lv.)

BULGARIA

🎭 ENTERTAINMENT

On summer evenings there's often a ■ **sound and light show** above Tsarevets Hill—huge projectors light up the ruins for an unforgettable sight. (30min. show starts between 9:45 and 10pm.) Check at **Interhotel Veliko Tarnovo** (☎63 68 28), off Hristo Botev, for dates, although they may not know if the show will go on until two hours before. **Bar Poltava** (Бар Полтава) on pl. Maika Bulgaria houses a three-tiered disco. It's dead during the week, but jamming on weekends. (Bar open daily 7am-5am, disco open daily 11pm-5am. Cover 1-3lv.)

🗓 DAYTRIPS FROM VELIKO TARNOVO

ETURA (ЕТЪРА)

Buses from Veliko Tarnovo (45min., 13 per day, 2.50lv) and Kazanluk (40min., 5 per day, 1.40lv) stop in Gabrovo. From the bus station, turn right at the end of the building, and make another right to reach the center. Take trolley #32 or 36 or bus #1 from the center to the last stop, Bolshevik (20min., 0.40lv), then take bus #7 or 8 and ask to be dropped off at Etura (10min. 4 per day, 0.40lv). Buses are rare on weekends; take a taxi (☎126, 3lv) from the Bolshevik bus station. All buses stop by Hotel/Restaurant Etura, a white building with dark wooden trim.

Midway between Kazanluk and Veliko Tarnovo sits a small village where blacksmiths still pound goatbells by hand and nothing is a lost art. If you want to experience Bulgaria's past and see the best Revival architecture in the country, visit Etura, an **outdoor ethnographic museum** 8km south of Gabrovo. Sixteen of the houses have been turned into workshops, revealing the talent of the Revival craftsmen. Climb through tiny doors and up narrow staircases into workshops where artisans make woodcarvings, metalwork, jewelry, icons, musical instruments, herbal medicines, and pottery just as they've done for centuries. At the **Vuzrozhdenska Mehana** (Възрожденска), you can watch the chef prepare your food. (☎427 88; www.tourinfo.bg/etar. Open daily May-Sept. 8:30am-6pm; Oct.-Apr. 9am-4:30pm. 6lv, students 4lv. English tours 7lv.)

TRYAVNA (ТРЯВНА)   ☎(0)677

Take a train from Veliko Tarnovo (1hr., 6 per day, 1.70lv) or a minibus from Gabrovo (45min., every 30min., 1.50lv). From the train station, go right 50m to reach the bus station. From the back of the bus station, turn right on Angel Kunchev (Ангел Кънчев) and follow it 10min. to the center. When you reach a tree-lined square, turn right at the yellow building and continue to follow Angel Kunchev to pl. Kapitan Dyado Nikola (Капитан Дядо Никола) and the site.

A center of wood-carving, icon painting, and unique architecture, Tryavna is itself a museum of National Revival arts (see **The Arts**, p. 105). Works of the 17th-century Tryavna School of Woodworking and Icon Painting endure as reminders of the settlement's greatest years. The **Church of the Archangel Michael** (Църквата Св. Архангел Михаил; Tsurkvata Sv. Arhangel Mihail), Angel Kunchev 9, which dates back to the Middle Ages, stands across the street and a little way down from the post office. It holds the treasured **Tsar's Crucifix** (Царскят Кръцт; Tsarskiyat Krutst), a wooden relic on which 12 scenes from the Gospels are carved—ask the priest to remove it from its locked case for you. (Open daily 7am-noon and 3-6pm.) To the left when facing the church, the **Museum of the Old School** (Музей Школо; Muzey Shkolo; ☎25 17) stands at pl. Kapitan Dyado Nikola 7, the only preserved National Revival square in Bulgaria. The museum displays a comprehensive collection of art, both modern and classical, including pieces from Japan, the USA, Western Europe, and Bulgaria. (Open Apr.-Sept. M-F 9am-6pm, Sa-Su 9am-1pm and 2-6pm; Oct.-Mar. daily 8am-noon and 1-

5pm. 2lv, students 1lv.) To find the **Museum of the Tryavna School of Icon Painting** (Музей Тревненска Иконописна; Muzey Trevnenska Ikonopisna), turn right out of the old square when your back is to the Museum of Old School and cross the small bridge. Take a left on Slaveikov (Славеиков), the next street, then take the first right. Continue uphill over the railroad tracks. Take a left on Breza (Бреза), and after the buildings, head up the stairs on the right through the woods; the museum will be to the right. It has icon-making tools, instructions on the requirements of the Eastern Orthodox canon, and over 160 icons. (Open June-Sept. M-F 9am-6pm, Sa-Su 9am-1pm and 2-6pm; Oct.-May daily 8am-noon and 1-5pm. 2lv, students 1lv.) For more active recreation, **Stara Planina,** Angel Kunchev 22 (☎22 47), rents bikes (1lv per hr., 2.50lv per 3hr., 5lv per 8hr., 7.50lv per 24hr.), provides routes for daytrips, and gives info about the area. (Open June-Sept. M-F 9am-noon and 2-5pm, Sa-Su 10am-noon and 4-5pm.)

At **Restaurant Pri Maistora ❶** (При Майстора), the chef creates amazing dishes. With your back to the Museum of the Old School in the old square, take the street in the upper left-hand corner of the square to its end and turn right on Kaleto (Калето). Green signs with the friendly chef's name lead to the restaurant. Maistora's personal version of traditional Bulgarian dishes will reinvigorate your senses. Try his *shopska salad* (1.80lv)—you haven't seen or tasted anything like it—or his specialty: veal, pork, and cheese in the form of a pyramid. (☎32 40. 6lv. Open daily 11am-3pm and 6pm-midnight.)

RUSE (РУСЕ) ☎(0)82

Voyagers have drifted down the Danube for centuries, bringing music, art, and architecture to ports along the way to Ruse (ROO-seh), meaning "river," or "flow." The city's fortune continues to depend on the Danube and the ships it carries. In the late 1990s, the war in Serbia and Montenegro cut important links with Central Europe and greatly affected Ruse's shipping livelihood, but the tide is slowly turning. Ruse's fountain-filled center remains one of the most beautiful in Bulgaria, reminiscent of its better-known Danubian brothers and sisters.

▛ TRANSPORTATION

Trains: To: **Burgas** (7hr., 1 per day, 9.70lv); **Plovdiv** (8½hr., 1 per day, 8.20lv); **Sofia** (7hr., 4 per day, 9.70lv); **Varna** (4hr., 2 per day, 6.20lv); **Bucharest, ROM** (3hr., 1 per day, 11.80lv). **Rila,** Knyazheska 33 (☎22 39 20), sells international train tickets. Open M-F 10am-4:30pm.

Buses: To: **Pleven** (2½hr., 3 per day, 5lv) and **Varna** (3hr., 2 per day, 6.50lv). **Group Travel,** pl. Svoboda (Свобода; ☎82 29 29), next to the Dunav Hotel. To **Sofia** (4½hr.; 7 per day; 10-12lv, students 9-11lv). Open M-F 9am-6:30pm, Sa 10am-2:30pm.

Public Transportation: Buy 0.40lv tickets on board **buses** and **trolleys.**

Taxis: (☎189) 0.40lv per km.

▟ ORIENTATION

Despite its size, Ruse is very easy to navigate. The **train** and **bus stations,** a 20min. walk from the center, are connected to the main **pl. Svoboda** (Свобода) by **Borisova** (Борисова). Take bus #11 to the stop after the traffic circle and walk straight from the monument. The main street is **ul. Aleksandrovska** (Александровска), which cuts through the main square. The **Freedom Monument,** a Greco-Roman style statue sculpted by Arnolde Zocci in 1908, looks toward the Danube, which runs parallel to Aleksandrovska, a 5min. walk away. A few blocks to the right of the square (facing the same direction as the statue), intersecting Aleksandrovska and running south toward the stations, is the main drag, **Tsar Osvoboditel** (Цар Освободител).

🛈 PRACTICAL INFORMATION

Tourist Office: Dunav Tours (Дунав Турс), pl. Han Kubrat 5 (Хан Кубрат; ☎22 30 88 or 22 52 50; fax 22 30 85). From pl. Svoboda, take ul. Aleksandrovska in the direction indicated by the statue's left hand to the next small square. The office is on the left. Arranges **private rooms ❷** (singles US$15; doubles US$20). English spoken. Open M-F 9:30am-6pm.

Currency Exchange: Bulbank, pl. Sv. Troitsa 5 (Св. Троица; ☎231 34 80), in an old yellow house on a small square at the upper left-hand corner of pl. Svoboda, when your back is to the rear of the statue, to the left of the opera house. Exchanges **AmEx Traveler's Cheques** for 1.4% commission and a US$3 minimum. Open 8:30am-4:30pm. **ATMs** are in front of Bulbank, the post office, and Hali (Хали; see **Food,** below).

Luggage Storage: At the train station. 0.80lv per day. Open daily 7am-1:30pm and 2-8:30pm.

24-Hour Pharmacy: Apteka Avitsena (Авицена), ul. Aleksandrovska 106 (☎22 50 92).

Telephones: At the post office. Open daily 7am-9:45pm.

Internet Access: Alfa Internet Center, ul. Tsurkovna Nezavisimost (Църковна Независимост; ☎27 70 86). From pl. Svoboda, go down the street in front of the statue; it's on the left. 7am-midnight 0.80lv per hr.; midnight-7am 0.60lv. Open 24hr.

Post Office: Sredets 1 (Средец), on the lower left side of pl. Svoboda when facing the river. Open M-F 10am-5pm, Sa 10am-noon. **Faxes** (fax 82 36 00) to the U.K. (1.68lv per page) or to the U.S. (1.80lv per page) are sent and received daily 7am-8pm.

Postal Code: 7000.

🏠 ACCOMMODATIONS

Private rooms or dorms are the best option; go to Dunav Tours (see above). Small hotels are few, and the former state ones have fallen into ruin during privatization.

■ **Hotel Petrov** (Петров; ☎/fax 22 24 01), in Prista Park, 8km west of the city center by the Danube. Take bus #6 or 16 to the "Camping" stop, but continue past the campground, take a right at the auto service station on the cobblestone road, and follow it to the end (20min.). Take a taxi (3-4lv) at night. Don't be discouraged by the secluded location, because you won't regret staying at this small, family-run hotel when you gaze out of your sparkling clean room at the Danube. Laundry, ironing board, even complimentary slippers and toiletries. English spoken. Breakfast included. Reception 8:30am-10:30pm. Singles with private bath 30lv; doubles 45lv. ❷

Campground Ribarska Koliba (Рибарска Колиба; ☎22 40 68), also in Prista Park. Follow directions to Hotel Petrov (see above). While you should avoid the campground during the nightly bug bomb, you'll be glad they detonate it. Spartan but clean bungalows and trailers at 8lv per bed (get one in the shade). Tents 5lv per person. ❶

🍴 FOOD

Food in Ruse centers around ul. Aleksandrovska. The **Hali** (Хали) supermarket on the corner of Tsar Osvoboditel (open M-Sa 7:30am-8:30pm, Su 7:30am-2pm).

■ **Restaurant Panorama** (Панорама; ☎2 21 81, ext. 1614), in Hotel Riga. From pl. Svoboda, take ul. Tsurkovna Nezavisimost, the street the statue faces, to its end and turn right. Hotel Riga will tower in front of you. Inside, head up one flight of stairs and turn right at the top to the special restaurant elevator; press "T" to reach the restaurant. Enjoy a candlelit dinner, live piano music, and a spectacular view of the Danube. Entrees 7.50-10lv. Open daily noon-1am. ❷

Mehana Chiflika (Уифлика; ☎82 82 22), Otets Paisii 2 (Отетс Пайсий). Head down Aleksandrovska from pl. Svoboda in the direction indicated by the statue's left hand. When the street ends, hang a right and Chiflika will be on the right. Enjoy fish dishes (3.80-6.90lv) under the mirrored ceiling. Open daily 11am-3am. ❶

Restaurant Petrov, in Hotel Petrov (see **Accommodations** above). Provides the rare opportunity to dine on the banks of the Danube. An English menu and pictures of the dishes should help you choose among home recipes (4.50-7.90lv) like stuffed pork filet (6.90lv). Open daily 8:30am-10:30pm. ❷

◉ SIGHTS

Ruse centers around **pl. Svoboda,** which is marked by elegant and colorful Baroque, Renaissance, and Art Deco architecture. This peaceful square is filled with fountains and cafes. On the right side lies another square, **pl. Sv. Troitsa** (Св. Троица), which houses the **Opera House.** (☎23 43 03. Box office open M-F 9am-1pm and 3-6pm.) To the right of the Opera House is **Sveta Troitsa** (Holy Trinity Church), erected in 1632 during the Ottoman occupation. (Open daily 6:30am-7pm.) **Sveti Pavel** (Свети Павел; St. Paul's), one of the few Catholic churches in Bulgaria, is on a small street off Knyazheska. (Services M-Sa at 6pm, Su at 10am.) In the evening, locals head to the popular **Mladezhka Park** (Младежка Павел; Mladezhka Pavel) on the east side of the city to stroll or swim in its **outdoor pool** (0.50lv). At night, try one of the **movie theaters** on ul. Aleksandrovska or the **discos** in the Riga and Dunav Hotels. Buy theater tickets through the Kontsertno Byuro (Концертно Бюро) on pl. Svoboda. (☎22 53 64. Season runs Sept.-June. Tickets US$2.) And don't forget the annual **March Music Days,** Bulgaria's symphonic music festival. (Mar. 12-31; see the Kontsertno Byuro for info.) Close by is **Basarbovo Monastery** (Басарбово Манастир); take bus #8 from Iv. Dimitrov (Димитров). Ask Dunav Tours for info.

PLEVEN (ПЛЕВЕН)　　　　☎(0)64

Bulgaria's final liberation from Turkish rule took place in Pleven after a war that took five months and claimed over 25,000 lives. Roughly 200 memorials commemorate the Russo-Turkish war of 1877, including a common grave for thousands of Russian soldiers in Skebelev Park, but an afternoon in the verdant main squares may make visitors forget the town's historical strife.

■ **TRANSPORTATION.** Trains go to: **Gorna Oryahovitsa** via **Veliko Tarnovo** (1½hr., 16 per day, 3-4lv); **Ruse** (3½hr., 4 per day, 4.80-7lv); and **Sofia** (3hr., 12 per day, 4.60-6.20lv). **Buses** run to **Ruse** (3hr., 5 per day, 4lv) and **Sofia** (2½hr., 14 per day, 5-7lv).

■ **ORIENTATION.** Pleven's focal points are its two spacious squares, **pl. Vuzrazh-dane** (Възраждане; Revival) and **pl. Svoboda** (Свобода; Freedom). **Ul. Vasil Levsky** (Васил Левски) connects the two squares. From the train station, go through the park and walk down **bul. Danail Popov** (Данаил Попов), which runs perpendicular to the front of the train station and becomes **Osvobozhdenie** (Освобождение; Liberation). It eventually intersects with pl. Svoboda (10min. walk). Kiosks on Vasil Levsky sell excellent English site **maps** (4lv).

■ **PRACTICAL INFORMATION.** There is **no tourist office** in town. Store **luggage** at the train station. (0.80lv. Open 24hr., except 8:15-8:45am, 8:15-8:45pm, and 11:30pm-midnight.) **Bulgarian Post Bank** (Българска Пощенска Банка), bul. Danail Popov 18, just before the name change to Osvobozhdenie, **exchanges currency.** (☎80 13 33. Open M-F 8am-5pm.) **Biohim Bank** (Биохим), ul. Kosta Hadzhipakev 1 (Коста Наджипакев), is the green and white building on the right behind the mar-

BULGARIA

FROM THE ROAD

BULGARIAN WITHOUT VERBS

No offense, but you are probably not going to master the Bulgarian language. Well, maybe if you can already decipher the Cyrillic alphabet (created by two monks of Bulgarian origin, Cyril and Methodius) and are familiar with another Slavic language, then you stand a chance. However, many foreigners' verbal skills remain at a rudimentary level (think: caveman), even after spending considerable time in the country. My father's greatest linguistic feat—after living in Bulgaria for six months—was a triumphant exchange with a hotel maid letting her know it was okay to clean the room; his phrase translates to "Now...good."

I suppose I have not really applied myself to Bulgarian, because I quickly learned that a simple, functional form of the language, **Bulgarian Without Verbs (BWV)**, is enough to get by. Just consult a phrase book, point, add a clause like *kolka* (how much?) for flare, and smile. You'll find that the effort is appreciated, as I did when I elicited a "Bravo" from a shopkeeper after pointing to a yogurt and saying strawberry." Of course, a potential snag is that the response to your question will be in Bulgarian, but you might get lucky and meet an anglophone of the younger generation. In any case, brush up on your German, Russian, or French as well.

I must warn you, however, about getting too confident with your quasi-Bulgarian. While my BWV has plateaued during my months in the country, I've greatly improved faking comprehension—in fact, I'm too good.

(continued on next page)

ket as you head up Osvobozhdenie to pl. Svoboda. The bank cashes **traveler's checks** for 1% commission. (☎88 02 22. Open M-F 8:30am-4:30pm.) There are **pharmacies** in every square; one sits across San Stefano (Сан Стесфано) from Gradska Poliklinika. (☎4 80 74 or 3 95 59. Open M-F 7:30am-8pm, Sa 8am-8pm, Su 10am-2pm and 4-7pm.) **Gradska Poliklinika** (Градска Поликлиника), San Stefano 1 (☎2 40 97), to the right when facing the post office, provides **medical assistance. Internet access** is available at **Lik** (Лик), bul. Danail Popov 2, near the park in front of the train station (open 24hr; 1lv per hr). The **post office** at pl. Vuzrazhdane, to the left when entering the main squares from Osvobozhdenie, has **telephones** inside and an **ATM** out front. (Open M-F 7am-7:30pm. Telephones open M-Su 7am-1:45pm and 2-9:50pm.) **Postal Code:** 5800.

ACCOMMODATIONS AND FOOD. Rostov na Don ❹ (Ростов на Дон), Osvobozhdenie 2, on the left as you enter pl. Svoboda, is a tower hotel with TVs, phones, and clean private baths. (☎80 10 95. Reception 24hr. Check-out noon. Singles US$31; doubles US$48. MC/V 5% surcharge.) **Hotel Pleven** ❷, pl. Republica 2 (Република), to the left of the train station when facing the park, is drab inside and out, but has private baths. (☎3 01 81. Breakfast included. Reception 24hr. Check-out noon. Singles US$19; doubles US$32.) Vendors sell vegetables at the **outdoor market** (0.3-3lv per kg) on Osvobozhdenie before Rostov na Don.

SIGHTS. Of all of Pleven's sights, the **Panorama** (Панорама) attracts the most attention. It depicts the third Russo-Turkish Battle of Pleven and the liberation of Bulgaria (see **History**, p. 102). From the center, take bus #1 (7min., 0.30lv) away from the train and bus stations and ask for the Panorama; get off, take a left, and follow the windy road to the top of the hill. You can also take a cab from the center for 1-2lv. (☎3 02 51. Open daily 9am-noon and 12:30-5pm. 3lv, students 1lv with ISIC; Th free. Guided tour 5lv.) Down the path from the main entrance of the Panorama is the old battlefield, now **Park Skobelev** (Парк Скобелев). Soldiers' graves and guns remind visitors of the price Bulgarians paid for their freedom. Built in 1834, **St. Nicholas's Church** (Св. Николай; Sv. Nikolai), on Vasil Levski between the Museum of the Liberation of Pleven (see below) and the train station, was sunk 2m to comply with Ottoman laws that no church be higher than local mosques. (☎3 72 08. Open daily 8:30am-6:30pm.) The **Museum of the Liberation of Pleven** (Музей Освобождението на Плевен; Muzey

Osvobozhdenieto na Pleven), in the fenced-in park on the right as you walk down Vasil Levsky toward the train station away from the main square, gives a detailed history of the Battle of Pleven. (Open Tu-Sa 9am-noon and 1-6pm. 3lv, students 1lv with ISIC; Th free.) The **Historical Museum** (Исторически Музей; Istoricheski Muzey), Sv. Zaimov 3 (Св. Заимов), stretches across two floors in several buildings, taking you through archaeology, ethnography, and National Revival exhibits. To get there, exit pl. Vuzrazhdane past the post office onto ul. San Stefano. Take the second right onto Zaimov and the museum will be the black dome on the left. (☎2 35 62. Open Tu-Sa 9am-noon and 1-5pm. 3lv, students 1lv with ISIC card; Th free.) Named after a famous Bulgarian caricaturist, the **Iliya Beshkov Art Gallery** (Художествена Галерия "Илия Бешков"; Hudozhestvena Galeria "Iliya Beshkov"), bul. Skobolev 1 (Скоболев), opposite the Historical Museum, exhibits Bulgaria's best painters. (☎80 20 91. Open Tu-Sa 9am-5pm. Knock if door is locked. Free.) Now an **art gallery,** the Old Public Bathhouse, Doiran 75 (Дойран), the white building with red brick stripes on pl. Vuzrazhdane, offers a melange of Bulgarian and international painting. On the third floor, look for pieces by Picasso and Dalí. (☎3 83 42. Open Tu-Sa 10:30am-6:30pm.)

▶ DAYTRIP FROM PLEVEN

TROYAN MONASTERY
(ТРОЯНСКИ МАНАСТИР)   ☎(0)69

Buses run from Pleven to Troyan (1½hr., 2 per day, 3.50lv). Troyan can also be reached from Pleven via Lovech (1hr., 1 per hr. 7am-6pm, 2.50lv). From Lovech, take a bus to Troyan (50min., 1 per hr., 2lv). In Troyan, catch the bus to the monastery outside the station (30min., every hr., 0.70lv).

Located in the tiny mountain village of Oreshka (Орешка), the **Troyan Monastery** (Троянски Манастир; Troyansky Monastir) was an active participant in the 19th-century independence movement, hiding revolutionary leader Vasil Levsky (see **History,** p. 102). The largest monastery in the Balkans, it contains a wide range of murals by master artist **Zahari Zograf** (see **The Arts,** p. 105). His work *Last Judgment*, representing Death leading damned souls to hell, welcomes you at the church entrance. Zograf's brother, Dimitev, contributed icon paintings to the collection, most of which are in the main church. The **Three-Handed Holy Virgin,** the church's oldest icon, is believed to work mira-

While staying in a private home in Varna, the elderly proprietress beckoned me into her kitchen where two cups of coffee and a plate of cookies lay on the table. While I appreciated my hostess's hospitality, my palms began to sweat when I realized that she wanted conversation in addition to coffee. Earlier in the day, I had managed to answer questions about my name, age, and origin (using the BWV method), but perhaps had given a false impression of my linguistic skills. Realizing that I was beyond the point of no return, I sat down with her as she began her monologue. The only words I understood were "capitalism," "communion," and "pension," but I let Baba Gina soliloquize as I smiled and nodded.

That's another thing—be wary of head movements in Bulgaria. At some point in the country's social history, a nod of the head became equivalent to "no" and a shake became "yes." Although it is difficult to change ingrained body language, it is possible with concentration. Communication becomes a comedy of errors when Bulgarians try to compensate for the gesticulator differences by switching their nods and shakes too. My advice: wait for the verbal affirmation *da* or *ne*. Does this mean you'll get the information you want? Will you get on that *autobus* in the right direction for the *autogara*? Will you successfully order your pizza *bez yaitsei anshwa*? I'm just going to nod my head and let you figure out the rest.

—Stephanie Videka Sherman

cles. (Open in summer daily 7:30am-7:30pm; in winter daily 7:30am-6pm. 3lv. Tour 4lv.) If you decide to stay the night, you can sleep in a **monastic cell ❶** (12lv in the new building, with private bathrooms; 10lv in the old building). Across the street, the **Manastirska Bara Restaurant ❷** (Манастирска Бара) serves tasty Bulgarian fare above a bubbling brook. (☎52 31 05. Entrees 2.50-8.50lv. Open daily 8:30am-midnight.)

SHUMEN (ШУМЕН)   ☎(0)54

Shumen (pop. 106,400) is notable only for its proximity to archaeological sites at Preslav, Pliska, and Madara, which are as old as the Bulgarian state itself. The city is mainly an industrial center—indeed the name of the town translates as "noisy." The town has little to offer tourists other than worn buildings well on their way to becoming archaeological relics themselves.

▐ TRANSPORTATION. Shumen can be reached by **train** from: **Ruse** (3hr., 1 per day, 4-6lv); **Sofia** (6hr., 5 per day, 9-12lv); **Varna** (1½hr., 10 per day, 3-4lv); and elsewhere via **Gorna Oryahovitsa** (2hr., 10 per day, 4-5lv). **Group Travel** (☎6 27 13), in a kiosk next to the **bus station** and opposite the train station, sends **buses** to **Sofia** (6hr., 4 per day, 13lv) and **Varna** (1hr., 3 per day, 5lv).

▟ ORIENTATION. Everything you need in Shumen is located between the cobblestone **Tsar Osvoboditel** (Цар Освободител) and **bul. Slavyanski** (Славянски), the city's main pedestrian drag. To get to the origin of these two streets from the train station, take bus #1, 4, or 10 (0.30lv) and get off at Hotel Shumen; this is **pl. Oborishte** (Оборище). **Hristo Botev** heads uphill from the square and becomes Slavyanski at pl. Osvobozhdenie (Освобождение).

▟ PRACTICAL INFORMATION. The tourist office inside Hotel Shumen arranges **private rooms ❶** (US$8 per person), sells maps (3lv), and provides info. (☎5 53 13. Open M-F 8:30am-6pm.) You can also buy maps from kiosks on bul. Slavyanski (2lv). Down Slavyanski, a **BulBank** cashes **traveler's checks** for 1.4% commission with a US$3 minimum. (Slavyanski 64. ☎5 55 92 or 5 72 89. Open M-F 8:45am-4:30pm.) There's an **ATM** at the United Bulgarian Bank on Tsar Osvoboditel. **Pharmacy Siana** is right outside of the hotel. (☎5 00 11. Open daily 8am-8pm.) An **Internet** office, ul. Dimitar Blagoev 9, stands off Slavyanski after the post office. (☎5 81 88; www.icon.bg. Open M-Sa 9am-midnight. 1.20lv per hour.) **The post office** (Open M-F 7:30am-noon and 1-5pm), at the beginning of Slavyanski on pl. Osvobozhdenie, has **telephones** inside. (Open daily 7am-10pm.) **Postal Code:** 9700.

With bare rooms and an inconvenient location, **Hotel Orbita ❷**, in Kyoshkovete Park (Кьошковете Парк), at the western end of town near the Shumen Brewery (Шуменско Пиво), is the least expensive place in town. Take bus #10 from the train station to the last stop. With your back to the stop, take the road to your left for five minutes to reach the park entrance. Walk down the paved path, and head up another paved path in the park to the right, across from the green brewery buildings. The hotel will be at the end, next to a small zoo. (☎5 23 98. Private bath. Singles 30lv; doubles 40lv.) On nights or weekends, take a **Tikko Cab.** (☎52 252. 0.19lv per km.) Bul. Slavyanski and Hristo Botev are lined with restaurants and vendors. The **mehana ❶** inside Hotel Shumen has the best food in town. Come for the authentic Bulgarian food and stay for the fake village decor, including a well and a bridge. (☎5 91 41. English menu. Entrees 3-8lv. Open daily 11am-2am.)

⚡ DAYTRIPS FROM SHUMEN

VELIKI PRESLAV (ВЕЛИКИ ПРЕСЛАВ)

Buses run to Preslav, 18km south of Shumen via Kochovo (Кочово; 45min., 7 per day, 1.20lv). Facing the bus station, walk to the left up the main street, then take a left on the road just before the plaza with big stone statues and a church. Staying to the left, pass the food market (пазар; pazar) to reach the park that contains the museum and the ruins. To get to the museum, enter the park, walk past the statue of a man and woman, and bear right at the next intersection. Walk to the parking lot, then take a sharp left on a paved path (20min.). ☎ 538 26 30; fax 45 37; preslavcap@yahoo.com. Open Apr.-Sept. M-F 9am-6pm, Sa-Su 9am-5pm; Oct.-May daily 9am-5pm. 3lv, students 1.50lv. Film 1.50lv. English guide 2lv.

Veliki Preslav (Veh-LEEK-ee PRES-lav) was the second capital of the Bulgarian Kingdom (AD 893-972), and is now an archaeological site from Bulgaria's Golden Age. The first white-clay icons in Europe were made here and this craft remains a popular local pastime. The **Archaeological Museum** (Археологически Музей; Arheologicheski Muzey) exhibits artifacts found in the area and shows three short films in English about the town's history. Ask the curator to unlock the safe to see the museum's most valuable exhibit: a golden treasure that once belonged to a noblewoman. The **ruins** are down the road from the museum through a stone gate. Be sure to view the remains of the **Golden Temple** (AD 908) and its well-preserved floor mosaic. Parts of the city's fortress wall and the **King's Palace** still stand.

MADARA (МАДАРА)

To get to Madara, 16km east of Shumen, take a bus (20min., 2 per day, 0.90lv) or any slow train (путнически; putnicheski; 20min., 4 per day, 3 stops, 0.80lv) to Varna. After you get off the bus, continue on the same road in the direction of the bus. Cross the tracks and keep left. The road leads to the horseman (2km). From the train station, face the tracks and go left on the small path toward town (10min.). Turn left at the 1st paved street, which crosses the tracks next to the post office, stay to the left when the road splits, and follow the winding road uphill (30min.). After you pass the motel and non-functioning restaurant, take the stairs on the right to the horseman. At the top, take the small path on the left. (Open daily Apr.-Sept. 8am-6pm; Oct.-Mar. 8am-4pm. 2lv, student 1lv.)

Madara (mah-DAH-rah) is home to the famous **Madara Horseman** (Мадарски Конник; madarski konnik) stone relief. The large figure features a horse with a rider, lion, and dog—an ensemble so legendary it graces the backs of all leva coins and the labels of Shumen beer. There is debate concerning the origins of the monument. Some think it was created in the 8th century and symbolizes the victories of Bulgarian ruler Han Tervel over the Byzantine Empire. Others maintain that the horseman is much older and trace its origins back to Thracian times. A path leads methodically through the **caves** (3500 BC). The largest one served as the **Temple of Three Thracian Nymphs** (Тракически Светилище; Trakicheski Svetilishchte; 1st-4th century BC) and now hosts the annual June festival **Madara Music Days** (Мадарски Музикални Дни; Madarski Musikalni Dni). Symphonic orchestras play in the cave every Thursday. **Motel Madarski Kennik ❸** lies on the left side of the main road leading to the Horseman. A room comes with huge beds, a large couch, a fireplace, and private baths. (☎ 313 20 63. Breakfast included. 24hr. reception. Doubles 50lv; bungalows with bath 30lv.) There are some popular **campsites ❶** to the right of the mountain road, past the Restaurant Madarski Kennik (5lv per person). Take the path marked by the "Къмпинг" sign and stay to the right when the path splits (10min). Small **cafes** abound in front of the Horseman.

CROATIA (HRVATSKA)

KUNA

AUS$1 = 4.10KN	1KN = AUS$0.24
CDN$1 = 4.78KN	1KN = CDN$0.21
EUR€1 = 7.32KN	1KN = EUR€0.14
NZ$1 = 3.49KN	1KN = NZ$0.29
UK£1 = 11.52KN	1KN = UK£0.09
US$1 = 7.43KN	1KN = US$0.13
ZAR1 = 0.70KN	1KN = ZAR1.43

Croatia is a land of unearthly beauty, endowed with thick forests, barren mountains, sun-kissed beaches, and crystal-clear waters. Positioned at the convergence of the Mediterranean, the Alps, and the Pannonian plain, it has also been situated in the middle of dangerous political divides—between the Frankish and Byzantine empires in the 9th century, the Catholic and Orthodox Churches beginning in the 11th century, Christian Europe and Islamic Turkey during the 15th through 19th centuries, and its own fractious ethnic groups in the past decade. Experiencing independence for the first time in 800 years after the devastating war of 1991-1995, Croatia is finally at peace.

CROATIA AT A GLANCE

OFFICIAL NAME: Republic of Croatia

CAPITAL: Zagreb (pop. 1 million)

POPULATION: 4.3 million (78% Croat, 12% Serb, 1% Bosniak, 9% other)

LANGUAGE: Croatian (Latin script)

CURRENCY: 1 kuna (kn) = 100 lipas

RELIGION: 77% Catholic, 11% Orthodox, 1% Muslim, 11% other

LAND AREA: 56,414km²

CLIMATE: Mediterranean and continental

GEOGRAPHY: Mountainous coast; numerous islands; lowlands in the north

BORDERS: Bosnia and Herzegovina, Hungary, Serbia and Montenegro, Slovenia

ECONOMY: 71% Tourism and Services, 19% Industry, 10% Agriculture

GDP: US$5800

COUNTRY CODE: 385

INTERNATIONAL DIALING PREFIX: 00

HISTORY

HERE COME THE SLAVS! The Slavic ancestors of Croatia's present inhabitants settled the region in the 6th and 7th centuries, partly expelling and partly assimilating the indigenous Illyrian (Latin) population. **Catholicism** arrived slowly over the next two centuries. In the 9th century, an independent Croatian state emerged, and was consolidated by **King Tomislav** (910-28 BC), who earned papal recognition for his country. King Zvonimir was crowned by Pope Gregory in 1076, decisively strengthening Croatia's orientation toward Catholic Europe.

Croatia

UNDER THE HUNGARIAN YOKE. In 1102, the Croatian Kingdom entered into a dynastic union with Hungary. While at first Croatia maintained its sovereignty, it was soon stripped of both its independence and its territory, effectively disappearing for 800 years. Following Hungary's defeat in 1526, the **Austrian Habsburgs** took over what remained of Croatia and turned it into a buffer zone against the Ottomans. Orthodox Christians from the Ottoman-controlled area migrated to the region, laying a foundation for the Serbian minority in Croatia. Desperate for autonomy, the Croats, led by **Josip Jelačić,** sided with the Austrians and demanded self-government when Hungary revolted in 1848.

BITTERSWEET UNION. As part of Austria-Hungary, Croatian troops fought on the side of the Germans during **World War I.** After Austria-Hungary's defeat, the Croatians declared **independence** on December 1, 1918, and announced its incorporation into the **Kingdom of the Serbs, Croats, and Slovenes** with Serbian King Alexander I as its head. The Croats preferred a federation, but the government soon became centralized in Belgrade. In 1934, Alexander was assassinated by Croatian nationalists from the **Ustaše (Insurgents),** a terrorist organization demanding the complete independence of Croatia.

FASCISM. The Ustaše finally achieved Croatia's "independence" in 1941 in the form of a fascist puppet state. The ruthless regime sought to eliminate the country's Jewish and Serbian populations, killing more than 350,000 people in massacres and concentration camps. Croatia's support of the Axis powers during **World War II** would become the principle reason behind the international community's reluctance to support Croatian independence in the 1990s. The majority of Croats, however, joined the communist-led **Partisan** resistance early on in the war. The Partisans, led by **Josip Brož Tito,** demanded the creation of a federal Yugoslav state. In 1945, the **Socialist Federal Republic of Yugoslavia** declared its independence as communist regimes took power across Eastern Europe.

TITO AND NOTHING ELSE. Tito, Yugoslavia's first president, placed all industry and natural resources under state control and suppressed ethnic rivalries. During his rule, Yugoslavia broke away from Moscow's control in 1948 and walked down its own communist path, which allowed economic trade with the West. Despite these apparent improvements, the Croats were upset over growing numbers of Serbian nationals in the government. In 1971, the Croatian leadership demanded greater autonomy within Yugoslavia, which led to its dismissal and replacement. After Tito's death in 1980, Yugoslavia descended into confusion.

A COSTLY FREEDOM. The rotating presidency established upon Tito's death was unable to curb nationalist sentiments. In April 1990, Croatian nationalist **Franjo Tudjman** was elected President of Croatia, and on June 25, 1991, the people of Croatia declared **independence.** Tensions arose between the Croats and their large Serbian minority and soon escalated. Claiming to protect Serbian nationals, the Serb-controlled **Yugoslav National Army** invaded Croatia. In a few months, it expelled hundreds of thousands of Croatians from Eastern Slavonia and shelled Vukovar, Zagreb, and Dubrovnik. Meanwhile, the Serbian minority declared their own independent republic, the **Serbian Krajina,** around Knin in central Croatia. Not until the world witnessed the senseless destruction of Dubrovnik did the international political leadership realize that Croatia was indeed occupied. On January 15, 1992, Croatia's independence was recognized by the EU. A UN military presence kept further fighting at bay. In May 1995, Croatia, frustrated with its lack of control over more than half its territory, seized the Serb-controlled Krajina, expelling over 150,000 Serbs. This did not stop the Croatian leadership from making claims on Bosnia and Herzegovina, sending troops and participating in the massacres of Bosnian Serbs and Muslims. The **Dayton Peace Accords,** negotiated by American Richard Holbrooke in 1995, brought a cease-fire in Bosnia and Herzegovina and stabilized the situation in the disputed areas of Croatia.

TODAY

Croatia is a parliamentary democracy with extensive executive powers invested in the president, who is elected by popular vote for a 5-year term. The **Sabor** acts as a parliament; deputies are elected for four years. For better or worse, **Franjo Tudjman** led Croatia as President from 1991 until his death in December 1999. During his eight-year tenure, Tudjman and his nationalist **Democratic Party** (Hrvatska demokraticka zajednica; HDZ) established Croatia as a sovereign state, but their corruption, abuse of power, and censorship of the media also isolated the country from the West. The 2000 elections transferred power to the democratically thinking left, headed by a reformed communist **Social Democratic Party (SDP).** A pro-Western liberal, **Stipe Mesić,** became President and immediately began accession talks with the EU and NATO. With an economy dependent upon tourism, Croatia suffered severely from the recent war. **Unemployment** rates skyrocketed to over 20%. The country's hopes for recovery were halted by the Kosovo crisis in 1999, which once again discouraged Western tourists from travel to the Balkans. Economic reforms have met with strong resistance from both the parliament and the public, further hindering growth and reconstruction. As the political situation continues to calm, Croatia has now focused its resources on rebuilding the nation's infrastructure to support Croatia's booming tourism industry.

PEOPLE AND CULTURE

DEMOGRAPHICS AND RELIGION

Croatia retains a substantial (12%) **Serbian** minority despite an exodus as the war ended in 1995. Tensions between Serbs and Croats still run high, but outbreaks of violence are now rare. Both ethnic communities remain relatively closed to the other, and the Serbian population suffers from stigmatization and unemployment. Croatia's **Bosnian** minority (1%) also suffers from discrimination, albeit to a much milder extent than the Serb population. Nearly 100% of the ethnically Croat population is **Catholic.** Serbian nationals remaining in the country after the massive exodus of 1995 belong to the **Serbian Orthodox** church, while the Bosnian minority practices **Islam**.

LANGUAGE

Croats speak Croatian, a South Slavic language written in Roman characters recently redefined from Serbo-Croatian. Only a few expressions differ from Serbian, but be careful not to use the Serbian ones in Croatia—you'll make few friends. Words are pronounced exactly as they are written; "č" and "ć" are both "ch" (only a Croat can tell them apart), "š" is "sh," and "ž" is "zh." The letter "r" is rolled, except in the absence of a vowel, in which case it makes an "er" sound as in "Brrrr!" The letter "j" is equivalent to "y," so jučer (yesterday) is pronounced "yuchur." Street designations on maps often differ from those on signs by "-va" or "-a" because of grammatical declensions (see p. 160). The most useful phrase to learn is "Može?" which means, literally, "Is it possible?" and serves as an all purpose phrase, whether asking to take a brochure or asking for the bill (račen). See **Bosnia: Language** (p. 83) and **Say What?** (p. 192) for the differences between Bosnian, Croatian, and Serbian. **German** is the most common second language among adults; most Croatians under 25 speak some **English**. For a phrasebook and glossary, see **Glossary: Croatian,** p. 875.

FOOD AND DRINK

CROATIA	❶	❷	❸	❹	❺
FOOD	under 30kn	31-60kn	61-120kn	121-200kn	over 200kn

Croatian cuisine is defined by the country's varied geography; in continental Croatia around and east of Zagreb, heavy meals featuring meat and creamy sauces dominate. *Purica s mlincima* (turkey with pasta) is the regional dish near Zagreb. Also popular is the spicy *Slavonian kulen,* which is considered one of the world's best **sausages** by the panel of German men who decide such things. On the coast, textures and flavors change as **seafood** blends with Italian influences. In this region, don't miss out on *lignje* (squid) or *Dalmatinski pršut* (Dalmatian smoked ham). The **oysters** from Ston Bay have received a number of awards at international competitions. If your budget does not allow for such treats, *slane sardele* (salted sardines) are a tasty substitute. Croatia offers excellent **wines;** price is usually the best indicator of quality. Mix red wine with tap water to get the popular *bevanda*, and white with carbonated water to get *gemišt*. *Šlivovica* is a hard-hitting plum brandy found in many small towns. *Karlovačko* and *Ožujsko* are the two most popular beers. For more information on Croatia's wine industry, see **Croatian Wine** (p. 164).

CUSTOMS AND ETIQUETTE

Tipping is not expected, although it is appropriate to round up when paying; in some cases, the establishment will do it for you—check your change. Fancy restaurants often add a hefty service charge. **Bargaining** is reserved for very informal transactions, such as hiring a boat for a day or renting a private room directly from an owner. If a price is posted they usually mean it. If you wear **shorts** and **sandals,** you'll stick out as a tourist in the cities, but will blend in along the coast. Though southern Croatia is dominated by a beach-oriented mentality, remember that this land of skin and shorts is also quite Catholic. Avoid jumping from the beach to the cathedral without a change of clothes (long pants or skirts and close-toed shoes). Croats have few qualms about **drinking** and **smoking,** but abstain in buses, trains, and other marked areas. When you clink glasses with someone before drinking, look them in the eye, even if there are a dozen people at the table. Otherwise, local superstition holds you will have seven years bad luck.

THE ARTS

HISTORY

Croatian texts first emerged during the 9th century, but for the next 600 years literature consisted almost entirely of translations from other European languages. In southern Dalmatia, Dubrovnik was the only independent part of Croatia after 1102 and produced literature that had a lasting impact on Croatian culture. After the city's 1667 devastation by an earthquake, the nexus of Croatian literature shifted north. The 16th-century dramatist **Martin Držić** and the 17th-century poet **Ivan Gundulić** raided Italy for literary models, combining them with traditions from back home. During Austrian and Hungarian repressions of the Croatian language, **Ljudevit Gaj** led the movement to reform and codify the vernacular. **August Šenoa,** Croatia's dominant 19th-century literary figure, played a key part in the formation of a literary public and in completing the work that Gaj had begun.

CURRENT SCENE

Croatian prose sparkled in the late 20th century. **Dubravka Ugresić's** personal, reflective novels, which discuss nostalgia and the revision of history, have become instant best-sellers in Croatia. **Slavenka Drakulić,** another novelist, is more popular abroad than at home. Croatian visual arts have also come into their own very recently. Characterized by the rejection of conventional and "civilized" depictions of subjects, **naive art** presides as the most popular painting style. Highly influenced by folk traditions, it eliminates perspective and uses only brilliant and vivid colors. The works of Croatia's most famous modern sculptor and architect, **Ivan Meštrović** (see **Zagreb: Sights,** p. 164 and **Split: Sights,** p. 199), have achieved fame outside Croatia; his wooden religious sculptures can be seen at London's Tate Gallery and New York City's Metropolitan Museum of Art. **Vinko Bresan** is Croatia's recent contribution to the international film scene. His 1996 comedy, *How the War Started on My Island (Kako je poceo rat na mom otoku)*, won multiple awards and has proven enormously popular both at home and abroad.

HOLIDAYS AND FESTIVALS

NATIONAL HOLIDAYS IN 2003	
January 1 New Year's Day	**June 22** Anti-Fascist Struggle Day
January 6 Epiphany	**August 5** National Thanksgiving Day
April 20-21 Easter	**August 15** Assumption
May 1 May Day	**November 1** All Saints' Day
May 30 Independence Day	**December 25-26** Christmas

Croatian summer brings out the country's best, including a large number of festivals. Check out the entertainment listings for each city, and the highlights below, to get an idea of the celebrations Croatia has to offer. Stores may close on holidays, but buses and trains still run.

CEST IS D'BEST. Zagreb's own version of Woodstock is held each year during the second week of June. An easygoing philosophy keeps revelers and street musicians on city streets from dusk to dawn.

CHILDREN'S FESTIVAL. Featuring everything from a children's demolition derby to puppet performances, this festival, held during the last week of June and the first week of July, is an annual highlight in Sibenik.

ADDITIONAL RESOURCES

GENERAL HISTORY

Croatia: A Nation Forged in War, by Marcus Tanner (1998). A British journalist's powerful, if somewhat pro-Croat, take on the nation's troubled history.

The Balkans, by Misha Glenny (2000). An engaging survey of the history of the Balkans over the past century, with a special emphasis on the recent fall of Yugoslavia.

FICTION, NONFICTION, AND FILM

Balkan Ghosts: A Journey Through History, by Robert Kaplan (1994). A travel narrative guiding the reader through the political complexities of Croatia and its neighbors.

Black Lamb and Grey Falcon, by Rebecca West (1941). Written just before Europe plunged into World War II, this classic weaves history and personal experience into a captivating narrative.

How We Survived Communism and Even Laughed, by Slavenka Drakulic (1993). A series of perceptive essays on everyday life before and after the Balkan conflict.

How the War Started on My Island, directed by Vinko Bresan (1996). This unusually comedic film about recent Balkan violence was hugely successful in Croatia.

CROATIA

CROATIA ESSENTIALS

ENTRANCE REQUIREMENTS

Passport: Required of all travelers.
Visa: Required of citizens of South Africa.
Letter of Invitation: Not required.
Inoculations: None required. Recommended up-to-date on MMR (measles, mumps, and rubella), DTaP (diptheria), Polio booster, Hepatitis A, Hepatitis B.
Work Permit: Required of all foreigners planning to work in Croatia.
International Driving Permit: Required of all those planning to drive.

DOCUMENTS AND FORMALITIES

EMBASSIES AND CONSULATES

Embassies of other countries in Croatia are all in Zagreb (see p. 156). Croatia's embassies and consulates abroad include:

Australia: 14 Jindalee Crescent, O'Malley, Canberra ACT 2606 (☎06 286 6988; fax 286 3544; croemb@dynamite.com.au).

Canada: 29 Chapel Street, Ottawa, ON K1N 7Y6 (☎613-562-7820; fax 562-7821; www.croatiaemb.net). **Consulate:** 918 Dundas St. East Suite 302, Mississauga, Toronto, Ontario LAY 2B3 (☎905-277-9051; fax 277-5432).

New Zealand: Consulate: 131 Lincoln Rd., Henderson, Auckland (☎09 836 5581; fax 836 5481).

South Africa: 1160 Church St., Colbyn, Pretoria; P.O. Box 11335, Hatfield 0028 (☎012 342 1206; fax 342 1819).

UK: 21 Conway St., London W1P 5HL (☎020 7387 2022; fax 7387 0310).

US: 2343 Massachusetts Ave. NW, Washington, D.C. 20008 (☎202-588-5899; fax 588-8936; www.croatiaemb.org).

VISA AND ENTRY INFORMATION

Citizens of Australia, Canada, Ireland, New Zealand, the UK, and the US do not need visas for stays of up to 90 days. Visas are required of South African citizens; send your passport, a visa application, two passport-sized photos, a document proving your intent of tourism (i.e. invitation, voucher, or receipt of business arrangements), and a personal check or money order (US$29 for single-entry, US$37 for double-entry, US$59 for multiple entry) to the nearest embassy or consulate. Visas take anywhere between two business days to six weeks to process, depending on the country. Only seven-day transit visas can be purchased at the border, at wildly varying prices.

Citizens of countries that don't require visas who wish to stay more than 90 days should fill out an "extension of stay" form at a local police station. **All visitors must register with the police within two days of arrival,** regardless of their length of stay. Hotels, campsites, and accommodation agencies should automatically register you, but those staying with friends or in private rooms must do so themselves to avoid fines or expulsion. Police may check foreigners' passports anywhere. There is no required entry fee. The most direct way of entering or exiting Croatia is to take a direct bus or train between Zagreb and a neighboring capital.

TRANSPORTATION

BY PLANE. Croatia Airlines flies from many cities, including **Chicago, Frankfurt, London, New York, Paris,** and **Toronto,** to Zagreb, Dubrovnik or Split. Rijeka, Zadar, and Pula also have tiny international airports.

BY TRAIN. Trains travel to Zagreb from **Budapest, Ljubljana,** and **Vienna,** continuing on to other destinations throughout Croatia. Due to the destruction of railways during the recent war, train connections are *very* slow, and nonexistent south of Split. *Odlazak* means departures, *dolazak* arrivals.

BY BUS. For domestic travel, buses are by far the best option, running faster and farther than trains at comparable prices. Tickets are even cheaper if you buy them on board, bypassing the 2kn "service charge" at station kiosks. In theory, luggage must be stowed (3kn), but this is only enforced on the most crowded lines.

BY FERRY. If you're on the coast, take one of the **ferries** run by **Jadrolinija.** Boats sail the Rijeka-Split-Dubrovnik route, stopping at islands along the way. Ferries also float from Split to **Ancona, Italy,** and from Dubrovnik to **Bari, Italy.** Although slower than buses and trains, ferries are more comfortable. A basic ticket provides only a place on the deck. Cheap beds sell out fast, so purchase tickets in advance. If the agency will only offer a basic ticket, you'll need to *run* to get a bed.

BY CAR. Anyone over 18 can rent a car in larger cities (350-400kn per day), but downtown parking and gas are expensive. Roads in the country are in atrocious condition, and those traveling through the Krajina region and other conflict areas should be cautious of off-road land mines. Traveling by car can get especially expensive when island-hopping—Jadrolinija (see **By Ferry,** above) charges obscene amounts for decking your wheels. **Moped** and **bicycle rentals** are a good and cheap option in resort or urban areas.

BY TAXI. Taxi drivers are generally honest. Prices are set; there is no haggling.

BY THUMB. *Let's Go* does not recommend hitchhiking. No, really. Don't hitchhike in Croatia, it's a bad idea.

TOURIST SERVICES AND MONEY

Even the smallest towns have a branch of the excellent and resourceful **state-run tourist board** *(turistička zajednica)*. The staffs speak English, almost always Italian, and sometimes German, and give out amazing free maps and booklets. Private accommodations are handled by private agencies *(turistička/putnička agencija)*, the largest of which is the ubiquitous **Atlas.** Local outfits are generally cheaper and worth a call in the summer. Most banks, tourist offices, hotels, and transportation stations exchange currency and traveler's checks. Banks usually have the best rates. Croatia's monetary unit, the **kuna** (kn)—divided into 100 lipa— is pretty much impossible to exchange abroad, except in Hungary and Slovenia. The South African rand (ZAR) is not exchangeable in Croatia. **Inflation** hovers around 6.8%, so prices may change a little over the next year. Most banks give MC/V **cash advances,** and credit cards are widely accepted. **ATMs** are everywhere.

HEALTH AND SAFETY

 EMERGENCY NUMBERS: Police: ☎092 **Fire:** ☎093 **Emergency:** ☎094 **Roadside Assistance:** ☎987

HEALTH AND SAFETY. Pharmacies are well-stocked with Western products, including condoms. Tapwater is normally chlorinated, and while relatively safe, may cause mild abdominal upsets. **Bottled water** is readily available. Milk is pasteurized. The official age limit for **alcohol** consumption is 18, but—as far as natives are concerned—what's a couple of years between friends? Nonetheless, *Let's Go* does not recommend or condone underage drinking. Travel to the Slavonia and Krajina regions remains dangerous due to **unexploded mines.**

WOMEN AND BGLT TRAVELERS. Croatians are friendly toward foreigners and sometimes a little too friendly to **female** travelers; going out in public with a companion will help to ward off unwanted displays of machismo. Croatians are just beginning to accept **homosexuality,** so discretion is best.

ACCOMMODATIONS AND CAMPING

SYMBOL	❶	❷	❸	❹	❺
ACCOM.	under 90kn	91-140kn	141-200kn	201-300kn	over 300kn

HOTELS. Hotels in Croatia are wildly expensive—a cheap overnight stay in a Zagreb hotel will run you at least US$80. If you opt for a hotel, call a few days in advance, especially in summer along the coast.

HOSTELS. For info on the country's five **youth hostels** (in Zagreb, Pula, Zadar, Dubrovnik, and Punat), contact the **Croatian Youth Hostel Association** in Zagreb (☎1 482 92 94; fax 482 92 96; hfhs@alf.tel.hr).

PRIVATE ROOMS. Apart from hostels, private rooms are the only budget accommodations options. Look for *sobe* signs, especially near transportation stations. English is rarely spoken by room owners. Agencies generally charge 30-50% more if you stay fewer than three nights. All accommodations are subject to a tourist tax of 5-10kn (one reason the police require foreigners to register). In private lodging, hot water is often heated in a barrel and then fed into the house's pipes.

CAMPING. Renowned for its natural beauty, Croatia has become one of the top camping destinations in Europe—33% of travelers to Croatia stay in campgrounds. Facilities usually meet Western standards concerning space and utilities and prices are among the cheapest along the Mediterranean. Camping outside of designated areas is illegal. For more information, contact the **Croatian Camping Union,** HR-52440 Poreč, Pionirska 1 (☎52 451 324; fax 52 451 279; www.camping.hr).

KEEPING IN TOUCH

MAIL. The Croatian Post is quite reliable. Standardized letters abroad cost 5kn, express 9.50kn. Postcards abroad cost 3.50kn. Mail from the US arrives in seven days or less; mail addressed to **Poste Restante** will be held for 90 days at the main post office. Address envelope as follows: Nick (first name) GOSSEN (last name), POSTE RESTANTE, Pt. Republike bb (post office street address), Dubrovnik (city) 200 00 (postal code), CROATIA. *Avionski* and *zrakoplovom* both mean "airmail" in Croatian.

TELEPHONES. Post offices usually have **public phones;** pay after you talk. All phones on the street require *telekartas* (phone cards), sold at all newsstands and post offices. 50 "impulses" cost 23kn (1 impulse equals 3min. domestic, 36 seconds international; 50% discount 10pm-7am and Sundays and holidays). Technically, operator assistance is free, but some phones demand a *telekarta.* Calls to the US and Europe are expensive (20kn per min.).

INTERNET ACCESS. Most towns, no matter how small, have at least one Internet cafe. Connections on the islands are slower and less reliable than on the mainland.

ZAGREB   ☎(0)1

Although many visitors treat it as little more than a stop-over on the way to the Croatian Coast, those who choose to explore Zagreb (pop. 1,000,000) find them-selves enthralled. Zagreb's magnificent churches, colorful museums, and lively outdoor cafes are filled with more locals than foreign visitors. Despite its spacious Austro-Hungarian boulevards and its sprawling public parks, the city maintains a distinctive small-town feel. The stern Habsburg architecture belies the city's sleepy Mediterranean air. Come nightfall a stillness descends, broken only by the throbbing bass of underground nightclubs. The external scars of the recent civil war have all but vanished as rapid renovations transform the city into a thriving cultural center, attracting a plethora of international festivals and conventions. Hold back from the tourist route for a few days and follow the lead of the *Zagrebčani* by relaxing and enjoying this city.

✈ INTERCITY TRANSPORTATION

Flights: The international airport (☎626 52 22) is about 30min. from city center. **Buses** (☎615 79 92) run between the bus station and the airport (every 30min. M-F 5:30am-7:30pm, after 7:30pm following flight arrivals; 25kn). **Taxis** to the center should cost no more than 200kn. **Croatia Airlines,** Zrinjevac 17 (toll free ☎0800 77 77, reservations 062 77 77). Inquire here to book flights on other airlines as well. Open M-F 8am-8pm, Sa 9am-noon. No luggage yet? **Lost and found** ☎456 22 29.

Trains: Glavni kolodvor (main station), Trg kralja Tomislava 12 (☎06 033 34 44, inter-national info 457 32 38). From the bus station, take tram #2, 3, or 6 and get off at the 3rd stop. To: **Rijeka** (3hr., 3 per day, 65kn); Split (9hr., 2 per day, 76kn); **Budapest, HUN** (7hr., 4 per day, 140kn); **Ljubljana, SLN** (2½hr., 4 per day, 81kn); **Venice, ITA** (7hr., 2 per day, 260kn); **Vienna, AUS** (6½hr., 2 per day, 320kn); **Zurich, SWI** (8hr., 1 per day, 625kn). No trains to **Dubrovnik** or **Sarajevo, BOS.** AmEx/MC/V.

Buses: Autobusni kolodvor (bus station), Držiceva bb (☎060 313 333, domestic info 615 79 86, international info 615 79 83). Information, tickets, and luggage storage are on the 2nd floor. To: **Dubrovnik** (11hr., 3 per day, 134kn); **Rijeka** (4hr., 5 per day, 100kn); **Split** (6½-9hr., 5 per day, 133kn); **Berlin, GER** (15hr., 2 per day, 702kn); **Ljubljana, SLN** (2hr., 2 per day, 115kn); **Sarajevo, BOS** (9hr., 3 per day, 500kn); **Vienna, AUS** (8hr., 2 per day, 200kn).

Ferries: Jadrolinija, Zrinjevac 20 (☎487 33 07; fax 487 31 41; www.jadrolinija.tel.hr). Reserves tickets for travel along the Dalmatian coast to **Dubrovnik** and **Split,** as well as to **Ancona, ITL.** Pick up one of their comprehensive schedules if you plan on taking any ferries later in your trip. Open M-F 8am-4pm.

CROATIA

◢ ORIENTATION

Despite a great deal of urban sprawl, the center of downtown Zagreb is easily walkable. To the north, historic **Gornji Grad** (Upper Town) is composed of **Kaptol** and **Gradec** hills. The central **Donji Grad** (Lower Town) is home to most of the museums, squares and parks. The **Sava River** separates these neighborhoods from the modern residential area **Novi Zagreb** (New Zagreb). Both Gornji and Donji Grad are bustling centers of activity. Most shopping occurs around the city's central square, **Trg bana Josipa Jelačića** (Ban Josip Jelačić Square) and on **Ilica,** the commercial artery that runs through the square.

> **THE NAME GAME.** Finding your way around Zagreb can be tricky at times, for a number of reasons. First, many street names in Zagreb appear differently on street signs than on maps and in addresses because of grammatical declensions. The root of the name remains the same, but the ending changes, often dramatically. For example, on a street sign you might find ul. kralja Držislava; addresses and maps, however, will usually list the street as Držislavova. In general, the case declension from proper street name to an address or map changes the ending from -a to -ova or from -e to -ina. Also, "bb" after a street name indicates that buildings on the street are not numbered. Second, street names change from block to block. While it may look like the same street to you, each section may have a different name and a different numbering system, none of which necessarily appears on any of the maps you have. Third, names themselves change more than you might think. For example, Trg Žrtava Fašizma will appear as Trg Hrvatskih Velikana in some tourist maps you pick up. The Victims of Fascism Square was renamed Square of the Great Croatians in 1990 as nationalism grew. It was returned to its old name in 2000, but confusion remains on many maps. And finally, there is always the possibility that the street sign, or the map, is just wrong. So when finding your way around, try to rely on landmarks to find your way and count streets when necessary. As always, the best way to avoid frustration is to retain a sense of humor.

◲ LOCAL TRANSPORTATION

Trams: Trams are sweat-boxes in the summer and packed year-round, but do cover the entire city. Buy tickets at any newsstand (6kn) or from the driver (7kn). Day pass 15kn. Punch them in the boxes near the doors. 150kn fine for riding ticketless, and they do check. From midnight-4am trams run less frequently, when tickets cost 20% more.

Buses: Buses pick up where the trams stop, beyond the city center. All the same rules and fares apply as for trams.

Taxis: Cabs congregate at the stand on Gajeva and at the corner of Trg b. Jelačića and Bakačeva. Rates are generally fair, averaging 15kn to start plus 6kn per km, but prices increase by 20% 10pm-5am and Su. Large companies like **Radio Taxi** (☎ 668 25 05) are the most reliable, but speak little English.

◪ PRACTICAL INFORMATION

TOURIST AND FINANCIAL SERVICES

Tourist Office: Tourist Information Center (TIC), Trg b. Jelačića 11 (☎ 481 40 51, 52, or 53; fax 481 40 56; www.zagreb-touristinfo.hr). Friendly, resourceful staff will ply you with free maps and pamphlets. Ask for the invaluable *Zagreb Info A-Z* pamphlet, which is also available on the website. Pick up a **Zagreb Card** (valid 3 days; 60kn), which covers all bus and tram rides and provides great discounts in restaurants and museums. Open M-F 8:30am-8pm, Sa 9am-5pm, Su 10am-2pm.

Embassies: Australia, Kršnjavoga 1 (☎483 66 00, emergency 098 41 47 29), inside Hotel Opera. Open M-F 8:30am-4:20pm. **Bosnia and Herzegovina,** Torbarova 9 (☎468 37 61). Open M-F 8am-4pm. **Canada,** Prilax Dure Deželica 4 (☎488 12 00; fax 488 12 30). Open M-F 8am-4pm. **Hungary,** Krležin Gvozd 11a (483 49 90). Open M-F 8am-4pm. **Slovenia,** Savska 41 (☎631 10 14). Open M-F 8am-4pm. **UK,** Vlaška 121 (☎455 53 10; fax 455 16 85). Open M-Th 8:30am-5pm, F 8:30am-2pm. **US,** Hebrangova 2 (☎661 22 00). Open M-F 8am-4:30pm.

Currency Exchange: Zagrebačka Banka, Trg b. Jelačića 10 (☎480 82 18). Open M-F 7am-8:30pm, Sa 7:30am-noon. Cashes traveler's checks (1.5% commission). Banks and hotels throughout the city offer similar rates. **ATMs** *(bankomat)* can be found at the bus and train stations and city center.

American Express: Zrinjevac 17 (☎487 30 64). Open M-F 8am-7pm, Sa 8am-noon.

LOCAL SERVICES AND COMMUNICATIONS

Luggage Storage: At the **train station:** 10kn per piece per day. Open 24hr. At the **bus station,** 2nd fl.: 1.20kn per bag per hour, 2.30kn for bags over 15kg. Open 24hr.

English-Language Bookstore: Algoritam, Gajeva 1 (☎481 86 72; fax 481 74 97), next to Hotel Dubrovnik. Carries international newspapers, magazines, and music on the ground floor. The basement holds Croatian phrase books, English classics, and travel guides. Open M-F 8:30am-9pm, Sa 8:30am-3pm. AmEx/MC/V.

Laundromat: Predom, Draškoviceva 31 (☎461 29 90). 2-20kn per item, next day pickup 50% more. No English spoken, but English price list available. Open M-F 7am-7pm, Sa 8am-3pm.

Sports Facilities: ŠRC Šalata. From the intersection of Vlaška and Draškoviceva, cross the square and head up the stairs; continue up the road until you smell the chlorine. Pool open M-F 1:30pm-6pm, Sa-Su 11am-7pm. M-F 20kn, Sa-Su 30kn; discounts after 4pm. Changing rooms and lockers are underneath the cafe.

Police: Department for Foreign Visitors, Petrinjska 30 (☎456 36 23, after hours 456 31 11). Room 103 on the 2nd floor of the central police station. To **register,** use Form #14. Open M-F 8am-4pm.

Pharmacy: Gradska Liekarna Zagreb, Zrinjevac 20 (☎487 38 73). Open M-F 7am-8pm, Sa 7am-2:30pm. **Night service** available at Ilica 43 (☎484 84 50). AmEx/D/MC.

Medical Services: Hospital REBRO, Kišpaticeva 12 (☎238 88 88). Open 24hr.

Telephones: Pay phones are scattered throughout the city but they only take prepaid cards, not coins. Buy these from any news kiosk. Or call from the **post office** and pay afterwards. All rates, international and domestic, are expensive, so bring your calling card from home.

Internet Access: Art Net Club, Preradoviceva 25 (☎455 84 71). Fast connections 16kn per hr. Seconds as a creative underworld with photo exhibits, TV, bar, and live music (Sept.-Nov.). Open M-Sa 9am-9pm. **Charlie Net,** Gajeva 4 (☎488 02 33), through the courtyard and on the right. Great connection. 16kn per hr., 12kn with ISIC. Open M-Sa 8am-10pm. **Sublink Cyber Cafe,** Teslina 12 (☎481 13 29), through the courtyard, up the stairs, and to the left. So dark you can barely see the keyboard. 14kn per hr. 10% ISIC discount. Open M-Sa 9am-10pm, Su 3-10pm.

Post Office: Branimirova 4 (☎484 03 45), next to the train station. From Branimirova, turn left up the stairs. **Poste Restante** on 2nd floor (desk #3). Desk #1 exchanges cash and **traveler's checks** for the standard 1.5% commission. Open 24hr.

Postal Code: 10000.

CROATIA

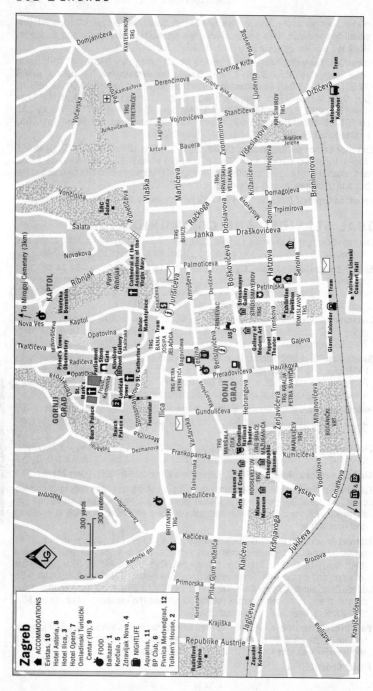

Zagreb

♠ ACCOMMODATIONS

Evistas, 10
Hotel Astoria, 8
Hotel Ilica, 3
Hotel Opera, 7
Omladinski Turistički
Centar (HI), 9

♥ FOOD

Baltazar, 1
Korčula, 5
Zdravljak Nova, 4

■ NIGHTLIFE

Aquarius, 11
BP Club, 6
Pivnica Medvedgrad, 12
Tolkien's House, 2

ⓘ ACCOMMODATIONS

Cheap accommodations are scarce in Zagreb; fortunately, so are budget travelers. If the hostel is full or you would prefer something a little less like summer-camp, head straight to **Evistas ❷**, Šenoina 28, for a private room. From the train station, take a right on Branimirova, a quick left onto Petrinjska, and then a right onto Šenoina. This friendly husband and wife travel agency can register and reserve you a bed in private rooms or some hotels, even at the height of festival season. (☎483 95 46; fax 483 95 43; evistas@zg.hinet.hr. Open M-F 9am-8pm, Sa 9:30am-5pm. Singles 175kn; doubles 240kn; apartments 140-180kn per person. Minimum stay 3 days; 20% more for 1 night only, 30% more during festivals; under 26 15% off. 7kn tax.) Foreigners just entering Croatia and staying in private accommodations must **register** at the Police Station (see above) within 2 days of arrival. Hostels and hotels will register you automatically.

Hotel Ilica, Ilica 102 (☎377 75 22 or 377 76 22; fax 377 77 22; www.hotel-ilica.hr). Walk down Ilica from Trg b. Jelačića, past Trg Britanki. From the train station, take tram #6 toward Črnomerec and get off the 2nd time it stops on Ilica. Satellite TV and telephones grace every room in this small private hotel. German and English spoken. Breakfast and parking included. Reception 24hr. Check-out noon. Call ahead. Singles 349kn; doubles 449kn; 3-person apartments 749kn, 4-person 889kn. ❷

Hotel Astoria, Petrinjska 71 (☎484 12 22; fax 484 12 12). Just a few steps past the HI hostel. Enter through the Chinese restaurant. This sparkling clean, dimly-lit hotel is superbly situated but has small rooms. TV and phone in all 120 rooms. English spoken. Excellent breakfast included. Reception 24hr. Check-out noon. Singles 330kn; doubles 500kn; triples 600kn. AmEx/D/MC/V. ❷

Omladinski Turistički Centar (HI), Petrinjska 77 (☎484 12 61; fax 484 12 69). With your back to the train station, walk right on Branimirova; Petrinjska will be on your left. Despite the peeling paint, nothing beats this state-run hostel's central location and great price. Stop in at the grocery store just to the left as you walk out the door for a sandwich the size of your forearm (10-15kn). Reception 24hr. Check-in 2pm-1am. Check-out 9am. No reservations necessary. 6-bed dorm 67kn, non-members 72kn; singles 149kn, with bath 202kn; doubles 204kn/274kn. ❶

Hotel Opera, Kršnjagova 1 (☎489 20 00; fax 489 20 01; www.opera-zagreb.hr). For a splurge at the end of a long trip, check into the plush Hotel Opera. The prices are lower than most of the other large hotels in town and the views are unbeatable. There are a number of excellent (and expensive) restaurants on the ground floor, as well as all the amenities you would expect from a fine hotel. Reception 24hr. Singles 1230kn; doubles 1520kn. AmEx/MC/V. ❺

ⓕ FOOD

Zagrebčani adore meat, and restaurant menus reflect their carnivorous tastes, offering local specialities like *štruca*, grilled veal scallop stuffed with Dalmatian ham, mushrooms, and cheese. While these dishes dominate restaurant menus all year, most Croatians opt for lighter fare in the summer. Behind Trg b. Jelačića in Gornji Grad lies Zagreb's liveliest open-air market, **Dolac.** (Open M-Sa 6am-3pm, Su 6am-noon.) There are grocery stores throughout the city, including **Konzum** at the corner of Preradoviceva and Hebrangova. (Open M-F 7am-8pm, Sa 7am-3pm. AmEx/MC/V.) For an extensive list of the best restaurants and pubs, pick up the free *Zagreb Info A-Z* from the tourist office.

🏶 Baltazar, Nova Ves 4 (☎466 68 24). Follow Kaptol till it turns into Nova Ves, about 5 minutes past the Cathedral. The feeling in the garden courtyard of Baltazar is relaxed,

CROATIA

THE HIDDEN DEAL

CROATIAN WINE

International critics are taking notice of Croatia's high-quality wines, and it won't be long before they are priced out of the range of even the most lavish budget traveler. But with prices still reasonable for even the best Croatian wines, now's your chance to do some exploration.

The wine-growing regions of Croatia can be divided into two main areas. The Adriatic Coast (particularly Pelješac, Hvar, and the Istria Peninsula) produces fine red wines, with dense, full-bodied tastes and a high alcohol content. The eastern parts of the country produces lighter white wines. (The best reds come from the plavac mali grape, which is unique to the Croatian Adriatic.) The high end of the Croatian wine industry is populated by about 100 very small producers, many of whom produce only 10,000-20,000 bottles a year. After years under socialist production rules which stifled competition and creativity, and a war that destroyed much of the industry's infrastructure, wine makers must work hard to make their mark with quality products.

The best place to explore Croatian wines in **Zagreb** is in the dark, vaulted basement of ⊠**Vinoteka Bornstein.** Vlado and Slavica Borošic, the owners, have brought together the best wines of Croatia in a beautiful cellar. Vlado will help you find what suits you best, but also offers advice on hunting great Croatian wine in its natural habitat. The best way to find good wines, he says, is to stay away from the chain supermarkets and just go to a village and ask for the best local wine in the area. A very good bottle of wine sells in the shop for 75-100kn and is marked up as much as 150-200% in restaurants. (Kaptol 19. ☎ 481 23 61. Open M-Sa 9am-7pm.)

—A. Nicholas Gossen

but the food is serious. Big helpings of juicy sausages and steaks make up most of the menu at this traditional Croatian restaurant. Try the *pljeskavica sa kajmakom* (seasoned hamburger with fresh cheese; 50kn); it's unlike any cheeseburger you've ever imagined. Entrees 35-80kn. Open daily noon-midnight. AmEx/MC/V. ❶

Korčula, Teslina 17 (☎487 21 59). From Trg b. Jelačića, walk down Gajeva to Teslina. Named after the Adriatic island, Korčula brings a taste of the sea to inland Zagreb with its Dalmatian specialties. The *crni rizoto* (black risotto; 60kn) is a particularly delicious squid dish that is colored with squid ink. Entrees 50-80kn. Restaurant open daily 10am-11pm, bar open daily 8am-11pm. AmEx/MC/V. ❹

Zdravljak Nova, Ilica 72/1 (☎484 71 19). Go into the passageway, enter the building on the right and walk up one flight into a world of peace, love, and polenta. This combined health store and restaurant serves up Asian-influenced vegan cuisine that serves as a nice change from Croatian chunks of meat. Entrees 39-59kn. Open M-Sa noon-10pm. AmEx/DC/MC/V. ❸

◎ SIGHTS

The best way to see Zagreb is on foot. A short walk up any of the streets behind Trg b. Jelačića leads to **Gornji Grad,** where you can wander through winding cobblestone streets and visit most sights in a single day. To give your weary feet a rest, hop on the **funicular,** an entertaining but peculiarly inefficient way of getting up the short hill. (Open 6:30am-9pm; 2.50kn or free with your Zagreb Card.) To get to it, walk down Ilica from Trg b. Jelačića; it will be on your right. The funicular puts you in a great position to explore Gornji Grad. Carry a copy of *Zagreb: City Walks,* available at the TIC (see **Tourist and Financial Services,** p. 160).

CATHEDRAL OF THE ASSUMPTION. (Katedrala Marijina Uznesenja.) Also known simply as the Cathedral, its first incarnation was built in 1217. After being destroyed by the Tartars, rebuilt, remodelled, and restored a number of times throughout the centuries, it finally gained its current glimmering appearance in 1880-1902, when the distinctive towers were added. (Kaptol 1. Services daily 7, 8, and 9am. Open daily 10am-5pm. Free.)

ST. MARK'S CHURCH. (Crkva Sv. Marka.) The most striking aspect of St. Mark's is the dazzling roof, which is hard to miss. The multi-colored tiles depict the coat of arms of Croatia, Dalmatia, and Slavonia on the left side and that of Zagreb on the right. This sparkling display makes the dark stone interior feel dank, but if you squint you can make out the newly restored frescoes on the walls. *(From the top of the funicular, turn right and then left onto Cirilometodska; the church is straight ahead. Entrance to the left. Open daily 7am-5pm. Free.)*

LOTRŠČAK TOWER. (Kula Lotrščak.) This 13th-century tower, constructed to guard against Tartar attacks, is marked by a 19th-century addition—a peculiar staircase that winds up halfway on the outside, and halfway on the inside. The view from the top is spectacular. The cannon near the top of the tower has fired every day at noon since 1877. Go a few minutes before noon to meet the cannoneer. *(At the corner of Strossmayerovo and Dverce, right at the top of the funicular. Open May-Sept. Tu-Su 11am-8pm. 5kn.)*

ST. CATHERINE'S CHURCH. (Crkva sv. Katrinski.) Built by Jesuits between 1620 and 1632, St. Catherine's modest facade does nothing to prepare you for its inner elegance. Decorated with the gifts of Croatian nobles, the church's most striking feature is the intricate pink and white stucco on the vault, the walls of the chapel, and the shrine—all fashioned by the Italian master Anton Joseph Quadrio from 1721 to 1726. The unstained windows let natural light bounce off the sculptures with gold leaf and delicate pink designs. *(From the top of the funicular, the first church on your right. Open M-F and Su 7am-11pm, Sa 7am-6:30pm.)*

MIROGOJ CEMETERY. Set at the edge of the city, this beautiful cemetery is so big you wonder if its population rivals that of Zagreb itself. Wander through the serene park composed of cyprus trees, wide avenues, and endless rows of gravestones. Beyond the grand mausoleum at the entrance, you'll find the massive grave of Croatia's first president, Franjo Tudjman, who died of cancer in the fall of 1999. *(Take a bus from Kaptol in front of the Cathedral (8min., every 15min). Photography not allowed. Open M-F 6am-8pm, Su 7:30am-6pm.)*

PARK RIBNJAK. Park Ribnjak offers the chance for a peaceful walk without leaving the city. Come here to enjoy a cheap picnic or to watch the entire canine population of Zagreb play in the grass. *(Behind the Cathedral. From Trg b. Jelačća, turn down Jurisceva, then right on Palmoticeva. The entrance is on your left after one block.)*

🏛 MUSEUMS

While you won't find any Picassos or Monets in Zagreb, there are plenty of interesting collections and exhibits to occupy the art lover for a day or two. For a complete list of museums, consult the free monthly *Zagreb: Events and Performances*, available at the TIC (see **Tourist and Financial Services,** p. 160). It also lists galleries, plays, festivals, concerts, and sporting events. Many of the museums lie in Donji Grad below Ilica. Trams #12, 13, 14, and 17 all reach the Mimara, the Arts and Crafts Museum, and the Ethnographic Museum (see below).

MUSEUM OF ARTS AND CRAFTS. (Muzej za Umjetnost i Obrt.) From timepieces to furniture, glass to graphic art, this museum, with its eclectic mix of periods and media, keeps you wondering what the next room will hold. Particularly interesting is an exhibit on Croatian photography from the 1850s to the 1930s. *(Trg Maršala Tita 10. ☎ 482 69 22. Open Tu-F 10am-6pm, Sa-Su 10am-1pm. 20kn, students 10kn.)*

KLOVIČEVI DVORI GALLERY. (Galerija Klovičevi Dvori.) Situated in a beautifully converted monastery, the exhibitions change monthly and usually feature Croatian artists. Regardless of the exhibit, it is worth visiting just for the building itself. After visiting the gallery, enjoy a coffee in the elegant central courtyard. *(Jesuitski Trg 4, immediately to the left of St. Catherine's (see p. 165). ☎ 485 14 26. Open Tu-Su 11am-7pm. 20kn, students 10kn.)*

CROATIA

GALLERY OF MODERN ART. (Moderna galerija.) Features rotating exhibitions of Croatia's best artists in a small, attractive gallery. A great way to get a feel for the thriving modern art scene. *(Hebrangova 1, across from the US embassy.* ☎ *492 23 68. Hours and prices vary with each exhibition.)*

MIMARA MUSEUM. (Muzej Mimara.) A vast and varied collection from Egyptian art to Raphael, Velasquez, Rubens, and Rembrandt, although little background information is provided. *(Rooseveltov Trg 5.* ☎ *482 81 00. Open Tu-W and F-Sa 10am-5pm, Th 10am-7pm, Su 10am-2pm. 20kn, students 15kn.)*

STROSSMAYER GALLERY. (Strossmayer Galerija Starih Majstora.) Two flights up inside the beautiful Croatian Academy of Arts and Science. Founded by Bishop Josip Juraj Strossmayer in 1884, the permanent collection includes works from 20 Italian schools of painting from the Renaissance through Baroque. The in-progress student reproductions sprinkled throughout the gallery highlight the excellence of the originals. *(Zrinjskog Trg 11.* ☎ *489 51 17. Open Tu 10am-1pm and 5-7 pm, W-Su 10am-1pm. 10kn, students 5kn.)*

ETHNOGRAPHIC MUSEUM. (Ethnografski Muzej.) This small museum offers a unique look at the traditional culture of Croatia. Exhibits include costumes from various regions and etchings of local architecture. Don't miss the "Cultures of the World in Three Rooms" gallery. *(Mažuranićev Trg 14, across the street from the Mimara.* ☎ *482 62 20. Open Tu-Th 10am-6pm, F-Su 10am-1pm. 15kn, students 10kn.)*

◘ FESTIVALS

Zagreb hosts an impressive array of festivals. Each year kicks off with a **blues festival** in January, while April 4-11, 2003 will bring the **Biennial International Music Festival.** Streets burst with performances during the second week in June for the annual Zagreb street festival **Cest is d'Best** ("The Streets are the Best"). Folklore fetishists will flock to Zagreb on July 16-20, 2003 for the 37th **International Folklore Festival,** the premier gathering of European folk dancers and singing groups. The end of October sees Zagreb's **International Jazz Days,** and the huge **International Puppet Festival** occurs at the beginning of September. Every year, mid-December is filled with the colorful **Christmas Fair.** For up-to-date, detailed information and schedules, check out www.zagreb-touristinfo.hr.

◙ NIGHTLIFE

The lively outdoor **cafes** lining both sides of the street along **Tkalčićeva,** in Gornji Grad, beckon to an older, classier crowd, while **Opatovina,** a parallel street, hosts a slightly younger and more budget-minded group. Most of the cafes in Donji Grad are indistinguishable, but pleasant. Many **discos** are open all week; the best ones lie outside the center. For a complete listing of all discos and nightclubs in Zagreb, consult *Zagreb Info A-Z.*

▨ **Aquarius,** on Lake Jarun. Take Tram #17 from the center and get off on Srednjaci at the 3rd unmarked stop (15min.). Turn around, cross the street, and follow one of the dirt paths—they all lead to the lake. At the lake, walk along the boardwalk to the left; Aquarius is the last building. This lakeside cafe/nightclub offers something for everyone. Boogie inside or out, or take a late-night dip in the artificial lake. Live jazz some Tu, funk W, Latin Th, house Su, and a grab-bag on weekends. Drinks 15-35kn. Cover 30kn. Cafe open daily 9am-9pm, club open W-Su 10pm-4am.

▨ **Pivnica Medvedgrad,** Savska 56. Take tram #13, 14, or 17 from Trg b. Jelačića to the corner of Avenija Vukovar and Savska cesta. The best (and cheapest) beer in town. This microbrewery's long, wooden tables, dim lights, and good beer attract crowds of students and business people. Four kinds of beer (15kn/liter). When the munchies kick in, try the whole-grain bread and *čevapčici* (small sausages served with raw onion; 22kn) Open M-Sa 10am-midnight, Su noon-midnight.

BP Club, Teslina 7. Head for the right side of the courtyard, then down the yellow stairs. *The* venue for jazz (loosely interpreted to include blues, trance, and U2), BP keeps it cool year round. Live music during the Oct. and Apr. festivals. Open daily 5pm-2am.

Tolkien's House, Vsanicanijeva 8. From St. Mark's, go down Cirilometodska to a right on Vsanicanijeva. Quirky Irish pub festooned with memorabilia from J.R.R. Tolkien's fantasy books and a healthy dose of posters from the recent films. Tolkienana aside, the Irish music and the pints of Guinness (27kn) make this a great place to relax. Drinks 13-27kn. Open M-Sa 9am-11pm, Su 10am-11pm.

▶ DAYTRIPS FROM ZAGREB

Defining the crests of Zagreb's surrounding hilltops are the 56 mysterious **castles** of Hrvatsko Zagorje (the region north of Zagreb), formerly owned and constructed by warring Croatian nobles. They now lie in various states of disrepair, waiting to be conquered with cameras instead of cannons. The following two are in the best shape and are the most popular; consult *Zagreb and Surroundings*, available at the TIC in Zagreb (see **Tourist and Financial Services,** p. 160) to explore the rest.

▨ TRAKOŠČAN

From the Zagreb bus station, take a bus to Varaždin (1¾hr., 20 per day, 40kn), and change to a local bus (1.25hr.; 11 on weekdays, 7 on weekends; 22kn). Leave early in order to make the connection and still have plenty of time at the castle. ☎042 79 62 81. Open April-Oct. daily 9am-6pm; Nov.- Mar. daily 9am-3pm. 20kn, students 10kn. English booklet 20kn. Free guided tours in English; reservations necessary.

Trakoščan's magical white walls rise high above the surrounding deep forests and untouched rolling hills as if out of a fairy tale. Built as a defense tower in the 13th century, it passed to the Drašković nobility in 1584, who enlarged its structures, refurbished its rooms, and retained the castle until World War II. Today family portraits, tapestries, a collection of firearms and suits of armor from the 15th through the 19th centuries are on display. Leave time to wander around the quiet lake and to hike through the hills, if only to get away from the crowds of Croatian schoolchildren. All the food options are absurdly overpriced, so bring a sandwich or be prepared to lighten that wallet.

MEDVEDGRAD

From Trg b. Jelačića, take tram #14 or 8 to Mihaljevac (the last stop); transfer to bus #102 and get off at the 5th stop, just past the church. Or, take bus #102 from Britanski Trg and ask the driver where to get off. Walk back past the church and take the road that runs next to the graveyard. Continue on up the curvy road for 1hr. to the right or take the steep hike through the woods straight up the hill. Free.

Officially still part of Zagreb city district, Medvedgrad is a royal fortress that has guarded Mount Medvednica since the 13th century. The incredible views of the city from here make the trek worthwhile, and on weekends dozens of Zagreb teenagers and families take to the mountain for a break from the city. Visit the Dolac market before you go and picnic on the castle walls or visit the somewhat overpriced cafe in the castle itself. It is free and open to the public except on Independence Day (May 30), when the president lays flowers next to the eternal flame on the **Altar of the Homeland,** a monument to national war heroes.

CROATIA

PLITVICE LAKES NATIONAL PARK   )(0)53

Buses run from Zagreb (2½hr., every 30min., 39kn) and Zadar (3hr., every 30min., 50kn); ask the driver to drop you at one of the park entrances. Tourist office ☎75 10 15 or 75 10 14; fax 75 10 13; www.np-plitvice.tel.hr/np-pltivice. Park open daily 7am-7pm. July-Aug. 60kn, students 40kn; May-June and Sept.-Oct. 50kn/30kn; Jan.-Apr. and Nov.-Dec. 40kn/ 20kn. Tourist centers at each of the 3 park entrances provide maps and a comprehensive guide. Store your luggage at the center while you explore the lakes.

Plitvice Lakes National Park lies in the Krajina region, where Croatia's bloody war of independence began. Throughout the conflict (1991-95), the area was held by the Serbs, who planted **landmines** in the ground. There are over a million landmines in the surrounding area. **Under no circumstances should you leave the road and marked paths.** Don't let this warning stop you from visiting the natural wonder of the Plitvice lakes; just be intelligent about where you walk.

Though a bit of a trip from Zagreb, the Plitvice Lakes National Park (Nacionalni park Plitvička jezera) is definitely worth the transportation hassle. Some 30,000 hectares of forested hills, dappled with 16 lakes and hundreds more waterfalls, make up this pocket of paradise. Declared a national park in 1949, Plitvice was then added to the UNESCO World Heritage list in 1979 for the unique evolution of its lakes and waterfalls, formed through the interaction of water and petrified vegetation. A system of wooden pathways hovering just above the iridescent blue surface of the lakes leads up to the waterfalls. Two bus routes (every 20min.) help you get around the park, while one boat runs on the largest of the lakes (every 30min.). While most tourists circulate around the four lower lakes (Donja Jezera) to snap pictures of Plitvice's famous 78m waterfall, **Veliki Slap** (2-3hr.), the true wanderer explores the hidden falls of the 12 upper lakes, Gornja Jezera (4hr.).

ISTRIA

The Istrian Peninsula lies on the northern part of the Adriatic Coast, where the Mediterranean kisses the foot of the Alps. Influenced throughout history by its rather pushy neighbor, the region today seems almost more Italian than Croatian. According to some Italians, Istria is indeed more like heaven than earth: a Roman chronicler almost 2000 years ago remarked, "In Istria, Roman patricians feel like gods." Today, the mosaics of Poreč, ruins of Roman Pula, picturesque 19th-century Rovinj, and clear craters of the Adriatic make this area a true paradise.

PULA   ☎(0)52

An enormous billboard at the threshold of Pula's Old Town welcomes visitors to a "3000 year-old town." The Roman amphitheater, the second largest in the world, has been a center for entertainment since ancient times, featuring everything from gladiatorial combat to rock concerts. Pula still remains a town fit for lazy strolls through winding medieval alleys and jaunts out to the Brijuni Archipelago, where Tito built his palace. Relax on the rocky coast, mingle with locals in outdoor cafes, and soak in the vibrant culture of one of Istria's richest destinations.

▐ TRANSPORTATION

Trains: Kolodvorska 5 (☎54 19 82). Ticket window open daily 8am-4pm. To: **Rijeka** (2½hr., 4 per day, 41kn); **Zagreb** (7hr., 4 per day, 97-120kn); **Ljubljana, SLN** (7½hr., 3 per day, 120kn).

Buses: Matta Balotta 6 (☎21 89 28), for regional and international service. Ticket office open M-Sa 4:30am-8:30pm; tickets can also be purchased on board. To: **Opatija** (2hr., 16 per day, 47kn); **Poreč** (1½hr., 21 per day, 59kn); **Rijeka** (2½hr., 14-21 per day, 59kn); **Rovinj** (1hr., 17-23 per day, 21kn); **Šibenik** (9hr., 3 per day, 195kn); **Zagreb** (5-6hr., 15 per day, 137kn); **Trieste, ITA** (3¾hr., 4 per day, 98kn); **Venice, ITA** (6hr., 1 per day, 164kn).

Ferries: Jadroagent Riva 14 (☎21 04 31; fax 21 17 99). Open M-Th 7am-8pm, F 6am-8pm. To: **Zadar** (8hr., 4 per week, 88kn); **Trieste, ITA** (5hr., 1 per day, 60kn); **Venice, ITA** (6hr., 2 per week, 264kn).

Public Transportation: Purchase tickets on the bus for 10kn or at any newsstand for 8kn. Each ticket is good for two trips; just punch the other end of the ticket when you get on the second time. Most local buses pass by the garden on Giardini, next to the regional and international bus station (see above) and stop running around 10:30pm.

Taxis: ☎22 32 28. Catch one across from the bus station on Via Carrara. Average fare starts at 20kn plus 8kn per km and 3kn per piece of luggage.

▐ ORIENTATION

Sergijevaca, Pula's main street, circles around the central hill in **Stari Grad** (Old Town) and turns into **Kandlerova** after **Trg Forum. Castropola,** a parallel street higher up, also circles the hilltop. To get to Sergijevaca from the **train station,** walk on Kolodvorska for 5min., keeping the sea to your right. Turn right onto **Istarska** at the **amphitheater.** Follow Istarska through its name change to **Giardini,** passing the inter-city and local **bus stations** on your right. After the park, a right through the **Slavoluk Sergijevaca** (Arch of the Sergians) leads to Sergijevaca, which runs down to both the forum and the waterfront.

▐ PRACTICAL INFORMATION

Tourist Office: Tourism Office Pula, Forum 3 (☎21 29 87 or 21 91 97; fax 21 18 55; www.pulainfo.hr). Friendly English-speaking staff provides useful city maps and information about hotels, apartments, and private rooms. Ferry and bus schedules. Open M-Sa 9am-8pm, Su 10am-6pm.

Currency Exchange: Zagrebačka Banka (☎21 47 44), at the corner of Giardini and Flanatička, exchanges cash for free and **traveler's checks** for 1.5% commission. Open M-F 7:30am-7pm, Sa 8am-noon. There is a currency exchange machine outside **Kaptol Banka,** Istarska 5, next to the bus station.

American Express: Atlas Travel Agency, Starih Statuta 1 (☎21 41 72; fax 21 40 94). Open Apr.-Oct. M-Sa 8am-2pm and 5:30-8pm, Su 9am-12:30pm and 6-8pm. Nov.-March M-F 8am-2pm and 5:30-8pm.

Luggage Storage: At the bus station. 7kn per hr., over 15kg 13kn per hr. Open M-F 4:30-9:30am, 10am-6pm, and 6:30-11:30pm; Sa 5am-11pm; Su 5:30am-11pm.

English-Language Bookstore: Istarske Knjižare, Giardini 9 (☎21 81 85). A sparse selection of books from Agatha Christie to John Grisham, plus **maps** of Croatia and books on the history of the region. Open M-F 8am-noon and 5-8pm, Sa 8am-1pm.

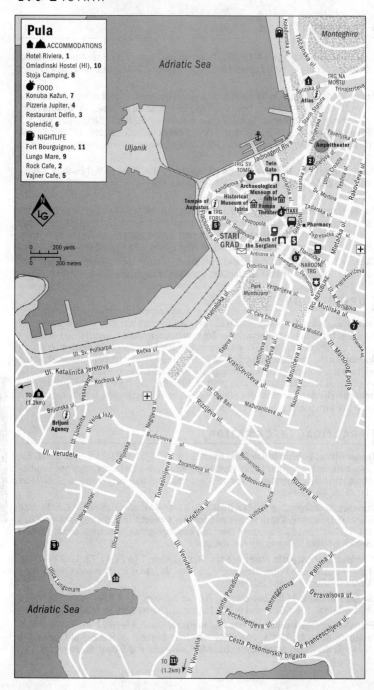

Pula

▲▲ ACCOMMODATIONS

Hotel Riviera, **1**
Omladinski Hostel (HI), **10**
Stoja Camping, **8**

🍎 FOOD

Konuba Kažun, **7**
Pizzeria Jupiter, **4**
Restaurant Delfin, **3**
Splendid, **6**

🍺 NIGHTLIFE

Fort Bourguignon, **11**
Lungo Mare, **9**
Rock Cafe, **2**
Vajner Cafe, **5**

Police: Trg Republike (☎53 26 29 or 53 26 28). Open 24hr.

Pharmacy: Ljekarna Centar, Giardini 15 (☎22 25 44). Open 24hr.

Hospital: Clinical Hospital Center, Zagrebačka 34 (☎21 44 33).

Internet Access: DIGI, Glaminićev uspon 2 (☎38 00 88; www.digi-hr.com). Entrance off Sergijevaca just below the Arch of the Sergians, up the stairs to the right. 20kn per hr., students 18kn. Happy hour (1-6pm) 10kn per hr. Open daily 9am-9pm. **Cyber Café,** Flanatička 14 (☎21 53 45). Facing away from the Arch of the Sergians, walk up Flanatička past the market area. New chic cafe with 3 terminals. 23kn per hr. Open M-Th 7am-10pm, F-Sa 7am-1am.

Post Office: Danteov Trg 4 (☎22 22 50 or 22 24 21; fax 21 89 11). Go to the left for mail and to the right for Poste Restante and telephones. Open M-F 7am-8pm, Sa 7am-2pm, Su 8am-noon.

Postal Code: 52100.

ACCOMMODATIONS

Several agencies help tourists find reasonably priced **private rooms.** The **tourist office** offers the best deals. **Arenaturist,** Giardini 4, keeps lists of private rooms in Zagreb with good locations. (☎21 86 96; fax 21 22 77; www.arenaturist.hr. July-Aug. singles 68kn; doubles 116kn. June and Sept. 63kn/110kn. 50% more for 1 night, 25% for 2-3 nights. Registration 9kn. Open M-Sa 8am-8pm, Su 8am-1pm. ❷)

Omladinski Hostel (HI), Zaljev Valsaline 4 (☎39 11 33; fax 39 11 06; www.nncomp.com/hfhs). From the bus station, turn right and follow the street to a small park on Giardini where local buses stop. Take bus #2 to "Veruda" and ask the bus driver where to get off. Follow the signs downhill to this slice of paradise. This hostel has its own private cove, a bar, table tennis, a giant trampoline, and very clean communal rooms. Simple breakfast included. Reception open 8am-9pm. Call ahead. July-Aug. 97kn; June and Sept. 82kn; May and Oct. 66kn; Nov. and Apr. 63kn. Camping 30kn. ❶

Hotel Riviera, Splitska 1 (☎21 11 66; fax 21 91 17). Across the park from the amphitheater, by the waterfront. Hotels in Pula are expensive, but at least at Hotel Riviera you get your money's worth. This elegant old yellow hotel has views of the waterfront (for which, of course, you have to pay extra) and a wonderful terrace for coffee or cocktails. Singles 280-360kn; doubles 460-640kn. ❸

Stoja Camping (☎38 71 44, reservations 22 20 43; fax 38 77 48). From Giardini (see directions to hostel above), take bus #1 toward Stoja to the end. Within walking distance of town, with dozens of pitches of different sizes. Also sports facilities and beaches. June-Aug. 42kn; Sept.-May 28kn. ❶

FOOD

Fresh fish, meat, and cheese are available in the market building. (Fish market open M-Sa 7am-1:30pm, Su 7am-noon; meat and cheese markets open M-Sa 7-noon, Su 7am-2pm). **Puljanka** grocery store has several branches throughout the town, including one at Sergijevaca 4. (Open M-F 6am-8pm, Sa 8am-1:30pm, Su 7am-noon.) Buffets and fast-food restaurants line **Sergijevaca.** There is an open-air fruit and vegetable **market** at Trg Narodni, off Flanatička. (Open daily 6am-2pm.)

Konuba Kažun, Vrtlavska 1 (☎22 31 84). From Trg Republike, walk up Mutilska Ulica; Vrtlavska is to the right. Konuba serves up simple, excellent Istrian specialties (35-80kn). Grilled pork sausages 35kn. Seafood 40-100kn. Open M-F 9:30am-midnight, Sa-Su noon-midnight. ❷

THE BIG SPLURGE

VALSABBION

Perhaps the best meal you'll ever have. Rated the best restaurant in Istria every year from 1996 to 2001 and the best restaurant on the Croatian Coast in 1998, Valsabbion is a Slow Food restaurant, part of a growing number of restaurants and groups of individuals throughout the world who reject the dominance of pre-prepared "fast food." At Valsabbion, every dish is prepared from scratch after you order it, which makes for long waits and excellent food. The menu features an extensive list of specialties, and emphasizes local produce and styles of cooking. A polite note in the menu informs guests that if they really want the best meal, and the best wine to go with it, they'll just listen to what the waiters have to suggest rather than deciding on their own. They're right; the waiters know everything about all the dishes, which ingredients are freshest, what the weather's like that day, and how that all adds up to the perfect meal for you. *(Pješčana uvala IX/26. To get there, take the #2 bus from Giardini, toward the hostel. Instead of turning right down the hill after getting off, turn left and walk along Premorskih Brigada for about five minutes, then turn right on the first unnamed road that leads down to Veruda Marina. Walk along the marina for about 20 minutes until you round the tip of the peninsula; Valsabbion will be on your right 100m after you leave the marina. ☎21 80 33. Open daily for lunch and dinner. Appetizers 45-115kn, entrees 95-140kn.* ❹ *)*

—A. Nicholas Gossen

Restaurant Delfin, Trg sv. Tome 1 (☎22 32 89), across from the 4th-century cathedral. The fish-themed decor doesn't detract from Delphin's cheap, delicious seafood. In nice weather, sit on the patio with a pleasant view of the cathedral. Entrees 35-55kn. Open daily 11am-10pm. ❷

Pizzeria Jupiter, Castropola 42 (☎21 43 33). Walk behind the bus station along Carrarina Ulica, past the Archaeological Museum. Curve around sharply to the left up the ramp; the pizzeria will be on your left. Lauded by Pulians young and old, this place is the perfect spot for a bite to eat before a concert at the amphitheater. Pizza 20-39kn. Open M-F 9am-11pm, Sa-Su 1-11pm. AmEx. ❶

Splendid, Trg Privoga Svibvija 5 (☎22 32 84). Across from the far side of the market building at Narodni Trg. For really cheap eating, a Croatian version of the school lunch lady will fill your tray with delights in this cafeteria-style restaurant—meat, fish, soup, sausage, and salad for 6-22kn. Open M-F 9:30am-9pm, Sa-Su 9:30am-3pm. ❶

👁 SIGHTS

🏛 AMPHITHEATER. Built in the first century AD during the reign of the Roman Emperor Vespasian, the arena was used for gladiatorial combat until sport killing was outlawed in the 4th century. Although the blood has long since dried and the amphitheater has suffered through centuries of neglect, it's easy to imagine the battles that took place in this impressive stone structure. Today, this venue houses entertainment of a different sort, showcasing the area's big-ticket concerts. An underground system of passages originally constructed as a drainage system now serves as a **museum** of local wine production. *(From the bus station, take a left on Istarska. Open daily 8am-9pm. 16kn, students 8kn. English booklet 30kn.)*

ARCH OF THE SERGIANS. (Slavoluk obitelji Sergii.) The arch was built in 29 BC for three local members of the Sergii family, one of whom had commanded a Roman battalion at the battle of Actium between Mark Antony and Octavius. The sturdy stone arch now serves as a gateway to Sergijevaca, Pula's main street. *(From the bus station, follow Istarska as it turns into Giardini; the arch is on the right.)*

THE FORUM. The Forum, at the end of Sergijevaca, was the central gathering place for political, religious, and economic debates in Roman days. Today the original cobblestones lie buried safely 1.2m beneath the ground and the square is used primarily for cafe lounging and gazing at the nearby Temple of Augustus.

TEMPLE OF AUGUSTUS. (Augustov hram.) This remarkably preserved temple, constructed between 2 BC and AD 14, was dedicated to Roman Emperor Augustus. There were originally two similar temples nearby. The larger one was destroyed but the rear wall of the smaller one, the Temple of Diana, now serves as the facade of the City Hall. Inside the Temple of Augustus you'll find a very small **museum** containing pieces of Roman statues and stone sculpture from the first and second centuries AD. *(At the Forum. Open M-F 9:30am-1:30pm and 6-9pm, Sa-Su 9:30am-1:30pm. 4kn, students 2kn.)*

OTHER SIGHTS. Up the street from Sergijevaca, the **Citadel** has guarded Pula since Roman times. Last year it lay down its guns to house the **Historical Museum of Istria,** an unimpressive maritime and military history exhibit. *(Open daily 10am-10pm. 10kn, students 5kn.)* On the nearby hilltop stand the remains of a **Roman Theater,** and, farther down, the **Twin Gate** (Dvojna vrata). If ancient history excites you, you'll be ecstatic about the **Archaeological Museum of Istria** (Arheološki Muzej Istre). The museum offers an overview of Istria's history, with an emphasis on Roman stone artifacts. *(☎ 21 86 09. Open M-Sa 9am-8pm, Su 10am-3pm.)*

▮ ⚑ FESTIVALS AND BEACHES

Amphitheater shows are impressive and the highlight of a trip to Pula. Open seating allows you to sit or stand wherever you can climb; grab a seat and snack on toasted pumpkin seeds and a pint of *Ožujsko.* Buy tickets at the theater, from the bookings agency **Lira Intersound** (☎ 21 78 01; open M-F 8am-3pm; prices vary), or from a tourist agency. Agencies also sell tickets to the popular **Biker Days Festival** during the last few days of July (150kn). Exhibitions at this chrome and leather celebration have included female mud wrestling. The **Pula Film Festival** (www.pulafilmfestival.com) during the last week of July and the **Art and Music Festival** during the first week of August offer fun for fewer kunas (40-100kn). The **International Accordian School** hits town in the second half of July. Take some classes or just stop by for a few concerts. Keep your eyes open for fliers advertising the annual **Punk Festival "Monte Paradiso,"** which turns an old army barracks into a stage and mosh pit in the first weekend in August. **Kino Zagreb,** Giardini 1, the only permanent cinema in Pula, shows nightly Hollywood movies with Croatian subtitles. (Screenings nightly at 7 and 9pm. 15-20kn, M night special 12kn.)

You wouldn't guess it when looking at the shipyards, but Pula is riddled with private coves and **beaches.** Take bus #1 to the Stoja campground. Facing the sea, walk left down the coastline. For quieter, less crowded beaches, head to **Fažana** (see the **Brijuni Archipelago,** below). A pleasant pebble beach curves in front of the hostel offers paddle boats (40kn per hour) and scuba diving (30min. novice dive 200kn).

▮ NIGHTLIFE

▩ **Fort Bourguignon,** Zlatne Stijene 6c. Take bus #2 or 7 from Giardini to the last stop; walk straight toward the sea, curving around to the left. Continue past the cheesy illustrated Pyramid disco to the pulsing stone building. A cafe, club, and art gallery sit in a 135-year-old stone fort overlooking the Adriatic. Hosts crazy raves (10pm to noon; 70kn) about once a month. Open M-F 8am-midnight, Sa 11am-4am, Su 6am-noon.

Lungo Mare, Cortanova Ujula bb (☎ 39 10 84). Take bus #2 or 7 from Giardini, get off at Verud, walk right on Verudela to the Hotel Pula and then go down to the sea. Cafe by day, raging club by night, this outdoor chameleon blasts music over its own cove. 1L *Favorit* 25kn. On the beach and along the road below the club, hundreds of young Pulians gather for raucous Croatian tailgates most Th, F, and Sa nights in summer. BYOB. No cover. Open M-Su 10am-4am.

Rock Cafe, Scallerova 8 (☎21 09 75). Not to be confused with the "harder" worldwide chain, this sturdy oak bar with pool tables and pictures of Hendrix and Morrison has real rock 'n roll character and a lively local scene. 0.5L *Pivo Točeno* (draft) 10kn. Beer-sponsored parties some F-Sa nights. Open M-Sa 8am-midnight, Su noon-midnight.

Vajner Cafe, Forum 2 (☎21 65 02). Modern art hangs on the walls while outdoor tables provide a perfect view of the Temple of Augustus. Check out the bank vault next to the bar. Dupli cappuccino 8kn, mixed drinks 15-25kn. Open daily 7:30am-midnight.

🎒 DAYTRIP FROM PULA

🏛BRIJUNI ARCHIPELAGO

Unless you're staying at the Brijuni Hotel, the only way to see the island is with a guided tour run by the Brijuni Agency, Brijunska 10 (☎52 58 83 or 52 58 82; fax 52 11 24; www.np.brijuni.hr.), in Fazana. Tours daily 11:30am; call the day before to reserve a spot and to check if they're offering a tour in your language. Round-trip ferry and a 4hr. tour 160kn. Open daily 8am-7pm. To get to Fazana, take a local bus from the station on Istarske Divizije in Pula (20min., 1 per hr., 10kn).

The Brijuni Archipelago, just a short bus and a lovely ferry ride away from Pula, is one of Croatia's most fascinating and beautiful regions. Even if you're only spending a few days in Istria, make sure to reserve one for Brijuni. It's got something for everyone—animals for the kids, ruins for the historians, politics for the governmentally inclined, medical history for the doctors, and a general sense of mystery. The archipelago's largest island, **Veli Brijun,** was once home to a Roman resort and a Venetian colony. More recently, this region has seen the discovery of how to prevent malaria, and the construction of former Yugoslav president Josip Brož Tito's residence—if you can call the opulent complex that Tito erected a "residence." The mini-trolley tour includes a ride through a safari park inhabited by such curiosities as a pair of elephants given to Tito by Indira Ghandhi. The walking part of the tour leads through a picture gallery full of photos of Tito in all his publicity-grubbing glory. After the tour ends, stay and explore the island on your own for a few hours. It's worth the steep 25kn per hour to rent a bicycle (located on the far side of the Hotel Neptune from the pier) and pedal off to some of the deserted beaches that surround the island.

POREČ ☎(0)52

Poreč sits on a tiny peninsula that juts out into the Adriatic, little more than a stone's throw away from Slovenia and Italy. The town is brimming with Gothic and Romanesque houses, unique 6th century Byzantine mosaics and the ruins of Roman temples. Unfortunately, it is also brimming with tourists. Poreč is surrounded by resorts and full of hotels, to the point that in peak season tourists can literally outnumber locals by more than two-to-one. But if you're prepared to pay the high prices and brush up on your German, Poreč is definitely a worthwhile stop as you island-hop down the coast.

🚍 TRANSPORTATION. The **bus station** is at Rade Končara 1 (☎43 21 53). To reach the central Trg Slobode, turn left out of the bus station, walk down the street, and take a right onto the pedestrian Milanovića. To: **Pula** (1hr., 14 per day, 29kn); **Rijeka** (2hr., 8 per day, 49kn); **Rovinj** (1hr., 7-10 per day, 23kn); **Zagreb** (6hr., 8 per day, 139kn); **Ljubljana, SLN** (5hr.; June-July and Sept. 3 per day, Aug. 4 per day, Oct.-May 1 per day; 88kn); **Trieste, ITA** (2hr., 2 per day, 51kn).

■ 7 ORIENTATION AND PRACTICAL INFORMATION. Poreč is easy to navigate. The main pedestrian walkway, **Decumanus,** runs through Stari Grad (Old Town) and is lined with shops, cafes, and restaurants. The **tourist office,** Zagrebačka 9, is right up the road from Trg Slobode and should be your first stop. (☎45 12 93; fax 45 16 65. Open May-Oct. M-Sa 8am-10pm, Su 9am-1pm and 4-10pm; Nov.-April daily 8am-4:30pm. **Zagrebačka Banka,** Obala M. Tita bb, by the sea, **exchanges cash** for no commission and cashes **traveler's checks** for 1.5% commission. (☎45 11 66. Open M-F 7:30am-7pm, Sa 8am-noon.) There is a MC **ATM** and a **currency exchange** machine outside. MC/V ATMs are available throughout the old town. Other services include: **luggage storage,** at the bus station (open daily 5-9am, 9:30am-5:30pm, and 6-9pm. 5kn.); a **pharmacy,** Trg Slobode 13 (☎43 23 62; open M-Sa 7:30am-8pm; **Internet Access** at **Cybermac,** around the corner from the tourist office (☎42 70 75; open M-Sa 8am-noon, Su 10am-noon. 42kn per hr.); and the **post office,** opposite the church at Pino Brudičin 1 (☎43 18 08; open M-F 8am-3pm, Sa 8am-1pm). **Postal Code:** 52441.

■ ■ ACCOMMODATIONS AND FOOD. Sol Avis ❶, Zagrebačka 17, books **private rooms.** (☎43 40 00; fax 45 33 77; rex-porec@pu.tel.hr. Open June-Aug. daily 8:30am-2pm and 5-9pm; Sept.-May 8:30am-1pm and 5-9pm. Singles 70-120kn; doubles 85-200kn; apartments 155-230kn per person. 30% more for stays under 4 nights.) **Hotel Poreč ❸,** R. Končara 1, has modern and clean rooms with TVs, fridges, and telephones. (☎45 18 11; fax 45 17 30; www.hotelporec.com. Singles 210-304kn; doubles 294-504kn. 20% more for stays under 3 nights. AmEx/MC/V.) **Camping** is by far your pocket's best friend. Both of the following camps offer a wide range of services, including grocery stores, restaurants, and sports facilities. The large **Lanterna Camp ❶** is 13km to the north and has a 3km beach. (☎40 45 00. Open Mar.-Oct. 17-34kn per person; tents 24kn, with electricity 42kn.) Save on your laundry bill at the nudist camp and apartment-village **Solaris ❶.** (☎40 40 00. Open Mar.-Oct. No tents rented. 14-34kn per person; apartments 100-200kn per person.) Both camps are accessible by the same bus from the station (25min., 9 per day, 12kn).

There is a **supermarket** at Zagrebačka 2, next to the church. (Open M-Sa 7am-9pm, Su 7am-noon). **Ulixes ❹,** Decumanus 2, just off the main tourist strip, offers a daily selection of fresh meat and seafood, such as grilled calamari (60kn). The beautiful outdoor terrace overlooks the stone walls of Stari Grad. (☎45 11 32. Open daily noon-midnight.) **Gostionica Istra ❸,** Milanovića 30, by the bus station, offers similar fish and meat fare, as well as a selection of pasta dishes. (☎43 46 36. Open daily noon-10pm.)

■ SIGHTS. Starting at Trg Slobode, walk down to the **Pentagonal Tower** (Peter-okunta Pula), built in 1447. Continuing down Decumanus, turn right on Sv. Eleuterija to find ■ **St. Euphrasius's Basilica** (Eufrazijeva bazilika), which was placed on UNESCO's World Heritage list in 1997 for its beautifully preserved mosaics. Across from the basilica entrance stands the octagonal **baptistry** and **bell tower,** which you can climb for a view of the tiled roofs of Poreč. Don't miss the **museum,** to the right of the basilica entrance. Housed in the ancient Bishop's palace, the museum displays fragments of the intricate floor mosaics from the original chapel floor. *(Services held Su 11am and 7pm; open M-Sa 10am-6pm, Su 11am-8pm. Basilica free, chapel museum 10kn, belltower 10kn.)* Back on Decumanus, head down through Trg Marator and to the right. Here are the remains of the Roman **Temple of Neptune,** from the first century AD. Finish up by returning along Obala m. Tita, next to the ocean, to the **Round Tower,** a 15th-century defensive structure. Climb to the top for a macchiato (5kn) at the Caffe Torne Rotunda. (Open daily 10am-1am.)

CROATIA

◪⬗ BEACHES AND ENTERTAINMENT. Beaches in Poreč—and along most of the Istrian coast—are steep and rocky, but offer convenient tanning shelves cut into the shoreline. The best sites near town are south of the marina. Hop on the passing mini-train or face the sea on Obala m. Tita, turn left, and head along the coast for about 15min. to reach the **Blue Lagoon** (Plava Laguna). Walk for another 10min. to get to the **Green Lagoon** (Zelena Laguna). These resorts offer waterslides, tennis, and minigolf, most of which are open to non-guests. The only real way to escape the crowds is to continue past the Green Lagoon towards the marina (30min.). A **ferry** (every 30min. 7am-1am; round-trip 15kn at kiosk nearby) leaves from the marina for the less popular, quieter beaches on **Saint Nicholas Island** (Sveti Nikola), just across the harbor. To see more of the coast, rent a bike for 15kn an hr. from **Ivona**, Prvomajska 2, across the square and down a block from the information office. (☎43 40 46. Open M-Sa 8am-1pm and 4pm-7pm, Su 8am-1pm.) Ask for a **free bike map.** Its two marked trails take you through more than 50km of olive groves, forests, vineyards, and medieval villages.

◪ NIGHTLIFE. Any beach that has a name also has a hotel complex and a disco, invariably frequented by (mostly German) tourists of all ages. In Stari Grad, ▨ **Capitol,** Vladimira Nazora 9, attracts large crowds and good times but doesn't really get rolling each week until Thursday. (☎41 51 51. Cover 20kn. Open nightly 10pm-5am.) To dance with a more local crowd take a 10min. walk south down the beach to the open-air, Roman-columned **Colonia Iulia Parentium.** (Open June-Oct. daily 10pm-4am.) **Club No. 1,** Marafor 10, the coolest of a cluster of little bars and cafes in the square at the end of Decumanus, stays lively throughout the week. (*B-52* or *Blow Job* 8kn. 0.3L *Favorit* 8kn. Open nightly 6pm-4am.) With smoky portraits hanging on the walls, **Bar Casablanca,** Eufrazijeva 4, pays homage to Humphrey Bogart. (☎45 31 31. Open daily 9am-1am.)

ROVINJ ☎(0)52

At the beginning of the 19th century, Rovinj (ro-VEEN; pop. 15,000) became a favorite summer resort for the Austro-Hungarian emperors and their friends. Modern vacationers still find a special resort hideaway here. Once the most important fishing settlement in Istria and a fortress for the Venetian Navy, Rovinj and its crystal-clear waves provide a pleasant setting for a quiet getaway.

⯊ TRANSPORTATION

With no train station, Rovinj sends **buses** to: **Poreč** (1hr., 7-10 per day, 23kn); **Pula** (1hr., every 30min., 21kn); **Rijeka** (3½hr., 8-11 per day, 70kn); **Zagreb** (5-6hr., 9 per day, 126kn); **Ljubljana, SLN** (5hr., 1 per day in high season, 120kn); **Trieste, ITA** (2½hr., 2-3 per day, 82kn). **Bikes** are available at **Bike Planet,** Trg na Lokvi 3, across the street from the bus station. (☎81 11 61. 20kn per hr., 70kn per day. Open M-Sa 8:30am-12:30pm and 5-8pm.) The tourist office (see below) has **maps** for suggested bike routes 22-60km in length.

◪⯊ ORIENTATION AND PRACTICAL INFORMATION

Turn left out of the bus station and walk down Nazora toward the marina or up on Karera to the **Stari Grad.** Orientation can be tricky at first, as street signs and numbers are often difficult to find or non-existent. Tourist agencies offer free miniscule **maps,** but they're impossible to read. Buy a large map for 15-20kn at any agency and save your eyesight, or just wander; it's not that big of a town.

Tourist Office: Turistička Zajednica Rovinj, Pino Budičin 12 (☎81 15 66; fax 81 60 07; www.istra.com/rovinj.). From the bus station, walk down Nazora to the sea and follow the waterfront on your right for about 10min. The official tourist agency. Open June 16-Aug. daily 8am-8pm; Sept.-June 15 daily 8am-4pm.

Currency Exchange: Istarska Banka, on Aldo Negri (☎81 32 33), cashes **traveler's checks** and **exchanges currency** for no commission. Open M-F 7:30am-7pm, Sa 7:30am-noon.

Luggage Storage: At the bus station, on M. Benussi (☎81 14 53), offers **luggage storage.** 10kn up to 30 kg, 15kn for heavier bags. Open 6:30am-9pm.)

Pharmacy: (☎81 35 89). With your back to the bus station, turn right on M. Benussi. Open M-F 8am-9pm, Sa 8am-4pm, Su 9am-noon.

Internet Access: Planet, Svetog Križa 1 (☎84 04 94), a little place past the tourist agency and right before Veli Jože (see **Food,** below). 4kn per 10min. Open M-Sa 10am-12:30pm and 5-9:30pm, Su 5-9:30pm. **Caffe Bar "Aurora,"** Prolaz M. Maretic 8 (☎83 03 33). From the bus station, walk up Carducci, past the little church on your right and turn left on Lorenzetto. The cafe is set back from the road on your right, across the park. Try a Campari-esque Istra bitter vodka for 10kn. 30kn per hr. Open daily 9am-9pm.

Post Office: (☎81 14 66). To the right from the bus station, with **telephones** inside and out. Open M-Sa 7am-8pm, Su 7am-2pm.)

Postal Code: 52210.

⌂⌂ ACCOMMODATIONS AND FOOD. As usual, your best bet for a budget room is to avoid the hotel scene and search around for a **private room.** Across the street from the bus station, **Natale ❷,** Carducci 4, offers decent prices and friendly service; call ahead in the summer. It also *exchanges cash* and *traveler's checks* for no commission. (☎81 33 65; fax 83 02 39; www.natale.hr. Singles 80-130kn; doubles 100-160kn; 2-person apartments 192-290kn. 100% more for only 1 night; 50% for 2; 30% for 3. Tax 7kn. Registration 15kn.) Simple, clean rooms are available in the massive **Hotel Monte Mulini ❷.** Facing the sea at the end of Nazora, walk to the left all the way around past the marina and then up the stone steps on your left. (☎81 15 12; fax 81 58 82. Breakfast included. Singles 150-220kn; doubles 300-440. AmEx/MC/V.) For those with tents, **Camping Polari ❶,** 2.5km east of town, also has a supermarket and several bars. To get there, take one of the frequent buses (6min., 9kn) from the bus station. (☎80 15 01; fax 81 13 95. June 74kn per person, July-Aug. 87kn. Closed Oct.-Mar.)

Buy **groceries** at Nazora 6, between the bus station and the sea. (Open M-Sa 6:30am-7:30pm, Su 7-11:30am.) There is an **open-air market** on Trg Valdibora. (Open daily 6am-10pm.) Don't miss the local seafood hot spot ▨ **Veli Jože ❸,** Svetog Križa 3, located at the end of the marina toward the tip of the peninsula. Enjoy some of the best food around amid funky maritime artifacts, including a primitive deep-sea diving suit. Prices vary by season, but you can usually get first-rate fish for 240kn per kilo. (☎81 63 37. Open M-Su noon-2am. AmEx/DC/MC/V.) For a great deal, head across the street to **Stella di Mare ❶,** S. Croche 4, with its terrace overlooking the ocean and pizzas that barely fit on the plate. (Pizzas and pasta 25-45kn. Open daily 10am-11pm. AmEx/MC/V.)

◙ SIGHTS. Although Rovinj has been surrounded by walls since the 7th century, only three of the original seven gates—**St. Benedict's, Holy Cross,** and **the Portico**—survive today. When entering the Old Town, you'll probably walk through the **Balbijer Arch** (Balbijer luk), a Baroque structure built on the site of the 17th-century outer gate that now serves as the principal threshold of the Old Town. Perhaps the best view of town is from a distance: old houses packed on the tiny peninsula lead up to the 18th-century **St. Euphemia's Church** (Crkva sv. Eufemije), built when

FROM THE ROAD

NO PLACE LIKE *SOBE*

Any budget traveler in Croatia will end up spending at least some time in private rooms, which are often the only vaguely affordable accommodations available. But I've found that private rooms are more than just a financial necessity in Croatia; they're also a chance to glimpse beyond typical tourism into the private lives of people you otherwise only see working behind shop counters or walking down the street.

Perhaps the most entertaining aspect of staying in private rooms is the variety of situations in which you find yourself. Some hosts invite you into their living room for coffee and whiskey at 10am; others demand payment with an outstretched hand, toss you the key, and slam the door behind them as they leave, never to be seen again. Some rooms are so cavernous that you could play tennis in them; others are so small you're more likely to giggle than complain when you see them.

(continued on the next page)

Rovinj was a fortress under the Venetian Navy. Most people trek here to see the 6th-century Byzantine **sarcophagus** containing the remains of St. Euphemia, the 3rd-century patron of Rovinj. During Roman Emperor Diocletian's reign, Euphemia and other Christians were imprisoned and tortured for refusing to deny their faith. The 15-year-old martyr survived the wheel, but not the pack of lions. Amazingly, the beasts left her body intact and her fellow Christians then encapsulated it in a sarcophagus. The vessel made its way to Constantinople but disappeared from there in AD 800—only to float mysteriously to the shoreline of Rovinj later that year. Today it lies behind the right-hand altar, often visited by locals, particularly on St. Euphemia's Day (Sept. 16). It's definitely worth the 10kn to climb up the rickety stairs to the **bell tower** (6lm), for a majestic view of the city and sea. Atop the tower there is a 4m copper statue which changes direction with the winds. During the summer, the lawn outside hosts many classical music performances. (Services Su at 10:30am and 7pm. Open M-Sa 10am-2pm and 4-6pm, Su 4-6pm.)

The excellent **City Museum of Rovinj**, Trg Maršala Tita 11, has changing exhibits including local modern art, archaeological exhibits, and three millennia worth of local paintings. (Open M 9am-12:30pm, Tu-Sa 9am-12:30pm and 6-9:30pm. 10kn.) Boats anchored in the harbor are raring to take off on trips to the 22 nearby **islands** (around 50kn) or to the **Lim Fjord** (around 90kn), a sea inlet that separates Rovinj from Poreč. You can buy tickets at the tourist office or from boat owners.

◪ BEACHES. For the prettiest **beaches** in the area, take a ferry to **Red Island** (Crveni Otok; 17 per day, 20kn). Nude sunbathing is permitted. On the mainland, reach natural rock shelves by walking past the marina for 30 minutes (facing the sea, go left) and cutting through **Golden Cape** (Zlatni vrt). Alternatively, join locals on the patios cut into the tip of the peninsula for sunset seating. Ferries from the marina also go to beaches on **Katarina Island** (1 per hr., 10kn).

◪ ENTERTAINMENT. At night, Rovinj takes on a mellow, laid-back air. Most of the action takes place along the marina. **Bar Sax Caffe,** Ribarski Prolaz 4, tucked away in a an alley just off the marina, hosts lively patrons inside and out. There's a bar but no sax. (Open daily 8am-3am.) Recline in neo-colonial decadence at **Zanzi Bar,** also along the marina. This hip new bar offers a wide range of high-octane cocktails for 20-40kn as well as other drinks. (Open daily 8am-1am.) **Cayenne Disco Club,** Ob. Aldorizmondo bb, is a moored ferry boat-turned-party house that offers drinks upstairs and dancing in the hull. The rolling of the boat provides a convenient excuse when you're no longer able to walk. (☎81 73 67. Open Apr.-Sept. nightly 6pm-5am, but things don't really start up until 11pm. Cover 20kn.)

On August 23-24, Rovinj takes to the sky for **Rovinjska noć** (Rovinj Night), its famous annual night of fireworks. International artists come to display their work at the traditional open-air art festival **Grisia**, held on the street of the same name (second Sunday of Aug.). **Kanfanar** (July 25th), a folk festival dedicated to St. Jacob, features traditional Istrian music played on the *mih* (bagpipes) and the *roženice* (Istrian flute), as well as a healthy spread of regional cuisine.

GULF OF KVARNER

Blessed by long summers and gentle sea breezes, the islands just off the coast of mainland Croatia are natural tourist attractions. Larger Krk bears the brunt of the invasion. Farther south and away from the mainland, Rab is less visited, less disturbed, and well worth the longer trip.

RIJEKA ☎(0)51

A typical sprawling Croatian port town, Rijeka (ri-YE-kah) is a functional transportation hub but not exactly the prettiest stop on the Croatian coast. It earns its keep by providing access to the islands in the Gulf of Kvarner and much of the Dalmatian coast—destinations that warrant a trip through as many Rijekas as necessary.

TRANSPORTATION

Trains: Kralja Tomislava 1. Info desk open daily 7am-6:45pm. Escape to: **Split** via Ogulin (7hr., 2 per day, 123kn); **Zagreb** (3½hr., 7 per day, 77-117kn); **Berlin, GER** (11¾hr., 3 per day, 1185kn); **Budapest, HUN** (9hr., 1 per day, 254kn); **Ljubljana, SLN** (2½hr., 4 per day, 78kn); **Vienna, AUS** (9hr., 1 per day, 1250kn).

Buses: Žabica 1, down Krešimirova, a right from the train station. (☎33 88 11. Open daily 5:30am-9pm.) To: **Dubrovnik** (12hr., 3 per day, 223kn); **Krk Town** (1½hr., 13 per day, 33kn); **Pula** (2½hr., every hr., 56kn); **Split** (8hr., 12 per day, 171kn); **Zagreb** (4hr., every hr., 93kn); **Ljubljana, SLN** (3hr., 2 per day, 60kn); **Sarajevo, BOS** (13hr.; 2 per week, F and Su; 240kn); **Trieste, ITA** (2hr., 4 per day, 58kn).

Ferries: For tickets, face the sea from the bus station and go left to **Jadrolinija**, Riva 16. (☎66 61 00. Open

Some commonalities, however, are equally striking as you move from room to room. First are the hideous, battleship-sized armoires that take up half of every Croatian bedroom, large or small. Second is the overbearing presence of Catholic kitsch art in nearly every Croatian home. In any given room, odds are there will be a massive, life-size portrait of the Holy Family, usually in pastel colors and featuring cuddly animals.

Then, there's the ubiquitous and mysterious Weeping Child, a maudlin Balkan tradition that extends throughout Serbia and Montenegro and Albania. The portrait usually features a young girl with an enormous, glistening tear tumbling down one rosy cheek. It's not entirely clear to me what, exactly, the Weeping Child is supposed to signify, and I have as yet to get a straight answer. They're sort of the equivalent of the Norman Rockwell posters in the United States; everyone has one, but no one's quite sure why. So wherever you are and whatever the room, sit back and enjoy the unique experience of the Croatian *sobe*.

—A. Nicholas Gossen

M and W-F 7am-6pm, Tu and Sa 7am-8pm.) To: **Dubrovnik** (18-24hr.; June-Sept. 5 per week, Oct.-May 2 per week; 144kn); **Hvar** (10-15hr., 9 per week, 118kn); **Korčula** (15-18hr., 8 per week, 130kn); **Sobra** (21hr., 2 per week, 144kn); **Split** (12hr., 7 per week, 107kn); **Zadar** (6hr., 4 per week, 72kn). All prices listed are for June; Sept.-May 20% less, August and July about 10% more.

▲ PRACTICAL INFORMATION

Luggage storage in the train station is open 24hr. (10kn for 24hr.). It's also available at the bus station (9kn, 10kn for backpacks; open 5:30am-10:30pm), along with a **24hr. restaurant, grocery store,** and **currency exchange.** There is a 24hr. **pharmacy** across from the train station. In the train station you'll find a **bank** that exchanges **cash** and **traveler's checks** for no commission and an AmEx/MC/V **ATM.** (☎21 33 18. Open M-Sa 8am-8pm, Su 8am-12:30pm.)

▲ ACCOMMODATIONS AND FOOD

If you need to spend the night in Rijeka, the closest and cheapest hotel to the train and bus stations is **Prenocište Rijeka ❷**, 1. Maja 34/1. With your back to the train station, turn right on Krešimirova and left on 1. Maja, continuing up the hill for about 5min.; a sign on the right directs you through an archway to the hotel. A concrete monster from the outside, it provides clean but well-worn rooms with balconies. (☎55 12 46. Reception 24hr. Singles 109kn; doubles 218kn. AmEx/MC.) For food, try the grilled specialties (45-55kn) and pizza (14-26kn) at **Viktorija ❶**, Manzoni 1a, on your left heading up to the hotel. (☎33 74 16. Open M-Sa 7am-11pm, Su noon-11pm.)

KRK ISLAND ☎(0)51

Croatia's largest island, Krk is only a short ride across the Krk Bridge from the mainland. Its mountains and valleys are most stunning toward the southern end, in the town of Baška. While both Krk Town and Baška reel in a large catch of tourists, their small streets, scuba diving, hiking trails, and hidden coves give the island a wild, undiscovered feel.

⌐ TRANSPORTATION. Buses run from Rijeka to **Krk Town** (1½hr., 13 per day, 31kn); most continue to **Baška** (1hr., 10 per day, 11kn). **Jadrolinija** operates a **ferry** between Baška and **Lopar** on the northern tip of **Rab Island.** (1hr.; 4 per day; 22.30kn, car 130kn, bike 24.10kn. June-Aug. only.)

KRK TOWN

Krk Island's gateway to the rest of Croatia and the main intra-island transport hub, Krk Town is a well located base for visits to the rest of the island. This drowsy town's primary attraction is the 14th-century fortification, still visible today at the **South Town Gate** (Mala Vrata), the entrance to Stari Grad right on the marina. The waters around Krk Town offer more excitement than the town itself. **Fun Diving Krk,** Lukobran 8, leads a variety of underwater expeditions throughout the year. (☎/fax 22 25 63. Dive 148kn; full day trip with 2 dives 300kn; novice dive 320kn; night dive 172kn; snorkel trip 100kn. Equipment rental 24-40kn. Open daily 8am-7pm.) The town's only **beach** is next to the diving center. Less populated beaches are farther away in Autocamp Ježevac (see below).

The **bus station** is on Šetalište sv. Bernardina 1 (☎22 11 11). A short walk to the left along the sea leads to Stari Grad and its main square, **Vela placa**. The tourist and travel agency **Autotrans,** Šetalište sv. Bernardina 3, next to the bus station, **exchanges currency** and cashes **traveler's checks** for no commission. (š22 26 61; fax 22 21 10. Open M-Sa 8am-9pm, Su 9am-1:30pm.) **Riječka Banka,** on Trg b. Josipa Jelačića, has a MC/V **ATM;** another stands outside the **supermarket** on Šetalište sv. Bernardina bb, behind the bus station. (Open daily 7am-9pm.) There's a **pharmacy** at Vela pl. 3. (☎22 11 33. Open M-F 7:30am-9pm, Sa 7am-1pm and 6-8pm, Su 9am-noon.) **Internet Access** is available at **Multilink Internet Center Krk,** at the corner of Strossmayera and Vitezića (open M-Sa 4pm-10pm). The **post office,** Trg b. Josipa Jelačića bb, gives MC **cash advances** and has **telephones.** (☎22 11 25. Open M-F 7am-8pm, Sa 7am-2pm.) **Postal Code:** 51500

Autotrans ❷ (see above) books **private rooms,** but it's cheaper to look for a room yourself. (Autotrans singles July-Aug. 128-144kn; doubles 168-210kn. Off-season 20% cheaper. 30% surcharge for less than 3 days. Tourist tax 7kn. Registration 8kn.) *Sobe* and *apartman* signs line Slavka Nikoliča (the road to the bus station from Rijeka) and Plavnička. **Autocamp Ježevac ❶,** Plavnička bb, is a 10min. walk from the bus station away from Stari Grad. (☎/fax 22 10 81. Open April-Oct. and July-Aug. 24kn per person; April-June and Sept.-Oct. 19kn. Tent 16kn. Car 14kn. Registration 8kn. Daily tax 7kn.) **Galeb ❶,** Obala hrvatske mornarice bb, serves Adriatic standards on a terrace overlooking the marina. (Meat entrees 25-65kn, vegetarian 25kn. Open daily 9am-midnight.)

RAB ISLAND ☎(0)51

Having endured Byzantine, Venetian, Hungarian, and Croatian rulers, Rab still boasts ruins from the original Roman city constructed under Emperor Augustus's reign during the first century BC. If the whitewashed stone houses and the scent of rosemary from backyard gardens don't seduce you, the beaches will. Unlike rocky-shored Krk, Rab is blessed with long stretches of sandy coastline, making it a worthwhile stop along the coast.

⌐TRANSPORTATION. Getting to Rab is inexplicably difficult, so be prepared for frustration. **Buses** connect Rab Town with **Rijeka** (3hr., 2-3 per day, 84kn) and **Zagreb** (5½hr., 3 per day, 127kn). To head south along the coast, catch a Zagreb- or Rijeka-bound bus to **Živi Bunari** (45min., 5 per day, 34kn). Tell the driver your destination, and he'll drop you off on the *magistrala* (highway) where southbound buses stop. To ensure that there will indeed be a south-bound bus to your destination to pick you up along the highway, have the Rab ticket office check the mainland bus schedules. The only buses that are guaranteed to come are those serving major cities such as Zadar or Split. (Office open M-Sa 5:30-10:15am and 10:45am-1pm, Su 11am-4pm.) Mid-June through Sept. a Jadrolinija **ferry** runs daily between **Rijeka** and **Novalja** via **Rab.** (Rijeka 1½hr., 90kn; Novalja 35min, 35kn). In June and September, a ferry runs between **Baška** on Krk and **Lopar** on the northern tip of Rab Island (1hr., 2-5 per day, 23kn). From the ferry drop-off, walk 5min. down the road to the bus stop to catch the bus to Rab Town (20min., 9 per day, 11kn).

◼❼ ORIENTATION AND PRACTICAL INFORMATION. Rab Town is the historical center and main destination on the island. The peninsular Stari Grad is organized around three parallel streets: **Gornja** (Upper), **Srednja** (Middle), and **Donja** (Lower). To reach these from the **bus station** on Mali Palit (☎72 41 89), turn left and walk downhill until you reach the sea. The friendly staff at the **tourist**

office Turistička Zajednica, on the other side of the bus station building at Mali Palit, provides free maps of the town and island and can decipher tricky ferry schedules. (☎77 11 11; fax 77 11 10. Open daily 8am-10pm.) **Riječka Banka**, also on Mali Palit, **exchanges currency.** (Open M-F 8-11:30am and 5:30-8pm, Sa 8am-noon.) There is an AmEx/MC/V **ATM** outside the bank and another one off Trg sv. Kristofora. The **pharmacy** is next to the bus station. (☎/fax 72 54 01. Open M-Sa 8am-9pm, Su 9-11:30am.) **Internet access** is available at **Digital X,** Donja 4 (☎77 70 10. 0.50kn per min. Open daily 11am-2pm and 5pm-1am.) Head toward the water from the tourist office to reach the **post office,** Palit bb, which gives MC **cash advances** and exchanges currency and **traveler's checks** for 1.5% commission. **Telephones** are located inside. (Open M-F 7am-8pm, Sa 7am-2pm.) **Postal Code:** 51280.

⌂⌘ACCOMMODATIONS AND FOOD. Katurbo ❶, M. de Dominisa bb, between the bus station and the center, arranges **private rooms.** (☎/fax 72 44 95; katurbo-tourist-agency@ri.tel.hr. Open Sept.-June daily 8am-1pm and 4-9pm; July-Aug. 8am-9pm. July-Aug. singles 60-90kn; June and Sept. 50-70kn; Oct.-May. 50kn. 30% more for stays under 3 nights. Tourist tax 7kn.) **Hotel Istra ❸,** M. de Dominisa bb, is the most reasonably-priced hotel option in town. Rooms are modern and clean, but otherwise unremarkable. (☎724 134; fax 724 050. Breakfast included. 160-289kn per person.) **Camping Padova ❶** has its own sandy beach. To get there, take the bus that heads to Barbat (10min., 7 per day, 8kn), or walk left along the shore for 2km. (☎72 43 55; fax 72 45 31. 22kn per person; 20kn per tent. Registration 4kn. Daily tax 7kn.) Restaurant **St. Maria ❷,** Dinka Dokule 6, a continuation of the street Srednja, specializes in such Hungarian pleasures as *gulaš* (goulash; 30kn) and *punjena paprika* (stuffed bell pepper; 45kn), served either in the medieval courtyard or nautical interior. (☎72 41 96. Entrees 45-85kn. Open daily 11am-2pm and 4pm-midnight.) **Buffet Harpun ❷,** Donja bb, treats you to friendly service and to a wide assortment of dishes; try tasty fish specialties for 40-70kn or landlubber meat specialties for 30-40kn. (☎82 27 43. Open daily 10am-midnight.) There's a **supermarket** in the basement of Merkur, Palit 71. (Open daily 7am-9pm.)

◉⌘ SIGHTS AND NIGHTLIFE. The best way to see the sights of Rab is to take a stroll along **Gornja Ulica.** Walking down Gornja takes you from the remains of **St. John's Church** (Crkva Sv. Jvana), a Roman basilica, to the ruins of the **Church of the Holy Cross** (Crkva Sv. Križa), where, according to legend, the icon of Jesus once wept on the cross. Farther down, Gornja leads to Trg Slobode and to **St. Justine's Church** (Crkva Sv. Justine), which houses a museum dedicated to Christian art. (Open daily 9am-noon and 7:30-10pm. 7kn.) Climb the steep ladders to the top of the bell tower of the 13th-century **St. Mary's Church** (Crkva Sv. Marije) and peek into the nuns' lush garden. (Open daily 7:30-10pm. 5kn.) The 12th-century **Virgin Mary Cathedral** (Katedrala Djevice Marije) and the nearby 14th-century **St. Anthony's Monastery** (Samostan Sv. Antuna), farther down Gornja, complete the tour of the historical quarter. For more information, pick up a free pamphlet from the tourist office (see above).

Komrčar, a wooded park and cemetery, lies at the base of Stari Grad peninsula and offers shade as well as a rock beach. To reach a local favorite beach named **"Sahara,"** take a bus to San Marino (25min., 9 per day, 11kn) and ask someone to point you in the right direction. Signs mark the **hiking trail** to the bathing suit-optional **beach** (20min.). Other beach choices include **Supetarska Draga, Kampor,** and **Barbat,** all of which can be reached by bus and a 20- to 30-min. walk, or by rented bicycle from one of the local vendors (ask at the tourist office for a map). In general, sand beaches are on the north of the island, rocky beaches are on the west and pebble beaches are on the east.

Cafes abound in Rab. The most popular spot among local youth is **Le Journal,** on Donja just off Kristofor Trg Hipsters gather here to throw back a few heavy-hitting "Le Journal" cocktails (25kn) and hear the latest underground music. (0.33L Heineken 15kn. Open nightly 10pm-5am.) Closer to the waterfront, **San Antonio,** Trg Municipium Arbae, throws a fine fiesta with two bars. (☎72 11 45. Coffee 4kn. DJs spin on weekends. Open daily 8am-4am.) The **Grand Restaurant,** just past Trg sv. Kristofora, hosts live cover bands and an older crowd on its outdoor terrace. (Open daily 8am-midnight.)

DALMATIAN COAST

After his last visit to Dalmatia, George Bernard Shaw wrote: "The gods wanted to crown their creation and on the last day they turned tears, stars and the sea breeze into the isles of Kornati." Shaw's words speak to the entire Dalmatian Coast—a stunning seascape of unfathomable beauty set against a backdrop of dramatic mountains. With more than 1100 islands (only 66 of which are inhabited), Dalmatia is not only Croatia's largest archipelago, but also has the cleanest and clearest waters in the Mediterranean. Zadar and its preserved environs are excellent starting points for exploring smaller wonders: Pag's remarkable lace; Brač's phenomenal beach; the astonishing Krka waterfalls near Šibenik; Hvar, one of the most beautiful islands in the world; and the winding streets of the UNESCO-protected town of Trogir. Farther south, the nightlife of Split and vibrant culture of Korčula are preludes to Dubrovnik.

ZADAR   ☎(0)23

Zadar (pop. 76,000), the center of northern Dalmatia, hides its many scars well. Allied attacks destroyed Zadar during World War II and the recent war (1991-1995) saw the destruction of much of what had been rebuilt. Residents have restored their homes yet again and the city stands as beautiful as the coiling, shoreline leading to it. With the extraordinary Kornati Islands and Paklenica National Park both near enough for daytime excursions and a history so well preserved that Roman ruins serve as city benches, Zadar is the quintessential Dalmatian city.

▐ TRANSPORTATION

Trains: Ante Starčevića bb (☎43 05 99). To **Zagreb** (5-7hr., 3 per day, 80-120kn).

Buses: Ante Starčevića bb (☎21 19 38). More reliable than trains. To: **Dubrovnik** (8hr., 9 per day, 133-137kn); **Korčula** (4 hr., 1 per day, 115kn); **Rijeka** (4½hr., 1 per hr., 95-107kn); **Split** (3hr., 2 per hr., 70-80kn); **Zagreb** (5hr., 1 per hr., 93-105kn); **Ljubljana, SLN** (8hr., 1 per day, 180kn); **Trieste, ITA** (7hr., 2 per day, 130kn).

Ferries: Depart from Liburnska Obala, 5min. up the peninsula from the pedestrian bridge. **Jadrolinija** stands (☎25 48 00; fax 25 03 51) provide ferry information and sell tickets. The one on the tip of the peninsula handles ferries operating beyond the local islands of Ugljan and Dugi Otok. Open M-F 7am-8pm and 11pm-1am; Sa 7am-6pm; Su 7am-noon, 5-10pm, and 11:30pm-1am. To: **Dubrovnik** (16hr., 3-5 per week, 138kn); **Korčula** (12hr., 4 per week, 107kn); **Rijeka** (7hr., 4 per week, 72kn); **Split** (6hr., 4 per week, 61kn); **Arcona, ITA** (8hr., 3-5 per week, 238 kn).

Public Transportation: Schedules for buses (daily 6am-11pm) are posted at the main bus station and at most stops. Station names are rarely posted at each stop, so ask for help. Buy tickets from the driver for (6kn) or a round-trip ticket from any kiosk (10kn).

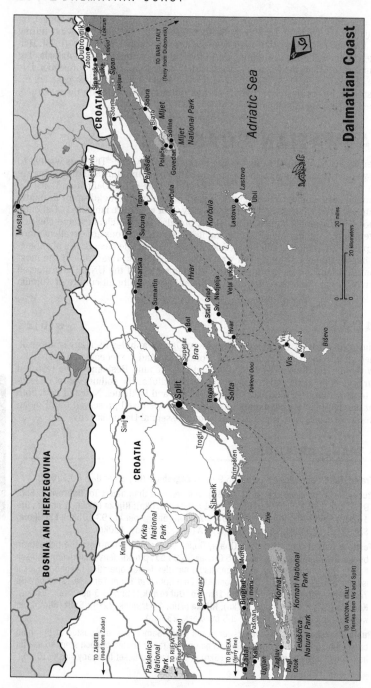

Dalmatian Coast

⊞ 🛈 ORIENTATION AND PRACTICAL INFORMATION

Most of the city's businesses and sights are scattered along **Široka,** the main street in Stari Grad. The **bus** and **train stations** are on Ante Starčevića. To get to Široka from these main stations, with your back to the main entrance, go through the pedestrian underpass and continue straight until you hit **Zrinsko-Frankopanska.** Follow this street (and the signs to the "Centar'") all the way to the water, then walk along the left side of the harbor to the gate of Stari Grad. Široka branches off **Narodni Trg** after you pass through the gate.

Tourist Office: Ilija Smiljanica bb (☎21 22 22; fax 21 17 81; tzg-zadar@zd.tel.hr). Once inside the main gate of Stari Grad, turn left on Don Ive Prodana, then another left at the street's end. The office offers detailed maps, but little else. Open daily 8am-8pm.

Currency Exchange: Dalmatinska Banka, Trg sv. Stošije 3 (☎25 11 36), on Široka, exchanges currency and cashes **traveler's checks** for no commission. Open M-F 8am-8pm, Sa 8am-noon.

American Express: Atlas, Obla Kneza Branimira 12 (☎23 58 50; fax 23 57 72; atl.zadar@atlas.tel.hr). On the waterfront to the right of the pedestrian bridge. Holds marked client mail for up to a month. Books flight tickets, rooms, and arranges excursions. Open M-F 8am-3pm, Sa 9am-noon.

Luggage Storage: At the bus station; follow the *Garderoba* signs. 1.20kn per hr. 2.20kn per hr. over 15kg. Open daily 7am-9pm. Closer to Stari Grad, **Bagul Garderoba,** opposite the Jadrolinija office on the waterfront. 3kn per hour, 15kn all day. Open Su-F 7am-8pm, Sa 7am-3pm.

Pharmacy: Barakovića 2 (☎21 33 74). Open M-F 7am-8pm, Sa 8am-noon.

Internet Access: Free at the **Gradska Knjižnica Zadar** (Zadar City Library), Stjepana Radića 116 (☎31 57 72). Cross over the pedestrian bridge and continue straight for two blocks away from Stari Grad; the library is on your left. Open M-F 8am-noon and 6-8pm, Sa 8am-1pm. **Cyber Caffe Cyber-Net,** Špire Brusine 8. From Narodni Trg, walk down M. Klaića and take a left. 0.50kn per min. Open daily 7am-midnight.

Post Office: Nikole Matafara 1 (☎25 05 06), off Široka, has **telephones** inside and gives MC **cash advances. Poste Restante** at the main post office, Kralja Držislava 1 (☎31 60 23). Open M-Sa 7am-9pm.

Postal Code: 23000.

▐ ACCOMMODATIONS

Zadar is blessed with a youth hostel, but it's far from Stari Grad. If you're a party animal, your best option might be a **private room** in the center of town. Occasionally, *sobe* (room) signs crop up on the waterfront, but a more reliable option is the **Aquarius Travel Agency ❷,** inside the main gate at Nova Vrata bb. (☎/fax 21 29 19; jureska@zd.tel.hr. Open daily 7am-10pm. Singles 100-120kn; 2-person apartments 200-250kn. Tourist tax 5.50-7kn.)

Omladinski Hostel Zadar, Obala Kneza Trpimira 76 (☎33 11 45; fax 33 11 90), on the waterfront near the outskirts of town. From the station, take bus #5 heading to Puntamika (15min., 6kn) or bus #8 to Diklo (20min., 6kn), and get off at the first stop after Autocamp Borik (see below). This huge complex has plenty of dorm rooms along with a bar and sports facilities. Breakfast included. Reception 24hr. Check-out 10am. Call ahead. July 15-Aug. 20 85kn per person; June 1-July 14 and Aug. 21-Sept. 16 75kn; May and Sept. 16-Oct. 30 70kn; Jan.-Apr. and Nov.-Dec. 65kn. Tourist tax 4.50-7kn. ❶

CROATIA

Autocamp Borik, Gustavo Matoša bb (☎ 33 20 74; fax 33 20 65), on the beach. Follow the directions to the hostel; look for large signs to the camp on the right. Clean, ample site. July-Aug. 23kn per person, 20kn per tent, 39kn per car. Tourist tax 7kn. May-June and Sept. 16kn per person, 16kn per tent, 31.50kn per car. Tourist tax 5.50kn. ❶

◖ FOOD

The **Zadranka supermarket** has branches around town, including one at Široka 10 and one at J. Štrossmayerova 6. (Both open daily 6:30am-9pm.) There is a fruit and vegetable **market** at Zlatarska, below Narodni Trg. (Open daily 6am-2pm.)

Foša, Kralja Dmitra Zvonimira 2 (☎ 31 44 21), located outside the city walls, grills up sizeable portions of fish (45-100kn) and meat (55-75kn) on a patio overlooking the bay. Open M-Sa 11am-midnight, Su 5pm-midnight. ❷

Gostionica Zlati Vrtič, Borelli 12 (☎ 21 30 76), serves meat (35-55kn) and fish dishes (45-100kn) in a pebbled courtyard to the sounds of traditional Croatian music. Open daily 7am-11pm. ❷

Restaurant Dva Ribara (Two Fishermen), Blaža Jurjeva 3 (☎ 21 34 45), off Plemića Borelli, is a local favorite. Serves vegetarian options (27kn) in addition to standard Croatian fare. Open daily 10:30am-midnight. ❶

◉ SIGHTS

The most legendary area in Zadar is the ancient **Forum,** located on Široka in the center of the peninsula. Built in Byzantine style at the beginning of the 9th century, **St. Donat's Church** (Crkva sv. Donata) sits atop the ruins of an ancient Roman temple that is still visible from inside. Today, the building remains one of only three circular Catholic churches in the world. Although no longer a place of worship, it is still used by Zadarians for the occasional high-school graduation. (Open daily 9am-1pm and 5-9pm. 5kn.) **St. Mary's Church** (Crkva Sv. Marija), Trg Opatice Čike 1, across the square from St. Donat's, is a more traditional place of worship; it also houses the fabulous **Permanent Exhibition of Religious Art** (Stalna Izložba Crkvene Umjetnosti). The gold and silver busts, reliquaries, and crosses kept here are regarded as some of Croatia's most precious artifacts—shrewd nuns keep a close watch. (☎ 21 15 45. Buy tickets to the left of the church. Open M-Sa 10am-12:30pm and 6-8pm, Su 10am-12:30pm. 20kn, students 10kn.) Next to St. Mary's stands the **Archeological Museum** (Arheološki Muzej), which documents the history of Zadar, including aerial photographs of towns and archeological sites, beautiful medieval stonework, and innumerable shards of prehistoric pottery. Though smaller, the **National Museum** (Narodni Muzej Zadar) offers a more accessible and entertaining view of the city's history. The scale models of Zadar that chronicle the city's development through the centuries are particularly interesting. From St. Mary's, follow the same street to the other side of peninsula; the museum will be on your right. (☎ 25 18 51. Open M-Tu and Th-F 9am-2pm, W 9am-2pm and 5pm-7pm. 5kn, students 3kn.) Though it may strain your pocketbook, consider taking a guided boat tour of **Kornati National Park.** The going rate for a full daytrip (8:30am-6:30pm) is 250kn and includes unlimited cocktails, breakfast, and lunch. Each of the dozen or so agencies that offer trips do essentially the same tour for the same price. Try to talk it down and consult the tourist office (above) for details. These tours remain the only way to venture into the only European park of its kind—365 islands, almost completely uninhabited, and home of the famous salt-water Silver Lake.

🔊🎵 NIGHTLIFE AND ENTERTAINMENT

Although Zadar is not a rave town, you can always find a late-night party at **Central Kavana**, Široka 3, the trendiest and liveliest venue around. CK is a kaleidoscope of funky lights and decor including hanging blue bicycles, orange TVs, and sewing machines. Live music on weekends ranges from jazz to reggae. (☎21 10 41. Open M-Th 7:30am-midnight, F-Su 7:30am-1am.) **Caffe Bar Forum**, on Široka at the Forum, has comfortable chairs and fantastic outdoor seating overlooking the ruins. (0.33L *Karlovačko* 10kn. Open daily 7:30am-midnight.) For a loud 20-something scene, check out the cafes along **Varoška**, just off of Špire Brusine. Every night, **Kino Pobjeda**, on Jurja Dalmatinca just off Narodni Trg, shows English-language movies with Croatian subtitles in an enormous theater. (Screenings 6:30-11pm. 12-20kn; the later the screening, the more expensive the ticket.)

🏛 DAYTRIP FROM ZADAR

PAKLENICA NATIONAL PARK

*Buses run from Zadar (50min., 2 per hr., 25kn). Make it clear you're going to the "Nacionalni Park" and ask the driver to let you off at the road to the park entrance. The actual entrance is about 1km off the main road. If you're coming from Zadar, continue in the same direction to the well-marked road to the park on the left. The entrance office has excellent rock-climbing information compiled by former visitors, detailed route maps, and general hiking maps. There is also a **tourist office** across the street from the bus stop that offers similar camping and hiking advice. ☎/fax 36 92 02; www.tel.hr/paklenica. Open M-F 8-11am and 4-7pm. Park open Apr.-Oct. daily 7am-8pm; Nov.-Mar. 8am-4pm. 30kn, students 15kn. Cave tours Sept.-June M, W, F 10am-1pm; July-Aug. daily 10am-1pm. Tunnel tours Th 9am-1pm and Su 10am-1pm. Each tour 10kn.*

> **!** There are **landmines** around the park; stay on the marked paths. Bring water and hiking boots. For more info, see **Essentials: Camping and the Outdoors**, p. 39.

The craggy peaks of the **Velebit Massif** mountain range loom over most of Paklenica's 3657 hectares, an area that's home to several species of bear, fox, snake, wild flowers and endangered birds, including the enormous **Griffon Vulture**, which has a wingspan of up to 2.7m (don't worry—it's not predatory). The mountains are a playground for the hard-core hiker as well as for the amateur nature appreciator. Visitors can take part in a wide range of activities, from swimming in mountain streams and cave-crawling to challenging hikes and advanced, world-famous rock climbs on routes that bear names such as **Psycho Killer.**

There are two main attractions in the park: **Mala Paklenica** (Small Canyon) and **Velika Paklenica** (Big Canyon). Velika Paklenica is more popular, with easy access to spectacular cliffs and caves. Mala Paklenica is every bit as impressive, but the steep trail and boulder-scrambling it takes to get up tend to keep the crowds away. If you have a full day, the best way to see the park is to hike up Velika Paklenica and cross over the crest and head down Mala Paklenica (6-7hr.). The trail maps handed out at the entrance office are somewhat useful and the park is clearly marked. Be sure to ask at the office about trail conditions in Mala Paklenica, as it can become slippery and dangerous during rainy seasons. For an extended visit, spend the night at a **mountain hut ❶**. A 2hr. hike from the main road, the hut is a great spot to start the 4hr. hike to **Vaganski Vrh.**, which is the highest peak in the Velebit Mountain range at 1757m. (☎21 37 92. Bunk and blanket provided, but bring sheets or sleeping bag. Call ahead for reservations. 45kn.) There are also many campgrounds and some *sobe* (room) signs along the main road.

CROATIA

PAG ISLAND

Pag is a strange mix of barren expanses and lush green coastline. Pag Town is made up of low white buildings set dramatically on one side of an artificial isthmus wedged between the mountains. Novalja, the "Beverly Hills of Croatia," attracts famous Croatians looking to soak up some sun during the summer months. Often overlooked by tourists, Pag retains an authentic Croatian flare.

PAG TOWN
☎(0)23

While Pag Town's terrain appears harsh in the daytime sun, it gains an unearthly beauty as dusk falls. The town and its traditions have been left largely unaltered by the tourist economy, making it a pleasant change from the coast. *Paška čipka*, the famous local lace, is still sold straight from the skilled hands of its elderly makers.

TRANSPORTATION. Pag Town has a **bus stop**, but no station. The best way to get to Pag is to take a bus from **Zadar** (1hr., 1 per day, 24kn). Buses also come from **Rijeka** (4hr., 2 per day, 100kn) and **Zagreb** (6hr., 4 per day, 120kn). If you're on a southbound bus along the coast, you'll need to ask the driver to drop you off at **Prizna.** Walk 2km down to the water and catch a **ferry** to **Zigljen** on Pag Island. Buses to Pag Town meet the incoming ferries.

ORIENTATION AND PRACTICAL INFORMATION. To get to the center from the bus stop, face the sea and walk left along the waterfront. Turn left on Vela Ulica to reach the main square, **Trg Kralja Krešimira IV.** The center of Pag is miniscule, so getting around is easy. For those less in touch with their internal compasses, **maps** are available at the official **tourist office**, Katine bb, on the waterfront by the pedestrian bridge. (☎/fax 61 13 01. Open daily 7am-9pm.) **Riječka Banka,** on the way to the main square at Vela Ulica bb, has an **ATM** outside. (Open M-F 8-noon and 6-9pm, Sa 8am-noon.) There's a **pharmacy** on the waterfront just beyond the tourist office, on S. Radića bb. (☎61 10 43. Open M-Sa 7:30am-1pm and 5-9pm, Su 8am-noon.) Hook up to the **Internet** and grab a drink at **Gea,** Frankopanska 3, just above the main square. (☎61 25 74. 0.30kn per min. Open daily 10am-2pm and 6pm-1am.) The **post office**, two streets behind the bus stop at A.B. Šimića, **exchanges cash** and cashes **traveler's checks** for no commission. There are **telephones** inside. (☎61 10 04. Open M-Sa 7am-9pm.) **Postal Code:** 23250.

ACCOMMODATIONS AND FOOD. Since Pag is not a beach resort, there are few hotels or low priced **private rooms. Meridijan 15 Travel Agency ❶,** A. Starčevića 1, next to the bus stop in the same building complex as Hotel Pagus, books rooms. (☎61 21 62 or 61 21 65; fax 61 21 61; meridijan-15@zd.tel.hr. Open May-Oct. daily 8am-9pm. Singles 60-80kn; doubles 100-200kn. 30% more for stays under 3 nights. Tourist tax 5.50-7kn.) Those with tents can head down to **Autocamp Šimuni ❷,** which offers some of the best camping beaches on the island, although it's a long way to either Pag Town or Novalja. To get there from the town, grab a Zagreb-bound bus; ask the driver to let you off at Šimuni (20min., 5 per day), then follow the signs downhill. (☎69 82 08. Open May-Sept. July-Aug. 96kn per person; May-June and Sept. 56kn. Tourist tax 4kn.) Follow the locals to **Na Tale ❸,** S. Radića 2, next to the pharmacy, and eat well outside amid boisterous Croatian families. Choose from pasta and risotto (25-45kn), *Kotlet sa žara* (grilled cutlet; 44kn), and many other tasty entrees. (☎61 11 94. Open daily 8am-11pm.) Behind the main square, the terrace restaurant **Tamaris ❶,** Križevaćka bb, serves up the local favorite *Pileći Batak* (chicken leg with bacon and cheese; 30km), in addition to typical island fare. (☎61 22 77. Open daily 6:30am-11pm. AmEx.) Swing by the **fruit and vegetable market** in front of Tamaris. (Open daily 6am-10pm.)

LACED LABOUR LOST Four hundred years ago, nuns from the Venetian island of Burano arrived in Pag and founded the industry that now puts the island town on Croatia's cultural and historical maps—*Paška čipka* (lace from Pag). In Croatia, lace is only produced in Pag. While the designs and patterns have changed over the centuries, the Pag women are taught to employ the same methods as their pious predecessors. The process requires a supreme amount of patience; producing a frisbee-sized piece of lace can take up to 6 months. The results are beautifully intricate and dauntingly expensive: that same delicate cloth fetches anywhere from 800 to 2000kn. You needn't worry about shopkeepers overpricing the goods, as all lace is only sold out of private homes or from the **Lace Gallery** near the main square, Kralja Zvonimira 1. (Open nightly 7:30-11pm. Free.) For more information on *Paška čipka*, contact Pag's **Cultural Center** at Franijevački Trg. (☎61 10 25. Open M-F 8am-3pm.)

🎭 🎷 ENTERTAINMENT AND NIGHTLIFE. On the last weekend in July, Pag's main square hosts the town's **summer carnival.** Locals dress up in traditional garb called *Paška Naškja* to perform the dance *Paška Kolo.* On the last day, watch the ceremonial "Burning of Marco"—the burning of a sealed coffin symbolizing the year's sins. If you can't find your own spot of sand between the reclining bodies on the **beach,** try the pebbly **Gradska Plaža,** right across the bridge from Stari Grad. For more secluded tanning spots, walk farther down the coast. Alternatively, follow the waterfront past Hotel Pagus to reach the beaches on the opposite side of the bay, or take a daytrip to the island near Novalja.

Bars and cafes line the waterfront between the bus stop and the tourist office. Join a young crowd at ▨ **Kameriengo,** Jadrulićeva Br. 1. Soothing green lighting, mellow dance music, and the self-described "most comfortable chairs in Croatia" mix nicely with a 10kn pint of *Karlovačko* or *Ožujsko.* (Open daily 8am-1am.) Most cafes close around 1am, but fear not: the party marches on across the bridge at the newly renovated **Saloon Club.** The 500-year-old party zone comes complete with ancient stone walls, disco balls, and all of the late-nighters of Pag Island. Just past the disco, on the water, the **Cohiba Havanna Beach Bar** is a great place to watch night fall over the mountains. (Open daily 8pm-2am.)

NOVALJA ☎(0)53

With its famous Croatians and equally famous sandy beaches, this lush summer resort town stands in contrast to more modest Pag. Once a Roman port, Novalja now hosts a healthy nightlife scene, making it an old favorite of Croatians and an up-and-coming destination for foreigners.

📧 TRANSPORTATION. Buses run from the **Autotrans bus station** on Petra Krešimira IV to: **Pag Town** (40min., 5 per day, 18kn); **Rijeka** (3hr., 2 per day, 100kn); **Zagreb** (5hr., 3 per day, 120kn); **Zadar,** via **Pag Town** (1½hr., 2 per day, 24kn). Mid-June through Sept., a Jadrolinija **ferry** runs from Novalja to **Rijeka** (2hr., 1 per day, 100kn) with a stop at **Rab Town** along the way (30min., 35kn). A small boat runs from **Lun** on the northern tip of the island to **Rab Town** (1hr., 1 per day, 35kn), but you'll need to catch a taxi to Lun (20min.).

📧 🔃 ORIENTATION AND PRACTICAL INFORMATION. To reach the town center from the bus station, face the sea and walk right along **Petra Krešimira IV** to **Trg Loža. St. Maria Travel Agency** (see **Accommodations,** below) serves as the bus station and offers **maps** and info. The agency's English-speaking staff also books rooms and apartments. **Exchange currency** and cash **traveler's checks** for no commission at

CROATIA

Croatia Osiguranje, just past Trg Loža on Krešimira IV. (Open daily 7:30am-2:45pm and 3-9:30pm.) An AmEx/MC/V **ATM** stands next door, in front of **Riječka Bank.** There is a **pharmacy** at Dalmatinska 1, off Krešimira IV. (☎66 13 70. Open M-Sa 8am-noon and 5-8pm, Su 10am-noon.) For **Internet access,** head to **Cafe Paloma,** just off the main square and across from the vegetable market. The connection is spotty, but it's the only option in town. (☎66 19 60. 20kn per hr. Open daily, although hours vary by season.) The **post office** is around the corner from Riječka Bank, facing the water. There are **telephones** inside. (☎66 11 22. Open M-F 7am-8pm, Sa 8am-4pm.) **Postal Code:** 53291.

⌐⌐ ACCOMMODATIONS AND FOOD. There are two hotels in Novalja, but you can save money by shopping around for **private rooms** or **apartments.** Start at the **St. Maria Travel Agency ❶.** (☎66 16 55; fax 66 21 50; sv.marija@gs.tel.hr; www.donat.com/marija. Open July-Aug. Su-M and W-F 7am-1pm and 5-10pm, Tu and Sa 7am-10pm. July-Aug. Singles 70-90kn; doubles 120-160kn. 30% more for stays under 3 nights. Tax 7kn.) Or try **Pansion Maria ❶,** Krešimira IV, which offers comfortable rooms with balconies and private bathrooms. (☎66 13 73. Breakfast included. Singles 90kn; doubles 140kn.) Campers can head to **Auto-camp Straško ❶,** which has its own rock beach and nude camping area. Bring your own tent; leave your inhibitions. To get there from the bus station, face the sea, walk left on Krešimira IV, and follow the signs to the right toward the water (25min. ☎66 12 26; fax 66 12 25. Open May-June and Sept. 22kn per person, 46kn for both car and tent; July-Aug., 32kn/66kn. Tax 5.5-6kn.) **Hotel Loža ❹** offers a more upscale and modest option than bearing it all on the beach. Along the shore by Trg Loža. (☎66 13 26; fax 66 13 04. Breakfast included. Singles 202-237kn; doubles 322-392kn.)

A local favorite, **Bistro Stefani ❸,** opposite the bus station, serves grilled turkey breast with fresh sage and dill (*Navavni Odreznak,* 60kn) and other house specialties. (☎66 16 97. Open daily 7am-midnight. AmEx/DC.) Through town past the post office along Brače Radić on your right, **Starac I More ❷** ("Old Man and the Sea") serves seafood favorites (50-100kn), pasta, and risotto (50-70kn) in a stone courtyard. (☎66 24 23. Open daily noon-midnight. AmEx/MC/V.) Eat cheap and tasty brick-oven pizza (18-35kn) at **Moby Dick ❶,** near the bus station on Krešimira IV. (☎52 11 39. Open daily 11am-2am.) There is an open-air **fruit and vegetable market** in the center of town on Trg Bazilike. (Open daily 7am-10pm.)

◢▪ ENTERTAINMENT AND NIGHTLIFE. June 13th is **Novalja/St. Anton's Day,** a holiday that honors the town's patron saint. Local dancers perform to the *mih,* a sheepskin bagpipe-like instrument unique to Pag and Dalmatia. **Zrće** is the most famous beach near Novalja; take advantage of **paddleboating, kayaking, parasailing,** and the **Blato,** a natural mineral spa. In July and Aug. a minivan runs from the front of the bus station to Zrće and other beaches every 15min (7kn). Out of season, get there by renting a bicycle or scooter. Walk left along the water from the bus station to reach the sandy beach, **Plaža Lokunje,** or around the coast to **Straško** (15min.). In July and Aug., people go out every night, starting around midnight. Head to **Cocomo,** opposite the bus station at Krešimira IV 9. This Carribbean-themed bar and disco keeps the night alive. (Drinks 15-20kn. Open daily 8am-5am.) **Calypso** is the most popular club on Zrće beach. (Open daily 7:30pm-5am.)

ŠIBENIK
☎ (0)22

Facing the magnificent bay of Šibenicka Luka at the mouth of the Krka River, Šibenik (pop. 40,000) seems to have slipped under the radar of the average tourist. The few who find themselves here are rewarded with a town of nightlife-loving locals, steep medieval streets free of tourist shops, and one of the most beautiful cathedrals on the Adriatic. Much enlarged since its establishment as the Diocese of Šibenik in 1298, this town has kept itself a hidden delight well worth finding.

▐ TRANSPORTATION. The **bus station** is at Drage bb. (☎21 20 87. Open daily 6:30am-9pm.) Buses go to: **Dubrovnik** (6hr., 10 per day, 100kn); **Split** (1½hr., 20 per day, 31kn); **Zadar** (1½hr., 20 per day, 31kn); **Zagreb** (6hr., 10 per day, 100kn); and **Ljubljana, SLN** (7hr., 1 per day, 140kn).

▰ ▱ ORIENTATION AND PRACTICAL INFORMATION. While much of new Šibenik sprawls across the hills rising from the harbor, the **Gorica Grad** (Old Town) is packed tightly on a steep face against the water. To get to Gorica Grad from the **bus station,** face the water and walk right along the waterfront (5min.). Gorica Grad's confusing maze of alleyways is cut by **Kralja Tomislava,** which runs diagonally up the hill from the waterfront to **Cathedral of St. Jacob.** The road leads to the main traffic artery, **Kralja Zvonimira,** which serves as a border between the Old and New Towns. **Vladimira Nazora** runs uphill from the water near the bus station and connects with Kralja Zvonimira.

The **tourist office,** Fausta Vrančića 18, is just above Trg Palih Šibenskih Boraca, one of the squares traversed by Kralja Tomislava. The enthusiastic staff hands out **maps** and provides info about excursions. (☎21 20 75; fax 21 90 73; www.summernet.hr. Open June-Aug. M-Sa 8am-8pm, Su 8am-noon; Sept.-May M-F 8am-3pm.) **Jadranska Banka,** on Trg Kralja Držislava, **exchanges currency** and cashes **traveler's checks** for no commission. (☎33 33 88. Open M-F 7:30am-8.30pm, Sa 7am-1pm.) There is a free-standing MC/V **ATM** on the far side of Kralja Zvonimira, diagonally opposite Trg Poljana. **Luggage storage** is available at the bus station. (3.70kn per day. Open daily 6am-10pm.) The **pharmacy Ljekarna Varoš** is at Kralja Zvonimira 2. (☎21 22 49. Open M-F 7am-8pm, Sa 7am-2pm.) Check email at **Da Noi Internet Club,** Trg Jurja Barakovića 3; follow signs off Kralja Tomislava. (0.30kn per min. Open daily 9am-2pm and 5-10pm.) The **post office,** Vladimira Nazora 5, has **telephones.** (☎21 49 90. Open M-Sa 7am-9pm, Su 7am-2pm.) **Postal Code:** 22000.

▐ ▱ ACCOMMODATIONS AND FOOD. Private rooms are the best option in town. To find one, try **Cromovens Travel Agency ❷,** Trg Republike Hrvatske, by the cathedral. (☎21 25 15; fax 21 25 16; www.cromovens.hr. Singles 100-150kn; doubles 150-220kn. Prices depend upon date of stay. Open daily 9am-2pm and 5-8pm.) Tent folk should make their way to **Autocamp Solaris ❶,** on the Zablaće peninsula across the bay, where **beaches** abound. Take a local bus from the station to Solaris (10min., every 2 hr. 8am-10pm, 8kn) or Zablaće and ask the driver to drop you off at the camp. (☎36 40 00; fax 36 44 50; www.dalmacija.net/solaris/solaris.htm. July-Aug. 24kn per person, 43kn with tent or car. Tax 8kn. May-June and Sept.-Oct. 15.50kn/32kn. Tax 6kn.)

The town's food options are not overwhelming. **Pizzeria Kike ❶** (kee-kay), Durija Sižgorića 3, serves up pizza (27-50kn) in a quiet courtyard off Kralja

FROM THE ROAD

SAY WHAT?

Not so long ago, no one spoke Croatian. At least, not officially. Under Tito's rule, everyone in Yugoslavia spoke an awkwardly-named language called Serbo-Croat (except the Slovenians, who were allowed to continue speaking Slovene). Now, of course, Croats speak Croatian (*Hrvatski*), Serbs speak Serbian (*Srpski*), and Bosnian Muslims, for the most part, speak Bosnian (*Bosanski*).

During and after the war, the politics of language became a sensitive and important issue in Croatia. While Croatian is written in Latin script and Serbian is written in Cyrillic, they are linguistically almost identical. But as Croatia struggled to liberate itself politically from Yugoslavia (and Serbia in particular), it also tried to separate itself linguistically. The handful of words that distinguished the two dialects from each other became the basis for claims that Croatian was, in fact, an entirely separate language from Serbian.

(continued on next page)

Tomislava. (☎33 01 41. Open M-Sa 7am-11pm, Su 3-11pm.) When you can't stand the thought of another pizza or pile of french fries, head to **Steak House No. 4 ❶,** Trg Dinka Zavorivića, for one of their light and tasty fresh mozzarella salads for 25kn. (☎21 75 17. Open daily 8am-1am.) There's a **supermarket,** Poljana 3, at the top of Vladimira Nazora. (Open daily 6:30am-10pm.)

◨ ◫ SIGHTS AND ENTERTAINMENT. Šibenik's pride is the Gothic-Renaissance **Cathedral of St. Jacob** (Katedrala Sveti Jakova). This massive, white stone masterpiece by Croatian sculptor **Juraj Dalmatinac** commands a view of Gorica Grad. A native of Zadar, Dalmatinac took over construction of the cathedral in 1432, but it wasn't until 1536 that his pupil, Nikola Firentinac, completed it. Both the intricate dome designed by Firentinac and the frieze of 71 heads on the exterior walls of the apses are striking. (Open May-Oct. daily 8am-noon and 6-8pm. Services daily 9am, Su also at 9:30, 11am, 7:30pm.) For an incredible view of the town, harbor, outlying islands, and the distant Kornati, climb up to the crumbling **St. Ana Fortress** above Gorica Grad. (Open 24hr. Free.)

Šibenik has no seaside sand, but a short bus ride to Zablaće (10min., 1 per hr., 8kn) across the harbor takes you to a number of **pebble beaches.** The cultural event of the year is the **Children's Festival** held in during the last week of June and the first week of July. The line-up includes a tot demolition derby, a nightly program of children's films, puppet performances, and children's theater. International performers headline during the first week, while dancers and local comedians take over during the second. Daily boat excursions to **Kornati** (see **Zadar: Sights,** p. 186) are available from the nearby town of **Murter,** which is accessible by bus (15min., 8 per day, 15kn). Contact the **Kornata Agency** in Murter, Rudina 1, one day in advance. (☎43 54 47. Open daily 8am-10pm. Excursions daily 9am-6pm; 220kn per person, including lunch, a drink, and park ticket.)

◪ NIGHTLIFE. Welcome to one of the best nightspots on the Dalmatian Coast. For the wildest dance club on the Coast, take a nighttime excursion to **◪ Aurora.** To get there, take a bus (18kn) to **Primošten,** 35min. south of Šibenik on the way to Split, and follow the stream of partiers up the hill (15-20min. from the bus stop). Fliers advertise Aurora's special weekend events that feature house and techno DJ masters from around the world. (☎57 08 36. Open Th-Sa 11pm-6am. Call ahead to check event schedule.) Šibenik parties every night of the week and the party happens at **Dolac,** a neighborhood by the waterfront.

Facing the water from Gorica Grad, turn right and walk along the harbor straight into the crowds and the competing beats. In July and Aug. it feels like Croatian Mardi Gras. For techno, try **Domald,** Obala Prvoboraca 3. (0.5L Guinness 40kn. Live music Tu, DJs Th-Sa. Open daily 7am-late.) For a cool scene minus the crowds, check out **Papa Dolpo,** Obula Prvoboraca 28, past Dolac and opposite the marina. The bar serves a wide range of coladas (24-26kn) to loungers on its wicker chairs. (☎21 77 12. Open daily 10am-2pm and 5pm-3am.)

ⓑ DAYTRIP FROM ŠIBENIK

KRKA NATIONAL PARK

Take the bus from Šibenik to Skradin (20min., 5 per day, 12kn) and ask the driver to let you off at either Lozovac, the first park entrance, or Skradin, the second park entrance. From the Lozovac entrance, buses run every 20min. to the Krka River and the Skradinski buk waterfalls. From the Skradin entrance, a boat (1 per hour, included with park ticket) will take you up the river to Skradinski buk. Park office ☎21 77 20 or 21 77 30; fax 336 836; www.npkrka.hr. Open June-Aug. daily 8am-8pm; Mar.-May 8am-7pm. Call ahead in Sept.-Feb. July-Aug. 45kn, students 24kn; Mar.-June 40kn/22kn.

Croatia's youngest national park surrounds and protects the Krka River as it winds and cascades 72km through canyons and hills, dropping a total of 242m. Like the more impressive (and more crowded) Plitvice National Park, the falls at Krka are formed by *karst,* a sedimentary limestone that builds up on underwater objects. The impressive **Skradinski buk Waterfalls** are the park's highlight and walking around them only takes about an hour. Bring your bathing suit, as swimming is allowed in some of the crystal-clear pools at the base of the falls. You can take a boat tour (4 hr., 1 per day, 100kn) to the Franciscan monastery on Visovac Island and the Roški Slap waterfall, but the trip is long and over-priced.

TROGIR . ☎(0)21

Trogir (pop. 1500), a tiny island between the mainland and the much larger Otok Čiovo, is a sheltered spot along the coast. Here, medieval buildings crowd winding streets and palmed promenades open onto well-maintained parks and the calm, blue sea. Now a popular hang-out for sailors exploring Dalmatia, Trogir has always been an attractive destination. As early as the 13th century, Gothic and Renaissance artists ventured here and stayed, building countless churches. In 1997, Trogir earned a coveted place on the UNESCO World Heritage List.

In schools, children were taught the uniquely Croatian words that "proved" this distinction, and in some cases words were either invented or dredged up from obscurity to fill the role. Parents found themselves in the peculiar position of not knowing some of the vocabulary their 10 year-olds were studying.

Since the election of the current moderate government in 2000, much of this linguistic nationalism has taken a back seat to more pressing issues like correcting the country's massive unemployment and rebuilding the tourist industry. As the country's political independence has become ever more secure and accession to the EU becomes the Holy Grail of Croatian policy, efforts to actively differentiate the language may fade altogether. But the past decade has left lasting marks on the language; a language that is unquestionably known as Croatian.

—A. Nicholas Gossen

▛ TRANSPORTATION. The **bus station** is on the mainland. Many **buses** from **Rijeka, Zadar,** and **Zagreb** stop in Trogir on their way south to **Split** (30min., 22kn to Split); buses stop in front of the bus station, so make sure to wait outside. You can also take local bus #37 from Trogir to **Split** (30min., 3 per hr., 15kn). All the buses that pass through Trogir heading north stop in **Šibenik** (45min., 31kn). There are **no ferries** to or from Trogir. To check **bus schedules** and find out about ferries to other towns, head across the Čiovski bridge to **Atlas,** Obala kralja Zvonimira 10. The staff clears up bus confusion and sells tickets for boats and flights to and from Split. (☎88 42 79 or 88 13 74; fax 88 47 44. Open M-Sa 8am-9pm, Su 6-9pm.)

▛▛ ORIENTATION AND PRACTICAL INFORMATION. The town spills from the mainland across short bridges to two islands. The **Stari Grad** (Old Town) is on the small island of Trogir; behind it lies Čiovo, which has the town's best beaches, accessible by the Čiovski bridge. The main street, **Kohl-Genscher,** is a short walk from the bus station across the tiny bridge, the next street to the left of the stone **North Gate.** It leads past the central square, **Trg Ivana Pavla,** to the Čiovski bridge. The **tourist office, Turistička Zajednica Grada Trogir,** Obala b. Berislavića 12, at the end of Kohl-Genscher, gives out free **maps** of the city. (☎/fax 88 14 12. Open M-F 8am-2pm and 4-7:30pm, Sa 8-11am.) **Zagrebačka Banka,** Gradska Vrata 4, just past the North Gate, **exchanges currency** for no commission and cashes **traveler's checks** for 1.5% commission. (Open M-F 7:30am-7pm, Sa 8am-noon.) There is a MC/V **ATM** outside the bank and an AmEx/MC/V **ATM** at Kohl-Genscher 15, near the tourist office. The **pharmacy** is at Kohl-Genscher 23. (☎88 15 35. Open M-F 7am-8pm, Sa 7am-2pm.) Log onto the **Internet** at **Online Club,** Matije Gupa 4, past Zagrebačka; follow the signs. (20kn per hr. Open daily 10am-1pm and 5-9pm.) **Cyber Cafe,** at ACI Marina across the Čiovski bridge, is also wired, and Internet is free from 7-8am and 1-2pm. (Otherwise 1kn per min., 0.60kn per min. after the first 30min; students 0.40kn/0.30kn. Open daily 7am-midnight.) **Telephones** are inside the **post office,** B. Jurjeva Trogiranina 1. The post office also gives MC **cash advances,** exchanges cash for 1.5% commission, and cashes **traveler's checks** for no commission. (☎88 14 52 or 88 14 70. Open M-Sa 7am-10pm, Su 8am-1pm.) **Postal Code: 21220.**

▛▛ ACCOMMODATIONS AND FOOD. The best deals in town are **private rooms,** arranged by **Čipko ❷,** Kohl-Genscher 41, opposite the Cathedral and through an archway. (☎/fax 88 15 54. Open daily 8am-8pm. July-Aug. singles 96-112kn; doubles 192-228kn. Tourist tax 6kn. May-June and Sept. 80-96kn/160-192kn. Tourist tax 4.50kn.) To get to beachside **Prenoćište Saldun ❶,** Sv. Andrije 1, cross the Čiovski bridge and walk straight on Pt. Balana, which winds up the hill; keep to the right and Saldun will be at the top (about 10min.). Half of their small rooms have balconies overlooking the harbor and all of their shared bathrooms are clean. Call ahead for reservations. (☎80 60 53 or 80 60 85. Breakfast 28kn. Reception 24hr. 70kn per person. Tax 6kn.) **Vila Sikaa ❺,** Obala Kralja Zvonimira 13, sits on the waterfront just across the Čiovski Bridge. It's well worth the extra cash to bask in this lap of luxury—modern rooms have baths, telephones, Internet, A/C, and satellite TV. (☎88 12 23 or 88 56 60; fax 88 51 49; stjepan.runtic@st.tel.hr. Breakfast included. Reception 24hr. Luxury rooms have saunas and jacuzzis. Reserve at least 10 days ahead. Singles 420kn; doubles 450-550kn.)

Stari Grad is filled with tourist-oriented eateries of similar price and quality. For something different, head over the Čiovski bridge and take a right to find **Bistro Lučica ❷,** Kralja Tomislava. A favorite among the marina crowd, this bistro grills seafood and meat delights (35-120kn) on the outdoor BBQ and plays country favorites in the background. (☎ 88 56 33. Open M-F 9am-midnight, Sa-Su 4pm-midnight.) The small **Ćiovka Supermarket,** Obala v. Bakarvića 11, next to Atlas (see above) has all the groceries you need. (Open M-Sa 5:30am-9pm, Su 6:30am-8pm.)

🖾 🖪 **SIGHTS AND NIGHTLIFE.** A statue of Trogir's patron, St. Ivan Orsini, tops the **North Gate,** a beautiful Renaissance arch that forms the entrance to Stari Grad. Most sights, including the **Cathedral of St. Lawrence** (Crkva sv. Lovre), are in **Trg Ivana Pavla,** at the center of the old quarter. Begun in 1213 as a Romanesque basilica, it was not completed until 1598. Croatian Master Radovan chiseled its famous entrance in 1240. Inside the Cathedral is the Renaissance **Chapel of St. John of Trogir,** a work built from 1461 to 1497 guided chiefly by Florentine architect Nikola Firentinac. The Cathedral is currently being restored, and although it was scheduled to be completed in 2001, the actual date of completion remains anyone's guess. For other examples of Trogir's spectacular tradition of stone-carving, visit the **City Museum of Trogir,** housed in two buildings. The first, near the Cathedral at Gradska 45, exhibits photographs and documents from the city's past, as well as miscellany, like a giant wooden chicken taken as a war-trophy from a Turkish ship at the Battle of Lepanto. The **lapidary,** through the arch directly in front of the North Gate, and features stone sculptures by Firentinac, among others. (Open M-Sa 9am-noon and 6pm-9pm. 10kn, students 5kn.) If it's religious art you crave, head to **"Kairos,"** a collection in the convent of St. Nicholas off Kohl-Genscher past Trg Ivana Pavla. The centerpiece of the exhibition is a 3rd-century BC Greek relief of a figure symbolizing Kairos, god of the "fleeting moment." Also be sure to step outside the city walls and admire the intricate lattice-work on the bell-tower of the monastery. (☎ 88 16 31. Open M-Sa 9am-12:30pm and 4-6:30pm. 10kn, students 5kn.) At the tip of the island lie the remains of the **Fortress of Kamerlengo.** Originally built in 1380 by Genoans to defend the city, it now it serves as Trogir's only **cinema,** showing the latest Hollywood flicks beneath the night sky during the summer. (Open M-Sa 9am-6pm. 10kn, students free. Movies 20kn.)

The rocky **beach** starts at Hotel Saldun, across the Čiovski bridge and on the other side of the hill (15min. walk). The beach then winds around the larger island. Cafes of similar atmosphere, prices, and menus line Kohl-Genscher and the waterfront, but there's only one named **Big Daddy,** Obala b. Berislavića 14. It will fill you with 0.33L bottles of *Karlovačko* (11kn) while you rock on swing chairs. (Open daily 8am-3am.) On weekend nights, all the action goes down on this stretch. For a Cathedral view, try **Radovan,** Trg Ivana Pavla 2, which has seating on a quiet terrace. (☎ 88 23 80. 0.5L *Karlovačko* 12kn; coffee 5kn. Open daily 7am-midnight.)

SPLIT ☎ (0)21

Metropolitan, busy, and dusty, Dalmatia's capital, Split (pop. 200,000), is by no means a typical Dalmatian town. As Croatia's second-largest city, it is more a cultural center than a beach resort, boasting a wider variety of activities and nightlife than any of its neighbors. Stari Grad, wedged between a high mountain range and a palm-lined waterfront, is framed by a luxurious palace where Roman Emperor Diocletian used to spend his summers. In the 7th century, the local Ilyrian population fled to the palace to escape the attacks of marauding Slavs and built a town there, incorporating the walls and arches of the palace into their houses and public squares. The result is perhaps the most puzzling piece of architecture in Europe, and surely one of the most interesting.

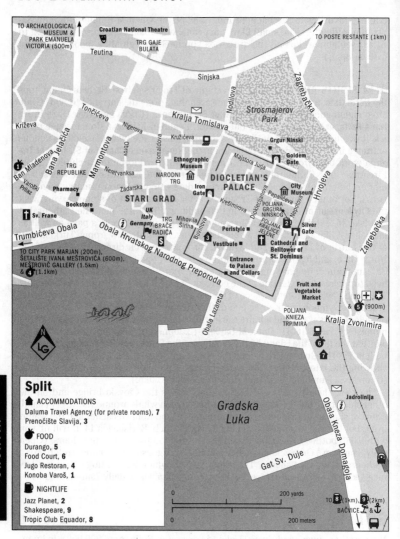

Split

♦ ACCOMMODATIONS
Daluma Travel Agency (for private rooms), 7
Prenoćište Slavija, 3

♠ FOOD
Durango, 5
Food Court, 6
Jugo Restoran, 4
Konoba Varoš, 1

◖ NIGHTLIFE
Jazz Planet, 2
Shakespeare, 9
Tropic Club Equador, 8

▣ TRANSPORTATION

Flights: Split Airport (☎20 35 55; fax 20 34 22). A bus runs between the airport and the waterfront near where the passe nger catamarans dock 90min. before every departure. **Croatia Airlines,** Obala hrvatskog narodnog preporoda 9 (☎36 29 97). Open M-F 8am-8pm, Sa 9am-noon.

Trains: Obala Kneza Domagoja 10 (☎33 85 35). Due to the destruction of railways during the recent war, trains are very inefficient; use buses. Trains do not run south of Split. Ticket office open daily 6am-10pm. To: **Rijeka** (12hr., 2 per day, 123kn) via **Oguli;**

Zadar (6½hr., 1 per day, 63kn) via **Knin; Zagreb** (7½hr., 4 per day, 124kn). For international destinations, go to **Croatia Express** (see **Budget Travel**, below), next to the train station. To **Budapest, HUN** (16hr., 1 per night, 320kn) and **Ljubljana, SLN** (12hr., 2 per week, 200kn).

Buses: Obala Kneza Domagoja 12 (☎33 84 83 or 33 84 86, schedule info 050 32 73 27). Domestic tickets sold outside, international *(medunarodni karte)* inside. Open daily 5am-11pm. To: **Dubrovnik** (4½hr., 17 per day, 110kn); **Rijeka** (7hr., 13 per day, 171kn); **Zadar** (3½hr., every 30min., 70-80kn); **Zagreb** (8hr., every 30min., 114-134kn); **Ljubljana, SLN** (11hr., 1 per day, 233kn); **Sarajevo, BOS** (7½hr., 6 per day, 171kn). Buses to **Trogir** (30min.; 3 per hr.; 15kn, round-trip 23.50kn) leave from the **local bus station** on Domovinskog rata, an extension of Zagrebačka.

Ferries: Obala Kneza Domagoja bb (☎33 83 33; fax 33 82 22). To: **Dubrovnik** (8hr., 5 per week, 72kn); **Korčula** (6hr., 6per week, 31kn); **Rijeka** (10½hr., 5 per week, 107kn); **Ancona, ITA** (10hr., 4 per week, 256kn); **Bari, ITA** (25hr., 3 per week, 256kn).

Public Transportation: Buy tickets (5kn) from the driver and punch them on board. Buses run all night, but are few and far between after midnight.

Taxis: ☎34 77 77. Many wait in front of Diocletian's Palace on Obala hrvatskog narodnog preporoda. Average fare 18kn, plus 9kn per km.

■ ORIENTATION

Split is the most important ferry port in Croatia, serving the nearby islands of Brač, Hvar, and Vis, as well as Dubrovnik, Rijeka, and more distant destinations in Italy and Greece. The **train** and **bus stations** lie across from the **ferry** terminal on **Obala Kneza Domagoja.** Leaving the stations, follow Obala Kneza Domagoja, often referred to simply as **Riva,** to the right along the water until it runs into **Obala hrvatskog narodnog preporoda,** which runs roughly east to west. To the north lies **Stari Grad** (Old Town), packed inside the walls of Diocletian's Palace (Dioklecijanova Palača). To reach Stari Grad from the local bus station, turn right on **Domovinskog Rata,** which turns into **Livanjska** and then **Zagrebačka.** Turn right on **Kralja Zvonimira** at the end of Zagrebačka and follow it to the harbor.

■ PRACTICAL INFORMATION

Tourist Office: Turistički Biro, Obala hrvatskog narodnog preporoda 12 (☎/fax 34 21 42 or 34 25 44), hands out detailed **maps** of Stari Grad and sells larger maps of Split (25kn). Open M-F 7:30am-8:30pm, Sa 8am-2pm.

Budget Travel: Croatia Express, Obala Kneza Domagoja 9 (☎33 85 25; fax 33 84 70; croatia-express@st.tel.hr), sells bus, plane, and train tickets. Student discounts for train tickets. Open daily 6am-10pm.

Consulates: UK (☎24 14 64, emergency 34 14 64; public hours M-F 9am-1pm), **Italy,** and **Germany** share a building at Obala hrvatskog narodnog preporoda 10, above Zagrebačka bank. There are no **US, Canadian,** or **Australilan** consulates in Split.

Currency Exchange: Zagrebačka Banka, Obala hrvatskog narodnog preporoda 10 (☎34 78 10), exchanges currency for no commission and cashes **traveler's checks** for a 1.5% commission. Open M-F 8:30am-2pm and 3-7:30pm, Sa 8:30am-12:30pm.

American Express: Atlas Travel Agency, Nepotova bb (☎34 30 55; fax 36 20 12). Open M-Sa 8am-8pm, Su 8am-noon.

Luggage Storage: At the bus station: 2.50kn per hr. Open daily 6am-10pm. At the train station: 10kn per day. Open daily 5:30-10:30am, 11am-4:30pm, and 5-9:30pm.

Pharmacy: Marmontova 2 (☎48 84 00). Open M-F 7am-8pm, Sa 7am-1pm.

CROATIA

Police: Trg hrvatske bratske zajednice 9 (☎30 71 11). From Stari Grad, take Kralja Zvonimira and bear right onto Pojišanka; the station is on the right.

Hospital: Clinical Hospital Center, Spinčiceva 1 (☎55 61 11). From Stari Grad, follow Kralja Zvonimira until it runs into Pozjička Cesta. Then turn right onto Pt. Iza Nove Bolnice; the hospital is on the right.

English-Language Bookstore: Obala hrvatskog narodnog preporoda 21 (☎34 16 26). Good selection of foreign-language magazines and newspapers. Open M-Sa 8am-8pm, Su 8am-12:30pm.

Internet Access: Žute Stranice, Obala Kneza Domogoja (☎33 85 48). Friendly Aussie proprietor Steve hooks you up to the Internet for 30kn per hr., sells used English-language paperbacks, and gives advice on getting around. **Cyber Caffe Mriža,** Kružićeva 3 (☎32 13 20). 20kn per hr. Open M-F 9am-9pm, Sa 9am-2pm.

Post Office: Ul. Kralja Tomislava 9 (☎36 14 21). Mail through the main doors; **telephones** and **fax** through the doors to the left. Also **exchanges currency** for 1.5% commission. Open M-F 7am-8pm, Sa 7am-1pm. **Poste Restante** at Hercegovačka 1 (☎38 33 65). Take Zagrebačka from Stari Grad to Domovinskog Rata to a left onto Pt. Stinica (20min.). Hang a right onto Hercegovačka. Open M-Sa 7am-8pm.

Postal Code: 21000

▚ ACCOMMODATIONS

For a city its size, Split has a paltry selection of accommodations—especially budget ones—as many hotels are still recovering from the war. Two of the largest hotels have recently closed, although attempts are being made to reopen them. **Daluma Travel Agency ❷,** Obala Kneza Domogoja 1, near the bus and train stations, can help find central **private rooms.** (☎33 84 84; ☎/fax 33 84 39; www.tel.hr/dalumatravel. Open M-F 8am-8pm, Sa 8am-12:30pm. May-Oct. singles 120kn; doubles 240kn. Nov.-Apr. 90kn/180kn.) People at the bus station and ferry landing also offer rooms. **Prenoćište Slavija ❸,** Buvinova 2, recently renovated, has 70 beds in high-ceilinged, clean rooms in the middle of Stari Grad. It's right next to some of the hippest (and loudest) cafes in town. Follow Obala hrvatskog narodnog preporoda to a right on Trg Braće Radića, then take another right on Mihovilova Širina. Signs lead up the stairs. (☎34 70 53; fax 59 15 58. Breakfast included. Reception 24hr. Check-out 11am. Singles 180kn, with shower 220kn; doubles 210kn/260kn; triples 250kn/300kn; quads 280kn/360kn. Tax 5.50-7kn. Registration 9kn.)

◖ FOOD

There are **supermarkets** inside the Jadrolinija complex across from the bus station (open M-Sa 6am-9pm, Su 7am-9pm) and at Svačićeva 4 (open daily 7am-10pm). The **food court ❶** at Obala Kneza Domogoja 1, between Stari Grad and the stations, is incredibly cheap. (Pizza 8kn; sandwich 10kn.) Across Kralja Zvonimira from the food court is an **open-air market** that sells everything from fruit and vegetables to clothing and cigarettes. (Open daily 6am-8pm.)

▨ **Jugo Restoran,** Uvala Baluni bb (☎34 12 12). Facing the water on Obala hrvatskog narodnog preporada, walk right along the waterfront (10min.) to Branimirova Obala. Signs to the restaurant lead up the hill. This modern restaurant overlooking the marina attracts local celebrities with its excellent seafood, brick-oven pizza, and homemade sausage. Large menu. Entrees 30-65kn. Open daily 9am-midnight. AmEx/MC/V. ❷

Konoba Varoš, Ban Mladenova 7 (☎39 61 38). Facing the water on Obala hrvatskog narodnog preporoda, head right on Varoški Prilaz and then left on Ban Mladenova. A true Dalmatian feast, prepared and served in a den adorned with fishing nets and wine racks. Prepare your taste buds for something different—frogs with prosciutto (*žabe na žaru s pršutom;* 215kn per kg) and calves' brains (*mozak pohani;* 53kn)—or stick with pasta (30-44kn). Open M-F 9am-1am, Sa-Su noon-1am. ❷

Durango, Dubrovačka 1a (☎53 10 26). Follow Kralja Zvonimira from the waterfront until it becomes Poljička, then turn left on Dubrovačka. While it's far from authentic, the Tex-Mex food served up at Durango provides a welcome change to the taste buds. A margarita (20kn) goes nicely with the burritos and the blues playing in the background. Entrees 25-60kn. Open daily noon-midnight. ❶

SIGHTS

DIOCLETIAN'S PALACE (DIOKLECIJANOVA PALAČA)

Across from the taxis on Obala hrvatskog narodnog preporoda and to the right down into the cool, dark corridor.

The eastern half of Split's Stari Grad occupies the one-time fortress and summer residence of the Roman Emperor Diocletian. The palace, built between AD 395 and 410, has seen its fair share of empires—and refugees. Having first protected Roman royalty, it later served as sanctuary for Galla Placidia, daughter of Byzantine Emperor Theodosius, and her son Valentinius III, who were dodging the blades of usurpers. In the 7th century, local residents were forced into the fortress to protect themselves from Slavic raids. They later built their city within its walls. Today, it's a living museum of classical and medieval architecture.

CELLARS. The city's cellars are located near the entrance to the palace; turn through either gate to wander around this haunting labyrinth. Nearly two millenia ago, the dark stone passages constituted a flat floor for the emperor's apartments. The central hall runs from Obala hrvatskog narodnog preporoda to the Peristyle and holds booths that sell the work of local artists, some of it quite good. The hall on the left houses a brand-new computer that gives a wealth of history about the palace and city while it entertains visitors with Renaissance music. Some of the archaeological finds are displayed in hallways to the left of the entrance. The airier right side is used to display artwork. Every year the palace becomes more complete as more rooms (some from right under local residences) are excavated. *(Cellars open daily 10am-7pm. 6kn, students 3kn.)*

CATHEDRAL. The Cathedral on the right side of the Peristyle is one of architecture's great ironies: it's the oldest Catholic cathedral in the world, but was originally the mausoleum of Diocletian, who was known for his violent persecution of Christians. The small circular interior, which contains intricately wrought stonework, leaves almost no room for tourists who come to wonder at the magnificent inner door and altar. The cathedral **treasury,** up the stairs to the right, displays 15th-century ecclesiastic garments, delicate 13th-century books, and a mass of silver busts and goblets. The adjoining **Bell Tower of St. Domnius** (Zvonik Sv. Duje), begun in the 13th century, took 300 years to complete. The view from the top is incredible, but the climb is a bit unnerving. *(Cathedral and tower open daily 8:30am-9:30pm. Tower and treasury 5kn.)*

OTHER SIGHTS IN STARI GRAD

Stari Grad is framed on the eastern side by the **Silver Gate** (Srebrna Vrata), which leads to the main open-air market (see above). Outside the north **Golden Gate** (Zlatna Vrata) stands Ivan Meštrović's rendering of **Gregorius of Nin** (Grgur Ninski), the 10th-century Slavic champion of commoners. The western **Iron Gate** (Željezna Vrata) leads onto Narodni Trg. Medieval architecture also dominate this side of town, though there aren't any excavations in progress. Many of the medieval houses are crumbling with age and drop stones here and there. Why dig to find history when it finds you? **Park Emanuela Victoria,** off Zrinsko-Frankopanska on the way to the Archaeological Museum (see below), is a great place for a stroll.

🏛 MUSEUMS

▨ **MEŠTROVIČ GALLERY.** (Galerija Ivana Meštrovića.) The gallery has a comprehensive collection of works by Ivan Meštrović (see **The Arts,** p. 154), as well as tremendous views of the ocean. The entrance fee gets you into both the gallery, housed in a stately villa that the artist built for himself, and the Kaštelet, decorated with wood carvings that depict the life of Jesus. *(Šetaliste Ivana Meštrovica 46, a 25min. walk along the waterfront. ☎35 84 50. Open June-Aug. Tu-Sa 10am-6pm, Su 10am-3pm; Sept.-May Tu-Sa 10am-4pm, Su 10am-2pm. 15kn, students 10kn. English booklet 20kn.)*

ARCHAEOLOGICAL MUSEUM. (Arheološki Muzej.) One of the oldest museums in Croatia, this venerable institution makes shards of pottery fascinating with well-written English descriptions. The beautiful garden outside is filled with an impressive hodgepodge of Roman statuary. *(Zrinsko-Frankopanska 25. From the waterfront, follow Marmontova to Trg Gaje Bulata, turn left on Teutina and then take the first right, which leads up to Zrinsko-Frankopanska. ☎31 87 21 or 31 87 62. Open M-F 9am-noon and 5-9pm, Sa-Su 9am-noon. 10kn, students 5kn.)*

CITY MUSEUM. (Muzej Grada Splita.) Houses a minimal selection of artifacts, but tells the history of Split in detail. The building is a 15th-century construction by Juraj Dalmatinac, the architect of Šibenik's Cathedral. *(Papaliceva 1. From the Golden Gate, enter Stari Grad and turn left on Papaliceva. ☎34 12 40. English placards. Open Tu-F 9am-noon and 6-9pm, Sa-Su 10am-noon. 10kn, students 5kn.)*

ETHNOGRAPHIC MUSEUM. (Etnografski Muzej.) This museum displays artifacts of Croatian domestic and ceremonial life in times past. Great if you enjoy intricate old clothing; otherwise, stick to the other museums. *(Iza lože 1, in Narodni Trg. ☎34 41 64. Open Tu-F 9am-noon and 6pm-9pm, Su-M 9am-noon. 10kn, students 5kn.)*

🌊 🎭 BEACHES AND ENTERTAINMENT

The rocky cliffs, green hills, and pebbly beaches on the west end of Split's peninsula make up **City Park Marjan,** a great spot for walking or jogging. From Obala hrvatskog naraodnog preporoda, face the water and head right (15min.). Paths are indicated on the map; you can find your own way, but watch for signs indicating that a trail leads to private lands, as the dogs are known to bite. The closest beach to downtown Split is sandy **Bačvice,** a favorite of local nocturnal skinny dippers and the starting point of a great strip of bars along the waterfront that make up the heart of Split's nightlife. From mid-July to mid-Aug., Split hosts an annual **Summer Festival,** when the city's best artists and international guests perform ballets, operas, plays, and classical concerts in the town's churches and ruins. A three-day **Folk Concert** is held at the open-air stage in Zvončac at the beginning of July.

CROATIA

NIGHTLIFE

▨ **Tropic Club Equador,** Kupalište Baćvice bb. Just past Baćvice beach (see above), on the second level of the club complex. A Latin terrace bar that plays the rumba. Sip on not-so-subtly named cocktails—go see for yourself (20-50kn). Open daily 9am-1am.

Shakespeare, Cvetna 1 (☎51 94 92). Follow the waterfront past Tropic Club Equador for another 20min. The bard might turn over in his grave now that 2 floors of raging techno bear his name. 30kn cover. Open Th-Su 11pm-until you drop.

Jazz Planet, Grgura Ninskoga 3 (☎34 76 99). Hidden on a tiny back street opposite the City Museum, Jazz Planet has comfy chairs outside and soothing blue lighting inside that mixes well with jazz and beer. 0.5L Guinness 25kn, 0.5L *Bavaria* 15kn. Open Su-Th 8am-midnight, F-Sa 8am-2am.

BRAČ ISLAND: BOL ☎(0)21

Central Dalmatia's largest island, Brač (BRAtch; pop. 1500), particularly the town of Bol on its southern coast, is an ocean-lover's paradise. Most visitors come here for Zlatni rat, a peninsula just a short walk from the town center that packs the crowds on its white pebble beach and in the emerald waters that kiss the shore. Brač has more to offer than location, though: churches, galleries, lively nightlife, and more water sports than you can imagine will keep you busy for as long as you choose to stay.

▐ TRANSPORTATION. The **ferry** from **Split** docks at **Supetar** (1hr.; July-Aug. 13 per day, Sept.-June 7 per day; 23kn). From there, take a **bus** to Bol (1hr., 5 per day, 13kn). The last bus back to the ferry leaves at 5:50pm; the last ferry to Split leaves June-Aug. at 8:30pm and Sept.-May. at 7:30pm. A **catamaran** runs directly to Bol from Split (40min.; departs M-Sa from Bol 6:30am, from Split 4pm; Su from Bol 7:30am, Split 4pm; 70kn, round-trip 120kn). Buy tickets on board.

▟ ▞ ORIENTATION AND PRACTICAL INFORMATION. The town is organized around the many-named waterfront: at the bus stop and marina, it's called **Obala Vladimira Nazora;** to the left of the bus station (facing the water) it becomes **Riva,** then **Frane Radića,** then **Porat bolskih pomorca;** to the right it's called **Pt. Zlatnograta.** The **tourist office,** Porat bolskich pomorca bb, is a 5min. walk to the left of the bus station on the far side of the small marina. It offers **Internet access** (25kn per hr., 15kn per 30min.) and dispenses a Bol guide and large **maps.** (☎63 56 38; fax 63 59 72; tzo-bol@st.tel.hr.) **Zagrebačka banka,** Uz Pjacu 4, uphill from Frane Radića, **exchanges currency** for no commission and cashes **traveler's checks** for a 1.5% commission. (☎/fax 63 56 11. Open M-F 8am-2pm, Sa 8am-noon.) **Adria Tours,** Obala Vladimira Nazora 28, to the right of the bus station facing the water, **rents motorcycles** (150kn per half-day, 250kn per day) and **cars** (400kn per day including mileage). The Adria office also books rooms and organizes excursions (see **Accommodations,** below). There's a **pharmacy** and **clinic** on Porat bolskich pomorca bb. (☎63 51 12. Open M-Sa 8am-9pm, Su 8am-noon.) The **post office,** Uz Pjacu 5, has **telephones.** (☎63 52 35; fax 63 52 53. Open M-Sa 7am-9pm.) **Postal Code:** 21420.

▛ ▢ ACCOMMODATIONS AND FOOD. Your cheapest bet is to call one of the local residence numbers listed in the tourist office's booklet and arrange a **private room.** This method generally saves you 10-20% by bypassing agency prices. If the locals are all at the beach, **Adria Tours ❶** will find you a room. (☎63 59 66; fax 63 59 77; www.tel.hr/adria-tours-bol. Open daily 8am-9pm. 60-136kn per person. Tax 5.50kn. 20% surcharge for stays under 3 nights.) If it's a **hotel room** you're after, going through an agency can save you 10-15% off the price at the desk for reasons unknown. Adria Tours offers special deals on local hotel rooms starting at 250kn per person. There are five **campsites** around Bol; the largest is **Kito ❶**, Bračka Cesta bb, on the road into town. (☎63 54 24 or 63 55 51. Open May 1-Sept. 30. 38kn per person; tent included.)

Konoba Gušt ❷, Frane Radića 14, offers shady respite among hanging fishing gear and local diners, along with an array of fresh seafood. (☎63 59 11. Entrees 40-100kn. Open daily noon-2am). If you're sick of bringing picnic lunches to the beach, the picnic-table **cafeteria ❶**, under the pines off Zlatni Rat, is the answer. (Salads and grilled specialties 20-50kn. Open daily 10am-6pm.) **Pizzeria Topolino ❶**, A. Radića, on the waterfront in the center of town, has good pizza and pasta for 25-40kn. (Open daily 8am-2am.) **Supermarket Vrtić**, on Uz Pjacu up the hill from the post office, can slice up a sandwich for around 10kn. (Open daily 6:30am-9pm.)

◨ 🎭 **SIGHTS AND ENTERTAINMENT.** The free **map** distributed by the tourist office (see above) shows all the town's sights, the most important of which is the 1475 **Dominican Monastery,** located on the eastern tip of Bol. Facing the water, walk left for 15min. The highlight of the monastery is Tintoretto's altar painting of the Madonna with Child. Apparently concerned they might need a refund, the monks kept the invoice for the masterpiece, which is on display in the **museum,** among other artifacts of local history. (Open daily 10am-noon and 5-7pm. 10kn.) The **Dešković Gallery,** on Porat bolskih pomorca, next to the bus station, exhibits contemporary Croatian art in a small 17th-century Renaissance-Baroque mansion. (Open daily 5-10pm. 5kn.) More art comes to town during **Bol Cultural Summer** (Bolsko Kulturno Ljeto; June-Sept.). **Big Blue Sport,** Podan Glavice 2, on the way to Zlatni rat, organizes **scuba diving** and **windsurfing.** (☎/fax 63 56 14; www.tel.hr/bigblue-sport. Open daily 8:30-11:30am and 6-10pm. One-day dive or night dive with equipment rental 240kn. 8hr. windsurfing course 780kn; rentals 300kn per day, 230kn per ½ day.) **Boat rentals** are available through Adria Tours (see above) or along the waterfront past the bus station. The **outdoor cinema** opposite the bus station has nightly showings (15-18kn), weather permitting.

VIS ISLAND: KOMIŽA   ☎(0)21

A bit farther from the mainland than Dalmatia's most popular islands, Vis's relative isolation has preserved its natural beauty and traditional character in the island slow pace of life. Residents continue to fish, grow olives, and make wine as they have for centuries, with only a passing nod to tourism. However, Vis offers stunning natural attractions for the bold tourist to explore, with boat rides through the blue grotto on nearby Biševo and scuba diving through sunken shipwrecks.

🚆 **TRANSPORTATION.** A **ferry** runs to Vis Town from **Split** (2½hr., June-Sept. 1-2 per day, 22kn). There is also a **catamaran** that makes the trip more quickly (1 per day, 22kn). Take a day excursion from **Hvar Town** (1hr.; 1 per week; 100kn, round-trip 70kn). **Buses** to Komiža meet the ferry (30min., 7 per day, 12kn).

▉ 🖫 **ORIENTATION AND PRACTICAL INFORMATION.** The town of Komiža is tiny enough that you can't get lost. The bus stops on **Hrvatskih Mučenika,** a few steps from **Riva** (the waterfront). A right turn on Riva leads to **Ribarska** and to the **beach,** while a left takes you to most services and sights. To get to the **tourist office,** Riva 1, face the water and walk left along the waterfront until the end of the harbor. (☎/fax 71 34 55. Open July-Aug. M-Sa 8am-9pm; Sept.-June M-Sa 8am-2pm and 3-9pm, Su 9am-noon.) On your way you'll pass the **bus station** and the **tourist agency**

Darlić & Darlić, Riva 13. Mother Darlić, brother Darlić, or sister Darlić will arrange **private rooms** (see below), and **exchange currency** for no commission. You can also connect to the **Internet** with their fast computer for a pricey 30kn per 15min. (☎71 37 60; fax 71 72 06; www.pl-print.tel.hr/darlic. Open in summer daily 8am-9pm; in winter 8am-1pm.) **Splitska Banka,** Trg Kralja Tomislava 10, on the waterfront, exchanges cash for no commission and **traveler's checks** for a 2% commission. (☎71 82 88. Open M-F 8am-1pm, Sa 8-11:30am.) There are **no ATMs** on the island. The **pharmacy,** San Pedro 11, is the only tricky place to find; from the waterfront, turn on Hrvatskih Mučenika, then take the second left. When the street curves to the left, curve with it and then walk up a ramp that leads behind a long white building; the pharmacy is at the end of the ramp and up the stairs. (☎71 34 45. Open M-F 8am-1pm and 7-8pm, Sa 8:30-10:30am.) The **post office,** Hrvatskih Mučenika 8, next to the bus station, **exchanges currency,** cashes **traveler's checks** for 1.5% commission, and gives MC **cash advances.** There are **telephones** inside. (☎71 30 20; fax 71 35 98. Open M-Sa 8am-2pm.) **Postal Code:** 21485.

⌐⌐ ACCOMMODATIONS AND FOOD. The only budget option around is a **private room** arranged by **Darlić & Darlić ❷** (see above). The family will find you a bed by any means necessary—even in their own home. (July 15-Aug. 19 singles 90-130kn; doubles 130-180kn. July 1-10 and Aug. 19-Sept. 10 65-105kn/90-150kn. June and Sept. 60-80kn/75-105kn. 30% surcharge for stays under 3 nights. Tourist tax 3.50-6kn.) The one hotel in town is the **Hotel Biševo ❹,** Ribarska 72. To get there, turn right as you face the water from anywhere in town and keep walking; it's next to the beach. Small modern rooms offer TV, phone, and fridge. (☎71 30 95; fax 71 30 98. Breakfast included. Singles 200-330kn; doubles 320-540kn.) Restaurants are pricey, but excellent. Don't miss the local favorite ▨ **Konoba Bako ❷,** Gundulićeva 1. In its own little cove in town, Konoba Baka sets up tables and benches right on the water. (☎71 37 42. Seafood and meat dishes 55-120kn. Open daily 6pm-midnight.) For a more central location, head to **Riblji Restoran Komiža ❸,** on the waterfront next to Darlić & Darlić. (Entrees 50-80kn. Open daily 7am-11pm.) There's a **supermarket** on Riva. (Open M-Sa 6:30am-9pm.)

◪ SIGHTS. St. Nicholas Church (Crkva sv. Nikole), called *muster* (monastery) by the locals, overlooks Komiža. Built as part of a Benedictine monastery in the 12th century, it now holds services every Sunday, the only time you'll be able to get inside to take a look. To get there, follow any side street uphill from the waterfront. Right on the beach sits the **Pirates' Church** (Gusarica). According to legend, pirates stole a Madonna from this church, but were soon caught in a storm so fierce that only the Blessed Virgin made it back to shore. (Open daily morning and evening during the summer.) Several agencies organize daytrips to neighboring islands; try the Darlić & Darlić-organized excursions (see above). Trips include the **Green Cave** on Ravnik Island (daily, 120kn), the incredible **Blue Cave** on Biševo Island (2 per day, full or half-day 80kn), and **St. Andrew,** which includes fishing with a local fisherman and then cooking up your catch (1 per day, 230kn). According to legend, the Illyrian queen Teutha was banished to the island of St. Andrew for murdering her lover. She brought with her a royal stash of gold—treasure that has yet to be found. If you'd rather spend a few days exploring with local fishermen, inquire at the tourist office. Fishing excursions take three to four days at a time.

   The **Fisherman's Museum** (Ribarski muzej) is on Riva next to the tourist office (see above). You never knew rope could be tied in so many ways. The museum lacks English placards, but the weathered seaman/curator will give you the lowdown. The museum's roof offers a splendid view of the town and of the marina. (Open M-Sa 10am-noon and 7-10pm, Su 7-10pm.)

🎵 **ENTERTAINMENT.** Komiža's **beach** is small and crowded, but that makes little difference when you're floating in water so clear you can see your toes. Both **Issa Diving Center,** Ribarska 91 (☎/fax 71 36 51; www.diving-hr/idc), on your left before the beach, and **Manta Diving Center,** at the far end of the beach (☎ 098 26 59 23; fax 52 23 48; manta@st.tel.hr) offer 30min. intro dives (300kn) and advanced dives to sunken shipwrecks. The most popular cafe-bar is **Speed,** Škor 12, though the name belies the town's lazy, easygoing nightlife. (Open daily 6am-1am.) Don't miss the **Voga Disco Bar,** Trup 9, on the water between the hotel and the center. This 800-year-old building became Croatia's first disco in 1969 and hasn't slowed down since. The action picks up at 1am. (Open in summer daily 8am-4am.)

HVAR ISLAND ☎(0)21

In 1997, *Traveller* magazine named Hvar (hVAR) one of the ten most beautiful islands in the world. The thin, 88km-long island affords breathtaking views of the mainland mountains from its high, rugged hills. A favorite summer getaway for chic urbanites from Split, the town plays host to the tanned masses from mid-July through August. Luckily, the nearby Pakleni Otoci (Hellish Islands) provide enough beach for everyone. Many resort hotels actually guarantee the weather—if the temperature dips too low or it begins to snow, rooms are on the house.

📧 **TRANSPORTATION. Ferries** make the trip from Split to Hvar's **Stari Grad** (2hr.; June-Aug. M-Th 3 per day, F-Su 5 per day; 28kn, with car 182kn). From there, **buses** scheduled around the ferry take passengers to **Hvar Town** (15min., 11kn). Alternatively, head from Split directly to Hvar Town: there's a fast boat in the morning (1hr., 1 per day, 22kn) in addition to a regular ferry (2hr., 2 per day, 28kn). Pelegrini Tours (see below) runs a **catamaran** between Hvar and **Komiža** for day excursions during the summer (1hr.; 1 per week; 100kn, round-trip 170kn). You can also come from Bol on Brač to **Jelsa** on Hvar (1hr., 4 per week, 60-100kn). Contact Adiva Tours in Bol (see **Bol Island,** p. 201). A bus runs to Hvar Town from Jelsa (40min.; M-Sa 5 per day, Su 2 per day; 19kn). To reach the **bus station,** walk through Trg sv. Stjepana from the marina and to the left of the church; the station is on your left. **Jadrolinija,** Riva bb, on the left tip of the waterfront, sells **ferry** tickets. (☎ 74 11 32; fax 74 10 36. Open M-Sa 5:30am-12:30pm and 2-9pm, Su 8am-pam and 2pm-5pm. Opening hours may vary according to ferry schedule). During the summer **Pelegrini Tours,** Riva bb, **rents cars** (380kn per day, unlimited mileage) and **bikes** (50kn per day, 10kn per hr.) for exploring the rest of the island. (☎/fax 74 22 50. Open daily 8am-10pm, off-season 8:30am-12:30pm and 6-9pm.)

🖥📋 **ORIENTATION AND PRACTICAL INFORMATION.** Hvar Town has virtually no street names and even fewer signs. The main square, **Trg sv. Stjepana,** directly below the bus station by the waterfront (Riva), is the one place graced with a name. Facing the sea from the main square, take a left along the waterfront in order to reach the **tourist office, bank,** and ferry terminal; a right leads to the major hotels and beaches. The tourist office, **Turistička Zajednica,** Trg sv. Stjepana 21, is on the corner of the main square closest to the water. The smiling staff has detailed **maps** (15kn) and bus schedules. (☎/fax 74 10 59; www.hvar.hr. Open M-Sa 8am-2pm and 5-10pm, Su 9am-noon and 6-9pm; off-season daily 8:30am-noon.) **Splitska Banka,** Riva 4, **exchanges currency** for no commission and cashes **traveler's checks** for a 2% commission. (Open M-F 7:30am-1pm and 2-8pm, Sa 8-11:30am.) There's a Visa **ATM** outside the bank and an AmEx/MC **ATM** across the harbor in front of **Zagrebačka Banka.** There's a **pharmacy** at Trg sv. Stjepana. (☎ 74 10 02. Open

M-F 8am-9pm, Sa 8am-1pm and 5:30-8:30pm, Su 9am-noon.) The **post office** is a bit of a walk; it's easier to buy stamps at a kiosk and drop mail into a yellow post box. If necessary, walk straight away from Trg sv. Stjepana, past the bus station, and fork left on the road going to Vira. It's the last building on your left and has **telephones** and **Poste Restante.** (☎74 24 13. Open M-Sa 7am-9pm.) **Postal Code:** 21450.

☎ ⬚ ACCOMMODATIONS AND FOOD. As in other Croatian resort towns, the only budget accommodations are **private rooms,** and even these are expensive. **Pelegrini Tours ❷** (see above) can make arrangements. (May 1-June 26 and Sept. 25-Oct. 23 singles 97kn; doubles 124kn. June 26-July 24 and Aug. 28-Sept. 25 113kn/156kn. July 24-Aug. 29 125kn/170kn. 30% surcharge for stays under 3 nights.) Many locals hang around the bus station offering rooms for less, and some even make the trip to Stari Grad to meet the ferries and offer you a ride. If all else fails, try your luck finding *sobe* (room) signs down the waterfront from the main square. Overpriced restaurants line the waterfront and the square. For a cheaper and better meal, head one block up the steps leading from the main square to the fortress to visit **Luna ❷.** The enchanting rooftop terrace lets you dine by moonlight on excellent fish and meat standards. (Entrees 55-90kn.) On a hot day, don't miss the ice-cold gazpacho (18kn. ☎74 86 95. Open daily 12-3pm and 6pm-midnight.) Dine under hanging lanterns and grapevines at **Alviz ❷,** opposite the bus station. Vegetable lasagne (38kn) and salad *Nicoise* (20kn) to satisfy hungry leaf-eaters. (☎74 27 97. Open daily 6pm-1am. Cash only.) There's an **open-air market** between the bus station and the main square. (Open daily 7am-8pm.) The **supermarket** on Trg sv. Stjepana is small but well-stocked. (Open M-Sa 6.30am-10pm, Su 7am-noon.)

⬚ SIGHTS. The stairs to the right of the square (as you face the sea) lead to a 13th-century **Venetian fortress.** Although Turkish attacks weakened the fortress, a lightning bolt that once struck the powder-room proved even more devastating. (Open daily 8am-midnight. 10kn.) Inside, you'll find a **marine archaeological collection** *(hidroarheološka zbirka),* that consists primarily of Greek and Byzantine amphorae. (Open daily 10am-1pm. Free.) Any remaining museum-going thirst can be quenched at the **Gallery Arsenal,** up the stairs next to the tourist office (open daily 10am-noon and 8-11pm; 10kn, students free), or at the **Last Supper Collection** in the **Franciscan monastery,** which includes the *other* famous *Last Supper,* an oil-painting by Matteo Ignoli. (Open daily 10am-noon and 5-6pm. 10kn.)

⬚ ⬚ FESTIVALS AND NIGHTLIFE. The Franciscan monastery hosts many outdoor performances during the **Hvar Summer Festival.** Some of the indoor performances take place above the Arsenal in one of Europe's oldest **community theaters,** dating from 1612. (Festival performances 30-50kn.) For 10 days every July or August, Hvar hosts the **Shakespeare Days Festival,** a celebration of the bard's work by international actors and directors, including performances and workshops at the monastery. Inquire at the tourist office (see above) for more information.

The most crowded bars are along the waterfront. For something smaller and more intimate, head to **Caffe Bar Jazz,** Burak bb, on a side street uphill from Splitska Banka. The bar's multi-colored interior and local crowd make this a worthy spot. (Vodka juice 15kn. Open daily 9am-1pm and 6pm-2am). At the end of Rira, past the Jadrohhja office, **Carpe Diem** has loud live DJs and beach drink specials during the summer, like *bellini* for 23kn. (Open daily 9am-2am.) Walk all the way around to the opposite side of the marina and up the garden path on your right to the local **disco,** which has dancing indoors and outside around a big fountain. (Open daily 10pm-5am.) Earlier in the evenings, this same space functions as an **open-air cinema.** Keep your eyes out for posters advertising what's playing.

CROATIA

◢🏊 **BEACHES AND ISLANDS.** Some of the Adriatic's clearest waters surround Hvar, but to enjoy them you'll have to brave the loud, crowded, gravel **beaches** and fearsome aquatic hedgehogs. Less crowded beaches are a 20min. walk to the left down the waterfront. Or, head to Jevolim, Ždrilca, and Palmižana, known collectively as the **Hellish Islands** (Pakleni Otoci). The last island is home to **Palmižana beach,** which has waterside restaurants, rocks for tanning, sparse sand, and a nudist area at the far tip of the cove. Boats run a **taxi service** between the islands. (Every 30min. 10am-6:30pm, round-trip 15-30kn.) The cheery family staff of the **diving center** in Hotel Amfora, on the beach, offers diving and rentals. (☎/fax 74 24 90. Open daily 10am-6pm. Shore dives including equipment 133-150kn; boat dive with equipment 122kn; 2 dives 245kn. Bike rental 54kn per day. Motorboats 200kn per day. Snorkel equipment 31kn per day. Kayaks 30kn per hr.)

KORČULA ISLAND ☎ 020

Korčula (KOR-chu-lah) got its name from the Greek words *korkyra melaina* (black woods) because of the dark macchia thickets and woods that cover the island. Korčula Town (pop. 4000) faces the stunning mountains of the Croatian mainland, which are just a short ferry trip away. More attractive than its location, however, is its distinctive personality. Weekly sword dances in the summer, a superb local music scene, and the friendly locals combine to create the small town's unique atmosphere. A healthy crop of tourists has also made it significantly more developed than its neighbors Vis and Mljet.

🚆 **TRANSPORTATION.** Korčula is one of the few islands served by buses (which board a ferry to the island). The **bus station** is at Porat bb. (☎71 12 16. Ticket window open M-Sa 6:30-9am, 9:30am-4pm, and 4:30-7pm, Su 2-7pm). **Buses** run to: **Dubrovnik** (3½hr., 1 per day, 62kn); **Split** (5hr., 1 per day, 90kn); **Zagreb,** via **Knin** or **Zadar** (11-13hr., 1 per day, 190kn); and **Sarajevo, BOS** (6½hr., 4 per week, 145kn). For **ferry information** and tickets, check the **Jadrolinija** office, 20m toward Stari Grad from the ferry landing. (☎71 54 10; fax 71 11 01. Open M-F 8am-8pm, Sa 8am-1pm, Su 8am-1pm.) **Ferries** run from Korčula Town to **Dubrovnik** (3½hr., 5 per week, 64kn); **Hvar** (3hr., 1-2 per day, 62kn); **Split** (4½hr., 1 per day, 74kn). Ferries arrive in **Vela Luka** on the opposite side of the island. A bus meets the ferries and transports you to Korčula Town (1hr., 5 per day, 22kn). For a **taxi,** call ☎71 54 52 or 71 11 95.

◢🔋 **ORIENTATION AND PRACTICAL INFORMATION.** The town is situated beside the sea on the end of the island. **Stari Grad** (Old Town) was built on a small oval peninsula, and its streets are arranged in a herringbone pattern. Outside the city walls, medieval, baroque, and modern houses blend together, tapering off into hotels farther down the coastline. Street addresses are rare, but the town is small and easily navigable. The **tourist office,** Turistička zajednica, is on the opposite side of the peninsula from the bus and ferry terminals. To get there, face the water and walk left, following the main street as it curves away from the marina. Then head right along the water toward the peninsula to Hotel Korčula; the office is just before the hotel in a glass building. (Open M-Sa 8am-3pm and 4-9pm, Su 9am-1pm.) **Splitska Banka,** in front of the stairs leading to Stari Grad, **exchanges currency** for no commission, cashes **traveler's checks** for 2% commission, gives Visa **cash advances,** and offers **Western Union** services. (☎71 10 52. Open M-F 7:30am-7:30pm, Sa 7:30-11am.) There is a Visa **ATM** outside Splitska Banka and another around the corner toward Stari Grad. The **pharmacy,** Trg Kralja Tomislava bb, is at the foot of the Stari Grad stairs. (☎71 10 57. Open M-F 7am-8pm, Sa 7am-noon and 6-8pm, Su

9-11am.) For **Internet access**, head to **Tino Computers**, before Stari Grad, on a little street heading away from the marina. (☎71 60 93. 30kn per hr. Open M-Sa 8am-noon and 5-9pm, Su 5-11pm.) Alternatively, try the **bike rental kiosk** in front of the Hotel Park (see below), which has a computer with a fast connection (25kn per hour). It also, of course, rents great new bicycles for 15kn per hr. The **post office**, Trg Kralja Tomislava 1, **exchanges currency**, cashes **traveler's checks** for 1.5% commission, and has **telephones** inside and out. (☎71 11 32. Open M-F 7am-9pm, Sa 8am-8pm.) **Postal Code:** 20260.

⌐⌐ ACCOMMODATIONS AND FOOD. Private rooms are the only budget accommodations available. **Marko Polo ❶**, Biline 5, on the waterfront where the ferry docks, will arrange one for you. (☎71 54 00; fax 71 58 00; marko-polo-tours@du.tel.hr. Open daily 8am-10pm. Singles 76-160kn; doubles 100-212kn; triples 140-272kn. Prices depend on the season. Tourist tax 4.50-7kn.) Or, look for *sobe* (room) signs uphill from the bus station away from Stari Grad. While not exactly budget, **Hotel Park ❸** offers pleasant rooms near the beach at the best prices in town. From the bus station, walk away from Stari Grad along the waterfront and follow the signs. (☎72 03 36; fax 71 17 46. Breakfast included. Singles 210-395kn; doubles 320-560kn.) There's camping at **Autocamp Kalac ❶**, with nice views of the mainland across the water. (☎71 11 82; fax 71 17 46. Reception open daily 7am-10pm. 24kn per person, 12kn per car; tourist tax 7kn.) A bus shuttles people to the camp from the station (10min., every hr., 5kn).

Restaurants in Korčula are expensive and tourist-driven. For the frugal, there's a **supermarket** next to Marko Polo (see above; open M-Sa 6:30am-10pm, Su 7am-9pm) and a **market** to the right of the Stari Grad stairs (open daily 6am-9pm). ■ **Adio Mare ❸**, Marko Polo bb, next to Marco Polo's house, packs in visitors interested in sampling authentic local specialties like *korčulanska pasticada* (beef stewed in vegetables and plum sauce with dumplings) for 60kn or *Ražnjic Adio Mare* (mixed meats skewered with apples, onions, and bacon) for 60kn. (Entrees 40-70kn. Open M-Sa 1-11pm, Su 6-11pm.) Up the double staircase by the Hotel Korčula, **Pizzeria Agava ❷**, Cvit. Bokšic 6, caters to hungry local youths. (Pizzas 22-35kn. Open daily 8am-midnight.) For a late-night snack, have a hamburger (15kn), a hot dog (9kn), and a beer (8-12kn) at **Fast Food Agara ❶**, set back from the street between Olea and Amadeus. (Open M-Sa 6:30am-2am, Su 6:30am-10pm.)

◪ SIGHTS. Korčula's grandest tribute to its patron, **St. Mark's Cathedral** (Katedrala Sv. Marka), is at the highest point of the Stari Grad peninsula. Planning began in the 14th century, inspired by the founding of the Korčula Bishopric and confidence in the economy, but construction wasn't completed until 1525. The Gothic-Renaissance cathedral is complemented by the older **bell tower**. (Services daily 6:30pm and Su 7am, 9:30am, and 6:30pm.) The **Abbey Treasury of St. Mark** (Opatska Riznica Sv. Marka), next to the cathedral, houses collections of 12th-century manuscripts, Renaissance and Baroque drawings, contemporary paintings and sculptures, and coins from all periods. (Open M-Sa 9am-1pm and 5-6:30pm, Su 11pm-1am. 8kn.) The **Town Museum** (Gradski Muzej) sits opposite the treasury in the Renaissance Gabrielis Palace. Four floors display nearly five millennia of Korčula's history and culture, including everything from 5000-year-old knives to a 19th-century wedding dress. (Open M-Sa 9am-1pm and 7-9pm. 10kn, students free.) **Marco Polo's House**, the supposed birthplace of the explorer (though the history remains vague), is a late Gothic ruin to the left of the cathedral. You won't find any Polo artifacts, but the tower offers a great view of the city and cathedral. (Open daily 9am-1pm and 5-9pm. 5kn.)

CROATIA

EN GARDE The traditional Moreška sword dance, first recorded in Korčula in the 17th century, may have begun after the Turkish siege of 1571. Over the next few centuries it became popular throughout the Mediterranean, but only in Korčula has it survived to the present day. It is characterized by simple, fluid movements, swordsmanship, and a folk drama symbolizing a battle between Christians and Muslims. The dance is performed by two groups of young men called *moreškanti*. They are led by kings and fight for Bula, the Christian king's fiancée, who was kidnapped by the Muslim King Moro. After a dialogue between the kings and Bula's subsequent refusal of Moro, the armies collide; the wind orchestra accompanying the dance quickens its tempo as the clashing of the swords grows fiercer. Predictably, the Christians win and Bula is returned. Today, you can catch the dance (updated, with dancers flying the Croatian flag above their heads), during the **Festival of Sword Dances** in July and August.

🎭 **ENTERTAINMENT AND NIGHTLIFE. Carnival celebrations,** including weekly masked balls (maškare), are held from Epiphany to Ash Wednesday. All events are free. The **Festival of Sword Dances** (Festival Viteških Igara) takes place every July and August. The Moreška, Moštra, and Kumpanija sword dances are performed throughout the island. In the city of Korčula, you can catch a performance of the Moreška every Tu and Th evening. Tickets are available at any major tourist agency (40kn), but to save money, plan to come for the free shows at the end of July (ask the tourist office for details). The first two weeks of September are dedicated to the **Marco Polo Festival.** Events include folk entertainment and a grand reconstruction of the famous 1298 naval battle in the Pelješac channel between Korčula and the mainland. The September 7 battle brought Signore Polo and the forces of Venetian Korčula into combat with Genoa's navy.

The late-night cafe scene happens at **Olea,** just off the marina on a small street between the bus station and Stari Grad. (Open M-Sa 7am-2am, Su 9am-2am.) For a clubbier atmosphere, try **Gaudi.** There's a cafe outside, but the real action happens inside the stone cocoon of sound and colored lights behind it. Go up the ramp to the right of the steps that lead to Stari Grad and it will be on your left. (Open daily 11pm-3am.) The techno crowd gathers near the bus station at **Amadeus,** Pt. Brodo-graditelja bb. (Draft beer 10kn. Open M-Sa 6am-2am, Su 7am-2am.)

DUBROVNIK ☎(0)20

Those who seek Paradise on Earth should come to Dubrovnik.
—George Bernard Shaw

Countless epithets have been used to describe Dubrovnik, including "the pearl of the Adriatic" and "the city of stone and light." Although it would be hard for any location to live up to such adulation, this walled city, wedged between the Adriatic Sea and the Dinaric Alps, very nearly does. Ravaged by war in 1991 and 1992, Dubrovnik is miraculously almost scarless; only close inspection reveals bullet holes and the burned brown of once-green hillsides. Instead, as its 30,000 fiercely proud residents will attest, Dubrovnik is defined by its Mediterranean grace. Azure waters, golden sunsets, and glistening Italian marble of the central plaza have made this ancient port a popular tourist destination for decades.

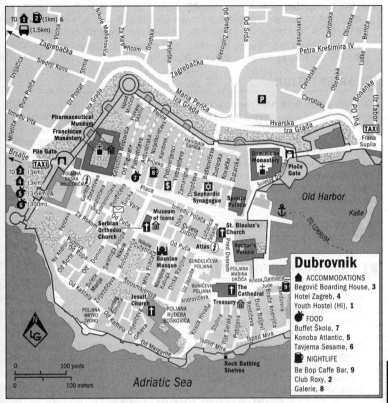

TO **1**, **2** (1km) & (1.5km)

Zagrebačka

Za kapelicom

Nikole Mašanovića

Grudska

Peljeska

Za Grada

Od Srđa

Lokrumska

Cavtatska

Obodska

Lužke

Beritica

Petra Krešimira IV

Izvojlatica

Srednji Kono

Sirna

Uz Postat

Zagrebačka

Maria Perića
Iza Grada

Od Greba Zlidiluum

Ivslsuriluum

Cavtatska

Obodska

Cavtatska

Put Od Bosanke

Uz Tabor

Đura Pulića

Iza Grada

P

Hvarska
Iza Grada

TAXI
Frana
Supila

Između Vrta

Miletića

Brsalje

Pile Gate

TAXI

TO **3** (3km),
4 (3km),
5 (3.5km) &
6 (300m)

Garištica

Zlatarićeva

Dubrovničko

POLJANA
PAŠKA
MILIĆEVIĆA *i*

Svara

Od Sigurate

Celestina Medovića

Od Puča

**Pharmaceutical
Museum**
**Franciscan
Monastery**

Peline

Antuninska

Prijeko

Boškovićeva

Zudioska

Kovačka

Zlatarska

Nalješkovićeva

Palmotićeva

Žudioska

Placa

7

8

Između Polača

**Sephardic
Synagogue**

Sponza
Palace

**Dominican
Monastery**

**Ploče
Gate**

Svetog Dominika

Old Harbor

Kaše

TO LOKRUM

Za Rokom

Od Šone

Za Rupa

Na Andiji

Puljiva

Od Domina

Boldarvev

Nikole
Gučetića

Od Puča

**Museum
of Icons**

**Serbian
Orthodox
Church**

Od Puča

Cvijete
Zuzorić

Lučarica

Marojice

Između Polača

Dropčeva

**St. Blasius's
Church**

Atlas *i*

Pred Dvorom

**Rector's
Palace**

Dubrovnik

Svetog Marije

Svetoga Đurđa

Za Rokom

Ferićeva

Vijeković

Strosmajerova

Miha Pracata

Kabužić

Dinka Ranjina

Bošković

**Bosnian
Mosque**

GUNDULIĆEVA
POLJANA

POLJANA
MARINA
DRŽIĆA

Kneza Damjana

9

Kneza Hranoja

Androvićeva

**The
Cathedral**

Jude
Brde Andrijta

Bunićeva

POLJANA
MRTVO
ZVONO

POLJANA
RUĐERA
BOŠKOVIĆA

BUNIĆEVA
POLJANA

**Jesuit
Church**

Androvićeva

Treasury

Đura Baljevi

Restićeva

Pobijana

Ispod Mira

Đilla Saraka

Stulina

Od Margarite

Od Kaštela

Od Kaštela

Crijevićeva

Gradića

**Rock Bathing
Shelves**

Adriatic Sea

0   100 yards

0   100 meters

N
LG

ACCOMMODATIONS
Begović Boarding House, **3**
Hotel Zagreb, **4**
Youth Hostel (HI), **1**

FOOD
Buffet Škola, **7**
Konoba Atlantic, **5**
Tavjerna Sesame, **6**

NIGHTLIFE
Be Bop Caffe Bar, **9**
Club Roxy, **2**
Galerie, **8**

⬗ TRANSPORTATION

Buses: Pt. Republike 38 (☎35 70 88). To get to Stari Grad, face the bus station, walk around to the other side of the building, and turn left onto Ante Starčevića. Follow this road uphill to the Pile Gate (25min.). Local buses running to Stari Grad stop at a number of places along Ante Starčevića. To: **Rijeka** (12hr., 6 per day, 242kn); **Split** (4½hr., 17 per day, 103kn); **Zadar** (8hr., 7 per day, 138kn); **Zagreb** (11hr., 7 per day, 190kn); **Frankfurt, GER** (27hr., 2 per week, 740kn); **Ljubljana, SLN** (14hr., 1 per day, 300kn); **Medugorje, BOS** (2½hr., 1 per day, 77kn); **Mostar, BOS** (3hr., 3 per day, 54-85kn); **Sarajevo, BOS** (6hr., 2 per day, 156kn); **Trieste, ITA** (15hr., 1 per day, 210kn).

Ferries: Jadrolinija, Obala S. Radića 40 (☎41 80 00; fax 41 81 11). Open M, Tu and Th 8am-8pm; W and F 8am-8pm and 9-11pm; Sa 8am-2pm and 7-8pm; Su 8-10am and 7-8:30pm. The ferry terminal is opposite the Jadrolinija office. To reach the terminal, face away from the bus station and head left; when the road forks, bear right (5min.). To: **Rijeka** (22hr., 1 per day, 182kn); **Sobra** (2hr., 1-2 per day, 18kn); **Split** (8hr., 1 per day, 72kn); **Zadar** (16hr., 1 per week, 118kn); **Bari, ITA** (9hr., 5 per week, 257kn). With your back to the ferry dock, walk left 50m along Gruška obala to the bus stop and take bus #1a, 1b, or 3 to "Pile Gate" (last stop) to reach Stari Grad.

Public Transportation: All buses except #5, 7, and 8 go to Stari Grad's Pile Gate. Tickets 7kn at newsstands, 10kn from the driver. Exact change required except on buses #1a and 1b. No cheating the system here; the driver checks everyone's ticket.

Taxis: ☎35 70 44. In front of the bus station, the ferry terminal, and Pile Gate. 25kn plus 8kn per km. 50kn from the bus station to Stari Grad.

■ ORIENTATION

The walled **Stari Grad** (Old Town) is the city's cultural, historical, and commercial center. Its main street, called both **Placa** and **Stradun**, runs from the **Pile Gate,** the official entrance to Stari Grad, to the **Old Port** at the tip of the peninsula. The main traffic arteries, **Pt. Republike** and **Ante Starčevića**, sandwich the **bus station** from the front and rear, respectively, merge into Ante Starčevića, and end at the Pile Gate. The new **ferry terminal** in Gruž is a 10min. bus ride from Stari Grad. Dubrovnik has no train station. To the west of Stari Grad, two hilly peninsulas—**Babin Kuk** and **Lapad**—jut out from the mainland. Both are home to modern settlements, sand beaches, and numerous hotels.

> ▌ Do not explore the beautiful bare mountains rising above Dubrovnik—these peaks may still harbor concealed **landmines.**

▐ PRACTICAL INFORMATION

Tourist Offices:

Tourist Board, Ante Starčevića 7 (☎41 69 99; fax 42 62 84). From the bus stop at Pile Gate, take Ante Starčevića away from Stari Grad; the office is on your left. Distributes free **maps** and arranges **private rooms** (see below). Open M-Sa 8am-7pm, winter 8am-3pm.

Turistička Zajednica Grada Dubrovnika, Cvijete Zuzoric 1/2, 2nd fl. (☎32 38 87; fax 32 37 25; tzgd@du.del.hr). From the end of Placa, turn right between St. Blasius's Church and cafe Gradska Kavana, and take the 1st right. The English-speaking staff answers questions and hands out the invaluable (and free) *City Guide.* Open M-F 8am-3pm, Sa 9am-1pm, Su 9am-noon.

Turistički Informativni Centar (TIC), Placa bb (☎42 63 54; fax 42 63 55). Next to the fountain at the head of Placa. Arranges private rooms, **exchanges currency** for 2% commission, and sells **maps** (20kn). Open June-Aug. daily 9am-9pm; Sept.-May 9am-7pm.

Budget Travel: Atlas, Lučarica 1 (☎44 25 28; fax 42 02 05; www.atlas-croatia.com). Next to St. Blasius's Church at the end of Placa. Arranges accommodations, sells plane and ferry tickets (student discounts with *Euro 26* card), **exchanges currency** for 1% commission, and cashes and sells AmEx **Traveler's Cheques**. Organizes expensive but convenient tours to: **Elafiti Islands** (2 per week, 210kn); **Mljet National Park** (2 per week, 320kn); **Mostar, BOS** (1 per week, 240kn); **Neretva River Delta** (1 per week, 330kn with lunch). **Branches** at sv. Durda 1 (☎44 25 74; fax 44 25 70), near the Pile Gate, and at Grušla Obala (☎41 80 01; fax 41 83 30), near the ferry terminal. All open June-Aug. M-Sa 8am-8pm, Su 9am-1pm; Sept.-May M-Sa 8am-7pm.

Currency Exchange: Dubrovačka Banka, Placa 16 (☎32 10 45). Exchanges currency for no commission and cashes **traveler's checks** for 1% commission. Open M-F 7:30am-1pm and 2-8pm, Sa 7:30am-1pm. **Branch** next to the bus station, Pt. Republike 9. Open M-F 7:30am-1pm and 2-9pm, Sa 7:30am-1pm.

Luggage Storage: At the bus station. 1kn per hr. for bags under 15kg, 2kn per hr. for bags over 15kg. Open daily 4:50am-9pm.

Pharmacy: Ljekarna Mala Braća, Placa 2 (☎32 14 11), inside the Franciscan monastery just within the Pile gate—the oldest working pharmacy in Europe. Open daily 8am-2pm. **Night service** (8pm-8am) at either Ljekarna Gruž, Gruška Obala bb (☎41 89 90), the ferry terminal, or Ljekarna Kod Zvonika Placa 1 (☎32 15 03).

Internet Access: Cyber Club DuNet, Pt. Republike 7, room 206 (☎35 68 94). With your back to the bus station, turn right and walk past Dubrovačka Banka to the black building next to it; it's upstairs. 14kn per hr., 5kn per 10min., students 7kn/2.5kn. 5kn per 10min., students 2.5kn. Open M-F 8am-2pm and 6pm-midnight, Sa-Su 10am-10pm.

Post Office: Pt. Republike 28 (☎41 39 68). Leaving the bus station, walk right for 70m. Turn left on the small street that runs between a stone wall and a pink building. **Poste Restante** open M-F 8am-9pm, Sa 8am-7pm, Su 8am-noon. A **branch** in Stari Grad, on Široka, has **telephones.** Open M-F 8am-9pm, Sa 9am-1pm and 6-9pm.

Postal Code: 20000.

ACCOMMODATIONS

Dubrovnik offers accommodations in a wide range of locales: city center, beachside in Lapad, or close to the ferry terminal. For two or more people, a **private room** is the cheapest option; arrange one through the **Tourist Board ❶** (80-120kn), the TIC, or **Atlas ❷**. (Singles 100-150kn; doubles 120-180kn.) For cheaper rooms, try your luck with the women hovering around the bus and ferry terminals. They'll start by asking absurd prices, but will drop to very reasonable rates with some haggling (doubles about 100-130kn). There are campgrounds 20km from town.

Youth Hostel (HI), B. Josipa Jelačića 15/17 (☎42 32 41; fax 41 25 92; hfhs-du@du.hinet.hr). From the bus station, walk 10min. along Ante Starčevića, turn right at the lights, and right again after 40m onto b. Josipa Jelačića. Look for a well-concealed HI sign on your left immediately before #17. From the ferries, take bus #12 toward "Pile" and get off at the stop after the bus station. One of Croatia's best hostels. Clean doubles, quads, and 6-person dorms. Hall bathrooms with spotless blue-tiled floors, an outdoor terrace, and a TV/dining room. Helpful, friendly staff. Breakfast included. Check-out 10am. Curfew 2am. July 15-Aug. 87kn; June 1-July 14 and Aug. 21-Sept. 15 79kn; May and Sept. 16-Oct. 30 73kn; Nov.-Dec. 65kn. ❶

Begović Boarding House, Primorska 17 (☎43 51 91; fax 45 27 52). From the bus station, take bus #6 toward Dubrava and tell the driver you want to get off at post office Lapad. Facing the walkway, turn right at the intersection. Go left at the fork, and take the 1st right onto Primorska. Call ahead and the hospitable owner, Sado, will pick you up at the bus or ferry terminal. A cozy villa with 10 doubles, kitchenettes, and a spectacular terrace view. Call ahead. July-Aug. 100kn per person; Sept.-June 80kn. ❶

Hotel Zagreb, Šetalište Kralja Zvonimira 31 (☎43 61 46; fax 43 60 06). Follow directions to post office Labad (see **Begović Boarding House,** above). Walk through the 1st intersection and proceed onto the pedestrian Šetalište Kralja Zvonimira. The hotel is on the left. Near the beach, with a wonderful veranda. Clean rooms with hardwood floors, bath, TV, phone, and large windows. Breakfast included. Reception 24hr. Singles 165-290kn; doubles 260-490kn, depending on season. Tourist tax 4.50-7kn. ❷

FOOD

Most establishments feature seafood-oriented menus, risotto, and pasta. **Prijeko,** the first street parallel to Placa on the left when coming from Pile Gate, is lined with cookie-cutter *konobi* (taverns). The **outdoor market,** on Gundulićeva Poljana, sits behind St. Blasius's Church. (Open daily 7am-8pm.) **Supermarket Mediator,** Od puča 4, faces the market. (Open M-Sa 6:30am-9pm, Su 7am-9pm.)

Konoba Atlantic, Kardinala Stopinga 42 (☎43 58 911). Take bus #6 to post office Labad and walk straight on the walkway; it's on the right near Hotel Kompas. This family-run restaurant by the beach is worth the ride. Konoba Atlantic makes some of the best pasta in Croatia (28-45kn), bakes its own bread and cakes, and offers a wide range of seafood (40-120kn). Open daily noon-11pm. AmEx/V. ❷

CROATIA

IN RECENT NEWS

WAR AND TOURISM

Tourism is more than just a business in Croatia. It's *the* business—the only one that makes serious money, anyway. In the 1970s and 1980s Croatia used to attract vast numbers of vacationers from within Yugoslavia and from around the world with its spectacular natural beauty. Wars, however, are not good for tourism. In Dubrovnik, for example, the number of tourists has been increasing 10-15% every year for the last three years, but has yet to reach 50% of what it was in 1990.

With the end of the Kosovo conflict in 1999, the Balkans have been on the front pages less and less, which means that tourists are more and more willing to come back to their former playground. But after nearly 10 years of virtual non-existence, it's hard for the tourism industry to get back into the swing of things. Around Dubrovnik, the biggest draw on the Croatian coast, a dozen hotels sit empty and decaying, damaged by the war or by a decade of neglect. Repairs are underway on several of them, but the government lacks the money to finance larger projects, and foreign investors are returning only hesitantly.

(continued on next page)

Tavjerna Sesame, Dante Alighieria bb (☎41 29 10). A 5min. walk from the Pile Gate toward the hostel along Starčeviča, on the left. Much closer to town than Konoba Atlantic, Sesame also specializes in excellent pasta dishes (35-50kn). The dining area is on a porch above the cafe; hanging vines and candles create a romantic dinner atmosphere (if you ignore the traffic noise). For a splurge, order a bottle of wine made by Frane Miloš, the most celebrated of Croatia's wine makers from nearby Pelješac (85kn). Entrees 60-95kn. Open M-Sa 8am-midnight, Su 10am-midnight. ❹

Buffet Škola, Antuninska 1 (☎41 67 90), just off Placa. This cafe is *the* place to go for an excellent sandwich. Try the local favorite *sir iz ulje* (oily cheese) or the famous *dalmatinski pršut* (Dalmatian ham) layered between thick slices of homemade bread (19kn). Open daily June-Aug. 7am-1am; Sept.-May 9am-midnight. ❶

🅶 SIGHTS

Stari Grad is packed with churches, museums, palaces, and fortresses—every angle is an eyeful. The popular sights are those along the broad Placa, but much of Dubrovnik's history is off the beaten path.

CITY WALLS. (Gradske zidine.) Nearly 2000 uninterrupted meters of limestone (25m tall at points), with an average thickness of 1.5m, connect four round towers, two corner towers, three fortresses, 12 quadrilateral forts, five bastions, two land gates, two port gates, and a partridge in a pear tree. Walls enclosed the entire city as early as the 13th century. When Dubrovnik was liberated from Venetian rule, extensive work was carried out on its wall in order to protect against potential Turkish attacks. Once you've seen the sunset from the top of the walls, you'll feel like writing poetry. *(Entrances to the walk on the walls are through the Pile gate on the left and at the old port. Open daily 9am-7:30pm. 15kn, children 5kn.)*

CATHEDRAL OF THE ASSUMPTION OF THE VIRGIN MARY AND TREASURY. (Riznica Katedrale.) This Baroque structure was erected after the previous Romanesque cathedral, built from the 12th to 14th centuries, was destroyed in the massive 1667 earthquake. In 1981, the foundation of a 7th-century Byzantine cathedral was found beneath the cathedral floor, necessitating considerable revision of Dubrovnik's history. The cathedral treasury houses religious relics collected by Richard the Lionheart, Roman refugees, and a few centuries of fishermen.

Crusaders in the 12th century brought back a silver casket from Jerusalem that contains 2000-year-old cloth material alledgedly worn by Jesus—don't miss the 'Diapers of Jesus,' the small swath of black cloth in the center of the treasury. *(Kneza Damjana Jude 1. From Pile gate, follow Placa to the Bell Tower and turn right to Poljana Marina Džića. Cathedral open daily 6:30am-8pm. Treasury open daily 9am-7pm. 5kn.)*

FRANCISCAN MONASTERY AND PHARMACEUTICAL MUSEUM. (Franjevački Samostan.) Stunning stonework encases this 14th-century monastery. The southern portal that opens on the Placa includes a Pietà relief by the Petrović brothers, the only relic from the original Franciscan church. The cloister was built in 1360 by Mihoje Brajkov; no two capitals of the colonnade are the same. The monastery also houses the oldest working pharmacy in Europe, established in 1317—the small museum displays elegant medicinal containers and historical tools along with a collection of gold and silver jewelry. *(Placa 2. On the left side of Placa, just inside Pile gate next to the entrance to the city walls. Open daily 9am-6pm. Museum 5kn.)*

ORTHODOX CHURCH AND MUSEUM OF ICONS. (Pravoslavna Crkva i Muzej Ikona.) Around 2000 Serbs live in Dubrovnik—approximately a third of the population that existed here before the 1991-1995 civil war—and their church stands as a symbol of Dubrovnik's continued ethnic and religious tolerance. The museum houses a wide variety of 15th- to 19th-century icons gathered by local families. Traditionally each Serb household is protected by a specific saint and any member of the family traveling abroad collects icons depicting that saint. *(Od Puča 8. From Pile gate, walk 100m down Placa and turn right onto Široka, the widest side street. Turn left down Od Puča. Church open daily 8am-noon and 5-7pm. Museum open M-Sa 9am-1pm; 10kn.)*

MOSQUE. (Džamija.) This former apartment serves Dubrovnik's 4000 Bosnian Muslims. The beautifully carpeted room is divided in two: one half contains an Islamic school for children and the other is used for prayer. A small antechamber serves as a social center for the Bosnian community. Members are glad to let tourists in as long as you take off your shoes. *(Miha Pracata 3. From Pile gate, walk down Placa and take the 8th street on the right, M. Pracata. The mosque is marked by a small sign on the left side of the street. Open daily 10am-1pm and 8-9pm.)*

In order to compensate for the lack of hotel capacity, the government and tourist board have encouraged families to make private rooms available in their houses (which accounts for all the cries of "sleeping rooms! *zimmer!*" greeting you at the bus station) and have tried to stretch the season by increasing the availability of outdoors-oriented activities. Currently, the period from June to September accounts for 71% of the total tourist flow through Dubrovnik, worsening the housing crunch and making for a very lopsided business year.

But developing tourist infrastructure is about a lot more than just making sure that you can get a room in Dubrovnik in the middle of August. With a 25% national unemployment rate, new hotels and restaurants mean new jobs for the thousands of Croatians that are currently unemployed. As the only major growth industry in Croatia, its success is imperative for the economic future of the country. The goals for growth are ambitious, aiming to return to the glory days of the 1980s. So if you want to find a spot on the beach, you'd better go now, before they succeed.

—A. Nicholas Gossen

SEPHARDIC SYNAGOGUE. (Sinagoga.) Round off your tour with a visit to the 2nd-oldest Sephardic synagogue in Europe (the oldest one is in Prague). The city's 46 Jews have their offices inside. Most of Dubrovnik's Jewish archives were lost during the Nazi occupation, but a number of families risked their lives to hide much of the synagogue's interior in their own homes. (*Žudioska 5. From the Bell Tower, walk toward Pile gate and take the 3rd right onto Žudioska. Open M and Th-F 10am-noon.*)

BEACHES AND FESTIVALS

For sand, palms, and crowds, hop on bus #6 toward Dubrava and ask to get off at post office Lapad. Head straight through the intersection onto the pedestrian boulevard and follow the bikinis. Right outside the fortifications of Stari Grad there are a number of rock shelves for sunning and swimming. Walk down Pobijana, go to the left of the cathedral entrance, and continue through the small door that leads into the wall to find a great place to watch the sunset. (Open 9am-8pm.) For a truly surreal seaside experience, take a swim in the cove at the foot of the wreckage of the old **Hotel Libertas,** still marked on most maps. The hotel was damaged during the war and then abandoned. Now it looks like a post-apocalyptic movie set, but the great location still draws the youth of Dubrovnik to swim in the pristine water and play soccer in the abandoned swimming pool. You can also continue on the path to the beach below the Hotel Bellevue. To get there, walk along Starčevića for about 10min., then take a left shortly after the hotel. Another option is the nearby island of **Lokrum,** which features a **nude beach** for both naturists and naturalists. Ferries shuttle daily from the Old Port. (15min.; every hr. 9am-8pm; 25kn round-trip, children 15kn.) Once there, stroll through the **botanical garden.**

From mid-July to mid-August, the **Dubrovnik Summer Festival** (Dubrovački Ljetni Festival) transforms the city into a cultural mecca and a crazy party scene. The Festival office on Placa hands out schedules and sells tickets. (☎42 88 64; fax 42 79 44. Open during the festival daily 8:30am-9pm, tickets 9am-2pm and 3-7pm. 50-300kn.) For off-season information and reservations, contact the head office at Poljana Oaska Miličevica 1. (☎41 22 88; fax 42 63 51; www.dubrovnik-festival.hr.)

NIGHTLIFE

Young hipsters and cafe loungers congregate in **Stari Grad. Buničeva Poljana** and **B. Josipa Jelačića,** near the Youth Hostel, are also known as "Bourbon Streets" and are lined with cafes.

▨ **Divinae Follie,** Pt. Vatroslava Lisinskog 56, Babin Kuk (☎43 56 77). From Stari Grad, take bus #6 and ask the driver to let you off near the disco; follow the beat down the street and around to the left. The bus stops running at 1:45am, but cabs gather in front of the disco (60kn to Stari Grad). Slam draft beer (15kn), stroll through the adjacent woods, or watch the lovely dancers in the floor show. Cover 70kn. Open June-July and Sept. Sa 11pm-5am, daily in Aug., but call ahead to make sure.

Be Bop Caffe Bar, Kneza Damjana Jude 6. Walk down the narrow side street opposite the cathedral entrance. A mini rock museum, with every inch of the walls covered with holy relics, including posters signed by Carlos Santana and Jimi Hendrix. Plays a great selection of rock and blues. Open daily 9am-2pm and 6pm-4am.

Club Roxy, B. Josipa Jelačića 11. Here the Bourbon Street scene begins: loud music, tables that invade the street, and a whole lot of skin. Only a short stumble away from the hostel. 0.5L domestic draft 15kn, 0.33L Guinness 18kn, coffee 5kn. Open daily 8am until you pass out.

Galerie, Kunićeva 5. If you come early, don't be deceived. This tiny bar overflows with locals around 10pm. They sit on the street, hang from windows, and talk it up over bottles of *Ožjusko* (0.33L, 10kn). Open daily 9am-2pm and 6pm-midnight.

DAYTRIPS FROM DUBROVNIK

LOPUD ISLAND

A ferry runs from Dubrovnik to Lopud and the Elafiti islands (50min.; summer M-Sa 4 per day, Su 1 per day; round-trip 25kn). The beach is on the opposite side of the island from the village. From the ferry dock, face the water, walk around to the left for 5min., and turn left onto the road between the high wall and the palm park, following signs for the beach and "Konoba Barbara." Continue over the hill for 15min.; when the path forks, keep right, and follow the stairs down to the beach.

 Beautiful as it is, parts of Lopud are still rife with **landmines.** Stick to the paved paths and the beach, and do not wander off into the wilderness.

Less than an hour from Dubrovnik, Lopud is an enchanting island. The tiny village, dotted with white buildings, chapels, and parks, stretches along the island's waterfront *(obala)*. Currently under renovation, **Dorđić Mayneri** remains among the most beautiful parks in Croatia. Signs from Kavana Dubrava on the waterfront point to the **museum,** which is the meeting place for tours of the church, museum, and monastery (Th 9am). A 15min. stroll along the waterfront leads to a gazebo with a breathtaking view of the white cliffs and a dark blue sea. A short walk in the other direction leads you to the abandoned **monastery.** Although slated for reconstruction and development at some point in the future, its current semi-ruined state makes for wonderful exploring. Be careful, though, as many of the floors have fallen in. The **beach** is the island's highlight. **Plaža Šunj,** arguably the best beach in Croatia, has that special quality that most of the Dalmatian Coast lacks: sand.

MLJET NATIONAL PARK

During the summer (June-Sept.), the best way to visit Mljet is to take one of the passenger ferries operated by Atlantagent, Obala S. Radića 26 (☎41 90 44), behind the Jadrolinija office. The ferry (1½hr., 1 per day, 35kn) leaves in the morning and drops passengers off in Pomena from Dubrovnik at one of the park entrances, then returns in the evening. During the winter, the Jadrolinija ferry from Dubrovnik drops passengers in Sobra, on the eastern side of the island (2hr., 2 per day, 29kn). The bus that meets the ferry in Sobra travels to its western end, Pomena (1hr., 12kn). Entrances to the park are in Polače and Pomona. 50kn with ticket to the St. Maria island, 25kn without; students 25kn. Atlas and numerous other travel agencies offer one-day excursions to the park. Private rooms are available in Sobra or Pomena; inquire at the cafe or where you see a sign (75-100kn).

Mljet's relative isolation and correspondingly small population make it an ideal location for a national park. The Croatian government agreed and decided to preserve the western-most third of the island in 1960. Scarce transport has kept tourism at bay and the island's mystery intact. The island's mystique has earned it a place in the literary imagination since the *Odyssey* and the writings of St. Paul. The saltwater **Large** and **Small Lakes** (Veliko and Malo Jezero), created by the rising sea level 10,000 years ago, are the most unique formations on the island. Every 6hr. the direction of flow between the lakes changes with the tides, so the water is constantly cleansed. In the center of Veliko Jezero sits the **Island of St. Maria** (Sv. Marija). The island is home to a beautiful, white-stone **Benedictine monastery,** built in the 12th century and abandoned 700 years later when Napoleon conquered the area. Today it houses a restaurant and a church.

If you plan on spending the night, **Polače** is worth a stop for its Roman ruins and Christian basilica, once part of the second-largest Roman city in Croatia (the first being Diocletian's palace in Split). Unfortunately, most of the city is now under water. Get off at Polače (which also has a tourist office), walk 2km to Pristanište, where the park's info center is located, and jump on the boat to St. Maria (5min., every hr.). To return, take the boat to Mali Most (2min.), and walk another 3km to Pomena. When you get tired, a minivan run by park management will give you a ride; if you miss it, catch one of the Atlas-operated buses.

CZECH REPUBLIC
(ČESKÁ REPUBLIKA)

CZECH CROWN

AUS$1 = 16.78Kč	10Kč = AUS$0.60
CDN$1 = 19.55Kč	10Kč = CDN$0.51
EUR€1 = 29.94Kč	10Kč = EUR€0.33
NZ$1 = 14.29Kč	10Kč = NZ$0.70
UK£1 = 2.87Kč	10Kč = UK£0.21
US$1 = 47.17Kč	10Kč = US$0.33
ZAR1 = 30.43Kč	10Kč = ZAR3.49

From the Holy Roman Empire through the USSR, the Czechs have long stood at a crossroads of international affairs. Unlike many of their neighbors, the citizens of this small, landlocked country have rarely resisted as armies marched across their borders, often choosing to fight with words instead of weapons; as a result, Czech towns and cities are among the best-preserved and most beautiful in Europe. Today the Czechs face a different kind of invasion, as enamored tourists sweep in to savor the magnificent capital, the welcoming locals, and the world's best beers.

CZECH REPUBLIC AT A GLANCE

OFFICIAL NAME: Czech Republic

CAPITAL: Prague (pop. 1.2 million)

POPULATION: 10.3 million (81% Czech, 13% Moravian, 3% Slovak, 3% other)

LANGUAGE: Czech

CURRENCY: 1 crown (Kč) = 100 halers

RELIGION: 40% Catholic, 40% Atheist, 4% Protestant, 26% other

LAND AREA: 78,866km²

GEOGRAPHY: Plateaus and mountains

BORDERS: Austria, Germany, Hungary, Poland, Slovak Republic

ECONOMY: 55% Services, 42% Industry, 3% Agriculture

GDP: US$12,900 per capita

COUNTRY CODE: 420

INTERNATIONAL DIALING PREFIX: 00

HISTORY

IN THE BEGINNING... As legend has it, the Czech nation was born when Father Čech (Czech) climbed the Říp mountain near present-day Prague and instructed his people to settle the land. According to textbooks, however, the civilization traces back to the first century settlement of the Celtic Boii. By the 6th century, Slavs had settled in the region. By the end of the 10th century the Czechs were united under the **Přemyslid Dynasty.** The good king and legendary patron saint of Bohemia, **Wenceslas** (Václav), was one of the dynasty's earliest rulers. In 1114, the Holy Roman Empire invited the Czech kings to join as electors.

Czech Republic

FROM THE GOLDEN AGE TO THE DARK AGE. The reign of Holy Roman Emperor **Charles (Karel) IV** (1346-1378) was a Golden Era for the Czechs. The many accomplishments that distinguished his reign included the promotion of Prague to an Archbishopric and the founding of the first university in Central Europe (Charles University). Charles's son, Václav "the Lazy," was unable to attain the golden heights of his father, however, and dissent emerged. It was during his reign that **Jan Hus** (1369-1415) openly protested the corruption of the Catholic hierarchy and, for his heresy, was burnt at the stake. In response to the execution, the proto-Protestant **Hussite movement** took shape and organized the **First Defenestration of Prague** in 1419, in which protestors threw the royalist mayor out the window of the Council House. The strategy clearly had some merit: nearly two centuries later, the **Second Defenestration of Prague** set off the **Thirty Years' War** (1618-1648). The Czech Protestants' defeat was sealed when they suffered an early, harsh blow in the **Battle of White Mountain** in November 1620. Their loss led to the absorption of Czech territory into the **Austrian Empire** and three centuries of oppressive rule.

CZECHOSLOVAKIA. The spirit of nationalism that swept across Europe during the nineteenth century did not leave the Bohemian peoples untouched. This sentiment was crushed, however, in the imperial backlash that followed the **1848 revolutions.** While **World War I** did little to increase harmony among the nationalities of the Habsburg Empire, mutual malcontent did help unite the Czechs and Slovaks. In the post-war confusion, **Edvard Beneš** and **Tomáš Garrigue Masaryk** convinced the victorious Allies to legitimize a new state that combined Bohemia, Moravia, and Slovakia into **Czechoslovakia.** This **First Republic** brought another golden era for the Czechs. Czechoslovakia enjoyed remarkable economic prosperity, only to be torn apart as Hitler exploited the Allies' **appeasement** policy. The infamous **Munich Agreement** of 1938 handed a Czech border region, the Sudetenland, over to Germany, ignoring Czechoslovak pleas that it would destroy the country. The following year, Hitler annexed the entire country. Most of Czechoslovakia's substantial Jewish population was murdered by the Nazis.

RISING UP AND MOVING OUT. Following liberation by the Allies, the Communists won the 1946 elections, seizing permanent power in 1948. In 1968, Communist Party Secretary **Alexander Dubček** sought to dramatically reform the country's nationalized economy and ease political oppression during the **Prague Spring.** Displeased, the Soviets invaded the country. **Gustáv Husák,** who became president in 1971, introduced an even more repressive regime that lasted for the next 18 years.

Czech intellectuals protested Husák's violations of human rights with **Charter 77,** a nonviolent movement. Most of its leaders were imprisoned and persecuted, but they nonetheless fostered increasing dissidence. After the demise of Communism in Hungary and Poland, and the fall of the Berlin Wall in 1989, the **Velvet Revolution** hit Czechoslovakia, named for the almost entirely bloodless transition from Communism to a multi-party state system. The Communist regime's violent suppression of a peaceful demonstration outraged the nation, which immediately went on strike. Within days the Communists resigned, and **Václav Havel,** the long-imprisoned playwright and leader of both Charter 77 and the Velvet Revolution, became president. However, Slovak calls for independence soon grew strong; after much debate, the Czech and Slovak nations parted ways on January 1, 1993.

TODAY

The Czech Republic is a parliamentary democracy. The president, who is elected by Parliament to a five-year term, retains symbolic powers, while the prime minister, who chooses members of the cabinet, is a more significant political figure. Appointed by the president, the prime minister is typically a leader of the majority political party. The country enjoyed a rapid revival after Communism, but has recently experienced economic stagnation and rising unemployment. In 1997, the poorly conceived economic policies of Prime Minister **Václav Klaus** resulted in a tremendous depreciation of the koruna's value, and the 1998 elections allowed **Miloš Zeman,** leader of the **Social Democrats,** to form the first left-wing government since 1989. **Vladimir Spidla** recently replaced Zeman as head of the Social Democrats and, in June 2002, the party again topped the polls and Spidla became prime minister. However, having won only 70 of 200 seats in Parliament, the Social Democrats have been forced to ally with a number of centrist parties in order to form a tiny 101-seat majority. Playwright and former dissident **Václav Havel,** who was re-elected president in 1998 by only one vote, will remain the country's official head of state until the 2003 presidential election. The Czech Republic joined **NATO** in March 1999 and is expected to be invited to join the **EU** in 2004. However, concern has been raised over Czech policies toward the Roma (Gypsies) who suffer disproportionately high poverty and unemployment, as well as a shaky record in European relations. In 2000, the Czech Republic and Austria disagreed over a Czech nuclear power plant near the countries' shared border, and in 2002 Germany objected strongly to Czech refusal to revoke the Benes decree, which legalized the confiscation of property from the millions of German civilians expelled from the country after World War II. In August 2002, the country suffered a major economic setback due to severe flooding. Much of the western half of the country was inundated, causing damage to roads, railway lines, and a number of Prague's historic landmarks.

PEOPLE AND CULTURE

LANGUAGE

Czech is a Western Slavic language, most closely related to Slovak and Polish. **English** is widely understood, and **German** phrases may be useful, especially in the western spas. **Russian** is also commonly understood, but tread carefully as the language is not always welcome. The trick to good pronunciation is to pronounce every letter. Stress is always placed on the first syllable. However, don't confuse stress with elongation. When there is a diacritical over a vowel—such as *á, é, í, ó, ú, ů,* and *ý*—this simply means you hold the vowel sound for longer, without placing emphasis on it. "*C*" is pronounced "ts"; "*g*" is always hard, as in "good"; "*ch*", which is considered one letter, is a cross between "h" and "k" but "h" is a comprehensible approximation; "*j*" is "y"; "*r*" is slightly rolled; and "*w*" is "v." The letter "*ě*" softens the preceding consonant: "*dě*" (also written "*ď*") becomes "dy," as in *děkuji* (DYEH-koo-yee-ee, not DEH-koo-yee-ee); "*mě*" is "mnye," as in *město* (MNYEH-stoh, not MEH-stoh); "*ně*" (also written "*ň*") is "ny," as in *něco* (NYEH-tsoh, not NEH-tso); and "*tě*" (also written "*ť*") is "ty," as *tělo* (TYEH-loh, not TEH-loh). All other diacriticals soften the consonant: "*č*" is "ch," "*ř*" is "rzh" (see **The World's Most Difficult Sound,** below), "*š*" is "sh," and "*ž*" is "zh." For phrasebook and glossary, see **Glossary: Czech,** p. 877.

FOOD AND DRINK

CZECH	❶	❷	❸	❹	❺
FOOD	under 80Kč	81-100Kč	101-140Kč	141-200Kč	over 200Kč

Appreciation for true Czech cuisine starts with learning to pronounce *knedlíky* (KNED-lee-kee). These thick loaves of dough, feebly known in English as dumplings, are a Czech staple, soaking up *zelí* (sauerkraut) juice and other sauces. Meat, however, lies at the heart of almost all main dishes; the Czech **national meal** is *vepřové* (roast pork), *knedlíky,* and *zelí* (known as *vepřo-knedlo-zelo*). If you're in a hurry, grab *párky* (frankfurters) or *sýr* (cheese) at a streetside food stand. **Vegetarian** restaurants serving *bez masa* (meatless) specialties are uncommon, and at traditional restaurants vegetarians will be limited to *smaženy sýr* (fried cheese) and *saláty* (salads). Ask for *káva espresso* rather than just *káva* to avoid the unappealing brew Czechs call coffee. *Koblihy* (doughnuts), *jablkový závin* (apple strudel), and *ovocné knedlíky* (fruit dumplings) are favorite sweets, but the most beloved is *koláč*—a tart filled with poppy-seed jam or sweet cheese. Moravian **wines**

THE WORLD'S MOST DIFFICULT SOUND

Not quite a Spanish "r" and simply not the Polish "rz," Czech's own linguistic blue note, the letter "*ř,*" lies excruciatingly in between. Although many of Prague's expats would sacrifice a month of Saturdays at Jo's Bar to utter the elusive sound just once, few manage more than a strangely trilled whistle. Most foreigners resign themselves to using the "*ž*" in its place, but what we consider a subtle difference often confuses Czechs. For all those linguistic daredevils in the audience, here's a sure-fire method of tackling the randy Mr. Ř: roll your tongue and quickly follow with a "*ž*".

are generally of high quality. Wine is typically drunk at a *vinárna* (wine bar) that also serves a variety of spirits, including *slivovice* (plum brandy) and *becherovka* (herbal bitter), the **national drink**. However, it is local brews, such as *Plzeňský Prazdroj* (Pilsner Urquell), *Budvar*, and *Krušovice*, that truly dominate the Czech drinking scene.

CUSTOMS AND ETIQUETTE

Firmly established customs govern wining and dining in the Czech Republic. When beer is served, wait until all raise the common *"na zdraví"* ("to your health") toast before drinking, and always look into the eyes of the individual with whom you are toasting. Similarly, before biting into a sauce-drowned *knedlík* wish everyone *"dobrou chut"* ("to your health"). It is customary to **tip** 10-20% in restaurants; if a service charge has already been included on your bill, you should still add 10%. It is still acceptable to **bargain** for goods at outdoor markets, but not in stores. When it comes to **public transport,** younger people are expected to give up their seats to older people, especially older women.

THE ARTS

HISTORY

LITERATURE. The Czech Republic is a highly literate country in which writers hold a privileged position as important social and political commentators. From the first Czechoslovak president, **T.G. Masaryk,** to current incumbent **Václav Havel,** literary figures have proven to be the nation's most powerful citizens and political figures. The Habsburgs oppressed Czech literature during the 18th century, but the 19th century saw a nationalist literary renaissance. In 1836, **Karel Hynek Mácha** penned his celebrated epic *May (Máj),* considered a lyric masterpiece. The founding of the literary journal *Máj*—named after Mácha's poem—in 1856 marked the beginning of the **National Revival,** during which nationalist literary output exploded. One of its brightest stars, **Božena Němcová,** introduced the novel to modern Czech literature with *Granny (Babička;* 1855). The 20th century saw the creation of **Jaroslav Hašek's** satire, *The Good Soldier Švejk (Dobrý voják Švejk;* 1921-23), which became a classic commentary on life under Habsburg rule. While he wrote in German, **Franz Kafka's** work is pervaded by the dark circumstances of his position as a German-speaking Jew in his native Prague. **Jaroslav Seifert** and **Vítězslav Nezval** explored Poetism and Surrealism, producing image-rich meditations; in 1984, Seifert became the first Czech author to receive the **Nobel Prize.**

FINE ARTS. Marie Černinová Toyen, a notable surrealist, immigrated to Paris in the 1920s and worked closely with André Breton. One of the most important Czech artists of the early 20th century, **Alfons Mucha,** also worked in Paris and helped develop the **Art Nouveau** style of painting. **Jozef Čapek** was an important Cubist and caricaturist best known for his satire of Hitler's ascent to power.

ARCHITECTURE. While few Czech architects have become household names, the country itself overflows with architectural treasures. Both **Český Krumlov** (see p. 273) and **Kutná Hora** (see p. 258) have been declared protected cultural monuments by UNESCO for their medieval buildings and winding streets. **Telč** (see p. 292) also enjoys protected status for its Renaissance gables and arcades. Within **Prague** (see

CZECH REPUBLIC

p. 226), architectural styles intermingle, juxtaposing the one-thousand-year-old **Prague Castle** (see p. 248) with daring examples of Art Nouveau and Cubism.

MUSIC. The National Revival of the 19th century brought out the best in Czech music. The nation's most celebrated composers, **Antonín Dvořák, Leoš Janáček,** and **Bedřich Smetana,** are renowned for transforming Czech folk tunes and tales into 19th-century symphonies and operas. Dvořák's *Symphony No. 9, "From the New World,"* which combines Czech folk tradition with the author's experience of America, is probably the most famous Czech masterpiece. Among Czechs, however, Smetana's symphonic poem *My Country (Má vlast)* remains more popular.

FILM. For such a small country, the Czech Republic has been very successful in the film industry. In 1966, director **Jiří Menzel's** *Closely Watched Trains (Ostře sledované vlaky)*, won the Academy Award for Best Foreign Film. Director **Miloš Forman** immigrated to the US in 1968 and exploded into the film industry with the critically acclaimed *One Flew Over the Cuckoo's Nest* (1975).

CURRENT SCENE

The Czech literary tradition remains strong today. The late 20th-century novels of **Milan Kundera** and **Josef Škvorecký** drew international attention to Czech literature, and continue to be popular both at home and abroad. The country's current president, **Václav Havel,** is a well-known playwright with a number critically acclaimed dramas to his name. Film has become an increasingly popular medium in the Czech Republic, and Karlovy Vary (see p. 265) hosts one of the world's most star-studded film festivals. In 1997, an Oscar traveled to the Czech Republic for Jan Svěrák's film **Kolya** (1996), about a young boy's relationship with his stepfather.

HOLIDAYS AND FESTIVALS

NATIONAL HOLIDAYS IN 2003	
January 1 New Year's Day	**September 28** St. Wenceslas Day
April 20-21 Easter	**October 28** Independence Day
May 1 May Day	**November 17** Day of Student Struggle for Freedom and Democracy
May 8 Liberation Day	
July 5 Cyril and Methodius Day	**December 24-25** Christmas
July 6 Jan Hus Day	

The Czech Republic plays host to a number of internationally renowned festivals. While this provides a feast of activities for the traveler, it also means that accommodations become even more crowded than usual; if you are planning to attend any major festivals, be sure to reserve both a room and your tickets well in advance.

SPRING FESTIVAL. Classical musicians and orchestras from around the world descend on **Prague** (see p. 226) for this massive festival held from mid-May until the beginning of June. Tickets may sell out up to a year in advance.

FIVE-PETALED ROSE FESTIVAL. Held each June, this boisterous medieval festival in Český Krumlov (see p. 273) features music, dance, and a jousting tournament.

MASOPUST. This Moravian version of Mardi Gras is celebrated in villages across the Czech Republic from Epiphany to Ash Wednesday. Revelers dressed in animal masks feast, dance, and sing until Lent begins.

ADDITIONAL RESOURCES

GENERAL HISTORY

The Coasts of Bohemia, by Derek Sayer (2000). Weaving together politics and culture, Sayer's lively narrative is scholarly, but accessible to the general reader.

Prague in Black and Gold, by Paul Dementz (1998). A comprehensive, yet engaging, account of the complicated past of Central Europe.

FICTION AND TRAVEL BOOKS

The Garden Party, by Václav Havel (1993). A collection of the Czech president's renowned dramas.

Pink Tanks and Velvet Hangovers: An American in Prague, by Douglas Lytle (1995). One of the first and most engaging tales of expatriate life in the Czech Republic.

Prague: A Traveler's Literary Companion, by Paul Wilson, ed. (1995). A series of essays and short stories by various Czech authors illuminating the historical and literary significance of Prague's monuments and cityscapes.

The Spirit of Prague, by Ivan Klima (1995). These essays by a prominent dissident writer during the communist era explore the highs and lows of Prague's recent history.

The Unbearable Lightness of Being, by Milan Kundera (1984). A lyrical novel of two couples that has become a classic of high Modernism, and one of the most famous works to emerge from the Czech Republic.

FILM

Kolya, directed by Jan Svěrák (1996). The Academy Award-winning story of a Czech musician who finds himself in charge of his stepson after his wife leaves the country.

Closely Watched Trains, directed by Jiří Menzel (1966). Another Oscar-winner, this film recounts the lives and loves of Czech railway employees during World War II.

CZECH ESSENTIALS

ENTRANCE REQUIREMENTS

Passport: Required of all travelers.

Visa: Required of citizens of Australia, Canada, and South Africa.

Letter of Invitation: Not required.

Inoculations: None required. Recommended up-to-date MMR (measles, mumps, rubella), DTaP (diptheria), Polio booster, Hepatitis A, and Hepatitis B.

Work Permit: Required of all foreigners planning to work.

International Driving Permit: Required of all those planning to drive.

DOCUMENTS AND FORMALITIES

EMBASSIES AND CONSULATES

Embassies of other countries in the Czech Republic are all in Prague (see p. 320). The Czech Republic's embassies and consulates abroad include:

Australia: 8 Culgoa Circuit, O'Malley, Canberra, ACT 2606 (☎02 6290 1386; fax 6290 0006; canberra@embassy.mzv.cz).

Canada: 251 Cooper St., Ottawa, ON K2P 0G2 (☎202-274-9100; fax 966-8540; ottowa@embassy.mzv.cz).

Ireland: 57 Northumberland Rd., Ballsbridge, Dublin 4 (☎01 668 1135; fax 668 1660; dublin@embassy.mzv.cz).

New Zealand: 48 Hair St., Wainuiomata, Wellington (☎04 939 1610; fax 564 9022).

South Africa: 936 Pretorius St., Arcadia 0083, Pretoria; P.O. Box 3326, Pretoria 0001 (☎012 342 3477; fax 430 2033; www.icon.co.za/czmzv).

UK: 26 Kensington Palace Gardens, London W8 4QY (☎020 7243 1115; fax 7243 7926; london@embassy.mzv.cz).

US: 3900 Spring of Freedom St. NW, Washington, D.C. 20008 (☎202-274-9103; fax 363-6308; www.mzv.cz/washington).

VISA AND ENTRY INFORMATION

Citizens of Ireland, New Zealand, and the US may visit visa-free for up to 90 days, and UK citizens for up to 180 days. Australians, Canadians, and South Africans must obtain 30-day tourist visas. Visas are available at embassies or consulates. You cannot obtain a Czech visa at the border. Processing takes seven to ten days when materials are submitted by mail, five days when they are submitted in person. With the application, you must submit your passport; one photograph (two if applying to the Czech consulate in Los Angeles) glued—not stapled—to the application; a self-addressed, stamped envelope (certified or overnight mail); and a cashier's check or money order. Single-entry visas cost US$41 for Australians, US$53 for Canadian citizens, and US$24 for citizens of most other countries, while 90-day multiple-entry visas cost US$41/US$106/US$88. Prices for single-entry transit visas are the same as those for other single-entry visas; double-entry transit visas cost US$41/US$59/US$35. A multiple-entry transit visa costs US$88. The maximum stay in the Czech republic is five days per transit and all transit visas are valid for 90 days. Travelers on a visa must **register** with the Czech Immigration Police within three days of arrival; hotel guests are registered automatically.

TRANSPORTATION

BY PLANE. Air France, Alitalia, British Airways, Continental, ČSA, KLM, Lufthansa, and **Swissair** are among the major carriers with flights into Prague.

BY TRAIN. The easiest and most economical way to get around is by train. **Eastrail** is accepted in the Czech Republic, but **Eurail** is valid only with a special supplement. The fastest international trains are *EuroCity* and *InterCity* (*expresní*, marked in blue on schedules). *Rychlík* trains, also known as *zrychlený vlak*, are fast domestic trains, marked in red on schedules. Avoid slow *osobní* trains, marked in white. *Odjezdy* (departures) are printed in train stations on yellow posters, *příjezdy* (arrivals) on white. Seat reservations (*místenka;* 10Kč) are recommended on express and international trains and for first-class seating.

BY BUS. Czech buses are efficient and convenient, but their schedules can be confusing (see **Czech Buses 101,** p. 276). **ČSAD** runs national and international bus lines, and a number of European companies operate international service. Consult the timetables posted at stations or buy your own bus schedule (25Kč) from kiosks.

BY THUMB. Though popular in the Czech Republic, *Let's Go* does not recommend hitchhiking.

TOURIST SERVICES AND MONEY

Municipal tourist offices in major cities provide information on sights and events, distribute lists of hostels and hotels, and often book rooms. **CKM**, a national student tourist agency, is helpful for young travelers, booking hostel beds and issuing ISICs and HI cards. Most bookstores sell a national hiking map collection, *Soubor turistických map*, with an English key.

The Czech unit of currency is the **koruna** (crown; Kč), plural *koruny*. **Inflation** is around 4.7%, so prices should be relatively stable. **Banks** offer good exchange rates. **Komerční banka** and **Česká spořitelna** are common bank chains. **ATMs** are everywhere—look for the red-and-black *"Bankomat"* signs—and offer the best exchange rates. **Traveler's checks** can be exchanged almost everywhere, though rarely without commission. MasterCard and Visa are accepted at most expensive places, but many hostels and lower-priced establishments remain wary of plastic.

HEALTH AND SAFETY

 EMERGENCY NUMBERS: Police: ☎ 158 **Fire:** ☎ 150 **Ambulance:** ☎ 155

HEALTH AND SAFETY. The greatest risk of illness comes from **food**—bodies accustomed to a lighter diet tend to rebel against mass quantities of sausage and sauerkraut. Vegetables and fruits should be washed thoroughly. Medical services are quite good, and major foreign insurance policies are accepted. *Lékárna* (pharmacies) and supermarkets carry international brands of *náplast* (bandages), *tampóny* (tampons), and *kondomy* (condoms). Petty **crime** has increased dramatically since 1989; beware pickpockets prowling among the crowds in Prague's main squares and tourist attractions.

WOMEN AND BGLT TRAVELERS. Women traveling alone should experience few problems in the Czech Republic. However, caution should be exercised while riding public transportation, especially after dark. **Homosexuality** is legal in the Czech Republic, but public displays of it are not common; travelers should expect to encounter stares and are advised to remain cautious in public situations.

ACCOMMODATIONS AND CAMPING

CZECH	❶	❷	❸	❹	❺
ACCOM.	under 300Kč	301-500Kč	501-800Kč	801-1200Kč	over 1200Kč

HOSTELS AND HOTELS. Hostels, particularly in **university dorms,** are the cheapest option in July and August; two- to four-bed rooms cost 200-300Kč per person. Hostels are consistently clean and safe throughout the country. Showers and bedding are included. **Pensions** are the next most affordable option; expect to pay 600Kč, including breakfast. **Hotels** tend to be both more luxurious and more expensive than hostels or pensions, starting at around 1000Kč. From June to September reserve at least one week ahead in Prague, Český Krumlov, and Brno. If you can't keep a reservation, call to cancel so that some weary backpacker won't be sleeping on the street—at some point, that weary backpacker might be you.

HOMESTAYS. Private homes are not nearly as popular (or as cheap) as in the rest of Eastern Europe. Scan train stations for *Zimmer frei* signs. As quality varies, do not pay in advance.

CAMPING. There are many **campgrounds** strewn about the country; however, most are open only from mid-May to September.

CZECH REPUBLIC

KEEPING IN TOUCH

MAIL. The Czech Republic's postal system is reliable and efficient. A postcard to the US costs 9Kč, to Europe 7Kč. When sending by **airmail**, stress that you want it to go on a plane *(letecky)*. Go to the customs office to send packages heavier than 2kg abroad. Mail can be received through **Poste Restante.** Address envelopes as follows: Dali (first name), SNYDER (last name), POSTE RESTANTE, Jindřišská 14 (post office street address), Praha (city) 110 00 (postal code), CZECH REPUBLIC.

TELEPHONES AND INTERNET ACCESS. Card-operated phones (175Kč per 50 units; 320Kč per 100 units) are simpler to use than coin phones. You can purchase phone **cards** at most *Tábaks* and *Trafika* (convenience stores). Calls run 31Kč per minute to the UK; 63Kč per minute to Australia, Canada, or the US; and 94Kč per minute to New Zealand. Dial ☎1181 for English information, ☎0800 12 34 56 for the international operator. **Internet access** is readily available throughout the Czech Republic. Internet cafes offer fast connections for about 2Kč per min.

PRAGUE (PRAHA)   ☎(0)2

I see a grand city whose glory will touch the stars.
 —Countess Libuše

From Countess Libuše's mythological prophecy to the present, visionaries have placed Prague (pop. 1,200,000) on the cusp of the divine. Envisioning a royal seat worthy of his rank, King of Bohemia and Holy Roman Emperor Charles IV refashioned Prague into a city of soaring cathedrals and lavish palaces. Its maze of shady alleys and demon-haunted houses lend it a dark and dreamy atmosphere. As the 21st century now rises upon Prague, an ethereal magic still hangs over this city, where the clocks run backwards or not at all.

The magic has been well tested in recent years. Since the fall of the Iron Curtain, hordes of foreigners have flooded the venerable capital. In summer, most locals leave for the country and the foreigner-to-resident ratio soars above nine-to-one. The beer runs cheaper and faster than water in these streets, but you'll have to look elsewhere to find the city's true magic. Walk a few blocks from any of the major sights and you'll be lost in the labyrinthine cobblestone alleys. But even in the hyper-touristed Old Town, Prague's majesty gleams: the Charles Bridge, packed so tightly on a summer's day that the only way off is to jump, is still breathtaking at sunrise and eerie in a fog. Though Prague's spell may be fading, there's still plenty of stardust left in its cobblestone cracks.

✈ INTERCITY TRANSPORTATION

Flights: Ruzynw Airport (☎20 11 32 59), 20km northwest of the city. Bus #119 operates between the airport and Metro A: Dejvická (5am-midnight; 12Kč, 6Kč per bag). Tickets sold in kiosks or machines but not on board. An **airport bus** (☎20 11 42 96; every 30min.) collects travelers outside the Metro stations at Nám. Republiky (90Kč) and Dejvická (60Kč). **Taxis** to the airport are extremely expensive but may be the only option at night. Try to settle a price before starting out (400-600Kč). Airlines include: **Air France,** Václavské nám. 57 (☎24 22 71 64); **British Airways,** Ovocný trg 8 (☎22 11 44 44); **Czech Airlines** (ČSA), V Celnici 5 (☎20 10 43 10); **Delta,** Národní třída 32 (☎24 94 67 33); **KLM,** Na Příkopě 13 (☎33 09 09 40); **Lufthansa,** Ruzyně Airport (☎20 11 44 56); **Swissair,** Pařížská 11 (☎24 81 21 11).

Trains: ☎24 22 42 00, international info 24 61 52 49; www.cdrail.cz. English spoken. Prague has 4 main terminals. **Hlavní nádraží** (☎24 22 42 00), Metro C: Hlavní nádraží, is the largest, but most international service runs out of **Nádraží Holešovice** (☎24 61 32 49), Metro C: Nádraží Holešovice. Domestic trains leave from **Masarykovo nádraží** (☎24 61 51 54; Metro B: Nám. Republiky), on the corner of Hybernská and Havlíčkova, and from **Smíchovské nádraží** (☎24 61 72 55), Metro B: Smíchovské nádraží). International trains run to: **Berlin, GER** (5hr., 5 per day, 1400Kč); **Bratislava, SLK** (5½hr., 7 per day, 400Kč); **Budapest, HUN** (10hr.; 5 per day; 1300Kč); **Kraków, POL** (8½hr., 1 per day, 730Kč); **Moscow, RUS** (30¼hr., 1 per day, 2500Kč); **Munich, GER** (6hr., 3 per day, 1700Kč); **Vienna, AUS** (4½hr., 3 per day, 750Kč); **Warsaw, POL** (9½hr., 3 per day, 870Kč). **BIJ Wasteels** (☎24 61 74 54; fax 24 22 18 72; www.wasteels.cz), on the 2nd floor of Hlavní nádraží, to the right of the stairs, sells discounted international tickets to those under 26, books couchettes, and also sells bus tickets. Open in summer M-F 7:30am-8pm, Sa 8-11:30am and 12:30-3pm; off season M-F 8:30am-6pm. Wasteels tickets are also available from the **Czech Railways Travel Agency** (☎24 23 94 64; fax 24 22 36 00) at Nádraží Holešovice. Open M-F 9am-5pm, Sa-Su 8am-4pm.

Buses: Schedule information (☎1034, open daily 6am-9pm; www.vlakbus.cz or www.jiznirday.cz). The state-run **ČSAD** (Česká státní automobilová doprava; Czech national bus transport) has several bus terminals. The biggest is **Florenc**, Křižíkova 4 (☎24 21 49 90). Metro B or C: Florenc. Info office open daily 6am-9pm. Buy tickets in advance. To: **Berlin, GER** (8hr., 1 per day, 850Kč); **Budapest, HUN** (8hr., 1 per day, 1050Kč); **Paris, FRA** (18hr., 1 per day, 2200Kč); **Sofia, BUL** (26hr., 4 per day, 1600Kč); **Vienna, AUS** (8½hr., 1 per day, 800Kč). 10% student discount. The **Tourbus** office (☎24 21 02 21; www.eurolines.cz) upstairs sells tickets for **Eurolines** and airport buses. Open M-F 7am-7pm, Sa 8am-7pm, Su 9am-7pm.

■ ORIENTATION

Shouldering the river **Vltava**, greater Prague is a mess of suburbs and maze-like streets. Fortunately, nearly everything of interest to the traveler lies within the compact downtown. The Vltava runs south-northeast through central Prague, separating **Staré Město** (Old Town) and **Nové Město** (New Town) from **Malá Strana** (Lesser Side). On the right bank of the river, the Old Town's **Staroměstské náměstí** (Old Town Square) is Prague's focal point. From the square, the elegant **Pařížská ulice** (Paris Street) leads north into **Josefov**, the old Jewish ghetto in which only six synagogues and the Old Jewish Cemetery remain. In the opposite direction from Pařížská, **Nové Město** houses **Václavské náměstí** (Wenceslas Square), the administrative and commercial core of the city. West of Staroměstské nám., **Karlův most** (Charles Bridge) spans the Vltava, connecting the Old Town with **Malostranské náměstí** (Lesser Town Square). **Pražský Hrad** (Prague Castle) looks over Malostranské nám. from **Hradčany** hill.

Prague's **train station, Hlavní nádraží**, and **Florenc bus station** sit in the northeastern corner of Václavské nám. All train and bus terminals are on or near the excellent **Metro** system. To get to Staroměstské nám., take the Metro A line to Staroměstská and head down Kaprova away from the river. Kiosks and bookstores sell an indexed *plán města* (map), which is essential for newcomers to the city.

■ LOCAL TRANSPORTATION

Public Transportation: Prague's **Metro, tram,** and **bus** services are excellent and share the same ticket system. Buy tickets from newsstands, *tabák* kiosks, machines in stations, or DP (*Dopravní podnik;* transport authority) kiosks. The DP office, by the Jungmannovo nám. exit of the Můstek Metro stop (☎24 22 51 35; open daily 7am-9pm) and

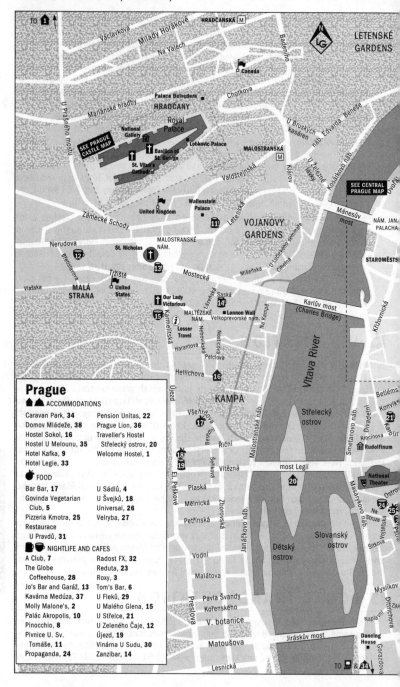

Prague

🔺🔺 ACCOMMODATIONS

Caravan Park, **34**
Domov Mládeže, **38**
Hostel Sokol, **16**
Hostel U Melounu, **35**
Hotel Kafka, **9**
Hotel Legie, **33**
Pension Unitas, **22**
Prague Lion, **36**
Traveller's Hostel
Střelecký ostrov, **20**
Welcome Hostel, **1**

🍎 FOOD

Bar Bar, **17**
Govinda Vegetarian
Club, **5**
Pizzeria Kmotra, **25**
Restaurace
U Pravdů, **31**
U Sádlů, **4**
U Švejků, **18**
Universal, **26**
Velryba, **27**

🌙☕ NIGHTLIFE AND CAFES

A Club, **7**
The Globe
Coffeehouse, **28**
Jo's Bar and Garáž, **13**
Kavárna Medúza, **37**
Molly Malone's, **2**
Palác Akropolis, **10**
Pinocchio, **8**
Pivnice U. Sv.
Tomáše, **11**
Propaganda, **24**
Radost FX, **32**
Reduta, **23**
Roxy, **3**
Tom's Bar, **6**
U Fleků, **29**
U Malého Glena, **15**
U Střelce, **21**
U Zeleného Čaje, **12**
Újezd, **19**
Vinárna U Sudu, **30**
Zanzibar, **14**

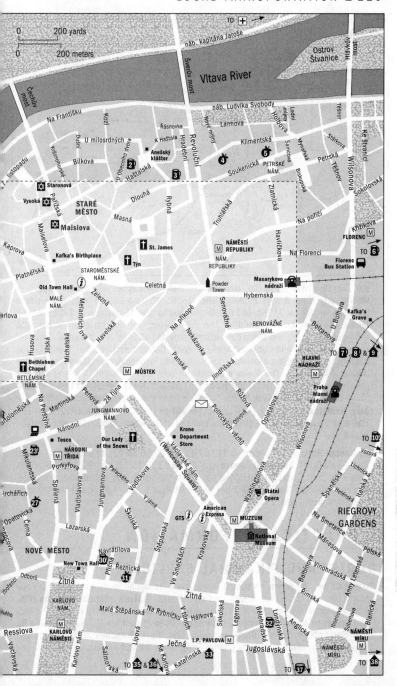

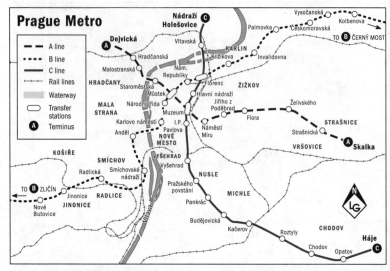

the 24hr. tourist office in Old Town Hall sell **multi-day passes** valid for the entire network (1 day 70Kč, 3 days 200Kč, 1 week 250Kč, 15 days 280Kč). A 30-day **student pass** is available for 210Kč. 8Kč tickets are good for one 15min. ride or 4 stops on the Metro. The 12Kč ticket is valid for 1hr, during which you can travel anywhere, with unlimited bus, tram, and Metro connections, provided all travel is in the same direction. Large bags, bikes, and baby carriages 6Kč each; babies travel free. Validate tickets in the machines above the escalators, as plainclothes inspectors roam the transport lines issuing 400Kč fines. The **Metro's** 3 lines run daily 5am-midnight: A is green on the maps, B is yellow, C is red. **Night trams** #51-58 and **buses** run all night after the last Metro (12:30-4:30am); look for the dark blue signs with white letters at bus stops.

Taxis: Radiotaxi (☎ 24 91 66 66) or **AAA** (☎ 140 14). 30Kč flat rate plus 22Kč per km. Hail a cab anywhere on the street, but call one of the above numbers to avoid getting ripped off.

Car Rental: Hertz, at the airport (☎ 312 07 17; fax 20 56 34 72). Open M-F 8am-10pm, Sa-Su 8am-8pm). **Branch** at Karlovo nám. 28 (☎ 22 23 10 10; fax 22 23 10 15). Open daily 8am-8pm. Cars start at 1006Kč per day for the first 4 days with unlimited mileage. Weekend specials (Th-Su) 700Kč per day. Must have a valid 3-year-old driver's license and major credit card. 21+.

🔢 PRACTICAL INFORMATION

TOURIST AND FINANCIAL SERVICES

Tourist Office: The green "i"s around Prague mark the myriad tourist agencies that book rooms and sell maps, bus tickets, and guidebooks. **Pražská informační služba** (PIS; Prague Information Service), in the Old Town Hall (☎ 54 44 44), sells **maps** (39-49Kč) and tickets to shows and for public transport. Open in summer M-F 9am-7pm, Sa-Su 9am-6pm; off season M-F 9am-6pm, Sa-Su 9am-5pm. **Branches** at Na příkopě 20, Hlavní nádraží, and the tower by Charles Bridge have the same hours.

Budget Travel:

CKM, Mánesova 77 (☎22 72 15 95; fax 22 72 63 40; ckmprg@login.cz). Metro A: Jiřího z Poděbrad. Sells budget air tickets to those under 26. Also books accommodations in Prague starting from 250Kč. Open M-Th 10am-6pm, F 10am-4pm.

GTS, Ve smečkách 27 (☎22 21 12 04). Metro A or C: Muzeum. Offers student discounts on airline tickets. Open M-F 8am-7pm, Sa 11am-3pm.

Lesser Travel, Karmelitská 24 (☎57 53 41 30; www.airtickets.cz). Sells student airfares. Open M-F 9:30am-5:30pm.

Passport Office: Foreigner police headquarters at Olšanská 2 (☎683 17 39). Metro A: Flora. From the Metro, turn right on Jičínská with the cemetery on your right and go right again on Olšanská. Or take tram #9 from Václavské nám. toward Spojovací and get off at Olšanská. To obtain a **visa extension**, get a 90Kč stamp inside, line up at doors #2-12, and prepare to wait up to 2hr. Little English spoken. Open M-Tu and Th 7:30-11:30am and 12:15-3:00pm, W 8:00am-12:15pm and 1-5pm, F 7:30-11:30am.

Embassies:

Australia (☎51 01 83 50) and **New Zealand** (☎22 51 46 72) have consulates, but citizens should contact the UK embassy in an emergency.

Canada, Mickiewiczova 6 (☎72 10 18 00). Metro A: Hradčanská. Open M-F 8:30am-12:30pm.

France, Velkopřerovské nám. 2 (☎57 53 27 56). Metro A: Malostranská.

Germany, Vlašská 19 (☎57 11 31 11). Metro A: Malostranská.

Hungary, Badeniho 1 (☎33 32 44 54). Metro A: Hradčanská. Open M-W and F 9am-noon.

Ireland, Tržiště 13 (☎57 53 00 61). Metro A: Malostranská. Open M-F 9:30am-12:30pm and 2:30-4:30pm.

Poland, Valdštejnské nám. 8 (☎57 53 03 88). Metro A: Malostranská. Open M-F 9am-1pm.

Russia, Pod Kaštany 1 (☎33 37 15 49). Metro A: Hradčanská. Open M-F 8am-5pm.

Slovak Republic, Pod Hradební 1 (☎33 32 54 43). Metro A: Dejvická. Open M-F 8:30am-noon.

South Africa, Ruská 65 (☎67 31 11 14). Metro A: Flora. Open M-F 9am-noon.

UK, Thunovská 14 (☎57 53 02 78). Metro A: Malostranská. Open M-F 9am-noon.

US, Tržiště 15 (☎57 53 06 63, after-hours emergency 53 12 00). Metro A: Malostranská. Open M-F 9am-4pm.

Currency Exchange: Exchange counters are everywhere; their rates vary wildly. Don't bother with the expensive hotels, and don't ever try changing money on the streets. **Chequepoints** are open quite late, but charge unpredictable commissions and may try to rip you off, so know your math. Try bargaining. **Komerční banka,** Na příkopě 33 (☎22 43 21 11), buys notes and checks for 2% commission. Open M-F 8am-5pm. **E Banka,** Václavské nám. 43 (☎22 11 55 90). Open M-F 8am-8pm, Sa 9am-noon.

ATMs: All over the place; look for the green and orange "*Bankomat*" signs.

American Express: Václavské nám. 56 (☎22 80 02 37; fax 22 21 11 31). Metro A or C: Muzeum. AmEx **ATM** outside. Grants MC/Visa **cash advances** for 3% commission. Open daily 9am-7pm. **Branches** at Mostecká 12 (☎57 31 36 38; open daily 9:30am-7:30pm), Celetná 17 (☎/fax 24 81 82 74; open daily 8:30am-7:15pm) and Staroměstské nám. 5 (☎24 81 83 88; fax 24 81 83 89; open daily 9am-8:30pm).

Work Opportunities: Unless you are fluent or near fluent in Czech, many establishments are reluctant to hire foreign short-term workers. The best option for short-term work is to place advertisements on bulletin boards in cafes, Internet cafes, laundromats, or even in the local newspaper offering language, sports, or music lessons.

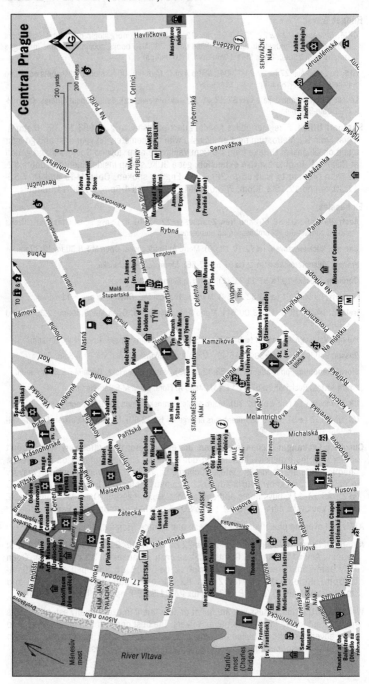

Central Prague

Havličkova

Masarykovo nádraží

V. Celnici

Hybernská

NÁM.
REPUBLIKY M
NÁMĚSTÍ
REPUBLIKY

Municipal House
(Obecní dům)

American
Express

Powder Tower
(Prašná brána)

Kotva
Department
Store

Rybná

Revoluční

U Obecního domu

Kralodvorská

Truhlářská

Na Poříčí

Senovážná

SENOVÁŽNÉ
NÁM.

Dlážděná

Nekázanka

Panská

Jubilee
(Jubilejní)

Jeruzalémská

St. Henry
(sv. Jindřich)

Museum of Communism

Na příkopě

Rámová

Masná

Dlouhá

Kozí

Vezeňská

Masná

Dušní

Vzkolovná

Rybná

TO 1 & 2

Malá
Štupartská

St. James
(sv. Jakub)

Jakubská

House of the
Golden Ring

Templova

TÝN

Týn Church
(Panna Marie
před Týnem)

Týnská

Celetná

Czech Museum
of Fine Arts

OVOCNÝ
TRH

Estates Theatre
(Stavovské divadlo)

Havířská

Provaznická

MŮSTEK M

Goltz-Kinský
Palace

Kamzíková

Museum of
Torture Instruments

STAROMĚSTSKÉ
NÁM.

Jan Hus
Statue

Zelezná

Karolinum
(Charles University)

St. Gall
(sv. Havel)

Havelská
Ulička

Na můstku

Rytířská

Spanish
(Španělská)

Dušní

sv. Duch

St. Salvator
(sv. Salvátor)

Košostná

American
Express

Melantrichova

Michalská

V. kotcích

Kožná

Kamzíková

El. Krásnohorské

Dušní

Image
Theater

Jáchymova

Maisel
(Maiselova)

Pařížská

Cathedral of St. Nicholas
(sv. Mikuláš)

Old Town Hall
(Staroměstská
radnice)

MALÉ
NÁM.

Hlavsova

Jilská

St. Giles
(sv. Jiljí)

Zlatá

Břehová

Pařížská

Old-New
Synagogue
(Staronová)

High
(Vysoká)

Jewish
Ceremonial
Hall

Maiselova

Kafka
Museum

Žatecká

Široká

Maisel Town Hall
(Židovská radnice)

Široká

Kaprova

Valentinská

Platnéřská

Linhartská

Husova

MARIÁNSKÉ
NÁM.

Seminářská

Karlova

Jalovcová

Husova

Řetězová

Husová

Bethlehem Chapel
(Betlémská kaple)

Zlatá

Liliová

Klementinum and sv Kliment
(St. Clement Church)

Museum of
Medieval Torture Instruments

Náprstkova

ANENSKÉ
NÁM.

Na Zábradlí

Theater at the
Balustrade (Divadlo na
zábradlí)

Decorative
Arts Museum
(Umělecko-
průmyslové)

Rudolfinum
(Dům umělců)

NÁM. JANA
PALACHA

17. listopadu

STAROMĚSTSKÁ M

Pinkas
(Pinkasova)

Klaus
(Klausová)

Řísé
Loutek
Theater

Old Jewish
Cemetery (Starý
židovský hřbitov)

Veleslavínova

Thomas Cook

Křižovnická

St. Francis
(sv. František)

Smetana
Museum

Karlův
most
(Charles
Bridge)

River Vltava

Mánesův
most

Dvořákovo nábř.

Alšovo nábř.

200 yards
200 metres

N
LG

0 200 meters
0 200 yards

i

Central Prague

🏠 ACCOMMODATIONS
Dům krále Jiřího, **18**
Hotel Junior, **20**
Pension Týn, **6**
Ritchie's Hostel, **14**
Traveller's Hostel Dlouhá 33, **2**
Traveller's Hostel Husova 3, **25**
U Lilie, **16**

🍴 FOOD
Cafe Bambus, **5**
Country Life, **19**
Klub Architektů, **23**
Pizza Express, **21**
Roma Due, **15**
Shalom, **9**
U Rozvarilů, **8**
U Špirků, **13**

🌙☕ NIGHTLIFE AND CAFES
Cafe Marquis de Sade, **11**
Dobrá Čajovna, **24**
Jazz Club Železná, **12**
Karlovy Lázně, **17**
Kavárna Imperial, **7**
Kozička, **4**
Le Chateau, **10**
Roxy, **1**
U Staré Paní, **22**
Žiznivý Pes, **3**

LOCAL SERVICES

Luggage Storage: Lockers in train and bus stations take two 5Kč coins. If you forget the locker number or combination, you'll be charged 20Kč. For storage over 24hr., use the luggage offices to the left in the basement of **Hlavní nádraží** (under 15kg 15Kč per day; larger bags 30Kč per day; open 24hr.) or along the stairs at **Florenc** (under 15kg 10Kč per day; larger bags 25Kč per day; 100Kč for lost tickets; open daily 5am-11pm).

English-Language Bookstores: Abound throughout Prague.

The Globe Bookstore, Pštrossova 6 (☎26 20 32 86). Metro B: Národní třída. Exit Metro left on Spálená, make the first right on Ostrovní, then turn left on Pštrossova. The coffeehouse sells new and used books, periodicals, and **Internet** access (1Kč per minute).

Anagram Bookshop, Týn 4 (☎24 89 57 37; fax 24 89 57 38; www.anagram.cz). Metro A: Staroměstská. Behind Týn Church in the Ungelt passageway. Offers trade-ins for used books. Open M-Sa 10am-8pm, Su 10am-6pm.

Big Ben Bookshop, Malá Štupartská 5 (☎24 82 65 65; fax 24 82 65 59). Metro A: Staroměstská. Near the Church of St. James. Open M-F 9am-6:30pm, Sa-Su 10am-5pm.

U Knihomola International Bookshop, Mánesova 79 (☎627 77 67; fax 627 77 82). Metro A: Jiřího z Poděbrad. Open M-F 10am-9pm.

Laundromat: Laundry Kings, Dejvická 16 (☎33 34 37 43), one block from Metro A: Hradčanská. Cross the tram and railroad tracks, then turn left on Dejvická. A social center-*cum*-laundromat; travelers flock here at night to watch CNN and to pick each other up. Bulletin board for apartment seekers, English teachers, and "friends." **Internet access** (55Kč/30min). Wash 60Kč per 6kg; dry 15Kč per 8min. (usually takes 45min.; use the spinner to save on drying). Soap 10-20Kč. Full-service 30Kč more and takes 24hr. Dry cleaning (M-F 7am-7pm, Sa 8am-noon) 41-225Kč depending on garment. Beer 15Kč. Open M-F 6am-10pm, Sa-Su 8am-10pm. **Laundromat/Internet Cafe,** Korunní 14 (☎22 51 01 80). Metro A: Nám. Míru. Kill two birds with one stone. Washer 65Kč, dryer 65Kč per load. Soap 20Kč. Internet 30Kč per 15min. Open daily 8am-8pm.

EMERGENCY AND COMMUNICATIONS

 Don't be fooled by the different lengths of telephone numbers ranging from 4 to 8 digits. Prague is continuously updating its phone system, and has scheduled a major phone number change for September 22, 2002. If numbers listed here are no longer in service after this date, call the city's telephone information line for an update (☎14111).

24-Hour Pharmacy: U Andwla, Štefánikova 6 (☎57 32 09 18). Metro B: Anděl. Exit toward Anděl and follow Nádražní until it becomes Štefánikova.

Medical Services: Na Homolce (Hospital for Foreigners), Roentgenova 2 (☎57 27 11 11; after hours 57 77 20 25). Major foreign insurance plans and credit cards accepted. **American Medical Center,** Janovského 48 (☎87 79 73). Major foreign insurance policies accepted. **Canadian Medical Centre,** Veleslavínská 30 (☎35 36 01 33). BUPA and MEDEX insurance accepted.

CZECH REPUBLIC

Telephones: Virtually everywhere. Card phones are most common and convenient. Phone cards sell for 175Kč per 50 units and 320Kč per 100 units at kiosks, post offices, and some exchange establishments; don't let kiosks rip you off.

Internet Access: Prague is an Internet nirvana. Jump on the web in libraries, hostels, posh cafes, and trendy bars. Národní is home to several lab-like cyber cafes.

Bohemia Bagel, Masna 2 (☎24 81 25 60; www.bohemiabagel.cz). Metro A: Staroměstská. Internet 1.5Kč per min. Open M-F 7am-midnight, Sa-Su 8am-midnight. **Branch** at Újezd 16. Open daily 9am-midnight.

Cafe Electra, Rašínovo nábřeží 62 (☎24 92 28 87). Metro B: Karlovo nám. Exit on the Palackého nám. side. Extensive menu. Internet 80Kč per hr. Open M-F 9am-midnight, Sa-Su 11am-midnight.

Cafe Net, Havelská 27 (☎24 21 32 65). Metro A: Staroměstská. See directions to U Špirků restaurant (p. 238). Friendly staff. Internet 20Kč per 15min. Open daily 10am-10pm.

Internet Cafe, Národní třída 25 (☎21 08 52 84; www.internetcafe.cz). Metro B: Národní třída. Across from Tesco inside the Pasáž paláce Metro. Internet 120Kč per hr. Open daily 10am-midnight. **Branch** at Liliova 18, near the Charles Bridge through Pension Salieri.

Post Office: Jindřišská 14 (☎21 13 14 45). Metro A or B: Můstek. **Poste Restante** available. Tellers close at 7pm. Open daily 2am-midnight. **Postal Code:** 110 00.

⚆ ACCOMMODATIONS

While hotel prices have risen exponentially, hostel prices have stabilized around 250-600Kč per night. Smaller hostels with familial atmospheres tend to be cheaper than large hostels in the center of town. Reserve rooms at least two days in advance and even earlier in July and Aug. Most accommodations have 24hr. reception and require check-in after 2pm and check-out by 10am. Though far less common than in other parts of Eastern Europe, a growing number of Prague residents rent out affordable rooms.

ACCOMMODATION AGENCIES

Hawkers, most of whom are mere hired agents, besiege visitors at the train station. Many offer legitimate deals, but some just want to rip you off. The going rates for **apartments** hover around 600-1200Kč per day, depending on proximity to the city center; haggling is possible. If you're wary of bargaining on the street, try a private agency. Staying outside the center is convenient if you're near public transport, so ask where the nearest tram, bus, or Metro stop is. If in doubt, ask for details in writing. You can often pay in US dollars, but prices are lower if you pay in Kč. Some travel agencies will book accommodations (see **Tourist and Financial Services,** p. 230).

Ave., Hlavní nádraží (☎236 25 60; fax 236 29 56; ave@avetravel.cz), on the 2nd floor of the train station. Two locations; English spoken at the location on the left. Hundreds of rooms (shared and private) starting at 800Kč per person. Books hostels from 290Kč. Open daily 6am-10pm. AmEx/MC/V.

HOSTELS

If you're schlepping a backpack in Hlavní nádraží or Holešovice, you *will* be bombarded by hostel runners. Many of these hostels are university dorms that take in travelers from June to August. These rooms are easy options for those arriving without reservations. For more than a mere bed, there are plenty of smaller, friendlier alternatives. Most places have an English-speaking staff.

STARÉ MĚSTO

Ritchie's Hostel, Karlova 9 (☎22 22 12 29; fax 602 206 711; www.mujweb.cz/www/praguehostel). Metro A: Staroměstská, down Karlova from the Charles Bridge. Enter through the souvenir shop. Great facilities and convenient location. Next to several bars and clubs. 10% discount in summer. 20% discount during the rest of the year if you book through a travel agent. 20Kč extra fee per night for taxes. 9-bed dorm 360Kč per person for 4 nights or more, 400Kč for 3 nights or less; 4-bed dorm 485Kč/535Kč; doubles 1310Kč/1460Kč; triples 1760Kč/1940Kč. ❷

Pension Týn, Týnská 19 (☎/fax 24 80 83 33; backpacker@razdva.cz). Metro A: Staroměstská. From Staroměstské nám., head down Dlouhá, bear right at Masná, and take another right on Týnská. A quiet getaway conveniently located in the center of Old Town. No common room, but immaculate facilities and a friendly staff. Breakfast not included, but a special bagel rate is offered from 6-9am at **Bohemia Bagel** (see p. 234). Dorms 400Kč; doubles 1100Kč. 30Kč ISIC discount. ❷

Traveller's Hostels (☎24 82 66 62; fax 24 82 66 65; www.travellers.cz). These big-dorm specialists round up travelers at bus and train stations around the city and herd them into one of their hostels for beds and beer. Price varies with proximity to the center, but breakfast is included at all hostels. As guest turnover is rapid, the hostels often have space for those without reservations.

Dlouhá 33 (☎24 82 66 62; fax 24 82 66 65). Metro B: Nám. Republiky. Exit the Metro and walk towards Hotel City Centre following Revoluční toward the river. Turn left on Dlouhá; the hostel will be on your right. Unbeatable location right off Staroměstské nám. In the same building as the Roxy Club, but with good soundproofing. The only Traveller's Hostel that stays open year-round has social dorms and more private, newly renovated apartments. Internet access 27Kč per 15min. Laundry 150Kč per load. Hostel: 6-bed dorm 430Kč; 10-bed 370Kč; doubles 620Kč; triples 1440Kč. Apartments: 2-3 beds 2400Kč; 4 beds 2900Kč; 2 rooms with 4 beds 3000Kč; 2 rooms with 5/6 beds 3500Kč. 40Kč ISIC discount. ❷

Husova 3 (☎22 22 00 78). Metro B: Národní třída. Turn right on Spálená (which turns into Na Perštýně after Národní), and then Husova. In the middle of the Old Town. Satellite TV. Open July-Aug. Dorms 400Kč. ❷

Újezd, U Lanove Drahy 3 (☎57 31 24 03). Metro B: Národní třída. Follow Národní across Most Legií bridge until it becomes Vitězná. Turn right on Újezd; the hostel is on the left next to Lanovka Draha. A converted gymnasium next to the cable car running up to Petrin Gardens. Outdoor sports facilities, park, indoor and outdoor picnic area. Open June-Sept. Dorms 220Kč. ❶

Střelecký ostrov (☎24 91 01 88). Metro B: Národní třída. Located on an island beneath Legií bridge. Holds frequent barbecues for its guests. Tennis courts available. Open June 10-Sept. 15. Spacious dorms 300Kč. ❶

NOVÉ MĚSTO

Hostel u Melounu (At the Watermelon), Ke Karlovu 7 (☎/fax 24 91 83 22; www.hostelumelounu.cz). Metro C: IP Pavlova. Follow Sokolská to Na Bojišti and turn left at the street's end on Ke Karlovu. An "oasis of rest," this former hospital provides the ideal environment in which to recuperate from the city's wild pace. Facilities include a bar and a private garden. Provides a list of the top 5 clubs, bars, and restaurants in Nové Město, but the grounds are so peaceful you won't want to leave. Breakfast included. Laundry 100Kč. Dorms 380Kč; singles 500Kč; doubles 420Kč. 30Kč ISIC discount. ❷

Prague Lion, Na Bojišti 26 (☎/fax 96 18 00 18; www.praguelion.com). Metro C: IP Pavlova. Follow Sokolská to Na Bojišti. Good location, clean rooms, but a little pricey. Internet 3Kč per min. Breakfast included. Singles 1250Kč; doubles 1400Kč; triples 1750Kč; quads 1950Kč. Prices lower Sept.-May. ❹

Hotel Junior, Senovážné nám. 21 (☎24 23 17 54 or 22 10 55 36; fax 24 22 15 79; euroagentur@euroagentur.cz). Metro B: Nám. Republiky. Follow Revoluční toward the Powder Tower, turn left to Senovážná at the tower, then left again to Senovážné nám. Down a beer while bowling a perfect game and reward yourself with a cheap, tasty pizza in the pizzeria downstairs. Breakfast included. Check-in 2pm. Reservations recommended 1-2 weeks in advance. June-Aug. dorms 550Kč; Sept.-May 450Kč. ❸

MALÁ STRANA

Hostel Sokol, Nosticova 2 (☎57 00 73 97; fax 57 00 73 40). Metro A: Malostranská. From the Metro, take tram #12 or 22 to Hellichova; or walk from Malostranské nám. down Karmelitská about 300m. Take a left on Hellichova then the last left on Nosticova and watch for the signs. Reception is on the 3rd fl. Clean dorms in the Malá Strana sports club. Nice rooftop terrace. Communal kitchen. Safes and lockers. Reception 24hr. Check-in and check-out 11am. Weekend rooms are often unavailable due to athletic competitions. Dorms 300Kč; doubles 660Kč. ❶

VINOHRADY

Domov Mládeže, Dykova 20 (☎/fax 22 51 17 77; jana.dyrsmidova@telecom.cz). From Metro A: Jiřího z Poděbrad, follow Vinohradská toward the huge clock, then go right on Nitranská and left on Dykova. It's 2 blocks down on the right. 100 beds in the tree-lined Vinohrady district; so peaceful you might forget you're in Prague. Breakfast included. Reserve 1-2 weeks in advance. 2- to 7-person dorms 350Kč; doubles 440Kc. 10% ISIC discount. When there are no beds, the staff will check you in at their sister hostel, **Košická,** Košická 12. Metro A: Nám. Míru. Same hours and prices. ❷

OUTSIDE THE CENTER

🏠 **Hostel Boathouse,** Lodnická 1 (☎41 77 00 57; fax 41 77 68 88; www.aa.cz/boathouse,). Take tram #21 from Národní třída south toward Sídliště. Get off at Černý Kůň (20min.) and follow the yellow Boathouse signs from the tram stop down to the Vltava. As Věra, the owner, says, "This isn't a hostel; it's a crazy house." Despite the madness, she manages to remember almost everyone's name. A young, energetic crowd and 70 beds make this hostel the perfect fusion of nurturing home and summer camp. The Boathouse serves meals (hot breakfast or dinner 70Kč) and offers board games, Internet access, satellite TV, and laundry service (100Kč per load). Free welcome gift of postcards and a pen. Call ahead; if they're full, Věra might let you sleep in the hall. E-mail reservations preferred. 3- to 5-bed dorms perched above a working boathouse 320Kč; 8-bed dorm 300Kč. ❶

🏠 **Penzion v podzámčí,** V podzámčí 27 (☎/fax 41 44 46 09; evacib@yahoo.com). From Metro C: Budějovická, take bus #192 to the 3rd stop—ask the driver to stop at Nad Rybníky. The hostel is just up the hill behind the bus stop. The friendly staff makes this the homiest hostel in Prague, with extraordinary laundry service (100Kč per load)—they *iron* your socks—and daily clothes-folding and bed-making. Communal kitchen, satellite TV, comfy beds, warm hot chocolate, friendly cats, and great stories. Internet access 40Kč per 15min. Dorms 280Kč; doubles 320Kč; triples 300Kč. ❶

Welcome Hostel, Zíkova 13 (☎24 32 02 02; fax 24 32 34 89; www.bed.cz). Metro A: Dejvická. Exit the Metro on Šolinova and turn left on Zíkova. Great if you're arriving from the airport late at night; if they don't have room at Zíkova, they might at their sister hostel at Strahov Complex (see below). Some of the cheapest beds in town in a tidy, spacious, and convenient university dorm. Breakfast included. Check-in 2pm. Check-out 9:30am. June 20-Nov. 1 250 beds; Nov. 2-June 19 50 beds. Singles 400Kč; doubles 270Kč per person. 10% ISIC discount. ❷

Welcome Hostel at Strahov Complex, Vaníčkova 5 (☎33 35 92 75; fax 24 32 34 89). Take bus #217 or 143 from Metro A: Dejvická to Koleje Strahov. Right by an enormous stadium, Strahov is 10 concrete blocks of high-rise dormitories that open annually.

(June 20-Nov. 11; some beds available all year.) Newly renovated building only 10min. by foot from Prague Castle. Not terribly convenient to the center, but there's always space and a free beer to greet you at check-in. Singles 300Kč; doubles 480Kč. 10% ISIC discount. ❶

HOTELS AND PENSIONS

As tourists colonize Prague, hotels are upgrading their service and their prices; budget hotels are now quite scarce. Call several months ahead to book a room for the summer months and confirm by fax with a credit card.

STARÉ MĚSTO

Dům Krále Jiřího, Liliová 10 (☎22 22 09 25; fax 22 22 17 07; www.kinggeorge.cz). Metro A: Staroměstská. Exit the Metro to Nám. Jana Palacha. Walk down Křížovnická toward the Charles Bridge and turn left on Karlova; Liliová is the 1st street on the right. Capturing the antique character of the Old Town, Krále Jiřího offers gorgeous rooms with private bath. Buffet breakfast included. May-Dec. singles 2000Kč; doubles 3300Kč. Dec.-May 1500Kč/2700Kč. ❺

U Lilie, Liliová 15 (☎22 22 04 32; fax 22 22 06 41; pensionulilie@cz). Metro A: Staroměstská. Follow the directions to Dům Krále Jiřího (above). U Lilie boasts a lovely courtyard. Satellite TV, telephone, and minibar in every room. Breakfast included. Singles with shower 1850Kč; doubles 2150Kč, with bath 2800Kč. ❺

Pension Unitas/Cloister Inn, Bartolomějská 9 (☎232 77 00; fax 232 77 09; cloister@cloister-inn.cz). Metro B: Národní třída. Cross Národní, head up Na Perštýně away from Tesco and hang a left on Bartolomějská. Rooms in renovated cells of a former Communist jail. Stay in the multi-bedded "pink prison" downstairs for a (brightened) glimpse into what life might have been like when Havel was incarcerated here. Comfortable rooms with communal bathrooms. Parking available for 250Kč per night. Breakfast included. Reception 24hr. Reservations via fax or Email only. Singles 1100Kč; doubles 1400Kč; triples 1750Kč; quads 2000Kč. ❹

NOVÉ MĚSTO

Hotel Legie, Sokolská 33 (☎24 26 62 31, reservations 24 26 62 40; fax 24 26 62 34; www.legie.cz). Metro C: IP Pavlova. From the Metro, turn left on Ječná; the hotel is across the street. Clean rooms with private showers, phone, and cable TV; some offer great views of Prague Castle. Breakfast included. May-Oct. and Jan. doubles 3000Kč; triples 3900Kč. Feb.-May and Nov.-Dec. 2300Kč/3100Kč. ❺

OUTSIDE THE CENTER

Hotel Kafka, Cimburkova 24 (☎22 78 13 33; fax 22 78 04 31), in Žižkov near the TV tower. From Metro C: Hlavní nádraží, take tram #5 toward Harfa, #9 toward Spojovací, or #26 toward Nádraží Hostivař; get off at Husinecká. Head uphill along Seifertova 3 blocks and go left on Cimburkova. Brand-new hotel amid 19th-century buildings, close to plenty of beerhalls. Breakfast included. Apr.-Oct. singles 1700Kč; doubles 2200Kč; triples 2600Kč; quads 2800Kč. Nov.-Mar. 1200Kč/1600Kč/1800Kč/2000Kč. MC/V for 5% commission. ❺

B&B U Oty (Ota's House), Radlická 188 (☎/fax 57 21 53 23 or 57 21 53 25; www.bbuoty.cz). Metro B: Radlická. Exit the Metro up the stairs to the left and go right past Bistro Kavos on Radlická, and walk 400m. Ota is the charming proprietor of this pension. Reserve 2 weeks in advance. Free parking. Breakfast included. Kitchen facilities. Laundry free after 3 nights. Singles 700Kč; doubles 770Kč; triples 990Kč; quads 1300Kč. 100Kč extra per person if staying only one night. ❸

⚑ CAMPING

Campsites have taken over both the outskirts and the centrally located Vltava islands. Bungalows must be reserved in advance, but tent space is generally available without prior notice. Tourist offices sell a guide to sites near the city (15Kč).

Caravan Park, Císařská louka 599 (☎57 31 86 81; fax 57 31 83 87), on the Císařská louka peninsula on the Vltava. Metro B: Smíchovské nádraží, then any of the buses numbered in the 300s to Lihovar. Take a left on the shaded path as you head to the river (500m). Alternatively, a ferry service leaves every hour on the hour from the small landing, 1 block over from Smíchovské nádraží (10Kč). 90-140Kč per tent, plus 95Kč per person; 2-bed bungalows 480Kč; 4-bed 720Kč. Local tax 15Kč per person, plus 5% national tax. Children and students are exempt from local taxes. ❶

Sokol Troja, Trojská 171 (☎/fax 33 54 29 08). Prague's largest campground, north of city center in the Troja district. From Metro C: Nádraží Holešovice, take bus #112 to Kazanka, the 4th stop. If the manicured grounds are full, at least 4 similar establishments line the same road. Pitch a tent in the yard and admire the beautiful houses located in one of Prague's wealthiest neighborhoods. Bathing facilities so clean you could eat off them. July-Aug. tents 90-180Kč plus 130Kč per person; dorms 270Kč; bungalow 230Kč per person. Oct.-June 70-150Kč/240Kč/200Kč. ❶

Na Vlachovce, Zenklova 217 (☎/fax 688 02 14). Take bus #102 or 175 from Nádraží Holešovice to Okrouhlická. Cross the street, and continue in the same direction up the hill. Enter through the restaurant. If you've ever felt like crawling into a barrel of Czech beer, try these outdoor beds in romantic 2-person barrels. Great view of Prague. Breakfast included. Reserve a week ahead. Discounts for extended stays. If the barrels (200Kč) invoke claustrophobia, the attached *pension* has doubles for 975Kč. ❶

◧ FOOD

The nearer you are to the center, the more you'll pay. In less touristed areas, however, you can have pork, cabbage, dumplings, and a beer for 50Kč. Always bring cash and check the bill, as you'll pay for everything the waiter brings, including ketchup and bread, and some restaurants may try to massage bills higher than they should. At lunchtime, *hotová jídla* (prepared meals) are cheapest. Though vegetarian establishments are quickly multiplying, the options often remain limited to fried cheese and cabbage. For fresher alternatives, look out for the **daily market** at the intersection of Havelská and Melantrichova in Staré Město.

STARÉ MĚSTO RESTAURANTS

Klub architektů, Betlémské nám. 52 (☎24 40 12 14). Metro B: Národní třída. Take Spálená until it becomes Na Perštýně, then turn left on Betlémské nám. Walk through the gate immediately on your right and descend underground. A 12th-century cellar thrust into the 20th century, with sleek table settings and copper pulley lamps. Try the delicious pork steak and other tantalizing meat dishes (140-150Kč). Veggie options 90-100Kč. Open daily 11:30am–midnight. Kitchen closes at 11pm. MC/V. ❸

Cafe Bambus, Benediktská 12 (☎24 82 81 10). Metro B: Nám. Republiky. See directions to Hostel Dlouhá 33 (see **Accommodations,** p. 234) and take a left on Benediktská. Step out of the Prague jungle into this African oasis where masks, statuettes, and crocodiles adorn the walls. Asian and international cuisine with Czech flavors 80-140Kč; sandwiches 45Kč. Open M-F 9am-midnight, Sa-Su 11am-midnight. ❷

U Špirků, Kožná ulička 12 (☎24 23 84 20). Metro A: Staroměstská. With your back to the astronomical clock on Staroměstské nám., go through the archway down narrow Melantrichova and take the first left on Kožná. The restaurant is on the right. Sit next to hungry locals and devour some of the city's biggest portions of good, cheap food. Salads 20-40Kč; steak, potatoes, and cabbage 105Kč. Open daily 11am-midnight. ❶

Country Life, Melantrichova 15 (☎ 24 21 33 66). Metro A: Staroměstská. See directions to U Špirků (above). Country Life's salad bar answers those green, vegetarian cravings that emerge after days of a Czech dumpling and fried cheese diet. Pay by weight for a mix of greens (19Kč per 100g) and a variety of light, dairy-free dishes. Open M-Th 9am-8:30pm, F 9am-6pm and Su 11am-8:30pm. ❷

Shalom, Maiselova 18 (☎ 231 90 02). Metro A: Staroměstská. Head down Kaprova away from the river and go left on Maiselova; the restaurant is inside the town hall on the right. Fine kosher lunches in the old Jewish Quarter. Set menu 270-600Kč. Buy tickets beforehand across the road at Legacy Tours (☎ 232 19 51; open M-F and Su 9am-6pm). Order tickets in advance for Jewish holidays and group dinners. Open M-Sa 11:30am-2pm. ❺

NOVÉ MĚSTO RESTAURANTS

▨ **U Sádlů,** Klimentská 2 (☎ 24 81 38 74). Metro B: Nám. Republiky. From the square, walk down Revoluční toward the river, then go right on Klimentská. The armor by the bar promises portions bountiful enough to sustain a full day of knight-errantry. Or touristing. Call ahead for reservations. Menu in Czech only, but the staff can help you order traditional Czech meals (115-230Kč). Open daily 11am-midnight. ❸

Velryba (The Whale), Opatovická 24 (☎ 16 10 30 50). Metro B: Národní třída. Cross the tram tracks and follow the narrow Ostrovní and then take a left on Opatovická. The establishment is opposite the church. Enjoy a cheap Czech or international dish (80-140Kč) among a diverse crowd of locals, expats, business types, and tourists, or slip back to the plush cafe for coffee or wine. An art gallery hides under the cafe floor. Descend the spiral staircase and leave your mark in the belly of the whale by signing the guestbook. Open M-Th 11am-midnight, F 11am-2am. Cafe and gallery open M-F noon-midnight, Sa 5pm-midnight, Su 3-10pm. ❷

Universal, V jirchářích 6 (☎ 24 93 44 16). Metro B: Národní třída. Follow the directions to Velryba (see above), but head right around the church to V jirchářích. The French quote on the wall reads "full of colors, full of noise, full of people, full of joy." A perfect description of Universal. Enjoy the biggest and freshest salads in Prague (115-165Kč) or more traditional meat dishes (165-335Kč) in a spacious dining room. Open M-Sa 11:30am-1am, Su 12:30pm-1am. ❹

IN RECENT NEWS

ROAD BLOCKS AND RADIO BROADCASTS

Do not be alarmed by the military vehicles and armed guards blocking the streets of Prague outside of Radio Free Europe; the communists have not retaken the country. Since the terrorist attacks on the World Trade Center in New York on September 11, 2002, the Czech Republic has paid closer attention to the security of one of its best-known buildings. Radio Free Europe broadcasts throughout Europe giving news updates and information on global news and world affairs. They advocate peace and an end to regional conflict. Worried that the broadcasts may anger terrorist groups and make it a target for attack, the American embassy requested military protection of the building that sits just 100m from one of Prague's most commercial areas, Václavské Náměsti. The Czechs complied, and brought in soldiers and armed vehicles.

The decision has been controversial. Many Czechs are unhappy with a military presence in Prague, and complain that the road blocks cause unnecessary traffic jams. The issue has caused so much unrest that Czech officials offered to move Radio Free Europe outside of the city. However, since it has been broadcasting from the corner of Wilsonova and Vinohradská since WWII, Radio Free Europe is reluctant to leave Prague. They argue, and many locals agree, that the risk of an attack on the building is minimal and that the military budget would be better spent elsewhere.

—Dalibor Eric Snyder

Pizzeria Kmotra, V jirchářích 12 (☎24 93 41 00). Metro B: Národní třída. Follow the directions to Universal (see above). One of the first pizza places to open in Prague, this cellar overflows at dinner time. Huge salads, pasta, and pizzas 69-149Kč. Open daily 11am-midnight. ❷

Restaurace U Pravdů, Žitná 15 (☎22 23 08 61). Metro B: Karlovo nám. Walk through Karlovo nám. on Ječná, go left on Vodičkova and right on Žitná. Traditional Czech cuisine (Entrees 75-180Kč) offered alongside veggie options (40-100Kč). Good luck finding a seat at the bar after 7:30pm. Beer 18Kč. Open daily 10:30am-11pm. ❷

Govinda Vegetarian Club, Soukenická 27 (☎24 81 66 31). Metro B: Nám. Republiky. Walk down Revoluční, away from the Obecní Dum, and turn right on Soukenická. Statues of Hindu gods gaze upon diners and delicious vegetarian stews. Set daily menu 80Kč. Second helpings of the main dish are free. Open M-Sa 11am-5:30pm. ❶

U Řozvarilů, Na Poříčí 26 (☎25 76 83 79). Metro B: Nám. Republiky. As you exit the station on Na Poříčí, take a sharp right around the church to arrive at this cafeteria-style establishment. Quality dining doesn't come much cheaper—the Czech regulars gorge on traditional meals like meat with cream sauce (48Kč) and potato dumplings (13-15Kč). Open M-Sa 7:30am-8:30pm, Su 10am-6pm. ❶

MALÁ STRANA RESTAURANTS

▦ **U Švejků,** Újezd 22 (☎57 31 32 44). Metro A: Malostranská. From the Metro, head down Klárov and go right on Letenská. Bear left through Malostranské nám. and follow Karmelitská until it becomes Újezd. Converted to a restaurant in 1993, this former inn dates back to 1618 and hosted President Masaryk during WWI. After a few beers you might attempt to dance with the accordionist (nightly after 7pm). Chuckle at murals and cartoon pictures of Svejk and see why this inn-turned-restaurant was named after the lovable cartoon hero of Hašek's novel, *The Good Soldier Svejk.* Entrees 98-158Kč. Open daily 11am-midnight. ❸

Kajetanka, Hradčanské nám. (☎57 53 37 35). Metro A: Malostranská. Exit the Metro and walk down Letenská, through Malostranské nám. Climb Nerudova until it curves around to Ke Hradu. Kajetanka is about 100m uphill. The cafe offers a spectacular view over the red-tiled roofs of Prague. Meat dishes (129-289Kč) and salads (49-69Kč). Gaze through telescopes for a closer look at Prague's beautiful skyline (20Kč per 2min.). Open in spring and summer daily 10am-9pm; in fall and winter 10am-6pm. ❹

El Centro Bar y Bodega, Maltézské nám. 9 (☎57 53 33 43). Metro A: Malostranská. From the Metro, walk towards the Charles Bridge; at the bridge, take a right on Mostecká and a left on Lazenská. El Centro will be in Maltézské nám. Decorative fans and portraits of matadors decorate the walls of this Spanish-themed restaurant. Enjoy authentic Spanish cuisine (135-245Kč) and other international dishes (85-140Kč) in the vaulted interior of a 15th-century house. Chug *Gambrinus* (13Kč) or sip one of over 80 cocktails on the menu. Veggie options 95-140Kč. Open daily 11am-midnight. ❸

Bar bar, Všehrdova 17 (☎57 31 22 46). Metro A: Malostranská. Follow the tram tracks from the Metro station down Letenská, through Malostranské nám., and down Karmelitská. Take the left on Všehrdova after the museum. A diverse menu of meats (80-209Kč), fish, cheese, and veggie dishes (70-90Kč), as well as some delicious pancakes (70-109Kč). Order a fine whiskey (from 55Kč), sit back, and appreciate the jazz music and photo gallery. Open daily noon-2am. ❷

LATE-NIGHT EATING

4:45am. Charles Bridge. Karlovy Lázně's house disco beat is still pumping ferociously, but all you can hear is your stomach growling. Rather than catching the night bus home and going to bed hungry, grab a *párek v rohlíku* (hot dog) or a *smažený sýr* (fried cheese sandwich) from a vendor on Václavské nám. or a gyro from a stand on Spálená or Vodičkova. Or, even better, make a morning of it and discover Prague's developing late-night cuisine.

▨ Radost FX, Bělehradská 120 (☎ 24 25 47 76). Metro C: IP Pavlova. Indulge in a dish from Radost's highly imaginative menu (karma chameleon wrap 150Kč) and lounge on the zebra print sofas with the coolest cats in town as they emerge from the throngs of sweaty dancers in the club below. Brunch Sa-Su (95-140Kč). Italian night Su 5pm-2am. Open daily 11am-late (at least 3am on weekdays and 5am on weekends). ●

Roma Due, Liliová 18 (☎ 28 79 43). Metro A: Staroměstská. From the Charles Bridge, take the 2nd right off Karlova on Liliová. Hay rides in the wagon over the bar are not permitted. Perfect for capping off a night out in Malá Strana or Karlovy Lázně. Pasta (119-179Kč) until 11pm; pizza (99-150Kč) until 5am. Open 24hr. ●

Pizza Express, Na mustku 1 (☎ 602 37 02 60). Metro A or B: Můstek. 100m from Můstek, across from the Prague Tourist Center. Pizza, sandwiches, and pastries 39-49Kč. Open Tu-Su 24hr. ●

SUPERMARKETS

Head to the basement of Czech department stores for food halls and supermarkets. Small *potraviny* (delis) and vegetable stands can be found on most street corners.

Tesco, Národní třída 26 (☎ 22 00 31 11). Right next to Metro B: Národní třída. Open M-F 7am-10pm, Sa 8am-8pm, Su 9am-9pm.

Krone department store (☎ 24 23 04 77), Václavské nám., at the intersection with Jindřišská. Metro A or B: Můstek. Open M-F 9am-8pm, Sa 9am-7pm, Su 10am-6pm.

Kotva department store (☎ 26 23 17 35), at the corner of Revoluční and Nám. Republiky. Metro B: Nám. Republiky. Open M-F 9am-8pm, Sa 9am-6pm, Su 10am-8pm.

◪ CAFES

When Prague journalists are bored, they churn out yet another "Whatever happened to cafe life?" feature. The answer: it turned into *čajovna* (tea house) culture. Tea is all the rage, and many tea houses double as bars or clubs in the evening.

▨ Dobrá čajovna U čajovníka (Good Tearoom), Boršov 2 (☎ 22 22 13 24). Metro A: Staroměstská. Follow Křížovnická past Charles Bridge, then bear left on Karoliny Světlé. Boršov is a tiny street on the left. Ring the bell to be let in. Tea connoisseurs and novices alike will revel in this mysterious tea house. Relax with locals in the exotic Moroccan saloon or sip on one of over 90 teas (12-150Kč) from all over the world. Open M-Sa 10am-midnight, Su noon-midnight.

Kavarná Imperial, Na Poříčì 15 (☎ 25 78 04 25). Metro B: Nám. Republiky. Lofty ceilings and mosaic tiles lend a refined demeanor to this pillared cafe. Listen to Louis Armstrong blow his horn while Ella Fitzgerald serenades. For 1943Kč, you can disturb the courtly air by purchasing a "bowl of yesterday's doughnuts that you can throw at other customers" (provided you're passably sober). Live jazz F-Sa 9pm. Open M-Th 9am-midnight, F-Sa 9am-1am, Su 9am-11pm.

Kavárna Medúza, Belgická 17 (☎22 51 51 07). Metro A: Nám. Míru. Go down Rumunská, and turn left at Belgická. Mismatched lamps, musty sofas, and murky mirrors mark this antiquated coffee shop. Locals sip coffee (19-30Kč) and peruse the daily paper. Open M-F 11am-1am, Sa-Su noon-1am.

U Malého Glena, Karmelitská 23 (☎57 53 17 17). From Metro A: Malostranská, take tram #12 to Malostranské nám., or walk down Letenská. The motto "Eat, Drink, Drink Some More," indicates that this place has consumption down to a science. Entrees include veggie plates (80-160Kč) and sandwiches (95Kč). Killer margaritas 90Kč. After 9pm, descend to the Maker's Mark basement bar for nightly jazz or blues (cover 100-150Kč). Open daily 10am-2am.

The Globe Coffeehouse, Pštrossova 6 (☎26 20 32 86), near the Globe Bookstore (see p. 233). Black coffee (20Kč), gazpacho (35Kč), and fruit smoothies (60Kč), plus plenty of English speakers seeking love connections. Open daily 10am-midnight.

Propaganda, Pštrossova 29 (☎24 93 22 85). Metro B: Národní třída. Near the Globe Bookstore, (see p. 233). The menu warns: "Propaganda is a type of social manipulation based on simplicity." Chill out in their low-slung chairs with a *Budvar* (25Kč) or an espresso (19Kč). Open M-F 3pm-2am, Sa-Su 5pm-2am.

U zeleného čaje, Nerudova 19 (☎57 53 00 27). Metro A: Malostranská. Follow Letenská to Malostranské nám. Stay right of the church and head on Nerudova. The sweet aroma of over 60 varieties of fragrant tea (28-62Kč) will please the senses and calm the mind. Sandwiches 25Kč. Open daily 11am-10pm.

◎ SIGHTS

The only major Central European city unscathed by both natural disaster and by World War II, Prague is a well-preserved combination of labyrinthine alleys and Baroque buildings. You can easily find respite from the throngs of tourists by heading outside of Staroměstské nám., the Charles Bridge, and Václavské nám. Best traveled by foot, central Prague—Staré Město, Nové Město, Malá Strana, and Hradčany—is compact enough to be traversed in one day, but deserves more. Don't leave the city without strolling through the synagogues of Josefov, exploring the heights of Vyšehrad, and meandering through the streets of Malá Strana.

NOVÉ MĚSTO

Nové Město (New Town) has become the commercial core of Prague and has embraced the global chains that such growth seems to entail. There's little else new in Nové Město, which Charles IV established in 1348 (see **History,** p. 217) as a separate municipality. Visitors can pay homage to its inception with a walk down historic Wenceslas Square, or worship the gods of globalization by grabbing a Big Mac.

WENCESLAS SQUARE. (Václavské náměstí.) Not so much a square as a boulevard running through the center of Nové Město, **Wenceslas Square** owes its name to the equestrian statue of 10th-century Czech ruler and patron St. Wenceslas (Václav) that stands in front of the National Museum. At his feet in solemn prayer kneel smaller statues of the country's other patron saints: St. Ludmila, St. Agnes, St. Prokop, and St. Adalbert (Vojtěch). The perfectionist-sculptor

Josef Václav Myslbek completed the statue after 25 years of deliberation. As others gasped at its 1912 unveiling, poor Myslbek just mumbled, "It could have been bigger." The inscription under St. Wenceslas declares, "Do not let us and our descendants perish." The spot has proven the impact of these words upon the nationalist spirit: a new Czechoslovak state was proclaimed here in 1918, Jan Palach set himself on fire here to protest the 1968 Soviet invasion, and it was from atop this statue that proclamations against the Communist regime were voiced in 1989. The square sweeps down from the statue past department stores, discos, posh hotels, trashy casinos, and Art Nouveau architecture. In spite of the commercialization, the view of the statue from the Můstek stop remains hypnotic at full moon. *(Metro A or B: Můstek serves the bottom of the square; Metro A or C: Muzeum serves the top of the square by the statue and the museum.)*

FRANCISCAN GARDEN. (Františkánská zahrada.) No one is quite sure how the Franciscans have managed to maintain such a bastion of serenity in the heart of Prague's bustling commercial district. An ideal escape from Wenceslas Square, the immaculate rose garden provides a perfect spot to relax, read the paper, and yes, smell the roses. *(Metro A or B: Můstek. Enter through the arch to the left of the intersection of Jungmannova and Národní, behind the Jungmannova statue. Open Apr. 15-Sept. 14 daily 7am-10pm; Sept. 15-Oct. 14 7am-8pm; Oct. 15-Apr. 14 8am-7pm. Free.)*

CHURCH OF OUR LADY OF THE SNOWS. (Kostel Panny Marie Sněžné.) Founded by Charles IV in 1347, this church was meant to be the largest in Prague. The Gothic walls are, indeed, higher than those of any other house of worship, but there wasn't enough in the coffers to complete the plan. The result: extraordinarily high ceilings in a church of strikingly short length. *(Metro A or B: Můstek. From the bottom of Wenceslas Square, turn left on Jungmannovo nám.; the entrance is behind the Jungmannova statue.)*

THE DANCING HOUSE. (Tančící dům.) Built by American architect Frank Gehry, of Guggenheim-Bilbao fame, in co-operation with Slovene architect Milunic, the building—known as "Fred and Ginger" to Western visitors and as the "Dancing House" to Czechs—is one of Prague's most controversial landmarks. It opened in 1996 next to President Havel's former apartment building amid a stretch of remarkable Art Nouveau buildings. Since its unveiling, the Dancing House has frequently been called an eyesore, yet some claim that it is a shining example of postmodern design. Its undulating glass wall and paired cone and cube evoke a dancing couple. *(Metro B: Karlovo nám. Exit to Karlovo nám. and head down Resslova toward the river. It's at the corner of Resslova and Rašínovo nábřeží.)*

VELVET REVOLUTION MEMORIAL. Under Národní's arcades stands a memorial to the hundreds of Czech citizens beaten on November 17, 1989. On that day, police attacked a march organized by students at the Film Faculty of Charles University (FAMU) to mourn the Nazi execution of nine Czech students some 50 years earlier. The event sparked the mass protests that led to the collapse of Communist Czechoslovakia. The simple, moving plaque depicts a wall of hands. The inscription—*Máme holé ruce* ("Our hands are empty")—was the protesters' slogan as they were being beaten by the police. At the nearby **Magic Lantern Theater** (Laterna magika divadlo; Národní 4), Revolutionary leader Havel once plotted to overthrow the old regime. *(Metro B: Národní třída. Exit the Metro and head down Spálená, taking a left on Národní. The memorial is in the arcade on the left side of the street across the street from the Black Theatre.)*

CZECH REPUBLIC

STARÉ MĚSTO

Settled in the 10th century, Staré Město (Old Town) is a labyrinth of narrow streets and alleys. It's easy to get lost, but doing so is the best way to appreciate the neighborhood's charm. Eight magnificent towers enclose **Old Town Square** (Staroměstské nám.) in the heart of Old Town. The vast stone plaza fills with blacksmiths, carriages, and ice cream vendors in summer. As soon as the sun sets, the labyrinth of narrow roads and alleys fill with a younger crowd seeking midnight revelry at Staré Město's jazz clubs and bars.

CHARLES BRIDGE. (Karlův most.) Charles IV built this 520m bridge to replace the wooden Judith, the only bridge crossing the Vltava, which washed away in a 1342 flood. Defense towers border the bridge on each side; the smaller *Malostranská mostecká věž* (Malá Strana Bridge Tower) dates from the 12th century as part of Judith's original fortification, while the taller *Staroměstská mostecká věž* (Old Town Bridge Tower) was erected in the 15th century. Both towers offer splendid views of the river and of Prague's most precious sites. Over the years, the bridge has acquired 16 Baroque statues, but don't be fooled—those are replicas that you see. The originals are locked away in local museums, safe from tourists and pigeons alike. *(Open daily 10am-10pm. 30Kč, students 20Kč.)*

When darkness falls, take care not to incur the wrath of the mobs and the musicians lining the bridge, lest they tie you in a goatskin and throw you off the bridge. This happened to the hapless St. Jan Nepomuk, who was tossed over the Charles for concealing the extramarital secrets of his queen from a suspicious King Wenceslas IV. Torture by hot irons and other devices failed to loosen Jan's lips, so the King ordered that he be drowned. A halo of five gold stars appeared as Jan plunged into the icy water. The right-hand rail, from which Jan was supposedly ejected, is now marked with a cross and five stars between the 5th and 6th statues. Place one finger on each star and make a wish: it's guaranteed to come true. *(The best way to reach Charles Bridge is on foot. The nearest Metro stops are A: Malostranská on the Malá Strana side and A: Staroměstská on the Old Town side.)*

OLD TOWN HALL. (Staroměstská radnice.) Next to the grassy knoll in Old Town Square, Old Town Hall is the multi-facaded building with the bit blown off the front. Partially demolished by the Nazis in the final days of World War II, the original pink facade now juts out from the tower. Prague's Old Town Hall has long been a witness to violence—crosses in front of it mark the spot where 27 Protestant leaders were executed on June 21, 1621 for staging a rebellion against the Catholic Habsburgs. Crowds throng on the hour to watch the **astronomical clock** chime as the skeletal Death empties his hourglass and a procession of apostles marches by. They say the clock-maker Hanuš's eyes were put out so he couldn't design another. The clock's operation stops for the night at 9pm. Inside the hall, you can climb (or take the lift) to the top of the tower to take in the spectacular view, which includes Prague's best view of Týn Church. *(Metro A: Staroměstská; Metro A or B: Můstek. In Staroměstské nám. Open summer Tu-Su 9am-5:30pm, M 11am-5:30pm. Clock tower open daily 10am-6pm. 30Kč, students 20Kč.)*

JAN HUS STATUE. Burned at the stake in 1415 for his invocations against the indulgences of the Catholic Church, Jan Hus now stands as a symbol of Czech nationalism. Today his statue in Old Town Square serves not as a rallying place for war, but as a meeting place for friends. *(In the center of Staroměstské nám.)*

TÝN CHURCH. (Chrám Matky Boží před Týnem.) Across from Old Town Hall, the spires of the Gothic Týn Church rise above a mass of medieval homes. Although the church is open only for mass, you can catch a glimpse of its amazing Baroque gold and black interior from the entrance. Buried inside the church's hallowed halls is famous astronomer Tycho Brahe, whose overindulgence at one of Emperor

Rudolf's lavish dinner parties cost him his life. Since it was deemed most improper to leave the table unless the Emperor himself did so, poor Tycho had to remain in his chair while his bladder filled and finally burst. *(In Staroměstské nám.; enter through Cafe Italia. Mass M-F 2pm-6pm, Sa noon-2pm, Su 11am-1pm and 8pm-10pm.)*

ST. JAMES'S CHURCH. (Kostel sv. Jakuba.) Creamy marble, pastel paintings, and ornate sculptures are a feast for the eyes, but think twice before touching anything. Legend has it that 500 years ago a thief tried to pilfer a gem from the Virgin Mary of Suffering, whereupon the figure came to life, seized the thief's arm, and wrenched it off. Taking pity on the bleeding soul, the monks invited him to join their order. He accepted and remained pious; the arm remains at the church entrance, a dangling reminder that Mary is not averse to the occasional steel-cage maneuver. *(Metro B: Staroměstská. On Malá Štupartská, off Staroměstské nám. behind Týn Church. Open M-Sa 9:30am-12:30pm and 2-4pm; Su mass 7:30am-noon and 2-4pm.)*

POWDER TOWER AND MUNICIPAL HOUSE. (Prašná brána, Obecnídům.) The contrasting designs of the Gothic Powder Tower and the Art Nouveau Municipal House are a fitting entrance to Staré Město. Though the Powder Tower was rendered a useless fortification by the establishment of Nové Město, you can still appreciate the expansive views from its topmost lookout. *(Metro B: Nám. Republiky. Open Apr.-Oct. daily 10am-6pm. Top of tower 30Kč, students 20Kč.)* On the former site of the royal court next door, the Municipal House captures the opulence of Prague's 19th-century cafe culture. The new Czechoslovak state proclaimed its independence here on October 28, 1918. Today, Czech culture continues to thrive with concerts, art exhibitions, and salons adorned with the work of Czech artist Alfons Mucha. Consider a visit to the Mucha Museum (see p. 252) to see more of his work. *(Nám. Republiky 5. Metro B: Nám. Republiky. Open daily 10am-6pm. Guided tours Sa noon and 2pm, 150Kč.)*

JAN PALACH SQUARE. (Náměstí Jana Palacha.) Down river from the Charles Bridge, Jan Palach Square offers a peaceful view of the Vltava and Prague Castle. Originally called Red Army Square in honor of the Russians who liberated Prague in 1945, the square was renamed in 1990. It now honors one of the Red Army's great opponents, the late Jan Palach, who burned himself to death on Václavské nám. to protest the 1968 Soviet invasion. On the river banks, lions guard the entrance to the Rudolfinum, a famous concert hall that hosts the annual festival of classical music *Pražské jaro* (Prague Spring; see **Entertainment,** p. 253). Across the tram tracks from the Rudolfinum, the main building of the Faculty of Arts of Charles University (Filozofická fakulta Univerzity Karlovy) shelters a post-mortem mask of Jan Palach by its outside wall. The stunning view of the castle from the faculty classrooms has kept many a daydreaming student awake throughout the years. A beautiful path from Jan Palach Square hugs the Vltava, but you can also cruise the river in paddle boats, which you can rent just under the Mánesů for 80Kč per hour. *(Metro A: Staroměstská. Just off the Metro exit on Křížovnická.)*

BETHLEHEM CHAPEL. (Betlémská kaple.) Although the current chapel is a 1950s reconstruction, its unadorned walls and accessible pulpit help you imagine how Jan Hus achieved such a powerful following at the turn of the 14th century. The second floor contains an informative history exhibit on the life and work of the great Czech hero. *(Metro A or B: Můstek. From the Metro, walk down Národní třída toward the river and turn right on Na Perštýně; the Chapel is in Betlémské nám., which will appear on your left. Open daily 9am-6pm. 30Kč, students 20Kč.)*

GOLTZ-KINSKÝ PALACE. The flowery 14th-century Goltz-Kinský Palace is the finest of Prague's Rococo buildings. It is also the official birthplace of Soviet Communism in the Czech Republic; on February 21, 1948, Klement Gottwald declared Communism victorious from its balcony. *(At the corner of Staroměstské nám. and Dlouhá, next to Týn Church. Open Tu-F 10am-6pm; closes early in summer for daily concerts.)*

JOSEFOV

Metro A: Staroměstská. From the Metro, walk down Maiselova, which is parallel to Kaprova.
☎ *22 32 51 72; education@jewishmuseum.cz. Synagogues and museum open Su-F 9am-6pm. Closed Jewish holidays. Admission to all six synagogues except Staronová Synagogue 300Kč, students 200Kč. Staronová Synagogue 200Kč/140Kč. Museum only 300Kč/200Kč.*

Prague's historic Jewish neighborhood and the oldest Jewish settlement in Central Europe, Josefov lies north of Staroměstské nám., along Maiselova and several side streets. Its cultural wealth lies in five well-preserved synagogues, all that remains of this former Jewish ghetto. In 1179, the Pope decreed that all good Christians avoid contact with Jews and a year later Prague's citizens complied by constructing a 12-foot wall. The gates were opened in 1784, but the walls didn't come down until 1848, when the city's Jews were first granted limited civil rights. The closed neighborhood bred exotic legends, many surrounding the famed **Rabbi Loew ben Bezalel** (1512-1609), whose legendary *golem*—a creature made from mud that came to life to protect Prague's Jews—predates Frankenstein's monster by 200 years. Rabbi Loew lived at Široká 90, now a private residence. The century following 1848 was not a happy one for Prague's Jews. The open quarter quickly became a disease-racked slum. In an ill-conceived attempt to turn Prague into a small Paris (evident in today's Pařížská), the whole quarter, save the synagogues, was demolished. Then the Nazis rose to power and deported most of Prague's Jews to Terezín and the death camps. Ironically, Hitler's decision to create a "museum of an extinct race" led to the preservation of Josefov's old Jewish cemetery and synagogues.

PINKAS SYNAGOGUE. (Pinkasova synagoga.) Some 80,000 names line the walls of Pinkas Synagogue, in requiem for the Czech Jews persecuted during the Holocaust. This incredibly moving display reminds visitors of the tremendous horror and the loss dealt to the community and the world at large. Upstairs, drawings by children interred at the Terezín camp further memorialize the inhumanity of Hitler's Nazi armies. *(On Široká, between Žatecká and Listopadu 17.)*

OLD JEWISH CEMETERY. (Starý židovský hřbitov.) This cemetery remains Josefov's most popular attraction. Between the 14th and 18th centuries, 20,000 graves were dug in 12 layers. The striking clusters of tombstones result from a process by which the older stones were lifted up from underneath. Rabbi Loew is buried by the wall opposite the entrance—you'll recognize his grave by the piles of stones with wishes placed on his tomb. *(At the corner of Široká and Žatecká.)*

OLD-NEW SYNAGOGUE. (Staronová synagoga.) The oldest operating synagogue in Europe and the earliest Gothic structure in Prague, the 700-year-old Old-New Synagogue is still the religious center of Prague's Jewish community. Behind the iron gates flies a tattered remnant of the Star of David flag flown by the congregation in 1357 when Charles IV first allowed them to display their own municipal emblem. Prague's Jews were the first to adopt the Star of David as their official symbol. *(On the corner of Maiselova and Pařížská. Services 8pm.)*

SPANISH SYNAGOGUE. (Španělská synagoga.) The youngest and most ornate synagogue in Josefov, the Spanish Synagogue was built in 1868 and modeled after Grenada's Alhambra. Today it displays a history of Czech Jews from the 18th century to the present day. *(On the corner of Široká and Dušní.)*

MAISEL SYNAGOGUE. (Maiselova synagoga.) This synagogue displays treasures from the extensive collections of the Jewish Museum, which were only returned to the city's Jewish community in 1994. Its exhibits render an excellent history of the Jews in Bohemia and Moravia, including Prague's ghetto and the events that took place within it. *(Maiselova, between Široká and Jáchymova.)*

KLAUS SYNAGOGUE. (Klausová synagoga.) Built in the 1690s in a notorious red-light district, Klaus Synagogue now displays rotating exhibits on Judaica. *(Next to Ceremony Hall on Červená, just off Maiselova.)*

CEREMONY HALL. (Obřadní dům.) Originally a ceremonial hall for the Jewish Burial Society, Ceremony Hall now houses exhibits devoted to the themes of illness and death in the ghetto, Jewish cemeteries in Bohemia and Moravia, and the activities of the Prague Burial Society. *(On Červená, just off Maiselova.)*

JEWISH TOWN HALL. (Židovská radnice.) Once the administrative center of Josefov, the Jewish Town Hall was one of the few Jewish administrative centers in Europe to survive World War II. The Hebrew clock in the Rococo town hall runs counterclockwise. On the other side of the building, a statue of Moses by František Bílek was hidden from the Nazis during the war. *(Next to the Old-New Synagogue, on the corner of Maiselova and Červená. The building is closed to the public.)*

HIGH SYNAGOGUE. (Vysoká synagoga.) Now a working synagogue closed to the public, this 16th-century synagogue housed massive collections of textiles and Judaica during the war for Hitler's "museum of an extinct race." *(On Červená.)*

MALÁ STRANA

The hangout of criminals and counter-revolutionaries for nearly a century, the cobblestoned streets of Malá Strana have become the most prized real estate on either side of the Vltava. Yuppies dream of flats overlooking St. Nicholas's Cathedral, while affluent foreigners sip beer where Jaroslav Hašek and his bumbling soldier Švejk once guzzled suds (see **The Arts,** p. 220). Malá Strana seems to have realized the vision of its 13th-century designer, King Přemysl Otakar II, who dreamed of a powerful economic and cultural quarter. In the 15th century, the Austrian nobility built great churches and palaces here. Now carefully restored, Malá Strana is home to some of Prague's most impressive architecture.

ST. NICHOLAS'S CATHEDRAL. (Chrám sv. Mikuláše.) The towering dome of the Baroque St. Nicholas's Cathedral, Malá Strana's centerpiece, is one of Prague's most discernible landmarks. The father-son team of Kristof and Kilian Ignaz Dienzenhofer, who also built the Church of St. Nicholas in Staré Město and the Břevnov Monastery (see **Outer Prague,** p. 251) near Hradčany, constructed St. Nicholas's as their crowning achievement. Expensive classical music concerts take place here each night. *(Metro A: Malostranská. Follow Letenská from the Metro to Malostranské nám. ☎ 57 53 42 15. Open daily 9am-4pm. 50Kč, students 25Kč. Concert tickets 390Kč/290Kč.)*

JOHN LENNON WALL. Hroznová, a tiny street on Kampa Island, is home to the infamous John Lennon Wall. The mural, a crumbling memorial to John Lennon, became much remarked upon when Communist authorities attempted to suppress it. In summer 1998, the wall was whitewashed and it is now covered with an unimpressive portrait of John Lennon and unimaginative tourist graffiti. *(Metro A: Malostranská. From the Metro, walk down U Lužického semináře to the Charles Bridge. Descend the stairs leading to Na Kampě and take the first right on Hroznová. Stay close to the wall and bear right over the bridge on Velkopřerovské nám.)*

⧉ PETŘÍN HILL AND GARDENS. (Petřínské sady.) Petřín Gardens, on the hill beside Malá Strana, provide spectacular views of the city. To avoid the steep climb, take a cable car to the top from just above the intersection of Vítězná and Újezd. *(Look for* lanovka dráha *signs; 8Kč.)* It stops once along the way to deposit visitors at **Nebozízek,** Prague's most scenic cafe. *(☎57 31 53 29. Open daily 11am-11pm. Entrees 240-360Kč.)* A plethora of delights await you at the summit: a small Eiffel tower *(open daily 10am-10pm; 40Kč, students 30Kč),* the city's observatory, the **Church of St. Lawrence,** and a befuddling maze of mirrors at **Bludiště** that will leave you in hysterics. Ever seen yourself with a forehead as tall as your torso? *(☎57 31 52 72. Open daily 10am-10pm. 30Kč, students 20Kč.)* Just east of the park is Strahov Stadium, the world's largest, covering the space of 10 soccer fields.

WALLENSTEIN GARDEN. (Valdštejnská zahrada.) A simple wooden gate opens into Wallenstein Garden, one of Prague's best-kept secrets. This tranquil, 17th-century Baroque garden is enclosed by old buildings that glow on sunny afternoons. General Albrecht Wallenstein, owner of the famous Prague palace of the same name and hero of Schiller's grim plays (the *Wallenstein* cycle), held parties here among Vredeman de Vries's classical bronze statues. When the works were plundered by Swedish troops in the waning hours of the Thirty Years' War, Wallenstein replaced the original casts with facsimiles. Frescoes inside the arcaded loggia depict episodes from Virgil's *Aeneid. (Letenská 10. Metro A: Malostranská. Exit the Metro and turn right on Letenská. The garden will be on the right. Open Apr.-Oct. daily 10am-6pm. Free.)*

CHURCH OF OUR LADY VICTORIOUS. (Kostel Panny Marie Vítězné.) Not known for its exterior, the modest Church of Our Lady Victorious contains the famous polished-wax statue of the **Infant Jesus of Prague** that is said to perform miracles for the faithful. The statue first arrived in town in the arms of a 16th-century Spanish noblewoman who married into the Bohemian royalty; mysteriously, the plague bypassed Prague shortly thereafter. In 1628, the Carmelite abbey gained custody of the statue and allowed pilgrims to pray to it. The public has been infatuated ever since. Six times per year this babe of over 75 outfits is swaddled anew by the nuns of a nearby convent. Enter the museum to see a display of a few of the spectacular robes and crowns. *(Metro A: Malostranská. Follow Letecká from the Metro through Malostranské nám. and continue on Karmelitská. ☎57 53 36 46. Open M-F 9:30am-5:30pm, Sa 9:45am-8pm. Su Mass in six languages. Call for schedules. Museum open daily 10am-5pm. Free.)*

PRAGUE CASTLE (PRAŽSKÝ HRAD)

Take tram #22 or 23 from the center, get off at "Pražský Hrad" and go down U Prašného Mostu past the Royal Gardens and into the Second Courtyard. Alternatively, hike up the steep, picturesque Nerudova street or climb the Staré zámecké schody (Old Castle Stairs) from Malostranské nám. ☎ 24 37 33 68. Open Apr.-Oct. daily 9am-5pm; Nov.-March 9am-4pm. Ticket office opposite St. Vitus's Cathedral, inside the castle walls. The 3-day ticket gains access to the Royal Crypt, Cathedral Tower, Old Royal Palace, Powder Tower, and Basilica of St. George. 220Kč, students 110Kč.

Prague Castle has been the seat of the Bohemian government since it was founded over 1000 years ago. In this century, liberal presidents, Nazi despots, and communist officials have all held court here. After the declaration of independent Czechoslovakia in 1918, first President Tomáš Garrigue Masaryk invited renowned Slovene architect Josip Plečnik to rebuild his new residence, which had suffered from centuries of Habsburg neglect. Plečnik not only restored all the castle's buildings and redesigned its gardens, but also added fountains, columns, and embellishments characteristic of his style. Try to arrive on the hour to catch the changing of the guards, which takes place 5am-midnight.

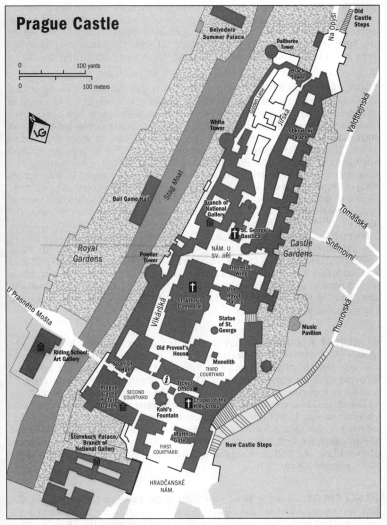

Prague Castle

0   100 yards

0   100 meters

Old Castle Steps

Belvedere Summer Palace

Dalliborka Tower

Na Opyši

Black Tower

Golden Lane

Jiřská

White Tower

Lobkovický Palace

Valdštejnská

Ball Game Hall

Stag Moat

Branch of National Gallery

St. George's Basilica

Castle Gardens

Tomaššká

Royal Gardens

Powder Tower

NÁM. U SV. JIŘÍ

Theresian Wing

Sněmovní

St. Vitus's Cathedral

Vikářská

Old Royal Palace

U Prasného Mosta

Statue of St. George

Music Pavilion

Thunovská

Old Provost's House

Riding School; Art Gallery

Spanish Hall

Monolith

THIRD COURTYARD

Prague Castle Picture Gallery

SECOND COURTYARD

ℹ️

Ticket Office

Chapel of the Holy Cross

Kohl's Fountain

Šternberk Palace; Branch of National Gallery

Matthias Gate

FIRST COURTYARD

New Castle Steps

HRADČANSKÉ NÁM.

HRADČANY SQUARE AND FIRST CASTLE COURTYARD. Outside the Castle gates at Hradčany Sq. is the **Šternberk Palace,** home to the National Gallery's Collection of European Old Masters, including works by Rembrandt, El Greco, Goya, and Rubens. (☎ 20 51 46 34. Open Tu-Su 10am-6pm. 50Kč, students 20Kč.) The Baroque **Matthias Gate** (Matyášská brána), inside the First Castle Courtyard, is the castle's official entrance. Plečnik designed the two wooden flagpoles next to it.

SECOND CASTLE COURTYARD AND ROYAL GARDEN. (Královská zahrada.) After passing through Matthias Gate, turn left in the Second Castle Courtyard for access to the lush Royal Garden. Recently opened to the public after years as a private paradise for only the highest Communist functionaries, the serene Royal Garden offers a luxurious respite in the midst of one of the city's most popular tourist attractions. Past the tulip beds, the **Singing Fountain** spouts its watery tune before the **Royal Summer Palace**. Follow the hordes of school children and place your head under the fountain to hear the chiming water. *(Royal Garden open Apr.-Oct.)*

THIRD CASTLE COURTYARD. In the Third Castle Courtyard stands Prague Castle's centerpiece, the colossal **St. Vitus's Cathedral** (Katedrála sv. Víta or Svatovítská katedrála), which was completed in 1929, some 600 years after construction began. To the right of the high altar stands the silver **tomb of St. Jan Nepomuk**. A statue of an angel holds a silvered tongue that many believed to belong to Jan, whose tongue was reputedly silvered after he was thrown into the Vltava by King Charles IV (see **Charles Bridge,** p. 244). It remains on display, though the story was officially proven false in 1961. The walls of **St. Wenceslas's Chapel** (Svatováclavská kaple) are lined with precious stones and paintings depicting the legend of this saint. In an adjoining but inaccessible room, the real crown jewels of the Bohemian kings are behind a door with seven locks, the keys to which are in the hands of seven different religious and secular Czech leaders. If you have strong legs, attack the 287 steps that spiral up to the roof of the **Cathedral Tower** for one of the city's best views. Alternatively, descend underground to the **Royal Crypt** to visit the tomb of Emperor Charles IV. All four of Charles's wives are tactfully buried together in the grave to his left, along with a handful of other Czech kings. To the right of St. Vitus, the **Old Royal Palace** (Starý královský palác) houses the lengthy **Vladislav Hall,** where jousting competitions were once held.

ST. GEORGE'S SQUARE. Across the courtyard from the Old Royal Palace stands the Romanesque **St. George's Basilica** (Bazilika sv. Jiří) and its adjacent convent. Built in 921, the basilica enshrines the tomb of St. Ludmila, complete with skeleton on display. A mason who stole the thighbone supposedly activated a vicious curse that killed three before the mason's son restored the bone to the grave. The convent houses the **National Gallery of Bohemian Art,** which displays art ranging from Gothic to Baroque. In the medieval galleries, Master Theodorik's ecclesiastical portraits, the relief from *Matka Boží před Týnem,* and the so-called Kapucínský Cycle of Christ and the Apostles stand out; upstairs, Michael Leopold Willmann's paintings warrant a visit. *(Open Tu-Su 9am-5pm. 40Kč, students 20Kč.)*

JIŘSKÁ STREET. Jiřská begins to the right of the basilica. Halfway down, the tiny and colorful **Golden Lane** (Zlatá ulička) heads off to the right. Alchemists once worked here; their attempts to create gold inspired the street's name. **Franz Kafka** lived at #22, where today a small herd of cramped souvenir shops feed off of his fame. Above the shops is a hallway displaying replicas of the Bohemian court's armory; visitors are sometimes permitted to shoot the crossbow for 50Kč. Back on Jiřská, the **Lobkovický Palace** contains a replica of Bohemia's coronation jewels and a history of the Czech lands. *(Open Tu-Su 9am-5pm. 40Kč, students 20Kč.)* At the end of the street is the **Museum of Toys** (Muzeum hraček), the collection of cartoonist, artist, and film maker Ivan Steiger. *(☎ 24 37 22 94. Open daily 9:30am-5pm. 50Kč, students 30Kč.)* The **Old Castle Steps** (Staré zámecké schody) at the end of the street descend down to Malostranská.

OUTER PRAGUE

If you have more than two days in Prague, explore the city's outskirts to find green fields, majestic churches, and panoramic vistas, all hidden from the touring hordes.

PRAGUE MARKET. (Pražskátrznice.) An old-school Eastern European market remains Prague's best place to haggle over clothing, fresh produce, jewelry, and everything else. Rows of stalls and Czechs of all ages make this shopping experience feel truly authentic. *(Take tram #3 or 14 from Nám. Republiky to Vozovna Kobylisy; get off at Pražskátrznice.)*

BŘEVNOV MONASTERY. The oldest monastery in Bohemia was founded in 993 by King Boleslav II and St. Adalbert, who were both guided by a divine dream to build a monastery atop a bubbling stream. **St. Margaret's Church** (Kostel sv. Markéty), a Benedictine chapel, waits inside the complex. Beneath the altar rests the tomb of the vegetarian St. Vintíř. Czechs claim that on one particular diplomatic excursion, St. Vintíř dined with a German king who, being a fanatical hunter, served up a main course of pheasant slain by his own hand. The saint prayed for deliverance from the myriad *faux pas* possibilities, whereupon the main course sprang to life and flew out the window. The monastery's green bell tower and red roof are the only parts of the original Romanesque structure to be spared when the Dienzenhofers redesigned the complex in a High Baroque style. Pack a lunch and take a stroll along the stream leading to the small pond to the right of the church. Guided tours lead you through the monk's quarters as well as the monastery crypt. *(Metro A: Malostranská. Take tram #22 uphill to Břevnovský klášter (15 min.). Church open daily 7am-6pm. Czech guided tours Sa 9am; Sa-Su 10:30am, 1, 2:30, and 4pm. 50Kč, students 30Kč.)*

NEW JEWISH CEMETERY. Although less visited than the Old Jewish Cemetery, the New Jewish Cemetery is one of Central Europe's largest burial grounds. **Kafka** is interred here; obtain a map and, if you're male, a mandatory head covering from the attendant before hunting for his tombstone. *(Metro A: Želivského. Open Apr.-Sept. Su-Th 9am-5pm, F 9am-3pm; Oct.-Mar. Su-Th 9am-3:30pm, F 9am-12:30pm. Free.)*

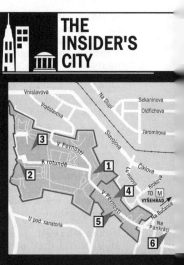

THE INSIDER'S CITY

VYŠEHRAD

The former haunt of Prague's 19th-century Romantics, Vyšehrad is a storehouse of nationalist myths and imperial legends. Quiet paths wind among the crumbling stone walls of this historic settlement, offering respite from Prague's busy streets. (Metro C: Vyšehrad.)

1 Stroll by the Romanesque **St. Martin Rotunda**, Prague's oldest building

2 Indulge in an elegant Czech meal at **Na Vyšehradě** (Open daily 10am-10pm)

3 The **cemetery** holds the remains of the Czech Republic's most famous citizens

4 Relax in the sun with ice cream from **Obcerstveni Penguin** (Open daily 11am-7pm)

5 A small **gallery** exhibits the work of local disabled children (Open daily 10am-5pm)

6 Pass through the **Tábor Gate** to reach **Nad Vyšehradem**, a beer hall packed with locals (Open M-Th 10am-10pm, F-Su 11am-11pm)

TROJA. Located in one of the most beautiful neighborhoods surrounding Prague, Troja is the site of French architect J. B. Mathey's masterful **chateau.** The pleasure palace, overlooking the Vltava, includes a terraced garden, an oval staircase, and a magnificent collection of 19th-century Czech artwork. The tourist office carries schedules of **free concerts** in the chateau's great hall. (*Bus #112 winds from Metro C: Nádraží Holešovice. You'll see the colossal palace as the bus approaches. Open Apr.-Oct. Tu-Su 10am-6pm; Nov.-March Sa-Su 10am-5pm. 120Kč, students 60Kč*). If the castle doesn't excite, venture next door to the Prague Zoo. (*Open daily 9am-7pm. 60Kč, students 30Kč.*)

🏛 MUSEUMS

Prague's magnificence is not in her museums; if the weather's good, you may want to stick to the streets. On one of the city's many rainy days, however, peruse some of its interesting and quirky museum collections. Keep your eyes open for special exhibits, and check out the work of local artists at the private galleries off Národní třída and Staroměstské nám. Most museums are closed on Mondays.

MUCHA MUSEUM. This is the only collection devoted entirely to the work of Alfons Mucha, the Czech Republic's most celebrated artist, who gained his fame in Paris for his posters of "la divine Sarah," Sarah Bernhardt. It was within this series of posters that Mucha pioneered the Art Nouveau Movement. Be sure to see the collection of Czech and Parisian posters, as well as Mucha's panel paintings. (*Panská 7. Metro A or B: Můstek. Head up Václavské nám. toward the St. Wenceslas statue. Hang a left on Jindřišská and turn left again on Panská. ☎ 62 84 162; www.mucha.cz. Open daily 10am-6pm. 120Kč, students 60Kč.*)

MUSEUM OF MEDIEVAL TORTURE INSTRUMENTS. This is not a museum for the weak of stomach. The collection includes numerous pain-inducing devices, such as the Head Crusher, thumbscrews, the iron gag, and the Masks of Shame and Infamy. The highly detailed explanations are guaranteed to nauseate. (*Staroměstské nám. 20. Metro A: Staroměstská. In Old Town Square. ☎ 24 21 55 81; torture@post.cz. Open daily 10am-10pm. 140Kč.*)

EXHIBITION OF SPIDERS AND SCORPIONS. Just in case the torture instruments do not give you nightmares, the spiders, centipedes, and scorpions next door will. Get up-close and personal with the largest, hairiest, most venomous spiders and scorpions in the world. (*Staroměstské nám. 20. ☎ 24 21 55 81. Open daily 10am-10pm. 100Kč, children 80Kč.*)

MUSEUM OF COMMUNISM. This new gallery is committed to exposing the flaws of the Communist system that suppressed the Czech people from 1948-1989. The exhibition is divided into three parts: the dream (the origins of Communism); the reality (the impact of Communism on the Czech people); and the nightmare (the despair that led to the Velvet Revolution). A model factory and an interrogation office send you behind the iron curtain. (*Na Příkopě 10. Metro A: Můstek. Exit the Metro and turn right on Na Příkopě. ☎ 24 21 29 66. Open daily 9am-9pm. 180Kč, students 90Kč*)

MONUMENT TO NATIONAL LITERATURE. (Památník národního písemnictví.) The star attraction here is the **Strahov Library,** with its magnificent **Theological and Philosophical Halls.** The frescoed, vaulted ceilings of the Baroque reading rooms were intended to spur monks to the loftiest peaks of erudition. (*Strahovské nádvoří 1. Metro A: Hradčanská. From the Metro, take tram #8 toward Bílá Hora to Malovanka. Turn around, follow the tram tracks, then turn right on Strahovská. The museum is inside the monastery on the left. ☎ 20 51 66 95. Open Tu-Su 10am-5pm. 20Kč, students 10Kč.*)

RUDOLFINUM. The Czech Philharmonic Orchestra shares this space with one of Prague's oldest galleries. Rotating exhibits, as well as an elegant cafe, fill the huge Art Nouveau interior. *(Alšovo náb. 12. ☎ 24 89 32 05; galerie.rudolfinum@telecom.cz. Open July-May Tu-Su 10am-6pm. 100Kč, students 50Kč.)*

NATIONAL GALLERY. (Národní galerie.) The National Gallery runs nine museums in different locations throughout Prague; the notable **Šternberský palác** and **Klášter sv. Jiří** are within the **Prague Castle** complex (see p. 248). All museums carry a pamphlet describing the collections of the other galleries, most of which are in suburban Prague and not worth the trek. The **Trade Fair Palace and the Gallery of Modern Art** (Veletržní palác a Galerie moderního umění) display the National Gallery's impressive collection of 20th-century Czech art. The seven-story functionalist building is almost as stunning as the art inside; even Le Corbusier approved. *(Dukelských hrdinů 47. Metro C: Holešovice. Tram #5, 12, or 17 to Veletržní. ☎ 24 30 10 03. Open Tu-Su 10am-6pm. 150Kč, students 70Kč.)*

HOUSE OF THE GOLDEN RING. (Dům u zlatého prstenu.) A collection of 20th-century Czech art in a refreshing gallery that emphasizes installations and technological art. Four floors, each with a separate theme. The 2nd-floor exhibit, "In the Distorted Mirror," might sound interesting, but the first floor collection, "Dream, Myth, and Ideal," and the basement collection of 1990s Czech art are the museum's true showpieces. *(Týnská 6. Metro A: Staroměstská. Behind Týn Church in Old Town Square. ☎ 24 82 80 04. Open Tu-Su 10am-6pm. Top 3 floors 60Kč, students 30Kč; entire museum 70Kč. First Tu of the month free.)*

CZECH MUSEUM OF FINE ARTS. (České muzeum výtvarných umění.) The building itself, the House of the Black Madonna (Dům u Černé matky boží), is one of Prague's first—and finest—examples of Cubist architecture. The collection continues the theme, devoting two floors to a history of Czech Cubism. The downstairs gallery exhibits works of Western European Modernists. *(Celetná 34. Metro A: Nám. Republiky. Walk through the Powder Tower down Celetná. ☎ 24 21 17 32. Open Tu-Su 10am-6pm. 35Kč, students 15Kč. The museum was closed due to reconstruction in 2002, but is scheduled to reopen in 2003.)*

🔛 ENTERTAINMENT

For a list of current concerts and performances, consult *The Prague Post*, *Threshold*, or *Do města-Downtown* (the latter two are free and distributed at many cafes and restaurants). Most performances begin at 7pm; unsold tickets are sometimes available 30min. before show time. The majority of Prague's theaters close in July and August, but the selection is rather extensive during the rest of the year—particularly in mid-May and early June when the **Prague Spring Festival** draws musicians from around the world. Tickets (400-3500Kč) may sell out up to a year in advance. Try **Bohemia Ticket International,** next to Čedok. (Malé nám. 13. ☎ 24 22 78 32; fax 21 61 21 26. Open M-F 9am-5pm, Sa 9am-2pm.) **Národní divadlo, Stavovské divadlo,** and **Státní opera** (see below) all stage operas; while performances rarely scintillate, the staggeringly low prices do. **Cinemas** showing English-language blockbusters abound. Prices depend on the movie's popularity; ask at a tourist office for a list of current films. The **Kino Cafe-bar** shows Czech films with English subtitles, as do many theaters in town. Look for a sign posted on the ticket booth. (Karlovo nám. 19. ☎ 24 91 57 65. Tickets around 100Kč.)

🔳 **Říše loutek** (Marionette Theater), Žatecká 1 (☎ 24 81 93 22). Metro A: Staroměstská. On the corner of Žatecká and Mariánské nám. The world's oldest marionette theatre ensures that puppetry is taken seriously in the Czech Republic. The hilarious version of

Mozart's *Don Giovanni* brings the audience to tears. The marionette cast springs to life as the curtains rise, and a delightfully drunk Mozart marionette interacts with the audience during interludes. June-July performances Su-Tu and Th-Sa 8pm. Box office open daily 10am-8pm. 490Kč, students 390Kč.

Národní divadlo (National Theater), Národní třída 2/4 (☎ 24 92 15 28). Metro B: Národní třída. Features theater, opera, and ballet. Box office open M-F 10am-6pm, Sa-Su 10am-12:30pm and 3-6pm, and 30min. before performances. Tickets 100-1000Kč.

Stavovské divadlo (Estates Theater), Ovocný trg 1 (☎ 24 92 15 28). Metro A or B: Můstek. Left on the pedestrian Na Příkopě. *Don Giovanni* premiered here years ago; the theater features mainly classical performances, opera, and ballet. Use the Národní divadlo box office (see above) or turn up 30min. before the show.

Image Theater, Pařížská 4 (☎ 231 44 48). Metro A: Staroměstská. From the Metro, walk down Křížovnická toward Josefov. Turn right on Široká and continue straight until you hit Pařížská. Features silent, black-light performances. Enter the public experimental laboratory of gene manipulation in *Clonarium*. Learn more about the human body through endoscopic penetration, macroscopic image transfers, and musical monitoring of organ functions. Visitors may be used as a source of biological material. Shows daily 8pm. Box office open daily 9am-8pm. 350Kč.

Státní opera (State Opera), Wilsonova 4 (☎ 24 22 72 66). Metro A or C: Muzeum. Box office open M-F 10am-5:30pm, Sa-Su 10am-noon and 1-5:30pm. Tickets 50-600Kč.

■ NIGHTLIFE

The most authentic way to experience Prague at night is through an alcoholic fog. With some of the best beers in the world on tap, pubs and beer halls are understandably the city's favorite places for nighttime pleasures. These days, however, authentic pub experiences are often restricted to the suburbs and outlying Metro stops; in central Prague, Irish pubs and American sports bars are cropping up everywhere, charging high prices for foreign beers. You may have to look a bit harder for them, but a few trusty Czech pubs remain scattered throughout Staré Město and Malá Strana.

Prague is not a clubbing city, although there are enough dance clubs pumping out techno to satisfy those craving the Euro-club scene. More popular among Czechs are the city's many jazz and rock clubs, which host excellent local and international acts. Otherwise, you can always retreat to the Charles Bridge to sing along with aspiring Brit-pop guitarists. Whichever way you indulge in Prague nightlife, swig a few pints of *pivo*, grab some 4am snacks (see **Late-Night Eating,** p. 241), and forego the night bus for the morning Metro.

BEERHALLS AND WINE CELLARS

▨ Vinárna U Sudu, Vodičkova 10 (☎ 22 23 22 07). Metro A: Můstek. Cross over Václavské nám. to Vodičkova and follow it as it curves left. The bar is on your left. As of yet undiscovered by tourists, this Moravian wine bar looks quite plain from its 1st-floor entrance, but beneath the veneer sprawls a labyrinth of catacombs and cavernous cellars, where the carafes of smooth red wine (120Kč) go down frighteningly fast. Isolate yourselves in one of the many cellars or challenge locals to a match of foosball. Open M-F noon-midnight, Sa-Su 2pm-midnight.

U Fleků, Křemencova 11 (☎ 24 93 40 19). Metro B: Národní třída. Hang a right on Spálená, away from Národní, then right on Myslíkova and right again on Křemencova; the bar is on the left. Prague's oldest beer hall, founded in 1499. Live brass bands play

"Roll out the Barrel" nightly. Home-brewed beer 49Kč. Open daily 9am-11pm. Brewery tours 9am-4pm. 50kč.

Pivnice u Sv. Tomáše, Letenská 12 (☎57 53 18 35). Metro A: Malostranská. Walk downhill on Letenská. The mighty dungeons echo with boisterous revelry. Sing drunken ballads with a beer in one hand and meat off the roasting spit in the other. (Roasting spit meats must be ordered a day in advance.) Beer 40Kč. Live brass band nightly 7-11pm. Open daily 11:30am-midnight.

BARS

Kozička, Kozí 1 (☎24 81 83 08). Metro A: Staroměstská. Take Dlouhá from the square's northeast corner, then bear left on Kozí. Giant cellar bar is always packed. You'll know why after your first *Krušovice* (18Kč). A hot spot where young Czechs come early and stay all night. Open M-F noon-4am, Sa-Su 6pm-4am.

Molly Malone's, U obecního dvora 4 (☎24 81 88 51). Metro A: Staroměstská. Turn right on Křižovnická, away from the Charles Bridge. After Nám. Jana Palacha, turn right on Široká, which becomes Vězeňská; at its end, turn left. The Irish prove they're the most fun at this pub, where overturned sewing machines double as tables. Grab three friends, four pints of Guinness (80Kč), and head for the loft. Irish and British newspapers on Su. Live music Th 9pm-midnight. Open Su-Th 11am-1am, F-Sa 11am-2am.

Cafe Marquis de Sade, Melnicka 5 (☎24 81 75 05). Metro B: Nám. Republiky. From the Metro, go down U Obecního Domu to the right of the Obecního Dum. Take a right on Rybna, a left on Jakubska, and hang a left on Melnicka. This spacious bar envelops you in rich red velvet and considerable pleasure. Ascend the wrought-iron spiral staircase to the loft, slug a *Velvet* beer (27-35Kč), and scope out the crowd below. Happy hour M-F 4-6pm. Open daily noon-2am.

Jo's Bar and Garáž, Malostranské nám. 7. Metro A: Malostranská. If you can't bear the idea that the people at the next table might not speak English, Jo's Bar is the perfect spot for you. Foosball, darts, card games, and a dance floor downstairs. Some of Prague's best DJs spin acid jazz, techno, house, and dance. Long Island iced tea 115Kč. Happy Hour 6-10pm (beer 20Kč). Open daily 11am-2am.

Újezd, Újezd 18 (☎53 83 62). Metro B: Národní třída. Exit the Metro on Národní and turn left toward the river. Cross the Legií bridge, continue straight on Vítězná, and turn right on Újezd; the bar is on your right. The gremlins escape from the dungeon in the basement to take over the upper 2 floors as well. Local Czechs keep the tempo mellow. Order a rounds of suds (*Budvar* 25Kč) to down with the buds. Open daily 11am-4am.

Zanzibar, Saská 6. Metro A: Malostranská. From the square, head down Mostecká toward the Charles Bridge, turn right on Lázeňská, and left on Saská. The tastiest, priciest, and most exotic cocktails this side of the Vltava (110-150Kč). Cuban cigars 600-1200Kč. Open daily 5pm-3am.

Žíznivý pes (Thirsty Dog), El. Krásnohorské (☎22 31 00 39). Metro A: Staroměstská. Walk up Pařížská, next to St. Nicholas's Church, away from Staroměstské nám. Hang a right on Široká, then left on Krásnohorské. The inspiration for the Nick Cave song, this bar is a watering hole for crazy expats (Kiefer Sutherland) and Czech regulars (Václav Havel). Full English breakfast for 165Kč. Open M-F 11am-2am, Sa-Su noon-2am.

Le Chateau, Jakubská 2 (☎232 62 42). Metro B: Nám. Republiky. From the Metro, walk through the Powder Tower to Celetná, then take a right on Templová. On the corner of Templová and Jakubská. Red lighting grows softer as Czech voices grow louder, drink by drink. Non-stop techno-rock keeps the place pumping until the wee hours. Open M-Th noon-3am, F noon-4am, Sa 4pm-4am, Su 4pm-2am.

CLUBS AND DISCOS

Radost FX, Bělehradská 120 (☎24 25 47 76; www.radostfx.cz). Metro C: IP Pavlova. Heavily touristed, but still plays only the hippest techno, jungle, and house music. Hi-tech laser lights, Nintendo, and twistedly creative drinks (Sex with an Alien 150Kč.) will expand your clubbing horizons. Also serves brunch (see **Late-Night Eating,** p. 241). Cover 80-150Kč. Open M-Sa 10pm-dawn.

Roxy, Dlouhá 33 (☎24 82 62 96). Metro B: Nám. Republiky. Walk up Revoluční to the river; go left on Dlouhá. Hip locals and in-the-know tourists come to this converted theater for experimental DJs and theme nights. Watch out for swooping butterflies and falling clubgoers from the balcony above. Beer 30Kč. Cover 100-350Kč, depending on the show. Open M-Tu and Th-Sa 9pm-late.

Palác Akropolis, Kubelíkova 27 (☎96 33 09 11; www.palacakropolis.cz). Metro A: Jiřího z Poděbrad. Take Slavíkova and turn right on Kubelíkova. Live bands several times per week. Top Czech act Psí Vojáci is an occasional visitor. Open daily 10pm-5am.

Karlovy Lázně, Novotného Lávka 1 (☎22 22 21 56). An irresistible location under the Charles Bridge. The teenagers and early 20-somethings in line at the door stare eagerly at televisions broadcasting from inside this 4-story complex. Cover 100Kč, 50Kč before 10pm and after 4am. Open nightly 9pm-late.

JAZZ CLUBS

Jazz Club Železná, Železná 16 (☎24 23 96 97). Metro A or B: Staroměstská. From Old Town Square, follow Železná, opposite the clock. Vaulted cellar bar attracts both young and old for live jazz. Beer 30Kč. Happy hour 3-7pm 18-24Kč. Cover 80-150Kč. Shows 9-11:30pm. Open daily 3pm-1am.

Ungelt, Týn 2 (☎24 89 57 48). Metro A or B: Staroměstská. From Old Town Square, follow Týnska and take a right on Týn. Two-floor music room and bar in a subterranean vault. Jazz a la B.B. King. Live concerts daily from 9pm-midnight. Cover 150Kč, or listen from the jazz pub for free. Open daily noon-midnight.

U staré paní (The Old Lady's Place), Michalská 9 (☎/fax 24 22 80 90). Metro A or B: Můstek. Walk down Na můstku at the end of Václavské nám. through its name change to Melantrichova. Turn left on Havelská and right on Michalská. Showcases some of the finest jazz vocalists in Prague in a tiny, yet classy, downstairs venue. Shows W-Sa 9pm-midnight. Cover 160Kč, includes 1 drink. Open daily 7pm-1am.

Reduta, Národní 20. (☎24 93 34 87) Metro A: Národní třída. Exit on Spalena, take a left on Národní, and go through the facade of the Louvre. An old haunt of Presidents Clinton and Havel, as the photos attest. Cover 200Kč. Open daily 7:30pm-12:30am.

U malého Glena II, Karmelitská 23 (☎57 53 17 17). The cellar club of U malého Glena (see **Cafes,** p. 241) hosts smoky jazz, throaty blues, and Stan the Man's nightly funk. Sunday jam sessions feature local amateurs straining or entertaining the local crowd. Beer 30Kč. Cover 100-150Kč. Call ahead for weekend tables. Open daily 8pm-2am.

THE FAGUE AND THE DRAGUE OF PRAGUE

Prague's gay and lesbian scene is developing fast and in many directions: transvestite shows, stripteases, discos, bars, cafes, restaurants, and hotels aimed at gay and lesbian travelers can be easily found. At any of the places listed below, you can pick up a copy of the monthly *Amigo* (40Kč), an English-heavy guide to gay life in the Czech Republic, or *Gayčko* (60Kč), a glossier mag mostly in Czech.

U střelce, Karolíny Světlé 12 (☎24 23 82 78). Metro B: Národní třída. Exit the Metro and take a right on Spalena, a left on Národní, and a right on Karolíny Světlé. U střelce is under the arch to the left. The club draws crowds to its cabarets, where magnificent female impersonators lip-sync on-stage. Cover 80Kč. Shows after midnight. Open W-Sa 9:30pm-5am.

A Club, Milíčova 25 (☎22 78 16 23). Metro C: Hlavní Nádraží. Take tram #5, 9, 26, or 55 uphill. Get off at Lipsanká and head back down Seifertova, veering right on Milíčova. Prague's only nightspot for lesbians welcomes men as well, though they will receive a few glances. Classy wire sculptures, soft light, and deep couches by the bar. Beer 20Kč. Disco starts 10pm. Open nightly 7pm-dawn.

Tom's Bar, Pernerova 4 (☎24 81 38 02). Metro B or C: Florenc. Walk down Křižíkova past the Karlin Theater, pass under the tracks, and go right on Prvního pluků. Follow the tracks as they veer left to become Pernerova. Men of all ages rip up the dance floor or lounge in the video screening rooms. Clothing optional Th. Men only. Open Tu-Th 8pm-4am, F-Sa 8pm-late.

Pinocchio, Seifertova 3 (☎22 71 07 76; www.pinocchio-club.cz). See directions to A Club above; exit tram at Husinecka and walk back downhill. The Pinocchio complex includes poker machines, live strip shows, and video arcades. Beer 25Kč. Open daily 3pm-late.

▶ DAYTRIPS FROM PRAGUE

When you're in the city, it's easy to forget that Prague isn't the only place worth visiting in the Czech Republic. But even if you're only spending a few days in the capital, take the time to explore the towns and sights in the surrounding Bohemian hills. A day spent wandering through the magnificent castles of Karlštejn and Křivoklát or exploring the former concentration camp of Terezín will afford you a fuller experience and more complete understanding of the Czech Republic.

TEREZÍN (THERESIENSTADT)   ☎(0)416

Buses run from Prague-Florenc (45min., 9 per day, 59Kč). Exit at the second Terezín stop by the tourist office, which sells maps (30Kč; open Tu-Su 9am-12:30pm and 1-4pm). Around the corner from the bus stop, the museum sells tickets to Terezín's sights (☎78 22 25; fax 78 23 00; manager@pamatnik-terezin.cz). Open Apr.-Sept. daily 9am-6pm; Oct.-Mar. 9am-5:30pm. Tickets to the museum, barracks, and fortress 160Kč, students 120Kč. Crematorium and graveyard open Mar.-Nov. Su-F 10am-5pm. Free.

The fortress town of Terezín (Theresienstadt) was built in the 1780s on Habsburg Emperor Josef II's orders to safeguard the northern frontier. In 1940, Hitler's Gestapo set up a prison in the Small Fortress, and in 1941 the town itself became a concentration camp. By 1942, the entire pre-war civilian population had been evacuated, and the town became a waystation for over 140,000 Jews who were to be transferred farther east. Overpopulation, malnourishment, and death chambers killed over 30,000 people in the camp. Terezín was twice beautified in order to receive delegations from the Red Cross, who never realized the camp's true purpose. Terezín was one of Hitler's most successful propaganda ploys: Nazi films described the area as a resort where Jews were "allowed" to educate their young, partake in arts and recreation, and live a "fulfilling" life. Terezín has been repopulated since the war and life goes on in the former concentration camp. Families now live in the barracks and supermarkets occupy former Nazi offices. The population, however, has yet to reach its pre-war levels, when the town counted over 4000 Czechs and Germans—by the last census, there were fewer than 2000 residents.

CZECH REPUBLIC

THE LOCAL STORY

INSIDE TEREZÍN

An interview by Let's Go Researcher Dalibor Eric Snyder with Petra Penickova, tour guide at Terezín, a former concentration camp.

Q: Is there a particular tour of Terezín that you enjoy giving most?

A: I like giving tours of the Small Fortress, because here I can take people into the cells; they can touch it, they can feel.

Q: How do most people react?

A: I tour with students 16-20 years old. They are very interested and sometimes shocked. A few girls cry. They are very quiet here, and don't expect such horrible conditions.

Q: What was the town like before the Nazis took over?

A: It was a garrison town of the Czech-oslovakian army, so soldiers and civilians lived here together.

Q: Has the town recovered?

A: The people who left Terezín during the war never came back. Terezín is now an empty town. It's like a death town. We need more young people to come here, but they don't want to come.

Q: Do any concentration camp survivors come back to visit?

A: I have met many survivors. Some of them survived Terezín or Auschwitz. They come here with relatives to show them.

Q: How did Communism affect this memorial?

A: This history was changed. During the Communist era, the guides here were not allowed to talk about the Jews. There was no museum. In the

(continued on next page)

THE TOWN AND CEMETERY. To walk the streets of Terezìn is to confront its ghosts; every building here was used to house and monitor Jews during the war. The former school has been converted into a **museum** of ghetto life. It displays mountains of documents that place Terezín in the wider context of the war. East of the marketplace, the **Magdeburg Barracks** portray the lives of Jews within their prison walls. Outside the walls lie Terezìn's **Cemetery and Crematorium,** where the Nazis disposed of the remains of the executed. *(Open Mar.-Nov. Su-F 10am-5pm. Free.)*

SMALL FORTRESS. The Small Fortress sits across the river. Much of the fortress is left bare and untouched for visitors to explore freely. Permanent exhibitions chart the town's development from 1780 to 1939 and the story of the Fortress during WWII. Above the entrance lies the ironic epitaph of the Nazi concentration camps: *"Arbeit macht frei"* ("Work makes you free"). A walk through the dimly lit underground passage brings you to the excavation sight where you discover just how free work made those imprisoned here. Liberators uncovered mass graves after the war and transferred many of the bodies to the memorial cemetery. *(Open Apr.-Sept. daily 8am-6pm; Oct.-Mar. 8am-4:30pm. Closed Dec. 24-26 and Jan. 1.)*

KUTNÁ HORA ☎ (0)327

Buses run from Prague-Florenc. Bus times can be sporadic, so check with information at the station. (1½hr., 6 per day, 60Kč.) The chapel is 2km from the bus station. Exit the station and turn left on Benešova. Continue through the rotary until it becomes Vítězná, then go left on Zámecká. The ossuary will be in front of you. Open Apr.-Oct. daily 8am-6pm; Nov.-Mar. 9am-noon and 1-4pm. 30Kč, students 20Kč. Cameras 30Kč, video 60Kč. The rest of Kutná Hora's sights lie in the opposite direction from the station. Head right on Benešova, left on Vocekoca, and then continue on Vladislavova to Palackeho nám., the town square.

An hour and a half east of Prague, the former mining town of Kutná Hora (Mining Mountain) has a history as morbid as its famous bone church. Founded in the late 13th century when lucky miners hit a vein of silver, the city boomed with greedy diggers, but the Black Plague halted the fortune-seekers dead in their tracks. A few years later, a local monk sprinkled soil from Jerusalem's Golgotha Cemetery on Kutná Hora—this religious infusion made the superstitious rich eager to be buried there. When neighbors began to complain about the stench from the over-crowded graveyard, the Cistercian Order built a chapel and started cramming in bodies. In a fit of whimsy (or possibly insanity), one monk began designing flowers from pelvi and crania. He never finished the ossuary, but the artist František Rint eventually completed the project in 1870, decorating the chapel from floor to ceiling with the bones of over 40,000 people. Look for the femur crosses, and the grotesque chandelier made from every bone in the human body.

Kutná Hora's less macabre sights derive from its prosperous past, when the miners pooled their money to build a cathedral to rival Prague's St. Vitus (see p. 250). **St. Barbara's Church** (Chram Sv. Barbory) aptly honors the patron saint of miners. *(Open May-Sept. Tu-Su 9am-5:30pm; Mar.-Apr. and Oct.-Nov. 9-11:30am and 1-3:30pm. 30Kč, students 20Kč.)* To learn about mining methods from nearly 500 years ago, continue through the town square to the **mining museum** in Hrádek, which leads tours down through the old silver mines. *(☎51 21 59. Open July-Aug. Tu-Su 10am-6pm; May, June, and Sept. Tu-Su 9am-6pm; Apr. and Oct. Tu-Su 9am-5pm. 120Kč, students 60Kč. Call ahead for tour reservations.)*

MĚLNÍK   ☎(0)206

Buses run from Prague-Holešovice (45min., every 30min., 32Kč). From the bus station, make a right on Bezručova and bear left uphill at the fork on Kpt. Jaroše; this brings you to the town center. Enter Nàm Míru, the Old Town Square, through the passage under the clock tower. The chateau and the Cathedral will be to the left on Svatovaclvska.

Perched dramatically above the confluence of the Vltava and Elbe Rivers is Mělník, Bohemia's fertile wine-making region. In one day, you can visit its ossuary, tour its stately Renaissance chateau, sample the castle's homemade wines, and savor your favorite vintage over lunch in the old schoolhouse overlooking the Ríp Valley. The town's viniculture was honed about 1000 years ago, when Princess Ludmila, later St. Ludmila, planted the first vineyards for communion wine. Legend says that her grandson, St. Wenceslas, the patron saint of Bohemian wine-makers, was introduced to the secrets of winemaking in the vineyards of Mělník.

The **castle** tour winds through the heavily decorated rooms of the Lobkowicz family, but its highlight is wine-tasting in the chateau's Gothic cellars, where the floor is composed of upside-down wine bottles. Winetasting with Martin the wine master (110K⁻) is available by reservation. *(☎62 21 08; www.lobkowicz-melnik.cz. Open daily 10am-6pm. Tours 60Kč, students 40Kč.)* Opposite the chateau is the 15th-century **St. Peter and Paul Cathedral.** You can't enter the cathedral, but you can visit the crypt below, which houses the bones of 10,000 medieval plague victims, all stacked neatly to form morbid messages, like "Look, the Death!" Indeed. *(Open Tu-Su 10am-4pm. 30Kč, students 15Kč.)*

cemetery there was no Jewish star. And the history was changed so that only Soviet soldiers liberated this area.

Q: Since 1989 have more people come to the memorial?

A: Yes, many visitors from other countries began coming. Before visitors were from the former Yugoslavia, the Soviet Union, Hungary, and the Communist countries of the Eastern Block.

Q: How many people survived the camp?

A: About 5000 survived. Because it was not a liquidation camp, there was a chance to survive if people were strong not only physically, but in their mind.

Q: Did anyone ever escape?

A: I know about three cases, three young men who escaped in 1944 and survived.

Q: What happened to the officers that ran the camp?

A: Some of them were caught. The commander and his assistant were executed, but most were never found, changed their name, identity.

Q: Were a lot of the records from this complex destroyed?

A: Yes, most of them were destroyed. We have parts of them because prisoners who worked in the offices made copies for us. And it is possible to find relatives of people in the camp, search their memories of it, and try to find other survivors' letters and records.

KARLŠTEJN ☎(0)311

Trains run from Praha-Smíchov (45min., 1 per hr., 50Kč round-trip). Hang a right out of the train station and take your first left over the Berounka river. Turn right after crossing the bridge and walk through the village toward the castle. ☎68 16 17or 61 80 95. Open July-Aug. Tu-Su 9am-6pm; May-June and Sept. 9am-5pm; Apr. and Oct. 9am-4pm; Nov.-March 9am-3pm. Czech tour 120Kč, students 60Kč; English tour 200Kč/100Kč. 7-8 tours per day. Chapel tours by reservation only. ☎02 74 00 81 54; rezervace@spusc.cz. Open Tu-Su 9am-5pm. Tours 300Kč, students 100Kč; in English 600Kč/200Kč.

Karlštejn is Bohemia's gem, a walled and turreted fortress built by Charles IV as a country home and storehouse for crown jewels and holy relics. Charles originally banned women from entering the castle, but soon changed his mind when his wife snuck inside dressed as a castle guard and managed to spend the night. He later built a secret passage that allowed him to go directly from his bedroom to the queen's chambers. Most of the interior decorations were stolen during one war or another, but the **Chapel of the Holy Cross** (excluded from the basic tour) is decorated with more than 2000 precious stones and 129 apocalyptic paintings by medieval artist Master Theodorik. The castle's surroundings are as impressive as the castle itself, so take some time to walk along the Berounka River, or venture into the surrounding forest. But beware: obscure trail markers may lead you astray.

KŘIVOKLÁT ☎(0)313

Take a train from Prague-Smíchov to Beroun and switch trains to Křivoklát (1¾hr., 1 every 1-2 hours, 99Kč round-trip). From the train station, take a right down the path and across the bridge into town. Walk left for about 15m and turn right up the hill. ☎55 84 40. Open June-Aug. Tu-Su 9am-5pm; May 9am-4pm; March-Apr. and Sept.-Dec. Sa-Su 9am-3pm. Closed noon-1pm. Last tour at closing time. Czech tours 70Kč, students 40Kč; English tours 140Kč/70Kč. Tours given in Czech offer the English translation for free.

Křivoklát's main attraction was originally a 12th-century hunting lodge, but later became the royal residence of such families as the Luxembourgs, Hapsburgs, and Furstenburgs. Throughout the centuries, the castle's royal inhabitants were obsessed with preserving youth; Rudolf II imprisoned alchemist Edward Kelley for failing to concoct a potion to make him younger, and noblewoman Elisabeth Bathory bathed in the blood of young girls to steal their beauty. Although its history is filled with bone-chilling stories, the castle is rich with culture. The Furstenburg library houses over 50,000 titles, making it one of the largest libraries in the country. Paintings by Rubens and portraits of royalty hang from the castle's walls. As you wait for the tour to begin in the castle's first courtyard, take the time to meet the castle woodcarver, the blacksmith, and the collection of hawks and owls.

WEST BOHEMIA

Bursting at the seams with curative streams of all sorts, West Bohemia is a Czech oasis for those in search of a good bath or a good beer. Over the centuries, emperors and intellectuals alike soaked in the waters of Karlovy Vary (Carlsbad in German). Today, tourists follow their lead, flocking to the town's bubbling springs and wandering through its delicate colonnades. It's beer rather than water that tourists seek in Plzeň (Pilsen in German), home to the one of the world's finest brews, Pilsner Urquell.

PLZEŇ ☎ (0)19

Tell Czechs you're going to Plzeň (PIL-zenyuh; pop. 175,000), and they might say *"to je škoda"* ("what a pity"), making an unfortunate pun on "Škoda", the name of a car company. After the car manufacturer set up base here, Plzeň quickly became one of Bohemia's most polluted areas. Recent attempts to clean up the city, however, have left its beautiful architecture and gardens looking surprisingly fresh and new. But it's not the architecture that lures so many to Plzeň—it's the world-famous beer. Between the Pilsner Brewery, Burgher's Brewery Museum, and the countless beerhalls around town, Plzeň is the beer-lover's utopia.

TRANSPORTATION

Trains: On Sirková between Americká and Koterovská (☎ 701 46 90). To **Prague** (1¾hr., 12 per day, 140Kč) and **Český Krumlov** (4hr., 2 per day, 204Kč) via **České Budějovice.** Domestic tickets on the 1st level; international tickets on the 2nd. Open M-F 6am-10pm, Sa-Su 6am-7pm.

Buses: Husova 58 (☎ 723 72 37). Many Eurolines buses pass through en route to **Prague** (2hr., at least 1 per hr., 66Kč) from **France, Germany,** and **Switzerland.** To **Karlovy Vary** (1¾hr.; 17 per day, less frequently on weekends; 76Kč). Open M-Sa 5am-10:30pm, Su 5am-8pm.

Public Transportation: Tram #2 goes to the train and bus stations, Nám. Republiky, and the hostel. Tram #4 runs north-south along Sady Pětatřicátníků. Get tickets from any *tabák* and punch them on board (8Kč, backpacks 4Kč). 200-1000Kč fine for riding ticketless. **Trams** stop running at 11:45pm; identically numbered **buses** take over at night.

Taxi: Radio Taxi (☎ 22 77 02). Taxis wait outside the bus and train stations, and at Nám. Republiky.

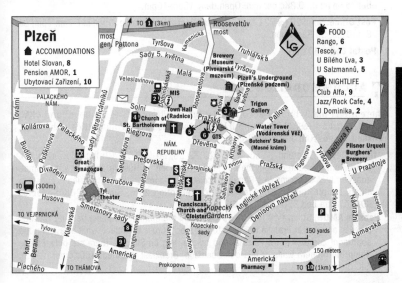

■ ⚡ ORIENTATION AND PRACTICAL INFORMATION

Nám. Republiky (Republic Sq.), the main square, lies amid a grid of parks and streets. Restaurants and cafes are clustered outside the square. The city's sights branch out from this area, but the happening nightlife is concentrated around **Americká** street. From the **train station**, turn right on **Sirková** and enter the pedestrian underpass. Turn left on **Pražská** and bear right to reach Nám. Republiky. From the **bus station**, turn left on **Husova**. After it becomes **Smetanovy Sady**, hang a left on **Bedřicha Smetany** and follow it to the square (15min.).

Tourist Office: Městské Informační Středisko (MIS), Nám. Republiky 41 (☎803 27 50; fax 803 27 52; infocenter@mmp.city.cz). Offers free **maps**, books rooms (from 300Kč), and sells phone cards (175Kč). **Internet access** 2Kč per min. Open Apr.-Sept. daily 9am-6pm; Oct.-Mar. M-F 10am-5pm, Sa-Su 10am-3:30pm.

Budget Travel: GTS Int, Pražská 12 (☎732 86 21; fax 732 52 46). Arranges plane and train tickets. Open M-F 9am-6pm.

Currency Exchange: Plzeňská Banka, Nám. Republiky 16 (☎723 53 54). Cashes **traveler's checks** for 2.5% commission. Open M-F 8am-5pm. A 24hr. **currency exchange** machine sits at **Československá Ochodní Banka,** Americká 60, by the train station.

ATM: There's a MC/V machine at **Bank Austria,** Františkánská 7.

Luggage Storage: On the 1st fl. of the train station behind the staircase. 10Kč per bag, 20Kč for bags over 15kg. Lockers 5Kč per day. Open 24hr.

Pharmacy: Lekarna, Pařížská 15. On the corner of Americká and Pařížská, 200m from the train station. Open M-F 8am-6pm, Sa 8am-noon.

Medical Services: Emergency ☎27 38 10 or 155.

Internet Access: Alien Club, Dominikánská 3, 3rd fl. 1Kč per min. Open M-F 11am-11pm, Su 2-11pm. **Internet Kavarna Arena,** Františkánská (☎722 04 02). Ring the bell to be let in. 0.8Kč per min. Open daily 10am-10pm.

Post Office: Solní 20 (☎721 11 11). **Poste Restante** available. Open M-F 7am-7pm, Sa 8am-1pm, Su 8am-noon.

Postal Code: 301 00.

⌂ ACCOMMODATIONS

There aren't many budget accommodations in Plzeň. **MIS** (see above) and **CKM,** Dominikánská 1 (☎723 63 93), both book **private rooms ❷** (from 300Kč). Otherwise, **pensions** range from 300 to 600Kč.

Hotel Slovan, Smetanovy Sady 1 (☎722 72 56; fax 722 70 12; hotelslovan@iol.cz), 5min. from the center. From the bus station, turn left on Husova and follow it to Smetanovy sady. A sweeping Neo-Renaissance stairway adorned with mirrors leads guests to clean, simple rooms. Breakfast 150Kč. Reception 24hr. Singles 620Kč; doubles 990Kč. Extra bed 350Kč. MC/V. ❸

Pension AMOR, Stikova 14 (☎752 99 86). From the train station, take tram #1 towards Bolevec and exit at Pražská (the 2nd to last stop). Cross the street, walk away from the apartment complex down Pražská, and take a right on Stikova. There are only 7 beds within the modern walls of this quiet pension. Breakfast included. 400Kč per person. ISIC discount. ❷

Ubytovací Zařízení, Zahradní 21 (☎/fax 744 32 62). Take tram #1 from the train station toward Slovany and get off at the 2nd stop, Jedlová. Head right on Jedlová and then left on Zahradní. The bathrooms need maintenance, but the rooms are quite clean and comfortable. 177Kč per person. ❶

FOOD

Every meal in Plzeň should include a glass of *Pilsner Urquell* or its dark brother, *Purkmistr.* If you can't decide, have a *řezané*, a Czech black and tan. For groceries, try **Tesco,** Americká 47. (Open M-W 7am-7pm, Th-F 7am-8pm, Sa-Su 8am-6pm.)

U Salzmannů, Pražská 8 (☎ 723 58 55). Walk through the original Renaissance portal to the city's oldest beerhouse, where hearty Czech pub food has yet to grow old. Entrees 62-163Kč. Beer 20Kč. Open M-Sa 11am-11pm, Su 11am-10pm. MC/V. ❷

Rango, Pražská 10 (☎ 732 99 69). Descend a stone staircase into this romantic 16th-century vaulted cellar. Sip fine wines (bottles from 350Kč) while feasting on Greek specialties (155-240Kč) and mouthwatering Italian deserts (50Kč). An extensive salad (60-135Kč) and pasta (80-135Kč) menu caters to vegetarians. Open M-F 11am-11pm, Sa-Su noon-11pm. MC/V. ❹

U Bílého Lva (At the White Lion), Pražská 15 (☎ 722 69 98). Enter around the corner on Perlová. With its animal skin decor and savory meat dishes (70-185Kč), this restaurant could pass as a hunter's cabin. If the antlers frighten you, sit outside on the peacefully secluded patio. Open daily 10am-11pm. ❷

SIGHTS

Aside from the Brewery, the town's attractions all lie near Nám. Republiky.

PILSNER URQUELL BREWERY. (Měšťanský Pivovar Plzeňský Prazdroj.) In 1842, over 30 independent brewers plied their trade in the beer cellars of Plzeň. They eventually formed a union called the Pilsner Urquell Burghers' Brewery, intent on creating the best beer in the world. Many would agree that they succeeded with the legendary Pilsner Urquell. As you walk through the huge gate and spot the famous Prazdroj sign behind the billowing smoke, it's hard not to feel like you've won the golden ticket to Willy Wonka's land of beer. The knowledgeable guides provide intricate explanations of why their beers taste so good and lead thirsty tourists to the fermentation cellars for samples straight from the barrel. After the tour, head to **Na spilce,** the on-site beerhouse, where Pilsner pours forth at 20Kč per pint. *(300m from Staré Město over the Radbuza River, where Pražská becomes U Prazdroje. ☎706 28 88. 1hr. tours June-Aug. daily 10:30am, 12:30, 2, 3pm; Sept.-May daily 12:30pm. 120Kč, students 60Kč.)*

REPUBLIC SQUARE. (Náměstí Republiky.) Imperial dwellings loom over this marketplace, but none overshadow the belfry of the **Church of St. Bartholomew** (Kostel sv. Bartoloměje), the tallest in the country. Inside, Gothic statues and altars bow to the stunning 14th-century statue **Plzeňská Madona.** Look from the entrance for free, or pay to walk around the interior. *(Open W-F 10am-4pm, Sa 10am-5pm, Su noon-4pm. 20Kč.)* Tourists climb 60m to the observation deck of the tower for a dizzying, if dazzling, view of the town. *(Open daily 10am-6pm. 20Kč, students 15Kč.)* You can get to the 1607 **Kaiser House** (Císařský dům) through Plzeň's Renaissance **town hall,** which has a golden clock at its top. *(Nám. Republiky 39.)*

WATER TOWER COMPLEX. Head down Pražská from the square to reach the **water tower** (vodárenská věž), which once stored the crystal-clear water needed for fine beer. *(Pražská 19.)* A 40min. tour of the tower and **Plzeň's underground** (Plzeňské podzemí) winds through the cellars where the town's burghers used to covertly brew their beers. *(Perlová 4. ☎722 52 14. Open June-Sept. Tu-Su 9am-5pm; Apr.-May and Oct.-Nov. W-Sa 9am-5pm. Tours every 20min. Last tour leaves 4:20pm. 35Kč, students 25Kč.)* The **Trigon Gallery** next door features a collection of early 20th-century drawings, which includes the work of Vachal, Capek, and Kupka. *(Pražská 19. ☎732 54 71. Open M-Th 10am-6pm, F 10am-5pm, Sa 10am-noon. 10Kč, students 5Kč.)*

GREAT SYNAGOGUE. Built in 1892 by Plzeň's once prosperous Jewish community, this temple is the third largest in the world. Due to the Holocaust and the subsequent flight of the Jewish people, there are fewer than 50 Jews in Plzeň today. A captivating photo exhibit depicts Jewish sights and people from the past fifty years. *(From the south end of Nám. Republiky, go down Prešovská to Sady Pětatřicátníků and turn left; the synagogue is on the right. Open Su-F 11am-5pm. 20Kč, students 10Kč.)*

OTHER SIGHTS. The sprawling ■ **Brewery Museum** exhibits beer paraphernalia from medieval taps to a coaster collection. Learn about the history of brewing through miniature brewing plants, reconstructed malthouses, chemical laboratories, and simulated pub environments. The zaniest room, labeled "the room of curiosities," showcases steins of all sizes and a statue of Shakespeare's most famous drunk, Sir John Falstaff. You can even buy a souvenir glass (45Kč) and sample the beer to enhance the exhibit's effect. *(Veleslavínova 6. From the square, go down Pražská and turn left on Perlová, which ends at Veleslavínova. ☎722 49 55; fax 723 55 74. Open daily 10am-6pm. English text available. 60Kč, students 30Kč.)* The black iron gate of the **Franciscan Church and Cloister** (Františkánský kostel a klášter) leads to a quiet cloister garden with statues. Inside, the highlight is the 15th-century **Chapel of St. Barbara**, which is covered with brilliant frescoes and protected by its strangely vaulted roof. *(Enter at Františkánská 11, south of Nám. Republiky. Open Tu-Su 10am-6pm. 30Kč, students 15Kč.)* Join the locals at the edge of the old town, as they stroll and relax in the immaculate **Kopecký gardens** (Kopeckého sady) while brass bands perform. *(Františkánská runs into the park south of Nám. Republiky.)*

◙ NIGHTLIFE

Thanks to students from the University of West Bohemia, Plzeň abounds with bars and late-night clubs. Things heat up around 9:30pm. For more options, check with the young summer staff at the tourist office.

Club Alfa (☎722 70 70), at the intersection of Americká and Jungmannova. Follow B. Smetany until it becomes Jungmannova and turn right on Americká. Teens and early 20-somethings sweat the night away to techno-pop in this beautiful Renaissance ballroom. Bowling 150Kč per hr. Bowling open 11am-closing. Cover F-Sa 20Kč. Open M-Th and Su 7:30pm-5am, F-Sa 7:30pm-6am.

Jazz/Rock Cafe, Sedláčova 18. From the square, go down Solní and take the first left on Sedláčova. A chill crowd of regulars lounges in this underground cellar cafe. Beer 26Kč. Live music every W Sept.-June. Open M-F 10am-4am, Sa-Su 9pm-4am.

U Dominika, Dominikánská 3 (☎22 32 26), off Nám. Republiky's northwest corner past the town hall. Dance to techno around the bonfire in the beer garden, or groove to jazz in the pub above. Beer (16Kč) and coffee (16Kč) are the drinks of choice. Open M-F 10-1am, Sa 1pm-1am, Su 1-11pm.

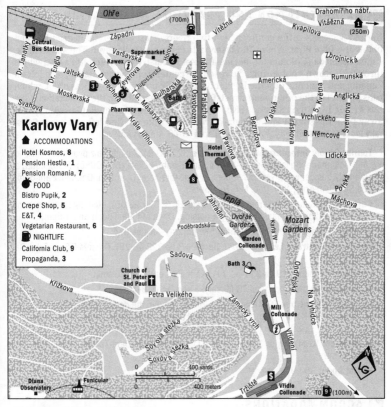

Karlovy Vary

🏠 **ACCOMMODATIONS**
Hotel Kosmos, 8
Pension Hestia, 1
Pension Romania, 7
🍎 **FOOD**
Bistro Pupik, 2
Crepe Shop, 5
E&T, 4
Vegetarian Restaurant, 6
📺 **NIGHTLIFE**
California Club, 9
Propaganda, 3

KARLOVY VARY   ☎ (0)35

From the bus station, Karlovy Vary (pop. 60,000) doesn't look like much, but a stroll into the spa district elucidates why Johann Sebastian Bach, Peter the Great, Sigmund Freud, and even Karl Marx frequented salons here. Along the Teplá, the town evokes serenity: swans, ducks, and fish populate the gurgling river, while ornate pastel buildings and weeping willows line its banks. The town now hosts mostly older Germans and Russians seeking the springs' therapeutic powers.

🚌 TRANSPORTATION

Trains: Horní nádraží (☎391 35 59), northwest of town. Connections are inconvenient; buses are more efficient. To **Prague** via **Chomutov** (4½hr. plus 1-2hr. layover in Chomutov, 4-5 per day, 250Kč) and **Berlin, GER** (6-8hr., 1 per day, 1300Kč).

Buses: Dolní nádraží (☎391 35 50), on Západní. Buy tickets on board. To: **Plzeň** (1½hr., 12 per day, 80Kč) and **Prague** (2½hr., 25 per day, 100-130Kč).

Public Transportation: All local buses pass through the main stop on Varšavská (8Kč). Buses run 4am-10pm; night buses are infrequent.

Taxi: Centrum Taxi (☎322 30 00). 24hr. service at Zeyerova 9. Taxis wait outside the main bus stop on Varšavská and in front of the train station.

⚡ 🛈 ORIENTATION AND PRACTICAL INFORMATION

Karlovy Vary sits at the confluence of two rivers. The commercial district lies just below the **Ohře River,** where **TG Masaryka** leads to the **Teplá River.** The spa district, called **Kolonáda** (Colonnade), begins at **Hotel Thermal,** from which **IP Pavlova** winds through the town's hot springs. To reach the center from the **bus station,** turn left on Západní and continue past the Becher building. Bear right on T. G. Masaryka, which runs parallel to the other main street, **Dr. Davida Bechera.** From the **train station,** take bus #11 or 13 to the last stop (8Kč). By foot, it's 15min. downhill. Cross the street away from the station and go right on **Nákladní.** Take the first left and cross **Ostrovský most** at the highway. Follow the Teplá to TG Masaryka.

Tourist Office: Infocentrum, Lazenská 1 (☎322 40 97; kurinfo@plz.pvtnet.cz), next to Mill Colonnade. Sells **maps** (30-169Kč) and theater tickets (60-400Kč). *Promenada,* a monthly booklet with event schedules, is available here. Open Jan.-Oct. M-F 8am-6pm, Sa-Su 10am-6pm; Nov.-Dec. M-F 7am-5pm.

Currency Exchange: Komercní banka, Tržiště 11 (☎322 22 05), exchanges currency for 2% commission and has a MC/V **ATM** outside. Open M-F 9am-noon and 1-5pm.

Luggage Storage: In the train station. 5Kč per day; lockers 5Kč.

Pharmacy: Centralni Lekarna, Dr. D. Bechera 3 (☎322 48 20). Open M-F 8am-6pm, Sa 8am-noon.

Hospital: Bezrucova 19 (☎311 51 11). Northwest of the spa district.

Telephones: At the junction of TG Masaryka and Dr. D. Bechera.

Internet: Vir Centrum, TG Masaryka 12, 2nd fl. Through the door that doesn't lead to the bookstore. 20Kč per 15min. Open daily 10am-10pm. **W.D. Group,** IP Pavlova 19 (☎322 76 41). 80Kč per hr. Open M-F 9am-noon, Sa 8:30am-noon.

Post Office: TG Masaryka 1 (☎316 11 01). Open M-F 7:30am-7pm, Sa 8am-1pm, Su 8am-noon.

Postal Code: 360 01.

🛏 ACCOMMODATIONS

Budget accommodations are hard to come by in Karlovy Vary. Come festival time, most rooms have been booked 4-5 months in advance. **Infocentrum ❷** (see above) books rooms (from 400Kč). Private agencies can also help you out. **City Info ❸,** at the kiosk at TG Masaryka 9, offers singles in pensions from 600Kč and hotel doubles from 860Kč. (☎322 33 51. Open daily 9am-6pm.)

Hotel Kosmos, Zahradní 39 (☎322 54 76; fax 322 31 68). In the center of the spa district. Follow the directions from the bus station to TG Masaryka (see **Orientation,** p. 266) and bear right at the post office. Comfortable and convenient, with simply furnished rooms overlooking the Teplá River. Singles 700Kč, with bath 890Kč; doubles 1150Kč/1450Kč. Oct.-Apr. 100Kč off. ❸

Pension Hestia, Stará Kysibelská 45 (☎322 59 85; fax 322 04 82; hestiakv@volny.cz). Take bus #6 4 stops from the main stop on Západní toward Stará Kysibelská. Get off at Blahoslavova. The pension is up the street to the left. Cheap, spacious rooms make it worth the trip. 2 baths per fl. Reception 24hr. Singles 320Kč; doubles 640Kč. ❷

Pension Romania, Zahradní 49 (☎322 28 22; fax 322 25 01). Next to the post office at the corner of Zahradní and TG Masaryka. Offers luxurious, modern rooms with bath, TV, phone, and fridge, right on the Teplá. Breakfast included. Singles 1365Kč; doubles 1980Kč; triples 3095Kč. Student singles 865Kč. Nov.-Apr. 100Kč less per bed. ❺

⚑ FOOD

Karlovy Vary is known for its sweet *oplatky* (wafers), which are especially enjoy-able with the therapeutic spa waters. Many vendors sell them on the street (5Kč). If you are looking for something even sweeter, check out the **crepe shop** on Zeyerova, where you can design your own dessert for 13-23Kč. (Open M-F 9am-7pm, Sa 9am-noon.) A **supermarket,** Horova 1, occupies the large building with the "Městská tržnice" sign near the local bus station. (Open M-F 6am-7pm, Sa 7am-5pm, Su 9am-5pm. AmEx/MC/V.) Meals in the spa district are expensive, but the ambiance and delicious food may be worth the extra money; cheaper options lay hidden in the commercial district.

E&T, Zeyerova 3 (☎322 60 22). Between D. Bechera and TG Masaryka. Faithful regulars dine inside under posters of James Dean and American culture, while a hipper crowd occupies the patio, chatting on cell phones and watching passersby. Entrees 70-235Kč. Open M-F 9:30-2am, Sa-Su 11-2am. ❸

Bistro Pupik, Horova 2 (☎322 34 50). Across from the local bus stop on Varšavská. Delicious meals (40-79Kč) in a cafeteria-like setting fill your stomach without emptying your wallet. Open M-F 7:30am-7pm, Sa-Su 8am-5pm. ❶

Vegetarian Restaurant, IP Pavlova 25 (☎322 90 21). From Hotel Thermal, head away from the Spa district on Pavlova. Despite its name, this restaurant serves both meat and vegetarian dishes in a traditional Czech interior. Entrees 40-75Kč. Open daily 11am-9pm. ❶

◉ SIGHTS

The beauty of Karlovy Vary is that one must indulge in order to sightsee. The **spa district** begins with the Victorian **Bath 5** (Lázně 5), Smetanovy Sady 1, across the street from the post office. Thermal baths (340Kč) and underwater massages (475Kč) are among the services offered here. (☎322 25 36; infor@spa5.cz; www.spa5.cz. Make reservations 1-2 days in advance. Pool and sauna open M-F 8am-9pm, Sa 8am-6pm, Su 10am-6pm. 90Kč. Treatments M-F 7am-3pm, Sa 8am-1pm.) Cross the bridge on TG Masaryka, turn right, and continue along the river. The path crosses back over the Teplá and leads through the **Dvořák** gardens to the Victorian **Garden Collonade** (Sadová kolonáda). Here you can sip the curative waters of the **Snake Spring** (Hadí pramen) from a serpent's mouth and of the **Garden Spring** (Sadový pramen) from a marble peasant woman. While it's free to drink, you may be able to manage only a few sips of the metallic water—it sure isn't Perrier. Bring your own cup or buy a porcelain one from the kiosks (75-220Kč). At Mlýnské nábř. 5, **Bath 3** offers full-body massages to complement the healing springs. (☎322 56 41; www.lazneIII.cz. Neck and shoulders 442Kč; full body 714Kč. Treatments daily 7-11:30am and noon-2:30pm. Pool and sauna open M-F 3-7pm, Sa 1-6pm. 110Kč.) Next door, the **Mill Collonade** (Mlýnská kolonáda) shelters five separate springs. Farther along, the former **market** (tržiště) appears by the white **Market Collonade** (Tržní kolonáda), where two springs bubble to the surface. The **Zawojski House,** now the Živnostenská Banka, is a gorgeous Art Nouveau building from the early 20th century. Next door, **Strudel Spring** (Vřídlo pramen) inside the **Strudel Collonade** (Vřídelní kolonáda) spouts 30L of water each second at 72° Celsius, making it Karlovy Vary's hottest and highest-shooting spring. (Open daily 6am-7pm.)

At the end of Stará Louka sits **Grandhotel Pupp.** Founded in 1774 by Johann Georg Pupp, the Grandhotel was the largest hotel in 19th-century Bohemia. From the right side of the hotel, follow the narrow walkway Marianska to the funicular, which leads to the **Diana Observatory**. (Funicular runs every 15min. 9am-7pm. 25Kč, round-trip 40Kč. Tower open daily 9am-7pm. 10Kč.) Follow the paths of Petra Velikého back to town to see a statue of **Karl Marx** commemorating his visits to the bourgeois spa between 1874 and 1876. He apparently needed to experience the luxuries of wealth before he could denounce it in good conscience. Around the corner on Krále Jiřího, the turquoise-and-gold Russian Orthodox **Church of Saints Peter and Paul,** built in the 19th century, offers an inspiring spectacle of painted domes, icons galore, and an enormous chandelier. Escape to the 12th-century **Loket Castle,** perched above the Ohře River 12km to the west. Originally constructed to help protect trade routes, the castle now displays bleak dungeon cells and bright porcelain manufactured in nearby Loket nad Ohří. (☎016 868 46 48. Open daily Apr.-Oct. 9am-4:30pm; daily Nov.-Mar. 9am-3:30pm. Admission 70Kč, students 50Kč.)

ENTERTAINMENT AND NIGHTLIFE

Across the river from Loket Castle, the outdoor **amphitheater** hosts **opera** productions in late July and early August. Inquire at Infocentrum (see **Practical Information,** p. 266) for ticket information. **Buses** to Loket leave from platform nine at the main bus station (30min., every 25min., 20Kč), but the **hike** is half the fun. Follow the 17km **blue trail** from the steps of Diana Rozhleda Observatory entrance in Karlovy Vary. Two-thirds of the way into the trail you'll find the magnificent rocks of **Svatošské skály,** supposedly an inspiration to both Goethe and the Brothers Grimm.

Promenáda, a brochure available at the tourist office, lists the month's concerts and performances; it includes info for Karlovy Vary's **International Film Festival,** which screens independent films from all over the globe. The event is held in early July and attracts some of the world's biggest stars. It you plan to attend, buy a pass to see five films per day inside **Hotel Thermal,** the festival's center. Tickets go quickly, so get to the box office early. The town's hotels and pensions fill up months in advance, so reserve accommodations early or camp outside of town.

Like its restaurants, Karlovy Vary's nightlife is geared toward older tourists. Although clubs are sparse, expensive cafes abound. **Propaganda,** Jaltská 5, off Bechera, attracts Karlovy Vary's hippest crowd to its trendy blue steel interior. (☎323 37 92. Cocktails 40-100Kč. Beer from 11Kč. Pool table. Open daily 5pm-late.) It's a steep hike up Kolmi from behind the Church of Mary Magdalen to **California Club,** Tyrsova 2, but the club's late hours and hot dancing make it worth the trek. (☎322 20 87. Beer from 12Kc. Open daily 6pm-5am.)

SOUTH BOHEMIA

Truly a rustic Eden, South Bohemia is a scenic medley of scattered villages, unspoiled brooks, virgin forests, and soaring ruins. Its hills have made the region a favorite of Czech bicyclists and hikers, who now flock to the countryside to traipse through castles, observe wildlife, and guzzle *Budvar* straight from the brewery.

ČESKÉ BUDĚJOVICE   ☎(0)38

More convenient than scenic, this transportation hub located deep in the heart of the Bohemian countryside is a great base from which to explore the surrounding region. It may lack the charm of Český Krumlov, its neighbor to the south, but it does provide plenty of fun and beer; the city is home to the great *Budvar* brewery. So grab your stein and head to the pub, because a few brews may be just what you need to pronounce České Budějovice (CHESS-kay BOOD-yeh-yoh-vee-tsay).

☐ TRANSPORTATION

Trains: Nádražní 12 (☎ 785 24 62). To: **Brno** (4½hr., 2 per day, 250Kč); **Český Krumlov** (50min., 8 per day, 46Kč); **Plzeň** (1½hr., 11 per day, 162Kč); **Prague** (2½hr., 11 per day, 204Kč); **Milan, ITA** (2330Kč); **Munich, GER** (1494Kč); **Rome, ITA** (3201Kč). Info office open June-Sept. M-F 9am-6pm, Sa 9am-4pm; Oct.-May M-F 9am-5pm.

Buses: On Žižkova (☎ 635 44 44), around the corner from the trains. To: **Brno** (4½hr., 6 per day, 180-220Kč); **Český Krumlov** (45min, 15 per day, 30Kč); **Plzeň** (3hr., 2 per day, 110Kc); **Prague** (2½hr., 10 per day, 120-144Kč); **Milan, ITA** (14hr., 3 per week, 2030Kč); **Munich, GER** (5½hr., 3 per week, 970Kč).

Public Transportation: You can get around České Budějovice via **buses** and **trolley-buses.** Buy tickets (6Kč) at kiosks or *tabaks* and punch them as you board.

Taxis: Taxi-Budejovice ☎ 140 14.

◪ ☐ ORIENTATION AND PRACTICAL INFORMATION

Staré Město (Old Town) centers around the gigantic **Nám. Přemysla Otakara II.** From the train station, turn right on **Nádražní** and hang a left at the first crosswalk on the pedestrian **Lannova třída.** This stretch, which becomes **Kanovnická** after it passes the moat, soon meets the northeast corner of Nám. Otakara II (10 min.). The **bus station** is on **Žižkova,** just around the corner from the train station. To get to the center, turn left on Žižkova and then right on **Jeronýmova.** Go left on Lannova třída, which leads to the center.

Tourist Office: Turistické Informační Centrum (TIC), Nám. Otakara II 2 (☎/fax 635 94 80; www.c-budejovice.cz). English-speaking staff gives out free **maps,** books private rooms, and organizes tours. Open May-Sept. M-F 8:30am-noon and 12:30-6pm, Sa 8:30am-noon and 12:30-5pm, Su 10am-noon and 12:30-4pm; Oct.-Apr. M-F 9am-noon and 12:30-5pm, Sa 9am-noon and 12:30-3pm.

Currency Exchange: Komerční Banka, Krajinská 15 (☎ 774 11 47). Off Nám. Otakara II. Cashes **traveler's checks** for 2% commission. Open M-F 8am-5pm.

ATMs: MC/V machines are along Nám. Otakara II.

Luggage Storage: Along the right wall of the **train station.** 10Kč per day for 15kg. Lockers 10Kč per day. Make sure to set the combination on the inside of the locker door before you shut it. Open daily 4:30am-10:45pm.

English-Language Bookstore: Omkiron, Nám. Otakara II 25 (☎ 635 89 48). Sells English books and newspapers. Open M-F 8am-6pm, Sa 8am-noon.

Pharmacy: Nám. Otakara II 26 (☎ 635 30 63). Open M-F 7am-6pm, Sa 8am-noon.

Hospital: Nemocnice, B. Nemcove 54 (☎ 787 11 11).

Emergency Service: (☎ 635 55 55); **for children:** (☎ 787 86 25).

Internet Access: Internet Club, Průmyslova 1656 (☎ 635 04 58). From the train station, go left on Nádražní and right on Průmyslova (behind the bus station). 0.70Kč per min. Open M-F 9am-9pm, Sa 10am-9pm. **X-Files@Internet Cafe,** Senovážné nám. 6 (☎ 635 04 04). 1Kč per min. Open M-F 10am-10pm, Sa-Su 4-10pm.

Post Office: Senovážné nám. 1 (☎ 773 41 22). South of Lannova as it enters Staré Město. The large pink- and peach-colored building. Open M-F 7am-7pm, Sa 8am-noon.

Postal Code: 37001.

IN RECENT NEWS

THIS BUD'S FOR EU

In years past, many Yanks, having tasted the malty goodness of *Budvar* brew, return home to find that the beer from Budweis is conspicuously unavailable. The fact that *Budvar* is the Czech Republic's largest exported beer, beating out even *Pilsner Urquell* by 1995, made its absence from American store shelves stranger still. So where's the *Budvar*? The answer lies in a tale of town names. České Budějovice (Budweis in German) had been brewing its own lager for centuries when the Anheuser-Busch brewery in St. Louis, MO marketed its own Budweiser-style beer in 1876. It wasn't until the 1890s, however, that the Budějovice Brewery began producing beer labelled "Budweiser." A 1911 non-competition agreement sought to end international trademark conflicts: Budějovice Brewery got European markets, while Anheuser-Busch took North America. But the story continues. When Anheuser-Busch tried to end the confusion by buying a controlling interest in the makers of *Budvar*, the Czech government refused. Anheuser-Busch then sued for trademark infringement in Finland, while Budějovice Brewery petitioned the EU to make the moniker "Budweiser" as exclusive as "Champagne," so that any brand sold in the EU under that name would have to come from the Budweis region. In spite of on-going name games and debates, Budvar has finally assumed its place on the beer shelves in American stores. Since 2000, it has been sold in the US as Czechvar. America, this Czechvar's for you.

—Dalibor Eric Snyder

ACCOMMODATIONS

Accommodations in České Budějovice don't come cheap. If price is a priority, a short bus or trolley ride beyond the confines of Staré Město's walls will aid you in your search. **Private rooms** are the best option; TIC ❶ has listings (250Kč and up).

Penzion U Výstaviště, U Výstaviště 17 (☎724 01 48, mobile 0602 84 09 06). Take bus #1 from the bus station 5 stops to U parku and follow the street that branches to the right behind the bus stop (200m). Fall asleep under the cloud-patterned sheets of this friendly, quiet, hostel-style pension. Only 12 beds, so call ahead. Dorms 250Kč 1st night, 200Kč thereafter. ❶

University of South Bohemia, Studentská 15 (☎777 44 00). Take bus #1 from in front of the bus station 5 stops to U parku. Turn back from the bus stop and head down Husova to a right on Studentská. The university dorms are in the 4 large buildings at the end of the street. Full of students. Open July-Sept. 5. Doubles 300Kč. 20% ISIC discount. ❷

Vzdělávací Centrum PVT, Žižkova 1 (☎731 22 08; fax 731 22 09; www.pvt.cz/vcu). From the bus station, head left on Žižkova. The hotel is 3 blocks down, just through the parking lot on the right. All the rooms in this modern, centrally located budget hotel have baths; some have TVs. Breakfast 40Kč. Singles 560Kč; doubles 690Kč. ❸

AT Penzion, Dukelská 15 (☎731 25 29). From Nám. Otakara II, make a right down Dr. Stejskala. At the first intersection, turn left and follow Siroka, veering right on Dukelská. Follow Dukelská past Na Sadech and Alesova. Private baths and beautifully furnished rooms make this small, residential pension well worth the extra crowns. Singles 600Kč; doubles 1200Kč. ❸

FOOD

The small streets around the center shelter a number of restaurants; most have terraces and hearty fare. Get groceries at **Večerka,** Palachého 10. (Enter on Hroznova. Open M-F 7am-8pm, Sa 7am-1pm, Su 8am-8pm.)

Restaurant Rio, Hradební 14 (☎635 05 72). Right off ul. Černé věže. Despite the Brazilian name, this restaurant serves cheap Czech cuisine on an alleyway terrace. Entrees 45-75Kč. Open M-F 11am-11pm, Sa 6pm-midnight. ❶

Restaurace Ameno, Riegrova 8 (☎ 636 07 33). Head up ul. Černé věže from the center of town, cross over the moat to Jírocova. Ameno sits on the corner. With sombreros, Italian dishware, and soft candlelight, Ameno successfully mixes Europe and Central America, satisfying both your pasta (65-110Kč) and chimichanga (95Kč) cravings. Open M-Sa 11am-midnight. ❷

Ceska Rychta, Nám. Otakara II 30. Under Grand Hotel Zvon. A Pilsner Urquell original restaurant serving delicious Cordon Bleu, steaks, and other entrees (104-252Kč). Dine in the wooden interior among beer-guzzling merriment, or relax on the patio overlooking Nám. Otakara II. Open M-Sa 10am-midnight, Su 10am-11pm. ❸

🔘 SIGHTS

The city's most famous attraction, the **Budvar Brewery,** Karoliny Světlé 4, can be reached from the center by buses #2 and 4. The inner workings of the functioning brewery are extremely interesting, especially for beer connoisseurs, but beware of the strong fumes emanating from the hops. Try to book a tour ahead of time, although those who show up early often get in as well. English guidebooks make it easy to join non-English groups. (☎ 770 53 41. Tours 9am-4pm. Czech tasting tours 70Kč; English tours 120Kč, students 70Kč.)

If you have half an hour to spare, you shouldn't miss the **Museum of Motorcycles.** Situated next to the Church of the Sacrifice of the Virgin Mary in historic Piaristické Nám., this magnificent exhibit showcases over 100 motorcycles, racing trophies, and other motorcycle paraphernalia from the early 1900s to today. The museum's highlight is a WWII exhibit incorporating a model aircraft, barbed wire, and a mini-jeep. (☎ 720 08 49. Open daily 10am-1:30pm and 2-6pm. 40Kč, students 20Kč.)

Encased by colorful Renaissance and Baroque architecture, the cobblestone **Nám. Otakara II** is the largest square in the Czech Republic. **Samson's Fountain** (Samsonova kašna; 1726), which towers over the center of the square, makes a great point for orientation. Behind the fountain, the square's ornate 1727-1730 Baroque **town hall** *(radnice),* built by architect Antonius Martinelli, stands a full story above the square's other buildings. Samson's right eye looks to the 72m **Black Tower** (Černá věž). It's free to climb up, but it costs 15Kč to get to the 360° balcony after the climb. The steep stairs can be treacherous. (☎ 635 25 08. Open July-Aug. daily 10am-6pm; Apr.-June and Sept.-Oct. Tu-Su 10am-6pm.) The tower once served as a belfry for the neighboring 17th-century Baroque **Cathedral of St. Nicholas** (Chrám sv. Mikuláše). Concerts now make use of the cathedral's acoustics—check the posted schedules. (Open daily 7am-6pm.)

🔘 NIGHTLIFE

Posters around town advertise summertime open-air **concerts** around the lakes.

MotorCycles Legend Pub (☎ 635 49 45), Radniční 9. For the leather wearin', bleached-blond, tattooed, pierced crowd. Join the regulars beneath the skeleton lampshades at this hard-core club. Open M-Th 1pm-1am, F-Su 5pm-3am.

Restaurant Heaven Club Zeppelin, Nám. Otakara II 38, 3rd fl. (☎ 635 26 81). A younger crowd chills to classic rock in this great venue, and you can still hear yourself think. *Budvar* 25Kč. Open M-Th 11am-1am, F 11am-late, Sa 6pm-late.

Lucerna, on the corner of Nádraží and Skuherského. For those Budějovicers who just have to dance. 2 floors of disco. Cover 50Kč. Open M-Sa 9pm-7am.

▶ DAYTRIPS FROM ČESKÉ BUDĚJOVICE

HLUBOKÁ NAD VLTAVOU

*Buses run from České Budějovice to Hluboká nad Vltavou (25min.; frequently during the week, less so on weekends; 14Kč); look for buses with Týn nad Vltavou as their final destination. Get off of the bus at Pod Kostolem in Hluboká nad Vlatavou. As you exit the bus, head left on Nad parkovištěm, take the first right on the hill on Zborovskám and then a right to Bezručova at the street's end. Head uphill, bearing right at the fork in the path. Alternatively, take a 2hr. hike or a 30min. bike ride along the road from České Budějovice. The castle is on the right. ☎796 70 45. **Castle** open July-Aug. daily 9am-noon and 12:30-5pm; May-June Tu-Su 9am-noon and 12:30-5pm; Apr. and Sept.-Oct. Tu-Su 9am-noon and 12:30-4:30pm. Czech tours 80Kč, students 40Kč. English tours (approx. 3 per day) 150Kč/80Kč. **Armory** tours 100Kč/50Kč. **Grand tour** (armory, main tour, and theater) 90Kč/50Kč. In English 200Kč/120Kč. **Gallery** (☎796 70 41) open daily 9-11:30am and 12:30-6pm. 30Kč, students 15Kč.*

Hluboká is an ordinary town blessed with an extraordinary castle. The structure owes its appearance to Eleonora Schwarzenberg, who, after a visit to fashionable England, transformed the original Renaissance-Baroque castle into a Windsor-style fairytale stronghold in the 19th century. The 45min. tour winds through 20 of the castle's 141 rooms. Along the way, you'll find tapestries, paintings (including copies of Raphael and da Vinci), ostentatiously ornate wooden furniture, and more Schwarzenberg portraits than you can shake a stick at. Tours of Bohemia's second-largest **armory** are also available. If you aren't completely exhausted by the end of the tour, check out the **gallery** opposite the castle entrance, which shelters a fascinating display of Gothic Dutch and modern Czech sculptures and paintings.

TŘEBOŇ ☎(0)384

*Buses run from České Budějovice (40min.; every 30min., less on weekends; 22Kč). From the bus station, turn left on Sportovní and right on Svobody, which curves to the right. At Palackého nám., turn left and follow Sokolská out of the square, past the gardens, and through the underpass. Once Sokolská becomes Husova, take the first right to Březinova, which leads to the castle. The ticket booth is around the corner and under the clock. ☎72 11 93. Open June-Aug. Tu-Su 9am-5pm; Apr.-May and Sept.-Oct. Tu-Su 9am-4pm. There are 3 Tours: **Tour A** (45min.; 45Kč, students 25Kč); **Tour B** (45min.; 60Kč/30Kč); **Tour C** (30min.; 50Kč/25Kč). Last Tour 45min. before closing. English tour prices double. Groups should call 2 days ahead to reserve an English-speaking guide.*

The Třeboň Estate is ideally located in a town graced by a colorful center, shady parks, and a refreshing lake. The castle first belonged to the Rožmberk family, but was passed on to the Schwarzenbergs when last of line Petr Vok died in 1611. After being evicted from his Český Krumlov estate in 1602, Vok moved his court to Třeboň, which he constantly redecorated until death. His additions can be seen only through Tour A, which takes you through the medieval armories and kitchens before ending in a colorful salon decorated with smiling bears and 36 coats of arms. Tour B leads through the elegantly decorated 19th-century Schwarzenberg rooms, while Tour C uncovers the dog's kitchen, castle stables, and underground corridors. A more frightening exhibit introducing mythical characters of Bohemian legend, such as the woman of the woods, wild huntsmen, and werewolves, lies just beneath the foundation of the estate (20Kč).

CZECH REPUBLIC

TABOR TEL ☎(0)361

Buses run from České Budějovice (1hr.; about every hr., less on weekends; 59Kč). From the bus station, head right along Husov nám. with the park on your left. At the end of the park, go right on 9 Kvetne and continue through the commercial district until the road ends. Cross the small parking lot on Palackého. Follow it as it becomes Prazska and leads to Žižkovo nám. The museum is at Žižkovo nám 1. ☎25 42 86. Open May-Aug. daily 8:30am-5pm; Sept.-Apr. M-F 8:30am-5pm. Gallery and tunnel tour each 40Kč, students 20Kč. Tower open May-Oct. daily 8:30am-5pm. 32Kč, students 16Kč.

When the Catholic Church condemned heretic Jan Hus to death in 1415, a massive anti-Church movement took flight, upsetting the political balance of the 15th century and establishing Tabor as a Hussite stronghold. Today, a reconstructed Tabor offers gorgeous Renaissance and Baroque edifices edging its rambling cobblestone streets, but the Hussite influence perseveres throughout town. An enormous statue of war hero Jan Žižka guards the square, while military fortifications loom over the Luznice River. The **Hussite Museum** documents the history of the movement, and leads to the entrance of the 14km of **underground passageways.** The tunnels once housed the entire town for a full year following a disastrous fire. Follow Klokotská from the museum to the 13th-century **Ketnov tower** on the outskirts of town.

ČESKÝ KRUMLOV ☎(0)380

This once hidden gem of the Czech Republic has finally been discovered—some might say besieged—by tourists seeking refuge from Prague's hectic pace and overcrowded streets. Český Krumlov (TSCHes-kee KRUM-lov) still won't disappoint those who wander its medieval streets, raft down the meandering Vltava, and explore the enormous 13th-century castle that looms over it all. Weeks could be spent exploring and enjoying this UNESCO-protected town and its surrounding hills. Apart from hiking, horseback riding, and kayaking, the town lures visitors with affordable accommodations and burgeoning nightlife.

▐ TRANSPORTATION

Trains run from Nádražní 31 (☎71 14 77), 2km uphill from the center, to **České Budějovice** (50min., 9 per day, 46Kč). A bus runs from the station to the center of town (5Kč). **Buses** run from Kaplická 439 (☎71 54 15) to **České Budějovice** (30-45min.; M-F 24 per day, Sa 8 per day, Su 11 per day; 25Kč). For **taxis** call **Krumlov Taxi** (☎71 27 12) or **Taxi Růže** (☎71 17 11), or catch one in Nám. Svornosti.

▟ ORIENTATION

The curves of the winding **Vltava** River form the pocket that contains the central square, **Náměstí Svornosti.** The main **bus station** lies on **Kaplická,** southeast of the square. To get to Nám. Svornosti from the bus station, head up the path behind the terminal, near stops #20-25. Go downhill at the path's intersection with Kaplická. At the light, cross the highway and head straight on **Horní,** which leads into the square. If you get off at the **Špičák** stop north of town, it's an easy downhill march to the center. From Špičák, take the overpass, continue through **Budějovice Gate,** and follow **Latrán** past the castle and over the Vltava. It becomes **Radniční** as it enters Staré Město and leads to Nám. Svornosti.

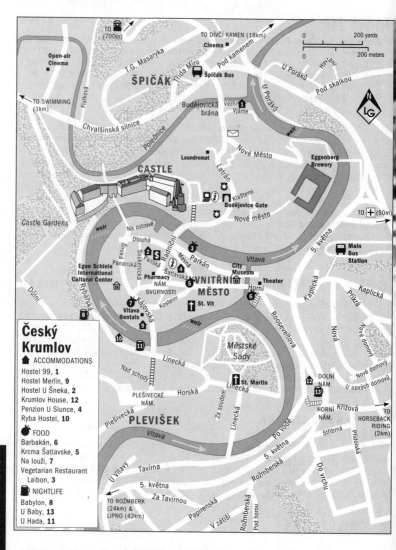

Český Krumlov

⌂ ACCOMMODATIONS
Hostel 99, **1**
Hostel Merlin, **9**
Hostel U Šneka, **2**
Krumlov House, **12**
Penzion U Slunce, **4**
Ryba Hostel, **10**

🍎 FOOD
Barbakán, **6**
Krcma Šatlavske, **5**
Na louži, **7**
Vegetarian Restaurant
Laibon, **3**

🍷 NIGHTLIFE
Babylon, **8**
U Baby, **13**
U Hada, **11**

🛈 PRACTICAL INFORMATION

Tourist Office: Nám. Svornosti 1 (☎ 70 46 22; fax 70 46 19; www.ckrumlov.cz/infocentrum). Books accommodations, sells trail **maps** (80-90Kč), and rents audio guides (2hr. 150Kč, students 100Kč; 3hr. 180Kč/120Kč; 500Kč deposit). Open July-Aug. daily 9am-8pm; May-June and Sept. daily 9am-7pm; Oct.-Aug. daily 9am-6pm.

Currency Exchange: Bank SMW, Panská 22 (☎ 71 22 21) cashes **traveler's checks** for 0.75% commission. 100Kč min. Open M, W, F 8:30am-5pm, Tu and Th 8:30am-4pm.

ATM: The ATM on the left side of Horní just before Nám. Svornosti accepts MC/V.

Luggage storage: At the **train station,** across from the ticket booths (15Kč per day). Open daily 6am-9pm.

Laundromat: Lobo, Latrán 73 (☎71 31 53). Part of the Lobo Pension. Wash 100Kč per load, dry 10Kč per 6min. Detergent and softener included. Open daily 9am-6pm.

Pharmacy: Nám. Svornosti 16 (☎71 17 87). Open M-F 8am-noon and 1-5pm.

Hospital: Horní Braná, Hřbitovní 424 (☎76 19 11, emergency 71 76 46). Just behind the bus station.

Telephones: Card-operated **telephones** outside post office. Buy cards inside and at local *tabaks*.

Internet Access: At the **tourist office** (see above). 10Kč per 10min. The **Internet Café** (☎71 22 19) in the castle courtyard offers 18 computers at 1.5Kč per min. Open June-Sept. daily 9am-10pm; Oct.-May 10am-10pm. The bar on the 2nd floor of **U Šneka** (see **Accommodations,** below) has another 3 computers for 1Kč per min.

Post Office: Latrán 193 (☎71 66 10). **Poste Restante** at window #2 on the right side as you enter. Open M-F 7am-6pm, Sa 7-11am.

Postal Code: 38101.

ACCOMMODATIONS

Krumlov's stellar hostels undoubtedly offer the best beds in town. They fill up quickly in summer, so make reservations at least four days in advance. **Private rooms** (*Zimmer frei* or *ubytování*) abound; look for signs on ul. Parkán or contact the **tourist office ❷** (see **Practical Information,** above; *pensions* start at 600Kč; private rooms doubles 800Kč).

Krumlov House, Rooseveltova 68 (☎71 19 35; zukowski3@hotmail.com). Follow the directions to Nám. Svornosti, turn left on Rooseveltova after the traffic lights, and follow the signs. Pay homage to the beautiful dragons emblazoned on its doors, and cross the threshold into the backpacker's Shangri-La. This former bakery is now a legendary hostel with a huge kitchen and a comfortable living room. The staff will do your laundry (100Kč per 5kg) and arrange everything from massages to horseback riding. 6-bed dorms 250Kč; doubles 600Kč; suites 750Kč. ❶

Hostel 99, Vezni 99 (☎71 28 12; fax 71 28 12; www.hostel99.com). From Nám. Svornosti, head down Radniční to its name change to Latrán and continue to the 13th-century red-and-yellow gate, then turn right on Vezni. Rock to the sounds of the gypsy band at affiliated Hospoda 99, or chill to the mellow beats of jazz on calmer nights. The outdoor terrace hosts barbecues and "free keg Wednesdays." When you finally decide to catch some z's, sleep in beds acquired from a 4-star hotel. Laundry service (200Kč), Internet (80Kč per hr.), and bike rental (200Kč per day) available. 4- to 10-bed dorm 300Kč; doubles 600Kč. ❷

Hostel U Šneka (Snail Hostel), Panská 19 (☎71 28 62, www.krumlos.cz). Follow the directions from the main bus station to Nám. Svornosti. Turn away from Horní, go to the right corner of the square, then head down Panská; it's on the right. Check in with the bartender and meet the tank of African snails. The immaculate, centrally located dorm stays quiet despite the rock club below, and is being expanded in 2003. Dorms 250Kč.

FROM THE ROAD

CZECH BUSES 101

Traveling by yourself can be lonely. A good book only kept me company for so long, and photographs of the places I visited seemed empty without smiling faces as their focal point. Some people enjoy traveling alone, but while it's nice to set your own pace, a little human contact is necessary to keep anyone sane. After weeks in the Czech Republic, I finally discovered a failsafe method for meeting people. Once I mastered the bus system, my lonely days in the Czech Republic were over. In fact, I not only made friends, I was idolized by my companions and seen as a savior of their lost souls. Once I knew the system, I became a knight in shining armor, a super-hero of sorts. When I saw a fellow tourist in need, I ran to help. When I unveiled the mystery of the bus system, astonished travelers refused to leave my side. I soon had lunch partners and dinner companions, and again became the subject of my own photographs, along with three or four of my new best friends. I was invited to visit their hometowns and kissed on the cheek by both men and women. My hard work should not be wasted, so here are the keys that will ensure you never spend a lonely day in the Czech Republic: "Czech Buses 101."

First, check the main schedule when you arrive at the station and locate the departure time of the bus to your destination. Then head to the ticket counter and ask them to confirm you have the correct information.

(continued on next page)

Hostel Merlin, Kájovská 59 (mobile ☎0606 25 61 45; www.ckrumlov.cz/nahradbach). Set out from the right-hand corner of Nám. Svornosti, across from the tourist office, drift left on Kájovská. Merlin is just before the bridge. The most peaceful hostel in town with a caring staff that respect your needs and your privacy. Right in the center. Full of modern rooms and newly remodeled bathrooms. Laundry 100Kč. 5-bed dorms 250Kč; doubles 500kč; triples 750Kč. ❶

Ryba Hostel (Fish), Rybářská 5 (☎71 18 01). Overlooking the Vltava across from the town center. See directions to Hostel Merlin (see above), and from there head over the bridge and take a right on Rybářská. The laid-back atmosphere allows you to forget that there are only 2 bathrooms in this 29-bed establishment. Sleep downstairs for 250Kč or in the rafters for 200Kč. 7th night free. ❶

Penzion U Slunce, Nám. Svornosti 2 (☎70 46 21; fax 70 46 19; www.ckrumlov.cz/uslunce). See directions to tourist office (see **Practical Information**, p. 274). The perfect melange of space and comfort. Huge, fully furnished rooms come with private bath, satellite TVs, and free coffee or tea. Located in the main square. Singles 590Kč; doubles 890-990Kč. 10% discount after 5 nights. Off-season discount. ❸

🍴 FOOD

While many restaurants unabashedly pander to the tourist masses, a few still manage quality and distinction in their cuisine. If you prefer to do it yourself, the central supermarket in town is **SPAR**, Linecká 49. (Open M-Sa 7am-6pm, Su 9am-6pm.)

🔲 **Na louži,** Kájovská 66 (☎71 74 46). From the square, go down Na louži opposite the tourist office and hang a right on Kájovská. Sizeable portions of great Czech cooking in a small wooden dining room with antique beer ads. Always packed with a mix of locals and tourists. Entrees 85-135Kč. Veggie options 54-71Kč. Open daily 10am-10pm. ❷

Krcma v Šatlavske, Horní 157 (☎71 33 44). On the corner of Šatlavská and Masná, just off the square. A roaring fire prepares the banquet for your medieval feast. Period music, waiters in medieval dress, and occasional performances by musketeers and swordfighters. Grilled meat 95-210Kč. Reservations recommended. Open daily noon-midnight. ❷

Barbakán, Kaplická 26 (☎71 26 79). Here you can savor the best meat dishes in town. Dine on the patio overlooking the river or inside the converted 13th-century battlement. Entrées 69-195Kč. Open daily June-Sept. noon-midnight; Oct.-May 3pm-11pm. ❶

Vegetarian Restaurant Laibon, Parkán 105 (☎72 84 56). Facing away from Horní in Nám. Svornosti, turn right on Radniční. Take the 2nd right on Parkán; the restaurant is on the left. Heaping portions of vegetarian dishes on a stone porch overlooking the Vltava. Entrees 50-110Kč. Open daily 11am-11pm. ❶

🔄 SIGHTS

Towering above Krumlov's houses from the other side of the Vltava since the 1200s, the **castle** has been home to a succession of Bohemian and Bavarian noble families. Follow Radniční across the river to the castle's main entrance on Latrán. Climb the stairs on the left and exit through the gate into the **stone courtyards.** It is free to see the sparkling Renaissance frescoes and the **garden** above the castle. Two tours take you into the castle: the first covers the older Renaissance rooms and the decadently Baroque **Schwarzenberg chambers,** before concluding in the festive excess of **Masquerade Hall.** The second tour gives the history of the Schwarzenberg family and their 19th-century homes. (Enter through the 3rd stone courtyard, just after the moat with the bears. ☎70 47 21; castle@ckrumlov.cz. Open June-Aug. Tu-Su 9am-6pm; May and Sept. Tu-Su 9am-noon and 1-5pm; Apr. and Oct. Tu-Su 9am-noon and 1-4pm. Last tour 1hr. before closing. 1hr. Czech tour 70Kč, students 40Kč. English tour 140Kč/70Kč. Garden open daily June-Aug. 8am-7pm; May and Sept. 8am-6pm; Apr. and Oct. 8am-5pm.) Tours of the **Mansion Baroque Theater** cover the rest of the structure. The majority of the tour is dialogue, so tours in English are recommended. (English tour 170Kč, students 90Kč; Czech tour 100Kč/50Kč.) From the castle **tower** you can take in a fine view of the town. (Open daily June-Aug. 9am-5:30pm; May and Sept. 9am-6pm, last admission 5:35pm; Oct. and Apr. 9:30am-4:30pm. 30Kč, students 20Kč.) More hardy souls should wander among the eerie melodies and distorted sculptures of the **crypt.** (Open June-Aug. daily 10am-5pm. 20Kč, students 10Kč.) Less creepy, though no less controversial, the 🎨 **Egon Schiele International Cultural Center,** Široká 70-72, highlights the work of Austrian painter Egon Schiele (1890-1918), who set up shop here in 1911. The citizens ran him out of town, however, when he started painting burghers' daughters in the nude. The infamous nudes now share wall space with top-notch exhibitions of other 20th-century art. (☎70 40 11. Open daily 10am-6pm. 150Kč, students 75Kč.)

Next, go to the departure stand and check the schedule there. This is often difficult, as there are numerous sheets outlining various bus routes forcing you to look at all of them to find the time corresponding to your destination. If all three times match, then you're on the right track. Before basking in your success, look above the initial departure time of the scheduled route to check for special symbols. Crossed mallets indicate buses that run only on weekdays. The number six inside a circle means that the bus runs only on Saturdays, unless it is accompanied by the two mallets, which means that it also runs Monday through Friday. A cross or a seven inside a circle indicates buses running on Sundays. A "K" or "L" accompanied by a number corresponds to notes at the bottom of the schedule which detail periods of time during which the bus does not run as scheduled. You should also check the arrival time at your destination: if you see a vertical or zig-zagged line running through it, this means that the bus is an express, and passes through but does not stop at this destination. As a final precaution, check with the driver to make sure the bus is going where you think it is. Remember that patience is a virtue when dealing with Czech buses, and even the most savvy traveler should be prepared to wait once in a while. However, if you master the secrets of the bus schedule and use your knowledge to help others, at least you'll never have to wait alone.

—Dalibor Eric Snyder

📻🎭 ENTERTAINMENT AND FESTIVALS

Hike into the hills for a pleasant afternoon of **horseback riding** at **Jezdecký klub Slupenec,** Slupenec 1. Rides take you through trails high above Český Krumlov. Follow Horní from the town center to its intersection with the highway. At the second light, turn left on Křížová and follow the red trail to Slupenec. (☎71 10 52; www.jk-slupenec.cz. Open Tu-Sa 9am-6pm. 250Kč per hr. Full-day trip with refreshments from 2000Kč. Call ahead.) Most hostels rent out inner-tubes so you can drift the day away on the river. Jump out under the arched bridge before you float into Budějovice. **Vltava,** Kájovská 62, rents all kind of boats and bikes, and transports you to the departure point or from your destination. (☎/fax 71 19 78; www.ckvlatava.cz. **Kayaks** from 390Kč per day; **canoes** from 640Kč per day; **rafts** from 960Kč per day. Open Apr.-Sept. **Mountain bikes** 200Kč per 6 hr. or 300Kč per day, plus a 3000Kč deposit or a credit card. Open June-Aug. daily 9am-8pm; Sept.-May 9am-6pm. AmEx/MC/V.) If you're not up for a swim in the Vltava, check out the town's **indoor pool** (*plavecky bazen*) and **steambaths** (*para*). For 20Kč per hour, you can plunge into the icy-cold waters and then sweat off your beers in a steamroom. From the town square, take Radniční to Latrán. Once past the castle and the post office, turn left on the highway *Chvalšinská* and swing right on Fialková after the stream and across from the tennis center. (Pool open Tu and Th 7-8:30am, 2-5pm, and 6-10pm; W and F 6-8:30am, 1:30-4pm, and 6-10pm; Sa 1-10pm; Su 1-9pm. Steambaths open W and F-Sa 6-9pm. 20Kč per hr. 20Kč lock deposit.)

The **Revolving South Bohemia Theater** (Otáčivé Hlediště) in the castle garden hosts opera, Shakespeare, and classic comedies. Sitting in the bleachers as they rotate to face the different sets is as entertaining as the Czech-only shows. (Open June-Sept. Shows at 9pm. The tourist office lists current showings and sells tickets. 260-390Kč.) If you'd prefer English entertainment, the **cinemas** in town usually show English-language films with Czech subtitles. **Kino J&K,** Highway 159 next to the Špičák bus stop, shows the latest Hollywood blockbusters year-round. (☎71 18 92. Shows at 7 and 9:30pm. 54-69Kč.) The same company runs the town's summer **open-air cinema.** Follow the directions to the swimming pool until you see the **Letni Kino** on your right. (Shows at 9:30pm. 59-69Kč.) The **Five-petal Rose Festival,** Krumlov's hip medieval gig the third weekend of June, is a great excuse to wear tights and joust with the locals. The weekend is one big party, so book accommodations months in advance. Krumlov also hosts two world-class music festivals: both the **Early Music Festival** in the second week of July and the mid-August **International Music Fest** attract renowned classical performers.

🍸 NIGHTLIFE

Party animals in Český Krumlov enjoy the city's full array of bars and cafes, many of which line Rybářská. The night tends to start early here, around 8pm.

U Hada (Snake Bar), Rybářská 37 (☎71 58 95). The live snakes that slither beneath the bar feast on mice while a younger crowd sociably searches for drinks, lost in the thick smoky haze. 0.5L beer 22Kč. Open M-Th 7pm-3am, F-Sa 7pm-4am, Su 7pm-2am.

U baby (Granny's), Rooseveltova 66 (☎71 23 00). Next-door to Krumlov House (see **Accommodations,** p. 275). Pronounced "Ooh Bah-bee" and not "ooh Baby," as the regulars will growl over their beers (15-22Kč) at this medieval bar. As the drinks flow, the locals grow less gruff, joining the nearby hostel-goers as they jam to Creedence Clearwater Revival and the Grateful Dead. Open Tu-Su 6pm-late.

Babylon, Rybářská 6, by Ryba Hostel (see **Accommodations,** p. 275). A bar where anything goes: bikers and hippies toss down beers together at the bar and out on the terrace, while the locals discuss Czech politics. Occasional live music. *Budvar* 18Kč. Open daily noon-late. Kitchen closes 10pm.

OUTDOORS

Local firms rent mountain bikes (see **Entertainment**, p. 278). There are a couple of routes that begin in Český Krumlov itself. The first is a 70km loop along the banks of the Vltava, the second a much shorter, hillier trip. Check the weather before heading out.

LONG ROUTE (70KM). For a ride along the Vltava, turn right on the bridge from Vltava Travel. Cross the river, turn left on Linecká, and then turn right as it crosses the river again to intersect Po vodě. At the highway intersection, turn right on Května, cross the river, and follow the signs to **Rožmberk** (24km). This winds through the towns of **Vetřní** and **Záton**, which is so little that only the church perched atop the hill tells you you're in a town. Follow the banks of the river until you see a pale fortress on the left. Rožmberk, seat of the mighty **Rožmberks Castle**, is around the bend. (☎74 98 38. Open June-Aug. Tu-Su 9am-5:15pm; Apr.-May and Sept.-Oct. Tu-Su 9am-5:15pm. Tours every hr. Czech tour 60Kč, students 35Kč. Call ahead for English tour; 120Kč, students 70Kč.) **Lipno** lies another 18km upstream, and the "up" part of "upstream" becomes particularly evident here. On the way, look for the ancient **Cistercian monastery** at **Vyšší Brod**. More pleasant than Lipno, **Frýmburk** sits along the lake shore 8km west. Complete with a waterside church, this town is very Swiss. From here a road leads back to Český Krumlov; the next 22km are mostly downhill. If you can't make it this far, head back the way you came: there's no alternate route. Travelers daunted by the hills can take a **bus** from Krumlov to Rožmberk (20Kč) or Lipno (27Kč) from the main bus station. Bikes are not allowed on buses.

SHORTER ROUTE (40KM). Unlike the road that curves around the Vltava, this route north heads through hillside meadows. Take Horní across the river to its intersection with the highway. Turn left at the light and follow the highway as it veers left and crosses the river. At the sign toward Budějovice, hang a right and head uphill, turning toward **Srnín;** two gas stations and a supermarket point the way. Be careful crossing rail tracks. Turn right when the road splits near a factory and head into the meadow. From here, you'll whiz through Srnín, following the signs to **Zlatá Koruna.** The long descent ends in front of the 1263 **monastery,** where a tour winds through massive courts, halls, a convent, a church, and the second-largest library in the Czech Republic. Over the course of its tumultuous history, the local order of monks was abolished several times before being stripped of its property in 1785. Since then, the building has been a pencil factory and an unappreciated tourist attraction. (☎74 31 26. Open June-Aug. Tu-Su 8am-noon and 1-5pm; Apr.-May and Sept.-Oct. Tu-Su 9am-noon and 1-4pm. Last tour 45min. before closing. Minimum 5 people; available in English. 55Kč, students 25Kč.) From here, walk your bike back uphill. At the T-junction, go straight toward **Křemže.**

After entering **Třísov,** take the second right (by the village notice board) and cross the railway line just below the station. Continue down this stone path toward the river. After 10min. you'll reach the river bank, where the stone path becomes a sidewalk and comes to a metal bridge. Lock your bike, cross the bridge, and head left. Be sure not to cross the second metal bridge. Up the steps on the right, you'll find the 1349 ruins of the castle **Dívčí kámen.** Climb atop the ruins for a gorgeous view of the Šumava region. Getting out of Dívčí kámen can be brutal. Once out of Třísov, however, the trip home is mostly downhill.

SHORTEST ROUTE (17KM). A third option is to catch a train with your bike from Český Krumlov to Horní Planá (1hr., every 2-3hr., 37Kč) and enjoy the downhill 17km coast with a gorgeous vista of the countryside. Facing away from the train station, turn right on the dirt path, left on the first road, and then right at the intersection with the highway. Signs point the way back to Český Krumlov.

CZECH PARADISE (ČESKÝ RÁJ)

Centuries of volcanic activity, erosion, and other environmental factors carved Cesky Raj into the fairy-tale landscape it is today. Picturesque valleys, towering rock towns, and dense forests typify what Czechs affectionately call their Bohemian Paradise. A State Nature Preserve since 1951, Český Ráj offers spectacular views, some stellar climbing, and a dense network of trails perfect for hikers.

JIČÍN   ☎(0)433

While attractive Renaissance and Baroque buildings line its streets, Jičín's architectural beauty remains second to that of its sister city, Prague. Yet visitors flock to this Bohemian village considered the gateway to Český Ráj. Its convenient location just minutes from the park makes it the perfect base camp for nature lovers.

⊑ TRANSPORTATION. Trains run from **Prague** (2½hr., 8 per day, 66Kč), but usually require a stopover. **Buses** from Prague-Florenc to Jičín (1¾hr., 7 per day, 85Kč) are the best means of transportation to the town. As bus and train schedules in Jičín change frequently, it's a good idea to call or to visit the station in advance.

▓✷ ORIENTATION AND PRACTICAL INFORMATION. Valdštejnovo náměstí (Wallenstein Square) is the center of town. It meets **Žižkovo náměstí** through Valdice Gate. Shops, cafes, and restaurants line **Husova,** which stretches out from Valdštejnovo nám. Just off Husova, **Šafaříkova** leads to the **bus station.** The **train station** is at Dělnická 297. (☎53 11 11. Office open daily 6am-5:30pm.) The **tourist office** at Valdštejnovo nám. 1 sells **maps** (39Kč) of the town and various hiking areas in Český Ráj. It also organizes river rafting, rock climbing, mountain biking, and hiking excursions. (☎/fax 53 43 90; ceskyraj@consultour.cz. Open M-Sa 9am-5pm, Su 9am-noon and 4-6pm.)

GE Capital Bank, Žižkovo nám. 4, **exchanges currency** for 2% commission. (☎53 54 92. Open M and W 8am-noon and 1-5pm, Tu and Th-F 8am-noon and 1-4pm.) An **ATM** sits next to the tourist office. The **police station** is at Balbínova 27. (☎58 41 11. **Emergency** ☎158. Open M and W 8am-5pm; reception open daily 7am-3:30pm.) There's a **pharmacy** at Tylova 812, just off Žižkovo nám. (☎53 16 59. Open M-F 8am-5pm, Sa-Su 8am-noon.) **Telephones** are in the main square. **Internet Cafe Jičín,** Husova 1058, has some of the best rates in the country. (☎52 34 12. 1Kč per min., students 47Kč per hr. Open M-F 10am-10pm, Sa-Su 6-10pm.) The **post office** is at Šafaříkova 141. (☎58 51 11. Open M-F 8am-6pm, Sa 8-noon.) **Postal Code:** 506 01.

▛⬔ ACCOMMODATIONS AND FOOD. The cheapest beds are 10min. from town at **Motel Rumcajs ❶,** Koněva 331, where camping spaces and beds are always available. Don't be turned off by the broken-down cars at the attached service garage; the rooms are clean and comfortable. From Valdštejnovo nám., take Nerudova to B. Němcové and turn right. Head through Komenského nám., then bear left on Kollárova, which becomes Koněva. (☎53 10 78; www.rumcajs.cz. Doubles 240Kč; triples 405Kč; quads 540Kč. Camping 25Kč per person, 30-50Kč per tent.) The 11-story **Hotel Start ❷** towers above the trees at Revoluční 863. Follow Žižkovo nám. and then take Havlíčkova until it becomes Revoluční. A Czech version of Club Med, Hotel Start offers dining, swimming, water slides, bowling, tennis, and an outdoor track. Sore hikers can enjoy a massage or a dip in the jacuzzi next door. (☎52 38 10; fax 52 39 16; www.hotelstartjc.cz. Breakfast included. Dorms 240Kc; singles 690Kč; doubles 990Kč. AmEx/MC/V.) **Hotel Paříž ❷,** Žižkovo nám. 3, is a great deal in a great location. Spacious rooms hold 1970s revival decor—swivel chairs, orange lamps, and tablecloths to match. It also houses a buffet-style restaurant. (☎53 27 50. Singles 450Kč; doubles 790Kč.)

Most of Jičín's restaurants serve decent food at affordable prices. **Restaurant Lucie ❷**, Fügnerova 197, bathes its trendy clientele in class and candlelight, offering an international menu highlighted by ice-cream desserts. (☎53 11 92. Entrees 70-110Kč, dessert 30-45Kč. Reservations required. Open M-Th 10am-10pm, F-Sa 10am-11pm. AmEx/MC/V.) For a more relaxed meal, head over to **U Matěje ❸**, Nerudova 45. A dining room decorated with hunting gear and mounted animals serves Greek cuisine (125-140Kč) and Czech specialties (130-160Kč). If the dining hall's regulars intimidate you, chill in the beer garden with a more youthful crowd. (Open daily 10:30am-10pm.) Grab groceries at **Fa Market**, Komenského nám. 57. (Open M-F 6am-6pm, Sa 6am-noon, Su 7am-11am.)

◙ ◘ **SIGHTS AND ENTERTAINMENT.** The entrance to the main square is through **Valdice Gate**. Ascending the **gate-tower** via its steep, creaky stairs provides a view of town. (Open Mar.-Sept. daily 9am-5pm. 10Kč.) Next door is the **Church of St. James**. Constructed between 1627 and 1634, this magnificent church boasts a mesmerizing painted dome. (Open daily 9am-5pm.) Enter the Italian-designed **chateau** through the wooden doors in the arcade by the church. The building is home to a **museum** dedicated to archaeological finds from the Jičín region. The Renaissance, Outdoor Life, Prussian-Austrian War, and WWI rooms are worth a peak. (Open M 9am-5pm, Tu-Su 8am-4pm. 50Kč, students and children 30Kč.) The main square draws crowds to its outdoor markets, but if you prefer to stay in, Hotel Start offers **bowling** and **swimming** facilities to the public. (Bowling 180Kč per hr. Open M-F 2pm-2am, Sa-Su 11am-2am. Swimming 30Kč, students 20Kč per hr. Open M 2-9pm, Tu-Sa 10am-9pm, Su 10am-8pm. Sauna 50Kč, students 40Kč.)

◪ **HIKING AND OUTDOORS.** Numerous **trails** cross **Český Ráj National Preserve.** Red signs mark the long **Golden Trail,** which connects Prachovské skály (Prachovské Rocks) to Hrubá skála (Rough Rock). Green and yellow signs guide hikers to additional vistas and sights, while triangles denote vistas off the main trails.

To hike in **Prachovské skály,** catch a bus from Jičín to Český Ráj (15min., several per day, 9Kč). Check with the tourist office to see if buses are running less frequently than scheduled, as they sometimes do. You can also walk to the park along the relatively easy 6km trail, beginning at the Motel Rumcajs in Jičín (see p. 280). The **ticket office** sells trail guides (35Kč) at the base of the rocks; follow the red trail to get there. Hiking trails wind through Prachovské skály's sandstone formations, the ruins of the 14th-century rock **castle** Pařez, and the rock pond Pelíšek. (Open daily 8am-5pm. Park entrance 25Kč, students 10Kč. Castle open Apr.-Oct. Swimming in rock pond May 1-Sept. 1.)

To get to **Hrubá Skála**, take a **train** from Jičín (45min., 12 per day, 43Kč round-trip). At Hrubá Skála, follow the signs to the blue trail, which leads behind the train station to the right, over the tracks, and uphill to the castle. This rock town surrounds a hilltop castle-turned-hotel, where hikers can enjoy some of the best views of the famous Trosky sandstone rocks (entrance to the hotel 15Kč). The roadside trails tend to be more level than those in Prachovské skály, but offer similarly breathtaking views. The red trail leads from the castle up to the ruins of **Valdštejnský hrad** (Wallenstein Castle), a contested commodity during the Hussite Wars of the 15th century. A peek through the archers' window evokes romantic visions of knights defending the castle from the enemy below.

CZECH REPUBLIC

EAST BOHEMIA

From the fertile lowlands of the Elbe to the mountain ranges that create a natural border with Poland, the often-overlooked East Bohemia has skiing, sightseeing, and swimming opportunities to spare. Under Habsburg rule, the Czech language was kept alive among the people of East Bohemia. Consequently, it was within these villages that many of the 19th-century Czech intellectuals and nationalists were born. Today, Hradec Králové, the region's administrative and cultural center, combines marvelously preserved medieval buildings with a lively urban pace.

HRADEC KRÁLOVÉ ☎ (0)49

At the confluence of the Elbe and the Orlice Rivers, Hradec Králové (HRA-dets KRAh-loveh), literally "Queens' Castle," once served as a depository for royal widows, but now caters to a much younger crowd. Cyclists and university students rule the avenues and boulevards of this East Bohemian town, one of the most lively areas in the Czech Republic. In fact, bicycles are so popular that the town developed a separate road for them, complete with stoplights and traffic signs. Though the students disappear during the summer months, the town's energy does not. Hradec prides itself on its ability to entertain, scheduling numerous cultural events, festivals, and outdoor activities throughout the year. Lacking the dizzying tempo of Prague, Hradec Králové offers a more relaxed atmosphere and the leisure to explore its rivers, historic squares, and fine architecture at your own pace.

▐ TRANSPORTATION

Trains: Riegrovo nám. 914 (☎553 75 55). To **Prague** (2hr.; every hr. 6am-8pm; 140Kč one-way, 2-5 person group rate 138Kč round-trip per person). Open daily 3am-11:30pm; info center open daily 6am-7pm.

Buses: S.K. Neumanna 1138 (☎553 35 30), next to the train station. Buses to **Prague** (2hr., every hr., 75-80Kč) leave from in front of the train station. Info center open M-F 5:30am-6pm.

Public Transportation: Tickets (8Kč) sold at kiosks, at the station, and on board (10Kč).

Taxi: Sprint Taxis (☎140 14) wait in front of the train station.

■✳❷ ORIENTATION AND PRACTICAL INFORMATION

Hradec Králové feels like two separate towns separated by the **Labe** (Elbe) River. On the west side, the pedestrian-only **Čelakovského** is a favorite local drag along the shop-infested **Nové Město** (New Town). The east side is home to the churches and cafes of **Staré Město** (Old Town). The **train** and **bus stations** are next to each other, on the edge of Nové Město away from the river. To get to **Velké náměstí** (Great Square) from the stations, take a right on Puskinova and then a left on **Gočárova**. Follow Gočárova through Nové Město to the river, cross the bridge, and continue for one block. When you hit **Čs. armády,** head left and then turn right on **V kopečku,** which leads to Velké nám. Alternatively, buses #1-3 and 5-17 go to the center from the train station.

Tourist Office: Information Center, Gočárova třída 1225 (☎553 44 82; fax 553 44 85; www.ic-hk.cz). English-speaking staff arranges accommodations and sells tickets for events in town. Free maps and information on town festivals. Open June-Aug. M-F 8am-6pm, Sa 9am-3pm; Sept.-May M-F 8am-6pm.

Budget Travel: GTS, Čelakovského 623 (☎551 58 25), next to the pharmacy. Discounted airline and bus tickets for students. Open M-F 8:30am-5:30pm.

Currency Exchange: Komerční Banka, Čelakovského 642 (☎581 55 50), at Masarykovo nám. 2% commission on currency exchange. **ATM** inside. Open M-F 8am-5pm.

Luggage storage: At the train station. 10Kč per bag. Lockers 5Kč. Open daily 5am-10pm.

International Bookstore: Skippy Bookstore, Střelecká 748 (☎61 57 24). Small English section. Open M-F 8am-6pm, Sa 8am-noon. MC/V.

Police: Haškova, near the train station. **Emergency** ☎158. Open 24hr.

Pharmacy: Centrální lékárna, Masarykovo nám. 637 (☎551 16 14), across from Komerční Bank. Open M-F 7am-6pm, Sa 8am-noon.

Hospital: (☎583 11 11). On Sokolská, south of the old town.

Internet Access: Jowin Digital, Gočárova 1261 (☎553 65 95; www.joiwn.cz), across from the tourist office, 2nd fl. 59Kč per hr., includes a cup of coffee. 1Kč per min. otherwise. Open M-F 8am-8pm, Sa 9am-noon.

Post Office: (☎553 37 15). On Riegrovo nám., next to the train station. Get a ticket from the machine in the waiting area. Send packages at window #7 or 8. Card **telephones** in front. Cards can be purchased inside. Open M-F 7am-7pm, Sa 7am-1pm.

Postal Code: 500 02.

ACCOMMODATIONS AND FOOD

You won't find budget accommodations in the center of town. The best rooms for your buck are at **Hotel Dům ❶,** Heyrovského 1177, a 10min. walk from Staré Město. From the train station, take bus # 1, 9, 21, or 28 to Heyrovského, cross Sokolská, and take the first right on Heyrovského. Incredibly clean and cheap, and all rooms come complete with fridges and desks. (☎551 11 75; fax 551 13 21; www.hotelovydum.cz. Reception 24hr. Singles 230Kč; doubles 320Kč.) Outside the center, **Hotel Garni ❷,** Na Kotli 1147, is a step up: all rooms have baths. Take bus #1, 9, or 28 from the station to Hotel Garni; it's to the right of the bus stop. (☎576 36 00; fax 526 25 91; hotel.garni@worldonline.cz. Breakfast included. Reception 24hr. Dorm singles 400Kč; apartment singles 550Kč (apartment singles include TV, fridge, telephone); doubles 1000Kč. Discounts for HI members.) **Hotel Stadion ❸,** Komenského 1214, has more expensive rooms directly in Staré Město, as well as a pool and a weight room. Take bus #2 or 16 from the station to Fortna, then backtrack on Komenského. (☎551 46 64; fax 551 46 67. Breakfast included. Reception 24hr. Singles 670Kč; doubles 770Kč; triples 990Kč; quads 1170Kč. MC/V.)

Staré Město boasts many pubs and restaurants that offer traditional Czech cuisine. In Nové Město, **Pivnice Gobi ❶,** Karla IV 522, is an underground hangout with inexpensive meals but a limited menu. This student haven features pool, darts, foosball, and a big-screen TV. (☎551 10 03. Entrees 30-84Kč. Open M-Th 2:30pm-1am, F 2:30pm-3am, Sa 5pm-3am, Su 5pm-1am.) The best lunch option is **Jídelna Praha ❶,** Gočárova 1229, a local favorite serving high-quality food and large portions at low prices. (☎618 97. Entrees 33-50Kč. Open M-F 6:30am-4pm, Sa 9am-12:30pm.) The **supermarket** giant Tesco, Nám. 28. října 1610, sells groceries. (☎507 21 11. Open M-F 7am-8pm, Sa 7am-7pm, Su 8am-6pm.)

SIGHTS AND ENTERTAINMENT

Most sights in Hradec Králové are in **Velké nám.,** the center of Staré Město. Here, the 1307 **Church of the Holy Spirit** (Kostel Svatého Ducha) attests to the town's royal past, with priceless items such as a 1406 tin baptismal font (one of the oldest in Bohemia) and tower bells affectionately named Eagle (Orel) and Beggar (Žebrák). (Open M-Sa 10-11am and 2:30-3:30pm, Su 2-3:30pm.) Climb up the 71m **White Tower** (Bílá věž) beside the church to see Bohemia's second-largest bell. Keep your clapper-meister tendencies to yourself, however—eight burly men have been assigned

CZECH REPUBLIC

to perform the honor on special occasions only. (Open Tu-Su 9am-noon and 1-5pm. 15Kč.) In the middle of the square, the excellent **Gallery of Modern Art** (Galerie moderního umění), at #139, showcases 20th-century Czech painting and sculpture. The ascending floors lead chronologically through Czech stabs at Impressionism, Cubism, Expressionism, and more recent works. (☎ 55 14 89 36. Open Tu-Su 9am-noon and 1-6pm. 20Kč, students 10Kč.) Walk across the square from the museum to the **Church of the Assumption of the Virgin Mary** (Kostel Nanebevzetí Panny Marie), constructed by Jesuits from 1654 to 1666. Prussian soldiers destroyed its interior in 1792, but 19th- and 20th-century renovations have revived this Baroque beauty. (Open daily 10am-5pm. 20Kč, students 10Kč.) Fish lovers can find peace at the **Ohří Aquarium**, Baarova 1663. To get there from Velké nám., cross the Elbe River on Gočárova and bear left on to V. Lipkách. After you cross Střelecká, Baarova will be on the left. Walk across the tropical rain forest bridge or through the tank while 40 species of fish swim above and therapeutic music plays in the background. (☎ 553 45 55. Open Th-Su 9am-6pm. 60Kč.)

In late October, Hradec Králové's largest festival, **"Jazz Goes to Town,"** features musicians from all over the world. The action takes place at the Aldis Center, Eliščino náb. 357 (☎ 505 21 11), and at pubs all over town, but you can buy tickets at the tourist office (www.jazzgoestotown.com). The **Theater Festival of European Regions** is usually held in the last two weeks of June. Classic and modern plays are performed daily all over town by professional groups from the Czech Republic and surrounding regions. If you're looking for a relaxing pub, **Hogo Fogo Bar**, 19 Eliščino náb., is where the students flock when night falls. (☎ 551 55 92. Beer 17Kč. Open M-Th 1pm-1am, F 1pm-3am, Sa 4pm-3am, Su 4pm-1am.)

■ DAYTRIPS FROM HRADEC KRÁLOVÉ

LITOMYŠL ☎ (0)464

Buses run from outside the train station in Hradec Králové (1hr., 1 per hr., 54Kč). Trains are infrequent and inconvenient. From the bus station, turn left on Mařákova and follow it over the river to Tyršova. Turn left and then bear left again at Braunerovo nám. to get to Smetanovo nám., the main square. The tourist office, at Smetanovo nám. 72, provides free maps of the town. (☎/fax 61 21 61; www.litomysl.cz. Open Tu-Su 9am-5pm.)

Birthplace of "Bartered Bride" composer **Bedřich Smetana** and the only small town to have hosted seven Central European presidents at once, tiny Litomyšl has made a big name for itself in the world of art and politics. It maintains its historic local feel with its magnificent chateau, pristine gardens, and banana-shaped Staré Město (Old Town). Vratislav of Perštejn built Litomyšl's magnificent **chateau** between 1568 and 1581 after the supreme chancellor ordered its construction for his wife Marie Manrique de Lara of the Spanish Mendoza family, who missed the Renaissance architecture of her home. The elegant arcades are adorned by thousands of *sgrafitti*, which, like snowflakes, are wholly unique geometrical shapes. Tours wind through the chateau's salons and parlors but the main attraction is the 1797 wooden **theater** inside. To get here from the square, ascend Váchalova, take a right, and hang a quick left up the covered stairs. (☎ 61 10 66. Open May-Sept. Tu-Su 9am-noon and 1-5pm; Apr.-Oct. Sa-Su 9am-noon and 1-5pm. Full tour 100Kč, students 50Kč. English tours 200Kč. English info available.) During the last weeks of June, the courtyard houses the **Smetana Opera Festival** (June 20-July 1; ticket office ☎ 61 60 70). Visitors can also stroll through the birthplace of composer **Bedřich Smetana** on the castle grounds. (☎ 61 52 87. Open May-Sept. Tu-Su 9am-noon and 1-5pm; Oct.-Apr. Sa-Su only or by appointment. 20Kč, students 10Kč.) Opposite the chateau, locals lounge among the garden statues of **Klášterní Zahrady.** Two blocks away, on Terezy Novákové 75, lies the **Portmoneum House,** decorated by experimental painter **Josef Váchal** in the 1920s. (Open May-Sept. daily 9am-noon and 1-5pm. 20Kč.)

THE ZOO AT DVŮR KRÁLOVÉ NAD LABEM ☎(0)437

Štefánikova 1029. ☎82 95 15; zoodkr@dk.fairnet.cz; www.zoodk.cz. Buses run from outside the train station in Hradec Králové (45min., 6 per day, 37Kč). Turn right out of the bus station on Listopadu, walk 2 blocks, and turn left on Švehlova. Cross the town square diagonally and take your 1st left downhill to Husova. From there, follow the zoo signs to the park. Alternatively, take a local bus from the station to the zoo. (Every 30min., 8Kč). Open May-Sept. daily 9am-6pm; Feb.-Apr. and Oct.-Nov. 9am-4pm; Dec.-Jan. 9am-7pm. 100Kč, students 65Kč, parking 50Kč. Ticket price includes park and safari bus.

Founded in 1946, the zoo at Dvůr Králové nad Labem is the largest animal park in the Czech Republic and houses all of your favorite quadrupeds and monkeys. In the summer (May 15-Sept. 30, weather permitting) follow the signs to the **safari bus** (15-20min., every 25min.), which embarks on a journey through the wild side of the park where the herds roam free. Between the gallery and the summer exhibit, you'll find monkeys, birds, and the popular carnivores. While the 2km walk to the safari past the zebra and rhino enclosure is the highlight, there is also a **mini-train** (5-10min., 25Kč) that leaves from outside the restaurant "Rotunda" to transport you there. To the left of the main entrance, a **gallery** displays various natural history exhibits alongside some colorful dinosaur portraits. (Open daily 10am-6pm. 10Kč.) For a great lunch, grab a tray at **U Lemura ❶**, at the zoo's entrance, and fill up on its home-style meals for 52-64Kč. (☎66 70 66. Open daily 9am-6pm.) The **ticket office** at the main entrance has zoo **maps** (5Kč) and sells a handy English **guidebook** (55Kč).

MORAVIA

Wine-making Moravia makes up the easternmost third of the Czech Republic. Home of the country's finest folk-singing and two leading universities, it's also the birthplace of a number of Eastern European notables, including Tomáš G. Masaryk, first president of Czechoslovakia, psychoanalyst Sigmund Freud, and chemist Johann Gregor Mendel, who founded modern genetics in a Brno monastery. Tourists have yet to weaken Brno's cosmopolitan vigor or disrupt Olomouc's cobblestoned charm. Outside the city, the low hills of the South Moravian countryside harbor the remarkable caves of Moravský Kras and the architectural pearls of Telč.

BRNO ☎(0)5

The Czech Republic's second-largest city, Brno (berh-NO; pop. 388,900) has been an international marketplace since the 13th century. Brno's grocers today sell fruits and vegetables at the very same sites their ancestors have used for 800 years. The market has grown: today, emissaries of global corporations compete for space and sales among local produce stands. The result is a dynamic and spirited city where historic churches soften the glare from the clubs that line some of its streets.

▐ TRANSPORTATION

Trains: Nádražní (☎42 21 48 03 or 41 17 44 43). Trains connect to every major city in the Czech Republic. To: **Prague** (3hr., 16 per day, 257Kč); **Bratislava, SLK** (2hr., 9 per day, 203Kč); **Budapest, HUN** (4½hr., 2 per day, 864Kč); **Vienna, AUS** (2hr., 1 per day, 543Kč).

Buses: (☎43 21 77 33). On the corner of Zvonařka and Plotní. Follow Plotní from the trains past Tesco and take the pedestrian underpass. Buses connect to every major city in the country. To **Prague** (3hr., several per day, 112-167Kč) and **Vienna, AUS** (2½hr., 3 per day, 250Kč).

Public Transportation: Trams, trolleys, and **buses** cost 12Kč, 15Kč if purchased on board; 24hr. pass 48Kč. Luggage 5Kč. Buy tickets at a *tábak* or any kiosk. The fine for riding ticketless is 600-1000Kč and ticket checks are common. Tram routes #90 and above run all night; the rest run daily 5am-10pm.

Taxis: Impulse Taxi (☎45 21 66 66). Taxis line the corner of Starobrněnská and Husova.

■✷🛈 ORIENTATION AND PRACTICAL INFORMATION

Brno's compact center makes everything in town accessible by foot. Its main streets radiate from **Nám. Svobody** (Freedom Square). From the entrance to the **train station,** cross the tram lines on **Nádražní,** take a left, walk 15m, and then turn right on **Masarykova,** which leads to Nám. Svobody. From the bus station, follow **Plotní** over **Zvonarka** to the train station and go left on Nádražní; Masarykova is on the right.

Tourist Office: Kulturní a informační centrum města Brna, Radnická 8 (☎42 21 10 90; fax 42 21 07 58). From Nám. Svobody, go down Masarykova and turn right on Průchodní. The office is inside the town hall. Sells city **maps** (7Kč). Open M-F 8am-6pm, Sa-Su 9am-5pm.

Budget Travel: GTS International, Vachova 4 (☎42 22 19 96; fax 42 22 10 01). English spoken. ISIC 250Kč. Open M-F 9am-6pm, Sa 9am-noon.

Currency Exchange: Komerční banka, Kobližná 3 (☎212 71 11), just off Nám. Svobody. Gives V **cash advances,** cashes **traveler's checks** for 2% commission (50Kč minimum), and has an AmEx/MC/V **ATM.** Open M-F 8am-5pm.

Luggage Storage: At the train station. 13Kč per bag per day. Lockers 10Kč per day.

Laundromat: Kavarna Pradelna, Hybesova 45. Take tram #1 or 2 from the train station to "Hybesova." 25m ahead on the left. Wash 60Kč, dry 40Kč, detergent 20Kč. Offers **Internet** access for 30Kč per hr. Open daily 10am-10pm.

Pharmacy: Kobližná 7 (☎42 21 21 10). Open M-F 7am-7pm, Sa 8am-1pm. MC/V.

Hospital: Urazova Nemocnice, Ponavka 6 (☎45 53 81 11). From Nám. Svobody take Kobližná to Malinovského nám. Continue on Malinovského nám. to Cejl (300m) and take a left on Ponavka.

Internet Access: Internet Center Cafe, Masarykova 2/24. 52 quick computers in the center of town. 40Kč per hr. Open daily 8am-midnight.

Post Office: Poštovská 3/5 (☎42 15 36 27). **Poste Restante** at the corner entrance. Open M-F 7am-7pm, Sa 8am-noon.

Postal Code: 601 00.

▐ ACCOMMODATIONS

Brno's hotel scene is geared toward the business suit, so it comes as no great surprise that one of the city's budget hotels was recently replaced by the "Moulin Rouge Erotic Night Club Disco." Though few and far between, budget options are available, especially in the summer. Off-season, the staff at the local tourist office (see **Tourist Office,** above) can arrange **private rooms** ❶ (from 400Kč).

Hotel Astorka, Novobranská 3 (☎42 51 03 70; fax 42 51 01 06; astorka@jamu.cz). Head up Masarykova from the train station and take the 1st right on Josefská. At the fork, veer right on Novobranská, and cross Orli. This brand-new, centrally located hotel has incredibly clean and modern facilities, a beautiful outdoor terrace, shared bathrooms, and a restaurant. Reception on the third floor. Doubles 420Kč per person, students 210Kč; triples 315Kč/158Kč. ❷

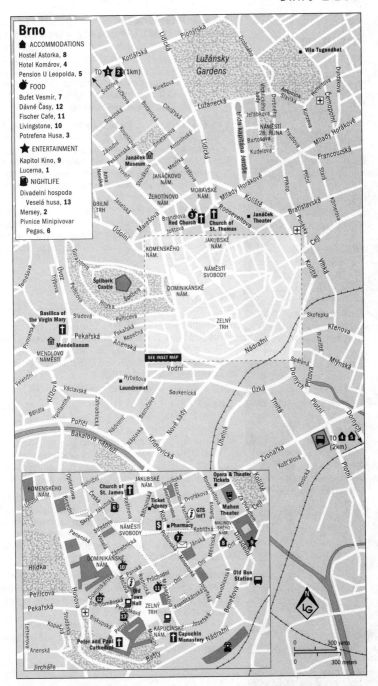

Brno

🏠 **ACCOMMODATIONS**
Hostel Astorka, **8**
Hotel Komárov, **4**
Pension U Leopolda, **5**

🍴 **FOOD**
Bufet Vesmír, **7**
Dávné Časy, **12**
Fischer Cafe, **11**
Livingstone, **10**
Potrefena Husa, **3**

⭐ **ENTERTAINMENT**
Kapitol Kino, **9**
Lucerna, **1**

🎵 **NIGHTLIFE**
Divadelní hospoda
    Veselá husa, **13**
Mersey, **2**
Pivnice Minipivovar
    Pegas, **6**

IN RECENT NEWS

THE ROMA DILEMMA

While cycling through the small own of Vetřní, near Český Krumlov, I suddenly saw an onion hit the pavement right in front of my bicycle. When I lifted my eyes from the smashed vegetable, I saw a young Roma boy running from the scene in hysterical laughter. I began to watch my surroundings more carefully and noticed that many of the people in his small town were Roma. Alongside the road, Czech police officers were separating two Roma men who continued to scream insults at each other. This was not the first time I'd encountered Roma during my trip. In Brno, I'd noticed an elderly Czech man scolding a group of young Roma children on a bus, as well as two Roma women who began fighting in the main square while observers stood shaking their heads. And in almost every city I visited, hostel owners warned me to watch my wallet around the gypsies.

The Roma dilemma stares Czech society in the face everyday; situations and stereotypes like those I've witnessed serve as a constant reminder that something must be done. Around 75-90% of Roma in the Czech Republic are unemployed, giving them a standard of living far below that of the average citizen.

(continued on next page)

Pension U Leopolda, Jeneweinova 49 (☎45 23 30 36; fax 45 23 39 49). Take tram #12 or bus #A12 to the last stop (Komárov). Take a left behind the *tábak* huts on Studnicni. At the end of Studnicni, turn right on Jeneweinova. Beautifully furnished rooms with TV and private bath. The ground floor houses an intimate restaurant with a cozy fireplace. Singles 577.50Kč; doubles 750.80Kč; triples 981.80Kč. ❸

Hotel Komárov, Brati Zurku 5 (☎45 23 31 97; fax 45 23 41 87). Take tram #12 or bus #A12 to the last stop (Komárov). Continue toward the overpass on the opposite side of the street. Take the 2nd-to-last turn before the overpass on the unmarked Pompova. Walk 200m, go right on Lomena, and then take the 1st left to the hotel, which is marked by a large sign. A high-rise dormitory well out of the center. Plain doubles with showers and baths. Currently being renovated, but should be open in 2003. Temporary facilities located down the road at Lomena 48. Open July-Sept. 15. Doubles 390Kč. ❷

🍴 FOOD

Street-side pizza joints far outnumber traditional *párek* peddlers. The fruit and vegetable **market** (open M-F 9am-6pm) still thrives on Zelný trh., while the supermarket **Tesco** offers a somewhat larger selection at Dornych 4, behind the train station. (☎43 54 31 11. Open M-F 7am-8pm, Sa 7am-7pm, Su 8am-6pm.)

Dávné Časy, Starobrněská 20 (☎42 21 52 92). Located up Starobrněnská from Zelný trh. As the Czech inscription at the entrance reads, forget your problems and revisit the world of heroic knights and medieval feasts. Dig into huge portions of Czech cuisine (99-189Kč) amid medieval stone walls, suits of armor, and dungeon gates. Open daily 11am-11pm. AmEx/V. ❸

Livingstone, Dominikánské nám. 5 (☎/fax 42 21 00 90). Take Zámečnická from Nám. Svobody and head left on Dominikánské nám. An angsty student population chills to American music under the African decor at this multicultural pub. Entrees 50-110Kč; beer 20Kč. Open M-F 10am-2am, Sa-Su 5pm-2am. ❷

Potrefena Husa, Moravské nám. 8 (☎42 21 31 77). Follow Rašinova from Nám. Svobody 3 blocks to the corner of Joštova. It ought to be hard to start a night in style at a place named "The Messed-Up Goose," yet the trendy Czechs at the sleek monochrome bar do just that. Bar food 70-95Kč. Beer 20Kč. Open daily 11am-1am. MC/V. ❷

Fischer Cafe, Masarykova 8/10 (☎ 42 22 18 80). Filled with beautiful people busy chatting on cell phones, sipping bottled water, and ignoring one another, this cafe serves up a touch of New York, along with some ingenious entrees (110-200Kč) and salads (60-95Kč). Open M-F 8am-10pm, Sa 9am-10pm, Su 10am-10pm. ❸

Bufet Vesmír, Kobližná 8. From Nám. Svobody, head down Kobližná; Vesmír is on the right. Great for a quick, cheap, and filling meal (45-60Kč), but be prepared to stand over your plate in this chair-less establishment. Open M-F 7am-7pm, Sa 8am-1pm. ❶

🔅 SIGHTS

PETER AND PAUL CATHEDRAL. (Biskupská katedrála sv. Petra a Pavla.) Brno was allegedly saved from the Swedish siege of 1645 in one day. The attacking general promised to retreat if his army didn't capture the city by noon, so when the townsfolk learned of his claim, they rang the bells one hour early and the Swedes slunk away. The bells have been striking noon at 11am ever since. Although the retreating Swedes burnt the cathedral as they withdrew, some of it was left intact, and the remains of the earliest Romanesque church on Petrov are still visible in the current cathedral's crypt. *(On Petrov Hill. Climb Petrska from Zelný trh. Cathedral open M-Sa 6:15am-6:15pm, Su 7am-6pm. Chapel, towers, and crypt open M-Sa 10am-5:30pm, Su 1-5:30pm. Cathedral free. Chapel 10Kč, students 7Kč. Towers 25Kč/20Kč. Crypt 10Kč/7Kč.)*

ŠPILBERK CASTLE. (Hrad Špilberk.) Once home to Czech kings and later a mighty Habsburg fortress, Špilberk has had quite a past. After a brief stint as the city's main fortress against the Swedes, the castle served as a prison for convicted criminals, as well as for Hungarian, Italian, Polish, and Czech revolutionaries of the 18th and 19th centuries. During World War II, the Nazis imprisoned their own unwanteds here. The castle's corridors are now extensive galleries detailing the history of the prison and of Brno. Trek through the moat's tomb-like encasements, where the most dangerous criminals were imprisoned. *(From Nám. Svobody, take Zámečnická through Dominikánské nám. and go right on Panenská. Cross Husova and follow the paths uphill. ☎ 42 21 41 45; muzeum.brno@spilberk.cz. Open May-Sept. Tu-Su 9am-6pm; Oct. and Apr. 9am-5pm; Nov.-Mar. W-Su 9am-5pm. Call ahead to reserve an English tour. 90Kč, students 45Kč. Castle tower 20Kč/10Kč.)*

The Roma's illiteracy rates are also high, and unlikely to improve, as schooling for Roma children is poor. Many never attend school, and those who do are often relegated to schools for the mentally challenged. The situation worsens as Roma families are pushed outside city centers into run-down homes where they are less visible to tourists and secluded from society.

The European Union (EU) has urged the Czech Republic to provide better services for the Roma and to halt the blatant discrimination they face. In fact, the EU has gone so far as to warn the Czech Republic that they will not be offered membership until they have addressed the Roma question. As the country is eagerly hoping to join the EU by 2004, the Czech government has begun to make a serious effort to improve Roma living conditions. However, among most members of Czech society, the perception that the Roma are second-class citizens has diminished little.

—Dalibor Eric Snyder

CAPUCHIN MONASTERY CRYPT. (Hrobka Kapucínského kláštera.) If bones and bodies catch your fancy, you'll love this morbid resting place. The monks at the Capuchin Monastery Crypt developed a revolutionary embalming technique and preserved more than 100 18th-century monks and assorted worthies. The displayed results now enlighten the living: the crypt opens with the Latin inscription, "Remember death!" and ends with the dead monks's dark reminder: "What you are, we were. What we are, you will be." *(Just to the left of Masarykova from the train station.* ☎ *42 21 32 32. Open May-Sept. M-F 9am-noon and 2-4:30pm, Sa 11-11:45am and 2-4:30pm. Free English brochures are available. 40Kč, students 20Kč.)*

AROUND MENDEL SQUARE. (Mendlovo náměstí.) In the heart of Old Brno, the high Gothic **Basilica of the Assumption of the Virgin Mary** (Basilika Nanebevzetí Panny Marie) houses the 13th-century **Black Madonna,** the Czech Republic's oldest wooden icon, which purportedly held off the Swedes in 1645. *(From Špilberk, walk downhill on Pelicova and take the stairs to Sladová. Go left on Úvoz to Mendlovo nám. Open M-Sa 6-7:15pm, Su 7am-12:15pm and 6-7:15pm.)* The Augustinian monastery next door was home to **Johann Gregor Mendel,** the father of modern genetics. The newly renovated and expanded **Mendelianum,** Mendlovo nám. 1a, features slide shows, audio presentations, and exhibits of Mendel's genetic work that document the monk's life and experiments. While the Nazis and the Lysenkoist Communists distorted his theories after his death, visitors James Watson and Francis Crick redeemed Mendel by proving his hypotheses almost a century later. By 2003, the Mendelianum will include a bee house and a modern version of Mendel's greenhouse. The hops and barley grown within it will be used by the brewery next door where, by tasting the beer, you'll be able to fully appreciate Mendel's work. *(☎ 43 42 40 43. Open Tu-Su 10am-6pm. English info book 85Kč. 80Kč, students 40Kč.)*

OLD TOWN HALL. (Stará radnice.) The stuff of old legends fills the crannies of the the Old Town Hall. Its crooked Gothic portal supposedly took on its shape after the carver blew his commission on too much Moravian wine. As for the dismayed stone face looking out on Mecova from the back of the hall, rumor has it that it's the petrified head of a burgher who met his doom there after siding with the Hussites in 1424. The most famous tale involves the stuffed "dragon" hanging from the ceiling in the passageway. Legend says that the dragon perished after devouring an ox carcass that had been stuffed with quicklime. As thirst began to overwhelm him, he downed a whole river—and his belly burst. In actuality, however, the dragon is an Amazonian crocodile Archduke Matyáš gave Brno to garner favor among the burghers. *(Radnická 8, just off Zelný trh. Open Apr.-Oct. daily 9am-4:30pm. 20Kč, students 10Kč.)*

AROUND NÁMĚSTÍ SVOBODY. The partially gold **Plague Column** (Morový sloup) in the square has successfully warded off infections for the last 300 years. North of Nám. Svobody along Rašínova, the **Church of St. James** (Kostel sv. Jakuba) was built for Brno's medieval Flemish and German communities. The French Huguenot Raduit de Souches, who helped save Brno from Swedish invasion in 1645, rests within the church. On the way back to the square, go left along Koblížná and turn left on Rooseveltova for a game of comparative architecture. On the right is the grand **Mahen Theater** (Mahenovo divadlo), built by the Viennese duo Helmer and Fellner in the 19th century. Two blocks down, the 1960s **Janáček Theater** (Janáčkovo divadlo) is Brno's opera house.

🎵 🎭 ENTERTAINMENT AND NIGHTLIFE

The Old Town Hall hosts frequent summer **concerts;** buy tickets at the tourist office's ticket agency, Běhounská 16. (☎42 21 08 63. Open M-F 8am-noon and 1-6pm.) Get **theater** and **opera** tickets at Dvořákova 11. (☎42 32 12 85. Open Sept.-June M-F 8am-noon and 1-4:30pm.) **Cinemas** that play Hollywood flicks abound (80-140Kč). **Kapitol Kino,** Divadelní 3 (☎42 21 33 51), features American blockbusters; **Lucerna,** Minská 19 (☎74 70 70), shows British and American indie films. Look for posters advertising **techno raves,** Brno's hottest summer entertainment. While it's easier to find a beer hall than a wine pub in the heart of wine-producing Moravia, there is an occasional *vinárna* (wine cellar; bottles 80-120Kč).

Divadelní hospoda Veselá husa (Merry Goose Theatrical Pub), Zelný trh 9 (☎42 21 16 30). Just behind the theater, this pub attracts an artsy group of regulars; the largest crowd gathers right after performances in the attached Merry Goose Theater. *Pilsner* 23Kč. Open M-F 11am-1am, Sa-Su 3pm-1am.

Pivnice Minipivovar Pegas, Jakubská 4 (☎42 21 01 04). This modern microbrewery has a loyal following among the young crowd tossing back homemade brews at the wooden bar inside. Pints 15.60Kč. Open daily 9am-midnight. MC/V.

Mersey, Minská 14 (☎41 24 06 23). Take tram #3 or 11 from Česká to Tábor and continue down Minská. Features live bands and DJs, sometimes from overseas, playing a variety of genres from funk to disco to reggae to rock depending on the night. Large crowds gather for theme events such as U2 night. Beer 19Kč. Occasional cover F-Sa 30Kč. Open M-Sa 8pm-late.

📷 DAYTRIPS FROM BRNO

🏛 MORAVSKÝ KRAS CAVES   ☎(0)506

Take a train (30min., 7 per day, 43Kč round-trip) from Brno to Blansko. From there, either hike the 8km on the green trail from Blansko to Skalní Mlýn or take the bus (15min., 5 per day, 8Kč) from the station up the road from the trains. Get there early, as tours are likely to sell out. If you can't get to the caves until later, call ahead to reserve a spot on the tour. At Skalní Mlýn, there's a ticket and info office (☎41 35 75; fax 41 53 79; www.cavemk.cz) and a shuttle to the cave (round-trip 40Kč, students 30Kč). You can also walk to the caves along the road (1.5km). The BVV travel agency in Brno, Starobrněnská 20, organizes afternoon tours. (☎42 21 77 45. 640Kč per person, 4-person minimum.)

Inside the forested hills of Southern Moravia sits the network of caves that comprises Moravský Kras (MO-rahv-skee krahs). The most popular is **Punkevní,** where tour groups pass magnificent stalactites and stalagmites to emerge at **Stepmother Abyss** (Propast Macocha). Legend has it that a wicked stepmother threw her stepson into the gaping hole. When villagers found the boy hanging by his trousers, they saved him and threw in the woman instead. The tour concludes with a chilly boat ride down the eerily calm underground Punkva river. (Apr.-Sept. tours 8:20am-3:50pm; Jan.-Mar. and Oct.-Dec. tours 8:20am-2pm. Buy tickets for the tour at Skalní Mlýn's bus stop or in the entrance. 80Kč, students 40Kč. Cameras 10Kč, video 50Kč.) Those craving more can explore the other caves in the area: **Balcarka** (45min. tour; open Apr.-Sept. M-F 7:30am-3:30pm, Sa-Su 8:30am-3:15pm; Oct. M-F 7:30am-1:30pm, Sa-Su 8:30am-2:30pm;

Feb.-Mar. 9 11am and 1:30pm tours; 40Kč, students 20Kč); **Kateřinská** (30min. tour; open Apr.-Sept. 8:20am-4pm; Oct. 8:20am-2pm; Feb.-Mar. 10am, noon, 2pm tours; 40Kč, students 20Kč); **Sloupskošošůvské** (1hr. tour; open Apr.-Sept. 7:30am-3:30pm; Oct. 8am-1:30pm; Feb.-Mar. 10am, noon, 1pm tours; 40-60Kč, students 20-30Kč). Visitors may also take a cable car to the top of **Stepmother Abyss** (60Kč, students 40Kč) and marvel at the view, or set out on the leisurely hiking trails of the **Moravský Kras Reserve.**

TELČ
☎ (0)66

Buses from Brno to České Budějovice stop at Telč (2hr., 8 per day, 80-85Kč). The bus station lies 5min. from Nám. Zachariáše z Hradce. Follow the walkway and turn right on Tyršova, then left on Masarykovo. Pass under the archway on the right to enter the square. Castle open May-Aug. Tu-Su 9am-noon and 1-5pm; Mar.-Apr. and Sept.-Oct. Tu-Su 9am-noon and 1-4pm. Final tour leaves 1hr. before closing. Tour 60Kč, students 30Kč; English tour 120Kč. Museum open same hours as castle. Last admission 30min. before closing. 20Kč, students 10Kč. Gallery open May-Aug. Tu-Su 9am-5pm; Apr. and Sept.-Oct. Tu-Su 9am-noon and 1-4pm; Nov.-Mar. Th-F and Su 9am-noon and 1-4pm, Sa 9am-1pm. 20Kč, students 10Kč. Tower open June-Aug. Tu-Sa 10-11:30am and 12:30-6pm, Su 1-6pm; May and Sept. Sa-Su 1-5pm. 15Kč, students 10Kč.

The Italian aura of Telč (TELCH) stems from a trip **Zachariáš of Hradec,** the town's ruler, took to Genoa, Italy, in 1546. He was so enamored of the new Renaissance style that he brought back a battalion of Italian artists and craftsmen to spruce up his humble Moravian castle and town. Stepping over the cobblestone footbridge into the main square makes it easy to see why UNESCO named the gingerbread town of Telč a World Heritage Monument; the square is flanked by long arcades of peach-painted gables, lime-green Baroque bays, and time-worn terra-cotta roofs.

It's easy to get caught up browsing the center's porticos and watching local children perform traditional Moravian songs and dances, but it's well worth tearing yourself away for a tour of Telč's castle. There are two options—tour A and tour B, both 45min. Tour A goes through the Renaissance hallways past tapestries, exotic hunting trophies, through the old chapel, and under extravagant ceilings; tour B leads through the rooms decorated in the 18th and 19th centuries that have been left untouched since the Czech state seized control of the castle in 1945. Any of the guidebooks on sale around town (from 15Kč) provides useful commentary in English; the ticket office also has some free English pamphlets. In the arcaded courtyard, a **museum** displays examples of Telč's folklore. The **gallery** is a memorial to artist **Jan Zrzavý** (1890-1977), who trained as a neo-Impressionist, dabbled in Cubism, and produced some religious paintings (see **History,** p. 217). This eclectic collection of work is definitely worth a glimpse.

Beside the castle grounds stands the town's **tower.** If you can bear the winding stairs and unstable ledges, climb to the top to take in a magnificent view of Telč. Those who prefer to stay closer to the ground can rent **rowboats** from **Půjčovna lodí,** and enjoy the view in the company of swans. (Open June 20-Aug. daily 10am-8pm. 20Kč per 30min.) For further information, there's a **tourist office** in the town hall, Nám. Zachariáše Hradce 10. (☎ 724 31 45; fax 724 35 57; info@telc-etc.cz. Open M-F 8am-6pm, Sa-Su 9am-6pm.)

OLOMOUC
☎ (0)68

More charming than Brno and less touristed than Prague, Olomouc (OH-lo-mohts; pop. 103,372), the historic capital of Northern Moravia, is a city that embodies the best aspects of the Czech Republic. By day, locals enjoy the masterfully rebuilt town center where Baroque architecture lines cobblestone paths. At night, the student population takes over, keeping the clubs thumping well into the morning light.

▐ TRANSPORTATION

Trains: Jeremenkova 23 (☎548 21 75). To **Brno** (1½hr., 7-8 per day, 112Kč) and **Prague** (3hr., 19 per day, 224Kč).

Buses: Rolsberská 66 (☎531 38 48). To **Brno** (1½hr., 10 per day, 84Kč) and **Prague** (4hr., 3 per day, 215Kč).

Public Transportation: The city's **trams** and **buses** all require 6Kč tickets, sold at kiosks by the station.

Taxis: Eurotaxi (☎522 47 70). Taxis congregate in front of the train station and at the intersection of Riegrova and Národních hrdinů.

▋ ORIENTATION

Olomouc's Staré Město (Old Town) forms a triangle, in the center of which is the enormous **Horní náměstí** (Upper Square). Behind the *radnice* (town hall), **Dolní nám.** (Lower Square) connects with Horní nám. **Masarykova třída** leads west from the train and bus stations to the town center, though not before changing its name to **1. máje** and then to **Denišova.** Trams or buses marked "X" shuttle between the **train station** and the center (5 stops, 6Kč per ticket). Get off at Koruna and the gigantic **Prior** department store, then follow **28. října** to Horní nám. Alternatively, trams #1-6 stop just outside the center. Get off at **Nám. Hrdinů** and follow **Riegrova** to the center. The **bus station,** beyond the train station, is connected to the center by trams #4 and 5.

▐ PRACTICAL INFORMATION

Tourist Office: Horní nám. (☎551 33 85; fax 522 08 43; inforcentrum@olomoucko.cz), in the *radnice*. Sells **maps** (20Kč), and books hotels, hostels, and private rooms. English spoken. Open daily Mar.-Nov. 9am-7pm; Dec.-Feb. 9am-5pm.

Budget Travel: CKM, Denišova 4 (☎522 21 48; fax 522 39 39). Sells ISICs (200Kč) and train tickets. Open M-F 9am-5:30pm.

Currency Exchange: Komerční banka, Svobody 14 (☎550 91 11) and Denišova 47 (☎550 91 69), cashes most **traveler's checks** for 1% commission and gives MC **cash advances** for 2% commission. Denišova branch gives AmEx/MC **cash advances** for a 2% commission. Open M-F 8am-5pm.

Luggage Storage: At the **train station.** 10Kč per piece per day; 24hr. lockers 5Kč. At the **bus station.** Lockers 5Kč.

English Bookstore: Votobia, Riegrova 33 (☎522 39 98). A few shelves of English titles in the back of the store. Open M-F 8:30am-6pm, Sa 9am-noon.

Pharmacy: Lekarná, on the corner of Ostružnická and Horní nám. behind the town hall. Open M-F 7:30am-6pm, Sa 8am-noon.

Hospital: Fakultni Nemocnice, IP Pavlova 6 (☎585 11 11; fax 541 38 41). Located southwest of the center off Albertova.

Internet Access: Internet Cafe, Denišova 35 (☎523 30 81). Dirt-cheap Internet access (40Kč per hr.). Open M-F 9am-8pm, Su 1-7pm. **Synapse,** 1. máje. (☎522 52 94). 1Kč per 2min. 10am-5pm; 1Kč per min. after 5pm. Funky blue lights and lounge booths make typing comfortable. Open M-F 9am-midnight, Sa-Su 7pm-late.

Post Office: Horní nám. 27. Open M-F 7am-6pm, Sa 8am-noon.

Postal Code: 772 00.

ACCOMMODATIONS

The cheapest beds (200Kč) pop up in summer when **university dorms ❶** open to tourists. Inquire at the **tourist office** for more information on arranging these accommodations, as well as **private rooms ❶** (from 200Kč).

Hostel Betánie, Wurmova 5 (☎523 38 60; fax 522 11 27). Take tram or bus "X" to U Domu on 1. máje. Wurmova is on the left. Spacious sleeping quarters off 2 large common rooms (one with a TV and one with dining facilities) on each floor. Bathrooms are pristine, and bedrooms are cozy. Reception 6am-10pm. Singles 420Kč; doubles and triples 300Kč per person. ❷

Pension na Hradbách, Hrnčílská 14 (☎/fax 523 32 43; aquaveria@iol.cz). From Horní nám., head down Školní, go straight along Purkrabská, and turn right on Hrnčílská. A small *pension* in the quiet streets of the town center. Like living at home, except no one bothers you. Worth calling ahead for one of the 3 rooms. Luxurious singles with private bath and TV 600Kč; doubles 800Kč; triples 900Kč. ❸

Penzion Best, Na Strelnici 48 (☎/fax 523 14 50). Take tram #1 or 4-7 to Nám. Hridinů, then hop on bus #17, 18, or 22 to Na Strelnici. Continue in the same direction until the hotel appears on your right (10min.). An excellent deal, as all rooms have bathrooms and TVs. Breakfast 40Kč. Singles 380Kč; doubles 620Kč. MC/V. ❷

Národní Dům, 8. května 21 (☎522 48 06; fax 522 49 83). From Horní nám., head down 28. října past Prior department store and bear left. Slightly outdated decor, but each room comes with TV, radio, telephone, and private bath. Centrally located. Singles 515Kč; doubles 730Kč; triples 945Kč. ❸

FOOD

Good food is easy to find in Olomouc, which offers everything from Czech fare to Chinese food. Pick up essentials at the **24hr. grocery** at Komenského 3. (☎522 43 64.)

U červeného volka (At the Red Bull), Dolní nám. 39 (☎522 60 69). A treat for vegetarians; these tofu pioneers serve delicious soy and pasta dishes (50-70Kč). Open M-Sa 10am-11pm, Su 11am-11pm. ❶

Cafe Caesar, Horní nám. (☎522 92 87), in the town hall. They say Caesar was the founder of Olomouc. He could have fed (and protected) his armies on the garlicky pizzas (30 varieties; 25-130Kč) and cheap plates of pasta (45-95Kč) at this cafe. Open M-Sa 9am-1am, Su 9am-midnight. V. ❷

U Kejklire (The Juggler), Michalská 2 (☎523 05 19), behind the town hall. Fashionable ambiance and elegant dining characterize this restaurant. Serves healthy portions of steak (87-181Kč), other meats (80-150Kč), and veggies (37-82Kč). Open M-Sa 10:30am-10pm, Su 11am-9pm. MC/V. ❸

SIGHTS

The massive 1378 **town hall** *(radnice)* and its spired clock tower dominate the town center. The tourist office arranges trips up the tower for 10Kč. (Daily at 11am and 3pm.) A wonderful **astronomical clock** is set in the town hall's north side. In 1955, communist clockmakers replaced the mechanical saints with archetypes of "the people"; since then the masses strike the hour with their hammers and sickles. The 35m black-and-gold **Trinity Column** (Sloup Nejsvětější Trojice) soars higher than any other Baroque sculpture in the country. One of Europe's largest Baroque organs bellows each Sunday in the **Church of St. Maurice** (Chram sv. Mořice), 28. října; it also stars in Olomouc's **International Organ Festival** each September.

Going back to Horní nám., take Mahlerova to the intimate **Jan Sarkander Chapel** (Kaple sv. Jana Sarkandra) on the right, which honors a Catholic priest tortured to death by Protestants in 1620 after he refused to divulge a confessee's secret. There's an exhibit on his "threefold torture" inside. (Open daily 9am-4pm. Free.) Continue on Mahlerova, turn left on Univerzitní, and then right on Denišova. The **Museum of National History and Arts** (Vlastivědné Muzeum), Nám. Republiky 5, chronicles the history of the astrological clock and displays beautiful time pieces from the 17th to the 19th centuries. Visit the zoological exhibit to see lifelike creatures of the forest in natural poses. (☎551 51 11; www.vmo.cz. Open Apr.-Sept. Tu-Su 9am-6pm; Oct.-Mar. W-Su 10am-5pm. 40Kč, students 20Kč.)

From Nám. Republiky, continue away from the center on 1. máje and then climb Dómská on the left to reach Václavské nám. Let the spires of **St. Wenceslas Cathedral** (Metropolitní Kostel sv. Václava) lead the way. The church interior is in impeccable condition, having been reworked virtually every century since it was damaged by fire in 1265. The crypt exhibits Christian paraphernalia, including the gold-encased skull of St. Pauline (Sv. Pavlína), Olomouc's protectress. (Open M-W and F-Sa 9am-5pm, Th 9am-4pm, Su 11am-5pm. Free.) Next door to the cathedral, the walls of the wondrous **Přemysl Palace** (Přemyslovský palác) are covered in pristine, if fading, frescoes. Across the square sits the former **Capitular Deaconry** (bývalé Kapitulní děkanství), where an 11-year-old Mozart composed his *Symphony in F major* while his peers were learning to tie their shoelaces. Continue away from the center on 1. máje and go right on Kosinova to reach the path that runs through **Bezrucovy sady,** the city park. For a peaceful afternoon, stroll through the beautifully manicured grounds and sculptures of the Botanical Garden located across the stream. (Open Apr. 9:30am-4pm, May-Sept. 9:30am-6pm. 15Kč, students 10Kč.)

▧ NIGHTLIFE

Dance the night away at **Exit Discoteque,** Holická 8, the Czech Republic's largest outdoor club. From Horní nám., walk to Dolní nám., then follow Kateřinská to 17 Listopadu (400m). Turn left, then take a right on Wittgensteinova and follow it across the bridge (200m). The club will be on the right. Eight bars ensure that you'll never wait for a drink, and the terraces are perfect for sipping a drink while watching the dancing below. (☎523 05 73. Cover 50-60Kč. Open June-Sept. F-Sa 9pm-5am.) The popular **Depo No. 9,** Nám. Republiky 1, pours *Staropramen* (20Kč) in three underground rooms with metallic decor and comfy seats. In the wee hours, the basement becomes Olomouc's most happening student dance club, with frequent live rock performances. (☎522 12 73. Occasional cover 50-100Kč. Open M-Th 10am-2am, F 10am-6am, Sa 7pm-6am, Su 7pm-midnight.) Closer to town is **Barumba,** Mlýnská 4, which churns out the techno along with the beer. Follow Pavelčákova out of Horní nám. then turn left on Mlýnská. (☎520 84 25; www.barumba.cz. Beer 14Kč. Cover men 30-60Kč, women free. Open M-Th 7pm-2am, F 9pm-6am.)

ESTONIA (EESTI)

KROONS

AUS$1 = 8.76EEK	1EEK = AUS$0.11
CDN$1 = 10.21EEK	1EEK = CDN$0.10
EUR€1 = 15.65EEK	1EEK = EUR€0.06
NZ$1 = 7.47EEK	1EEK = NZ$0.13
UK£1 = 24.65EEK	1EEK = UK£0.04
US$1 = 15.90EEK	1EEK = US$0.06
ZAR1 = 1.50EEK	1EEK = ZAR0.67

Happy to forget its Soviet past, Estonia has been quick to revive its historical and cultural ties to its Nordic neighbors, as Finnish tourism and investment revitalizes the nation. The material wealth that has accumulated in Tallinn, however, masks the declining living standards that lurk outside of big cities, as well as the chagrin of the ethnically Russian minority over Estonia's Finnish leanings. Still, having overcome successive centuries of domination by the Danes, Swedes, and Russians, Estonians are now proud to take their place as members of modern Europe.

ESTONIA AT A GLANCE

OFFICIAL NAME: Republic of Estonia

CAPITAL: Tallinn (pop. 408,608)

POPULATION: 1.4 million (68% Estonian, 26% Russian, 6% other)

LANGUAGES: Estonian (official), Russian

CURRENCY: 1 Estonian kroon (EEK) = 100 cents

RELIGION: Evangelical Lutheran, Russian Orthodox, Estonian Orthodox

LAND AREA: 45,226km^2

CLIMATE: Maritime

GEOGRAPHY: Lowlands; 1520 islands

BORDERS: Latvia, Russia

ECONOMY: 66% Services, 30% Industry, 4% Agriculture

GDP: US$10,000 per capita

COUNTRY CODE: 372

INTERNATIONAL DIALING PREFIX: 800

HISTORY

THOR, BJÖRN, AND THE GANG. Estonia's newfound freedom stands in contrast to a long history of foreign domination and repression. Ninth-century **Vikings** were the first to impose themselves on the Finno-Ugric people who had settled the area long before. In 1219, King Valdemar II of **Denmark** conquered northern Estonia. Shortly thereafter, Livonia, now southern Estonia and northern Latvia, fell to German knights of the **Teutonic Order,** who purchased the rest of Estonia in 1346.

TERRIBLE IVAN AND KINDER SWEDISH KINGS. German domination continued until the emergence of Russian Tsar Ivan IV (the Terrible), who, in the **Livonian War** of 1558, crushed many of the tiny feudal states that had developed in the region. In an attempt to force Ivan out, the defeated states searched for foreign assistance: northern Estonia capitulated to Sweden in 1629, while Livonia joined the Polish-Lithuanian Commonwealth. During the **Swedish Interlude** (1629-1710), a number of Estonian-language schools and **Tartu University** (p. 326) were established.

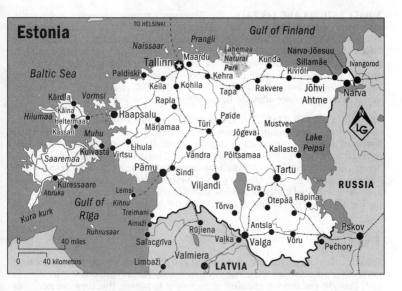

THE RUSSIANS, TAKE TWO. The Russians invaded once more and the 1721 **Peace of Nystad** concluded the Great Northern War, handing the Baltics to Peter the Great. Russian rule reinforced the power of the nobility and serfs lost all rights until Estonian serfdom was finally abolished by **Tsar Alexander I** in 1819, 45 years earlier than in Mother Russia herself. Benefitting from a wave of Enlightenment reforms and the reforms of Tsar Alexander II, by the end of the 19th century Estonian peasants owned two-fifths of all private land. Following the coronation of reactionary **Tsar Alexander III** in 1881, however, Russia clamped down on its privileged borderlands, replacing the Baltic civil and criminal codes with Russian ones and making Russian the language of instruction. Russification prompted an Estonian nationalistic backlash, led by **Konstantin Päts** and peaking in a brutally repressed bid for independence during the Russian Revolution of 1905.

WAR: WHAT IS IT GOOD FOR? At the outbreak of **World War I,** Estonians were caught in a difficult position. Most of the Estonian-German population sympathized with Prussia, but had to fight in the Russian army. The **1917 Russian Revolution** spurred Estonian nationalism, but by the time the state declared **independence** in 1918 it was already under German occupation. It was soon recaptured by the Red Army. With British and Finnish help, the Estonians fought off the Soviets and embarked upon self-rule. From 1919 to 1933, a succession of some 20 coalition governments ruled. The country prospered, but the **Depression** of the 1930s allowed extreme right-wing parties, led by veterans from the war for liberation, to gain public support. The circumstances drove President **Konstantin Päts** to proclaim a state of emergency in 1934. He ruled as a benevolent dictator until he won a referendum on his rule in 1938. Päts's tenure was cut short by the Soviets, who occupied Estonia in 1940 under the **Nazi-Soviet Non-Aggression Pact.** Päts and other Estonian leaders, as well as a significant portion of the Estonian population, were arrested, deported, or killed. When **Hitler** reneged on the pact he annexed Estonia, stationing German troops there from 1941 to 1944. When the Red Army returned, thousands of Estonians fled and thousands more died trying to escape as Estonia became part of the **USSR.**

SOVIET ESTONIA AND ITS FALL. The 1950s saw extreme repression and Russification under **Soviet rule,** when internal purges removed the few native Estonians left in the ruling elite. It was not until *glasnost* and *perestroika* in the 1980s (see **Russia: History,** p. 624) that Estonians won enough freedom to establish a political renaissance. In 1988, the **Popular Front** emerged in opposition to the Communist government, pushing a resolution on independence through the Estonian legislature. Nationalists won a legislative majority in the 1990 elections and successfully declared independence after the failed 1991 coup in the Soviet Union.

ESTONIA'S RISING STAR. The 1992 general election, the first following Estonia's declaration of independence, saw the rejection of the government of **Edgar Savisaar,** who had founded the Popular Front in the twilight of Soviet rule. Savisaar's regime was replaced by a coalition of parties committed to radical economic reform, a trend which has continued to the present day under **Lennart Meri.** The government has managed to privatize most industries, lower trade barriers, and add a balanced budget amendment to its constitution. Its success in eliminating the old planned economy made the country the darling of Western investors.

TODAY

Estonia today is a parliamentary democracy, with a much weaker presidency than most other post-Soviet states. The most recent **Riigikogu** (Parliament) elections in 1999 brought yet another coalition government to power, this time composed of three center-right parties: **Pro Patria,** the **Reform Party,** and the **Moderates.** After independence, relations with **Russia** grew troubled, mainly because the Estonian government tried to promote Estonian language and culture by denying citizenship to those unable to speak Estonian. The discriminatory practice, which targeted the 30% Russian minority, brought pressure on the Estonian government from Russia and the European Union. In 1998 citizenship was automatically extended to the children of Russian speakers born in Estonia. Officials finally approved border protocols in St. Petersburg in 1999, but the final Estonian-Russian border agreement still has yet to be signed. Over the past few years Estonia has entered a variety of agreements bringing the Baltic states closer together economically, politically, and strategically. Under the second Estonian **President Arnold Rüütel,** elected November 2001, and **Prime Minister Siim Kallas,** elected spring 2002, the government has made 2003 **NATO** and 2004 **EU** accession its top priorities.

PEOPLE AND CULTURE

LANGUAGE AND RELIGION

Estionian is a **Finno-Ugric** language, closely related to **Finnish.** Estonians speak the best **English** in the Baltic states; most young people know at least a few phrases. Many also know **Finnish** or **Swedish,** but **German** is more common among the older set and in the resort towns. **Russian** used to be mandatory, but Estonians in secluded areas are likely to have forgotten much of it since few Russians live there. Estonians are usually adverse to using Russian (forty-odd years of occupation can do that). Always try English first, making it clear you're not Russian, and then switch to Russian if necessary. The clear exception to this is along the border in eastern Estonia, where many prefer Russian to Estonian. Before Soviet occupation, **Lutheranism** was the dominant faith, claiming 80% of the population as adherents. Under later Soviet occupation religious practice was discouraged, but since independence the Lutheran faith has grown stronger. The next largest faith, the

Estonian Apostolic-Orthodox Church, counts much smaller numbers. Small **Catholic** communities still practice, bolstered by the visit of Pope John Paul II in 1993. For a phrasebook and glossary, see **Glossary: Estonian,** p. 879.

FOOD AND DRINK

ESTONIA	❶	❷	❸	❹	❺
FOOD	under 40EEK	40-80EEK	81-100EEK	101-140EEK	over 140EEK

Although Estonia has managed to move past the days when it was plagued by drab Soviet cuisine, some things still haven't changed. *Schnitzel* (a breaded and fried pork fillet) still figures prominently in nearly every restaurant—much to the dismay of **vegetarians** and those trying to keep **kosher.** Most inexpensive Estonian cuisine is fried and doused with sour cream. Estonian specialties include the typical Baltic *seljanka* meat stew and *pelmenid* dumplings, as well as smoked salmon and trout. Bread is usually dark and dense. If you visit the islands, try picking up some *Hiumaa leib;* a loaf of this black bread easily weighs a kilo. Pancakes with cheese curd and berries are a delicious and common dessert. The national brew *Saku* is excellent, as is the darker *Saku Tume.* Local beers, like *Saaremaa* in Kuressaare, are less consistent. The Estonian brand of carbonated **mineral water,** *Värska,* is particularly salty.

THE ARTS

HISTORY

LITERATURE. The oldest book in Estonian is the **Wanradt-Koell Lutheran Catechism** from 1535, but true literature didn't appear until the Estophile period (1750-1840) centuries later. The most notable publication of this period was **Anton Thor Helle's** 1739 translation of the Bible, which created a common Estonian language based on the northern dialect. Folklore provided the basis for **Friedrich Reinhold Kreutzwald's** *Kalevipoeg* (1857-61), an epic that became the rallying point of Estonian national rebirth in the Romantic period and is still a major influence on Estonian style. Toward the end of the century, the Neo-Romantic nationalist **Noor-Eesti** (Young Estonia) movement appeared. Led by the poet **Gustav Suits** and the writer **Friedebert Tuglas,** the writers of the movement played with form and looked for a national spirit. **Anton Tammsaare's** prose evolved from the Noor-Eesti approach toward Realism. His *Truth and Justice* (*Tõde ja õigus;* 1926-33), is essential to the Estonian canon, and Tammsaare has been praised as Estonian's foremost writer. The strictures of the official Soviet style of **Socialist Realism** sent many authors abroad or into temporary exile in Siberia, but creativity blossomed once more under Khrushchev's thaw in the early 1960s. This period saw the introduction of Modernism via the work of **Artur Alliksaar, Lydia Koidula,** and **Juhan Viidng.** Frequent Nobel nominee **Jaan Kross** managed to criticize the realities of Soviet life despite USSR censors in *The Tsar's Madman* (1978). In the same year, **Aimée Beekman** addressed plight of women in *The Possibility of Choice.*

FINE ARTS. Woodcarvers **Elert Thiele** and **Christian Ackermann** are Baroque masters, the former for the 1667 **Tallinn Town Hall Frieze** and the latter for his ornate altars. Not until 1803 was the first Estonian art school founded at Tartu University (p. 326). The first nationally conscious Estonian art emerged at the close of the 19th century with painters **Johann Köler** and **Amandus Adamson** and sculptor **August Weizenberg.** Realism was initially dominant, but with the turn of the century artists began to turn to symbolism and surrealism. The Neo-Impressionist paintings of

Konrad Mägi and the landscapes of **Nikolai Triik** moved increasingly toward abstraction at the end of the 19th century, while the later painting of the 1920s and 1930s was heavily influenced by European trends, including Cubism and the principles of the German *Bauhaus*. Visual art also suffered under Soviet rule, but is now reviving with fresh, young talent.

CURRENT SCENE

With the rise of nationalism and the dissolution of the Soviet Union, literature took on an increasingly important role in the re-established independent Estonia. In the last decade, several Estonian writers have been nominated for the Nobel prize. Among them are poet and essayist **Jaan Kapinski** and novelist **Emil Tode**, whose 1993 *Border State (Piiririik)* was internationally acclaimed as a great postmodern text. **Aarne Ruben** has attracted the public's attention with the book *The Volta Works Whistles Mournfully (Volta annab Kaeblikku vilet;* 2001). The most popular writer in Estonia today is **Andrus Kivirähk**, best known for his humorous tale *Old Barvy (Rihepaap)*. Popular contemporary Estonian **composers** include **Arvo Pärt,** known for *Tabula rasa* and *St. James's Passion*, pieces reminiscent of medieval compositions; **Veljo Tormis,** who revived the **runic,** an ancient chanting-style of choral singing; and **Alo Mattisen,** whose pop rock songs became pro-independence anthems.

HOLIDAYS AND FESTIVALS

NATIONAL HOLIDAYS IN 2003	
January 1 New Year's Day	**June 23** Victory Day
February 24 Independence Day	**June 24** Jaanipäev (St. John's Day, Midsummer)
April 18 Good Friday	
April 20 Easter	**August 20** Restoration of Independence
May 1 May Day	**December 25** Christmas
June 8 Pentecost	**December 26** Boxing Day

SUMMER MUSIC AND FILM SEASON. Conductors and musical groups from around the world are drawn to Pärnu, the so-called "summer capital" of Estonia.

NATIONAL SONG FESTIVAL (2004). Estonia's biggest event, a folk festival so large that it only occurs once every five years.

ADDITIONAL RESOURCES

GENERAL HISTORY

Baltic Revolution: Estonia, Latvia, Lithuania and the Path to Independence, by Anatol Lieven (1994). Provides a solid background in Baltic history.

Estonia: Independence and European Integration, by David Smith (2001). Examines Estonia's recent past and EU prospects.

FICTION AND NONFICTION

Border State, by Emil Tode (1993). A look at tensions between East and West as played out in post-Communist Estonia.

The Tsar's Madman, by Jaan Kross (1978). A historical novel about a 19th-century Baltic nobleman. Arguably the best Estonian fiction available.

ESTONIA

ESTONIA ESSENTIALS

ENTRANCE REQUIREMENTS
Passport: Required of all travelers.
Visa: Required of citizens of Canada and South Africa.
Letter of Invitation: Required to obtain a visa.
Inoculations: None required. Recommended up-to-date on MMR (measles, mumps, and rubella), DTaP (diptheria), Polio booster, Hepatitis A, Hepatitis B
Work Permit: Required of all foreigners planning to work in Estonia.
International Driving Permit: Required of all those planning to drive.

DOCUMENTS AND FORMALITIES

EMBASSIES AND CONSULATES

Embassies of other countries in Estonia are all in Tallinn (see p. 301). Estonia's embassies and consulates abroad include:

Australia: Honorary Consulate: 86 Louisa Rd., Birchgrove, NSW 2041 (☎02 9810 7468; fax 9818 1779; eestikon@ozemail.com.au).

Canada: Honorary Consulate: 958 Broadview Ave., Suite 202, Toronto, ON M4K 2R6 (☎416-461-0764; fax 461-0353; estconsu@inforamp.net).

Ireland: Merlyn Park 24, Ballsbridge, Dublin 4 (☎01 269 1552; fax 260 5119).

South Africa: Honorary Consulate: 16 Hofmeyer St., Welgemoed, Belville 7530 (☎021 913 3850; fax 913 2579).

UK: 16 Hyde Park Gate, London SW7 5DG (☎020 7589 3428; fax 7589 3430; www.estonia.gov.uk).

US: 2131 Massachusetts Ave. NW, Washington, D.C. 20008 (☎202-588-0101; fax 588-0108; www.estemb.org).

VISA AND ENTRY INFORMATION

Citizens of Australia, Ireland, New Zealand, and the US can visit Estonia visa-free for up to 90 days in a six month period; UK citizens for 180 days in a year. Canadians and South Africans must obtain a **visa** at the nearest Honorary Consulate or have a visa to Latvia or Lithuania. To apply for a visa you need a passport, a photo, an invitation or letter from a contact in Estonia, proof of solvency (such as plane tickets or hotel reservations from a state-recognized institution), and a health insurance policy valid in Estonia with a coverage of at least 160,000EEK for the duration of your stay. Single-entry visas (valid for 30 days) are €13, multiple-entry (maximum continuous stay 90 days) €65—pay in Euros. Visa **extensions** are not granted, and visas cannot be purchased at the border. For visa information, consult the Estonian Ministry of Foreign Affairs (www.vm.ee/eng). The easiest means of crossing the **border** is to take a direct bus or train from Tallinn to Moscow, St. Petersburg, or Rīga. There is no fee to enter or exit the country, but passing through Estonian customs may take several hours.

TRANSPORTATION

BY PLANE, TRAIN, OR FERRY. Several international airlines offer flights to Tallinn; try **SAS** or **AirBaltic**. If you're coming from another Baltic state or **Russia**, trains may be even cheaper than **ferries**—which connect to **Finland** and **Sweden**—but expect more red tape when crossing the border.

BY BUS. Domestically, buses are the best means of transport, as they are much cheaper and more efficient than trains. It's even possible to ride buses from the mainland to island towns (via ferry) for less than the price of the ferry ride. During the school year (Sept.-June 25), students receive half-price bus tickets. Internationally, buses can be a painfully slow choice as clearing the border may take hours.

BY TAXI OR THUMB. Taxis are a safe means of transportation. The average rate is 7EEK per km. *Let's Go* does not recommend **hitchhiking.** Those who choose to do so should stretch out an open hand or call the agency **Vismutar** (☎37290 01 050), which matches passengers with drivers going the same way.

TOURIST SERVICES AND MONEY

Most towns have well-equipped tourist offices with literature and English-speaking staff. Generally, such offices are quite knowledgeable about accommodations and the local scene, but less so about transportation. Booths marked with a green "i" sell maps and give away brochures. The unit of currency is the **kroon** (EEK), divided into 100 **senti.** The kroon is pegged to the Euro at €1=15.65EEK. **Inflation** is around 4.4%, so prices and exchange rates should be relatively stable. The biggest and most stable banks in the country, **Hansapank** and **Eesti Ühispank,** cash **traveler's checks.** Many restaurants and shops take credit cards, mostly **MasterCard** and **Visa. Visa ATMs** are common; **MasterCard** ATMs are harder to find. When purchasing an item, cash is not usually passed between hands, but is instead put in a small tray.

HEALTH AND SAFETY

 EMERGENCY NUMBERS: Police, Fire, and **Ambulance:** ☎112

HEALTH AND SAFETY. **Medical services** for foreigners are few and far between, and usually require cash payments. **Pharmacies** (look for the "Apteek" sign) are usually well-equipped Scandinavian chains. They only sell medicine; try grocery stores for toiletries. Public **toilets** *(tasuline)*, marked by "N" or a triangle pointing up for women and "M" or a triangle pointing down for men, usually cost 3EEK and include a very limited supply of toilet paper. While Tallinn's tap water is generally safe to drink, **bottled water** is worth the extra money and is necessary in the rest of the country. The petty **crime** rate is low.

WOMEN, MINORITY, AND BGLT TRAVELERS. **Women** should not have a problem traveling alone, though you might want to dress conservatively. **Minorities** in Estonia are rare; they receive stares but generally experience little discrimination. For English-speaking help in an emergency, contact your embassy. **Homosexuality** is legal in Estonia, but public displays are not socially accepted.

ACCOMMODATIONS AND CAMPING

ESTONIA	❶	❷	❸	❹	❺
ACCOM.	under 200EEK	200-400EEK	401-550EEK	551-600EEK	over 600EEK

HOTELS, HOSTELS, AND HOMESTAYS. Each **tourist office** has accommodations listings for its town and can often arrange a bed for visitors. There is little distinction between **hotels, hostels,** and **guesthouses;** some upscale hotels still have hall toilets and showers. The word *võõrastemaja* (guesthouse) in a place's name usually implies that it's less expensive. Many hotels provide laundry services for an extra charge. Some hostels are part of larger hotels, so be sure to ask for the cheaper rooms. **Homestays** are common and inexpensive. For info on HI hostels around Estonia, contact the **Estonian Youth Hostel Association,** Tatari 39-310, Tallinn (☎6461 455; fax 6461 595; www.baltichostels.net).

CAMPING. Camping is the best way to experience Estonia's islands and unique selection of fauna and flora. Camping outside designated areas is illegal and a threat to wildlife. Farm stays are gaining in popularity. For more information visit Estonia's stellar **Rural Tourism** website, www.maaturism.ee.

KEEPING IN TOUCH

MAIL. Mail can be received general delivery through **Poste Restante.** Address envelopes as follows: Dunia (first name) DICKEY (last name), POSTE RESTANTE, Narva mnt. 1 (post office address), Tallinn (city) 0001 (postal code), ESTONIA. An airmail letter costs 6.50EEK to Europe and the CIS, and 7.50EEK to the rest of the world. Postcards cost 6EEK/8EEK.

PHONE MAYHEM The phone system in Estonia proves that the universe tends toward chaos. Tallinn numbers all begin with the number 6 and have 7 digits. Numbers in smaller towns, however, often have only 5 digits. Tallinn, unlike other Estonian cities, has no city code; to call Tallinn from outside Estonia on the digital system, dial Estonia's country code (372) and then the number. To call any city besides Tallinn from outside the country, dial the country code, the city code, and then the number. The 0 listed in parentheses before each city code need only be dialed when placing calls within Estonia.

TELEPHONES AND INTERNET ACCESS. Telephones take digital cards, available at any kiosk. Cards come in denominations of 30, 50, and 100EEK. Calls to the Baltic states cost 5EEK per min., to Russia 10EEK. Phoning the US runs US$1-4 per min. **Internet access,** which is common, usually costs 30-60EEK per hour.

TALLINN ☎(0)

Medieval buildings, German spires, and Danish towers loom alongside each other in Tallinn (pop. 399,850), the self-proclaimed "Heart of Northern Europe." The capital's trendy bars, bustling shops, and cosmopolitan youth point to the success of Estonia's economic liberalization, which, as its rapid convergence toward membership in the EU attests, is almost complete. Tourists from all over Europe may have invaded Tallinn, but when the sun sets over the church steeples that pierce the pink evening sky, any doubt of the city's beauty and energy fades.

ⴹ TRANSPORTATION

Flights: Tallinn Airport, Lennujaama 2 (☎605 88 88, 24hr. info 605 88 87; www.tallinn-airport.ee). Bus #2 runs to Vanalinn. **Copterline** (☎610 18 18; www.copterline.com) runs a **helicopter** service between Tallinn and **Helsinki** (18min.; 1 per hr. 8:30am-9:30pm; US$75, US$150 if reserved in advance). Airlines include: **Estonian Air,** Lennujaama tee 13 (☎640 11 01; www.estonian-air.ee); **Finnair,** Roosikrantsi 2 (☎611 09 50; fax 611 09 45; www.finnair.ee); **LOT,** Lembitu 14 (☎646 60 51; fax 645 42 98); **SAS,** Rävala pst. 2 (☎666 30 30; fax 666 30 31; www.scandinavian.net).

Trains: Toompuiestee 35 (☎615 68 51; www.evrekspress.ee). Trams #1 and 5 travel between the station and the center. Get international tickets on the 2nd fl. (open on

ESTONIA

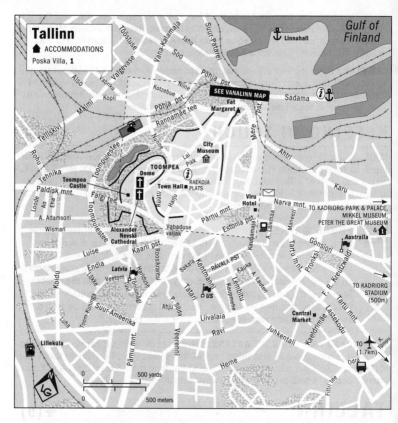

Tallinn
▲ ACCOMMODATIONS
Poska Villa, 1

⚓ Linnahall

Gulf of Finland

TOOMPEA

Dome

Town Hall

Alexander Nevski Cathedral

Viru Hotel

SEE VANALINN MAP

Fat Margaret

City Museum

RAEKOJA PLATS

Narva mnt. TO KADRIORG PARK & PALACE,
MIKKEL MUSEUM,
PETER THE GREAT MUSEUM

TO KADRIORG STADIUM
(500m)

Central Market

0   500 yards

0   500 meters

odd dates 9am-7:15pm, even dates 9am-11pm) and domestic tickets on the ground floor. English spoken at info desk. To: **Moscow, RUS** (16½ hr., 1 per day, 718EEK) and **St. Petersburg, RUS** (10hr., 1 per day on even dates, 225-387EEK).

Buses: Lastekodu 46 (☎680 09 00), just south of Tartu mnt. and 1.5km southeast of Vanalinn. Trams #2 and 4 and bus #2 connect the bus station to the city center. Catch trams at the Viru stop on the side of Hotel Viru; get off at "Bussijaam." Open daily 6:30am-11:30pm; ticket office open daily 6:30am-9:15pm. To: **Berlin, GER** (27hr., 1 per week, 1360EEK); **Kaliningrad, RUS** (15hr., 1 per day, 300EEK); **Munich, GER** (36hr., 1 per week, 1680EEK); **Riga, LAT** (6hr., 4 per day, 200EEK); **St. Petersburg, RUS** (9hr., 7 per day, 180-260EEK); **Vilnius, LIT** (10½hr., 2 per day, 400EEK).

Ferries: (☎631 85 50). At the end of Sadama, 15min. from the center. 4 different terminals. Boats, hydrofoils, and catamarans cross to **Helsinki. Eckerö Line,** Terminal B (☎631 86 06; fax 631 86 61; www.eckeroline.ee). 3½hr.; 1 per day; 220EEK, students 180EEK. MC/V. **Nordic Jet Line,** Terminal C (☎613 70 00; fax 613 72 22; www.njl.info). 1½hr.; 6 per day; 280-580EEK. MC/V. **Silja Line,** Terminal D (☎611 66 61; fax 611 66 65; www.silja.ee). 1½hr.; 4 per day; 230-590EEK, students 180-540EEK. MC/V. **Tallink,** Terminals A and D (☎640 98 08; www.tallink.ee). 3¼hr.; 3 per day; 315-345EEK, students 284-310EEK. Express ferries 1½hr.; 7 per day; 235-425EEK, students 212-384EEK. MC/V.

Public Transportation: Buses, trams, and **trollies** run 6am-midnight. **Minibuses** run until 4am. Buy tickets *(talong)* from kiosks for 10EEK or from drivers for 15EEK. Validate them in the metal boxes on board. 600EEK fine for riding ticketless.

Taxis: Silver Takso (☎ 648 2300) or **Tulika Takso** (☎ 1200). 7EEK per km. Call ahead to avoid the 8-50EEK "waiting fee."

ORIENTATION

Tallinn's **Vanalinn** (Old Town) is an egg-shaped maze ringed by five main streets, all running into one another: **Rannamäe tee, Mere pst., Pärnu mnt., Kaarli pst.,** and **Toompuiestee.** The best entrance to Vanalinn is through the 15th-century **Viru ärarad,** the main gate in the city wall, located across from **Hotel Viru,** Tallinn's central landmark. **Viru,** the main thoroughfare, leads directly to **Raekoja plats** (Town Hall Square), the scenic center of Old Town. It has two sections: **All-linn,** or Lower Town, and **Toompea,** a rocky, fortified hill.

PRACTICAL INFORMATION

TOURIST AND FINANCIAL SERVICES

Tourist Office: Tourist Information Center, Raekoja pl. 10 (☎ 645 77 77; fax 645 77 78; www.tourism.tallinn.ee). Opposite the town hall. Offers city **maps** and sells *Tallinn In Your Pocket* (35EEK). Open June-Aug. M-F 9am-8pm, Sa-Su 10am-6pm; Sept.-May M-F 9am-5pm, Sa-Su 10am-4pm. **Branch** at Sadama 25 (☎/fax 631 83 21), at the harbor (Terminal A). Open daily 8am-4:30pm.

Embassies: For a complete embassy directory, check out the foreign ministry's website (www.vm.ee) or consult *Tallinn This Week.* **Australia,** Kopli 25 (☎ 650 93 08; fax 667 84 44; mati@standard.ee). Open M-F 9am-5pm. **Canada,** Toom-kooli 13 (☎ 627 33 11; fax 627 33 12; canembt@zzz.ee). Open M, W, F 9am-noon. **Finland,** Kohtu 4 (☎ 610 32 00; fax 610 32 81; www.finemb.ee). Open M-F 9am-noon. **Latvia,** Tõnismägi 10 (☎ 646 13 13; fax 631 13 66). Open M-F 10am-noon. **Lithuania,** Uus 15 (☎ 631 40 30; fax 641 20 13). Open M, Tu, Th 9am-10:30am, F 9am-10am. **Russia,** Pikk 19 (☎ 646 41 75; fax 646 41 78). Open M-F 9am-5pm. **UK,** Wismari 6 (☎ 667 47 00; fax 667 47 23; www.britishembassy.ee). Open Tu-Th 2:30-4:30pm. **US,** Kentmanni 20 (☎ 668 81 00; fax 668 81 34; www.usemb.ee). Open M-F 9am-noon and 2-5pm.

Currency Exchange: Located throughout the city, although the bus station offers poor exchange rates. **ATMs** are located throughout the city.

American Express: Suur-Karja 15 (☎ 626 62 11; fax 626 62 12; www.estravel.ee). Books hotels and tours, sells airline, ferry, and rail tickets, and arranges visas to former Soviet republics and Russia. Open June-Aug. M-F 9am-6pm, Sa 10am-5pm; Sept.-May M-F 9am-6pm, Sa 10am-3pm.

LOCAL AND EMERGENCY SERVICES

Luggage Storage: 10EEK per day at the **bus station.** Open daily 6:30am-11:30pm. Also at **Rotermanni Shopping Center,** Mere pst 4. Open M-Sa 9am-8pm, Su 9am-5pm.

English-Language Bookstore: Apollo Raamatumaja, Viru 23 (☎ 654 84 85; fax 610 17 61), has a small collection. Open M-F 10am-8pm, Sa 10am-6pm, Su 11am-4pm.

Laundromat: Sauberland, Maakri 23 (☎ 661 20 75). Self-service. Wash 62EEK, dry 22EEK. Open daily 7am-10pm. MC/V.

Pharmacy: *Apteeks* are common. **Raeapteek,** Raekoja plats 11 (☎ 631 48 30), has been in business since 1422. Open M-F 9am-7pm, Sa 9am-5pm, Su 9am-4pm.

Hospital: Tallinn Central Hospital, Ravi 18 (☎602 70 00, 24hr. info 620 70 15).

Internet Access: @5 Kaubamaja, Gonsiori 2, in the Kaubamaja department store (☎667 33 22; fax 667 32 05). 40EEK per hr. Open M-F 9am-9pm, Sa 9am-8pm, Su 10am-6pm. **Kohvik@Grill,** Aia 3 (☎627 12 29). 25EEK per hr. Open daily 10am-11pm.

Post Office: Narva mnt. 1 (☎661 66 16), opposite Hotel Viru. **Poste Restante** in the basement. Open M-F 7:30am-8pm, Sa 8am-6pm.

Postal Code: 10101.

⚓ ACCOMMODATIONS

Tallinn's hostels fill quickly in summer; it's wise to book in advance. **Rasastra ❸,** Mere pst. 4 (☎/fax 661 62 91; www.bedbreakfast.ee), finds **private rooms** in Tallinn. (Breakfast 30EEK. Singles 260EEK; doubles 460EEK; triples 639EEK; apartments from 800EEK. Open daily 9:30am-6pm.)

Hostel Vana Tom (HI), Väike-Karja 1, 2nd fl. (☎631 32 52; fax 612 05 11; www.hostel.ee), in Vanalinn. From Hotel Viru, head toward Raekoja plats and turn left on Sauna. Turn right on Väike-Karja, and look for an archway on your right. Clean, and located in the heart of Old Town, but you might hear some noise from the 3rd fl. strip club. Laundry 20EEK per kg. Breakfast included. Reception 24hr. Dorms 225EEK, with HI card 210EEK; doubles with shared bath 590EEK. MC/V. ❷

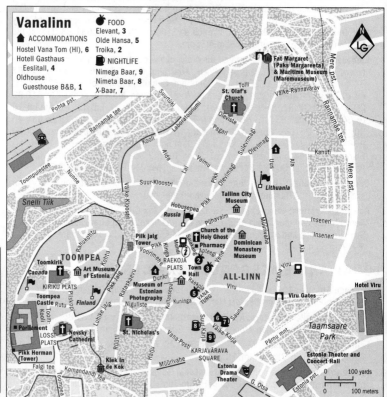

Vanalinn

🍴 FOOD
Elevant, 3
Olde Hansa, 5
Troika, 2

♠ ACCOMMODATIONS
Hostel Vana Tom (HI), 6
Hotell Gasthaus
   Eeslitall, 4
Oldhouse
   Guesthouse B&B, 1

🍸 NIGHTLIFE
Nimega Baar, 9
Nimeta Baar, 8
X-Baar, 7

Oldhouse Guesthouse Bed & Breakfast, Uus 22/1 (☎/fax 641 14 64; www.old-house.ee). From Raekoja plats, follow Viru and turn left on Uus. This quiet guesthouse offers immaculate rooms. Shared kitchen. Breakfast included. Reception daily 8am-11pm. 6-bed dorm 290EEK; singles 450EEK; doubles 650EEK; quads 1300EEK. 10% ISIC discount. ❷

Poska Villa, Poska 15 (☎601 36 01; fax 601 35 74; www.hot.ee/poskavilla). From Vanalinn, follow Gonsiori and make a left on Poska; the hotel will be on the left. Located within a residential neighborhood, this luxurious guesthouse provides respite from the hustle and bustle of Old Town. The rooms are small, but have private baths. Breakfast included. Singles 650EEK; doubles 760-980EEK. MC/V. ❺

Hotell Gasthaus Eeslitall, Dunkri 4, 3rd fl. (☎631 37 55; fax 631 32 10; www.eesli-tall.ee). From Raekoja plats, walk along Dunkri and look to the right. Prime location with bright, clean rooms. Breakfast 36EEK. Singles 450EEK; doubles 585EEK. ❸

▷ FOOD

There are **24hr.** eateries located near the bus and train stations. To stock up on easy-to-prepare foods, drop by **Kaubahall** on Aia and Inseneri. Walking out of Vanalinn on Viru, it's on the left. **Stockmann,** on the corner of Liivalaia and A. Laut-eri, is a mammoth Finnish supermarket. (Open M-F 9am-9pm, Sa-Su 9am-8pm.) The **market,** Keldrimäe 9, will be on the right as you take Lastekodu toward the bus station. (Open M-Sa 7am-5pm, Su 7am-4pm.)

Troika, Raekoja plats 15 (☎627 62 45). This extravagant Russian restaurant combines large portions, good service, and an interior that takes you back in time. Live music daily 6-10pm. Entrees 106-168EEK. Open daily 10am-11pm. MC/V. ❹

Elevant, Vene 5 (☎631 31 32). An ecologically sound establishment that serves tasty Indian fare with an Estonian twist. Entrees 84-278EEK. 90EEK lunch special M-F noon-4pm. Open daily noon-11pm. ❸

Olde Hansa, Vana turg 1 (☎627 90 20), near Raekoja plats. Enjoy live music (Tu-Su from 6pm) while you munch on portions sized for "mild hunger" or "great hunger" at this medieval restaurant. For dessert, don't miss the rose pudding, "the velvet delight of the nobility" (58EEK). Entrees 188EEK-540EEK. MC/V. ❺

◎ SIGHTS

ALL-LINN. Tallinn's 14th-century **town hall** is the oldest in Europe. (☎645 79 00. Tower open June 1-Aug. 31 Tu-Su 11am-6pm. Town hall 30EEK, students 20EEK; tower 25EEK/15EEK.) To reach the 14th-century **Church of the Holy Spirit,** cross the square and follow Mündi to the intersection of Pikk and Pühavaimu. The church houses a 15th-century bell tower and an intricate 17th-century wooden clock. (☎646 44 30. Open May-Sept. M-Sa 10am-4pm; Oct.-Apr. M-Sa 10am-2pm. 10EEK, students 5EEK.) **St. Olaf's Church** (Oleviste kirik) is the tallest church in town. From the Church of the Holy Ghost, walk up Pikk; St. Olaf will be near the end of Pikk on the left, though the entrance is on the parallel street Lai—just walk down Oleviste and walk in. The murals inside the adjoining chapel illustrate the architect's fatal fall from the tower. (☎641 22 41. Open June-Sept. daily 10am-2pm.) To reach south Vanalinn's **St. Nicholas Church** (Niguliste kirik) and its mighty spire, take Kullasseapa from the corner of the square and turn right on Niguliste. (☎631 43 27. Open W-Su 10am-5pm. Free organ concerts Sa-Su 4-4:30pm. 35EEK, students 20EEK.)

IN RECENT NEWS

SELLING ESTONIA

If you've spent time in Estonia, you've probably noticed the posters that exclaim "Subversively Chic" and "Positively Transforming." These words were carefully chosen by Enterprise Estonia, a state-funded foundation that launched the Brand Estonia campaign in 2002. Its main goals are to promote Estonian businesses, increase foreign investment, and attract more tourists to the country.

The Brand Estonia concept is aimed at creating a consistent identity that Estonia can present to foreigners. The slogans were developed based on foreign and Estonian perceptions of the country. "Nordic with a twist" and "Ecological haven" hope to lure tourists to Estonia's natural beauty. "No establishment," "The freest economy in Europe," and "A real self-starter" are aimed to bring in foreign business, highlighting the country's continuing economic transformation.

Estonia's campaign seems to be succeeding; Tallinn is packed with tourists and the Estonian economy continues to grow. Though some worry that the independent spirit the slogans glorify will soon be lost when Estonia joins the European Union, the Brand Estonia campaign itself has met with almost universal acclaim; under its influence, the country does seem to be "Positively Transforming."

—Dunia Dickey

TOOMPEA. Castle Square (Lossi plats) sits at the center of Toompea. From St. Nicholas Church, turn left on Niguliste kirik, which turns into Lühike jalg. Uphill, Toompea leads to the Castle Square. The **Alexander Nevsky Cathedral,** located in the center of the square, was begun under Tsar Alexander III and finished just in time for the Bolshevik Revolution. *(Open daily 8am-7pm. Services 9am and 6pm.)* **Toompea Castle,** the present seat of the Estonian **Parliament** (Riigikogu) also faces the square, but is closed to visitors. Directly behind it, a fluttering Estonian flag tops **Tall Hermann** (Pikk Hermann), Tallinn's tallest tower and most impressive medieval fortification. To get to **Toomkirik,** Toom-Kooli 6, head down either Piiskopi or Toom-Kooli for a block; this will lead you to Kiriku plats, the square within which the church is framed. The 13th-century spires of this Lutheran Cathedral tower over Toompea. (☎644 41 40. Services Su 10am. Open Tu-Su 9am-5pm.) To get to **Kiek in de Kök,** a 1483 tower-turned-museum, walk on Toompea away from Lossi plats and turn left on Komandandi tee. Its name, which means "peep in the kitchen," comes from the views it provides through the windows of neighboring houses. (☎644 66 86. Open Tu-Su 10:30am-6pm. 15EEK, students 7EEK.) The two **best views** of the lower town are at the end of Kohtu and at Patkuli vaate plats.

KADRIORG. Quiet paths, shady trees, and fountains adorn Kadriorg Park. Its jewel is ▨ **Kadriorg Palace,** designed in 1718 by architect Niccolo Michetti for Tsar Peter the Great. The palace's sumptuous grand hall is considered to be one of the best Baroque rooms in Northern Europe. The palace is also home to a **Foreign Art Museum,** which holds a strong collection of Dutch and Flemish works. (☎606 64 00; www.ekm.ee. Open May-Sept.Tu-Su 10am-5pm; Oct.-Apr. W-Su 10am-5pm. 35EEK, students 20EEK.) Cross the **flower garden** to see the **President's Palace,** housed in a pink building. *(Flower garden open May 1-Aug. 31 daily 9am-8pm; Sept. 1-Oct. 31 M-Th 9am-8pm, F-Su 9am-9pm. Free. President's Palace closed to the public. To reach Kadriorg Park from Old Town, follow Narva mnt. and veer right on Weizenbergi when it splits from Narva mnt. Trams #1 and 3 also run to Kadriorg.)*

ROCCA-AL-MARE. Rocca-al-mare is a peninsula 10km west of central Tallinn. It contains the **Estonian Open Air Museum** (Eesti Vabaõhumuuseum), a park full of 17th- to 20th-century wooden mills and homesteads that were collected from all over Estonia and rebuilt here. Visitors can duck into log cabins, climb rickety stairs, and explore stables and dirt paths leading to the sea. The museum has 68 buildings, including **Sutlepa Chapel** (kabel), where a choir sings in Estonian and Swedish during holidays. Intricately attired Estonian folk troupes perform regularly. *(Take bus #21 or tram #7 to the zoo stop. Keeping the carnival to your right, walk away from the street. Turn left onto the path. The museum is at Vabaõhumuuseumi 12, 100m past the schoolhouse. ☎654 91 00. Museum and chapel open May-Aug. daily 10am-6pm; Sept. and Nov.-Apr. 10am-5pm; Oct. daily 10am-4pm. 25EEK, students 9EEK.)*

🏛 MUSEUMS

🏛TALLINN CITY MUSEUM. (Tallinna Linnamuuseum.) The looming door opens on a particularly visitor-friendly, three-storied museum charting the city's history from its founding in 1219 through the Soviet occupation to its current role as the capital of independent Estonia. Children (and others) will enjoy pulling on strings to move models of medieval Tallinn citizens; you can even make a monk hit a lazy pupil over the head. *(Vene 17. ☎644 65 53; www.linnamuuseum.ee. Open May-Sept. W-M 10:30am-5:30pm; Oct.-Apr. W-M 11am-4:30pm. 25EEK, students 10EEK.)*

MIKKEL MUSEUM. (Mikkeli Muuseum.) The private art collection of Johannes Mikkel is now available for all to see. Housed within the former kitchens of Kadriorg Palace (see p. 308), the museum features works from Western Europe, Estonia, and China, as well as a number of Russian icons. *(Weizenbergi 28, near Kadriorg Park. ☎601 34 30; www.ekm.ee. Open W-Su 11am-6pm. 15EEK, students 5EEK.)*

PETER THE GREAT MUSEUM. (Muuseum Peeter 1 Maja.) This simple residence, where Peter stayed before a palace in Tallinn was completed, houses many of its original furnishings, as well as an imprint of Peter's extremely large hand. *(Mäekalda 2, near Kadriorg Park. ☎601 31 36; www.linnamuuseum.ee/peeter1maja. Open W-Su 10:30am-5:30pm. 10EEK, students 5EEK.)*

ART MUSEUM OF ESTONIA. (Eesti Kunstimuuseum.) An all-Estonian collection housing classics of the 19th and 20th centuries, including symbolic art based on the national epic *Kalevipoeg*, the mythical redeemer of the Estonian people. *(Kiriku plats 1. ☎644 93 40; www.ekm.ee. Open W-Su 11am-6pm; last admission 5:30pm. 20EEK, students 5EEK.)*

MUSEUM OF PHOTOGRAPHY. (Raevangla-Fotomuuseum.) An excellent exhibit featuring Estonian photographs and interesting 19th-century views of Tallinn. The upper floor has a collection of old cameras; temporary exhibits are in the basement. *(Raekoja 4/6, behind the town hall. ☎644 87 67; www.linnamuuseum.ee. Open Apr.-Sept. Th-Tu 10:30am-5:30pm; Oct.-Mar Th-M 10:30am-5:30pm. 10EEK, students 5EEK.)*

DOMINICAN MONASTERY MUSEUM. (Dominiiklaste Kloostri Muuseum.) Look for the *domini canes* (Lord's hounds) on Vene to guide you to the oldest building in Vanalinn. A thorough history of the Dominicans in Tallinn awaits inside, along with an "energy column" to test one's extra-sensory powers. *(Vene 16. ☎644 46 06. Open May 12-Sept. 23 daily 9:30am-6pm. 30EEK, students 15EEK.)*

🎵 🎭 ENTERTAINMENT AND FESTIVALS

Tallinn This Week, free at tourist offices, lists performances. The premier theaters in town, the **Estonia Concert Hall** and the **Estonian National Opera,** both at Estonia pst. 4, offer opera, ballet, musicals, and chamber music. (Concert Hall ☎614 77 60; www.concert.ee. Box office open M-F noon-7pm. Tickets 30-150EEK. Opera ☎626 02 60; www.opera.ee. Box office open daily noon-7pm. Tickets under 200EEK.) The **Forum Cinema** at Coca-Cola Plaza, Hobujaama 5, shows Hollywood films in English. (☎1182. Tickets 40-100EEK.) On Sundays, Tallinn converges on the **beach** at Pirita (buses #1, 1a, 8, 34, or 38 from the post office).

During the **Old Town Days,** usually the last week of May and the first week of June, the city hosts open-air concerts throughout Vanalinn, as well as fashion shows, singing, and skits at Raekoja pl. The **Grillfest,** in late June, is a huge midsummer celebration in Kadriorg Park featuring the world's largest bonfire (www.grillfest.ee). The first week of July provides just one more excuse (as if one were necessary) to loose the taps in Tallinn bars, as **Beersummer,** always hopping, celebrates the power of barley. Mid-July brings the **Sun Dance Music Festival,** in the Kadriorg area, during which hundreds of DJs come to Tallinn to ply their trade (www.vibe.ee). Every February, the **Student Jazz Festival** brings prodigies from all over northern Europe. The **National Song Festival,** which occurs once every four to five years (next in 2004), proved instrumental to Estonia's drive to independence in the "singing revolution" of 1990-91. In the midst of bleak December, the international **Dark Nights Film Festival** showcases exceptional cinematic talent.

🎭 NIGHTLIFE

Bars dot every street of Vanalinn. The town's popular wine bars provide an elegant alternative to cocktails and beer.

Nimeta Baar (The Pub with no Name), Suur-Karja 4/6 (☎641 15 15). Draws a boisterous crowd on weekend nights, especially when it broadcasts Eesti (Estonian) soccer matches. Soccer nights often end in shot-drinking competitions. Beer 32EEK. 2-for-1 beers during Happy Hour (6-7pm). Open Su-Th 11am-2am, F-Sa 11am-4am. MC/V.

Nimega Baar (The Pub with a Name), Suur-Karja 13 (☎620 92 79). This bar draws less of an expat crowd than its nameless counterpart. Cushy couches and a dance floor. Beer 32EEK. Open M-Th 11am-2am, F-Sa 11am-4am, Su noon-2am. MC/V.

X-Baar, Sauna 1 (☎620 92 66). Easily located by the rainbow flag outside, this small bar offers a relaxed atmosphere to its gay clientele. Beer 27EEK. Open daily 2pm-1am.

COASTAL ESTONIA

Sun, sand, natural preserves...and mud baths. East of Tallinn, Lahemaa National Park shelters precious coastline, historic villages, and endangered species from the ravages of tourism. Hip Pärnu and quiet Haapsalu welcome weary travelers with open—albeit muddy—arms and act as a gateway to the Estonian islands.

LAHEMAA NATIONAL PARK ☎(0)232

Founded in 1971, Lahemaa was the USSR's first national park; today it's one of Europe's largest. It covers nearly 500 sq. km, 75% of them woodland, and frames a jutting and rocky coastline. Four peninsulas stretch out from the mainland, sheltering quiet bays and beaches from caprices of the Baltic Sea. Farther inland, eight nature trails lead through forest clearings and bogs flecked with purple lupin and white tufts of grass. The park serves as a cultural and ecological reserve, protecting fishing villages, 18th-century country estates, and 838 plant species.

■ ⁊ **ORIENTATION AND PRACTICAL INFORMATION. Palmse** is the most convenient base for exploring the park, as it's home to the **Lahemaa National Park Visitor Center.** (☎955 30; fax 955 31; info@lahemaa.neti.ee. English spoken. Open May-Aug. daily 9am-7pm; Sept. daily 9am-5pm; Oct.-Apr. M-F 9am-3pm.) To get to the park from Tallinn, take the **Rakvere** bus to **Viitna** (1hr., 28 per day, 15-45EEK; ISIC discount available). From there, catch a bus to Palmse Mõis or walk the 7km road. Call the visitor center for the bus schedule from Viitna to Palmse Mõis. Most buses are infrequent and run only on alternate days; biking and hiking are the only ways to get around if you don't want to wait. For direct access to the **coast** and the **Palmse Manor House,** inquire at the Tallinn station about buses to **Võsu** via **Loksa** (3 per week). See below for details on **bike rental,** available at the hostel Sagadi Mõis (50EEK per hr., 200EEK per day) and at the Park Hotell Restaurant (100EEK per day). **Postal Code:** 45202.

⁊ ◖ **ACCOMMODATIONS AND FOOD.** Near Palmse, the best bet is the **Ojaäärse Hostel ❶.** From Viitna, turn right about 500m before the visitor center. Clearly marked, the hostel is located in a spacious clearing 1.5km down the road. (Singles 100EEK.) Situated a scenic 8km hike from Võsu in the village of Käsmu, **Lainela Puhkemajaad ❶,** toward the end of Neema, offers small, tidy rooms close to the sea. A basketball court, two tennis courts, and a sauna are on the premises. (☎/ fax 381 33. Singles 170EEK; doubles 340EEK. Tent space 40EEK per person.) For more luxurious, inland lodging, try **Sagadi Mõis ❺,** which offers rooms with phone and private bath. (☎588 88; fax 588 80. Breakfast included. Singles 600EEK; doubles 750EEK. MC/V.) In Viitna proper, the lakeside **campground ❶** is 400m past the bus stop, through the wooden arch on the right. Tent space and rooms in log cabins are available. (☎936 51. Tent space 20EEK per person. Doubles 180EEK.)

In the wilds of Palmse Mõis, the **Park Hotell Restaurant ❷** prepares fresh salads for 15EEK and *schnitzel* for 60EEK. (☎236 26. Open daily 11am-10pm.) The **restaurant ❷** inside Sagadi Mõis (see above) offers savory meals (50-100EEK) and a full vegetarian menu. The **tavern ❷** in Viitna, opposite the bus stop, sells hearty dishes for 50-100EEK. (☎586 81. Open daily 8am-11pm.)

◖ ⁊ **SIGHTS AND ENTERTAINMENT. Palmse Manor** is among the best restored and most historically significant estates in Lahemaa. The von Pahlen family resided here among the manor's ostentatious gazebos and swan ponds from 1677 until 1923, when the government reclaimed all private land. Peter Ludwig was involved in the 1801 assassination of Russian Tsar Paul I and Alexander initiated the building of the Tallinn-St. Petersburg railroad in 1879. The estate itself includes eclectic furniture from all over the country. The manor grounds include period gardens, stables, and servants' quarters that now house a small museum with vintage cars and motorcycles. The **Museum of Forestry,** the first white building on the left through the gates, explores the park's plant and tree life. (☎688 88. Manor open May-Aug. daily 10am-7pm; Sept. daily 10am-6pm; Oct.-Apr. Tu-Su 10am-3pm. 25EEK, students 15EEK. Car museum open May-Aug. daily 10am-7pm; Sept. 10am-5pm. 20EEK/10EEK. Forestry museum open May 15-Sept. 30 daily 11am-6pm. 20EEK/15EEK. Combined ticket for manor and forestry museum 30EEK.)

The **famine stones** are 1km past the tourist office just outside the town limits sign for Palmse. These large mounds of limestone were piled up by serfs picking rocks from the fields to prepare them for plowing. They're a testament to peasant toil. Next to the Lainela Puhkemajaad, the **Kásmús Maritime Museum,** Kásmús Merekööl

FROM THE ROAD

AN OLD FRIEND

I arrived in Pärnu on one of the busiest weekends of the year—in late July when the festival **Watergate** brought various water sports and concerts to the beach, and **Guild Days** jammed Rüütli street with Estonian crafts and souvenirs. This also meant that all the hostels and hotels in Estonia's summer capital were booked. Luckily, I managed to get a room in a private home, which is often the best option for backpackers on their own. Such homes tend to be inhabited by elderly, garrulous ladies who may or may not speak English. If you are able to find a common language (Russian in my case), they can tell about the inside story of wherever you are staying—usually over a comforting pot of tea. They have lived through a decade of independence, and can tell you what life was like during Soviet times.

My host had some mixed feelings about the rapid changes taking place. There is no question that Estonia is more free today and its economy is booming, but there is less stability and only a meager pension for the elderly. I heard similar views echoed by older people throughout the Baltics. Although the country is generally better off, pensioners gripe that they have been largely forgotten, and many must do whatever they can in order to make ends meet. This economic crunch has had unexpected benefits for travelers like me, though; I have made some wise and hospitable friends that I otherwise may never have gotten a chance to chat with.

—Dunia Dickey

3, introduces visitors to the history of the surrounding fishing village, which once served as a ship-building center and a school for sailors. Ask the proprietor, Aarne Vaik, for a tour. (☎529 71 35. Open daily 9am-9pm. Free.) On the far side of the Puhkemajaad Neemetee, a path through the woods opens to a rocky beach where the **stone hill** grants wishes to those who contribute new rocks to the mound. Ice Age glaciers carried boulders all the way from Finland; they remain here, 8m tall in the sand. During the 1950s, the Soviets closed off much of the northern coast with barbed wire and banned fishing; **Altja** is one of the few fishing villages remaining. The fishing huts on the cape are part of an open-air **museum.** (Open 24hr.) As you continue around the cape and cross the river, white stripes on the trees mark a short trail that runs through the forest and back to town. The new harbor visible is **Vergi,** connected to the cape by a land bridge 2.5km farther along the road. In the first half of July, the **Vihula Folklore Festival** summons storytellers from around the world. In July 2003, the **International Bagpipe Festival** (and its heavy Scottish contingent) will fill the woodland expanse with its din.

PÄRNU   ☎(0)44

The summer capital of Estonia, Pärnu (PAER-noo; pop. 45,040), long a Hanseatic trade center, got its makeover as a resort in the early 19th century and hasn't looked back since. After toiling long under its Soviet stepmother, the "Cinderella of the Baltics" has gone from sooty to glamorously muddy, drawing crowds to its famous mud baths, beaches, and breezes.

▮ TRANSPORTATION

Trains: The station is 3km east of the center, near the corner of Riia and Raja; take bus #15 or 40 to Raeküla Rdtj (6EEK). To **Tallinn** (3hr., 2 per day, 40EEK).

Buses: Ringi 3 (☎720 02, Eurolines 278 41; fax 417 55). To: **Haapsalu** (2½hr., 1 per day, 76EEK); **Kuressaare** (2½hr., 5 per day, 100-120EEK); **Tallinn** (2hr., 46 per day, 30-80EEK); **Tartu** (2½hr., 24 per day, 45-180EEK); **Rīga, LAT** (3½hr., 4 per day, 110-150EEK); **St. Petersburg, RUS** (11hr., 1 per day, 240EEK).

Taxis: Pärnu Takso (☎412 40) and **E-Takso** (☎311 11). 6-7EEK per km.

Bike Rental: Rattapood, Riia 95 (☎324 40). 75EEK per day. Open M-F 10am-6pm, Sa 10am-2pm. June-Aug. also at various stands on the beach.

■▮ ORIENTATION AND PRACTICAL INFORMATION

The **River Pärnu** neatly bisects the city. The town center is on the seaside, stretching from the inlet **Vallikraav** to the bus station on **Ringi**. The main street is **Rüütli**. A short walk down **Nikolai** and **Supeluse** from the center of town leads to the **mud baths** and the **beach**. **Ranna pst.** runs along the beach and becomes **Mere pst.** on its way back into town. Be sure not to confuse the two streets **Aia** and **Aisa**.

Tourist Office: Rüütli 16 (☎730 00; fax 730 01; www.parnu.ee). Hands out the invaluable *Pärnu In Your Pocket* and **maps** for free. Open May 15-Sept. 15 M-F 9am-6pm, Sa 9am-4pm, Su 10am-3pm; Sept. 16-May 14 M-F 9am-5pm. If the office is closed, get info from Hotel Pärnu, Rüütli 44.

Currency Exchange: Eesti Ühispank, Rüütli 40a (☎771 00; fax 771 10). Cashes AmEx **Traveler's Cheques** for 25EEK commission, and others for 1% commission. Also gives **cash advances** and has a MC/V **ATM.** Open M-F 9am-6pm, Sa 9am-2pm.

American Express: Estravel, Kuninga 34 (☎737 71; fax 310 63; www.estravel.ee), on the street parallel to Rüütli. Open M-F 9am-6pm, Sa 10am-3pm.

Luggage Storage: Outside the **bus station,** opposite the terminals. 3-10EEK for 24hr. depending on weight. Open M-F 8am-7:30pm, Sa 8am-1pm and 1:45-7pm, Su 9am-1pm and 1:45-7pm.

Hospital: Pärnu Hospital, Sillutise 6 (☎731 01; fax 761 02; www.ph.ee).

Internet Access: Rüütli Internetipunkt, Rüütli 25 (☎315 52). The entrance is through the courtyard in the yellow building. 13 fast connections for 20EEK per hr. Open M-F 10am-9pm, Sa-Su 10am-6pm. **Hallo,** Rüütli 5 (☎730 25), past the post office. 2 connections for 20EEK per hr. Open M-F 9am-6pm, Sa 9am-3pm.

Post Office: Akadeemia 7 (☎711 11). The west end of Rüütli. Open M-F 8am-6pm, Sa 9am-3pm.

Postal Code: 80010.

▮ ACCOMMODATION

Pärnu has become a popular vacation spot, and rooms fill up quickly, so reserve far in advance. **Tanni-Vakoma Majutusbüroo ❶,** Hommiku 5, behind the bus station, rents **private rooms.** The office is only open from May to August but can be reached by phone year-round. (☎310 70, mobile 051 853 19; fax 275 86; tanni@online.ee. Open May-Aug. M-F 10am-8pm, Sa-Su 10am-3pm. 130-330EEK per person.)

Külalistemaja Delfine, Supeluse 22 (☎269 00; fax 269 01; www.delfine.ee). From the bus station, turn left on Ringi, left on Pühavaimu, and left again on Supeluse. Delfine is the yellow building on the right. Great rooms with bath, TV, and phone in a cheerful guesthouse very close to the beach. Sauna 150EEK per hr. Breakfast included. Singles 550EEK; doubles 700EEK; triples 850EEK. MC/V. ❸

Hostel Lõuna, Lõuna 2 (☎309 43; fax 309 44; hostellouna@hot.ee). From the bus station, walk down Ringi, turn right on Rüütli, left on Vee, and right on Lõuna; the hostel is at the end of the block on the 2nd fl. Bright comfortable rooms near the beach and the city center. Breakfast 30EEK. Dorms 250EEK. ❷

Linnakämping Green, Suure-Jõe 50b (☎387 76; fax 358 11; matti@estpak.ee), is 3km from the town center. Take bus #9 or 40 from the bus station along Riia to Tammsaare. Backtrack, turn right on Kastani, and hang another right on Suure-Jõe. Pärnu's cheapest and most basic accommodations. Facilities include gnome-sized cabins, a bar, a basketball court, and bathrooms in the boathouse. Boat rental 30EEK per hr. Call ahead. Breakfast 30EEK. Open June-Aug. Tent site 60EEK; cabin bed 60-95EEK. ❶

ESTONIA

◘ FOOD

A *turg* (market) is on the corner of Sepa and Karja. (Open M-F 8am-6pm, Sa 8am-4pm, Su 9am-3pm.)

Trahter Postipoiss, Vee 12 (☎648 64; 648 61; www.restaurant.ee). This child-friendly restaurant serves diminutive but delicious portions of Russian treats such as *blini* and *borscht,* as well as meat and fish dishes. Entrees 45-175EEK. Live music and dancing F-Sa from 9pm. Call ahead. Open Su-Th noon-midnight, F-Sa noon-2am. MC/V. ❷

Mandarin, Mere pst. 22 (☎648 75 or 394 69). Serves tasty and filling Chinese food right by the beach. Vegetarian options available. Entrees 60-150EEK. 18% service charge. Open daily noon-midnight. ❷

Georg, Rüütli 43 (☎311 10), at the corner with Hommiku, is a cafeteria-style joint that's dirt cheap and packed with locals. Entrees under 35EEK. Open M-F 7:30am-10pm, Sa-Su 9am-10pm. V. ❶

◎ SIGHTS

Mud has never looked or felt better than at Pärnu's Neo-Classical **Mudaravila,** Ranna pst. 1, a health resort that celebrated its 75th anniversary in 2002. Get covered with mud for 90-130EEK. (☎255 20; www.mudaravila.ee. Massages 220EEK. "Curative" bath or shower 60-75EEK. Open daily 8am-3pm.) If you don't want to get dirty, head to one of several local museums. The **Museum of New Art,** Esplanaadi 10, also known as the Chaplin Center, exhibits unorthodox contemporary art. Look for the statue of a headless Lenin with a red police light on its nape, entitled *Bye-bye to the 20th Century!* (☎307 72; fax 307 74; www.chaplin.ee. Open daily 9am-9pm. 15EEK, students 10EEK.) The **Pärnu Regional Museum** (Pärnu Rajoonide Vaheline Koduloomuuseum), Rüütli 53, houses rotating exhibitions on the first floor and displays everything from taxidermy to Stone Age tools on the second. The final display case contains heart-wrenching letters from local children to their exiled parents in Siberia. (☎332 31; fax 332 32. Info in Estonian and Russian only. Open July daily 10am-6pm; Aug.-June W-Su 10am-6pm. 30EEK, students 15EEK.) The **Lydia Koidula Museum,** Jannseni 37, across the River Pärnu, commemorates the 19th-century poet who revived Estonian verse and drama. (See **The Arts,** p. 299; ☎416 63. Open W-Su 10am-5pm. 5EEK, students 3EEK.)

At the corner of Uus and Vee one block north of Rüütli, the Russian Orthodox **Catherine Church** (Ekateriina kirik), Vee 8, is a multi-spired, silver-and-green structure built in the 1760s by order of Catherine the Great. The interior, which shimmers with icons, is even more astonishing than the outer facade. (☎431 98. Open M-F 11am-6pm, Sa-Su 9am-6pm. Services Sa 8:30am and 6pm, Su 9am.) Rüütli ends at an **open-air theater,** where local artists perform in the summer, beginning in July. Turn left off Rüütli before you reach the open-air theater to pass through **Tallinn Gate** (Tallinna värav). A broad, tree-lined street stretches south from the gate to the white-sand **beach.** Women can bathe **nude** on the right side of the beach; watch for the sign. Swings, jungle-gyms, and trampolines are set up on the sand, and a free waterslide is open from June to August.

◘ ♬ FESTIVALS AND NIGHTLIFE

In mid-June, the **Estonian Country Dance Festival** takes place at Sassi Horse Farm, near Pärnu, and ends with a line dance that stretches down the length of Rüütli (☎500 70; www.noorusemaja.ee). The end of June, when **Hello, Pärnu Summer!** hits the city, marks the beginning of the festival season (☎764 91). The **Pärnu David Oistrakh Festival,** which spans the end of June and early July, draws musicians and conductors from the international scene to Pärnu's outdoor venues. (☎665 40; www.hot.ee./oistfest.) The **International Film Festival,** in early July, features documentaries and anthropological films. (☎307 72; www.chaplin.ee.) Artists from around the world come to the Pärnu Jazz Festival during late June and early July. (www.parnujazz.com.) The news-breaking Watergate festival brings every water activity imaginable to Pärnu in mid-July. (☎919 66; www.watergate.ee.) On summer evenings, the temporary bars that set up along the beach draw both drinkers and sunset-gazers. **Mirage,** Rüütli 40, the current top dog of the discos, appeals to booty-shakers of all ages. (☎446 70; www.mirage.ee. Open Sa-Th 10pm-3am, F-Sa 10pm-4am. Cover around 50EEK.) On the beach, **Sunset Club,** Ranna pst. 3, offers sand as well as a dance floor, and hosts bands. (☎306 70. Open W-Th 10pm-4am, F-Sa 10pm-6am.) For a more sedate atmosphere, try **Tallinna Värav,** Vana-Tallinna 1, a stone tavern atop the grand Tallinn Gate. (☎450 73. Entrees 20-80EEK. *Saku* 20EEK. Open daily 11am-11pm.)

HAAPSALU ☎(0)47

Haapsalu (HAAP-sa-loo), once the seat of the Saare-Lääne bishopric that ruled most of western Estonia in the 13th century, now reigns as a point for relaxation, sailing, and a healthy mud wash. In the 19th century Haapsalu was famed throughout the Russian Empire for its curative mud baths, but its reputation faded in the 20th century when the Soviets planted a military base here. After years of abandonment, Haapsalu is coming back into its own as a resort.

▐ TRANSPORTATION. The **bus station,** Raudtee 2, occupies the tsars' former train station. The massive covered platform (at 216m, the longest in Europe) was built by Nicholas II to ensure that his party wouldn't get wet while disembarking. (☎347 91. Ticket office open daily 5am-1pm and 2-7pm.) To: **Kärdla** (3hr., 3 per day, 65EEK); **Pärnu** (2-3hr., 3 per day, 76EEK); and **Tallinn** (1½-2hr., 25 per day, 30-51EEK). **Trains** no longer run to Haapsalu. **Taxis** (☎335 00) charge 5EEK per km.

▐▐ ORIENTATION AND PRACTICAL INFORMATION. To reach the center from the bus station, take Jaama and turn left on Posti. At the **tourist office,** Posti 37, just down the street, the English-speaking staff provides **maps.** (☎33 248; fax 33 464; www.haapsalu.ee. Open May 15-Sept. 15 M-F 9am-6pm, Sa-Su 10am-3pm; Sept. 16-May 14 M-F 9am-5pm.) **Exchange currency** or use the **24hr. ATM** at **Hansapank,** Posti 41. (☎202 00. Open M-F 8:30am-5:30pm, Sa 9am-2pm.) The **Läänemaa Pharmacy** is at Karja 1 (☎370 73; open M-F 9am-7pm, Sa 9am-4pm, Su 10am-2pm), while the local **hospital** is at Vaba 6 (☎112, emergency 258 70, info 258 75). Free **Internet access** is available upstairs at the library, Posti 3. (☎355 99. Open M-F 10am-6pm, Sa 11am-4pm.) If you don't want to wait in line, head to **Hallo,** Posti 26. (☎204 80. 20EEK per hr. Open M-F 9am-6pm, Sa 10am-3pm.) The **post office** is at Nurme 2. (☎204 00. Open M-F 7:30am-6pm, Sa 8am-3pm.) **Postal Code:** 90 501.

▐▐ ACCOMMODATIONS AND FOOD. For a great deal, head to **Jahtklubi ❷** (Yacht Club), Holmi 5a, at the end of the peninsula. Follow Posti past the tourist office as it turns into Karja and turn left on Ehte. With the lake on your left, turn right on Sadama, then veer left on Uus-Sadama. Finally, make a right on Kaluri and another right on Holmi. Jahtklubi is accessible by the infrequent bus #2, but your best bet is to walk. The hotel offers basic but clean rooms with hall baths, a bar, a small outdoor restaurant, and miniature golf. (☎356 32; fax 356 27. Restaurant open daily 7am-2am. Internet access 20EEK per hr. Bike rental 140EEK per day. All rooms 350EEK.) For more convenient housing, try **Rong-Hotell ❶** (Train-Hotel), a train-turned-hostel located on the tracks of the old train station. (☎346 64. Open June-Sept. Linen 25EEK. Singles 99EEK; doubles 198EEK; lux coupe 150EEK.) The

ESTONIA

Paralepa Puhkemaja ❶ lies on a gorgeous beach behind the Fra More Sanatorium, 10min. from the bus station. Small, clean rooms with bunkbeds, and tent sites. (☎051 067 35; fax 558 49; bjumest@webs.ee. Open June 1-Sept 1. Doubles 280EEK; triples 420EEK; quads 560EEK. Tent site 35EEK for one person, 55EEK for two, and 90EEK for three.) The **outdoor market** *(turg)* is one block from the bus station, on the corner of Jürlöö and Jaama. (Open Tu-Su 7am-2pm.) **Säästu market,** Jaame 12, is a well-stocked supermarket on the way from the bus station. (Open daily 9am-9pm. MC/V.) **The Central Restoran ❸,** Karja 12, has meat and fish entrees (55-145EEK) and veggie options. The mellow beer cellar downstairs lacks the garish green decor of the restaurant upstairs. (☎355 95. Beer 15-20EEK. Open Su-Th noon-midnight, F-Sa noon-2am.) **Laterna Bar ❶,** Lahe 12, offers a 10% ISIC discount. (☎333 48. Open M-F 11am-midnight, Sa-Su noon-midnight.)

🟦 SIGHTS. The **Estonian Railway Museum** (Eesti Raudteemuuseum), Raudtee 2, at the train station, contains old train schedules, devices salvaged from trains, and even a three-wheel bike designed to run on tracks. A photo from Sept. 22, 1995 captures the last voyage of a passenger train on the Haapsalu-Riisipere line. (☎345 74; www.jaam.ee. Open W-Su 10am-6pm. 15EEK, students 5EEK.) For a look at the turrets and fortifications of old, head to **Bishop's Castle** (Piiskopilinnus), about halfway up the peninsula. First built in 1265, the building was home to the powerful ruler-bishops of Saare-Lääne bishopric from 1302 until 1358, when the head honcho relocated with the rest of the clerics to Saaremaa. A large portion of the castle has since been restored and now houses a **museum,** which exhibits period costumes, a scale model of the old castle, and informative plaques about the town's history. (Open Tu-Su 10am-6pm. 15EEK, students 5EEK.) The museum and the fortification itself are less impressive than the **Castle Park** and the dazzlingly renovated chapel in the **Episcopal Church** next door. Climb the steep and ragged steps of the castle tower for a view of Haapsalu and the seas. To get to the castle, follow Kalda or Posti from the bus station to the town center. When they converge onto Karja and merge into Lossiplats (Castle Square), which opens onto the castle grounds. (Park open daily 7am-9pm. Chapel admission included in museum ticket. Tower 10EEK.) From there, head back on Karja, hang a right on Ehte, then turn left on Valkne Kallas and follow Lahe around the lake; veer right on Väike-Viigi and the yellow house with the red roof on your left will be the **Cyrillus Kreek Apartment Museum** (Cyrillus Kreegi Kortermuuseum), Vaike-Viigi 10. Kreek (1889-1962), the famous composer of choral and national music, also collected folk songs from villages throughout Estonia and directed several song festivals. He lived in this tiny two-room apartment with his family from 1939 to 1962. (☎370 65; www.muuseum.haapsalu.ee. Open May 1-Oct. 1 W-Su 2-6pm.) Great **walking** paths stretch near the castle: the **Africa Beach** (Aafrikarand) promenade, northeast of the castle at the end of Rüütli, runs 2km to the yacht club, while **Kaluri,** farther east, winds past wooden houses and marshland.

🟦 FESTIVALS. Haapsalu's grand celebrations center around the **White Lady Days,** which occur annually at the beginning of August. Concerts, waltzes, open-air theater, and a number of ladies clothed in white mark the festivities. (☎355 16; www.daam.haapsalu.ee.) In early July, the **Old Music Festival** brings in noted interpreters of medieval tunes and the **Haapsalu Fire Night** lights up town with fireworks. The bi-annual **Interteaterfest** will be drawing amateur and semi-professional theater companies for performances in July 2004. (☎356 52; www.haapsalu/itf.) Early August brings blues and American cars to the Bishop's Castle as part of the **Augustibluus Blues Festival.** (☎056 48 90 166; www.haapsalu.ee/augustibluus.) The **Baltic/Nordic Jazz Festival** "Only Girls in Jazz" brings female jazz musicians to Haapsalu. (☎050 977 95; www.kuursaal.ee.) In mid-August, the **Pjotr Tchaikovsky Music Festival** celebrates the music of the famous composer, who spent a summer in Haapsalu in 1867 (☎050 324 68).

ESTONIAN ISLANDS

Estonia's 1521 islands, which extend far into the Baltic Sea, preserve much that is distinctive about Estonia. The largest three—Saaremaa, Hiiumaa, and Muhu—are becoming popular with vacationers, but don't yet feel like modern resorts. Afraid the islands would become an escape route out of the USSR, Soviet officials isolated the region from outside influence, and the tourists are just now returning.

SAAREMAA ISLAND

The largest and most visited of the Estonian islands, Saaremaa (SAA-reh-maa; pop. 38,760) is often considered more Estonian than mainland Estonia. Mysterious meteorite craters, bubbling springs, rugged coasts, and formidable cliffs testify that natural beauty is everywhere in largely forested Saaremaa. Come summer, young Estonians from the mainland arrive in increasing numbers to party beachside, adding a surge of energy and revelry to the otherwise austere serenity of the island. As distances are long and buses infrequent, the best way to see the entire island is to rent a car in Kuressaare.

KURESSAARE   ☎ (0)45

Kuressaare (KOO-res-saa-re; pop. 15,820), on Saaremaa's southern coast, is the island's largest town, and is currently experiencing a tourism revival. When the Soviets shut the town off from visitors they slowed the pace of life, but luckily left the landscape alone. Looking much as it did in its first incarnation as a resort, Kuressaare is rapidly rising in popularity.

TRANSPORTATION. Direct **buses**, which get priority on the ferries, are the fastest way to the mainland. From the station, Pihtla tee 2 (☎316 61), at the corner of Tallinna, buses head to: **Pärnu** (3½hr., 5 per day, 99-120EEK); **Tallinn** (3-4hr., 10 per day, 100-160EEK); and **Tartu** (5½-6½hr., 5 per day, 170-184EEK). A new **ferry** route island-hops between **Triigi** on Saaremaa and **Sõru** on Hiiumaa (1hr.; 3 per day in summer, 2 per day in winter Th-Tu; 50EEK, students 30EEK). **Taxis** run from the town hall, the bus station, and Smuuli pst. (☎533 33. 6EEK per km.) Visitors can rent **bikes** from **Õu Bivarix,** Tallinna 26, near the bus station (☎571 18; bivarix@saar-lane.ee; 135EEK per day; open M-Sa 10am-6pm) or **cars** from **Polar Rent,** Tallinna 9. (☎336 99; www.polarrent.ee. From 790EEK per day.)

ORIENTATION AND PRACTICAL INFORMATION. The town is centered around the narrow **Raekoja pl.** (Town Hall Square). The **tourist office,** Tallinna 2, inside the Town Hall, sells **maps** (10EEK) and books **private rooms.** (☎/fax 331 20; www.visitestonia.com. Open May-Sept. 15 M-F 9am-7pm, Sa 9am-5pm, Su 10am-3pm; Sept. 16-Apr. M-F 9am-5pm.) **Exchange currency,** cash traveler's checks, and get MC/V cash advances at **Eesti Ühispank,** Kauba 2. (☎215 00; fax 215 33. Open M-Sa 9am-5:30pm, Sa 9am-2pm.) **Luggage storage** is available outside the bus station. (3-5EEK for 24hr. Open M-F 7:15am-2pm and 2:30-8pm, Sa 7:15am-2pm and 2:30-6pm.) Access the **Internet** for free at **Hallo,** Komandandi 6 (☎211 11; fax 211 12; www.hallo.ee) or at the **Interneti Punkt** in the Piljardisaal, Raekoja 1, where beer and billiards are also available. (☎541 96. 15EEK per 30min. Open daily noon-11pm.) The **post office,** Torni 1, is on the corner of Komandandi. (☎240 80. Open M-F 8am-6pm, Sa 8:30am-3pm.) **Postal Code:** 93 801.

ACCOMMODATIONS AND FOOD. The **tourist office** ❷ (see p. 317) can arrange **private rooms** (200-250EEK). **Transvaali 28 B&B** ❸, Transvaali 28, is a 5min. walk from the town center. All rooms are renovated and have bath and TV. (☎333 34; fax 246 16; www.saaremaa.ee/transvaali28. Breakfast included. 250EEK per

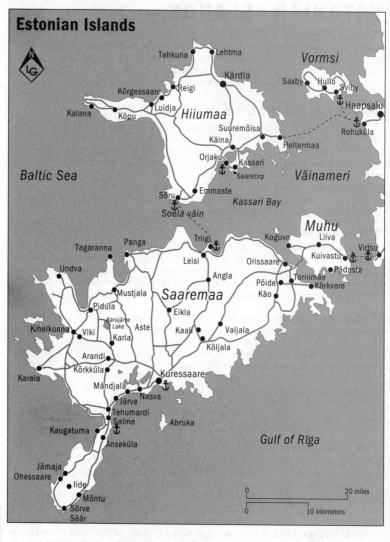

Estonian Islands

person.) **Mändjala Puhkeküla ❶**, Kuressaare Vald, 11km out of town by the "Kämping" stop on the Kuressaare-Järve bus, offers tent space and big cabins along a beach. (☎441 93; fax 442 01. Open May-Sept. Dorms 180EEK. Camping 40EEK.) **Vanalinna ❹**, Kauba 8, serves delicious fish for 99-130EEK and wild boar for 160-180EEK. (☎/fax 553 09. Open daily noon-midnight. MC/V.) The 100-year old **Restoran Veski ❷**, Pärna 19, in the old windmill, serves steak and seafood (56-170EEK) to four floors of diners. (☎337 76. Live music M-Sa 9pm. Open Su-Th noon-midnight, F-Sa noon-2am.) **Supermarket EDU**, Tallinna 1, sells meat and fresh produce. (Open M-F 8am-4pm, Sa 8am-3pm.)

COPS AND ROBBERS Mention hooliganism and soccer in the same sentence and most people will conjure up visions of brawls between drunk fans. Rarely would anyone picture a soccer team *made up* of hooligans, let alone a group of ne'er-do-wells who annually organize themselves into a soccer team. But then again, not many people have visited Kuressare in June. A few years back, an Estonian policy-maker had the bright idea to let the troublemakers and lawmakers vent their pent-up aggression on the playing field. Since then, every June, the cops with their badges and the punks with their rainbow mohawks have had at each other with a flurry of slide tackles and obscenities. The quality of the footballing is usually rather poor—especially by the end of the game, after the keg of beer on the punks' sideline has had its effect—but the game is a town spectacle that draws crowds of fans. Perhaps not surprisingly, almost everyone who attends supports the underdogs against the long leg of the law.

🔘📱 **SIGHTS AND FESTIVALS. Town Hall Square** (Raekoja pl), is lined by 17th-century buildings, the most notable of which is the 1670 **Town Hall** *(raekoda)*, built by Swedish landowner Marcus Gabriel de la Gardie. Inside, a gallery presents temporary exhibitions by Estonian artists, and the second floor has a newly reinstalled 17th-century ceiling painting brought back from Tallinn. (☎332 66. Open June-Aug. M-Sa 10am-6pm, Su 10am-3pm; Sept.-May Tu-Sa 11am-5pm.) Past the square's south end stands a **statue** commemorating the 1918-20 struggle for independence. It's actually a 1990 replica of the original, which was erected in 1928 but destroyed by the Soviets. The massive ▨ **Bishopric Castle** (Piiskopilinnus), down Lossi from the tourist office, is through a sleepy park and across a moat. Built in 1260 after the Teutonic Order conquered the island, the castle was renovated in the 1300s for the Bishop of Saare-Lääne, who liked it so much that in 1358 he declared it the bishopric's administrative center. The eclectic **Saaremaa Museum**, located in the castle, chronicles the island's history with intricately carved coats-of-arms, carriages, and military and maritime objects. Practice your archery skills outside on the castle grounds. (☎563 07. Open May 1-Sept.1 daily 10am-6pm; Sept.-Apr. W-Su 11am-6pm. 30EEK, students 15EEK. 2hr. audio tours in English, Russian, or Estonian 60EEK. Archery open daily 10am-5pm. 4 arrows 10EEK, 15min. 50EEK.) On weekends in July, there's **live music** in the park around the castle. (Shows at 6pm. Sa brass band, Su orchestra. In late July, **Õlletoober,** a beer festival, peps up Leisi, while an **Opera Festival** takes over Kuresaare and the **Mustjala Classical Music Festival** hits nearby Mustjala (see **West Saaremaa,** below). Early August brings sailing competitions and musical performances during the **Maritime Days.**

WEST SAAREMAA

To get to **Karujärve Lake,** take the road to Kinelkonna about 18km. From the main road, you will see a sign to Kärla; turn right on a dirt road. At the main intersection, go right on the paved road. You should see a sign for Karujärve at the intersection. After 5km, you'll see the Karujärve **Campground** on the left. It has campsites, small cabins for two, and access to nearby swimming and horseback riding. (☎421 81; fax 420 34. Open May 15-Sept. 1. Horseback riding 80EEK per hr. Campsites 35EEK; 2-person cabins 270EEK.) If you head back to Kärla and then to the main road, it will take you toward **Kihelkonna** past the **Mihkli Farm Museum** (Mihkli Talumuuseum) in Viki, where 19th-century farmhouses cluster around a garden. (☎466 13. Open May-Sept. daily 10am-6pm. 15EEK, students 10EEK.) Farther along the road, turn left down the hill to Kihelkonna, where the 13th-century **Kihelkonna Church** depicts a relief of Archangel Michael fighting a dragon and boasts an impressive Baltic bell tower built separately from a church. Turn around and pass the Kihelkonna-Kuressaare road to reach the quietly bubbling **Odalästi Springs,** rumored to bring eternal youth, on your left. Keep

ESTONIA

going toward **Pidula** and you will find the **Pidula fish farm** ❹ on your left. Here they raise 'em, release 'em, catch 'em, and fry 'em. (☎465 13. If you catch it yourself, plain 100EEK per kg; salted 110EEK per kg; grilled 135EEK per kg. Open daily 9am-11pm.)

From **Mustjala** you can reach two peninsulas: **Tagaranna** has an impressive shoreline, and **Panga** has an amazing 25m drop (you might recognize it from the back of the 100EEK note). If you go to Tagaranna, skirt the tip of the peninsula to reach a former **Soviet training facility,** complete with trenches and barbed wire now overgrown with lupines. The facility is one of the venues used during the **Mustjala Classical Music Festival** that hits town at the end of July every year. If you choose Panga, climb up the **"lighthouse,"** a ladder enclosed by scaffolding. Be careful: the steps are steep and the wind strong.

SOUTHWEST SAAREMAA

Renting a bike (see **Orientation and Practical Information,** p. 317) is one of the best ways to explore Southwest Saaremaa, which starts at Kuressaare and stretches down to the Sõrve peninsula. The first stops on the route south from Kuressaare are the quiet beaches of **Mändjala** and **Järve,** 8-12km west of town. To reach Mändjala, take the first left after the "Mändjala 1" bus stop. For the beach in Järve, turn left after the "Ranna" bus stop. At **Tehumardi,** a giant concrete sword and rows of memorials mark the location of a 1944 World War II battle. Farther on, **Salme,** 17km out of Kuressaare, makes a good lunch stop. About 2km from Salme, a sign points along an unpaved road to **Lide,** which cuts over to the west side of **Sõrve poolsaar** (the peninsula). There, the choppy waters of the open Baltic meet rocky beaches. The "cliffs" at **Kaugatuma** (often overrated by tourist offices) border fossil-strewn beaches and pastures with grazing cows. About 5km down the road, the ruins of the **World War II defense line** are visible. At **Sõrve säär,** the tip of the peninsula, clear weather reveals a view of Latvia, 25km south across the Baltic. The 1960 **Sõrve lighthouse** can also be found here. On the trip back, the road through **Mõntu** (in the opposite direction from Jämaja) passes through the **national park.**

MUHU ISLAND

Between Saaremaa and the mainland, Muhu bears witness to centuries of Estonian religious history. The first sight you'll see on the island is **Eemu Tuulik,** a large windmill just off the coast. (Open Apr. 15-Oct. 1 W-Su 11am-6pm. 5EEK, students 3EEK.) Farther on, **Muhu Katariina Church** in Liiva is an edifice dating from at least 1267. With no steeple and bright asymmetrical stained-glass, it looks a bit avant-garde. Portions of the early-Gothic church's 13th-century murals are still visible through the layers of whitewash with which they were plastered during the Reformation. The trapezoidal tombstones in the churchyard recall the pagan religions that found a refuge on these islands when mainland Estonia was converted to Roman Catholicism. (Church open daily 10am-6pm.) Slightly east of Liiva and off the main highway, a dirt road veers right 8km to Muhu's **south shore** and the 17th-century **Pädaste Manor** (Pädaste Mõis), which is currently under renovation. To get to Muhu, you can **bike** across the bridge from Saaremaa. Though the ride is short, it's viciously windy. **Buses** run from Kuressaare to **Kuivastu** on Muhu (1hr., 11 per day, 30EEK) and also stop in Liiva. **Vanatoa Tunsmitalu** ❷, on Muhu vald in Koguva, next to the Muhu Open-Air Museum, offers sunny accommodations and good meals at very moderate prices. (☎488 84. Breakfast included. 275EEK per person.) **Aki Kõrts** ❷, in Liiva near Muhu Church, has small but clean cabins, tent sites, and a restaurant that serves hearty fare. (☎981 04; www.muhu.ee/aki. Breakfast 35EEK. Laundry 25EEK per load. Entrees 42-125EEK. Open daily 8am-midnight. Singles 140EEK; doubles 250EEK; quads 500EEK.)

HIIUMAA ISLAND

By restricting access to Hiiumaa (HEE-you-ma; pop. 11,497) for 50 years, the Soviets unwittingly preserved many rare plant and animal species, as well as the island's pre-Communist way of life. Native residents speak of ghosts, giants, trolls, and devils who inhabited Hiiumaa before them, and the unadorned churches, history-laden lighthouses, and shrines support such claims. With endless groves ringing the few spots of habitation, Hiiumaa is a restful haven for all weary spirits.

KÄRDLA ☎(0)246

The Swedish settlers who stumbled across this sleepy spot on Hiiumaa's north coast named it "Kärrdal," meaning "lovely valley." Home to many more creeks and trees than houses, Kärdla (pop. 4118) is hardly an urban center, but with easy access to the beach and bike rentals, the town remains the gateway to Hiiumaa.

 More than two-thirds of all the plant species native to Estonia exist only on Hiiumaa. Due to this biodiversity, much of the island now belongs to the **West Estonian Islands Biosphere Reserve.** Hiking and camping are permitted and encouraged; just be sure to pick up info at the tourist office about off-limits regions. Motor vehicles are not allowed on the seashore and campfires and smoking are prohibited in some areas due to dry conditions.

TRANSPORTATION. Catch a **bus** to the mainland. (Ticket price includes the ferry). The **bus station** is at Sadama 13. (☎320 77. Open daily 7am-7pm.) Buses run to **Haapsalu** (2½hr.; 3 per day, Sa-Su 2 per day; 65EEK) and **Tallinn** (4½hr.; M-F 3 per day, Sa-Su 2 per day; 140EEK) as well as to points around the island (0.40EEK per km). A **shuttle** from the station runs to **Heltermaa** (1hr., 5 per day, 20EEK) and **Sõru** (1hr., 2 per day, 25EEK). **Ferries** go to **Heltermaa** from Rohuküla, south of Haapsalu (1½hr.; Su-F 7 per day, Sa 6 per day; 45EEK, students 20EEK, W and Su 137-150EEK, 98EEK per car) and **Sõru** from Triigi (1hr.; 3 per day; 50EEK, students 30EEK, 150EEK per car). For a **taxi** call ☎314 47.

PRACTICAL INFORMATION. The island's **tourist office,** Hiiu 1, in **Keskväljak,** the main square, sells **maps** (15-40EEK) and the indispensable biking guide "The Lighthouse Tour." (25EEK; ☎222 32; fax 222 34; www.hiiumaa.ee. Open May-Sept. M-F 9am-6pm, Sa-Su 10am-2pm; Oct.-Apr. M-F 10am-4pm.) **Eesti Ühispank,** Keskväljak 7, **exchanges currency,** cashes **traveler's checks,** and has an **ATM.** (☎320 40; fax 320 47. Open M-F 9am-4pm.) Rent **bikes** (100EEK per day) from **Kerttu Sport,** Sadama 15, across the bridge past the bus station. (☎321 30; fax 320 76. Open M-F 10am-6pm, Sa 10am-3pm.) The **Keskväljaku Apteek,** Põllu 1, is a **pharmacy** just off the main square. (☎321 37. Open M-F 9am-6pm, Sa 10am-2pm. MC/V.) The cultural center, Rookopli 18, has free **Internet access.** (☎321 82. Open M-F noon-6pm, Su 10am-1pm.) The **post office** is on the main square at Keskväljak 3. (☎320 13. Open M-F 8am-5:30pm, Sa 8:30am-1pm.) **Postal Code:** 92 412.

ACCOMMODATIONS AND FOOD. Eesti Posti Puhkekeskus ❶, Posti 13, has private, modern, and comfortable rooms 5min. from the center of town and near the beach. Hall showers are large and clean, and there is a kitchen guests can use. From Kekväljak, turn onto Uus; it will be the pink building on your left at the intersection with Posti. (☎91 871. Sauna 25EEK per hr. Bike rental 40EEK per day. Call ahead. 150EEK per person.) A bit farther from the center is **Nuutri Matkamaja ❶,** Nuutri 4. From Keskväljak, walk away from the bank and take a right on Põllu. Continue past the tracks and turn right onto either of the paired footbridges; the hostel is the red house on your far right after you cross. Nuutri has 12 beds in three rooms, as well as a common room, a sauna, a kitchen, and a fireplace. (☎987 15; fax 311 78; www.hot.ee/nuutri. Breakfast 50EEK. Sauna 200EEK for first hr., 100EK per hr. thereafter. Beds 200EEK per person.) **Hausma Hostel ❷** is far from town but near the ocean. From the town square, take Uus past Ranna until it ends. Hang a right and continue for 2km; Hausma will be on your right. This hostel boasts large rooms, cabins, and camping space. (☎291 90; www.hausma.ee. Breakfast included. Reservations recommended. 240EEK per person; cabins 170EEK per person; camping 35EEK per person.) The **Konsum supermarket** is in Keskväljak. (Open daily 9am-9pm. MC/V.) The reasonably priced **Arteesia Kohvik ❷**, Keskväljak 5, serves standard fare for 30-65EEK. (☎321 73. Open M-Th 9am-11pm, F-Sa 9am-midnight, Su 11am-10pm.) **Rannapaargu ❷**, at the end of Lubjaahju, is a great spot for a bite by the sea. (☎051 442 66. Entrees 40-75EEK. Open Su-Th noon-8pm, F-Sa noon-8pm and 10pm-4am.)

🔘 **SIGHTS.** On a nice day, head to **Rannapark**, at the end of Lubjaahju, to enjoy a shallow **beach**, walking trails, and an obstacle-less miniature golf course. (20EEk per hr. Open 10am-10pm.) If you just can't get enough of regional exhibitions, **Hiiumaa Museum**, Vabrikuväljak 8, details the history of Kärdla and the island in general, including authentic period furniture. (☎320 91. English descriptions. Open June-Aug. Tu-Sa 10am-5pm; Sept.-May M-F 10am-5pm, Sa 10am-2pm. 10EEK, students 5EEK.) Just outside Kärdla at the main crossroads is a large stone **memorial** to the Soviet soldiers who defeated the Germans in WWII. Nicknamed "Jüri" by the locals, it is jokingly called the last Russian soldier remaining on Hiiumaa. The ruined **Palugüla Church,** built in 1820 by the Ungern-Sternberg family, served as a landmark for sailors and later as target practice for Soviet soldiers. You can still see the hundreds of rusty bullet shells scattered on the ground. Palugüla lies about 4km outside Kärdla on the edge of the Kärdla crater, created by an ancient meteorite. (From Kärdla, take the road to Heltermaa for about 3km until it splits; veer left toward the airport. On your left you'll see an informational sign about the formation of the Kärdla crater; the church will be about 1km ahead on your right.)

🔼 **BIKING TO KÖPU.** Heading west out of Kärdla toward Kõrgessaare, you'll encounter the spooky **Hill of Crosses** (Ristimägi) on your left after about 6km. The crosses, which seem to emerge from the surrounding forest, were placed here to commemorate the Hiiumaa Swedes who were deported to Ukraine by Catherine the Great in 1781. However, local folklore has it that the crosses are a result of two wedding parties who met on this spot, but fought because the road was too narrow for both to pass. The bride of one couple and the groom of the other were killed in the squabble, but the families made the best of it and married the remaining bride and groom to each other. Just past the Hill of Crosses, a right turn leads to the **Tahkuna Lighthouse** (11km), built in Paris in 1874. Be aware that after 7km, the road is unpaved. The lighthouse was consistently ineffective in warning ships about the coast's shallow waters, but no one seemed to mind, since salvaging loot and rescuing passengers from the ships was quite profitable. Near the lighthouse is a bell memorializing those lost in the 1994 sinking of the ocean liner *Estonia.* The surrounding sands are still occupied by the gun emplacements and bunkers of the former Soviet occupants. On your way back to the main road, consider a detour to the **Mihkli Farm Museum** on your left, just off the lighthouse road, on a plot of land that's been cultivated since 1564. The museum staff and its goat, Yoshu, are quite friendly. (☎320 91. Open May 15-Sept. 15. M-F 10am-6pm.)

Go back to the main road and make a right in the direction of Kõrgessare. Near the 43km marker you'll see **Reigi Church,** built in 1800-1802 by Count Ungern Sternberg to commemorate his son who committed suicide because of growing debts. After a few kilometers, turn right into Kõrgessare where you can take a break at the excellent **Restoran Viinaköök ❸**, Sadama 2. "Edgar's piggy-widdy fillet" (90EEK) sounds almost too cute to eat, but this pork fillet with fried potatoes, vegetables, and mushroom sauce is a delectable dish. The restaurant is housed in the old Viskoosa building, an artificial silk factory that was completed just before 1914 but never used because of the outbreak of WWI. (☎933 37. Entrees 30-130EEK. Open daily noon-2am.) Continue about 20km past Kõrgessare to reach the most impressive sight in Western Hiiumaa, the 16th-century **Kõpu Lighthouse**. From the top, take in a panoramic view of the Baltic Sea. (15EEK, students 5EEK.)

KÄINA   ☎(0)246

Käina, southwest of Suuremõisa, remains Hiiumaa's second most populous area (pop. 2448) and an excellent point from which to explore the island's southern tip.

[⎯🔢 TRANSPORTATION AND PRACTICAL INFORMATION. The main **bus stop** in town is located at Hiiu mnt. 11, outside Tondilossi in the center of Käina. Buses run daily to **Haapsalu** and **Soru,** where a ferry connects to **Saaremaa.** Local buses also go to **Kärdla** several times daily. (Info ☎320 77; fax 320 65.) The best place for local information is the **cultural center,** Maë 2, which also has free **Internet access** on two machines upstairs. (☎362 31. Open M-F 10am-5pm, Sa 10am-2pm.) **Hansapank** and an **ATM** are on the first floor. (Open daily 8:30am-12:30pm and 1-4:30pm.)

🛏🏠 ACCOMMODATIONS AND FOOD. Tondilossi öömaja, Hiiu mnt. 11, in Käina center, has 16 beds, a sauna, extremely friendly proprietors, and a pub next door. (☎/fax 363 37; kylvi.rannu@mail.ee. Breakfast included. Sauna 150EEK per hr. Beds 200EEK.) To get to **Puulaiu Matkamaja ❶** (Campground Puulaid), just a short distance from Käina on the way to Kassari, take Hiuu mnt. in the direction of Emmaste. Take a left toward Kassari, and you'll see a sign on your right. Or, take the bus toward Jausa and ask the driver to let you off at Puulaiu. In the middle of the wilderness, Puulaiu has 40 beds, cozy fireplaces, and a sauna. You can also **rent boats** or **bikes** here for 20EEK per hr. (☎291 70; fax 361 26; www.hiiumaa.ee. Breakfast 40EEK. Sauna 150EEK per hr. Rooms 200EEK per person; cabins 130EEK per person; camping 25EEK per person.) Hiiumaa's best restaurant, **🔲 Lilia Restoran ❸,** Hiiu mnt. 22, serves high-society dishes at *hoi polloi* prices. (☎361 46; www.hot.ee/liiliahotell. Entrees 50-120EEK. Open daily noon-11pm.)

🔳 BIKING TO SUUREMÕISA AND KASSARI. Pühalepa Church, in Suuremõisa, contains the graves of the Baltic-German Count Ungern-Sternberg's family. The Count, who came to the island in 1781, wanted to acquire the entire island, but his shipping and salvage business was cut short when he was killed by one of his ship captains during a dispute. From the church parking lot, take a right onto a gravel road and continue about 150m to the mysterious **Contract Stones** (Põhilise leppe kivid), piled up centuries ago. Some believe they were placed here in the 6th century to mark the grave of a Swedish king, while others think sailors stacked the boulders to mark the "contract" they'd made with God for their safety during voyages. From the stones, head back to the highway and take a left directly before the bridge over the river. The **Suuremõisa Palace,** about 12km from Käina, was built on the estate of the Swede Jakob de la Gardie, who purchased the island in 1624. (☎943 91. Open July 1-Aug. 16 M-W 8am-4pm, Th-F 8am-6pm, Sa 8am-2pm, Su 8am-6pm; Aug. 17-July 1 M-F 9am-4pm. 10EEK, students 5EEK.)

The ride to 🔳 **Kassari** (ka-SA-ree; pop. 286), a tiny village on its own island southeast of Käina, passes through some fantastic forest scenery. Roads from the east and the west feed into Kassari; a circular ride allows you to see all the sights. Follow Hiiu mnt. in the direction of Emmaste to reach the **Rudulf Tobias House Museum** (R. Tobiase Maja-Muuseum), Hiiu mnt. 33, in the house where the composer and organist was born in 1873. (Open June-Aug. daily 11am-5pm. 5EEK, students

ESTONIA

3EEK.) If you enter Kassari from the west, the **Hiiumaa Museum,** in the middle of the island, is about a 7km ride from the turn to Kassari village. From the turn to Kassari, go about 6km and take a left at the signs for the museum. The exhibit chronicles the history and wildlife of the island. (☎971 21. English captions. Open May-Sept. daily 10am-5:30pm; Oct.-Apr. M-Th 10am-3pm. 5EEK.) Backtrack to the freeway, head straight and to the right, and follow the road to the most beautiful of the island's sights, **Sääretirp,** a 1.3m wide peninsula lined with wild strawberry and juniper bushes that jut 3km into the sea. Legend holds that this peninsula is all that remains of an ancient bridge between Hiiumaa and Saaremaa. Supposedly, the giant Leigerso built the link so his brother Suur Tõll could come for a visit.

INLAND ESTONIA

All roads inland from Tallinn lead to Tartu, the intellectual and historic heart of Estonia. However, the countryside should not be overlooked. Visitors can immerse themselves in the mystical town of Otepää or daytrip to Viljandi to see the mountainous landscape and the medieval castle that still protects the town.

TARTU ☎(0)27

Tartu (pop. 100,000) may be the oldest city in the Baltics, but it's had a couple of face-lifts, having been razed and rebuilt five times since its founding in 1030. The university, a wellspring of Estonian nationalism, is the source of the youthful verve that keeps the city going. Even when the students leave in summer, plenty of music, theater, museums and nightlife fill Estonia's second-largest city.

▢ TRANSPORTATION

Trains: Vaksali 6, at the intersection of Kuperjanovi and Vaksali, 1½km from the city center. Although the station itself is closed, a few lone trains still run through here. Call ☎615 68 51 or check out www.edel.ee for info. To **Tallinn** (3½hr., 3 per day, 70EEK).

Buses: Turu 2 (☎47 72 27). On the corner of Riia and Turu, 300m southeast of Raekoja plats along Vabaduse. To: **Pärnu** (4hr., 20 per day, 50-95EEK); **Tallinn** (2-5hr., 46 per day, 50-80EEK); **Rīga, LAT** (5hr., 1 per day, 190EEK); **St. Petersburg, RUS** (10hr., 2 per day, 160EEK). 30-50% ISIC discount on some routes. Info open daily 8am-8pm.

Public Transportation: Bus tickets 6EEK from kiosks, 8EEK on board. Buses #5 and 6 go from the train station to Raekoja plats and the bus station. Bus #4 travels down Võru. Buses #2 and 22 travel away from the river on Riia; # 6, 7, and 21 head toward it; #3, 8, and 11 go both ways. Bus routes converge at the Kaubamaja on Riia.

Taxis: ☎42 04 20 or 36 65 66. 10EEK base fare plus 6EEK per km; 25EEK minimum.

✳ ▢ ORIENTATION AND PRACTICAL INFORMATION

The **bus** and **train stations** border the center of town on opposite sides. The main artery, **Riia mnt.,** runs into the center from the southwest. It becomes **Narva mnt.** and **Fortuna mnt.** after crossing the river and then ends by the bus station. **J. Kuperjanovi** leads into the city center from the train station, intersecting the cobblestone street **Vallikraavi** in town. **Raekoja plats** (Town Hall Square), the city's geographical and social center, stretches west from the **Emajõgi River** toward the old castle hills. **Rüütli** heads north from the square to **Lai,** forming the boundary of the historic center. Behind the town hall, **Lossi** meanders uphill between the two peaks of **Toomemägi** (Cathedral Hill) and intersects Vallikraavi, which circles the hills.

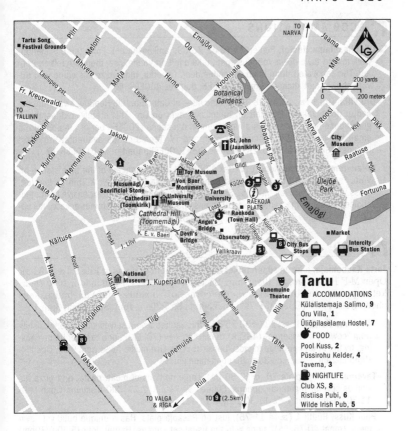

Tartu

■ ACCOMMODATIONS
Külalistemaja Salimo, 9
Oru Villa, 1
Üliõpilaselamu Hostel, 7

🍖 FOOD
Pool Kuss, 2
Püssirohu Kelder, 4
Taverna, 3

🍺 NIGHTLIFE
Club XS, 8
Ristiisa Pubi, 6
Wilde Irish Pub, 5

Tourist Office: Raekoja plats 14 (☎/fax 44 21 11; www.visitestonia.com). Arranges guides, rental cars, and **private rooms** (15EEK surcharge for some rooms). Also sells **maps** (10-90EEK) and the helpful semi-annual *Tartu Today* (15EEK). Open Sept.-May M-F 9am-5pm, Sa 10am-3pm; June-Aug. M-F 9am-5pm, Su 10am-2pm.

Currency Exchange: Hansapank, Ülikooli 1 (☎44 72 30), cashes AmEx and Thomas Cook **traveler's checks** for 1% commission. 24hr. **ATM** inside. Open M-F 9am-4pm.

American Express: Estravel, Vallikraavi 2 (☎44 03 00; fax 44 03 01; www.estravel.ee). Open M-F 9am-6pm, Sa 10am-3pm.

Luggage Storage: In the **bus station.** 4-12EEK per bag for 24hr. Open M-F 6am-3pm and 3:30-9pm, Sa 7am-3pm and 3:30-9pm.

24-Hour Pharmacy: Raekoja Apteek (☎43 35 28), the Toomemägi side of Town Hall.

Internet Access: Hallo, Küüni 5b (☎37 77 73; www.hallo.ee), in the glass building. 20EEK per hr. Open M-F 9am-7pm, Sa 10am-5pm. **Internet,** Küütri 3, on the 3rd fl. inside the Rüütli Keskus Gallery. 4 speedy machines for 20EEK per hr., students 15EEK. Open daily 10am-10pm.

Post Office: Vanemuise 7 (☎41 06 00). Open M-F 8am-7pm, Sa 9am-4pm.

Postal Code: 51003.

ACCOMMODATIONS

■ **Üliôpilaselamu Hostel,** Pepleri 14 (☎42 76 08; janikah@ut.ee). From the bus station, walk toward town down Vabaduse pst., take a left on Vanemuise, then turn left on Pepleri. This renovated dorm is an incredible deal. Cheerful, modern rooms come with private shower and kitchen. Singles 250EEK; doubles 400EEK. ❷

Oru Villa, Oru 1 (☎/fax 42 28 94), on the edge of Cathedral Hill. Heading away from the center down Jakobi, turn left on Baeri, and right on Oru. This stately, old-fashioned guesthouse has a TV room, a dining room, and a sauna (200EEK per hr.) in addition to small but comfortable rooms with bath and TV. Tennis courts available. Breakfast included. Singles 450-850EEK; doubles 800-1200EEK; apartment 1000EEK. ❸

Külalistemaja Salimo, Kopli 1 (☎/fax 47 08 88), 3km southeast of the train station off Võru. Take bus #4 from Riia opposite the Kaubamaja to Alasi. Walk 25m to your left, cross Võru, and turn left on Kolpi. Salimo is bright, clean, and less expensive than other choices closer to the center. Every 2 rooms share a bath. Free Internet access. Reception 24hr. Singles 200EEK; doubles 400EEK; triples 600EEK. ❶

FOOD

Tartu Kaubamaja, a large **supermarket** and department store, is at Riia 2. (☎47 62 31. Open M-F 10am-8pm, Sa 10am-6pm, Su 11am-5pm. MC/V.) The indoor *turg* (market), opposite the bus station on the corner of Vabaduse and Vanemuise, sells cheap fresh food. (Open M-F 7:30am-5:30pm, Sa 7:30am-4pm, Su 7:30am-3pm.)

Püssirohu Kelder, Lossi 28 (☎30 35 55). This vaulted tavern serves international dishes from "cowboy's casserole" (48EEK) to chicken kiev (70EEK). For a taste of home-cooking, try the potato porridge in cross buns (35EEK). Live music Tu-Sa from 9pm. Open M-Th noon-2am, F-Sa noon-3am, Su noon-midnight. ❸

Taverna, Raekoja plats 20 (☎42 30 01). Large portions of meat, pasta, and pizza, as well as several vegetarian options. Entrees 39-79EEK. 7.5% ISIC discount. Open M-Th 11:30am-midnight, F-Sa 11:30-1am, Su 1-11pm. ❷

Pool Kuss, Rüütli 1 (☎44 11 75), just off Raekoja plats. Has a unique build-your-own menu (meat 40-75EEK), along with the usual set entrees. Happy Hour (5:30-6:30pm) has 25EEK beer. Don't be too excited if you spot the hour of glee on the wall—all the clocks are permanently set for 5:30. 10% ISIC discount. Open daily 11am-4am. ❷

SIGHTS

TOWN HALL SQUARE. (Raekoja plats.) The 1775 Town Hall Square is the social center of Tartu. The **town hall** was constructed in Dutch style. In front stands a fountain of a couple kissing in the rain, one of Tartu's icons. Near the bridge, the **Tartu Art Museum** (Tartu Kunstimuuseum), Raekoja plats 18, hosts exhibits in a building that leans (like the city's student population) a little to the left. (☎44 10 80. Open W-Su 11am-6pm. 10EEK, students 5EEK; F free. Call ahead for a guided tour 100EEK.)

TARTU UNIVERSITY. (Tartu Ülikool.) In 1632, the Swedish King Gustauvas II established the first university in Estonia (Academia Dorpatensis) on this spot. The school didn't become Tartu University until 1919 when Estonia achieved independence from the Russian Empire. Today, it is one of the country's main institutions of higher learning. The three-room **Museum of Classical Art** is in the main building, graced with copies of Greek and Roman statues. The recently renovated

Assembly Hall is used for lectures, concerts, and special occasions. The ▓**student lock-up** *(kartser)* in the attic was used to detain students for breaking school rules until 1892. Insulting a lady would earn you four days here, while dueling or defrauding a shopkeeper would land you here for three weeks. You can still see the drawings and inscriptions left by involuntary guests. Tartu was the only university in the Russian empire with the right to have fraternities after the Great Northern War, and it used the privilege well: in 1870, the **Estonian National Awakening** began here with the founding of the Estonian Student Association (Eesti Üliõpilaste Selts). So many nationalists in the fraternity were central to Estonia's struggle for independence that when the country won its freedom in 1919 the national flag was designed using the frat's colors: blue, black, and white. *(Ülikooli 18. With the town hall behind you, follow Ülikooli right. ☎ 37 53 84. Open M-F 11am-5pm. Classical Museum 7EEK, students 4EEK; Assembly Hall 10EEK/4EEK; student lock-up 5EEK/2EEK.)*

CATHEDRAL HILL. (Toomemägi.) The hill's central site is the once-majestic 15th-century **Cathedral of St. Peter and Paul,** which is now in ruins. A sign warns: "Be cautious! The building is liable to fall down." An adjoining building houses the **Tartu University History Museum** (Museum Historicum Universitatis Tartuensis), featuring scientific instruments. *(Lossi 25. ☎ 37 56 74; fax 37 56 79. Open W-Su 11am-5pm. 20EEK, students 5EEK. English tours 120EEK.)* Near the church are two 17th-century Swedish cannons. **Kissing Hill** (Musumägi), once part of a prison tower, is the site of an ancient pagan sacrificial stone. Each April, the university choirs compete on the two bridges that lead to the east hump of Toomemägi. Women crowd onto the pink wooden **Angel's Bridge** (Inglisild), while men stand on the concrete **Devil's Bridge** (Kuradisild). Cathedral Hill is also littered with **statues.** Nikolai Pirogov, a 19th-century pioneer in the field of anesthesia, stands at the bottom of the hill, while the national poet Kristjan Joak Peterson is on the hill itself. Embryologist Karl Ernst von Baer, who graces the 2EEK banknote, is at the peak, awaiting the biology students who annually douse him with champagne. An **observatory,** built in 1808-1810 by architect J.W. Krause, is on the site of the former bishop's castle.

OTHER MUSEUMS. The **Tartu City Museum** (Tartu Linnamuuseum), Narva mnt. 23, has well-organized and informative exhibits detailing the city's history. It displays the table on which the Peace Treaty of Tartu was signed in 1920 with the USSR, guaranteeing Estonian independence, and hosts occasional concerts. *(☎ 46 19 11; fax 46 19 12; www.tartu.ee/linnamuuseum. Open T-Su 11am-6pm. 20EEK, students 5EEK; free last F of the month, May 18, and Oct. 30. Tours 120EEK.)* The **Estonian National Museum** (Eesti Rahva Muuseum) displays folk costumes, furniture, and model houses. *(J. Kuperjanov 9. Follow Riia uphill from the bus station. Turn right on Pepleri and follow it around the bend to the left as it becomes Kuperjanov. ☎ 42 13 11. Open W-Su 11am-6pm. 12EEK, students 8EEK.)* The **Tartu University Botanical Gardens,** Lai 40, is a peaceful area in which to relax with a book. *(Open daily 10am-5pm. 10EEK, students 5EEK.)*

🎵 🔍 ENTERTAINMENT AND FESTIVALS

The **Vanemuise Concert Hall** (Vanemuise Kontserdimaja), Vanemuise 6, stages classical concerts. *(☎ 37 75 30; www.vkm.ee.)* The 1870 theater **Vanemuine,** Venemuise 6, holds theater performances and operas. *(☎ 44 01 65; www.vanemuine.ee.)* **Eesti Suve Teater** (Summer Theater; ☎ 42 74 71) hosts performances in July and August outside and in the medieval church on Cathedral Hill. February brings the **Tartu Maraton,** which features a 63km cross-country ski race as well as non-competitive 31 and 16km group jaunts. *(☎ 42 16 44; fax 42 25 36; tartumaraton@tartumaraton.ee.)* On March 18, the **International Day of Museums,** all of Tartu's museums open their doors for free. The **Dionysia Arts Festival,** held from late March to early

April, features drama and dance performances, film screenings, and art exhibitions. Everyone makes a port call during the **Hanseatic Days** in mid-June, when the Middle Ages return with craft fairs and folk dancing in Raekoja plats. (www.tartu.ee/hansa.) In mid-November and again in early May, Tartu celebrates its university with **Student Days,** featuring boat races, contests in the town square, and car races (www.ut.ee/studentdays).

ⓢ NIGHTLIFE

▨ **Wilde Irish Pub,** Vallikraavi 4 (☎30 97 64; fax 30 97 61; www.wilde.ee). A bronze Oscar Wilde meets his Estonian counterpart Eduard on the bench outside this Wildely popular haunt. Irish and Estonian victuals served with local and foreign brews. Vegetarian options available. Entrees 45-170EEK. Live music M-Sa from 9 or 10pm. Open M-Tu 11am-midnight, W-Th 11am-1am, F-Sa 11am-3am, Su noon-midnight.

Ristiisa Pubi (Godfather Pub), Küüni 7 (☎30 39 70; fax 30 39 74; ristiisapubi@hot.ee), just down the street from Raekoja plats. Portraits of notorious gangsters decorate the walls of this large mafia-themed bar. 0.5L *Saku* 20EEK. Open Su-Tu 11am-midnight, W-Th 11-1am, F-Sa 11-3am.

Club XS, 21 Vaksali (☎30 36 40; micro@online.ee), directly across from the railroad tracks that run parallel to Vaksali. One of the more popular clubs, with an industrial feel, a spacious dance floor, and the usual techno-dance-pop mix. Th "Students' Rock Club." 18+. Cover Su-Th 30EEK, F-Sa 60EEK. Open Tu-Th 10pm-3am, F-Sa 10pm-4am.

ⓓ DAYTRIPS FROM TARTU

OTEPÄÄ   ☎(0)76

Buses run between Tartu and Otepää (1hr., approx. every hr., 18EEK). The tourist office, Lipuväljak 13, sells maps for 10EEK and gives out free booklets. (☎553 64; fax 612 46; www.visitestonia.com/otepaa. Open Apr. 1-May 14 M-F 9am-6pm; May 15-Sept. 15 M-F 9am-6pm, Sa-Su 10am-3pm; Sept. 16-Jan. 1 M-F 9am-5pm; Jan. 2-Mar. 31 M-F 9am-5pm, Sa 10am-3pm.) Bikes available for 230EEK per day at: Hotell Bernhard, Kolga tee 22a (☎696 00); Scandic Hotel Karupesa, Tehvandi 1a (☎615 00); and Pühajärve Hotell (☎655 01).

Otepää, the highest town in Estonia (152m), is a scenic retreat that becomes a mecca for skiers in winter. Named after the shape of Linnamägi Hill, which resembles the town's emblem, a bear's head, Otepää was first mentioned in historical texts in 1116. Before 1922, however, it was known as Nuustaku. Long ago when the town was rich with hazelnuts, the local Prussian squire organized "Nusstag," the day of nuts, to pick the nuts in the fall. Today the town depends on **Pühajärve** (Holy Lake) for its livelihood. To reach the lake, which is about 3km from Otepää's center, follow Pühajärve tee until you reach the parking lot. Take the small rocky path that hugs the shores of the lake, passing the amphitheater and going onto the beach. Pühajärve, blessed by the Dalai Lama in October 1991, is surrounded by forests so lush they seem almost primeval. A day spent exploring the many inlets and islands of the lake by canoe makes a welcome reprieve from city life. You can **rent boats** at Pühajärve beach. (Boats 80EEK per hr.; waterbikes 60EEK per hr. Open daily 10am-7pm.) Or, from the boatlaunch on the side of the lake opposite the beach, motorboats leave for a 35min. tour of the lake every hour—no oars required. (30EEK. Open daily 10am-7pm.) On your way back from the beach, be sure to stop behind the amphitheater at the Wheel of Life that is the **Dalai Lama monument.** Returning to Otepää on Pühajärve tee, a quick detour brings nirvana— or at least a glimpse at the "Energy Column" that marks the region's positive vibe.

(Turn right on Mäe and walk 500m.) Heading into town, continue up Pühajärve tee as it becomes Tartu mnt., following the signs for a wide right. To the right on Võru will be the 1890 **Lutheran Church.** (☎550 75. Open by appointment only.) Near the church gates is a path leading to **Otepää Linnamägi,** the partially buried hilltop remains of Otepää's 18th-century fortress. If you're here in the second week of June, check out the **Pühajärve Beach Party,** a two-day music festival on the hip, holy lake itself. (www.beachparty.ee.)

VILJANDI   ☎(0)43

Buses arrive from Tartu (1½hr., 26 per day, 40-45EEK). The Tourist Info Center, Tallinna 2b (☎/fax 337 55), gives out free maps and walking tours, and provides free Internet. Open May-Aug. M-F 9am-6pm, Sa-Su 10am-3pm; Sept.-Apr. M-F 10am-5pm, Sa 10am-2pm. To get to the castle from the bus station, walk down Tallinna, and go through Vabaduse plats (the main square) toward the river. The road becomes Tasuja pst. Follow it to its end. The path just to your left leads to the castle. St. John's Church ☎330 00; viljandi.jaani@eelk.ee. Open May 15-Sept. 15 daily 10am-5pm; Sept. 15-May 15 M-F noon-1pm. Free entry. Museum ☎333 16. Open W-Su 10am-5pm. 10EEK, students 5EEK.

Viljandi, a small, hilly town littered with old stone buildings and wooden foot-bridges, is a change from the flat lands that make up most of Estonia. Its imposing **Order's Castle** (Ordulinnuse varemed), constructed by the Knights of the Sword in the 13th century, was once one of the largest in the Baltics, spanning three hilltops connected by bridges. It's in ruins today, but still affords an impressive view of **Viljandi Lake** *(järv)*. The stone archway leads to the last remaining wall of the **keep,** which now acts as a backdrop for spooky summer productions. Around the back is the candy-colored 1879 **suspension footbridge** *(rippsild)*, which leads to town. It was sent to Viljandi in 1931 by a German count to stop his daughter from racing her horses over it. In the central castle park is the medieval **St. John's Church** (Jaani kirik), Pikk 6, a plain white structure erected in 1446-1472. In the center of town, the **Viljandi Museum,** Kindval Laidoneri plats 10, includes a reconstructed model of the Order's Castle as well as the first-ever model of an Ericsson phone, dating from 1892. Viljandi is known for its **Folk Music Festival,** which takes place in late July every four or five years; the last one was in 2002 (www.folk.ee).

ESTONIA

HUNGARY
(MAGYARORSZÁG)

FORINT

AUS$1 = 136.79FT	1FT = AUS$0.73
CDN$1 = 159.53FT	1FT = CDN$0.63
EUR€1 = 244.24FT	1FT = EUR€0.41
NZ$1 = 116.67FT	1FT = NZ$0.86
UK£1 = 384.80FT	1FT = UK£0.26
US$1 = 248.25FT	1FT = US$0.40
ZAR1 = 23.41FT	1FT = ZAR4.27

Communism was a mere blip in Hungary's 1100-year history of repression and renewal and today the nation appears well at ease with its new-found capitalist identity. Budapest remains Hungary's social and economic keystone, and provincial capitals rife with cultural attractions lie within a three-hour train ride. Nonetheless, with luscious wine valleys nestled in the northern hills, a rough-and-tumble cowboy plain in the south, and a luxurious beach resort in the east, the beauty of the countryside should not be forsaken for a whirlwind tour of the capital. Otherwise, you'll have seen the heart of Hungary, but missed its soul entirely.

HUNGARY AT A GLANCE

OFFICIAL NAME: Republic of Hungary

CAPITAL: Budapest (pop. 1.9 million)

POPULATION: 10 million (90% Magyar, 4% Roma, 3% German, 2% Serb, 1% other)

LANGUAGE: Hungarian (Magyar)

CURRENCY: 1 forint (Ft) = 100 filler

RELIGION: 68% Roman Catholic, 20% Calvinist, 5% Lutheran, 7% other

LAND AREA: 92,340km²

CLIMATE: Continental

GEOGRAPHY: Mostly plains; low mountains and hills on Slovakian border

BORDERS: Austria, Croatia, Romania, Serbia and Montenegro, Slovak Republic, Slovenia, Ukraine

ECONOMY: 60% Services, 35% Industry, 5% Agriculture

GDP: US$11,200 per capita

COUNTRY CODE: 36

INTERNATIONAL DIALING PREFIX: 00

HISTORY

THE MIGHTY MAGYARS. In the third century BC, **Celtic tribes** forced their way onto the territory of what is now Hungary, only to be followed by the land-hungry **Romans** (see **Aquincum,** p. 353), who founded the provinces of Pannonia and Dacia, which they held through the 4th century AD. The **Magyars,** warrior tribes from Central Asia, arrived in AD 896. Led by **Prince Árpád,** they quickly conquered the middle basin of the Danube River. Árpád's great-great-grandson, **Stephen I,** was crowned King of Hungary with the papal benediction on Christmas Day, 1000. Canonized in 1083, Stephen is considered the founder of the modern Hungarian state.

HUNGARY

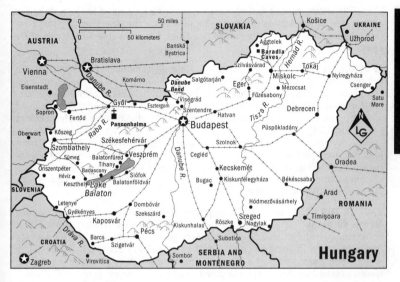

THOSE GOLDEN YEARS. As Hungary grew stronger, the nobility forced the king to sign the **Golden Bill,** granting rights to the people and restricting the powers of the monarchy. Less than two decades later, a devastating Mongolian invasion swept through the land and by 1301 the Árpáds' reign had come to an end. As leadership changed throughout the 13th and 14th centuries, Hungary enjoyed its **Golden Age,** marked by both economic prosperity and military repute.

ONLY THE GOOD DIE YOUNG. Unfortunately, royal infighting was to gradually weaken the country and tarnish its golden hue. In the mid-15th century, claimants to the throne imprisoned Mátyás Hunyadi, known as **Matthias Corvinus** (1458-1490). An angry nobility freed and coronated Corvinus, who went on to reign over Hungary's Renaissance, stressing the importance of art and science and cultivating an extensive library. His successors to the throne, however, made sure to undo nearly all of Corvinus's reforms. The unhappy peasantry finally attempted an unsuccessful **rebellion** in 1514, the repercussions of which lingered for hundreds of years. With the country in great disarray, the Turks easily conquered the Hungarian army at **Mohács** in 1526.

THE RISE AND DEMISE OF THE AUSTRO-HUNGARIAN EMPIRE. Conflict among the Protestant nobility, the Ottomans, and the Holy Roman Empire plagued Hungary for the next 150 years, until the Austrian Habsburgs took over in the early 17th century. A new war of independence began in 1848, led in spirit by the young poet **Sándor Petőfi** and in law by **Lajos Kossuth.** Together, they convinced the Diet (parliament) to pass a series of reforms that became known as the **April Laws.** Kossuth's state held out for one year, but in the summer of 1849, Habsburg Emperor Franz Josef I regained Budapest with the support of Tsar Nicholas I of Russia. Though heavily repressed throughout the following years, Hungary (under the leadership of Ferenc Deák) did make some headway as the nation was granted its own government by the **Compromise of 1867.** Thus the **dual monarchy** of the **Austro-Hungarian Empire** was born. Magyarization in both the cultural and political realms provoked opposition movements among Romanians, Serbs, Croats, and Slovaks.

HUNGARY

These divisions erupted during World War I, which resulted in the permanent destruction of the Austro-Hungarian Empire. After the war, Hungary lost two-thirds of its territory to countries of the Allied Powers in the 1920 **Treaty of Trianon.**

APOCALYPSE. As the empire collapsed, a bourgeois democratic revolution rose to power in 1918, and was replaced in less than six months by the Communist Hungarian Republic of Councils under Bolshevik **Béla Kun.** Counterrevolutionary forces eventually took control, though, brutally punishing those involved with the Communist administration. **Admiral Miklós Horthy** settled in for a rather paradoxical 24 years of dictatorial control (1920-1944) over a (hardly) democratic government. A tentative alliance with Hitler in **World War II** led to a year-long Nazi occupation and the near-total destruction of Budapest during the two-month Soviet siege of 1945. Two-thirds of Hungary's Jews, whose pre-war population numbered close to one million, were murdered in the Holocaust. Nearly all survivors fled the country.

BACK IN THE USSR. In 1949 Hungary became a People's Republic under **Mátyás Rákosi** and the Hungarian Workers' Party. He tied Hungary to the USSR economically and politically; the country often served as a "workshop" for Soviet industry. Rákosi lost control in the violent **1956 Uprising** in Budapest, in which **Imre Nagy** declared a neutral, non-Warsaw Pact government. Soviet troops crushed the revolt and executed Nagy and his supporters.

FIGHT FOR YOUR RIGHT (TO PARTY). Over the next three decades Nagy's replacement, **Janos Kádár,** oversaw the partial opening of borders and a rising national standard of living. Inflation and stagnation halted progress in the 1980s, but democratic reformers in the Communist Party pushed Kádár aside in 1988, seeking a market economy and increased political freedom. Hungary broke free of the Soviet orbit in 1989 and in 1990 power was transferred to the Hungarian Democratic Forum in the first free elections. Slow progress, sky-rocketing inflation, and burgeoning unemployment greatly eroded the Forum's popularity. The renamed-and-revamped Socialists returned to power in 1994 as **Gyula Horn** of the **Hungarian Socialist Party** was elected Prime Minister by promising a moderate course.

TODAY

Hungary has come a long way from its once-communist state. Hungary now boasts a **president,** who serves a five-year term as commander-in-chief of the armed forces but has authority over little else. The 386-member National Assembly elects the president, the **prime minister,** and the **cabinet ministers** that comprise the Council of Ministers. Members are elected to parliament every four years. Six parties participate regularly in parliament: the Hungarian Democratic Forum, the Alliance of Free Democrats, the Independent Smallholders' Party, the Christian Democratic People's Party, the Federation of Young Democrats, and the Socialist Party. In the years since the 1994 elections, Hungary has gradually recouped economic and social stability as its borders have opened to the Western world. Though wages and inflation continue to concern the budding capitalists, Hungary has managed to lower inflation, stem unemployment, and approach consistent GDP growth. Hungary held its fourth round of post-Communist parliamentary elections in April 2002. A Socialist-liberal coalition has replaced the former right-wing majority by a small margin, and this new government plans to lead Hungary into the **EU** by 2004.

PEOPLE AND CULTURE

LANGUAGE

Hungarian, a **Finno-ugric** language, is distantly related to Turkish, Estonian, and Finnish. After Hungarian and **German, English** is Hungary's third language. *"Hello"* is often used as an informal greeting or farewell. *"Szia!"* (sounds like "see ya!") is another greeting—you'll often hear friends cry: "Hello, see ya!" A few starters for pronunciation: *"c"* is pronounced "ts" as in "pots;" *"cs"* is "ch" as in "which;" *"gy"* is "dy" as in *"adieu;" "ly"* is "y" as in "yak:" *"s"* is "sh" as in "shard;" *"sz"* is "s" as in "cell-phone;" *"zs"* is "zh" as in "fusion;" and *"a"* is "a" as in "paw." The first syllable is always stressed. For a phrasebook and glossary, see **Glossary: Hungarian,** p. 881.

FOOD AND DRINK

HUNGARY	❶	❷	❸	❹	❺
FOOD	under 400Ft	401-800Ft	801-1300Ft	1301-2800Ft	over 2800Ft

Hungarian food is more flavorful and varied than many of its Eastern European culinary cohorts. **Paprika,** Hungary's chief agricultural export, colors most dishes red. In Hungarian restaurants (*vendéglő* or *étterem*), begin with *halászlé,* a delicious spicy fish stew. Alternately, try *gyümölcsleves,* a cold fruit soup topped with whipped cream. The Hungarian national dish is *bográcsgulyás* (goulash), a stew of beef, onions, green pepper, tomatoes, potatoes, dumplings, and plenty of paprika. *Borjúpaprikás* is veal with paprika and potato-dumpling pasta. Vegetarians can often find recourse in the tasty *rántott sajt* (fried cheese) and *gombapörkölt* (mushroom stew). Delicious Hungarian fruit and vegetables abound in the summer. Veggie-lovers look for *salata* and *sajt* (salad and cheese) on the menu, as these will be the only options in many small town restaurants. *Túrós rétes* is a chewy pastry filled with sweetened cottage cheese, while *Somlói galuska* is a fantastically rich sponge cake of chocolate, nuts, and cream, all soaked in rum. The Austrians stole the recipe for *rétes* and called it "strudel," but this delicious concoction is as Hungarian as can be.

Hungary produces a diverse array of fine wines (see **A Mini-Guide to the Wines of Tokaj,** p. 409). *Sör* (Hungarian beer) ranges from the first-rate to the merely acceptable. *Dreher Bak* is a rich, dark brew. Lighter beers include *Dreher Pils, Szalon Sör,* and licensed versions of *Steffl, Gold Fassl, Gösser,* and *Amstel.* Hungary also produces different types of *pálinka,* a liquor that resembles brandy. Among the best tasting are *barackpálinka* (similar to apricot schnapps) and *körtepálinka* (pear brandy). *Unicum,* advertised as the national drink of Hungary, is a herbal liqueur that was used by the Hapsburg kings to cure digestive ailments.

CUSTOMS AND ETIQUETTE

Rounding up the bill as a **tip** is standard etiquette—especially in restaurants, but also for everyone from taxi-drivers to hairdressers. Be sure to check the bill, as gratuity may be included. In restaurants, it's considered rude to leave tips on the table, so hand it to your server. Waiters usually expect foreigners to tip 15%, although locals never give more than 10%. At a meal, **toasts** are usually made and should be returned. A useful word is *egészségünkre* (pronounced Ay-gash-ay-goonk-gre), meaning "your health." The frequency and extent of public displays of affection among young and old alike may be startling, or at least distracting—every bus has a couple exchanging bodily fluids. Taste in **clothing,** especially for men, is casual and unpretentious; you may see men over 50 wearing Speedos. Women's fashions can be similarly revealing, though people in smaller towns tend to dress more conservatively. Certain monasteries, churches, and synagogues require covered knees and shoulders. From the look of things, **smoking** seems to be the national pastime. As paprika is one of Hungary's most important commodities, exporting it is illegal. Border patrol will accost you—on trains, they check under every seat.

THE ARTS

HISTORY

LITERATURE. The generation of writers that lived through the Revolution of 1848 played an important role in Hungary's history. Most notably, the Populist, anti-Romantic **Sándor Petőfi** fueled the nationalistic rhetoric that drove the revolution. Hungarian literature owes much to the work of **Ferenc Kazinczy,** who struggled to promote a national literature in the Hungarian language rather than its previous Latin forms. Hungarian literature gained greatly in focus with the founding of the *Nyugat* (West) literary journal in 1908, and with the (unrelated) work of avant-garde poet and artist **Lajos Kassák,** who concerned himself with Hungarian working-class life. After World War II, the Communist regime forced Magyar writers to adopt the doctrines of Socialist Realism, but eventually a new generation appeared that was able to develop individual styles more freely. The novels of **György Konrád,** one of the most important Hungarian authors of the century, were most influential in defining the dissident movements of Central Europe.

FINE ARTS AND MUSIC. The growth of the fine arts in Hungary was significantly influenced by evolution in the rest of Europe. Nevertheless, Hungary was sure to add its own character. Renaissance and Medieval frescoes on buildings were the most widely practiced art forms, which later gave birth to historical painting and impressive portraiture. The 20th century saw **Lajos Kassák** and **László Moholy-Nagy** emerge as internationally significant avant-garde painters and **Miklós Jancscó** and **István Szabó** stand as pioneers in Hungarian **film.** One staple of Hungarian culture is **folk dancing. Csárdás,** the national dance, includes a women's circle and men's boot-slapping dances. All begin with a slow section (*lassu*) and end in a fast section (*friss*). Dancers don embroidered costumes and perform music in double time.

It has been in **music** that the Hungarian cultural tradition has gained the most international acclaim. The greatest piano virtuoso of his time, **Franz Liszt** (1811-1886), was the most prolific musician in Hungary's history. Liszt's contributions to music range from advancing the technique of piano composition to giving the piano a fuller sound to inventing the **symphonic poem.** Although he spoke German, not Hungarian, his heritage shines through in his Hungarian Rhapsodies. These 19 pieces are based on the spirit of Hungarian folk music. Similarly, **Béla Bartók** (1881-1945) was noted for his use of folk material to create music that expressed a deep sense of nationalism. His most famous works include string quartets and *Concerto for Orchestra.*

CURRENT SCENE

Less concerned with social issues than with the postmodern exploration of the meaning and use of words, the contemporary work of author/novelist **Péter Esterházy** marks a new cultural movement in Hungarian literature. In the architectural arena, organic influences have given many budding artists new inspiration. Among these is **Imre Makovecz,** whose pavilion for the Seville expo won him international acclaim in 1992. Other burgeoning modern architects include **József Finta** and **György Vadász.** In recent years, from late August to early September, Hungary has hosted the **Millenium Music Theater Festival.**

HOLIDAYS AND FESTIVALS

NATIONAL HOLIDAYS IN 2003	
January 1 New Year's Day	**June 8** Pentecost
March 15 National Day	**August 20** Constitution Day
April 20-21 Easter	**October 23** Republic Day
May 1 Labor Day	**December 25-26** Christmas

FERENCVAROS FESTIVAL. Usually held between June and July in Budapest, this festival celebrates music at its most diverse. Enjoy symphony concerts, rock operas, and ballets at this popular gala.

BUDAPEST FAREWELL FESTIVAL. Remembering the day the last Russian soldier left the country, the celebration includes parades, pop concerts, a fancy dress competition, and other jovial affairs.

ADDITIONAL RESOURCES

GENERAL HISTORY

A History of Hungary, ed. by Peter Sugar, Peter Hanak, and Tibor Frank (1994). More exhaustive than most books of its kind in its treatment of Hungarian history.

A History of Modern Hungary 1867-1994, by Jorg K. Hoensch (1996). Provides a brief summary of Hungarian history.

FICTION AND NONFICTION

Battlefields and Playgrounds, by Janos Nyiri (1995). A highly acclaimed recent novel on the Holocaust in Budapest.

The Bridge at Andau, by James Michener (1988). An account of the 1956 Uprising.

The Glance of Countess Hahn-Hahn, by Peter Esterházy (1999). Provides a rich cultural history of Hungary in a fictional journey down the Danube River.

A Little Hungarian Pornography, by Peter Esterházy (1995). A satirical and engaging account of life in Hungary in the Kadar era.

The Melancholy of Rebirth: Essays from Post-Communist Central Europe 1989-1994, by Gyorgy Konrad (1995). Both humorous and depressing views of Communism in Hungary through 26 essays.

HUNGARY ESSENTIALS

ENTRANCE REQUIREMENTS
Passport: Required of all travelers.
Visa: Required of citizens of Australia and South Africa.
Letter of Invitation: Required of citizens of Ukraine and Venezuela.
Inoculations: None required. Recommended up-to-date on MMR (measles, mumps, and rubella), DTaP (diphtheria), Polio booster, Tetanus, Typhoid, Hepatitis A, and Hepatitis B.
Work Permit: Required of all foreigners planning to work in Hungary.
International Driving Permit: Required of all those planning to drive.

DOCUMENTS AND FORMALITIES

EMBASSIES AND CONSULATES

Embassies of other countries in Hungary are located in Budapest (see p. 344). Hungary's embassies and consulates abroad include:

Australia: 17 Beale Crescent, Deakin, ACT 2600 (☎02 6282 2226; fax 6285 3012) **Consulate:** Edgecliff Center, Suite 405/203-233, New South Head Road, Edgecliff, NSW 2027 (☎02 9328 7859; fax 9327 1829).

Canada: 299 Waverley St., Ottawa, ON K2P 0V9 (☎613-230-2717; fax 230-7560; www.docuweb.ca/Hungary). **Consulate:** 302 Metcalfe Street, Ottawa, ON K2P 0V9, (☎613-230-2717; fax 230-8887).

Ireland: 2 Fitzwilliam Pl., Dublin 2 (☎01 661 2903; fax 661 2880). **Consulate:** 35B Eaton Place, London SW1X 8BY (☎020 7235 2664; fax 7235 8630; www.docuweb.ca/Hungary/).

New Zealand: 151 Orangi Kaupapa Rd., Wellington 6005 (☎644 938 0427; fax 938 0428; www.geocities.com/CapitolHill/Lobby/1958/ContentsEn.htm). **Consulate:** Edgecliff Center, Suite 405/203-233, New South Head Road, Edgecliff NSW 2027.

South Africa: 959 Arcadia St., Hatfield, Arcadia; P.O. Box 27077, Sunnyside 0132 (☎012 430 3020; fax 430 3029; hunem@cis.co.za).

UK: 35 Eaton Pl., London SW1X 8BY (☎020 7235 5218; fax 7823 1348; www.huemblon.org.uk).

US: 3910 Shoemaker St. NW, Washington, D.C. 20008 (☎202-362-6730; fax 966-8135; www.hungaryemb.org).

VISA AND ENTRY INFORMATION

Citizens of Canada, Ireland, South Africa, the UK, and the US can visit Hungary without **visas** for up to 90 days, provided their passport does not expire within six months of their journey's end. Australians and New Zealanders must obtain 90-day tourist visas from a Hungarian embassy or consulate. For US residents, visa prices are as follows: Single-entry US$40, double-entry US$75, multiple-entry US$180, and 48hr. transit US$38. Non-US residents pay US$65/US$100/US$200/US$50. Visa processing takes a few days and requires the application; proof of transportation (such as an airplane ticket); a valid passport; three photographs (5 for multiple-entry visas); a money order; and a self-addressed, stamped (certified mail) envelope. Hungarian visas are occasionally available at the border, but always priced exorbitantly; it is safer and cheaper to arrange a visa before visiting. Visa extensions are rare; apply at local police stations. There is no fee for crossing a Hungarian **border.** In general, Hungarian border officials are efficient; crossing should add no more than 30 minutes to your journey.

TRANSPORTATION

BY PLANE. Hungary's national airline, **Malév,** has daily direct flights from **New York** and **London** to **Budapest.** It also flies to neighboring countries. Many international airlines fly into Budapest.

BY TRAIN. Most trains *(vonat)* pass through Budapest and are generally reliable and inexpensive. **Eurail** and **EastRail** passes are valid in Hungary. Students and travelers under-26 are sometimes eligible for a 30% discount on train fares; inquire ahead and be persistent. An **ISIC** commands discounts at IBUSZ, Express, and station ticket counters. Flash your card and repeat "student," in Hungarian (*diák; DEE-ahk*). Book international tickets in advance.

Személyvonat trains are excruciatingly slow; *gyorsvonat* (listed on schedules in red) cost the same and move at least twice as fast. Large provincial towns are accessible by the blue *expressz* lines. Air-conditioned *InterCity* trains are the fastest. A *potegy* (seat reservation) is required on trains labeled "R." The fine for boarding an *InterCity* train without a reservation is 1000Ft in addition to the cost of the reservation; purchasing the reservation on board will double the price of the ticket. Some basic vocabulary will help you navigate the rail system: *érkezés* (arrival), *indulás* (departure), *vágány* (track), and *állomás* or *pályaudvar* (station, abbreviated *pu*). The *peron* (platform) for arrivals and departures is rarely indicated until the train approaches the station, and will be announced in Hungarian only. Many train stations are not marked; ask the conductor what time the train is expected to arrive (just point at your watch and say the town's name) and watch for a stop at that time.

BY BUS. Buses are best for travel between the outer provincial centers. The cheap, clean, and crowded bus system links many towns that have rail connections only to Budapest. The **Erzsébet tér** bus station in Budapest posts schedules and fares. Purchase *InterCity* bus tickets on board (arrive early if you want a seat). In larger cities, tickets for local transportation must be bought in advance from a newsstand and punched when you get on; there's a fine if you're caught without a ticket. In smaller cities, you pay when you board.

TOURIST SERVICES

Tourinform has branches in most cities, and is the most useful tourist service in Hungary. They can't make reservations, but they'll check on vacancies, usually in university dorms and private *panzió*. Tourinform should be your first stop in any Hungarian town, as they always stock maps and tons of local info, and employees generally speak both English and German. In smaller towns, you might only find German-speaking services. Most **IBUSZ** offices throughout the country book private rooms, exchange money, sell train tickets, and charter tours, although they are generally better at assisting in travel plans than at providing information about the actual town. Pick up the pamphlet *Tourist Information: Hungary* and the monthly entertainment guides *Programme in Hungary* and *Budapest Panorama* (all free and in English). **Express,** the former national student travel bureau, reserves hostel rooms and changes money. Regional agencies are most helpful in outlying areas.

MONEY

The national currency is the **forint** (Ft), divided into 100 **fillérs,** which have mostly disppeared from circulation. **Inflation** is hovering around 6.8%, so expect prices to increase a little over the next year. Rates are generally poor at exchange offices with extended hours. The maximum legal commission for cash-to-cash exchange is 1%. Never change money on the street. Currency exchange machines are popping up all over and have excellent rates, although they tend to be slow. **American Express** offices in Budapest and IBUSZ offices around the country exchange **traveler's checks** for a steep commission; banks, such as **OTP Bank** and **Postabank,** offer the best exchange rates. Most OTP branches provide **cash advances,** but with the ever-increasing ubiquity of **ATMs,** many banks no longer give them. Major **credit cards** are accepted at expensive hotels and many shops.

HEALTH AND SAFETY

 EMERGENCY NUMBERS: Ambulance, Fire, and Police: ☎112

HEALTH AND SAFETY. Medical assistance is most easily obtained in Budapest, where embassies carry a list of Anglophone doctors, and most hospitals have English-speaking doctors on staff. Outside Budapest, try to bring a Hungarian speaker with you. **Tourist insurance** is valid—and often necessary—for many medical services. **Tap water** is usually clean and drinkable (except in the town of Tokaj, where it bears an uncanny resemblance to the neighboring Tisza River). Bottled water is sold at every food store. Public bathrooms vary tremendously in cleanliness: pack soap, a towel, and 30Ft to pay the attendant. Carry a roll of **toilet paper** with you, as many hostels do not provide it and the single square you get in a public restroom is not always enough. Gentlemen should look for *Férfi*, and ladies for *Női* signs. Many *gyógyszertar* **(pharmacies)** stock Western brands and carry tampons and condoms. In bigger towns, there are usually 24hr. pharmacies. Violent **crime** in Hungary is low, but in larger cities, especially Budapest, foreign tourists are prime targets for petty thieves and pickpockets. In an emergency, your embassy is a better bet than the police.

WOMEN, MINORITY, AND BGLT TRAVELERS. Many **women** travel alone in Hungary, as do families with children and the elderly. **Minorities** are generally well-accepted, though some discrimination against Roma still remains, and dark-skinned travelers that resemble Roma may encounter prejudice. **BGLT** travelers will come up against serious discrimination, especially outside of Budapest.

ACCOMMODATIONS AND CAMPING

HUNGARY	❶	❷	❸	❹	❺
ACCOM.	under 1000Ft	1001-3000Ft	3001-6000Ft	6001-10,000Ft	over 10,000Ft

PRIVATE HOMES. Many travelers stay in private homes booked through a tourist agency. Singles are scarce—it's worth finding a roommate, as solo travelers must often pay for a double room. Agencies may try to foist off their most expensive rooms on you. Outside Budapest, the best and cheapest offices are region-specific (e.g. EgerTourist in Eger). These agencies will often make advance reservations for your next stop. After staying a few nights, you can make arrangements directly with the owner, thus saving yourself the agencies' 20-30% commission. **Panzió** (pensions), run out of private homes, are the next most common option, although not necessarily the cheapest.

HOTELS AND HOSTELS. Hotels exist in some towns, but most have disappeared. As the industry develops and room prices rise, staying in **hostels** is becoming more attractive, although it is rare outside Budapest. Hostels are usually large enough to accommodate summer crowds, and **HI cards** are increasingly useful. Many hostels can be booked through **Express,** the student travel agency, or sometimes through the regional tourist office. From June through August, university **dorms** become hostels. Locations change annually; inquire at Tourinform and always call ahead.

CAMPING. More than 300 campgrounds are sprinkled throughout Hungary; most sites stay open from May through September. If you rent a bungalow you must pay for unfilled spaces. Tourist offices offer the annual booklet *Camping Hungary* for free. For more info and maps, contact Tourinform in Budapest (see **Tourist and Financial Services,** p. 344).

KEEPING IN TOUCH

MAIL. The Hungarian mail system is somewhat reliable; airmail *(légiposta)* takes 5-10 days to the US and the rest of Europe, and two weeks to Australia, New Zealand, and South Africa. Mail costs hover around 25-35Ft domestically, and 110-220Ft internationally. Mail can be received general delivery through **Poste Restante.** Address envelopes as follows: Sandra (first name) NAGY (last name), POSTE RESTANTE, Varoshaz u. 18 (post office address), Budapest (city) 1052 (postal code), HUNGARY.

TELEPHONES. For intercity calls, wait for the tone and dial slowly; "06" goes before the phone code. **International calls** require red phones or new digital-display blue ones. Although the blue phones are more handsome than their red brethren, they tend to cut you off after 3-9 minutes. Phones increasingly require *telefonkártya* (phone cards), available at kiosks, train stations, and post offices in denominations of 800Ft and 1600Ft. Direct calls can also be made from Budapest's phone office.

INTERNET ACCESS. Internet access has spread throughout the country, and is ubiquitous in Budapest and major provincial centers. The Hungarian keyboard differs significantly from English-language keyboards. When you first log on, go to the bottom right-hand corner of the screen and look for the "Hu" icon; click here to switch the keyboard setting to "Angol." Depending on the location, service usually costs 500-700Ft per hour.

BUDAPEST ☎ 1

Budapest (pop. 1.9 million) doesn't always feel Hungarian, and has been aptly described as the Paris of the East. While some other parts of Hungary seem uninterested in adopting the hectic pace of modern life, Budapest has steamrolled its way into the very nucleus of European *très chic.* Urban modernity gleams throughout the city's crowded streets, drawing energy from its racy nightclubs, towering apartment buildings, and flourishing corporations. World War II ravaged Budapest, but the proud Hungarians raised their city from the rubble and restored much of its architectural majesty. The same pride resonated throughout the city as it fomented the ill-fated 1956 Uprising and weathered the Soviet invasion. Budapest is reassuming its place as a major European capital; even 40 years of Communism couldn't kill the Magyar spirit. Originally two separate cities, Budapest was created in 1872 with the union of Buda and Pest, and thereafter became the Hapsburg Empire's number-two city. No toyland Prague, Budapest is bigger, dirtier, and more vibrant than its Czech contemporary.

■ INTERCITY TRANSPORTATION

Flights: Ferihegy Airport (☎ 296 96 96, departures 296 70 00, arrivals 296 80 00, lost and found 296 81 08). **Malév** (Hungarian Airlines; reservations ☎ 296 72 11). The cheapest way to the center from the airport is to take **bus** #93 (20min., every 15min. 4:55am–11:20pm), then take M3 to Kőbanya-Kispest (15min. to Deák tér, which is in downtown Budapest). To catch this bus, turn right from outside Terminal A or left from B and find the *"BKV Plusz Reptér Busz"* sign. Purchase tickets from the newsstand inside Terminal B or the vending machines outside Terminal A (106Ft). The **Airport Minibus** (☎ 296 85 55) runs 24hr.; call 1 day in advance. One-way 1800Ft; round-trip 3300Ft.

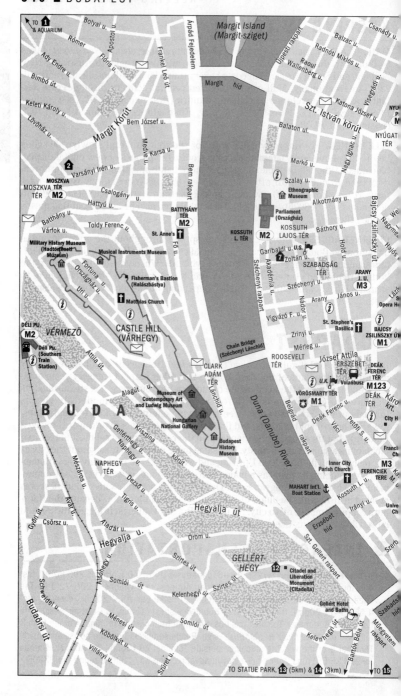

TO & AQUARIUM

Bolyai u.

Römer

Apostol u.

Ady Endre u.

Flóris u.

Frankel Leó út

Árpád fejedelem

Margit Island
(Margit-sziget)

Újpesti rakpart

Csanády u.

Balzac u.

Radnóti Miklós u.

Raoul Wallenberg u.

Bimbó út.

Keleti Károly u.

Lövőház u.

Margit Körút

Bem József u.

Medve u.

Margit híd

Balaton ul.

Markó u.

Szt. István körút

Katona József u.

Visegrádi u.

NYU
P
M

NYÚGAT
TÉR

Bajcsy Zsilinszky út

MOSZKVA
TÉR M2

MOSZKVA TÉR

Varsányi Irén u.

Karsa u.

Bem rakpart

Szalay u.

Nagy Ignác u.

Ethnographic Museum

Csalogány u.

Alkotmány u.

Batthyány u.

Hattyú u.

BATTYHÁNY
TÉR M2

Parliament (Országház)

Báthory u.

Várfok u.

Toldy Ferenc u.

St. Anne's

Fő u.

KOSSUTH
L. TÉR M2

KOSSUTH
LAJOS TÉR

Hold u.

Military History Museum (Hadtörténeti Múzeum)

Fortuna u.

Garibaldi u.

Zoltán u.

SZABADSÁG
TÉR

ARANY
J. U. M3

Musical Instruments Museum

Országház u.

Úri u.

Akadémia u.

Széchenyi u.

Opera He

Fisherman's Bastion (Halászbástya)

Széchenyi rakpart

Arany
János u.

DÉLI PU.
M2

VÉRMEZŐ

Mattbias Church

CASTLE HILL (VÁRHEGY)

Vigyázó F. u.

St. Stephen's Basilica

BAJCSY
ZSILINSZKY ÚT
M1

Déli Pu. (Southern Train Station)

Attila út.

Zrinyi u.

Mérleg u.

ROOSEVELT
TÉR

József Attila

DEÁK
FERENC
TÉR M123

Alagút u.

Museum of Contemporary Art and Ludwig Museum

Chain Bridge (Széchenyi Lánchíd)

ERZSÉBET
TÉR

B U D A

Gellérthegy u.

Krisztina

Naphegy u.

CLARK
ADÁM
TÉR

Lánchíd u.

VÖRÖSMARTY TÉR
M1

U.K.

Volánbusz

DEÁK
TÉR

Károly krt.

NAPHEGY
TÉR

Dezső u.

Hungarian National Gallery

Deák Ferenc u.

Petőfi S u.

Váci u.

City H

Mészáros u.

Avar u.

Tigris u.

Budapest History Museum

Duna (Danube) River

Belgrád rakpart

Franci
Ch

FERENCIEK
TERE M3
M

Győri út.

Csörsz u.

Aladár u.

Hegyalja út

Inner City Parish Church

Kossuth L. u.

Irányi u.

Unive
Ch

Hegyalja u.

Orom u.

MAHART Int'l. Boat Station

Szirtes út

Szt. Gellért rakpart

Erzsébet híd

Alsóhegy u.

GELLÉRT
HEGY

Szerb

Schweidel u.

Somlói út

Kelenhegy u.

Szirtes út

12

Citadel and Liberation Monument (Citadella)

Budaörsi út.

Ménesi út.

Köbölkút u.

Somlói út

Villányi u.

Süget u.

Gellért Hotel and Baths

Kelenhegy u.

Bartók Béla út

Szabads
híd

Műegyetem rakpart

TO 15

TO STATUE PARK, 13 (5km) & 14 (3km)

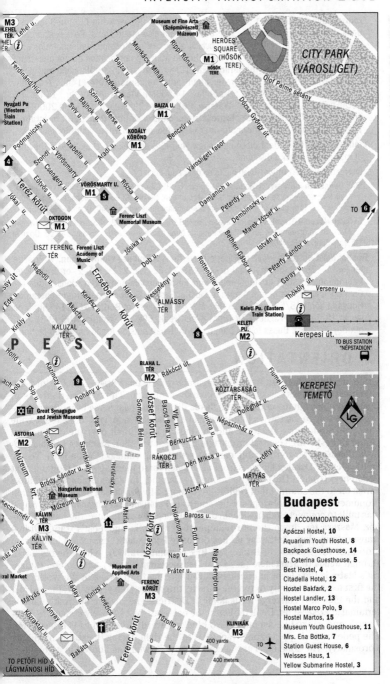

Budapest

🏠 ACCOMMODATIONS

Apáczai Hostel, **10**
Aquarium Youth Hostel, **8**
Backpack Guesthouse, **14**
B. Caterina Guesthouse, **5**
Best Hostel, **4**
Citadella Hotel, **12**
Hostel Bakfark, **2**
Hostel Landler, **13**
Hostel Marco Polo, **9**
Hostel Martos, **15**
Museum Youth Guesthouse, **11**
Mrs. Ena Bottka, **7**
Station Guest House, **6**
Weisses Haus, **1**
Yellow Submarine Hostel, **3**

Trains: International ☎461 55 00, domestic 461 54 00; www.mav.hu. The 3 main stations—**Keleti pu., Nyugati pu.,** and **Déli pu.**—are also Metro stops. Railway stations are the favorite haunts of thieves and pickpockets, so be careful. Most international trains arrive at and depart from Keleti pu., but trains to and from a given location do not necessarily stop at the same station. To: **Berlin, GER** (12hr.; 1 per day; 22,900Ft: night train 15hr.; 1 per day; 36,000Ft; 1500Ft reservation fee); **Bucharest, ROM** (14hr.; 7 per day; 17,400Ft); **Prague, CZR** (8hr.; 4 per day; 14,000Ft); **Vienna, AUS** (3hr.; 17 per day; 7000Ft; 700Ft reservation fee); **Warsaw, POL** (11hr.; 2 per day; 13,950Ft; 2000Ft reservation fee). The daily **Orient Express** stops on its way from **Paris, FRA** to **İstanbul, TUR.** Prices listed are approximate—they vary depending on where your buy your ticket.

Train Tickets: For student discounts, show your ISIC and tell the clerk *"diák."* They may or may not give you a discount.

International Ticket Office, Keleti pu. Open daily 8am-6pm.

MÁV Hungarian Railways, VI, Andrássy út 35 (☎/fax 322 8405; www.mav.hu), with branch offices at all train stations, sells domestic and international tickets. Check the website for up-to-date ticket prices. They often offer 30-40% off international fares with an ISIC. Open M-F 9am-5pm.

Carlson Wagonlit Travel, V, Dorottya u. 3 (☎483 33 85; fax 266 25 85; agent@carlsonwagonlit.hu), off Vörösmarty tér. 15% off international fares for travelers under 25 and over 65. Open M-F 9am-5pm. AmEx/MC/V.

Buses: Most buses to Western Europe leave from **Volánbusz main station,** V, Erzsébet tér (☎117 29 66, international tickets 485 21 62, ext. 211). M1, 2, or 3: Deák tér. International cashier upstairs helps with **Eurail passes** and reservations. Open M-F 6am-6pm, Sa 6:30am-4pm. Buses to most of Eastern Europe depart from **Népstadion,** Hungária körút 48/52 (☎252 18 96). M2: Népstadion. To: **Berlin, GER** (14½hr.; 5 per week; 19,900Ft); **Prague, CZR** (8hr., 4 per week, 6990Ft); **Vienna, AUS** (3-3½hr., 5 per day, 5790Ft). Buses to the Danube Bend depart outside Árpád híd Metro station.

■ ORIENTATION

Originally Buda and Pest, two cities separated by the **Duna River** (Danube), modern Budapest preserves the distinctive character of each. The tree-lined streets of **Buda** wind through the cobblestone **Castle District** and past some breathtaking vistas on the way to the town's hilltop citadel. On the east side, grid-like streets, wide shopping boulevards, theaters, and the Parliament spread over the commercial center of **Pest.** Three central bridges tie Budapest together. **Széchenyi Lánchíd** connects **Roosevelt tér** to the cable car that scurries up **Várhegy** (Castle Hill). To the south, slender **Erzsébet híd** runs from near **Petőfi tér** to the St. Gellért monument at **Gellért-hegy** (Gellért Hill). Farther along the Danube, the green **Szabadság híd** links **Fővám tér** to the south end of Gellért-hegy, topped by **Szabadság Szobor** (Liberation Monument). The other bridges to the south are **Petőfi híd** and **Lágymánosi híd,** which was built to connect Buda residents to Budapest's newest theatre, the **Nemzeti Színház. Moszkva tér,** down the north slope of Várhegy, is Budapest's tram and bus transportation hub. **Batthyány tér** lies opposite **Parliament** (Országház), one Metro stop past the Danube in Buda. The **HÉV commuter railway,** which heads north through **Óbuda** to **Szentendre** (see **Local Transportation,** below), starts here. Budapest's **Metro** is the oldest in continental Europe, the third oldest in the world, and the first to use electricity to run the cars. Its three lines (the yellow M1, the red M2, and the blue M3) converge at **Deák tér** in District V, beside the international bus terminal at **Erzsébet tér.** Deák tér lies at the center of Pest's loosely concentric boulevards and spoke-like avenues. Two blocks toward the river lies **Vörösmarty tér.** The pedestrian shopping zone, **Váci u.,** is to the right, facing the statue of Mihály Vörösmarty. The zone ends at the central market, which is housed in a gorgeous building roofed in multi-colored tiles. **Addresses** in Budapest begin with a Roman numeral representing one of the city's 23 **districts**. Central Buda is I; central Pest is V. The middle two digits of postal codes also indicate the district in which the address lies. The **American Express** and **Tourinform** offices provide free maps.

⌐ LOCAL TRANSPORTATION

Commuter Trains: The **HÉV commuter railway** station is near the Parliament, 1 Metro stop past the Danube in Buda. Trains head to **Szentendre** (40min., every 15min. 5am-9pm, 268Ft). Purchase tickets at the station for transport beyond the city limits or be prepared to pay the hefty fine.

Public Transportation: Budapest's public transportation is inexpensive, convenient, and easy to navigate—it's by far the best way to get around. Open daily 4:30am-11:30pm.

Budapest Public Transport (BKV; ☎ 80 40 66 86; www.bkv.hu) offers toll-free transportation information in Hungarian. Open M-F 7am-3pm. All public transport uses the same tickets (106Ft; no transfers), sold in Metro stations, *Trafik* shops, and kiosks. Punch them in the orange boxes at the Metro gate and on buses and trams. **10 tickets** are 950Ft; 20 tickets 1850Ft. There is also a 70Ft ticket *(metrószakaszjegy)* valid for 3 Metro stops, a 110Ft ticket *(metrószakaszszállójegy)* valid for 5 Metro stops with a transfer, and a 160Ft ticket *(metróátszállójegy)* valid for 1hr. with one transfer between Metro lines. Buy a **pass** if you're going to be in town for more than a day.

Budapest Public Transport

Day-pass 850Ft; 3-day 750Ft; 1-week 2100Ft; 2-week 2650Ft; 1-month 4050Ft. Monthly passes require a transport ID card (100Ft), so bring a photo. Budapest transport tickets are good on HÉV suburban trains within city limits. Otherwise purchase separate HÉV tickets.

Night Transportation: The Metro stops around 11:30pm, but gates may lock at 10:30pm. All Metro stops post the 1st and last trains of the day by the tracks. Buses and trams stop at 11pm. Buses with numbers ending in an "É" run midnight-5am. Bus #7É and 78É follow the M2 route, #6É follows the 4/6 tram line, and bus #14É and 50É run the same route as M3.

Fines: Riding ticketless will cost you 1500–3000Ft if you can't pay on the spot. The inspectors, who wear red armbands, prowl Deák tér looking for victims, so be sure to punch a new ticket when switching lines. They also issue fines for losing the cover sheet to the 10-ticket packet.

Car Rental: There are several reliable rental agencies in Budapest, which charge roughly US$40-50 per day for the cheapest cars. Few agencies rent to those under 21.

Taxis: Be wary of taxi scams; check that the meter works and is running. Before getting in, ask how much the ride usually costs. Prices should not exceed the following: 6am-10pm base fee 200Ft, 200Ft per km, and 50Ft per min. waiting; 10pm-6am base fee 280Ft, 280Ft per km, and 70Ft per min. waiting. Taxis ordered by phone charge less than those hailed on the street. **Budataxi** (☎233 33 33) has some of the best rates at 135Ft per km by phone and 200Ft per km on the street. They will take you to the airport for 3500Ft from Pest and 4000Ft from Buda. **Fötaxi** (☎222 22 22) offers competitive rates at 140Ft per km by phone and 160Ft per km on the street. **6x6 Taxi** (☎266 66 66), **City Taxi** (☎211 11 11), **Rádió Taxi** (☎377 77 77), and **Tele 5 Taxi** (☎355 55 55) are also reliable companies with decent rates.

🛈 PRACTICAL INFORMATION

TOURIST AND FINANCIAL SERVICES

Tourist Offices: All tourist offices, Metro stations, and travel agencies sell the **Budapest Card** (Budapest Kártya). You get public transportation, entrance to all museums—including the zoo and Pál-Völgyi caves—reduced rates on car rental and the airport mini-bus, and discounts at shops and restaurants. (2-day card 3700Ft; 3-day card 4500Ft.) Pick up 📖 *Budapest in Your Pocket* (www.inyourpocket.com; 750Ft), an up-to-date guide of the city.

Tourinform, V, Vigadó u. 6 (☎235 44 81; fax 235 45 70), toward the river from the Metro. M1: Vörösmarty tér. Open 24hr. **Branch** at V, Sütő u. 2 (☎317 98 00, 24hr. hotline 0690 66 00 44; fax 356 19 64; www.hungarytourism.hu), off Deák tér behind McDonald's. M1, 2, or 3: Deák tér. The best place for event and tour info. Open daily 8am-8pm.

Vista Travel Center: Visitor's Center, Pauley Ede 7 (☎429 99 50; incoming@vista.hu). Arranges tours and accommodations, and has **luggage storage.** Open M-F 9am-8pm, Sa 10am-4pm.

Travel Agency, Andrássy út. 1 (☎429 97 51; tourop@visa.hu). M1, 2, or 3: Deák tér. Exit on Bajcsy-Zsilinszky u. Arranges accommodations, books transportation, handles car rentals, gives advice on travel outside Budapest. Open M-F 9am-6:30pm, Sa 9am-2:30pm.

IBUSZ, V, Ferenciek tér 10 (☎485 27 00). M3: Ferenciek tér. Books cheap tickets and sightseeing tours (basic 3hr. tour 6000Ft, with Budapest Card 3000Ft), finds rooms (see **Accommodations,** p. 346), and **exchanges currency.** Open M-F 8:15am-6pm; Sa 9am-1pm for currency exchange only. AmEx/MC/V accepted for some services.

Budget Travel: Express, V, Zoltán út 10 (☎311 98 98). Focuses on student travel. Offers the same youth discounts on rail travel available at the train station. Open M-Th 8:30am-4:30pm, F 8:30am-3pm. **Malév Airlines,** V, Dorottya u. 2 (☎235 35 65; fax 266 27 84; malew@malev.hu). M1: Vörösmarty tér. Youth discounts for those under 24. Open M-W and F 8:30am-5:30pm, Th 8:30am-6pm.

Embassies and Consulates: New Zealand and **Irish** citizens should contact the UK embassy.

Australia, XII, Királyhágo tér 8/9 (☎457 97 77; fax 201 97 92; austembbp@mail.datanet.hu). M2: Déli pu., then bus #21 or tram #59 to Királyhágo tér. Open M-F 9am-noon.

Canada, XII, Budakeszi út 32 (☎392 33 60). Take bus #158 from Moszkva tér to the last stop. Entrance at Zugligeti út 51-53. Open M-F 8:30am-11am and 2-3:30pm.

South Africa, II, Gárdonyi Géza út 17 (☎392 09 99, emergency 0620 955 80 46; fax 200 72 77). M2: Batthyány tér, then take bus #11 to "Móricz Zsigmond Gynasium." Open M-F 9am-noon.

UK, V, Harmincad u. 6 (☎266 28 88; fax 266 09 07), near the intersection with Vörösmarty tér. M1: Vörösmarty tér. Open M-F 9:30am-noon and 2:30-4pm.

US, V, Szabadság tér 12 (☎475 44 00, after hours 475 47 03, 24hr. emergency 266 28 88 93 31, visas 90 52 05 20; fax 475 47 64). M2: Kossuth tér. Walk 2 blocks down Akademia and turn on Zoltán. Open M-F 8:15am-5pm.

Currency Exchange: The best currency exchange rates are found at banks. Try to avoid the steep premiums at the airport, train stations, and small currency exchange shops. **Citibank,** V, Vörösmarty tér 4 (☎374 50 00; fax 374 51 00). M1: Vörösmarty tér. Cashes **traveler's checks** for no commission and, if you bring your passport, provides MC/V **cash advances. Budapest Bank,** V, Váci u. 1/3 (☎328 31 55; fax 267 30 40). M1: Vörösmarty tér. Offers credit card **cash advances,** cashes **traveler's checks** into US$ for 3.5% commission, and has great exchange rates. Open M-F 8:30am-5pm, Sa 9am-2pm. The ubiquitous **OTP** and **K&H** banks also have good exchange rates.

American Express: V, Deák Ferenc u. 10 (☎235 43 30; fax 235 43 49; travel@amex.hu). M2 or 3: Deák tér. Open M-F 9am-5:30pm, Sa 9am-2pm.

LOCAL SERVICES

Luggage storage: At **Keleti pu.** large yellow lockers sit across from the international cashier (200Ft). **Nyugati pu.** has a 24hr. luggage desk in the waiting room next to the ticket windows. 140Ft per day, 280Ft for large bags. At **Déli pu.,** luggage storage open daily 3:30am-11:30pm. 150Ft, 300Ft for large items. Lockers in the main hall cost 200Ft per day. The **Volánbusz** bus station has small lockers for 90Ft per day. Open M and F-Sa 6am-8pm, Tu-Th and Su 6am-7pm. **Vista Travel Center** (see **Tourist Offices,** p. 344) has lockers big enough to hold a pack. 100Ft per hr.

English-Language Bookstores: Atlantisz, Piarista Köz 1 (☎/fax 267 62 58; atl-book@matavnet.hu), just off Váci u. M3: Ferenciek tér. Terrific selection of nonfiction. Open M-Sa 10am-6pm, Su 10am-2pm. AmEx/MC/V. **Bestsellers,** V, Október 6 u. 11 (☎312 12 95; fax 302 30 26; www.bestsellers.hu), off the intersection with Arany János u. M1, 2, or 3: Deák tér or M3: Arany János út. Carries international publications, as well as *The Phone Book,* a free English-language business directory handy for long stays. Open M-F 9am-6:30pm, Sa 10am-5pm, Su 10am-4pm.

Gay Hotline: GayGuide.net Budapest (☎0630 932 33 34; fax 351 20 15; www.gayguide.net/europe/hungary/budapest). This volunteer organization posts an on-line guide and runs a hotline (operator guaranteed daily 4-8pm) with info and reservations at gay- and lesbian-friendly lodgings. See also **Gay Budapest,** p. 359.

EMERGENCY AND COMMUNICATIONS

Tourist Police: V, Vigadó u. 6 (☎235 44 79). M1: Vörösmarty tér. Walk toward the river from the Metro to reach the station, just inside Tourinform. Open 24hr.

24-Hour Pharmacies: II, Frankel Leó út 22 (☎212 44 06); **III,** Szentendrei út 2/a (☎388 65 28); **IV,** Pozsonyi u. 19 (☎389 40 79); **VI,** Teréz krt. 41 (☎311 44 39); **VII,** Rákóczi út 39 (☎314 36 95); **VIII,** Üllöi út 121 (☎215 38 00). Look for a tan-and-white motif with *Gyógyszertár, Apotheke,* or *Pharmacie* in black letters in the window. 100-200Ft for after-hours service.

Medical Assistance: For an **ambulance,** call ☎104. **Falck (SOS) KFT,** II, Kapy út 49/b (☎200 01 00 or 275 15 35). Ambulance service US$120. **American Clinic,** I, Hattyú

u. 14 (☎224 90 90; www.americanclinics.com), accepts walk-ins during clinic hours. Open M-Th 8:30am-7pm, F 8:30am-6pm, Sa 8:30am-1pm. The US embassy maintains a list of English-speaking doctors.

Telephones: Domestic operator ☎191; **international operator** ☎190. **Domestic Information** ☎198; **international information** ☎199. Most phones use **phone cards,** available at newsstands and Metro stations. 50-unit card 800Ft, 120-unit card 1800Ft.

Internet Access: Cyber cafes litter the city, but access can get expensive and long waits are common. Internet access is available at many of Budapest's hostels.

Ami Internet Coffee, V, Váci u. 40 (☎267 16 44; www.amicoffee.hu). M3: Ferenciek tér. 200Ft per 10min., 400Ft per 30min., 700Ft per hr. Open daily 9am-10pm.

Eckermann, VI, Andrássy út 24 (☎269 25 42). M1: Opera. Free. Call a week ahead during summer. Open M-F 8am-10pm, Sa 9am-10pm.

Libri Könyvpalota, VII, Rákóczi út 12 (☎267 48 43; www.libri.hu). M2: Astoria. Reserve in advance. 200Ft per 30min., 350Ft per hr.

Matav Office, Petőfi Sandor 17/19 (☎485 66 12; fax 485 66 16). 500Ft per hr., 300Ft per 30min.

Post Office: V, Városház u. 18 (☎318 48 11). **Poste Restante** (Postán Mar). Open M-F 8am-8pm, Sa 8am-2pm. **Branches** at Nyugati pu.; VI, Teréz krt. 105/107; Keleti pu.; VIII, Baross tér 11/c; and throughout the city. Open M-F 8am-9pm, Sa 8am-2pm.

Postal Code: Depends on the district (1052 for post office listed above).

ACCOMMODATIONS

Tourists fill the city in July and August; save yourself some blisters by phoning first or storing luggage while you seek out a bed for the night. Tourists arriving at Keleti pu. enter a feeding frenzy as hostel solicitors jostle each other for guests. Don't be drawn in by promises of free rides or special discounts: some hostel-hawkers may stretch the truth.

ACCOMMODATION AGENCIES

Private rooms are slightly more expensive than hostels (2000-5000Ft per person; prices decrease with longer stays), but offer what hostels can't: peace, quiet, and private showers. Accommodation agencies appear everywhere in town. Be there when they open and haggle to secure cheaper rooms. Before you accept any room, make sure the hostel is easily accessible by public transportation. Bring cash.

Budapest Tourist, I, Deli pu. (☎/fax 212 46 25). M2: Déli pu. Well-established. Singles in Central Pest 5000-7000Ft; doubles 6000-10,000Ft; triples 6000-12,000Ft. Off-season prices considerably lower. Apartments for stays over 1 week 3000-7000Ft per day, less for stays over 2 months. Open M-F 9am-5pm. ❸

IBUSZ, V, Ferenciek tér (☎485 27 67; fax 337 1205). M3: Ferenciek tér. Doubles 5000Ft; triples 5000-6000Ft. 1800Ft surcharge if staying fewer than 4 nights. Also rents centrally located Pest apartments with kitchen and bath. 1-bedroom flat from 7000Ft; 2-bedroom flats from 14,000Ft. Reservations by email. Open M-Th 8:15am-4pm, F 8:15am-3pm. **Branch** at VIII, Keleti pu. (☎342 95 72). Open M-F 8am-6pm. ❸

Non-Stop Hotel Service, V, Apáczai Csere J. u. 1 (☎266 80 42; fax 266 81 59). M1, 2, or 3: Déak tér. Rooms in Pest. 6000Ft and up. Open 24hr. ❹

HOSTELS AND HOTELS

Budapest's hostels are backpacker social centers, each with its own quirks. You may find some hostel common rooms as exciting as the city's expat bars and clubs. Many hostels are now run by the **Hungarian Youth Hostels Association,** which operates from an office in Keleti pu. Their representatives wear Hostelling International T-shirts and will—along with legions of competitors—accost you as you get off the train. Take the free transport; it doesn't commit you.

BUDA

▨ **Backpack Guesthouse,** XI, Takács Menyhért u. 33 (☎209 84 06; backpackguest@hotmail.com), 12min. from central Pest. From Keleti pu., take bus #7 or 7a toward Buda. Get off at Tétenyi u. and walk back under the railway bridge to a sharp left turn. Take the 3rd right at Hamzsabégi út. Themed rooms with murals and weekly spelunking trips (2900Ft). Get to know the helpful staff and be sure to exploit the CD and video collections, as well as the cheap beer. Internet access (15Ft per min.) and laundry service (1000Ft). Reception 24hr. Reserve in advance. 4- to 5-bed dorms 2300Ft; double 5600Ft; mattress in the gazebo 1500Ft. ❷

Citadella Hotel, XI, Citadella Sétány (☎466 57 94; fax 386 05 05). Take bus #27 to Búsuló Juhász and walk 5min. to the top of Gellért Hill. This hotel boasts private showers, spacious rooms, and knock-out views—even if it does lack the warmth and energy of a hostel. No TV, no kitchen. Call ahead. 14-bed dorm 2060Ft; doubles 9000Ft, with shower 11,300Ft, with bath 12,300Ft. ❹

PEST

▨ **Station Guest House (HI),** XIV, Mexikói út 36/b (☎221 88 64; fax 383 40 34; www.stationguesthouse.hu). Near the train station. From Keleti pu., take bus #7 or night bus #78É 4 stops to Hungária Körút, walk under the railway pass, and take an immediate right on Mexikói út. Set up to party, with free billiards, satellite TV, a common room, live music twice a week, beer at the reception, and a friendly staff. Ask for a kitchen-floor room if you plan to sleep. Well-kept rooms with private lockers. Internet access 20Ft per min. Breakfast 500Ft. Laundry service 600Ft per 4kg. Reserve 1 day in advance. Attic 1700Ft per person; 6- to 8-bed dorms 2200Ft; quads 2500Ft; 2- to 3-bed rooms 3000Ft. All prices drop 100Ft with each extra night you stay, up to 5 nights. ❷

▨ **Hostel Marco Polo,** VII, Nyár u. 6 (☎413 25 55; fax 413 60 58; www.hotelmarcopolo.com). M2: Astoria or Blaha Lujza tér. This is the luxury hotel of hostels—and the prices reflect it. Internet access 500Ft per 30min. Laundry 500Ft. Reception 24hr. Book 1-2 days in advance in July-Aug. Dorms 4700Ft; singles 13,000Ft; doubles 17,000Ft; triples 19,800Ft; quads 22,400Ft. HI and ISIC discount. ❸

Best Hostel, VI, Podmaniczky u. 27, 1st fl. (☎332 49 34; fax 269 29 26; www.besthostel.hu). Ring bell #33 in the building opposite Nyugati pu. This hostel offers large dorms, a common room, and a kitchen. Breakfast included. Laundry 1000Ft. Internet access 10Ft per min. Dorms 2800Ft; doubles 8000Ft. 10% HI discount. ❷

Yellow Submarine Hostel, VI, Teréz Körút 56, 3rd fl. (☎/fax 331 98 96; www.yellowsubmarinehostel.com). Across from Nyugati pu. Basic dorms with bunked beds and lockers—bring your own padlock. Most doubles and triples are in nearby apartments. Internet access 9Ft per min. after 6pm. Breakfast included. Laundry 1000Ft. Check-out 9am. 8- to 10-bed dorms 2500Ft; 4-bed dorms 2800Ft; doubles 5500Ft; triples 9000Ft. 10% HI discount. MC/V. ❷

Aquarium Youth Hostel, IX, Alsoérdósor u. 12 (☎322 05 02; aquarium@budapesthostels.com). Close to Keleti pu. Run by a hospitable, fun-loving staff, this hostel is decorated with an underwater motif. Free use of Internet and kitchen. Laundry 1200Ft. Reception 24hr. 4- to 5-bed dorms 2500Ft; doubles 8000Ft. 250Ft HI discount. ❷

Museum Youth Guesthouse, VIII, Mikszáth Kálmán tér 4, 1st fl. (☎318 95 08 or 266 88 79; museumgh@freemail.c3.hu). M3: Kálvin tér. Take the left exit from the stop onto Baross u.; when it forks, take the left branch, Pevieczky u. At the square, go to the far right corner and ring the buzzer at gate #4. The lofts, bunks, and single beds hide its capacity, but the morning line for the single shower and electric kettle will soon remind you. Internet 800Ft per hr.; free after 7pm. Laundry 1200Ft. 500Ft locker deposit. English spoken. Reception 24hr. Check-out 10am. Reservations recommended. Dorms 2500Ft, 2000Ft after the second night. ❷

SUMMER HOSTELS

Many university dorms moonlight as hostels during July and August. The majority are clustered around Móricz Zsigmond Körtér in district XI. Unless otherwise noted, all have kitchens, luggage storage, and a TV in the common room.

Hostel Bakfark, I, Bakfark u. 1/3 (☎329 86 44). M2: Moszkva tér. From the Metro, walk along Margit krt. with Burger King to the right. Take the 1st right after passing Mammut. Among the most comfortable dorms in town, with lofts instead of bunks. The sparkling showers are a trek from the rooms. Breakfast 700Ft. Check-out 10am. Call ahead. Open June 15-Aug. 28. 6-bed dorms 3300Ft. 10% HI discount. ❸

Apáczai Hostel, V, Papnövelde 4/6 (☎267 03 11). One of the best locations in Budapest—only steps away from the major venues in Pest. A friendly staff and clean rooms. Open June-Aug. 3- to 6-bed dorms 3600Ft; doubles 4300Ft. 10% HI discount. ❸

Hostel Landler, XI, Bartók Béla út 17 (☎463 36 21). Take bus #7 or 7A across the river, and get off at Géllert. A short walk from the river on Bartók Béla út; the hostel is on the right. A rare find in a cheerful, antiquated building with big staircases and natural light. Free transport from the bus or train station. Laundry available. Check-out 9am. Open July 5-Sept. 5. Singles 5850Ft; triples 11,700Ft; quads 15,600Ft. 10% HI discount. ❸

Hostel Martos, XI, Stoczek u. 5/7 (☎209 48 83; reception@hotel.martos.bme.hu). From Keleti pu., take bus #7 to Móricz Zsigmond Körtér and go 300m toward the river on Bartók Béla út. Turn right on Bertalan Lajos and take the 3rd right on Stoczek u.; it's on the corner. This student-run hostel has cheap, clean rooms and a kitchen on each floor. Free Internet. Satellite TV. Laundry available. Check-out 9am. Reserve a few days in advance. Singles 3500Ft; doubles 4400Ft, with shower 8000Ft; triples 6600Ft; 2- to 4-bed apartments with bath 14,000Ft. ❸

GUEST HOUSES

For a few more forints than a hostel bed, you can enjoy the personal touch of a guest house or a private home. Friendly owners will usually pick travelers up at the train station or at the airport and allow them to use the kitchen. Visitors receive keys to their rooms and the house; while trying not to wake a sleeping household as you tiptoe down the hall might trigger high-school flashbacks, you'll be free to come and go as you please. Guest houses should not be confused with *panzió* (pensions), which are larger and start at 6000Ft per person.

Mrs. Ena Bottka, V, Garibaldi u. 5 (☎/fax 302 34 56, mobile 0630 951 87 63; garibaldiguest@hotmail:com). M2: Kossuth tér. From the Metro, head away from Parliament along Nádor u., and take the first right on Garibaldi u. Close to Parliament. Charming Ena offers a suite of spacious rooms in her apartment, though there are some basic doubles as well. Most include kitchenette, TV, showers, and towels. Rooms 3500Ft per person. Apartments 6000-10,000Ft. Prices decrease with longer stays. ❸

B. Caterina Guesthouse and Hostel®, VI, Andrássy út 47, apt. #18, ring bell #11. (☎342 08 04; fax 352 61 47; www.extra.hu/caterin). M1: Oktogon. Or trams #4 or 6. This century-old building on Andrássy near central Pest is the home of Caterina Birta. Fresh linens, a squeaky-clean kitchen floor, and quiet hours after 10pm. TV in all rooms. Free Internet access. Outings in the family minivan 2500Ft. Laundry 700Ft per 5kg.

English understood. Reception 24hr. Check-out 9am. Lockout 10am-2pm. Reserve by fax or email. Dorms 2400Ft per person; 2-bed lofts 7000Ft; triples 8300Ft. ❷

Weisses Haus, III, Erdőalja út 11 (☎/fax 387 82 36, mobile 0630 432 36 28; weisses_haus@excite.com). M3: Árpád híd. Continue on Béci ut.-bound tram #1 to Floriantér; from there, take bus #137 to the Iskola stop, which is right in front of the guesthouse. A family-owned villa in a pleasant neighborhood 30min. from the city center. Breakfast prepared by family matriarch Mama Zsuzsa. You may occasionally be rewarded with freshly baked goodies. English spoken. Laundry 1200Ft per 4kg. No curfew, but bus #137 stops running at 11:30pm. 6 doubles with a great view of distant Pest. Doubles in summer US$30; in winter US$20; 6-bed suites US$50. ❸

CAMPING

Római Camping, III, Szentendrei út 189 (☎368 62 60; fax 250 04 26; www.camping.hu/romai). M2: Batthyány tér, then take the HÉV to "Római fürdő" and walk 100m toward the river. This huge complex pampers its guests with a grocery store and tons of restaurants. Enjoy the swimming pool (300Ft) and the vast shady park and Roman ruins nearby. Bungalows are ranked by class according to amenities included. Complex is guarded. Communal showers and kitchen. Laundry 800Ft. Tents 1990Ft per person; bungalows 1690-15,000Ft. Tourist tax 3%. 10% HI discount. MC/V. ❷

Zugligeti "Niche" Camping, XII, Zugligeti út 101 (☎/fax 200 83 46; camping.niche@matavnet.hu). Take bus #158 from Moszkva tér to the last stop, Leszállóhely. An easy commute from central Budapest, located right next to the János Negyi chairlift. A grassy campsite with shady walks and friendly people. Quality communal showers, an on-site restaurant, and a safe. English spoken. 850Ft per person. Tents 500Ft, large tents 900Ft. Cars 700Ft. Caravans 1800Ft. Electricity 450Ft. MC/V. ❶

🖸 FOOD

Explore the cafeterias beneath "Önkiszolgáló Étterem" signs for something greasy and cheap (meat dishes 300-500Ft) or seek out neighborhood *kifőzés* (kiosks) or *vendéglő* (vendors) for a real taste of Hungary. **Non-Stop** stores and corner markets stock basics. The king of them all, the 🖾**Grand Market Hall,** IX, Fővamtér 1/3, next to Szabadság híd (M3: Kálvin tér), was built in 1897; it now boasts 10,000 square meters of stalls, making it a tourist attraction in itself. Find fresh produce, baked goods, and meat on the first floor, while the second floor boasts every type of Hungarian souvenir you can possibly imagine. For a wide array of ethnic restaurants, try the upper floors of **Mammut Plaza,** just outside of the Moskva tér Metro stop in Buda, or the **West End Plaza,** accessible from the Nyugati Metro stop in Pest.

🖾 Gandhi, V, Vigyázó Ferenc u. 4 (☎269 16 25). From the yoga classes to the trickling waterfall, Gandhi takes customers to a higher plane. This superior restaurant cuts the fat, meat, and fried cheese out of traditional Hungarian food, but it cuts back on the portions too. Even carnivores will enjoy their luscious green concoctions. Entrees 980-1680Ft. Open M-Sa noon-10:30pm, kitchen open until 10pm. AmEx/MC/V. ❸

🖾 Marquis de Salade, VI, Hajós u. 43 (☎302 40 86). M3: Arany János. At the corner of Bajcsy-Zsilinszky út, 2 blocks from the Metro. Huge menu with dishes from Azerbaijan, France, India, Italy, Japan, and Hungary. Barry White croons to guests in the subterranean dining room. Entrees 1300-2300Ft. Open daily 11am-1am. Cash only. ❹

🖾 Robinson Mediterranean-style Restaurant and Cafe, Városligeti tér (☎422 02 22; fax 422 00 72). This spectacularly scenic restaurant on a platform on top of the lake in City Park is infused with special charm, though the service can be excruciatingly slow. Vegetarian options. Entrees 2300-6000Ft. Open daily noon-4pm and 6pm-midnight. ❹

THE BIG SPLURGE

GOLDEN GUNDEL

Gundel, Hungary's most highly regarded restaurant serves scrumptious dishes in golden-age opulence. The a la carte restaurant is laden with paintings by some of Hungary's most famous artists. Have a drink and a cigar at the elegant bar, and taste the famous Gundel pancake (a crepe filled with raisin-walnut cream, covered in chocolate and flambéed). Have you fallen in love with the place yet? Its banquet halls have served up elegant meals for the rich and famous—both Queen Elizabeth II and Pope John Paul II have dined here. As if that isn't enough to make you feel like royalty, the subterranean wine cellar is a connoisseur's dream. Sample wines from every one of Hungary's famous regions—and do it in style. The elegance and professionalism of the cellar is apparent even to the undiscerning eye.

The Sunday brunch buffet (3900Ft) and the outdoor cafe (sandwiches 400-600Ft; coffee 300Ft) best suit the tight budget, but if money's no object, try the 13,000Ft and 17,500Ft seven-course fixed menus or a banquet of unmatched proportions. (*XIV, Állakerti út 2. M1: Hősök tere. Behind the Museum of Fine Arts. ☎468 40 40; fax 363 19 17; info@gundel.hu. Reservations necessary; jacket required in evening. Entrees 3900-17,500Ft. Open daily noon-4pm and 6:30-midnight. Sunday brunch 11:30am-3pm. Bar open daily 9pm-midnight.* ❺)

—Sandra Nagy

Carmel Pince Étterem, VII, Kazinczy út 31 (☎342 45 85). This subterranean restaurant in the Jewish quarter near the Dohany Synagogue serves up generous Jewish-Hungarian delicacies. Entrees 1000-3000Ft. 10% student discount. Open daily noon-11pm. ❸

Remiz, II, Budakeszi út 5 (☎275 13 96). Take bus #22 from Moszkva tér to Szépilona. Known for its outdoor BBQ, where sumptuous ribs and steaks are cooked on lava stone. Entrees 980-1780Ft. Open daily 9am-1am. BBQ May-Sept. AmEx/MC/V. ❶

Marxim, II, Kisrókus u. 23 (☎316 02 31; www.marxim.hu). M2: Moszkva tér. Walk along Margit krt. facing away from the castle-like building, then turn left down the industrial road. Hip local teens unite at this tongue-in-cheek Communist-themed pizzeria. Though barbed-wire "iron curtains" separate the booths, there's no Checkpoint Charlie: just dig in. Great pizzas 450-900Ft. Open M-F noon-1am, Sa noon-2am, Su 6pm-1am. ❷

Marcello's, XI, Bartók Béla út 40 (☎466 62 31). Before Móricz Zsigmond Körtér. With "cigarette" breadsticks, fresh flowers, and classy servers, this is pizza grown up. Great salad bar. Reservations recommended. Pizzas 700-1600Ft. Open M-Sa noon-10pm. ❷

Borpatika (Wine Pharmacy), XI, Bertalan L. út 26 (☎204 26 44). Take tram #47 or 49 from Deák tér to Bertalan Lajos. Aptly named, this tavern lures patrons to its boisterous Happy Hour. Dining downstairs. Entrees 630-1800Ft. Open daily 8am-11pm. ❷

Falafel Faloda, VI, Pauley Ede u. 53 (☎267 95 67; www.falafel.hu). M1: Opera. From the Metro, cross Andrássy, head straight on Hajós u., and turn left on Pauley Ede. Fast food at its best: falafel with tahini and fresh vegetables. Falafel 450Ft, sandwich 440Ft, salad 380Ft. Open M-F 10am-8pm, Sa 10am-6pm. ❶

Okay Italia, XII, Szent István krt. 20 (☎390 29 91). Also at Nyugati tér 6 (☎332 69 20). M3: Nyugati pu. Delectable pizzas (990-1490Ft) and pastas (990-1590Ft) draw the crowds. Pastas are labeled "first course," but they're full meals. Open daily noon-midnight; kitchen closes at 11:30pm. ❸

◪ CAFES

The former haunts of the literary, intellectual, and cultural elite as well as political dissidents, Budapest's cafes boast rich histories. Currently, the "hip" cafes can be found at Ferencz Liszt tér (M2: Oktogon). These upscale cafes are frequented by expats and yuppy Hungarians, and English is commonly spoken. Each cafe has a large summer patio—come early to get a great people-watching post.

Gerbeaud, V, Vörösmarty tér 7 (☎ 429 90 00). M1: Vörösmarty tér. This Budapest institution has been serving its layer cakes (520Ft) and homemade ice cream (95Ft) since 1858. The large terrace sprawls over the end of Vörösmarty tér. Open daily 9am-9pm.

Muvész Kávéház, VI, Andrássy út 29 (☎ 352 13 37). M1: Opera. Diagonally across from the Opera. The name means "artist cafe" and, unlike most remaining Golden Age coffeehouses, the title fits. Enjoy a *Muvész torta,* a slice of deliciously sinful cake (290Ft) and cappuccino (260Ft) at the polished stone tables. Open daily 9am-midnight.

Ruszwurm, I, Szentháromság 7 (☎ 375 52 84). Just off the square on Várhegy in the Castle District. This teeny cafe has been confecting since 1827, when it made sweets for the Habsburgs. Pastries and cake 120-220Ft. Open daily 10am-7pm.

Faust Wine Cellar, I, Hess András tér 1-3 (☎ 488 68 73). Enter the Hilton in the Castle District, head left and descend deep into the 13th-century Dominican cloisters to the monks' former wine cellar. An overwhelming array of excellent Hungarian vintages served straight from the source. 300-3900Ft per glass. Open daily 4-11pm.

◎ SIGHTS

In 1896, Hungary's 1000th birthday bash prompted the construction of what are today Budapest's most prominent sights. Among the works commissioned by the Habsburgs were **Heroes' Square** (Hősök tér), **Liberty Bridge** (Szbadság híd), **Vajdahunyad Castle** (Vajdahunyad vár), and continental Europe's first **Metro** system. Slightly grayer for wear, war, and Communist occupation, these monuments attest to the optimism of a capital on the verge of its Golden Age. See the sights, gain an orientation of the city, and meet other travelers with **The Absolute Walking & Biking Tours.** Their basic tour (3½hr.; 3500Ft, 26 and under 3000Ft) meets May 16-Sept. 30 daily at 9:30am and 1:30pm on the steps of the yellow church in Déak tér and at 10am and 2pm in Heroes' Square. They also hold off-season tours Oct. 1-Jan. 6 and Feb. 1-May 15. These leave at 10:30am from Deák tér and at 11am from Heroes' Square. You can also choose from a range of specialized tours that focus on everything from communist Hungary to pub-crawling Budapest. (☎ 211 88 61; www.budapesttours.com. Specialized tours 2½-5½hr.; 4000-5000Ft.)

BUDA

CASTLE HILL (VÁRHEGY)

M1, 2, or 3: Deák tér. From the Metro, take bus #16 across the Danube. Once over the river, get off at the base of the Széchenyi Chain Bridge and take the funicular (sikló) up the hill (400Ft). Runs daily 9:30am-5:30pm; closed 2nd and 4th M of the month. The upper lift station is just inside the castle walls, only a few meters from the Hungarian National Gallery (Nemzeti Galéria). Alternatively, take the Metro to M2: Moszkva tér, and walk up to the hill on Várfok u. Vienna Gate (Becsi kapu) marks the Castle entrance.

Towering above the Danube, the castle district has been razed and rebuilt three times over 800 years, most recently in 1945 when the Red Army decimated most of Castle Hill. With its winding, statue-lined streets and breathtaking views, the UNESCO-protected district appears as it did in Hapsburg times, with the addition of tourists and gift shops. Visit in the evening to see the beautiful area in lights.

THE CASTLE. (Vár.) Built in 1242, Budapest's original castle was razed by a Mongol invasion. Centuries later, **Good King Mátyás** (see **History,** p. 330) choose Buda for the site of his Renaissance palace, but restless Turks seized the castle in 1541. Nearly a century and a half later, Habsburg forces leveled the castle in order to oust the Ottomans. Another reconstruction was completed just in time to be destroyed by the Germans in 1945. Determined Hungarians cemented the castle together once more, only to face the Red menace; today, bullet holes in the facade are reminders of 1956 Uprising (see **History,** p. 330). In the post-Soviet period, much-needed resources have been channeled toward restoration, but little is left to restore: the hill is mostly a reproduction of its former self. The World War II bombings unearthed artifacts from the original castle; they are now housed in the **Budapest History Museum** (Budapesti Történeti), in the Royal Palace (Budavári palota). For a description of Castle Hill museums, see **Museums,** p. 355.

MATTHIAS CHURCH. (Mátyás Templom.) The Gothic Matthias Church is one of the most-photographed buildings in Budapest, largely due to its multicolored roof. The church still bears the marks of Turkish rule: when Ottoman armies seized Buda on September 2, 1541, the church was converted into a mosque overnight. In 1688, the Habsburgs defeated the Turks, sacked the city, and reconverted the building into a church. Ascend the spiral staircase to reach the **Museum of Ecclesiastical Art,** but explanations of the permanent exhibits are in Hungarian only. The stunning marble bust of Hapsburg Queen Sissy guards the entrance to the adjacent **St. Stephen's Chapel** (Szent István Kápelna). A second chapel contains the **tomb of King Béla III,** the only sepulcher of the Árpád dynasty not looted by the Ottomans. (*l, Szentháromság tér 2. M1, 2, or 3: Deák tér. From the Metro, take bus #16 to the top of Castle Hill.* ☎ *355 56 57. Open M-Sa 9am-5pm, Su 1-5pm. High mass daily 7, 8:30am, 6pm; Su and holidays 10am and noon. Orchestra and chorus concerts most W and F 7:30pm. Free. Call Tourinform (see* p. 344*) for info. Church and museum 600Ft, students 300Ft.)*

FISHERMAN'S BASTION. (Halászbástya.) The grand equestrian monument of **King Stephen,** bearing his trademark double cross, sits in front of the Fisherman's Bastion. The stone wall supports a squat, fairy-tale **tower,** built as a romanticized reconstruction of the original. The amazing view is still the same, although you pay to see across the Danube. (*Behind Matthias Church. Tower 240Ft, students 120Ft.)*

CASTLE LABYRINTHS. (Budvári Labirinths.) The caverns beneath the Castle, formed by thermal springs, were created when Budapest's only residents were unicellular. There's no minotaur in the center, but children under 14, young mothers, and people with heart conditions are advised not to participate in this spooky, off-beat trip through the city's subterranean world. Some hostels such as the **Backpack Youth Hostel** (see p. 347) can arrange spelunking excursions. (*Úri u. 9.* ☎ *212 02 07; labrint@elender.hu. Open daily 9:30am-7:30pm. 900Ft, students 700Ft.)*

OTHER SIGHTS IN BUDA

More disjointed than young Pest, older Buda tumbles down from Castle and Gellért Hills on the east bank of the Danube, sprawling out into Budapest's main residential areas, where there are plenty of great parks, lush hills, and islands.

GELLÉRT HILL. The Pope sent Bishop Gellért to the coronation of King Stephen, the first Christian Hungarian monarch, to assist in the conversion of the Magyars (see **History,** p. 330). Unconvinced by his message, the people hurled the good bishop to his death from atop the hill that now bears his name. Watching over the city from atop Gellért Hill (Gellért-hegy), the **Liberation Monument** (Szabadság Szobor) was erected to honor Soviet soldiers who died "liberating" Hungary; the Soviet star and the smaller military statues have only recently been removed. The adjoining **Citadel** was built as a symbol of Hapsburg power after the failed 1848 Revolution. The view from the top of the hill is breathtaking at night, when the Danube and its bridges shimmer in black and gold (300Ft). Only a short way down from the Citadel, the **statue of St. Gellért,** complete with glistening waterfall, overlooks Erzsébet híd. At the base of the hill sits the **Gellért Hotel and Baths,** Budapest's most famous Turkish bath. (*See Baths, p. 357. Take tram #18 or 19 to Hotel Gellért. Follow Szabó Verjték u. to Jubileumi Park, and continue on the marked paths to the summit. Alternatively, take bus #27 to the top; get off at Búsuló Juhász, and walk 5min. to the peak.*)

MARGIT ISLAND. (Margitsziget.) Off-limits to private cars but not to buses, Margit Island offers garden pathways and numerous shaded terraces. It is named after King Béla IV's daughter, whom he vowed to rear as a nun if the nation survived the Mongol invasion of 1241. The Mongols left Hungary decimated, but not destroyed, and poor Margit was confined to the island convent. Now, visitors can come and go as they wish. The outdoor **pools** are especially popular with Hungarian children. You can **rent bikes** or **bike-trolleys,** a Flintstone-esque way to pedal around the island (750Ft per 30min., 1250Ft per hr.). **Golf carts** allow you to put-put about the island (2500Ft per 30min.). At night, **open-air clubs** entertain the crowds. See **Insider's City: Margit Island,** to the left, for a walking tour of the island. (*M3: Nyugati pu. Continue from the Metro on bus #26 or 26A; get off on Margit híd or on the island itself. Or, take the HÉV from Batthyány tér to Margit híd and walk across the bridge. Pools open daily May-Aug. 8am-7pm; Sept.-Apr. 10am-6pm*)

AQUINCUM. In northern Budapest, the ruins of the Roman garrison town Aquincum crumble in the outer regions of the third district. The most impressive vestiges of a 400-year Roman occupation have been reduced to large stones scattered by the highway. The settlement's significance increased steadily over time; eventually, it attained the status of *colonia* and became the capital of Pannonia Inferior, a region covering most of Western Hungary. Unfortunately, the remains don't reflect the site's former grandeur. The **museum** on the grounds contains a model of the ancient city. (*Szentendrei út 139. From M2: Batthyány tér, take the HÉV to Aquincum; facing the Danube, the site is 100m to the right of the HÉV stop, across the overpass. ☎ 368 42 60. Open Apr. 15-Oct. 9am-6pm. 700Ft, students 300Ft.*)

PÁL-VÖLGYI CAVES. These popular caves give first-time spelunkers a taste of the real thing. There's a 500m route with tricky paths, challenging climbs, and stalactites impressive enough and pressing close enough to bring out the claustrophobe in anyone. Be sure to wear warm clothing, even in the summer. (*Take bus #86 from Batthyány tér to Kolosyi tér, then bus #65 to the caves (5 stops). ☎ 325 95 05. Open Tu-Su 10am-4pm; last admission 3pm. Tours every hr. 400Ft, students 300Ft.*)

THE INSIDER'S CITY

MARGIT ISLAND

Outdoor enthusiasts will find plenty to do in the gorgeous scenery of this oasis north of Budapest. Catch the #26 or 26A bus in Pest at Nyugati pu., and take it to the famous Grand Hotel on the island.

1 Rent bikes, in-line skates, and pedal carts at Bringóvár. (☎329 27 46. Open daily 8am-dusk.)

2 Visit the Palatinus Strandfürdo, dubbed Budapest's Beach. Huge pools and waterslides provide respite from the heat.

3 Stop and have a bite to eat at Europe Grill Kert. (Open daily 11am-10pm.)

4 Stroll or bike through the beautiful Rose Garden.

5 Next to the garden is the Artist's Walk, a sculpture park dedicated to Hungary's cultural icons.

6 King Béla IV once bet on his daughter's freedom and lost, and St. Margaret's Monastery Ruins are named after the unfortunate girl.

7 End with a historical tour of the infamous Grand Hotel.

PEST

Pest has become Budapest's commercial and administrative center. Although downtown Pest dates back to medieval times, its overall feel is decidedly modern. Its streets were constructed in the 19th century; today, they meander past scores of shops, cafes, and restaurants, as well as Hungary's biggest corporations. The old-world architecture of Inner City (Belváros), centered around the pedestrian Váci u. and Vörösmarty tér, is animated by 21st-century life.

■ **PARLIAMENT.** (Országház.) Standing 96m tall, a number that symbolizes the date of Hungary's millennial anniversary, the palatial Gothic Parliament was modeled after Britain's, right down to the riverside location and churchly facade. The architect Steindl Imre's design won first place in a competition, and his masterpiece is truly one of the most beautiful buildings in Europe. The massive 692-room structure is oversized for the Hungarian government; the legislature uses only 12% of the building. The **Hungarian crown jewels,** housed here since 1999, were moved from the National Museum to the center of the Cupola Room amidst national controversy. *(M2: Kossuth Lajos tér.* ☎ *268 49 04. English tours M-F 10am and 2pm; Sa-Su 10am only—come early. Purchase tickets at gate #10; enter at gate #12. Reservations recommended. Ticket office opens at 8am. 1500Ft, students 750Ft.)*

ST. STEPHEN'S BASILICA. (Sz. István Bazilika.) The city's largest church, St. Stephen's Basilica was decimated by Allied bombs in World War II. Its Neo-Renaissance facade is under reconstruction, but its spectacular ornate interior continues to attract both tourists and worshippers. The 360° balcony of the Panorama Tower, Pest's highest vantage point, offers an amazing view. The church's oddest attraction is St. Stephen's mummified right hand, one of Hungary's most revered religious relics. A 100Ft offering in the box will light up the hand, allowing 2min. of closer inspection. *(M1, 2, or 3: Deák tér. Open May-Oct. M-Sa 9am-6pm; Nov.-Apr. M-Sa 10am-4pm. Mass M-Sa 7, 8am, 6pm; Su 8:30, 10am (High Mass), noon, 6pm. See the "Hand" M-Sa 9am-4:30pm, Su 1-4:30pm. Tower open daily June-Aug. 9:30am-6pm; Sept.-Oct. 10am-5:30pm; Apr.-May 10am-4:30pm. Tower 500Ft, students 400Ft.)*

GREAT SYNAGOGUE. (Zsinagóga.) The largest synagogue in Europe and the second largest in the world, the Moorish Great Synagogue, built in 1859, was designed to hold 3000 worshippers. It has been under renovation since 1988, and much of its artwork remains hidden from view. In the garden, the **Holocaust Memorial,** an enormous metal tree unveiled in 1991, sits above a mass grave for thousands of Jews killed near the war's end. Each leaf bears the name of a family that perished. The Hebrew words above the monument read "Whose pain can be greater than mine?" The Hungarian words below say "Let us remember." *(M2: Astoria. At the corner of Dohány u. and Wesselényi u. Open May-Oct. M-Th 10am-5pm, F 10am-3pm, Su 10am-2pm; Nov.-Apr. M-F 10am-3pm, Su 10am-1pm. Admissions often don't start until around 10:30am. Admission includes entrance to the **Jewish Museum** (see **Museums,** p. 355). 600Ft, students 300Ft.)*

ANDRÁSSY ÚT AND HEROES' SQUARE. (Hősök tere.) Hungary's grandest boulevard, Andrássy út, extends from Erzsébet tér in downtown Pest to Heroes' Square. Built in 1872, this area's elegant balconies and gated gardens evoke Budapest's Golden Age. Perhaps the most vivid reminder of this era is the gorgeous Neo-Renaissance **Hungarian National Opera House** (Magyar Állami Operaház). If you can't actually see an opera, be sure to take a tour. Make sure to take a close look at the magnificent paintings in the main *Bufé* that depict the sounds of nature. *(Andrássy út 22. M1: Opera.* ☎ *332 81 97. 1hr. English tours daily 3 and 4pm. 1500Ft, students 600Ft. 20% off with Budapest Card.)* Andrássy út's most majestic stretch lies near Heroes' Square, where the **Millennium Monument** (Millenniumi emlékmu) dominates the street. The structure, built in 1896 for the city's 1000-year anniversary, commemorates the nation's most prominent leaders. The seven horsemen at the statue's base represent the Magyar tribes who settled the Carpathian Basin. The Archangel Gabriel overhead offers St. Stephen the Hungarian crown. *(Andrássy út. stretches along M1 from Bajcsy-Zsilnszky út to Hősök tere.)*

CITY PARK. (Városliget.) The shaded paths of City Park are perfect for lazy strolls by the lake. Inside, balloon men and hot dog stands herald the presence of a permanent circus and a respectable zoo. You can rent ice skates in the winter or bike-trolleys and rowboats in the summer (pedal boats 980Ft per hr.; rowboats 500Ft per hr.; ice skates 500Ft per 4hr.). Amidst all this, the lakeside Vajdahunyad Castle sits in the park's center. Created for the millennium celebration of 1896, the facade is a collage of Romanesque, Gothic, Renaissance, and Baroque styles that chronicles the history of Hungarian architecture. Outside the castle broods the hooded statue of Anonymous, King Béla IV's scribe and the country's first historian, who recorded everything about medieval Hungary but his own name. A park legend says that if you go to the bridge of love with your sweetheart and kiss, you will marry within three years. If you are already married, kiss anyway to secure eternal love. *(M1: Széchenyi Fürdő. Zoo ☎ 343 60 75. Open Apr.-Aug. daily 9am-6pm; Sept.-Mar. 9am-3pm. Pedal boat rentals May 1-Aug. 20 daily 10am-8pm. Rowboat rental May-Aug. 20 daily 10am-9:30pm. Ice skate rental Oct.-Feb. daily 10am-2pm and 4-8pm.)*

NEMEZETI SZINHAZ. This new theater, which just opened in 2002 is still undergoing final touches, but is still worth visiting just for the gorgeous park around it. Just north of the new Lágymánosi híd on the Pest side, this area is sure to be better developed by 2003 and will be accessible by public transportation. *(Check with Tourinform, p. 344, for the most up-to-date details.)*

🏛 MUSEUMS

The magnificent buildings that house Budapest's eclectic museums often delight as much as their contents. Thoughtful visitors can find backroom gems and hidden masterpieces that a see-the-sights plan of attack will surely miss. Fortunately for travelers, the museums attract little attention here—you'll have space to enjoy paintings that would be mobbed in any other European capital.

MUSEUM OF FINE ARTS. (Szépmuvészeti Múzeum.) This magnificent building hosts a spectacular collection of European art. From Raphael to Rembrandt, Gauguin to Goya, these paintings are never seen in books. *(XIV, Hősök tere. M1: Hősök tere. ☎ 363 26 75, English 06 90 369 300. Open Tu-Su 10am-5:30pm; last entrance 5pm. 500Ft, students 200Ft. English audio guide 950Ft/600Ft. Tours up to 5 people 2000Ft.)*

STATUE PARK MUSEUM. (Szoborpark Múzeum.) This park features an arresting outdoor collection of communist statuary from Budapest's parks and squares after the collapse of Soviet rule. The indispensable English guidebook explains the statues' past and present. *(XXII, on the corner of Balatoni út and Szabadkai út. Take the express bus #7 from Keleti pu. to Étele tér. From there take the Volán bus from terminal #2 to Diósd (15min., every 10min.). ☎ 424 75 00; www.szoborpark.hu. Open in good weather Mar.-Nov. daily 10am-dusk, Dec.-Feb. weekends and holidays only. 300Ft, students 200Ft.)*

MUSEUM OF APPLIED ARTS. (Iparmuvészeti Múzeum.) The eclectic collection of impressive handcrafted *objets d'art*—including Tiffany glass, furniture, and ironware—warrants diligent exploration. Excellent temporary exhibits highlight specific crafts, while the video demonstration shows artists at work. Built for the 1896 millennium celebration, the Hungarian Art Nouveau design of the building is as important as the pieces. *(IX, Üllői út 33-37. M3: Ferenc körút. ☎ 456 51 00. Open Mar. 15-Oct. Tu-Su 10am-6pm; Nov.-Mar. Tu-Su 10am-4pm. 500Ft, students 250Ft.)*

NATIONAL MUSEUM. (Nemzeti Múzeum.) Two well laid-out, extensive exhibitions chronicle the history of Hungary. The first extends from the founding of the state to the 20th century, while the second covers Hungary in the 20th century—a cheery Stalin reaches out to guide you to rooms devoted to Soviet propaganda. Descriptions have English translations and helpful historical maps. *(VIII, Múzeum krt. 14/16. M3: Kálvin tér. ☎ 338 21 22; www.origo.hnm.hu. Open Mar. 15-Oct. 15 Tu-Su 10am-6pm; Oct. 16-Mar. 14 Tu-Su 10am-5pm; last admission 30min. before closing. 600Ft, students 300Ft.)*

JEWISH MUSEUM. (Zsidó Múzeum.) This museum presents a celebration of Hungary's rich Jewish past with a haunting exhibit about the Holocaust. Admission includes entrance to the Great Synagogue. *(See Sights, p. 354. VII, Dohány u. 2-8. M2: Astoria. ☎ 342 89 49; bpjewmus@visio.c3.hu. Open M-Th 10am-2pm, F and Su 10am-2pm. Closed on Jewish holidays. 600Ft, students 250Ft.)*

BUDA CASTLE. Leveled by the Soviets and the Nazis, the reconstructed palace now houses fine museums in several wings. Featuring mostly contemporary art and historical artifacts, there is no way you will be able to traverse this complex in one day. *(I, Szent György tér 2. M1, 2, or 3: Deák tér. From the Metro, take bus #16 across the Danube to the top of Castle Hill (see Sights, p. 351). ☎ 375 75 33.)* **Wing A** houses both the **Museum of Contemporary Art** (Kortárs Muvészeti Múzeum) and the smaller upstairs **Ludwig Museum,** and is devoted to Picasso, Warhol, Lichtenstein, and other big names in modern art. The highlight, however, is the impressive collection of works by Eastern European artists, many of which were suppressed under Soviet rule. *(☎ 375 91 75; www.ludwigmuseum.hu. Open Tu-Su 10am-6pm. 400Ft, students 200Ft.)* **Wings B-D** hold the huge **Hungarian National Gallery** (Magyar Nemzeti Galéria), a definitive collection of the best in Hungarian painting and sculpture. Its treasures include works by realist Mihály Munkácsy and impressionist Pál Mersei, Károly Markó's Neoclassical landscapes, gold medieval altarpieces, and many depictions of national tragedies. *(☎ 375 75 33. Open Tu-Su 10am-6pm. 600Ft, students 300Ft. English tour by appointment.)* **Wing E** houses the well-organized and interesting **Budapest History Museum** (Budapesti Történéti Múzeum). It seems to inadvertently imply that the history of Hungarians is one of Hungarians losing wars and making ill-fated alliances. *(☎ 375 75 33. English info. Open May 16-Sept. 15 daily 10am-6pm; Sept. 16-Oct. and Mar.-May 15 M and W-Su 10am-6pm; Nov.-Feb. M and W-Su 10am-4pm. 600Ft, students 300Ft.)*

🎭 ENTERTAINMENT

Budapest's cultural life flourishes with a series of performance events throughout the year (for more info on festivals, see **Tourinform,** p. 346). In August, **Óbudai Island** hosts the week-long **Sziget Festival,** Europe's largest **open-air rock festival.** (☎ 372 06 50. Call for ticket prices.) The best of all worlds come together in the last two weeks of March for the **Budapest Spring Festival** (☎ 486 33 00), a showcase of Hungary's premier musicians and actors. The new **Danube Festival** in June celebrates the building of the Chain Bridge that links Buda and Pest. Highlights of the free festival include musical acts, sports events, and fireworks at night. Budapest fills with racing enthusiasts who zoom into the suburb of Mogyoró to attend the **Formula 1 Hungarian Grand Prix** each August. (☎ 266 20 40; www.hungaroinfo.com/formel1/e.) Many of the world's biggest shows pass through Budapest. Prices are reasonable; check the **Music Mix 33 Ticket Service,** V, Váci ú. 33. (☎ 317 77 36; www.musicmix.hu. Open M-F 10am-6pm, Sa 10am-1pm.) *Budapest Program, Programme in Hungary, Budapest Panorama, Pesti Est,* and *Budapest in Your Pocket* (750Ft) are the best English-language entertainment guides, detailing everything from festivals to art showings. All are available at most tourist offices and hotels. The "Style" section of the *Budapest Sun* (www.budapestsun.com; 300Ft) features comprehensive 10-day calender listings and an English section with film reviews. (Movie tickets 550-1000Ft.)

■ **State Opera House** (Magyar Allami Operaház), VI, Andrássy út 22 (☎332 81 97). M1: Opera. One of Europe's leading performance centers. For 3000-9800Ft, you can enjoy an opera in the splendor of Budapest's Golden Age. The box office (☎353 01 70) sells unclaimed tickets at great prices 30min. before show time. Open M-Sa 11am-7pm, Su 4-7pm; cashier closes at 5pm on non-performance days.

Philharmonic Orchestra, V, Vörösmarty tér 1 (☎/fax 318 44 46). Ticket office at V, Mérleg u. 10; look for the "Jegyroda" sign. Grand music in a slightly more modest venue. Concerts most evenings Sept.-June, some weekend performances July-Aug. 2000-5000Ft. off on the day of the show. Open daily 9am-3pm.

Városmajor Open-Air Theater (☎375 59 33), XII, Városmajor. M1: Moszkva tér. Performances in this lovely open-air theater include musicals, operas, and ballets.

Buda Park Stage (☎466 98 94), XI, Kosztolányi Dezső tér. An eclectic line-up of music and theater acts perform at this outdoor theater. Tickets 90-350Ft. Box office at V, Vörösmarty tér 1. Open M-F 11am-6pm.

Pesti Vigadó (Pest Concert Hall), V, Vigadó tér 2 (☎318 99 03; fax 375 62 22). On the Danube near Vörösmarty tér. Flashy costumes and lots of vibrato. Hosts operettas every other night. Box office open M-Sa 10am-6pm.

⌐BATHS

Soak away weeks of city grime, crowded trains, and yammering tourists in the essential Budapest experience, a thermal bath. Some baths are meeting spots for Budapest's gay community—for more info, check www.gayguide.net/Europe/Hungary/Budapest. Ticket windows close an hour before the baths.

■ **Széchenyi,** XIV, Állatkerti u. 11/14 (☎321 03 10). M1: Hősök tere. This welcoming bath is in the center of City Park. Play on floating chessboards in the outdoor pool or lounge in the sun. July-Aug. thermal baths are men only Tu, Th, and Sa; women only M, W, and F. Open May-Sept. daily 6am-7pm; Oct.-Apr. M-F 6am-7pm, Sa-Su 6am-9am. 1000Ft deposit is returned if you leave in 5hr.; keep your receipt. 15min. Massage 1200Ft.

Gellért, XI, Kelenhegyi út 4/6 (☎466 61 66). Bus #7 or tram #47 or 49 to Hotel Gellért, at the base of Gellérthegy. One of the most elegant baths in Budapest. Enjoy a rooftop sun deck, an enormous wave pool, and a huge range of inexpensive a la carte options, including mud baths, and the new "Thai massage," featuring "the world famous masseuses of the Bangkok *wat po*" (7500Ft, call for reservations). Open May-Sept. M-F 6am-6pm, Sa-Su 6am-4pm; Oct.-Apr. M-F 6am-6pm,

THE BIG SPLURGE

BUCK-NAKED IN BUDAPES

The baths were first built in 1565 b Arslan, a Turkish ruler of Buda wh feared that a siege of the city woulc prevent the population from bathing Thanks to his anxiety, nothing will keep you from bathing either: the range o services—from mud baths to mas sage—are cheap enough to warran indulgence without guilt. Treatment a a Budapest bath is royal, if somewha intimidating for the virgin bather Upon arrival, you may be handed a bizarre apron with strings that is nc bigger than a dish-rag and no les dingy. Modesty requires that you tie i around your waist. After depositing your belongings in a locked stall (the attendant keeps the key), proceed to the baths. In general, women set the apron aside as a towel while mer keep theirs on. Bring your bathing suit, as customs vary greatly by estab lishment, but it's a good idea to do a the locals do—there's nothing more conspicuous than a Speedo-clad tour ist among the naked natives. Once you've cycled through the sauna and thermal baths, repeat for good mea sure, and enter the massage area. I you're looking for a good scrubbing go with the sanitary massage *(vízi);* i you're a traditionalist, stick to the medical massage *(orvosi).* In botl cases, the masseuse will chatter away in Hungarian or talk on his cell phone while pummeling your back. Mos baths provide a much-needed res area once the process is complete Refreshed, smiling, and somewha sleepy, tip the attendant, lounge ove mint tea, and savor your afternoon o guilt-free pampering. *(700-8000Ft.)*

Alicia DeSantis was a Researcher fo Let's Go: Eastern Europe 2000.

Sa-Su 6am-1pm. Pools open May-Sept. daily 6am-6pm; Oct.-Apr. M-F 6am-6pm, Sa-Su 6am-4pm. Thermal bath and pool 2000Ft. Towel, bathrobe, and swimsuit rental 500Ft each with a 3000Ft deposit. 15min. massage 1100Ft. MC/V.

Király, I, Fő u. 84 (☎202 36 88). M2: Batthány tér. Basic baths encased in Turkish architecture. Men only M, W, F 9am-9pm; women only Tu, Th, Sa 7am-5pm. 700Ft. 15min. massage 1000Ft, 30min. 2000Ft.

Rudas, Döbrentei tér 9 (☎356 13 22). Take bus #7 to the 1st stop in Buda. Right on the river under a dome built by Turks 400 years ago, this is the gorgeous bath you see in all the brochures. Unfortunately, centuries haven't altered the dome, the bathing chamber, or the "men-only" rule. This is more of an old-boys-club than a boys' club, though—Rudas has a reputation for being one of the straightest baths in Budapest. Steam baths open M-F 6am-8pm, Sa-Su 6am-1pm; baths M-F 6am-7pm, Sa 6am-1pm; pool M-F 6am-6pm, Sa-Su 6am-1pm. Baths 1000Ft. Pool (open to women) 750Ft.

NIGHTLIFE

On any given night out in Budapest, you can experience an amazing variety of scenes, from the lively atmosphere of all-night outdoor parties to the ubiquitous thumping of discos to the decadent elegance of an after-hours club. Despite the throbbing crowds in the city's clubs and pubs, the streets themselves are surprisingly empty at night. The chic cafes and restaurants in **VI, Ferencz Liszt tér** (M2: Oktagon) have become the newest night-time retreat for Budapest's up-and-coming youth. In the summer, on the Buda side of **Peötlfi híd,** two bars rock all night every night; **Zold Pardon** (open 9-6am) and **Rio** (open 10am-5am). Music varies widely, but the drinks are always cheap and the view is great. See **Entertainment**, p. 356, for a list of publications that will get you to the most happening scenes.

PUBS

Old Man's Music Pub, VII, Akácfa u. 13 (☎322 76 45; www.oldmans.hu). M2: Blaha Lujza tér. Popular with locals, expats, and tourists alike, this hopping underground institution features live blues and jazz every evening 9-11pm—check the schedule and arrive very early. Then relax in the restaurant (open 3pm-3am) or hit the small yet populous dance floor (11pm-late). No cover. Open M-Sa 3pm-4:30am.

Fat Mo's Speakeasy, V, Nyári Pal u. 11 (☎267 31 99). M3: Kálvin tér. "Spitting prohibited" in this homage to Prohibition bars. Drinking, however, isn't. 14 varieties of draft

AN OFFER YOU CAN'T REFUSE. Fellas, watch out! You may meet her—an English-speaking Hungarian hottie—at a swank bar or on the street around Váci u. She nonchalantly suggests meeting at a venue, where you chivalrously offer buy her a drink. The bill comes accompanied by some impressively sized thugs. US$1000 for a single Slow Gin Fizz? No mistake, they assure you. And what do you give a gigantic gorilla? Whatever he wants. Ask to see the menu and there it is, written in black-and-white. Not enough cash in your wallet? Don't worry, the post-Soviet mafia now accepts major credit cards—or, if needed, accompanies victims home to fetch more cash. The names of these establishments change frequently. For the most current list of establishments about which complaints have been received, check with the US Embassy in Budapest or view their list on the web at www.usembassy.hu/conseng/announcements.html.

beer (0.5L 350-750Ft) and live jazz (Su, M, Th 9-11pm) to make the booze flow quicker. Th-Sa DJ from 11:30pm. Open M-F noon-2am, Sa noon-4am, Su 6pm-4am.

Crazy Cafe, VI, Jokai u. 30 (☎302 40 03). M3: Nyugati pu. A great place to start a long evening on the town. With belly-baring waitresses serving 40 kinds of whisky (shots 450-1190Ft), 13 kinds of tequila (350-550Ft), and 17 kinds of vodka (280-450Ft), the scene at this underground, vaguely jungle-themed bar has been known to get a little rowdy. Live music nightly 9pm. Karaoke Su and Tu. Open daily 11am-1am.

Morrison's Music Pub, VI, Révay u. 25 (☎269 40 60). M1: Opera. Just left of the opera. An older crowd stakes out the bar, while a younger set hits the dance floor; wherever you go, there's a party. The British telephone booth inside actually works but moonlights as a make-out spot. June-Aug. cover men 500Ft; women free. Open F-Sa 9pm-4am.

CLUBS

▧ Undergrass, VI, Ferencz Liszt tér 10 (☎322 08 30). M2: Oktogon. Or, tram #4 or 6. The hottest club in Pest's trendiest area. Behind the bank vault door, the underground bar has little seating, but most patrons happily stand, kiss cheeks, and express the giddiness of beautiful youth. The soundproof door allows bar talk while the disco spins funk and pop. Open daily 8pm-4am; disco Tu-Su 10pm-4am.

Piaf, VI, Nagymező u. 25 (☎312 38 23). A much-loved afterhours place and the final destination for many. Guests are admitted into the red velvet lounge after knocking on an inconspicuous door and meeting the approval of the club's matron. Cover 500Ft, includes 1 beer. Open daily 11pm-6am, but don't come before 1am.

Club Seven, Akácfa u. 7 (☎478 90 30). M2: Blaha Lajos tér. A local favorite, this underground club is upscale but crowded. Funk, jazz, soul, and disco. Cover Sa-Su men 1000Ft, women free. Open daily 9pm-6pm, dance floor 10pm-5am.

Jazz Garden, V, Veres Páiné u. 44a (☎266 73 64). It's all about the music. The "garden" is actually a vaulted cellar with Christmas lights, but the effect works surprisingly well. The jazz is so good that the touristy surroundings become less obvious and the company doesn't matter. Live jazz every night at 10:30pm. Beer 420-670Ft. Open Su-F noon-1am, Sa noon-2am.

GAY BUDAPEST

An underground world for decades, gay Budapest is only beginning to appear in the mainstream. It's still safer to be discreet, however, as the city has its share of those who disapprove of homosexuality. If you run into problems of any sort or are simply looking for information on gay venues or accommodations, call the **gay hotline** (☎0630 932 33 34; fax 351 20 15; budapest@gayguide.net), and take advantage of the knowledgeable staff. The establishments below are either gay-friendly or have gay clientele. Unfortunately, the gay scene in Budapest generally excludes women, and the lesbian scene is growing at a frustratingly slow pace. Ask around about clubs that occasionally sponsor special nights or events, such as the women-only parties on the second Saturday of every month at **Cafe Elektika,** V, Semmelweis u. 21. (☎266 30 54. Open in summer M-F 10am-midnight, Sa-Su 5pm-midnight; in winter M-F noon-midnight, Sa-Su 5pm-midnight.)

Capella, V, Belgrád rakpart 23 (☎318 62 31; www.extra.hu/capellacafe). The glow-in-the-dark graffiti illuminates lip-syncing transvestites. Women welcome, though the staff is mostly gay. Cover 1000-1500Ft. Open Tu-Su 9pm-5am.

Limo Cafe, V, Belgrád rakpart 23 (☎266 54 55; www.extra.hu/limo). From the owners of Capella comes this pretty 3-level cafe down the street. Sometimes has drag queen staff. The crowd is more mixed upstairs. Beer 350-700Ft. Open daily noon-5am.

Angyal (Angel) Bar, VII, Szövetség u. 33 (☎351 64 90). The 1st gay bar in Budapest. Until a few years ago, the club moved weekly; now this huge 3-level disco, cafe, and bar is packed for its weekend programs: F and Su nights bring drag shows. Sa is men only. Cover F-Sa around 600Ft. Open Th-Su 10pm-dawn.

Heaven 51, Ó út 51 (www.heaven51.hu). Near M2: Oktogon. This 2-level cellar bar attracts a mixed gay/lesbian/straight crowd. You are given a consumption card when you enter and pay when you leave—don't lose it or you'll be fined 10,000Ft. W-Th and Su bar only. Club nights with a show F-Sa. Open W-Su 10:30pm-6am.

THE DANUBE BEND

North of Budapest, the Danube sweeps into the arc known as the Danube Bend (Dunakanyar), one of the finest travel destinations in Hungary. Colorful towns and cities sit along the Danube's banks in an idyllic European landscape. Ruins of first-century Roman settlements cover the countryside, Esztergom's cathedral and Visegrád's castle cast shadows on the river, and an artists' colony thrives in Szentendre. The towns along the Danube offer a breath of beauty and fresh air.

SZENTENDRE ☎(0)26

Not far from Budapest, Szentendre (sen-TEN-dreh) appears at first to be just another picturesque rural town. Upon closer inspection, though, the abundance of upscale art galleries and overpriced restaurants reveal a hidden truth: this is a modern city. Wander through the cobblestone streets and enjoy the artistry as a daytrip from Budapest—or stay overnight and relax in the city's slow pace.

⊑ TRANSPORTATION. HÉV travels from **Budapest's** Batthyány tér (45min., every 10-15min., 286Ft). **Buses** run from **Budapest's** Árpád híd Metro station (30min., every 20-40min., 196Ft); many continue on to **Esztergom** (1½hr. from Szentendre, 476Ft) and **Visegrád** (45min., 246Ft). **MAHART boats** leave from a pier 20min. north of the town center; with the river on the right, walk along the water to the sign. Late May-Aug. boats run to: **Budapest** (3 per day, 830Ft); **Esztergom** (1 per day, 870Ft); and **Visegrád** (3 per day, 830Ft). For **cabs,** call **Dunakanyar Taxi** (☎21 12 11). A taxi from the station to the center of town should not cost more than 700Ft.

▮▯ ORIENTATION AND PRACTICAL INFORMATION. The **HÉV, train,** and **bus station** is a 10min. walk from **Fő tér,** the main square. Descend the stairs past the end of the HÉV tracks, go through the underpass, and head up Kossuth út. At the fork in the road, bear right on Dumsta Jenő út. **Tourinform,** Dumsta Jenő út 22, offers free **maps** and brochures. (☎/fax 31 79 65; www.szentendre.hu. Open Oct. 16-Mar. 15 M-F 9:30am-4:30pm; Mar. 16-Oct. 15 M-F 9am-4:30pm, Sa-Su 10am-2pm.) **OTP Bank,** Dumsta Jenő út 6, has great **exchange** rates and cashes **traveler's checks** for no commission. A MC/V **24hr. ATM** stands outside. (☎31 90 62. Open M 7:45am-6pm, Tu-Th 7:45am-5pm, F 7:45am-4pm.) **Szentendrei Magvető Könyvesbolt** offers a decent-sized selection of **English-language books.** (☎31 12 45. Fő tér 5. Open Apr.-Sept. daily 10am-10pm; Oct.-Mar. 10am-6:30pm.) The **post office** is just off Fő tér. (Open M-F 8am-4pm, Sa 9am-3pm, Su 10am-3pm.)

▮▯ ACCOMMODATIONS AND FOOD. Although Szentendre can be visited in a day, it has a number of lodging options. If you plan on staying during July or August, make reservations. **IBUSZ ❹,** Bogdányi út 11, will hook you up with a private double for 8000Ft. (☎31 01 81; fax 50 01 77. Open M-F 9am-4pm, Sa-Su 10am-3pm.) **Ilona Panzió ❸,** Rákóczi Ferenc út 11, in the center of town, rents doubles with private baths. The friendly proprietors serve breakfast on their terrace. (☎31 35 99. Breakfast included. Doubles 5600Ft.) An English-speaking staff welcomes guests at **Centrum Panzió ❺**, Bem út and Dunakorzó, just a few minutes north of Fő tér. The large rooms and clean showers complement the service, but the steep prices may deter budget travelers. (☎/fax 30 25 00 or 31 51 51; www.hotels.hu/centrumpanzio. Doubles 13,000Ft.) The popular **Pap-szigeti Camping ❷** sits 1km north of the center on its own island in the Danube. Walk along the water with the river on your right to the bridge to the island. Try to call two days ahead for reservations in summer. (☎31 06 97; fax 31 37 77. Open May-Oct. 15. Tent sites 2500Ft; 2-person caravan 3300Ft. Each additional person 1200Ft. *Panzió* (pension) doubles with shower 5000Ft; triples 6000Ft; quads 7000Ft.)

Many *bufés* (snack bars) litter the city streets, some with salad bars and others selling burgers or "Dixie" fried chicken—eat at your own risk. One proven tasty option is **Kedvenc Kifőzde ❶**, Bükköspart 21. (☎31 91 86. Entrees 300-460Ft. Open M-F noon-5pm, Sa noon-3pm.) Enjoy a cappuccino at ▉**Nostalgia Cafe ❷**, Bogdányi út 2. The internationally recognized opera-singing owners sometimes host concerts in the outdoor courtyard. Try the Special Nostalgia Coffee, made with orange liqueur, bits of chocolate, and whipped cream. (☎31 16 60. Pastry or coffee 350Ft and up; wine 840-5000Ft. Open Th-Su 10am-10pm.) **Kaiser Supermarket** is by the rail station. (Open M-W 7am-7pm, Th-F 7am-8pm, Sa-Su 7am-3pm. AmEx/MC.)

■❗ **SIGHTS AND FESTIVALS.** Start your visit by climbing **Church Hill** (Templomdomb), above the town center in Fő tér, to visit the 13th-century Roman Catholic Church, one of the few medieval churches left in Hungary and host to the best view in town. Facing it, the **Czóbel Museum** exhibits the work of Béla Czóbel, Hungary's foremost post-Impressionist painter, including his bikini-clad "Venus of Szentendre." (Templom tér 1. ☎31 27 21. Open W-Su 10am-6pm. Cashier closes at 5:30pm. 300Ft.) Across Alkotmány út, the museum at the red Baroque **Serbian Orthodox Church** (Szerb Ortodox Templom) displays the art of Szentendre's Serbian community. The church's ornate interior, an Orthodox take on Baroque, is also worth a look. (Museum open Tu-Su 10am-6pm. Church open Tu-Su 10am-5pm. Cashier closes at 4:30pm. 200Ft.) Szentendre's most popular museum, **Margit Kovács Museum**, Vastagh György út 1, exhibits whimsical ceramic sculptures and tiles by the 20th-century Hungarian artist. (☎31 02 44, ext. 114; fax 31 07 90. Open Mar.-Oct. daily 10am-6pm; Nov. daily 9am-5pm; Dec.-Feb. Tu-Su 10am-5pm. Ticket office closes 30min. earlier. 400Ft.) **Szabó Marzipan Museum and Confectionary**, Dumtsa Jenő út 7, is an edible summary of all the other museums in Hungary—folk art, treasuries, icons. From storybook characters to Michael Jackson in 80kg of white chocolate, your sweet tooth is sure to be aroused. Purchase chocolate marzipan in the shop or indulge in decadent pastries in the cafe. (☎31 19 31. Chocolates and pastries 120-240Ft. Open daily 10am-6pm. 200Ft.)

Hungary's ethnological **Open Air Village Museum** (Szabadtéri Néprajzi Múzeum) is about 3km from Szentendre's center. Buses leave about once every hour until 7pm; the morning bus takes 20min. while the afternoon bus follows a 40min. route. Take the "Skanzen" bus from terminal #7 (☎31 20 89; 72Ft). The museum reconstructs traditional settlements and architecture from various regions of Hungary. On weekends, craftsmen and artisans bring life to the place with displays of basket-weaving, butter-making, and other traditional skills. (☎31 23 04; fax 50 25 02; www.sznm.hu. Open Apr.-Oct. Tu-Su 9am-5pm. Ticket office closes at 4:30pm. 500Ft, students 250Ft.)

Held from mid-March to late April, the annual **Danube Carnival** celebrates regional folk art with performances by dance groups. In the summer months, the **Szentendre Summer Festival** (Szentendrei Nyár Fesztivál) draws music and theater performances, while the **Ister Days** light up July with concerts, markets, and fireworks. Tourinform (see **Practical Information**, p. 360) has a printed schedule and more info on events in town.

VISEGRÁD ☎(0)26

Seat of the royal court in medieval times, Visegrád (VEE-sheh-grad) has declined in the ranks of Hungarian towns since the 15th century. The town was truly devastated when the Habsburgs destroyed its citadel in an early 18th-century struggle against freedom fighters; since then, its only claim to fame has been its archaeological importance. The slumbering town's slow pace and splendid views make it an ideal retreat from Budapest, its bustling successor.

□ TRANSPORTATION. There is no train station in Visegrád. **Buses** from **Budapest's** Árpád híd Metro station (1½hr., 30 per day, 430Ft) and **Esztergom** (45min., every hr., 250Ft) pass through on route #11 along the Danube. The bus from Budapest will drop you off in front of a large parking lot, the unofficial bus station. **MAHART boats** run to: **Budapest** (2½-3hr., 5 per day, 870Ft); **Esztergom** (2hr., 3 per day, 830Ft); and **Szentendre** (1¼hr., 3 per day, 830Ft).

◼◪ ORIENTATION AND PRACTICAL INFORMATION. To get to the center from the bus stop, cross the parking lot and turn right on Fő út, which runs parallel to the river. After about 5min. you'll reach the Catholic church at the town center, where Rév út and Fő út intersect. **Visegrád Tours,** Rév út 15, offers visitor and accommodations information and sells **maps** (300Ft). Turn right at the church; the office is at the very end of the street. (☎39 81 60; fax 39 75 97. Open Apr.-Oct. daily 8am-7pm; Nov.-Mar. M-F 10am-4pm.) **OTP Bank,** Fő út 36, **exchanges currency** and has a MC/V **ATM** outside. **Vár Pharmacy,** Fő út 44, on the corner with Rév út, stocks Western products. (☎39 83 65. Open M and W-Sa 8:30am-noon and 1-5pm, Tu 8:30am-noon.) The **post office,** Fő út 77, is open M-F 8am-4pm. **Postal Code:** 2025.

⌐◖ ACCOMMODATIONS AND FOOD. Visegrád Tours arranges **private rooms** ❸ (see above; doubles 5500Ft). If you prefer to find a room on your own, look for *Zimmer frei* signs along Fő út outside the center. Private rooms hover around 2000Ft per person. The traditional-style **Haus Honti ❸,** Fő út 66, offers beautiful, spacious doubles with TVs, showers, and fans. (☎39 81 20; fax 39 72 74; hotelhon@matavnet.hu. Breakfast 750-1000Ft. Singles 4000Ft; doubles from 5000Ft.) **Hotel Visegrád ❹,** Rév út 15, lets you enjoy a first-class hotel with views of either the Visegrád Castle or the Danube at a reasonable price. (☎39 70 34; fax 59 70 88; hotelvisegrad@visegradtours.hu. Sauna, jacuzzi, and 2 restaurants. Breakfast included. Doubles 6000Ft.) The cozy family restaurant **Gulás Csárda ❸,** Nagy Lajos út 4, prepares five excellent Hungarian dishes daily; you can smell the garlic from the garden outside. (☎39 83 29. Entrees 950-1990Ft. Open daily noon-10pm.) On a sunny day, the grassy banks of the Danube provide a perfect picnic spot. Pick up the basics at **CBA Élelmiszer supermarket,** across from Visegrád Tours at the end of Rév út. (Open M 7am-6pm, Tu-F 7am-7pm, Sa 7am-3pm, Su 7am-noon. MC.)

◖◢ SIGHTS AND ENTERTAINMENT. The 13th-century **citadel** is Visegrád's main attraction. Perched above the Danube, this former Roman outpost commands a dramatic survey of the river and surrounding hills. A local bus shuttles back and forth from town three times a day (2hr.; 9:30am, 12:30, 3:30pm; 100Ft); if you can afford it, save time with a minibus (☎39 73 72; 2000Ft) to the fortress. Otherwise, make the arduous 30min. hike up Kalvária út. The citadel also has a **wax museum** where medieval torture techniques now petrify waxen victims. (Open Apr.-Nov. daily 9:30am-6pm. 600Ft, students 250Ft.) Considered a mythic construct until archaeologists uncovered it in 1934, King Matthias's **Royal Palace** (Királyi Palota) sprawls across the foothills above Fő út. The impressive exhibits inside include a computerized reconstruction of the castle as it was in 1259. (☎39 80 26; fax 39 82 52. Open Tu-Su 9am-5pm. 400Ft, students 200Ft.) During the second weekend of July, the grounds relive their glory days during the **Visegrad Palace Games** with parades, jousting tournaments, concerts, and a crafts marketplace. (☎209 34 59.) Named for a king imprisoned here in the 13th century, the Romanesque **Solomon's Tower** (Alsóvár Salamon Torony), at the end of Salamontorony út, provides a fine view of Hungary's one-time Camelot. Inside, the **King Matthias Museum** displays artifacts from the palace ruins. (☎39 80 26; fax 39 82 52. Open Apr.-Oct. Tu-Su 9am-5pm; last admission 4:30pm. 400Ft, students 200Ft; Su students free.) For adventure in the great outdoors, **Nyári Bobpálya** hosts a popular alpine slide. (From the citadel's parking lot, go left up Panorama út. ☎39 73 97. Open daily 9am-6pm. Weekdays 280Ft, children 230Ft; weekends 320Ft/250Ft.)

ESZTERGOM ☎(0)33

One thousand years of religious history have revolved around a solemn hilltop cathedral in Esztergom (ESS-ter-gom), "the Hungarian Rome." Religious pilgrims still flock to the winding streets of this town. The birthplace of King (and Saint) Stephen and the site of the first Royal Court of Hungary, Esztergom remains central to Catholicism in modern Hungary.

▐ TRANSPORTATION. Trains go to **Budapest** (1½hr., 22 per day, 804Ft). Catch **buses** three blocks from Rákóczi tér on Simor János út to **Szentendre** (1½hr., every hr., 476Ft) and **Visegrád** (45min., every hr., 246Ft). **MAHART boats** (☎41 35 31) depart from Gőzhajó út on Primas Sziget Island for: **Budapest** (4hr., 3 per day, 890Ft); **Szentendre** (2¾hr., 1 per hr., 870Ft); and **Visegrád** (1½hr., 1 per hr., 830Ft).

▰▱ ORIENTATION AND PRACTICAL INFORMATION. The train station is an easy 10min. walk from town. Facing away from the station, go left on the main street. Turn right at Kiss János Altábornagy út, which becomes Kossuth Lajos út as it proceeds toward the square. From the **bus station**, walk up **Simor János u.** toward the **street market**, which brings you to Rákóczi tér. **IBUSZ**, Kossuth út 5 (☎41 16 43; fax 41 25 52) can reserve decent rooms for 10-15% commission and book bus, train, and plane tickets. (☎41 16 43; fax 41 25 52. Open May-Aug. M-F 9am-5pm; Sept.-Apr. M-F 10am-4pm.) **Grantours**, Széchenyi tér 25, at the edge of Rákóczi tér, sells **maps** (200-500Ft) and reserves accommodations. (☎/fax 41 70 52 or 41 37 56; grantour@mail.holop.hu. Open July-Aug. M-F 8am-6pm, Sa 9am-noon; Sept.-June M-F 8am-4pm, Sa 9am-noon.) **K&H Bank**, on Rákóczi tér, has the best **exchange** rates in town and cashes **traveler's checks** for no commission. (Open M 8am-5pm, Tu-Th 8am-4pm, F 8am-3pm.) There's a **currency exchange machine** and an AmEx/MC/V **ATM** outside. **Szent István Pharmacy** is at Madách tér, one block up Bajcsy-Zsilinszky út from Rákóczi tér. (Open M-F 8am-6pm, Sa 8am-noon.)

▐▐ ACCOMMODATIONS AND FOOD. IBUSZ ❷ (see above) arranges private rooms and pensions (2500Ft-10,000Ft), as does **Grantours ❸** (private rooms 3500Ft; pension doubles 8500Ft). **Pension RIA ❸**, Batthány út 11/13 (☎31 31 15; fax 40 14 29), is about 50m from the basilica and close to the shops and restaurants. This quaint pension welcomes guests with open arms. Rooms are clean and comfortable, and the generous breakfast is served on the patio. (Reception 24hr. Breakfast included. Bike rental available. Doubles 10,500Ft.) **Alabardos Panzió ❸**, Bajcsy-Zsilinszky út 49, has tidy doubles with TVs and clean showers. (☎/fax 31 26 40. Reception 24hr. Doubles 10,000Ft.) **Gran Camping ❶**, Nagy-Duna Sétány, in the middle of Primas Sziget, is a lush park on the Danube's banks. The grounds boast a restaurant, grocery store, swimming pool, and beach. (☎ 40 25 13; fax 41 19 53. Reception 24hr. 950Ft per person. Tents 800Ft. Bungalows 6500Ft.) Nearby, **Szalma Csárda ❸**, on Primas Sziget by the pier at the end of Gőzhajó út, serves fried Hungarian fare and fish fresh from the Danube. (☎ 31 53 36. Entrees 900-1600Ft. Open daily noon-10pm.) **Csülök Csárda ❷**, Batthány út 9, offers fine Hungarian cuisine, adding creative variations to the usual repertoire of roasts and stews. (☎ 31 24 20. Entrees 480-1800Ft. Open daily noon-midnight.) **Match supermarket** is just off of Rákóczi tér. (Open M-F 6:30am-6:30pm, Sa 6:30am-1pm.)

◪ SIGHTS. A basilica was originally built in Esztergom in 1010, but the present Neoclassical colossus, **Hungary's largest cathedral,** was consecrated in 1856. The treasury houses one of the premiere collections of Hungarian religious iconography, while the basilica offers one of Hungary's most sublime views. Ascend the interminable spiral staircases to the top of the cathedral cupola (100Ft) for an incredible echo and the best view of the Bend; on clear days, you can see as far as the Slovak Low Tatras. The solemn **crypt** below the cathedral holds the remains of Hungary's archbishops. The **cathedral treasury** (kincstáv) hosts Hungary's most extensive ecclesiastical collection, a treasure trove of ornate relics and textiles spanning a millennium. The jewel-studded cross in the case near the entrance is the 13th-century **Coronation Oath Cross** (Koronázási Eskűkereszt) on which Hungary's rulers pledged their oaths until 1916. The red marble **Bakócz Chapel,** to the left of the nave as you face the altar, is a masterwork of Tuscan Renaissance craftsmanship. Dismantled during the Turkish occupation, the chapel was reassembled from 1000 separate pieces. (Cathedral open Mar.-Oct. daily 9am-4pm; Nov.-Dec. M-F 11am-3:30pm, Sa-Su 10am-3:30pm. 300Ft. English guidebook 100Ft.) Beside the cathedral, the restored 12th-century **Esztergom Palace** and **Castle Museum** (Vár Múzeum) displays segments of St. István's original palace and medieval fresco fragments. (☎ 31 59 86. Open May-Sept. Tu-Su 9am-4pm; Oct.-May Tu-Su 10am-3:30pm. 300Ft.) At the foot of the cathedral hill, the **Christian Museum** (Keresztény Múzeum), Berenyi Zsigmond út 2, houses a marvelous collection of Renaissance and medieval religious art. (☎ 41 38 80. Open Tu-Su 10am-5:30pm; last admission 5pm. 400Ft.)

THE ŐRSÉG

The western corner of Hungary shelters the pastoral region known as the Őrség (EWR-shayg) or Western Transdanubia. During the Cold War, authorities discouraged visitors and Hungarians alike from entering the Őrség, as they believed capitalist Austria and Tito-era Yugoslavia were too close for comfort. Thus a region that had always been a bit behind the times—electricity didn't arrive until 1950—fell even farther beyond modernity's reach, and much of the countryside remains unspoiled today. The rolling hills and stretches of farmland are perfect for leisurely strolls, bicycle rides, and hiking.

GYŐR ☎ (0)96

The streets of Győr's (DYUR) inner city wind peacefully around a wealth of religious monuments, illustrious museums, and stunning displays of late 17th- and 18th-century architecture. The large population that lives within the old town brings life to the storybook beauty of its winding streets. Parks, pedestrian passageways, terrace restaurants, and a popular water park prove that recreation and relaxation abound in one of Hungary's most pleasant cities.

▛ TRANSPORTATION

The **train station,** Révau út 4-6 (domestic ☎31 16 13, international 52 33 66) lies about 3min. from the city center; as you exit the station, turn right. Turn left just before the underpass and cross the street to get to the pedestrian **Baross Gabor út.** Trains run from to **Budapest** (2½hr., 26 per day, 1130Ft) and **Vienna, AUS** (2hr., 13 per day, 4450Ft). The **bus station,** Hunyadu út 9 (☎31 77 11), is connected to the train station by the same underpass that links the rail platforms. Buses head to **Budapest** (2½hr., 1 per hr., 1300Ft).

▟ PRACTICAL INFORMATION

Tourist Office: Tourinform kiosk, Árpád út 32 (☎31 17 71), Baross Gabor u. Provides accommodations info and free **maps.** Open June-Aug. M-F 8am-8pm, Sa-Su 9am-6pm.

Budget Travel: IBUSZ, Kazinczy út 3 (☎31 17 00). A few blocks farther up Baross Gabor út, turn left on Kazinczy út. Extensive accommodations info and assistance. 10% discount on international train and bus tickets for those under 26. Open June-Aug. M-F 8am-6pm, Sa 8am-noon; Sept.-May M-F 8am-4pm. AmEx/MC/V.

Currency Exchange: OTP Bank, Teleki L. út 51, at the corner of Bajcsy-Zsilinszky u., has good exchange rates. Open M 7:45am-6pm, Tu-Th 7:45am-5pm, F 7:45am-4pm. MC/V **ATM** and **currency exchange machine** outside. The *Postabank* desk in the post office (see below) cashes AmEx **Traveler's Cheques** for no commission.

Luggage Storage: At train station. 100Ft for under 6hr., 200Ft overnight. Open 8am-midnight.

Pharmacy: Jedlik Á. út 16 (☎32 88 81). Open M-F 7am-6pm, Sa 7am-2pm. The sign in the window posts local pharmacies with emergency hours.

Internet Access: Different Internet Cafe & Club, Liszt Ferenc út 20 (☎51 68 10; fax 31 76 75; www.different.hu), in the courtyard. 250Ft per 30min.

Post Office: Bajcsy-Zsilinszky út 46 (☎31 43 24). Open M-F 8am-8pm, Sa 8am-2pm.

Postal Code: 9021.

▛ ACCOMMODATIONS

Accommodations in downtown Győr may overflow in July and August, so it's essential to make a reservation before arriving. Tourinform (see **Tourist Office,** p. 365) can help you find a *panzió* or hotel room and will make reservations if you call ahead. **IBUSZ ❷** (see p. 365) offers a few **private rooms,** but expect to pay a 30% surcharge for stays under four nights. (Prices vary based on room size and amenities, starting at 2000Ft.) Tourinform keeps an up-to-date listing of **campsites** outside the city. Call ahead and they will help you find a site that meets your needs.

▩ **Katalin's Kert (Yard),** Sarkantyú köz 3 (☎/fax 45 20 88, mobile 302 77 55 92). Off Bécsi Kapu tér. Huge modern rooms hidden in a quaint courtyard include TV and shower. A restaurant downstairs has live music most nights. Breakfast included. Singles 5800Ft; doubles 7500Ft; triples 9500Ft; quads 11,000Ft. ❸

Széchenyi Istvan Főiskola Egyetem, Hédevári út 3, entrance K4 (☎50 34 00). Across the Moscow-Dune River. Heading up Baross Gabor út from the train station, turn right on Bajcsy-Zsilinszky út and left on Czuczor Gergely út, which becomes Jedlik Ányos. Hang a left on Kúlóczy tér once over the bridge and continue until the parking lot; cross the lot and head to the left toward the Bufé. Entrance K4 is on the left; after 9pm enter at K3. Standard dorms in modern buildings. Private showers; toilets in the hall. Reception 24hr. Check-out 9am. Open July-Aug. Doubles 2700Ft; triples 2950Ft. ❷

FOOD

Kaiser's supermarket sprawls across the corner of Alany János út and Aradi út. (Open M 7:30am-7pm, Tu-F 6:30am-7pm, Sa 6:30am-2pm.)

Matróz Restaurant, Dunakapu tér 3 (☎32 49 55). Off Jedlik Ányos facing the river. More fancy than the folksy tavern decor or dwarf-sized wooden chairs might lead you to believe, this local favorite fries up succulent fish dishes. Entrees 500-1100Ft. Open Su-Th 9am-10pm, F-Sa 9am-11pm. ❷

Teátrum Étterem, Scweidel út 7 (☎31 06 40 or 32 68 27). An upscale eatery with medium-scale prices. Enjoy candle-lit dining in a luxurious atmosphere. Entrees 700-1850Ft. Open daily noon-midnight. ❷

John Bull Pub, Aradi út 3 (☎61 83 20). Offers brief respite from the Hungarian diet with Italian options, meat grilled in a lava stone oven, and salads (250-460Ft). Sidewalk cafe tables rest on a pleasant street while a real English pub atmosphere thrives indoors. Entrees 810-1500Ft. Open daily 9am-midnight. ❸

SIGHTS

Head uphill on Czuczor Gergely út, which runs parallel to Baross Gabor út, to reach **Chapter Hill** (Káptalandomb), the oldest sector of Győr. The striking **Ark of the Covenant statue** (Frigylada Szobov), built in 1731, was bankrolled by taxes King Charles III levied on his impoverished mercenaries to keep them in line. The **Episcopal Cathedral** (Székesegyház), at the top of the hill, has suffered constant additions since 1030; its exterior is now a motley medley of Romanesque, Gothic, and Neoclassical styles. Gilded cherubim perch above the magnificent frescoes that illuminate the splendid Baroque interior. Seeking refuge from Oliver Cromwell's bloody forces in the 1650s, a priest brought the miraculous **Weeping Madonna of Győr** all the way from Ireland. Legend has it that on St. Patrick's Day 1697 the image wept blood and tears for three hours for the persecuted Irish Catholics. The statue rests to the left of the cathedral entrance. In the opposite corner of the cathedral, the Hédeváry chapel holds the **Herm of King St. Ladislas,** a medieval bust of one of Hungary's first saint-kings. It also contains the **tomb of Baron Vilmas Apor,** a Győr martyr revered for his anti-Nazi and anti-Communist stance—he was eventually assassinated by Russian soldiers. Packed away in a small alley behind the cathedral, the **Diocesan Library and Treasury** (Egyházmegyei Kincstáv), Káptalandomb 26, displays 14th-century gold and silver religious artifacts; the illuminated 15th-century manuscripts are worth a peek. It also includes a 19th-century priceless gold reliquary with about 30 saints' fingernail clippings visible inside. (☎31 21 53. English captions. Open Tu-Su 10am-4pm. 300Ft, students 150Ft.)

The **Imre Patkó Collection** (Patkó Imre Gyűjtemény), Széchenyi tér 4 (enter on Stelczera út), contains two floors of modern Hungarian art and an attic full of Asian and African works that Patkó amassed in his travels. The museum is housed in the **Iron Log House** (Vastuskós ház), a centuries-old inn for traveling craftsmen. (☎31 05 88. Open Tu-Su 10am-6pm. 200Ft, students 100Ft.) A short walk down Kenyér Köz from Széchenyi tér, the **Margit Kovács Museum** (Kovács Margit Gyűjtemény), Apácu út 1, displays the Győr-born artist's expressive ceramic sculptures and tiles. (☎32 67 39. Open Mar.-Oct. Tu-Su 10am-6pm; Nov.-Feb. Tu-Su 10am-5pm. 300Ft, students 150Ft.)

🎵 🎭 ENTERTAINMENT AND NIGHTLIFE

In summer, do as the locals do: splash in the water and bask in the sun. Across the river from the center of town, thermal springs serve as the basis for a large **water park** *(furdő)*, Cziráky tér 1, which seems to draw the whole city to its streams. (From Bécsi kapu tér, take the bridge over the island and take the first right on the other side. Hang another right on Cziráky tér; the park is to the left. Open daily 8am-7pm. 500Ft, students 400Ft; after 3pm 400Ft/300Ft.) Győr flits away the summer months of June and July with **Győri Nyár,** a festival of concerts, drama, and the city's famous ballet. Schedules are at Tourinform and IBUSZ (see **Practical Information,** p. 365); buy tickets at the box office on Baross Gabor út or at the venue.

At night, music and young people spill out from cellar bars onto Győr's streets. **Komédiás Biergarten,** Czuczor Gergely út 30, boasts a fabulous patio that invites laughing and drinking. (☎52 72 17. Beer 250-420Ft. Open M-Sa 11am-midnight.) If you're wistful for the Emerald Isle, **Dublin Gate Irish Pub,** underground at Bécsikapu tér 8, across from the Carmelite Church, taps a lively young crowd and whole lot of beer. (☎31 06 88. Guinness 340Ft. Open M-Sa noon-midnight, Su noon-11pm.) The wine selection at **Trófea Borozó,** Bajcsy-Zsilinszky út 16, promises to bring out the wine snob in anyone and a guaranteed hangover the next day. (Wine 40Ft. Open M-F 8am-8pm, Sa 8am-10pm, Su 9am-8pm.) Győr's bold and beautiful head to **The 20th Century,** Schweidel út 25. (Beer 250-480Ft; cocktails 480-980Ft. Live jazz F 9pm. Open M-Sa 8am-midnight, Su 5pm-midnight.) For a mellow night, try **Patio Belvárosi Kávénaz,** Baross út 12. Popular among locals for its beer, wine, and delectable desserts, Patio is a low-key place to spend any evening drinking. (☎31 00 96. Beer 400-600Ft; desserts 98-400Ft. Open daily 11am-midnight.)

🔁 DAYTRIP FROM GYŐR

🏛 ARCHABBEY OF PANNONHALMA ☎(0)96

Pannonhalma is an easy daytrip from Győr. Take the bus from stand #11 (45min.; 7 per day; 246Ft one-way, 369Ft return). Ask the driver for Pannonhalma vár and get off at the huge gates. Abbey open daily 8:30am-4pm. Hungarian tour 1000Ft, students 300Ft; English tour 2000Ft/1000Ft. Tickets at Pax Tourist (☎57 01 91; fax 57 01 92; pax@osb.hu) in Győr. AmEx/MC/V.

Visible at a distance from Győr, the hilltop Archabbey of Pannonhalma (Pannonhalmi Főapátság) has seen ten centuries of destruction and rebuilding since the Benedictine order established it in AD 996. Now a UNESCO World Heritage Site, the working abbey houses a 13th-century basilica, an opulent 360,000-volume library, a small art gallery, and one of the finest boys' schools in Hungary. The treasures to be found here include a 1055 deed founding a Benedictine Abbey, the oldest document written in Hungarian, a charter from 1001 bearing St. Steven's signature, and a mosaic picture of the Madonna created using naturally bright stones. Although renovations in honor of the Pope's visit in 1996 left the abbey halls looking spiffy, Hungary's oldest graffiti is still visible: a soldier defending the hill against the Turks "was here" in 1578. Legend has it that if you fit into St. Steven's wooden throne in the Gothic-Romanesque crypt, the wish you make there will be granted. You can hear **Gregorian chants** every Sunday at the 10am mass and classical music concerts, which take place frequently in the halls of the abbey; inquire at **Pax Tourist** (see **Practical Information,** p. 365). To see the abbey, join an hourly tour group at the office to the left of the entrance. English-speaking guides are available in summer for the mandatory 1hr. tour at 11am and 1pm. English texts are available if you arrive when an English tour is not being offered.

SOPRON
☎ (0)99

With soaring spires and winding cobblestone streets, Sopron's (SHO-pron) medieval quarter feels decidedly Austrian. However, as any local will remind you, Sopron is considered "Hungary's most loyal town." In 1920, the Swabians of Ödenburg (as Sopron was then called) voted to remain part of Hungary, rather than join their linguistic brethren in Austria. German and Hungarian are both widely spoken by the friendly denizens of this charming town.

■ ⑦ ORIENTATION AND PRACTICAL INFORMATION

Belváros (Inner Town), the historic center, is a 1km long horseshoe bounded by three main streets: **Ógabona tér** and **Várkerület u.** form an arc, while **Széchenyi tér** connects the two longer roads near the train station. At the center farthest from the train station, several museums and notable edifices line the edges of **Fő tér**. To get to the center from the **train station**, veer to the left following **Mátyás Király ú.** which leads to Széchenyi tér and becomes Várkerület as it curves around the Inner Town. The **bus station** is 5min. from the center. Exit the station and turn right on **Lackner Kristóf ú.**; turn left at Ógabona tér to reach Várkerület near Fő tér.

Transportation: Trains head to: **Budapest** (3-4hr., 6 per day, 2100Ft); **Győr** (1½hr., 20 per day, 700Ft); and **Vienna, AUS** (1-2hr., 13 per day, 2300Ft). **Buses** leave from Lackner Kristóf út 9 (☎31 10 40). To **Budapest** (4hr., 5 per day, 2370Ft) and **Győr** (2hr., 1 per hr., 930Ft).

Tourist Office: Tourinform, Előkapu út 11 (☎/fax 33 88 92). Follow the signs to the office off Várkerület út. Free **maps** and accommodations info. Open May-Oct. M-F 9am-7pm, Sa-Su 9am-6pm; Nov.-Apr. M-F 9am-4pm.

Currency Exchange: Posta Bank, on Várkerület, offers good exchange rates and cashes traveler's checks. There's a 24hr. MC/V **ATM.**

Pharmacy: There are 3 pharmacies in town: Deák tér 35, Magyar út 6, and Mâtyâs kirâl út 23. A sign in the window lists emergency services available.

Internet Access: ISE, Üjut 3 (☎31 02 52), in the center of Belváros. 400Ft per hr., students 200Ft. Open M-F 11am-8pm, Sa 11am-5pm.

Post Office: Széchenyi tér 7/10 (☎31 31 00). Outside Belváros. Open M-F 8am-8pm, Sa 8am-noon. **Telephones** are in the post office.

Postal Code: 9400.

▐ ACCOMMODATIONS

Tourinform (see **Tourist Office,** above) can settle you into a comfy **private room ❸** or *panzió* ❹ near the center. (Private room singles 2000Ft; doubles 4000Ft. *Panzió* singles 5000Ft; doubles 8000Ft.) **Ciklámen Tourist,** Ógabona tér 8, between the bus station and the town center, can also set you up with a private room. (☎31 20 40; fax 31 41 83. Rooms vary by size and location. Open M-F 8am-4:30pm, Sa 8am-1pm.) **Locomotiv Turist,** Várkerület 90, helps locate the cheapest *panzió* rooms in town. (☎31 11 11; fax 31 98 37; loktur@gysev.hu. Prices depend on size, location, and amenities. Open M-F 8:30am-4:30pm, Sa 8:30am-noon.)

Ringhofer Panzió, Balfi út 52 (☎32 50 22; fax 32 60 81). From Széchenyi tér, go down Várkerület u. and take a right on Torna út. Follow the street as it becomes Bem út to a left on Balfi út. Large rooms with clean showers. Breakfast 500Ft. Bike rental 1000Ft per day. Reception 24hr. Check-out 10am. Doubles 5000Ft. Tourist tax 300Ft. ❸

Wieden Panzió, Sas tér 13 (☎52 32 22; fax 52 32 23; www.wieden.hu), close to the center. The charm of this *panzió* overcomes its outdated scenery. Helpful staff offers advice on biking, hiking, and sightseeing daytrips, and even lend their bikes for free.

Breakfast included. Reception 24hr. Doubles 7900-9900Ft; triples 11,300-13,900Ft; 4-person apartment 12,500-15,900Ft. ❹

Ozon Camping, Erdei Malomkőz 3 (☎33 11 44; fax 33 11 45; www.ozoncamping.tsk.org). The best way to reach this camping site is by bus #10B. The beautiful grounds offer scenic views of Hungary and Austria. Swimming pool on site. Tennis, angling, and riding facilities 2km away. Sauna 2800Ft per hr. Breakfast 350-400Ft. Reception 24hr. Tents 440Ft, plus 1020Ft per person; bungalow for 1-2 people 2100-2970Ft, 3-4 people 3600-5100Ft. ❷

FOOD

The large **Smatch supermarket** at Várkerület 100/102 stocks groceries. (Open M-F 6:30am-8pm, Sa 6:30am-6pm. MC/V.)

Fórum Pizzeria, Szt. György út 3 (☎34 02 31). In a quiet courtyard off one of the inner city's main drags, this Italian eatery provides a refreshing break from Hungarian fare. Choose from among 41 different pizza options (480-1250Ft), 18 different pastas (440-880Ft), and a salad bar (320-470Ft) in an ornate dining room or on the summer terrace. Open M-Th noon-11pm, F-Su 11am-11pm. ❷

Várkerület Restaurant, Várkerület 83 (☎31 92 86). Near Széchenyi tér. Spices up a traditional Hungarian menu with its own "house-proud dishes." The efficient staff brings meaty entrees (600-2150Ft) and vegetarian options to warmly lit tables in the dining room and beer garden. Open M-Sa 9am-1am, Su 11am-1am. ❸

Pince Csárda, Széchenyi tér 5 (☎34 9 276; fax 24 00 08). Has a tremendous array of chicken, venison, and veal dishes. Comfy canvas seats surround distinctive wooden tables. English menu available. Entrees 690-1440Ft. Open M-Th 11am-11pm, F-Sa 11am-midnight, Su 11am-4pm. ❸

SIGHTS

Most of Sopron's sights are located in the inner city. Pick up a map at Tourinform (see p. 368) to help navigate the cobblestone streets.

TRINITY COLUMN. The first prominent sight on at Fő tér and one of Europe's first corkscrew column sculptures, Trinity was commissioned by Eva Katalin Thőkőly and her husband Sakab Louenberg to commemorate the great plague of 1695-1701.

FIRE-WATCH TOWER. (Tűztorony.) The symbol of Sopron, this tower consists of a 17th-century spire atop a 16th-century tower on a 12th-century base that straddles a Roman gate. The clock's chimes still sound the hour. Squeeze up the spiral staircase to the balcony for a view of the surrounding hills. *(From Fő tér, just to the left after the passage under the tower. Open Tu-Su 10am-6pm. 300Ft, students 150Ft. Binoculars 100Ft.)*

FABRICIUS HOUSE. The upper floor of the former Gotchi chapel contains a well-organized archaeological museum. The underground **Roman Lapidarium** (Római Kőtár) houses tombs and statues that date back to Sopron's origins as the Roman colony of Scarbantia. *(Fő tér 6. Open Tu-Su 10am-6pm. Museum 200Ft, students 20Ft. Lapidarium 200Ft/100Ft.)*

BENEDICTINE CHURCH. (Bencés Templom.) Built in the 13th century by a herder whose goats stumbled upon a cache of gold, the Benedictine Church has been the site of royal coronations for two queens and one king. Visitors can enter its Chapter Hall, a room full of Gothic architecture decorated with allegorical sculptures of human sin. Information sheets (available in several languages) explain their meaning, while taped Gregorian chants add atmosphere. *(On Fő tér. Open daily 10am-noon and 2-5pm. Holy Mass M-F 8am, Su 9:30am.)*

OLD AND NEW SYNAGOGUES. Two of the few medieval synagogues to survive the Holocaust, these are now museums depicting the daily life of the local Jewish community, which was expelled in 1526. The **Old Synagogue** (Középkori Ó-Zsinagóga) was first built around 1300, and contains a stone Torah ark, a wooden *bima*, and a ritual bath well. *(Új út 22. Open W-M 9am-5pm. 200Ft, students 100Ft.)* The **New Synagogue** (Új-Zsinagóga), only 50 years newer, is now being restored after centuries of neglect. Its exterior is visible through the courtyard at Szent György út 12, on the opposite side of the block. *(Új út 11. Open M 1-5pm, W-Th 9am-3:30pm, F 9am-noon. Free.)*

BAKERY MUSEUM. (Pékmúzeum.) Illustrating the history of professional baking from the 15th to 20th centuries in the restored shop of a 19th-century baker, the Bakery Museum unfortunately denies patrons the full sensory experience—there are no samples to be seen. *(Bésci út 5. From Várkerület, enter Ikva h. út near the small branch of the post office. Take the 2nd left on Jégverem Halász út and follow it through Sas tér as it becomes Bésci út. ☎ 31 13 27. Open Tu-Su 10am-noon. 300Ft, students 250Ft.)*

⏏ ▣ ENTERTAINMENT AND FESTIVALS

Sopron is a perfect starting point for the outdoor enthusiast. Bike trails begin just north of the city center, leading to Lake Fertő-Hanság National Park (recently declared a UNESCO World Heritage Site), and Fertőd (see p. 370). Bike maps are free at Tourinform (see **Tourist Office,** p. 368), where there are also listings of bike rental shops. Horse shows and daytrips to mineral springs are also available. For information on cultural events, pick up a free copy of the monthly *Soproni Ünnepi Hetek* (Sopron Program). During the **Sopron Festival Weeks** (from late June to mid-July), the town hosts opera, ballet, and concerts. Some are set in the **Fertőrákos Quarry,** 10km away, reached by hourly buses from the terminal. (Quarry 30Ft for students. Concerts 3000-8000Ft.) Buy tickets for all events from the **Festival Bureau** (☎ 51 17 30), on Széchenyi tér, opposite the post office. (Open mid-Aug. to mid-July M-F 9am-5pm, Sa 9am-noon.) **Cinema City** at Sopron Plaza shows both Hungarian and English-language films.

▣ NIGHTLIFE

Cézár Pince, Hátsókapu 2 (☎31 13 37). Near Fő tér. You may never want to leave this spacious 17th-century home, converted into a classy local hangout. Wine 550-950Ft; 0.5L *Gösser* 290Ft. Open M-Tu 11am-11pm, W-Sa 11am-1am, Su 4-11pm.

La Playa Cafe and Bar, Várkerület 22 (☎52 40 18). Sopron youth pack the place so tight that it's hard to appreciate the eclectic decor, complete with a sombrero, a sewing machine, and a *Gone With the Wind* poster. Beer 220-290Ft; cocktails 700-1400Ft. Open F-Sa 6pm-2am, Su-M and W-Th 6pm-1am.

The Ex-Rockline Freestyle Music Club, Ágfalvi út 2 (☎34 23 46). The best place for clubbing, if you can still bust a move after the long trek out here. Despite its inconvenient location, the Freestyle is swamped nightly by a devoted crowd of regulars. Beer 250-350Ft; shots 200-500Ft. Open W-Sa 9pm-4am.

▣ DAYTRIP FROM SOPRON

FERTŐD ☎(0)99

Buses leave for Fertőd from platform #11 in Sopron's station (45min., every hr., 294Ft). Ask the driver if he is going to the Castle (Kastély). ☎37 09 71. Palace open Mar. 16-Sept. 30 Tu-Su 10am-6pm; Oct. 1-Mar. 15 F-Su 10am-4pm. Tours run on the hour and the half hour in the summer, variably off-season. Last tour 1hr. before closing. 1000Ft, students 600Ft. Concerts 5000Ft/8000Ft.

Twenty-seven kilometers east of Sopron, Fertőd (FER-tewd) is home to the magnificent **Eszterházy Palace,** Joseph Haydn 2, nicknamed the "Hungarian Versailles." Prince Miklós Eszterházy, a.k.a. Miklós the Sumptuous before he squandered his family's fortune, ordered its construction in 1766 to host his extended bacchanalian feasts. The reason for such excess? "What the emperor can afford, I can afford as well." The hour-long Hungarian tour explains everything from the marble floors to the painted ceilings, including the cleverly concealed door in the prince's bedroom (English information sheet available). The mansion was used as a stable and then a hospital during World War II; government funding helped restore the mansion shortly after the 1957 revolution. ■**Concerts** are held at the castle as part of the annual **Haydn Festival,** which celebrates the most famous works of Josef Haydn, who spent over 30 years here.

SZOMBATHELY ☎ (0)94

The seat of Vas county and a major commercial crossroads between Transdanubia and Austria, Szombathely (SOM-ba-tay; "Saturday's Place") hides 2000-year-old ruins beneath the cover of modern storefronts and Baroque facades. Though it's one of the oldest towns in Hungary, the modern sheen of lively cafes, cheap rooms, and year-round festivals lures tourists from both near and far.

⌁ TRANSPORTATION. Trains (☎ 31 14 20) run to: **Budapest** (3¾hr., 9 per day, 1928Ft; *Intercity* 2¾hr., 4 per day, 2316Ft plus 400Ft reservation fee); **Győr** (2hr., 4 per day, 926Ft; 1¼hr., 4 per day, 1326Ft plus 400Ft reservation fee); and **Keszthely** (2½hr., 3 per day, 1242Ft). Buy tickets in the train station or at Király út 8/a. (Open M-F 8am-5pm, Sa 8am-noon.) **Buses** (☎ 31 20 54) run to: **Budapest** (3½hr., 6 per day, 2360Ft); **Győr** (2½hr., 8 per day, 1100Ft); and **Keszthely** (2½hr., 6 per day, 910Ft).

⊞⃗ ORIENTATION AND PRACTICAL INFORMATION. Szombathely spreads out from several squares, the largest of which is **Fő tér,** home to the main **tourist office.** As you exit the **train station,** turn left and then take the next left on **Széll Kálmán út.** Follow this until you reach **Mártírok tér.** Turn left on **Király út,** which ends in the small square of **Savaria tér.** The **bus station** sits on the opposite side of the inner city; turn left on the street parallel to the station and follow it as it curves to the left and

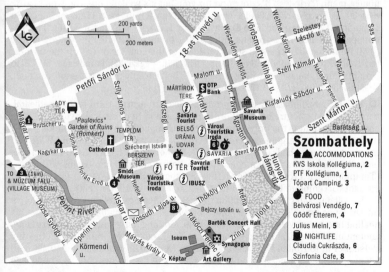

Szombathely

▲▲ ACCOMMODATIONS
KVS Iskola Kollégiuma, **2**
PTF Kollégiuma, **1**
Tópart Camping, **3**

🍴 FOOD
Belvárosi Vendéglo, **7**
Gödör Étterem, **4**
Julius Meinl, **5**

🌙 NIGHTLIFE
Claudia Cukrászda, **6**
Szinfonia Cafe, **8**

HUNGARY

enters town. Cross **Kiskar út** and then head straight to the narrow pedestrian **Belsikátor,** which ends in Fő tér.

Városi Touristikai Iroda, Belsikátor 1, off Fő tér, has English info. (☎51 12 66; www.szombathely.hu. Open M-F 10am-5pm.) **Savaria Tourist** offers info and free maps at three locations: Király út 1 (☎50 94 85; fax 32 58 30), Mártírok tér 1 (☎51 14 35 or 51 14 36), and Berzsenyi tér 2 (☎51 14 46; fax 51 14 45). All locations **exchange currency** and cash **traveler's checks** for no commission. (Open M-F 8:30am-4:30pm, Sa 8am-noon.) **OTP Bank,** Fő tér 4, exchanges currency and has a MC/V **ATM** outside. (Open M 7:45am-6pm, Th-F 7:45am-5pm.) A **pharmacy** is at Fő tér 9. (☎31 24 66. Open M-F 7:30am-6:45pm, Sa 8am-1pm.) A **doctor** is on call at Wesselényi Miklós út 4 (☎31 11 00). The **post office** is at Kossuth Lajos út 18. (☎31 15 84. Open M-F 8am-8pm, Sa 8am-2pm.) **Postal Code:** 9700.

ⓘⓒ ACCOMMODATIONS AND FOOD. To book one of Szombathely's few **private rooms,** visit either **Savaria Tourist ❸** (see above; central doubles starting at 3500Ft) or **IBUSZ ❸,** Fő tér 44. (☎31 41 41; fax 31 04 40; szombath@iroda.ibuisz.hu. Open June-Aug. M-F 8am-5pm, Sa 9am-noon; Sept.-May M-F 8am-4pm. Singles from 5000Ft; doubles 5200Ft.) **Kereskedelma és Vendéglátói Szakképzö Iskola Kollégiuma ❶,** Nagykar út 1/3, is next to the bus station. Its pristine rooms are more spacious than most dorm accommodations. (☎31 23 75. Open July-Aug. 6-bed dorms 700Ft, with toilet 1000Ft, with TV and shower 2500Ft.) **Puskás Tivadar Fém és Villamosipari Szakközépiskole Kollégiuma ❶,** Ady tér 2, is in the park opposite the bus parking lot. This hostel with a big name has small but clean rooms. (☎31 21 98. Ask for Dr. Öri Imréné (EW-ry EEM-ray-nay). Open July-Aug. Dorms 900Ft.) To get to **Tópart Camping ❹,** Kenderesi út 14, take any bus going to Berkovic Lakó and ask the driver to bring you to the campsite. This campsite offers peace, quiet, and a few swans in a picturesque setting. (☎50 90 38; fax 509 039. Open May-Sept. 300Ft per tent plus 600Ft per person. Doubles 3000Ft; 2-bed bungalows 5000Ft; 3-5 bed 8000Ft; 5-bed 10,800Ft. Electricity 500Ft. Tourist tax 120Ft.)

Most of the town's restaurants line Fő tér's pedestrian walkway. **Julius Meinl supermarkets** are at Fő tér 17 (open M-F 7am-8pm, Sa 7am-2pm) and behind the bus station (open M 6am-6pm, Tu-F 6am-7pm, Su 6am-noon; MC/V). ▧**Gődőr Étterem ❸,** Hollán Ernő 10/12, dishes up huge portions of Hungarian specialties from an honest menu ("fried; so it's not good for you, but it's so delicious you won't care"; ☎51 00 78. Entrees 750-2000Ft. Open M-Th 11am-11pm, F-Sa 11am-midnight, Su 11am-3pm.) **Belvárosi Vendéglo ❸,** Savaria tér 1, is near the end of Fő tér. This nononsense kitchen races out heaping plates of meat (620-1620Ft). Enjoy a beer (0.5L Heineken 400Ft) and a steak (1340Ft) at the counter or out on the terrace. (☎31 49 67. Open daily 8:30am-10pm.) The name **Égszínkék Paradicsom ❷,** Belső Urdánia udvar, means "sky-blue paradise." The heavenly pasta will send you high. (Pastas 430-880Ft. ☎34 20 12. Open daily 11am-11pm.)

ⓖ SIGHTS. Szombathely is the proud home of Hungary's third-largest **cathedral,** a magnificent structure built in 1797 in Baroque and Neoclassical styles. The little chapel to its right is the only portion of the original edifice that still stands today; the building is undergoing extensive restoration to repair damage from WWII. To the right of the cathedral, the **Paulovics Garden of Ruins** (Paulovics Romkert) was once the center of a Roman colony, as the ruins and fading mosaics will attest. (Templom tér 1. From Fő tér, go left on Széchenyi út, right on Szily János út, and straight to Templom tér. ☎31 33 69. Open Mar. 1-Dec. 15 M-F 9:30am-3:30pm, Sa 9:30-11:30am. 200Ft, students 100Ft.) The **Smidt Museum,** Hollán Ernő u. 2, shows off Dr. Lajos Smidt's obsessive collection of just about anything he could get his healing hands on: weapons, watches, coins, clothing, tableware, Roman artifacts, ancient maps, and Franz Liszt's pocket watch. (From Fő tér, walk through the tiny Belsikátor út to Hollán E. út, the main street. ☎31 10 38. Open Jan. 8-Feb. 28 Tu-F 10am-5pm; Mar. 1-Dec. 20 Tu-Su 10am-5pm. 300Ft, students 150Ft.) The **Village**

Museum (Vasi Múzeum Falu), on the outskirts of town, displays authentically furnished 200-year-old farmhouses, which have been transplanted from villages throughout the region. Take bus #7 from the train station to the lake, go left on Árpád út, and follow the shore to the parking lot. (Árpád út 30. ☎31 10 04. English tours Tu-F and Su. Open Apr.-Nov. Tu-Su 10am-5pm. 400Ft, students 200Ft.)

🔊🎵 **ENTERTAINMENT AND NIGHTLIFE.** A series of gorgeous **parks** surround the lake, where you can rent a boat and paddle merrily along its bank. (Boat rentals 500-1000Ft per hr.) Szombathely's active spirit has brought a range of new activities to the region, including golf, tennis, rock climbing, and the ever-popular paintball. Around the summer solstice, the **Szentivánéji Festivities** light up the parks on the west side of town with bands, beer-drinking contests, and magic shows. In the first weekend of June, the **Sovalia Dance Competition** tangos into town, while the **Sovalia Carnival,** held in Fő tér during the last week of August, features dramatic performances and an open-air market. Nightlife in Szombathely centers around **Fő tér.** The square hosts summer performances, impromptu concerts, and ice cream stands that stay open late into the night. Enjoy a gooey pastry (100-320Ft) or an ice-cream concoction (300-670Ft) at the charming and cozy **Claudia Cukrászda,** Savaria tér 1. (☎31 33 75. Open daily 9am-8pm.) Next to the synagogue, the **Szinfonia Café,** Rákóczi út 3, is a meeting place for musicians who perform in Bartok Hall. The pleasant, if subdued, crowd that gathers here lounges in plush seats and enjoys coffees from the black-and-white piano-key bar. (☎32 26 89. Open daily 8am-midnight.) The younger element flocks to **Murphy's Mojo Cafe,** Semmelweis Ignác út 28. Enjoy beer (280-500Ft) and friendly conversation with the regulars. (☎31 58 91. Open M-Su 11am-1am.)

LAKE BALATON

Lake Balaton has become one of Central Europe's most coveted vacation spots. The freshwater lake is so warm that it feels more like a bath than a "Hungarian sea." Although villas first sprouted along its shores under Roman rule, it was when the railroad finally linked the lake to its surrounding towns in the 1860s that the area took shape as a playground for the European elite. More recently, it has become a favorite spot for budget-conscious Austrian and German university students, who spend debaucherous weeks enjoying the twin pleasures of liquor and the lake. The south shore sports flashy resorts such as Siófok, while the north offers outdoor adventures and the historic landscapes of Badacsony and Tihany.

SIÓFOK   ☎ (0)84

There are more tourist offices per square kilometer in Siófok than in any other Hungarian city—a fact that attests to the number of vacationers who visit here annually; Siofok's population grows from 20,000 to 200,000 in the summer. The lake provides ample excuse for the bikinis, beer, and bacchanalia that rule this summer capital. An eclectic mix of students, families, elderly people, and everyone in-between take in the sun and party together.

🚌 TRANSPORTATION

Trains: To **Budapest** (2½hr., every hr., 926Ft, 400Ft reservation fee). Siófok is a stop on the Budapest line to: **Ljubljana, SLN; Split, CRO; Venice, ITA; Zagreb, CRO.**

Buses: Express buses *(gyorsjárat)* leave for **Budapest** (1½hr., 9 per day, 1320Ft) and **Pécs** (3hr., 4 per day, 2456Ft).

Ferries: The quickest way to north Balaton is the hourly **MAHART ferry,** 10min. from the train station in the Strand center. To **Tihany** (1¼hr., 700Ft).

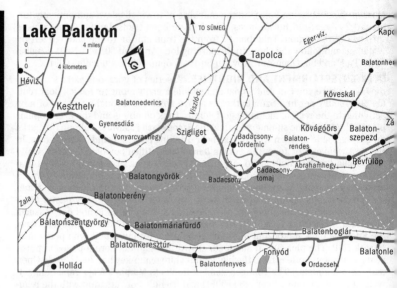

 ORIENTATION AND PRACTICAL INFORMATION

Siófok's excellent transportation services make it an ideal base from which to explore the lake. The **train** and **bus stations** are next to each other, near the center of town. The main street, **Fő út,** runs parallel to the tracks in front of the station. **FA canal** runs perpendicular to the tracks, connecting the lake to the Danube and dividing the town. The eastern **Arany-part** (Gold Coast), to your left as you exit the train station, is home to older, larger hotels, while the **Ezüst-part** (Silver Coast), to your right, has newer and slightly cheaper accommodations. The elevated walkway at **Hock János Koz,** by Ezüst-part, leads to the shore.

> **!** Storms roll in over Lake Balaton in less than 15min., raising dangerous whitecaps on the usually placid lake. Yellow lights on top of tall buildings at Siófok's harbor give **weather warnings;** 1 revolution per 2 sec. means stay within 500m of shore; 1 revolution per sec. means swimmers must return to shore.

Tourist Offices: Tourinform, Fő út. at Szabadság tér (☎31 53 55; fax 31 01 17; www.siofok.com), in the base of the water tower opposite the train station. English-speaking staff finds cheap accommodations and free maps. Open July-Aug. M-Sa 8am-8pm, Su 9am-6pm; Sept.-June M-F 9am-4pm. **IBUSZ,** Fő út. 61, 2nd fl. (☎51 07 20; fax 31 52 13), on the left, exchanges currency for no commission and books private rooms. Open M-F 8am-8pm..

Currency Exchange: OTP, Szabadság tér 10 (☎31 04 55), exchanges currency for no commission. A MC/V **ATM** is outside. Open M 7:45am-6pm, Tu-Th 7:45am-5pm, F 7:45am-4pm. **Postabank,** Fő út. 174-6 (☎31 04 00 or 31 08 33), exchanges currency and cashes **traveler's checks** for no commission. A MC/V **ATM** and currency exchange machine are outside. Open M-F 8am-noon and 12:30-6pm, Sa 10am-1pm.

Emergency: Police: Sió u. 14 (☎31 07 00). **Coast Guard** (☎31 09 90).

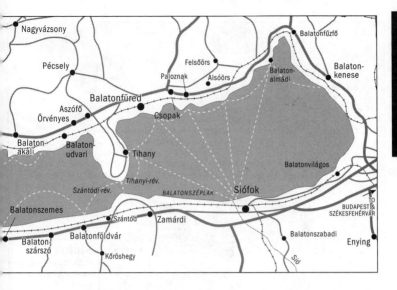

Pharmacy: **Régi Pharmacy,** Fő út. 202 (☎31 00 41). Open M 8am-7pm, Tu-F 8am-6pm, Sa 8am-2pm. Extra 200Ft per item for after-hours service. AmEx/MC/V.

Post Office: Fő út. 186 (☎31 02 10), opposite the train station. Open M-F 8am-7pm, Sa 8am-noon. **Telephones** outside.

Postal Code: 8600

ACCOMMODATIONS

Due to the preponderance of affluent Western tourists, sojourns in Balaton have grown increasingly expensive. Several agencies offer **private rooms.** Your best bets are **Tourinform ④** (see above), which will find rooms and negotiate rates with hotels (doubles 6000-15,000Ft), and **IBUSZ ❸** (doubles 4000Ft; tourist tax 200Ft per night; 30% surcharge for fewer than 4 nights). If you prefer to try your own luck, search streets close to the water for *Panzió* and *Zimmer frei* (room available) signs. Start hunting on **Erkel Ferenc u.,** on the far side of the canal, and **Szent László u.,** to the left when leaving the train station.

■ **Hotel Park,** Batthány u. 7 (☎31 05 39). This hotel, located close to the Strand's cheesy nightlife, is a 5min. walk to the center. Modern wood-paneled rooms, some with A/C. Reception 24hr. Sept.-June doubles 8000-10,000Ft; July-Aug. 10,000-15,000Ft. ④

Hotel Viola, Bethlen Gabor u. 1 (☎31 28 45; ☎/fax 31 01 57; www.siofok.com/viola). From the train station, follow Fő út. with the tracks on your right; cross at Bethlen Gabor u. The white building on your left houses comfortable doubles with baths just blocks from the beach. Breakfast included. Reception 24hr. July to Aug. reservations recommended. May-June and Sept.-Oct. doubles 3200Ft; July-Aug. 4600Ft. ❸

Hotel Azúr, Vitorlás u. 11 (☎31 24 19; fax 31 26 52), entrance on Erkel Ferenc u. From the train station, go right on Fő út, then right on Mártirok u. before the bridge. Go left on Indóház u. and cross the bridge on the far side of the tracks. Continue as the street become Vitorlás u., and turn left at Erkel Ferenc u. Immensely popular complex hosts a beer garden, tennis courts, and a weight room. Reserve 2 weeks in advance. Apr. 27-

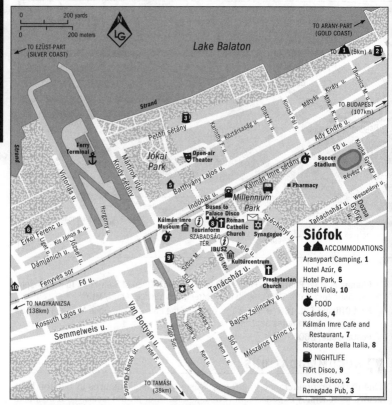

June 15 singles 4400Ft; doubles 5800Ft; triples 7800Ft. June 16-July 6 and Aug. 24-Sept. 14 6400/8600/11600Ft. July 7-Aug. 25 8500/11200/15200Ft. MC/V. ❹

🏕 **Aranypart Camping,** Szent László u. 183/185 (☎35 25 19; fax 35 28 01). 5km from the town center. Take bus #2 to the camping sign (15min.). The most affordable option, if you don't mind the commute to the beach. Infrequent bus service stops at 9:30pm, so the lively crowd brings the party back to camp. Open late Apr. to late Sept. Tents 1050Ft plus 1380Ft per person; 4-person bungalows 21,510Ft. Tourist tax 200Ft. ❷

🍴 FOOD

Stock up on beach supplies at **Plus Supermarket,** Fő út. 156-160, at the intersection of Sió u. (Open M-F 7am-8pm, Sa 7am-3pm, Su 8am-noon. MC/V.)

🍝 **Ristorante Bella Italia,** Szabadság tér 1 (☎31 08 26). The statue-flanked restaurant dishes out enticing entrees with surprising speed and stellar service. Sit on the spacious terrace and enjoy fresh-squeezed orange juice from the adjacent fruit stand (140Ft per dL). Pizza 530-1200Ft; pasta 480-980Ft. Open daily 9am-midnight. ❸

Csárdás, Fő u. 105 (☎31 06 42). Tasty Hungarian dishes. The warmly lit terrace has a romantic atmosphere. Entrees 690-2300Ft. Open daily 11am-11pm. AmEx/MC/V. ❸

Kálmán Imre Cafe and Restaurant, Kálmán Imre sétány 13 (☎310 651). At the far end of Kálmán Imre sétány on the corner of Fő tér, on the left as you exit the train station. Offers the usual fried fare in an unusually pleasant setting. A female vocalist sings nightly 6pm. Entrees 590-2300Ft. Open daily 10am-midnight. ❸

ENTERTAINMENT

Siófok's other daytime attractions pale in comparison with the **Strand,** a series of park-like lawns running to the sandless shoreline. There are public and private sections; entrance to a private area costs around 200-400Ft per person, depending on its location and the owner. The most popular section is the town park, where swimming isn't allowed. Be careful where you sit in this area lest you are accosted by whistle-blowing security guards yelling at you to get off the grass. The largest private beach lies just right of town as you face the water. (400Ft. Open M-F 8am-7pm.) Most sections rent an assortment of water vehicles, including paddleboats and kayaks. (200-400Ft per hr.) Drink stands and "party cafes" line the streets.

For a taste of culture beyond the *Elvis Goes to Hawaii* variety, check out the German operettas held nightly in the **Kultúrcentrum,** Fő tér 2, by the water tower. Get tickets at Tourinform (see **Tourist Offices,** p. 374). In the first week of July, the annual, weeklong **Golden Shell International Folklore Festival** (phsiofok@mail.datanet.hu) celebrates folk music and dancing. The **Kálmán Imre Múzeum,** Kálmán Imre sétány, next to the train station, displays the native composer's piano and playbills from his shows. The second floor hosts rotating art exhibitions. (Open Apr.-Oct. Tu-Su 9am-5pm; Nov.-Mar. 9am-4pm. 300Ft.) For something more solemn, the **church** at Fő u. 57 holds biweekly organ concerts (600Ft, students 450Ft).

NIGHTLIFE

Come nightfall, the excessive displays of skin, drunkenness, and debauchery shift from Siófok's beaches to its bars. **Nightclubs** line the lakefront; many feature semi-nude dancers and sexy murals. Disco lovers hop on the **disco boats** (☎31 00 50) and DJs, live pop, and plenty of Bee Gees and ABBA keep the party alive. (Cover 1500Ft, 18 and under 1000Ft. Departs nightly June 30-Aug. 31 9pm.)

Renegade Pub, Petőfi sétány 3 (www.renegade-pub.com). In the center of the Strand, this casual bar and dance club draws a large crowd nightly. Feast your eyes on the beautiful people dancing on tables to the latest Euro-pop hits. Enough beer (270-450Ft; 0.5L Kaiser 750Ft) and liquor (.4cL 500-700Ft) to float you home in the morning. No cover. Open June 1-Sept. 1 daily 8pm-5am.

Palace Disco, Deák Ferenc sétány 2 (☎35 06 98). Ticket information near the beach at Petőfi sétány 3. Free buses depart every hr. from behind the water tower. A party complex—discos, bars, restaurants (pizza 800-950Ft), and a 3rd fl. "erotic bar"—surrounds a well-lit courtyard. Cocktails 980-1750Ft. Cover 1500-3500Ft. Disco open May to mid-Sept. 10pm-5am. Pizzeria open 11am-5am.

Flört Disco, Sió u. 4 (☎333 33 03; www.flort.hu). Follow the spotlights to this 2-story Balaton institution (pronounced "flirt"). Admire yourself and the young crowd shaking to house music on the mirrored walls. Beer 420-700Ft. Cover 1500-3000Ft. Open mid-June to late Aug. daily 10pm-8am.

FROM THE ROAD

JOURNEY TO THE PAST

As the daughter of Hungarian emigrants, I grew up hearing stories about the Communists—the lines for food, the tanks in the streets, crossing the border by foot. I can even remember being here when buying cake at Gerbaud (see p. 351) was a sin. But nothing prepared me for seeing the apartment my father grew up in—the place from which he, my aunt and my grandparents fled in 1956.

The building lies on the main street in Miskolc (a gateway town into and out of the Slovak Republic), and is merely a door with a buzzer that leads into a small courtyard. I walked in, with my dad by my side. It was exactly the same as it was then—the balconies looked ready to fall on my head, the windows that he had smashed with his soccer ball were still broken, and the woman whose husband my family hid from the Russian police was still alive.

He reminisced about the families that used to live in these 65 square meter apartments—4 to 7 people in each. He told me the story of how a Russian soldier almost killed him because he pretended to shoot him with a make-believe gun, and how scared his father was that day. He spoke with the last remaining "original" resident and learned the whereabouts of his childhood friends. Every memory unleashed many emotions for him, and something became clear to me.

(continued on next page)

⚡ DAYTRIPS FROM SIÓFOK

SZÉKESFEHÉRVÁR   ☎(0)22

Trains run from Budapest (1hr., 21 per day, 498-1084Ft) and from Siófok (1hr., 21 per day, 324-724Ft). From the train station (☎31 22 93), on Béke tér, follow the "Centrum" sign to Deák Ferenc u., which runs perpendicular to the tracks. After 15min., turn left on the Budai út and then right on Varkörút. The red brick gates will appear on your left after 5min.; Koronázo tér leads from the gates to Városház tér. Buses run from Budapest (1hr., 4 per day, 463Ft). From the bus station (☎31 10 57), on Piac tér, veer left of terminal #2 and take a right on Liszt Ferenc u., which becomes Városház tér. Alternatively, take local bus #13, 34, or 35 from the train station and get off at the Rigi Mozi (Old Movie) cinema stop on Varkörút (tickets from the train station paper shop 86Ft, from the driver 120Ft). Follow Varkörút in the direction of the bus to the city gates. To reach the castle museum, take bus #32 from the train station to the intersection of Kassai u. and Vágújhelyi u. From here, turn left on Vágújhelyi u. and go left on Mária Völgyi u. to Bory tér. Castle open M-Su 9am-5pm. 300Ft, students 150Ft.

Known as the place where Árpád—the nation's Magyar forefather—first set up camp, Székesfehérvár is technically Hungary's oldest town. Today, those traveling from Budapest to Balaton stop in this friendly, unpretentious city to visit the extraordinary ▨ **Bory Castle** (Bory-vár). Over the course of 40 summers, architect and sculptor Jenő Bory built this iron, concrete, and brick mansion by hand in honor of his wife, his art, and his country's history. The rector of the Academy of Fine Arts from 1911 to 1945, Bory filled Bory-vár's towers, gardens, crooked paths, winding staircases, and stone chambers with dozens of his renowned sculptures. He decorated every inch of this eccentric retreat, lining colonnades with sculptures of historic Hungarians and erecting a chapel for his wife as the ultimate "monument to marital love." Today his descendents tend the **castle museum.**

If you have the time, explore Székesfehérvár's cobblestone streets as they thread between 18th-century civic buildings and historic churches. Pick up a walking tour guidebook and free maps at **Tourinform**, Városház tér 1 (☎31 28 18; fax 50 27 72). In the center, the **King St. Stephen Museum** (Szent István Király Múzeum), Fő u. 6., houses an archaeology exhibit that showcases fantastic Roman artifacts. (☎31 55 83. Open Mar. 4-Apr. 28 Tu-Su 10am-2pm; Apr. 29-Sept. 30 Tu-Su 10am-4pm. 200Ft, students 100Ft.) The **Budenz House: Ybl Collection** (Budenz-ház: Ybl Gyűjtemény), Arany János u. 12, includes exquisite 18th- to 20th-century Hungarian art and furniture from the Ybl family collection. Brave the heavily gesticulated German tour of the collection to learn more about Miklos Ybl, one of Budapest's preeminent architects. (☎31 30 27. Open May 1-Oct. 1 Tu-Su 10am-4pm; Oct. 1-27 and Mar. 5-Apr. 31 Tu-Su 10am-2pm. 200Ft, students 120Ft.) Founded in the early 13th century, **St. Stephen's Cathedral** (Szent István Király Bazilika), Városház tér 1, was converted into a mosque under Turkish rule. The 18th-century renovations lent stunning Baroque designs and magnificent frescoes to this spired church. (☎31 28 18; fax 50 27 72. Open M-F 9am-6pm, Sa 9am-2pm.)

TIHANY PENINSULA   ☎(0)87

MAHART ferries are the fastest way to reach Tihany from Siófok (1-1¼hr., every hr., 700Ft, round-trip 1400Ft); land transport can take up to 5hr. To reach the town from the ferry pier and neighboring Strand, walk toward the elevated road. Pass underneath and follow the "Apátság" signs up the steep hill to the abbey. Tihany's main drag, Kossuth Lajos u., is just beyond the church at the top of the hill.

The beautiful Tihany (TEE-hahn) Peninsula is known as the pearl of Balaton. Although just as heavily touristed as the rest of the lake, Tihany retains a historical weight and outdoorsy charm that makes this little place seem more mature than its debauchery-laden peers. (Bencés Apátság.) The small but magnificent **Benedictine Abbey** draws over a million visitors each year. The abbey's outdoor views of the surrounding region pale in comparison with the luminous frescoes and intricate Baroque altars within. Below the abbey, the **András I crypt** (I. András kriptája) contains the remains of King András I, one of Hungary's earliest kings and the abbey's founder. In the **Tihany Museum** next door, a former 18th-century monastery exhibits an odd combination of contemporary art exhibits and Roman archaeological finds, all on display in the subterranean lapidarium. *(To get to the crypt from the abbey, pass through the door next to the altar and go downstairs. Abbey and museum open Mar.-Oct. M-Sa 9am-5:30pm, Su 11am-5:30pm. Church and crypt 260Ft, students 130Ft, families 650Ft; Su free.)* The pleasantly shaded **Rege Kávézó**, Kossuth Lajos u. 22, offers visitors delectable pastries along with panoramic views of Lake Balaton. *(☎44 82 80. Pastries 350-480Ft. Coffee 280-600Ft. Ice cream 300-950Ft. Open daily 10am-9pm.)* **Hiking** across the peninsula through hills, forests, farms, and marshes takes only an hour or two. For an even shorter hike, take the red-cross trail around Belső-tó Lake and turn right on the red-line trail on the opposite side. The path will take you to the summit of Kiserdő Teto (Little Wood), from which you can see both of Tihany's interior lakes. The green-line trail, which covers the eastern slope of Óvár, snakes past

Though I always thought that leaving Hungary was the best thing that ever happened to my parents, coming "home" for them is painful and bittersweet. Whereas being uprooted to travel is something I hunger for, for them it meant survival, freedom, and the chance for their children to live in peace.

Many Hungarians I meet ask me if life is better in North America. I can say that I am thankful that my parents were able to leave when they felt the need to, and I think I would never be where I am today otherwise. This is not to say that no one can succeed here, especially when so much positive change is happening. It is merely a reflection on how 30 to 40 years ago, the decision to leave was a huge step. These personal stories of escape may not be detailed in history books, but they're alive in the families that have lived to tell them.

—Sandra Nagy

Barátlakáksok (the Hermit's Place), where cells and a chapel hollowed out in the rocks by 11th-century Greek Orthodox hermits are still visible. If you're lucky, you'll never see another person on these trails, save for the occasional vineyard gardener. *(Get a map (350Ft) by the church before you start your hike, or pick up a free, less detailed one at Tourinform, Kossuth Lajos u. 20. ☎43 80 16; fax 44 88 04; tihany@tourinform.hu.)* Follow the "Strand" signs along the promenade behind the church and descend to the **beach.** *(Beach open daily 9am-8pm. 200Ft.)* A bit farther along the walkway rises **Echo Hill.**

KESZTHELY   ☎(0)83

Sitting at the lake's west tip, Keszthely (KESS-tay) was once the toy-town of the powerful Festetics family. The family left a legacy of architectural design, grand parks, and an opulent mansion. Keszethely's amusements have gone down-market since then, but it still attracts a sizeable crowd of visitors. Today, the main promenade hosts an eclectic mix of street cafes, rogue tattoo parlors, and pricey restaurants, while the nearby healing thermal spring attracts both locals and tourists.

▐ TRANSPORTATION

The **train station** is about 250m from the water on Kazinczy u. *Intercity* trains run to **Budapest** (3hr., 13 per day, 1556Ft plus 400Ft reservation fee), while slow trains *(személyvonat)* serve **Szombathely** (3hr., 1 per day, 1084Ft). The **bus terminal** is next to the train station. Buses beat trains for local travel to **Balatonfüred** (1½hr., 9 per day, 700Ft) and **Pécs** (4hr., 5 per day, 1486Ft). Some buses leave from the terminal while others use stops at either Fő tér or Georgikan u. Each departure is marked with an "F" or a "G" to indicate which stop it uses; check the schedules. In summer, boats run to **Badacsony** (1¾hr.; May 28-June 30 1 per day, July-Sept. 4 per day; 840Ft) from the pier at the end of the dock.

▐ ORIENTATION AND PRACTICAL INFORMATION

The main **Kossuth Lajos u.** runs parallel to the shore, from **Festetics Palace** (Festetics Kastély) to the center at **Fő tér.** To reach the main square from the train station, walk straight up **Mártirok u.** to its end at Kossuth Lajos u., and turn left to reach Fő tér. If you're coming from the pier, walk toward the shore and, after the tracks, turn left on **Kazinczy u.** This leads directly to the train and bus stations.

Tourinform, Kossuth Lajos u. 28, on the palace side, off Fő tér, gives out free **maps** and info. (☎/fax 31 41 44. Open July-Aug. M-F 9am-8pm, Sa-Su 9am-6pm; Oct.-June M-F 9am-5pm, Sa 9am-1pm.) **IBUSZ,** Fő tér 6/8, **exchanges currency** and books **private rooms** in town for 16% commission. (☎31 43 20. Open June-Aug. M-F 8am-6pm, Sa 9am-1pm; Sept.-May M-F 8am-4pm.) **OTP Bank,** at the corner of Kossuth Lajos u. and Helikon u., **exchanges currency** and cashes **traveler's checks** for no commission. There's a 24hr. MC/V **ATM** outside. (Open M-Tu and Th-F 7:45am-4pm, W 7:45am-5pm.) **Park gyógyszertar** is a sunscreen-packed **pharmacy** at Kossuth Lajos u. 64. (☎31 31 49. Open M-F 7:45am-7pm, Sa 8am-noon.) There are card **telephones** outside of the **post office** at Kossuth Lajos u. 48. (☎51 59 60. Open M-F 8am-6pm, Sa 8am-noon.) Access the **Internet** at **Stone's Cyber-cafe,** Kisfaludy u. 17, at the intersection of Bem József u. (☎51 01 09; www.stones-cafe.hu. Before 6pm 1200Ft per hr., after 6pm 800Ft per hr. Open M-Th 9am-2am, F-Sa 9am-4am, Su 10am-2am.) **Postal Code:** 8360.

HUNGARY

⚡ 🏠 ACCOMMODATIONS AND FOOD

Homes with *Zimmer frei* (rooms available) signs abound near the Strand, off Fő tér on Erzsébet Királyné u., and near Castrum Camping (see below) on Ady Endre u. Head up Kossuth Lajos u. and turn right on Szalasztó u. immediately before the palace entrance; Ady Endre is a few streets down on the right. **IBUSZ ❸** (see above) books central, private doubles with showers (starting at 5000Ft) and for longer stays, apartments with kitchen (starting at 7000Ft). If you'd like to avoid finder's fees, the folks at **Tourinform ❸** (see above) offer a few private rooms near the center (starting at 3000Ft). **Zalatour ❸,** Kossuth Lajos u. 1, rents rooms with baths. (☎31 25 60; fax 31 43 01. Singles 4500Ft; doubles 5500Ft. Open June-Aug. M-F 9am-5pm, Sa 9am-1pm; Sept.-May M-F 9am-4pm, Sa 9am-1pm.) The immaculate and spacious rooms at **Admiral Panzió ❹,** Pázmány P. u. 1, all include a free welcome cocktail and breakfast. The extremely helpful staff speaks German and English. (☎31 43 68; fax 31 41 43; www.admiralpanzio.hu. Reception 24hr. Singles 5600-9800Ft; doubles 7000-11,200Ft; extra bed 3500-4900Ft. Tax 324Ft per person.) **Castrum Camping ❶,** Móra Ferenc u. 48, boast large sites with all the amenities: tennis courts, beach access, a restaurant, and the most happening nightspots in town. (☎31 21 20. July-Aug. tents 580Ft, with electricity 680Ft, plus 680Ft per person; Sept.-June non-electric sites drop to 450Ft. Tourist tax 250Ft.)

There's been a fruit and flower **market** on Piac tér since medieval times. At the center of the market, **Jééé supermarket** (pronounced "yay") provides everything else you could possibly need. (Open M-F 6:30am-7pm, Sa 6:30am-4pm, Su 7:30am-1pm. MC/V.) Most of the restaurants around Fő tér and on Kossuth Lajos u. are relatively overpriced, but there are more reasonable options a bit farther from the center. The smell of baked sweetbreads (90-120Ft) wafting from **Helyben Süly Finompékáruk ❶,** on the corner of Kossuth Lajos u. and Balaton u., lures crowds. (Open M-F 6am-6pm, Sa 7am-6pm.) The buffet of fresh, homemade dishes at **Oázis-Reform Restaurant ❶,** Rákóczi tér 3, is no mirage; there's not a trace of meat at this lunchtime haven. (☎31 10 23. 210Ft per 100g. Open M-F 11am-4pm, Sa 11am-2pm.) **Donatello ❷,** Balaton u. 1/A, serves pizza and pasta in a sun-drenched courtyard. The eatery manages to maintain its dignity despite the Teenage Mutant Ninja Turtle sign out front. (☎31 59 89. Pasta 410-950Ft; pizza 440-1200Ft. Open daily noon-11pm.) **Corso Restaurant ❸,** Erzsébet Királyné u. 23, closer to the Strand in the Abbázia Club Hotel, draws on Balaton's rich fish stock for its culinary concoctions. Live music all year. (☎31 25 96. Entrees 650-1600Ft. 3-course lunch 699Ft, pizza from 550Ft. Open M-Sa 7am-11pm.)

👁 🎵 SIGHTS AND ENTERTAINMENT

Keszthely's pride is the ▨ **Helikon Palace Museum** (Helikon Kastélymúzeum) in the **Festetics Palace.** Follow Kossuth Lajos u. from Fő tér past the Tourinform office until it becomes Keszthély u. Built by one of the most powerful Austro-Hungarian families of the 18th century, the storybook Baroque palace boasts fanciful architecture and a fascinating history. The site of Hungarian literary events hosted by György Festetics, the palace was named "Helikon" after Helicon Hill, the mythical Grecian home of the nine muses. Of the 360 rooms, visitors may visit only the central wing, but its mirrored halls, parquet floors, and extravagantly furnished chambers are captivating enough: visitors can access the 90,000-volume, wood-paneled Helikon Library, an exotic arms collection that spans 1000 years, and an exhibit of the Festetics's elaborate porcelain pieces. Pick up an English guidebook (700Ft) at the bookstore as you enter, as there are no English translations. A new Islamic art exhibition was installed in 2001 as part of the permanent collection. It spans the 18th-20th centuries and has English translations. The well-kept **English park** around the museum provides photo-worthy vistas for mid-afternoon promenades. (Open Tu-Su 9am-6pm; ticket office closes at 5:30pm. 1500Ft, students 700Ft. English tours, for groups booked in advance only, 5000Ft.) Popular chamber music **concerts** are frequently held in the mirrored ballroom; inquire at Tourinform (see above) for tickets. (5500Ft; in summer reserve seats 2 weeks in advance.)

Families throng to Keszthely's **Strand**, which lies to your right as you exit the train station. From the center, walk down Erzsébet u. as it curves right into Vörösmarty u. Go through the park on the left after the train tracks to reach the beach beyond. Though rocks replace the sand and swamp restrains the waves, this arcade-lined strip manages to draws many to its shores. (Open May 15-Sept. 15 daily 8:30am-7pm. 370Ft, children 250Ft. After 4pm 320Ft/220Ft.) The 1896 pastel green tower of the **Church of Our Lady** on Fő tér conceals the main structure, which dates from 1386 and remains a shining example of Gothic architecture in Hungary. Spectacular stained glass and 14th-century paintings adorn the dark sanctuary.

⚡ DAYTRIPS FROM KESZTHELY

HÉVÍZ
☎(0)83

Buses leave from Keszthely's Fő tér (30min., every 30min., 100-200Ft).

Six kilometers outside Keszthely, Hévíz is home to the world's largest ▧ **thermal lake.** Covered in gigantic lilies, the sulphurous and slightly radioactive water is rumored to have miraculous healing powers—according to legend, it once cured the beautiful, crippled daughter of the lord of Tátika Castle. With waters heated to a soothing 26-33°C (77-91°F), you too can seek longevity alongside the algae. The 11-acre lake is large, but the spring that fills it pumps so fast that the water is entirely replaced every 28 hours. To take advantage of this amazing spot, head to the *fin de siècle* **bathhouse,** which sits on stilts above the center of the lake; the entrance is at Dr. Schülhof Vilmos sétány 1, across from the bus station. Look for the sign that reads "Tó Fürdö." Massages and pedicures are available at various prices. (☎50 17 00; fax 34 04 64. 600Ft for 3hr. Open daily 8:30am-6pm, cashier closes at 5pm.) If the bathing makes you hungry, dine at **Grill Garden Restaurant,** Kölesal u. 4, on a side street near the bus station. The log-cabin restaurant serves delicious Hungarian dishes. Ask for the English menu. (☎34 39 70. Entrees 790-1490Ft. Open daily 11am-11pm.)

SÜMEG
☎(0)87

Buses run from Keszthely (1¼hr., approx. every hr., 386Ft). From the station at Flórián tér, cross Petőfi Sandor u. to Kossuth Lajos u., the town's central street. To reach the castle from the town center, walk up Vak Bottyán u. from Kossuth Lajos u., bear right at Szent István tér, and continue up the steep street.

Though only a short distance from the Balaton shore, Sümeg feels worlds away. This cobblestoned town doesn't attract the same racy crowds that frequent most of Balaton's resorts. Trek up the stone path to visit Sümeg's **castle** (vár), one of Hungary's largest and best-preserved strongholds, strategically perched 270m above the town. Built as a last defense against the invading Mongols, the 13th-century fortress also resisted the Turks, standing until the Hapsburg army burned it down in 1713. The stony walls were diligently restored in the 1960s, and the atmosphere inside is kitschy, with magic shows, pony rides, archery ranges, and costumed characters performing to mandolin music. (☎35 27 37. Open May-Oct. daily 8am-8pm. 700Ft, students 350Ft.) The **museum** inside displays medieval armor and the requisite torture chamber, full of grisly reconstructions of applied justice.

The castle's festivities may be the headliner in Sümeg, but it's the **Church of the Ascension**, at the corner of Deák Ferenc u. and Széchenyi György u., that steals the spotlight. To get there, follow Deák Ferenc downhill from the intersection across from the OTP bank on Kossuth Lajos u. Its mundane exterior conceals a frescoed marvel known to locals as the Hungarian Sistine Chapel; the comparison is slightly hyperbolic, but one can't help but be impressed by Franz Anton Maulbertsch's 1757 Rococo masterpiece. It seems that Maulbertsch knew how magnificent his work was: he's the one mugging for you in the first fresco to the right as you enter the church (the cheese in his hand is supposedly a symbol of humility).

BADACSONY ☎(0)87

Buses pass through the town from Keszthely (1hr., 7-8 per day, 340Ft). Badacsony also lies on the tram lines but buses are far more convenient.

Although four resort towns lie at the foot of Balaton Hill (Badacsonyhégy), Badacsony and **Badacsony-tomaj** (BAD-uh-chone TOE-my) are by far the most popular, and are within easy walking distance from each other. The town's main draw is the cluster of **wine cellars** on the southern face of the hill, where you can sample a vintage or purchase it by the 5L plastic jug (600Ft and up). If you don't enjoy a 3km walk uphill on a blazing Balaton day, the jeep parked in front of the post office offers rocky rides up the slope. (600Ft per person, 3600Ft per car. Discounts on round-trip. Jeep leaves whenever 6 customers arrive.) Get off at the **Kisfaludy Ház** restaurant and sip the region's finest wines in a somewhat touristy setting. (☎43 10 16. Open daily 10am-11pm.) Less pricey cellars sit on the cobblestone Hegyalya u. (part of the yellow-cross hiking trail). **Bormúzeum Pince** (Wine Cellar Museum), Hegyalya 6 (☎43 12 62), serves sweet and dry wines; Grey Monk, a demi-sweet, is their most famous vintage. (3 1dL samples and Hungarian cold plate 1020Ft. Open daily 10am-10pm.)

If the round of "samples" hasn't done you in, head farther uphill—about 100m past the spring next to Kisfaludy Ház—to try one of the Badacsony's pleasantly shaded **hikes.** Pick up a map of the hiking routes, available at Tourinform and most hotels. Fill up before you set off as the soda stands end here. A short trek on the red trail leads to **Rose Rock** (Rózsa-kő), where legend has it that a couple that sits facing away from the water will be married within a year. An hour's hike farther up rocky stairs will bring you to **Kisfaludy Tower** (Kisfaludy kiláto) and a gorgeous, sweeping vista. Walk toward the right when facing the Rose Rock, and follow the Hegyeto trail. For those willing to make a day of it, the **stone gate** *(kőkapu)*, a dramatic cliffside basalt formation, awaits farther along the trail. Although Badacsony's **beach** is small and swampy (open daily 8am-9pm; 250Ft, children 150Ft), the carnival-esque **marketplace** around it captures the party atmosphere. If the combination of wine and hiking makes a return to Keszthely impossible, head to **Tourinform Badacsony,** Park u. 6 (☎13 10 46), for free **maps** and advice on rooming options. Accommodations in July and August are limited on weekends, so call ahead. (Open July-Aug. daily 8am-8pm; Sept.-May 9am-5pm.)

SOUTHERN TRANSDANUBIA

Framed by the Danube to the west, the Dráva River to the south, and Lake Balaton to the north, Southern Transdanubia is known for its rolling hills, sunflower fields, mild climate, and delicious wine. Once the southernmost portion of the Roman province of Pannonia, the region later suffered through the Turkish occupation until the bloody 1566 Battle of Szigetvár halted the Ottoman advance. To reward the people for their bravery, the Austro-Hungarian Empire erected magnificent churches and elegant buildings throughout the region.

HUNGARY

PÉCS

☎ (0)72

Safely nestled at the southern base of the Mecsek mountains, Pécs (PAYCH) slows down the pace of life with a warm climate, incomparable vistas, and captivating architecture. Its monuments reveal a 2000-year-old legacy of Roman, Ottoman, and Hapsburg, while its fine collections of modern art pick up where the sights leave off. Add nightlife fueled by university students, and bountiful outdoor activities in the surrounding Baranya region, and it's no surprise that Pécs is one of Hungary's most popular weekend destinations.

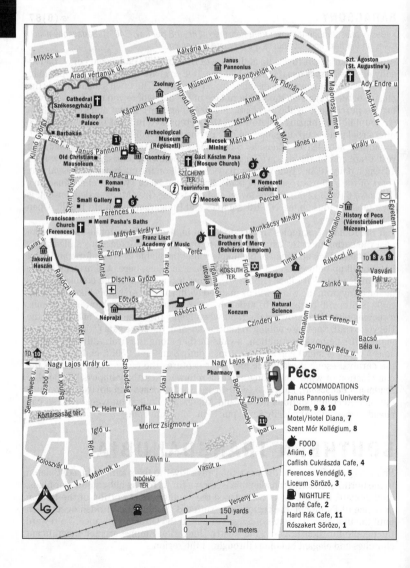

Pécs

ACCOMMODATIONS
Janus Pannonius University
 Dorm, **9 & 10**
Motel/Hotel Diana, **7**
Szent Mór Kollégium, **8**

FOOD
Afiúm, **6**
Caflish Cukrászda Cafe, **4**
Ferences Vendéglő, **5**
Liceum Söröző, **3**

NIGHTLIFE
Danté Cafe, **2**
Hard Rák Cafe, **11**
Rószakert Sörözo, **1**

⌐ TRANSPORTATION

Trains: The station is just beyond the bottom of the historic district. Take bus #30, 32, or 33 from the center, or walk 20min. from Jókai u. to Széchenyi tér. To **Budapest** (3½hr., 3 per day, 1996Ft) and **Villány** (45min., 10 per day, 316Ft). 4 trains leave daily for various Lake Balaton towns; get tickets at the MÁV office in the station (☎21 50 03; www.elvira.hu) or at Jókai u. 4 (☎21 27 34). Both open M-F 9am-5pm.

Buses: ☎21 52 15; www.agria.hu. To: **Budapest** (4½hr., 7 per day, 2088Ft); **Keszthely** (4hr., 4 per day, 1506Ft); **Szeged** (4½hr., 7 per day, 1992Ft).

Public Transportation: Bus tickets cost 105Ft at kiosks and 130Ft on the bus.

Taxis: Don't enter any taxis except Volán and Euro brands, as others usually overcharge.

⚑ ⁊ ORIENTATION AND PRACTICAL INFORMATION

Pécs rests on the knees of the Mecsek mountain range; conveniently, north and south corresponds to uphill and downhill. Tourists throng about the historic **Belváros** (inner city), a rectangle bound by the ruins of the city wall. The center is **Széchenyi tér,** where most tourist offices are located. Belváros takes less than 20min. to cross going downhill, but be wary of the steep incline.

Tourist Offices: Tourinform, Széchenyi tér 9 (☎21 26 32; fax 21 33 15), offers **maps,** phone cards, and stamps. Open June 16-Sept. 30 M-F 9am-7pm, Sa-Su 10am-6pm; Oct. M-F 8am-4pm, Sa 9am-2pm; Nov. 1-Apr. 30 daily 8am-4pm; May 1-June 15 Su-F 8am-4pm, Sa 9am-2pm. **Mecsek Tours,** Széchenyi tér 1 (☎51 33 70; fax 21 48 66), arranges travel, sells phone cards, **exchanges currency,** books rooms, and has an **ATM.** Open M-F 9am-4:30pm.

Currency Exchange: OTP Bank, Rákóczi út 44 (☎50 29 00), cashes **traveler's checks** and **exchanges currency** for no commission. Open M 7:45am-6pm, Tu-F 7:45am-4pm. A 24hr. MC/V **ATM** is outside.

24-Hour Pharmacy: **Zsolnay Gyógyszertár,** Zsolnay V. u. 8 (☎/fax 51 67 60). Open M-F 7:30am-7:30pm, Sa 7:30am-1:30pm. Ring bell after hours (100Ft extra per item).

Internet Access: Fortuna Étterem and Internet Cafe, Ferences u. 32 (☎52 65 76; www.netcafepecs.hu). 160Ft per 15min. Open daily 10am-11pm. **Mac Cafe,** Janus Pannonius u. 11, in the same building as the Csontváry Museum. 10am-3pm 100Ft for the first 10min., 6Ft per additional min.; 3pm-1am 100Ft for 10min., 8Ft per additional min. Open daily 10am-1am.

Post Office: Jókai Mór u. 10 (☎50 60 00). Its 2 floors offer so many services there's an info desk to guide you. Open M-F 7am-8pm, Sa 8am-2pm.

Postal Code: 7621.

⌐ ACCOMMODATIONS

For central accommodations, **private rooms** are the best budget option. Pécs's efficient bus system, however, makes cheaper rooms outside of town almost as convenient. It's best to call ahead, especially in the summer and on weekends.

Motel/Hotel Diana, Timár u. 4a (☎328 59; fax 33 33 73). Right off Kossuth tér in the center of town, this pricey hostel offers tiny, well-kept singles and doubles. A more luxurious hotel will open next door in 2003. Singles 5600Ft; doubles 8600Ft. MC/V. ❸

Szent Mór Kollégium, 48-as tér 4 (☎50 36 10). Take bus #21 from the main bus terminal to 48-as tér. This gorgeous old university building houses spiffy triples. Laundry by request. Reception 24hr. Check-out 10am. Curfew midnight. Ring the bell after 10pm. Open July-Aug. 30. 1000Ft per person. ❶

Janus Pannonius University, Universitas u. 2 (☎31 19 66; fax 32 44 73). Take bus #21 from the bus terminal to the wooded 48-as tér. The dorm is to the right, behind McDonald's. Clean, inhabitable rooms. Reception 24hr. Open June-Sept.; call ahead June and Sept. 3-bed dorms 1000Ft. Several branches available around the city. ❶

🄵 FOOD

The countless restaurants, cafes, and bars that line Pécs's streets are among the city's biggest attractions. Reservations are necessary at more popular restaurants on Friday and Saturday nights, but a walk down Király u., Apáca u., or Ferences u., should yield a table and an excellent dinner. **Konzum,** is the main supermarket on Kossuth tér. (Open M-F 6:30am-7pm, Sa 6:30am-2pm.).

Afiúm, Irgalmasok u. 2 (☎51 44 34). This subterranean restaurant is eclectically furnished with mismatched chairs and tablecloths. Old-time relics, from radios to sewing machines, decorate the corners of the restaurant. Italian and Hungarian menu with veggie options. Entrees 830-1950Ft. Open M-Sa 11am-1am, Su 11am-midnight. ❸

Ferences Vendéglő, Ferences út 24 (☎32 52 39), serves delicious Hungarian specialties indoors or at sidewalk tables. Entrees 790-1550Ft. Vegetable dishes 500-800Ft; beer 260-360Ft. Open daily 11am-10pm. ❸

Liceum Söröző, Király u. 35 (☎32 72 84). Opposite the Liceum Church and through a courtyard; restaurant is downstairs. Low prices make this a favorite of the student community. Everything is fried, but with 0.5L of *Gold Fassl* at 300Ft no one seems to mind. Entrees 400-780Ft. Open M-Th noon-10pm, F 11am-11pm, Sa 6-11pm. ❷

Caflisch Cukrászda Café, Király u. 32 (š31 03 91). Sink your sweet teeth into pastries (from 79Ft) and sinful sundaes (210-550Ft) at one of the best joints in town. Check out the Herend (famous Hungarian China) espresso machine. Open daily 8am-10pm. ❶

🄾 SIGHTS

MOSQUE OF GHAZI KASSIM. (Gázi Khasim Pasa dzsámija.) Nicknamed the "Mosque Church," the elegant green-domed building is a former Turkish mosque, built on the site of an earlier Christian church. Verses from the Koran decorate the interior walls, and a former ablution basin—where the Turks washed their feet before entering the mosque—now serves as a baptismal font. The largest structure from the Ottoman occupation still standing in Hungary, the church is a dynamic and somewhat jarring fusion of Christian and Muslim traditions; as such, it has become a symbol of the city. *(Széchenyi tér. ☎32 19 76. Open Apr. 16-Oct. 14 daily 10am-4pm; Oct.15-Apr. 15 10am-noon. There is no admission fee, but it is polite to buy a postcard or souvenir as a donation.)*

CATHEDRAL AND BISHOP'S PALACE. The 4th-century neo-Romanesque Cathedral *(bazilika)*, with its ornate altarpiece and chapels, stands as Pécs's centerpiece. Together with the elegant Bishop's Palace, it makes the hilltop a peaceful refuge. A tiny museum showcasing church relics is worth a peek. *(On Dóm tér. From Széchenyi tér, walk left on Janus Pannonius u., take the 1st right, and then go left on Káptalan to Dóm tér. ☎51 30 30. Cathedral open M-Sa 9am-1pm and 2-5pm, Su 1-5pm. 500Ft, students 250Ft. Palace not open to the public.)*

SYNAGOGUE. The stunning 1869 synagogue, with intricate paintings covering the ceiling and a fabulous Ark of the Covenant, holds services for the city's Jewish population, which now numbers a meager 140. *(On Kossuth tér. Walk downhill from*

Széchenyi tér on Irgalmasok u.; Kossuth tér is on the left. Open Su-F 10-11:30am and noon-5pm. 200Ft, students 100Ft.)

ROMAN RUINS. The 4th-century Roman ruins near the cathedral in the neighboring Szent István tér stand as a testament to Pécs's past. Underneath lies the largest burial site in Hungary, and a chilly crypt with barely-there Roman Christian paintings. *(Cross Janus Pannonius from the cathedral or walk 5min. from Széchenyi tér; the ruins lie in the left-hand corner of the park. Open Tu-Su 10am-6pm.)*

🏛 MUSEUMS

CSONTVÁRY MUSEUM. This museum displays the works of Tivadar Csontváry Kosztka (1853-1919), a local artist who gained an international reputation in his relatively short 20 years of work. The impressively designed exhibit highlights the master's thematic interests and his luminous, expressionistic skies, making it clear why he is known as the Hungarian Van Gogh. This exhibit highlights journeys to Israel, Italy, Morocco, and Athens. *(Janus Pannonius u. 11. Follow Janus Pannonius to the left from Széchenyi tér. ☎31 05 44. Open Tu-Sa 10am-6pm. 400Ft, students 300Ft.)*

ZSOLNAY MUSEUM. There's nothing mass-produced at this museum, where a family workshop has hand-crafted the world-famous Zsolnay porcelain since the mid-19th century. *(Káptalan u. 2. Walk up Szepessy I. u. behind the Mosque Church and turn left at Káptalan u. ☎32 48 22. Open Tu-Sa 10am-6pm, Su 10am-4pm. 450Ft, students 200Ft. Photographs 200Ft, video 450Ft.)*

VASARELY MUSEUM. Houses works of one of Hungary's most important 20th-century artists, Pécs-born Viktor Vasarely (1908-97), who founded the Pop Art movement. *(Káptalan u. 3, next to the Zsolnay Museum. ☎32 48 22, ext. 21. Open Apr.-Oct. Tu-Su 10am-6pm. 400Ft, students 200Ft. Photographs 200Ft, video 400Ft.)*

🎭 FESTIVALS AND NIGHTLIFE

Festivals in Pécs are concentrated in September. Choir music and wine pleasantly mingle at Pécs's 🌟 **World Festival of Wine Songs** in late September. For information, contact Pécsi Férfikar Alapitvány, Színház tér 2 (☎/fax 21 16 06). Other festivals include the **Gastronomic Pleasures of the Pécs region,** the **Pécs City Festival** and the **Mediterranean Autumn Festival.** Pick up the festival brochure at Tourinform. Pécs's **nightlife** scene is one of the best in Hungary. Hit the crowded, colorful bars near Széchenyi tér, especially on the first two blocks of Király u., for brain-busting beats and body piercings aplenty. Clubs are closer to the train station and pack in a lively, fun-loving crowd.

🌟 **Dante Cafe,** Janus Pannonius u. 11 (☎21 06 61), in the same building as the Csontváry Museum. The cafe was originally founded to finance the Pécs literary magazine *Szép Literaturari Ajándék.* It now plays host to an artsy clientele, plus a small crowd of Hungarian youth. Beer 290-390Ft. Open daily 10am-1am, later on weekends.

Hard Rák Cafe, Ipar u. 7 (☎50 25 57). Turn left at the corner of Bajcsy-Zsilinszky u. The door is somewhat camouflaged so keep your eyes open. The name refers to the music, not the American chain. If the cave paintings in this dimly lit club don't inspire your primal urge, the drinks will. Live rock performances in summer F-Sa nights. Cover Th-Sa 500Ft. Open M-Sa 7pm-6am.

Rózsakert Söröző, Janus Pannonius u. 8/10 (☎31 08 62). Locals and a slightly older crowd come here to enjoy the evening zephyr, live Hungarian Gypsy music, and a lantern-adorned terrace. 0.5L *Gold Fassl* 260Ft. Open daily noon-midnight.

THE GREAT PLAIN (NAGYALFÖLD)

Romanticized in tales of cowboys and bandits, the grasslands of Nagyalföld stretch southeast of Budapest, covering almost half of Hungary. Also called the *puszta*, meaning "plain," this tough region is home to arid Debrecen, fertile Szeged, and the vineyards of Kecskemét, which rise out of the flat soil like Nagyalföld's legendary mirages. Brimming with universities, fine art museums, and elegant architecture, these civilized spots offer Hungarian high culture at its best.

DEBRECEN   ☎(0)52

Protected by the mythical phoenix and dubbed the festival capital of Hungary, Debrecen (DE-bre-tsen; pop. 210,000) has risen from the ashes of over 30 devastating fires, the fate of a landlocked city on the dry Great Plain. Happily, recent reconstructions have bestowed lush parks and wide boulevards upon the city; 19th-century architecture comfortably mingles with modern designs. This unofficial capital of eastern Hungary, and of Hungarian Protestantism, is famed for its Reformed College, one of the country's oldest and largest universities. The student population fills Debrecen's streets by day and its pubs by night.

▐ TRANSPORTATION

Trains: (☎32 67 77), at Petofi tér. To: **Budapest** (3hr., 13 per day, 1850Ft; *InterCity* 2½hr., 5 per day, 2192Ft); **Eger** (3hr., 6 per day, 1323Ft) via **Fúzesabony; Miskolc** (2½-3hr., 5 per day, 1087Ft); **Szeged** (3½hr., 7 per day, 2040Ft) via **Cegléd.**

Buses: (☎41 39 99; www.agriavolan.hu) at the intersection of Nyugari u. and Széchenyi u. To: **Eger** (2½hr., 4 per day, 1392Ft); **Kecskemét** (5½hr., 1 per day, 2390Ft); **Miskolc** (2hr., every 30min.-1hr., 994Ft); **Szeged** (4-5½hr., 4 per day, 2390Ft); **Tokaj** (2hr., 2 per day, 894Ft).

Public Transportation: Public transport is the most convenient way to navigate the city. Tram #1 runs from the train station through Kálvin tér, loops around the park past the university, and heads back to Kálvin tér. Ticket checks are frequent and fines are menacing (2000-5000Ft); buy tickets from the kiosk by the train station (92Ft) or pay the driver (120Ft). Prices change frequently; current prices are posted on the back of the driver's seat. Once on board, validate your ticket in the blue punchers. Trams only stop on the way in; to return to the center of town you must ride the loop. Get off at *Varashaza* for tourist offices and most other necessities.

Taxis: ☎44 44 44 or 44 45 55.

▟✦▟ ORIENTATION AND PRACTICAL INFORMATION

The town center is a 15min. walk from the train station. Facing away from the station, head down Petofi tér, which becomes **Piac u.,** a main street which runs perpendicular to the station. Piac u. ends in **Kálvin tér,** where the huge yellow **Nagytemplom** (Great Church) presides over the center. Debrecen's other main hub lies about 3km farther along Piac u., which becomes **Péterfia u.** at Kálvin tér running north to **Nagyerdei Park** and **Kossuth Lajos Tudományegyetem** (KLTE; Kossuth Lajos Technical University). Trams and buses run to the center. Check with the info desk to the left of the ticket booths in the station for schedules and prices. The **bus station** is 10min. from the center. Exiting the station, turn right on **Széchenyi,** then make a left on Piac u., which opens into Kálvin tér.

Tourist Office: Tourinform, Piac u. 20, (☎41 22 50; fax 53 53 23; tourinform@ph.debrecen.hu), above Széchenyi u., under the eves of the cream-colored building to the right of the train station. Free maps and info on accommodations, food, and daytrips. Open May 15-Sept. 15 daily 8am-8pm; Sept. 16-May 14 M-F 9am-5pm.

Currency Exchange: Banks abound on Piac u. **OTP,** Hatvan u. 2/4 (☎50 65 00), **exchanges cash,** gives MC **cash advances,** accepts most **traveler's checks,** and has a 24hr. MC/V **ATM.** Open M-Tu and Th-F 7:45am-4pm, W 7:45am-5pm.

Pharmacy: Hatvan u. 1 (☎41 51 15). Open M-F 8:30am-6pm, Sa 8:30am-1pm.

Medical Assistance: Emergency room (☎41 43 33), at the intersection of Erzsébet u. and Szoboszlój u.—look for the blue-and-white *"Mentok, orro si ügyelet"* sign.

Internet: Hajdu Online Net Cafe, Kossuth u. 8 (☎53 67 24; www.haon.hu). 4-6Ft per min. Open daily 9am-midnight.

Post Office: Hatvan u. 5/9 (☎41 21 11). Open M-F 7am-7pm, Sa 7am-1pm.

Postal Code: 4025

⌐ ACCOMMODATIONS

Hajdútourist ❸, Kálvin tér 2 (☎41 55 88; fax 31 96 16), arranges centrally located **private rooms.** (Doubles 3000Ft. Tourist tax 120Ft. Open M-F 8am-5pm. AmEx/MC/V.) **IBUSZ ❷** does the same on Széchenyi u. near Piac u. (☎41 55 15; fax 41 07 56. Doubles 2800Ft; triples 3400Ft. Open M-F 8am-5:30pm, Sa 8am-noon. AmEx/MC/V.) In July and Aug., many **university dorms ❷** rent rooms (1300-2000Ft per person)—ask at Tourinform (see above), but be forewarned: many of the dorms it lists rent rooms to groups only; call first. Book rooms early during festival season, especially during the Flower Carnival (see **Sights and Entertainments,** below).

> **Pansio Stop,** Batthány u. 18 (☎42 03 01). From Kossuth tér, head down Piac u. and go left on Kossuth u.; Batthány u. will be on the right. The Pansio is located in a lovely courtyard. Clean and bright rooms. Breakfast 700Ft. Reception 24hr. Check-out 11am. Doubles with shower 5400Ft; triples with shower and TV 6900Ft. ❸

> **Hotel Fönix,** Barna u. 17 (☎41 30 54; fax 53 21 74). Close to the train station, right off Piac u. Rooms are spotless, albeit far from town and a bit stuffy. Breakfast 600Ft. Free luggage storage. Reception 24hr. Singles 2800Ft, with shower 4300Ft; doubles 4800Ft/7400Ft; extra bed 1000Ft. 200Ft tourist tax. MC/V. ❸

THE HIDDEN DEAL

WINE WITH A VIEW

Before or after a day of hiking, muster up the energy to climb the 3km hill to get to Panorama Etterem Panzio, Hegalya u. #14.

Share a visit with the owner of this peaceful and breathtakingly beautiful viewpoint. Tastings here are as cheap as they get; taste 5 1dL glasses for 400Ft. Skip the cheese plate and order the bread with eggplant spread or the Palacsinta with homemade jam—both house specialties. The winery has been located here for 150 years, and the cellar is worth a peek. Though Tibor has only been the proprietor for 15 years, he prides himself on upholding the traditions of the cellar.

There is no skimping at Panorama; if the wine makes your trip back down the hill difficult, have no fear! This *panzio* is clean, comfortable and extremely affordable. *(Hegalya u. 14. Climb 3km uphill until you reach Hegalya u. Instead of stopping at the first winery, the Barmúzeum Pince, continue along the road, past the part where the cobblestone ends. Keep walking until you see the sign on your left. ☎43 15 93. Quads 12000-13200. Breakfast included. Reservations recommended.)*

—Sandra Nagy

Termál Camping, Nagyerdei Körút 102 (☎41 24 56; fax 53 20 46; hajdutourist@matav-net.hu), hidden in Nagyerdei Park. From the train station take tram #1 or bus #10 or 14. Get off the tram once in the park—you'll see Hotel Termál on the left—follow the tracks until you hit Nagyerdei Körút. Turn right; the campground is 5min. down the road. A restaurant on the premises serves breakfast (600Ft), lunch (1100Ft), and dinner (1000Ft). Reserve 1 month ahead for July and Aug. Open May-Sept. Tent 1150Ft; bungalows 3200Ft, with shower 6000Ft plus 200Ft per person. May-June and Sept. bungalows 2800Ft/4400Ft. Tourist tax 200Ft. AmEx/MC/V. ❷

Centrum Pension, Péterfia u. 37/a. Uniquely decorated, comfortable, and air-conditioned. Peaceful green and floral garden with lounge chairs, swings, and a shower among the many amenities. The owners offer horse rides with a trainer on their horse farm. All rooms have baths. Breakfast 900Ft. Horse rides 2000Ft per hr. Singles 6500Ft; doubles 6900-7600Ft; 2-bed apartment 8600-10,600Ft; 3- to 4-bed apartment 10,000-16,000Ft. Tax 12%. ❺

🍴 FOOD

The **Match Supermarket** at the Debrecen Plaza, Péterfia u. 18, is well stocked. (Open M-F 7am-9pm, Sa 6am-9pm, Su 7am-8pm.) The tiny **supermarket** at Hatvan u. 8 is open 24hr.

Csokonai Söröző, Kossuth u. 21 (☎41 08 02), in a classy, candle-lit cellar. The city's easiest menu includes English translations and photographs of its excellent meals. Entrees 750-1200Ft. Veggie soups and salads 450-800Ft. Open daily noon-11pm. ❷

Sütöde, off Kossuth u. Walk down Kossuth u. from Piac u. Make a right down the small alley across from the parking lot or follow the delicious aroma from several blocks away. Sütöde is a small, store-front bread stand where locals get their daily supply of sweet-smelling breads. Bread 100Ft per kg. Open M-F 7am-7pm, Sa 8am-2pm. ❶

University Dining Halls, Egyetm tér. Keeping to the right, walk behind the main university building on Egyetem tér, and then head to the right of the white-pillared buildings. Once under the cross-bridge, you'll find the "Menza" on the 2nd floor of the white building. Offers lunch for 100-250Ft during the school year, with cheap leftovers until approximately 4pm for 50-100Ft. Open Sept. to mid-June daily 11:30am-2:30pm. ❶

👁 SIGHTS

GREAT CHURCH. Hungary's largest Protestant church and Debrecen's town symbol, the twin-spired 1863 Great Church (Nagytemplom) looms over Kálvin tér's northern end. The bell tower offers a great view of the town, if you get that far—the narrow wooden stairs become progressively steeper and more rickety toward the top. Hear the huge organ in action every F at noon. (☎41 26 94. Open Apr.-Oct. M-F 9am-noon and 2-6pm, Sa 9am-noon, Su 1-4pm; Nov.-Mar. M-F 10am-noon, Su 1-3pm. 60Ft, students 30Ft. Concerts 1hr., free.)

REFORMÁTUS KOLLÉGIUM. The Református Kollégium, Kálvin tér 16, behind the church, was established in 1538 as a center for Protestant education. The present building housed the government of Hungary twice—in 1849, when Lajos Kossuth led the Parliament in the Oratory, and again in 1944. Today it houses Calvinist schools, as well as a collection of religious art; the highlight, though, is the 650,000-volume library with 16th-century Bibles and other Bibles in 214 languages. (☎41 47 44. Open Tu-Sa 9am-5pm, Su 9am-1pm. 160Ft. English info 200Ft.)

DÉRI MUSEUM. The Déri Museum displays a collection ranging from local tinware-craft to Japanese lacquerware. Awe-inspiring murals by Hungarian artist **Mihály Munkácsy** depicting Christ's trial and crucifixion are displayed upstairs.

Spot the artist's self-portrait in *Ecce Homo* as an old man in the crowd, next to the arch. Coming from Kossuth tér, steer left of the Great Church and turn left on to Múzeum u.—the museum is on the right, flanked by the sculpture garden. (☎41 75 77. *Open Nov.-Mar. Tu-Su 10am-4pm; Apr.-Oct. Tu-Su 10am-6pm. 300Ft, students 200Ft; special exhibits 100Ft. No cameras.*)

♫ ENTERTAINMENT

Most of Debrecen's youths congregate in **Nagyerdei Park,** where bike lanes, bars, tattoo salons, paddle boats, and leering young men lounging in tank tops speckle the land. There is also an **amusement park.** At the park's **municipal thermal bath,** you can soak in the steamy baths with nude Debreceners. (☎51 41 00; fax 34 68 83. Open M-F 7:45am-noon and 12:45-5pm. Thermal bath 550Ft, students 460Ft. Sauna open Sept.-May M 1-10pm, Th-F 11am-10pm, Sa-Su 6-8pm. 650Ft for 2hr.)

The official festival season runs from June to August, but really gets kicked off every spring when the **Jazz Days** bring well-known musicians and bands to town. In July on even years, the **Béla Bartók Choir Festival** attracts choirs worldwide. The season culminates in the popular **Flower Carnival** parade on August 20. For more information on any of these festivals, call ☎31 93 11. **Tourinform** (see p. 368) can provide schedules and often tickets for all festivals.

At night, head to the smoky **El Tornado,** Pallagi u. 2, in Nagyerdei Park. This saloon-style pub cranks out country music when the mood strikes. (☎34 05 90. 0.5L *Borsodi* 200Ft. Open daily 5pm-4am.) The **John Bull Pub,** Piac u. 28, makes patrons believe they are really in England. In the fall and winter, enjoy live music on Friday and Saturday. From May to Oct., an open patio sets the stage for weekend cocktail parties. (☎42 20 36. Guinness 350-1750Ft. Lager 290-1450Ft. Open M-Sa 10am-1am, Su 10am-midnight.) The more mellow **Yes Jazz Bár,** Kálvin tér 4, is usually filled with quiet conversation set in time to live jazz and blues. (☎41 85 22. Budweiser 390Ft; Guinness 410Ft. Open M-Sa midnight-4am, Su 5pm-4am.) With its nine air-conditioned theaters, **Cinema City,** Pétrifia u. 18 (☎45 61 11), on the 2nd floor of Debrecen Plaza, offers refuge from the oppressive summer heat.

SZEGED ☎(0)62

The easygoing charm of the Great Plain's cultural capital has prompted some to describe Szeged (SAY-ged) as a Mediterranean town on the Tisza. After an 1879 flood practically wiped out the city, streets were laid out in orderly curves punctuated by large, stately squares. The result of this reconstruction is a quiet, cosmopolitan atmosphere that more closely resembles Europe's seaside cities than anything else to be found in landlocked Hungary. Instead of the usual Baroque facades, rows of colorful art nouveau buildings evince a lively and lovely architectural mood that complements Szeged's swinging social scene.

▐ TRANSPORTATION

Trains: Szeged pu. (☎42 18 21 or 42 44 83; www.elvira.hu), on Indóház tér on the west bank of the Tisza. International ticket office on 2nd floor. Open daily 6am-5:45pm. To: **Budapest** (2½hr., 15 per day, 1556Ft); **Debrecen** (3-4hr., 3 per day, 2040Ft) via **Cegléd; Kecskemét** (1-1¼hr., 15 per day, 678Ft).

Buses: (☎55 11 66 and 55 11 60), on Mars tér. To reach the bus station, continue 2 more stops from the train stop at Széchenyi tér to the corner of Pacsirta u. and Kossuth L. sugárút. Continue in the same direction as the tram, turning left on Pacsirta u. and walk 2 blocks to reach Mars tér. From the station, cross the street at the lights and follow Mikszáth Kálmán u. toward the Tisza. This intersects Széchenyi tér after becoming

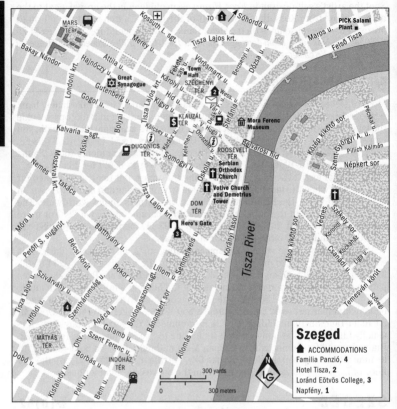

Szeged

■ ACCOMMODATIONS
Familia Panzió, **4**
Hotel Tisza, **2**
Loránd Eötvös College, **3**
Napfény, **1**

Károlyi u. To: **Budapest** (3½hr., 7 per day, 1688Ft); **Eger** (5hr., 2 per day, 2260Ft); **Debrecen** (5¼hr., 2-4 per day, 2390Ft); **Győr** (6hr., 2 per day, 2670Ft); **Kecskemét** (1¾hr., 10-14 per day, 894Ft); **Pécs** (4½hr., 7 per day, 1936Ft).

Public Transportation: Tram #1 connects the train station with Széchenyi tér (4-5 stops). Otherwise it's a 20min. walk. Tickets from kiosks 90Ft; from the driver 110Ft. The fine for riding ticketless is 1500Ft.

Taxis: ☎ 44 44 44, 47 04 70, or 48 04 80. 100Ft base fare plus 150Ft per km. Students approx. 100Ft per km with no base fare.

■✴ 🛈 ORIENTATION AND PRACTICAL INFORMATION

Szeged is divided by the **Tisza River,** with the city center on the west bank and the parks and residences of **Újszeged** (New Szeged) to the east. The city center forms a semicircle against the river, bounded by **Tisza Lajos krt** and centered at **Széchenyi tér,** the main square. Across **Híd u.** (Bridge St.) from Széchenyi, shops and cafes cluster on the pedestrian **Klauzál tér.** Large multilingual **maps** are sold in kiosks.

Tourist Office: Tourinform, Dugonics tér 2 (☎/fax 48 86 90; szeged@tourinform.hu). From the tram stop at Széchenyi tér and Vár u., head back along the tracks for 3 blocks and turn left on Oroszlán u. Offers free maps and accommodations info. Open M-F 10am-6pm.

Currency Exchange: OTP, Klauzál tér 5 (☎48 03 80), cashes **traveler's checks** for no commission and gives MC/V **cash advances.** Open M-W and F 7:45am-4pm, Th 7:45am-5pm. **Budapest Bank Ltd.,** Klauzál tér 4 (☎48 55 85), doubles as a **Western Union** and has a 24hr. MC/V **ATM** outside. Open M-F 8am-5pm.

Luggage Storage: At the train station. 100Ft per bag 4am-4pm, 200Ft 4-11pm. Open daily 4am-11pm.

24-Hour Pharmacy: Kígyó Richter Referenciapatika, Klauzál tér 3 (☎420 131). Ring bell outside 8pm-7am.

Medical Assistance: Kossuth Lagos sgt. 15/17 (☎47 43 74). From the Town Hall, walk up the center of Széchenyi tér, turn left on Vörösmarty u., and continue as it becomes Kossuth Lagos sgt. The **medical center** is at the intersection with Szilágyi u. Open M-F 5:30pm-7:30am, Sa 7:30am-M 7:30am. Ring bell after hours.

Internet Access: Cyber Arena, Híd u. 1 (☎92 28 15). 8am-midnight 5Ft per min.; midnight-8am 4Ft per min. Open 24hr. **Matrix Internet Cafe,** Kárász u. 5 (☎42 38 30). 10am-10pm 5Ft per min.; 10pm-10am 4Ft per min.; Sa 10pm-M 10am 3Ft per min. Open 24hr.

Post Office: Széchenyi tér 1 (☎47 62 76), at the intersection with Híd u. Open M-F 8am-8pm, Sa 8am-2pm, Su 8am-noon.

Postal Code: 6720.

ACCOMMODATIONS

Tourinform (see above) has info on **pensions** and other accommodations. **IBUSZ ❸,** Oroszlán u. 3 (☎/fax 47 11 77), will hook you up with a private room in a flat (3000-3500Ft; additional 30% for stays fewer than 4 nights). University dorms are generally cheapest, but are only available in July and August.

Hotel Tisza, Széchenyi tér 3 (☎/fax 47 82 78; www.tiszahotel.hu). In the center of town, this elegant 1886 hotel was once frequented by the artistic elite: Béla Bartók performed in its concert hall and its restaurant was a favorite among Hungarian literary figures. Today, it offers a few rooms at reasonable prices. Breakfast included. Reception 24hr. Check-out noon. Singles 5880Ft, with shower and sink 7480Ft; doubles 9800/11900Ft; triples 17,900Ft-19,900Ft. ❹

Familia Panzió, Szentháromság u. 71 (☎44 18 02; fax 44 16 16). About a 15min. walk from the center, but buses and trams run regularly. A few hundred meters from the train station, this family-run pension is clean and comfortable. Nice-sized rooms clad in wooden paneling. Breakfast included. Doubles 4000Ft, with bath 5400Ft; triples and quads offered, but prices vary. ❸

Loránd Eötvös College, Tisza Lajos krt. 103 (☎54 41 24). The hostel is to the left of Hero's Gate; its entrance is hidden from the street, to the left of the restaurant. Cheap, central dorms with mosquito-proof screens and clean bathrooms. Well-lit and pleasant. Laundry service included. Open July-Aug. Doubles 2100Ft. ❷

Napfény, Dorozsmai u. 4 (☎42 18 00; fax 46 75 79). Take tram #1 to the last stop, go up the overpass, then turn right. After 10min. you'll see Napfény on the left. Next to route E75, this hotel and campground feels like a typical highway motel. An agreeable place to crash for the night with 2 restaurants to boot. Reception 24hr. Singles 2900-7600Ft; doubles 9900Ft; tent space 3800Ft. ❸

THE LOCAL STORY

ESCAPE FROM HUNGARY

Gyuri was born and raised in a small village 30km from Miskolc, and is now a restaurant proprietor in Budapest. He is one of the last members of his family remaining in Hungary and was interviewed by Let's Go Researcher Sandra Nagy.

Q: Can you describe what it meant to live under Communist rule, and to have to escape Hungary?

A: Along with [Communism] came serious restrictions about travel, which severely inhibited the ability to escape. I will tell you the story of my cousins and how they got out...

Back then, in 1970, getting out of the country for a vacation was only granted every three years. You had to apply for a vacation voucher and there were restricted allowances. However, football [soccer] games, which were often played in Austria, were special circumstances. You could be guaranteed an allowance to go to a game in Austria if you went over the border in the morning and came back at night. The buses were checked as they left, lists were made of those on board, and each person was checked off as they returned. As times became a bit more lax, you were sometimes able to leave for three days at a time, which didn't count against your three-year vacation allowance. My cousins escaped by going to a soccer game in Graz [Austria] and never returning.

(continued on next page)

⚑ FOOD

Szeged is home to Hungary's finest lunchmeat—always pick salami—and is the best place for *halászlé* (spicy soup made with fresh Tisza fish). Keep in mind that it is taboo to order water with your soup, as it takes away the paprika flavor; it tastes better with wine or beer anyway. The 24hr. **ABC market** on Mars tér, near the corner of Londoni krt. and Mikszáth Kálmán u., provides late-night sustenance. **Szeged Pick Korzó Márkaáruház,** at the corner of Karasz u. and Kölcsey u., sells all sorts of salami. (☎42 65 17. Open M-F 6am-8pm, Sa 7am-2pm.)

▨ **Roosevelt téri Halászcsárda,** Roosevelt tér 14 (☎42 41 11 or 55 59 80). Next to the river, across from the Móra Ferenc Museum. Sit on the peaceful shaded terrace or in the vaulted dining room and let the famously spicy *szegedi halászlé* or any of the *hallé* (fish soup) dishes with fiery green paprika and delicious bread on the side appease your tastebuds. Vegetarian options. Entrees 500-3400Ft. Open daily 11am-11pm. ❸

Belvárosi Kikötö, Stefánia 4 (☎43 22 33), across from Roosevelt tér. This kitschy, ship-like restaurant specializes in "lava rock grilling," a process in which gravy is steamed with meat. Great veggie options, and the kids' meal names are good for a laugh. Live jazz almost every night. Outdoor performances in summer. Entrees 850-2450Ft. Restaurant open daily 11am-midnight; bar open daily noon-3am. ❹

Roxy Cafe and Pizzeria, Deák Ferenc u. 24 (☎42 34 96). Chic restaurant serves pizza (350-800Ft), pasta (500-600Ft), and a daily vegetarian platter (600Ft) to Szeged's hippest university students. A perfect post-party, pre-hangover stop. Closed for renovations in 2002, but reopening by 2003. Open M-Th 10am-midnight, F 10am-2am, Sa noon-2am, Su noon-midnight. ❷

Aranykorona Étterem, Victor Hugo u. 6 (☎42 57 04). Traditional Hungarian and vegetarian dishes served in the dining room, garden, and sidewalk cafe. Entrees 590-1750Ft. Open M-F 11:30am-10pm, Sa 11:30am-midnight, Su 11:30am-5pm. ❸

◉ SIGHTS

▨ **SYNAGOGUE.** (Zsinagóga.) Widely acknowledged as the most beautiful of its kind in Hungary, and ranked one of the ten most beautiful in Europe, this 1903 synagogue is an awe-inspiring display of craftmanship and an amalgam of styles, with Moorish altars and gardens, Romanesque columns, Gothic domes, and Baroque facades. The cupola, decorated with symbols of infinity and faith, symbolizes the world, and it grows more profound the longer you look up at it. The Hebrew script on the supporting pillars testifies to the three fundamental principles of Jewish liturgy: Torah, Sermons, and Philanthropy. Its 24 columns stand for both the 24 hours in a day and the 24 books of the Old Testament. The vestibule walls are lined with the names of the 3100 members of the congregation killed in concentration camps. Today's small Jewish community still comes here to worship each Sabbath. *(Jósika u. 8. From Széchenyi tér, walk away from the river along Híd u. through Bartók tér; turn left on Jósika. The synagogue is on the left. Open Su-F 10am-noon and 1-5pm. Closed on holy days. 200Ft, students 100Ft.)*

MÓRA FERENC MUSEUM. This riverside museum houses an eclectic collection of 18th- to 20th-century folk art in a gorgeous Neoclassical palace. The first floor details the life of the long-vanished Avar tribe with an impressive series of yarn-haired papier-maché mannequins. Check out Spányi Béla's Forest *(Erdö)* paintings in the hall on the way to the Avar Display, and be sure to take a look at the panoramic paintings depicting Szeged during the great flood of 1879. *(Roosevelt tér 1/3. From Széchenyi tér, turn right on Vár u., which brings you to Roosevelt tér. Open July-Sept. Tu-Su 10am-6pm; Oct.-June Tu-Su 10am-5pm. Hours are subject to change; call before making the trip. 300Ft, students 150Ft.)*

VOTIVE CHURCH. (Fogadalmi Templom.) This neo-Romanesque, red-brick church pierces the skyline with its two 91m towers, each with four clocks displaying the wrong time. The church was built after the 1930 flood in the hope that the architecture would ward off future deluges. Hungary's fourth-largest church houses a 9740-pipe organ that sometimes performs afternoon concerts. The dome at the front of the church, above the first set of pews, sends even the non-religious imagination to a majestic and mystic place. The 12th-century **Demetrius Tower** (Dömötör Torony) is all that remains of the church that originally stood on the site. On the walls surrounding the church, in bright colors laden with gold, the **National Pantheon** portrays Hungary's great political, literary, and artistic figures. *(From Széchenyi tér, turn left on Híd u., then right on Oskola u., which leads to Dom tér. Open Tu-Sa 8am-6pm, Su 12:30-6pm.)*

OTHER SIGHTS. The yellow **Town Hall** (Városháza), reshingled with red-and-green ceramic tiles after the 1879 deluge, overlooks grassy Széchenyi tér. A bridge

Q: So, what happened when someone was missing from the bus when it returned to Hungary?

A: You had to predetermine and plan the act. I went to meet the bus to pretend as though I had no idea that they were not coming back. I waited until the bus emptied and went to the guard to inquire about the whereabouts of my cousins. They told me that they never came back. Somehow, and I really don't know how, I mustered up tears—I think they were of joy! You had to pretend you knew nothing, or they would throw you in jail. The whole family had to put on this charade of ignorance, especially my uncle, who was taken into the police station for questioning the next day. He had to act sad and horrified that anyone would want to leave the "great" Hungarian lifestyle.

Q: So, how did you find out that they were okay? When did you speak with them next?

A: About three weeks after they left, one of my cousins wrote an apology letter to her father in an effort to clear him of any repercussions. She praised Hungary as a country and said that she was not leaving because of anything bad here. She said that she wanted to explore the world, and escaping was the only way to achieve her goal. Writing the letter was a way of further enhancing the smokescreen around their escape. At one point, they were able to call and talk in a predefined code so that no one would catch on. We were all so happy to hear from them and were relieved that the plan had worked.

joining the bright building to the drab former tax office next door was built so Hapsburg Emperor Franz Joseph wouldn't have to take the stairs. *(Széchenyi tér 10.)* The 1778 Serbian Orthodox Church (Palánki Szerb Templom) features impressive artwork. The iconostasis holds 80 gilt-framed paintings, while the ceiling fresco of God creating the Earth is covered with stars. *(Somogyi u. 3a. ☎32 52 78. Open by request.)* **Hero's Gate** (Hősök Kapuja) was erected in 1936 to honor Horthy's White Guards, who brutally cleansed the nation of "Reds." *(Start at Dóm tér and head away from the center to reach the gate, in the adjacent Aradi Vértanuk tér.)*

🎵 📷 ENTERTAINMENT AND NIGHTLIFE

The **Szeged Open Air Festival,** held from early July to late Aug., is Hungary's largest outdoor performance event. International troupes perform folk dances, operas, and musicals in the amphitheater, with the looming church as a backdrop. Buy tickets (700-3000Ft) at Tourinform (see **Orientation and Practical Information,** p. 392) or at Deák u. 28/30. (☎47 14 66; fax 47 13 22; www.tiszanet.hu/szabadteri. Open M-F 10am-5pm.) Other festivals make their way to Szeged's streets from early spring until late autumn. From the **wine festival** to the **jazz jamboree,** the vivacity of Szeged fails to go unnoticed. Swimming pools and baths line the **Partfürdo Strand;** from Szeged, cross the Belváros bridge and walk left along the river. Most of these establishments are open daily and charge 300-600Ft admission. **Bike paths** line the city streets, and **kayaking** is available along the Tisza River. Though the green water looks less than appealing, locals claim it's safe enough for a dip. To rent equipment, contact **Vizisporttelep** at Felsö-Tisza purt 4 (☎42 55 74). Shop for Communist-era relics at Szeged's vintage clothing stores, such as **Ciánkáli Underground Second Hand,** Déák Ferenc u. 26. (Open M-F 10am-6pm, Sa 10am-2pm.) Ask at Tourinform for info on **gay and lesbian nightlife.**

Grand Cafe, Deák Ferenc u. 18, 3rd fl. (☎42 05 78). Skip the strobes and save your voice at Sophisticate Central. Here you can watch films in the art movie theater or sip red wine to mellow jazz. Open Sept.-June M-F 3pm-midnight, Sa-Su 5pm-midnight.

Gin-tonic Club, Wesselényi u. 1 (☎55 95 59), in the Tisza Hotel building. Terrifically chic and well-decorated underground vault where the stylish get drunk and get down. Beer 230-520Ft. W karaoke. Sa live music. Cover F-Sa 500Ft. Open W-Sa 8pm-late.

HBH Bajor Serfőzde (Beer House), Deák Ferenc u. 4 (☎42 03 94). In the center of the city. A major sponsor of Szeged's annual beer festival, this local pub also serves fried grub. 168-380Ft. Open M-Sa 11:30am-midnight, Su 11:30am-11pm.

Sing-Sing, on Mars tér. The DJ churns out popular beats for a ready-to-rave crowd. W and Sa brings a young, dance-loving group. 0.5L Amstel 400Ft. Open daily 11pm-dawn.

KECSKEMÉT ☎(0)76

Surrounded by vineyards, fruit groves, and dusty *puszta* (plains), Kecskemét (KETCH-keh-MATE) lures tourists with its park-like central square, its famous *barack pálinka* (apricot brandy), and the musical genius of native composer Zoltán Kodály (1882-1967). First described in 1368 as a market town, "the garden city" sprung up as the crossing point of trade routes between Istanbul and Hamburg. Today, Kecskemét is celebrated for its exceptional and eclectic architecture, best epitomized in its pink art nouveau town hall, which was inspired by the motto of the contest for which it was designed: "Neither height nor depth deter me."

HUNGARY

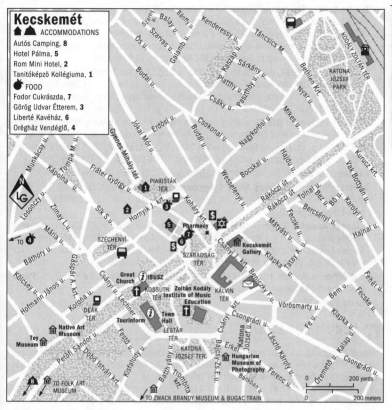

Kecskemét

▲▲ ACCOMMODATIONS
Autós Camping, 8
Hotel Pálma, 5
Rom Mini Hotel, 2
Tanítóképző Kollégiuma, 1

🍎 FOOD
Fodor Cukrászda, 7
Görög Udvar Étterem, 3
Liberté Kavéház, 6
OreghÁz Vendéglő, 4

TRANSPORTATION

Trains: (☎32 24 60; www.elvira.hu), on Kodály Zoltán tér, at the end of Rákóczi út. To: **Budapest** (1½-2hr.; 13 per day; 926Ft, *InterCity* 880Ft); **Pécs** (5hr., 12 per day, 2326Ft) via **Kiskunfélegyháza; Szeged** (1¼hr., 17 per day, 678Ft).

Buses: (☎32 17 77; www.agria.hu/agriavolan), on Kodály Zoltán tér. To: **Budapest** (1½hr., 26 per day, 894Ft); **Debrecen** (5hr., 1 per day, 2390Ft); **Eger** (2½hr., 3 per day, 1884Ft); **Pécs** (5hr., 3 per day, 1992Ft); **Szeged** (1¾hr., 13 per day, 894Ft).

Public Transportation: The main local **Volán** bus terminal is a block away from Kossuth tér; turn right from the terminal on Sík S. Timetables are posted at most stops—service ends around 10pm. 90Ft from kiosks, 105Ft from the driver. Prices change frequently.

ORIENTATION AND PRACTICAL INFORMATION

The town sprawls around a loosely connected string of squares. The largest, **Szabadság tér** (Liberty Square), is orbited by three satellite squares, **Kossuth tér, Kálvin tér,** and **Széchenyi tér.** To get to Szabadság tér from the **train station,** turn left as you exit the station, head straight, and then make a right on Rákóczi út. as the road turns. Follow the street for 10min. until you hit the square. The **bus station** is around the corner on the right from the train station.

Tourist Office: Tourinform, Kossuth tér 1 (☎/fax 48 10 65; kecskemet@tourinform.hu; www.kecskemet.hu). From the train station, follow Rákóczi út. through the park at Szabadság tér, then head toward the corner of the pink town hall. Staff sells maps, arranges accommodations, and provides information on local events. Open July-Aug. M-F 8am-6pm, Sa 9am-1pm; Sept.-June M-F 8am-5pm, Sa 9am-1pm.

Budget Travel: IBUSZ, Kossuth tér 3 (☎/fax 480 557), in the Aranyhomok hotel. Assists with visas, books rooms, and arranges international bus, train, and plane tickets. Student discounts on certain international planes, trains, and buses. Open summer M-F 8am-12:30pm and 1-4:45pm. MC/V.

Currency Exchange: OTP, Szabadság tér 1/a (☎51 74 78), at Arany János u., has the best rates in town and cashes traveler's checks for no commission. Open M-W and F 7:45am-4pm, Th 7:45am-5pm. There's a 24hr. MC/V **ATM** outside. A **branch** is by the old synagogue on Koháry I. krt. Open M-W and F 7:45am-5pm, Th 7:45am-6pm.

Luggage Storage: At the train station. 150Ft per day. Open daily 7am-7pm.

24-Hour Pharmacy: Mátyás Kírály Gyógyszertár, Szabadság tér 1 (☎48 07 39). Open M-F 7:30am-8pm, Sa 8am-4pm, Su 8am-2pm. Ring bell after hours. 100Ft extra if you aren't filling a prescription.

Internet Access: Piramis Internet Cafe, Csányi u. 1-3 (☎41 83 14; piramis-cafe@yahoo.com), in the Hotel Udvarház courtyard. 480Ft per hr. Open M-F 10am-8pm, Sa-Su 1-8pm. **Katona József Library,** Piaristák tér 8 (☎50 05 60; fax 50 05 70; www.kjmk.hu). Become a member (600Ft) to get 1hr. online per day.

Post Office: Kálvin tér 10/12 (☎48 65 86). Open M-F 8am-8pm, Sa 8am-2pm. **Poste Restante** available.

Postal Code: 6000.

▟ ACCOMMODATIONS

Winter brings all sorts of bargains, but summer travelers should consider booking ahead. While some are overpriced, pensions are the best deal in town. Most tourist agencies (see **Orientation and Practical Information,** p. 397) can help you locate an affordable bed. **IBUSZ ❸** rents private 4-bed flats near the center, and can locate equally convenient pensions. Prices range from 3500 to 9000Ft.

Hotel Pálma, Arany János u. 3 (☎/fax 32 10 45), in the heart of the city. From Tourinform, turn left 1 block past McDonald's; the hotel is in the sea-green building on the right. This calm, ex-college dorm with beachy decor offers great service and clean, well-sized rooms. First-class rooms are larger and air-conditioned. English spoken. Breakfast 400Ft. Reception 24hr. Check-out 10am. Book ahead 1-2 days. 1st class: Singles 5400Ft; doubles 7000Ft; triples 8100Ft. 2nd class: 3500Ft/5800Ft/6200Ft. ❹

Rom Mini Hotel, Széchenyi tér 14 (☎/fax 48 31 74). The clean and air-conditioned rooms of Rom Mini, equipped with private baths, are coupled with a central location. The owner is extremely helpful in providing information about activities around the area. Breakfast available at the Sörözo (500Ft). Doubles 5000Ft. ❸

Tanitóképzö Kollégiuma (Teacher's College), Piaristák tér 4 (☎48 69 77; fax 48 07 67), 5min. from Kossuth tér. Coming from the train station, turn right on Koháry I. krt. and follow it to where it forks at Piaristák tér. The Kollégiuma is on the right. Serviceable and convenient. Laundry 150Ft. Reception 8am-2am. Call 1-2 days ahead. Rooms are let in triples and quads on a per-person basis; 1600 Ft, students 1200Ft. ❷

Autós Camping, Csabay Gréza Krl. 5 (☎32 93 98). 15min. southwest of town on Volán bus #1 or 11. Get off at the swimming pool and follow the signs to this somewhat sandy site. Open Apr. 15-Oct. 15. 600Ft per person; tents 500Ft; 2-person caravans 1500Ft; 4-bed bungalows 5500Ft. Tax 100Ft per person; students and seniors not taxed. Electricity 600Ft. AmEx/MC/V. ❶

◉ FOOD

Kecskemét is the home of apricots; not surprisingly, it is also the home of apricot brandy *(Palinka)*. Don't let the sweet name fool you: it may taste great, but even small amounts have been known to put the biggest drinker under the table. **Coop supermarket,** Deák tér 6, fulfills more practical culinary needs; there's a drugstore and cafe inside as well. (☎48 17 11. Market open M-F 6:30am-7pm, Sa 6am-1pm.)

⊠ **Liberté Kavéház,** Szabadság tér 2 (☎48 03 50), offers outdoor dining on the park and formal dining inside. Hungarian specialties served in a plush, leafy atmosphere perfect for lingering. English menu. *Goulash* 650Ft. Entrees 490-1990Ft. Open daily 9am-11pm. AmEx/MC/V. ❸

Görög Udvar Étterem, Hornyik J. 1 (☎49 25 13). This Greek oasis serves terrific *souvlaki* (1000Ft), *gyros* (850Ft), veggie pita (800Ft), and traditional Hungarian fare. Entrees 800-1800Ft. Open daily 10am-11pm. ❸

Öregház Vendéglő, Hosszú ut. 27 (☎49 69 73). From Széchenyi tér, follow Mária ut. for 2 blocks to the intersection with Hosszú ut. Large portions of Hungarian-style meat 'n potatoes in a spacious neighborhood restaurant. *Öregháztáls* are platters of food fit to feed 2-3 people. Entrees 500-690Ft; 20% off Sa-Su 11am-3pm. Open daily 11am-10pm; last seating 10:15pm. ❷

Fodor Cukrászda, adjacent to Liberté Kavéház (see above). Tasty dessert (100-450Ft) or ice cream (60Ft). Open June-Aug. daily 9am-8:30pm; Sept.-May 9am-6:30pm.

◎ SIGHTS

The salmon-colored **town hall,** Kossuth tér 1, was built in 1897 during the height of the Hungarian art nouveau movement; its pink facade and painted Gala Hall serve as excellent examples of the style. It dominates Kecskemét's main square, and its glockenspiel bells chime the songs of the Kecskemét-native composer Zoltán Kodály. The **Zoltán Kodály Institute of Music Education** is nearby at Kéttemplom-Köz 1/3, set back from the street in what was once a Franciscan monastery. The 1806 Roman Catholic **Great Church** asserts itself with marble columns and an interior of elaborate frescoes. (Usually open Tu-F 9am-noon and 3-6pm.) From the entrance of the right side of the Church you can climb the tower to get a good view of Kecskemét. (Open daily 10am-8pm. 200Ft, students 100Ft.)

The cupola-topped synagogue at Rákóczi ú. 2 is now the **House of Science and Technics.** The former synagogue irreverently boasts 15 fake Michelangelo sculptures. (☎48 76 11. Open M-F 10am-4pm. Free.) The **Lekowsky Musical Instrument Collection,** Zimay u. 6/a, houses a private collection of Hungarian and European instruments. (Open M-Sa 9am-5pm. 500Ft, students 300Ft.)

🏛 MUSEUMS

MUSEUM OF NATIVE ARTISTS. (Naív Művészek Múzeum.) This museum fills halls with the often-intriguing work of local amateurs. *(Gáspár András u. 11. ☎32 47 67. Follow Déak Ferenc tér away from the Great Church. At the second major intersection of Deák Ferenc, turn right on Dobó István Körút; the entrance is on the left behind the strip mall. Open Tu-Su 10am-5pm. 150Ft, students 50Ft.)*

TOY MUSEUM. (Szórakaténusz Játékmúzeum és Műhely.) Houses a fun collection of antique miniature trains, castles, and dolls and offers hands-on workshops for children. *(Gáspár András u. 11. ☎48 14 69. Museum open Mar. 15-Dec. 31 Tu-Su 10am-12:30pm and 1-5pm. Toymaker's workshop open Mar. 15-Dec. 31 W and Sa 10am-12:30pm and 2:30-5pm, Su 10am-2pm. 200Ft, students 100Ft; Su free.)*

MUSEUM OF HUNGARIAN APPLIED FOLK ART. (Magyar Népi Iparművészet Múzeuma.) The extensive collection of costumes, furniture, ceramics, horse whips, and high-concept gingerbread fosters appreciation for Hungarian folk art. *(Serfőző u. 19. ☎/fax 32 72 03. From Tourinform (see p. 398), turn left on the main street and follow it as it becomes Petőfi Sandor and Dózsa Gy. út. Take the first right after the Arpád Körút onto Lajita u. and go left on Serfőző; the museum is on the right (10min.). Open Jan. 15-Dec. 14 Tu-Sa 10am-5pm. 200Ft, students 100Ft.)*

HUNGARIAN MUSEUM OF PHOTOGRAPHY. (Magyar Fotográfiai Múzeum.) The only one of its kind in Hungary, this photography museum features constantly changing exhibits. *(Katona József tér 12. ☎48 32 21; www.c3.hu/~fotomuz. Open W-Su 10am-5pm. 150Ft, students 100Ft.)*

KECSKEMÉT GALLERY. (Kecskeméti Képtár.) Once a boarding house with a casino and ballroom, the gallery now features undulating walls with ultra-modern tiles and colorful peacock reliefs. While it also displays the work of local artists, the gallery's gorgeous-if-gaudy building is the main attraction. *(Rákóczi ú. 1. ☎48 00 76, across the square from the town hall. Open Tu-Sa 10am-5pm, Su 1:30-5pm; last admission 30min. before closing. 200Ft, students 60Ft.)*

▐▌ ▐▌ ENTERTAINMENT AND NIGHTLIFE

Shakespeare may lose something in translation, but the elegant stage at the **Katona József Theater** *(Színhaz)*, Katona tér 5, lends grace to any script. (☎48 32 83; www.kecskemet.hu/szinhaz. Tickets 1300Ft and up. Box office open Sept.-June M-F 10am-7pm.) Kecskemét's artistic tradition continues each March with the **Kecskemét Spring Festival,** which features music, theater, and literary readings. During the last week of Aug. and early Sept., the Hungarian food industry dishes out its best culinary creations at the **Hírös Food Festival.**

At **Xtreme Music Club,** the latest and greatest DJ spins tunes for the "hip" crowd in town. (☎50 09 27. Call ahead for DJ line-up and opening hours.) For a more laid-back evening, try **Kilele Music Cafe,** Jokai 34. The sign outside may suggest a raging inferno, but the downstairs is more cool than hot, with live jazz on Thursday and disco on Saturday. (☎32 67 74. Beer 150-380Ft. Cover Sa only 400Ft. Open M-F 5pm-2am, Sa 6pm-3:30am, Su 6pm-1am.)

NORTHERN HUNGARY

Hungary's northern upland is dominated by a series of six low mountain ranges running northeast from the Danube Bend along the Slovak border. The mountains' soils yield unique wines and their terrain provides endless opportunities for outdoor exploration. From the famous wines of Eger and Tokaj to the Lipizzaner ponies of Szilvásvárad, it seems every town has its own distinctive export. Meanwhile, Bükk and Aggtelek National Parks beckon hikers with scenic trails and magnificent caves.

EGER ☎(0)36

The siege of Eger Castle and István Dobó's subsequent defeat of the Ottoman army figure prominently in Hungarian lore. The key to victory: the strengthening powers of local *Egri Bikavér* (Bull's Blood) wine. The legacy lives on today in the vibrant cellars of the Valley of the Beautiful Women and in the historical monuments scattered throughout the city. Eger (EGG-air) continues to seduce visitors with its quaint cobblestone streets, delicious delicacies, and infectious friendliness.

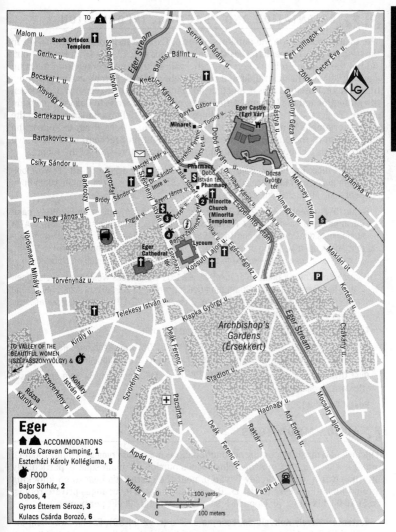

Eger

▲ ▲ ACCOMMODATIONS
Autós Caravan Camping, **1**
Eszterházi Károly Kollégiuma, **5**

🍎 FOOD
Bajor Sörház, **2**
Dobos, **4**
Gyros Étterem Sérozc, **3**
Kulacs Csárda Borozó, **6**

0   100 yards
0   100 meters

▭ TRANSPORTATION

Trains: Vasút u. (☎31 42 64). To: **Budapest** (2hr.; 21 per day, 6 direct; 1036-1242Ft); **Szeged** (4½hr., 12 per day, 2326Ft); **Szilvásvárad** (1hr., 9 per day, 262Ft). Budapest direct trains split in Hatvan—confirm with the train conductor or other passengers that your car is heading to Budapest. Non-direct trains to **Keleti station** via **Füzesabony.**

Buses: Barkóczy u. (☎511 706 or 511 701; www.agriavolan.hu). To: **Aggtelek** (3½hr., 8:45am, 1092Ft); **Budapest** (2hr., 15-20 per day, 1296Ft); **Debrecen** (3hr., 5-6per day, 1296Ft); **Szilvásvárad** (45min., every ½-1hr., 294Ft).

Taxi: City Taxi ☎55 55 55.

HUNGARY

✦ 🛈 ORIENTATION AND PRACTICAL INFORMATION

The **train station** lies on the outskirts of town. Exit the train on the right to get to the train station. To reach the **bus station,** catch bus #11, 12, or 14 (110Ft) right outside of the station on Deák Ferenc út. To walk to the town center from the train station (20min.), head straight and take a right on Deák Ferenc út. After 10min., turn right on Kossuth Lajos u. and take an immediate left on Széchenyi u., between the Cathedral and the Lyceum. A final right on Érsek u. leads to **Dobó tér,** the main square. To get to the center from the bus station, turn right on **Barkcózy u.** from the exit at terminal #10 and right again at the next main street, **Brody u.** Follow the stairs down to the end of the street and turn right on **Széchenyi u.**; a left down Érsek u. leads to Dobó tér. Most sights are within a 10min. walk of the square.

Tourist Office: Tourinform, Bajcsy-Zsilinszky u. 9 (☎51 77 15; fax 51 88 15; www.tourinform.hu/eger). **Maps** available. Open June-Sept. M-F 9am-7pm, Sa-Su 10am-6pm; Sept.-June M-F 9am-5pm, Sa 9am-1pm.

Bank: OTP, Széchenyi u. 2 (☎31 08 66; fax 31 35 54), gives AmEx/MC/V **cash advances** and cashes AmEx **Travelers Cheques** for no commission. A MC/V **ATM** stands outside. Open M-Tu and Th 7:45am-5pm, W 7:45am-6pm, F 7:45am-4pm; currency desk open M, Tu, Th until 2:45pm, W until 4:30pm, F until noon. There is a 24hr. currency exchange machine next to the OTP ATM opposite the church on Dobó tér.

Pharmacies: Zalár Pakka, Zalár Jósef u. (☎31 01 91), stocks Western products. Open 24hr.; between 8pm and 7:30am, ring bell for service (110Ft extra). AmEx/MC/V. The smaller **Dobó tér Kigyó Patika,** Dobó tér 2 (☎/fax 31 22 19), is slightly more accessible. Open M-F 7:30am-6pm, Sa 8am-12:30pm.

Telephones: Inside the post office and all over the town.

Internet: Egri Est Cafe, Széchenyi u. 16 (☎41 11 05; www.agria.hu/cafe). Cafe has computers in the back. 500Ft per 30min. Open Su-Th 11am-midnight, F-Sa 1pm-2am.

Post Office: Széchenyi u. 22 (☎31 32 32). Open M-F 8am-8pm, Sa 8am-1pm. **Poste Restante** available.

Postal Code: 3300.

⌂ ACCOMMODATIONS

The best and most welcoming accommodations are **private rooms** (around 2000Ft); look for *Zimmer frei* or *szòba eladò* signs outside the main square, particularly on Almagyar u. and Mekcsey István u. near the castle. It's best to go knocking around lunchtime. **Eger Tourist ❸,** Bajcsy-Zsilinszky u. 9, arranges private rooms. (☎51 70 00; fax 51 02 70. Open M-F 9am-5pm. Around 3000Ft per person.)

Eszterházi Károly Kollégiuma, Leányka u. 2/6 (☎52 04 30). Facing away from the church at Dobo tér, exit the square to the right, walking over the river and past the outdoor cafes. Turn right on Dobó u., walk along Dózsa Gry. tér, and turn left at the castle. Take the stairs to the right of the castle gate (Var Köz), go through the underpass and emerge on Leanyka u.; the Kollégiuma is the multi-level cement building on the left. The path isn't well-marked, but the stay is cheap and well worth the walk. Open July-early Sept. Reservations recommended. 1200Ft per person; bungalows 2000Ft. Camping 900Ft, students 700Ft. ❷

Autós Caravan Camping, Rákóczi u. 79 (☎/fax 41 05 58), 20min. north of the center on bus #5, 11, or 12. Get off at the Shell station and follow the signs. Call ahead or reserve through Eger Tourist. Open Apr. 15-Oct. 15. 320Ft per person; tents 250Ft. ❶

FOOD

There are plenty of options along **Széchenyi u.** A super-sized **ABC supermarket** dominates its own square off of Széchenyi u., between Sandor u. and Szt. Janos u. (Open M-F 6am-6pm, Sa 6am-1pm. AmEx/MC/V.) A daily **market** is hidden just off Széchenyi u.—go right on Arva Köz; it's on the right at Katona I tér. (Open M-F 6am-5pm, Sa 6am-1pm, Su 6-10am.)

Kulacs Csárda Borozó (☎/fax 31 13 75), in the Valley of the Beautiful Women. The vine-draped courtyard adds a rich atmosphere to a menu of Hungarian cuisine. Try the house specialty—boar stew. Meals 950-1600Ft. Open Tu-Su noon-10pm. ❹

Gyros Étterem Sérozc, Széchenyi u. 10 (☎41 37 81), serves gyros (350-380Ft) and roasts (750-1800Ft) in a bright, well-kept setting that offers patio seating in the summer. Open daily 9am-10pm. ❸

Dobos, Széchenyi u. 6. Offers a mouth-watering selection of decadent pastries and desserts. Try a marzipan snail or rose (250-280Ft), a candy frog (135Ft), or another creative confection (100-180Ft). Delicious ice cream 80Ft. Open daily 9:30am-9pm. ❶

Bajor Sörház, Bajcsy-Zsilinsky u. 19 (☎31 63 12), off Dobó tér, near the pharmacy. The English menu helps visitors navigate a selection of "Hungarian standards" such as cold brains, ham knuckles, and liver. Other less daring, yet authentically Hungarian options are also available. Entrees 900-2950Ft. Open daily 10am-10pm. AmEx/MC/V. ❹

SIGHTS

VALLEY OF THE BEAUTIFUL WOMEN. (Szépasszonyvölgy.) After exploring Eger's historical sights during the day, spend the evening in the wine cellars of the Valley of the Beautiful Women. Following World War II, cheap land prices allowed hundreds of wine cellars to sprout on this volcanic hillside. Most of the 25 open cellars consist of little more than a tunnel and a few tables and benches, but each has its own personality: some are hushed while others burst with Hungarian and Roma sing-alongs. Eger is Hungary's red wine capital; its most popular reds are the famous *Bikavér* and the sweeter *Medok* or *Medina*. The valley is for people serious about buying, but many linger for hours in the smoky cellars, chatting with wine-filled tupperware in hand. Sample the Bull's Blood alongside the friendly proprietors of **Cellar #17.** Alternatively, take in a drink at the less rowdy, but equally congenial **Cellar #20.** After 10pm the back of the cellar becomes an after-hours bar, with DJ and live music. Tasting fee of 50-80Ft. *(Start out on Széchenyi u. with Eger Cathedral to your right. Turn right on Kossuth Lajos u. and then left on Deák Ferenc út. Ignore the signpost on Kossuth Lajos u. and continue on Deák u., making the 1st right on Telekessy u. Continue until you arrive at Szépasszony-völgy (20min.) Cellars open at 9am, but closing times vary; in July-Aug., some stay open until midnight. Afternoon visits are best. 100mL for 50-80Ft; 1L 350Ft.)*

EGER CASTLE. (Egri Vár.) Egri Vár's interior includes subterranean barracks, catacombs, a crypt, and a wine cellar. Walking around the perimeter of the castle yields a 360° view of the city of Eger. One ticket buys admission to the castle's three museums: a **gallery** with Hungarian paintings from the 15th century onwards; the **Dobó István Vármúzeum,** which displays excavated artifacts, armor, and an impressive array of weapons; and the **dungeon exhibition,** a collection of torture equipment that will either inspire the sadist within or horrify more innocent hearts. The 400-year-old **wine cellars** are also open to the public for tastings. Be wary as you sip, however: the bar is in the same room as the hands-on archery exhibit, which features longbows with real arrows. *(☎31 27 44 or 31 15 21; info 439 28 13; varmuzeum@div.iif.hu; www.div.iif.hu. Castle open daily 8am-8pm. Museums open Mar.-*

Oct. Tu-Su 9am-5pm; Nov.-Feb. 9am-3pm. Wine cellars open daily 10am-7pm. Underground passages open M only. Castle 200Ft, students 100Ft. All 3 museums Tu-Su 500Ft/250Ft; M 250Ft/ 120Ft. Wine cellars offer free admission but charge 140Ft per tasting. English tour 400Ft.)

LYCEUM. The fresco in the library on the first floor of the Rococo Lyceum displays an ant's-eye-view of the Council of Trent. History buffs will recall the meeting wherein the edicts of the Counter Reformation were established. Upstairs, a small **astronomical museum** houses 18th-century telescopes and instruments from the building's old observatory. A marble line in the floor represents the meridian; when the sun strikes the line through a pin-hole aperture in the south wall, it is astronomical noon. In earth time, it's closer to 11:30am. Two floors up, a *camera obscura* projects a live picture of the surrounding town onto a table, providing a godlike view of the world below. *(At the corner of Kossuth Lajos u. and Eszterházy u. Open Apr.-Oct. Tu-Su 9:30am-1:30pm; Oct.-Dec. and Mar.-Apr. Th-F 9:30am-1pm, Sa-Su 9:30am-1:30pm. 200Ft, students 100Ft. Museum 200Ft. Tickets sold until 30min. before closing)*

EGER CATHEDRAL. Completed in 1837 by Joseph Hild and designed to be the largest cathedral in Hungary, the only Neo-Classical building in Eger was quickly eclipsed by Hild's larger church in Esztergom. The soaring architecture, soft pastel hues, and intricately painted domes are more liberating than most Baroque interiors. **Concerts** (30min.) are held here from May to mid-October. *(On Eszterházy tér just off Széchenyi u. Concerts M-Sa 11:30am, Su 12:45pm. 350Ft.)*

OTHER SIGHTS. The pink Baroque **Minorite Church** (Minorita Templom) in Dobó tér was built in 1758. The facade of the elaborate carved wooden interior overlooks a statue of Captain Dobó and two Hungarian defenders. (☎31 27 44. Open Apr.-Oct. Tu-Su 9am-5pm.) From Dobó tér, walk down Mescet u. on the right to reach the 40m, 17th-century **Minaret**, the Ottomans' northernmost building in Europe. The steep spiral staircase is not much wider than the average 20th-century person—only the intrepid make it to the top. (☎41 02 33. Open Apr.-Oct. M-Su 10am-6pm. 50Ft.) The 18th-century **Serbian Orthodox Church** (Szerb Ortodox Templom), on Vitkovics u. at the center's northern end, drips with gilt ornamentation. Follow Széchenyi u. from the center and enter at #15. *(Open Tu-Su 10am-4pm.)*

🎵📷 ENTERTAINMENT AND FESTIVALS

In summer, the **open-air baths** (swimming pools) offer a desperately needed respite from the sweltering city. To get there from Dobó tér, take Jókai u. to Kossuth Lajos u. and continue down Egészségház u. Make a right on Klapa György u.; the baths will be on the right after you cross the stream. (☎41 16 19. Open May-Sept. M-F 6am-7pm, Sa-Su 8:30am-7pm; Oct.-Apr. daily 9am-7pm. 500Ft, students 350Ft.)

Eger hosts musical evenings on Small Dobó tér, every night at 6pm. From late July to mid-August, Eger revels in its heritage during the **Baroque Festival.** Nightly performances of operas, operettas, and medieval and Renaissance court music take place on Dobó tér, at the Basilica, and around the city. Buy tickets at the venue. (☎41 03 24.) The **Eger Bull's Blood Festival** is celebrated in the beginning of July. An international folk dance festival, **Eger Vintage Days,** is held in early September. Tourinform (see **Practical Information,** p. 402) has festival schedules.

📍 DAYTRIPS FROM EGER

LILLAFÜRED   ☎(0)36

*From Eger, hop on a **bus** heading to Miskolc (45min., 7-10 per day, 1300Ft). When you arrive, ask someone to direct you to Buza tér; from there catch bus #1, 101, or 1a to Diosgyor. From the stop in Diosgyor catch bus #5 or 15 to Lillafüred. **Neptune Rental** rowboats 250Ft per person, pedal boats 300Ft. **Trail map** available at Miskolc Tourinform,*

Rákóczi út 2 (☎35 04 25; miskolc@tourinform.hu), or inquire at hotels. **Scenic train tour** *☎37 03 45 for schedule. 170Ft.* **Stalactite Cave** *(☎33 41 39) open Apr. 16-Oct. 15 9am-5pm; Oct. 16-Apr. 15 daily 9am-4pm. Tours start on the hour.* **Lime Cave** *(☎33 41 30) open Apr. 16-Oct. 31 daily 10am-3pm. Tours start on the hour.*

A short distance from Eger and Miskolc, Lillafüred is the perfect base from which to explore the Bükk Mountains and National Park. Whether you are in Lillafüred for a day or more, take advantage of Hungary's outdoor playground. Rent **row** or **pedal boats** on Lake Hamori from Neptune Rentals, directly across from Tókert Panzió (see below). If hiking is more your style, the varied *karst* (rock) surfaces, excellent lookouts, and labyrinthine **cave system** in the Bükk will satisfy all your naturalistic desires. **Hikes** within the park vary in length from 5 to 36km. For those who appreciate nature without the strenuous activity, hop on the **narrow-gauge railway** (the station is to the left of Tókert Panzió). This 30min. tour takes you into the mountains, meanders through lush forests, and crosses Hungary's largest viaduct. The **Szent István Stalactite Cave** has a 170m visitation area, in which the natural stalactite formations can be examined. The cave's unique climate has also been rumored to have a curative effect on respiratory diseases. The **Lime Tuff Anna Cafe** is in the hanging garden and waterfall park of Hotel Palota (see below). The formations and materials in the cave make it unique in the world.

The dominant structure in Lillafüred is the **Hotel Palota ❹**. Built between 1927 and 1930, this castle-like hotel overlooks the man-made Lake Hamori and the Bükk Mountain range. Call far in advance. (☎33 14 11; fax 53 32 03; reserve@hotelpalota.hunguesthotels.hu. Breakfast included. Rooms 6000-26,000Ft.) Next door **Tókert (Garden Lake) Panzió ❸** offers affordable rooms, also overlooking Lake Homari. The staff helps travelers plan expeditions into the Bükk. (☎53 35 60; fax 53 12 02; www.tokert.hu. Dorms 3600Ft; singles 6400-8800Ft; doubles 8200-11,100Ft. Tax 300Ft.)

If the outdoor fun has given you an appetite, eat well at the **King Matthias Restaurant ❷** in the basement of Hotel Palota. Abundant portions of wild game, fruit, and potatoes will fill you to the gills. Although cutlery is available, it is customary to eat as the king did—with your hands. (☎33 14 11. Entrees 600-4000Ft. Reservations recommended. Open daily 11am-midnight.)

▨ BARADLA CAVES ☎(0)48

The **bus** *leaves Eger daily at 8:45am, whizzes through Szilvásvárad at 9:23am, and arrives in Aggtelek at 11:25am. The returning bus leaves from the same stop at 3pm; the bus to Miskolc is at 5pm. To get to the cave from the bus stop, head left, walk behind the hotel, and go downstairs to the white gravel path. Cut across the field toward the street. Once on the road, the national park is to your right. ☎/fax 35 00 06. Mandatory 1hr. Hungarian* **tours** *daily 10am, 1pm, 3pm; in the high-season also 5pm and whenever more than 10 people assemble. 1200Ft, students and seniors 600Ft. Tours covering the entire main branch of the cave (5hr., 7km) can be arranged through the ever-helpful staff of Tourinform (☎34 30 73); call ahead. 4500Ft, students 2250Ft.*

The spectacular Baradla Caves, which have been declared a UNESCO world heritage site, are well worth the trip from Eger or Miskolc. The caves wind for 25km, straddling the Hungarian-Slovak border. The entrance in Hungary is at **Aggtelek** (AWG-tel-eck). In each chamber, a forest of dripping stalactites, stalagmites, and fantastically-shaped stone formations loom over visitors. A large chamber inside the cave with perfect acoustics has been converted into an auditorium, and the tour takes a dramatic pause here for a **light show**. Another hall contains an **Iron Age cemetery** where 13 people, thought to be recent crime victims when the cave was first discovered, are buried. The temperature is 10°C year-round, so bring a jacket. If you find the cavernous hollows echoing the rumble of your hungry stomach, **Barlang Vendéglö** (☎34 71 77), just inside the park, offers reasonably priced Hungarian favorites (entrees 390-1390Ft) in a pleasant outdoor setting.

SZILVÁSVÁRAD ☎(0)36

Renowned for its carriages, Lipizzaner horses, and surrounding national parks, Szilvásvárad (SEAL-vash-vah-rod) trots along at its own dignified clip. One of only four places in the world to breed prize-winning Lipizzaners, Szilvásvárad takes pride in its international prominence. Locals are warm and hospitable, attempting to bridge language barriers whenever possible.

⚡ TRANSPORTATION. Trains run to **Eger** (1hr., 7per day, 262Ft). Szilvásvárad has two stations; get off at the first, "Szilvásvárad-Szalajkavölgy." There is no bus station. **Buses** are generally the most convenient transport, running to **Eger** (45 min., every 30min.-1hr., 294Ft) and **Aggtelek** (1¾hr., 9:23am, 744Ft). Don't get off at the first bus stop in town, unless you want to investigate the *Zimmer frei* (rooms available) signs. The second stop is on Egri út, within sight of Szalajka u.

⚡🐴 ORIENTATION AND PRACTICAL INFORMATION. The town's main street **Egri út** extends from the Szilvásvárad-Szalajkavölgy train station and bends sharply at the race course's ticket office. The booth marks the entrance to **Szalajka u.,** which leads directly to the national park. Farther north, Egri út turns into **Miskolci út.** There's no tourist office in town, so get information and a basic map at the **Eger Tourinform** (see **Eger: Orientation and Practical Information,** p. 402) before heading out. The women at Hegy camping (see **Accommodations,** below) provide a wealth of information about the area, as well as free maps. **Hiking maps** are posted throughout the park. Maps of the surrounding mountains are available at the **bike shop** on Szalajka u., just past the stop sign at the park entrance. (☎30 3 35 26 95. Open daily 10am-7pm. There's a **pharmacy** at Magyar Korona, Egri út 4. (☎35 51 28. Open M-Th 8am-noon and 1-4pm, F 8am-1:30pm.) A small **bank** stands behind the bus stop on Egri út. (☎35 41 05. Open M-F 8am-noon and 12:30-3:30pm.)

🐴🍴 ACCOMMODATIONS AND FOOD. Although Szilvásvárad makes a perfect daytrip, it can be a relaxing place to stay and rejuvenate. **Private rooms** are the cheapest option (from 2000Ft), but their price rises during the Lipicai Festival (see below). **Hegy Camping,** Egri út 36a, offers great views of the valley from the groomed campground. (☎35 52 07. Open Apr. 15-Oct. 15. Tent space for 2 people 1800Ft, students 1100Ft; each additional person 900Ft/550Ft. Bungalow doubles with bath 3900Ft; triples 4900Ft; quads 5600Ft.) Houses are being built in the area to provide tourists with additional accommodations, expected to open in 2003. There are some restaurants on Szalajka u. and on Egri u., but your best bet may be the **Nagy ABC,** Egri u. 6. (Open M-F 6am-6pm, Sa 6am-1pm, Su 8am-noon.)

📷🎭 SIGHTS AND ENTERTAINMENT. Outdoor opportunities abound in this one street town, from leisurely biking in the Szalajka Valley to arduous hikes through the low Bükk mountains. At the arena on Szalajka u., just right of the park entrance, which hosts weekend **horse shows** (800Ft per person), you can learn how to drive a carriage, brandish a whip, or ride a steed. Each July, the hugely popular **Lipicai Festival** (call the stables for info) at the arena draws carriage drivers from across the globe for a three-day competition. Many farms offer horse riding, especially in the summer. Péter Kovács, Egri út 62 (☎35 53 43; mobile 20 372 0722), **rents horses** (1500Ft per hr.), and **two-horse carriages** (4500Ft per hr.). **Lipicai Stables,** the stud farm for Szilvásvárad's Lipizzaner breed, is where it all begins. Heading away from the park entrance on Egri út, turn left on Enyves u. and follow the signs to the farm. (☎35 51 55. Open daily 8:30am-noon and 2-4pm. 80Ft.)

Shaded walks through the **Bükk mountains** and the **Szalajka valley** are beautiful, but not always relaxing—in June the trails swarm with school and tour groups and families whose children can't get enough ice cream. At the **Fátyol waterfall,** the lazy trail side stream transforms into the most dramatic—and most popular—of the park's attractions. It only takes 45min. to walk here at a leisurely pace by the green trail, or 15 minutes by the open-air train, which departs from the white gravel driveway at the park's entrance. (160Ft, students 80Ft. Train departs daily 9:25, 10:35, 11:30am, 1:35, 2:25, 3:10, 4:10pm. Trains only leave when there are a sufficient number of people around.) A 30min. hike along the green trail beyond the waterfalls leads to the **Istálósk Cave,** home to a bear cult during the Stone Age (see **History,** p. 330). After clearing the brook, the trail becomes extremely steep, so either bring a walking stick or wear shoes with good traction. Avoiding crowds by **renting a bike** at Szalajka u., just past the stop sign at the park entrance. Pick up one of their excellent free **cycling maps** and tourist guides, and hit the trails. The paths are just rough enough to make it fun. For the cost of a day's rental, the shop arranges trips to the local plateaus for groups of 10 or more. They can also arrange other outdoor activities. An **outdoor goods store** has been opened across the street. (☎35 26 95. 600Ft 1st hr., 200Ft thereafter; 1600Ft per day. Open daily 10am-7pm.)

TOKAJ ☎(0)47

King Louis XIV of France called Tokaj (toke-EYE) "the wine of kings and the king of wines." One of many small towns at the foot of the Kopasz Mountains (a.k.a. hills), Tokaj is bordered by the volcanic Zemplen hills on the north, and by the Tisza and Bodrog rivers on the south. The scent of its rich grapes drifts through the streets of the town and bends of the Tisza River. If Tokaj gives the wine its name (Tokaji Féherbör), the wine gives Tokaj its flavor, with days split between exploration of the famed local cellars and outdoor activity in the hills and waters.

▐ TRANSPORTATION. Trains run from the station at Baross G. u. 18 (☎35 20 20; www.elvira.hu) to **Debrecen** (2hr., 8 per day, 646Ft) via **Nyíregyháza** and **Miskolc. Buses** departing from the train station serve local towns.

▐▐ ORIENTATION AND PRACTICAL INFORMATION. To get to the center from the **train station,** take a left from the station entrance and follow the railroad tracks to an underpass, then turn left on the main **Bajcsy-Zsilinszky u.** Bear left as the road forks by Hotel Tokaj (15min.). Bajcsy-Zsilinszky ú. becomes **Rákóczi u.** after the Tisza bridge and after **Kossuth tér** becomes **Bethlen Gábor u.** The staff at **Tourinform,** Serház u. 1, on the right side of Rákóczi u. as you walk into town, arranges **private** and **hotel rooms** for no fee and can set you up with a horse, canoe, or rafting tour. (☎/fax 35 22 59; tokajṣtourinform.hu. Open June 15-Sept. 15 M-F 9am-6pm, Sa-Su 9am-5pm; Sept. 16-June 14 M-F 9am-4pm.) **Exchange currency,** cash **traveler's checks,** and get MC/V **cash advances** at **OTP,** Rákóczi u. 35. (☎35 25 21. Open M-Th 7:45am-3:15pm, F 7:45am-noon and 12:25-2:15pm.) A MC/V **ATM** sits outside. **Paracelsus Pharmacy** is on Kossuth tér; ring after hours for emergencies. (Open M-F 8am-5pm, Sa 8am-4pm, Su 8am-noon and 12:30-4:30pm.) There are **telephones** in the **post office** at Rákóczi u. 24 and in the center of town. (Post office ☎35 36 47. Open M-F 8am-5pm, Sa 8am-noon.) **Postal Code:** 3910.

▐ ACCOMMODATIONS. See what **Tourinform ❸** has to offer (see above), but *Zimmer frei* and *Szoba Kiadó* (rooms available) signs abound—your best bet is to walk along Rákóczi u. and venture down the small side streets to choose where to rest. (Singles 1500-2000Ft; doubles 3000-5000Ft.) Don't be afraid to bargain, but beware: your host may well talk you into sampling—and buying—expensive homemade wine. The plush **Toldi Fogado ❺,** Rákóczi u., has six rooms that can sleep up to 15 people. The rooms are new, large, and extremely comfortable. (☎35

34 03; fax 35 34 02; www.hotels.hu/toldi. Full breakfast included. Doubles 10,000Ft; triples 12,500Ft.) **Lux Panzió ❸**, Serház u. 14, provides sunny rooms with pink-infused interiors. To get there, turn right on Városháza-köz from Rákóczi u., just after OTP. Ask for the double with the shower—it's the same price as those that share a shower. (☎35 21 45. Breakfast 500Ft. Reception 8am-10pm. Doubles 4500Ft; triples with TV 5900Ft. Tax 125Ft.)

The convenient **Makk Marci Panzió ❹**, Liget Köz 1, in the center, basks in its location just steps from some of the town's best wine cellars. (☎35 23 36; fax 35 30 88. Breakfast included. Reception 24hr. Singles 3960Ft; doubles 6200Ft; triples 9200Ft; quads 10,700Ft. Tax 125Ft.) **Vizisport Turistahotel ❷**, over the Tisza River, offers hostel accommodations to weary travelers. Its proprietor also rents canoes and bikes and arranges tours on request. (☎35 26 45; www.tokaj-hostel.hu. 1200Ft per person, with bath 1500Ft.) If you'd rather camp out with the mosquitoes, cross the Tisza bridge to reach the enormous **Camping Tisza ❶**, where guests stay in waterfront campsites or small bungalows. (Check-out 10am. Camping 600Ft per person. Bungalow 1200Ft per person.) **Spori Sport Camping ❶**, down the road from Camping Tisza, is a more peaceful ground set back from the main road. Bungalows and camping available with common kitchens and bathrooms. (☎/fax 425 063 04; www.spori.sport.hu. Camping 650Ft, bungalows 1400Ft.)

❏ FOOD. Soak up regional wines at **Toldi Fogado ❸**, Hajdú Köz, at Rákóczi u., which serves up Hungarian dishes in a pleasant dining room and garden setting. (☎35 34 03. English menu available. Entrees 690-1800Ft. Open daily 11am-10pm.) The **restaurant ❸** downstairs from Toldi Fogado serves delicious Hungarian specialties (entrees 690-1800Ft). There's also a **pizzeria ❷** downstairs from Makk Marci Panzió. (Pizzas 430-780Ft. Open daily 10am-10pm.) **Bacchus Etterem ❷**, centrally located at Kossuth tér 17, is a local diner. (☎35 20 54. Breakfast 250-300Ft. *Goulash* 400Ft. Open M-Sa 8am-10pm, Su 9am-10pm.) The **Coop supermarket** is on Kossuth tér. (Open M-F 6:30am-6:30pm, Sa 6:30am-1pm, Su 7-11am.)

◉ ♫ SIGHTS AND ENTERTAINMENT. *Bor Pince* signs herald **private wine cellars** whose owners are generally pleased to let visitors sample their wares (about 1000Ft for 5 or 6 1dL samples). Ring the bell if a cellar looks closed. Cellars on the main road are usually more touristy—on the side streets you'll find higher-quality wines and more homey environs. Serious tasting and wine-knowledge building takes place in the 1.5km-long tunnel cellar of **◪Rákóczi Pince,** Kossuth tér 15. Five hundred years worth of dripping, spongy fungus chill in the 10°C cellar; in 1526, János Szapohjai was elected king of Hungary in the elegant subterranean hall. Wine tastings and group tours of the cellar and hall are arranged on the hour, but can be preempted by tour groups. Individual tours can be arranged at any time. English-speaking guides may be available in July and August. (☎35 20 09; fax 35 27 41. Open 10am-8pm. 1800Ft for 30min. tour and 6-glass tasting. AmEx/MC/V.) The young **Tokaji Hímesudvar Cellars,** Bem u. 2, produce phenomenal *Aszú* wines—their 1993 *5-puttonyos* received several international awards. The friendly Várhelyi family happily guides you through the history of the region and the subtleties of the Tokaj wines. To get to the royal hunting lodge where the cellar is located, take the road to the left of the church in Kossuth tér and follow the signs to the cellar. (☎35 24 16. Open daily 9am-9pm. Tastings 1100Ft for 5 wines.) The **Tóth family cellar** at Óvár út. 40 produces five exceptional whites, including a 1988 *6-puttonyos Aszú*. Take the street that begins opposite Tourinform at Rákóczi u. Ring the bell to be let in. You will then be guided into a small, yet thoroughly authentic mold-infested cellar. (5 glasses 500Ft, 1L of *6-puttonyos* 4000Ft.)

When you are ready to take a break from tasting, venture down Rákóczi u., going to the right when facing the church, and you will come across the **Tokaj**

A MINI-GUIDE TO THE WINES OF TOKAJ

Wine connoisseurs have admired Hungarian wines for years. Enjoy the prices in Tokaj, as you can pay six times more for the same bottle when exported. The exotic names on the labels, however, might intimidate those used to wine-in-a-box. In order from driest to sweetest (and lightest to darkest), the main varieties are:

Furmint, a basic dry white that goes well with seafood, fish, and game dishes.

Szamorodni, which comes in dry (Száraz) and sweet (Édes) varieties, has a more complex flavor. While the dry can accompany most main meals, the sweet goes well with pâté, delicate cheeses, and ice cream.

Aszú, Furmint sweetened with Aszú grapes (grapes which ripen and dry out more quickly than others in the same bunch) is the most famous. According to local lore, Aszú wine was invented when Máté Szepsi Laczkó neglected his harvest in 1630—fearing Turkish invasion, he left his grapes to rot on the vine. The fruit produces an extremely sweet dessert wine that is popular among farmers. Sweetness is measured in 3, 4, 5, or 6 puttonyos, or the number of baskets of Aszú grapes added to a particular barrel of wine. (Szamorodni is a mix of both Aszú and regular grapes.)

Aszú Eszeneia, the "imperial elixir," is too sweet to be described in terms of puttonyos; drink it alone or accompanied by great Havana cigars.

1972, 1975, 1983, 1988, 1993, and 1999 are considered good vintages. Some vintners believe the overall quality of their wines increased after the privatization of the vineyards in 1991. To be an expert, or just look like one, sample wines in order from driest to sweetest. In the opposite order, dry wines will taste bitter or acidic.

Museum. The building was built in 1790 by Greek vintners. The stairs inside are originals, and the frescoes on the walls are refurbished replicas. Ask for the English guide and then explore the different rooms. From the history of Tokaj wine to a Catholic priest's collection of iconography, this museum runs the gamut of Tokaj's rich history and culture. (☎35 26 36. Open Tu-Su 10am-4pm. 200Ft, students 100Ft.) From the museum, continue down Rákóczi u. until it meets Josef Atilla u. Turn right, and on the next block you'll find the largest structure in Tokaj, the **Synagogue.** The Jewish population in Tokaj was significantly larger before WWII; now, only two Jews remain. While the synagogue is closed to visitors, try to spot someone lurking around and ask to be given a tour.

Outdoor recreation in Tokaj is as popular as the wine that draws people here. **Vízisport Centrum,** at the campground over the bridge, rents bikes (800Ft per day) and canoes (500Ft per day) and arranges horseback riding (1200Ft per hr., 2500Ft with trainer, must be arranged 1 day ahead). **Spori Sport,** to the right of Camping Tisza, also rents canoes. (☎48 17 16 or 31 60 67; fax 31 15 78. 2-seater 900Ft per day; 4-seater 1600Ft per day.) **Tourinform** can also arrange outdoor activities. **Murphy's Mühely Söröző,** Rákóczi u. 30/32, is an Irish pub that packs in students for an after-dinner round. (Beer 80-130Ft. Pool 60Ft per game. Open daily 2pm-2am.)

LATVIA (LATVIJA)

LATS

AUS$1 = 136.64LS	1LS = AUS$3.02
CDN$1 = 159.54LS	1LS = CDN$2.59
EUR€1 = 244.22LS	1LS = EUR€1.69
NZ$1 = 116.54LS	1LS = NZ$3.54
UK£1 = 384.82LS	1LS = UK£1.07
US$1 = 248.29LS	1LS = US$1.66
ZAR1 = 23.41LS	1LS = ZAR17.63

At the Baltic crossroads, Latvia has been caught for hundreds of years in the political struggles between Germany, Russia, Sweden, Lithuania, and Poland. The country has been conquered and reconquered so many times that the year 2003 will only be Latvia's 34th year of independence—ever. However, national pride abounds, from patriotically renamed streets draped with crimson-and-white flags, to a rediscovery of native holidays predating even the Christian invasions. Rīga, Latvia's only large city, is a westernized capital luring more and more international companies. The rest of the country is mostly a provincial expanse of green hills dominated by tall birches and pines, dairy pastures, and quiet towns.

LATVIA AT A GLANCE

OFFICIAL NAME: Republic of Latvia

CAPITAL: Rīga (pop. 874,000)

POPULATION: 2.4 million (57% Latvian, 30% Russian, 5% Belarussian, 5% Polish and Ukrainian)

LANGUAGES: Latvian or Lettish (official), Lithuanian, Russian

CURRENCY: 1 Lat = 100 santimi

RELIGION: Lutheran, Roman Catholic, Russian Orthodox

LAND AREA: 64,589km²

CLIMATE: Maritime

GEOGRAPHY: Low plains

BORDERS: Belarus, Estonia, Lithuania, Russia

ECONOMY: 62% Services, 33% Industry, 5% Agriculture

GDP: US$7200 per capita

COUNTRY CODE: 371

INTERNATIONAL DIALING PREFIX: 00

HISTORY

INVASION, ANYONE? Like its Baltic sisters, Latvia has consistently struggled under the yoke of foreign rule. The Germans arrived in the late 12th to convert the locals to Christianity. In 1237, the Teutonic Knights established the **Confederation of Livonia,** which ruled over the territory for nearly 300 years. The confederation collapsed when Russian Tsar **Ivan IV** (the Terrible) invaded, beginning the 25-year **Livonian War** (1558-83) and a half-century of partition.

AND NOW FOR A SWEDISH INTERLUDE. The 1629 **Truce of Altmark** brought an extended period of relative stability and freedom known as the **Swedish Interlude,** achieved by ceding control of eastern Livonia (present-day Latvia and Estonia) to the Poles and giving Rīga and the northern regions to Sweden. Sweden, however, was forced to cede the Livonian territories to **Peter the Great** under the Peace of Nystad in 1721, and with the second partition of Poland in 1795 the entire country fell under

410

Russian control. The Latvian peasantry, which became increasingly prosperous after the **abolition of serfdom** in 1861, continued to struggle for freedom from the Russian empire throughout the 19th century. **Nationalism** flared with particular strength during the Russian Revolution of 1905, when Latvians began to envision a state of their own.

THE WAR YEARS. Reacting to the Bolshevik coup of November 1917, the **Latvian People's Council** proclaimed independence on November 18, 1918, establishing a government in Rīga led by **Kārlis Ulmanis.** Over the next few years, the country was overrun by battling foreign armies, and by 1920 the Latvians were in control. The **Constitution of 1922** provided for a republic governed by a president and a unicameral parliament, but the large number of political parties in the legislature, or **Saeima,** kept the political situation unstable. Ulmanis encountered increasing problems as German elements within Latvia became sympathetic to the Nazi party, and in 1934 he declared a state of emergency. Under the secret provisions of the **Nazi-Soviet Nonaggression Pact,** Latvia fell under the control of the USSR in 1938. However, Germany reneged on the Pact and occupied Latvia in 1941, only to be driven back in 1945 by the Red Army, which annexed its smaller neighbor.

SUPREMELY SOVIET. Latvia entered the **Soviet Union** as one of its wealthiest and most industrialized regions. Under Soviet rule, the state was torn by radical economic restructuring, political repression, and a thorough Russification of its national culture. Some 35,000 Latvians, including many members of the intelligentsia, were deported to Russia during the first year of the occupation, just as immigrants, encouraged by the Soviet state, poured in from the rest of the USSR. Foreigners soon dominated local politics and within four decades ethnic Latvians accounted for only half the population.

ALL LATVIAN, ALL THE TIME. Under *glasnost* and *perestroika* (see **Russia: History,** p. 624), Latvians protested en masse against the Communist regime and created the **Popular Front** in 1988. Faced with competition, the Communists were trounced in the 1990 elections. On May 4, 1990, the new legislature declared independence, but Soviet intervention sparked violent clashes in Rīga in 1991. Following the failed Moscow coup in August, the Latvian legislature reasserted independence. Soon after, the world recognized the legislature's sovereignty.

TODAY

Internal politics remain turbulent, with numerous parties, including the **For Fatherland and Freedom Party, the People's Party,** and **the Latvian Way Party,** jockeying for position in the Saeima (Parliament). **Coalitions** have come and gone—on April 12, 2000, Prime Minister **Andris Skele** resigned for the third time. The rapid political turnover, spurred in part by conflict over the pace of privatization of large government holdings in telecommunications and energy, has caused delays in economic reform. The current president, **Vaira Vike-Freiberga,** a psychology professor who spent most of her life in Canada, was elected in June 1999 after seven rounds of voting in the Saeima. The next round of presidential elections will be in 2003. Latvia expects to join the EU in 2004, but if future reforms are slowed by domestic political woes, many observers expect that date to slip to 2005 or 2006. Relations with **Russia** remain thorny. Tension flared especially over the **Latvian State Language Law** (1999), which set stringent requirements for residents to gain proficiency in Latvian and for business to be conducted in Latvian. The law was seen by Moscow as undermining the rights of the ethnic Russian population in Latvia, and the Russian Duma threatened, but did not enact, economic sanctions. Under pressure from both Russia and the EU, Latvia eased up on the Russian minority.

PEOPLE AND CULTURE

DEMOGRAPHICS AND LANGUAGE

A surprisingly large number of Latvian inhabitants aren't actually **Latvian.** In fact, nearly 30% of the country's population is **Russian,** leaving a mere 56% majority for the native Latvians. **Belarussians** constitute a sparse 5% portion, and **Poles** and **Ukrainians** make up an additional 5%. Heavily influenced by German, Russian, Estonian, and Swedish, **Latvian** is one of two languages (the other is Lithuanian) in the Baltic language group. Life, however, proceeds bilingually. **Russian** is in disfavor in the countryside but still spoken; it is much more acceptable and widespread in Rīga. Many young Latvians study **English;** the older set knows some **German.** For a phrasebook and glossary, **see Glossary: Latvian,** p. 883.

FOOD AND DRINK

LATVIA	❶	❷	❸	❹	❺
FOOD	under 2Ls	2-3Ls	4-5Ls	6-7Ls	over 7Ls

Latvian food is heavy and starchy, but tasty. Big cities offer foreign cuisine, and Rīga is one of the easiest places to be a vegetarian in all the Baltics. Tasty national specialties include the holiday dish *zirņi* (gray peas with onions and smoked fat), *maizes zupa* (bread soup usually made from cornbread, currants, cream, and other goodies), and the warming *Rīgas* (or *Melnais*) *balzams* (a black liquor great with ice cream, Coke, or coffee). Dark rye bread is a staple. Try *speķa rauši*, a warm pastry, or *biezpienmaize*, bread with sweet curds. Dark-colored *kaņepju sviests* (hemp butter) is good but too diluted for "medicinal" purposes. Latvian beer, primarily from the Aldaris brewery, is great, particularly *Porteris*.

CUSTOMS AND ETIQUETTE

If a **tip** is expected where you're dining, it will usually be included in the bill. Expect to be bought a drink if you talk with someone awhile; repay the favor in kind. If you're invited to a meal in someone's home, bring a **gift** for the hostess (an odd number of flowers is customary). **Handshaking** is expected when meeting new people or greeting a friend. **Shops** sometimes close for a break between noon and 3pm. Try not to get Latvians and Lithuanians confused; both consider it quite insulting.

THE ARTS

HISTORY

The legacy of the ancient Balts is the foundation of Latvian literature. The mid-19th century brought a national awakening as the country asserted its literary independence in works such as *Lāčplēsis (Bearslayer)*, **Andrējs Pumpurs**'s 1888 national epic. Realism and social protest became important with the arrival of the **New Movement** in the last years of the 19th century. Writer **Jānis Rainis** used folk imagery to depict contemporary problems, while his wife, **Aspazija**, fought for women's rights. New literary forms diversified Latvia's literature after the country achieved independence in 1918. **Aleksandr Caks**'s most outstanding work was *Marked by Eternity (Muzibas skartie)*, a haunting account of the Latvian riflemen of World War I. Many Latvian writers turned to psychological detail in the 20th century: in particular, **Anslavs Eglitis** reveled in intensifying human traits to the point of absurdity. Following World War II the Soviets imposed **Socialist Realism** on Latvian literature, mandating that texts promote revolutionary ideals. Their censorship, however, was not always successful. **Jānis Medenis**, exiled to a labor camp in Siberia, longed for a free Latvia in his poetry. **Martis Ziverts**, famous for his one-act plays, is regarded as the best 20th-century Latvian dramatist. Using the folk tradition of Latvia in their late 19th century works, **Jazeps Vitols** and **Andrejs Jurjans** became the country's first and most famous composers.

CURRENT SCENE

The contemporary art scene in Latvia owes much of its growth to the pioneers of Latvian history, whose ideas continue to resonate in modern works. In architecture, the **Latvian National Library** in Rīga was the recipient of the 2000 Architecture Award for its unique and modern design. **Miervaldis Polis** has begun to enjoy international acclaim for his hyper-realist art and is best known for *A Golden Man*. **The International Chamber Choir Festival,** held annually in Rīga, commemorates the ever-present choral appreciation and religious allusions of Latvian music. **Rīga** is the **Art Nouveau** capital of Europe, with blocks upon blocks of buildings designed with this style—look along **Elizabetes Street, Strelnieku Street,** and **Alberta Street.**

HOLIDAYS AND FESTIVALS

NATIONAL HOLIDAYS IN 2003

January 1 New Year's Day	**June 24** St. John's Day
March 29 Good Friday	**November 18** Independence Day
April 20 Easter Sunday	**December 25** Christmas
May 1 Labor Day	**December 31** New Year's Eve
June 23 Ligo Day	

LATVIA

ADDITIONAL RESOURCES

GENERAL HISTORY

Baltic Revolution: Estonia, Latvia, Lithuania and the Path to Independence, by Anatol Lieven (1994). A solid background to 20th-century Baltic history.

Historical Dictionary of Latvia, by Andrejs Plakans (1997). A detailed survey of Latvia's history, and an analytical view of its present situation.

FICTION AND NONFICTION

Latvia in Transition, by Juris Dreifelds (1996). An excellent look at the early years of Latvian independence.

The Testimony of Lives: Narrative and Memory in Post-Soviet Latvia, by Vieda Skultans (1998). Eloquently examines the recent difficulties experienced by Latvians.

LATVIA ESSENTIALS

ENTRANCE REQUIREMENTS

Passport: Required of all travelers.
Visa: Required of citizens of Australia, Canada, New Zealand, and South Africa.
Letter of Invitation: Not required.
Inoculations: None required. Recommended up-to-date on MMR (measles, mumps, and rubella), DTaP (diptheria), Polio booster, Hepatitis A, Hepatitis B.
Work Permit: Required of all foreigners planning to work in Latvia.
International Driving Permit: Required of all those planning to drive.

DOCUMENTS AND FORMALITIES

EMBASSIES AND CONSULATES

Embassies of other countries in Latvia are all in Rīga (see p. 419). Latvia's embassies and consulates abroad include:

Australia: Consulate: 38 Longstaff Street, East Ivanhoe, Victoria 3079 (☎03 9499 6920; fax 9499 7088).

Canada: 280 Albert Street, Suite 300, Ottawa, ON K1P 5G8 (☎613-238-6014; fax 238-7044; www.magmacom.com/~latemb).

UK: 45 Nottingham Pl., London W1M 3FE (☎020 7312 0040; fax 7312 0042).

US: 4325 17th St. NW, Washington, D.C. 20011 (☎202-726-8213; fax 726-6785; www.latvia-usa.org).

VISA AND ENTRY INFORMATION

Citizens of Ireland, the UK, and the US can visit Latvia **visa-free** for up to 90 days. Citizens of Australia, Canada, New Zealand, and South Africa require 90-day visas, available at a Latvian consulate and valid for travel through Lithuania and Estonia as well. Although visas are not available at the border, travelers from these countries may purchase 10-day single-entry visas at the airport in Rīga (12Ls). Transit visas (US$10; valid for 48hr.) are available for those who already have visas for their destination country. Standard single-entry visas (valid for 30 days) cost US$15; double-entry US$20; multiple-entry US$30-80, depending on length of validity (maximum 90 days). For two-day processing the fee is doubled, and for 24hr. processing it is quadrupled. Allow 10 days for standard processing. Send the application with your passport, one photograph, and payment by check or money order. If you plan on staying longer than 90 days, apply to the Department of Citizenship and Immigration (see **Rīga: Passport Office,** p. 419) for temporary residency. There is no fee for crossing a Latvian **border.** The best way to enter Latvia is by taking a plane, train, or bus to the capital. Allow extra time for crossing **borders;** even crossing to or from Latvia's friendly Baltic sisters can take hours.

TRANSPORTATION

BY PLANE. Airlines flying to Latvia use the **Rīga** airport. **Air Baltic, SAS, Finnair, Lufthansa,** and others make the hop to Rīga from their hubs.

BY TRAIN. Trains link Latvia to **Berlin, Lviv, Moscow, Odessa, St. Petersburg, Tallinn,** and **Vilnius.** Trains are cheap and efficient, but stations aren't well-marked, so make sure to always have a map. The **commuter rail** system renders the entire country a suburb of Rīga. For daytrips from Rīga, you're best off taking the **electric train;** as a rule, a crowded train is more comfortable than a crowded bus.

BY FERRY OR BUS. Ferries go to **Kiel, GER** and **Stockholm, SWE,** but are slow and expensive. Latvia's efficient long-distance bus network reaches **Prague, CZR; Tallinn, EST; Vilnius, LIT;** and **Warsaw, POL.** Buses, usually adorned with the driver's bizarre collection of Christian icons, stuffed animals, and stickers, are quicker than trains for travel within Latvia. Beware the standing-room-only long-distance jaunt.

BY THUMB. Hitchhiking is common, but hitchers may be expected to pay at least the cost of the comparable bus fare. *Let's Go* does not recommend hitchhiking.

TOURIST SERVICES AND MONEY

Look for the green "i" marking official tourist offices, which are rather scarce. Private tourist offices such as **Patricia** (see p. 419) are much more helpful. The Latvian currency unit is the Lat (Ls), which divides into 100 santîmi. **Inflation** averages around 3%. There are many MC/Visa **ATMs** in Rīga, and at least one or two in larger towns. Larger businesses, restaurants and hotels accustomed to Westerners accept **MasterCard** and **Visa. Traveler's checks** are harder to use; both AmEx and Thomas Cook can be converted in Rīga, but Thomas Cook is a safer bet outside the capital. It's often difficult to exchange currencies other than US dollars or Euros.

HEALTH AND SAFETY

 EMERGENCY NUMBERS: Police: ☎02 **Fire:** ☎01 **Ambulance:** ☎03

HEALTH AND SAFETY. Latvia has been hotlisted by the World Health Organization for its periodic outbreaks of incurable varieties of **tuberculosis;** drink **bottled water** (available at grocery stores and kiosks, although it is usually carbonated) or boil tap water before drinking. **Medical facilities** do not meet Western standards. **Pharmacies** are well-stocked with German brands of tampons, condoms, and band-aids. Most **restrooms** require you to bring your own toilet paper. They are marked with an upward-pointing triangle for women, downward for men. With Rīga's cosmopolitan glitz comes cosmopolitan **crime;** foreigners in particular are targets for petty theft and street assaults. Beware of pickpockets during daylight hours and drunken crowds around the bars and casinos at night. Both men and women should avoid walking alone at night. If you feel threatened, *"Ej prom"* (EY prawm) means "go away;" *"Lasies prom"* (LAH-see-oos PRAWM) says it more offensively; and *"Lasies lapās"* (LAH-see-oos LAH-pahs; "go to the leaves"), poetic though it may sound, is even ruder. You are more likely to find English-speaking help from your **consulate** than from the police.

WOMEN AND BGLT TRAVELERS. Women should not experience many difficulties in Latvia, even when traveling alone. However, it is best to take precautions when out after dark in Rīga and take a cab home. **Gay and lesbian** clubs advertise themselves as such freely in Rīga. Outside the city, there is less tolerance.

ACCOMMODATIONS AND CAMPING

LATVIA	❶	❷	❸	❹	❺
ACCOM.	under 10Lv	10-14Lv	15-19Lv	20-24Lv	over 24Lv

HOSTELS, HOMESTAYS, AND DORMS. There are four HI hostels in Rīga and a scattering of hostels around the beaches. Contact the **Latvian Youth Hostel Association,** Aldaru 8, Rīga 1050 (☎371 921 8560; fax 722 4030; www.hostellinglatvia.com), for more information. **College dormitories**—and the occasional circus dorm (literally)—are often the cheapest places to sleep, but are only open to travelers in the summer. In Rīga, the **Patricia Agency** arranges homestays and apartment rentals for around US$15 per night (see **Rīga: Tourist Offices,** p. 419).

HOTELS. Rīga's wide array of hotels satisfy any budget, from 10Ls dives to the glamorous Hotel de Rome. Many towns outside the capital have only one hotel (if any) in the budget range; expect to pay 3-15Ls per night.

CAMPING. Camping isn't very popular in Latvia; campgrounds do exist in the countryside, but keep in mind that camping beyond marked areas is prohibited.

KEEPING IN TOUCH

MAIL. Ask for *gaisa pastu* to send something by **airmail.** The standard rate for a letter to Europe is 0.30Ls, to anywhere else 0.40Ls; for a postcard 0.20Ls/0.30Ls. **Mail** can be received general delivery through **Poste Restante.** Address envelopes: Audrey (first name) BOWER (last name), POSTE RESTANTE, Stacijas laukums 1 (post office address), Rīga (city) LV-1050 (postal code), LATVIA.

TELEPHONES AND INTERNET ACCESS. Latvia is by far the most difficult of the Baltic states from which to **call** abroad; there's no way to make a free call on a Latvian phone to an international operator. Most telephones take **cards** (available in 2, 3, 5, or 10Ls denominations) from post offices, telephone offices, kiosks, and state stores. **International** calls can be made from telephone offices or booths. If a number is only six digits long, you must dial a 2 before the number; if it's seven digits, you needn't dial anything extra before the number. To call abroad from an analog phone, dial 1, then 00, then the country code. From a digital phone, simply dial 00, then the country code. The phone system has been undergoing changes; phone offices and *Rīga in Your Pocket* have the latest information. **Internet access** is only available in Rīga, where 24hr. cafes abound and average 0.5Ls per hr.

RĪGA

☎ 8(2)

Founded in 1201 by the German Bishop Albert, Rīga (pop. 756,000) just celebrated her 800th birthday in August 2001, and has every reason to do so. After a long history of occupation by Germans, Swedes, Russians, and Soviets, Rīga is once again free and experiencing a rebirth. The self-proclaimed capital of the Baltics, Rīga envisions itself as the Russian-speaking "Paris of the East." Rīga is not only larger than both Tallinn and Vilnius, but is also more urbane and cultured: the number of museums, concerts, plays, and various annual festivals in the city is staggering. Today, all of Rīga's treasures might seem newly rebuilt, renovated, or restored; but luckily, the city has not yet been flooded with camera-toting tourists, which makes the "Paris of the East" all the more appealing.

LATVIA

 The phone code in Rīga is 2 for all 6-digit numbers; there is no phone code for 7-digit numbers. Dial ☎ 116 for a Latvian operator and ☎ 115 for an international operator. Still confused? Call ☎ 800 80 08 for information or ☎ 118, 722 22 22, or 777 07 77 for directory services.

◼ INTERCITY TRANSPORTATION

Flights: Lidosta Rīga (Rīga Airport; ☎ 720 70 09), 8km southwest of Vecrīga (Old Riga). Take bus #22 from Gogol iela (0.20Ls). Taxi to Vecrīga 6Ls. **Air Baltic** (☎ 720 77 77; fax 720 75 05; www.airbaltic.lv) flies to many European capitals. **Lufthansa** (☎ 750 77 11; fax 750 77 13) flies to **Frankfurt, GER** while **Finnair** (☎ 720 70 10; fax 720 77 55; www.finnair.com) flies to **Helsinki, FIN.**

Trains: Centrālā Stacija (Central Station), Stacijas laukums (☎ 583 30 95), down the street from the bus station. Long-distance trains depart from the larger of the 2 buildings. Departures *(atiešanas)* are on the board to the right as you enter. Open daily 4:30am-midnight. To reach **Berlin, GER** or **Warsaw, POL** on the **Baltic Express,** you must go via Vilnius. To: **Moscow, RUS** (16hr., 2 per day, 12.78Ls); **St. Petersburg, RUS** (13hr., 1 per day, 10.69Ls); **Vilnius, LIT** (8hr., 3 per day every other day, 6Ls).

Buses: Autoosta (Bus station), Prāgas 1 (☎ 900 00 09). 200m from the train station in along Prāgas iela. Across the canal from the central market. Open daily 5am-midnight. To: **Kaunas, LIT** (4-5hr., 2 per day, 5.20Ls); **Minsk, BLR** (10-12hr., 3 per day, 6.20-6.90Ls); **Tallinn, EST** (4-6hr., 9 per day, 7-8.50Ls); **Vilnius, LIT** (5hr., 6 per day, 3.80-6Ls). Book buses to **Prague, CZR** (25½hr.; 2 per week; 28Ls, students 24Ls) through **Ecolines** (☎ 721 45 12; www.ecolines.lv). Other international destinations can be booked through **Eurolines** (☎ 721 40 80; fax 750 31 34; www.eurolines.lv).

◼ ORIENTATION

The city is neatly divided in half by **Brīvības bul.**, which leads from the outskirts to the **Freedom Monument** in the center and continues through **Vecrīga** (Old Rīga) as **Kaļķu iela.** To reach Vecrīga from the **train station,** turn left on Marijas iela and right on one of the small streets beyond the canal. **K. Valderāma iela** cuts through Vecrīga roughly parallel to Brivibas; from the river, it passes the National Theater on its left and the Art Museum on its right. **Elizabetes iela** surrounds Vecrīga and its adjoining parks in a semicircle. The information-packed *Rīga In Your Pocket* (1.20Ls), available at kiosks and travel agencies, has **maps** and up-to-date listings. Look out for the free *Rīga This Week*, which covers current and cultural events.

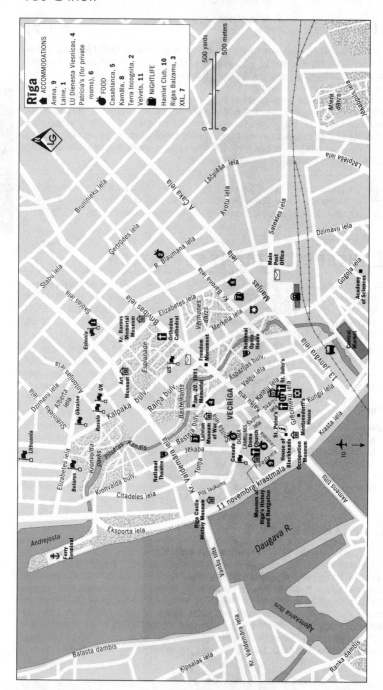

Rīga

ACCOMMODATIONS
Arena, 9
Laine, 1
LU Dienesta Viesnicas, 4
Patricia's (for private rooms), 6

FOOD
Casablanca, 5
Kamala, 8
Terra Incognita, 2
Velvets, 11

NIGHTLIFE
Hamlet Club, 10
Rīgas Balzams, 3
XXL, 7

▐ LOCAL TRANSPORTATION

Trains: Suburban trains, running as far as the Estonian border at **Valka/Valga,** leave from the smaller building of the train station. The Lugaži line includes **Cēsis** and **Sigulda.** Buy same-day tickets in the halls or advance ones in the **booking office** (☎583 33 97) off the right side.

Public Transportation: Buses, trams, and **trolleybuses** run daily 5:30am-midnight. Buy tickets on board (0.20Ls). Local bus booking office open daily 6am-10:50pm.

Taxis: Private taxis have a green light in the windshield. **Taxi Rīga** (☎800 10 10) charges 0.30Ls per km during the day, 0.40Ls per km at night.

▐ PRACTICAL INFORMATION

TOURIST AND FINANCIAL SERVICES

Tourist Office: Tourist Information Center, Ratslaukums 6 (☎703 79 00; fax 703 79 10; www.rigatourism.com), next to the House of Blackheads and the Occupation Museum. Sells **maps** and gives helpful English-speaking advice. Open daily 10am-7pm.

Embassies: Australia: Alberta iela 13 (☎733 63 83; fax 733 63 14; acr@latnet.lv). Open M-F 10am-noon and 3-5pm. **Belarus:** Jēzusbaznīcas 12 (☎732 25 50; fax 732 28 91). Open M-F 9am-1pm. **Canada:** Doma laukums 4, 3rd and 4th fl. (☎722 63 15; fax 783 01 40; canembr@bkc.lv). Open Tu and Th 10am-1pm. **Estonia:** Skolas iela 13 (☎781 20 20; fax 781 20 29; embassy@estemb.lv). Open M-Tu and Th-F 10am-1:30pm. **Ireland:** Brīvības iela 54 (☎702 52 59; fax 702 52 60). Open M-Tu and Th-F 9:30am-noon. **Lithuania:** Rūpniecības iela 24 (☎732 15 19; fax 732 15 89). Open M-F 9:30am-12:30pm. **Russia:** Antonijas iela 2 (☎721 01 23; fax 783 02 09), entrance on Kalpaka bul. Open M-F 9am-5:30pm. **UK:** Alunāna iela 5 (☎777 47 00; fax 777 47 07; www.britain.lv). Open M-F 9am-1pm and 2-5pm. **US:** Raiņa bul. 7 (☎703 62 00; fax 782 00 47; www.usembassy.lv). Open M-Tu and Th 9-11:30am.

Currency Exchange: At any of the common **Valutos Maiņa** kiosks. **Unibanka,** Pils iela 23 (☎800 80 09; fax 721 53 36; www.unibanka.lv) gives MC/V **cash advances** and cashes AmEx and Thomas Cook **traveler's checks** for free. Open M-F 9am-5pm. **24hr. exchange desks** are at the branches at Basteja bul. 14, Brīvības 30, and Marijas 2.

American Express: Latvia Tours, Kaļķu iela 8 (☎708 50 01; fax 782 00 20; www.latvi-atours.lv), has a representative. Open M-F 9am-6pm.

LOCAL SERVICES AND COMMUNICATIONS

Luggage Storage: At the **bus station,** near the Eurolines office. 0.20Ls per 10kg for 2hr. Open daily 6:30am-10:30pm.

English-Language Bookstore: Globuss, Vaļņuiela 26 (☎722 69 57). Open daily 8am-10pm. MC/V.

Bi-Gay-Lesbian Organizations: Puškina 1a (☎951 95 51; info@gay.lv). Open daily 9am-11pm; call before stopping by.

Laundromat: Nivala, on Akas iela between Ģertūdes iela and Lāčplēša iela. Self-service 3Ls per load; 2hr. laundry service 4Ls. Open 24hr.

24-Hour Pharmacy: Mēness aptieka, Brīvības bul. 121 (☎737 78 89). MC/V.

Telephone Office: Brīvības bul. 19 (☎701 87 38). MC/V **ATM.** Open M-F 7am-11pm, Sa-Su 8am-10pm. Smaller **branch** at the post office by the train station. Open 24hr.

Internet Access: Delat, Baznicas iela 4a (☎722 05 10). 14 fast connections, tea, and beer. 0.40Ls per hr. Open 24hr. **Elik,** Kaļķu iela 11 (☎722 70 79), smack in the center of Vecrīga, with 47 machines. 0.50Ls per hr. 3Ls if you want to spend the day here (8am-10pm). 4Ls for 24hr. Open 24hr. **Branch** at Čaka iela 26 (☎728 45 06).

Post Offices: Stacijas laukums 1 (☎ 701 88 04; www.riga.post.lv), near the train station. **Poste Restante** at window #3. Open M-F 8am-8pm, Sa 8am-6pm, Su 8am-4pm. **Branch** at Brīvības 19 (☎ 701 87 38). Open M-F 7am-11pm, Sa-Su 8am-10pm. **Postal Code:** LV-1050.

ACCOMMODATIONS

Rīga's prices for decent rooms are the highest in the Baltics. To arrange a private room, try **Patricia ❸**, Elizabetes iela 22 (☎ 728 48 68; fax 728 66 50; www.rigalatvia.net. Homestays from US$25; apartments from US$40. Open M-F 9:15am-6pm, Sa-Su 11am-1pm.)

Laine, Skolas iela 11 (☎ 728 88 16; fax 728 76 58; www.laine.lv). Heading away from Vecrīga on Brīvības bul., make a left on Dzirnavu iela and a right on Skolas iela. A tastefully decorated modern hotel with Latvian artwork on the walls. Rooms are comfortable and come with bath, phone, satellite TV, and minibar. Economy rooms share hall bathrooms. Breakfast included and served in the elegant, classic dining room. Call ahead. Singles 15-60Ls; doubles 25-70Ls. MC/V. ❸

Arena, Palasta iela 5 (☎ 722 85 83). The cheapest place in Vecrīga, Arena hides in an unmarked building by Dome Cathedral with a beautiful view of the old town. Hall shower and kitchen. Rooms are small but clean, and usually equipped with sinks. Call ahead. Open May-Sept.—circus performers live here Oct.-Apr. 3- to 4-bed dorms 4.50Ls. ❶

LU Dienesta Viesnicas, Basteja bul. 10 (☎ 782 03 60; fax 721 62 21). From the bus station, cross under the railroad tracks and take the pedestrian tunnel. Bear right on Aspazijas bul., which becomes Basteja bul. Enter through the Europcar Interrent office. Great location in Vecrīga. Singles 10Ls, with private bath 20Ls; doubles 16Ls/30Ls. ❷

FOOD

Look for 24hr. food and liquor stores along Elizabetes iela, Marijas iela, and Ģertrūdes iela. The central supermarket **Rimi,** Audēju 16, stocks just about everything you could ever want. (☎ 701 80 20. Open daily 8am-10pm. MC/V.) Occupying five enormous zeppelin hangars behind the bus station, **Centrālais Tirgus** (Central Market) is the largest market in Europe. It has the best selection at the cheapest prices; remember to haggle. (Open daily 8am-6pm.)

Terra Incognita, Blaumaņa iela 27 (☎/fax 728 0063; terraincognita@log.lv). Walk past the art for sale in this spirited African restaurant and art gallery. The menu offers African specialties, such as tasty couscous with vegetables (2Ls). Lounge on the comfortable sofas in back and soak in the live music W-Sa 8pm; African music F. Entrees 2-4Ls. 1Ls cover some nights. Open M noon-11pm, Tu-Sa 11am-11pm. ❷

Velvets, Skārņu iela 9 (☎ 721 50 75), just off Kaļķu iela in Vecrīga. This stylish French restaurant features moderately priced meals (entrees 1-7Ls) and a large dessert selection (1-3Ls). Try the delicious field mushroom cream soup (1.45Ls). Open Su-Th 10am-2am, F-Sa 10am-4am. MC/V. ❶

Kamāla, Jauniela iela 14 (☎/fax 721 13 32; kamala@delfi.lv), around the corner from the Dome Cathedral. An intimate Indian vegetarian restaurant named after the goddess of peace and prosperity. A decadent setting with soft couches, pillows, Indian rugs, and bejewelled lamps. Entrees 2-4Ls. Open M-Sa noon-11pm, Su 2pm-10pm. MC/V. ❷

Casablanca, Smilša iela 1/3 (☎ 721 24 20; ☎/fax 722 76 60), near Doma lamkums. Munch on hummus and falafel, or try the "oasis" lamb skewer marinated in fresh herbs and chili (3.90Ls) amid a colorful interior supported by Egyptian columns. Entrees 2-6Ls. Live music in summer Th; cover F 2Ls to dance. Open M 10am-1am, Tu 10am-2am, W-Th 10am-3am, F-Sa 10am-5am, Su 10am-midnight. MC/V. ❸

◎ SIGHTS

Most of Rīga's sights are clustered in Vecrīga, but even the "modern" parts of town, which generally date from the mid-19th century, offer their own architectural pearls. An exploration of Vecrīga should begin with the towering Freedom Monument, then branch out slowly to the side streets. Consider buying a **Rīga Card,** sold at most hotels and travel agencies, for restaurant and museum discounts and free rides on trams and trolleys. (☎/fax 721 72 17. 8Ls for 24hr., 12Ls for 48hr., 16Ls for 72hr.)

FREEDOM MONUMENT. (Brīvības Piemineklis.) Recently renovated, this beloved monument—affectionately known as "Milda"—stands proudly in the city center, raising her arms skyward as three gold stars seem to levitate above her fingertips. Dedicated in 1935, during Latvia's brief period of independence, she survived the subsequent Russian occupation by masquerading as a Soviet symbol. Mighty Milda depicts Liberty raising up the three main regions of Latvia (Vidzeme, Latgale, and Kurzeme), but Soviets claimed it represented Mother Russia supporting the three Baltic states. Two steadfast honor guards protect Milda daily 9am-6pm; the changing of the guard occurs on the hour. *(At the corner of Raiņa bul. and Brīvības iela.)*

BASTEJKALNS. Rīga's central park, surrounded by the old city moat (Pīlsētas kanāls), houses ruins of the old city walls. Across and around the canal, five red stone slabs stand as **memorials** of January 20, 1991, when Soviet special forces stormed the Interior Ministry on Raiņa bul. The dead included a schoolboy and two cameramen recording the events. At the north end of Bastejkalns, on K. Valdemāra iela, two sculpted men bear the weight of the **National Theater** on their shoulders. It was here that Latvia first declared its independence on November 18, 1918. *(Kronvalda bul. 2. ☎732 27 59. Open daily 10am-7pm.)*

DOME SQUARE. (Doma Lamkums.) Vecrīga's cobblestoned central square may feel timeless, but it actually only dates from 1936, when Latvian prime minister Kārlis Ulmanis (see **History,** p. 410) built the square so his voice could be heard during a speech. On the far side is the largest cathedral in the Baltics, **Dome Cathedral** (Doma Baznīca), begun in 1226. Unfortunately, only 12 of its original magnificent stained-glass windows survived the bombing of World War II. The immense pipe organ, which contains 6768 pipes ranging from 7mm to 10m in height, is put to use every July for the **International Organ Music Festival.** *(Follow Kaļķu iela from the Freedom Monument, then turn right on Šķūņu iela. ☎721 32 13. Cathedral open Tu 11am-6pm, W-F 1pm-6pm, Sa 10am-2pm. 0.50Ls, students 0.10Ls. Call for the concert schedule.)*

ST. PETER'S CHURCH. (Sv. Pētera Baznīca.) St. Peter's dark spire is visible throughout Rīga. Firs built in 1209, the church as it is now dates from 1408. Its tower, for a long time the tallest in Europe, hasn't fared as well: it has caught fire several times throughout the centuries. Destroyed again by artillery fire during World War II, it was rebuilt—complete with an elevator—in the 1970s. From the top of the 123m spire, you can see the entire city and the Baltic—don't miss this truly breathtaking view. *(Follow Kaļķu iela from the Freedom Monument and hang a left on Skārņu iela. Open in summer Tu-Su 10am-7pm; off-season Tu-Su 10am-5pm. Church free. Tower 1.60Ls, students 1Ls. Exhibitions 0.50Ls. Camera 0.50Ls, video 3Ls.)*

THE BOY WHO CRIED "NAPOLEON!" In 1812,

Rīga was devastated by a single herd of cattle. Traveling happily through the countryside, the oblivious bovines raised a cloud of dust that was clearly visible to the city's residents. Believing the herd to be Napoleon's army, the people set fire to the city, razing 740 buildings and hundreds of acres of farmland. The citizens later realized that the fearsome marauders had only been looking for grass and a good milking. As it turned out, Napoleon chose a different route into Latvia and wreaked his own havoc.

ART NOUVEAU. (Jugendstil.) The newer areas of Rīga showcase fantastic examples of Art Nouveau architecture. Figure-entwined buildings dot the city, but the largest grouping is on Alberta iela: works by the renowned architect **Mikhail Eisenstein,** father of the Russian filmmaker Sergei Eisenstein, are at #2, 2a, 4, 6, 8, and 13. Others are at Elizabetes iela 10b and Strelnieku iela 4a. Particularly spectacular are the gorgeous cream-colored building at Alberta iela 13 and the 1905 blue-and-white Stockholm School of Economics at Strelnieku iela 4a.

HOUSE OF BLACKHEADS. (Melngaluju Nams.) You can't wander through Vecrīga without noticing the striking, intricate Dutch facade of the city's reconstructed medieval Assembly Hall, now used for meetings of state by the president as well as for occasional concerts. The museum in the basement traces the building's stormy history; originally erected in 1334 for the use of town councilors and merchants, it became the property of the Blackheads company in 1687 (hence its name). Completely blown up in 1948 by the Soviets, it was just newly rebuilt in time for Rīga's 800th birthday. *(Rautslaukums 7, in the town square by the Occupation Museum. ☎ 704 43 00; fax 704 43 12; melngalv@rcc.lv. Open Tu-Su 10am-5pm. 1Ls. Camera 1Ls. Call ahead for tours in German, Russian, and English, 5Ls.)*

ORTHODOX CATHEDRAL. (Pareizticigo Katedrāle) Originally built in 1876-1884 by the architect R. Pflug in the Byzantine style of the 6th century, it was closed in 1961 and rebuilt as a "house of atheism," which contained a cafe, lecture hall, library, and planetarium. Restoration work is well underway to restore it to its original splendor. *(Brīvības iela 23, on the left past the Freedom Monument, walking away from Vecrīga. ☎ 721 29 01. Services M-F 8am and 5pm; Sa-Su 7, 10am, and 5pm. Open daily 7am-6pm. Donation requested.)*

BIĶERNIEKI FOREST. Erected in 2001 by the German War Graves Commission, this beautiful, powerful memorial remembers the Jews who were murdered here from 1941 to 1944. A central altar holds the inscription from Job, "O earth, do not cover my blood, and let there be no resting place for my cry." Around the altar rocks jut out of the ground representing the cities from which Jews were brought here. *(Take tram #14 from Brīvības to "Keguma," just before Biķernieki forest. Walk straight ahead, and on your right you will see a white gate leading to the memorial.)*

SOVIET SIGHTS. Outside the Occupation Museum stands the **Latvian Riflemen Monument** (Latviešu Strēlnieku Laukums), which depicts three granite soldiers guarding the square. Dedicated during Soviet times, the figures honor the team that served as Lenin's bodyguards during and after the Revolution. The statue was one of the few Soviet monuments not torn down after independence, since the Rifleman gained fame in the fight for Latvia during World War I. Some still want it gone. More insulting to the eyes, as well as Latvian pride, is the orange-tiered tower of the **Academy of Sciences.** Its nicknames range from "the Kremlin" to "Stalin's birthday cake." *(Turgeņeva 19, visible from Janvara iela and A. Čaka iela.)*

🏛 MUSEUMS

◙ OCCUPATION MUSEUM. (Okupācijas Muzejs.) The museum is a very accessible collection detailing the Nazi and Soviet periods, with top-notch exhibits and multilingual explanations in excruciating detail. Allow several hours to see it all. The initial Soviet occupation is depicted so vividly that you can almost hear the Red Army marching. *(Strēlnieku laukums 1, in the black-walled building behind the Latvian Rifleman statue. ☎ 721 27 15; fax 722 92 55; www.occupationmuseum.lv. Open May 1-Oct. 1 daily 11am-6pm; Oct. 1-May 1 Tu-Su 11am-5pm. Free, donations accepted.)*

ART MUSEUM. (Valsts Mākslas Muzejs.) Opened in 1905, the building is as much of a treat as the art within. The museum's excellent collection showcases 18th- to 20th-century works by Latvian artists in a magnificent pale green Neoclassical interior. Occasional concerts take place here. *(Valdemāra iela 10a, near the Elizabetes iela intersection. ☎ 732 32 04. Open Apr.-Oct. W and F-M 11am-5pm, Th 11am-7pm; Oct.-Apr. W-M 11am-5pm. 0.50Ls, students 0.40Ls. Tours in English, German, or Russian 3Ls.)*

MUSEUM OF RĪGA'S HISTORY AND NAVIGATION. (Rīgas Vēstures un Kugniecības Muzejs.) Originally a 13th-century monastery, the building now holds well-organized permanent collection displays Riga's ancient, medieval, and modern history. Highlights include the grandiose statue of St. Christopher (the patron saint of travelers and seafarers) and an exhibition on the prosperous days of the Latvian Republic. *(Palasta iela 4, behind the Dome Cathedral. ☎ 721 13 58; www.rigamuz.lv. Open May 1-Oct. 1 W-Su 10am-5pm; Oct. 1-May 1 W-Su 11am-5pm. 1.20Ls, students 0.40Ls. Tours in English, German, or Russian 3Ls/2Ls.)*

KRISJĀNIS BARONS MEMORIAL MUSEUM. (Krisjāna Barona Memoriālais Muzejs.) This is the apartment where Krisjanis Barons, the famous collector and publisher of Latvian folk songs, spent the last years of his life. In addition to family photos, personal letters, and fragments of his work, you can see the cabinet where Barons kept the thousands of folk songs he accumulated and organized over the course of 40 years. *(Barona iela 3, top floor. At the corner of Elizabetes iela. ☎ 728 42 65. English descriptions available. Open W-Su 11am-6pm. 0.60Ls, students 0.40Ls.)*

OPEN-AIR ETHNOGRAPHIC MUSEUM. (Etnogrāfiskais Brīvdabas Muzejs.) Nearly one hundred 18th- and 19th-century buildings from all over Latvia have been gathered here, complete with artisans churning out traditional wares. *(Brīvības 440. Take bus #1 from Merķela iela to "Brīvdabas Muzejs." ☎ 799 41 06. Open May-Oct. daily 10am-5pm; Nov.-Apr. 10am-4pm. 1Ls, students 0.25Ls. Tours 8Ls/5Ls; call ahead.)*

HISTORY MUSEUM OF LATVIA. (Latvijas Vestures Muzejs.) The museum's intriguing collection explores Latvian history from prehistoric times through the 19th century. The focus is on ethnographic history; the display includes folk crafts, musical instruments, costumes, and a reconstructed 19th-century hut. *(Pils laukums 3, off Valdemāra iela. ☎ 721 24 66. Open W-Su 11am-5pm. 0.70Ls, students 0.40Ls; W free. Tours in English, German, or Russian 5Ls.)*

LATVIAN MUSEUM OF WAR. (Latvijas Kara Muzejs.) Located inside Powder Tower, which has nine cannonballs still lodged in its 14th-century walls (curiously enough on the side inside the city). It now jams the long history of war into eight floors. *(Smilšu iela 20. From the Freedom Monument, walk into Vecrīga and turn right on Valnu iela. ☎ 722 81 47. Open May-Sept. W-Su 10am-6pm; Oct.-Apr. 10am-5pm. 0.50Ls, students 0.25Ls. English tours 3Ls. Cameras 2Ls.)*

🎭 ENTERTAINMENT

Rīga offers the best and widest array of music and performance art in the Baltics. Theaters close during the off-season (mid-June through August), but the Opera House and Dome Cathedral host special summer events. The **Latvian National Opera** performs in the **Opera House,** Aspazijas bul. 3 (☎ 722 58 03; fax 722 82 40; www.opera.lv), where Richard Wagner once presided as director. The **Latvian Symphony Orchestra** (☎ 722 48 50) has frequent concerts in the Great and Small Guilds off Fīlharmonija laukums. Smaller ensembles perform throughout the summer in **Wagner Hall,** Vāgnera iela 4 (Vāgnera zāle; ☎ 721 08 17). At the **Dome Cathedral,** popular organ concerts (ērģeļmūzikas koncerts) employ the world's third-largest

IN CASE YOU MISS EUROVISION 2003...

Everyone and their Latvian mother knows that Latvia's Marija Naumova won the 2002 Eurovision song contest in Tallinn, which means Latvia will have the honor of hosting **Eurovision 2003.** The Eurovision Song Contest, annually one of the most widely-watched events in the world, inevitably whips up a fervor across Europe, and in May of 2003 it will be coming to Skonto Hall in Rīga.

This is undeniably a big deal, but besides Eurovision, Latvian folk festivals are some of the most anticipated events in Rīga. And if you happen to be here from June 29 through July 6 2003, you're in luck—the **Festival of Song and Dance,** which only takes place every four years, is scheduled for that week. The festival is a 130-year-old tradition honoring Latvian folk crafts and music, aimed at increasing both international and domestic awareness of the country's enduring cultural arts. The Opening Ceremony will take place on June 29 at Dom Square, to be followed by the first performance of Bernstein's *Mass* in Latvian. The festivities will continue with an exhibit celebrating Latvian culture through folk and fine art at the Kipsala Exhibition Center, concerts in Dome Cathedral and the National Opera, and the Grand Dance Performance Daugava Stadium on July 5th. city. So don't cry if you miss Eurovision 2003. Instead, check with the tourist office for more details and an entertainment schedule.

—Dunia Dickey

organ. Buy tickets at *koncertzales kase*, opposite the main entrance at Doma laukums 1 (☎721 32 13), or in Wagner Hall. The **Rīga Ballet** carries on the proud dancing tradition of native star Mikhail Baryshnikov. The **ticket offices** at Teātra 10/12 (☎722 57 47; open daily 10am-7pm) and Amatu iela 6 (☎721 37 98), on the first floor of the Great Guild, serve most local concerts.

■ NIGHTLIFE

The social scene is centered in **Vecrīga,** where 24hr. casinos and *diskotekas* are ever-multiplying. If you feel like a mellow evening, join the hundreds of Rīgans sipping beer at their favorite beer garden.

Hamlet Club, Jāņa Sēta 5 (☎722 99 38), in the heart of Vecrīga. Poor Yorick's skull sits in back, wearing a hat and soaking up the artsy atmosphere. Live jazz M-Tu and F-Sa nights at 9:30pm (2.50Ls), while W is improv night (1Ls). Open M-Sa 7pm-2am.

Rigas Balzams, Torņa iela 4 (☎721 44 94), in Vecrīga near the Powder Tower. You can order your *Black Balza*—the Latvian national drink—any way you like it, even hot (2Ls). Or, sit back in the wicker chairs and try the creamy *Nerainigais balzams* (2.60Ls), made with balsam, mango, peaches, and ice cream. Entrees 5-7Ls. Open daily noon-midnight. MC/V.

XXL, A Kalniņa iela 4 (☎728 22 76; www.xxl.lv). Off K. Barona iela; buzz to be let in. This gay and lesbian bar combines a good restaurant and bar with a pumping club. Admire the leather daddies on the wall or attend the special events, from gymnastics exhibitions and go-go dancing. Cover Tu-Sa 1-5Ls. Open daily 4pm-6am.

■ DAYTRIPS FROM RĪGA

JŪRMALA   ☎(8)77

The commuter rail runs to Jūrmala (30min., every 30min. 5am-11:30pm, 0.51Ls). Public buses (0.18Ls) and microbuses (0.20-0.30Ls) connect Jūrmala's towns.

Sun-bleached, powder-fine sand, warm waters, and festive boardwalks have drawn crowds since the late 19th century to this narrow spit of sand 20km from the capital. From Rīga, beachless Priedaine is the first train stop in Jūrmala (YOUR-ma-la). In 1959, 14 of the region's towns were incorporated into the giant city-resort of Jūrmala (pop. 60,000), which quickly became popular with the vacationing Soviet elite. Dealt an economic blow when Latvian independence stripped the city of its eastern visitors, Jūrmala is now recovering, as tourists rediscover its beaches and shops. In fact, Majori and Bulduri have received the all-important Blue Flag—a beach status symbol based on water quality, safety, and toilet facilities. Any of the towns between **Bulduri** and **Dubulti** are popular for sunning and swimming, but if you're looking for Jūrmala's social center, go to **Majori**. Trainloads of people file to the beach or wander along **Jomas iela,** which is lined with cafes, restaurants, and shops. Not the place to go for secluded stretches of virgin sand; like Jomas iela, the beach itself is loud and crowded. From the train station, cross the road, walk through the small park, and turn right. The **tourist office,** Jomas iela 42, has **maps,** brochures, and English-speaking employees willing to help with anything. (☎642 76; fax 646 72; www.jurmala.lv. Open in summer daily 10am-9pm; off-season 10am-5pm.) There's plenty of eating and drinking on **Jomas iela.** For dinner and a strategic people-watching position, try **De La Presse,** Jomas iela 57. Sip a cocktail after a long day at the beach and try the juicy pork *shashlik* (2.90Ls), prepared on coals outside. After 9pm, the upstairs lounge turns into a disco. (☎776 14 01. Entrees 2-12Ls. Open daily 10am-4am. MC/V.)

SALASPILS MEMORIAL

Electric trains run to Dārziņi (20min., 14 per day, 0.30Ls). Make sure the train stops at Dārziņi before leaving Rīga. Do not take the train to "Salaspils." Last train back to Rīga departs at 10:14pm. When you get off the train, turn around and face the station. Cross two tracks and walk directly past it, away from the railroad, until you reach a paved road. Turn right and continue for 15min. You'll see signs for Salaspils Memorial. Take a left after the soccer field.

The Salaspils Memorial marks the remains of the Kurtenhof concentration camp, which was primarily a place of transit to larger death camps from 1941 Oct. The inscription over the entrance reads, "Here the innocent walked the way of death. How many unfinished words, how many unlived years were cut short by a bullet." Four clusters of massive sculptures—Motherhood, Solidarity, The Humiliated, and The Unbroken—watch over the Way of the Suffering, the circular path connecting barrack foundations in which flowers now grow. A black box emits a low ticking, like the pulse of a beating heart.

PILSRUNDĀLE ☎(8)39

Take the bus to Bauska (1¾hr., 22 per day, 1Ls). From Bauska, buses run directly to Pilsrundāle (2min., 18 per day, 0.25Ls), though not always on schedule. The palace is around a hedge to the left. ☎621 97; www.rpm.apollo.lv. Open May-Oct. daily 10am-6pm; Nov.-Apr. 10am-5pm. 1.50Ls, students 1Ls. Cameras 1-3Ls. English guidebook 1.20Ls. Special exhibitions 0.50Ls each; park exhibition 0.10Ls.

Located in the heart of the Latvian countryside, the magnificent **Rundāles Palace** (Rundāles pils) long served as a summer retreat for the local nobility. In the late 18th century, **Ernst Johann von Bühren** employed 15,000 laborers and artisans to build his pleasure dome, a maze of 138 gilded ballrooms and cavernous halls. Bartolomeo Rastrelli, the Italian master who planned St. Petersburg's Winter Palace (see p. 677), designed the palace in 1736, but it wasn't completed until 1768, when Catherine the Great commissioned Johann Michael Graff to finish the wall decorations. At the top of the grand staircase is the **Gold Room** (Zelta Zāle), the marble-and-gold-leaf home to the throne, with dramatic murals and soldiers' graffiti from 1812. In the **White Room** (Baltā Zāle), which was once a ballroom, cherubs represent the seasons and the elements. The upstairs exhibition, "Restoration, 10 Years," gives a good idea of the amount of work and attention to detail that transformed the ruined palace into mint condition between 1972 and 2002.

INLAND LATVIA

SIGULDA   ☎ (8)29

Situated in the Gaujas Valley National Park, Sigulda couldn't feel more removed from hectic Rīga. The dramatic castle ruins and aged caves hearken back to an earlier era, and the primeval forests, rivers, and gorges almost take you back in time. The slower pace of life does not mean inactivity, however; Sigulda offers much to interest the adventurous nature lover, from bungee jumping to hot-air ballooning. The renowned Sigulda Opera Festival takes place here at the end of every July in the shadow of the ruins.

TRANSPORTATION. Trains run from **Rīga** on the Rīga-Lugaži commuter rail line (1hr., 15 per day, 0.85Ls). **Buses** (1hr., 15-20 per day, 0.80Ls) drop passengers off at a stop on the far edge of Sigulda, at the corner of Gātes and Vizdemes. Walking back toward Rīga, take the first right on Gātes and walk across the train tracks to reach the **bus station,** Raiņa iela 3. (☎721 06. Open daily 6am-8pm. Ticket office open M-Sa 8am-1:30pm and 2-5:30pm.) For **bike rental,** look for the hut behind the bus station (1Ls per hr., 5Ls for 24hr., 3Ls for each additional day).

PRACTICAL INFORMATION. From the **bus** and **train stations,** walk along Raiņa iela to the center. Continue as it turns into Gaujas iela, which, after the Gaujas Bridge, becomes the steep Turaidas iela and passes **Turaida Castle.** Bus #12 runs directly to Turaida Castle (0.20Ls) and a cable car runs from the Sigulda side of the Gauja to Krimulda (5min., every 30min. between 7:25am-6:25pm, 0.50Ls). The **Tourist Information Center (TIC),** Pils iela 6, in the Hotel Sigulda, gives out free **maps** and arranges bed and breakfast stays in Sigulda. (☎/fax 713 35; www.sigulda.lv. Open daily May-Oct. 10am-7pm; Nov.-Apr. 10am-5pm.) **Exchange money,** cash AmEx or Thomas Cook **traveler's checks,** and receive **Western Union** services at **Latvijas Krajbanka,** Pils iela 1. (Open M-F 9am-5pm, Sa 9am-1pm.) A pharmacy, **Centra Aptieka,** is next door at Pils iela 3. (☎709 10. Open M-F 7:30am-9:30pm, Sa 9am-8pm, Su 9am-6pm. MC/V.) Across the street is the **post office,** Pils iela 2. (☎721 77. Open M 8am-6pm, Tu-F 8am-5pm, Sa 8am-2pm.) **Telephones** are outside. (Open daily 7am-9pm.) **Postal Code:** LV-2150.

ACCOMMODATIONS AND FOOD. The **TIC ❶** arranges private rooms (see above; breakfast 1Ls; 7Ls). **Hotel Sigulda ❹,** Pils iela 6, is in the center of town near the bus station. It is absolutely the finest accommodation in Sigulda. The original late 19th-century stone building has a modern addition completed in 2001; all rooms have private baths, and some have phone and TV. (☎722 63; fax 714 42; www.hotelsigulda.lv. Breakfast included. Pool and sauna 3Ls per hr. Singles 24Ls; doubles 30Ls. MC/V.) **Viesu Nams Livonija ❷,** Pulkveža Brieža iela 55, is farther from town but conveniently close to the bus stop on the highway. With your back to the train station facing the tracks, cross the tracks and walk right on Stacijas iela, and make a left on Gātes. Make another left on P. Brieža iela and Livonija will be on your left. The hotel is small and peaceful, with comfy beds, a kitchen, and a sauna. (Breakfast 2Ls. Sauna 10-15Ls per hr. Singles 14Ls; doubles 16-20Ls.) Located inside the 19th-century Sigulda Dome, ⚑**Pilsmuižas Restorāns ❷,** Pils iela 16, is one of the best restaurants in the region, and serves delicious and generous portions. Ask to go up to the roof, from where you can see all of Sigulda and nearby castle ruins. (☎921 41 49; fax 714 90 33. Entrees 2.50-5Ls. Open daily noon-midnight.) **Trīs Draugi ❶** (The Three Friends), Pils iela 9, has full, economical meals. (☎737 21. Open daily 8am-10pm.) A **grocery store** is next to the Kafejnīca at Pils iela 4. (Open M-Sa 8am-10pm, Su 9am-8pm. MC/V.)

⊙ 🔲 **SIGHTS AND ENTERTAINMENT.** A caption outside ⚔ **Turaida Castle** (Turaidas Pils) proclaims, "The wheel of history with its many wars, damage, and suffering has rolled over our little land." Across the river from Sigulda and 2km up the road at Turaidas iela 10, the restored brick fortifications of the castle are visible throughout the Gauja Valley and surrounding hilltops. Work on the castle began in 1214, initiated by German crusaders in town to convert the Liivs. Climb the steep staircase of the main tower (restored in 1959) for views of the region (tower open daily 8am-9pm). The **History Museum** (Siguldas Novadpētniecības Muzeja), next door, details the history of the Liiv people. English info complements the ancient music. (Open in summer daily 10am-6pm; off-season 10am-5pm. Castle, tower, and museum M-Tu 1Ls, students 0.80Ls; W-Su 1.50Ls/0.80Ls. Cameras 0.50Ls, video 1Ls.)

Walk 10-15min. back down the hill along Turaidas iela to reach the legendary sacred **caves** of Sigulda. The chiseled mouth of **Gutman's Cave** (Gūtmaņa Ala) is inscribed with coats of arms and scribbling from as far back as the 16th century. Climb the wooden stairway behind the cave and walk along the high ridge above the valley to reach the ruins of the 13th-century **Krimulda Castle** (Krimuldas Pilsdrupas). There's barely anything left, as the bulk of it fell in the 1601 Polish-Swedish war, but the hints of magnificence make the walk pleasant. Perched on a ridge to the right of Gauja iela, on the near side of the gorge, is the **Sigulda Dome,** the "new" castle-palace where the Russian Prince Kropotkin once lived. Behind the palace lie the immense ruins of the formerly glorious **Siguldas Castle** (Siguldas Pilsdrupas). Constructed between 1207 and 1226 by the German order of the Knights of the Sword, it was destroyed in the Great Northern War (1700-1721) between Russia and Sweden. Now it forms the backdrop for the outdoor stage where the Opera Festival and other performances take place.

🏔 **OUTDOOR ACTIVITIES.** A 2km walk follows the Gauja River in the opposite direction from Turaida Castle, toward the steep **Piķenes Slopes,** home of the deep **Devil's Cave** (Velna ala) and **Devil's Little Cave** (Mazā Velnala). The nearby spring is purportedly a **Fount of Wisdom;** ambitious mothers have been known to bathe their babes here. Another good hike runs from Siguldas Castle down to the Gauja and upstream to cross Vējupite creek. A bit farther upstream, stairs rise to **Paradise Hill** (Paradīzes kalns) and the view made famous by 19th-century Latvian painter Jānis Rozentāls. The **Gaujas National Park Center,** Baznicas iela 3, has 2-3hr. guided English tours

THE HIDDEN DEAL

CASTLE, SWEET CASTLE

Sigulda is best known for the unusual number of castles, palaces, and ruins sprinkling its rolling hills. What better place to stay the night, then, than in the **Krimulda Rehabilitation Center ❶,** situated in one of Sigulda's "newer" castles, a yellow neoclassical structure built. in the 18th century built high on a cliff overlooking the Gauja River Valley. Worlds away from the nonstop bustle of Rīga, Krimulda Castle is so secluded that the best way to reach it is by cable car.

Lucky for the budget traveler, a night's stay won't cost a royal fortune. Singles go for 5-7Ls and doubles for 10-15 Ls. In summer, 5Ls dorms open directly on to the lush garden. The hidden treasure here is not the volleyball court, the sauna (5Ls per hr.), or the various massages and therapeutic procedures available (1.40-14Ls), but rather Krimulda's spectacular views of Sigulda's sweeping hills. *(Menieku iela 3. ☎ 797 22 32, after-hours mobile 911 16 19; fax 797 17 21; krimulda@lis.lv.)*

—Dunia Dickey

and helps arrange accommodations in the park. (☎713 45. Open M 9:30am-6pm. Tours 20Lt per group. Call ahead.) **Makars Tourism Agency**, Peldu 1, can arrange all kinds of outdoor excursions, including canoeing, rafting, camping, bungee jumping, and even bobsledding. (☎924 49 48; fax 701 64; www.makars.lv.)

Visible from the commuter rail, the Olympic-sized **bobsled** and **luge run** plummets from Sveices iela 13. You can take the plunge year-round; in summer, you'll be on wheels. (☎739 44; fax 790 16 67. Open Sa-Su 10am-8pm. 3Ls.) To go bungee jumping, go up to the cable car, sign a release, and battle gravity. (☎725 31; fax 722 53. Open Sa-Su 6:30pm until last customer. 13Ls for the first jump, 11Ls for each subsequent jump.) Watching from the bridge as jumpers take the plunge is a popular sport on weekend evenings. Try **Dukšte Gunars** for **hot-air balloon** rides. (☎761 16 14; fax 786 0206; www.altius.lv. 30-50min. 70Ls per person; 1-1½hr. 100Ls per person; exclusive charter flight for 2-3 people 350Ls.) The **International Ballooning Festival** floats out of town in late May. Next to the Turaidas Castle, **horses** are available for hire. (☎292 43 69. Open Tu-F noon-6pm, Sa-Su noon-7pm. 5Ls per hr.)

CĒSIS

Entrancing medieval streets, majestic castle ruins, and nearby hills and streams draw foreigners and Latvians alike to Cēsis (TSEH-siss; pop. 19,500). The conquering knights of the Livonian Order once made it their headquarters, constructing a magnificent castle. The town also has a bloody history with Russia: in 1703, Peter the Great invaded and in 1919 it was the site of a crucial battle in the Latvian rebellion against Russia. Now it's a quiet cluster of striking old buildings and ruins.

▣▨ TRANSPORTATION AND PRACTICAL INFORMATION. Cēsis is easily reached from **Rīga** via suburban **trains** (1½-2hr., 12 per day, 1.50Ls) and **buses** (2hr., 1-2 per hr. 6am-9pm, 1.30Ls). **Public transportation** consists of two buses (0.20Ls): bus #9 runs west to the Gauja River while bus #11 runs east along **Poruka iela** and down **Lapsu iela**. **Raunas iela** heads to the town center from the station and opens up on the main square, **Vienības laukums. Rīgas iela** and **Valnu iela** head downhill at the square's south end and meet at **Līvu laukums**, the original 13th-century heart of the town. **Lenču iela**, which leads away from Vienības laukums, travels to Cēsis Castle (Cēsu Pils). Free **maps** are available at the **Cēsis Hotel** (see below), Vienības laukums 1 (☎412 23 92). The **tourist office**, Pils laukums 1, across from the castle, has a helpful English-speaking staff who can arrange a bed and breakfast stay in Cēsis or its vicinity. (☎412 18 15; fax 410 77 77; info@cesis.lv. Open M-F 9am-7pm, Sa-Su 10am-5pm.) **Exchange currency** upstairs at **Unibanka**, Raunas iela 8, which cashes **traveler's checks** and gives MC/V **cash advances**. (☎220 31. Open M-F 9am-5pm.) Ask the cashier at the **bus** and **train station** (☎412 27 62) to **store luggage**. The **post office**, Raunas iela 13, is at the corner of Vienības laukums in a red brick building. (☎227 88. Open M-F 8am-6pm, Sa 8am-4pm.) **Postal Code:** LV-4100.

▌▐ ACCOMMODATIONS AND FOOD. Ask at the **tourist office ❶** for bed and breakfast listings (4-20Ls). The **Cēsis Hotel ❺**, Vienības Lakums 1, is pure luxury. Revel in the huge beds and sparkling private baths. (☎412 23 92; fax 412 2695; www.danlat-group.lv. English spoken. Breakfast included. Singles 30Ls; doubles 42Ls; apartment 52Ls. 25% discount Sept. 1-May 31 F-Su. MC/V.) **Putniukrogs ❶**, Saules iela 23, isn't bad as far as 70s-style Soviet accommodations go, and you can't beat the price. Leaving the train station, cross the tracks at the right end of the platform. Follow the unmarked road to your right through the low bushes until it becomes paved. The hotel is the second brick building on the right after the dirt bike track; enter around the back. (☎412 02 90,mobile 942 56 11. Showers 1Ls. Singles 4Ls; doubles 8Ls.) **Camping** can be found at **Cīrulīši ❶**, Cīrulīsū iela 70. (☎927

53 78. Tent space 0.25Ls per person.) There's a **market** on Uzvaras Bulvaris between Vienības laukums and the tourist office. (Open daily 8am-4pm.) **Cafe Popular ❶**, in the basement of Hotel Cēsis, sports loud music and fresh meals. Drop by after 6pm for their 50% off beer any pizza discount. (☎412 23 92. Entrees 2-3Ls; pizza 1.40-2Ls. Open Su-Th 10am-11pm, F-Sa 10am-midnight. MC/V.) The more elaborate **Restoran Alexis ❹**, Vienības laukums 1, in the hotel, serves Latvian and international cuisine, including delicacies such as elk roast in juniper berry sauce (8.10Ls; ☎412 23 92. Entrees 4-8Ls. Open M-Sa noon-11pm, Su noon-10pm.)

SIGHTS AND ENTERTAINMENT. Begun in 1206 by the Germans, the town's **castle** (*pils*; ☎226 15), with its 4m thick walls, was completed in the 1280s. By the late 16th century, the Livonian Order's power had lapsed. When Russia's **Ivan IV** (the Terrible) laid siege to the fortress in 1577, its defenders chose to fill the cellars with gunpowder and blow themselves up rather than surrender. The castle was later rebuilt, but in 1703 **Peter the Great** ordered the castle to be bombarded and the Russians left it in ruins. The ruins are closed indefinitely because of unsafe building conditions. **Cēsis History Museum** (Cēsis Vēstures Muzejs), Pils iela 9, in the newer of the two castles (the one with a roof and all four walls), details the history of Cēsis and its castle; the third floor contains temporary exhibitions. Ask an attendant to point out the **Lenin statue**, now resting under a giant wooden crate resembling a coffin in the garden. The roof gives a great view of the other castle's ruins. (☎412 26 15. Open May 15-Nov. 1 Tu-Su 10am-5pm; Nov. 2-May 14th W-Su 10am-5pm. Exhibition, tower, and garden 0.50Ls, students 0.30Ls. Temporary exhibitions 0.40Ls/0.20Ls. Excursion to castle prison 0.60Ls. Cameras 2Ls. English tour 10Ls.) To visit the town's older section, take Torņa iela from the parking lot by the castle. A number of **hiking** trails trace the cliffs that line the Gaujas River, which flows along the east side of town. Bus #9 from the hotel on Vienības laukums covers the 3km to the trails' base. The best cliffs are to the south. To reach **Araisu Ezerpils**, a 9th-century settlement of wooden houses and windmills on an island, take a bus in the direction of Rīga and get off at Araisu, 7km outside Cēsis; look for signs there. Cēsis is also host to a number of annual festivals, including the **Cēsis Town Festivity** and the **Beer Festival** in late July. In mid-August, the **Cēsis Music Festival** hits town. If you find yourself in Cēsis in late June, you can catch the closing of the **Baltic National Opera**'s season at the outdoor stage, near the castle ruins.

KULDĪGA ☎(8)33

Fantastic pastel streets, burbling streams, red-tile roofed architecture, and buried ruins make Kuldīga (kool-DEE-ga; pop 13,920) one of the prettiest stops in the Baltics. Originally the seat of the Duchy of Courland, Kuldīga fell to Russia during the Great Northern War and was consigned to provincial status. The town has enjoyed anonymity forever since and remains unscathed by former Soviet rule.

TRANSPORTATION AND PRACTICAL INFORMATION. **Buses** arrive from **Rīga** (2½-3½hr., 10 per day, 2.15Ls) at Stacijas iela 2. (☎332 20 61. Open daily 4:30am-9pm.) Kuldīga's main street, **Liepājas iela,** intersects **Baznīcas iela,** which heads downhill to the castle park and the Venta river. From the **bus station,** turn right and then left at the barn onto **Jelgavas iela.** After the street becomes **Mucenieku iela,** hang a right onto **Putnu iela,** which hits Liepājas iela. The **tourist office,** next to the Town Hall at Baznicas iela 5, sells **maps.** (☎/fax 332 22 59; www.kuldiga.lv. Open M-F 9am-5pm, Sa 10am-4pm, Su 10am-2pm.) **Exchange money** at **Hansa,** Liepājas iela 15, which also cashes AmEx **Traveler's Cheques** for 1Ls commission and gives MC **cash advances.** (Open M-F 10am-5pm.) The **post office** is at Liepājas iela 34. (Open M-F 8am-6pm, Sa 8am-4pm.) **Postal Code:** LV-3301.

▐▌░ ACCOMMODATIONS AND FOOD. The new **Jāṇa Nams Hotel ❹**, Liepājas iela 36, offers small but comfortable rooms with fresh pine furniture, TV, and private bath. (☎332 34 56; fax 332 37 85. Pool and sauna 10Ls per hr. Breakfast included. Singles 20Ls; doubles 22Ls; suite 40Ls.) **Viesnīca Kursa ❷**, Pilsētas laukums 6, harbors clean rooms. (☎332 24 30; fax 332 36 71. Singles 11Ls, with TV 12Ls; doubles 16Ls/18Ls; triples 20/22Ls.) To get back to nature, check into **Ventas Rumba ❶**, a hostel near the waterfall across the river from town. (☎332 41 68. Rooms 2.50-5Ls per person.) Jāṇa Nams Hotel's **cafe ❶** serves dishes in a colorful interior with a working cobalt-blue fireplace. (Entrees 1-3Ls. Open daily 7am-11pm.) Crowded **Staburadze Kafejnica ❶**, Liepājas iela 8, closer to the river, provides some of the town's best deals; most dishes are under 1Ls. (☎332 22 75. Open M-Sa 9am-7pm, Su 10am-6pm.) The **Karejnica Rumba ❶**, on Pils iela, serves light fare on a veranda overlooking the waterfall and bridge. (Open daily 11am-11pm.) **Tirdzniecības Centras,** in the town square, has **groceries.** (Open daily 8am-10pm.)

◙ ♫ SIGHTS AND ENTERTAINMENT. The most famous church in Kuldīga, **St. Katrina's** (Sv. Katrīnas baznīca), is on Baznīcas iela. Built in 1655 and rebuilt during the 19th and 20th centuries, this large white building was used as a museum by the Soviets. (Services Su 10am-noon.) Turn left onto the high bridge or bear right uphill for an impressive view of the river and its **waterfall.** Outside, the **Regional Museum** (Kuldīgas Novada Muzejs), Pils iela 5, a single-vaulted room of the castle, forms part of a **sculpture garden.** (☎332 23 64. Open May 1-Oct. 1 Tu-Su 11am-6pm; Oct. 2-Apr. 30 11am-5pm. 0.50Ls, students 0.30Ls.) The **Lutheran Church of St. Anne,** Dzirnavu iela 12, is a brick giant with green-coned tops. The stained glass near the pipe organ shows a Socialist Realist scene of bounty and family virtue. (Open occasionally.) Every July, the four-day **Kuldīga Town Festival** brings foot and bike races, fireworks, and an eggrace.

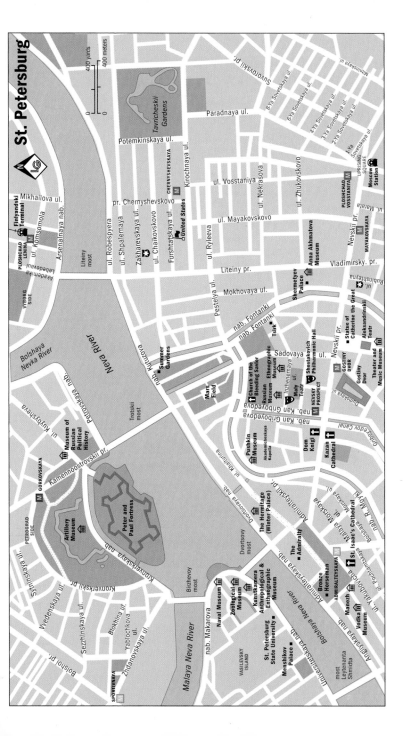

St. Petersburg

0   400 yards
0   400 meters

VYBORG SIDE

PLOSHCHAD LENINA Ⓜ

🚂 Finlyandskii Terminal

Akademika Lebedeva

Mikhaïlova ul.

ul. Komsomola

Arsenalnaya nab.

Liteiny most

Bolshaya Nevka River

Neva River

Petrovskaya nab.

ul. Kuybysheva

🏛 Museum of Russian Political History

Ⓜ GORKOVSKAYA

Kamennoostrovskii pr.

PETROGRAD SIDE

Kronverkskii pr.

🏛 Artillery Museum

Peter and Paul Fortress

Kronverkskaya nab.

SPORTIVNAYA 🚇

Ⓜ SPORTIVNAYA

Zhdanovskaya ul.

Bolshoi pr.

Sezzhinskaya ul.

Vedenskaya ul.

Blokhina ul.

Yablochkova ul.

VASILEVSKY ISLAND

St. Petersburg State University ■

Menshikov Palace ■

Malaya Neva River

nab. Makarova

🏛 Naval Museum

🏛 Zoological Museum

🏛 Kunstkamera Anthropological & Ethnographic Museum

Birzhevoy most

Universitetskaya nab.

most Leytenanta Shmidta

Bolshaya Neva River

Angliyskaya nab.

Admiralteyskaya nab.

Dvortsovy most

The Hermitage (Winter Palace) 🏛

The Admiralty

ADMIRALTEYSKAYA Ⓜ

🏛 Vodka Museum

Manezh 🏛

Bronze Horseman

🕍 St. Isaac's Cathedral

ul. Yakubovicha

Malaya Morskaya ul.

Bolsh. Morskaya ul.

Pochtamtskaya ul.

Galernaya ul.

Dvortsovaya nab.

ul. khalturina

Pushkin Museum 🏛

Akademicheskaya Kapella

Dom Knigi 🏛

🕍 Kazan Cathedral

nab. Kan Griboyedova

Konyushennaya

Summer Gardens ■

Mars Field

Church of the Bleeding Savior 🕍

Russian Museum 🏛

Ethnographic Museum 🏛

🎭 Maly Teatr

NEVSKY PROSPECT Ⓜ

Ⓜ GOSTINY DVOR

Gostiny Dvor

Theater and Music Museum 🏛

nab. Kanala Griboyedova

NEVSKY PROSPECT

Inzhenernaya ul.

Sadovaya ul.

Sadovaya

Tsirk

Shostakovich Philharmonic Hall

nab. Fontanki

nab. Fontanki

Sheremetyev Palace 🏛

Anna Akhmatova Museum 🏛

Liteiny pr.

Liteiny most

Mokhovaya ul.

Pestelya ul.

ul. Chaïkovskovo

ul. Shpalernaya

Zakharevskaya ul.

Furshtatskaya ul.

ul. Ryleeva

🏛 United States

pr. Chernyshevskovo

CHERNYSHEVSKAYA Ⓜ

Kirochnaya ul.

Kirochnaya ul.

Potemkinskaya ul.

Paradnaya ul.

Tavricheskii Gardens

Suvorovskii pr.

ul. Mirishnaya

1-ya Sovetskaya ul.

2-ya Sovetskaya ul.

3-ya Sovetskaya ul.

4-ya Sovetskaya ul.

6-ya Sovetskaya ul.

8-ya Sovetskaya ul.

ul. Vosstaniya

ul. Nekrasova

ul. Mayakovskovo

ul. Zhukovskovo

MAYAKOVSKAYA Ⓜ

Nevskii pr.

ul. Marata

PLOSHCHAD VOSSTANIYA Ⓜ

UPRISING SQUARE

🚂 Moscow Station

Kirochnaya ul.

Vladimirsky. pr.

ul. Rubinshteyna

Statue of Catherine the Great

Aleksandrinskii Teatr 🎭

Trotskii most

Troitskii most

Fontanki

Nevskii pr.

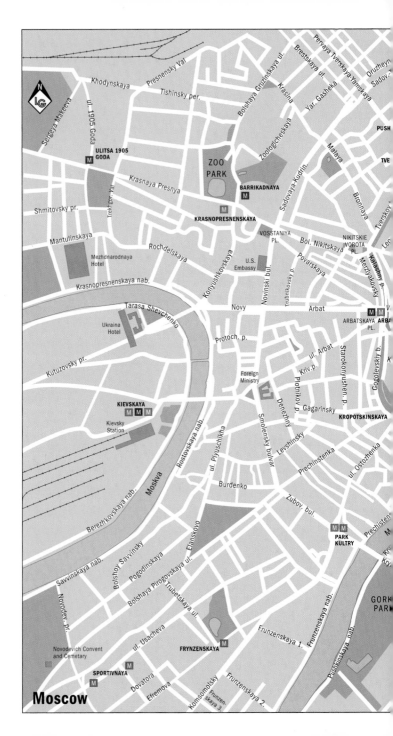

Moscow

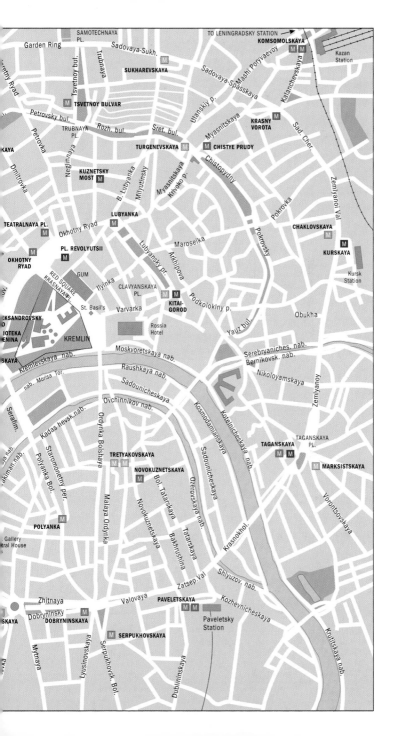

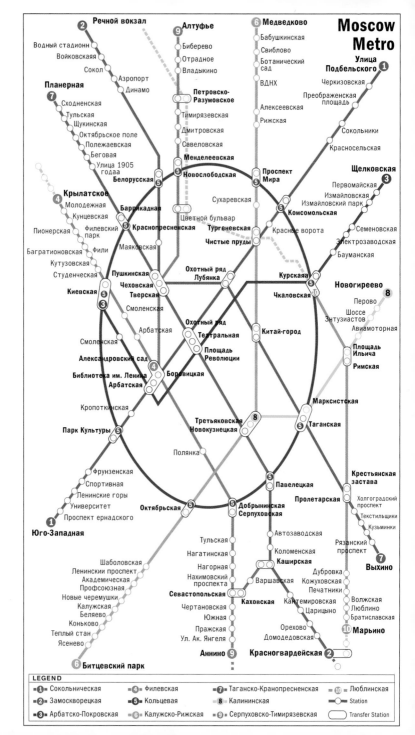

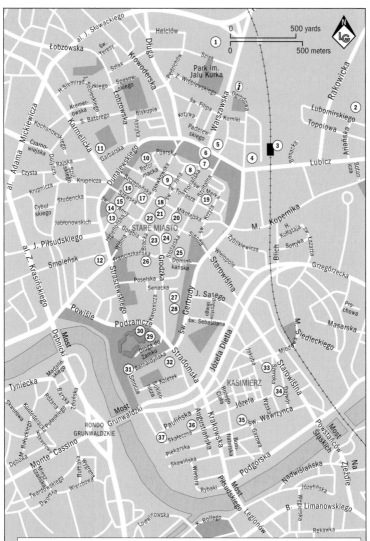

Central Kraków

Akademia Ekonomiczna, **2**
Almatur Office, **24**
Barbican, **6**
Bernardine Church, **32**
Bus Station, **4**
Carmelite Church, **11**
Cartoon Gallery, **9**
City Historical Museum, **17**
Collegium Maius, **14**
Corpus Christi Church, **35**
Czartoryski Art Museum, **8**
Dominican Church, **25**
Dragon Statue, **31**

Filharmonia, **12**
Franciscan Church, **26**
Grunwald Memorial, **5**
Jewish Cemetery, **33**
Jewish Museum, **34**
Kraków Glowny Station, **3**
Monastery of the
  Reformed Franciscans, **10**
Muzeum Historii Fotografii, **23**
Orbis Office, **19**
Pauline Church, **37**
Police Station, **18**
Politechnika Krakowska, **1**

St. Andrew's Church, **28**
St. Anne's Church, **15**
St. Catherine's Church, **36**
St. Florian's Gate, **7**
St. Mary's Church, **20**
St. Peter and Paul Church, **27**
Stary Teatr (Old Theater), **16**
Sukiennice (Cloth Hall), **21**
Town Hall, **22**
University Museum, **13**
Wawel Castle, **29**
Wawel Cathedral, **30**

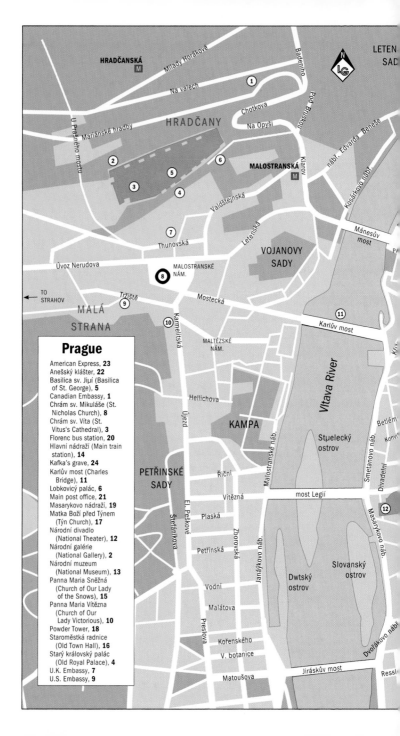

LETEN
SAD

N
LG

HRADČANSKÁ
M

Milady Horákové

Na valech

Badeniho

Pod Bruskou

U Prašného mostu

Mariánské hradby

Chotkova

Na Opyši

HRADČANY

nábř. Edvarda Beneše

MALOSTRANSKÁ
M

Klárov

Kosárkovo nábř.

Valdštejnská

Letenská

Mánesův
most

Thunovská

VOJANOVY
SADY

Úvoz Nerudova

MALOSTRANSKÉ
NÁM.

Tržiště

TO
STRAHOV

Mostecká

Karlův most

MALÁ
STRANA

Karmelitská

MALTÉZSKÉ
NÁM.

Prague

American Express, **23**
Anešský klášter, **22**
Basilica sv. Jiụí (Basilica
  of St. George), **5**
Canadian Embassy, **1**
Chrám sv. Mikuláše (St.
  Nicholas Church), **8**
Chrám sv. Víta (St.
  Vitus's Cathedral), **3**
Florenc bus station, **20**
Hlavní nádraží (Main train
  station), **14**
Kafka's grave, **24**
Karlův most (Charles
  Bridge), **11**
Lobkovicỵ palác, **6**
Main post office, **21**
Masarykovo nádraží, **19**
Matka Boží před Týnem
  (Týn Church), **17**
Národní divadlo
  (National Theater), **12**
Národní galérie
  (National Gallery), **2**
Národní muzeum
  (National Museum), **13**
Panna Maria Sněžná
  (Church of Our Lady
  of the Snows), **15**
Panna Maria Vítězná
  (Church of Our
  Lady Victorious), **10**
Powder Tower, **18**
Staroměstká radnice
  (Old Town Hall), **16**
Starý královský palác
  (Old Royal Palace), **4**
U.K. Embassy, **7**
U.S. Embassy, **9**

Hellichova

Újezd

KAMPA

Vltava River

Malostranské nábř.

Střelecký
ostrov

Smetanovo nábř.

Betlém

Konvi

Divadelní

PETŘINSKÉ
SADY

El. Peškové

Štefánikova

Říční

Vítězná

most Legií

Masarykovo nábř.

Plaská

Zborovská

Janáčkovo nábř.

12

Petřínská

Slovanský
ostrov

Dwtský
ostrov

Vodní

Malátova

Preslova

Kořenského

V. botanice

Jiráskův most

Matoušova

Ressl

Dvořákovo nábř.

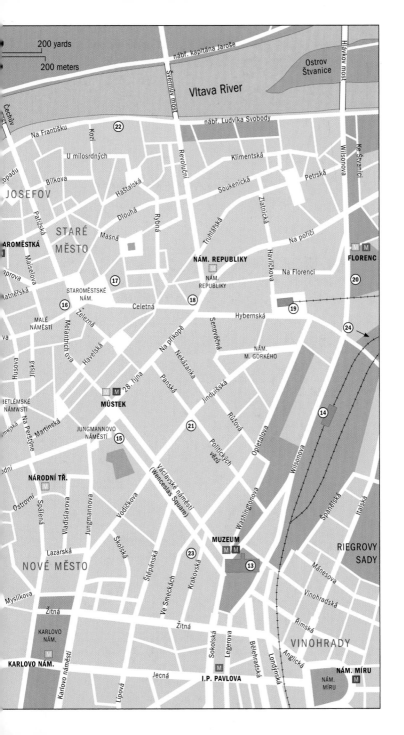

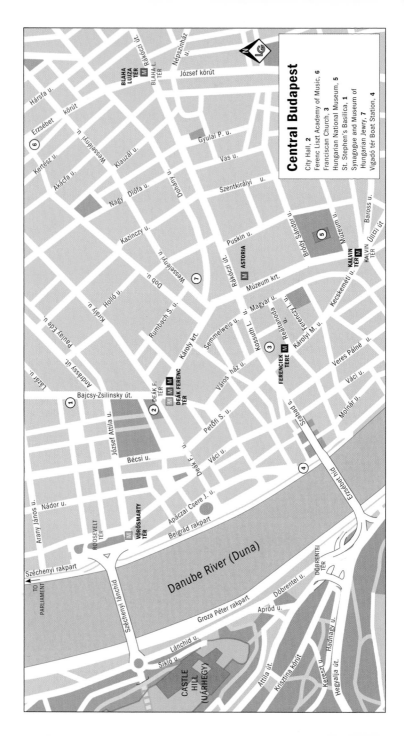

Central Budapest

City Hall, **2**
Ferenc Liszt Academy of Music, **6**
Franciscan Church, **3**
Hungarian National Museum, **5**
St. Stephen's Basilica, **1**
Synagogue and Museum of
Hungarian Jewry, **7**
Vigadó tér Boat Station, **4**

LITHUANIA
(LIETUVA)

LITA

AUS$1 = 1.93LT	1LT = AUS$0.52
CDN$1 = 2.26LT	1LT = CDN$0.44
EUR€1 = 3.45LT	1LT = EUR€0.29
NZ$1 = 1.65LT	1LT = NZ$0.61
UK£1 = 5.44LT	1LT = UK£0.18
US$1 = 3.51LT	1LT = US$0.28
ZAR1 = 0.33LT	1LT = ZAR3.02

Once part of the largest country in Europe, stretching into modern-day Ukraine, Belarus, and Poland, Lithuania has shrunk significantly as it has faced oppression from tsarist Russia, Nazi Germany, and the Soviet Union. The first Baltic nation to declare its independence from the USSR in 1990, Lithuania has become more Western with every passing year and now stands on the verge of joining the European Union. The spectacular capital city of Vilnius welcomes hordes of tourists into the largest Old Town in Europe, recently covered in a bright new coat of paint. In the other corner of the country, the mighty Baltic Sea washes up against Palanga and the towering dunes of the Curonian Spit.

LITHUANIA AT A GLANCE

OFFICIAL NAME: Republic of Lithuania

CAPITAL: Vilnius (pop. 590,000)

POPULATION: 3.6 million (81% Lithuanian, 9% Russian, 7% Polish)

LANGUAGES: Lithuanian (official), Polish, Russian

CURRENCY: 1 Lita = 100 centas

RELIGION: Roman Catholic, Lutheran

LAND AREA: 65,200km^2

CLIMATE: Maritime and continental

GEOGRAPHY: Lowlands with numerous lakes

BORDERS: Belarus, Latvia, Poland, Russia (Kaliningrad)

ECONOMY: 57% Services, 33% Industry, 10% Agriculture

GDP: US$7300 per capita

COUNTRY CODE: 370

INTERNATIONAL DIALING PREFIX: 810

HISTORY

PAGAN AND PROUD. The Baltic people settled in the region at the beginning of the Christian era. The Lithuanian tribes united under **Mindaugus,** who accepted **Christianity** in 1251 and was named the country's first Grand Duke by Pope Innocent IV in 1253. Mindaugas reverted to paganism, however, and was assassinated, along with two of his sons, in 1263. Lithuanian territory soon swelled to imperial proportions, swallowing modern Belarus and northern Ukraine, as **Grand Duke Gediminas** consolidated power in the 14th century.

Lithuania map showing cities including Rīga, Jūrmala, Sigulda in LATVIA; Klaipėda, Šiauliai, Panevėžys, Kaunas, Vilnius in Lithuania; Kaliningrad Region (Russia); Poland; and Belarus.

COME TOGETHER. Jogaila, Gedminas's grandson, married the 12-year-old Polish Princess Jadwiga and became Władisław II Jagiełło, King of Poland, in 1385. With this union, Jogaila introduced **Roman Catholicism** to Lithuania, converting the nobility. Turning his attention to Poland, Jogaila delegated control of Lithuania to **Vytautus Didysis** (the Great), most famous for his defeat of the Teutonic Knights (see **Trakai,** p. 448). Together, they expanded their empire until Vytautus's death in 1430, at which point Lithuanian territory stretched from the Baltics to the Black Sea, from Vilnius to a mere 160km away from Moscow. Lithuania solidified its ties to Poland with the 1569 **Union of Lublin,** which created the **Commonwealth of Two Peoples** (or Polish-Lithuanian Commonwealth), heralding a period of prosperity and cultural development. Along with the alliance came further division between the classes in Lithuania as the nobility became almost entirely Polanized while the peasantry held on to the old language and culture.

DECLINE AND FALL. In the 18th century the growing power of Russia and Prussia led to the three **Partitions of Poland** (see **Poland: History,** p. 476), which ceded most of Lithuania to Russia. By 1815, Russia had complete control of the territory. Nationalist uprisings in Poland in 1830-31 and 1863 provoked intensified campaigns of **Russification** in Lithuania; the tsars closed the 250-year-old University of Vilnius and banned the use of Lithuanian in public places. As Russia's empire began to crumble, Lithuania was subjected to the geopolitical whims of its mighty neighbors. German troops returned to Lithuania in 1915, 500 years after the defeat of the Teutonic knights. They left at the end of 1918, only to have the Soviets try to regain hold of the country. The Lithuanians expelled the Red Army in 1919 and declared **independence,** but during the confusion Poland took **Vilnius**—the population of the city was predominantly Polish—and refused to release it. A dispute also arose with Germany over the port of **Klaipėda,** a predominantly German city that was Lithuania's only viable harbor on the Baltic.

STUCK IN THE MIDDLE AGAIN. Deprived of its capital and primary port, Lithuania's independence was short-lived. A parliamentary democracy collapsed in 1926 in a coup, as dictator **Antanas Smetona** banned opposition parties. Whatever autonomy remained disappeared with the 1939 **Nazi-Soviet Non-Aggression Pact** and subsequent treaties, which invited the Soviets to invade. In June 1941, the Soviets began deporting Lithuanians and exiling them to remote regions of the USSR. Some 35,000 people were displaced. The Nazi occupation caused even greater hardship, as Lithuania lost another 250,000 citizens, including most of its Jewish population.

FINDING INDEPENDENCE. The Soviets returned in 1944, although they were opposed by Lithuanian guerrilla fighters—at their height 40,000 strong—into the early 1950s. It was not until the 1960s that **Antanas Sniečkus** managed to solidify Soviet rule, and resistance persisted through the stagnation of the 1970s and 1980s, as the republic generated more *samizdat* ("self-made" dissident publications) per capita than any other region in the Soviet Union. **Mikhail Gorbachev**'s reforms fell on dangerously fertile ground, and on March 1, 1990, Lithuania shocked the world when it seceded from the USSR. Moscow immediately retaliated, attempting futilely to disconnect the region's oil and gas resources. In a public relations disaster for Gorbachev, the Soviets launched an assault on Vilnius's radio and TV center, leaving 14 dead. Only in the wake of the failed Soviet *putsch* of August 1991 did Lithuania achieve independence. Despite internal divisions, the country rejoiced on August 31, 1993, when the last Russian soldiers left Lithuania.

TODAY

ECONOMIC WOES AND POLITICAL HOPES. Lithuania got off to an early start on economic reforms, and has been labeled by investors as one of Eastern Europe's economic "tigers." Recently, however, many of its reforms have run aground. Approximately 80% of the population is officially poor, and disenchantment with government institutions has grown. An associate member of the **European Union** since 1995, the country nonetheless remains heavily dependent on Russia for fuel and has therefore suffered from Russia's financial woes. Lithuania ranks first among the Baltic states in meeting EU membership requirements regarding the treatment of minorities, but it currently lags behind both Latvia and Estonia in economic categories. Still, Lithuania is currently projected to join the EU in 2004. Of the Baltic states Lithuania maintains the most cordial relations with its former ruler, due largely to the smaller Russian population on its soil. Among the Baltic states, its chances for **NATO** membership are thought to be the greatest, both because of its good relations with Russia and its ties to NATO-member Poland.

POLITICS. Prime Minister **Roland Paksas** resigned in 1999 to protest a deal to sell state oil control to US energy giant Williams Corp and was succeeded by the respected but relatively unpopular **Andrius Kublius.** The ruling right-center coalition, composed of the **Homeland Union-Lithuanian Conservatives** (TS-LK) and the conservative **Christian Democrats,** has attempted to catch up by implementing IMF austerity measures, but the resulting short-term decline in living standards has hurt the ruling coalition. The system of representation used in Lithuania's parliament has generally made it less fragmented than the legislatures of Latvia and Estonia, contributing to a lower turnover rate. The Lithuanian **presidency** is relatively weak; the President's primary power is in shaping foreign policy. **Valdas Adamkus,** elected in January 1998, currently holds the office.

PEOPLE AND CULTURE

LANGUAGE

Lithuanian is one of only two Baltic languages (Latvian is the other). All "r"s are trilled. **Polish** is helpful in the south, **German** on the coast, and **Russian** most places, although it is not as prominent as in Latvia. Russians aren't always well-received, so try English first before switching into Russian. If someone seems to sneeze at you, they're just saying *ačiu* (aa-choo; thank you). For a phrasebook and glossary, see **Glossary: Lithuanian,** p. 884.

FOOD AND DRINK

LITHUANIA	❶	❷	❸	❹	❺
FOOD	under 11Lt	11-20Lt	21-30Lt	31-40Lt	over 40Lt

Lithuanian cuisine is heavy and sometimes greasy. Keeping a **vegetarian** or **kosher** diet will prove difficult, if not impossible. Restaurants serve various types of *blynai* (pancakes) with *mėsa* (meat) or *varške* (cheese). *Cepelinai* are heavy, potato-dough missiles of meat, cheese, and mushrooms, served from street stands throughout Western Lithuania. *Šaltibarščiai* is a beet and cucumber soup prevalent in the east, *karbonadas* is breaded pork fillet, and *koldunai* are meat dumplings. Good Lithuanian **beer** flows freely. *Kalnapis* is popular in Vilnius and most of Lithuania, *Baltijos* reigns supreme around Klaipėda, and the award-winning *Utenos* is everywhere. Lithuanian **vodka** *(degtinė)* is also very popular.

CUSTOMS AND ETIQUETTE

Reserve informal greetings for those you know personally. Say *"laba diena"* (good day) whenever you enter a shop to ensure good feelings. In polite company, you can never say *"prašau"* too many times (both "please" and "you're welcome"). Handshakes are the norm for men; women get handshakes and perhaps a peck on the cheek. **Tipping** is not expected, but some Lithuanians leave 10% for excellent service. When eating in someone's home or, oddly enough, going to the doctor, bring a gift of flowers or chocolates. Feel free to **smoke** anywhere.

THE ARTS

HISTORY

LITERATURE. The earliest Lithuanian writings were the *Chronicles of the Grand Duchy of Lithuania*, written in an East Slavic dialect. During the Middle Ages and the Renaissance, Polish and Latin were the primary languages of Lithuanian literature. The first book in Lithuanian, a Lutheran catechism, was printed in 1547. The year 1706 saw the appearance of secular literature with the publication of *Aesop's Fables*. A Lithuanian translation of the **New Testament** was published in 1701 and a Lithuanian Bible in 1727. The first Lithuanian dictionary was the 1629 *Dictionarium trium linguarum* by **K. Sirvydas**. After 1864, many writers violated the tsarist ban on publishing Lithuanian works in Latin letters (as opposed to Cyrillic), seeking to overthrow Russian political and Polish cultural control. Known for both dramatic and lyric poetry, "the poet-prophet of the Lithuanian renaissance" was **Jonas Mačiulis,** whose 1895 *Voices of Spring (Pavasario balsai)* launched modern Lithuanian poetry. During the inter-war period, ex-priest **Vincas Mykolaitis-Putinas** pioneered the modern Lithuanian novel with *In the Altar's Shadow (Altorių šešėly)*. After the Second World War, Soviet rule gagged and shackled Lithuanian writers, but some literary voices managed to find alternate modes of expression. The poetry of **Alfonsas Nyka-Niliunas** and the novels of **Marius Katiliskis** flouted propagandistic Soviet Socialist Realism. *Pre-Dawn Highways*, by **Bronius Radzevicius,** which depicts an intellectual alienated from his national culture, is considered the strongest work of the late Soviet period.

MUSIC AND FINE ART. Both Lithuanian music and painting have been heavily influenced by the traditional folk culture. Much of the visual arts' development has centered around the **Vilnius Drawing School,** founded in 1866. Mikolojus Ciurlionis was one of the major figures in this artistic school (see **Kaunas,** p. 453). One of the major independent filmmakers of this century has been the Lithuanian-American artist Jonas Mekas, who is perhaps best known for his 1976 film *Lost Lost Lost*—an account of his arrival in New York and his contact with New York art-house figures like Allen Ginsberg and Frank O'Hara.

CURRENT SCENE

One of the best places to see and experience **wooden sculpture**—Lithuania's most prominent folk art form—is **Witch's Hill** (see p. 461), along the Curionian Spit. Life-sized sculptures evoke ancient myths and legends, carved in distinctive Lithuanian style. Lithuania's modern **architecture** has been greatly influenced by Finnish styles and the celebrated French architect Le Corbusier. The **art galleries** of **Vilnius** (see p. 444) and **Klaipėda** (see p. 460) are the best places to view works by up-and-coming Lithuanian artists.

HOLIDAYS AND FESTIVALS

NATIONAL HOLIDAYS IN 2003	
January 1 New Year's Day and Flag Day	**May 1** May Day
February 16 Independence Day	**July 6** Day of Statehood
March 11 Restoration of Independence	**August 15** Feast of the Assumption
April 20 Easter	**November 1** All Saints' Day
April 21 Easter Monday	**December 25-6** Christmas

KAZIUKAS FAIR. At this annual fair, held in Vilnius since the 19th century, craftsmen from around Lithuania and Eastern Europe gather to display their wares from February 28-March 2 in 2003.

WORLD LITHUANIAN SONG FESTIVAL. Held in Kalnu Park from July 1 to 7 in 2003, the festival attracts performers from around the world to Lithuania in a gigantic musical celebration.

ADDITIONAL RESOURCES

GENERAL HISTORY

The Baltic Revolution: Estonia, Latvia, Lithuania and the Path to Independence, by Anatol Lieven (1993). Contrasts the Baltic states' respective histories.

The Jews of Lithuania, by Masha Greenbaum (1995). A must for anyone interested in Lithuania's rich Jewish history.

FICTION, NONFICTION, FILM

The Issa Valley, by Czesław Miłosz (1998). This Nobel prize-winning poet (see **Poland: Literature,** p. 479) describes his childhood in the Vilnius of imperial Russia.

Native Realm, also by Miłosz (1968). In this phenomenal autobiography, Miłosz meditates upon the history of his home city and all of Eastern Europe.

There is no Ithaca: Idylls of Semeniskiai and Reminiscences, by Jonas Mekas (1996). A series of reflections from a Lithuanian who left the country to become an underground New York filmmaker.

Reminiscences of a Journey to Lithuania, dir. Jonas Mekas (1971-1972). A film diary of Mekas's first trip to his country of birth after 25 years of exile.

LITHUANIA ESSENTIALS

ENTRANCE REQUIREMENTS

Passport: Required of all travelers to Lithuania.

Visa: Required of citizens of South Africa.

Letter of Invitation: Not required.

Inoculations: None required. Recommended up-to-date on MMR (measles, mumps, and rubella), DTaP (diptheria), Polio booster, Hepatitis A, Hepatitis B.

Work Permit: Required for all foreigners planning to work in Lithuania.

International Driving Permit: Required of all those planning to drive.

DOCUMENTS AND FORMALITIES

EMBASSIES AND CONSULATES

Embassies of other countries in Lithuania are all in Vilnius (see p. 441). Lithuania's embassies and consulates abroad include:

Australia: Honorary Consulate: 40B Fiddens Wharf Rd., Killara, NSW 2071 (☎02 949 825 71).

Canada: 130 Albert St. #204, Ottawa, ON K1P 5G4 (☎613-567-5458; fax 567-5315; ltemb@storm.ca).

New Zealand: Honorary Consulate: 28 Heather St., Parnell Auckland (☎09 336 7711; fax 307 2911; saul@f1rst.co.nz).

South Africa Honorary Consulate: Killarney Mall, 1st fl., Riviera Rd., Killarney Johannesburg; P.O. Box 1737, Houghton 2041 (☎011 486 3660; fax 486 3650; lietuvos@iafrica.com).

UK: 84 Gloucester Pl., London W1U 3HN (☎020 7486 6401; fax 7486 6403).

US: 2622 16th St. NW, Washington, D.C. 20009 (☎202-234-5860; fax 328-0466; www.ltembassyus.org).

VISA AND ENTRY INFORMATION

Citizens of Australia, Canada, Ireland, New Zealand, the UK, and the US do not need a visa for visits up to 90 days. Citizens of South Africa who have visas from Estonia or Latvia can use those to enter Lithuania; otherwise, regular 90-day visas are required. Send a completed application, one recent passport-sized photo, your passport, the application fee (by check or money order), and a stamped, self-addressed envelope to the nearest Lithuanian embassy or consulate. Single-entry visas cost US$10 (valid for 90 days); multiple-entry visas US$20 (valid for 90 days); transit visas US$5 (valid for 48hr.); double-transit visas US$15. Regular service takes two weeks; rush service costs US$20 extra for 24hr. or US$15 extra for 72hr. service. "Special Visas" for temporary residence can be issued from the Migration Department of the Ministry of the Interior to those who wish to live in Lithuania for up to 1 year. There is no fee for crossing a Lithuanian **border.** Visas are not available at the border, but Estonian and Latvian visas can double as Lithuanian visas. Avoid crossing through Belarus to enter or exit Lithuania; not only do you need a transit visa for Belarus (US$20-30 at the border), but border guards will frequently demand an unofficial border-crossing "surcharge."

TRANSPORTATION

BY PLANE. Finnair, Lufthansa, LOT, SAS, and other, smaller, airlines fly into Vilnius from their hubs.

BY TRAIN. Trains are more popular for international and long-distance travel. Two major lines cross Lithuania: one runs north-south from **Latvia** through **Šiauliai** and **Kaunas** to **Poland** (via **Belarus**), and the other runs east-west from **Belarus** through **Vilnius** and Kaunas to **Kaliningrad,** or on a branch line from Vilnius through Šiauliai to **Klaipėda.**

BY BUS. Domestic buses are faster, more common, and only a bit more expensive than the often-crowded trains. Vilnius, Kaunas, and Klaipėda are easily reached by train or bus from **Belarus, Estonia, Latvia, Poland,** and **Russia.**

BY FERRY. Ferries connect Klaipėda with **Kiel, GER** and **Muhkran, GER.**

BY THUMB. Hitchhiking is common in Lithuania, although many drivers charge a fee comparable to local bus or train fares. Locals form a queue along major roads leaving large cities—be sure not to cut. *Let's Go* does not recommend hitchhiking.

TOURIST SERVICES AND MONEY

Major cities have official **tourist offices. Litinterp** is generally the most helpful organization for travel info; they will reserve accommodations, usually without a surcharge. Vilnius, Kaunas, and Klaipėda each have an edition of the *In Your Pocket* series, available at newsstands and some hotels.

The unit of **currency** is the **Lita** (1Lt=100 centas), plural Litai. In February 2002 the Lita was fixed to the Euro at €1 = 3.4528Lt. Prices are stable, with inflation hovering at just under 3%. Except in Vilnius, exchange bureaus near the train station usually have poorer rates than banks; it's often difficult to exchange currencies other than US dollars and Euros. Most banks cash **traveler's checks** for 2-3% commission. **Visa cash advances** can usually be obtained with minimum hassle. **Vilniaus Bankas,** with outlets in major cities, accepts major credit cards and traveler's checks for a small commission. If you're planning on traveling off the touristed path, be aware that most places catering to locals don't take credit cards. **ATMs,** especially **Visa,** are readily available in most cities.

HEALTH AND SAFETY

 EMERGENCY NUMBERS: Police: ☎02 Fire: ☎01 Ambulance: ☎03

HEALTH AND SAFETY. Well-stocked **pharmacies** are everywhere and carry most medical supplies and German or French brands of tampons, condoms, and toiletries. Drink bottled mineral water, and **boil tap water** for 10 minutes before drinking. A triangle pointing downward indicates men's **bathrooms;** an upward-pointing triangle indicates women's bathrooms. Many restrooms are nothing but a hole in the ground. Lithuania's **crime rate** is generally lower than most of Europe. Vilnius is one of the safer capitals in Europe, although street crime does occur on occasion. Lithuanian police are generally helpful but understaffed, so your best bet for English-speaking assistance is still your **consulate.**

WOMEN, MINORITY, AND BGLT TRAVELERS. Women traveling alone will be noticed but shouldn't encounter too much difficulty. Skirts, blouses, and heels are far more common than jeans, shorts, tank tops, or sneakers. **Minorities** traveling to Lithuania may encounter unwanted attention or discrimination, though most is directed towards Roma (Gypsies). **Homosexuality** is legal but not always tolerated. Lithuania has the most nightclubs, hotlines, and services for gays and lesbians in the Baltics (see **Vilnius: Practical Information,** p. 441).

ACCOMMODATIONS AND CAMPING

LITHUANIA	❶	❷	❸	❹	❺
ACCOM.	under 30Lt	31-80Lt	81-130Lt	131-180Lt	over 181Lt

HOSTELS, HOTELS, AND HOMESTAYS. Lithuania has several **youth hostels**. HI membership is nominally required, but an LJNN guest card (10.50Lt at any of the hostels) will suffice. The head office is in Vilnius (see **Vilnius: Practical Information,** p. 441). Their *Hostel Guide* is a handy booklet with info on bike and car rentals, hotel reservations, and maps. **Hotels** across the price spectrum abound in Vilnius and most major towns. **Litinterp,** with offices in Vilnius, Kaunas, and Klaipėda, assists in finding homestays or apartments for rent.

CAMPING. Camping is becoming increasingly popular, but is vigorously restricted to marked campgrounds by law, particularly along the Curonian Spit.

KEEPING IN TOUCH

MAIL. Airmail *(oro pastu)* **letters** abroad cost 1.70Lt (postcards 1.20Lt) and usually take about one week to reach the US. **Poste Restante** is available. Address envelope as follows: Carolyn (first name) KIMBALL (LAST NAME), POSTE RESTANTE, Laisves al. 102 (post office address), Kaunas (city) LT-3000 (postal code), LITHUANIA. **EMS** international mail takes three to five days.

TELEPHONES AND INTERNET ACCESS. There are two kinds of public phones: rectangular ones accept magnetic strip cards and rounded ones accept chip cards. Both are sold at phone offices and many kiosks in denominations of 3.54Lt, 7.08Lt, and 28.32Lt. Calls to **Estonia** and **Latvia** cost 1.65Lt per minute; **Europe** 5.80Lt; and the **US** 7.32Lt. Most cities have reliable **Internet** access.

VILNIUS ☎ 5

Deluged by new businesses and foreign investment, Vilnius (pop. 579,000) leads Lithuania's bid to join the EU in both name and spirit. Founded in 1321 after a prophetic dream by Grand Duke Gediminas, Vilnius grew and flourished throughout the centuries despite numerous foreign occupations from both East and West. Scarred but not destroyed by WWII, the Holocaust, and the iron grip of the Soviet Union, Vilnius remains a rich cultural center today. Its red roofs, cobblestone streets, and exquisite churches provide a dramatic setting for its vibrant commercial spirit, cellphone-toting youth, and eternal Lithuanian pride.

⊫ TRANSPORTATION

Flights: The **airport** (oro uostas), Rodūnės Kelias 2 (info ☎ 30 66 66, booking 75 26 00), 5km south of town. Buses #1 or 2 head to Old Town. Airlines include: **Air Lithuania** (☎ 13 13 22; www.airlithuania.lt); **Finnair** (☎ 33 08 10; www.finnair.com); **Lithuanian Airlines** (☎ 75 25 85; www.lal.lt); **LOT** (☎ 73 90 20; www.lot.com); **Lufthansa** (☎ 30 60 31; www.lufthansa.com); **SAS** (☎ 39 55 00; www.scandinavian.net).

Trains: Geležinkelio Stotis, Geležinkelio 16 (☎ 33 00 86; www.litrail.lt). Entering the station, domestic tickets are sold to the left and international (reservations for Western Europe 69 37 22) to the right. Tickets for trains originating outside of Lithuania can be bought no earlier than 3hr. before departure. Open daily 6-11am and noon-6pm. All international trains (except those heading north) pass through Belarus, which requires a Belarussian visa (see **Belarus: Essentials,** p. 69). To: **Berlin, GER** (22hr., 1 per day, 317Lt); **Kaliningrad, RUS** (7½hr., 2 per day, 70Lt); **Minsk, BLR** (5½hr., 2 per day, 57Lt); **Moscow, RUS** (17hr., 1 per day, 128Lt); **Rīga, LAT** (7½hr., 5 per day, 72Lt); **St. Petersburg, RUS** (18hr., 3 per day, 110Lt); **Warsaw, POL** (8hr., 4 per day, 115Lt).

Buses: Autobusų Stotis, Sodų 22 (☎ 90 16 61, reservations 16 29 77), opposite the train station. **Eurolines** (☎ 69 00 00; fax 69 06 90; www.eurolines.com) and **Varta Buses** (☎ 73 02 19 or 73 11 73; fax 72 38 84; www.5ci.net/varta) serve Western Europe. Windows #13-15 serve destinations outside the former Soviet Union. Open daily 7am-8pm. To: **Kaliningrad, RUS** (8hr., 2 per day, 38Lt); **Minsk, BLR** (5hr., 8 and 9am, 22Lt); **Rīga, LAT** (6hr., 5 per day, 30-40Lt); **Tallinn, EST** (11hr., 6am and 8:45pm, 90Lt); **Warsaw, POL** (8hr., 9am and 9:30pm, 80Lt).

Public Transportation: Buses and **trolleys** link downtown with the train and bus stations and the suburbs. All lines run daily 6am-midnight. Buy tickets at any kiosk (0.80Lt) or from the driver (1Lt); punch them on board to avoid the hefty fine—tickets are checked more often than you'd expect. Monthly passes are available for students (5Lt).

Taxis: Vilnius's cheapest companies are **Autvela** (☎ 15 05 05), **Fiakvas** (☎ 70 57 05), and **Kortesa** (☎ 73 73 73). 0.65Lt per km.

⊞ ORIENTATION

The **train** and **bus stations** are directly across from each other. **Geležinkelio** runs right from the train station, and leads to **Aušros Vartų,** which leads downhill through the **Aušros Vartai** (Gates of Dawn) into **Senamiestis** (Old Town). Aušros Vartų becomes **Didžioji** and then **Pilies** before reaching the base of Gediminas Hill. Here, the **Gediminas Tower** of Higher Castle presides over **Arkikatedros Aikštė** (Cathedral Sq.), and the banks of the river **Neris. Gedimino,** the commercial artery, leads west from the square in front of the Cathedral.

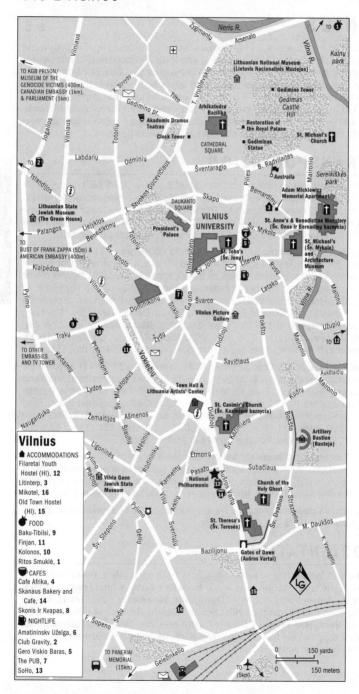

TO KGB PRISON/
MUSEUM OF THE
GENOCIDE VICTIMS (400m),
CANADIAN EMBASSY (1km),
& PARLIAMENT (1km)

Neris R.

Žygimantų

Arsenalo

Vilna R.

Kalnų
park

Lithuanian National Museum
(Lietuvis Nacionalinis Muziejus)

Gedimino Tower

Gedimas
Castle
Hill

K. Sirvydo

Tilto

T. Vrublevskio

Gedimino pr.

Vilniaus

Totorių

Akademis Dramos
Teatras

Arkikatedra
Bazilika

Restoration of
the Royal Palace

St. Michael's
Church

Clock Tower

Gediminas
Statue

CATHEDRAL
SQUARE

Labdarių

Odminių

Šventaragio

B. Radvilaitės

Maironio

Sereikiškės
park

Islandijos

Jogailos

Vilniaus

Pilies

Bernardinų

Australia

Adam Mickiewicz
Memorial Apartment

Lithuanian State
Jewish Museum
(The Green House)

Liejyklos

L. Stuokos-Gucevičiaus

DAUKANTO
SQUARE

Skapo

VILNIUS
UNIVERSITY

St. Anne's & Benedictine Monstery
(Šv. Onos ir Bernadinų baznycia)

Palangos

Benedktinų

President's
Palace

Šv. Mykolo

St. Michael's
(Šv. Mykolo)
and
Architecture
Museum

TO
BUST OF FRANK ZAPPA (50m) &
AMERICAN EMBASSY (400m)

Totorių

Universiteto

Šv. Jono

St. John's
(Šv. Jonu)

Literatų

Rusų

Klaipėdos

Šv. Ignoto

Pylimo

Vilniaus

Dominikonų

Stiklių

Ga ono

Švarco

Lataka

Vilna R.

Malūnų

Traku

Pranciškonų

Kėdainių

Žydų

Vokiečių

Vilnius Picture
Gallery

Didžioji

Bokšto

Savičiaus

Užupio

TO

TO OTHER
EMBASSIES
AND TV TOWER

Lydos

Šv. Mikalojaus

Ašmenos

Town Hall &
Lithuania Artists' Center

Aukštaičių

Maironio

Kudrų

Naugarduko

Žemaitijos

Šiaulių

Mėsinių

St. Casimir's Church
(Šv. Kazimiero baznycia)

Šv. Kazimiero

Didžioji

Bokšto

Artillery
Bastion
(Basteja)

Ligoninės

Rūdninkų

Etmonų

Subačiaus

A. Strazdelio

Pylimo

Plačioji

Vilvia Gaon
Jewish State
Museum

Karmelitų

Visu

Arklių

Pasažo
National
Philharmonic

Aušros Vartų

Church of the
Holy Ghost

M. Daukšos

Šv. Stepono

Gėlių

Šventųjų

St. Theresa's
(Šv. Teresės)

Šv. Dvasios

K. Vanagelio

Bazilijonu

Gates of Dawn
(Aušros Vartai)

N

LG

F. Šopeno

Sodų

TO PANERIAI
MEMORIAL
(15km)

Geležinkelio

TO
(5km)

0   150 yards

0   150 meters

Vilnius

■ ACCOMMODATIONS
Filaretai Youth
  Hostel (HI), 12
Litinterp, 3
Mikotel, 16
Old Town Hostel
  (HI), 15
● FOOD
Baku-Tibilsi, 9
Finjan, 11
Kolonos, 10
Ritos Smuklė, 1
● CAFES
Cafe Afrika, 4
Skanaus Bakery and
  Cafe, 14
Skonis Ir Kvapas, 8
■ NIGHTLIFE
Amatininskv Uželga, 6
Club Gravity, 2
Gero Viskio Baras, 5
The PUB, 7
SoHo, 13

⁊ PRACTICAL INFORMATION

> **PHONE CODE MANIA.** Navigating Vilnius's phone system can be more confusing than the winding alleys of Old Town. The city is in the process of switching to 7-digit phone numbers and a new city code, (8)5. Some numbers listed below will convert to the new system by dialing 2 before the 6-digit number; others will be completely changed. For more info, see www.telecom.lt.

TOURIST AND FINANCIAL SERVICES

Tourist Offices: Tourist Information Center, Didžioji 31 (☎/fax 62 07 62 or 62 64 70; www.vilnius.lt), in the Town Hall, provides information about travel and events throughout Lithuania, organizes tours, and sells *Vilnius in Your Pocket* (8Lt). Also posts train and bus schedules. English and Russian spoken. Open in summer M-F 9am-7pm, Sa-Su 10am-4pm; off-season M-F 10am-6pm. **Branch,** Vilniaus 22 (☎62 96 60; fax 62 81 69). Open daily 9am-noon and 12:45-6pm. **Kelvita Tourist Information,** Geležinkelio 16 (☎/fax 31 02 29), in a kiosk inside the station. German and English spoken. Obtains visas for Belarus, Ukraine, or Russia. Open M-F 8am-6pm, Sa 10am-2pm.

Budget Travel: Lithuanian Student and Youth Travel, V. Basanavičiaus 30, #13 (☎22 13 73). Great deals for travelers under 27. Sells student tickets for buses, trains, and planes. Open M-F 8:30am-6pm, Sa 10am-2pm.

Embassies and Consulates: Australia, Vilniaus 23 (☎/fax 22 33 69; aust.con.vilnius@post.omnitel.net). Visas M, W, F 11am-2pm. **Belarus,** Mindaugo 13 (☎66 22 00 or 66 22 11; fax 66 22 12; bpl@post.5ci.lt). Visas at Muitinės 41 (☎13 22 55; fax 33 06 26). Open M-Th 8am-noon and 1-4pm, F 8am-noon and 1-3pm. **Canada,** Gedimino pr. 64 (☎49 68 53; fax 49 68 98; vilnius@canada.lt). Visas M and W 9am-noon. **Estonia,** Mickevičiaus 4a (☎78 02 00; fax 78 02 01; sekretar@estemb.lt). Visas Tu-Th 10am-noon. **Latvia,** MK Čiurlionio 76 (☎13 12 60; fax 23 11 30; lietuva@latvia.balt.net). Visas M-F 9am-noon and 3-4pm. **Russia,** Latvių 53/54 (☎72 17 63; fax 72 38 77; rusemb@rusemb.lt). Visas M-F 8am-noon. **UK,** Antakalnio 2 (☎12 20 70; fax 72 75 79; www.britain.lt). Visas M-F 8:30am-11:30am. **US,** Akmenų 6 (☎66 55 00; fax 66 55 10; www.usembassy.lt). Visas M-Th 8:30-11:30am.

Currency Exchange: Geležinkelio 6 (☎33 07 63), left of the train station, has the best rates. Open 24hr. **Vilniaus Bankas,** Vokiečių 9 (☎/fax 62 78 69), gives MC/V **cash advances** at no commission and cashes AmEx and Thomas Cooke **traveler's checks.** Open M-F 8am-6pm. **Bankas Snoras,** A. Vivulskio 7 (☎16 27 70; fax 31 01 55), cashes **traveler's checks** and gives V **cash advances** for 2% commission at blue and white kiosks throughout town. Open M-F 8am-7pm, Sa 9am-2pm.

LOCAL SERVICES

Luggage Storage: At the bus station. 1.50Lt per bag. Open daily 7am-10pm. Also in the tunnels under the train station. 1.50-2.50Lt per bag; 2Lt for each extra day. Open 24hr.

English-Language Bookstore: Oxford Centre, Trakų 20 (☎61 04 16). Open M-F 10:30am-6pm, Sa 10:30am-3pm.

Bi-Gay-Lesbian Services: Gay Information Line, (☎33 30 31; www.gay.lt). Info about organizations, events, and accommodations for gay men. The **Lithuanian Gay and Lesbian Homepage** (www.gayline.lt) and **The Gay Club** (☎98 50 09; vgc@takas.lt) list gay and lesbian establishments in Lithuania.

Laundromat: Slayana, Latvių 31 (☎75 31 12), in Žvėrynas, 5min. west of Senamiestis across the Neris. Take tram #7 from the train station or tram #3 from Senamiestis. Self-service wash and dry 14Lt; full service 22Lt. Detergent 3Lt. Open M-F 8am-3pm.

LITHUANIA

EMERGENCY AND COMMUNICATIONS

24-Hour Pharmacy: Gedimino Vaistinė, Gedimino pr. 27 (☎61 01 35).

Medical Assistance: Baltic-American Medical and Surgical Clinic, Antakalnio 124 (☎34 20 20 or 76 71 01; fax 76 79 42; www.baclinic.com), at Vilnius University Hospital. Open 24hr.

Telephones: In the main post office (☎62 54 68) and on the streets. Phones take cards (from 8Lt) and allow direct dialing abroad.

Internet Access: Bazė, Gedimino 50 (☎49 77 01). 3-6Lt per hr, 20-25Lt per night. Open 24hr. **Spausk.lt,** Basanavičaus 18 (☎65 20 02). 8Lt per hr. Open daily 9am-midnight. **V002,** Ašmenos 8 (☎79 18 66). 8Lt per hr. Open 24hr.

Post Office: Centrinis Paštas, Gedimino 7 (☎62 54 68; www.post.lt), west of Arkikatedros aikštė. **Poste Restante** at the window "*iki pareikalavimo*"; 0.50Lt to pick up mail. Open M-F 7am-7pm, Sa 9am-4pm.

Postal Code: LT-2000.

▐ ACCOMMODATIONS

▧ **Litinterp,** Bernadinų 7/2 (☎12 38 50; fax 12 35 59; www.litinterp.lt). Beautiful, spacious rooms with wooden furniture. Spotless shared showers. Breakfast included, and delivered to your room. Helpful English-speaking staff. Reservations recommended. Reception M-F 8:30am-5:30pm, Sa 9am-2pm. Singles 80Lt-100Lt; doubles 120-140Lt. Apartment with kitchen and bath starts at 200Lt. 5% ISIC discount. MC/V. ❸

Mikotel, Pylimo 63 (☎60 96 26; fax 60 96 27; www.travel.lt/mikotel). From the train station, take a right and then a left on to Pylimo. Clean, cheery rooms with shower. Kitchen access. Friendly staff. Singles 180Lt; doubles 240Lt. MC/V. ❹

Old Town Hostel (HI), Aušros Vartų 20-15a (☎62 53 57; fax 22 01 49), 100m south of the Gates of Dawn. Little privacy with 8-10 people per room, but this is the place to meet fellow travelers. Complimentary coffee and tea, free Internet access, communal fridge, and shared showers. Reservations recommended, but they can usually squeeze guests in. Dorms 32Lt, non-members 34Lt; singles and doubles 40-60Lt. MC/V. ❷

Filaretai Youth Hostel (HI), Filaretų 17 (☎15 46 27; fax 12 01 49; filaretai@post.omnitel.lt). Same directions as Jaunujų Turistiu Centras (above). Kitchen, common room, TV, and VCR. Free bike rental. Luggage storage 3Lt. Linen 5Lt. Laundry 10Lt per load. Reception 7-11am and 2pm-midnight. Reservations recommended June-Sept. and weekends. Cozy, comfortable 2- to 8-bed dorms 24Lt per person; doubles 32Lt; triples and quads 28Lt. Non-members 3Lt fee. MC/V. ❶

◘ FOOD

Vilnius is home to a wealth of trendy, inexpensive restaurants that specialize in food from Georgian to Italian to Lithuanian. **Iki supermarkets,** which stock foreign brands, abound in Vilnius. The Iki at the bus station is the branch closest to Senamiestis. (Open daily 8am-10pm.)

▧ **Ritos Smuklė** (Rita's Tavern), Žirmūnų 68 (☎77 07 86; fax 31 65 15; www.rita.lt). Tram #12, 13, or 17. A favorite of various European presidents (check out the photos on the wall), Rita's attempts to embody the "spirit of Lithuania's past," recreating a traditional Lithuanian tavern, complete with thatched roof, wooden tables, and waiters in folk dress. "Strong Stomach Sweep" (7.20Lt) is for the brave only, but everyone should try the acorn coffee (3Lt) and something from the outside grill. Entrees 15-30Lt. English menu. Live folk music W-Sa 8-10pm. Open daily 10am-midnight. MC/V. ❷

■ **Finjan,** Vokiečių 18 (☎61 21 04). Offering a mix of Lebanese, Israeli, and Egyptian cuisine, Finjan serves authentic hummus (12Lt) and kebabs (26Lt). Vegetarian options. Entrees 24-45Lt. Post-meal water smoking pipe with flavored tobacco 20Lt. Belly dancer Th-Sa nights. Open daily 11am-midnight. MC/V. ❸

Baku-Tiblisi, Trakų 15 (☎12 31 54), serves Georgian and Azerbajiani specialities. Candles and live Russian ballads (nightly 6-11pm) create a romantic atmosphere enhanced by polite service. Try the *kiufte* soup (6Lt) and one of their excellent and inexpensive Georgian wines (6-11Lt). Entrees 10-25Lt. Open daily 10am-midnight. ❶

⌂ CAFES

■ **Skonis Ir Kvapas,** Trakų 8 (☎12 28 03). The perfect spot for a long chat with friends, serving delicious all-day breakfasts, desserts, and light meals. Try an exotic tea from the fan-shaped menu. Tea cups 2.50-6.60Lt, pots 3-10Lt. English menu. Open M-F 8:30am-11pm, Sa-Su 9:30am-11pm. MC/V.

Skaunaus Bakery and Cafe, Aušros Vartų 9. Cheap and tasty freshly-baked pastries. Sip quality coffee (2Lt) while people-watching from the tables outside. Great for a quick breakfast. Open M-F 8am-9pm, Sa-Su 10am-9pm. MC/V.

Cafe Afrika, Pilies 28 (☎61 71 90), fronts vibrant yellow decor and a purple-and-yellow zebra sign. Lithuanian treats with silly names, such as deep-fried chicken wings dramatically called "the last flight of the parrot" (11Lt). Soup, salad, and gourmet coffee for under 12Lt. Open daily 10am-11pm. MC/V.

◉ SIGHTS

SENAMIESTIS AND BEYOND

HIGHER CASTLE MUSEUM AND GEDIMINAS TOWER. (Aukštutinės Pilies Muziejus.) Behind the Cathedral, a winding path leads to the top of the hill, which has been crowned by a castle since 200 BC. The Higher Castle Museum details the history of the castle and city and displays old maps and scale models of the castle. Its main attraction, however, is the magnificent view of Senamiestis and Gedimino. *(Castle Hill, Arsenalo 5. ☎61 74 53. Open Mar.-Oct. daily 10am-7pm; Nov.-Feb. Tu-Su 11am-5pm. 4Lt, students 2Lt.)*

CATHEDRAL SQUARE. (Arkikatedros Aikštė.) A church has stood on this spot since 1387, when Grand Duke Jogaila converted his country to Catholicism to win the Polish throne (see History, p. 431)—

the site had previously stood as the principal temple to Perkūnas, Lithuanian god of thunder. The 18th-century Cathedral (Arkikatedra Bazilika) is white, restrained, and Neoclassical. Inside look for the richly-ornamented Chapel of St. Casimir (Šv. Kazimiero koplyčia), the royal mausoleum. In the square, the octagonal 1522 bell tower houses bells from throughout the country. The statue to the right is of Grand Duke Gedinimas, founder of Vilnius. To the right of the Cathedral the city is rebuilding the Royal Palace, to be completed in time for the 2009 millennial celebration of the first mention of Lithuania in written records. The controversial project may grind to a halt, however, due to dwindling funds and public protests of the cost. *(At the end of Pilies and Universiteto. ☎61 11 27. Cathedral open M-Sa 7am-1pm and 2:30-8pm, Su 7am-2pm.)*

TOWN HALL SQUARE. (Rotušės Aikštė.) Located on Didžioji, Town Hall Square is an ancient marketplace dominated by the columns of the 18th-century **town hall,** now home to the **Lithuanian Artists' Center** (Lietuvos Menininkv Rumai), with exhibits of local work in its gallery. *(Didžioji 31. ☎61 06 19. Open M-F 9am-6pm.)* Don't miss Lithuania's oldest church, **St. Nicholas's** (Šv. Mikalojaus Bažnyčia). Recently renovated, this Orthodox church, built in 1320 for the city's Hanseatic merchants, is rich in icons, crosses, and candles. *(Didžioji 12. ☎61 85 59. Open daily 10am-6pm.)*

ST. PETER AND PAUL CHURCH. (Sv. Apaštalv Petro ir Povilo Bažnyčia). Built in 1668-1676, St. Peter and Paul Church features an ornate Baroque interior decorated with over 2000 figures—note the chandelier styled like a sailing ship. The church's humble founder is buried next door; his tombstone reads *Hic jacet peccator*—"Here lies a sinner." Well worth the trip to the edge of Senamiestis. *(Antakalnio 1. Take tram #2, 3, or 4 from Senamiestis. ☎34 02 29.)*

VILNIUS UNIVERSITY. (Vilniaus Universitetas.) Founded in 1570, the Jesuit university was a major player in the Counter-Reformation and is the oldest university in Eastern Europe. **St. John's Church** (Šv. Jonų Bažnyčia), Šv. Jono 12, off Pilies, served as a science museum under the Soviets. The 17th-century **Astronomical Observatory,** once rivaled in importance only by Greenwich and the Sorbonne, sits through the arches opposite St. John's. With more than five million volumes, the university **library** remains Lithuania's largest library. *(Universiteto 3. ☎61 17 95.)* The nearby **Church of the Holy Spirit** (Šventosios Dvasios bažnyčia), a gold-and-marble Baroque masterpiece, was last rebuilt in 1770. *(Dominikonų 8, near the corner of Pilies and Šv. Jono. ☎62 95 95. Open daily 7-10am and 5-7pm.)*

ST. CASIMIR'S CHURCH. (Šv. Kazimiero Bažnyčia.) Named after the country's patron saint, St. Casimir's is Vilnius's oldest Baroque church. Built by the Jesuits in 1604, it has a spacious cream interior and a striking altarpiece. In 1832, it gained a Russian Orthodox dome; during World War II, the Germans made it Lutheran. After "liberating" Vilnius, the Soviets turned the light pink temple into a shrine to atheism. Both the town and the church returned to Catholicism in 1989. *(Didžioji 34. ☎22 17 15. Open M-Sa 4-6:30pm, Su 9am-1pm.)*

GATES OF DAWN AND BEYOND. (Aušros Vartai.) The Gates of Dawn, the only surviving portal of the old city walls, have guarded **Senamiestis** (Old Town) since the 16th Century. In 1671, a **chapel** (Koplyčia) was built inside the gates as a shrine for a portrait of the Virgin Mary, gilded with gold and reputed to have miracle-working powers. The gates remain a pilgrimage site for Eastern European Catholics. The Gates are currently undergoing renovation. *(Open daily 9am-6pm.)* **St. Theresa's Church** (Šv. Teresės bažnyčia), known for its Baroque sculptures, multi-colored arches, frescoed ceiling, and stained glass, is around the corner. The shockingly bright **Orthodox Church of the Holy Spirit** (Šv. Dvasios bažnyčia) is the seat of Lithuania's Russian Orthodox Archbishop. A working monastery, the church is the resting place of Saints Antonius, Ivan, and Eustachius, martyred in 1371. Their embalmed bodies, usually clad in red in a glass case under the altar, wear white for Christmas and black for Lent. *(Aušros Vartų 12. ☎ 12 35 13.)*

PARLIAMENT. In January 1991, the world watched as Lithuanians raised barricades to protect their parliament from the Soviet army. President Ladsbergis later said that all of the deputies expected to become martyrs on the night of the Soviet invasion. A section of the **barricade** remains as a memorial next to the main entrance; more sections, covered with graffiti and Soviet passports and medals, are housed at the Lithuanian National Museum (see **Museums,** p. 446). Concrete slabs remain from the barricade; next to the spray-painted remains stand crosses, flowers, and pictures to honor those who perished at the TV Tower (see below). One piece of graffiti depicts Moscow as a large crocodile devouring the sun, which is labeled "freedom." *(Gedimino 53, just before the Neris River.)*

HILL OF THREE CROSSES. (Trjių Kržių Kalnas). The Hill of Three Crosses is visible throughout Vilnius. White crosses were originally placed here during the 18th century to commemorate 13th-century Franciscans crucified on the hill by pagan tribes. The memorial has twice been replaced since then: once during Lithuania's first period of independence, 1919-1939, and again in 1989, since Stalin had ordered the symbol of Lithuanian national pride to be buried after WWII.

TV TOWER. (Televizijos Bokštas). Stretching to a height of 326.47m, the infamous tower is visible from the city center. Fourteen unarmed civilians were killed here on Jan. 13, 1991, as the Red Army forced the station off the air. Crosses and memorials surround the spot today, and the neighborhood's streets have been renamed in honor of the 14 martyrs. Take the elevator up to the revolving viewing platform and restaurant. *(Sausio 13-Osios 10. Take tram #11 from Skalvija on Žaliasis Bridge's south end toward Pašilaičai (14 stops). ☎ 45 88 77. Open daily 10am-9pm. 1½hr. excursions on the hr. 15Lt, children 6Lt.)*

FRANK ZAPPA MONUMENT. Not much to look at, this bust is perhaps the most random monument in Eastern Europe. It was installed in 1995 after the **Museum of Theater, Music, and Cinema** turned it away. *(Off Pylimo between Kalinausko 1 and 3.)*

JEWISH VILNIUS

Vilnius was once dubbed "The New Jerusalem," and was an international center of Jewish learning and culture, comparable only to Warsaw and New York. It held a Jewish population of 100,000 (in a city of 230,000) at the outbreak of World War II. Only 6000 survivors remained by the time the Red Army retook the city in 1944.

SYNAGOGUE. (Sinagoga.) Built in 1903, this is the only surviving reminder of Vilnius's pre-war status as the "Jerusalem of the North," a major center of Jewish culture which once boasted 105 synagogues. Newly restored to its former beauty, services are held F evenings and Sa mornings. *(Pylimo 39. ☎ 61 25 23. Open Su-F 8:30am-2pm and 6:15pm-8pm, Sa 9:30am-12:30pm.)*

PANERIAI GENOCIDE MEMORIAL. (Panerių Memorialas.) Hidden within beautiful, haunting forest, the Paneriai Genocide Memorial sits on the site of the former Paneriai Nazi death camp. Between 1941 and 1944, 100,000 people, including 70,000 Jews, were shot, burned, and buried here. Paneriai represents just a small part of the Holocaust in Lithuania, which exterminated 94% of the country's Jewish, or Litvak, population. Paved paths connect memorials, the pits that served as mass graves, and execution sites. A small museum holds artifacts and documents the excavation of the sites, but there is little need for description as the simple, somber plaques by the pits speak for themselves. *(Agrastų 15. A 10min. train ride* *from Vilnius in Paneriai (0.90Lt). Head right from the station and follow Agrastų to the memorial. Return by bus; cross the pedestrian bridge and catch bus #8 from the stop to the right of the bridge. ☎64 18 47. Open M and W-Sa 11am-6pm. English captions. Free.)*

JEWISH CULTURAL CENTRE. The only resident rabbi in Lithuania, American-born Shalom-Ber Krinsky, presides here. The Centre provides information on locating ancestors and learning more about the old Jewish Quarter, as well as kosher food and connections to the Jewish community. *(Šaltinių 12. ☎41 88 09 or 15 03 88; fax 15 03 89; office@chabad.ofc.lt. Open daily 9am-6pm.)*

◻ MUSEUMS

▨ MUSEUM OF GENOCIDE VICTIMS. (Genocido Aukų Muziejus.) A royal court for Tsar Nicholas II and a Gestapo outpost during WWII, the building became Vilnius's KGB headquarters. It remains today as it was when abandoned during the fall of the Soviet Union—shredded documents and all. The isolation cells, torture chambers, and execution room are disturbing, but the exhibition is eloquent and informative. One of the staff, G. Radžius, was a prisoner here; it's worth the effort to find a translator. *(Aukų 2a, at the intersection with Gedimino. ☎62 24 49. Tours in Lithuanian and Russian; captions in English. Open May 15-Sept. 15 Tu-Su 10am-6pm; Sept. 16-May 14 Tu-Su 10am-4pm. 2Lt.)*

LITHUANIAN NATIONAL MUSEUM. (Lietuvis Nacionalinis Muziejus.) Contains ethnographic exhibits detailing traditional Lithuanian life and exhibits on Lithuania's struggle for independence in 1990. The new wing at Arsenalo 3 has an excellent archeological exhibit on prehistoric Lithuania. *(Arsenalo 1, behind the Gedimino Tower. Enter Arsenalo 3 through the courtyard. ☎62 94 26. Some English captions. Open W-Su 10am-5pm. Each wing 4Lt, students 2Lt.)*

HOLOCAUST MUSEUM. "The Green House," as it is known locally, chronicles the destruction of the city's Jewish community. Ben-Zvi (1884-1963) and Š.Z. Šazaras (1889-1974), Israel's 2nd and 3rd presidents, were both born in Vilnius; their pictures now hang in the museum. *(Pamėnkalnio 12. ☎62 07 30. Self-guided tours in English. Open M-Th 9am-5pm, F 9am-4pm. Donation requested.)*

VILNIUS PICTURE GALLERY. (Vilniaus Paveikslų Galerija.) Housed in the beautifully restored 16th-century Chodkeviciai Palace, this museum displays late 18th- and early 19th-century works from the Vilnius Art School, which was shut down by the Tsarist government in 1831. Most interesting are the Neoclassical rooms on the top floor; also don't miss the various historical views of Vilnius. *(Didžioji 4. ☎22 42 58. Open Tu-Sa noon-6pm, Su noon-5pm. 5Lt, students 2.50Lt.)*

APPLIED ART MUSEUM. (Taikomosios Daliès Muziejus.) Home to the exhibit *Christianity in Lithuania's Art* until late 2003, the museum holds over 270 pieces of gold, silver, and jeweled religious objects hidden in the Cathedral walls on the eve of the Russian invasion in 1655 and only rediscovered in 1985. *(Arsenalo 3a, next to the National Museum (see above). ☎22 18 13. Open Tu-Su 11am-6pm. 4Lt.)*

VILNA GAON JEWISH STATE MUSEUM OF LITHUANIA. Named after Vilnius's famous 18th-century Jewish scholar Gaon, the museum contains exhibits on the remains of Lithuanian synagogues, Jews who fought the Nazis, and Jewish partisans who struggled against the Soviet Union. The **Gallery of the Righteous** (Teisuoliu Gallerija) honors Lithuanians who sheltered Jews during the war. The museum also arranges guided tours of Jewish Vilnius in English, Yiddish, Russian, and Lithuanian. If you meet the owner, ask him to show you his collection of 133,000 Jewish *ex libris* bookplates—the largest one of its kind. *(Pylimo 4. ☎61 79 17. Gallery ☎62 45 90 or 74 24 88. Open M-Th 9am-5pm, F 9am-4pm. 2Lt.)*

MICKIEWICZ MEMORIAL APARTMENT. (Mickevičiaus Memorialinis Butas.) The Lithuanian-Polish poet (see **Poland: Literature and Arts,** p. 479) lived here in 1822; his possessions remain. Although Adam Mickiewicz wrote in Polish, he is beloved by Lithuanians for penning their national epic, *Pan Tadeusz. (Bernardinv 11.* ☎ *61 88 36. English captions. Open Tu-F 10am-5pm, Sa-Su 10am-2pm. Free.)*

🔊 ENTERTAINMENT

Check *Vilnius in Your Pocket* or the Lithuanian morning paper *Lietuvos Rytas* for summer concert listings. The Tourist Information Center (see **Practical Information,** p. 441) has info on obtaining tickets. English-language movies are shown at **Lietuva Cinema,** Pylimo 17 (☎ 62 34 22), which has "seats for lovers" (two seats without an arm rest in-between). **Kino Centras Skalvija,** Goštauto 2 (☎ 61 14 03), shows the best non-Hollywood films. *Lietuvos Rytas* and www.kinas.lt list locations and show times. In July 2003, Vilnius will welcome the **World Lithuanian Song Festival,** a celebration of the 750th anniversary of the crowning of King Mindaugas.

Lithuanian National Philharmonic (Lietuvos Naciolinė Filharmonija), Aušros Vartų 5 (☎ 22 88 02 or 12 22 90; www.filharmonija.lt). Tickets 10-150Lt. Performances begin at 7pm. The office also organizes the **Vilniaus Festivalis** (www.filharmonija.lt/vilniaus-festivalis), a month of concerts that starts in late May. Box office open M-F 10am-6pm, Sa 11am-6pm, Su 11am-1pm. MC/V.

Opera and Ballet Theater (Operos ir Baleto Teatras), Vienuolio 1 (☎ 62 06 36; www.opera.lt). Housed in a beautiful 1970s Soviet building. Yes, you read that right. Box office open Tu-F 11am-6pm, Sa 10am-6pm, Su 11am-3pm.

Lithuanian National Drama Theater (Lietuvos Nacionalinis Dramos Teatras), Gedimino 4 (☎ 62 97 71; www.teatras.lt). Look for the 3 masked muses carved into black stone. Most performances in Lithuanian, with occasional shows in English. Dance performances and an annual summer festival of new drama. Box office open M-F 10am-5pm, Sa-Su 10am-noon and 2-5pm.

📍 NIGHTLIFE

Vilnius is home to a vibrant nightlife suitable for all ages and tastes, whether it be for mellow chatting over a beer or getting down on the dance floor. Look to the **Lithuanian Gay and Lesbian Homepage** or the **Gay Club** (see **Local Services,** p. 441) for the latest in Vilnius's gay nightlife scene.

Club Gravity, Jasinkio 16 (☎ 49 79 66; www.clubgravity.lt). Enter from Geležinis Vilkas. Don your finest Eurotrash attire and join Vilnius's young and beautiful at this ultra-modern, ultra-cool dance club. DJs spin great techno Th-Sa nights. Cover 25Lt, 15Lt for members (20Lt to join). Open Th-Sa 10pm-6am.

Gero Viskio Baras, Pilies 34 (☎ 62 98 19), in the center of town. With 3 different floors, options abound in this "good whisky bar." Stay above ground for drinks, or descend into the dark, pleasant basement for another drink and a small dance floor. Head to the top floor for—you guessed it—a drink. Basement 5Lt cover for men, women free. Open Su-Th 10am-3am, F-Sa 10am-5am. MC/V.

SoHo, Aušros Vartų 7 (☎ 12 12 10), next to the Filharmonic. A brand-new bar with a bright interior, a music-filled courtyard, and never a shortage of things to do. M 15% student discount, Tu finger painting, W cocktail night, Th live jazz, F 4-6pm All-You-Can-Eat (15Lt) and live music 8pm, Sa-Su live jazz 1-3pm, Su live classical music 3-10pm. M-F Happy Hour 4-6pm. Open Su-Th 10am-2am, F-Sa 10am-3am. MC/V.

The PUB (Prie Universiteto Baras), Dominikonų 9 (☎ 61 83 93; www.pub.lt), in the heart of Senamiestis, near the university. Traditional English pub with wooden interior and a cozy, 19th-century dungeon. Usually packed with expats and local students. Live music nightly 8pm. Open Su-Th 11am-3am, F-Sa 11am-5am. MC/V.

Amatininskv Užeiga, Didžioji 19, #2 (☎61 79 68). Mingle with locals at the bar or descend into the recently discovered medieval basement for a more intimate atmosphere and a 3Lt beer special. Open M-F 8am-5am, Sa-Su 11am-5am.

⚏ DAYTRIP FROM VILNIUS

TRAKAI CASTLE   ☎528

Buses run to Trakai, 28km west of Vilnius (30min., at least 1 per hr. 6:45am-9:30pm, 2.60Lt). The last bus back departs nightly at 8:30pm, but leaves early if full. Bus station (☎900 016 61) open daily 4am-midnight. Museum open daily 10am-7pm. Paddleboats and waterbikes for rent line the lake by the castle's footbridge (12Lt per hr.). Or, board a yacht in front of the castle for a 45min. guided tour (10Lt). 1hr. tours 40Lt, students 20Lt; foreign-language tours 50Lt. Castle and museum 8Lt, students 3.50Lt. Cameras 4Lt.

Trakai's red-brick fairy-tale castle has inspired legends since the beginning of the 15th century. In the summer of 1410 with the defeat of the Teutonic Order at the Battle of Grunwald, Trakai became the capital of what would become the Polish-Lithuanian Commonwealth (see **History,** p. 431). Vytautas's new digs were short-lived; in 1665 the Russians accomplished what the Germans could not, plundering the town and razing the castle. Perhaps out of a sense of guilt, the Soviets began restoring the castle in 1955; the original stone foundations are still visible. An admission ticket is valid for both the **Insular Castle**'s 30m brick watchtower and the **City and Castle History Museum,** which chronicles the history of Trakai and Lithuania. To discharge your aggression after close encounters with groups of tourists in the castle's narrow hallways, turn left as you exit the drawbridge to practice target shooting (5 shots for 1Lt) or try your hand at archery (1 arrow for 1Lt). The castle also forms a dramatic backdrop for a **summer concert series** (☎62 07 27; www.trakaifestival.lt). Outside the castle, stop by the **Karaite Ethnographic Museum,** Karaimų 22 (☎552 86), for insight into the Karaites, Lithuania's tiny ethnic minority brought by Vytautasas bodyguards to Trakai from Turkey in 1398. After, head over to **Kibininé,** Karaimų 65 (☎558 65), to sample *kiblinai* (a meat and onion pastry), the mouth watering traditional dish of Trakai's Karaites.

INLAND LITHUANIA

While flashier Vilnius has historically attracted foreign attention and investment, inland Lithuania has always been the bedrock of the country. Kaunas has come to set the standard of Lithuanian culture, just as in the north, Šiauliai and its Hill of Crosses has become a symbol of resistance to Communist rule.

KAUNAS   ☎37

Would-be dictators beware: staunchly nationalist Kaunas (KOW-nas; pop. 378,900) has proved that it's not easily subdued. During World War II, Hitler converted the city's Ninth Fort into a concentration camp, from which 64 prisoners and resistance fighters escaped in 1943—the only successful mass escape from the Nazi death camps. Stalin didn't have much luck either, as Kaunas resisted Sovietization to the point where Russian "colonists" planted in the city began speaking Lithuanian and adopting local customs. (The always-cuddly "Uncle Joe" responded by exiling the settlers to Siberia.) Through it all, serene Kaunas has remained the "most Lithuanian" city in the country and the cradle of Lithuanian culture.

☞ TRANSPORTATION

Trains: MK Čiurlionio 16 (☎29 22 60 or 22 10 93; www.litrail.lt), at the end of Vytauto, where it intersects with MK Čiurlionio. Open 24hr. To **Vilnius** (2hr., 11 per day, 9.80Lt) and **Rīga, LAT** (5hr., 1 per day, 29.30Lt). Schedule varies for other connections, including **Kaliningrad, RUS; Tallinn, EST;** and **Warsaw, POL.**

Buses: Vytauto 24/26 (☎40 90 60, international reservations 32 22 22; fax 40 90 72). Open daily 4am-11pm. To: **Klaipėda** (2½-6hr., 10 per day, 20-28Lt); **Palanga** (2½-6hr., 10 per day, 27-31Lt); **Vilnius** (1½hr., every 30min., 12.40Lt).

Hydrofoils: Raudondvario 107 (☎26 13 48), in the town of Vilijampolė, across the Neris. Take trolleybus #7 from the train and bus stations, or #10 or 11 from the stop at the west end of Laisvės; get off at Kedainių, the 3rd stop across the river. In summer, *Raketa* hydrofoils splash to **Nida** via **Nemunas** (4hr., 1 per day, 59Lt).

Funicular: Žaliakalnis (Green hill), between Putvinskio and Aušros. Open daily 7:30am-6:30pm. Aleksoto, across the Aleksoto bridge from Old Town and a left on Marvelės, takes you up the mountains. Open M-F 7am-7pm, Sa-Su 8am-noon and 1-5pm.

Public Transportation: Tickets for buses and trams are available from kiosks (0.80Lt) or the driver (1Lt). The best way to get around the city, however, is by one of the many **maršrutinis taksis** vans that speed along bus routes. Tell the driver where you want to get off (1Lt, 2Lt at night).

Taxis: State Taxi Co. (☎23 66 66). 1Lt per km. **Private Taxi** (☎23 98 80). Rates vary.

▄▉ ORIENTATION

At the confluence of the **Nemunas** and **Neris** rivers, Kaunas is on a peninsula pointing west, with **Senamiestis** (Old Town) at the western tip and the bus and train stations at the southeastern point. **Naujamiestis** (New Town) fills the middle, bisected by **Laisvės.** At the fork with **Šv. Gertrūdos,** Laisvės merges with **Vilniaus** at the entrance to Senamiestis and runs to **Rotušės.** The train station lies at the end of **Vytauto** where it intersects **MK Čiurlionio;** the bus station is about 300m from the train station on Vytauto Continue along Vytauto and **Kęstučio** and Laisvės are to the left. **Bus #7** runs parallel to Laisvės, never more than a block away. *Kaunas in Your Pocket* (8Lt), is available at Lintinterp (see p. 451) or the tourist office.

⁊ PRACTICAL INFORMATION

Tourist Office: Tourist Information Center, Laisvės 36 (☎32 34 36; fax 42 36 78; www.visit.kaunas.lt). Helpful staff sells **maps** and arranges tours. Open M-F 9am-6pm, Sa-Su 9am-1pm and 1-6pm.

Currency Exchange: Look for *Valiutos Keitykla* signs on Laisvės and Vilniaus. **Lietuvos Taupomasis Bankas,** Laisvės 82 (☎20 66 36), gives MC **cash advances** and cashes AmEx/MC/Thomas Cook **traveler's checks.** Open M-F 8am-4pm. **Hotel Taioji Neris,** K. Donelaičio 27, has a **24hr. currency exchange. ATMs** are everywhere.

Luggage Storage: In a tunnel under the train station. 1Lt per bag. Open daily 8:30am-2:15pm, and 3-8pm, and 8:30pm-8am.

English-Language Bookstore: Centrinis Knygynas, Laisvės 81 (☎22 95 72; fax 22 31 01), stocks classics and best-sellers. Open M-F 10am-7pm, Sa 10am-5pm.

Bi-Gay-Lesbian Services: Kaunas Organization for Sexual Equality (☎70 57 37) has info on gay clubs and events in Kaunas.

24-Hour Pharmacy: Vytauto 2 (☎32 44 44).

Telephones: To the left as you enter the post office. Open M-F 7am-7pm, Sa 7am-5pm.

LITHUANIA

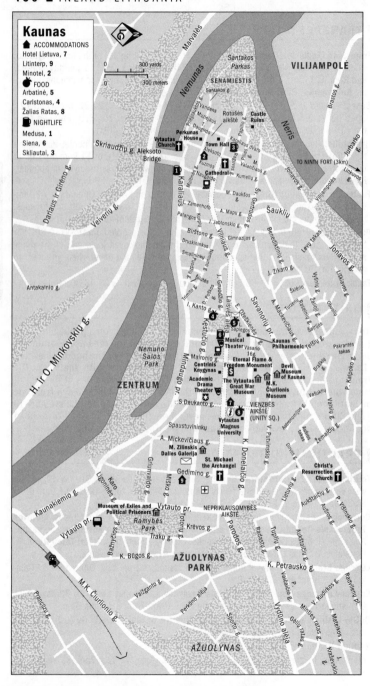

Kaunas

ACCOMMODATIONS
Hotel Lietuva, **7**
Litinterp, **9**
Minotel, **2**

FOOD
Arbatinė, **5**
Carlstonas, **4**
Žalias Ratas, **8**

NIGHTLIFE
Medusa, **1**
Siena, **6**
Skliautai, **3**

300 yards
0
0
300 meters

VILIJAMPOLĖ

Santakos
Parkas

SENAMIESTIS

Santakos g.

Vandens
Muziejaus

Rotušės
aikštė

Castle
Ruins

Perkūnas
House

Vytautas
Church

Town Hall

Cathedral

TO NINTH FORT (3km)

Skriaudžių g.   Aleksoto
Bridge

Kuzmos

Nemuno

ZENTRUM

Nemuno
Salos
Park

Maironio g.

Centrinis
Knygynas

Academic
Drama
Theater

S Daukanto g.

Spaustuvininku

A. Mickevičiaus g.

M. Zilinskis
Dalles Galerija

Gedimino g.

Museum of Exiles and
Political Prisoners

Ramybės
Park

Traku g.

K. Būgos g.

Kaunakiemio g.

Vytauto pr.

Krėvos g.

Musical
Theater

Eternal Flame &
Freedom Monument

The Vytautas
Great War
Museum

Vytautas
Magnus
University

VIENZBES
AIKŠTĖ
(UNITY SQ.)

Devil
Museum
of Kaunas

M.K.
Čiurlionis
Museum

Kaunas
Philharmonic

St. Michael
the Archangel

Christ's
Resurrection
Church

NEPRIKLAUSOMYBĖS
AIKŠTĖ

AŽUOLYNAS
PARK

K. Petrausko g.

AŽUOLYNAS

M.K. Čiurlionio g.

Internet Access: Interneto Svetaine, Laisvės 83a (☎/fax 20 60 13). Fast connections. English spoken. 4Lt per hr. Open daily 10am-10pm. **Kavinė Internetas,** Vilniaus 24 (☎40 74 27). English spoken. 4Lt per hr. Open daily 10am-midnight. **Internetas,** Maironio 22 (☎40 97 00). 4Lt per hr. Open M-Sa 9am-8pm, Su 10am-3pm.

Post Office: Laisvės 102 (☎32 42 86). **Poste Restante** window #11; 0.50Lt per package. Open M-F 7am-7pm, Sa 7am-5pm.

Postal Code: LT-3000.

ACCOMMODATIONS

Kaunas does not come cheap; the best option for the budget-conscious is to arrange a **private room** with ▨ **Litinterp ❸,** Gedimino 28. Most of their rooms and apartments have excellent locations, either in Senamiestis or on Laisvės. Call ahead for the best deals. (☎/fax 22 87 18, after hours 20 53 12; www.litinterp.lt. Open M-F 8:30am-5:30pm, Sa 9am-3pm. Singles 80-140Lt; doubles 140-260Lt.)

▨ **Minotel,** Vl. Kuzmos 8 (☎20 37 59; fax 22 03 55; minotel@kaunas.omnitel.net), in the heart of Senamiestis. From Rotušės, turn left on Muitinės. This quiet, beautiful hotel on the corner of Muitinės and Vl. Kuzmos has cheerful new rooms with bath, minibar, minisafe, phone, and TV. Breakfast included. Reception open daily 7am-10pm. Singles 160-300Lt; doubles 240-360Lt. 20% discount Sa; 10% discount for stays of 3 days or more; 15% ISIC discount (25% Sa). ❹

Hotel Lietuva, S. Daukanto 21 (☎20 62 69; metropol@takas.lt), just off Laisvės in the center of town. Older and darker than Minotel, Lietuva can put you up for the night in one of its small, but comfortable rooms if you don't mind the indelible smell of cigarette smoke. All rooms with bath and TV. Breakfast included. Reception open 24hr. Singles 100Lt; doubles 140-200Lt; triples 170Lt. ❸

FOOD

Žalias Ratas, Laisvės 36b (☎20 00 71). Entrance is around the corner. Locals come to this traditional Lithuanian tavern to find a retreat from the bustling Laisvės. Friendly waiters in linen costumes bring generous portions of quality local fare. Sit inside by the fireplace in winter, or outside under the thatched roof in summer. Entrees 5-28Lt. Live music F-Sa 8pm. English menu. Open daily 11am-midnight. MC/V. ❷

Carlstonas, Kęstučio 93 (☎20 29 93). A favorite of President Adamkus, Carlstonas is sumptuous in its decor and its Spanish and French cuisine. The small dining area defines decadence—you can order exquisitely-presented game entrees (28-43Lt) or splurge for caviar (69Lt). Accompany your meal with wine and live classical piano or jazz Tu-Th 7:30pm. English menu. Open daily noon-midnight. MC/V. ❹

Arbatinė, Laisvės 100 (☎32 37 32). The veggie-lover's dream. Decorated as a cabin—with a white picket fence to boot—Arbatinė offers a vegan menu (entrees 5.50-6Lt) and freshly-baked pastries (1.30-2Lt) so tasty you wouldn't guess they're vegan. Open M-F 8:30am-8pm, Sa 10am-6pm. ❶

SIGHTS

Sights in Kaunas cluster around the two ends of Laisvės, the city's main pedestrian boulevard. St. Michael's Church and Unity Square lie at one end, while Senamiestis and its cathedral, town hall, and smaller attractions are at the opposite end. Pažaislis Monastery and Church and the Ninth Fort are outside the city.

ST. MICHAEL THE ARCHANGEL CHURCH. The church was built for the Russian garrison that came to man the nine forts around Kaunas in the 1890s. The gorgeous, symmetric neo-Byzantine exterior and silver-blue domes are a feast for the eyes. *(Nepriklausomybės aikštė 14, at the end of Laisvės opposite Senamiestis. ☎ 22 66 76. Services M-F noon, Sa 10am, Su 10am and noon. Open M-F 9am-3pm, Sa-Su 8:30am-2pm.)*

UNITY SQUARE. (Vienybės aikštė.) On the south side, **Vytauto Didžiojo University** and the older **Kaunas Technological University** draw a student population of more than 16,000. Across the street, in an outdoor shrine to Lithuanian statehood, busts of famous Lithuanians flank a corridor leading from the **Freedom Monument** (Laisves paminklas) to an **eternal flame** commemorating those who died in the liberation struggle of 1918-20. These symbols of nationhood disappeared during Soviet occupation, but re-emerged at St. Michael's in 1989. On a hill behind the Čiurlionis Museum (see **Museums,** p. 453), **Christ's Resurrection Church** awaits completion. Begun in 1932, construction stopped in 1940 after Stalin and the Soviets swept in. The **Vytautas the Great War Museum** and the **Devil Museum** (see **Museums,** p. 453) are nearby. *(2 blocks down Laisvės from St. Michael's and right on Daukanto.)*

KAUNAS CATHEDRAL. (Kauno Arkikatedra Bažnyčia.) One of Lithuania's largest churches, Kaunas Cathedral is thought to have been built during the 1408-13 Christianization of Low Lithuania. Its breathtaking interior, dating from 1800, is a combination of Gothic, neo-Gothic, Baroque, and Renaissance styles. A pillar at the back of the church holds the **tomb of Maironis,** the beloved priest from Kaunas whose poetry was key in Lithuania's 19th-century National Awakening. Don't miss the incredible neo-Gothic Chapel of St. John the Baptist. *(Vilniaus 26. Where Laisvės ends and Senamiestis begins; follow Vilniaus through an underpass and inside the medieval city walls, and then 3 blocks farther to the cathedral. ☎ 22 75 46. Open daily 7am-7pm.)*

OLD TOWN SQUARE. (Rotušės aikštė.) Just past the cathedral, the **town hall,** a stylistically confused concoction constructed in stages from 1542 to 1771, presides over Old Town Square. Behind and to the left of the town hall stands a **statue of Maironis.** His hand hides his clerical collar, a ploy that duped the atheist Soviets into allowing the city to erect a statue of a priest. Up Karaliaus dvaro, which leads out of the square to the right of Maironis's statue, the Neris and Nemunas rivers meet at **Santakos Parkas.** The remains of the 13th-century **Kauno castle** (pilis) stand here. Next to it is the decaying late-Baroque **St. Francis Church and Jesuit Monastery.** Follow Aleksoto toward the river from the corner of Rotušės opposite Karaliaus to reach the quirky 15th-century **Perkūnas House** (Perkūnas namas), a late-Gothic edifice built for Hanseatic merchants on the site of a temple to Perkūnas, god of thunder. At the end of the street is the Gothic **Vytautas Church** (Vytauto bažnyčia), also built in the early 1400s.

NINTH FORT. (IX Fortas.) Across the Neris lies the town of **Vilijampolė,** which gained infamy during World War II as the Jewish Ghetto of Kaunas, vividly immortalized in Avraham Tory's *Kovno Ghetto Diary.* The Ninth Fort, a few kilometers north of the ghetto, was one of nine forts constructed around Kaunas as the first line of defense against the German Empire. The fort is infamous for its role as a Nazi death camp where 50,000 people, including 30,000 Jews, were murdered and buried in the surrounding fields. On December 25, 1943, 64 men burrowed their way out, though many were later caught or shot. Part of the museum allows access to the prison cells; look for the carved messages left by prisoners awaiting their execution in cell five. The looming memorial outside was erected in 1994. *(Žemaičių 73. Catch microbus #46 and ask to stop at IX Fortas (2-5 per hr. 6am-9pm). ☎ 37 77 50. Open W-M 10am-6pm. Each part of the museum 2Lt, students 1Lt. Tunnel connecting the prison with the barracks can be explored with a guide for 10Lt. Cameras 20Lt.)*

PAŽAISLIS MONASTERY AND CHURCH. This vibrant Baroque complex, which is filled with frescoes, sits on the right bank of the Nemunas 10km east of central Kaunas. Originally designed by three Florentine masters in the 17th century, the church was used as a KGB-run "psychiatric hospital" and then as a resort. The monastery was returned to the Catholic Church in 1990. Classical music concerts are held here, as is the much-touted **Pažaislis Music Festival** from late May through August. *(Kauno juros 31. Take tram #5 or 9 from the train station to the end of the line; the church is 1km down the road past a small beach. ☎75 64 85 or 45 64 85. Open daily 11am-5pm, but hours may vary, so call ahead. Free tour after 11am mass.)*

MUSEUMS

DEVIL MUSEUM. (Velnių Muziejus; formally the A. Žmuidzinavičiaus Art Collection.) Lithuanian artist, professor, and collector Antanas Žmuidzinavičiaus amassed more than 260 depictions of devils (20 devil dozens) in various media; the museum has grown to over 2000 devils from Lithuania, Africa, Asia, and the Americas. Most notable is "The Division of Lithuania," featuring Devil Hitler and Devil Stalin chasing each other across bone-covered Lithuania. Also, check out a carving of Žmuidzinavičiaus himself "hunting devils." *(V. Putvinskio 64, near Unity Square. ☎22 15 87. Open Tu-Su 10am-5pm; closed last Tu of the month. 5Lt, students 2.50Lt.)*

MUSEUM OF EXILES AND POLITICAL PRISONERS. (Tremties ir Rezistencijos Muziejus). This museum contains a collection of photographs and artifacts of the resistance to Soviet rule, as well as evidence of the life of Siberian exiles. The curator was an exile herself for ten years—get someone to translate her tour from Lithuanian, German, or Russian. *(Vytauto 46, near Ramybfs Park and a short walk from St. Michael's. ☎32 31 79. Brochure in English. Open W-Sa 10am-4pm. Donation requested.)*

M.K. ČIURLIONIS MUSEUM. (M.K. Čiurlionis Muziejus.) Displays works by the revered artist and composer who combined music and image to depict ideas in their early, pre-verbal state. Čiurlionis has been described as "a cross between Monet on acid and Dalí on valium," because of the combination of Symbolism, Impressionism, and Romanticism in his works. Upstairs, find 20th-century Lithuanian paintings, while the rest of the first floor houses folk art and distinctive wooden crosses. *(Putvinskio 55, in Unity Sq. behind the War Museum. ☎22 97 38. English captions. Open Tu-Su 11am-5pm. 5Lt, students 2.50Lt.)*

VYTAUTAS THE GREAT WAR MUSEUM. (Vytauto Didžiojo Karo Muziejus.) Houses all sorts of weapons and the aircraft *Lituanica*, in which two Lithuanian-Americans, Darius and Girėnas, attempted to fly from New York to Kaunas nonstop in 1933; they crashed in Germany. Another exhibit follows Napoleon's journey through the Baltics en route to his ill-fated Russian campaign. *(Donelaičio 64, in Unity Sq. behind 2 soccer-playing lions. ☎32 09 39. Open Mar. 15-Oct. 15 W-Su 10am-6pm; Oct. 16-Mar. 14 W-Su 9am-5pm. 2Lt, students 1Lt.)*

ENTERTAINMENT AND NIGHTLIFE

Muzikinis Teatras (The Musical Theater), Laisvės 91, performs operettas. (☎22 71 13. Box office open Tu-Su 10am-1pm and 3-6pm.) The **Academic Drama Theater** (Akademinis Dramos Teatras), Laisvės 71, stages dance and plays in Lithuanian and occasionally Russian. (☎22 40 64; fax 20 76 93; www.dramosteatras.lt. Box office open M-Sa 11am-2pm and 3-6pm, Su 4-6pm.) The **Kaunas Philharmonic,** Sapiegos 5, is known for its classical concerts. (☎22 25 58. Performances M-F at 6pm, Sa-Su at 5pm.) Check out www.kaunas.lt for info on the annual **Summer Song Festival** held at Song Valley (Dainų Siėnis). Cinemas dot Laisvės: **Kankės,** Laisvės 36 (☎20 58 90); the newly-renovated **Laisvė,** Laisvės 46a (☎20 52 03); and **Romuva,** Laisvės 54 (☎20 55 82). Show times are listed at www.cinemal.lt.

Medusa (☎75 05 75; www.meduza.lt), along the north bank of the Nemunas. From Rotušės, head down Aleksoto toward the river; Medusa is the ship docked just past the bridge. This newly opened bar/club consists of three floors and a boat-shaped bar with a statue of Medusa herself. Leave the kids at home for the rather risque variety show F-Sa nights (15Lt, students 10Lt). Open Su-Th 10am-2am, F-Sa 10am-4am.

Siena (The Wall), Laisvės 93 (☎42 44 24; www.siena.lt), beneath Miesto Sodas. The spacious dance floor fills quickly as local bands play and house DJs spin. Live jazz Su. Open Tu-Th 9pm-2am, F-Sa 9pm-4am.

Skliautai, Rotušės 26a (☎20 68 43). In a courtyard, this bar is more peaceful than the clubs along Laisvės. Older sophisticates mellow out and sip beer. Live jazz W-Th at 6pm. Open daily 9am-midnight. MC/V.

▣ DAYTRIP FROM KAUNAS

HILL OF CROSSES

Take a bus from Kaunas (3hr., 14 per day, 16-17.50Lt) to Šiauliai. From there, take any bus going toward Joniškis Meškuičiai from platform #2; ask the driver to stop at Kryžių. From the stop, follow the marked road for 2km. The last bus back leaves at 6:35pm.

On a sunny morning in 1236, the German Knights of the Sword were ambushed and massacred as they returned from a campaign to christianize Lithuania. The town founded on the site, Šiauliai (SEE-ow-oo-lee-eye; pop. 146,500), took its name from the shining sun *(saulė)* of that bloody day. To commemorate the bloodshed, local citizens established the **Hill of Crosses** (Kryžių Kalnas), 12km northwest of the city. After the Lithuanian uprisings of 1831 and 1863, people from across the country brought crosses to remember the dead and the deported. The collection grew, and by Soviet occupation the hill had been transformed into a mound of anti-Russian sentiment. Despite three encounters with a bulldozer, the memorial survived. Independence has brought a new eruption of crosses, as emigré Lithuanians and relatives of the exiled have returned to add their own monuments. In 1993, Pope John Paul II added a crucifix of his own. You can spend all day here and not finish reading the inscriptions on crosses of all sizes. Buy a small wooden cross (1-3Lt) from local vendors to add to the incredible collection.

COASTAL LITHUANIA

The chilly Baltic Sea dominates the secluded, thickly forested coast of Lithuania. The carnival resort town of Palanga fills its summer days and nights with fun, while the bustling port of Klaipėda enjoys economic prosperity and guards the gateway to Lithuania's share of the Curonian Spit (Neringa). Down the Spit, Juodkrantė showcases delightful Lithuanian art. Farther yet, near the border with Kaliningrad, Nida nestles among towering sand dunes, content in its isolation.

PALANGA   ☎(8)460

The water off Palanga (pop. 18,000) may be cold, but the town is the hottest summer spot in Lithuania—at least in the mind of the president, who chose Palanga for his summer residence. About 82,000 other summer settlers are also drawn to the magnificent beaches and rollicking nightlife. With the largest park in the country and over 20km of shoreline, there's room on the beach for all.

▤ TRANSPORTATION. The **bus station,** Kretinjos 1 (☎533 33), sends buses to: **Druskininkai** (7½hr., 1 per day, 42Lt); **Kaunas** (3hr., 11 per day, 31Lt); **Klaipėda** (30min., every 30min., 2.50Lt); and **Vilnius** (4hr., 10 per day, 40-44Lt). Speedier **microbuses** head to **Klaipėda** (20min., whenever microbuses are full, 3Lt).

⚡🔧 ORIENTATION AND PRACTICAL INFORMATION. Palanga's main streets are **Vytauto,** which runs parallel to the beach and passes the bus station, and **J. Basanavičiaus,** which runs perpendicular to Vytauto and becomes a boardwalk. The pedestrian **Meilės alėja** runs south of the pier alongside the beach, becoming **Birutės alėja** in the Palanga Park and Botanical Garden. **Tourist information** is available at Kretingos 1, to the right of the bus station. (☎488 11; fax 48 822; palangatur-info@is.lt. Open daily 9am-1pm and 2-7pm.) **Hansabankas,** Juratės 15/2, **exchanges currency,** cashes AmEx/MC/Thomas Cook **traveler's checks,** and processes MC **cash advances. Western Union** services are available inside and a **24hr. ATM** stands outside. (☎412 12. Open M-Sa 8am-6pm, Su 9am-1pm.) **Vilniaus Bankas,** Vytauto 61, also **exchanges currency.** (☎491 40. Open M-F 8am-5pm, Sa 9am-3pm.) **Palangos Vaistinė,** Vytauto 33, a renovated **pharmacy** from the 1800s, is still operating. (☎536 57. Open in summer daily 9am-9pm; off-season M-Sa 9am-8pm, Su 9am-4pm.) Find **Internet access** at **Jūra On-Line,** Vytauto 94a. (☎495 25. 9Lt per hr. Open daily 8am-11pm.) The **post office,** Vytauto 53, also has telephones. (☎488 71. Open M-F 9am-6:30pm, Sa 9am-4pm.) **Postal Code:** LT-5720.

🏠🍴 ACCOMMODATIONS AND FOOD. Make reservations in summer, as Palanga's beaches make this a hot spot. **Litinterp ❸** in Klaipėda (see **Practical Information,** p. 458) arranges **private rooms** in Palanga (singles 90-120Lt; doubles 140-180Lt). **Alanga Hotel ❹,** S. Nėries 14, has brightly colored rooms equipped with TV, phone, and minibar. Spacious modern bathrooms and candy on your pillow add an extra touch of class. From the bus stations, cross Vytauto, walk around the post office, and turn left on S. Nėries; it will be the pink building on your right, close to the beach. (☎492 15; fax 493 16; www.alang.lf. Breakfast 20Lt, children 12Lt. Nanny service 5Lt per hr. Doubles 120-160Lt; "lux" suite 190-250Lt; roomy apartment 340-390Lt. MC/V.) From the bus station, take a left on Vytauto, a right on J. Basanavičiaus, and another left on S. Daukanto to reach **Alka ❷,** S. Daukanto. 21. Come here for cheap rooms and a prime location between Vytauto and the beach. (☎562 77. Singles 25-30Lt; doubles 50-60Lt; triples 75-100Lt.)

The Palangan pedestrian will have no trouble finding food. **Vytauto** and **J. Basanavičiaus** are lined with cafes and restaurants offering outdoor seating and blaring music. Innumerable street vendors sell ice cream snacks (1-2.50Lt), *čeburekai* (meat-filled dough pastries; 3Lt), and waffles-dipped-in-chocolate-on-a-stick (3-4Lt). **Senoji Dorė ❸,** J. Basanavičiaus 5, at the end of the major pedestrian street, serves Lithuanian cuisine amid nautical decorations. (☎53 455. Entrees 16-28Lt. 5% service charge. Open daily 10am-midnight.) Serious carnivores will enjoy **Elnio Ragas ❷,** J. Basanavičiaus 25. This smoky hunting lodge—complete with fireplace and trophy boar's head—adds lots of deer, boar, and tongue to its dishes. (☎535 05. Entrees 8-30Lt. Open 11am until the last guest leaves; MC/V.) **Lašas,** J. Basanavičiaus 29, is another meat-lover's delight, complete with nightly live music in summer. (☎813 89. Open Su-Th 10am-midnight, F-Sa 10am-6am.) For an alternative to Palanga's many "themed" restaurants, try **Monika ❷,** J. Basanavičiaus 12, for some Lithuanian and Italian fare—namely, a large selection of pizzas. (☎525 60. Entrees 5-25Lt. Open daily 10am-midnight. MC/V.)

◎ SIGHTS. The beach is the hallmark of any Palanga excursion, as visitors flock here in the summer for fun in the sun. If the sun has got you down, or burnt, take a break at Palanga's pride and joy, the **Amber Museum** (Gintaro muziejus). Residing in a mansion built in 1897 by Count Tiškevičius, in the heart of the Botanical Gardens, this museum displays many of its 15,000 "inclusions," pieces of amber with primeval flora and fauna trapped inside. Check out Case 13 to see a rare example of a reptile skin frozen in time. (☎513 19. English captions. Open June-Aug. Tu-Sa

10am-8pm, Su 10am-7pm; Sept.-May daily 11am-4:30pm; ticket office closes 1hr. early in summer and 30min. early in winter. 5Lt, students 2.50Lt.) The **Palanga Botanical Gardens** include landscaped flower gardens, wooded paths, and a pond that hosts a family of trumpeter swans. Through the main entrance to the gardens, on the corner of Vytauto and S. Dariaus ir S. Girėno, stands **Eglė,** Queen of the Serpents, one of the most famous statues in Lithuania. Follow the path past the manor to the right to reach the **beach.** The pine-covered hill to the left before the boardwalk is **Birutė Hill,** once the site of a pagan shrine to Prau- rimė. The hill is named for a virgin of the shrine who was kidnapped and made a Grand Duchess; look for her grave nearby. A 19th-century octagonal **chapel** with brilliant stained-glass windows now invades Praurimė's turf. Leave the Botanical Garden through the main gate and walk along Vytauto to reach the **Dr. Jonas Šliūpas Memorial Gardens and House,** Vytauto 23a, where the Lithuanian patriot lived from 1930-1944. Šliūpas founded newspapers, participated in the Lithuanian government of the interwar period, and worked as a doctor, teacher, and brew-master. From 1884 to 1921, Šliūpas spent time in the US editing Lithuanian newspapers and establishing the American Lithuanians' national party "Santara" ("Concord"; ☎545 59. Captions in Lithuanian only. Open in sum- mer daily noon-7pm; off-season open daily 11am-5pm. 2Lt, students 1Lt. W Free.) To reach the **Antanas Mončys House-Museum,** S. Daukanto 16, near the cor- ner, continue on Vytauto toward the center, and go left on Kęstučio. The museum showcases the artist's work, a diverse collection of quirky chains, con- trasting forms, and statues. The entire exhibit is hands-on, due to specifications in Mončys's will. (☎493 66. Open Th-Su 12-5pm. 4Lt, students 2Lt.)

🚲📺 **ENTERTAINMENT AND FESTIVALS.** Street vendors rent **bikes** (5-10Lt per hr.) and a host of other wheeled vehicles. Alternatively, play **minigolf** (small course 10Lt, large course 15Lt) next to Ritos Virtuvė on J. Basanavičiaus, or **bumper boats** (5Lt for 3min.), next to Cafe Dviese, J. Basanavičiaus 22. The **Sum- mer Theatre** (Vasaraos Estrada) at Vytauto 43 hosts **concerts** by the Lithuanian National Philharmonic and the Klaipėda Philharmonic, as well as visiting per- formers. (☎522 10. Box office open daily 11am-noon and 1-8pm.) Many cafes on J. Basanavičiaus and Vytauto feature live bands and dancing at night. **Kinote- atras Naglis,** Vytauto 82, shows Hollywood flicks with Lithuanian subtitles (10Lt). Everyone congregates along the pier to watch the **sunset.** The **festival season** opens June 1-3, when bands and choirs compete, theater groups take to the street, fireworks light up the sky, and a giant feast runs long into the night. **Night Serenades,** evenings of classical music, are held every night July 27-August 5 at the Amber Museum (see **Sights,** p. 455). They let the dogs out the first week- end of August for the **Cup of Palanga,** a massive canine exhibition and competi- tion held in the town stadium at Sporto 1.

KLAIPĖDA
☎(8)46

With its fortress at the tip of the Neringa peninsula, Klaipėda (klai-PAY-da; pop. 194,000) stands guard over the Curonian Spit. Lithuania's third-largest city, however, has historically been too strategically located for its own good. Known as Memel until 1923, the great port city passed to Polish, Swedish, Rus- sian, and Prussian hands over the course of a few centuries. In 1807 it became the capital of Prussia while Napoleon roamed the continent and in 1919 it went to France in the Treaty of Versailles. Lithuania only reclaimed the city in 1923. All was well until Hitler personally stormed its shores in 1939, leaving only after Soviet eviction.

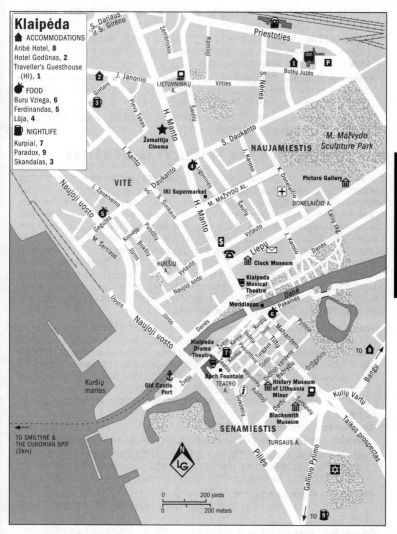

Klaipėda

🏠 **ACCOMMODATIONS**
Aribė Hotel, **8**
Hotel Godūnas, **2**
Traveller's Guesthouse
(HI), **1**

🍴 **FOOD**
Buru Vziega, **6**
Ferdinandas, **5**
Lūja, **4**

🍸 **NIGHTLIFE**
Kurpiai, **7**
Paradox, **9**
Skandalas, **3**

S. Dariaus ir S. Giréno

Priestoties

Žembrickio

Ramioji

Butkų Juzės

J. Janonio

Gintaro

LIETUVNINKŲ A.

Vilties

S. Nėries

Plevų Takas

Šaulių

H. Manto

M. Mažvydo Sculpture Park

Žemaitija Cinema

S. Daukanto

NAUJAMIESTIS

J. Karoso

K. Donelaičio

Picture Gallery

VITĖ

J. Zauerveino

S. Daukanto

Ligoninės

M. MAŽVYDO AL.

DONELAIČIO A.

IKI Supermarket

S. Šimkaus

H. Manto

Šaulių

Vytauto

Gegužės

Puodžių

Kroviejų

Bokštų

M. Šerniaus

Jūros

KURŠIŲ A.

Vytauto

Naujoji sodo

Clock Museum

Liepų

J. Karoso

Danės

Naujoji uosto

Naujoji uosto

Uosto

Jūros

Danės

Klaipėda Musical Theatre

Meridianas

Danė

Pakalnės

Pylimo

TO 8

Naujoji uosto

Kuršių marios

Old Castle Port

Žvejų

Žvejų

Klaipėda Drama Theatre

Teatro

Žvejų

Kurpių

Kaniaų

Vėžio

Kepėjų

Pasiuntinių

Jono

Turgaus

Tomo

Tiltų

Mažanderių

Didžioji Vandens

Bažnyčių

Grižgatvio

Bangų

TO SMILTYNĖ & THE CURONIAN SPIT (2km)

Mėsinnių

Aukštoji

Sukilėlių

Bach Fountain

TEATRO A.

History Museum of Lithuania Minor

Kuliu Vartu

Daržų

Šaltkalvių

Taikos prospektas

Blacksmith Museum

SENAMIESTIS

TURGAUS A.

Pilies

Gallinio Pylimo

Taikos prospektas

N

0   200 yards
0   200 meters

TO 9

LITHUANIA

◧ TRANSPORTATION

Trains: Geležinkelio stotis, Priestoties 1 (☎31 36 77). To: **Kaunas** (6½hr., 1 per day, 27-29.50Lt); **Vilnius** (5-8¾hr., 3 per day, 30-47Lt); **Moscow, RUS** (21¼hr., 1 per week, 191.20Lt). Station open daily 5:30am-10:30pm. *Kassa* open daily 6am-9:45pm.

Buses: Autobusų stotis, Butkų Juzės 9 (☎41 15 47, reservations 41 15 40). To: **Kaunas** (3hr., 14 per day, 28Lt); **Palanga** (30-40min., 23 per day, 2.50-3Lt); **Vilnius** (4-

5hr., 12 per day, 35-38Lt); **Kaliningrad, RUS** (4hr., 3 per day, 25Lt); **Riga, LAT** (6hr., 12 per day, 35Lt). Station open daily 3:30am-midnight.

Ferries: Old Castle Port, Žvejų 8 (☎31 42 17, info 31 11 57), sends ferries to **Smiltynė** (10min., every 30min. 5am-3am, free). Microbuses on the other side connect to **Juodkrantė** (30min., 5Lt) and **Nida** (1hr., 7Lt).

Public Transportation: City buses (0.60Lt) and the wonderfully convenient **maršrutinis taksis** (route taxis; 6am-11pm 1Lt, 11pm-6am 2Lt) run all over town. #8 travels from the train station down H. Manto through Taikos.

Taxis: State company (☎006). 1.20Lt per km is the standard fare. Several **private companies** roam the streets for 1-1.50Lt per km.

■✚ 🛈 ORIENTATION AND PRACTICAL INFORMATION

The **Danė River** divides the city into south **Senamiestis** (Old Town) and north **Naujamiestis** (New Town). Kuršių Marios (Curonian Lagoon) to the west cuts off **Smiltynė,** Klaipėda's Kuršių Nerija (Curonian Spit) quarter. **H. Manto,** the main artery, becomes **Tiltų** as it crosses the river into Senamiestis, and finally **Taikos** as it enters the more modern part of the city. For **maps** and info on Palanga, Juodkrantė, Nida, and the rest of the Spit, pick up *Klaipėda in Your Pocket* (4Lt). All of mainland Klaipėda lies close to the **bus** and **train stations,** which are separated by **Priestoties.** Facing away from the bus station, turn right on **Butkų Juzės,** and then left on **S. Nėries.** Follow S. Nėries away from the train station to its end, then take a right on S. Daukanto to reach the heart of the city. As you exit the ferry at Old Castle Port, turn left on **Žvejų** with the river behind you. From Žvejų, make any right after crossing Pilies to reach Senamiestis.

Tourist Offices: Tourism Information Centre, Tomo 2 (☎41 21 86 or 41 21 81; fax 41 21 85; www.klaipeda.lt). Dispenses **maps** and arranges English-language tours (100Lt for 2hr.). Open M-F 8am-6pm, Sa 9am-4pm. **Litinterp,** S. Šimkaus 21/4 (☎31 14 90; fax 41 18 15; klaipeda@litinterp.lt), arranges private rooms in: **Klaipėda** (singles 70-90Lt, in summer 90-120Lt; doubles 120-140Lt/140-180Lt; triples 180-210Lt; apartments 160-200Lt, in summer starting at 200Lt); **Palanga** (see p. 455); and **Nida** (see p. 461). Breakfast included. Call ahead. English spoken. Open M-F 8:30am-5:30pm, Sa 9:30am-3:30pm.

Currency Exchange: Hausabankas, Taikos 5 (☎522 41), cashes AmEx/Thomas Cook **traveler's checks** and offers **Western Union** services. **ATMs** are everywhere.

Luggage Storage: Lockers in the train station (2Lt for 24hr.; open daily 5:30am-10:30pm) or racks at the bus station (1.50Lt for 24hr.; open daily 3:30-11:30am and 12:30-8:30pm). The Tourist Information Centre (see above) will also store your bag.

Bookstores: Akaemija Knygynas, S. Daukanto 16 (☎/fax 31 08 20; www.akademijaştakas.lt), has a small selection of English books. Open M-F 10am-7pm, Su 10am-5pm. MC/V.

Telephones: Telephone Office, H. Manto 2 (☎41 10 33). Open daily 8am-10pm.

Internet Access: Bitas Interneto Svetainė, Tiltų 26a (☎41 16 59; www.bitas.lt), in the alleyway between Tiltų and the Blacksmith's Museum. 48 flat-screen machines. **Branch** at Šaulių 4-20 (☎41 10 49). Open M-F 10am-9pm, Sa-Su 10am-10pm. 3Lt per hr., students 2Lt. **JPC Interneto Salagas,** Lietuvininkų a. 11a (☎38 28 53), just off H. Mantog with 12 fast connections (2Lt per hr.). Open daily 8am-11pm.

Post Office: Central Post Office, Liepų 16 (☎31 50 22; fax 41 11 68). Houses a 48-bell carillon (the largest musical instrument in the country), which rings Sa-Su at noon. Open M-F 8am-7pm, Sa 9am-4pm.

Postal Code: LT-5800.

⌂ ACCOMMODATIONS

The ever-obliging folks at **Litinterp** (see **Tourist Offices,** above) arrange **private rooms** with local families and can set you up at the Litinterp **guest house** ❷ near M. Mažvydo. (Singles from 70Lt; doubles from 120Lt. MC/V.)

▨ **Klaipéda Traveller's Guesthouse (HI),** Butkų Juzės 7-4 (☎21 18 79; oldtown@takas.lt), 50m from the bus station. An absolute joy for the weary traveler, equipped with large, spacious dorms, hot showers, and a friendly staff. Make yourself a cup of tea, check your email (free), and chat with other backpackers. Laundry 12Lt per load. Free beer for reserving by email. 34Lt, HI members 32Lt. ❶

Aribė Hotel, Bangų 17a (☎49 09 40; fax 49 09 42; vitetur@klaipeda.omnitel.net). Heading away from the Danė River on Tiltų, make a left on Kulių Vartų, and another left on Bangų. This newly-opened hotel has simple, pleasant rooms, with bathroom, shower, phone, TV, and Internet connections. Breakfast included. Singles 120Lt, in summer 140Lt; doubles 160Lt/180Lt; "lux" suite 240Lt/260Lt. MC/V. ❸

Hotel Godūnas, Janonio 11 (☎/fax 31 09 00; godunas@klaipeda.omnitel.net), off H. Manto past Naujamiestis. Godūnas has large beds, roomy bathrooms with shower, and exceptionally large suites in a quiet part of town. Rooms have TV, phone, satellite TV, and minibars. Breakfast included. Singles from 190Lt; doubles from 240Lt. MC/V. ❹

⌷ FOOD

The **central market** is on Turgas aikštė; follow Tiltų through Senamiestis and take a hard right at the first rotary. (Open daily about 8am-6pm.) The **IKI supermarket,** M. Mažvyado 7/11, within walking distance of the Old Town, is the biggest in the Baltics. (Open daily 8am-10pm.) If you want more, go to the monstrous mall **Hyper Maxima,** Taikos 61—its name says it all. Follow H. Manto as it turns into Tiltų and then into Taikos pr. (Open daily 8am-midnight.)

▨ **Lūja,** H. Manto 20 (☎41 24 44; fax 41 25 55). Serves fine Lithuanian and international dishes in a sophisticated, sumptuous atmosphere. Quiet and romantic, with candlelit tables. Visiting dignitaries often dine here, so be sure to make reservations. 4-language menu and a friendly staff. Entrees 7-62Lt. 20% discount before 4pm. Open daily noon-midnight. MC/V. ❹

Ferdinandas, Naujoji Vosto 10 (☎31 36 84). From H. Manto, follow S. Daukanto in the direction of the river; it's at the corner of S. Daukanto and Naujoji Vosto. Munch on grilled roasts, stews, pelmeni, and *blini* (Russian-style pancakes), served by waiters in flashy purple-and-gold Russian attire. Tavern-like feel with Russian music Th 7pm, F-Sa 8pm. Entrees 6-35Lt. Open M-F 10am-midnight, Sa-Su noon-midnight. MC/V. ❸

Buru Vzeiga, Kepėju 17 (☎41 13 19), just off Tiltų in Senamiestis. Serves traditional Lithuanian fare, including eggs, curd, flour dishes, soups, and various meat, fish, and fowl. Tavern-like atmosphere, accentuated by the stuffed birds and animals (hopefully not the ones you're eating). Entrees 4-13Lt. English menu. Open daily 11am-11pm. ❶

◉ SIGHTS

MAINLAND KLAIPÉDA

One would never guess that the lush, cheery **M. Mažvydo Sculpture Park** (M. Mažvydo Skulptūrų Parkas), between Liepų and S. Daukanto, once served as the town's central burial ground. Sculptures by Lithuanian artists, as well as an art exhibition from Australia, New Zealand, and Oceania, await at the **Klaipėda Picture Gallery** (Paveikslų galerija), Liepų 33, across the park heading away from the bus station. (☎41 04 12. Info in Lithuanian only. Open Tu-Sa noon-6pm, Su noon-5pm. 4Lt, students 2Lt. "Common ticket," including the Clock Museum and Palanga's Amber Museum 4Lt.) Exiting the gallery, continue right down Liepų to the **Clock Museum** (Laikrodžių Muziejus), Liepų 12. Its bizarre collection includes every conceivable kind of timekeeping device, from Egyptian sundials to Chinese candle clocks to a modern quartz watch-pen. (☎41 04 13. Open Tu-Su noon-5:30pm. 4Lt, students 2Lt. English tour 40Lt.)

The 1857 **Klaipėda Drama Theater** (Klaipėdos Dramos Teatras), **Teatro aikštė**, on the other side of H. Manto, is famous as one of Wagner's favorite haunts and infamous as the site where Hitler personally proclaimed the incorporation of the town into the *Reich* in 1939. (Tickets ☎31 44 53; box office open Tu-Su 11am-2pm and 4-7pm.) In front, the **Simon Dach Fountain** spouts water over the symbol of Klaipėda, a statue of Ännchen von Tharau. The original statue disappeared in World War II; some say it was removed by the Nazis, who didn't want the statue's back to face Hitler during his speech. The copy standing today was erected by German expatriates in 1989. The **History Museum of Lithuania Minor** (Mažosios Lietuvos Istorijos Muziejus) is at Didžioji Vandens 6. (☎41 05 24. Open W-Su 10am-6pm. 2Lt, students 1Lt.) **Aukštoji**, near the history museum, is one of the best-preserved areas of Senamiestis, lined with examples of the exposed-timber *Fachwerk* buildings for which pre-war Klaipėda was well-known. Aukštoji feeds into the large market (Turgaus aikštė); take a right just before the market and then another right on Šaltkalvių to reach the **Blacksmith's Museum** (Kalvystės muziejus), Šaltkalvių 2, which showcases Lithuanian ironwork and sells modern pieces. (☎41 05 26. Open in summer W-Su 10am-5:30pm; off-season Tu-Sa 10am-5:30pm. 2Lt, students 1Lt.)

SMILTYNĖ

As you get off the ferry, make a right on Smiltynės and follow it along the river to the Tourist Information Center, Smiltynės 11. (☎/fax 40 22 57; www.nerija.lt. Open M-F 8am-5pm, Sa 10am-4pm, Su 10am-2pm.) Next door the **Nature Museum** (Kuršių nerijos nacionalinio parko gamtos muziejus), Smiltynės 9-12, exhibits the region's natural and human history, including dioramas of villages now buried by the shifting sand dunes. (Open May and Sept. W-Su 11am-5pm; June-Aug. Tu-Su 11am-6pm. 2Lt, students 1Lt.) The nearby **Fishermen's Village** (Ethnografinė Pajūrio Žvejo Sodyba) is a reconstruction of a 17th-century settlement. (Open 24hr. 2Lt.) Just down the road, four ships sit on pillars in the **Garden of Veteran Fishing Boats** (Žvejybos Laivai-veteranai). Forest paths lead west about 500m to the **beaches.** Signs mark gender-divided areas for **nude bathing**—women to the right, men to the left, and the **public beach** in between. Follow Smiltynės to the end for the main attraction here, the ▓ **Maritime Museum, Aquarium, and Dolphinarium** (Lietuvos Jūrų Muziejus), Smiltynė 3. Housed in an 1860s fortress that once guarded Klaipėda's bustling port, Baltic seals and sea lions now frolic in the moat, while the fort's inner sanctum houses the aquarium. (☎49 07 54; fax 49 07 50; www.juru.muziejus.lt. Open June-Aug. Tu-Su 10:30am-6:30pm; Sept. W-Su 10:30am-6:30pm; Oct.-May Sa-Su 10:30am-5pm. 8Lt, students 4Lt. Camera 5Lt.) Don't miss the highly amusing **sea lion show,** which features a huge North Sea sea lion and its trainer (11am, 1, 3pm; 3Lt). Dolphins leap, paint, and dance at the museum's **Dolphinarium.** (Shows noon, 2, 4pm. 12Lt, students 6Lt. Camera 5Lt.)

🎵 🎭 ENTERTAINMENT AND NIGHTLIFE

The best bar-hopping lies along H. Manto. The **Klaipėda Musical Theater** (Muzikinis teatras), Danės 19, hosts operas and other musical events. (☎41 05 56. Performances F 7pm, Sa-Su 6pm. Ticket office open Tu-Su 11am-2pm and 3-6pm.) **The Žemaitija Cinema**, H. Manto 31, shows Hollywood films with Lithuanian subtitles in a modern decor. (☎31 40 90; www.zemaitojskinas.lt. MC/V.) The **Sea Festival** brings

Hanseatic and handicraft fairs, as well as live entertainment, during the last week of July. In early June, a **Jazz Festival** swings.

Kurpiai, Kurpių 1a (☎/fax 41 03 33; www.jazz.lt), in the middle of Senamiestis. This excellent jazz club is a mix between a traditional tavern and a jazz museum. Live music nightly usually starting at 9:30pm. Cover F-Sa 5-10Lt. Open daily noon-3am. MC/V.

Paradox, Minijos 2 (☎31 41 05). From the rotary at the end of Tiltų, turn right on Gallnio Pylimo, which, after another rotary, becomes Minijos. Work your way up or down 3 floors, from the pulsing disco to the mellow pool room to the relaxed bar. Bar open M-Tu noon-3am, W-Su noon-6am. Disco open W-Su 9pm-6am. MC/V.

Skandalas, I. Kanto 44 (☎41 15 85; fax 41 15 84). Walking up H. Manto from the Danė River, turn left on S. Daukanto and make a right on I. Kanto. Walk past the full-sized car by the entrance to find American kitsch in the form of flags, license plates, and a working traffic light. Relax and gaze at the ceiling pasted with dollar bills. Open M-Th noon-1am, F-Sa noon-2am, Su noon-midnight. MC/V.

CURONIAN SPIT (NERINGA)

The great sandbar that is the Curonian Spit is lined with majestic dunes, crisscrossed by lush forests, and bordered by the Baltic Sea. The **Kuršių Nerija National Park,** which works to preserve this pristine natural wonder, charges a 3Lt "environmental tax" for all visitors entering the Spit by microbus or hydrofoil.

WITCH'S HILL

Goblins, devils, and amused mortals frolic on   Witch's Hill (Raganų Kalnas) in Juodkrantė. Set aside an hour to wander the worn trail (when in doubt, veer right; the path loops back to the beginning) through the dense magical wood lined with over 100 mythical wooden sculptures in high Lithuanian folk-art style. Knights slay dragons, fishermen sail to sea, imps throw a party, and Satan himself joins in on the fun. Visitors can mingle with the gnomes by frolicking on a seesaw, sliding down a giant tongue, or getting in a saddle seven feet off the ground. Don't miss the chance to cut in on a game of cards between the devil and a witch; they've left two seats free for you. Follow the "Sveikatingumo takas" path to the left or just head toward the sound of crashing water to find the **beach** on the Baltic side of the Spit. If you want a snack, try the tasty *žuvis* (smoked fish) that are sold along the boardwalk. While Juodkrantė is always a site of mirth and ritual, many locals claim Witch's Hill is *the* place to be on Midsummer's Eve and St. John's Day. Nearly all microbuses running between Klaipėda and Nida stop at Juodkrantė—ask the driver to be sure (30min., 5Lt).

NIDA   ☎(8)469

Wind-swept, white-sand dunes have long drawn summer vacationers to Nida (pop. 2000), just 3km north of the Russian Kaliningrad region. From the remains of the town's immense sundial—the highest point on the Spit—you can look down on the glorious vista of the dunes, the Curonian Lagoon, the Baltic, and nearby Russia.

⌐ TRANSPORTATION. The **bus station,** Naglių 18e (☎52472), is basically a schedule and a few chairs encased by four walls. **Microbuses** run to **Smiltynė** (1hr., every ½hr., 7Lt). A bus runs to Kaunas daily (4½hr., 1 per day, 39Lt).

⑦ PRACTICAL INFORMATION. From the water, **Taikos** runs west inland. Perpendicular to Taikos, **Naglių** eventually becomes **Pamario** The **Tourist Information Center,** Taikos 4, opposite the bus station, offers the standard Neringa **map,** arranges private rooms for a 5Lt fee, and has good transport info. (☎ 523 45; fax 525 38; www.ner-inga.lt. Open June 1-July 14 M-F 9am-1pm and 2pm-6pm, Sa 10am-6pm, Su 10am-3pm; July 15-Sept. 1 M-F 9am-1pm and 2-8pm, Sa 10am-8pm, Su 10am-3pm; in winter open M-F 9am-1pm and 2pm-6pm, Sa-Su 10am-3pm). **Hausabankas,** Taikos 5, **exchanges currency,** cashes **traveler's checks,** gives MC/V **cash advances,** and provides **Western Union** services. (☎ 522 41. Open M-Th 8am-4pm, F 8am-3:30pm.) and 1:30-5:30pm, Sa 9am-1pm and 2-7pm, Su 10am-4pm.) The **post office,** Taikos 13, lies up the road. (☎ 526 47. Open M-F 9am-noon and 1pm-5:30pm, Sa 9am-1pm.) The adjacent **telephone office** has card phones. (☎ 520 07. Open May-Sept. daily 9am-10pm; Sept.-May 9am-5:45pm.) **Postal Code:** LT-5870.

▛▟ ACCOMMODATIONS AND FOOD. The **tourist office ❷** (see above) arranges **private rooms** (30-50Lt per person), as does **Litinterp ❸** in Klaipėda (see **Tourist Offices,** p. 458; ☎ (26) 31 14 90; fax 41 18 15; www.litinterp.lt. Singles 90-120Lt; doubles 140-180Lt). The hostel, Taikos 26, is the cheapest place to stay in Nida. The rooms are damp, and be sure to BYOTP (Bring Your Own Toilet Paper). Shared shower downstairs. (☎ 526 32. 25Lt per person. 5Lt for linen.) **Urbo Kalnas ❺,** Taikos 32, on a pine-covered hill above town, rents large rooms with clean, hot showers, TVs, and fridges. Walk uphill along Taikos from the center. (☎ 524 28; fax 527 62. Breakfast 15Lt. Doubles 200Lt; apartments 250-400Lt.) The local specialty is *rūkyta žuvis* (smoked fish), which is best eaten with beer; selection varies from nondescript "fish" to eel and perch. **Seklyčia ❸,** at the end of Lotmiško, serves outstanding Lithuanian dishes. *Shashliks* and *blyni* are the cheapest meals. (☎ 529 45. Entrees 22-35Lt. Open daily 9am-midnight.) **Ešerinė ❸,** Naglių 2, is a wacky collection of thatched-roofed, glass-walled huts with wonderful views of the dunes. (☎ 527 57. Entrees 20-27Lt. Open daily 10am-midnight.) Nida's largest **grocery store** is **Kuršis,** Naglių 29. (Open daily 8am-10pm.) Kuršis also has an adjoining cafe that serves great breakfast for early rises. (Open daily 8am-midnight. MC/V.)

◪ SIGHTS. The ▧ **Drifting Dunes of Parnidis** rise south of town, across the bay from the shore-side restaurants at the end of Naglių and Lotmiško. Walk along the beach or through forest paths to reach the peak of the tallest sand dune, marked by the remains of an immense sundial with ancient Baltic carvings—it was smashed by a huge storm in 1999. After enjoying the wonderful views of the lagoon and Baltic Sea, roam the surreal, wind-carved mountains and gorges of white sand. The nature preserve farther south, along the border with Russia, is off-limits. All of the **wooden houses** clustered along Lotmiškio are classified as historic monuments; dozens more are buried somewhere under the sand. From the center of town, walk along the promenade by the water and bear right on Skruzdynės to reach the renovated **Thomas Mann House** (Thomo Manno Namelis) at #17. Mann built the cottage in 1930 and wrote *Joseph and His Brothers* here, but had to abandon it when Hitler invaded. The house now contains photos of Mann and his family and newspaper articles on the writer. (☎ 522 60. Open June-Aug. Tu-Su 10am-6pm; Sept.-May Tu-Sa 11am-5pm. 2Lt, students 0.50Lt.) The **Thomas Mann Cultural Center** puts on classical concerts for the **Thomas Mann Festival** in July. Head back to town along Skruzdynės and on your right you'll see the brand-new **Neringa Museum of History** (Neringos Istorijos Muziejus), Pamario 53. This lofted space presents a thoughtful exhibition of the various occupations of Neringa inhabitants. (☎ 511 62. Open Tu-Su 10am-6pm. 2Lt, students 0.50Lt.)

MOLDOVA

LEI

AUS$1 = 7.42 LEI	10 LEI = AUS$1.35
CDN$1 = 8.69 LEI	10 LEI = CDN$1.15
EUR€1 = 13.29 LEI	10 LEI = EUR€0.75
NZ$1 = 6.33 LEI	10 LEI = NZ$6.33
UK£1 = 20.95 LEI	10 LEI = UK£20.95
US$1 = 13.52 LEI	10 LEI = US$13.52
ZAR1 = 1.27 LEI	10 LEI = ZAR1.27

Although the country is historically part of Romanian Moldavia, Moldova endured Soviet rule for 45 years before gaining independence as the USSR fell apart. While 70% of Moldova's land and people are located on the west bank of the Dniester River, a high concentration of Russians and Ukrainians hold out for greater independence on the other side, in the Transdniester region. Not many tourists stumble over Moldova on their travels—if you do, look past the bleakness of the Soviet cities and discover the spirit of the Moldovan people.

MOLDOVA AT A GLANCE

CAPITAL: Chişinău (pop. 676,700)

POPULATION: 4.46 million

LANGUAGES: Moldovan (Romanian), Russian, Gagauz (Turkish dialect)

CURRENCY: 1 leu (plural lei) = 100 bani

RELIGION: 98.5% Eastern Orthodox

CLIMATE: Continental

GEOGRAPHY: Rolling steppe

BORDERS: Romania, Ukraine

ECONOMY: 40% Agriculture, 14% Industry, 46% other

GDP: US$2500 per capita

COUNTRY CODE: 373

INTERNATIONAL DIALING PREFIX: 810

HISTORY

BETWEEN A ROCK AND A RUSSIAN PLACE. Russia and Romania dominate Moldovan history, as both countries have long competed for the territories of **Bessarabia** and **Transdniester**. Bessarabia has been the most contentious region, controlled by Scythia (1000 BC), Kievan Rus (10th and 12th centuries), Galician princes (early 13th century), and the Tartars (1241-1300s). The region enjoyed temporary prosperity after its annexation by **Moldavia**, part of modern-day Romania, until the entire province was captured by the Turks. In the 15th century, **Ştefan cel Mare** (Stephen the Great) expanded Moldavia's frontiers, pushing back the Poles to the north and the Turks to the south. It was not long before covetous Russia cast eyes on the tasty little state. After invading five times beginning in 1711, the **Treaty of Bucharest** legitimized their claim to the region in 1812.

ROMANIAN UNIFICATION. Attempts to impose Russian culture on the region had little effect on the largely illiterate peasants who remained culturally aligned with Romania. The birth of the Romanian state in 1881 fueled nationalism that erupted into a Moldovan unification movement during the **Russian Revolution of 1905.** In December 1917, Bessarabia renounced Russian rule and declared its autonomy. In

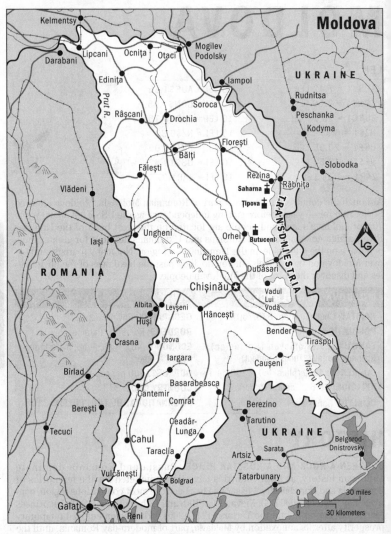

Moldova

response, the Bolsheviks invaded, only to be driven out by Romanian forces. The grateful Moldovan state joined Romania in 1918, despite Russia's refusal to acknowledge Moldova's cession.

RED MOLDOVA. In 1939, the Soviets invaded once again in an attempt to unite the Moldovan states under Communist rule. During **WWII,** Axis-aligned Romania won Bessarabia back and deported most Bessarabian Jews to Auschwitz in order to make room for Romanian peasants. After the Axis defeat, however, the Russians invaded (again) and integrated the region into the Soviet Union as the **Moldovan Soviet Socialist Republic.**

DOUBLE ALLEGIANCE. Nationalism grew as the USSR faltered in the 1980s, and on August 27, 1991, the **Republic of Moldova** declared independence. Finally free of Russia, a powerful nationalist movement reinstated the Latin alphabet and adopted Romania's national hymn as Moldova's own. These pro-Romanian tendencies alarmed the county's large Russian minority who feared reunification with Romania. Russian nationalists in **Transdniester** declared independence from Chişinău in September 1990. **Civil War** followed in 1992, with the Russian army aiding Transdniester and Romania backing the rest of Moldova. After a cease-fire in July of 1992, Transdniester emerged as an autonomous state with **Igor Smirnov** as its leader.

TODAY

AWAY FROM COMMUNISM... The Moldovan constitution was ratified in 1994, and gives executive power to the President and an appointed Council of Ministers. The Prime Minister is the head of the government, which consists of a parliament with 104 members elected for a four-year term. Moldovan politics are fraught with internal strife, a break-away province, and economic woes. On May 8, 1997, Moldovan President **Petru Luchinschi** (elected in December 1996) and Transdniester leader **Igor Smirnov** signed a **Memorandum of Understanding,** affirming a united Moldovan state with substantial autonomy for the Transdniester region. Nonetheless, the region remained firmly Russian and refused to acknowledge Moldovan authority. Russian troops in the region on an arms reduction mission only heightened tensions. Meanwhile, **Ion Sturza,** elected Prime Minister in 1999, had his hands full stabilizing an economy whose currency devalued 50% in 1998.

...AND BACK AGAIN. In 2001, the **Communist Party of Moldova (PRCM)** took control of both the parliament and the presidency. **Vladamir Voronin** is the new President, and **Vasile Tarlev** the new Prime Minister. The political question of the day is whether Moldova should align itself to Russia or Romania, as the current regime is trying to reinstate Russian as a state language and undo many of the pro-Romanian reforms passed by its predecessor. Mass demonstrations against the Communist regime have ground life in Chişinău to a halt periodically throughout 2002.

PEOPLE AND CULTURE

LANGUAGE

Despite a few differences, **Moldovan** and **Romanian** are the same language (see **What's in a Name?**, p. 472). About 60% of the country speaks Moldovan. For a phrasebook and glossary, see **Glossary: Romanian,** p. 887. Almost everyone in Chişinău speaks **Russian** (it is less popular in the countryside), so also check out the **Glossary**'s Russian section (p. 889).

ETIQUETTE

You're unlikely to encounter English speakers in your Moldovan travels. Moldovan customs are deeply rooted in Romanian history and culture. Moldovan women do not shake hands, while it is considered impolite for men not to. Due to Moldova's great wine tradition, it is also considered an insult to not finish one's glass of wine. Any shoes worn outdoors should be removed before entering someone's home. For more information on etiquette, see Romania: Customs and Etiquette, p. 579.

FOOD AND DRINK

MOLDOVA	❶	❷	❸	❹	❺
FOOD	under 5 lei	5-14 lei	15-29 lei	30-44 lei	over 45 lei

Moldovan **cuisine** is a combination of bland Russian dishes, Romanian *mamaliga* (cornmeal), and tasty Turkish kebabs. More uniquely Moldovan dishes can be found in the countryside; bean and sausage salad and noodles with poppy seeds and cheese are some examples. **Vegetarianism** is a rarity in Moldova, and those with eating restrictions will have a difficult time communicating their needs to natives with a very meaty diet. **Wine** is an integral part of Moldovan life; the country has some of the largest and most fertile vineyards in Europe. The country's most famous wine comes from **Cricova** (p. 473).

THE ARTS

HISTORY

Moldovan **literature,** like much of Moldovan history, is inextricably linked with that of Romania (see **Romania: The Arts,** p. 579). During the Soviet era, art in Moldova suffered under the yoke of **Socialist Realism.** One of the most notable writers to surface during this period was **Andrei Lupan,** who managed to enliven the otherwise bland praise for the Communist regime. **Ion Druta,** the greatest writer of the period, explored the psyche of the region's rural population in his 1963 novel *Ballad of the Steppes (Balade de câmpie).* Although both Lupan and Druta wrote in Moldovan, much of their work was published only in Russian translation by the Soviet-controlled press. Sovietization also indirectly reduced Moldova's **folk arts:** the state went to great lengths to preserve the native culture, but their efforts were negated by an economic program that eradicated much of their way of life. Distinctly Moldovan **architecture** is exemplified by the multitude of **churches** built by Ştefan cel Mare in the 15th century.

CURRENT SCENE

The Moldovan National Opera and Ballet Theatre reaps the benefits of Russian-trained ballet dancers like talented soloist **Cristina Terentiev.** Several fine art galleries in Chişinău feature some young Moldovan talent. Check out the **Holti Gallery,** Str. Columna 128 (☎ 24 37 03), or **L Gallery,** Str. Bucurest 64 (☎ 22 19 75).

HOLIDAYS AND FESTIVALS

NATIONAL HOLIDAYS IN 2003

January 1 New Year's Day	**May 1** Labor Day
January 7 Christmas (Orthodox)	**May 9** Victory Day
March 1 Martsishor (Moldova Day)	**August 27** Independence Day
March 8 International Women's Day	**August 31** National Language Day
April 21 Easter Monday (Orthodox)	**October 14** City Day

The vast majority of Moldovans are Eastern Orthodox, so most holidays and feasts are centered on the Christian calendar. Moldova also periodically celebrates international music and performance festivals. These include **Maria Bieshu Invites** (a week of opera and ballet performances featuring foreign guests), **Ukraine Culture Days,** and **Russian Culture Days.**

MARTSISHOR. Martsishor, or National Moldova Day, heralds the coming of spring according to an ancient folk legend. On March 1st, Moldovans give each other snowdrop flowers, the symbol of serenity. The **Martsishor Music Festival** was started in 1967 and runs from March 1-10th.

ADDITIONAL RESOURCES

GENERAL HISTORY AND FILM

Moldova and the Transdniester Republic, by Nicholas Dima (2001). Part of the East European Monographs series, with several good offerings on Moldovan history.

Studies in Moldovan: The History, Culture, Language, and Contemporary Politics of the People of Moldova, by Donald Dyer (1996). The broadest historical and cultural overview of modern Moldova.

The Gypsy Camp Vanishes Into the Heavens, directed by Emil Loteanu (1976). Moldova's most internationally acclaimed film, *Gypsy Camp* is a romantic and cultural tale amazingly produced in the dark, oppressive Communist era.

MOLDOVA ESSENTIALS

ENTRANCE REQUIREMENTS
Passport: Required of all travelers.
Visa: Required of all travelers.
Letter of Invitation: Required of citizens of Australia, New Zealand, and South Africa.
Inoculations: Recommended up-to-date on MMR (measles, mumps, and rubella), DTaP (diphtheria), Polio booster, Hepatitis A, and Hepatitis B.
Work Permit: Required of all foreigners planning to work in Moldova.
International Driving Permit: Required of all those planning to drive.

MOLDOVA

DOCUMENTS AND FORMALITIES

EMBASSIES AND CONSULATES

The US embassy and UK temporary diplomatic office in Moldova are in Chişinău (see p. 320). The only Moldovan embassy in an English-speaking country is in the **US,** 2101 S St. NW, Washington, D.C. 20008 (☎202-667-1130; fax 667-1204; moldova@dgs.dgsys.com). The embassy in **Belgium,** Ave. Max 175, Brussels (☎322 732 93 00 or 732 96 59; fax 732 96 60; moldovaşscynet.be), is also accredited to the **UK** and **EU.** For Moldovan embassies abroad, go to www.moldova.org.

VISA AND ENTRY INFORMATION

Citizens of Australia, New Zealand, and South Africa need both visas and invitations to enter Moldova; citizens of Canada, the EU, and the US need visas, but not invitations. Single-entry visas cost US$40 (valid one month); multiple-entry visas run US$50-200 (depending upon length of stay); and transit visas are US$20 for single-entry, US$40 for double-entry. The US$15 application fee is not included in these rates. Regular service takes seven business days; rush service is an additional 50% of the total visa cost. To apply for a visa you must submit an application, an invitation (if applicable), your passport, a photograph, and the fee by money order or company check to the nearest Moldovan embassy or consulate. Invitations can be obtained from acquaintances in Moldova, or from **MoldovaTUR** (see **Chişinău: Practical Information**, p. 470) after booking a hotel room. All foreign travelers to Moldova must **register** with the police within three days of arrival. **Borders** are not a problem in Moldova, but international buses to and from Odessa pass through Moldova's politically unstable breakaway **Transdniester Republic.** You will pass through an additional passport control at the Transdniester/Moldovan border, where you will be given a small slip of paper. The guards at the Transdniester/Ukrainian border demand this document and will not let you pass without it.

TRANSPORTATION

BY TRAIN. Trains are extremely inefficient in Moldova. The Iaşi-Chişinău train trip takes about six hours, of which only two are spent in motion; border controls and wheel-changing take up the rest. There are direct train and bus connections from Chişinău to **Bucharest, ROM; Kyiv, UKR;** and **Odessa, UKR.** Internally, trains from Chişinău go to Băltsi, Tiraspol, and Ungleni.

BY BUS. Buses are crowded and old, but provide a much cheaper and more comfortable way of getting in, out, and around Moldova.

TOURIST SERVICES AND MONEY

MoldovaTUR is the main tourist office. Its employees usually speak English and are a good resource. Do not confuse Moldovan lei with the Romanian currency of the same name. Moldovan lei are fully convertible (1 leu=100 bani). Moldovan inflation is about 6.5%, so rates and prices should remain fairly stable over the next year. **Bringing cash is necessary** since few places outside Chişinău take traveler's checks or give cash advances. There are only a few **ATMs** in the capital, and they only take Visa.

HEALTH AND SAFETY

 EMERGENCY NUMBERS: Fire: ☎901 **Police:** ☎902 **Ambulance:** ☎903

HEALTH AND SAFETY. Pharmacies in Moldova are generally well-equipped with Western products. The chain called **Farmacia Felicia** is open 24hr. In hospitals, pay with cash. Carrying **toilet paper** and **insect repellent** is always a good idea. In Chişinău, streets are poorly lit at night, and it is unwise to stay out late. The **water** is not safe to drink; boil it for 10 minutes or drink imported bottled water. Beware of unclean food, especially from street vendors. **Cholera** and **diphtheria** are problems in Moldova; talk with your doctor before going. **Avoid traveling through the Transdniester region if at all possible.**

WOMEN, MINORITY, AND BGLT TRAVELERS. Women should wear conservative clothing; stay away from tank tops, shorts, and sneakers that may draw unwanted attention. It is generally fine for women to travel alone in Moldova, but do not stay out after dark. Like most Eastern European countries, Moldovans harbor deep prejudice against Roma (Gypsies). Other foreign **ethnicities** may receive suspicious looks, and anti-Semitic attitudes are still very present. While most Moldovans are courteous, **homophobia** persists. Discretion is strongly advised.

ACCOMMODATIONS

MOLDOVA	❶	❷	❸	❹	❺
ACCOM.	under 100 lei	100-150 lei	151-250 lei	251-300 lei	over 300 lei

There are no **hostels** in Moldova. **Homestays** are the cheapest option in and around Chişinău, but you should have no problem finding quality **hotels** for under US$10.

KEEPING IN TOUCH

MAIL. Letters abroad cost 3.60-3.90 lei; **postcards** cost 2 lei. Delivery takes 10-14 days. Moldova has **Poste Restante** services. Address envelope as follows: Clay (first name) KAMINSKY (LAST NAME), POSTE RESTANTE, Bd. Ştefan cel Mare 134 (post office address), Chişinău (city) 2012 (postal code), MOLDOVA.

TELEPHONES AND INTERNET ACCESS. AT&T Direct and similar **telephone** services are not yet available; collect calls also remain impossible. Most local phones use Moldtelecom cards (from 12 lei), available at the post office or in kiosks. When calling Moldova from Ukraine and other former Soviet republics, you need only to dial the city code, not the country code. **Internet access** is cheap and widely available in Chişinău (5-8 lei per hr.).

CHIŞINĂU (KISHINEV) ☎(8)2

Once known as "the greenest city in the USSR," Chişinău (KEY-she-now; pop. 663,000) may surprise you. If you're looking for concrete monsters on a Stalinist scale, you'll find them here amid tranquil parks and colorful open-air markets. Indicators of the city's political, economic, and social future are as varied as the architecture as Chişinău struggles to reconcile its Romanian and Russian heritage and recover from 45 years of Soviet oppression.

▐ TRANSPORTATION

Flights: The **airport** (☎52 54 12) is 12km from downtown; take *marshrutka* (minitaxi) #165 to the corner of Ismail and Bd. Ştefan Cel Mare. Taxis to the city start at US$10; try to bargain down to US$5. **Voiaj Travel,** Bd. Negruzzi 10 (☎54 64 64), arranges flights. Open M-F 8am-8pm, Sa 9am-7pm, Su 9am-5pm. AmEx/MC/V.

Trains: Gara Feroviară (☎25 27 33), in the southwest corner of town. Buy international tickets on the 2nd fl. Open 24hr. To: **Bucharest, ROM** (12½hr., 2 per day, 130 lei); **Iaşi, ROM** (6 hr., 1 per day, 74 lei); **Kyiv, UKR** (12-18hr., 2 per day, 150 lei); **Moscow, RUS** (27-33hr., 2 per day, 430 lei); **Odessa, UKR** (5hr., 2 per day, 29 lei); **Sofia, BUL** (24hr., F, 707 lei); **St. Petersburg, RUS** (37hr., every other day, 4810 lei).

Buses: Autogara Chişinău, Str. Mitropolit Varlaam 58 (☎54 21 85, reservations 27 14 76). Ticket office open daily 9:30am-6:30pm. To: **Bucharest, ROM** (10-12hr., 4 per day, 144 lei); **Iaşi, ROM** (5hr., 4 per day, 43 lei); **Kyiv, UKR** (12hr., 3 per day, 97 lei); **Moscow, RUS** (34hr., 2 per day, 320 lei); **Odessa, UKR** (5hr., 12 per day, 33 lei); **Sofia, BUL** (24hr., Th, 450 lei); **St. Petersburg, RUS** (34hr., 1 per day, 330 lei).

Public Transportation: Chişinău has an extensive local **trolley** (0.75 lei) and **bus** (1.25 lei) system, which runs daily 6am-10pm (departures every 15min.). **Marshrutki** follow the same routes and are a quick alternative (2 lei) Many run until 11pm, some until 2am. Avoid overpriced **taxis** (☎907 or 908).

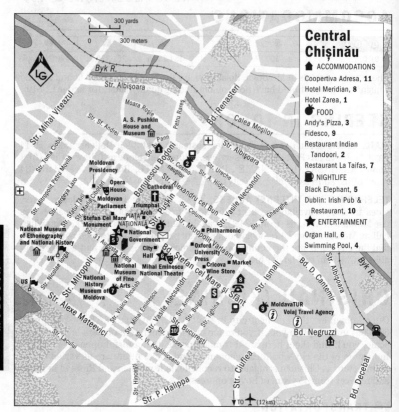

Central Chişinău

⌂ ACCOMMODATIONS
Coopertiva Adresa, **11**
Hotel Meridian, **8**
Hotel Zarea, **1**
🍴 FOOD
Andy's Pizza, **3**
Fidesco, **9**
Restaurant Indian
   Tandoori, **2**
Restaurant La Taifas, **7**
🍸 NIGHTLIFE
Black Elephant, **5**
Dublin: Irish Pub &
   Restaurant, **10**
★ ENTERTAINMENT
Organ Hall, **6**
Swimming Pool, **4**

✳ ORIENTATION

Chişinău is easy to navigate due to its grid layout. **Bd. Ştefan cel Mare şi Sfânt** (Stefan the Great and Saintly) crosses the city center from southeast to northwest. **Str. 31 Augusta 1989** runs parallel in the south. Both intersect **Str. Tighina** about 10min. from the **train station;** turn right to find the marketplace and the **bus station.** From the bus station, a 10min. walk along Bd. Ştefan cel Mare leads to the central **Piaţă Marii Adunari Naţională.** Trolleys #1, 4, 5, 8, and 22 run from the train station to the center, while #1, 4, 5, 8, 18, 22, and 28 run along Bd. Ştefan cel Mare.

❷ PRACTICAL INFORMATION

Tourist Office: MoldovaTUR, Bd. Ştefan cel Mare 4, 2nd fl. (☎54 03 01; fax 54 04 94; www.ipm.md/mtur), in Hotel Naţional. Arranges tours (US$10-20 per hr.), sells plane and train tickets, and provides free city **maps.** Open in summer M-F 8:30am-6:30pm, Sa 9am-3pm.; off-season M-F 8:30am-5pm.

Embassies: US, Str. Alexei Mateevici 10 (☎23 37 72 or 23 76 67). Open M-F 9am-6pm.
UK, temporary office at Str. Bănulescu Bodoni 57, Suite 320 (☎/fax 34 46 90; octa-

vian@be.moldline.net). The embassy will eventually be at Str. Nicolae Iorga 18. Citizens of other countries should contact their embassies in **Bucharest** (see **Embassies,** p. 588).

Currency Exchange: Look for обмен валют signs. **Moldindcombank,** Bd. Negruzzi (☎27 50 87), also exchanges AmEx **Traveler's Cheques** for 1.5% commission and offers **Western Union** services. Open daily 7:30am-1pm and 1:30-8pm.) **ATMS** are scattered along Bd. Ştefan cel Mare.

English-Language Bookstore: Oxford University Press, Str. Mihai Eminescu 64 (☎22 89 87). Books 45-150 lei. Open M-F 10am-6pm, Sa 10am-3pm.

24-Hour Pharmacy: Farmacia Felicia, Bd. Ştefan cel Mare 128 (☎22 37 25).

Medical Services: Hospitals at Str. Puşkin 51 (☎22 32 66 or 21 22 91) and Toma Ciorba 1 (☎21 06 93) treat foreigners. Pay with cash.

Internet Access: Moldtelecom, Bd. Ştefan cel Mare 65 (☎27 69 63). 5-8 lei per hr. for the fastest connection in the country. Open 24hr.

Post Office: Bd. Ştefan cel Mare 134, opposite city hall. Mail packages from the **branch** next to the train station. Open M-Sa 8am-7pm, Su 8am-6pm. **Fax** services at windows #9 and 10 open daily 9am-5pm.

Postal Code: 2012.

ACCOMMODATIONS

Hotels in the city center of Chişinău are generally quite expensive; hostels are nonexistent. All hotels levy a 10 lei **visa registration** fee. **Coopertiva Adresa,** Bd. Negruzzi 1, across from Hotel Cosmos, rents **private apartments ❸.** All rooms have TV and a bath with hot water; some have A/C. The helpful staff also organizes **homestays ❶** and arranges guided tours and daytrips. (☎54 43 92; fax 27 20 96; www.adresa.mdl.net. Open 24hr. Apartments US$12-70; homestays US$2.50.) At **Hotel Meridian ❸,** Str. Tighina 42, conveniently located next to the bus station. The friendly staff does laundry. Most "beds" are actually futons. (☎27 06 20. Shower 30 lei. Singles 125 lei, with toilet and sink 175 lei, with bath and fridge 270 lei; doubles 130 lei, with bath 250 lei; deluxe suite 510 lei.) **Hotel Zarea ❸,** Anton Pann 4, has bare rooms with TV, shared bath, and hot water. From Bd. Bodoni turn left on Alexandru cel Bun. Anton Pann is the first right. Pay for both beds to avoid sharing with a stranger. (☎22 76 25. Doubles 130 lei, with bath 240 lei.)

FOOD

Vendors sell fresh fruit and vegetables, *buterbrod* (open-faced sandwiches with meat and veggies; 3 lei), and pastries at the market in **Piaţa Centrala,** off Bd. Ştefan cel Mare. (Open daily 6am-6pm.) For groceries, look for **Alimentari** food stores or **Fidesco,** Bd. Ştefan cel Mare 6, next to Hotel National. (Open 24hr.) **Restaurant La Taifas ❶,** Str. Bucureşti 67, entrance on Str. Puşkin, offers stomach-warming Moldovan fare. Try the *mamăliguţă* (polenta; 2-27 lei), a national dish with various fillings. (Entrees 20-95 lei. Bottle of Cricova wine 45-55 lei. Open daily 8am-midnight.) **Restaurant Indian Tandoori ❷,** Bd. Renasteri 6, serves Indian and Persian classics. (☎24 50 23. Entrees 15-80 lei. Open M-F noon-midnight, Sa-Su 3pm-midnight. MC/V.) **Andy's Pizza ❸** serves slices at Bd. Ştefan cel Mare 152, behind the Opera House. (☎24 55 66. Pizza 25 lei. Open daily 8:30am-11:30pm.)

IN RECENT NEWS

WHAT'S IN A NAME?

To the visitor to Chişinău, it might not be immediately apparent that the national language is not Russian, but Moldovan, otherwise known as Romanian. More than likely, visitors won't find themselves in "Chişinău" but rather "Кишинев" (Kishinev). While the country on a whole is over 60% Romanian-speaking due to Moldova's historical, cultural, and former political ties to neighboring Romania, Chişinău itself is almost 60% Russian-speaking, the consequence of over 40 years as the seat to Moscow's puppet regime. The dissolution of the USSR in 1991 brought a wave of Moldovan nationalism as Romanian once again became the official language and Russian was stricken from school curriculums. The transition was not easy. In 2000, many radio stations lost their licenses due to violation of a law stipulating that two-thirds of programming had to be in Romanian.

(continued on next page)

🔘 SIGHTS

The 🏛 **National History Museum of Moldova** (Muzeul Naţional de Istorie a Moldovei), Str. 31 Augusta 1989, is so spectacular it might even make you believe that Moldova is the center of the universe. Archaeological and historical exhibits explore the ancient Moldovan kingdom of Bessarabia and end with the country's trials and tribulations during the 20th century. (☎24 04 26. Open Apr.-Oct. Sa-Th 10am-6pm; Nov.-Mar. Sa-Th 10am-4:30pm. Last entrance 1hr. before closing. 2 lei, students 1 lei.) The **National Museum of Ethnography and Natural History** (Muzuel Naţional de Ethnographie şi Istorie Naturală), Kogălniceanu 82, is a fascinating museum with exhibits on both the birth and destruction of Moldovan nature and culture. Check out the dinosaurs in the basement. (☎24 40 02 or 24 00 56. Open Tu-Su 10am-5pm. 2 lei, students 1 lei. They may charge foreigners US$1, students US$0.50. Cameras US$0.50. Call ahead to arrange an English tour, 10 lei.)

For the Moldovan take on Russian Pushkin-mania, visit the **A. S. Pushkin House and Museum** (Casa-Muzeu A.S. Puşkin), Str. Anton Pann 10. Pushkin was exiled here for writing poems that offended the Imperial Russian government. The poet lived in Chişinău from 1820 to 1823 while working on *Eugene Onegin*, the opening pages of which are set here. (☎29 26 86 or 29 41 38. Open Tu-Su 10am-4pm. Call ahead for a 1hr. English tour (100 lei). 20 lei, students 2 lei.) At the intersection of Bd. Ştefan cel Mare and Str. Puşkin is **Piaţa Naţională**, Moldova's main square. The 1841 **Triumphal Arch** stands in front of a park containing Chişinău's temple-like **Cathedral** (Catedrala Naşterea Domnului Clopotniţa). On one of the square's corners stands the cross-and sword-wielding statue of **Stephen the Great and Saintly** (Ştefan cel Mare şi Sfânt), who united greater Moldova (part of which now lies in Romania). For a bastion of serenity, walk five blocks up Str. Puşkin from the center to stroll around the **city park** or rent a boat from its small beach (12 lei per hr.). A statue of **Ion and Doina,** famous Moldovan folk singers, adorns the entrance to the park. The young pair, who perished in a tragic car accident, are credited with sparking the rebirth of Moldovan nationalism during *perestroika.*

🎵 ENTERTAINMENT

The biggest festival of the year is **Chişinău City Days,** on October 14. If you are looking to cool off on a hot summer day, check out the sparkling clean 50m outdoor **swimming pool** (Bazinul de inot) at Str. 31 Augusta 1989 #78. Walk up the alley opposite the National History Museum. (☎24 20 33. Pool 20 lei per hr. Entrance at

50min. after the hr., every hr. **Sauna** 100 lei per hr., up to 7 people. Reserve sauna in advance.) The **Organ Hall** (Sala cu Orgă), Ştefan cel Mare 81, holds concerts from September to June in an elegant turn-of-the-century concert hall with gorgeous chandeliers. (☎22 54 04 or 22 25 28. Box office open M-Sa 11am-5pm, until 6pm on concert days. Tickets 5-20 lei.) If you don't have time to tour the Cricova Vineyards (see **Daytrips: Cricova,** p. 473), stop by the beautiful **Cricova Wineshop,** Bd. Ştefan cel Mare 126. (☎22 27 75. Open M-F 10am-7pm, Sa-Su 10am-2pm.)

🔊 NIGHTLIFE

Black Elephant: The Underground Club, Str. 31 Augusta 1989 #78a, entrance off Bd. Bodoni, is Moldova's coolest club, with live rock and jazz music starting at 9pm. This club also houses a bar with a seating area, an Internet cafe (7 lei per hr.), and a billiard room. (☎23 47 15; www.freetime.md/slon. Cover 20-25 lei. Billiards 5-10 lei. Open daily 3pm-last customer.) **Dublin: Irish Pub and Restaurant,** Str. Bulgara 27, is an authentic Irish pub that packs in the crowds with live jazz and Irish music (Sa-Su 9pm-midnight). The food is overpriced (Irish breakfast 35 lei, entrees 30-95 lei), but the beer is reasonable (*Vitanta* beer 10 lei, Guinness 20 lei. ☎24 58 55; www.irishpub-md.com. Open daily noon-midnight. MC/V.)

🔊 DAYTRIPS FROM CHIŞINĂU

VADUL LUI VODĂ. About 12km northeast of Chişinău, this relaxing riverside resort is a summertime haven for Moldovans. On a hot summer day the **beach** is packed with Chişinău residents. Rent a small boat for 20 lei per hr. Small, basic 4-bed cabins near the beach rent for 25 lei per person. *(From behind the bus station, on Str. Bulgara, take the* marshrutki *marked "31A Vadul lui Voda" (45min., leave when full, 4 lei). Take* marshrutka *#130 to return; the last one leaves at 9pm.)*

CRICOVA. The **Crivoa Vineyards, Wine Factory, and Cellars,** producers of the famed Moldovan wine, are located in an old rock quarry north of Chişinău. Tiny Moldova once produced a staggering 20% of the wine in the USSR. You can buy wine from the barrel at 30 lei per 700g. View their extensive wine collection or just go for a drive in the old mine. Arrange a tour through MoldovoTUR (see **Moldova: Orientation and Practical Information,** p. 470) or head out on your own. *(Bus #2 from Str. V. Alecsandri, 3 blocks from the bus station (50min., 2 lei). From the bus stop bear right down a small hill.* ☎44 12 04 *or 46 37 27. Call ahead to arrange your visit. Tour and snack 180 lei; tour, snack, meal, and gift 320 lei. Open M-F 8am-4pm.)*

But times are changing. Since the 2001 elections brought the Russian Communists back to power, President Vladamir Voronin—who speaks Russian at home—has sought to ally Moldova once more with Moscow rather than Bucharest, as the previous administration had done. In the spring of 2002, the government reinstituted mandatory Russian classes in the schools, sparking protests in the streets of Chişinău. In May, however, the Parliament's attempt to require official documents to be kept in both Russian and Romanian was shot down, when the constitution court ruled that "the Moldovan language is the Republic's sole language."

The name of the "Moldovan" language is also a point of controversy. Critics contend that "Moldovan" was an artificial creation of the Stalinist regime. The current government's position is that "Moldovan" is a language distinct from Romanian, and they have legally changed the official name of the language from Romanian to Moldovan. The move, denounced by Romanian Foreign Minister Mircea Geoana as divisive propaganda, has been interpreted by observers as yet another political move eastward. As Yiddish linguist Max Weinreich once said, "A language is a dialect with an army and a navy." It's easy to tell what they're speaking in the breakaway Transdniester region of Moldova: it's held by the Russian 14th army.

—*Clay Kaminsky*

POLAND
(POLSKA)

ZŁOTY

AUS$1 = 2.27ZŁ	1ZŁ = AUS$0.44
CDN$1 = 2.66ZŁ	1ZŁ = CDN$0.38
EUR€1 = 4.07ZŁ	1ZŁ = EUR€0.25
NZ$1 = 1.94ZŁ	1ZŁ = NZ$0.52
UK£1 = 6.42ZŁ	1ZŁ = UK£0.16
US$1 = 4.14ZŁ	1ZŁ = US$0.24
ZAR1 = 0.39ZŁ	1ZŁ = ZAR2.56

Poles consider their homeland the last Western country on the threshold of the East, and as such, it has always been the site of international disputes and skirmishes. It is easy to forget that from 1795 to 1918, Poland simply did not exist on any map of Europe, and that its short spell of independence thereafter—like so many before it—was brutally dissolved. Ravaged by World War II and viciously suppressed by Stalin and the USSR, Poland has at long last been given room to breathe, and its residents are not letting the opportunity slip by. The most prosperous of the "Baltic tigers," Poland now has a rapidly expanding GDP, a new membership in NATO, and hopes to join the EU. With their new wealth, the legendarily hospitable Poles have been returning to their cultural roots.

POLAND AT A GLANCE

OFFICIAL NAME: Republic of Poland

CAPITAL: Warsaw (pop. 1.64 million)

POPULATION: 39 million

LANGUAGE: Polish

CURRENCY: 1 złoty (zł) = 100 groszy

RELIGION: 95% Roman Catholic (75% practicing), 5% Eastern Orthodox, Protestant, and other

LAND AREA: 312,685km²

CLIMATE: Harsh winters, wet summers

GEOGRAPHY: Plains, southern mountains

BORDERS: Belarus, Czech Republic, Germany, Lithuania, Russia, Slovak Republic, and Ukraine

ECONOMY: 68.3% Services, 26.6% Industry, 5.1% Agriculture

GDP: US$8500 per capita

COUNTRY CODE: 48

INTERNATIONAL DIALING PREFIX: 00

HISTORY

THE NASCENT STATE. When **Prince Mieszko I** converted to Catholicism in AD 966, he united many of the West Slavic tribes that had been occupying modern Poland since AD 800, but the union wasn't fully complete until his son, **Bolesław Chrobry** (the Brave), was crowned Poland's first king in 1025. The young conglomeration of states was devastated by the Mongols in 1241, but managed to recover by the 14th century, when it became far more prosperous and—particularly under **King Kazimi-**

POLAND

erz III Wielki (Casimir III the Great)—began to exhibit unprecedented religious and political tolerance. Poland became a refuge for Jews expelled from Western Europe, guaranteeing their freedom and prohibiting forcible baptism. The country also became a center of learning with the establishment in 1394 of **Jagiellonian University** in Kraków (see **Sights,** p. 508).

THE GRAND TEUTONS. After the death of Casimir III in 1370, Poland experienced greater difficulties with the **Teutonic Knights,** who took East Prussia and cut off the Baltic. To combat them, in 1386 Polish nobles allied themselves with the Lithuanians by marrying Casimir's only child, Princess Jadwiga, to the powerful Grand Duke of Lithuania, **Jagailo.** As part of the arrangement, Jadwiga's new husband was crowned King Wladyslaw II Jagiełło of Poland. This new **Polish Commonwealth** lasted 187 years and defeated the Teutonic Order in 1410 at the **Battle of Grunwald.**

THE GOLDEN AGE. In the 16th century, under King Zygmunt I Stary (Sigmund the Old), the **Renaissance** began to reach Polish territories. The knowledge and spirit of the age found particularly fertile ground at Jagiellonian University. One graduate, Mikołaj Kopernik, an astronomer from Toruń better known by his Latin name, **Copernicus,** built upon the scientific advances of the Renaissance and developed the **heliocentric model of the solar system,** changing humanity's perception of the universe. The Golden Age also saw the heyday of Polish literature (see **The Arts,** p. 479).

DELUGE. Poland and Lithuania drew even closer with the 1569 **Union of Lublin,** which established the **Polish-Lithuanian Commonwealth** with an elected king, a common customs union, and a shared legislature, but separate territories, laws, and armies. **King Zygmunt III Waza** moved the capital to Warsaw, and he and his successors embroiled the state in a series of wars with Sweden, Turkey, and Moscovy throughout the 17th century. This devastating period came to be known as the **"Deluge,"** and Poland was only saved by extraordinary military commanders like **Jan Zamoyski** and **Stanislaw Zolkiewski.** The bravery and perseverence of the Polish people during the wars was demonstrated in the defense of Częstochowa, the holy resting place of the Black Madonna icon, where a small force of monks and villagers threw off an invading Swedish army of 9000 (see **Częstochowa,** p. 528). Yet divisive nobles, separate Polish and Lithuanian administrations, and a weakened monarch hobbled the Polish state.

AUSTRIA, RUSSIA, AND PRUSSIA. To oppose Russian influence in domestic affairs and maintain the primacy of the Catholic faith, nationalist Poles formed the **Confederation of Bar** in 1768, precipitating a civil war that threw the nation into anarchy until 1772. France and Turkey aided the confederates, while Russia backed the monarchy. Fearful of losing its influence in the country, the Russian government began to support Prussian ruler Frederick the Great's schemes to partition Poland. In the **First Partition of Poland** (1772), Russia, Prussia, and Austria each took sizable chunks of the Commonwealth.

A STAB AT INDEPENDENCE. In 1788 Polish noblemen convened a special meeting of the *Sejm*, Poland's Parliament, to draft a constitution. After four years this "Great Sejm" produced a constitution calling for a parliamentary monarchy. Signed on May 3, 1791, the new constitution was only the second of its kind in the world; it established Catholicism as the national religion, set up a plan for the election of political leaders, and provided for a standing army. The prospect of a newly powerful state, however, made both Russia and Prussia very, very nervous.

POLAND IS DISSOLVED...AGAIN AND AGAIN. In response to these attempts at independence, Russia and Prussia incited the **Second Partition of Poland** (1793). The Polish government was forced to capitulate and many patriots fled abroad. The following year, **Tadeusz Kościuszko,** a hero of the American Revolution, led an uprising against Russian rule. He ended up in prison, and Poland was divided one last time in the **Third Partition** (1795). With this final partition, Poland **ceased to exist** as a state for 123 years, during which time Russia attempted to crush the nationalist spirit, fueling the rebellions of 1806, 1830, 1846, 1848, 1863, and 1905. Poland didn't regain its independence until 1918, after **Marshal Józef Piłsudski** pushed back an invasion by the Red Army. A Polish delegation led by **Roman Dmowski** worked **Polish statehood** into the Treaty of Versailles.

WORLD WAR II AND THE RISE OF COMMUNISM. The signing of the **Nazi-Soviet Non-Aggression Pact** in August 1939 rendered Poland's defense treaties worthless. In September, Nazi and Soviet forces attacked Poland simultaneously. Germany occupied the western two-thirds of the country, while the Soviet Union got the rest. More than six million Poles were killed during **World War II,** including three million Jews. At the end of the war, freedom fighters loyal to the government in exile in London initiated the **Warsaw Uprising** of 1944 to take back their city before the Soviets "liberated" it. The Germans retaliated ruthlessly, however, while the Soviets waited in the suburbs for the Germans to finish off the resistors. When Red tanks finally rolled in, they took Warsaw with little opposition and inaugurated 45 years of **communist** rule. The first few years brought mass migrations, political crackdown, and social unrest that led to the 1946 Jewish **pogrom** (massacre). Even after the country grudgingly submitted, **strikes** broke out in 1956 (see **Poznań,** p. 539), 1968, and 1970; all were violently quashed.

SOLIDARITY. In 1978 **Karol Wojtyła** became the first Polish pope, taking the name John Paul II. His visit to Poland the following year helped to unite Catholic Poles and was an impetus for the birth of **Solidarność (Solidarity)**, the first independent workers' union in Eastern Europe, in 1980. Led by the charismatic **Lech Wałęsa,** an electrician from Gdańsk, Solidarity's anti-Communist activities resulted in the declaration of **martial law** in 1981 by head of Polish government **General Wojciech Jaruzelski.** Wałęsa was jailed and released only after Solidarność was officially disbanded and outlawed by the government in 1982.

In 1989, Poland spearheaded the peaceful fall of Soviet authority in Eastern Europe. Solidarity members swept into all but one of the contested seats in the June elections, and **Tadeusz Mazowiecki** was sworn in as Eastern Europe's first non-Communist premier in 40 years. In December 1990, Wałęsa became the first elected president of post-Communist Poland. The government opted to swallow the bitter pill of capitalism all in one gulp by quickly eliminating subsidies, freezing wages, and devaluing the currency. This threw the antiquated economy into recession and produced the first true unemployment in 45 years, but Poland has rebounded toward economic and political stability.

TODAY

In Poland's tightly contested November 1995 presidential election, **Lech Wałęsa**—former leader of the Solidarity movement—lost to **Aleksander Kwaśniewski.** A 1980s Communist and head of the ex-Communist Democratic Left Alliance, Kwaśniewski was elected on a platform of moderately paced privatization and stronger ties with the West. Following Kwaśniewski's election, however, the **Solidarity Electoral Action Party (AWS)** saw success in local elections, marked by the ascendance of **Jerzy Buzek** to the post of Prime Minister in October 1997. The Solidarity-Freedom Union coalition government collapsed in June 2000, and Kwaśniewski was reelected in a landslide. Because of poor pollution control and concerns about subsidies for the free labor movement, Poland's planned accession to the **EU** in 2004 has been called into question. **Leszek Miller** was elected Prime Minister in 2001 on the platform of securing EU membership. A **NATO** member since 1999, Poland has been improving its military to meet NATO standards, and agreed to buy several thousand anti-tank missles in July 2002.

PEOPLE AND CULTURE

LANGUAGE

Polish varies little across the country (see **Glossary,** p. 885). The two exceptions are in the region of Kaszuby, where the distinctive, Germanized dialect is classified by some as a separate language, and in Karpaty, where the highlander accent is extraordinarily thick. In western Poland and Mazury, **German** is the most common foreign language, although many Poles in big cities, especially students, speak **English.** Many Poles understand but show an open aversion to speaking the language. Most can also understand other Slavic languages like **Czech** or **Slovak** if they're spoken slowly. Polish uses some letters not in the Latin alphabet: *"ł"* sounds like a "w"; *"ą"* is a nasal "on"; *"ę"* is a nasal "en." *"Ó"* and *"u"* are both equivalent to an "oo." *"Ż"* and *"rz"* are both like the "s" in "pleasure"; *"w"* sounds like "v." A few consonantal clusters are easier to spit out than they seem: *"sz"* is "sh," *"cz"* is "ch," and *"ch"* and *"h"* both sound like the English "h." *"C"* sounds like an English "ts," *"dż"* is "dg" as in "fridge," *"dź"* is "j" as in "jeep," *"ć"* or *"ci"* is "chyi," and *"zi"* or *"z"* is "zhy." One thing: "no" means "yes" in Polish (see **Just Say No!,** p. 522).

POLAND

RELIGION

Poland is one of the most uniformly **Catholic** countries in the world and the Catholic church enjoys both immense respect and tremendous political power. Polish Catholicism has been bolstered since 1978 by the election of the Polish Pope John Paul II, the first non-Italian pope since the 16th century. **Protestant** groups are generally confined to small geographic areas bordering Germany. Only a few traces of the rich **Jewish** culture that existed before WWII are still apparent.

FOOD AND DRINK

POLAND	❶	❷	❸	❹	❺
FOOD	under 8zł	8-15zł	16-25zł	26-35zł	over 35zł

Polish cuisine is a blend of dishes from the French, Italian, and Slavic traditions. A meal always starts with **soup**, usually *barszcz* (either beets or rye), *chłodnik* (cold beet soup with buttermilk and hard-boiled eggs), *ogórkowa* (slightly sour cucumber soup), *kapuśniak* (cabbage soup), *rosół* (chicken soup), or *żurek* (barley-flour soup loaded with eggs and sausage). Filling **main courses** include *gołąbki* (cabbage rolls stuffed with meat and rice), *kotlet schabowy* (pork cutlet), *naleśniki* (cream-topped crepes filled with cottage cheese or jam), and *pierogi* (dumplings with various fillings—meat, potato, cheese, blueberry). Some restaurants in Poland sell fish, poultry, and meat by weight; ask in advance how much the average weight is to avoid a nasty surprise when the check arrives.

Poland bathes in **beer, vodka,** and **spiced liquor.** *Żywiec* is the most popular strong beer (12% alcohol content); *EB* is its excellent, gentler brother. Also try *EB Czerwone*, a darker, heavier, stronger variety. Other beers include *Okocim* and *Piast*. Even those who don't like beer will like sweet ■ *piwo z sokiem*, beer with a shot of raspberry syrup, a Polish specialty. The popular brands of *Wódka* (vodka) are *Wyborowa*, *Żytnia*, and *Polonez*, and usually decorate private bars, while *Belweder* (Belvedere) is Poland's primary alcoholic export. "Kosher" vodka is rumored to be top-notch, although what makes it kosher remains a mystery. The herbal *Żubrówka* vodka comes with a blade of grass from Woliński, where the bison roam. It is sometimes mixed with apple juice (*z sokem jabłkowym*). *Miód* and *krupnik*—two kinds of mead—are beloved by the gentry, and many grandmas make *nalewka na porzeczce* (black currant vodka).

CUSTOMS AND ETIQUETTE

In restaurants, tell the server how much change you want back and leave the rest as a **tip** (10% is standard). If you're paying with a credit card, give the tip in cash. In any establishment, say *"dzień dobry"* to the owner as you enter, and *"do widzenia"* when you leave. Your waiter will often say *"smacznego"* (bon appétit) when he serves you food; reply with *"dziękuję"* (thank you). When arriving as a guest, bring a female host an odd number of flowers. When addressing a man, use the formal *"Pan"*; with a woman, use *"Pani."* **Drinking** on the street is common, but **smoking** is often prohibited indoors.

POLAND

THE ARTS

HISTORY

LITERATURE. Like its social and political history, the course of Polish literature changed forever when the nation chose to follow Roman—not Byzantine—Christianity. Poland's medieval texts, mostly religious works, were written in Latin. Self-taught 16th-century author **Mikolaj Rej,** the first to write consistently in Polish, is regarded as the father of Polish literature. His contemporary **Jan Kochanowski,** who remains one of the most important Slavic poets, shed the archaic elements present in Rej's work. His *Treny* (Laments), a cycle of poems about the death of his infant daughter, brought the Polish literary language to maturity.

Loss of statehood in 1795 paved the way for **Romanticism,** which held nationalism as a primary ideal. The most prominent writers of this great period—**Adam Mickiewicz, Juliusz Słowacki,** and **Zygmunt Krasiński,** exiles all—depict Poland as a noble, suffering martyr. The Lithuanian-born Mickiewicz is widely regarded as Poland's national poet and his *Pan Tadeusz* is still considered the country's primary epic.

The early 20th-century neo-Romantic **Młoda Polska** (Young Poland) movement was laden with pessimism and apathy. Painter and playwright **Stanisław Wyspiański**'s mystery-filled *Wesele* (The Wedding), one of the finest dramatic works of the period, addressed many of the problems that defined Poland in the era (to see his artwork, visit Kraków's **Franciscan Church,** p. 509). In the years immediately following World War II, a number of Polish writers published works abroad. Nobel Prize-winning poet **Czesław Miłosz** penned his controversial *Zniewolony Umysł* (The Captive Mind)—an essential commentary on communist control of individual thought—during the mid-1950s. It provides insight into the philosophical ramifications of the foreign occupation and brutal repression of Poland and Lithuania. The "thaw" following Soviet attempts to enforce **Socialist Realism** brought about an explosion of new work addressing life under communism's thumb. **Zbigniew Herbert** developed the character *Pan Cogito*, while **Tadeusz Różewicz** concentrated on very short, poignant lyric poems and plays. The **Generation of '68** ushered in a new wave of works tackling the dilemmas of living at a historical crossroads.

MUSIC AND FILM. The first Polish **opera,** Jan Stefani and Wojciech Boguslawski's *The Pretended Miracle;* or, *Cud mniemany czyli Karakowiacy i Górale* (The Krakovians and the Highlanders) appeared in 1794. Polish music is best defined by the 19th-century work of **Fryderyc Chopin** (in Polish, Fryderyk Szopen), a master composer and the first of many internationally acclaimed Polish instrumentalists (among them pianist **Artur Rubinstein**). Polish **films** have consistently drawn international acclaim. Filmmaker **Andrzej Wajda** is known for explorations of his country's internal conflicts in such films as *Pokolenie* (A Generation) and *Czlowiek z marmuru* (Man of Marble). He received an honorary Oscar in 2000 for his work. Polish directors **Roman Polański** and **Krzysztof Kieślowski** have achieved international recognition, the latter for his trilogy *Three Colors: Red, White and Blue*. Polański's first film, *Knife in the Water* (1962), made while he was at the acclaimed Łódź film school, was nominated for an Academy Award for best foreign language film. The Museum of Cinematography in Łódź (see p. 547) honors these and other artists.

POLAND

CURRENT SCENE

Poland is a jazz hotbed. The **Gdynia Summer Jazz Days** festival hits town every July (see p. 568), and jazz performances are regular occurrences in Kraków (see **Festivals and Entertainment,** p. 511). Popular contemporary composers include **Witold Lutoslawski** and **Krzysztof Penderecki.** Poland's art history has often been rocky and dissolute, but Kraków is now emerging as Poland's contemporary **fine arts** scene. Art galleries can be found throughout the city center, and the Kraków Academy of Fine Arts harbors some of the finest young talents in Europe today. In 1996 **Wisława Szymborska,** a female poet, became the second Polish writer in 16 years to receive the Nobel Prize.

HOLIDAYS AND FESTIVALS

NATIONAL HOLIDAYS IN 2003	
January 1 New Year's Day	**August 15** Assumption Day
April 20-21 Easter	**November 1** All Saints' Day
May 1 Labor Day	**November 11** Independence Day
May 3 Constitution Day	**December 25-26** Christmas
June 19 Corpus Christi	

Polish festivals are closely tied to Roman Catholic holidays, though a rich folk tradition adds variety that changes depending on region. Since 75% of the people are practicing Catholics, beware of closed businesses on Christian holidays like **Corpus Christi** (June 19th in 2003) and **Assumption Day** (August 15th) that are not as widely observed elsewhere in the world.

ADDITIONAL RESOURCES

GENERAL HISTORY

Heart of Europe: A Short History of Poland, by Norman Davies (1986). An easy read that provides a good sense of Polish history.

The Polish Way: A Thousand Year History, by Adam Zamoyski (1993). Focuses on the quirks and intricacies of Poland's past.

FICTION AND NONFICTION

Poland, by James Michener (1990). An outstanding fictional account of three Polish families over eight centuries.

Pan Tadeusz, by Adam Mickiewicz (ed. 1992). A classic by one of the founding fathers of Polish literature (see **The Arts,** p. 479).

The History of Polish Literature, by Czesław Miłosz (2nd ed. 1984). A fascinating overview of the poetic genre by one of Poland's literary masters.

In My Father's Court, by Isaac Bashevis Singer (ed. 1992). A Polish-born Jew who won a Nobel Prize for literature, Singer provides an engaging and unique view of the Poland of his childhood.

FILM

Poland: A Thousand Years of History and Culture, produced by the Center for International Studies at the University of Pittsburgh. A comprehensive documentary history.

Three Colors: Red, White, and Blue, directed by Krzysztof Kieslowski. Well-known and internationally acclaimed.

POLAND ESSENTIALS

ENTRANCE REQUIREMENTS

Passport: Required of all travelers.
Visa: Required of citizens of Australia, Canada, New Zealand, and South Africa.
Letter of Invitation: Not required of most visitors.
Inoculations: Recommended up-to-date on MMR (measles, mumps, and rubella), DTaP (diphtheria), Polio booster, Hepatitis A, and Hepatitis B.
Work Permit: Required of all foreigners planning to work in Poland. Must be obtained in conjunction with a work permit visa.
International Driving Permit: Required of all those planning to drive.

DOCUMENTS AND FORMALITIES

EMBASSIES AND CONSULATES

Embassies of other countries in Poland are in Warsaw and Kraków (see p. 484 and p. 501). Poland's embassies abroad include:

Australia: 7 Turrana St., Yarralumla, ACT 2600 Canberra (☎06 273 1208 or 273 1211; fax 273 3184; ambpol@clover.com.au).

Canada: 443 Daly St., Ottawa, ON, K1N 6H3 (☎613-789-0468; fax 789-1218; polamb@hookup.com).

Ireland: 5 Ailesbury Rd., Ballsbridge, Dublin 4 (☎01 283 0855; fax 269 8309).

New Zealand: 17 Upland Rd., Kelburn, Wellington (☎04 712 456; fax 712 455; polishembassy@xtra.co.nz).

South Africa: 14 Amos St., Colbyn, Pretoria 0083 (☎012 432 631; fax 432 608; amb.pol@pixie.co.za).

UK: 47 Portland Pl., London W1N 4JH (☎020 7580 4324; fax 7323 4018).

US: 2640 16th St. NW, Washington, D.C. 20009 (☎202-234-3800; fax 328-6271; www.polandembassy.org).

VISA AND ENTRY INFORMATION

Citizens of Ireland and the US can travel to Poland without a visa for up to 90 days and citizens of the UK for up to 180 days. Australians, Canadians, New Zealanders, and South Africans all need visas. Single-entry visas (valid for 180 days) are free of charge for US citizens, and cost US$60 for citizens of other countries (children and students under 26 pay US$45); multiple-entry visas cost US$100, students US$75; 2-day transit visas cost US$20, students US$15. A visa application requires a valid passport, two photographs, and payment by money order, certified check, or cash. Regular service takes four days with a US$10 surcharge; 24hr. rush service costs an additional US$35. To extend your stay, apply in the city where you are staying to the branch of the regional government (*voi vodine*) or to the **Ministry of Internal Affairs** at ul. Stefana Batorego 5, Warsaw 02-591 (☎022 621 02 51; fax 849 74 94).

TRANSPORTATION

BY PLANE. Warsaw's **Okęcie Airport** claims to be the best and most modern in Central Europe and is not far off the mark. **LOT,** the national airline, flies in from Chicago, London, Montreal, Newark, New York, and Toronto (among other cities).

BY TRAIN. It's usually more convenient to take a train than a bus, as buses are slower and tend to jostle their freight. Train stations have boards that list towns alphabetically and posters that list trains chronologically. *Odjazdy* (departures) are in yellow; *przyjazdy* (arrivals) are in white. *InterCity* and *Ekspresowy* (express) trains are listed in red with an "IC" or "Ex" in front of the train number. *Pośpieszny* (direct; also in red) are almost as fast, but not quite as expensive. *Osobowy* (in black) are the slowest and have no restrooms, but are 35% cheaper than *pośpieszny*. All *InterCity* and *ekspresowy* trains, and some *pośpieszny* trains, require seat reservations; if you see a boxed R on the schedule, ask the clerk for a *miejscówka* (myehy-TSOOF-kah; reservation). Buy surcharged tickets on board from the *konduktor* before he or she finds (and fines) you. Most people purchase *normalny* tickets, while students and seniors buy *ulgowy* (half-price) tickets. Beware: **foreign travelers are not eligible for discounts** on domestic buses and trains. You risk a hefty fine by traveling with an *ulgowy* ticket without Polish ID. On Sundays, tickets cost 20% less. Train tickets are good only for the day they're issued. **Eurail** passes are not valid in Poland. **Wasteels** tickets and **Eurotrain** passes, sold at Almatur and Orbis, get 40% off international train fares for those under 26. Allot time for long lines or buy your ticket in advance at the station or an Orbis office. Stations are not announced and are sometimes poorly marked. Thefts often occur on international overnight trains; try to sleep in shifts with a friend (for more on train safety, see **Safety and Security,** p. 39).

BY BUS. PKS buses are cheapest and fastest for short trips. Like trains, for buses there are both *pośpieszny* (direct; marked in red) and *osobowy* (slow; in black). In the countryside, PKS markers (steering wheels that look like upside-down, yellow Mercedes-Benz symbols) indicate bus stops, but drivers will often stop if you flag them down. Traveling with a backpack can be a problem if the bus is full, since there are no storage compartments. **Polski Express,** a private bus company, offers more luxurious service, but does not run to all cities.

BY FERRY. Ferries run from **Sweden** and **Denmark** to Świnoujście, Gdańsk, and Gdynia. Summer ferries connect Gdynia, Hel, and **Kaliningrad, Russia** (see p. 706).

BY TAXI OR THUMB. Either arrange the price before getting in or be sure the driver turns on the meter. The going rate is 1.50-2zł per km. Cabs arranged by phone are more reliable than those hailed on the street. Though legal, **hitchhiking** is rare and sometimes dangerous for foreigners. Hand-waving is the accepted sign. *Let's Go* does not recommend hitchhiking.

TOURIST SERVICES AND MONEY

City-specific tourist offices are generally more helpful than the bigger chains. You can count on all offices to provide free info in English and to be of some help with accommodations. Most provide good free maps and sell more detailed ones. **Orbis,** the state-sponsored travel bureau staffed by English speakers, operates luxury hotels in most cities and sells transportation tickets at about the same prices as station offices. **Almatur,** the Polish student travel organization, sells ISICs, arranges dorm rooms in the summer, and sells discounted transportation tickets. The state-sponsored **PTTK** and **IT** *(Informacji Turystycznej)* bureaus are probably the most helpful for basic traveling needs. The *Polish Pages,* a free annual information and services guide available at larger hotels and tourist agencies, is also helpful.

The Polish **złoty**—plural złote—is fully convertible (1 złoty = 100 grosze). Polish inflation is around 3.6%, so prices should be reasonably stable. For cash, private **kan-**

tor offices (except for those at the airport and train stations) offer better exchange rates than banks. **Bank PKO SA** also has fairly good exchange rates; they cash **traveler's checks** and give MC/V **cash advances** for a small commission. **ATMs** (bankomat) are everywhere except the smallest of villages, and are all in English. **MC** and **V** are the most widely accepted ATM networks. Budget accommodations rarely, if ever, accept **credit cards,** but some restaurants and upscale hotels do.

HEALTH AND SAFETY

 EMERGENCY NUMBERS: Police: ☎997 **Fire:** ☎998 **Ambulance:** ☎999

HEALTH AND SAFETY. Pharmacies are well-stocked, and at least one in each large city stays open 24hr. There are usually clinics in major cities with private, English-speaking doctors. Expect to plunk down 50zł per visit. Avoid the state hospitals. **Public restrooms** are marked with an upward-pointing triangle for men and a circle for women. They range from pristine to squalid, and can cost up to 0.70zł. Soap, towels, and toilet paper can cost extra. **Tap water** is theoretically drinkable, but **bottled mineral water,** available carbonated (*gazowana*) or flat (*nie gazowana*), will spare you from some unpleasant metals and chemicals.

WOMEN, DISABLED, MINORITY, AND BGLT TRAVELERS. It is safe for **women** to travel alone in Poland as long as the usual precautionary measures are taken. Wear skirts or khakis with boots and t-shirts or blouses to blend in with the native Poles; sneakers, shorts, and tank tops are rare. Travelers with physical **disabilities** will find sight-seeing irritating; though many hotels are wheelchair accessible, older palaces and museums are not. Travelers of different ethnicities may recieve unwanted attention. **Discrimination** is mostly directed towards Roma (Gypsies), but there may be lingering prejudice against Jews despite great efforts on the part of the government to resolve Polish-Jewish issues. **Homosexuality** is legal and a frequent topic of media debate, although its remains fairly underground. Discretion is advised.

ACCOMMODATIONS AND CAMPING

POLAND	❶	❷	❸	❹	❺
ACCOM.	under 35zł	35-60zł	61-80zł	81-100zł	over 100zł

HOTELS AND HOSTELS. Youth hostels (*schroniska młodzieżowe*) abound and average 15-40zł per night. They are often booked solid, however, by school or tour groups; call at least a week in advance. **PTSM** is the national hostel organization. **Dom Wycieczkowy** and **Dom Turystyczny** hostels, which are geared toward adults, usually cost around 50zł. **PTTK,** a tourist office, runs a number of hotels called **Dom Turysty,** which have multi-bed rooms as well as budget singles and doubles. Hotels generally cost 80-120zł per night.

HOMESTAYS AND DORMS. Private rooms are available in most towns; they are not regulated, so be careful what you agree to. When in doubt, ask the tourist office for recommendations. They should cost US$5-15 per night. **University dorms** transform into spartan budget housing in July and August; these are an especially good option in Kraków. The Warsaw office of **Almatur** can arrange stays in all major cities.

CAMPING. Campsites average about US$2.50 per person, US$4 with a car. **Bungalows** are often available; a bed costs about US$5. *Polska Mapa Campingów,* available at many tourist offices, lists all campsites. Almatur runs a number of sites in the summer; ask for a list at one of their offices. Be sure to only camp in campsites, however, or risk a night in jail.

POLAND

POLSKI PHONE HOME? After making a call from one of Warsaw's spiffy new magnetic card telephones, you may find yourself accosted by any number of locals—from young girls to elderly gentlemen—staring at your card longingly and trying to bargain with you in Polish. Before you write these poor souls off as freeloaders who couldn't bother to buy their own phone card, know that the opposite is more likely true: they probably have plenty of cards and are looking to add yours to their collection. If you need confirmation of this bizarre factoid, most collectors will whip out their collection with great pride if asked. The cards with pictures on the back are the most coveted; if you find you're holding the Honus Wagner of phone cards—a 1999 Pope John Paul II—you'll have to fend off an ugly mob to escape.

KEEPING IN TOUCH

MAIL. Mail is admirably efficient and most post offices have been modernized. Airmail *(lotnicza)* usually takes two weeks to reach the US. International ground mail is unreliable. Mail can be received general delivery through **Poste Restante.** Address the envelope as follows: Barb (first name) URBANCZYK (last name), POSTE RESTANTE, ul. Długa 22/25 (post office address), Gdańsk (city) 80-800 (postal code), POLAND. Letters abroad cost about 2.20zł. When picking up Poste Restante, pay a small fee (1.10zł) or show your passport.

TELEPHONES. Card telephones have become the public phone standard. Cards, which come in several denominations, are sold at post offices, Telekomunikacja Polska offices, and most kiosks. Before using a card, break off its perforated corner. In some cities Telekomunikacja Polska offices also offer **Internet access.** To make a **collect call,** write the name of the city or country and the number plus *"Rozmowa 'R'"* on a slip of paper and hand it to a post office clerk.

INTERNET ACCESS. Poland is wired. Most mid-sized towns have at least one Internet cafe and larger cities have several. The cost is about 5-10zl per hr.

WARSAW (WARSZAWA)   ☎ (0)22

According to legend, Warsaw (pop. 1.64 million) was founded when the fisherman Wars netted a mermaid *(syrena,* now the city's emblem). She begged him to release her and told him that if he and his wife established a city on the spot, she would protect it forever. She and the city's motto, *contemnire procellas* (to defy the storms), have been put to the test in the city's long history. Over the past millenium, invaders from the north, east, and west have all taken a shot at this fiercely proud capital city, which has been swallowed by neighboring empires more than once. Most recently, World War II saw two-thirds of the population killed and 83% of the city destroyed. It took decades to rebuild the ravaged capital, but Warsaw's inclusion on UNESCO's World Heritage list in 1980 shows the authenticity of its restoration as a beautiful city and a national emblem.

■ INTERCITY TRANSPORTATION

Flights: Port Lotniczy Warszawa-Okęcie, ul. Żwirki i Wigury (information desk ☎650 41 00, reservations 0801 300 952), referred to as "Terminal 1." Take bus #175, 174, or 192 to the city center (after 11pm, bus #611); buy tickets at the *Ruch* kiosk in the departure hall or at the *kantor* (currency exchange) outside (see **Local Transportation,** p. 488). Open M-F 8am-8pm. Hotel minibuses also run to the city center. Tickets are more expensive, but it is faster than the bus. Airlines include: **Aeroflot,** al. Jerozolimskie

29 (☎621 16 11; open M-F 8am-3:30pm); **Air France,** ul. Krucza 21 (☎628 12 81; fax 621 89 50) and at the airport (☎650 45 09; fax 650 45 06; open M-F 8:30am-5pm); **British Airways,** ul. Krucza 49, off al. Jerozolimskie (☎529 90 00; airport ☎650 45 03 or 650 45 20; open M-F 9am-5pm); **Delta,** ul. Królewska 11 (☎827 84 61; open M-F 9am-5pm); **KLM,** at the airport (☎622 80 00; open M-F 9am-5pm); **LOT,** al. Jerozolimskie 65/79 (☎95 72; open M-F 8am-8pm, Sa 8am-3pm), in the Hotel Marriott; **Lufthansa,** ul. Sienna 39 (☎338 13 00; www.lufthansa.pl; open M-F 9am-5pm).

Trains: There are 4 railway stations in Warsaw; the most convenient is **Warszawa Centralna,** al. Jerozolimskie 54 (☎94 36; www.pkp.com.pl). The station has a cafe, a **pharmacy, ATMs,** and **24hr. telephones.** International and **InterRail** *kasy* (counters) are upstairs, and domestic *kasy* are downstairs in the main hall. Lines can be long, and most employees speak only Polish. Write down where and when you want to go, along with "*Który peron?*" (Which platform?); the multilingual **IT** (see **Tourist Offices,** p. 488) is willing to help foreigners. Yellow signs list departures *(odjazdy),* white signs arrivals *(przyjazdy).* To: **Gdańsk** (3½-4½hr., 12 per day, 57-106zł); **Kraków** (2½-5hr., 10 per day, 55-101zł); **Poznań** (3hr., 13 per day, 55-101zł); **Szczecin** (6hr., 4 per day, 63-113zł); **Toruń** (3hr., 5 per day, 50-87zł); **Wrocław** (5hr., 9 per day, 60-112zł); **Berlin, GER** (6hr., 10 per day, 129zł); **Bratislava, SLK** (8-15hr., 2 per day, 163zł); **Bucharest, ROM** (16½hr., 1 per day, 120zł); **Budapest, HUN** (13hr., 2 per day, 216zł); **Kyiv, UKR** (23hr., 3 per day, 149zł); **Minsk, BLR** (11hr., 3 per day, 111zł); **Moscow, RUS** (22hr., 2 per day, 250zł); **Prague, CZR** (10hr., 4 per day, 185zł); **St. Petersburg, RUS** (28hr., 2 per day, 200zł); **Vilnius, LIT** (10hr., 2per day, 147zł).

Buses: Both PKS and Polski Express buses run out of Warsaw.

PKS Warszawa Zachodnia, al. Jerozolimskie 144 (☎822 48 11, domestic info and reservations 94 33, international info 823 55 70; open daily 6am-9:30pm), shares a building with the Warszawa Zachodnia train station (see p. 485). Take bus #127, 130, or 517 to the center; at night, when buses don't run, make the short train trip. To: **Gdańsk** (7hr, 3 per day, 50zł); **Kraków** (6hr, 4 per day, 37zł); **Toruń** (4hr., 9 per day). For international bus tickets, go to **Centrum Podróży AURA,** at the Zachodnia station (☎823 68 58; www.busnet.pl; open M-F 9am-6pm, Sa 9am-2pm) or at al. Jerozolimskie 63 (☎628 62 53), in the Marriott Hotel. International buses run to: **London, GRB** via the Chunnel (28hr., 1-5 per day, 360-550zł); **Lviv, UKR** (10hr., 4 per day, 75zł); **Paris, FRA** (25hr., 1 per day, 400-600zł); **Prague, CZR** (12hr., several per week, 129zł); **Venice, ITA** (20hr, 2-3 per day, 370-660zł). A few buses leave from **Warszawa Station** on Zieleniecka, on the other side of the river. Take bus #101 or 509 or tram #7, 8, 12 or 25 for the center.

Polski Express, al. Jana Pawła II (☎620 03 20), in a kiosk near Warszawa Centralna, the main train station. A private company that is faster and cushier than PKS. Domestic trips only. To: **Gdańsk** (6hr., 2 per day, 37zł); **Kraków** (6hr., 2 per day, 33zł); **Łódź** (2½hr., 7 per day, 17zł); **Lublin** (3hr., 7 per day, 17zł); **Szczecin** (9½hr., 2 per day, 33zł). Open M and Sa 6am-8:30pm, Tu-Th 6:30am-8:30pm, F and Su 6:30am-9:30pm.

■ ORIENTATION

The main part of Warsaw lies west of the **Wisła River.** Although the city is large, its grid layout and efficient public transportation system make it easy to navigate and explore. The main east-west thoroughfare is **al. Jerozolimskie.** Several north-south avenues, including **ul. Marszałkowska,** a major tram route, intersect this main drag. **Warszawa Centralna,** the busiest train station, is set in the thick of the city at the intersection of Al. Jerozolimskie and **al. Jana Pawła II.** A stone's throw away, the gargantuan **Pałac Kultury i Nauki** (Palace of Culture and Science) looms above **pl. Defilad** (Parade Square); its clock tower, visible from most anywhere near the city center, serves as an orientation point. To the east of these landmarks lies **Rondo Charles de Gaulle,** the traffic circle where a major, multi-named road intersects **al. Jerozolimskie.** Going north it becomes **Nowy Świat** (New World Street) and then **ul. Krakówskie Przedmieście** as it leads into **Stare Miasto.** Going south, the road becomes **al. Ujazdowskie** as it runs past embassy row, palaces, and gardens.

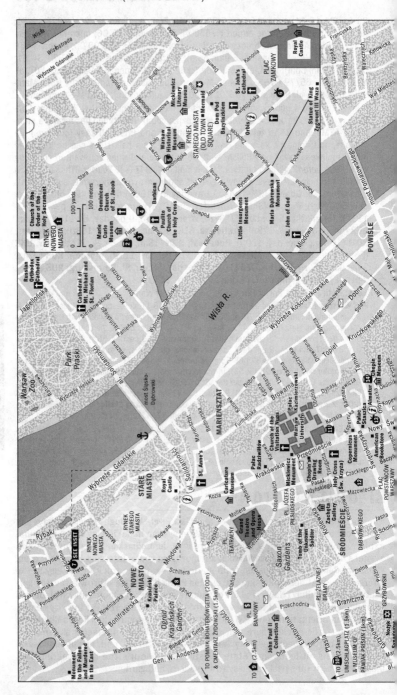

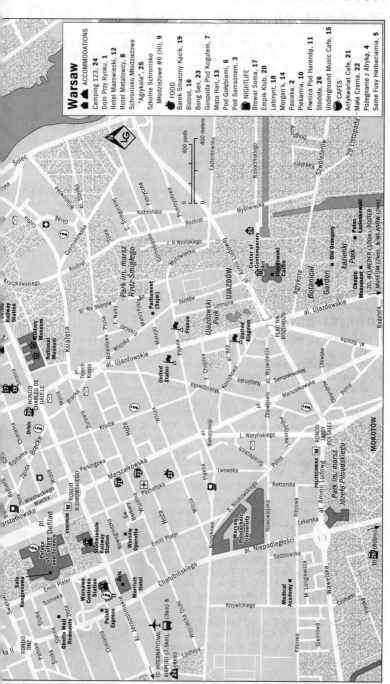

Warsaw

▲▲ ACCOMMODATIONS
Camping 123, 24
Dom Przy Rynku, 1
Hotel Mazowiecki, 12
Hotel Metalowcy, 8
Schronisko Młodzieżowe
"Agrykola", 25
Szkolne Schronisko
Młodzieżowe #6 (HI), 9

● FOOD
Barek Smaczny Kącik, 19
Bistrot, 16
Bong Sen, 23
Gospoda Pod Kogutem, 7
Mała Hari, 13
Pod Gołębiami, 6
Pod Samsonem, 3

■ NIGHTLIFE
Browar Soma, 17
Empik Klub, 20
Łabirynt, 18
Morgan's, 14
Pasieka, 2
Piekarnia, 10
Piwnica Pod Harendą, 11
Stodoła, 26
Underground Music Cafe, 15

☕ CAFES
Antykwariat Cafe, 21
Mała Czarna, 22
Pożegnanie z Afryką, 4
Same Fusy Herbaciarnia, 5

▐ LOCAL TRANSPORTATION

Public Transportation: (☎94 84; www.ztm.waw.pl). **Bus** and **tram** lines are marked on some maps. Day trams and buses, including express lines 2.40zł, with ISIC 1.25zł; large baggage needs a ticket of its own. Day pass 7.20zł/3.70zł. Weekly pass 26zł/ 12zł. Day and weekly passes are worth the money, as sights are spread out. Punch the ticket (on the end marked by the arrow and *tu kasować*) in the machines on board or face a 140zł fine, plus another 48zł for your pack. Bus #175 goes from the airport to Stáre Miasto by way of Warszawa Centralna and ul. Nowy Świat. Watch out for pickpockets. There are also 2 brand-new **sightseeing bus routes:** #100 and #180 hit many of the sights listed below. Warsaw's **Metro** has only 1 line; it connects the southern border of town, but it is not particularly convenient for tourists. Bus, tram, and subway lines share the same tickets and prices. Urban transport runs daily 5am-11pm.

Taxis: Try **MPT Radio Taxi** (☎919), **Euro Taxi** (☎96 62), or **Halo Taxi** (☎96 23). Overcharging is still a problem; if possible, call to arrange pickup. State-run cabs with the mermaid logo are generally the best. Fares start at 4zł, plus 1.60zł per km; the legal maximum is 2zł per km during the day, 2.40zł per km at night. MPT accepts MC/V.

Car Rental: Avis, (☎/fax 630 73 16) at the Marriott Hotel. Open daily 8am-6pm. Airport office (☎650 48 72) open daily 7am-10pm. Prices start at 256zł per day. **Budget,** (☎630 72 80) at the Marriott and the airport (☎650 40 62). Both branches open daily 8am-8pm. Prices start at 325zł per day.

▐ PRACTICAL INFORMATION

TOURIST AND FINANCIAL SERVICES

Tourist Offices: Informacji Turystyczna (IT), al. Jerozolimskie 54 (☎94 31; www.warsawtour.pl), inside the central train station. English-speaking staff provides **maps** (some free, some 6zł), **exchanges currency,** and arranges accommodations. Website has up-to-date information on cultural events. The indispensable *Warsaw Insider* (7zł) is on sale in kiosks just outside the office. Open May-Sept. daily 8am-8pm; Oct.-April daily 8am-6pm. **Branch** at ul. Krakówskie Przedmieście 89, opposite pl. Zamkowy. Open May-Sept. daily 8am-8pm; Oct.-Apr. 9am-6pm.

Budget Travel: Almatur, ul. Kopernika 23 (☎826 35 12; fax 826 45 92), off ul. Nowy Świat. Discount international bus and plane tickets. **ISIC** cards 44zł. English spoken. Open M-F 9am-7pm, Sa 10am-3pm. MC/V. **Orbis,** ul. Bracka 16 (☎827 07 30; fax 827 76 05), entrance on al. Jerozolimskie near ul. Nowy Świat. Sells plane, train, ferry, and international bus tickets. Open M-F 8am-6pm, Sa 9am-3pm. **Branch** at ul. Świętokrzyska 20 (☎827 80 33; orbis.bis@pbp.com.pl).

Embassies: Most are near ul. Ujazdowskie. **Australia,** ul. Nowogrodska 11 (☎521 34 44; fax 627 35 00). Open M-Tu and Th-F 9am-1pm and 2-4pm, W 9am-1pm. **Belarus,** ul. Ateńska 67 (☎/fax 617 32 12, visas 617 39 54). Open M-F 8am-4pm. **Canada,** al. Matejki 1/5 (☎584 31 00). Open M-F 8:30am-4:30pm. **Russia,** ul. Belwederska 49, bldg. C (☎621 34 53; fax 625 30 16). Open M-F 9am-6pm. **South Africa,** ul. Koszykowa 54 (☎625 62 28; fax 625 62 70). Open M-Th 8:30am-5pm, F 9am-3pm. **Ukraine,** al. Szucha 7 (☎625 01 27). Open M, W, and F 8am-noon. **UK,** al. Róż 1 (☎628 10 01; fax 621 71 61). Open M-F 10:30am-4:30pm. **US,** al. Ujazdowskie 29/31 (☎628 30 41; fax 628 82 98; www.usinfo.pl). Open M-F 8:30am-5pm.

Currency Exchange: *Kantori* have the best rates. **24hr. currency exchange** at Warszawa Centralna. **Bank PKO S.A.,** pl. Bankowy 2 (☎531 10 00), in the blue skyscraper, or ul. Grójecka 1/3 (☎658 82 17), in Hotel Sobieski, cashes AmEx/V **traveler's checks** for 1-2% commission and gives MC/V **cash advances.** Most branches have MC **24hr.**

ATMs. All branches open M-F 8am-6pm, Sa 10am-2pm. **Western Union,** ul. Długa 27 (☎636 56 89). Open M-F 9am-3pm. **Branches** in **Bank Przemysłowy Handlowy,** ul. Nowy Świat 6/12 (☎661 77 18), and **Bank Zachodni,** al. Jerozolimskie 91 (☎629 27 58). Both open M-F 8am-6pm.

American Express: al. Jerozolimskie 65/79 (☎630 69 52). Open M-F 9am-7pm, Sa 10am-6pm. **Branch** at ul. Sienna 39 (☎581 51 53). Open M-F 9am-6pm.

LOCAL SERVICES

Luggage Storage: At Warszawa Centralna train station, below the main hall. 4zł per item per day, plus 2.25zł per 50zł of declared value. Open 24hr. Storage also available in Zachodnia Station. 4zł for a large pack. Open daily 7am-7pm.

English-Language Bookstores: American Bookstore, ul. Nowy Świat 61 (☎827 48 52; american@americanbookstore.pl). Good but pricy selection of fiction, reference books, and periodicals. All open M-Sa 11am-7pm, Su 11am-6pm.

Bi-Gay-Lesbian Organizations: The Rainbow Helpline (☎628 52 22) in both English and Polish. Tu Gay Catholic, W lesbian support, F gay. Open Tu-W 6-9pm and F 4-10pm.

Laundromat: Ul. Karmelicka 17 (☎831 73 17). Take bus #180 or 516 north from ul. Marszałkowska toward Żoliborz and get off at ul. Anielewicza; backtrack 1 block to ul. Karmelicka. Some English spoken. Detergent 3zł. Wash and dry 26.60zł. Open M-F 9am-5pm, Sa 9am-1pm. Call ahead to make a reservation.

EMERGENCY AND COMMUNICATIONS

24-hour Pharmacy: Apteka Grabowskiego (☎825 69 86), at Warszawa Centralna.

Medical Services: CM Medical Center, al. Jerozolimskie 65/70, (**24hr. emergency line** ☎458 70 00, **ambulance** ☎630 30 30; fax 630 55 24; www.cm-lim.com.pl), at the Marriott. English speaking doctors. 80zł for an appointment. **Branch** at ul. Domaniewski 41. **Central Emergency Station,** ul. Hoża 56 (☎999) has a 24hr. ambulance. **Falck,** ul. Groszowicka 11/13 (☎535 91 51), is staffed by English-speaking paramedics.

Telephones: At the post office. Tokens and phone cards available at the post office and in many kiosks. For directory assistance, call ☎913.

Internet Access: e-cafe, ul. Marszałkowska, opposite Galeria Centrum, in "Kino Relax." 3zł per 15min., 5zł per 30min., 8zł per hr., 12zł per 2hr. Open daily 10am-9pm. **Piękna Internet Pub,** ul. Piękna 68A (☎622 33 77; www.piekna.pl). Beer 5zł. 3zł per 15min., 4zł per hr. Open M-F 10am-11pm, Sa noon-midnight, Su noon-11pm.

Post Office: Ul. Świętokrzyska 31/33 (☎827 00 52). The computer at the entrance doles out tickets; take a number and wait your turn. For stamps and letters, push "D." For packages, push "F." For **Poste Restante,** inquire at window #42 in the room to the left of the main hall. Open 24hr. *Kantor* (currency exchange) open daily 7am-10pm.

Postal Code: 00 001.

▛ ACCOMMODATIONS AND CAMPING

In the summer, rooms become scarce and prices high. Hostels are the first to fill up, so reserve at least a week in advance. **Biuro Kwater Prywatnych ❸** (Office of Private Quarters), ul. Krucza 17, off al. Jerozolimskie near Hotel Syrena, arranges **private rooms.** (☎628 75 40; fax 628 49 78. English spoken. Singles 79zł, 68zł per night for 3 or more nights; doubles 109zł/96zł. Open M-Sa 9am-7pm, Su 2-7pm.) **Almatur** and **IT** (see **Tourist Offices,** p. 488) can hook you up with a room in a **university dorm** if you're traveling during July and August. The city tourist offices maintain a list of all accommodations in the city and can help with reservations.

IN RECENT NEWS

WORLD CUP MANIA

Television commercials, radio announcements, and billboards all harnessed the world-wide momentum of World Cup 2002 and used football imagery to sell everything from cell phones to dog food. Pubs advertised "match specials" and hair salons even advertised "World Cup haircuts." But why all the commotion?

Football's (soccer's) popularity had been waning as Poland repeatedly failed to qualify for the World Cup. They last qualified in 1986, and made it to the second round before losing to Brazil. Unexpected success in 2002 roused the nation and gave birth to a new generation of football hooligans.

The first match ended in disaster, however, as Poland lost to major rival South Korea. Unruffled, fans consoled themselves, claiming the team still had another opportunity to advance and become World Champions. Unfortunately, Poland lost its second match to Portugal 0-4, and could not advance to the second round of competition. This did not discourage the proud fans who paraded through the streets of Kraków, sporting red and white garb, brandishing flags, and shouting "Polska" after the match. Poland's 3-0 victory over the United States in the third game further reassured fans that Poland's presence in the World Cup was deserved and that the next competition would end in victory.

All eyes are now fixed on World Cup 2006, and those die-hard fans who passionately cling to Poland's 1974 third-place finish now have a new legacy.

—Barbara Urbańczyk

HOSTELS

■ **Dom Przy Rynku,** Rynek Nowego Miasta 4 (☎/fax 831 50 33; www.strona.wp.pl/wp/dprhostel). Take bus #175 from the center to Franciszkańska. Turn right on Franciszkańska, then hang a right into the *rynek* (main square); the hostel will be on your left. Amazing location right in Nowe Miasto. Filled with book-lined rooms and sparkling bathrooms, some of which have potted plants. TV room, ping pong, and kitchenette. Reception 24hr. Lockout 10am-5pm. Open July-Aug. 2- to 5-bed dorms 45zł per person. ❷

Szkolne Schronisko Młodzieżowe #6 (HI), ul. Karolkowa 53a (☎632 88 29; fax 632 97 46; www.ptsm.com.pl/ssmnr6). Take tram #12, 22, or 24 west from al. Jerozolimskie or the train station to D. T. Wola and turn right at the underpass. Follow the green IYH signs. Prone to rambunctious school groups, but amenities and friendly staff compensate. Great bathrooms and cafe. Internet access 6-10pm (5zł per hr.). 140 beds. English spoken. Sheets 4zł. Reception 6-10am and 5-11pm. Lockout 10am-5pm. Curfew 11pm. 7- to 14-bed dorms 32zł, non-members 35zł, non-member students 16zł. Singles with bath 160zł; doubles with bath 260zł; triples and quads 50zł per person. ❷

Schronisko Młodzieżowe "Agrykola," ul. Myśliwiecka 9 (☎622 91 10 or 622 91 11; fax 622 91 05; www.hotelagrykola.pl). Near Łazienki Park. From train station, take bus #151, or from Marszałkowska, take bus #107, 420, or 520 to "Rozbrat." Continue as it turns into Myśliwiecka and turn right at the path to the Castle. Part hostel, part sports complex, Agrykola offers tidy rooms, a serene locale, and that new hostel smell. English spoken. In-line skate rental (for track use only) next door (6zł per hr.). Breakfast and cable TV included in rooms, but not in dorms. Dorms 40zł; singles 274zł; doubles 329zł; triples and quads 44-88zł per person. 10% discount with Euro 26 card. MC/V. ❷

HOTELS AND CAMPING

Hotel Metalowcy, ul. Długa 29 (☎831 40 21, ext. 29; fax 635 31 38; www.inhotel.pl). Take any tram along ul. Marszałkowska to pl. Bankowy, walk toward the tram, and turn right on Długa; the hotel is on the right. Or, take bus #175 from the train station to pl. Krasińskich, backtrack to ul. Długa, and turn right. Great location near Stare Miasto, with recently renovated bathrooms and quaint little rooms. Check-in 2pm. Check-out 10am. Reception 24hr. Singles 56zł; doubles 88zł; quads with bath 155zł. ❷

Hotel Mazowiecki, ul. Mazowiecka 10 (☎/fax 827 23 65, www.mazowiecki.com.pl), off ul. Świętokrzyska. Flanked by the Stare Miasto and modern-day Marszałkowska with newly-renovated bathrooms. Check-in 2pm. Check-out noon. Singles 150zł, with bath 210zł; doubles 200zł/270zł; triples 255zł. ❺

Camping "123," ul. Bitwy Warszawskiej 15/17 (☎822 91 21; fax. 823 37 48; http://friko6.onet.pl/wa/camp123/camp.htm), by the main bus station and opposite the hotel "Vera." Take bus #127, 130, or 517 to "Zachodnia" and cross the street at the traffic circle. Bitwy Warszawskiej is to the left. Surprisingly secluded. Close to the city center and well-shaded by trees. Swimming pool and tennis courts next door. Guarded 24hr. English spoken. Open May-Sept. 10zł per person, 10zł per tent. Electricity 10zł. Spartan 4-person bungalows: singles 40zł; doubles 70zł; triples 100zł; quads 120zł. ❷

🖸 FOOD

Countless food stands dot the square beneath the Pałac Kultury, and many more lie under the train station. Any **milk bar** *(bar mleczny)* or **cafeteria** *(stołowki)* will dish up a decent, inexpensive meal. **24hr. grocery stores,** often called *delikatesy,* are by the central train station and at ul. Nowy Świat 53. (☎826 03 22. Open 7am-5am.) Those plucky enough to cook for themselves will delight in **Domowy Okruszek,** a tiny store which sells ready-to-cook dishes like *naleśniki* (pancakes) and *pierogi* (dumplings) for 15-20zł. (Ul. Bracka 3, just south of Aleje Jerozolimskie. ☎628 70 77. Open M-Sa 10am-6pm, Su 10am-3pm.)

🔳 **Gospoda Pod Kogutem** (Under the Rooster), ul. Freta 48 (☎635 82 82; http://gospoda.pod.kogutiem.iport.pl). A shining star in Stare Miasto. Avoid tourist hordes and devour unmistakably local food among Poles and animal pelts in the barn-themed interior or, during the summer, outside along ul. Freta. Beer 5zł. Entrees 10-20zł. Open daily 11am-midnight. MC/V. ❷

🔳 **Pod Samsonem,** ul. Freta 3/5 (☎831 17 88). Between Stare Miasto and Nowe Miasto. Hearty Polish-Jewish cuisine that could satisfy even Samson's appetite. Interior is decorated with photos of Jewish life in pre-war Warsaw. Specialties include golden soup. Entrees 8-30zł. Open daily 10am-11pm. AmEx/MC/V. ❷

Bistrot, ul. Foksal 2 (☎827 87 07; fax 826 74 24), at the end of the street, through the gates. Nestled in a wing of the former Zamojski Palace, this elegant restaurant specializes in international gourmet cuisine. A delightfully formal wait staff provides excellent service, treating each of their patrons like royalty. The classy atmosphere and delicious food are worth treating yourself to. Entrees 35-80zl. English menu available. Open M-Sa 11am-midnight, Su noon-10pm. AmEx/MC/V. ❺

Mata Hari, ul. Nowy Świat 52 (☎620 98 29). Paper plates and cramped quarters don't deter budget-conscious omnivores from this incredibly cheap restaurant specializing in Indian vegetarian dishes. Soups and samosas 2.50-5.50zł. Takeout available. Open M-F 11am-7pm, Sa noon-6pm. ❶

Barek Smaczny Kącik ("Tasty Nook"), ul. Smolna 40, in the courtyard. This local favorite is one of the few places in the city where you can get a hearty, sit-down dinner for 12-19zł. Open M-F 10am-7pm. ❷

Pod Gołębiami, ul. Piwna 4a (☎635 01 56). A perfect stop for a quick and delectable lunch. Order from a variety of entrees inside (9-30zł), or partake in the house specialty, the best *naleśniki* in town (4-8zł). Order them from the window and drool while you watch them whipped up. Open daily 10am-11pm. AmEx/MC/V for orders over 50zł. ❶

Bong Sen, ul. Poznańska 12 (☎621 27 13), a few blocks south of the train station. Warsaw's first Asian restaurant, established by a Vietnamese chef, creates over 100 excellent dishes. Entrees 14-40zł. Open daily 11am-10pm. AmEx/MC/V. ❸

POLAND

▇ CAFES

▇ **Pożegnanie z Afryką,** ul. Freta 4/6 and ul. Dobra 56/66. The "Out of Africa" cafes brew incredible coffee (8-15zł). Worth the wait for 1 of 4 indoor tables: the burlap-clad interior lets you savor the heavenly smells. Cafe open July-Aug. 11am-10pm; Sept.-June 11am-9pm. Store open M-F 11am-7pm, Sa-Su noon-5pm.

▇ **Antykwariat Cafe,** ul. Żurawia 45 (☎629 99 29), 2 blocks south of Rondo de Gaulle. This tiny cafe mesmerizes patrons with its handsome interior and delicious coffee (5-10zł). Plush chairs welcome lingerers. Open M-F 11am-11pm, Sa-Su 1-11pm.

Same Fusy Herbaciarnia, ul. Nowomiejska 10 (☎635 90 14), in Stare Miasto. A cellar-joint-turned-earthy-teahouse with a forest-themed interior. 150 varieties of tea (10-35zł per pot, iced teas 6-11zł per glass). Open M-F 1-11pm, Sa-Su 1pm-late.

Mała Czarna (Little Black), ul. Hoża 54 (☎629 94 44), corner of ul. Marszałkowska. As chic as its namesake, the little black dress. Or does the cafe's name refer to small black coffees (5.50-12zł)? Either way, Mała Czarna pours out caffeine and exceptional smoothies (6-8zł). Open M-F 7:30am-9pm, Sa-Su 10am-9pm.

◎ SIGHTS

Razed during World War II to something resembling the surface of the moon, Warsaw had to be almost entirely rebuilt—and then had to withstand the wonders of Sovietization. Thanks to continuous renovations since World War II, buildings are impressively close to their pre-war state. Exploring the entire city takes several days since sights are very spread out. Convenient tourist bus route #100 begins at pl. Zamkowy and runs along pl. Teatralny, ul. Marszałkowska, al. Ujazdowskie, Łazienki Park, and back up the Royal Way, then loops through Praga before returning to pl. Zamkowy. Route #180 runs from Wilanów in the south past Łazienki and up the Royal Way before turning west to stop at the Jewish Cemetery.

STARE AND NOWE MIASTO

Warsaw's postwar reconstruction shows its finest face in the narrow, cobble-stoned streets and colorful facades of Stare Miasto. To get there, take bus #175 or E3 from the center to Miodowa.

STATUE OF ZYGMUNT III WAZA. Constructed in 1644 to honor the king who transferred the capital from Kraków to Warsaw, the statue stood atop a high column for 300 years before being destroyed in World War II. Now rebuilt, the kingly figure continues his vigil at the entrance to Stare Miasto. *(Stands proudly above the square in front of the castle.)*

ST. JOHN'S CATHEDRAL. (Archi-Katedra św. Jana.) Decimated in the 1944 Uprising, Warsaw's oldest church was rebuilt after the War in the Vistulan Gothic style, with pure white walls trimmed with brick vaulting. Documents from the 1339 case against the Order of Teutonic Knights, who had broken a pact with Duke of Mazovia Konrad Mazowiecki, are hidden within its walls. In its depths, **crypts** hold the dukes of Mazovia and such famous Poles as Nobel-winning author Henryk Sienkiewicz and Gabriel Narutowicz, the first president of independent Poland. A side altar contains the tomb of Cardinal Stefan Wyszyński, premier of Poland from 1948 to 1981. *(On ul. Świętojanska from pl. Zamkowy. Open daily 10am-1pm and 3-5:30pm. Entrance to crypts 2zł, students 1zł.)*

OLD TOWN SQUARE. (Rynek Starego Miasta.) A stone plaque at the entrance commemorates the reconstruction of the Renaissance and Baroque square, finished in 1953-54. The statue of the **Mermaid** (Warszawska Syrenka) marks the center of the square. On the square's southeast side at #3/9, **Dom Pod Bazyliszkiem** immortalizes the Stare Miasto Basilisk, a reptile famous for its fatal breath and a stare that instantly killed all those who crossed its path. Apparently, its fiery halitosis was no match for the modern firepower of World War II: the houses around the square were all but demolished during the 1944 Uprising, though large fragments of the ruins were used in reconstruction. *(On ul. Świętojańska.)*

BARBICAN. A rare example of 16th-century Polish fortification, the Barbican is a popular spot for locals and tourists to duck out of the traffic for a rest or to listen to the many street performers who cluster here. The **Little Insurgent Monument,** at the end of ul. Wąski Dunaj to the left (if your back is to Stare Miasto), is less a miniscule memorial than a symbolic marker of heroism; it honors the youngest soldiers of the 1944 Uprising. Around the Barbican are the crumbling walls that once enclosed Stare Miasto. The monument to author **Maria Dąbrowska** is at the intersection of Podwale and ul. Piekarska. *(Follow ul. Krzywe Koło (Crooked Wheel) from Stare Miasto.)*

NOWE MIASTO. The Barbican opens onto ul. Freta, the edge of Nowe Miasto. The "New Town," established at the beginning of the 15th century, had its own, separate town hall until 1791. Mostly destroyed during World War II, its 18th- and 19th-century buildings have enjoyed an expensive face lift. The great physicist and chemist **Maria Skłodowska-Curie,** winner of two Nobel prizes, was born at ul. Freta 16 in 1867 (see **Museums,** p. 496). Ul. Freta leads to New Town Square (Rynek Nowego Miasta), the site of the **Church of the Holy Sacrament** (Kościół Sakramentka), founded in 1688 to commemorate King Jan III Sobieski's 1683 victory over the Turks (see History, p. 474). Its interior is only a ghost of its past glory, but the Baroque dome still inspires awe. *(Open daily dawn-dusk.)*

TRAKT KRÓLEWSKI

The 4km Trakt Królewski (Royal Way) begins on pl. Zamkowy at the entrance to Stare Miasto. From ul. Krakówskie Przedmieście, Trakt Królewski becomes ul. Nowy Świat (New World Street). The Royal Way, so named because it leads to Poland's former capital of Kraków, is lined with palaces, churches, and convents built when the royal family moved to Warsaw. The name New World Street dates to the mid-17th century, when a new settlement composed mainly of working-class people was started here. It was not until the 18th century that the aristocracy started moving in and sprucing the place up with ornate manors and residences. Today, there's nothing working-class about it: it's the most fashionable street in town and the best urban route for a walk.

AROUND PL. ZAMKOWY. On the left as you leave pl. Zamkowy, **St. Anne's Church** (Kościół św. Anny), with its striking gilded altar and side altars, dates from the 15th century but was rebuilt in the Baroque style. *(Open daily dawn-dusk.)* Farther down the street, a monument to **Adam Mickiewicz,** Poland's national poet (see **The Arts,** p. 479), gazes west toward pl. Piłsudskiego and the **Saxon Garden** (Ogród Saski), which protects the **Tomb of the Unknown Soldier** (Grób Nieznanego Żołnierza). An **eternal flame** burns here in memory of Polish soldiers killed in battle and in the **Katyń Massacre,** when the Soviets murdered as many as 15,000 members of Polish intelligentsia in the spring of 1940. The changing of the guard takes place on Sundays at noon.

CHOPIN LEGACY. The next stretch of the Trakt is a requisite pilgrimage sight for fans of Frédéric Chopin (see **The Arts,** p. 479). Chopin spent his childhood in the neighborhood near ul. Krakówskie Przedmieście and gave his first public concert in **Pałac Radziwiłłów** (a.k.a. Pałac Namiestnikowski), ul. Krakówskie Przedmieście 46/48, the building guarded by four stone lions. Because it's now the Polish presidential mansion, these days a human guard stands alongside his feline counterparts. A block down the road, the **Church of the Visitation Nuns** (Kościół Wizytówek) once resounded with the romantic ivory pounding of the mop-topped composer. *(Open daily dawn-dusk.)* Before he left for France in 1830, Chopin wrote many of his best-known compositions in his last home, **Pałac Czapskich.** The palace now houses the **Academy of Fine Arts** and **Chopin's Drawing Room** (Salonik Chopinów), a room from the Chopins' home that has been preserved since the time when he gave concerts there. *(Enter through the gate at ul. Krakywskie Przedmieście 5; the entrance is on the left. ☎826 62 51, ext. 267. Open M-F 10am-2pm, closed holidays. 3zł, students 2zł.)* Chopin died abroad at the age of 39 and was buried in Paris, but his heart belongs to Poland: the organ now rests in an urn in the left nave of the **Holy Cross Church** (Kościół św. Krzyża), on your right as you walk further along. Nobel prize-winning author **Władysław Reymont** left his heart here, too.

UNIVERSITY OF WARSAW. (Uniwersytet Warszawski.) Opposite Kościół św. Krzyża and behind the swarms of students, a complex of rebuilt palaces belongs to the **University of Warsaw,** founded in 1816. **Pałac Kazimierzowski,** at the end of the alley leading from the main entrance to the university, now holds the rector's offices, but was once the seat of the School of Knighthood. Its alumni include **General Tadeusz Kościuszko,** who fought in the American Revolutionary War and later against the several partitions of Poland. The **Copernicus Monument** (Pomnik Mikołaja Kopernika) and **Pałac Staszica,** home of the Polish Academy of Sciences, mark the end of ul. Krakówskie Przedmieście and the beginning of ul. Nowy Świat.

ŁAZIENKI PARK

The park and the palaces within the park were built in the late 18th century for Stanisław August Poniatowski, the last king of Poland (see **History,** p. 474), but peacocks and pigeons rule the roost today. The sprawling grounds and meandering paths attract Varsovians eager for a weekend retreat. Amid a sea of roses and park benches are the oft-photographed **Chopin Monument** (Pomnik Chopina), a site for free concerts (Mar.-Oct. Su noon and 4pm), and the statue of Nobel Prize-winning author Henryk Sienkiewicz (see **The Arts,** p. 479). The park borders al. Ujazdowskie and Trakt Królewski. Take bus #100 from Marszałkowska, #116, 180 or 195 from ul. Nowy Świat, or #119 from the city center to Bagatela. The park is just across the street. Open daily dawn-dusk.

PAŁAC ŁAZIENKOWSKI. Farther into the park is the striking Neoclassical Pałac Łazienkowski, also called the **Palace on Water** (Pałac na Wodzie) or **Palace on the Isle** (Pałac na Wyspie). Surrounded by water and leafy boughs, this breathtaking building was the creation of benefactor King Stanisław August and his beloved architect Dominik Merlini. Rotating exhibitions await inside. *(Open Tu-Su 9:30am-4pm, closed in bad weather. Kasa closes at 3:15pm. 11zł, students 8zł. Guided tour in English 66zł.)*

OTHER SIGHTS. The **Old Orangery** (Stara Pomarańczarnia) houses both the rich 1788 Stanisławowski Theater and the Gallery of Polish Sculpture (Galeria Rzeźby Polskiej), which exhibits work from the 1500s through 1939. *(Orangery open Tu-Su 9am-4pm. Kasa closes at 3pm. 6zł, students 4zł.)* Just south of Łazienki, to the right as you face the entrance, is **Belweder,** a palace completed in 1818 for the Russian tsar and later converted into Józef Piłsudski's residence. Just north of Łazienki along al. Ujazdowskie is the **Ujazdowski Castle** (see **Museums,** p. 496), built in 1637 for King Zygmunt III Waza, and the soul-soothing **Botanical Gardens.** *(☎553 05 11. Open June-Aug. M-Th 9am-8pm, F-Su 10am-8pm; Sept. daily 10am-6pm; Oct. daily 10am-4pm. Kasa closes 1hr. before the gardens. 4zł, students 2zł.)* Continue back toward the center of town along al. Ujazdowskie and turn right on ul. Matejki to reach the **Sejm** (Parliament) and the **Senate building.** *(Both closed to the public.)*

THE FORMER WARSAW GHETTO

Still referred to as the Ghetto, the modern Muranów (literally, "walled") neighborhood, north of the city center, displays few vestiges of the nearly 400,000 Jews who once comprised one-third of the city's pre-war population. The building next to the Nozyk Synagogue houses **Our Roots,** ul. Twarda 6 (☎/fax 620 05 56), a Jewish travel agency that arranges English tours of Jewish Warsaw, Auschwitz, Treblinka, and Majdanek. (Open M-F 10am-5pm. Tours US$25-70.)

MONUMENTS. The **Umschlagplatz,** at the corner of ul. Dzika and ul. Stawki, was the railway platform where the Nazis gathered 300,000 Jews for transport to death camps. A large monument in Polish, Hebrew, and Yiddish now stands in its place. *(Take tram #35 from ul. Marszałkowska to Dzika.)* With the monument to the left, continue down Stawki and turn right on ul. DuBois, which becomes ul. Zamenhofa. You will pass a mound of earth with a monument on top marking the location of the underground command bunker of the **1943** ghetto uprising (see **History,** p. 474). In a large park to your right, the **Monument of the Ghetto Heroes** (Pomnik Bohaterów) pays homage to leaders of the uprising. Nearby, a marker commemorates the **Relief Council for Jews,** an organization sponsored by the government in exile that worked to rescue Jews from the Holocaust. The site is the future location of the **Museum of the History of Polish Jews,** expected by summer 2007. *(Ul. Jelinka 48. ☎833 00 21.)*

JEWISH CEMETERY. (Cmentarz Żydowski.) Built at the turn of the 19th century, this sprawling and thickly wooded cemetery is the final resting place of 250,000 of Warsaw's Jews. Sadly, many of the tombstones are shrouded in undergrowth and thousands have long since disappeared. 50m to your right as you enter, a bronze statue of **Janusz Korczak** commemorates the children's writer famous for his popular 1930s radio program and maintenance of two orphanages, one Catholic and one Jewish. He is perhaps best known for his courage during the early stages of the liquidation of the Ghetto. The Germans gathered everyone in his Jewish orphanage and, though several of his Gentile friends offered to help him escape, he chose to remain with the 200 children in his care and die with them in Treblinka. Of his actions Korczak said, "You do not leave a sick child in the night, and you do not leave children at a time like this." *(Ul. Okopowa 49/51, in the western corner of Muranów. From Dzielna, follow al. Jana Pawla II to Anielwicza and take a left. Alternatively, take tram #22 from the city center to Cm. Żydowski. ☎838 26 22; www.jewishcem.waw.pl. Open Apr.-Oct. Su-Th 9am-4pm; Nov.-Mar. 9am-3pm. 4zł.)* Nearby, the **Monument of Common Martyrdom of Jews and Poles** (Pomnik Wspólnego Męczeństwa Żydow i Polaków), ul. Gibalskiego 2, marks the site of mass graves from World War II. *(Facing the cemetery entrance, follow the street on the left of the cemetery to Gibalskiego, then turn left before the Nissenbaum building.)*

NOŻYK SYNAGOGUE. This beautifully restored building is a living artifact of Warsaw's Jewish life. Used as a stable by the Wehrmacht, it was the only synagogue to survive the war. Today it serves as the spiritual home for the few hundred observant Jews who remain in Warsaw. *(Ul. Twarda 6. From the city center, take any tram along ul. Jana Pawla II to Rondo ONZ. Turn right on Twarda (5min.) and left at the Jewish Theater (Teatr Żydowski). ☎620 43 24. Open Su-F 7am–8pm. Morning and evening services daily; contact the synagogue for a schedule. 5zł.)*

GHETTO WALL. Early in the occupation of Warsaw, the Nazis built a wall around the entire neighborhood, confining the Jews to the Ghetto until the Nazis liquidated the entire area in 1943 following the Jewish uprising. A small section of the original ghetto wall still stands between two apartment buildings on ul. Sienna and ul. Złota, west of al. Jana Pawła II and near Warszawa Centralna station. Enter the courtyard at ul. Sienna 55; the wall is on the left.

COMMERCIAL DISTRICT

PALACE OF CULTURE AND SCIENCE. (Pałac Kultury i Nauki.) The center of Warsaw's commercial district (southwest of Stare Miasto and adjacent to the train station) is dominated by the 70-story Stalinist Gothic Palace of Culture and Science, Poland's tallest structure. Originally christened the Joseph Stalin Palace, the building has since been dubbed "The Wedding Cake" because of its multi-tiered architecture. Locals claim "the cake" offers the best view of Warsaw. Not only are its views from 115km incomparable, it's the only place from which you can't see the building itself. This palatial eyesore, a 1955 gift from the Soviet Union, now houses over 3000 offices, a few exhibition and conference facilities, three theaters, several cinemas, a shopping center, a cafe, and two museums. *(☎656 71 36. Take a ride to the observation deck, "Taras Widokowy," for 15zł, students 9zł. After 9pm, 20zł. Open daily 9am-midnight.)* Below lies **pl. Defilad** (Parade Sq.), Europe's largest square. Yes, it's even bigger than Moscow's Red Square. *(On ul. Marszałkowska.)*

OTHER SIGHTS. Warsaw Insurgents' Square (pl. Powstańców Warszawy), is marked by a large memorial. On August 1, 1944, the valiant insurgents of the Warsaw Uprising began their heroic and ultimately doomed battle against the Germans here. *(On ul. Świętokrzyska, between ul. Marszałkowska and Krakówskie Przedmieście.)* **The Monument to the Fallen and Murdered in the East,** on pl. Sybiraków (Siberians' Square), remembers those who were exiled to Siberia. *(On the north end of Muranowska at the intersection with Andersa Marszałkowska's north end.)*

🏛 MUSEUMS

🏛 ROYAL CASTLE. (Zamek Królewski.) In the Middle Ages, the castle was home to the Dukes of Mazovia. In the late 16th century, it replaced Kraków's Wawel as the official royal residence; later it became the presidential palace, and in September 1939 it was burned down and plundered by the Nazis. Following its destruction, many Varsovians risked their lives hiding the castle's priceless works in the hope that one day the objects could be returned. Some of the treasures were retrieved when Poland gained independence in 1945, but it took another 40 years—and countless contributions from thousands of Poles, Polish expats, and dignitaries worldwide—to restore this symbol of national pride. The kingly abode, with its stately exterior and dazzling interior chambers, is an impressive example of restoration: it's a marvel that anything so regal was built in the 1970s. There are two routes for viewing: Route 1 snakes through the parliament chambers and apartments and is often home to temporary exhibits, while Route 2 hits the King's apartments, throne rooms, and the spectacular Marble Room. The sights along Route 2 are more visually arresting, although Route 1 does pass Jan Matejko's cycle of paintings *History of Civilization in Poland.* Each route takes about 30min. *(Pl. Zamkowy 4. ☎657 21 70; www.zamek-krolewski.art.pl. Tickets and guides at the kasa inside the courtyard. Kasa closes 1hr. before the museum. Route 1 open M 11am-4pm, Tu-Sa 10am-4pm. 8zł; students 3zł. Route 2 open M 11am-6pm, Tu-Sa 10am-6pm. 14zł, students 7zł. Highlights tour free Su 11am-6pm. English tour M-Sa 70zł per group.)*

WARSAW HISTORICAL MUSEUM. (Muzeum Historyczne Miasta Warszawy.) The tiny entrance belies the size of this massive museum, which occupies an entire side of the *rynek* (square). Artifacts from seven centuries of Warsaw's life adorn this museum, from meager 10th-century beginnings to the tragedies of the Nazi occupation. Some information is in English. *(Rynek Starego Miasta 42. ☎635 16 25. Excellent English-language film Tu-Sa noon. Open Tu and Th 11am-6pm, W and F 10am-3:30pm, Sa-Su 10:30am-4:30pm. 5zł, students 2.50zł. Su free.)*

POSTER MUSEUM. (Muzeum Plakatu.) This museum displays over 450 evocative posters from the last century, from Soviet propaganda to AIDS awareness. The museum store sells prints for 40-100zł. (Ul. Stanislawa Potockiego 10/16, by Palac Wilanowski. Branches at ul. Hoża 40 and Stary Rynek 23. ☎842 48 48; fax 842 26 06. Open Tu-F 10am-4pm, Sa-Su 10am-5pm. Last entrance 30min. before closing. 8zł, students 5zł. W free.)

CENTER OF CONTEMPORARY ART. (Centrum Sztuki Współczesnej.) Set inside the cavernous 17th-century Baroque Ujazdowski Castle, this gallery showcases the newest postmodern works of Polish and international artists. The sign above the entrance reads, "Far too many things to fit inside so small a box." A very unique and wonderfully bizarre little museum, it is definitely worth the trip for art lovers. English info is available at the *kasa* and placards throughout. (Al. Ujazdowskie 6. Take the same buses as to Lazienki, but get off at pl. Na Rozdrożu; the museum is past the overpass, 200m from the road. ☎628 12 71; www.csw.art.pl. Open Sa-Th 11am-5pm, F 11am-9pm. Last entrance 30min. before closing. 10zł, students 5zł.)

NATIONAL MUSEUM. (Muzeum Narodowe.) The impressive collection at Poland's largest museum traces the development of Polish and European art from early sacred pieces to contemporary artwork. (Al. Jerozolimskie 3. ☎629 30 93; English tour info ☎629 50 60. Open Tu-W and F 10am-4pm, Th noon-5pm, Sa-Su 10am-5pm; July-Aug. Tu-Su 10am-4pm. Kasa closes 45min. before museum. Closed the day after public holidays. 15zł, students 8zł, Sa permanent exhibits free. English tour 50zł. Call one week in advance.)

MUSEUM OF PAWIAK PRISON. (Muzeum Więzienia Pawiaka.) Built in the 1830s as a model prison for common criminals, Pawiak later served as Gestapo headquarters under the Nazis. From 1939 to 1944, over 100,000 Poles were imprisoned and tortured here; 37,000 were executed and another 60,000 were transferred to concentration camps. The Nazis leveled the prison during the 1944 Warsaw Uprising. One room has been converted into a museum, which exhibits a moving display of photographs and artifacts, including the letters, artwork, and poetry of many former prisoners. (Ul. Dzielna 24/26. ☎/fax 831 13 17. Open W 9am-5pm, Th and Sa 9am-4pm, F 10am-5pm, Su 10am-4pm. Donation requested.)

ZACHĘTA GALLERY. This internationally recognized gallery features dynamic contemporary art; don't be surprised if one or two of the sculptures are alive. (Pl. Malachowskiego 3. Buses #100 toward pl. Zamkowy and #160 toward Targowek from the center both stop at Zachęta. ☎827 58 54; www.zacheta-gallery.waw.pl. Open Tu-Su 10am-6pm. Guided tour in Polish 40zł, in English 60zł. Call 2 days in advance. 10zł, students 7zł. F free.)

POLISH MILITARY MUSEUM. (Muzeum Wojska Polskiego.) This museum could equip its own army with its collection of Polish weaponry and uniforms. Old planes and tanks litter the grounds. (Al. Jerozolimskie 3, opposite the Powisle rail station. ☎629 52 71 or 629 52 72. Open May 15-Sept. 30 W-Su 11am-5pm; Oct. 1-May 14 W-Su 10am-4pm. Last entrance 30min. before closing. Guided tours in English 20zł. 5zł, students 3zł. F free.)

FRYDERYC CHOPIN MUSEUM. (Muzeum Fryderyka Chopina.) A small but fascinating collection of original letters, scores, paintings, and keepsakes, including the composer's last piano and his first published piece—the Polonaise in G Minor, penned at the ripe old age of seven. The museum also hosts the International Chopin Festival, with concerts, usually at 7pm, on selected days July-Aug. Call for a schedule. (In Ostrogski Castle, ul. Okólnik 1. ☎827 54 71. Enter from ul. Tamka. Open May-Sept. M, W, F 10am-5pm, Th noon-6pm, Sa-Su 10am-2pm; Oct.-Apr. M-W and F-Sa 10am-2pm, Th noon-6pm. Audioguides in 5 languages 4zł. 8zł, students 4zł. Concerts 30zł, students 15zł.)

MARIA SKŁODOWSKA-CURIE MUSEUM. (Muzeum Marii Skłodowskiej-Curie.) Founded in 1967, on the 100th anniversary of the 2-time Nobel Prize winner's birth, the exhibit chronicles Maria Skłodowska's life in Poland, emigration to France, and marriage to scientist Pierre Curie, with whom she discovered radium, polonium, and marital bliss. (Ul. Freta 16, in Skłodowska's former house. ☎831 80 92. Open Tu-Sa 10am-4pm, Su 10am-2pm. 6zł, students 3zł.)

POLAND

THE LOCAL STORY

AN IRISHMAN IN WARSAW

Thomas Morgan is the owner of the popular Morgan's Pub in Warsaw. Over the music and din of his raucous patrons, Mr. Morgan tells Let's Go Researcher Barbara Urbańczyk about life in Poland, the World Cup, and how much he dislikes Guinness.

Q: So I'm wondering, why Poland?

A: Well, it wasn't planned. I was working in another pub here in Warsaw with Ollie, my dad. And well, I got bored with that. I couldn't make any decisions, so I opened up this place a couple years ago.

Q: Do you speak Polish?

A: (laughs) Very badly!

Q: (laughs) Have you learned the words to the *stolat* song?

A: Nearly! (sings) "Stolat! Stolat! Nie..." (trails off). Eh, I can hum along.

Q: Close enough. Do you ever run into problems communicating with the staff or customers?

A: Nah, the staff here speaks English. Most of the time I have no idea what the customers are saying or singing, but as long as they're happy and having a good time, that's all I care about.

Q: This is a very unique space for a pub—in a castle, under a Chopin museum...

A: Yeah, it's a great place. Upstairs, people don't even know there's a pub down here, which is good, you know, since we don't bother them. But that's the price I gotta pay for no ventilation!

(continued on next page)

JOHN PAUL II COLLECTION. Okay, so it's not a museum about the Pope, but the Carroll-Porczynski family started amassing a collection of paintings in 1980 and donated them all to the city of Warsaw in his name. Artists displayed here include Dalí, Titian, Rembrandt, Van Gogh, Goya, Rubens, Picasso, and others. *(Pl. Bankowy 1, in the Old Stock Exchange and Bank of Poland building. Enter from ul. Elektoralna. ☎620 21 81. Open May-Oct. Tu-Su 10am-5pm; Nov.-Apr. 10am-4pm. Kasa closes 1hr. before museum. 8zł, students 4zł. Polish tour 1zł per person.)*

ADAM MICKIEWICZ LITERARY MUSEUM. (Muzeum Literatury im. Adama Mickiewicza.) Old sketches, letters, books, and Mickiewicz's original inkpot recall the world of Poland's national poet. Information in Polish only. *(Rynek Starego Miasta 20. ☎831 40 61. Open M-Tu and F 10am-3pm, W-Th 11am-6pm, Su 11am-5pm. 5zł, students 4zł.)*

🎵 ENTERTAINMENT

Like any other major European capital, it's hard to take a step in Warsaw without seeing a notice about a performance. To get the latest schedule of events, call ☎94 31. Classical music aficionados will have a field day in Warsaw; it's possible to get standby tickets for major performances for under 10zł. Inquire about concerts at the **Warsaw Music Society** (Warszawskie Towarzystwo Muzyczne), ul. Morskie Oko 2 (☎849 56 51). Take tram #4, 18, 19, 35, or 36 to "Morskie Oko" from ul. Marsza-łkowska. The society is to your left as you pass the Japanese ambassador's residence on the right. The **Warsaw Chamber Opera** (Warszawska Opera Kameralna), al. Solidarności 76B (☎831 22 40), hosts a **Mozart Festival** each year during early summer. Nearby Łazienki Park hosts free Sunday performances at the **Chopin Monument** (Pomnik Chopina); different artists perform each week, but the score is always classical. (May-Oct. Su noon and 4pm.) **Teatr Wielki,** pl. Teatralny 1 (☎692 07 58; www.teatrwielki.pl), Warsaw's main opera and ballet hall, offers performances almost daily. (Tickets 10-100zł. AmEx/MC/V.) The **National Philharmonic** (Filharmonia Narodowa), ul. Jasna 5 (☎826 72 81, ext. 137), gives regular concerts, but is closed in summer. Jazz, rock, and blues fans also have quite a few options, especially in summer when Stare Miasto erupts with street music. **Sala Kongresowa** (☎620 49 80), in the Pałac Kultury on the train station side with the casino, hosts jazz and rock concerts with famous international bands. Enter from ul. Emilii Plater. Keep your eyes peeled in June for the annual **Warsaw Summer Jazz Days** (☎620 12 19; www.adamiakjazz.pl). For tickets to rock concerts, call **Empik Megastore** (☎625 12 19).

📧 NIGHTLIFE

Warsaw has much to offer in the way of evening revelry. A wide variety of pubs attract big crowds and often have live music, and the cafes (*kawiarnie*) around Stare Miasto and off ul. Nowy Świat stay open late into the night. During the summer, large beer gardens complement the pub scene. Warsaw is largely a community of conservative businesspeople, so those **bi, gay, and lesbian clubs** that do exist are often secluded and always discreet (on the outside, anyway). For the latest info, call the gay and lesbian **hotline** (see **Bi-Gay-Lesbian Organizations,** p. 489). Kiosks sell *Gazeta Wyborcza*, a magazine that lists some gay-oriented information.

BARS

📧 **Morgan's,** ul. Okólnik 1 (☎826 81 38; www.morgan-spub.com). Enter on ul. Tamka under the Chopin Museum. Thomas Morgan runs this comfortable, friendly Irish joint for expats and visitors. Says he pours the best Guinness in Poland, and he's probably right (0.5L, 15zł). Occasional live music, but usually not in summer. Raucous karaoke Tu. Open M-F 3pm-midnight, Sa-Su 2pm-midnight.

Pasieka, ul. Freta 7/9 (☎831 46 16). Specializes in mead, an alcoholic honey brew that singes your throat like the finest *wódka* and ends with a sweet soothing aftertaste. Before you go: *trójniak*, 1 part honey and 2 parts water, ages for 2½ years; *dwójniak*, half honey and half water, ages for 6 years; and *półtorak*, veritable nectar of the gods, 2 parts honey and 1 part water, ages for 10 years. Open daily 10am-10pm.

Piwnica Pod Harendą, ul. Krakówskie Przedmieście 4/6 (☎826 29 00), at Hotel Harenda. Enter from ul. Karasia. A ranch-like interior with pictures of the owners in bow ties doing chummy things. Escape the nostalgia and enjoy the huge outdoor beer garden, popular with students. Beer 10zł. Live music Tu and Th (cover only on Tu and Th 10-15zł). Disco F 10pm, Sa 9pm. Happy hour F-Sa 5pm. Open daily 8am-3am.

Empik Klub, ul. Nowy Świat 15/17 (☎625 10 86). In the basement and gardens outside of Empik Megastore; enter from al. Jerozolimskie. Hosts local bands. Save your Th night for Empik's shanty night, when everyone crams into the tiny club for the nautical singalong. Beer 9zł. Live music Tu-Sa 10pm-1am. Open M-Sa 9am-late, Su 11am-late.

Browar Soma, ul. Foksal 19 (☎828 21 33; fax 826 40 45). Warsaw's only micro-brewery is snazzy and hip, with decor so austere it could be Puritan—if you ignore the alcohol. Beer 9zł, early-bird specials 5zł. Open daily 11am-3am.

Q: That's unfortunate. Who's the mastermind behind the decorating scheme?

A: I put up a lot of the stuff myself. Ha! I did all the stuff that looks bad!

Q: Nah, it looks great. So what kind of people come here?

A: Jesus! All kinds. I get a lot of Poles who hear about this place and come wondering, "Hey, who's this crazy Irish fella?" Guys come in here and want to share a Guinness. To be honest, I don't really like the stuff. But I don't want to disappoint them, so I go along. (Imitates drinking and grimaces, but manages to crack a smile and give a thumbs up.)

Q: Does the Guinness sell well, or do the Poles stick to the local brews?

A: Yeah, it sells really well.

Q: What were the sales like during the World Cup?

A: Oh Jesus! This place was packed for the Ireland-England match. Everybody was drinking and cheering. There weren't any hooligans, though.

Q: Morgan's has become something of a legend here in Warsaw. Do you expect to stay here long?

A: Oh yeah. As long as the pub keeps doing well, I'll stick around. Poles are great. Love to sing and always telling stories. Very impatient, though. Almost too impatient...just like the Irish!

A: You said your brother owns a pub in Kraków. Whose is better?

Q: (laughs) Mine (winks) or maybe my brother's.

NIGHTCLUBS

■ **Piekarnia,** ul. Młocińska 11 (☎636 49 79). Take a tram to Rondo Babka and backtrack on ul. Okopowa. Make an immediate right on Powiązkowska, another right on Burakowa, and a 3rd right on Młocińska. The unmarked club will be on your left. A taxi from the center should cost 20-25zł. So hip it hurts. Packed dance floor and great music, often from top DJs. Cover F 20zł, Sa 25zł. Open F-Sa 10am-late.

Labirynt, ul. Smolna 12 (☎826 12 34), near ul. Nowy Świat. Resembling something of a jungle techno fest, with "cosmic bowling" (72zł), aquariums, and 3 dance floors to facilitate jungle boogie. Cover varies. Call ahead about specials. Open daily 3pm-late.

Underground Music Cafe, ul. Marszałkowska 126/134 (☎826 70 48). Opposite the Pałac Kultury; walk down the steps. Red lights illuminate the bar and an industrial-sized cage surrounds the stairs leading to the dance floor. Beer 8.50zł. Usually M, Tu, and Sa-Su House; W hip-hop and soul; Th dance; F disco. Cover W-Th 10zł, F-Sa 20zł. Open M-Sa 1pm-late, Su 4pm-late. Free for females W and F-Sa before 10pm, Th before 11pm.

Stodoła (The Barn), ul. Batorego 10 (☎825 86 25). Take the Metro south toward Ursynow and get off at Pole Mokotowskie. The student crowds from the Polytechnic and the School of Economics come here to get their groove on. Occasionally hosts big-name bands such as Megadeth and, recently, Tricky. Cover for big shows up to 100zł. Two crazily painted floors facilitate the madness. Cover 10zł. Open F-Sa 9pm-4am.

▶ DAYTRIPS FROM WARSAW

ŻELAZOWA WOLA

*Three **buses** pass daily through Żelazowa Wola (53km west of Warsaw). From the Warszawa Zachodnia (see p. 484), take the bus headed to Wyszogród. Żelazowa Wola is a regular stop on the route (7.80zł, but prices change frequently), but tell the driver where you want to get off ahead of time. Only the two earlier buses get there before the museum closes. There are no direct buses back after 4:30pm. The **commuter train** from Warszawa Śródmieście PKP, on al. Jerozolimskie, runs more frequently to the small town of Sochaczew (1hr., 25 per day, 8.50zł). A Sochaczew **city bus** heads to Żelazowa Wola (M-F every hr., Sa-Su every other hr.; 3zł.)*

They say you can still hear the strains of *études* and *waltzes* hanging in the air of Żelazowa Wola. Spirits? No; it's actually the Chopin-pumping speakers located in the nearby museum dedicated to the birth of this famous Polish composer. Although the family ultimately made their home in Warsaw just after Fryderyk's birth on February 22, 1810, they often spent summers in the cottage in Żelazowa Wola, and the city now houses the Chopin Birthplace Museum. Chopin enthusiasts realized the historical significance of this site at the turn of the century and refused to relinquish it to dilapidation, transforming the cottage and surrounding gardens into a shrine to the composer in 1939.

Visiting the Chopin house and museum is a literal walk in the park. Though the **museum** is respectable, it lacks the family's original furniture and features little more than rooms devoted to Chopin's parents, his birth certificate, and the cover page of his first published piece (dreamt up when he was seven). The expansive, well-maintained gardens, however, are worth the visit. Winding paths twist throughout the grounds, enveloping ponds, a small stream, and a black obelisk commemorating Chopin's birth. **Free concerts** take place in the garden as Polish musicians deliver Fryderyk's goods every Sunday (May-Sept. at 11am and 3pm). The frequently-changing schedule of music and performers is posted throughout Warsaw and at the Chopin Museum (see **Museums,** p. 497). Grab a bite near the entrance to the museum at **Restauracja "Pod Wierzbami"** ❸ (☎(46) 863 32 43; entrees 25zł), or pack a lunch and eat on one of the garden's many benches. (☎46 863 33 00; fax 863 40 76. 10zł, students 5zł. Park only 4zł/2zł. Open May-Sept. Tu-Su 9:30am-5:30pm; Oct.-Apr. Tu-Su 9:30am-4pm. English audio tour 20zł.)

POLAND

WILANÓW

Take bus #180, 410, or 414 from ul. Marszałkowska, or bus #519 from the train station south to Wilanów. Cross the street; the road to the palace is on the right. ☎842 81 01. Open June 15-Sept. 15 M and W-Sa 9:30am-2:30pm, Su 9:30am-4:40pm; Sept. 16-June 14 M and W-Su 9:30am-4pm. Last entrance 1hr. before closing. 15zł, students 8zł. English tour for fewer than 5 people 120zł; for 6-35 people 24zł per person. Video camera 40zł. Admission lands you a spot in a slow-moving Polish-language tour, but it is better to break off and explore on your own, letting the captions be your guide. Gardens open M and W-F 9:30am-dusk. 3zł, students 2zł. Orangery open M and W-F 9:30am-3:30pm.

Warsaw's answer to Versailles, this extraordinary residence lies just south of the city. In 1677, King Jan III Sobieski bought the sleepy village of Milanowo, had its existing mansion rebuilt as a Baroque palace, and named the residence Wilanów. Over the years, a long line of Polish aristocrats called the palace home. One of these bluebloods, Duke Stanisław Kostka Potocki, thought it might be nice to share it with his subjects. In 1805 he opened Wilanów to visitors, founding one of the first public museums in Poland. Since then, **Pałac Wilanówski** has functioned both as a museum and as a residence for the highest-ranking guests of the state. Inside are lovely frescoed rooms, countless 17th- to 19th-century portraits, and extravagant royal apartments. The surrounding **gardens** form strict, formal patterns in the French style and feature an array of elegant topiary creations. By the meandering river, the gardens merge with neighboring parks. Inside, the **Old Orangery** houses a collection of European porcelain, some of which is over 400 years old. Near the entrance to the grounds is a branch of the **Poster Museum** (see **Museums,** p. 496).

LESSER POLAND (MAŁOPOLSKA)

The Małopolska uplands, strewn with medieval castle ruins, stretch from the Kraków-Częstochowa Uplands in the west to Lublin in the east. Kraków, which suffered only minimal damage during World War II, remains Poland's cultural and social center, drawing a steady stream of travelers. The surrounding landscape is home to some of the most beautiful and most horrific of mankind's creations. The artistry of the salt caves at Wieliczka and the serenity of the castle at Pieskowa Skała lie in stark contrast to the remnants of the Auschwitz-Birkenau concentration camp, which lie south of the city, and the Majdanek camp, located on the outskirts of Lublin to the northeast.

KRAKÓW ☎(0)12

Although Kraków (KRAH-koof; pop 745,500) only recently emerged as a trendy, international city, it has long held a distinguished place in the heart and history of Poland. When the city served as the country's capital, it sheltered centuries of Central European kings and garnered astounding architectural achievements, many of which still stand in the maze of narrow streets in the multi-colored Old Town. Unlike other major Polish cities, Kraków miraculously managed to survive World War II and years of socialist planning almost intact. Of course, the city's current gloss and glamour don't completely hide the scars of the 20th century: the nearby Auschwitz-Birkenau death camps, located just 70km outside the city, are a sobering reminder of the atrocities committed by the Nazis. Home to scores of museums, galleries, underground pubs, and 100,000 students, Kraków alternately acts as the country's artist, pubber, scholar, historian, and cafe-lingerer. By no means undiscovered, Kraków remains the highlight of Poland.

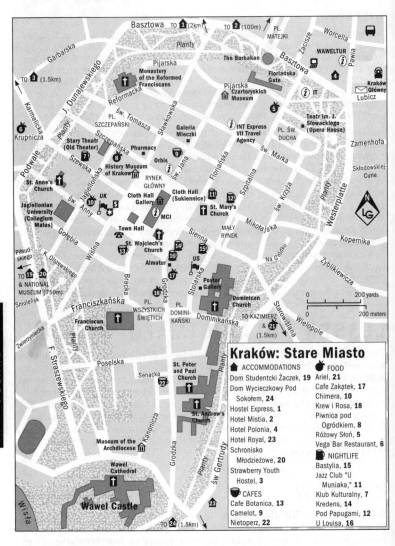

Kraków: Stare Miasto

ACCOMMODATIONS
Dom Studentcki Żaczek, **19**
Dom Wycieczkowy Pod
    Sokołem, **24**
Hostel Express, **1**
Hotel Mistia, **2**
Hotel Polonia, **4**
Hotel Royal, **23**
Schronisko
    Młodzieżowe, **20**
Strawberry Youth
    Hostel, **3**

CAFES
Cafe Botanica, **13**
Camelot, **9**
Nietoperz, **22**

FOOD
Ariel, **21**
Cafe Zakątek, **17**
Chimera, **10**
Krew i Rosa, **18**
Piwnica pod
    Ogródkiem, **8**
Różowy Słoń, **5**
Vega Bar Restaurant, **6**

NIGHTLIFE
Bastylia, **15**
Jazz Club "U
    Muniaka," **11**
Klub Kulturalny, **7**
Kredens, **14**
Pod Papugami, **12**
U Louisa, **16**

✈ INTERCITY TRANSPORTATION

Flights: Balice airport, ul. Kapitana Medweckiego 1 (☎411 19 55, ticket office 411 67 00; airport@lotnisko-balice.pl), 15km west of the center. Connected to the main train station by northbound **bus** #192 or 208 (40min.). A taxi to the center costs 30-50zł. Major carriers include Austrian Airlines, British Airways, LOT, and Swissair. Open daily 4am-midnight. **INT Express Travel Agency,** ul. św. Marka 25 (☎423 04 97; fax 421 79 06), books tickets on most airlines. Open M-F 8am-6pm, Sa 9am-2pm.

POLAND

Trains: Kraków Główny, pl. Kolejowy 1 (☎624 54 39, info 624 15 35). To: **Gdańsk** (destination "Gdynia"; 6½hr., 6 per day, 44-77zł); **Poznań** (6hr., 6 per day, 60zł); **Warsaw** (3hr., 34 per day, 51zł); **Zakopane** (5hr., 5 per day, 17-28zł); **Bratislava, SLK** (8hr., 1 per day, 95-135zł); **Budapest, HUN** (11hr., 1 per day, 114-1631zł); **Kyiv, UKR** (22hr., 1 per day, 200zł); **Lviv, UKR** (12½hr., 2 per day, 101zł) via **Odessa, UKR; Prague, CZR** (9hr., 1 per day, 100-160zł); **Vienna, AUS** (8½hr., 2 per day, 116-164zł).

Buses: Ul. Worcella (☎93 16), across from Kraków Główny. Open 5am-11pm. To: **Warsaw** (5hr., 3 per day, 40zł) and **Zakopane** (2hr., 33 per day, 10zł). **Sindbad,** in the main hall, sells international tickets. (☎421 02 40. Open M-F 8am-5:30pm, Sa 9am-2pm.) To: **Budapest, HUN** (11hr., 2 per week, 116zł); **Lviv, UKR** (10hr., 1 per day, 50zł); **Prague, CZR** (11hr., 3 per week, 139zł); **Vienna, AUS** (9hr., 7 per week, 100zł). **Polski Express** (☎022 620 03 30) buses depart from outside the PKS bus station. To: **Katowice** (1½hr, 3 per day, 19zł) and **Warsaw** (8hr., 2 per day, 45zł).

✴ ORIENTATION

For both tourists and locals, the true heart of the city remains the huge **Rynek Główny** (Main Marketplace), located in the center of **Stare Miasto** (Old Town). Stare Miasto is encircled by the **Planty** gardens and, a bit farther out, by a ring of roads that includes **Basztowa, Dunajewskiego, Podwale,** and **Westerplatte.** Just south of the Rynek Główny looms the gigantic **Wawel Castle** (see **Sights,** p. 507). The **Wisła** (VEE-swa) river snakes past the castle and borders the old Jewish village of **Kazimierz,** which is accessible from the *rynek* via ul. Starowiślna. The **bus** and **train** stations are located northeast of Old Town. A large, well-marked (and well-kiosked) underpass cuts beneath the road ring and into the Planty gardens; from there a number of paths cut into the *rynek* (10min.). Turn left from the train station and right from the bus station to reach the underpass.

▐ LOCAL TRANSPORTATION

Public Transportation: Buy tickets at kiosks near **bus** and **tram** stops (2.20zł) or on board (2.50zł) and punch them on board. Large backpacks need their own tickets. Night buses (from 11pm) 4zł. Day pass 9zł; weekly 22zł. 66zł fine if you're caught ticketless, 44zł if your bag is. Foreigners are fined frequently, so be sure your ticket is in order. Student fares for Poles only (though a good accent has been known to work).

Taxis: Cabs that display a call sign and phone number offer the most reasonable fares. Local companies include: **Barbakan Taxi** (☎96 61, toll-free 0800 400 400); **Euro Taxi** (☎96 64); **Express Taxi** (☎96 29); **Radio Taxi** (☎919); **Wawel Taxi** (☎96 66).

▐ PRACTICAL INFORMATION

TOURIST AND FINANCIAL SERVICES

Tourist Office: MCI (Małopolskie Centrum Informacji), Rynek Główny 1/3 (☎421 77 06; fax 421 30 36; info@mcit.pl; www.mcit.pl), in the middle of the square by the Cloth Hall. The knowledgeable, multilingual staff sells maps and the incredibly handy guide *Kraków in Your Pocket* (5zł, English version 10zł). 4hr. guided English tour of Kraków 280zł. Open May-Sept. M-F 9am-8pm, Sa 9am-3pm; Oct.-Apr. M-F 9am-6pm.

Budget Travel: Orbis, Rynek Główny 41 (☎422 40 35; fax 422 28 85; incoming@orbis.krakow.pl; www.orbis.krakow.pl). Sells domestic and international train tickets and arranges trips to the Wieliczka salt mines and Auschwitz (115zł, students 85zł). The staff also **exchanges currency, cashes traveler's checks,** and issues **cash advances.** Open M-F 9am-6pm, Sa 9am-2pm, Su 10am-2pm. AmEx/MC/V. **Almatur,** ul. Grodzka 2 (☎422 46 68; fax 428 45 20, www.almatur.pl) sells **ISIC** cards. English spoken. Open M-F 9am-6pm, Sa 10:30am-2pm.

Consulates: UK, św. Anny 9 (☎421 70 30; fax 422 42 64; ukconsul@bci.krakow.pl), 4th fl. Open M-F 9am-2pm. **US,** ul. Stolarska 9 (☎429 66 55, emergency 429 66 58; fax 421 8292; www.usconsulate.krakow.pl). Open M-F 8:30am-5pm.

Currency Exchange: *Kantory* (currency exchange), except those around the train station, have the best rates. **Bank PKO S.A.,** Rynek Główny 31 (☎422 60 22), cashes **traveler's checks** for 1-2% commission (10zł minimum) and gives MC/V **cash advances.** Open M-F 8am-6pm, Sa 9am-2pm. The **Forum Hotel,** ul. M. Konopnickiej 28 (☎261 92 12), has a **24hr. currency exchange.** There are **ATMs** all over the city.

American Express: Rynek Główny 41 (☎422 91 80), in the Orbis office (see above). Open Apr.-Oct. M-F 8:30am-6pm, Sa 9am-2pm, Su 10am-2pm; Nov.-Mar. M-F 9am-6pm, Sa 9am-1pm.

LOCAL SERVICES

Luggage Storage: At the train station. 1% of value per day plus 3.90zł for the first day and 2zł per bag for each additional day. Open 24hr.

English-Language Bookstore: Szawal, ul. Krupnicza 3 (☎421 53 61). Open M-F 10am-6pm, Sa 10am-2pm.

Laundromat: Ul. Piastowska 47 (☎622 31 81), in the basement of **Hotel Piast** (see **Accommodations,** below). 3hr. drop-off. Wash 9zł; dry 9zł. Open Tu, Th, Sa noon-6pm. **Betty Clean,** ul. Długa 17 (☎632 67 87), past the end of ul.Sławkowska. More of a dry cleaner than a laundromat, but the staff will clean all sorts of garments. Shirt 8.50zł, sweater 9zł, pants 12zł, nun's habit 20zł. Express service (6hr.) and super-express service (3hr.) available. Open M-F 9am-7:30pm, Sa 9am-2pm.

EMERGENCY AND COMMUNICATIONS

Pharmacy: Apteka Pod Zółtym Tygrysem (Under the Golden Tiger), Szczepańska 1 (☎422 92 93), just off Rynek Główny. Posts a weekly list of 24hr. pharmacies in its window. Open M-F 8am-8pm, Sa 8am-3pm.

Medical Assistance: Medicover, ul. Krótka 1 (☎422 76 33; after-hours emergency 430 00 34; fax 429 43 05). English-speaking staff can help you navigate the Polish medical system. Ambulance services available. Open M-F 8am-8pm, Sa 9am-2pm.

Telephones: At the post office (see below) and opposite the train station. Open 24hr. **Telekomunikacja Polska,** Rynek Główny 19 (☎429 17 11) sells phone cards. Open M-F 8am-10pm, Sa-Su 10am-10pm.

Internet Access: ◼ **Enter Internet Cafe,** ul. Basztowa 23/1 (☎429 42 25). 8am-11am 1.5zł per hr, 1zł per 30min., 0.5zł per 15min.; 11am-10pm, 3zł/2zł/1.50zł. Free tea. Open daily 8am-10pm. **Cafe Internet,** ul. Sienna 14 (☎431 23 94). 5zł per hr. Open Su-Th 9am-2am, F-Sa 24hr. **Club U Louisa,** Rynek Główny 13 (☎431 18 22). 5zł per hr. Open daily 10am-midnight.

Post Office: Ul. Lubicz 4. Go to one of the many *kasy* to send packges and letters and purchase stamps. **Poste Restante** at counter #5. Open M-F 7am-8pm; Sa 8am-2pm, and 2pm-4pm/8pm depending on service needed.

Postal Code: 31-075.

⌐ ACCOMMODATIONS AND CAMPING

Reservations are a good idea year-round, and are necessary in the summer. Call at least a few days ahead. **Waweltur ❸,** ul. Pawia 8 (☎422 16 40; fax 422 19 21), arranges **private rooms.** (Open M-F 8am-8pm, Sa 8am-2pm. Singles 75zł; doubles 118zł; triples 160zł. Stays over 1 week: singles 64zł; doubles 107zł.) Locals also rent rooms, though they vary wildly in quality; watch for signs and solicitors in the train station. **University dorms** open up in July and August. A few are listed below, but another worth checking is the **Strawberry Youth Hostel,** ul. Racławicka 9, which opens its doors in July and August. (☎636 15 00; www.strawberryhostel.com.)

HOSTELS AND DORMITORIES

▧ **Hostel Express,** ul. Wrocławska 91 (☎/fax 633 88 62; express.91@rodan.net). From the train station, take bus #130 five stops (10min.), walk half a block down the street, and turn right uphill. Travelers are lured here by the spacious bungalows, as well as sparkling baths, common rooms with TV, kitchens, and washing machines (7zł per load). Beware of the noisy train stop nearby. Friendly, English-speaking staff. Free storage. Reception 24hr. Check-in 3pm. Check-out 10am. No curfew. 6-bed dorms 29zł; doubles 70zł; triples 99zł. MC/V. ❶

Dom Wycieczkowy Pod Sokołem (Vacation Home Under the Falcon), ul. Sokolska 17 (☎292 01 99; ☎/fax 292 01 98; sokoldw@inetia.pl), across the river from Kazimierz. Take tram #8 or 10 from the train station towards "Łagiewniki" and get off at "Korona," the 1st stop after the bridge. Backtrack toward the river, then head down the stairs just before the bridge and take a left on ul. Sokolska. The hostel will be on your left. 12 extraordinarily clean rooms. Check-in noon. Check-out 10am. No curfew. Prices based on number of residents in one room: doubles 80zł; triples 110zł; quads 130zł; quints 145zł; sextets 165zł; septuplets 180zł; octets 206zł. ❷

Schronisko Młodzieżowe (HI), ul. Oleandry 4 (☎633 88 22). From the train station, take tram #15 toward "Cichy Kącik" and get off at "Cracovia," just after the National Museum. 15min. by foot from the center. Walk down Krupnicza, cross Mickiewicza, and turn left on Oleandry. The building will be on your right. This Socialist-era building has 350 cheap, mostly bunked beds in a good location. Caters to school groups, but plenty of backpackers pass through. Kitchenette and TV room. English spoken. Linen 2zł. Reception 6pm-noon. Flexible lockout 10am-5pm. Curfew midnight. 1- to 3-bed dorms 32zł; 4- to 5-bed dorms 28zł; 6- to 8-bed dorms 24zł; 8+ bed 20zł. ❶

Dom Studencki Żaczek, ul. 3-go Maja 5 (☎622 11 42; www.zaczek.com.pl). See directions for the Schronisko Młodzieżowe, above. By foot, walk down Piłsudskiego to the corner of Mickiewicza; building on your right just beyond the National Museum. Excellent location makes up for the noisy basement disco. 35 rooms open year-round, 350 in summer, except when they host visiting conferences; call ahead. Check-in 2pm. Check-out 10am. Singles 75zł, with bath 95zł; doubles 85zł/150zł; triples 105zł/165zł; quads 120zl; quints with bath 225zł. ❸

HOTELS

Hotel Royal, ul. Sw Gertrudy 26-29 (☎421 58 57; www.royal.com.pl). From the train station, take tram #10 toward "Łagiewniki" and get off at "Wawel." The hotel is on your right. Situated on the *planty gardens* and across the street from Wawel Castle and Cathedral, this 1898 hotel offers an excellent location and spotless, comfortable rooms. English spoken. Reception 24hr. Check-in and check-out 3pm. Wheelchair accessible. Singles 180-210zł; doubles 220-375zł; triples 360zł; quads 400zł. Single apartment 400zł; double 450zł. AmEx/MC/V. ❺

Hotel Polonia, ul. Basztowa 25 (☎422 12 33; fax 422 16 21; www.hotel-polonia.com.pl). Across from the train station. These elegant rooms are convenient if you arrive too early or late to check into more affordable accommodations. Reception 24hr. Check-in 2pm. Check-out noon. Singles 99zł, with bath 251zł; doubles 119zł/285zł; triples 139zł/329zł; quads 140zł. MC/V. ❹

Hotel Mistia, ul. Szlak 73a (☎633 29 26; fax 633 51 54; www.mistia.org.pl), corner of ul. Warszawska. Housed in an administrative building, this basic hotel won't impress you with decor or perks, but it has a great location: 10min. from the center and 5min. from the train station. Check-in 2pm. Check-out 10am. Singles with bath 150zł; doubles with sink 132zł, with bath 180zł; bed in a double 98zł; triples with bath 200zł. MC/V. ❹

🖸 FOOD

The restaurants and cafes on and around the *rynek* satisfy Kraków's huge tourist population. Grocery stores surround the bus and train stations and dot the city center. For less than a złoty, street vendors sell *obwarzanki*, round soft pretzels (get them fresh before they harden) with sesame seeds, poppy seeds, or salt. Any *bar mleczny* (milk bar) provides a hearty, inexpensive dose of Polish fare. Good ones are **Bar Mleczny Barcelona,** ul. Piłsudskiego 1 (open M-F 8am-6pm, Sa 8am-4pm) and **Pod Temidą,** Grodzka 43 (open daily 9am-9pm).

🖾 Cafe Zakątek, Grodzka 2 (☎429 57 25). This tiny *zakątek* (niche) provides sanctuary from the bustling *rynek*. Rub elbows with regulars and look through the vinyl records from Armstrong to ABBA while eating a fresh sandwich prepared just how you like it. Sandwiches 3zł, large 4.5zł; salads 3zł; breakfast 7zł. Open M-Sa 8:30am-8pm. ❶

🖾 Chimera, ul. św. Anny 3 (☎423 21 78). Sit downstairs in the cellar or, in summer, in the romantic ivy garden of the oldest and most famous salad joint in town. Huge sampler of 6 of their 29 cruciferous creations 10zł; smaller plate of 4 for 7zł. Live lyre music some nights 8pm. Open M-Sa 9am-11pm, Su 9am-10pm. ❷

Różowy Słoń (Pink Elephant), ul. Szpitalna 38 (☎422 14 16), near the train station, just opposite the giant Teatr Słowackiego. **Branches** at ul. Sienna 1 and ul. Straszewskiego 24. Batman speaks Polish! Or at least he does in the comic book murals on the walls of these popular, convenient fast food joints. Full meals—from Polish to pizza—under 5zł. Open M-Sa 9am-9pm, Su 10am-9pm. ❶

Vega Bar Restaurant, ul. Krupnicza 22 (☎430 08 46). The earthenware jugs and blue mosaic trim set the mood for munching on salads, soups, and vegetarian Polish cuisine (2-5zł). 36 varieties of tea 2.50zł. Open daily 9am-11pm. MC/V. **Branch** at ul. św. Gertrudy 7 (☎422 34 94). Open daily 10am-9pm. MC/V. ❶

Piwnica Pod Ogródkiem (Cellar Under the Garden), ul. Jagiellońska 6 (☎292 07 63; arton@kr.onet.pl). This subterranean restaurant puts a Polish twist on an old French favorite, serving nearly 30 varieties of crepe, from savory to sweet (8-12zł). Outdoor garden open June-Aug. Beer 6zł. 18+. Open daily noon-midnight, longer some weekend nights when there's music and disco. MC/V. ❷

Ariel, ul. Szeroka 18 (☎/fax 421 79 20), in the old Jewish district of Kazimierz, a 15min. walk south of the *rynek*. Elegant, antique interior full of paintings and hand-crafted dolls, with a creative, non-kosher mix of Polish and Jewish cuisine (8-35zł). English menu available. Jewish music nightly 8pm (cover 20zł). Open daily 9am-midnight. ❷

Krew i Roza, ul. Grodzka 9 (☎429 61 87; fax 429 60 17; krewroza@restauracja.com). This 15th century-style cellar restaurant serves up regional Polish cuisine, including wild game and roasted pork. Sit inside or in the garden and enjoy the live minstrel music performed F-Su. Entrees 20-70zł. Open daily noon-midnight. AmEx/MC/V. ❹

◪ CAFES

▩ **Camelot,** ul. Św. Tomasza 17 (☎421 01 23). One of Old Town's legends. Full of original paintings, soothing jazz, and the occasional 17th-century document. Sandwiches 3-6zł; salads 19-21zł; breakfast—including muesli with fresh fruit—9zł. Coffee 6-11zł. Music or cabaret W and F 8pm. Open daily 9am-midnight.

▩ **Nietoperz** (The Bat), ul. Senacka 7 (☎431 18 27). Wicker decor and dried flowers create an intimate woodsy atmosphere, perfect for a relaxing evening near Wawel. No, the parrot doesn't talk. Small dessert selection 3.50-5zł, Żywiec 6zl. Open M-Th 9am-midnight, F-Sa 10am-1am, Su 10am-midnight.

Cafe Botanica, ul. Bracka 9 (☎422 89 80). Metal vines and flower-bud lamps adorn this cafe, distinguishing it from the traditional *rynek* locale. Sip coffee or tea (3-8zł) or devour dessert (4.50-12zł). Open M-Sa 8:30am-11pm, Su 10am-10pm.

◎ SIGHTS

▩ WAWEL CASTLE AND CATHEDRAL

☎422 61 21; fax 422 16 97. *Castle* open Tu and F 9:30am-4:30pm, W-Th and Sa 9:30am-3pm, Su 10am-3pm. *Cathedral* open Apr.-Oct. M-Sa 9am-5:15pm, Su 12:15-5:15pm; Nov.-Mar. daily 9am-3:15pm. *Cathedral Museum* (Muzeum Katedralne) open Tu-Su 10am-3pm. *Dragon's Den* open May-Oct. daily 10am-5pm. *Royal chambers* Apr.-Oct. 15zł, students 12zł; Nov.-Mar. 12zł/10zł; *treasury and armory* 12zł/7zł; 10zł/6zł; *Oriental Collection* 6zł/4zł; 5zł/3zł; cathedral *tombs* and *Sigismund's bell* 6zł/3zł; *cave* 3zł. All Castle exhibits free M. Gates to Wawel open May-Sept. 6am-8pm; Oct.-Apr. 6am-5pm. English tours available (☎/fax 429 33 36); price varies with number of sights and size of the group. Call ahead. Enter all exhibits from the courtyard. English info and tickets to all buildings except the cathedral are available at the main kasa (window; open M 9:15-11:45am, Tu and F 9:15am-3:45pm, W-Th and Sa 9:15am-2:45pm, Su 9:45am-2:45pm). 10 tickets are dished out every 10min. to control the crowds, so you may have to wait. Cathedral **tickets** for sale at the kasa across the sidewalk from the cathedral entrance. Allow 1-4hr. to visit Wawel.

WAWEL CASTLE. One of the finest architectural works in Poland, the **Wawel Castle** (Zamek Wawelski) and Cathedral (Katedra) complex—arguably *the* sight to see in Poland—lies at the heart of the country's history and tradition. Begun in the 10th century but remodeled during the 1500s, the castle contains 71 chambers and a magnificent sequence of 16th-century tapestries commissioned by the royal family. Five different exhibits are offered, accessible from the **Dziedziniec** (Castle Courtyard). See the family's treasures in the **Komnaty** (State Rooms) and **Apartamenty** (Royal Private Apartments). The **Skarbiec** (Treasury and Armory), a paradise for the military-minded, features historical swords, spears, armor, guns, and cannons galore. The star of the collection is *Szczerbiec*, the coronation sword that touched newly-royal shoulders from 1230 to 1734. The **Oriental Collection** has an amazing display of 16th- to 19th-century porcelain from China and Japan, as well the spoils of battles the Poles fought with Turks near Vienna. Outside the castle courtyard, the **Lost Wawel** exhibit, which winds through archaeological digs, details the evolution of Wawel Hill, which was settled as early as the Stone Age.

WAWEL CATHEDRAL. Poland's monarchs were crowned and buried in the **Wawel Cathedral** (Katedra Wawelska), next to the castle. Back when he was still Archbishop Karol Wojtyla, Pope John Paul II was a member of the clergy here (see **Sights: Museum of the Archdiocese,** p. 509) The chapels that circle the cathedral house the ornate tombs of many kings. Note St. Jadwiga's miraculous crucifix on the far left as you enter—it is believed that the young queen asked whether she

P O L A N D

should marry King Ladislaus Jagiełło of Lithuania (who now rests in the first tomb on your right as you enter, not in a chapel). The crucifix spoke to the pious future queen and advised her to marry. Along with the union of the couple came the unification of their respective countries in 1386; much later, in 1997, Jadwiga was canonized. The splendid sarcophagus of King Kazimierz Jagiełłończyk was crafted by Wit Stwosz, who also designed the altar in **St. Mary's Church** (see p. 508). St. Maurice's spear, presented by German Emperor Otto III in 1000 to the Polish prince Bolesław Chrobry, commemorates a time of Polish-German friendship.

CATHEDRAL SIGHTS. Steep wooden stairs inside lead up to **Sigismund's Bell** (Dwon Zygmunta). The climb affords a great view of Kraków—and of the gargantuan ringer. Touch it for good luck or for a good spouse. Outside the Lipskich chapel, the underground **crypts** on your left as you enter house the resting places of poets Juliusz Słowacki and Adam Mickiewicz (see **The Arts,** p. 479). Enter the **tombs** through the Czartoryskich Chapel; this underground maze contains the graves of royals and a few outstanding military leaders, including heroic generals Józef Piłsudski, Tadeusz Kościuszko, and Stanisław Poniatowski (see **History,** p. 474). The small **Cathedral Museum** (Muzeum Katedralne) showcases selections from the Cathedral's treasury, including Papal gifts from Pope John Paul II and 18th-century popes. Exquisite embroidered textiles and a gold rose are on display.

DRAGON'S DEN. The entrance to Dragon's Den (Smocza Jama), residence of Kraków's erstwhile menace, is in the southwest corner of the complex. Legend has it that the dragon held the people of Kraków in terror until a clever young shepherd set a fake sheep full of sulfur outside its cave. Upon devouring the booby-trap, the troublesome reptile got so thirsty that it drank water from the Wisła until it burst. The cave opens onto the banks of the Wisła. It's a one-way trip so don't descend unless you're ready to leave. Or skip the cave to see the real treat, a fire-breathing sculpture of the dragon, on the banks of the Wisła below.

STARE MIASTO

At the center of the Stare Miasto spreads **Rynek Główny**, surrounded by beautiful, multi-colored row houses and replete with cafes, bars, pedestrians, and pigeons. It's a convenient central point for exploring the nearby sights.

JAGIELLONIAN UNIVERSITY. (Uniwersytet Jagielloński.) Over 600 years old, **Collegium Maius** of Kraków's Jagiellonian University ranks as the second oldest institution of higher learning in Eastern Europe (after Prague's Charles University). Astronomer Mikołaj Kopernik (Copernicus) and painter Jan Matejko are among its noted alumni. Tours of the Treasury, Assembly Hall, Library, and Commons start every 20min. Highlights include the oldest known globe showing the Americas: look for them near Madagascar. *(Ul. Jagiellonska 15. ☎422 05 49. Walk down sw. Anny in the corner of the rynek near the Town Hall and turn left onto Jagiellonska. Tours in English available by request. Open M-F 11am-2:20pm, Sa 11am-1:20pm. University Museum (30min.) 8zł, students 5zł; all rooms (60min.) 15zł/10zł; Sa free.)*

ST. MARY'S CHURCH. (Kościół Mariacki.) Deep blues and golds accent the black marble columns of the church's ornate interior. Vividly-colored walls surround the centerpiece of this famous cathedral, an amazing 500-year-old wooden altar carved by Wit Stwosz that portrays the joy and suffering of St. Mary. This gorgeous artifact, **the oldest Gothic altar in the world,** barely survived World War II. Dismantled by the Nazis, it was rediscovered by Allied forces at the war's end and only reassembled some time later. Every hour, the blaring *Hejnał* trumpet calls from the towers and cuts off abruptly, recalling the destruction of Kraków in 1241 when the invading Tatars shot down the trumpeter. The dissimilar towers also stand as monuments to ancient sibling rivalry. Built by two very different brothers, all was well until the hasty brother realized that the work of his careful sibling would put his own to shame and killed the meticulous craftsman in a fit of jealousy. However, overwhelmed with guilt, he mounted his own tower, publicly confessed to the murder, and stabbed himself with the same knife. The murder weapon is on display in the Cloth Hall. *(At the corner of the* rynek *closest to the train station. No photography. Covered shoulders and knees expected. Open daily 11:30am-6pm. Icon unveiled daily M-F 11:50am-6pm, Su and holidays 2-6pm. Altar 4zl, students 2zl. Video camera 5zl.)*

CLOTH HALL. (Sukiennice.) In the middle of the *rynek*, the yellow Italianate Cloth Hall remains as profit-oriented now as when cloth merchants actually used it: the ground floor is lined with wooden stalls hawking Krakoviana. Upstairs, the **Cloth Hall Gallery,** part of the National Museum (see below), houses a gallery of 18th- and 19th-century Polish sculptures and paintings. Of the many pastoral and military depictions, the most striking and famous are Jan Matejko's *Hołd Pruski,* Józef Chełmoński's *Four in Hand,* and Henryk Siemiradzki's enormous *Nero's Torches.* During the academic year, students cruise the area between Cloth Hall and St. Mary's and await their friends under the statue of **Adam Mickiewicz,** Poland's most celebrated Romantic poet. *(Cloth Hall ☎422 11 66. Open Tu-W and F-Su 10am-3:30pm, Th 10am-6pm. Last admission 30min. before closing. 7zl, students 4zl; Su free.)*

ROYAL ROAD. (Droga Królewska.) In medieval times, royals traversed this route on the way to coronations in Wawel. Today, it makes for a good, sight-packed walk through the city center. The route starts at the Barbakan (close to the train station) and runs through Floriańska Gate, the old entrance to the city and the only surviving remnant of the city wall, down ul. Floriańska to the *rynek*. The Barbakan and the Gate are the only remnants of the city's medieval fortifications, most of which were knocked down to make room for the Planty gardens. Inside the **Barbakan,** information in Polish and English along the walls chronicles the city's history. *(Open May-Oct. daily 10am-5pm. 4zł, students 2.5zł.)* On the south side of the *rynek*, the Royal route continues from the corner of *rynek* closest to the small St. Wojciech's Church (Kościół św. Wojciecha) along ul. Grodzka and the parallel Ul. Kanonicza. Many of its houses date from the 14th century. Near the end of the road, close to Wawel, is the **Museum of the Archdiocese** (Muzeum Archidiecezjalne). It is located in the building where Karol Wojtyla was archbishop of Kraków from 1951 to 1967, at which point he became Pope John Paul II in 1967. The one-room museum is well worth a visit for its furniture, its collections of sacred art, and its old typewriter, whose keys were once tapped by the Pope himself. *(Ul. Kanonicza 19/21. ☎421 89 63; fax 422 75 23; muzeumkra@diecezja.krakow.pl. Open Tu-F 10am-4pm, Sa-Su 10am-3pm. 5zl, students 3zl.)*

CZARTORYSKICH MUSEUM. Among other masterpieces, this branch of the National Museum displays Leonardo da Vinci's *Lady with an Ermine* and Rembrandt's *Landscape with a Merciful Samaritan.* Read a batch of letters written by Copernicus or peer into a Turkish ceremonial tent captured at the Battle of Vienna. Most of the exhibits came from the holdings of the well-educated Czartoryscy family. *(Ul. sw. Jana 19, runs parallel to ul. Florianska. From Rynek, head to the end of the street; the museum will be on the right. ☎422 55 66. Open Tu-Th and Su 10am-3pm, F-Sa 11am-5pm. Closed 3rd Su of every month. Last admission 30min. before closing. Cameras without flash 15zł. 7zł, students 4zł; Su free.)*

OTHER SIGHTS. The main branch of the **National Museum** has an excellent permanent exhibition on 20th-century Polish art and usually hosts one acclaimed temporary exhibition at a time. *(Al. 3 Maja 1 ☎634 33 77; www.muz-nar.krakow.pl. The museum is housed in the imposing building at the intersection of Józefa Pilsudskiego and Mickiewicza, across from Hotel Cracovia. Tram #15 goes to "Cracovia" from the train station. Open Tu and Th*

9am-3:30pm, W and F 11am-6pm, Sa-Su 10am-3:30pm. 8zł, students 5zł. MC/V.) The **History Museum of Kraków**, Rynek Główny 35, another branch of the National Museum, displays original ceiling frescoes and a variety of centuries-old documents from Kraków, as well as religious and military artifacts amid its rotation of temporary exhibits. *(☎422 99 22. Open W and F-Su 9am-3:30pm, Th 11am-6pm. Closed the second Sa and Su each month. 4zł, students 3zł; Sa free.)* The 🍀 **Franciscan Church** features vibrant colors and the amazing contemporary stained-glass window *God the Father* by Stanisław Wyspiański. *(pl. Wszystkich Świętych 5. ☎422 53 76; tours 422 71 15; www.semkrak.franciszkanie.pl. Call ahead to prevent a visit during one of the many daily masses. Open daily until 7:30pm. Free English tours available; donations encouraged).* For something more funky, visit the **Poster Gallery** for a glimpse of hundreds of Kraków-printed *plakaty. (Ul. Stolarska 8 ☎421 26 40. Open Su-F 11am-6pm, Sa 11am-2pm. AmEx/MC/V.)* **Galeria Autorska Andrzeja Mleczki,** simultaneously a store and gallery, is full of items decorated with the creations of renowned satirical cartoonist Andrzej Mleczko. *(Ul. Sw. Jana 14. Open M-F 11am-7pm, Sa 11am-4pm.)*

KAZIMIERZ: THE OLD JEWISH QUARTER

Kazimierz is southeast of the rynek and Wawel. Take tram #3, 13, or 24 towards "Bieżanow Nowy" from the train station and get off by the post office at the intersection of ul. Miodowa and Starowislna. Ul. Szeroka runs parallel to Starowislna, on the right if you're looking in the same direction as the tram. The 15min. walk from the rynek leads down ul. Sienna past St. Mary's Church. Eventually, ul. Sienna turns into Starowislna. After 1km, turn right on Miodowa and take the 1st left onto Szeroka. Open M-F 9am-6pm, Sa-Su 10am-6pm. Kazimierz tour 25zl per person, with ghetto 30zl; Schindler's List sights 45zl; Auschwitz 90zl, private tour 120zl. Discounts for students (20%) and groups larger than 8. Tours in English. AmEx/MC/V.)

South of the Stare Miasto lies Kazimierz, Kraków's 600-year-old Jewish quarter. Founded in 1335, Kazimierz was originally a separate town and was only linked directly to Małopolska's capital in 1495, when King Jan Olbrecht moved Kraków's Jews there in order to remove them from the city proper. On the eve of World War II, 68,000 Jews lived in the Kraków area—40,000 of them in Kazimierz—until occupying Nazis forced most of them out. The 15,000 remaining were resettled in the overcrowded Podgórze ghetto in 1941. All were deported by March 1943, many to the nearby Płaszów and Auschwitz-Birkenau concentration camps. While only about 100 practicing Jews now live here, Kazimierz today is a focal point for the 5000 Jews still living in Poland. The **Jarden Bookstore,** ul. Szeroka 2 (☎429 13 74; jarden@nova.kki.krakow.pl), organizes tours, including a two-hour tour of Kazimierz and the Płaszów concentration camp that traces the sites shown in the film *Schindler's List.* Płaszów, located in the south of Kraków, was completely destroyed by the Nazis on their retreat and is now an overgrown field.

OLD SYNAGOGUE. (Stara Synagoga.) A fine example of Jewish architecture, the Old Synagogue houses a museum depicting the history, traditions, and art of Kraków's Jews. Beautiful sacred art spans several centuries, while helpful information boards printed in Polish and English explain Jewish terminology and customs. *(Ul. Szeroka 24. ☎422 09 62; fax 431 05 45. Open Apr. 8-Oct. 13 Tu-Su 9am-5pm; Oct. 14-Apr. 7 W-Th 9am-3pm, F 11am- 6pm, Sa-Su 9am-3pm. Closed the 1st Sa-Su and open the 1st M of every month (free). 6zł, students 4zł.)*

REMUH SYNAGOGUE AND CEMETERY. The tiny Remuh Synagogue was established in 1553. The small, beautiful cemetery that surrounds it holds graves dating back to the plague of 1551-52. The 20m wall on your right as you enter—composed of tombstones recovered in 1959 after being scattered and shattered during the Nazi occupation—is a particularly moving sight. *(Ul. Szeroka 40. Open M-F 9am-4pm. 5zł, students 2zł. Services F at sundown and Sa morning.)*

CENTER FOR JEWISH CULTURE. The center, in the former Bene Emenu prayer house, was opened in November 1993 to organize cultural events, preserve the current Jewish culture in Kazimierz, and arrange heritage tours. *(Rabina Meiselsa 17, just off pl. Nowy. ☎ 430 64 49; fax 430 64 97; www.judaica.pl. Open M-F 10am-6pm, Sa-Su 10am-2pm. Closed Jewish holidays.)*

ISAAC'S SYNAGOGUE. (Synagoga Izaaka.) Haunting photographs from the permanent exhibit, "Memory of Polish Jews," are scattered throughout this 17th century synagogue. The synagogue also holds concerts and shows documentary films depicting Jewish life in Kazimierz before and after the Nazi occupation. *(Ul. Kupa 18. ☎ 430 55 77; fax 602 144 262. Open Su-F 9am-7pm. 7zł, students 6zł. Photos 10zł.)*

🎵 🎤 ENTERTAINMENT AND FESTIVALS

MCI (see **Practical Information,** p. 503) offers monthly brochures on cultural activities. The **Cultural Information Center,** ul. św. Jana 2 (☎ 421 77 87; fax 421 77 31), sells the monthly guide *Karnet* (3zł; www.karnet.krakow2000.pl) and tickets for upcoming events. (Open M-F 10am-6pm, Sa 10am-4pm.) Festivals abound in Kraków, particularly in summer. Notable among them are the **International Short Film Festival** (late May), the **Floating of Wreaths on the Wisła** (June), the **Festival of Jewish Culture** (early July), the **Street Theater Festival** (early July), and the **Jazz Festival** (Oct.-Nov.).

The city jumps with jazz; catch a good set at **Indigo,** ul. Floriańska 26 (☎/fax 429 17 43), **U Muniaka,** ul. Floriańska 3 (☎ 432 12 05), or **Harris Piano Jazz Bar,** Rynek Główny 28 (☎ 421 57 41; open daily 1pm-2am). Classical music buffs will appreciate the performances at **Sala Filharmonia** (Philharmonic Hall), ul. Zwierzyniecka 1. (☎ 422 94 77; www.filharmonia.krakow.pl. Box office open Tu-F 2-8pm, and Sa-Su 1hr. before performance. Closed June 9-Sept. 20.) The **opera** (www.opera.krakow.top.pl) performs at the **J. Słowacki Theater,** pl. Św. Ducha 1. (☎ 422 40 22; www.slowacki.krakow.pl. Box office open M-Sa 11am-2pm and 3-7pm, Su 2hr. before performance. Tickets 18-29zł, students 16-18zł.) The **Stary Teatr** has a few stages in the city. (Booking office at pl. Szczepański 1. ☎ 422 40 40; www.staryteatr.krakow.pl. Open Tu-F 8am-4pm, Sa 8am-1pm. Tickets 20-30zł, students 17-25zł.) Films in Poland are shown in their original language with Polish subtitles. Try **Kino Pod Baranani,** Rynek Główny 27 (☎ 423 07 68; tickets Tu-Th 14zł, students 12zł; F-Su 14zł, after 5pm 15zł), or **Kino Mikro,** ul. Lea 5 (☎ 634 28 97).

🎆 NIGHTLIFE

Kraków in Your Pocket, available at MCI and international bookstores, has up-to-date information on the *rynek* clubbing and pubbing scenes. For more info, see www.puby.krakow.pl. For tips about Kraków's **gay nightlife,** see http://gay-euro.com/krakow. The **Cocteau Gallery,** ul. Karmelicka 10, through the unmarked archway, is a quiet bar where gay men and a few women chat over a beer or coffee. (Beer 5zł. Open daily 7pm-4am.)

▨ **Pod Papugami** (Under the Parrots), ul. Mikołajska 2 (☎ 421 93 07). Laid-back disco with large booths and several conversation nooks. Beer 5zl. 18+. Cover F 8zl, ladies free; Sa 12zl. Open daily 7pm-3am.

▨ **Kredens,** Rynek Główny 20 (☎ 429 20 07). Convenient, casual, and packed with multinational partygoers who aren't too chic to sing along. *Żywiec* 6.60zł. Disco 10pm every night. 21+. Cover 5zł weekends. Open Su-W 4pm-2am, Th-Sa 4pm-4am.

Klub Kulturalny, ul. Szewska 25 (☎429 67 39; www.klubkulturalny.pl). Below ground and replete with blue lights and pulsing music. So hip it hurts. Maybe the gargoyle above the bar determines whether you pass the test? Beer 5.50zł. Open M-F noon-2am.

Bastylia, ul. Stolarska 3 (☎431 02 21). Storm the Bastille! 5 floors of brick pub grandeur. Mysterious doors line the brick walls; look through one of the peepholes for...a surprise. Beer 6.50zł. 18+. Open daily 3pm-3am. MC/V.

Jazz Club "U Muniaka," ul. Floriańska 3 (☎423 12 05). Run by renowned Polish jazz musician Janusz Muniak, this is the home of Kraków's jazz scene. Listen to Muniak jam with his friends. Wynton Marsalis played here once. Concerts M-W 10zł, Th-Sa 20zł. 50% student discount. Shows 9:30pm. Open F-Sa 3pm-1am, Su-W 3pm-midnight.

U Louisa, Rynek Główny 13 (☎431 18 22; www.louis.krakow.pl). This low-key pub draws a diverse crowd with funk and rock on weekends and a cyber cafe (see **Internet Access,** p. 504). Tasty *pierogi* and *naleśniki* (6-6.50zł) served late into the night. *Lech* 6zł. Live music on some weekends 9pm. Cover for shows 5zł. Open daily 10am-late.

◪ DAYTRIPS FROM KRAKÓW

AUSCHWITZ-BIRKENAU

Buses run to the town of Oświęcim from the central bus station. (1½hr., 10 per day, 7zł; get off at "Muzeum Oświęcim.") The bus back to Kraków leaves from a different stop across the parking lot. Trains leave from Kraków Główny (1¾hr., 3 per day, 8.70zł); times are inconvenient and trains may not be direct. More trains run from Kraków Płaszów. Tourist offices in Kraków organize trips that include transportation and knowledgeable guides. From outside the Oświęcim train station, buses #2-5, 8, 9, 24-29 drop visitors off at the "Muzeum Oświęcim" stop. By foot, turn right as you exit the station, go 1 block, and turn left onto ul. Więźniów Oświęcimia; the Auschwitz camp lies 1.6km down the road.

An estimated 1.5 million people, mostly Jews, were murdered, and thousands more suffered unthinkable horrors in the Nazi concentration camps at **Auschwitz** (Oświęcim) and **Birkenau** (Brzezinka). The largest and most brutally efficient of the death camps, their names are synonymous with the Nazi death machine. In 1979, the complexes were added to the UNESCO World Heritage List.

AUSCHWITZ I. This smaller camp was built by the Nazis in 1940 on the grounds of a Polish Army garrison. Ironically, the first transport consisted of 728 Polish political prisoners; Roma and Soviet POWs were killed here starting soon afterwards. In 1942, the Nazis began using the camp to systematically exterminate the European Jewish population. The eerily tidy rows of red brick buildings seem almost peaceful until the bitter irony of the inscription on the camp's gate—*Arbeit Macht Frei* (Work Makes You Free)—fully sinks in. As you walk through the barracks where the **museum** is housed, with nothing but a plate of glass between you and the remnants of thousands of lives—suitcases, shoes, glasses, and more than 45,360kg. of women's hair—the sheer enormity of the evil committed here comes into focus. Other rooms, such as the 2nd floor of Barrack 5, display horrifying details like the single pacifier atop a pile of children's clothing. At 11am and 1pm, the building through which visitors enter the grounds has an English-language showing of a 15min. **film** shot by the Soviet Army, who liberated the camp on January 27, 1945. Children under 14 are strongly advised not to visit the museum or view the film. *(☎843 20 22 or 843 20 77; fax 843 18 62. Open June-Aug. daily 8am-7pm; May and Sept. 8am-6pm; Apr. and Oct. 8am-5pm; Mar. and Nov.-Dec. 15 8am-4pm; Dec. 16-Feb. 8am-3pm. Film 2zł. Guided tour in English (3½hr.; daily 11:30am; 25zł, film included). English-language guidebook with maps 3zł. Free.)*

KEEPING FAITH It's difficult to visit the camps at Auschwitz and Birkenau without hearing the name of Maksymilian Kolbe, the priest who sacrificed his own life while he was a prisoner in Auschwitz. When another man was sentenced to death by starvation, Kolbe willingly took the man's place, submitting himself to even more ghastly torture than he was already enduring. He was able to keep up his strength and stave off death for two weeks, but then his efforts proved to be in vain—frustrated by how long it was taking to kill Kolbe, the Nazis shot him. After his death, Kolbe became a strong symbol within the Catholic Church of faith in the face of persecution: in 1971 he became the first Nazi victim to be proclaimed blessed by the Catholic Church, and was canonized by Pope John Paul II in 1982. The man whom Kolbe replaced, Franciszek Gajowniczek, lived to see not only the liberation of the camp, but also old age. He died in 1995. Kolbe's starvation cell (#18), located in barrack II of Auschwitz I, can be seen by visitors. A tribute to the priest lies inside.

AUSCHWITZ II-BIRKENAU. Konzentrationslager Auschwitz II-Birkenau lies 3km away from Auschwitz, and was built when massive numbers of Jews, Roma, Slavs, homosexuals, disabled people, and other "inferiors" were being brought to Auschwitz and a more "efficient" means of killing needed to be devised. Little is left of the camp as the Nazis attempted to destroy it to conceal the genocide before it was liberated by the Red Army on January 27, 1945. Endless rows of chimneys stretch across the grassy fields as haunting reminders of where the barracks once stood. The reconstructed railroad tracks run beneath the still-standing watch tower, gliding past the selection barrack where individuals were chosen for work. Ending between two gas chambers and crematoria, now nothing more than rubble, the morbid train made the first and final stop for the countless victims sent to the concentration camps. Just beyond the ruins, an international memorial pays tribute to those who died in the Auschwitz system. Near the monument lies a pond, still gray from the ashes deposited there a half century ago. *(Birkenau is a 3km walk away from Auschwitz I along a well-marked route. Between Apr. 15 and Oct. 31, a shuttle (1 per hr. 11:30am-5:30pm, 2zł) runs from the parking lot of the Auschwitz museum.)*

AUSCHWITZ JEWISH CENTER AND SYNAGOGUE. This new center, which is adjacent to the town's only surviving synagogue, serves as a starting point for people of Jewish descent. The regular exhibits focus on pre-war Jewish life in the town of Oświęcim, while the films center around survivors' testimonies. The knowledgeable, English-speaking staff provides guidance for those searching for family members from all over Europe. Resources available include a genealogy workroom and a reading room. Guides for Auschwitz available for hire. *(pl. Ks. Jana Skarbka 5, ☎33 844 70 02; fax 33 844 70 03; www.ajcf.org. Take bus #1, 3, 4, 5, 6, or 8 from the train station to the town center, get off at the first stop after the bridge, and backtrack to pl. Ks. Jana Skarbka; the Center will be on your right. Alternatively, take a taxi (about 15zł). Open Apr.-Sept. Su-F 8:30am-6pm, Oct.-Mar. Su-F 8:30am-8pm.)*

WIELICZKA

Ul. Daniłowicza 10. ☎278 73 66; www.kopalnia.pl. Many companies, including Orbis, organize trips to the mine. The cheapest way to go is to take one of the minibuses that leave from the road between the train and bus stations ("Lux-Bus" runs every 15min., 30min. 2zł). In Wieliczka, follow the old path of the tracks and then the "do kopalni" signs. Wheelchair accessible. Open Apr.-Oct. daily 7:30am-7:30pm; Nov.-March daily 8am-4pm. Closed Jan. 1; Easter Sunday; Nov. 4; Dec. 4, 24-26, and 31. Tours in Polish 30zł, students 15zł. English guide available 3 times per day in June, 5 times per day July-Aug. Foreign-language tour 35zł, students 25zł. MC/V.

POLAND

Thirteen kilometers southeast of Kraków and 100m below the tiny town of Wielic-zka, you'll find a ⬛**1000-year-old salt mine.** Centuries ago, miners and artists carved a complex of chambers, full of sculptures and carvings, entirely out of salt; in 1978, UNESCO declared the mine one of the 12 most priceless monuments in the world. The tour (2hr.) meanders past spectacular underground lakes. Favorite Poles, including Copernicus and Pope John Paul II, are immortalized in the sparkling salt, but the most spectacular sight is the breathtaking **Kinga's Chapel,** complete with chandeliers, an altar, and relief. At the end of the tour, take the lift 130m back to the surface or go to the **underground museum,** "Muzeum Żup Krakowskich," which gives a history of the mines and features 14 additional chambers (1hr. tours; 8zł, students 4zł, M free). It's possible to descend straight to the museum from ground level and bypass the tour. Take a sweater with you— it's cold in the depths.

LUBLIN   ☎ 0(81)

Lublin (LOO-bleen; pop. 400,000) can lull visitors with its picturesque skyline and quiet meandering streets, but residents know their city is anything but provincial. Long the birthplace of revolutionary social and religious movements, Małopolska's former capital served as the center of the Polish Reformation and Counter-Reformation in the 16th and 17th centuries. Later, the city housed the only independent institution of higher learning in the communist era, the Polish Catholic University. A bohemian atmosphere flourishes around the city's two universities and in the historic streets of the Old Town.

⌐ TRANSPORTATION

Trains: Pl. Dworcowy 1 (☎94 36). To: **Częstochowa** (6hr., 8 daily, 38.20zł); **Gdynia** via **Gdańsk** (7hr., 8 per day, 42-71zł); **Katowice** (6hr., 5 per day, 39.90zł); **Kraków** (4hr., 6 per day; 38.20zł, express 45zł); **Poznań** (8hr., 6 per day, 42.30zł); **Warsaw** (3hr., 8 per day, 29-57zł); **Wrocław** (8½hr., 8 per day, 41zł); **Zamość** (2½hr., 2 per day, 20zł); **Berlin, GER** (13hr., 1 per day, 157-193zł).

Buses: Ul. Tysiąclecia 4 (☎776 649, info 934). To: **Kraków** (6hr., 1 per day, 43zł); **Warsaw** (3hr., 2 per day, 12zł); **Wrocław** (8hr., 1 per day, 42zł); **Zamość** (2hr., 30 per day, 12zł). **Polski Express** (☎620 03 30; www.polskiexpress.pl.) goes to **Warsaw** (2hr., 7 per day, 30zł).

Public Transportation: Buy tickets for buses and trolleys at kiosks. 10min. ride 1.70zł, students 1.20zł; 30min. ride 1.90zł/1.40zł.

⬛⬛ ORIENTATION AND PRACTICAL INFORMATION

The city's main drag, **ul. Krakówskie Przedmieście,** connects **Stare Miasto** (Old Town) in east Lublin to the **Katolicki Uniwersytet Lubelski** (KUL; Catholic University of Lublin) and **Uniwersytet Marii Curie-Skłodowskiej** (Maria Curie-Sklodowska University) in the west, passing the urban oasis of the **Ogród Saski** (Saxon Garden), and becoming **al. Racławickie.** Take bus #5, 10, or 13 to town from the bus station. On foot, head toward the castle and climb **ul. Zamkowa,** which runs up to Stare Miasto. Changing names several times, Zamkowa emerges through **Brama Krakówska** (Kraków Gate) and intersects **ul. Krakówskie Przedmieście.** From the train station, take trolley #150 or bus #13 to the city center.

Tourist Office: IT, ul. Jezuicka 1/3 (☎532 44 12; loit@inetia.pl). Near the Kraków Gate, next to Hotel Victoria. Walk or take bus #8, 9, or 11 south on Narutowicza from the city center. Sells maps (7zł) and provides train and bus information. Some English spoken. Open May-Aug. M-Sa 9am-6pm; Sept.-Apr. M-F 9am-5pm, Sa 10am-3pm.

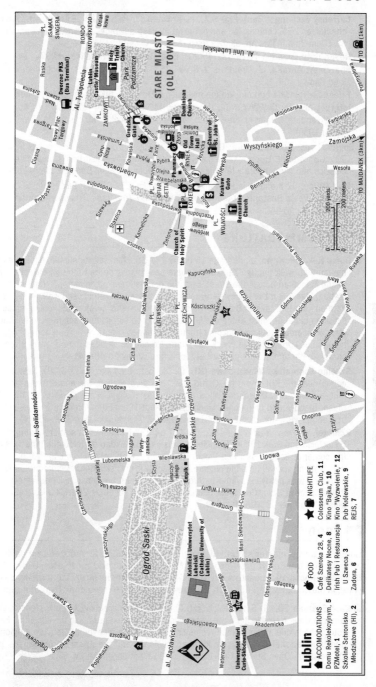

Lublin

▲ ACCOMODATIONS
Domu Rekolekcyjnym, **5**
PZMotel, **1**
Szkolne Schronisko
Mlodzieżowe (HI), **2**

● FOOD
Café Szeroka 28, **4**
Delikatesy Nocne, **8**
Irish Pub i Restauracja
U Szweca, **3**
Zadora, **6**

★ NIGHTLIFE
Colosseum Club, **11**
Kino "Bajka," **10**
Kino "Wyzwolenie," **12**
Pub Królewskie, **9**
REJS, **7**

Currency Exchange: Bank PKO S.A., ul. Królewska 1 (☎532 10 16) cashes **traveler's checks** for 1.5% commission and offers MC/V **cash advances.** Open M-F 7:30am-6pm, Sa 10am-2pm. **ATMs** are all over town.

Hospital: Ul. Staszica 16 (☎532 45 20). **Emergency:** ☎999. **Police:** ☎997

Pharmacy: Apteka, ul. Bramowa 2/8 (☎535 32 31). Open 24hr. Front window only 8am-8pm.

Telephones: Inside and outside the post office. Most only take Polish phone cards.

Internet Access: ■**WWW.Cafe,** Rynek 8 (☎442 35 80; www-cafe.lublin.pl), 4th fl. in the old square. 3zł per hr. Free coffee, tea, and hot chocolate for customers. Open daily 10am-10pm.

English-Language Bookstore: Empik, ul. Krakówskie Przedmieście 59 (☎/fax 534 30 99). Opposite ul. Lipowa. Carries a limited selection of English books, including both classics and contemporary favorites (25-40zł). Open M-F 9am-5pm, Sa 10am-2pm.

Post Office: Ul. Krakówskie Przedmieście 50 (☎/fax 532 20 71). **Fax** available at window #3. **Poste Restante** at window #2. Open daily 7am-9pm. **Branch** at Grodzka 7. **Postal Code:** 20 950.

ACCOMMODATIONS

■ **Domu Rekolekcyjnym,** ul. Podwale 15 (☎53 241 38; j.halasa@kuria.lublin.pl). From the bus station, walk through Zamkowy Square past the castle and through the gate. The hostel is located across the street. Buzz the doorbell marked "director." From the train station, take bus #1 or trolley #150 to ul. Lubartowska. Backtrack and walk through the gate on your left; take ul Bramowa, then ul. Grodzka. This comfortable resting place is set in an old abbey next to the castle gates. Don't be surprised to see nuns in full habit wandering around. All are welcome (though unmarried co-eds can't share rooms). Quiet hours after 10pm. Flexible check-out 10am. No curfew. 2-7 bed dorms; every 3 rooms share a bathroom. No set prices, but rooms are usually 20-40zł. ❶

Szkolne Schronisko Młodzieżowe (HI), ul. Długosza 6 (☎/fax 533 06 28), west of the center near the KUL. From the Ogród Saski bus stop, walk to the end of the park and take a right on ul. Długosza. Follow the blue hostel signs to the driveway on the left. Clean, friendly, and communal. Linen 6zł. Lockout 10am-5pm. Curfew 10pm. 6- to 22-bed dorms 18zł, non-members 24zł, over age 26 23zł; triples 28zł/31zł/30zł. ❶

PZMotel, ul. Prusa 8 (☎533 42 32; fax 747 84 93). From the bus station, turn right on Tysiąclecia and walk 10min. Tysiąclecia turns into al. Solidarnosci. Motel on the right on the corner of Solidarnosci and Prusa. From train station, take bus #1 to PKS bus station. Nothing special from the outside, but beauty is only skin deep. Comfortable rooms equipped with newly-renovated bathrooms. Continental breakfast included. Reception 24hr. Check-in 2pm. Check-out noon. Singles 150zł, doubles 200zł, triples 249zł. 2-person apartment 350zł. MC/V. ❺

FOOD

Lublin's eateries cluster around ul. Krakówskie Przedmieście. A dozen **beer gardens** are situated outside the gate to Stare Miasto, and several more are inside. The **Delikatesy Nocne,** ul. Lubartowska 3 (☎534 42 45), down the street from the Kraków Gate, is particularly popular with the late-night crowd. (Open daily 6am-midnight).

■ **Café Szeroka 28,** ul. Grodzka 21 (☎534 61 09; www.szeroka28.of.pl), close to the Grodzka Gate. Named after a pre-war Polish street, this cafe revels in the eccentric. Find your niche in one of the themed rooms or relax on the terrace for a great view. Regional and international cuisine. Live klezmer music Sa and theatrical performances Th. Entrees 20zł. Open Su-Th 11am-11pm, F-Sa 11am-midnight. MC/V. ❸

Naleśnikarnia/Kawiarnia "Zadora," Rynek 8 (☎534 55 34; www.zadora.com.pl). Zadora turns the traditional Polish dish into artwork that's as pleasing to the palette as it is to the eye. Enjoy your treat outside or in the antique and inviting interior. *Naleśniki* 4-12zł. Open daily 10am-11pm. AmEx/MC/V. ❶

Irish Pub i Restautacja U Szweca, ul. Grodzka 18 (☎532 82 84). An intriguing decor with bottles of Jack Daniels lining the walls and rows of shoes dangling from the shelves. Entrees 12-22zł. *Żywiec* (Polish beer) 5.50zł; Guinness 9zł. English menu. Open Su-Th noon-midnight, F-Sa noon-2am. MC/V. ❷

◐ ◖ SIGHTS AND FESTIVALS

The 19th-century ochre facades of **ul. Krakówskie Przedmieście** lead into medieval Stare Miasto, home of Lublin's historical sights. Pl. Litewski showcases an **obelisk** commemorating the 1569 union of Poland and Lithuania and a **Tomb of the Unknown Soldier.** Pl. Łokietka, east of pl. Litewski, is home to the 1827 **New Town Hall** (Nowy Ratusz), seat of Lublin's government. To the right begins ul. Królewska, which runs down around the corner to the grand **Cathedral of St. John the Baptist and St. John the Evangelist** (Katedra Sw. Jana Chrzciciela i Jana Ewangelisty; 1586-1596). The cathedral's frescoes, gilded altar, and barrel vault make it worthy of a visit.

Ul. Krakówskie Przedmieście travels through pl. Łokietka to the fortified **Kraków Gate** (Krakowska Brama), which houses the **Historical Division of the Lublin Museum** (Oddział Historyczny Muzeum Lubelskiego), pl. Łokietka 3. Exhibits on its four floors highlight the town's role in World War II and trace the changes in its appearance from 1585 to the present. (☎532 60 01. Open W-Sa 9am-4pm, Su 9am-5pm. Closed first and third Su of every month and second and fourth Tu. 2zł, students 1.5zł.) The top of the spiral staircase offers a **great view** of Lublin.

Across the gate, ul. Bramowa will lead you to the *rynek* amidst its early Renaissance houses. In *rynek's* center stands the 18th-century Neoclassical **Old Town Hall** (Stary Ratusz), which also houses a small history museum (Open W-F 8am-4pm, Sa 9am-5pm, Su 8am-4pm. 2zł, students 1.50zł). A walk along ul. Grodzka leads through the 15th-century **Grodzka Gate** (Brama Grodzka) to ul. Zamkowa, which runs to the massive **Lublin Castle** (Zamek Lubelski). Most of the structure was built in the 14th-century by King Kazimierz Wielki (see **History,** p. 474), but was restored in the 19th-century with a neo-Gothic exterior. During the Nazi occupation, the castle functioned as a Gestapo jail; the prisoners were shot en masse when the Nazis had to make a hasty retreat. Inside the castle, the **Lublin Museum** features historic paintings, armaments, and ornamental art. While its collection is interesting, the Russo-Byzantine frescoes in the attached **Holy Trinity Chapel** are truly stunning. The remarkably well-maintained panels, depicting various biblical scenes, were completed in 1418. (☎532 50 01, ext. 35. Castle museum open W-Sa 9am-4pm, Su 9am-5pm. 5zł, students 3zł. Chapel open M-Sa 9am-3:30pm, Su 9am-4:30pm. 6zł, students 4zł. Entry to both 9zł, students 5zł.)

Festivals abound in Lublin. In June, the city holds a month-long festival called **Odkryjmy Lublin: Dni Lublin** (Uncover Lublin: Lublin Days). The city hosts several musical performances, art exhibitions, and lectures throughout the entire month. Detailed schedules are available in the tourist office. For more information visit the **Nowy Ratusz,** pl. Łokietka 1 (☎444 55 55; fax 532 36 10; www.ym.lublin.pl).

◖ NIGHTLIFE

Tamer travelers can catch a **movie** at **Kino "Bajka,"** ul. Radziszewskiego 8, between the Colosseum Club and the ZNP hostel (☎/fax 533 88 72; open daily 3pm-10pm; 14zł, students 12zł) or **Kino "Wyzwolenie,"** ul. Peowiaków 6 (☎/fax 532 24 16; 14zł, students 12zł).

▨ **Colosseum Club,** Radziszewskiego 8 (☎ 534 43 00), near the University and near the ZNP hostel. This booty-shakin' students' favorite features a great bar and disco. Mostly techno, although one or two polka-inspired Polish tunes slip into the mix. Cover varies; usually F-Sa males 10zł, females 5zł. *Hevelius* 4.50zł. Open F-Sa 8pm-late.

REJS, ul. Krakówskie Przedmieście 55 (☎ 534 90 37), named after the famed Polish film of the same name. A popular student hangout close to the university. *Żywiec* 4zł. Live rock music every other weekend. Open M-F 9am-midnight, Sa-Su noon-midnight.

Pub Królewskie, Królewska 4 (☎ 534 57 06). A fledgling cellar joint popular with students and complete with dart board. Free live concerts are in the works. *Okocim* 4zł. 18+. Open M-F 10am-midnight, Sa-Su noon-midnight.

▶ DAYTRIP FROM LUBLIN

MAJDANEK

From Lublin, eastbound bus #28 from the train station, trollies #153 and 156 from al. Racławickie, and southbound trolly #156 from ul. Królewska all stop at the huge granite monument marking the entrance at Droga Męczenników Majdanka 67. Alternatively, you can walk the 4km down the road from Lublin to Zamość, the Droga Męczenników Majdanka (Road of the Martyrs of Majdanek; 30 min.). ☎ 744 26 48 or 744 19 55; fax 744 05 26; www.majdneak.pl. Museum open May-Sept. Tu-Su 8am-6pm; Mar.-Apr. and Oct.-Nov. Tu-Su 8am-3pm. Free; children under 14 not permitted. Dec.-Feb. visits by appointment 100zł. Tours in Polish 60zł; in English, German, and Russian 100zł per group. Call ahead for tours; the guides may not be available. A detailed English guide to the camp can be purchased at the ticket office for 7zł; maps are free.

During the Second World War, Majdanek was the largest concentration camp after Auschwitz. Approximately 235,000 people died here, including Jews, Poles, Soviets, and others from all over Europe. **Majdanek State Museum** (Panstwowe Muzeum na Majdanku) was founded in 1944 after the liberation of Lublin. The Nazis didn't have time to destroy the camp, so the original structures stand untouched, including the gas chambers, the crematorium, the prisoners' barracks, the watch-towers, the guardhouses, and the electrified barbed-wire perimeter. On November 3 each year, the camp holds a memorial service commemorating the day in 1943 when over 18,400 Jews were executed by the Nazis.

A visit to Majdanek begins in the information building, left of the large monument, whose staff supplies free information in several languages and shows a 25min. documentary that includes the first footage taken after the camp's liberation. (Available in English, last showing 2:30pm. 2zł per person; minimum 5 people per show.) Walking through the entire camp takes 1½-2hr. The actual tour begins with the gas chambers; signs in Polish, English, French, Russian, and German explain Nazi methods of extermination and experimentation. Guardhouses #43-45 contain historical exhibitions, including statistical displays, prisoners' clothes, instruments of torture, and a sample of the 730kg of human hair exported from Majdanek to a fabric factory in Germany. Perhaps the most overpowering exhibit is piled up in guardhouse #52: 260,000 shoes that the Nazis took from victims of Majdanek and neighboring camps fill the building. An especially sobering sight is the number of children's shoes in these masses; Majdanek had the highest percentage of children in any concentration camp. At the end of the main path, the intact crematorium ovens sit next to the concrete dome of the mausoleum, which stands as a massive mound of ash and human bone. The chilling inscription reads, "Let our fate be a warning for you."

THE CARPATHIANS (KARPATY)

Once known only to the reclusive and culturally distinct Górale (Highlander) peoples, the Carpathians now lure millions of Poles and foreigners every year to their superb hiking and skiing trails. Zakopane, the heart of the region, provides easy access to a number of excellent trails in the Tatry, while giving visitors a taste of local life in the Carpathians. The ancient town of Bielsko-Biala conserves the atmosphere of medieval Poland amidst a stunning backdrop of mountain scenery.

ZAKOPANE ☎ (0)18

Set in a valley surrounded by jagged Tatran peaks and alpine meadows, Zakopane (zah-ko-PAH-neh; pop. 33,000), Poland's premier resort, swells with hikers and skiers to a population of over 100,000 in the high seasons (from mid-June to Sept. and from late Dec. to early Feb.). The native highlander culture, however, endures in the region's architecture, folk costumes, and dialect, making a visit to Zakopane an experience not to be duplicated elsewhere in Poland.

▄ TRANSPORTATION

Trains: Ul. Chramcówki 35 (☎201 45 04). To: **Bielsko-Biała** (3¾hr., 5 per day, 30zł); **Kraków** (2¾hr., 8 per day, 27-40zł); **Warsaw** (8½hr., 3 per day, 62.5zł).

Buses: Ul. Kościuszki 25 (☎201 46 03). A better option than trains because of their inexpensive rates and frequency. To: **Kraków** (2hr., 22 per day, 11zł); **Warsaw** (8½hr., 1 per day, 49zł); **Poprad, SLK** (2¼hr., 2 per day, 15zł). A private **express bus** runs between Zakopane and **Kraków** (2hr., 15 per day, 10zł); buses leave from the "express" stop on ul. Kościuszki, 50m toward the center from the bus station. Call ahead, as schedules change frequently.

Taxis: Green Taxi ☎0603 22 09 11. **Radiotaxi** ☎919 or 125 60.

Bike Rental: Sukces, ul. Sienkiewicza 39 (☎201 41 97; fax 201 48 44; www.ski-sukces.zakopane.pl), near **IT** (see **Tourist Offices,** below). Mountain bikes 25zł per 4hr., 35zł per day. Open M-Sa 10am-5pm, but hours change with the weather, so call in advance. **Marek Malczewski Sport,** ul. Bronisława Czecha (☎201 20 05), near the "Pod Krokwią" campground. Turn right, take the first left, and walk 100m from the campground; the shop is a hut on your right. Mountain bikes 5zł per hr., 35zł per day. In-line skates 5zł per hr. Open daily 10am-5pm.

▄ �◪ ORIENTATION AND PRACTICAL INFORMATION

The **bus station** is on the corner of ul. Kościuszki and ul. Jagiellońska. The **train station** sits opposite the bus station on ul. Jagiellońska. The town center is a 10-15min. walk along **ul. Kościuszki,** which intersects **ul. Krupówki,** the dining and shopping hub. The **Tatras** lie just to the south of town.

Tourist Offices: Tourist Agency Redykołka, ul. Kościeliska 1 (☎/fax 201 32 53; info@tatratours.pl; www.tatratours.pl). Provides information on **private rooms ❷** (30-50zł), runs excellent English-language tours around Zakopane (60zł, 9am-1pm) and organizes Dunajec river-rafting expeditions (150zł, 9am-5pm). Email in advance for priority service. Open M-Sa 9am-5pm, Su 10am-5pm. **IT,** ul. Kościuszki 17 (☎201 22 11; fax 206 60 51), at the intersection with ul. Sienkiewicza. Walk right from the bus station

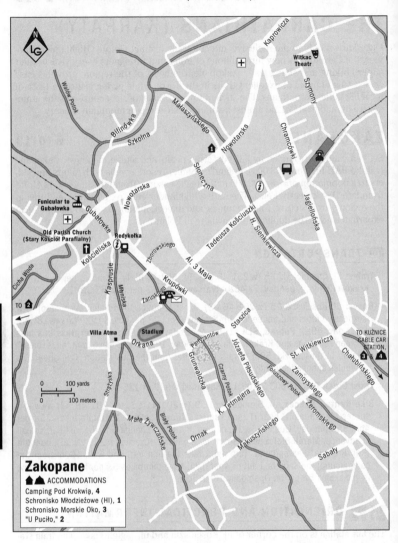

Zakopane

🏠🏠 ACCOMMODATIONS

Camping Pod Krokwią, **4**
Schronisko Młodzieżowe (HI), **1**
Schronisko Morskie Oko, **3**
"U Puciło," **2**

POLAND

along ul. Kościuszki and look for an alpine hut. The friendly staff sells **maps** (4-5zł) and arranges **private rooms** (30-45zł per person). Open daily 8am-8pm.

Budget Travel: erGuide Guiding Agency, ul. Zaruskiego 5, (☎/fax 20 140 05; erguide@meti.com.pl). Provides mountain guides, organizes rock climbing excursions, and arranges **private rooms ❷** (35-50zł). Open M-F 9am-5pm, Sa 10am-2pm.

Currency Exchange: Bank PKO SA, ul. Krupówki 71 (☎20 140 48), cashes **traveler's checks** for 1.5% commission and gives AmEx/MC/V **cash advances.** Open M-F 7:45am-7pm, Sa 7:45am-2pm. AmEx/MC/V **ATMs** line ul. Krupówki.

Luggage Storage: At the train station. 4zł per day. Open 24hr. At the bus station. 2zł per day. Open daily 8am-7pm.

Pharmacy: Ul. Krupówki 39 (☎206 33 31). Open M-Sa 8am-8pm. Posts addresses of other pharmacies in town.

Mountain Rescue Service: Ul. Piłsudskiego 63a (☎206 34 44).

Telephones: Ul. Zaruskiego 1 (☎/fax 201 44 21), by the "Telekomunikacja Polska" building behind the post office. Open M-F 7am-9pm, Sa-Su 8am-9pm.

Internet Access: Internet Cafe, ul. Krupówki 2. 1zł per 15min. Open M-F noon-8pm, Sa-Su 10am-8pm. **Dom Turysty Internet Cafe,** ul. Zaruskiego 5. 1zł per 30min. Open 24hr.

Post Office: Ul. Krupówki 20 (☎206 38 58). Open M-F 7am-8pm, Sa 8am-3pm, Su 9am-noon.

Postal Code: 34 500.

⌐ ACCOMMODATIONS AND CAMPING

During peak periods (June-Sept. and Dec.-Feb.), Zakopane can get crowded and prices rise 50-100%. More **private rooms ❶** become available during these periods, however, so few visitors have any real trouble locating a room. Just look for *pokój, noclegi*, or *Zimmer* signs (25-30zł). Hikers often stay in *schroniska* (mountain huts), but these fill quickly. Call 2-3 weeks ahead during peak season.

Schronisko Morskie Oko (☎207 76 09), 9km from Zakopane, by Lake Morskie Oko. Take the bus from the station to "Palenice Białczańska" (45min., 11 per day, 4zł) or a direct minibus from opposite the bus station (20min., 6-10zł). Hike the remaining distance to the hostel, or catch a horse-drawn carriage from the bus drop-off (round-trip 2½hr.; 30zł up, 15zł down). A gorgeous and immensely popular hostel in an ideal hiking location overlooking a mountain lake. Linen 7zł. Reception 8:30am-10pm. Check-out 10am. Reserve 2 months in advance during peak seasons. Dorms 30-40zł. ❶

"U Pucito" (The Puciło Family), ul. Za Strugiem 10 (☎206 29 20). From the bus station, go right on ul. Kościuszki toward the center, right on ul. Krupówki, and then left on Kościeliska. Ul. Za Strugiem is 10min. up the road on the left (15min. total). This friendly Highlander family provides clean rooms with original woodwork and embroidered curtains. Shared kitchenette and bathroom. Reserve 3 days in advance. High-season singles 40zł; doubles and triples 30zł per person; off-season 30zł/25zł. ❷

Schronisko Młodzieżowe (HI), ul. Nowotarska 45 (☎206 62 03 or 201 36 18). From the bus station, walk down ul. Kościuszki toward the center, take the 2nd right on ul. Sienkiewicza and walk 2 blocks. Comfortable accommodations in a newly renovated building. Breakfast included. Showers 5-10pm. Linen 4zł. **HI card required.** Reception 24hr. Check-out 10am. Curfew 10pm. Call one month in advance during the high season. 8- to 10-bed dorms 28zł; doubles 100zł; triples 150zł. ❶

Camping Pod Krokwią, ul. Żeromskiego (☎201 22 56; camp@regle.zakopane.pl), across the street from the base of the ski jump. From the train station, head left on ul. Jagiellońska and follow it as it becomes Chałubińskiego. Follow ul. Czecha from the rotary and turn right on ul. Żeromskiego. The remarkably well-kept grounds justify the price. Tents 20zł per person, students 18zł; bungalows 32-44zł per person. ❶

◖ FOOD

Highlanders sell the local specialty, *oscypek* (goat cheese; 1-3zł), in all shapes and sizes on the street. Keep in mind that no matter how artistically it's been carved, cheese will spoil after a few weeks. Beer and wine are often served warm, and locals love their *Herbate Ceperska* (25ml vodka with hot tea). Most restaurants cater to tourists and set their prices accordingly. To escape, try the **Delikatesy** grocery store, ul. Krupówki 41. (☎201 25 83. Open M-Sa 7am-10pm, Su 8am-10pm.)

Pizzeria Restauracja "Adamo," ul. Nowatarska 10d (☎201 28 54, delivery 201 52 90). Unassuming and enormously popular, this establishment off ul. Krupówki caters to both locals and tourists. Large portions of Polish dishes and pizza, as well as friendly service. *Danie dnia* (daily special) includes soup, entree, coffee, and dessert (13-16zł). Entrees 10-35zł. Open daily 11am-midnight. AmEx/MC/V. ❷

Bakowa-Zohylina, ul. Piłsudskiego 28a (☎201 20 45), serves up traditional dishes amid a mountain lodge atmosphere complete with animal pelts and an open hearth. Dine in the garden for an exceptional view of the Krokiew Mountain. Entrees 12-28zł. Open daily 1pm-midnight. ❸

Karczma Sopa, ul. Kościeliska 52 (☎201 22 16). Walk 20min. west along historic ul. Kościeliska. Serves traditional highland fare as well as delicious soups. On weekends, live Carpathian music starts at 7pm. Entrees 10-25zł. Open daily 5pm-midnight. ❷

🥾 HIKING

Poland's magnificent **Tatra National Park** (Tatrzański Park Narodowy) is not to be missed. Entrances to the park lie at the head of each trail. (2zł, students 1zł. Keep your ticket.) The best place to begin a foray into the mountains is **Kuźnice,** which can be reached on foot from the Zakopane train station (45min.). Take ul. Jagielloska and follow it as it becomes ul. Chałubińskiego. Then follow ul. Przewodników Tatrzańskich to the trailheads. Alternatively, take the 1987m **Kasprowy Wierch cable car,** which runs between Zakopane and Kuźnice. (Open daily July-Aug. 7:30am-6:30pm; June and Sept. 7:30am-5pm; Oct. 7:30am-3pm. Round-trip 28zł, students 18zł.) The **Gubałówka cable car** (1120m), in the northern part of the city, is also popular. To reach it, walk along ul. Krupówki to its end, take a left on Kościeliska and a very quick right onto Gubałówka, which leads to the cable car. (Open daily July-Sept. and Dec. 25-Feb. 6:45am-8pm; Oct.-Dec. and Mar.-June 8am-5pm. 8zł.) Breathtaking views of Zakopane await at the top, and highlander huts and sheep populate the mountain slopes. You can walk down to return to Zakopane (30min.), or take a leisurely stroll west on the blue, black, or red trail to **Butorowy Wierch** (30min.) and descend via the chairlift. (Open daily May-Sept. 9am-6pm; Mar.-Apr. and Oct. 9am-5pm; Jan.-Feb. and Nov. 9am-4pm; Dec. 9am-3pm. 5zł.) Before hiking, buy the map *Tatrzański Park Narodowy: Mapa turystyczna* (7zł) at a kiosk or bookstore.

Kościeliska Valley (Dolina Kościeliska; full day). An lovely hike between the peaks of Kościeliski. A bus runs from Zakopane to Kiry (every 30min., 2zł). From Kiry, a small road heads south along a river toward Schronisko Ornak. The road turns into a trail after about 30min.; another 1½hr. along the trail leads to various peaks and caves to explore. Considered one of the easiest hikes on the mountain.

Strazyska Valley (Dolina Strazyska; 4-5 hours). In Zakopane, take ul. Krupówki to ul. Kościeliska, and then make a left on Kasprusie, which leads to an entrance to Tatry National Park (30min.). Follow the path through this picturesque valley until you reach its end at the waterfall. Retrace your steps for about 10min. and follow the signs up Mt. Sarnia Skala. The climb is easy, and the splendid views of Zakopane and Mt. Giewont from the top are extremely rewarding.

Sea Eye (Morskie Oko; 1406m; 5-6hr.). The glacial Morskie Oko Lake dazzles herds of tourists every summer. Take a bus from Zakopane's bus station (45min., 11 per day, 4zł), or a private minibus (6-10zł) from opposite the station to Palenica Białczańska. Horses and carriages loiter in the parking lot, waiting to take tourists up the mountain's paved road. (Round-trip 2½hr.; 30zł up, 15zł down.) The trail is wildly famous and therefore quite crowded, but all is forgiven upon reaching the lake, where you'll suddenly realize why Poles love this region.

Red Peaks (Czerwone Wierchy; 2122m; full day). Take a right on the red trail at the top of the cable car at Kasprowy Wierch (see above), and follow it along the ridge separating Poland and the Slovak Republic. The ridge is part of the "West Tatras," a smoother, less rocky range. Four of the seven peaks along the way have paths that allow tired hikers to return to Zakopane. Taking a right onto the yellow trail at Kopakondracka (2005m) will lead to the blue trail that ends at Giewont, where you can catch a bus back to Zakopane. From the last peak, Ciemniak, the trail descends to Kiry. The heights of the ridge are known as "Red Peaks" because of the native *Boletus Bovinus* plants that blossom throughout the area each autumn, coloring the rocks.

Valley of the Five Polish Tarns (Dolina Pięciu Stawów Polskich; an intense full day). One of the most beautiful hikes in the area leads past 5 lakes: Wielki ("great one"), Czarny ("black one"), Przedni ("frontmost one"), Zadni ("rearmost one"), and Mały ("small one"). The hike begins at Kuźnice and leads along the blue trail to Hala Gąsienicowa. Refuel here at the mountain hut Schronisko Murowaniec, then continue to Czarny. On the incline to Zawrat Peak, you'll have to climb hand-over-hand up the chains. In the valley on the other side of Zawrat, another *schronisko* waits at Przedni to shelter those exhausted by the hike or overwhelmed by the scenery. After several steep climbs and descents, the blue trail ends 3km north at Morskie Oko, where you can eat, drink, or spend the night (see **Accommodations,** p. 521). From the lake, a road travels 2km farther down to a parking lot in Palenica Białczańska, where buses depart for Zakopane. A shorter version of the hike (4-5hr.) begins at Palenica Białczańska. Head in the direction of Morskie Oko (see above). A green path takes off to the right about 1hr. into the hike, after the Mickiewicza Waterfall, heading to the Valley of the Five Polish Tarns. Once you reach Wielki Staw (Great Tarn), take a left on the blue trail toward Przedni and follow the trail to its end before Morskie Oko.

Giewont (1894m; 6½hr.). Giewont's silhouette resembles a man lying down—hence the mountain's starring role in many Polish legends. The moderately difficult blue trail (7km) leads to the peak. Begin at the lower cable car station in Kuźnice and follow signs to the peak. The path becomes quite rocky as you reach Hala Kondratowa, where you can rest at the hostel and snack bar inside. From here, the trail begins to wrap around the ridge of Giewont's peak. Chains anchored into the rock help with the final ascent. The top affords an amazing view of Zakopane to the north and the highest Tatran peaks to the south and east. This peak is the most popular ascent, but also the most crowded. The summit's enormous cross was carried up the mountain by a local priest who decided that the Highlanders needed a permanent reminder of their faith.

Rysy (2499m; 8hr. from Morskie Oko, 12hr. from Zakopane). To claim you've climbed Poland's highest peak, follow the red trail from Schronisko Morskie Oko (see **Accommodations,** above) along the east lakeshore and up to Czarny Staw (Black Tarn). The arduous climb to Rysy begins in the lake's southeast corner. Only for the fittest in good weather after mid-July. You can also tackle Rysy from the Slovak Republic (see **Štrbské Pleso: Hiking,** p. 767) from July to September, when the peak becomes an official border crossing. Register your hike with the hostel where you will be staying to avoid any sort of legal wrangling with border officials.

👁🎵 SIGHTS AND ENTERTAINMENT

There are seven houses along **ul. Kościeliska** built by architect and artist **Stanisław Witkiewicz** (1851-1915). Having lived here for much of his life, he gave a name to Zakopane's architectural style, characterized by tremendous ornamentation on the interior and exterior of every building. Hugely popular, this became the Polish national style at the beginning of the 20th century. In the evening, check out the cafes on ul. Krupówki. At **Piano-Cafe,** ul. Krupówki 63, on the left behind the main walkway, you can burrow into a corner couch or sit at the glass-topped bar with Zakopane's youth. (0.5L *Żywiec* 4zł. Open daily 3pm-midnight.)

Air-Taxi (☎060 228 75 28; fax 201 37 95) arranges **paragliding** over the Tatras. If you've never jumped before, try a **tandem jump** (10-20min. flying time, 120zł) off Nosal Mountain. In the winter, you can make reservations at **Śliwa Snowboard,** Polana pod Nosalem, chair lift #4. Natural hot springs (1600m below ground) that bubble up at a cozy 30°C have been turned into the swimming pool complex **Basen Antalowka,** ul. Jagiellońska 18. (☎206 39 34. Open July-Sept. daily 8am-8pm. Day pass 9am-5pm, 12zł; night pass 5-8pm, 6zł). During the last week of August, Zakopane resounds with the **Festival of Highlander Folklore** (Micdzynardowy Festival Folkloro ziem Gòrskich), a week during which highland groups from around the world participate in dancing and music along ul. Krupówki.

BIELSKO-BIAŁA   ☎(0)33

As its name suggests, Bielsko-Biała (BYEL-skoh BYAH-wah; pop. 200,000) is a composite of two separate towns. Now divided only by a river, the towns were formerly politically divided: Bielsko spent centuries as part of Bohemia, while Biała was part of Poland. It was Austrian rule that first brought the towns together, though they were not officially united until 1951. Long known as "Little Vienna," the architectural and linguistic legacies of a Germanic presence that lasted for centuries are evident throughout Bielsko-Biała.

🚆 TRANSPORTATION

Trains: Ul. Warszawska 2 (☎94 36). To: **Katowice** (1½hr., 27 per day, 9zł); **Kraków** (3hr., 12 per day, 12zł); **Warsaw** (4hr., 4 per day, 76zł); **Zakopane** (4hr., 3 per day, 25zł); **Bratislava, SLK** (5½hr., 1 per day, 99zł).

Buses: Ul. Warszawska 7 (☎812 28 25). An overpass connects the bus station to the train station. To: **Kraków** (2½hr., 21 per day, 12-15zł) and **Oświęcim/Auschwitz** (1hr., 13 per day, 6.60zł). Leave plenty of time for your trips, as bus connections in the region can be unreliable.

✴🛈 ORIENTATION AND PRACTICAL INFORMATION

Bielsko-Biała has two centers: Biała's *rynek* in the east and Bielsko's castle and *rynek* in the west. The former is far more commercialized, with cafes and shops lining its streets, while the latter, filled with pubs, retains a more relaxed atmosphere. A 10min. walk along the city's main pedestrian artery, **ul. 11-go Listopada,** connects the two districts. To get to Biała center from the train station, turn left out of the station down **ul. 3-go Maja.** After 10min., head down the stairs past Hotel Prezydent to reach ul. 11-go Listopada. To reach Bielsko's *rynek*, go a bit farther on ul. 3-go Maja and turn right up **Wzgórze.**

Tourist Office: Miejskie Centrum Informacji Turystyczne, pl. Ratuszowy 4 (☎819 00 50; fax 819 00 61; www.it.bielsko.pl). From 11-go Listopada turn right onto Cechowa and left onto Ks. Stojałowskiego. The tourist office, over the river on the right, sells **maps** (4-7zł) and lists **private rooms ❷** (35-40zł). Open M-F 8am-6pm, Sa 8am-4pm.

Currency Exchange: Bank PKO SA, ul. 11-go Listopada 15 (☎816 52 31). Exchanges currency, cashes V **traveler's checks** for 1.5% commission (5zł minimum), and offers MC/V **cash advances.** Open M-F 8am-6pm, Sa 9am-1pm.

Pharmacy: Apteka Pod Korona, ul. Cechowa 4 (☎812 48 93), at the intersection with ul. 11-go Listopada. Open M-F 8am-9pm, Sa 8am-4pm.

Medical Assistance: ☎999. Ambulance service ☎812 34 12.

Internet Access: Cyber Czad, ul. 11 Listopada 7 (☎822 94 14). 30min. 3zł; 1hr. 6zł; 2hr. 10zł, every subsequent hr. 5zł. Open M-Sa 10am-10pm, Su 3pm-8pm. **Klub Internetowy,** ul. Sobieskiego 2-4, near St. Nicholas's Cathedral (☎819 35 38), is on the corner of Wzgorze and 3-go Maja. Though a bit out of the way, it rarely gets crowded. 2.5zł per 30min., 4zł per hr.

Post Office: Ul. 1-go Maja 2 (☎/fax 822 89 83). Open M-F 9am-8pm. **Poste Restante** at window #9. **Telephones** are nearby.

Postal Code: 43-300.

ACCOMMODATIONS

Schronisko Młodzieżowe "Bolka i Lolka," ul. Komorowicka 25 (☎816 74 66). Take the overpass as you head away from the bus and train stations. After crossing the tracks, continue in the same direction along Okrzge until it ends at ul. Grażyńskiego. Take a right and then a quick left onto Zmożk across the river. Veer right at Komorowicka and walk several blocks to reach the hostel (15 min.). Named after 2 local cartoon heroes, this playful hostel is run by a friendly and hospitable staff. 3- to 8-bed dorms. Sheets 3.50zł. Check-out 10am. Lockout 10am-5pm. Curfew 10pm. 16zł per person. ❶

PTTK Dom Wycieczkowy, ul. Krasińskiego 38 (☎812 30 19). Take the overpass from the train station toward the bus station to cross 3-go Maja. Take the stairs on your left and follow the street below. Turn right on ul. Piastowska; Krasińskiego is 2 blocks up on the left. Large, clean rooms in a peaceful area. Curfew 10pm-6am. Lockout 10am-2pm. Doubles 52zł, with bath 72zł; triples 75zł/108zł; quads and quints 20zł per person. ❷

Papuga Park Hotel, ul. Zapora 3 (☎818 58 60; fax 818 33 25; www.papuga.pl). Take bus #16 from the train station to the hotel. Set in idyllic surroundings, Papuga Park is pricey but luxurious. Check-in 2pm. Singles 195zł; doubles 290zł. AmEx/MC/V. ❺

FOOD

Grocery stores, bakeries, butchers, and bars are plentiful on and near the central ul. 11-go Listopada, but actual restaurants are tough to find. Traditional Polish fare is even more elusive. **Savia,** ul. 11-go Listopada 38, is one of the larger groceries. (☎812 35 44. Open M-F 6:30am-9pm, Sa 6:30am-8pm, Su 8am-4pm.)

Tawerna Rybna "Pirat," pl. Wojska Polskiego 14, just off ul. 11-go Listopada. This seaworthy restaurant serves up delicious fish and poultry. Fries, soup, and salad always included. Entrees 7-14zł. Open daily 9am-10pm. ❶

Pod Jemiolami, ul. Cechowa 6 (☎815 08 97), near the corner of ul. 11-go Listopada and ul. Cechowa. A cozy, traditionally decorated establishment that features magnificent Polish dishes from various regions. Entrees 12-30zł. ❷

Kawiarnia Murzynek, ul. 11-go Listopada 21 (☎812 21 71), serves up pizza (10-16zł) and coffee (2-3zł) in a lively outdoor cafe. Open daily 8am-midnight. ❷

◎ SIGHTS

Bielsko's modest 14th-century **castle** stands above pl. Chrobrego. From the main tourist office, turn right up Ks. S. Stojałowskiego. Cross ul. 3-go Maja into pl. Chrobrego and turn left onto Wzgórze. The entrance is located up the hill on the square's south end at ul. Wzgórze 16. Its **museum** houses a collection of European paintings and artifacts from the castle's past, including the works of several preeminent artists of the *Młodej Polski* (Young Poland) Movement. (☎822 06 56. Open Tu-W and F 10am-3pm, Th 10am-5pm, Sa 9am-3pm, Su 9am-2pm. 7zł, students 4zł.) Travel a bit off the beaten path to experience **Dom Tkacza,** ul. Sobiekiego 51, the 18th-century wooden home of a weaver. To reach this historic house from the castle, follow Wzgórze, take a right on Kopernika, and then hang a left onto Jana Sobieskiego. This house-turned-museum offers a glimpse into the industry that originally put Bielsko-Biała on the map. (☎11 71 76. Open Tu-W and F-Sa 8am-2pm, Th 10am-5pm. 2zł, students 1zł.) The steeple of the early 20th-century **St. Nicholas's Cathedral** (Katedra św. Mikołaja), pl. Mikołaja 19, is visible from most of the city. From the castle and continue up Wzgórze to the *rynek*, then turn left down Kościelna. The church was bumped up from provincial status only a few years ago, when the Pope made the parish a bishopric. The chapel's architecture and exterior facade make this church worth a secular scoping. The grounds of the **Lutheran Church** (Kościół Ewangelicko-Augsburski), pl. Lutra 8, feature Poland's only **statue of Martin Luther.** Follow directions to the castle, but go straight through pl. Chrobrego along Nad Niprem. Inquire at the church office to see the interior. (☎812 74 71. Office open M-F 9am-noon and 2-6pm, Sa 9-11am, Su after mass.)

A few kilometers south of Bielsko-Biała lies the sleepy town of Żywiec (ZHIH-vyets), home to Poland's best-known, hardest-hitting **brew** of the same name. **Trains** connect Bielsko-Biała and Żywiec (40min., 12 per day; 5.20zł, students 2.60zł). **Buses** also go there (40min., 10 per day, 4.30zł). Once you've arrived, the fastest and safest way to the **Żywiec Brewery**, a factory of bottled miracles, is to take bus #1 or 5 from the train station to the "Browarna" stop. Buy tickets at the kiosk next to the train station (2zł, students 1zł). **Trans-Trade Żywiec,** ul. Browarna 90, is unmistakable; just look for a modern complex of bright blue and white buildings with trucks and trains pouring in and out. Call in advance (☎861 99 03) and ask to speak to Master Duda to arrange a free tour of the brewery. Next door, **Żywiecka Pub,** Browarna 88, is a *piwarnia* (beer garden) that sells what is possibly the freshest, cheapest beer in Poland. All Żywiec products are sold at manufacturer's cost (0.5L 3.5zł) in a traditional pub setting. (☎861 96 17. Open Su-Th 11am-11pm, F-Sa 11am-midnight.)

◨ ENTERTAINMENT

Bazyliszek Pub and Gallery, ul. Wygórze 8, sits uphill from the castle. Original artwork adorns the walls, and the artists themselves might just be around to tell you about their work. The bar serves *Okocim* (0.5L 4.5zł), while the low-key clientele enjoys occasional live jazz and light rock in the back room. (Open M-Th noon-midnight, F-Sa noon-2am, Su 4pm-midnight.) At **Café Dziupla,** ul. Mickiewicza 15, a crowd of active drinkers mingles with more sedentary types. Enjoy the jukebox, foosball tables, and sports TV. (0.3L *Żywiec* 4zł. Open M-F 11am-11pm, Sa-Su 4-11pm. AmEx/DC/MC/V.) If it's dancing you're after, hit **Fabryka Rozrywki,** ul. Graiynskiego 38. A young crowd dances the night away in the swank interior of this former factory. (Beer 5zł. Open Su-Th 1pm-2am, F-Sa 9am-6am. MC/V.)

SILESIA (ŚLĄSK)

West of Kraków, Silesia became Poland's industrial heartland when uncontrolled Five-Year Plans depleted the land's resources, leaving much of it polluted. Farther west, Dolny (Lower) Śląsk has managed to provide some fresh air by protecting its forests, castles, and mountain spas. The regions' respective capitals, Katowice and Wrocław, reflect the varying impact of industrialization. Catholic pilgrims head toward Częstochowa, while hikers flock to Jelenia Góra and Karpacz, gateways to Karkonosze National Park.

KATOWICE   ☎(0)32

An industrial core and transportation hub, Katowice (ka-toe-VEE-tseh; pop. 367,000) is more a layover city than a final destination. Most travelers in Poland find themselves crossing through this major city at some point during their visit.

▐ TRANSPORTATION

Trains: The **train station**, pl. Szewczyka 1 (☎257 94 36). International tickets at tellers #12-14 downstairs only. To: **Częstochowa** (1-2hr., 32 per day, 10.40-18.50zł); **Kraków** (1½-3½hr., 29 per day, 11.40-18.50zł); **Poznań** (5½hr., 10 per day, 36.50zł); **Warsaw** (express 3hr., 16 per day, 63.30zł); **Wrocław** (2½hr., 14 per day, 31.50zł); **Berlin, GER** (8-9hr., 2 per day, 118-157zł); **Bratislava, SLK** (5½hr., 4 per day, 127zł); **Budapest, HUN** (8hr., 2 per day, 179zł); **Kyiv, UKR** (24hr., 1 per day, 203zł); **Lviv, UKR** (12hr., 1 per day, 115zł); **Prague, CZR** (6½hr., 4 per day, 148zł); **Vienna, AUS** (7hr., 2 per day, 157zł). AmEx/MC/V.

Buses: The **bus station** (☎258 94 65) is 3 blocks away on ul. Piotra Skargi. **PKS** buses run to: **Częstochowa** (2hr., 3 per day, 10-16zł); **Kraków** (1½hr., 12 per day, 12-15zł); **Warsaw** (4½hr., 1 per day, 36zł). Buses also run to many Western European countries, including Austria, France, Germany, Italy, and Norway. **Biuro Podróży Daniel** offers information about international travel; other *kasy* do not. (☎253 06 83. Open M-F 9am-5pm, Sa 9am-2pm.)

✦ ▐ ORIENTATION AND PRACTICAL INFORMATION

The **train station** is a traveler's haven with fast food, groceries (**Delikatesy Non-Stop** open 24hr.), telephones, *kantory*, and travel agencies galore. **Travel information** is available at **Biuro Obsługi Podróży**, in a booth upstairs. There is **luggage storage** in the lower level of the train station. (4zl plus 0.45zl for every 50zl of declared value. Open 24hr.) Exit the station via the overpass and walk straight across the street to reach the pedestrian strip, **ul. Stawowa**, full of fast food. Following Stawowa to its end at the Empik Megastore brings you within steps of the central **bus station**, which is just to Empik's left, on Piotra Skargi. **Bank PKO**, ul. Chopina 1, between the bus and train stations, gives **MC/V cash advances** and cashes **traveler's checks**. (☎357 98 78. Open M-F 8am-6pm, Sa 9am-1pm.) **Supernet Internet Cafe**, ul. Slowackiego 8, is around the corner from the bank. (☎781 58 80. 4zł per hr. Open M-F 8am-1am, Sa 8am-8am, Su 11am-10pm.)

⌂ ACCOMMODATIONS AND FOOD

Hotels in the city center are scarce and business-oriented. If you're staying the night, try **Hotel Brynów ❹**, ul. Sw. Huberta 11. Although Hotel Brynów is no diamond in the rough, its affordable rooms are unbeatable among Katowice's business hotels. From the train station, turn right until you get to the *rynek* (plaza). From there, take tram #6 or 16 toward "Brynów" and get off after 10min. at the last station. (☎257 59 55. Singles with bath and TV 97.37zł; doubles with sink 98.44zł, with bath and TV 173.34zł; triples with sink 136.96zł. Student discounts available.) **Bar Filipek ❷**, ul. Stawowa 9, serves basic Silesian fare. (☎258 99 50. Entrees 8-20zł. Open daily 8am-8pm.) **Restauracja Patio Grill ❷**, ul Stawowa 3, provides patrons with a romantic forest atmosphere and aesthetically pleasing dishes. (☎781 55 55. Entrees 10-30zł. Open M-Sa 10am-10pm, Su 1pm-7pm. AmEx/MC/V.) Vegetarians and health food buffs can stock up at the **Zdrowa Żywność** grocery, ul. Chopina 2, down Stawowa and to the left. (Open M-F 10am-5pm.)

CZĘSTOCHOWA ☎(0)34

In 1382, a haggard traveler arrived in Częstochowa (chen-sto-HO-va) weary from her trials and tribulations and scarred from a scuffle with Hussite thieves. The visitor, a Byzantine icon in the prime of her life at only 800 years old, soon found refuge from the world, settling claim atop the hill of Jasna Góra and entrusting herself to the care of the monks living there. Since she moved in, the city has been defined by little other than her presence. As the most sacred of Polish icons, she draws millions of Catholic pilgrims every year. They, and other visitors, descend upon the city to catch a glimpse of her, the famous Black Madonna (see p. 531).

⌷ TRANSPORTATION

Trains: Częstochowa Główna, ul. Piłsudskiego 38 (☎94 36). To: **Gdynia** (7hr., 4 per day, 42zł *pośpieszny)*; **Katowice** (1-2hr.; 35 per day; 11zł *osobowy*, 19zł *pośpieszny)*; **Kraków** (2-3hr.; 6 per day; 16zł, 26zł); **Łódź** (2hr., 5 per day, 28zł *pośpieszny)*; **Poznań** (5hr., 1 per day, 36.50zł *pośpieszny)*; **Warsaw** (2½hr.; 11 per day; 58zł *ekspres*, 33.20zł *pospieszny)*; **Wrocław** (2hr. *ekspres,* 3hr. *pośpieszny,* 4hr. *osobowy;* 4 per day; 55.50zł, 31.50zł, 19.30zł).

Buses: ul. Wolności 45/49 (☎324 66 16). Left on ul. Wolności from train station. To: **Katowice** (2hr., 10 per day, 11zł); **Kraków** (3hr., 6 per day, 12-33zł); **Warsaw** (3½hr., 3 per day, 30-39zł); **Wrocław** (4hr., 5 per day, 20-25zł). Info open daily 7am-6pm. **Polski Express** (☎022 620 03 30). To: **Katowice** (1½hr., 3 per day, 17zł); **Kraków** (3hr., 3 per day, 28zł); **Łódź** (2hr., 3 per day, 23zł); **Warsaw** (5hr., 2 per day, 28zł).

Taxis: Auto Radio ☎96 29, **Carex** ☎96 26, **Echo** ☎96 25, **Inter** ☎96 24.

✳❓ ORIENTATION AND PRACTICAL INFORMATION

Częstochowa is about 100km northwest of Kraków. The **train** and **bus stations** lie two blocks from each other and are between al. Wolności and ul. Piłsudskiego, by the town center. **Al. Najświętszej Marii Panny (NMP;** Avenue of Our Lady) links them to **Jasna Góra.** From either station, go right on al. Wolności to get to al. NMP. Take a left to reach Jasna Góra. You can see the basilica from the intersection.

Tourist Offices: CIT, al. NMP 65 (☎368 22 50; fax 368 22 60; www.czesto-chowa.um.pl), provides **maps.** English and German spoken. Open M-F 9am-5pm, Sa-Su 9am-2pm. **Jasnogórskie Centrum Informacji (IT),** ul. Kordeckiego 2 (☎365 38 88; fax 365 43 43; information@jasnagora.pl), inside the monastery near the cathedral. English-speaking staff sells maps and tours in English (110-170zł, depending on group size). Also makes reservations for Dom Pielgrzyma (see **Accommodations,** below). **MC/V ATM.** Open May 1-Oct. 15 daily 7:30am-7pm; Oct. 16-Apr. 30 8am-5pm.

Currency Exchange: *Kantory* (currency exchange kiosks) are throughout the city. **Bank PKO S.A.,** ul. Kopernika 17/19 (☎365 50 60), straight ahead from the train station, just off ul. Nowowiejskiego, cashes **traveler's checks** for 1% commission and gives MC/V **cash advances. 24hr. ATM** outside. Open M-F 8am-6pm, Sa 10am-2pm.

Luggage Storage: Lockers located at the train station, left of the ticket booths. 8zł per day, 4zł for smaller items. Open 24hr. Also at the monastery (for a donation)—ask at IT (see above). Open May-Oct. daily 6am-6pm; Nov.-Apr. 7am-5pm.

Pharmacy: Apteka Nobia, al. NMP 53 (☎324 68 52). Open M-Sa 8am-9pm.

Medical Assistance: At the monastery. Open Sept.-May M-Sa 7:30am-noon and 3:30-6pm; June-Aug. 6am-7:30pm; Su and holidays 7am-6pm. **Ambulance** ☎999.

Internet Access: Meganet, ul. Wilsona 8a. At the intersection of ul. Piłsudskiego and NMP, enter the Senka mall and go out the rear exit. Meganet is in the white building on the right. (1zł per 30min. Open daily 8am-10pm.)

Post Office: ul. Orzechowskiego 7 (☎324 29 59), between the bus and train stations. **Poste Restante** available at *kasa* 9 (window 9). Open M-Sa 7am-9pm.

Postal Code: 42-200.

ACCOMMODATIONS

Reservations are recommended year-round, but are a must for early May and mid-to late August, when pilgrims descend en masse. There is a **youth hostel ❶** (Internat TZN) at ul. Jasnogórska 84/96, but it's only open during July and August. (☎324 31 21, about 10zł.) Check at IT (see **Tourist Offices,** above) for more information.

Dom Pielgrzyma im. Jana Pawła II (The Pilgrim's House), ul. Wyszyńskiego 1/31 (☎377 75 64; fax 365 18 70; dp@jasnagora.pl). With your back to Jasna Góra, it's on the right side, adjacent to the parking lot opposite NMP. Walk through labyrinthine hallways to a clean and comfortable room. Frequently full. Check-in 3pm. Check-out 9am. Lockout 9am-3pm. Quiet hours 10pm-5:30am. Curfew 10pm. 4-bed dorms with sink 22zł; singles 70zł; doubles 90zł; triples with bath 105zł. ❷

Camping Oleńka, ul. Oleńki 10/30 (☎324 74 95). On the other side of Jasna Góra's parking lot from Dom Pielgrzyma. Oleńka's clean and comfortable bungalows boast free kitchen and laundry facilities. Good option year-round, as 1 bungalow stays open in winter. Call ahead for bungalows. Check-in 2pm. Check-out noon. Tent space 12zł per person, electricity 12zł. Singles with sink 25zł; doubles with sink 50zł; triples 80zł; quads with bath 100zł; quints with bath 125zł. ❶

Hotel Ha-Ga, ul. Katedralna 9 (☎324 61 73). From the train station go left onto Piłsudskiego, then right onto Katedralna for 1 block (5min.). The hotel is on the right, through the gate after the Ha-Ga bar. Reasonably clean, if nothing to go ha-ga over. All rooms have (ancient) radios. Check-in 2pm. Check-out noon. Singles 50zł, with bath and TV 70zł; doubles 60zł/90zł; triples 70zł/100zł; quads 80zł/110zł. ❸

◘ FOOD

If not fasting during your pilgrimage, satisfy your gluttony at one of Częstochowa's restaurants, or at the gigantic **Supermarket Billa,** in the red building across from the bus station. (Open M-F 8am-9pm, Sa 8am-8pm, Su 9am-4pm.)

Kawiarnia Stylowa, al. NMP 39/41 (☎365 20 52). An elegant cafe with a well-rounded dinner menu at reasonable prices. Entrees 6-26zł, scrumptious cakes and elaborate desserts 2.50-12zł. Outdoor seating available. Open daily 10am-10pm. ❷

Bar U Adasia, ul. Dąbrowskiego 15 (☎364 64 67). Walk up NMP toward Jasna Góra and turn right on Dąbrowskiego at the park; restaurant on your left through the archway. Take comfort in the home-style decor while dining on meals just like your Polish grandma used to make. Entrees 5.50-7zł. Open M-F 8am-5pm, Sa 9am-3pm. ❷

Pod Gruszką (Under the Pear), al. NMP 37 (☎365 44 90), next to Almatur in a court-yard. Good things happen under pear trees. This relaxed cafe/bar is a popular student hangout with a selection of salads (20zł per kg). Beer 4zł. Many varieties of coffee, tea, and hot chocolate 2.50-3.50zł. Open Su-Th 10am-10pm, F-Sa 10am-midnight. ❶

◙ SIGHTS

The Paulite Monastery (Klasztor Paulinów), on top of **Jasna Góra** (Bright Mountain), is *the* sight in town. The monastery, which resembles a Baroque fortress, was founded in 1382 by Duke Władysław Opolczyk, who also donated the painting *Blessed Mother and Child* in 1384. Despite its fortified exterior, Jasna Góra welcomes masses of pilgrims who come to see the reportedly miraculous **Black Madonna** (Czarna Madonna). The ornate 15th-century **Basilica** houses the icon inside the small **Chapel of Our Lady** (Kaplica Matki Bożej). Countless crutches, medallions, and rosaries strung up on the chapel walls attest to the pilgrims' faith in the painting's healing powers, while several jewel-encrusted nun-crafted robes decorate the Madonna herself. The icon is veiled and revealed several times a day, with solemn festivities. The ceremony is definitely worth seeing. (Chapel open daily 5am-9:30pm. Icon revealed Sept.-May M-F 6am-noon, 3-7pm, and 9-9:15pm; Sa-Su and holidays 6am-1pm, 3-7pm, and 9-9:15pm. June-Aug. M-F 6am-noon and 1-9:15pm; Sa-Su and holidays 2-9:15pm. Free, but donation encouraged.)

The monastery also houses several small museums, all of which are free to the public (donation requested). The **Skarbiec** (treasury) contains art donated by kings, nobility, clergy, and pilgrims, including chalices, liturgical vestments, and jewelry. (Open June-Aug. daily 9am-5pm; Sept.-May 9am-4pm.) The **Arsenal** exhibits weapons, military insignia, and medals commemorating the trials the monastery has weathered from the Middle Ages to World War II. (Open in summer daily 9am-5pm; off-season 9am-4pm.) Meanwhile, the **Museum of the 600th Anniversary** (Muzeum Sześćsetlecia), assembled in 1982 to commemorate the anniversary of the icon's arrival at Jasna Góra, highlights the work and history of the Paulite Fathers, as well that of **Lech Wełęsa,** whose Nobel Prize rests here. The museum also protects a copy of the Paulite Code from 1512, the Monastery's 1382 founding document, and an array of musical instruments used by the monks. (Open daily 9am-5pm.) The **Sala Rycerska** (Knight's Hall), which was once used to host parliamentary meetings, now features photographs of the Pope's travels abroad. Ascend the Basilica's tower for excellent views. (Tower open April-Nov. daily 8am-4pm.)

The largest crowds converge on the monastery during the **Marian feasts and festivals.** These include: May 3 (Feast of Our Lady Queen of Poland), July 16 (Feast of Our Lady of Scapulars), August 15 (Feast of the Assumption), August 26 (Feast of Our Lady of Częstochowa), September 8 (Feast of the Birth of Our Lady), and September 12 (Feast of the Name Mary).

BLACK MADONNA Jasna Góra's pilgrimage tradition dates to the monastery's founding in 1382. That year, Prince Władysław II of Opole invited Paulite monks from Hungary to Poland and set them up on top of the Jasna Góra hill, giving them land as well as the picture that is now known as the Black Madonna. According to legend, St. Luke painted the icon on a plank of the table at which the Holy Family prayed and dined in Nazareth. Historians, however, have surmised it is actually a 6th- or 7th-century Byzantine icon. She owes her name to an aging process which changed the color of her face over time, but her fame comes from the wounds she incurred. The story goes that two thieves—said to be followers of the Czech reformer Jan Hus, but more likely political opponents of the monastery's patron, King Władysław—tried to make off with her but were unable to because of her great weight. Frustrated, they slashed her face twice, immediately drawing a torrent of blood. Court painters painstakingly restored the Madonna and added on two painted slashes to remember the assault. Her legend grew further following the Swedish invasions of 1655 and 1705, when the monastery, defended by a few hundred monks and faced with an enemy numbering three thousand, remained unconquered while the surrounding countryside was overrun. Five million pilgrims come to Częstochowa each year to get a glimpse of the icon and ask for help in their own everyday battles.

⚡ DAYTRIP FROM CZĘSTOCHOWA

TRAIL OF EAGLES' NESTS

From Częstochowa, take bus #58 or 67 to Olsztyn-Rynek (30min.; every 15-30min.; 3zł, students 1.50zł) from ul. Piłsudskiego, across from the Częstochowa train station. Castle tower open daily 8am-8pm. 2zł, students 1zł.

Just when you've had it with crowded buses, churches, and regional history museums, a trip to the Trail of Eagles' Nests reminds you why you liked traveling in the first place. Numerous crags of Jurassic limestone erupt from rolling green hills along the narrow 100km strip of land known as the **Kraków-Częstochowa Uplands** (Jura Krakówska-Częstochowska). These outcroppings were often incorporated into the fortifications of 12th-century **castles** built in the area, whose perches high on the rocky crags earned them the name "eagles' nests." As artillery grew more powerful, the efficacy of the defensive walls diminished, and the fortifications proved no match for the invading Swedes. By the end of the 17th-century wars, the fortresses had seriously deteriorated. Today, only a few remain whole, including **Wawel Castle** in Kraków (see p. 507). The ruins of the rest still lie along the uplands, waiting to be discovered.

The two biggest attractions on the trail, the **Olsztyn Castle** and the **Pieskowa Skała Castle,** are easy half-day trips from Częstochowa and Kraków, respectively. Originally constructed in the 12th and 13th centuries, the castle that currently stands in the tiny, pastoral town of Olsztyn has lost much of its former glory. In 1655, the Swedish army ransacked the complex while, a century later, the locals appropriated bricks from the partially destroyed castle to rebuild the town church. The preserved sections—including two **towers**—are in the **upper castle.** Look out for signs of the two most famous castle ghosts; a young bride who got lost in the (since-destroyed) dungeon, and Maciek Borkowic, who was imprisoned in the circular tower for his rebellion against King Casimir the Great. An evening climb to the ruins allows for a great view of the illuminated spire of Jasna Góra. A **hiking trail** that runs along the entire 100km takes about seven days. PTTK in Kraków or Częstochowa can provide **maps.** The trail is marked by red blazes, and maps are posted regularly along the way. The route leads through many small towns where hikers can find tourist info, provisions, and accommodations.

WROCŁAW
☎(0)71

Wrocław (VROTS-wahv), the capital of Dolny Śląsk (Lower Silesia), straddles the Oder River. During World War II, it became *Festung Breslau*, one of the last Nazi battlegrounds en route to Berlin. After suffering heavily under communist control, Wrocław's architecture has been rejuvenated over the past ten years by local officials, and few scars are visible today. Although the city already captivates visitors with its colorful *rynek*, lush parks, and stone bridges, Wrocław has great plans for expansion—preparations are already underway for the 2010 Expo.

▊ TRANSPORTATION

Trains: Wrocław Główny, ul. Piłsudskiego 105 (☎368 83 33). **24hr. currency exchange** inside. Counters #17 and 18 handle international ticketing. MC/V. To: **Jelenia Góra** (3hr., 9 per day, 25.30zł); **Kraków** (4½hr., 8 per day, 34.80zł); **Poznań** (2hr., 21 per day, 29.40zł); **Warsaw** (5hr., 11 per day, 40zł); **Berlin, GER** (6hr., 2 per day, 141zł); **Budapest, HUN** (5hr., 1 per day, 209zł); **Dresden, GER** (5½hr., 4 per day, 119zł); **Moscow, RUS** (36hr., 1 per day, 290zł); **Prague, CZR** (7hr., 3 per day, 117zł).

Buses: Ul. Sucha 1 (☎61 22 99 or 61 81 22), behind the trains. Station open daily 5am-11pm. To: **Jelenia Góra** (3hr., 20 per day, 24zł); **Kraków** (7hr., 1 per day, 37zł); **Poznań** (3hr., 2 per day, 28zł); **Warsaw** (8hr., 3 per day, 40zł).

Public Transportation: Tram and **bus** tickets cost 2zł per person and per backpack (students 1zł). 1-day pass 6.60zł, students 3.30zł; 10-day pass 24zł/12zł. Express buses (marked by letters as opposed to numbers) 2.40zł. Night buses 2.80zł.

Taxis: ☎72 55 55, 96 21, or 96 29. The trip from the train station to the *rynek* should cost around 12zł.

▊▊ ORIENTATION AND PRACTICAL INFORMATION

The political and social heart of Wrocław is the *rynek* (main square). The **train** and **bus stations** lie 15min. southeast. With your back to the train station, turn left on **ul. Piłsudskiego,** take a right on **ul. Świdnicka,** and go past **pl. Kościuszki** (past McDonald's and Tutti-Frutti), over the **Fosa River,** and into the *rynek*. Alternatively, catch any tram in front of the Hotel Piast, just left of the station, going toward **pl. Dominikańska.** At the square, head down **Oławska** away from **ul. Janickiego** (2min.).

Tourist Office: IT, Rynek 14 (☎343 71 19 or 344 11 09; fax 344 29 62). Sells **maps** (4-6.50zł). English spoken. Open M-F 9am-5pm, Sa 10am-3pm.

Currency Exchange: Bank PKO, ul. Oławska 2 (☎344 44 54), cashes **traveler's checks** for 1.5% commission (10zł minimum) and gives MC/V **cash advances.** Open M-F 8am-6pm, Sa 9am-2pm.

24-Hour ATMs: ATMs are everywhere.

Western Union: 24-Hour services available at **Biuro Podróży,** ul. Kościuszki 27 (☎344 81 88). Open M-F 10am-4pm, Sa 10am-5pm.

Luggage Storage: At the **train station** to the right of the main hall. 10zł per day for up to 400zł of declared value; 14zł for up to 500zł, plus 2zł for every additional 100zł. Open 24hr. Also at the **bus station.** 5.50zł per day plus 1zł for every 50zł of declared value. Open daily 6am-10pm.

English-Language Bookstore: Empik Megastore, Rynek 50 (☎343 51 41). Sells foreign books and newspapers. Open M-Sa 9am-9pm, Su 11am-7pm. MC/V.

Emergency: ☎344 30 32. **Ambulance,** ul. Traugutta 112 (☎342 12 11 or 999).

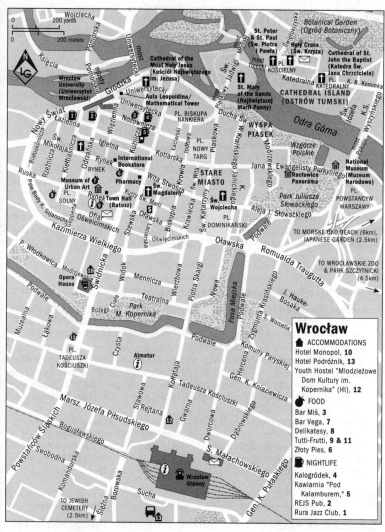

Wrocław

🏠 ACCOMMODATIONS
Hotel Monopol, **10**
Hotel Podróżnik, **13**
Youth Hostel "Młodzieżowe
    Dom Kultury im.
    Kopernika" (HI) **12**

🍎 FOOD
Bar Miś, **3**
Bar Vega, **7**
Delikatesy, **8**
Tutti-Frutti, **9 & 11**
Złoty Pies, **6**

🍸 NIGHTLIFE
Kalogródek, **4**
Kawiarnia "Pod
    Kalamburem," **5**
REJS Pub, **2**
Rura Jazz Club, **1**

POLAND

Hospital: Szpital Im. Babińskiego, pl. 1-go Maja 8 (☎341 00 00).

24-hour Pharmacy: Apteka Herbowa, ul. Wita Stwosza 3 (☎343 64 73).

Internet Access: Internet Klub Navig@tor Podziemia, ul. Kuźnica 11/13 (☎343 70 69). 5zł per hr., 7zł per 2hr. Open daily 9am-10pm. **Cafe Internet,** ul. Orzańska 20 (☎344 10 05) on the corner with ul. Barbary. 3.50zł per hr. Open daily 10am-9pm.

Post Office: Ul. Małachowskiego 1 (☎344 77 78), to the right of the train station. **Poste Restante** at window #22. **Telephones** inside and outside. Open M-F 6am-8pm, Sa-Su 8am-3pm. **Branch** at Rynek 28. Open 24hr.

Postal Code: 50 900.

♬ ACCOMMODATIONS

Check with the tourist office for info about **student dorms** ❶ that rent rooms July through August (15-35zł per person).

Youth Hostel "Mlodziezowy Dom Kultury im. Kopernika" (HI), ul. Kołłątaja 20 (☎343 88 56), opposite the train station on the road perpendicular to ul. Piłsudskiego. A cheerful hostel, plastered with children's artwork. Well-equipped kitchen and exquisite shared bathrooms. Sheets 7zł. Lockout 10am-5pm. Curfew 10pm. Call ahead. Dorms 22zł; doubles 28.40zł. Discount for stays two nights or longer. ❶

Hotel Podróżnik, ul. Sucha 1 (☎373 28 45), above the bus station. Skylights illuminate this immaculate white hotel. Breakfast included. Check-in 2pm. Check-out noon. Singles 88zł; doubles 130zł; triples 162zł; quads 196zł; quints 225zł. ❹

Hotel Monopol, ul. Modrzejewskiej 2 (☎343 70 41; fax 343 51 03; www.orbis.pl). From the stations, take tram "K" 2 stops to Kazimierza Wielkiego. Alternatively, from the station, turn left on ul. Piłsudskiego. Turn right on an unnamed street, then turn left on ul. Modrzejewskiej. The hotel is on the right. Monopol rolls out the red carpet for its guests, offering classy accommodations near the *rynek*. English spoken. All rooms include satellite TV, radio, telephone, and breakfast. Check-in and check-out 2pm. Singles 115zł, with bath 180zł; doubles 150zł/200zł; triples with bath 310zł. AmEx/MC/V. ❺

♫ FOOD

The **Delikatesy grocery store,** pl. Solny 8/9 (☎344 14 84), near the *rynek*, is open 24hr.

Bar Vega, Sukiennice 1/2 (☎344 39 34). A jungle-themed haven for veggie lovers. The menus differ by floor—the 2nd fl. has an international flair. Entrees under 8zł. 1st fl. open M-F 8am-7pm, Sa-Su 9am-5pm; 2nd fl. M-F noon-6pm, Sa noon-5pm. ❶

Bar Miś, ul. Kuźniczna 48 (☎343 49 63). The polar bear on the sign points to speedy service in this popular cafeteria. Entrees 10zł. Open M-F 7am-6pm, Sa 8am-5pm. ❷

Złoty Pies (Golden Dog), Rynek 41 (☎372 37 60; www.zlotypies.pl). In the corner of the *rynek*. Specializes in *grille* and *gryos* (hot sandwiches; 10-25zł). Has an extensive array of alcoholic refreshments. Try the *rura piwna* (beer cylinder, 30zł). Beer 6zł. Open daily noon-midnight. AmEx/MC/V. ❷

Tutti-Frutti, pl. Kościuszki 1/4 (☎344 43 06). This upscale restaurant serves endless arrays of ice cream desserts (7-13zł) and tortes (3-7zł). Though the color scheme is questionable, the quality of the desserts is not in doubt. Entrees 20-30zł. Bakery open M-Sa 9am-8pm, Su 9am-6pm; restaurant open daily 10am-10pm. **Branch** at Rynek 22 (☎342 80 03). Open M-Th 10am-11pm, F-Su 10am-midnight. ❺

◎ SIGHTS

RACŁAWICE PANORAMA AND NATIONAL MUSEUM. The 120-by-15m **Panorama** painting wraps viewers in the action of the 18th-century peasant insurrection against Russian occupation. The victory of the underdog Poles led by Tadeusz Kościuszko has achieved legendary status (see **History,** p. 474). Damaged by a bomb in 1944 and hidden in a Bernadine Monastery for safe-keeping, the painting was finally restored with the rise of Solidarity in 1980; previously it had been considered politically imprudent for the Poles to glorify independence from Russia. Thirty-minute showings include audio narration; headsets in 8 languages available. *(Ul. Purkyniego 11. Facing away from the town hall, bear left on Kuźnicza for 2 blocks and then right onto Kotlarska, which becomes ul. Purkyniego. The Panorama is several blocks down on the right. ☎/fax 343 36 39. Open Tu-Su 9am-4pm; reservations required for 10:30am, 1pm, 3:30pm ses-*

sions. Come early as sessions may sell out. 19zł, students 15zł.) The **National Museum** (Muzeum Narodowe) is in the massive ivy-clad building across the street and to the left. Permanent exhibits include a sprawling collection of Silesian paintings and modern artwork from around the country. *(Pl. Powstancyw Warszawy 5. ☎372 53 56; fax 343 36 39. Open Tu-W and F-Su 10am-4pm, Th 9am-4pm. 10zł, students 7zł. Free Sa.)*

CATHEDRAL SQUARE. (Pl. Katredralny.) Across the Oder lies the serene Cathedral Square. The sky-piercing spires of the 13th-century **Cathedral of St. John the Baptist** (Katedra Św. Jana Chrzciciela) dominates the skyline. Inside, light filters faintly through small stained-glass windows, shrouding much of the Gothic interior in shadow. Climb the **tower** for an excellent view of the surrounding churches. *(From the National Museum, turn left on Most Pokoju, then left again on Kardynala Boleslawa Kominka. Open daily 10am-5:30pm. 4zł, students 3zł. Donation requested for entrance to the chapel.)* Nearby, the **Church of St. Mary of the Sands** (Najświętszej Marii Panny) contains a 14th-century icon of Our Lady of Victory that medieval knights carried into battle.

WROCŁAW UNIVERSITY. (Uniwersytet Wrocławski.) This center of Wrocław's cultural life houses a number of architectural gems. **Aula Leopoldina**, an 18th-century lecture hall with magnificent frescoes, is the most impressive. *(Pl. Uniwersytecka 1, on the 2nd floor of the main university building. Entrance directly opposite ul. Więzienna. Go down Nankiera through its name change to Uniwersytecka. ☎375 22 71. Open Th-Tu 10am-3pm. 4zł, students 2zł).* Climb the **Mathematical Tower** for a sweeping view of the city. *(4zł, students 2zł.)* The adjoining 17th-century **Cathedral of the Most Holy Jesus** (Kościół Najświętszego im. Jezusa), replete with dramatic sculptures, is also worth a visit. *(Opposite ul. Kużnicza. Open to tourists M-Sa 10am-2pm. 2zł.)*

AROUND THE RYNEK. The *rynek* and its Renaissance and Gothic **Town Hall** (*ratusz*) are the heart of the city. Ul. Świdnicka, lining one side of the *rynek*, is a street so beautiful that the Germans tried to remove its cobblestones to destroy it during World War II. Inside the *ratusz* is the **Museum of Urban Art** (Muzeum Sztuki Mieszczańskiej), which features old and new art in an ancient building. Take time to look at the collections of old silver, including an amazing scepter, then enjoy the sights and sounds from a horse-drawn carriage. *(☎374 16 90. Open W-Sa 11am-5pm, Su 10am-6pm. Last admission 30min. prior to closing. 5zł, students 3zł. Horse-drawn carriage reservations ☎398 84 00. 5zł.)* Diagonal from the *rynek*, at the corner of ul. Ruska and ul. Gepperta, the smaller square, **pl. Solny**, is a calmer version of the bustling *rynek*. Its immaculately maintained, multi-colored buildings, flower vendors, and quiet fountains lend themselves to a picturesque stroll.

JEWISH CEMETARY. (Cmentarz Żydowski.) Recently opened to the public, the Jewish Cemetery contains the remains of Ferdinand Lasalle, the families of Max Born, Fritz Haber, and the wife of Thomas Mann. A walk around this shaded enclave reveals fragments of Jewish tombstones dating from the 12th and 13th centuries. *(Ul. Ślężna 37/39. From the train station, take bus #709 heading away from the center to Akademia Ekonomiczna. Get off at the corner of Ślężna and Kamienna; go farther down Ślężna and the cemetery will be on your right. ☎367 82 36. Gates open Apr.-Oct. daily 8am-6pm. Guided tours Su noon. 5zł, students 3zł.)*

JAPANESE GARDEN. (Ogród Japońskie.) Spend a meditative afternoon in this botanical haven created in 1913. Its harmonious elements fulfill the requirements of Japanese gardening art and its many winding paths twist past two waterfalls, a pond, and delicate wooden bridges. Several species of Japanese flowers flourish. *(Take tram #2 from pl. Dominikańska to the Hala Ludowa stop. Walk in the direction of the tram to the path on the left leading through the park. Continue through the park to garden entrance. ☎0601 743 563. Open Apr.-Oct. daily 9am-7pm. 2zł, students 1zł.)*

POLAND

🎵 🍷 ENTERTAINMENT AND NIGHTLIFE

For event info, pick up the free publication *Co jest grane?* (What's Going On?) at the tourist office. Wrocław is famous for its student and experimental theater; check out the **IT** to see what's going up when. May brings the international **Jazz nad Odrą Festival** (Jazz by the Oder) to Wrocław.

▨ REJS Pub, ul. Kotlarska 32a (☎343 19 42). Students and locals crowd this tiny bar, downing cheap beer and admiring the bear above the bar. Ask the barkeeper how to score a pair of free movie tickets. Beer 3.50zł. Open M-Sa 9:30am-late, Su 11am-late.

Rura Jazz Club, Łazienna 4 (☎344 30 20). The walls of Poland's first jazz club are lined with portraits of jazz greats. Live music 3 times per week, usually 9pm-midnight. Blues night W is a given; for other days, call ahead or pick up *Co jest grane?*. Cover varies; 20zł for popular acts. Open daily 4pm-1am. MC/V.

Kawiarnia "Pod Kalamburem," ul. Kuźnicza 29a (☎372 35 71; fax 341 94 62), in the university quarter. A decadent artists' corner that serves delicious doses of caffeine in the form of coffee, tea, and hot chocolate (4.50-9zł). Fine cheeses from 5zł. Open M-Sa 11am-midnight, Su 4pm-11pm.

Kalogródek, ul. Kuźnicza 29b. At the intersection with ul. Uniwersytecka in the center of the university district. Students crowd the large outdoor patio and play darts and foosball inside. Cheap beer (0.5L *Żywiec* 5zł). Open daily 10am-midnight.

JELENIA GÓRA ☎(0)75

At the foot of the Sudety's Karkonosze range lies the lovely town of Jelenia Góra, a natural stop along the way to hiking and skiing in Szklarska Poręba, but its most breathtaking attraction is the fabulous medieval **▨Chojnik Castle** (Zamek Chojnik). Standing guard over the Jelenia Góra Valley from its solitary mountaintop perch (627m), the well-maintained ruins, including a **tower** with magnificent view, are reminiscent of a fairy tale. To get there, take bus #9 from the train station or #7 or 9 from the ul. Wolności stop (follow ul. Długa from the *rynek* to Wolności) to Sobieszów (45min.). Hike 30min. on the red trail to the castle. Or, bike the red trail from Jelenia Góra. Check out the jousting tournament in August. (☎090 252 157. Open July-Aug. daily 10am-6pm; Sept.-May and Feb.-Apr. Tu-Su 10am-4pm; May-June and Sep. Tu-Su 10am-5pm. 3zł, students 1.50zł.)

The **train station,** ul. 1-go Maja 77 (☎94 36), is a 10min. walk from town. (Open 3am-12:15am.) Trains run to: **Kraków** (8hr., 1 per day, 44zł); **Szklarska Poręba** (40min., 7 per day, 6.30zł); **Warsaw** (9hr.; June-Aug. 3 per day, Sept.-May 2 per day; 44zł); and **Wrocław** (3hr., 16 per day, 16zł). Buses run to: **Kraków** (3hr., 2 per day, 42zł); **Poznań** (5hr., 2 per day, 38zł); **Szklarska Poręba** (1hr., 9 per day, 5zł); and **Wrocław** (3hr., 8 per day, 19zł). The *kasa* (ticket window), is open 8am-5pm. Tickets for city buses within town cost 2.20zł. **IT,** ul. Grodzka 16, lies near the *rynek* by the bus station. The friendly staff sells **maps** (4-6zł. ☎/fax 767 69 35; itratusz@box43.pl. Open M-F 9am-6pm, Sa 10am-2pm; July-Sept. also Su 10am-2pm.) **Luggage storage** is available at the train station (7zł per day; open 6am-7pm). **Bank Zachodni,** ul. J. Kochanowskiego 8, the second left after the train station, cashes AmEx **Traveler's Cheques** for 30zł commission. The bank also has **Western Union** services and a 24hr. MC/V **ATM.** (☎764 62 25. Open M-F 8am-5pm, Sa 8am-1pm.)

Youth Hostel Bartek ❶, ul. Bartka Zwycięzcy 10, is your best bet in Jelenia Góra. Head away from the train station on ul. 1-go Maja, go left on ul. Kochanowskiego, and turn right onto Bartka Zwycięzcy. The hostel's bunked beds and communal bathrooms teem with schoolchildren during tourist season, so call ahead. (☎752 57

46. Reception 7-10am, 5-9pm. Lockout 10am-5pm. 2- to 10-person dorms 13.50-16.50zł.) **Kurna Chata ❶**, pl. Ratuszowy 23/24, serves tasty *dolnoslaskie* (Lower Sląsk) dishes (4-8zł) in a barn-themed interior whose ceramic cows and pickle jars are curiously incongruent to the throbbing techno pouring from the speakers. (Open M-Sa 10am-late, Su noon-midnight.)

KARPACZ ☎(0)75

Going to Western Poland and not visiting Karpacz is like eating herring without vodka; both are simply unacceptable. Like nearby Szklarska Poręba, the town is an important gateway to Karkonosze National Park. Surrounding mountains throw long shadows over thickly forested valleys, and the raw beauty of the landscape—even from within Karpacz itself—is stunning.

⬛ TRANSPORTATION. There is no bus station in town. The winding main street, ul. 3-go Maja, is the main thoroughfare for PKS buses—eight stops dot the way to Karpacz Górny, the top of town, on their way to and from **Jelenia Góra** (45min., every 30min.-1hr., 5.20zł). Catch any of these buses to ride between stops within Karpacz (2.20zł). The poorly-marked stops are named after nearby landmarks. Keep your eyes open, as a missed stop could result in an exhausting climb.

⬛⬛ ORIENTATION AND PRACTICAL INFORMATION. Karpacz's streets are poorly marked and follow the contours of the mountain, meandering uphill along **ul. 3-go Maja.** Side streets provide steeply sloped shortcuts. Uphill from the Biały Jar stop, the road changes names to **Karkonoska.** Get off incoming buses at Karpacz Bachus and go uphill to the Karpacz **tourist office,** ul. 3-go Maja 52. They **exchange currency,** sell maps, and reserve rooms. You can also hire a hiking guide for 150zł per 8hr. (☎761 95 47; fax 761 95 53. English spoken. Open M-F 9am-5pm, Sa 9am-4pm., July-Aug. also Su 10am-4pm.) Ask at the tourist office about **biking, skiing, rock-climbing, horseback riding,** and **camping;** these are generally available at **Szkoła Górska,** ul. Obrońców Pokoju 6a (☎752 82 91; fax 761 99 09). Call ahead to make arrangements. **Bank Zachodni,** ul. 3-go Maja 43, cashes **traveler's checks** for 30zł commission. (☎/fax 753 81 20. Open M-F 9am-5pm.) It also has a Visa **ATM** and **Western Union** services. There's a **pharmacy, K-Med,** at ul. 3-go Maja 33. (☎761 86 69. Open M-F 9am-8pm, Sa 9am-5pm, Su 9am-1pm.) The **post office** is at ul. 3-go Maja 21. (☎761 92 20; fax 761 95 85. Open M-F 8am-6pm, Sa 8am-2:30pm.) **Postal Code:** 58-540.

⬛⬛ ACCOMMODATIONS AND FOOD. Reservations are unnecessary, except on New Year's Eve. **D.W. Szczyt ❶**, ul. Na Śnieżkę 6, is at the uphill end of town a few steps away from Świątynia Wang. Take the bus to Karpacz Wang—the uphill hike from the center of town takes an hour and is impossible with luggage. If the amazing view doesn't leave you breathless, the great prices will—as will the 200m haul from the bus stop. Make reservations at the Karpacz **IT** at ul. 3-go Maja 23 (see above); ring the doorbell if locked. (Singles through quads 25zł per person.) **Private pensions ❷** proliferate, especially on Kościelna street just downhill from Karpacz Bachus (30-70zł). Unfortunately, some are open only part of the year—inquire at the Karpacz tourist office or at IT (see above) for current info. **Pension Celina ❶**, in the center of town at ul. Kościelna 9, has all the comforts of Grandma's house, including a cozy sitting room, TVs in all rooms, and balconies in some. (☎761 94 55. Breakfast 10zł. Doubles with bath 50zł; triples 70zł.) **Camping Pod Brzozami ❶**, ul. Obrońców Pokoju 3, offers a quiet strip of greenery wedged between an abandoned swimming pool and the mountains. (☎0601 790 618. Check-in and check-out noon. Some English spoken. 7zł per person. 2-3 person tents 5zł, cars 5zł, buses 6zł, caravans 12zł. Electricity 5zł.) **Gospoda Karpacka ❷**, ul. Obrońców Pokoju 1, just downhill from IT, serves large, delicious meals (8-25zł) in a comfortable, rustic setting. Their specialty is *gołąbki* (14zł), rice and meat rolled in boiled cabbage leaves. (☎761 93 14. Open daily 10am-10pm.) The grocery store **Delikatesy**, ul. 3-go Maja 29, stocks everything necessary for a picnic in the mountains. (☎761 92 59. Open M-Sa 8:30am-9pm, Su 10am-8pm.)

◙ ♫ **SIGHTS AND OUTDOOR ACTIVITIES.** The uphill hike to **Wang Chapel** (Świątynia Wang), ul. Śnieżki 8, at the upper end of town, takes hours, but is worth the time. Follow 3-go Maja and side streets marked by a blue blaze to get there. (Or take the bus to Karpacz Wang and follow the signs.) This Viking church was built in southern Norway at the turn of the 12th century. In the early 1800s it sorely needed a restoration no one could afford, so Kaiser Friedrich Wilhelm III of Prussia had it sent to Karpacz for the Lutheran community to enjoy. Gaping dragons' mouths, stylized lions, and intricate plant carvings adorn the building. (☎752 82 91. Open Apr. 15-Oct M-Sa 9am-6pm, Su 11:30am-6pm; closes one hour earlier Nov.-Apr. 14. 3.50zł, students 2.50zł.)

Hikers of all ages aim for the crown of **Śnieżka** (Mt. Snow; 1602m), the highest peak in Poland. The border runs across the summit. Śnieżka and most of the trails lie within **Karkonosze National Park** (Karkonoski Park Narodowy; 3zł, students 1.50zł; 3-day pass 6zł/3zł). All the park's trails lead, more or less directly, to **Pod Śnieżka** (1394m), the last stop along the treeless ridge just beneath the rocky peak of Śnieżka. To get there as quickly (2-3hr.) and painlessly as possible, take the Kopa chairlift. (Follow the black trail from Hotel Biały Jar until you see the lift on the left. Lift runs daily June-Aug. 8:30am-5:30pm; Sept.-May 8am-4pm, weather permitting. Before 1pm 17zł, students 14zł; round-trip 22zł/18zł. After 1pm 13zł/9zł; round-trip 16zł/12zł.) If you want to hike all the way up, there are several routes:

Blue Trail (3hr.). The easiest way to reach Pod Śnieżka is to take the blue-blazed path starting at Świątynia Wang. This stone-paved road is also conducive to biking. Follow the blue route to Polana (1080m; 1hr.), then hike up to the scenic Mały Staw ("Small Lake"; 1hr.). From here, it's 35min. to Spalona Strażnica, above the tree line on the ridge, then an easy 30min. to the Pod Śnieżka pass.

Yellow Trail (2hr. 35min.). From Polana (see above), endurance hikers should continue along the yellow route to another petrified protrusion at Słonecznik (Sunflower; 35min.). This stretch, along a rocky stream bed, is a challenging, vertical haul not for the weak of ankle. Turning left here takes you to the red trail (see below), which leads to Pod Śnieżka (1hr.).

Red Trail (2½hr.). The scenic red trail begins behind Hotel Biały Jar's parking lot. It travels along the ridge to Spalona Strażnica, where it meets the blue trail (see above). Once you emerge above the tree line, it's a difficult hike up to Pod Śnieżka.

Black trail (2¼hr.). The most challenging of the trails, the black trail heads up from behind Hotel Biały Jar's parking lot. After splitting from the red trail, it shoots straight up the slope in an exhausting haul to the top.

From Pod Śnieżka, there are two trails up to Śnieżka itself. The black **Zygzag** goes straight up the north side; look for the cobblestone path (20-30min.). The blue trail, **Jubilee Way,** winds around the peak (45min.). Once there, if the breathtaking views of the Polish and Czech Sudety aren't enough, climb to the **observatory.** (Open June-Aug. 9am-5pm; Sept.-May 9am-3pm. 2zł, students 1zł.) Winter brings tons of snow and skiers seeking relaxation to Karpacz. Lift and equipment rental info is readily available (☎761 86 19; www.kopa.com.pl). A one-day pass costs 35-39zł, depending on the date; student rates are about 10zł less. The longest lift is 2229m long and has a vertical span of 530m; it leads to the Kopa peak.

GREATER POLAND (WIELKOPOLSKA)

A train ride through the *Wielkopolski* lowlands reveals green fields, rolling hills, and dense woodlands. Except for a trio of urban centers—multi-faceted Poznań, Copernicus's birthplace Toruń, and oft-neglected Łódź—Wielkopolska is as serene as it is culturally rich.

POZNAŃ ☎(0)61

Long influenced by the Prussians and the Germans, Poznań (POZ-nan; pop. 590,000) still retains close ties with its orderly Western neighbors. The city buzzes with economic efficiency, especially during its annual international trade fair. Though Poznań's primary interest lies in economic affairs, the capital of Wielkopolska maintains its traditional role as a center of political and cultural life. Rich music, art, and theater scenes lie just below Poznań's all-business surface, available to anyone willing to seek them out.

▐ TRANSPORTATION

Trains: Ul. Dworcowa 1 (☎866 12 12 or 869 38 11). To: **Gdynia** (4½hr., 7 per day, 44zł); **Katowice** (5hr, 11 per day, 41zł); **Kraków** (5½hr., 10 per day, 44zł); **Szczecin** (3hr., 12 per day, 25.32zł); **Warsaw** (3hr.; 19 per day; 56.30zł, add 17zł for reservation); **Berlin, GER** (3hr.; 8 per day; 95zł, students 85zł); **Moscow, RUS** (27hr., 2 per day, 250zł). Open 24hr.

Buses: Ul. Towarowa 17/19 (☎833 15 11, international travel office 833 16 55; fax 833 05 70;). To: **Kołobrzeg** (5½hr., 4 per day, 39zł); **Łódz** (4½hr., 4 per day, 36zł); **Berlin, GER;** (6½hr.; 5 per week; 110zł, students 99zł); **Paris, FRA** (18hr.; 11 per week; 314-399zł, students 283-359zł); **Prague, CZR** (8hr.; 2 per week; 129zł, students 116zł). International "autokar" trips available. Station open 5:30am-10:20pm; international office open M-F 9am-6pm, Sa 9am-1pm.

Public Transportation: 10min. 1zł; 30min. 2zł; 1hr. 3zł. Prices double 11pm-4am. 50zł fine for riding ticketless. Large baggage needs its own ticket.

Taxis: Radio Taxi (☎919, 951, or 96 66.)

▐▌▐▌ ORIENTATION AND PRACTICAL INFORMATION

Poznań is a huge city, but almost everything in town can be found in **Stare Miasto** (Old Town). The **train station,** Poznań Główny, occupies the dead end of **ul. Dworcowa** in Stare Miasto's southwest corner; the **bus station** is 500m down **ul. Towarowa.** To get to the **Stary Rynek** (Old Market) by foot, exit the main hall of the train station, climb the stairs, and turn right on **ul. Roosevelta.** After several blocks, turn right on **ul. Św. Marcin.** Continue to **al. Marcinkowskiego,** go left, and turn right on **ul. Paderewskiego** (30min. total). Alternatively, catch any **tram** heading down Św. Marcin (to the right) from the end of ul. Dworcowa. Get off at ul. Marcinkowskiego.

Tourist Offices: Centrum Informacji Turystycznej (CIT), Stary Rynek 59/60 (☎852 98 05; fax 855 33 79), sells maps (6zł), provides accommodations info, and arranges 3hr. tours (220zł). English and German spoken. Open Sept.-May M-F 9am-5pm; June-Aug. M-F 9am-5pm, Sa 10am-2pm. **Glob-Tour** (☎/fax 866 06 67), on ul. Dworcowa in the main lobby of the train station. Tourist info, maps (7zł), and **currency exchange.** English spoken. Open 24hr.

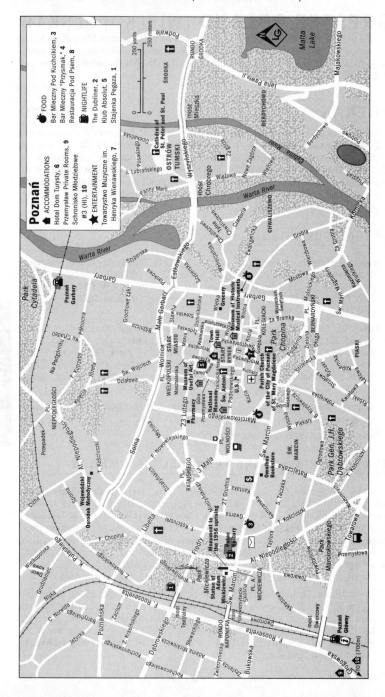

Poznań

ACCOMMODATIONS
Hotel Dom Turysty, 6
Przemysław Private Rooms, 9
Schronisko Młodzieżowe
#3 (HI), 10

ENTERTAINMENT
Towarzystwo Muzyczne im.
Henryka Wieniawskiego, 7

FOOD
Bar Mleczny Pod Kuchcikiem, 3
Bar Mleczny "Przysmak," 4
Restauracja Pod Psem, 8

NIGHTLIFE
The Dubliner, 2
Klub Absolut, 5
Stajenka Pegaza, 1

Currency Exchange: Bank PKO S.A., ul. Św. Marcin 52/56 (☎855 85 58), cashes **traveler's checks** for 1% commission. Open M-F 8am-6pm, Sa 10am-2pm. **Western Union** services available at **Bank Zachodni,** ul. Fredry 12. Open M-F 8am-4pm.

Luggage Storage: At the train station, opposite Glob-Tour. 2zł plus 0.15% of every 10zł of declared value. Open 24hr. with breaks from 7:45-8:15am and 7:45-8:15pm. Also in lockers at the train station. 8zł for a large bin, 4zł for a small one.

English-language Bookstore: Omnibus Bookstore, ul. Św. Marcin 39 (☎853 61 82). Open M-F 10am-7pm, Sa 10am-4pm. AmEx/MC/V.

24-Hour Pharmacy: Apteka Centralna, ul. 23 Lutego 18 (☎852 26 25).

Hospital: Ul. Szkolna 8/12 (☎999 or 852 72 11).

Internet Access: Internet Club, pl. Wolności 8 (☎852 79 33), opposite Empik on the 2nd fl.; take the stairs on your left once inside. 1zł per 10min., 5zł per hr. Open 24hr.

Post Office: Ul. Kościuszki 77 (☎853 67 43; fax 869 74 08). For **Poste Restante,** go to windows #6 or 7 upstairs. Open M-F 7am-9pm, Sa 8am-6pm, Su 9am-5pm. **Branch** next to the train station open 24hr.

Postal Code: 61 890.

ACCOMMODATIONS

During fairs (Mar., June, Oct.), tourists and businesspeople quickly fill the city. Prices rise 10%, and getting a decently priced room without calling ahead is virtually impossible. For **private rooms** contact ⊠**Przemysław ❷,** ul. Głogowska 16. The pleasant staff rents comfortably furnished rooms near the city center. (☎866 35 60; fax 866 51 63; przemyslaw@przemyslaw.com.pl. Singles 42zł, during fairs 68zł; doubles 64zł/96zł. Open M-F 8am-6pm, Sa 10am-2pm; closed some Sa July-Aug.)

Schronisko Młodzieżowe #3 (HI), ul. Berwińskiego 2/3 (☎866 40 40). Exit the train station through the tunnel and turn left onto ul. Głogowska; ul. Berwińskiego is 2 long blocks to the right. 2 rooms, 7 beds, and 1 entrance to the hallway. The hostel also separates foreign and Polish travelers. Sheets 4zł. Reception 5-9:30pm. Lockout 10am-5pm. Curfew 10pm. 2- to 10-bed dorms 20zł for Poles, 24zł for foreigners. ❶

Hotel Dom Turysty, Stary Rynek 91 (☎/fax 852 88 93; www.domturysty-hotel.com.pl). Entrance on ul. Wroniecka. Jan Dąbrowski and Józef Wybicki were guests in this former nobleman's residence. Join their ranks by exploiting the cheap dorms of this upscale inn right on Stary Rynek. English spoken. Breakfast included. Check-in noon. Check-out 10am. 4-person dorms 50zł per person; singles with bath 180zł; doubles 200zł, with bath 250zł; triples with bath 300zł. Discount for weekend stays. MC/V. ❷

FOOD

There are several **24hr. grocery stores.** In summer, enjoy the fruits of local farms at the **outdoor market** in pl. Wielkopolski, off ul. 23 Lutego.

Bar Mleczny "Przysmak," ul. Podgorna 2 (☎852 13 39). 2 floors of milk-bar mania. Order salads and pasta downstairs and hearty meals upstairs. Offers vegetarian soy renditions of several meals (4zł). Open M-F 9am-9pm, Sa 11am-7pm. ❶

Bar Mleczny Pod Kuchcikiem, ul. Św. Marcin 75. Traditional Polish food at unbeatable prices—so good this place earned the "Dobre bo Polskie" (Good because it's Polish) stamp of approval. Entrees 3-5zł. Open M-F 8am-7pm, Sa 8am-4pm, Su 10am-4pm. ❶

Restauracja Pod Psem, ul. Garbary 54 (☎851 99 70). Saddle up to the bar in this faux-farmhouse. Order traditional fare from 8 *odpasy* (courses). Grilled meat dishes 9-45zł, scrumptious soups 9zł. Open daily noon-10pm. AmEx/MC/V. ❷

◎ SIGHTS

Opulent 15th-century merchant homes, notable for their recent renovations and rainbow paint jobs, line **Stary Rynek**. The houses surround the **town hall** *(ratusz)*, a multicolored gem faithfully restored after World War II, and widely deemed the finest secular Renaissance structure north of the Alps. The museum within recalls Poznań's and Wielkopolska's history from the 13th century on, but the most captivating sight is the ornately painted ceiling. (☎852 56 13. Open M-Tu and F 10am-4pm, W noon-6pm, Th and Sa 9am-4pm, Su 10am-3pm. 5.50zł, students 3.50zł. Sa free.) The vast galleries of the **National Museum** (Muzeum Narodowe), ul. Marcinkowskiego 9, contain a marvelous collection of 13th- to 19th-century Flemish, Italian, and German paintings. (☎856 80 00; fax 851 58 98. Open Tu 10am-6pm, W 9am-5pm, Th and Su 10am-4pm, F-Sa 10am-5pm. 10zł, students 6zł; Sa free.) The National's daughter museums include the **Museum of Musical Instruments** (Muzeum Instrumentów Muzycznych), Stary Rynek 45/47, which holds a fascinating display of antique and foreign instruments, as well as the Chopin room, featuring a piano that once belonged to this son of Poland. (☎852 08 57. Open Tu-Sa 11am-5pm, Su 11am-4 3pm. 5.50zł, students 3.50zł. Sa free.) Its sister, the **Museum of Useful Art,** ul. Góra Przemysła 1, on the hill by Stary Rynek, features 13th- to 18th-century swords, clocks, and other utilities. (☎852 20 35. Open Tu-W and F-Sa 10am-4pm, Su 10am-3pm. 3.50zł. Sa free.)

In the **Parish Church of the City of Poznań,** at the end of ul. Świętosławska off Stary Rynek, sculpted ceilings and columns spiral heavenwards. (Free concerts M-Sa 12:15pm.) On the outskirts of town, in **Ostrów Tumski,** the oldest part of Poznań, stands the first Polish cathedral, **Cathedral of St. Peter and St. Paul** (Katedra Piotra i Pawła). The original 10th-century church is rumored to have been the site of Poland's symbolic baptism. The tombs of two famous Piasts are in the **Golden Chapel** (Kaplica Złota): Prince Mieszko I (d. 992) and his oldest son, Bolesław Chrobry (the Brave; d. 1025), the first king of Poland. (Open to tourists daily 9am-4pm, except during mass. Entrance to crypt 2.50zł, students 1.50zł.) **Pl. Mickiewicza** commemorates the 1956 clash over food prices between workers and government troops that killed 76 people. Two stark crosses knotted together with steel cable are emblazoned with the dates of five other workers' uprisings throughout Poland. An electronic recording tells the story from a console in front of the monument. (Free and in several languages.) In the hot summer months, escape to **Malta Lake** (Jezioro Maltańskie). From the train station, take tram #6 to Rondo Środka.

♫ ◎ ENTERTAINMENT AND FESTIVALS

Poznań's music and theater scene is lively but mercurial. The monthly *Poznań ski Informator Kulturalny, Sportowy i Turystyczny* (IKST) contains many useful phone numbers and a supplement in English on all cultural events (3.90zł; sold at bookstores and some kiosks). The **Towarzystwo Muzyczne im. Henryka Wieniawskiego** (Music Society), ul. Świętosławska 7, provides concert info. (☎852 26 42; fax 852 89 91. English spoken. Open M-F 9am-7pm.) It also hosts the huge **International Theater Festival** at Malta Lake in late June and early July. Other festivals include the **Jazz Festival** in early March, the **International Blues Festival** in late May and early June, and a **folk art festival** in July. For tickets and info on these and other cultural events contact **Centrum Informacji Miejskiej,** ul. Ratajczka 44, next to the Empik Megastore. (☎94 31. Open M-F 10am-7pm, Sa-Su 10am-5pm.)

◢ NIGHTLIFE

The Dubliner, ul. Św. Marcin 80/82 (☎853 60 81, ext. 147). Enter on al. Niepodłe-głości in the side of the Zamek. A warm and inviting pub full of warm and inviting spirits. Irish food 8-20zł. Guinness 12zł, *Lech* 8zł. Live music in summer, F-Sa 10pm. Open M-F noon-midnight or last guest, Sa-Su 4:30pm-midnight or last guest.

Klub Absolut, ul. Zamokowa 5 (☎505 38 87 27). Thread your way through the smoke and deafening techno to the tiny dance floor downstairs. Ask about vodka specials. Beer 5zł. Cover F-Sa for men 5zł. Women free. Open daily 4pm-late.

Stajenka Pegaza (☎851 64 18), at the corner of ul. Fredry and ul. Wieniawskiego. The mixed crowd and the numerous varieties of draft beers make up for the remote location. *Żywiec* 5.50zł. Open M-F 11am-late, Sa noon-late, Su 3pm-late.

TORUŃ ☎(0)56

Toruń (pop. 210,000; est. 1233), extols itself as the birthplace and childhood home of Mikołaj Kopernik, a.k.a. Copernicus, the man who "stopped the sun and moved the Earth" (see **History**, p. 474). Even before the local genius came to fame, the mercantile medieval city was known far and wide as "beautiful red Toruń" for its impressive brick and stone structures. Today, parishioners pray in 500-year-old churches and children scramble through the ruins of a Teutonic castle while visitors stroll through the city's cobbled streets and linger along the river promenade.

◢ TRANSPORTATION

Trains: Toruń Główny, ul. Kujawska 1 (☎94 36). International *kasa* (ticket window) sells Wasteels and InterRail. Open M-F 7am-5pm, Sa-Su 7am-2pm. To: **Gdańsk** (3hr., 6 per day, 36zł); **Katowice** (7hr., 2 per day, 42zł); **Kołobrzeg** (7hr., 3 per day, 41zł); **Kraków** (8hr., 3 per day, 46zł); **Poznań** (2½hr., 6 per day, 29zł); **Szczecin** (5hr., 1 per day, 43zł); **Warsaw** (3hr., 5 per day, 37zł); **Wrocław** (4hr., 2 per day, 49zł).

Buses: Dworzec PKS, ul. Dąbrowskiego 26 (☎655 53 33). To: **Gdańsk** (3½hr., 3 per day, 32zł); **Szczecin** (5½hr., 1 per day, 45zł); **Warsaw** (4hr., 5 per day, 36zł). **Polski Express** buses run from pl. Teatralny to **Kołobrzeg** (7hr., 1 per day, 60zł); **Szczecin** (5½hr., 2 per day, 56zł); **Warsaw** (3½hr., 16 per day, 20-37zł).

Public Transportation: 1.50zł at kiosks, 2zł from drivers. Luggage needs its own ticket.

Taxis: ☎91 91, wheelchair accessible transport 91 96. 4zł plus 1.60zł per km.

◢ ◢ ORIENTATION AND PRACTICAL INFORMATION

The tourist office and most sights are in and around **Rynek Staromiejski** (Old Town Square). To get to the *rynek* from the main train station, Toruń Główny, take the tunnel just outside and to your left and ride **bus** #22 or 27 across the **Wisła (Vistula) River** to the first stop over the bridge (Plac Rapackiego). Head away from the bus and through the little park, keeping the statue of Kopernik on your right, to find the square. On foot, take **ul. Kujawska** left from the train station, turn right onto **al. Jana Pawła II,** and hike over the Wisła. **Pl. Rapackiego** is on the right, after **ul. Kopernika.** From the bus station, walk through the park and take a left on **ul. Uniwersytecka.** Continue along the street until it intersects with **Wały Gen. Sikorskiego.** At **pl. Teatralny,** turn left onto **ul. Chełmińska,** which leads to **Rynek Staromiejski. Ul. Szeroka** and **ul. Królowej Jadwigi** run to **Rynek Nowomiejski** (New Town Square).

POLAND

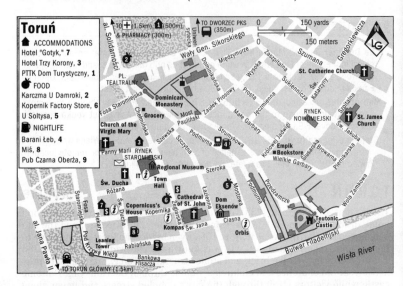

Toruń

♠ ACCOMMODATIONS
Hotel "Gotyk," 7
Hotel Trzy Korony, 3
PTTK Dom Turystyczny, 1
♦ FOOD
Karczma U Damroki, 2
Kopernik Factory Store, 6
U Sołtysa, 5
▮ NIGHTLIFE
Barani Łeb, 4
Miś, 8
Pub Czarna Oberża, 9

Tourist Offices: IT, Rynek Staromiejski 1 (☎ 621 09 31; fax 621 09 30; www.it.torun.pl), in the Old Town Hall. English-speaking staff sells **maps** (5.50zł). Open May-Dec. M and Sa 9am-4pm, Tu-F 9am-6pm, Su 9am-1pm. Sept.-Apr. closed Su.

Currency Exchange: Bank PKO, ul. Kopernika 38 (☎ 610 47 15), gives V **cash advances.** Open M-F 8am-6pm, Sa 9am-1pm. **ATMs** line ul. Szeroka.

English-Language Bookstores: Empik Megastore, ul. Wielkie Garbary 18 (☎ 622 48 95), sells English periodicals. Open M-F 10am-7pm, Sa 10am-4pm, Su 11am-5pm.

Pharmacy: Apteka Panaceum, ul. Odrodzenia 1 (☎ 622 41 59), is open later than most. Take ul. Chełmińska out of the *rynek.* Panaceum is on the corner with ul. Odrodzenia. Open M-F 8am-10pm, Sa 8am-3pm, Su 10am-2pm. MC/V.

Medical Assistance: Szpital Bielany, ul. Św. Józefa 53/59 (☎ 610 11 00). Take bus #11. **Private doctors** at ul. Szeroka 30/Szczytna 1 (☎ 652 12 32). Enter around the corner on ul. Szczytna. 50zł per visit. Open M-F 8am-9pm, Sa 9am-3pm. After hours call the **24hr. ambulance,** ul. Konstytucji 3 Maja (☎ 645 59 99).

Internet Access: Hacker Pub, ul. Podmurna 28 (☎ 663 54 21; www.hacker.komp.pl). 4zł per hr. Open M-Th 9am-midnight, F 9am-2am, Sa 10am-3am, Su 1pm-midnight.

Post Office: Rynek Staromiejski 15 (☎ 621 91 00). **Telephones** inside. **Poste Restante** at window #9. Open M-F 8am-8pm, Sa 8am-3pm. **Branch** at train station open 24hr.

Postal Code: 87 100.

◪ ACCOMMODATIONS

There are still a number of reasonably priced accommodations right in the old town, but vacancies fill up fast, so call ahead. **IT ❷** (see above) can help arrange rooms in hostels and in Mikołaj Kopernik University, which in summer offers dorm rooms near the city center (singles 45zł; doubles 60zł; triples 60zł).

▦ **Hotel Trzy Korony,** Rynek Staromiejski 21 (☎/fax 622 60 31). In the shadow of St. Mary's, this hotel is located right on the old market. Named "3 crowns" for the Polish royals who slept here. 24hr. reception. Breakfast 10zł. Singles 90zł, with bath 150zł; doubles 110zł/190zł; triples 140zł/230zł; apartments 250zł. AmEx/MC/V. ❸

Hotel "Gotyk," ul. Piekary 20 (☎658 40 00; fax 658 40 01; gotyk@ic.torun.pl). Though the gothic portal and burgundy walls may send you back a few centuries, the modern amenities of this fledgling hotel will bring you back. The impeccably-trained staff will escort you to beautiful rooms with carved wooden bedsteads and Internet access. Breakfast included. Check-in 2pm. Check-out noon. Reception 24hr. Singles 150zł; doubles 250zł; apartments 300-350zł. AmEx/MC/V. ❺

PTTK Dom Turystyczny, ul. Legionów 24 (☎/fax 622 38 55). From Rynek Staromiejski, follow ul. Chełmińska past pl. Teatralny to the 2nd right after the park (ul. Grudziądzka), then take a left on Legionów; it's on your right after 3 blocks. Or, take bus #10 from the train station to "Dekerta." The bus stops just outside the building. Close to the main bus station. Cheerful, well-appointed rooms and clean communal bathrooms make this student-filled *dom* worth the trek. Check-in 2pm. Check-out noon. Singles 70zł; doubles 80zł; triples 99zł; quads 120zł; quints 150zł. ❷

▌ FOOD

Toruń still offers its centuries-old treat: **gingerbread** *(pierniki)*. Originally sold by Copernicus's father to put his son through school, it is now hawked in various forms, including chocolate-coated and Copernicus-shaped. Ingest the genius for under 3zł. Supersam, a **24hr. grocery store,** sits at ul. Chełmińska 22. **Targowisko Miejskie,** composed of an international bazaar and a farmer's market, sprawls on ul. Chełmińska. From the rynek, walk up ul. Chełmińska past pl. Teatralny; the market will be on your left just after the "Universam" store. (Open daily 8am-4pm.)

▧ **U Sołtysa,** ul. Mostowa 17 (☎652 26 56, ext. 21). Look no further for quintessential Polish cuisine. The mock thatched roof might make you giggle, but the food won't. Deliciously plentiful entrees (6-19zł) are complemented by *naleśniki* (crepes; 7-8.50zł), 7 varieties of *pierogi* (dumplings; 7.50-13zł), and delectable soups (5-6zł). Open M-Sa 11:30am-midnight, Su 1pm-midnight. ❶

Karczma u Damroki, ul. Chełmińska 1 (☎622 36 60), in a renovated 18th-century hut right by the *Polski Express* station. In medieval times, a *karczma* was an eatery and watering hole for knights and peasants alike. U Damroki brings a little of that old Polish/Bavarian style to the 21st century. Entrees 9-24zł. Open daily 10am-1am. ❷

Kopernik Factory Store, ul. Żeglarska 25 (☎622 37 12), and Rynek Staromiejskie 6 (☎622 88 32). Enjoy gingerbread effigies of your favorite Polish heroes. Gets very crowded, so be patient while visions of gingerbread dance in your head. From 0.70zł for a small taste to 26zł for top-of-the-line historical figures. Available by the kg (around 12zł per kg) or in pre-packaged form. Open M-F 10am-6pm, Sa-Su 10am-2pm. ❷

◐ SIGHTS

An astounding number of attractions are packed into Toruń's ramparts, particularly in the 13th-century **Stare Miasto** (Old Town), built by the Teutonic Knights.

COPERNICUS'S HOUSE. (Dom Kopernika.) The birthplace of renowned astronomer Mikołaj Kopernik (b. 1473) has been meticulously restored and now showcases historical astronomical instruments, Kopernik family documents, and other artifacts from 16th-century Toruń. A surprisingly interesting sound and light show centered on a miniature model of the city circa 1550 plays every 30min. Choose from 8 languages, including English. *(Ul. Kopernika 15/17. ☎622 70 38 ext.13. Open Tu-Sa 10am-6pm, Su 10am-4pm. 6zł, students 4zł. Model of Toruń and audio show 8zł/5zł. Both 12zł/7zł. House free Su.)*

TOWN HALL. (Ratusz.) One of the finest examples of monumental Burgher architecture in Europe, this 14th-century building dominates the Old Town Square. The wings house 12 halls, 52 rooms, and 356 windows, while the 42m clock tower offers a grand bird's eye view of the city. The town hall now contains the **Regional Museum** (Muzeum Okręgowe), whose exhibits include a famous 16th-century portrait of Kopernik, an array of sacred art from the 15th and 16th centuries, and artifacts from Toruń's numerous craft guilds, including some 15th-century gingerbread tins. *(Rynek Staromiejski 1. ☎622 70 38. Some English info. Museum and tower open Tu-Sa 10am-6pm, Su 10am-4pm. 6zł, students 4zł; Su free. Medieval tower 6zł/4zł.)* Outside, it's impossible to miss the statue of Kopernik watching over the city. Another local "hero," the Raftsman, flanks the Ratusz on the other side. Legend has it that he charmed animals to deliver the city from a pesky frog plague.

TEUTONIC STRUCTURES. The 13th-century Teutonic Knights' Castle survived two centuries before a revolt by the burghers reduced it to the ruins that continue to draw visitors today. The remains of the building (on your left as you face the river) house a booth where you can try your hand at archery for 2zł. The 14th-century **toilet tower** served as indoor plumbing and as a kind of fecal defense, shooting more in the enemy's direction than the canons. *(Ul. Przedzamcze. Open daily 10am-6pm. 0.50zł.)* To the right as you face the river stands the Krzywa Wieża (Leaning Tower), built in 1271 by a knight as punishment for breaking the Order's rule of celibacy. The assumption was that the tower's "deviation" would remind the knight of his own. But the 15m tower, which is off by 1.5m at its top, doesn't lean enough to scare away entrepreneurs, who have opened up a bar and cafe inside. *(Ul. Krzywa Wieża 17.)*

CHURCHES. The **Cathedral of St. John the Baptist and St. John the Evangelist** (Bazylika Katedralna pw. Św. Janów) is the most impressive of the many Gothic churches in the region. Built from the 13th to the 15th centuries, it mixes Gothic, Baroque, and Rococo elements, giving a disjointed but rich look at medieval architectural development. Its great claim to fame does not concern its design, but rather its parishioners: the chapel witnessed baby Kopernik's baptism way back in 1473. *(At the corner of ul. Żeglarska and Sw. Jana. Open Jan. 4-Oct. 31 M-Sa 9am-5:30pm, Su 2-5:30pm. 2zł, students 1zł.)* The **Church of the Virgin Mary** (Kościół Św. Marii), with its delicately slender stained glass windows, has a less ornate feel than many Polish churches. The chancel holds the mausoleum of the Swedish queen Anna Wazówna. The church passed from one set of holy hands to another; the Bernardines, Franciscans, and Protestants each claimed the house of worship at one point. *(On ul. Panny Marii. Facing the front of the town hall, it's off the rynek to the left.)*

◨ ◧ FESTIVALS AND NIGHTLIFE

Toruń hosts a number of festivals, starting in May when **Probaltica**, the Baltic celebration of chamber music and arts, comes to town, followed later that month by the "Kontakt" **International Theater Festival.** In June and July, during the **Music and Architecture Festival**, classical concerts are held in different historical buildings each weekend. The **Song of Songs** Christian music festival hits town in early July and overlaps the annual **Summer Street Theater** series, which stages performances weekly in July and August. The season ends in November with **Blues Meeting**, a music festival for connoisseurs. Check **IT** (see **Tourist Offices**, p. 543) for more info.

▧ **Miś**, Św. Ducha 6 (☎622 30 49) in the basement. Don't let the record collage above the bar and oversized piano keys hanging from the ceiling scare you off. Despite the artsy reputation, patrons still take advantage of the dartboard and pinball machine in the corner. Żywiec 4zł. Live music nightly, DJs F-Sa. Open daily 6pm-late.

Barani Łeb, ul. Podmurna 28 (☎621 07 10). The patrons of this popular pub know how to party. Żywiec 4.80zł. Karaoke W, oldies Tu and Th, disco F-Sa. Open Su-M 3pm-midnight, Tu-W 3pm-3am, Th-F 3pm-4am, Sa 3pm-5am.

Pub Czarna Oberża (Black Inn), ul. Rabiańska 9 (☎621 09 63). A local student hangout with plenty of beer and billiards. Impressive selection of imported brew. Open M-Th 1pm-midnight, F-Sa 1pm-1am, Su 2pm-midnight.

ŁÓDŹ
☎ (0)42

Łódź (WOODGE; pop. 813,000), Poland's second-largest city, is overshadowed by international Warsaw to the northeast and picturesque Toruń to the north. This former textile town doesn't have many attractions that are easily placed on a postcard, but, after strolling down pedestrian ul. Piotrkowska—bustling by day and raucous by night—you'll understand why *Varsovians*, citizens of the capital city, come here to do business and party hard. At the crossroads of Polish, Jewish, and German culture, Łódź has many surprises in store.

⌐ TRANSPORTATION

Trains: There are two primary train stations in town. **Łódź Fabryczna:** ☎ 664 54 67, on pl. Sałacinskiego. To: **Częstochowa** (2hr., 4 per day, 27.40zł); **Katowice** (3hr., 4 per day, 33.20zł); **Kraków** (3¼hr., 1 per day, 35zł); **Warsaw** (2hr., 18 per day, 25zł). **Łódź Kaliska:** Al. Unii 3/5. To: **Kraków** (3hr., 2 per day, 33.50zł); **Poznań** (4hr., 5 per day, 34zł); **Toruń** (2½hr., 6 per day, 29.30zł).

Buses: Łódź Fabryczna PKS (☎ 631 97 06 or 631 93 16), pl. Sałacinskiego, is attached to the Fabryczna train station. To: **Częstochowa** (2½-3½hr., 2-8 per day, 17-24zł); **Kraków** (6hr., 6 per day, 37zł); **Poznań** (4½hr., 3 per day, 33-35zł); **Toruń** (3½hr., 4 per day, 25zł); **Warsaw** (2½-3hr., 7 per day, 18-25zł); **Wrocław** (4-5hr., 3 per day, 28-31zł). Comfortable **Polski Express** buses leave the front of the PKS station to: **Częstochowa** (2½hr., 3 per day, 26.40zł); **Katowice** (3½hr., 3 per day, 32zł); **Kraków** (5hr., 3 per day, 42.40zł); **Warsaw** (2½hr., 7 per day, 28zł).

Public Transportation: Trams and buses run throughout the city (10min. 1zł, 30min. 2zł; students 0.50zł/1zł). Prices vary by time on board and double at night. Daily passes available (8zł, students 4zł).

🔲 🔢 ORIENTATION AND PRACTICAL INFORMATION

Ul. Piotrkowska, the 3km main thoroughfare, is the city's hub. Its pedestrian-only section stretches from al. Pomorska to al. Marsz. Józefa Piłsudskiego. From **Łódź Fabryczna,** cross under ul. Jana Kilińskiego, the wide street with multiple tram lines, and head toward "Łódzki Dom Kultury," one of the large buildings just across the way. Continue on ul. Traugutta past Dom Kultury for two blocks to get to ul. Piotrkowska. From **Łódź Kaliska,** cross the parking lot and cross under al. Włókniarzy via the tunnel; the second exit on the left leads to the tram stop. Take tram #12 toward Stoki and get off at Piotrkowska.

Tourist Office: IT, ul. Piotrkowska 153 (☎/fax 638 59 55; it@uml.lodz.pl). Enter from al. Kościuszki. Free maps, foreign-language brochures, and accommodations info. English spoken. Open M-F 8:30am-4:30pm, Sa 9am-1pm.

Currency Exchange: Pekao SA, al. Piłsudskiego 12 (☎ 636 62 44), cashes **traveler's checks** for 1.5% commission (10zł minimum) and gives MC/V **cash advances. Branch** at al. Kościuszki 47. Both open M-F 8am-6pm, Su 10am-2pm.

Luggage Storage: There is a locked storage room at Łódź Fabryczna. 4zł per item; go to *Informacja.* Open daily 7:30am-10pm.

English-Language Bookstore: Empik, ul. Piotrkowska 81, 2nd fl. (☎ 632 83 55). Open M-Sa 10am-9pm, Su 11am-7pm. MC/V.

Pharmacy: Apteka Pod Białym Orłem, ul. Piotrkowska 46 (☎/fax 630 00 68). Boasts that it is one of the oldest pharmacies in Łódź. Open M-F 8am-8pm, Sa 10am-3pm.

Hospital: Szpital Bardickiego, ul. Kopcińskiego 22 (☎ 678 92 88).

Internet Access: Łódź is wired; Internet cafes dot Piotrkowska as well as nearby streets. **Gralnia Internet Cafe,** ul. Piotrkowska 143 (☎ 637 18 49), above Club Social Latino. Ask about their "Meganoc" option. 2.5zł per hr., 1.5zł per 30min., 1zł per 15min. Open

Łódź

🔺 ACCOMMODATIONS
Hotel Polonia, **3**
Hotel Reymont, **2**
PTSM Youth Hostel (HI), **1**

🍴 FOOD
Delikatesy, **5**
Piotrkowska Klub
  Zieliński i Syn, **7**
Presto Pizza, **4**
U Chochoła, **6**

🍸 NIGHTLIFE
Ale Kino, **10**
Klub Muzyczny Riff Raff, **9**
Łódź Kaliska, **8**

24hr. **Planeta Alfa,** ul. Piotrkowska 107 (☎ 639 88 48). After 10pm, enter from ul. Kościuszki. 3-9am 2zł per hr., 1.20zł per 30min., 0.70zł per 15min.; 9am-11am and 11pm-3am, 2.50zł/1.50zł/80zł; 11am-11pm 3zł/2zł/1zł. Open 24hr.

Post Office: ul. Tuwima 38 (☎ 633 94 52; fax 632 82 08). Take a ticket from the computer as you enter: "A/B" for stamps, "C" for *kantor* (currency exchange), "D" for **fax** services. **Telephones** are inside. Open 24hr. **Poste Restante** at window #19. Open M 7am-5pm, Tu-F 7am-3pm.

Postal Code: 90 001.

🏠 ACCOMMODATIONS

IT ❷ (see **Tourist Office,** p. 547) keeps a list of seasonal Uniwersyet Łódzki and Politechnika Łódzka (☎ 684 69 68) dorm rooms (40-50zł per person).

PTSM Youth Hostel (HI), ul. Legionów 27 (☎ 630 66 80; fax 630 66 83; youthhostel-lodz@wp.pl). Go north (as the street numbers descend) along ul. Piotrkowska to pl. Wolności, left on ul. Legionów. Or, take tram #4 toward Helenówek from the Fabryczna station to pl. Wolności. Clean and quiet with a *kawiarienka* (small coffee shop) in the basement (5pm-9pm). Free locked storage until 10pm. Linen 5zł. Reception 6am-11pm. Check-in 3pm. Check-out 10am. Flexible curfew 10pm. 4- to 6-bed dorms 25zł; singles with bath and TV 60zł; doubles and triples with TV 35zł per person. ❶

Hotel Reymont, ul. Legionów 81 (☎633 80 23; hotelreymont@infofirmy.pl), 4 blocks farther down Legionów from the youth hostel (see above). From pl. Wolności, take tram #43 toward Zdrowie to Cmentarna. A single bed in a double (56-99zł) or in a triple (45-75zł) is a good value, especially considering that a bathroom, phone, radio, and microfridge are included in every room. Breakfast 13zł. Singles 95-148zł; doubles 112-186zł; triples 135-234zł. Discount for weekend travelers. MC/V. ❹

Hotel Polonia, ul.Narutowicza 38 (☎632 87 73). From Fabryczna train station, take tram #1, 4, or 5 one stop to Narutowicza. Hotel Polonia offers an excellent location and cheerful rooms for reasonable prices. Reception 24hr. Check-in 2-10pm. Check-out 10am. Breakfast 15zł. Single 75zł, with bath 125zł; double 110zł/140zł. 10% discount on weekends. AmEx/MC/V. ❸

🍴 FOOD

A **24hr. grocery, Delikatesy,** is at ul. Traugutta 2 (☎633 46 54; AmEx/MC/V). Restaurants line ul. Piotrkowska.

U Chochoła, ul. Traugutta 3 (☎632 51 38). It may not be cheap, but you'll certainly get some cultural bang for your buck at U Chochoła. Specializing solely in the *góralskie* cuisine (15-35zł) of the Polish highlands, this restaurant takes advantage of the unique highlander culture in its decor. Prices increase after 5pm. Call ahead on weekends. Open Su-Th noon-11pm, F-Sa noon-midnight. AmEx/MC/V. ❸

Piotrkowska Klub Zieliński i Syn, ul. Piotrkowska 97 (☎632 24 78). You too can feel like one of the stars of "HollyŁódź" while you dine here. Choose from Polish standards such as *pierogi* (8zł) and *placki ziemniaczane* (potato pancakes; 6zł) for a filling meal. With fresh flowers on the tables and a 2-story terrace, Klub Zieliński i Syn lets you eat like a star without telling your wallet. Open M-Sa from 11am, Su from noon. ❶

Presto Pizza, ul. Piotrkowska 67 (☎630 88 83), in the courtyard marked by the "Kino Polonia" sign across from Hotel Grand. This pizzeria tests culinary limits (and your tastebuds) with some of its wood-oven pies, including the "San Francisco," topped with pineapples, ham, curry, and bananas. Small pizzas 7.50-14zł, large 8.50-16zł. Take-out available. Open M-Th noon-11pm, F-Sa noon-midnight. MC/V. ❷

👁 SIGHTS

JEWISH CEMETERY. (Cmentarz Żydowski.) The most stirring and beautiful sight in Łódź, the sprawling Jewish cemetery, established in 1892, is the largest in Europe. There are more than 200,000 graves and 180,000 tombstones, some quite elaborately engraved; especially noteworthy is the colossal Poznański family crypt with its gold-mosaic ceiling. Near the entrance to the cemetery is a memorial to the Jews killed in the Łódź ghetto. Signs lead the way to the **Ghetto Fields** (Pole Ghettowe), which are lined with the small, faintly marked graves of Jews who died there. *(Take tram #1 from ul. Kilinskiego, #15 from ul. Legionów, or #6 from ul. Kościuszki or Zachnodnia, north to "Strykowska" Inflancka at the end of the line (20min.). Continue up the street to the first corner, make a sharp left turn onto the cobblestone ul. Zmienna before the car lot, and continue until the small gate in the wall on your right. It is better to try this entrance than the main gate on ul. Bracka, which is usually locked for security purposes. ☎656 70 19. Open May-Sept. M-F and Su 9am-5pm; Oct.-Apr. M-F and Su 9am-3pm. Closed on Jewish holidays. 4zł; free for those visiting the graves of relatives.)* Back in the center of town, the **Jewish Community Center** (Gmina Wyznaniowa Żydowska) has info on those buried in the cemetery. Walk through the gates to the fourth door on the right. *(Ul. Pomorska 18. ☎633 51 56. Open M-F 10am-2pm. Services daily. English spoken.)*

THE LUCKY FEW   Established in 1940 as the largest Jewish ghetto in Europe, Łódź's ghetto was remarkably lucky (as far as ghettos go) during World War II. For the early part of the war, the ghetto doubled as a giant Nazi textile factory, supplying winter uniforms for German soldiers in Russia. As Nazi-controlled ghettos throughout Europe were being liquidated in 1942, only the elderly, the infirm, and the young of Łódź were deported to concentration camps; the ghetto had become too valuable as a source of labor for the Nazis to destroy. By 1944, it was the last remaining ghetto in Poland. As the Red Army loomed only 150km away in August 1944, though, the Nazis decided to liquidate the Łódź ghetto; its 70,000 residents were deported to Auschwitz, Birkenau, and Majdanek. Eight hundred "lucky" Jews remained as a cleaning crew, but as the Russians were about to capture Łódź, the Nazis decided to execute the remaining few and built a mass grave in anticipation. Fortunately, the swift advance of the Russians interrupted the execution, and the 800 ghetto residents were saved. Of those deported to concentration camps, some 20,000 survived—the highest number of survivors of any European ghetto. Their fortune was due to their late deportation; by the end of the war, the death camps were quickly declining in murderous "efficiency." Those interested in exploring the ghetto (many of whose buildings are still standing) or in seeking the graves of relatives buried in the ghetto's Jewish Cemetery should contact the Jewish Community Center.

POZNAŃSKI PALACE. On the corner of ul. Ogrodowa and ul. Piotrkowska stands the grandiose Poznański Palace. Named for a family of wealthy Jewish industrialists who lived there in the late 19th and early 20th centuries, the ornate gray building houses the **Łódź Historical Museum** (Muzeum Historii Miasta Łódźi). A visit to the museum begins in the vast and beautiful palace ballroom, winds through gorgeously furnished living rooms, and concludes with exhibits on Łódź's famous sons and daughters, including pianist Artur Rubinstein (see **The Arts**, p. 479) and Nobel Prize-winning author Władysław Reymont. *(Ul. Ogrodowa 15. Take tram #4 toward Helenówek or #6 toward Strykowskar to the intersection of ul. Nowomiejska and ul. Pół nocna. Turn left on Północna, which turns into Ogrodowa. ☎ 654 00 82. Open Tu and Th 10am-4pm, W 2-6pm, F-Su 10am-2pm. 6zł, students 3zł; Tu free. Tours in Polish 20zł.)*

MUSEUM OF CINEMATOGRAPHY. (Muzeum Kinomatografii.) International film giants Andrzej Wajda, Krzysztof Kieślowski, and Roman Polański (see **The Arts**, p. 479) all got their start at Łódź's famous film school—the city, sometimes called "Hollyłódź," has its own "Avenue of the Stars" on a block of ul. Piotrkowska. The Museum of Cinematography, which is housed in a mid-19th-century mansion on ul. Piłsudskiego, features rotating exhibits on Polish filmmaking and photography. *(Pl. Zwycięstwa 1. From the train station, take tram #1, 4, or 5 south to the intersection of ul. Kilinskiego and ul. Piłsudskiego. Turn left at Piłsudskiego; the museum will be behind a park on your right. ☎ 674 09 57. Open Tu noon-5pm, W-Su 10am-3pm; last entrance 30min. before closing. Closed last Su of each month and for a month around July. 4zł, students 3zł.)*

ŁÓDŹ FINE ARTS MUSEUM. (Muzeum Sztuki w Łódźi.) Holding the premier art collection in Łódź, the museum is home to 20th-century works by Polish artists like Stanisław Wiłkiewicz and Tadeusz Kantor, as well as such foreigners as Piet Mondrian and Max Ernst. Climb the ornate staircase with stained glass windows to the top floor, which opens up on the minimalist gallery. *(Ul. Więckowskiego 36. Four blocks west of ul. Piotrkowska along ul. Więckowskiego. ☎ 633 97 90; fax 674 99 82. Open Tu 10am-5pm, W and F 11am-5pm, Th noon-7pm, Sa-Su 10am-4pm; last entrance 30min. before closing. 6zł, students 4zł; Tu-Th free.)*

NIGHTLIFE

Łódź knows how to party. Ul. Piotrkowska turns into publand a little after 9pm.

Łódź Kaliska, ul. Piotrkowska 102 (☎630 69 55; www.lodzkaliska.pl). The place to be in the city, this pub is decked out with 2 floors, 2 bars, and funky art by the Łódź Kaliska art group on the walls. Spy on patrons while you do your business in the tinted glass bathrooms to make sure there's no funny business. Beer 7zł. Open daily noon-late.

Klub Muzyczny Riff Raff, ul. Roosevelta 9 (☎607 289 211). Pub/dance club Riff Raff blends foosball, rock, and beer to create an appealingly gritty atmosphere. Free concerts every Th; live DJ and dancing every F and Sa after 8pm. 18+. Open daily 4pm-late.

Ale Kino, in the Mega Bowling Center (☎639 58 48). On ul. Piłsudskiego at the intersection with Piotrkowska, this bar's interior is suggestive of a saloon from the Wild Wild West, complete with swinging doors. Pub grub 9-18zł. Open M 5pm-1am, Tu-Th 4pm-1am, F 3pm-4am, Sa 2pm-4am, Su 1pm-1am; disco open Th-Sa from 9pm.

POMORZE

Pomorze, literally "along the sea," encompasses the murky swamps and windswept dunes of the Baltic Coast. Centuries ago, fishermen battled the shifting sands and treacherous bogs to build villages here. A few hamlets grew into large ports—such as Szczecin on the lower Odra River. Others, like Świnoujście, are building themselves up around their shoreline assets. Woliński National Park, with its hiking trails and bison, extends from the popular beaches of Międzyzdroje.

SZCZECIN   ☎(0)91

Strategically situated at the mouth of the Oder River, the port of Szczecin (SHCHEH-cheen; pop. 420,000) has been the site of centuries of power plays at the hands of Sweden, Prussia, and finally Poland. Primarily an industrial and business center, the city serves as a major transportation hub with railways and waterways

POLAND

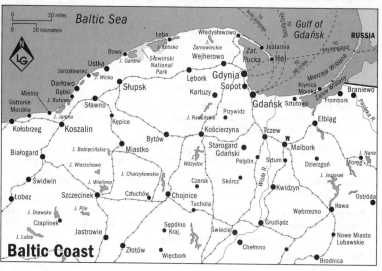

that sprawl kilometers from the center. Think twice, though, before you leave Szczecin to the businessmen. Rows of historic buildings and dense woods just outside of town beautify this industrious city, while the friendly attitude of the residents and the availability of budget accommodations encourage backpackers to visit.

▐ TRANSPORTATION. The **train station, Szczecin Główny,** sits at the end of ul. 3-go Maja. Trains run to: **Gdańsk** (5½hr., 5 per day, 44zł); **Kraków** (9hr., 3 per day, 40zł); **Poznań** (2½hr., 12 per day, 36zł); **Świnoujście** (2hr., 18 per day, 25zł); **Toruń** (5hr., 1 per day, 35zł); **Warsaw** (6hr., 6 per day, 42-81zł); and **Berlin, GER** (2hr.; 1 per day; 89zł, under 26 72zł). Purchase international tickets at *kasa* #15. The **bus station** is on pl. Tobrucki, a 2min. walk from the train station. Exit left out of the main hall and take the 1st left up the hill. Buses run to: **Kołobrzeg** (5hr., 3 per day, 20zł); **Międzyzdroje** (3hr., 4 per day, 15zł); **Świnoujście** (2½-3½hr., 3 per day, 17zł); and **Toruń** (6hr., 1 per day, 44zł). Tickets for international trains, buses, and ferries are available from **Euro Ster.** (☎/fax 489 38 78; www.e-bilety.pl; open M-F 9am-5pm.) The city's numerous **tram** and **bus** lines run along major roads. Tickets are sold in blocks of time rather than per ride. (1.70zł per 20min., 2.60zł per hr., 3.40zł per 2hr.; 7zł after 11pm; day pass 8.70zł. Student tickets half price.) For a cab, call **Express-Taxi** (☎96 25).

▐▌ ORIENTATION AND PRACTICAL INFORMATION. The city center is uphill from the stations, which lie by the river. Navigation can be confusing, so pick up a **map.** To reach the center from the train station, turn left and uphill onto **ul. Dworcowa.** Turn right onto ul. 3-go Maja, which runs into **al. Niepodległości,** the main north-south thoroughfare. For a quick ride into the city, take tram #3 toward Las Arkoński and get off at Brama Portowa. Al. Niepodległości stretches past the office to the right and heads to **pl. Brama Portowa,** the center of Szczecin and the best starting point for a tour of the city's sights.

Tourist Office: CIT, al. Niepodległości 1 (☎434 04 40; fax 433 84 20), on the corner with Dworcowa, provides free **maps** and English-language information about Pomorze. Open M-F 9:30am-5pm; July-Aug. also Sa 10am-2pm. A **branch** is located in the **castle** (☎489 16 30; fax 434 02 86).

Currency Exchange: Bank Pekao SA, pl. Żołnierza Polskiego 16 (☎440 06 23), cashes **traveler's checks** for 1.5% commission and gives MC/V **cash advances.** Open M-F 8am-6pm, Sa 10am-2pm. **ATMs** are all over town.

Luggage Storage: At the train station, downstairs by the exit to the platforms. 2zł, plus 0.50zł for every 50zł of declared value. Open daily 6am-10pm.

English-Language Bookstore: Empik, al. Niepodległości 60, 4th fl. (☎489 39 35), sells international books and **maps** (6zł). Open M-F 10am-10pm, Sa 10am-6pm, Su 10:30am-4:30pm. AmEx/MC/V.

24-Hour Pharmacy: Ul. Więckowskiego 1/2 (☎488 40 66), left of al. Niepodległości from the tourist office. Ring the bell 11pm-6am. 2.50zł extra for after hours service.

Internet Access: Bond Internet Cafe, ul. Narodowej, 2nd fl. (☎812 20 28), on the corner of Niepodległości. 3zł per hr. Open daily 9am-11pm.

Post Office: Ul. Bogurodzicy 1 (☎440 14 21), on the corner of Niepodległości, has **telephones** and **fax** services. For **Poste Restante,** go to the windows to the right of the entrance. Open M-F 7:30am-8pm, Sa 9am-2pm.

Postal Code: 70 405.

┌┐┌┐ ACCOMMODATIONS AND FOOD. For a complete list of Szczecin's summer youth hostels, contact the tourist office (see above). **Pocztylion ❷,** ul. Dworcowa 20 (enter from ul. Nowa), is an affordable hotel right between the stations and the center, and is adjacent to the mammoth "Poczta 2" post office. Have the guard let you through; it's in Building A on the third floor. Rooms are spacious and come with gigantic refrigerators. (☎ 440 12 11. Doubles 84zł; triples 126zł.)

The best cafe in the city, **▨Jazz Cafe Brama ❷,** pl. Holdu Pruskiego 1, has the competition licked in location with a cool and mellow atmosphere inside the King's Gate. (Live music F 9pm. Films Su 10pm. Coffee 4-6zł. Beer 4zł. Open Su-Th 10am-midnight, F-Sa 10am-2am.) **Haga ❷,** ul. Sienna, in the shadow of the old town hall, rolls out 200 varieties of delectable Dutch crepes (8.50-18zł), perfect for a snack or a meal. (☎ 812 17 59. Open July-Aug. daily 11am-11pm; Sept.-June M-Th and Su 11am-10pm, F-Sa 11am-11pm.) **Extra,** a large supermarket, is at ul. Niepodległości 27. (Open M-Sa 7am-9pm, Su 10am-6pm. MC/V.)

◨ SIGHTS. Walks through the city usually start at the **Port Gate** (Brama Portowa) in pl. Zwycięztwa off al. Niepodległości. Formerly called the Berlin Gate, it lends a Prussian flavor to the downtown area. The gate bears an inscription commemorating Emperor Friedrich Wilhelm I and a panorama of 18th-century Szczecin. Viadus, god of the Oder, leans against a jug from which the river's waters flow. Two blocks to the north (away from the train station), a right turn at pl. Żolnierza Polskiego leads to the Baroque **Pomeranian Parliament,** on the corner at ul. Staromłlynska 27/28. This branch of the **National Museum** (Muzeum Narodowe) exhibits Pomeranian art. Across the street is its sister museum, the **Museum of Modern Art.** (Muzeum Sztuki Wspołczesniej; ☎ 433 50 85. Open Tu-W and F 11am-6pm, Sa-Su and Th 10am-4pm. 6zł, students 3zł. Both museums 10zł/5zł; Th free.) Across Żolnierza Polskiego to the left lies another of the city's grand gates, **Brama Królewska** (Kings' Gate), now home to the city's hippest cafe. A block ahead rests the **Church of St. Peter and Paul,** built in the 15th century on 12th-century foundations with a unique wooden ceiling.

Farther on the right, on ul. Korsarzy, the enormous, newly restored **Castle of Pomeranian Dukes** (Zamek Książąt Pomorskich) overlooks the city from the site of Szczecin's oldest settlement. The seat of Pomeranian princes until 1630, the castle later belonged to Swedes and Prussians. Now it's occupied by an opera, a cinema, and a **museum** that displays the exquisitely decorated sarcophagi of dukes who once ruled Pomerania, as well as temporary exhibits (*wystawy;* usually fine art). The figurines on the clock face in the courtyard move every 30min. The **tower** offers a view of the city, river, and environs. (☎ 433 88 41; zamek@zamek.szczecin.pl. Open Tu-Su 10am-6pm. Tower open May-Sept. Museum 6zł, students 3zł; temporary exhibits 6zł/3zł. Tower 3zł/2zł.)

The **old town hall** (*ratusz*), ul. Mściwoja 8, dates from 1450, and now houses the **Museum of the History of the City of Szczecin.** Check out the giant 19th-century music box masquerading as a mirror and the vodka bottle from 1615. (☎ 488 02 49. Open Tu-W and F 10am-4pm, Th and Sa-Su 11am-6pm. 8zł, students 4zł; Th free.) Close to the river on ul. Wyszynskiego, one block from the *ratusz,* the **Cathedral of St. John the Evangelist** (Katedra Św. Jana Ewangelisty) rests on its 13th-century foundation. After all the stained-glass windows are restored, the church will finally shine again with all the Gothic splendor lost in World War II. (Open daily 7am until the end of the last service, around 8pm.) The huge **Basilica of St. James,** one block toward the center and across the overpass, has a striking altar and a large stained-glass window. The main building of the **National Museum** is on ul. Wały Chrobrego. (☎ 433 50 66. Open Tu-F 9am-3:30pm, Sa-Su 10am-4pm. 8zł, students 4zł; Th free.) The best area for walking is the raised **riverfront promenade.**

POLAND

MIĘDZYZDROJE
☎ (0)91

The resort town Międzyzdroje (MYEN-dzi-ZDROY-eh) stands out from the other developing coastal resorts along the Baltic Coast. Located on the edge of Woliński National Park—a pristine tract of Wolin Island that contains glacial lakes and a bison preserve—Międzyzdroje is remarkable for its gorgeous stretch of coast and its dramatic sandy cliffs. Pine-scented breezes stir the hiking trails that lead out of town into dense surrounding woodland. Whether you visit Międzyzdroje for the beach or the park, you'll find some of Poland's most calming natural scenery.

TRANSPORTATION. Trains run to: **Kraków** (8hr., 3 per day, 52zł); **Poznań** (4½hr., 6 per day, 49zł); **Świnoujście** (20min., 19 per day, 3.50zł); **Szczecin** (2hr., 17 per day, 14zł); and **Warsaw** (7hr., 2 per day, 48zł). **Buses** run to **Świnoujście** (20min.; July-Aug. 65 per day, Sept.-June 44 per day; 3.20zł) and **Szczecin** (3hr., 2 per day, 5zł). Buses also frequently travel to points along the hiking trails, including the towns of **Wisełka** and **Kołczewo** (10-30min., 6zł).

ORIENTATION AND PRACTICAL INFORMATION. PTTK, ul. Kolejowa 2, sells maps (3-6zł) and provides info about the park and accommodations. The PTTK city/park map (4.50zł) is useful for venturing deeper into the woods. (☎ 328 04 62; fax 328 00 86. Open M-F 7am-5pm, Sa 9am-1pm.) Maps are also available from reception in the attached hotel. (Open 24hr.) There is a MC/V **ATM** at ul. Zwycięstwa 1. **Luggage storage** is available at the train station. (5zł. Open daily 7:30am-noon and 1-9:30pm.) To get to town, turn right out of the train station and follow ul. Kolejowa down the hill to the center. A **pharmacy** is at ul. Zwycięstwa 9. (☎ 328 00 90. Open daily 8am-9pm; every other week daily 8am-midnight.) Hop on the **Internet** at **Internet Cafe Ole,** ul. Kolejowa 42. (☎ 328 05 40. 5zł per hr.) The **post office** is at ul. Gryfa Pomorskiego 7. (☎ 328 01 40. Open M-F 8am-8pm, Sa 8am-1pm.) **Postal Code:** 72 500.

ACCOMMODATIONS AND FOOD. Keep an eye out for *"wolne pokoje"* (available rooms) signs, particularly along ul. Gryfa Pomorskiego. Reserve ahead in July and August when singles are hard to come by. Week-long stays are usually required when the weather is nice during July and August. Alternatively, talk to **PTTK ❷** (see above), which arranges homestays in the summer (singles 32zł; doubles 40zł; triples 96zł) and runs the well-kept **PTTK Hotel ❷,** in the same building as the office. (☎ 328 03 82. July-Aug. dorms 35zł; singles 45zł; doubles 90zł; quads 180zł; Sept.-June 20zł/35zł/70zł/140zł.) **Camping Gromada ❶,** ul. Bohaterów Warszawy 1, has cabins (27zł per person, with bath 55zł) and tent sites (13zł per person) near the beach. Continue down Kolejowa as it becomes Gryfa Pomorskiego and later Dąbrówski; Gromada is at the end of the street on the right. Reception is through the gate to the right, on the hill behind the bungalows. (☎/fax 328 23 54; www.gromada.pl. 1- to 4-person cabins 27zł per person, with bath 55zł; tent sites 13zł per person. Open daily 8am-10pm.) Look for inexpensive food at the stands and restaurants along ul. Gryfa Pomorskiego and at the beach. Fried fish stands *(smażalnia ryb)* proliferate; some sell the local delicacy *wegorz wędzony* (smoked eel) for about 7zł. **Bistro Bar Pieróg ❶,** ul. Krasickiego 3, is tasty and cheap. (☎ 328 04 23. Great soups 3-3.50zł. Entrees 3.30-14.50zł. Open daily 9am-11pm.)

HIKING. Although Międzyzdroje draws crowds as a prime beach resort, the true accolades belong to adjacent ⊠**Woliński,** which shelters its own stretch of coastline. The park is immaculately kept, with four main **hiking trails** (black, red, green, and blue) marked on trees and stones; stick to them or risk an encounter with park officials. All four are accessible from Międzyzdroje—the red and black at the northeast end of **Promenada Gwiazd,** the green at the end of **ul. Leśna** (follow the signs to the bison preserve), and the blue off **ul. Ustronie Leśne.** These hikes are not very strenuous—don't expect Tatras trail-blazing. **Maps** are posted everywhere. Rent a **bike** at **Willa 5,** ul. Bohaterów Warszawy 16, close to the beach. (☎328 26 10. 5zł per hr. ID required. Open daily 8am-8pm.)

Black Trail. The trail quickly climbs up the seaside cliffs just off the beach to **Kawcza Góra** (61m), a lookout point in the pines that offers a breathtaking view of the Baltic Sea and the coast. Look closely and you just might glimpse one of the park's famed eagles *(bieliki).* Just after Kawcza Góra, the trail hits a dead-end drop-off and a closed military area; backtrack a few steps and follow the trail into the woods to the right and down the hill to the road, where the trail turns left. Just up ahead the black trail re-enters the woods; 2km later, it resumes and intersects the green trail (see below), then returns to Międzyzdroje.

Red Trail. Sea breezes keep hikers refreshed along the red trail, which starts at the beach in Międzyzdroje and includes a 15km stretch of coastline underneath the cliffs. Just 2km from the pier, the crowds disappear and the beach alternates between rocky and sandy. The trail passes under the highest of the Baltic's cliffs at **Góra Gosan** (93m), then turns back into the woods and passes the town of Wisełka and another scenic cliff at **Strażnica** (74m) before intersecting the green trail.

Green Trail. It's worth renting a bike to check out the green trail, which has an extensive set of **bike paths.** There are long stretches of less rewarding territory between the highlights, but the 15km route heads into the heavily forested heart of the park past glacial lakes. Just 1.2km from the trailhead is the small but popular **bison preserve** *(rezerwat żubrów),* home to deer, wild boar, eagles, and, of course, bison. (☎328 07 37. Open May-Sept. Tu-Su 10am-6pm; Nov.-Apr. 8am-4pm. 3zł, students 2zł.) At the village of Warnowo (7km), the trail runs along a paved road, then turns back into the woods by an area of saplings to the right. After you pass **Lake Czajcze,** continue to Kołczewo (7km) as the path turns away from the road and snakes around the different lakes. Alternatively, take the road onto Wisełka (3km). Buses run between the towns and from both towns to Międzydroje. The green trail ends where it hits the red trail, 3km past Kołczewo.

Blue Trail. This trail wanders south, covering more than 20km as it winds to Wolin, the island's southernmost point. It heads into the park right off ul. Ustronie Leśne by the train station; walk under the bridge and take a right. Less traveled than the other three trails, it's a great escape from the mobs of tourists in town.

KOŁOBRZEG

☎(0)94

Long known as the "Pearl of the Baltic," Kołobrzeg (koh-WOH-bzheg) has transformed itself from the modest salt-producing city of the 7th century into Poland's top vacation destination. But the glamour of this beachside resort belies the city's turbulent 1300-year history. Following occupations by Russians, Swedes, and even Napoleon, Kołobrzeg was under German control during WWII. In 1945, a two-week battle over the city left the Poles victorious and Kołobrzeg ruined. Despite the destruction, Kolobrzeg continues in its 200 year old saline tradition, treating visitors with its famed salt springs and microclimate. Kołobrzeg knows how to shake its assets, and was voted Poland's most popular holiday resort in 2001.

▆ TRANSPORTATION

Trains: Dworzec PKP, ul. Kolejowa (☎352 35 76). Open daily 5am-9pm. To: **Gdynia** (6hr., 7 per day, 37zł); **Katowice** (10hr., 3 per day, 48zł); **Kraków** (12hr., 1 per day, 51zł); **Poznań** (4hr., 6 per day, 40zł); **Szczecin** (3hr., 2 per day, 34zł); **Warsaw** (10hr., 7 per day, 49zł); **Wrocław** (7hr., 2 per day, 45zł).

Buses: Dworzec PKS, ul. Kolejowa (☎ 352 39 28). *Kasa* open daily 7am-10pm. To: **Darłowo** (3hr., 3 per day, 15zł); **Gdańsk** (6hr., 1 per day, 37zł); **Gdynia** (5hr., 2 per day, 33zł); **Poznań** (5hr., 4 per day, 40zł); **Świnoujscie** (3hr., 7 per day, 20zł); **Szczecin** (3hr., 2 per day, 22zł); **Warsaw** (11hr., 3 per day, 60zł).

Public Transportation: Local **bus** tickets 1.80zł at kiosks. Also available from driver.

✴ 🛈 ORIENTATION AND PRACTICAL INFORMATION

The majority of Kołobrzeg's sights lie near the town center or along the beach. To get to town from the train station, walk down **ul. Dworcowa**, which intersects **ul. Armii Krajowej**, the major east-west thoroughfare. Turn left down Armii Krajowej to reach the center (15min.), in the middle of which is the *ratusz* (town hall). Getting to the **beach** can be tough, as a tangle of train tracks separates the city from the beach. Turn left out of the train station (right out of bus station) and walk down **ul. Kolejowa.** To the right, the road turns into **al. Unii Lubelskiej.** On the left, behind a few shops, towers the overpass that leads to the beach. Walk down **ul. Norwida** two blocks until it dead-ends. To the left, the street is called **ul. Rodziewiczówny,** to the right **ul. Sikorskiego.** Any of the paths leading through the woods lead to the beach.

Tourist Offices: CIT, ul. Dworcowa 1 (☎/fax 352 79 39; www.kolobrzeg.turystyka.pl) opposite the train station. Free **maps** and English information about Kołobrzeg and the Pomorskie region. Open July-Aug. daily 8am-6pm; Sept.-May M-F 8am-4pm. **PTTK,** ul. Dubois 20 (☎/fax 352 32 87), in the tower, sells **maps** and provides 4hr. tours of Kołobrzeg (150zł). Open M-Sa 9am-4pm.

Currency Exchange: Bank PKO SA, ul. Źródlana 5 (☎ 354 68 50) gives MC/V **cash advances** and cashes **traveler's checks** (1.5% commission). Open M-F 9am-5pm. **Bank Zachodni WBK,** ul. Emilii Gierczak 44-45 (☎ 352 33 62), has **Western Union** services. Open M-F 9am-5pm. **24hr. AmEx ATM** in Lukas Bank, ul. Armii Krajowej 158/11.

Pharmacy: Apteka, ul. Mariacki 14 (☎ 354 24 50), near St. Mary's. Open M-F 8am-6pm, Sa 8am-2pm. Posts addresses of pharmacies open 9pm-8am.

Medical Assistance: Ul. Łopuskiego 3 (☎ 352 82 61).

Internet Access: M@trix, ul. Armii Krajowej 24/7, near the *ratusz* (☎ 354 43 30). 6zł per hr., 4zł per 30min. **NetSpin,** ul. Giełdowa 7c (☎/fax 354 73 66). 4zł per hr.

Post Office: Ul. Armii Krajowej 1 (☎ 354 43 02), on the corner with ul. Dworcowa. **Telephones** inside and outside. For **Poste Restante,** enter the room to the left of the entrance and inquire at either window. **Exchange** office open M-F 8am-1pm and 2-8pm. Open M-F 7:30am-8pm, Sa 9am-4pm.

Postal Code: 78 100.

🏠 ACCOMMODATIONS

Being one of Poland's top vacation destinations in July and August, cheap rooms are hard to come by without a reservation, especially anywhere near the beach. The best options are **private rooms,** and local Poles congregate near the stations brandishing *"wolne pokoje"* signs. Choose wisely: prices and standards vary wildly. A solid option is to arrange a room through **PTTK ❶** (see above). All rooms come with with TV, tea kettle, and bathroom (20-50zł per person).

Schronisko PTSM, ul. Śliwińskiego 1 (☎/fax 352 27 69). Take bus #3 or 6 from the station to Łopuskiego Szpital. Continue down Łopucińskiego until you reach Śliwińskiego. Sleep on cots in rooms labeled *"Biologia"* and *"Matematyka"* that have educational quotes on the walls. Communal bathrooms have no showers. Kitchenette available. Lockout 10am-5pm. Curfew 10pm. 8- to 12-cot dorms 13.40zł, students 8.70zł. ❶

Hotel New Skanpol, ul. Dworcowa 10 (☎352 82 11; fax 352 44 78; www.newskanpol.pl). Bask in the glory of Kołobrzeg's health spa status. Skanpol provides its guests with spacious and tastefully decorated rooms, many of which offer a spectacular view of Kołobrzeg's center. All rooms include breakfast, satellite TV, and telephone. Singles 166zł; doubles 218zł; suites 319zł. ❺

Camping Baltic 78, ul. IV Dyw. Wojska Polskiego 1 (☎/fax 352 45 69; www.baltic78.republika.pl). A quiet and secluded campsite with terrain ranging from wooded fields to concrete slabs. Reception open 8am-2:30pm and 3:30-8pm. 12zł per person; 1-5 person tent 6.50zł; 6-10 person tent 13zł; 1- to 6-person bungalows with bath and kitchenette, July-Aug. 200zł. Electricity 8zł. ❶

🄵 FOOD

Fried fish stands *(smażalnia ryb)* line the streets along the beach, particularly near the lighthouse and pier, and decent restaurants line the streets near the town hall. If those don't suffice, try the large **Delikatesy** sits at ul. Warzyńskiego 2. Open M-Sa 8am-midnight, Su 10am-midnight. MC/V.

Jadłodajnia Całoroczna, ul. Budowlana 28 (☎352 69 12). Facing away from the *ratusz*, turn left down ul. Armii Krajowej, then right down Budowlana. Pass through the arch and enter through the back. Just on the outskirts of the main town square, this delightful milk bar is so hidden some locals don't even know about it. Choose from daily *zestawy*, featuring a complete meal, from *zupa* to *kompot*, for 15zł. Open daily 10am-7pm. ❷

Bar Pod Winogronami (Beneath the Grapes), ul. Towarowa 16 (☎354 73 36; winogronami@wp.pl). Tuscany may be a long way from the Baltic but the vine-laden interior and extensive wine list of this restaurant bring it a little bit closer. Open daily 11am-midnight. AmEx/MC/V. ❸

Restauracja Fregata, ul. Dworcowa 12 (☎352 37 87). Though the glitzy decor may not be appealing at first, the meals at this disco/restaurant are top-notch. Try the phenomenal homemade soup (2-5zł). Open M noon-10pm, Tu-Su noon-2am. MC/V. ❶

👁 SIGHTS

Though the town of Kołobrzeg was practically razed to the ground during WWII, some of its medieval beginnings can be seen today around the town's center.

ST. MARY'S BASILICA. Built between the 14th and 16th centuries, this cathedral is an anomaly of Gothic architecture. The interior was torched during WWII, but its unique five-aisle structure remains, giving the Basilica a unique open feeling. A beautiful seven-sided chandelier from 1327 hangs from the center aisle. The most intriguing architectural features are the two towers that were fused together to form one gargantuan facade. Outside stands the monument commemorating the thousandth anniversary of Kołobrzeg's brief stint as the seat of the bishopric. *(On the corner of ul. Katedralna and ul. Armii Krajowej.)*

NAUTICAL NUPTIALS. On March 4-18, 1945, fierce battles raged between the Poles and Nazis over the small town of Kołobrzeg. The Poles reigned vicotrious and on the day of their triumph they vowed that the port city would forever remain on Polish soil. That day, the Poles threw a wedding ring into the Baltic during a ceremony that has become known as **"Poland's marriage to the sea"** (Zaślubiny z Morzem). A monument stands near the beach in commemoration of the wedding. The nearby **lighthouse,** built in 1745, overlooks the monument and offers an expansive view of the Baltic. *(☎0605 109 457. Open daily July-Aug. 10am-sunset; Sept.-June 10am-5pm. 3zł, students 2zł.)*

MUSEUMS. Muzeum Oręża Polskiego, ul. Emilii Gierczak 5, features an astounding array of Polish and international military uniforms. Wander outside for a glimpse of authentic military vehicles, such as tanks, jeeps, and the occasional helicopter. (☎ 352 52 53. *Open M-Tu and Th-Su 9:30am-5pm, W 9:30am-6pm. 6zł, students 3zł. Free W noon-6pm.*) A less impressive **branch,** ul. Armii Krajowej 13, features a permanent exhibit of Kołobrzeg artifacts found between the 13th and 15th centuries and an exhaustive array of salt-measuring scales. (☎ 352 52 54. *Open M-W and F 9am-3pm, Th noon-6pm. 3zł, students 1.50zł.*) The **Gallery of Modern Art** (Galeria Sztuki Współcz-esniej), ul. Armii Krajowej 12, in the *ratusz,* displays an exquisite collection of hand-crafted jewelry, paintings, and sculptures, mostly by Polish craftsmen. There are new exhibits monthly. (☎ 352 43 48. *Open Tu-Su 10am-5pm. 4zł, students 2zł.*)

FORTIFIED REMNANTS. The 1570 **Powder Tower,** ul. Dubois 20, is the only surviving tower of the many that once surrounded the fortified city, though in 1657 its survival was questionable. On May 3 of that year, lightning struck the tower, setting it ablaze and causing the gunpowder it stored to explode. Thoroughly repaired and restored, the most dangerous items the tower stores today are the PTTK tourist offices. The **Marshy Redoubt,** situated near the mouth of **Port Jachtowy,** was built in 1770 as part of an expensive port defense system. Today the brick fortification is home to restaurants and flocks of seagulls. (☎ 354 43 01.) A similar structure, the **Salt Redoubt,** stands guard over the nearby Wooden Canal (Kanal Drzewny).

♫ ◘ ENTERTAINMENT AND FESTIVALS

The **amfiteatr,** located near the beach, sporadically plays old Polish movies in summer evenings. For more information, contact **IT** (see p. 556). Though most visitors come to Kołobrzeg for its healing springs and stretches of sand, the fun doesn't stop with beach and brine. August brings **InterFolk,** an international dance festival to the streets of the city. From June through August, St. Mary's comes alive with the sound of music during **Music in the Cathedral** (Muzyka w Katedrze; performances at 7:30pm every Th; 10zł, students 8zł).

TRI-CITY AREA (TRÓJMIASTO)

The Tri-city area (pop. 465,000) on Poland's Baltic coast is rapidly becoming a major tourist destination. The cities of Gdańsk, Sopot, and Gdynia complement each other perfectly, forming a metropolis that is urban and cosmopolitan yet replete with beautiful beaches and stellar hiking. Gdańsk provides Old World charm, Gdynia a strong economy, and Sopot pleasant streets and the glitz of the beach. Efficient public transport makes it possible to find a bed in one city and explore the other two. Both the fishing village of Hel and the Teutonic castle of Malbork are within two hours of the cities.

GDAŃSK ☎ (0)58

Gdańsk's (gh-DA-insk) strategic location at the mouth of the Wisła (Vistula) River has enabled it to flourish as an international center of art and commerce for more than a millennium. As the free city of Danzig, it was treasured by Poles as the "gateway to the sea" during its years of occupation in the 18th and 19th centuries; as a port city, it acquired a rich international heritage. The city's success was threatened by World War II—it was the site of the first war casualties and of Germany's last stand—but it was quick to rebound. By the early 1980s, Gdańsk found itself perpetually in the international spotlight as the birthplace of Lech Wałęsa's Solidarity (see **History,** p. 477). Restored to its former splendor for the 1997 city millennium celebration, Gdańsk is once again an attractive, bustling Baltic city.

⊏ TRANSPORTATION

Trains: Gdańsk Główny, ul. Podwale Grodzkie 1 (☎94 36). To: **Katowice** (8hr., 10 per day, 42zł); **Kraków** (7hr., 11 per day, 43zł); **Poznań** (4½hr., 7 per day, 41zł); **Szczecin** (5½hr., 5 per day, 43.50zł); **Toruń** (3hr., 7 per day, 36zł); **Warsaw** (4hr., 18 per day, 66zł plus 7-17zł mandatory reservation); **Wrocław** (5½hr., 5 per day, 46zł); **Berlin, GER** (8hr., 1 per day, 205zł); **Kaliningrad, RUS** (8hr., 1 per day, 50zł); **Odessa, UKR** (32hr., every 2 days, 260zł); **Prague, CZR** (14hr., June-Aug. 1 per day, 218zł). **SKM** (Fast City Trains; ☎628 57 78) run to **Gdynia** (35min.; 4zł, students 2zł) and **Sopot** (20min.; 2.80zł/1.40zł) every 10min. during the day and less frequently at night. Punch your ticket in a yellow *kasownik* machine before boarding.

Buses: Ul. 3-go Maja 12 (☎302 15 32), behind the train station, connected by an underground passageway. To: **Kołobrzeg** (5hr., 8 per day, 36zł); **Krynica Morska** (2hr., 15 per day, 10zł); **Warsaw** (4½hr., 6 per day, 50-57zł); **Kaliningrad, RUS** (8½hr., 2 per day, 28zł). Comfortable **Polski Express** buses run to **Warsaw** (4½hr., 2 per day, 45zł).

Ferries: Passenger ferries run May-Sept. and depart from the Green Gate. (☎301 49 26; www.zegluga.gda.pl). To: **Gdynia** (1½hr.; 2 per day; round-trip 54zł, students 37zł; one-way 39zł/28zł); **Hel** (1-3hr.; 3 per day; round-trip 54zł/37zł, one-way 42zł/30zł); **Sopot** (1½hr.; 4 per day; round-trip 42zł/30zł, one-way 30zł/21zł); **Westerplatte** (50min.; Apr.-Oct. every hr. 10am-6pm; round-trip 31zł/17zł). **Polferries,** ul. Przemysłowa 1 (☎343 18 87), in Gdańsk-Brzeźno, sends ferries to **Nynäshamn, SWE** (19hr.; June-Sept. 1 per day, Oct.-May Tu, Th, Su 6pm; 385zł/225zł).

Public Transportation: Gdańsk has an extensive **bus** and **tram** system that charges per time period. 10min. 1.10zł; 30min. 2.20zł; 45min. 2.70zł; 1hr. 3.30zł; day pass 6.20zł. **Night buses:** 30min. 3.30zł; night pass 5.50zł. Large bags (over 60cm) need their own tickets. Fines for riding ticketless (71zł) or with ticketless bags (30.80zł).

Taxis: It's a bird, it's a plane, it's...**Super Hallo Taxi** (☎301 91 91). Not to be confused with the mild-mannered **Hallo Taxi** (☎91 97). Both 1.80zł per km.

⊞ ORIENTATION

While Gdańsk technically sits on the Baltic Coast, its center is 5km inland. From the **Gdańsk Główny** train station, the center lies just a few blocks southeast, bordered on the west by **Wały Jagiellońskie** and on the east by the **Motława River.** Take the underpass in front of the train station, go right, exit the shopping center, and then turn left on **ul. Heweliusza.** Turn right on **ul. Rajska** and follow the signs to **Główne Miasto** (Main Town), turning left on **ul. Długa.** Długa becomes **Długi Targ** as it widens near **Motława** and opens into the area that houses most of the city's sights. Gdańsk has several suburbs, all north of Główne Miasto. See the sights section for directions to **Westerplatte.** Closer to the center, bustling **Gdańsk-Wrzeszcz** was home to Nobel Prize-winning novelist Günter Grass.

⊠ PRACTICAL INFORMATION

Tourist Offices: IT Gdańsk, ul. Długa 45 (☎328 52 89; www.pttk-gdansk.com.pl), in Główne Miasto, provides free **maps.** Multilingual tour guides available (☎301 60 96). Open daily June-Aug. 10am-8pm; Sept.-May 10am-6pm. **Branch** on the top floor of the train station. Open daily 10am-6pm (☎328 52 89).

Budget Travel: Orbis, ul. Podwale Staromiejskie 96/97 (☎301 45 44; orbis.gdansk-pod@pbp.com.pl). International and domestic tickets. Open M-F 9am-6pm, Sa 10am-3pm. AmEx/MC/V. **Almatur,** ul. Długi Targ 11, 2nd fl. (☎301 29 31; www.almatur.gda.pl), in Główne Miasto. Sells **ISICs** (44zł), offers hostel info, and books international air and ferry tickets. Open M-F 10am-5pm, Sa 10am-2pm.

POLAND

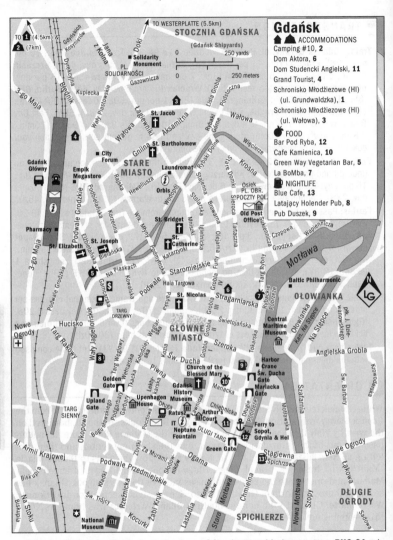

Gdańsk

⌂ ▲ ACCOMMODATIONS
Camping #10, **2**
Dom Aktora, **6**
Dom Studencki Angielski, **11**
Grand Tourist, **4**
Schronisko Młodzieżowe (HI)
  (ul. Grundwaldzka), **1**
Schronisko Młodzieżowe (HI)
  (ul. Wałowa), **3**

🍴 FOOD
Bar Pod Ryba, **12**
Cafe Kamienica, **10**
Green Way Vegetarian Bar, **5**
La BoMba, **7**

🍸 NIGHTLIFE
Blue Cafe, **13**
Latajacy Holender Pub, **8**
Pub Duszek, **9**

Currency Exchange: The train station has a 24hr. *kantor* with decent rates. **PKO SA,** ul. Garncarska (☎801 365 365) cashes **traveler's checks** for 1% commission and provides MC/V **cash advances** for no commission. Open M-F 9am-5pm and first and last Sa of every month 10am-2pm. **Orbis** (see **Budget Travel,** above) exchanges AmEx **Traveler's Cheques** for no commission.

Luggage Storage: In the train station. 4zł plus 0.50zł for every 50zł of value. Open daily 24hr. Also at the hostel on ul. Wałowa (see **Accommodations,** p. 561) for 1zł.

English-Language Bookstore: Empik Megastore, ul. Podwale Grodzkie 8 (☎301 62 88, ext. 115) at the underpass by the train station, also sells **maps** and *Gdańsk in Your Pocket* (10zł). Open M-Sa 9am-9pm, Su 11am-7pm.

24-Hour Pharmacy: Aptekus, at the train station (☎ 763 10 74). Ring the bell at night.

Medical Assistance: Private doctors, ul. Podbielańska 17 (☎ 301 51 68). A big blue sign on the building says "Lekarze Specjaliści." Internal medicine visit 35zł. For **emergency assistance,** go to **Szpital Wojewódzki,** ul. Nowe Ogrody 5 (☎ 302 30 31). From the train station, take a right out of the building and then the 1st right at the traffic circle; the hospital is on the left.

Laundromat: Hotel Hevelius, ul. Heweliusza (☎ 321 00 78), at the intersection with Lagiewniki. Enter through the basement door immediately to the right of the parking lot—just say *"pralnia"* (laundry) if the security guard gives you any grief—and head to the right. 5zł per kg. Ready in 24hr. Open M-Sa 7am-3pm.

Internet Access: Rudy Kot Internet Music Cafe, ul. Garncarska 18/20 (☎ 301 86 49), off Podwale Staromiejskie. 2.50zł per 30min. Open daily 10am-midnight. **Telekomunikacja Polska,** ul. Długa 22/27 (☎ 301 22 15), next to the post office, has free access. The wait is long; put your name on a list and come back later. Open M-F 10am-6pm; last Sa of every month 10am-3pm.

Post Office: Ul. Długa 23/28 (☎ 301 88 53). **Exchanges currency** and has **fax** service. Open M-F 8am-8pm, Sa 9am-3pm. For **Poste Restante,** use the entrance on ul. Pocztowa. **Telephones** inside.

Postal Code: 80 801.

ACCOMMODATIONS AND CAMPING

With Gdańsk's limited tourist infrastructure and increasing popularity, it's best to make reservations ahead of time, especially in summer. In July or August you can stay in a **university dorm.** Consult **IT, Almatur** (see p. 559), or *Gdańsk in Your Pocket* (10zł, available at some kiosks and at Empik) for info. Otherwise, **private rooms** are usually available and can be arranged through **IT ❷** or **Grand-Tourist ❷** (Biuro Zakwaterowania), ul. Podwale Grodzkie 8, downstairs in the City Forum complex, which is connected by the underground passage to the train station. (☎ 301 26 34; fax 301 63 01; tourist@gt.com.pl. Singles in the center 55zł, in the suburbs 43zł; doubles 90zł/73zł. Open July-Aug. daily 8am-8pm; Sept.-June M-Sa 9am-6pm.)

Schronisko Młodzieżowe (HI), ul. Wałowa 21 (☎ 301 23 13). Cross the street in front of the train station, head up ul. Heweliusza, turn left on ul. Łagiewniki, and right after the church onto Wałowa. These conveniently located rooms are popular with foreigners. Reception on 2nd fl. Kitchen available. Luggage storage 1zł. Showers until 10pm. Sheets 4.28zł. Lockout 10am-5pm. Curfew midnight. 5-6 bed dorms 14.40zł, nonmembers 16zł; singles 27zł/30zł; doubles 54zł/60zł. ❶

Dom Aktora, ul. Stragarniarska 55/56. This hotel combines European luxury and a home-style feel just a few steps from Długi Targ. Singles 200zł; doubles 250zł. ❺

Dom Studencki Angielski, ul. Chlebnicka 13/16 (☎ 301 28 16), 1 block off Długi Targ. Amazing location and unbeatable prices, but don't expect luxury: there's no toilet paper in the bathrooms and no linen. Sleeping bags required. Curfew midnight. Open July-Aug., but closed first week of Aug. Dorms 28zł per person, students 25zł. ❶

Schronisko Młodzieżowe (HI), ul. Grunwaldzka 244 (☎/fax 341 16 60). From the train station, take tram #6 or 12 north (to the left facing away from the station) and get off 14 stops later at Abrahama (unmarked); you'll see several tram garages on the left (20-25min.). Continue in the direction of the tram and turn right on ul. Abrahama. Walk several blocks, then turn right again on Grunwaldzka; the hostel entrance is by the track. Built only 5 years ago, it has immaculate rooms and bathrooms. The only down side is the remote location. Luggage storage 1zł. Sheets 3.21zł. Reception 24hr. Lockout 10am-5pm. Curfew 10pm. Dorms 18zł; doubles 30zł, with bath 41zł. ❶

Camping #10, al. Gen. J. Hallera 234 (☎343 55 31), in Gdańsk-Brzeźno. From the train station, take tram #13 or 63 north (to the left) toward Brzeźno. Stay on the tram past the last stop; after it turns around (and starts heading back on a different street), get off at Dworska (25min.). The entrance is next door. Owned by Grand-Tourist (see above), this complex is far from the center of town, but right by the beach. English spoken. Reception 24hr. Check-in 2pm. Check-out noon. 12zł per person, students 8.15zł, tents 8-15.50zł, bungalows 24zł per person. Electricity and parking 8zł each. ❶

🍴 FOOD

For fresh produce, try **Hala Targowa** on ul. Pańska, in the shadows of Kościół św. Katarzyny, just off Podwale Staromiejskie. (Open M-F 9am-6pm, first and last Sa of the month 9am-3pm.) If outdoor markets aren't your bag, head to **Esta,** ul. Podwale Staromiejskie 109/112, in Targ Drzewny. (Open M-Sa 10am-10pm, Su noon-10pm.) The cafes, restaurants, and beer gardens that flank **Długa** and **Długi Targ** provide prime people-watching opportunities and dish out *pierogi* late into the night.

🍽 **La BoMba,** ul. Rybackie Pobrzeże 5/7 (☎305 22 18). This tiny creperie, nestled on the banks of the Motława, delights patrons with its bohemian flare and creative-menu. Don't worry if the indoor tables are full on a chilly evening: warm yourself with a delicious cup of hot chocolate (5zł) and a complimentary blanket. Try each of the "Erotic Week" selections like "Whistling Breast" and "Disappointing Awakening" to earn your place in the "Regular Client" notebook near the door. Delectable crepes 4.50-15zł. Open daily June-Aug. 10:30am-10:30pm; Sept.-May 11am-9pm. ❷

🍽 **Cafe Kamienica,** ul. Mariacka 37/39. The best of the cafes in St. Mary's shadow. Tea lights softly illuminate the sea green interior, while a mural of Gdańsk's row houses adorns the loft. Coffee 5zł; tea 4zł; *szarlotka* (apple pie) 5zł. Entrees 12-19zł. ❷

🍽 **Green Way Vegetarian Bar,** ul. Garncarska 4/6 (☎301 41 21), serves vegetarian creations hearty enough for any carnivore. Stellar soups, samosas, stuffed pitas, and smoothies. Entrees 4-9zł. Open M-F 10am-8pm, Sa-Su noon-8pm. ❶

Bar Pod Ryba (Under the Fish), ul. Długi Targ 35/38 (☎305 13 07), serves huge baked potatoes with all sorts of fillings (6-15zł), as well as good fish (4-6zł per 100g) and chips. Open daily July-Aug. 11am-10pm, Sept.-June 11am-7pm. AmEx/MC/V. ❶

🎫 SIGHTS

GŁÓWNE MIASTO (MAIN TOWN)

DŁUGI TARG. The handsome main square, **Długi Targ** (Long Market), is at the heart of the painstakingly restored Główne Miasto. Cobblestone **ul. Mariacka, ul. Chlebnicka,** and **ul. Św. Ducha** are all lined by Gdańsk's unique row houses. Fanciful, gaping dragon's-head gutter spouts line the sides of the row houses, while stone steps lead up to their porches. The stone **Upland Gate**—so-named because it was upland of the city moat—and the elegant blue-gray **Golden Gate,** emblazoned with the shields of Poland, Prussia, and Germany, mark the entrance to ul. Długa. The 14th-century **Ratusz** (Town Hall), ul. Długa 47, towers over the spot where it al. Długa widens into Długi Targ and houses a branch of the **Gdańsk History Museum** (Muzeum Historii Gdanska). Baroque paintings, including an allegory of the marriage of Gdańsk and Poland, adorn the ceiling of the fantastic **Red Chamber,** while magnificent amber creations are displayed upstairs. Historical exhibits span from the first mention of the city to Gdańsk right after World War II—including some of the actual rubble. Nearby, the original 16th-century facade of **Arthur's Court** (Dwór Artusa), Długi Targ 43/44, faces out onto **Neptune's Fountain** (Fontanna Neptuna). Originally inspired by the court of King Arthur in Britain, it was fully restored in 1997 and now houses a second branch of the History Museum. The building's Renaissance interior and spiral wood staircase alone it worth the visit. Closer to the city gates, **Upenhagen House** (Dom Upenhagena), ul. Długa 12, showcases an 18th-century merchant's home. *(Town Hall ☎301 48 71. Arthur's Court ☎301 43 59. Upenhagen House ☎301 23 71. Each sight open Oct.-Apr. Tu and Th 11am-6pm, W 10am-4pm, F-Sa 10am-5pm, Su 11am-5pm. Last entrance 30min. before closing. Each branch 5zł, students 2.50zł. W free. Ticket for all three 10zł, students 5zł.)*

CHURCH OF THE BLESSED VIRGIN MARY. (Kościół Najświętszej Marii Panny.) The church was badly damaged during World War II, but has been almost completely rebuilt. Not all of the stained-glass windows are in place and only a few of the frescoes remain, but the intricate 1464 astronomical clock and the 1517 Dürer-inspired altarpiece still astound visitors. Legend has it that the king had the craftsman's eyes put out so he could never create another to match it. You can climb the 405 steps to the top of the steeple for a phenomenal view. *(Open June-Aug. M-Sa 9am-5:30pm, Su 1-5:30pm; off-season hours vary. 3zł, students 1.5zł.)* In the foreground on ul. Wielkie Młyny you'll find the 13th-century **St. Nicholas's Church** (Kościół św. Mikołaja); behind it is the 12th-century **St. Catherine's Church** (Kościół św. Katarzyny). Not only is St. Catherine's the final resting place of astronomer **Jan Heweliuz,** but its depths are also home to a Christian cemetary dating back to 997. Sixty-six steps above is the **Tower Clocks Museum,** which displays several clock tower mechanisms. The real draw, however, is one floor above where the 37 bell carrillon, open to the public, rings daily. *(Churches open for visiting daily between masses. Cemetary 1zł. Tower Clocks Museum open Tu-Su 10am-5pm. 4zł, W free.)*

NAUTICAL SIGHTS. The **Central Maritime Museum** (Centralne Muzeum Morskie) includes a main museum, the medieval **Żuraw** (Harbor Crane), and the ship **Sołdek.** The crane, which once loaded cargo ships, towers over the riverside promenade **Długie Pobrzeże.** You can go inside the crane to see the mechanism's inner workings, but the main exhibits are primitive boats from Asia, Africa, and South America. Passages from Polish authors are posted on the walls. Just across the Motława, the huge main museum building features all things nautical, from old diving equipment to cannons to paintings of the sea. The 1948 *Sołdek*, moored just outside, is now a playground for sea-happy visitors interested in ships, with machinery and models on display inside. To reach the *Sołdek*, take the shuttle boat or walk from the end of Długi Targ, cross two bridges, then bear left. *(☎301 86 11. All branches open June-Aug. daily 10am-6pm; Sept.-May Tu-Su 9:30am-4pm. Last entrance 30min. before closing. Crane 4zł, students 3zł. Museum 5zł/3zł. Sołdek 4zł/2.50zł. Shuttle boat round-trip 3zł/1.50zł. Ticket including all museums and ferry 12zł/7zł. English guide 15zł per group; call ahead.)*

NATIONAL MUSEUM. This large collection features 16th- to 20th-century art and furniture from Gdańsk, Polish art from the 19th-20th centuries, and numerous Flemish paintings. The jewel of the museum, Hans Menning's triptych "Last Judgment" altar, has a turbulent history. In 1473, it was captured by Gdańsk pirates en route from Italy to England during the continental blockade of England. In 1807, it was placed in the Louvre. Taken by Germans in 1815, it was reclaimed in 1817 and placed in St. Mary's Church in Gdańsk. After that, it was stolen by the Nazis in WWII, found by the Soviets in 1945, and placed in St. Petersburg's Hermitage for a decade. It was finally returned in 1956. *(Ul. Toruńska 1. ☎301 70 61. Follow the signs from the IT office opposite the Town Hall down Ławnicza and Żabi Kruk, under Podwale Przedmiejskie, to a right on Toruńska. Open from June to mid-Sept. Tu-F 9am-4pm, Sa-Su 10am-5pm; from mid-Sept. to May Tu-Su 9am-4pm.)*

OTHER SIGHTS. The legacy of **Solidarity** (*Solidarność*) will last long in the city from which it emerged. The flags of Lech Wałęsa's trade union (see **History,** p. 477) fly high at Gdańsk Shipyard (Stocznia Gdańska) and at the **Solidarity Monument,** which is located on pl. Solidarności, at the end of ul. Wały Piastowskie. The **Memorial to the Defenders of Post Office Square** (Obrońców Poczty), recognizes those postmen and women who bravely defended themselves at the start of World War II. On September 1, 1939 employees resisted the German army until the building was engulfed in

POLAND

flames. Those who survived the blaze were later executed or sent to concentration camps. A museum inside the reconstructed functioning post office commemorates the event, as well as the controversial establishment of a Polish postal service in occupied Gdańsk in 1920. *(From Podwale Staromiejskie, go north on Olejarna and turn right at Gdańsk Post Office #1 (Urzad Poctowy Gdańsk 1). ☎301 76 11. Open M and W-F 10am-4pm, Sa-Su 10:30am-2pm. 3zł, students 2zł.)*

BEYOND THE CENTER

WESTERPLATTE. When Germany attacked Poland on September 1, 1939, the little island fort guarding the entrance to Gdańsk's harbor gained the unfortunate distinction of being the first target of World War II. Its defenders held out for a week, until a lack of food and munitions forced them out. **Guardhouse #1** has been converted into a small museum with an exhibit about that fateful week. *(☎343 69 72. Open May-Sept. 9am-6pm. 2zł, students 1.50zł. English info booklet 6zł.)* The path beyond the exhibit passes the bunker ruins and the massive **Memorial to the Defenders of the Coast** (Pomnik Obrońców Wybrzeża). Follow the spiral path past the rose bushes for a closer look at the monument and a glimpse of the shipyard and the sea. Below the monument, giant letters spell "Nigdy Wiecej Wojny" (Never More War). On a clear day, you can see across the Baltic to the Hel Peninsula. *(From the train station, take bus #106 or 158 south to the last stop (20-25min.). The bus stop is just to the right of the station entrance. A ferry (50min.; every hr. 10am-6pm; round-trip 31zł, students 17zł) also runs to Westerplatte. Hop on by the Green Gate at the end of Długi Targ.)*

🎵 ENTERTAINMENT

Of the three cities that line this little stretch of the Baltic, Gdańsk draws the oldest and largest crowds to its activities. Elaborate street performances liven up Długi Targ. The **Baltic Philharmonic** (Philharmonia Bałtycka), ul. Ołowianka 1 (☎305 20 40), performs free outdoor concerts in summer. The audience listens from the other side of the Motława, near the end of Podwale Staromiejskie. Opera-lovers can check out the **Baltic Opera** (Opera Bałtycka), al. Zwycięstwa 15 (☎341 46 42). Consult the tourist office (see **Tourist Offices,** p. 559) for more information. **Church of the Blessed Virgin Mary** has organ concerts in July and August; call for details (tickets 15zł, students 10zł). Summer brings special events to the city, including a **Street Theater Festival** (early July), a **Shakespeare Festival** (early August), and the **International Organ Music Festival** at Oliwa. The first two weeks in August also see the arrival of the gigantic **Dominican Fair,** a centuries-old trading party.

🎭 NIGHTLIFE

When the sun goes down, the crowds party on Długi Targ, where bars and beer gardens abound. More pubbers than clubbers roam the city streets, but there's still plenty of dancing for those looking to shake their booties. Local magazines like *City* list events and venues in the Tri-city area.

■ **Latający Holender Pub,** ul. Waly Jagiellońskie 2/4 (☎802 03 63), in the basement of the LOT building near the end of ul. Długa; look for the flying Dutchman outside. Eclectically decorated with velvet couches and a hot-air balloon crashing through the ceiling. Beer 6zł; coffee 4zł; cocktails 7.50-22zł. Open daily noon-midnight.

Blue Cafe, ul. Chmielna 103/104 (☎346 38 61). Just across the first bridge at the end of Długi Targ, to the right. A new cafe decorated with Absolut paraphernilia, featuring occasional live music and an illuminated dance floor. Beer 7zł. Open daily 11am-late.

Pub Duszek (Goblin), ul. Św. Ducha 119/121 (☎802 03 04). The cultish fan club of Czech author Jaroslaw Haszek's "*Przygody Dobrego Wojaka Szwejka*" meets here to discuss the *Wojak's* adventures and plan trips to Prague, but most patrons come for the merry atmosphere. Beer 5.50zł. Open daily 10am-late.

▶ DAYTRIP FROM GDAŃSK

MALBORK ☎(0)55

Both trains (40-60min.; 37 per day; 9zł, express 21zł plus 7-17zł reservation) and buses (1hr., 8 per day, 7.20zł) run from Gdańsk to Malbork. Facing away from the station, walk right on ul. Dworcowa, then go left at the fork (sign points to Elbląg). Go up around the corner to the roundabout and cross to the street straight across the way, ul. Kościuszki, which runs between the pharmacy and the pizzeria. Follow it until you can veer right on ul. Piasłowska, where signs for the castle appear. Office ☎647 08 00, reservations 647 09 76; www.zamek.malbork.com.pl. Entire castle open May-Sept. Tu-Su 9am-8pm; Oct.-Apr. 9am-3pm. 19.50zł, students 11.50zł. Mandatory 3hr. tour in Polish included in ticket price. To make it intelligible, buy the red English booklet sold in the kiosks for 7zł or get an English guide for 126zł; call ahead and come early. Courtyards, terraces, and moats open May-Sept. daily 9am-6pm; Oct.-Apr. 9am-4pm. 6zł, students 4zł. Sound and light show May 15-Oct. 15 around 9:30-10pm. 10zł/5zł. AmEx/MC/V.

Malbork boasts the obscure distinction of being home to the **largest brick castle in the world.** Today's prevailing serenity, with children exploring the terraces and guides ushering visitors into every nook, belies the castle's violent history. Built by the **Teutonic Knights,** Malbork became the headquarters of the Teutonic Order in the 1300s. The Teutons first came to the region in 1230 at the request of Polish Duke Konrad Mazowiecki to assist the nation in its struggle against the heathen Prussians. The Teutons double-crossed the Poles, however, establishing their own state in 1309, with Malbork as its capital. The Polish victory over the Order at the **Battle of Grunwald** (see **History,** p. 475) in 1410 signaled the end of the great period of Teutonic castle-building. Malbork withstood several sieges, but the Poles finally defeated their arch-enemies in 1457. For the next 300 years, Malbork served as a stronghold for the Kingdom of Poland. In another wave of turbulence, it became part of Prussia after the first partition of Poland in 1772. It was still under German control in World War II, when it housed a POW camp (Stalag XXB). The mandatory tour snakes through the **High, Middle, and Low Castles,** including the spectacular **amber collection** and a **weapons collection** of the violent toys of the Polish hussars. The best point from which to see the entire castle is across the river. There's a **boat tour** (35min.; every hr. 9am-10pm; 11zł, students 7zł). An **IT** tourist office is outside the castle entrance at Piastowska 15. (☎272 92 46. Open June-Oct. Tu-F 10am-6pm, Sa 10am-2pm.) If you need to stay the night, consult the IT office or look for signs advertising **private rooms,** which are all over town.

SOPOT ☎(0)58

Though Sopot (pop. 50,000) is Poland's premier seaside spa town, the sun and sand are not its only attractions. On the way to the beach, along the famous pedestrian thoroughfare ul. Bohaterów Monte Cassino, you'll find shops, restaurants, bars, and street musicians. Be sure not to miss the area's best discos after you hit the golden sands or the famed 512m pier.

▬ TRANSPORTATION

Trains: The **commuter rail (SKM)** connects Sopot to **Gdańsk** (20min.; 2.80zł, students 1.40zł) and **Gdynia** (15min.; 2.80zł/1.40zł). Trains depart from platform #1 every 10min. during the day and less frequently at night. **PKP trains** run to: **Kołobrzeg** (5hr., 5 per day, 37zł); **Kraków** (6½-10hr., 10 per day, 48-79zł); **Poznań** (4½hr., 7 per day, 42-76zł); **Toruń** (3½hr., 6 per day, 33.20zł); **Warsaw** (4-5½hr., 18 per day, 38-76zł).

Ferries: ☎551 12 93. At the end of the pier. To: **Gdańsk** (1hr.; 1 per day; round-trip 46zł, students 32zł); **Gdynia** (35min., 4 per day, 45zł/34zł); **Hel** (1½hr., 4 per day, 45zł/31zł); **Westerplatte** (35min., 2 per day, 34zł/22zł).

THE LOCAL STORY

THE PARROT LADY

Katarzyna, a native of Sopot, tells fortunes in a most unusual fashion—with her two parrots, who draw fortunes out of a bowl using their beaks. Let's Go Researcher Barbara Urbańczyk couldn't resist learning more—it was in the stars.

Q: Where did this idea come from, using parrots for fortunetelling?
A: Well, it wasn't my idea. It's a tradition in my family to raise parrots. We've done it for over one hundred years. My grandmother used to do the same thing. She played the music box, the kind where you turn the handle.
Q: So how many parrots do you have at home?
A: Hah, I don't even know. Maybe a hundred?
Q: Are these the only two trained to read fortunes?
A: No, there are others.
Q: Can these two talk?
A: I could train them if I wanted to, but it's hard when there are two of them. They just talk amongst themselves. You can't get a word in edgewise. But if there's only one, it's easy to train.
Q: How do you train them?
A: I talk to them a lot. I stroke their feathers and give them little kisses when they do things correctly.

(continued on next page)

? PRACTICAL INFORMATION

Ul. Dworcowa begins at the train station and heads left to the pedestrian **ul. Bohaterów Monte Cassino,** which runs toward the sea and the *molo* (pier). Just about everything lies on ul. Bohaterów Monte Cassino or just off of it.

Tourist Office: IT, ul. Dworcowa 4 (☎550 37 83; fax 555 12 27; sts@sopot.pl), next to the train station. Sells **maps** of Sopot (3.50zł) and of the Tri-city area (4.50zł). Open June-Aug. M-F 8am-7pm, Sa-Su 9am-7pm; Sept.-May M-F 8am-4pm, Sa-Su 10am-6pm. The **private accommodations bureau** (☎551 26 17) is in the same office. Open June-Aug. M-F 8:30am-5pm, Sa-Su 9am-2pm; Sept.-May M-F 9am-2pm.

Currency Exchange: PKO Bank Polski, ul. Monte Cassino 32/34 (☎767 85 67). Gives MC/V **cash advances** (ID required), cashes **traveler's checks,** and has a MC/V **ATM.** Open M-F 8am-7pm, Sa 9am-1pm.

English-Language Bookstore: Empik, ul. Monte Cassino 55/57 (☎551 53 31). Open M-F 10am-8pm, Sa 11am-6pm, Su 11am-5pm. AmEx/MC/V.

24-Hour Pharmacy: Apteka pod Orlem, ul. Monte Cassino 37. Open M-Sa 10am-8pm, Su noon-8pm. Posts other 24hr. pharmacies in window.

Internet Access: NetCave, ul. Pulaskiego 7a (☎555 11 83; www.cave.hq.pl). Enter through arch at ul. Monte Cassino 32/34 and continue to Pulaskiego, where cyberspace meets the sub-aquatic. 3zł per 30min., 5zł per hr. Open daily noon-10pm.

Post Office: Ul. Kościuszki 2 (☎551 59 51). The 1st street on the right heading down ul. Monte Cassino. **Telephones** are inside. Open M-F 8am-8pm, Sa 9am-3pm.

Postal Code: 81 701.

⌂ ACCOMMODATIONS

Sopot is one of Poland's most popular and expensive resorts, so reservations are a must in the summer. Consider renting a **private room;** visit the bureau in IT ❷ (see **Tourist Offices,** above) for help. (June-Aug. singles 46zł; doubles 78zł; triples 90zł; Sept.-May 39zł/62zł/90zł.) If none of the following pan out, consider staying in Gdańsk, lest your złotys flutter away like a flock of seagulls.

▨ **Hotel Wojskowy Dom Wypoczynkowy (WDW),** ul. Kiliń skiego 12 (☎551 06 85; fax 626 11 33; www.wdw.sopot.pl), is a 10min. walk from the pier. Facing the sea, turn right on ul. Grunwaldzka; ul. Kiliń skiego is the 1st left after ul. 3-go Maja. Pass the guard and head for the 2nd building on your left, marked "Meduza." Pastel-colored rooms with well-kept bathrooms a stone's throw away from the beach. Breakfast included. Check-in 2pm. Check-out noon. Reserve a month ahead July-Aug. Singles 61zł, with sink 78zł, with bath 100zł; doubles 122zł/156zł/200zł; triples 183zł/234zł/300zł. ❸

Hotel Sopot, ul. Bitwy Pod Płowcami 62 (☎551 32 01; ☎/fax 551 55 33; www.hotel-sopot.pl). Facing the water, take a right on ul. Grunwaldzka from the pier, bear right at the fork on 3-go Maja, and then take a left. Walk down Bitwy and the hotel will be on your right (20min.). Gorgeous baths and spacious rooms. Most rooms with bath. Breakfast included. Check-in 2pm. Check-out noon. June-Sept. singles 99zł; doubles 198zł; triples 253zł; quads 363zł. Oct.-May 77zł/154zł/187zł/264zł. MC/V. ❹

Hotel Miramar, ul. Zamkowa Góra 25 (☎/fax 550 00 11; www.miramar.ta.pl). Take the commuter rail (3min., every 10-20min., 1.25zł) to the Sopot-Kamienny Potok station, then go down the right stairs and turn left. Cross the street and pass the gas station. Large rooms with spectacular bathrooms. Breakfast included for rooms with bath. Check-in 2pm. Check-out noon. Call ahead. Singles 50zł, with bath 150-200zł; doubles 100zł/190-240zł; triples 150zł/240-300zł; quads 200/320-400zł. AmEx/MC/V. ❷

🍴 FOOD

Ul. Monte Cassino is riddled with cafes and inexpensive food stands. A small **24hr. grocery,** ul. Monte Cassino 60 (☎551 57 62), is steps away from the pier.

🍴 **Błękitny Pudel** (Blue Poodle), ul. Monte Cassino 44 (☎551 16 72). The garden of this quirky cafe is lovely in summer, while the interior, chock-full of tapestried chairs and curiosities, is eclectically elegant. Entrees 18zł. Coffee 6zł. Open daily July-Aug. 9:30am-1am; Sept.-June noon-1am. ❷

🍴 **Przystań**, al. Wojska Polskiego 11 (☎550 02 41). Turn right at the last street before the pier or walk along the beach. The fabulous beach location with a view of Hel across the Baltic makes Przystań an unbeatable option. Fresh fish 3.80-6.40zł per 100g. *Hevelius* 5zł. Open daily 11am-11pm. ❶

Rotunda, ul. Powstancow Warszawy 2-6 (☎551 24 58; www.trojmiasto.pl/rotunda). Offers a varied menu of Polish fare, including vegetarian options that would satisfy the staunchest meat-eater (8-20zł). This airy restaurant offers a gorgeous view of Sopot's pier and the Baltic. Disco July-Aug. nightly 9pm. Restaurant open daily 11am-late. ❷

Q: What do parrots like to eat?
A: Seeds. Fruits and vegetables. For some reason, mine don't like fruit. They love vegetables though. They also like ham. I have to cut it up into tiny pieces for them.
Q: They won't fly away?
A: They do, every now and then. But they know that this is their home. Parrots always come back to their home, as long as they can recognize it. My windowpanes at home are painted in a special way so they can always come back when they want to. That's why this stand is red—it stands out. If they fly away while working, they always come back. I didn't paint it like this for customers, it's for the parrots! I would have painted it much nicer if it was for customers!
Q: Do they like doing this?
A: Yes, Polly more so than Kiri. Kiri is very lazy. He used to like it more, but all he wants to do now is sleep.
Q: Ah, a parrot after my own heart...
A: Ha ha, yes, he even sleeps between drawing fortunes. Look! He's sleeping now! But Polly always enjoys drawing the cards. She's very good at it. It's because she's a girl.
Q: Have any famous people ever asked you for a fortune?
A: Some actors and actresses. A senator once asked me for a fortune. Even the mayor of Lublin wanted his fortune read.

🎵🔲 ENTERTAINMENT AND FESTIVALS

Sopot's popularity is due largely to its **beach,** with its white sands and ample recreational facilities, from waterslides to an outdoor theater. The most popular and extensive sands lie at the end of ul. Monte Cassino, where the longest **pier** *(molo)* on the Baltic begins. (M-F 2.50zł, Sa-Su 3.30zł.) The town is just beginning to realize that the fun doesn't have to end when the tides come in, as evidenced by the growing number of streetside **cafes, pubs,** and **discos** along ul. Monte Cassino. **Galeria Kiń ski,** ul. Kościuszki 10, to the right when coming from the station, is a smoky tribute to the actor Klaus Kiński, who was born upstairs. Posters of Nosferatu and a full-scale mural adorn the walls. (☎802 56 38. Beer 5zł. Open daily 11am-3am.) **Galaxy Music Club,** to your left when facing the pier, in the seaside park Lazienki Północne at ul. Mamuszki 14, lets you dance all night in the blacklight and then admire the morning views of the Baltic. (☎555 03 76. Restaurant open daily 10am-8pm. Disco open daily 9pm-morning. Cover Th-Sa 10zł.) Posters spread the word about the clubs just out of town, which are accessible by commuter rail.

Opera Leśna ("Forest Opera"), an open-air theater, is a good place to get in on the local scene. Its **rock and pop music festival** (☎551 18 12) dominates the area in mid-August. For tickets or information about other festivals, call the theater or contact **Orbis** (see **Budget Travel,** p. 566). If you can't bear to leave the beach, then beeline to **Teatr Atelier,** ul. Franciszka Mamuszki 2 (☎550 10 01), which stages shows on the sands; IT (see **Tourist Office,** p. 566) has an event schedule.

GDYNIA   ☎(0)58

Young Gdynia (gh-DIN-ya; pop. 253,500), built mostly in the 20th century, is in no hurry to grow up. Happy to sink its teeth into modern business, it leaves history to nearby Gdańsk. Gdynia's residents are the wealthiest of any city in Poland, thanks to its position as a major port. Gdynia's prosperity, however, hasn't caused the city to forget its simple maritime history. Evening strolls along the waterfront reveal a little slice of nautical heaven, recalling the time when the Gdynian life was not one of cyberspace, but of the sea.

⌐ TRANSPORTATION

Trains: ☎94 36. Trains to: **Hel** (2hr., 18 per day, 10zł); **Kołobrzeg** (3hr., 6 per day, 37zł); **Kraków** (10hr., 10 per day, 49zł); **Poznań** (4-5hr., 8 per day, 38-76zł); **Szczecin** (5hr., 5 per day, 42zł); **Toruń** (3½hr., 6 per day, 36zł); **Warsaw** (4½hr., 18 per day, 38-76zł); **Wrocław** (6hr., 6 per day, 47zł); **Berlin, GER** (9½hr., 1 per day, 130zł). SKM commuter trains *(kolejka)* are the cheapest and easiest way to get to **Gdańsk** (35min.; 4zł, students 2zł) and **Sopot** (15min.; 2.80zł/1.40zł). They depart every 10min. from the *peron* (platform) #1. Punch your ticket in a yellow *kasownik* box.

Buses: ☎620 77 47. To: **Hel** (2hr., 26 per day, 10zł); **Świnoujście** (8hr., 2 per day, 47zł); **Toruń** (5hr., 1 per day, 34zł). **Polski Express** heads to **Warsaw** (6½hr., 2 per day, 37zł). But tickets at the PKS *kasa* or Orbis (see **Budget Travel,** below).

Ferries: Depart from al. Zjednoczenia 2 (☎620 26 42; www.zegluga.gda.pl), on Skwer Kościuszki. To: **Gdańsk** (1½hr.; 3 per day; 39zł, students 28zł); **Hel** (1hr.; 10 per day; 42zł/30zł); **Sopot** (30min.; 4 per day; 18zł/11zł); **Kaliningrad, RUS** (3hr., July-Aug. 2 per week, 110zł) via **Hel. Stena Line,** ul. Kwiatkowskiego 60 (☎660 92 00; fax 660 92 09), sends ferries to **Karlskrona, SWE** (8½-10½hr., 1 per day, 300-385zł).

Public Transportation: Rides cost 1.80zł, students 0.90zł. If kiosks are closed, buy a book of 5 tickets (9zł, students 4.50zł) from the driver.

POLAND

▓▐ ORIENTATION AND PRACTICAL INFORMATION

Any of the roads running away from the train station on your right will take you toward the waterfront; **ul. 10-go Lutego,** farthest to the right, takes you directly to the fountain-filled main square, **Skwer Kościuszki.** If you end up on **ul. Jana Kolna, ul. Wójta Radtkiego,** or **ul. Starowiejska,** take a right and walk until you can take a left on ul. 10-go Lutego. To shop, explore **ul. Świętojańska,** which intersects ul. 10-go Lutego at the top of Skwer Kościuszki. The **beach** is to the right of the pier.

Tourist Office: IT, pl. Konstytucji 1 (☎628 54 66), in the train station, has free small **maps** and a list of accommodations. Open May-Sept. M-F 8am-6pm, Sa 9am-4pm, Su 9am-3pm; Oct.-Apr. M-F 10am-5pm, Sa 10am-4pm.

Budget Travel: Orbis, ul. 10-go Lutego 12 (☎620 48 44; orbis.gdynia@pop.com.pl). Sells budget plane, train, bus, and ferry tickets, and arranges hotel stays. Open Sept.- June M-F 9am-5pm, Sa 10am-2pm; July-Aug. M-F 9am-6pm, Sa 10am-3pm.

Currency Exchange: Bank Gdański S.A., Skwer Kościuszki 14 (☎620 41 25), gives AmEx/MC/V **cash advances** and cashes **traveler's checks** for 0.5% commission. Open M-F 9am-6pm.

Luggage storage: In the main hall of the bus/train station. 2zł plus 1% declared value.

24-Hour Pharmacy: Apteka Pod Gryfem, ul. Starowiejska 34 (☎620 19 82).

Medical Assistance: Medicor, ul. Starowiejska 45 (☎660 88 90). Private doctors and English-speaking staff. 60-80zł. Open M-F 8am-8pm.

English-Language Bookstore: Ksiegarnia Językowa, ul. Świętojańska 14 (☎61 25 61). Open M-F 10am-6pm, Sa 10am-3pm.

Internet Access: TOMNet, ul. Świętojańska 69. 4zł per hr. Open M-F 9am-1pm, Sa-Su 10am-10pm.

Post Office: Ul. 10-go Lutego 10 (☎620 82 72), near Skwer Kościuszki. Open M-F 7am-8pm, Sa 9am-3pm. **Telephones** outside. For **Poste Restante** go to window #28. **Postal Code:** 81 301.

▐ ACCOMMODATIONS

Cheap rooms are hard to come by in the city center; look for **private rooms. Turus ❷,** ul. Starowiejska 47, opposite the train station, will help you find one. (☎621 82 65; fax 620 92 87. Singles 56zł; doubles 86zł. Open M-F 8am-6pm, Sa 10am-6pm.)

Dom Studencki Marynarza. From the train station, go through the tunnels under the platforms toward ul. Morska to the next-to-last exit. Take any numbered bus 3 stops or any express bus (marked by a letter) 2 stops to "Stocznia SKM-Morska." Backtrack, then head right up the hill on ul. Wojciecha Surmana. Veer right up the hill past the park. Dorms in these large apartment buildings provide a number of options.

#1, ul. Beniowskiego 24/24a (☎621 68 01). Last building on your right. Suites with kitchen, bath, and TV. Open year-round. 60zł per person 1st night, 50zł until 4th, 45zł after. ❷

#3, ul. Beniowskiego 15/17 (☎621 89 51). 1st building on your left. Open from mid-July to mid-Sept. Dorms 24zł per person; renovated rooms 32zł; hotel-style rooms 62zł 1st night, 52zł until 4th night, 46zł after. ❷

Schronisko Młodzieżowe (HI), ul. Energetyków 13a (☎627 10 05). From the train station, bear right from the main entrance to ul. Jana z Kolna. Take bus #128, 150, 152, or 182 from the middle bus stop (there are 3 in a row across from Hala Rybna) 2 stops to "Energetyków." Backtrack 20m and take a left; it'll be on your right. Located next to the shipyard's entrance, this brand-new hostel offers great rooms. Sheets 3.21zł. Lockout 10am-5pm. Curfew 10pm. Dorms 20zł. ❶

Dom Marynarza, Pilsudskiego 1 (☎ 622 00 25). This upscale hotel is nestled at the base of a wooded hillside, lending a sense of privacy and seclusion despite its location near the heart of Gdynia. Freshly painted rooms and stellar service complement the fabulous location, just 150m away from the beach. TV, telephone, and breakfast included. Check-in 2pm. Check-out 11:30am. Reception 24hr. Singles 140zł; doubles 180zł; triples 225zł. AmEx/MC/V. ❺

⟨ FOOD

One of the most extensive markets in the Tri-city area, **Hala Targowa** stretches between ul. Jana Kolna and ul. Wójta Radtkiego. For a full sensory experience, check out the pungent **Hala Rybna** (Hall of Fish; open M-F 9am-6pm, Sa 8am-3pm). The food stands lining the waterfront serve full meals for less than 6zł.

Kawiarnia Artystyczna Cyganeria, ul. 3 Maja 27 (☎ 699 90 15), just off ul. 10-go Lutego. Offers excellent coffee (3.50-5.50zł) and a mellow atmosphere, with velvet-covered couches, black-and-white photographs, and smoking students. Salads 7zł; burritos 10zł. Open M-Th 10am-12:30am, F-Sa 10am-midnight, Su 1pm-12:30am. ❷

Bistro Kwadrans, Skwer Kościuszki 20 (☎ 620 15 92). Packs in the people with cheap pizza (4.50-13zł), Polish fare (8.50-12zł), and breakfast (6.50zł). Open M-F 9am-10pm, Sa 10am-10pm, Su noon-10pm. ❷

Green Way, ul. Abrahama 24 (☎ 620 12 53), on the corner of ul. 10-go Lutego. Great samosas, pitas (6-9zł), and carrot cake. Open daily 11am-10pm. ❶

⟨ ♪ SIGHTS AND ENTERTAINMENT

Those looking to get nautical or naughty won't be disappointed by the city's massive pier off Skwer Kościuzki, where military history, marine biology, drinking, and dancing are all given their due. Ship tours replace history museums in this coastal city; the highlight is the destroyer **Błyskawica** ("Lightning"), the only Polish ship built before World War II. Sailors guide tourists through exhibitions covering Polish naval history, including the ship's role in combat. (☎ 626 37 27. Free English info at the *kasa*. Open Tu-Su 10am-12:30pm and 2-4pm. 4zł, students 2zł.) The 1909 sailboat **Dar Pomorza** (Gift of Pomerania), once known as the "fastest and most beautiful ship of the seas," served as a school at sea for the Polish navy between 1930 and 1981, and, in its competing days, took first honors at the Cutty Sark Tall Ships Contest. (☎ 620 23 71. Open daily June-Aug. 10am-6pm; Sept.-May 10am-4pm. Last entry 30min. before closing. 5zł, students 3zł; June-Aug. Sa free.) At the end of the pier sits the gargantuan **Muzeum Oceanograficzne i Akwarium Morskie** (Museum of Oceanography and Aquarium), a marine biologist's paradise featuring displays of Baltic ecology and a fascinating collection of live sea creatures. (☎ 621 70 21; www.mir.gdynia.pl/akw. Open daily 9am-7pm. 8.50zł, students 5zł. Last ticket sold 30min. before closing.)

Just upland of the waterfront, the forested hill **Kamienna Góra** makes an excellent observation point for those willing to scale its few hundred steps. Walking down ul. Świętojańska with the sea to your left, turn left on ul. Armii Krajowej, right on pl. Grunwaldzki, and follow the signs. Atop the summit, a towering steel cross dedicated to the **Defenders of Pomerania** (Obrońców Pomorza) overlooks the Gdańsk Bay and the Hel peninsula.

Gdynia Musical Theater (Teatr Muzyczny w Gdyni), pl. Grunwaldzki 1 (☎ 621 60 24 or 621 78 16) puts on productions and hosts concerts during the **Gdynia Summer Jazz Days** festival in early July. Consult the tourist office for a schedule (see p. 569). Crowds hang around after meals to relax by the sea. **Bul. Nadmorski im F. Nowowiejskiego,** which heads to the right when facing the water, provides particularly good views along the beach. The most intimate pub is 🏠 **Cafe Strych** (Attic), with antique radios and turn-of-the-century furniture littering the rafters. (Pl. Kaszubski 76, at the end of ul. Jana z Kolna. ☎ 620 30 38. Live piano music Th-F and Su 6:30-10:30pm. Open June-Aug. daily 4pm-1am; Sept.-May Tu-Su noon-midnight.)

HEL ☎(0)58

Go to Hel—really. For almost a millennium, the sleepy village of Hel has lived off the fish of the Baltic Sea and booty from boats stranded on Poland's only peninsula (Mierzeja Helska). Recently, the town has awakened to the sound of tourists walking its clean, wide beaches. Hel opens the gates to a day of relaxation, serving up outstanding fish and a heavenly change of pace from crowded resorts.

▤ TO HEL AND BACK. Hel on earth exists on the tip of a peninsula jutting into the Baltic, northeast of the Tri-city area. **Trains** go to **Gdynia** (2hr., 15 per day, 11zł); **Kraków** (9hr., 1 per day, 51zł) and **Warsaw** (6-7hr., 3 per day, 45zł). Buses go to **Gdynia** (2hr., 28 per day, 11zł). Hel can also be reached by the **Zegluga ferry** (☎ 675 04 37; www.zegluga.gda.pl) from: **Gdańsk** (3hr.; 5 per day; one-way 46zł, students 32zł; round-trip 56zł/39zł); **Gdynia** (1hr.; 8 per day; one-way 33zł/22złm, round-trip 46zł/32zł); **Sopot** (2hr.; 4 per day; one-way 35zł/23zł, round-trip 48zł/34zł). The **Merlin jet-ferry** (☎/fax 661 21 01) also runs to **Gdynia** (25min.; 7 per day; one-way 32zł/21zł, round-trip 45zł/31zł) and **Sopot** (30min.; 3 per day; one-way 32zł/21zł, round-trip 45zł/31zł). From July to September, a plain old **ferry** makes the short trip to **Kaliningrad, RUS** (3hr., 2 per week, 110zł). It departs from Hel's dock on **Bulwar Nadmorski,** just down the hill from ul. Wiejska. Charon sells tickets in the white kiosk by the ferry landing. (☎ 605 551 470. Open daily 9am-6pm.) Ferries don't run when Hel freezes over (Nov.-Mar.). For Hel on wheels, call a **taxi** ☎ 675 77 57.

⊞ 🔢 ORIENTATION AND PRACTICAL INFORMATION. The **train station,** opposite the first of the town's two bus stops, is a short walk from **ul. Wiejska,** the main street. Facing away from the station, take **ul. Dworcowa** to the right as it follows a small park to intersect ul. Wiejska, then turn left to head into town. The Gdańsk Bay and the ferry landing are on the right, while a strip of forest on the left separates the center from the Baltic shore. The **tourist office** (Miejska Informacja Turystyczna), ul. Wiejska 78, offers information about the Kaszubian culture that once flourished in Hel. (☎ 675 10 10. Open Tu-Su noon-6pm.) Even email reaches Hel at **Kawiarnia Internetowa Praetoria,** ul. Leśna 9c. (☎ 0 501 273 327. 3zł per 30min., 5zł per hr. Open M-Sa noon-late.) Send a postcard from Hel at the **post office,** ul. Wiejska 55 (☎ 675 04 05), which also **exchanges currency.** (Open M-F 8am-6pm, Sa 9am-1pm; *kantor* open M-F 8-11am and 2:30-6pm.) A MC/V **ATM** is across the street. **Postal Code:** 84 150.

⌐ ACCOMMODATIONS. The cheapest accommodations in Hel are **private rooms.** Look for the *wolne pokoje* (available rooms) signs along the road from the train station through town. It's hard to find a single; if you're in limbo, try the **tourist office** ❶ (see above). They can arrange a **private room** (25-50zł) or a stay in a *pensjonat* (75-100zł). **Foka** ❷ (Seal), ul. Leśna 9a, on the way to the beach, has inexpensive older rooms. Flashier renovated rooms come with a fridge and a color TV. (☎ 675 05 91; www.maxmedia.pl/foka. Doubles 40-70zł, renovated 80-100zł; triples 75-105/120-150zł; quads 100-150zł/160zł.) To reach **Camping Helska Bryza,** ul. Bałtycka 5, bear left at the end of ul. Wiejska. Near the lighthouse and 300m from the beach, this clean campground is a cheap place to rest your weary bones. (☎ 675 08 93. Guarded 24hr. English spoken. Check-in noon. Check-out 11am. Open May-Aug. 20zł per person; tents 7zł; 1- to 6-person bungalows 28zł per person, with 3 meals 55zł. AmEx/MC/V.)

POLAND

📮 **FOOD.** It'll be a cold day in Hel before anyone starves; the town feeds its guests well. Most restaurants flank ul. Wiejska. For Hel in a handbasket, prepare for a picnic at the central **supermarket "Marina,"** ul. Wiejska 70. (☎675 00 30. Open M-Sa 6am-10pm, Su 8am-10pm.) **Izdebka ❶,** ul. Wiejska 39, near the ferry landing in a white-and-brown fisherman's hut built in 1844, sells fresh fish for 3.50-10zł per 100g. (☎0 600 356 199. Open daily 10am-10pm.) If you're in the mood for downright sinful dessert, enjoy coffee (3-20zł) and sweets (6-20zł) among gaping blowfish and nautical knick-knacks at **Maszoperia ❷,** ul. Wiejska 110, a 200-year-old hut with a traditional half-door. (☎675 02 97. Open daily May 15-Sept. 15 10am-midnight; Sept. 16-May 14 10am-10pm.)

🔲 **SIGHTS.** If, like Odysseus, you arrive in Hel by boat, the first thing you'll see after the harbor is its oldest building. Hel's bells top the red-brick **Church of St. Peter and Paul** (Kościół św. Piotr i Pawła; 1417-32), on Bulwar Nadmorski, which now houses the **Fishing Museum** (Muzeum Rybołówstwa). Check out the fishermen's ice skates, the net-mending needles, and the giant eel-catching combs. (☎675 05 52. Open daily July-Aug. 9:30am-6pm; Sept.-June 8am-4pm. 4zł, students 2.50zł. Bell tower 1.50zł.) Facing the bay, head right to see one Hel of a seal. "Balbin" has lived in the pool of the town **Fokarium,** ul. Morska 7, since 1992. He and his playmates never fail to draw crowds with their frisky tricks, especially during feeding times at 10am and 3pm. (☎675 08 36; www.univ.gda.edu.pl. Open daily 8:30am-9pm. 1zł.)

One of the Baltic Coast's best-kept secrets is the **beach** at the end of ul. Leśna. Take a left off ul. Wiejska onto ul. Leśna, from which a footpath continues through a park to the other side of the peninsula (15-20min.). If you bear left on ul. Bałtycka at the end of ul. Wiejska, following the signs to "Latarni Morska," you can reach the octagonal red brick lighthouse. Climb up to see the tiny slip of peninsula from on high. (Open May-Aug. daily 10am-2pm and 3-7pm. 2zł, students 1.50zł.) On ul. Leśna, signs point to a path that leads to a "place of national memory" (*Miejsce Pamięci Narodowej*), a concrete fortification where the defenders of Hel trained their anti-aircraft artillery in 1939. Following ul. Wiejska as it becomes ul. Kuracyjna eventually leads to a military area. There, on the tip of the peninsula, sits the **Headland Battery,** site of the Polish defense at the beginning of World War II, but you have a snowball's chance in Hel of getting in as the area is closed off to civilians. On **ul. Wiejska** itself, check out the low-set **19th-century fishermen's houses** at #29, 33, 39 and 110. All face the street sideways. Have a Hel of a good time.

MAZURY

East of Pomorze, forested Mazury lives up to its nickname, "land of a thousand lakes." The region is actually home to about 4000 lakes; the largest, Śniardwy and Mamry, each cover an area of more than 100 sq. km. Small towns like Mikolajki greet both visitors in search of quiet time by the shores and those venturing out into the wild, beautiful waters to canoe, kayak, and sail.

MIKOŁAJKI   (0)87

Mikołajki has the distincion of being located near Poland's largest lake, Lake Sniardwy. Though not yet a thriving tourist town, Mikołajki pleases visitors with its peaceful surroundings and abundant fish. However, the fish were not always abundant. Legend has it that the residents of Mikołajki were terrorized by a giant whitefish called Krol Sielaw who broke their nets and capsized boats until a clever fisherman caught him in a steel net. Krol Sielaw begged for his life and promised that if he were spared, he would ensure that Lake Mikołajki would always be full of fish. Krol Sielaw was good to his word and to show their appreciation, the fishermen tied him to the bridge where he resides to this day.

TRANSPORTATION. The small town of Mikołajki is poorly connected to the rest of the country. The nearby town of Olsztyn provides more options. **Trains** run to Mikołajki from: **Białystok** (3-4hr., 1 per day, 19.10zł); **Ełk** (1½hr., 2 per day, 10.50zł); **Gdynia** (6hr., 1 per day, 40.84zł); and **Olsztyn** (1hr., 4 per day, 18.50zł). **Buses** run to: **Lublin** (8hr., 1 per day, 67zł) and **Warsaw** (5hr., 5 per day, 56zł).

ORIENTATION AND PRACTICAL INFORMATION. The train station is relativly close to the town center. To get there, hang a right out of the station and walk along **ul. Kolejowa.** The **bus stop** is about 1km down the road on the right, in the parking lot of the Protestant church. A left down **ul. 3-go Maja** will lead you to **pl. Wolnosci,** the center of town. To get to the **lake,** take any right out of the square to reach the shore a block away. **Al. Kasztanowa** and **al. Spacerowa** border the lake. In the center of town, the **IT** office provides visitors with **maps** (5zł) as well as info about accomodations, sporting, and cultural events. (☎421 68 50; www.mikolajki.pl. English spoken. Open M-Sa 10am-6pm, Su 10am-5pm.) **Bank PKO BP,** in pl. Wolnosci, cashes **traveler's checks** for 1.5% commission and provides MC/V **cash advances.** (☎421 69 36. Open M-F 9am-4pm.) A **pharmacy** sits at ul. 3-go Maja 3. (☎421 63 16. Open daily 8am-7pm. MC/V.) Surf the **Internet** at **Kawiarenka Internetowa,** ul. Szkolna 1, a left off ul. Kolejowa on the way to town from the train station. (0.08zł per min. Open M-Sa 4pm-9pm.) **Phones** are located outside the **post office,** ul. 3-go Maja 8. (Open M-F 8am-6pm, Sa 8:30am-2:30pm.) **Postal Code:** 11 730.

ACCOMMODATIONS AND FOOD. Mikołajki is just beginning to develop into a burgeoning tourist town, but it still retains its quiet and relaxed atmosphere that is problematic for those seeking hotel accommodations. Yellow street signs point the way to private rooms and pensions. **Pensjonat Mikołajki ❸,** ul. Kajki 18, is a family-run business providing guests with stellar service and an amazing location on the banks of Lake Mikołajskie. Ask about kayak and bike rentals. (From pl. Wolnosci, continue down ul. 3-go Maja until it turns into ul. Kajki. ☎421 64 37; fax 421 68 75. Singles July-Aug. 70zł, with bath 90zł; doubles 90zł/120zł, with view of lake 150zł. Prices approximately 25zł cheaper during the off-season.) **Camping Wagabunda ❶,** ul. Lesna 2, offers a breathtaking panorama of Lake Mikołajskie. Some cabins include a full bath and a kitchenette. (From the bus station, turn right on ul. Kolejowa and cross the bridge. Hang a left on ul. Warszawska and continue for 15min. until you see the Wagabunda signs. ☎421 60 18, www.wagabunda.w.pl. 4- to 6-person cabins 100-230zł; tent sites 8-10zł per person; electricity 10zł.) **U Aldon** (☎421 52 25), is a **24hr. grocery store** at ul. Szkolna 4f. Stocks fresh fish and some produce. For delicious fish in a rustic atmosphere, head to **Restauracja Sielaw ❶,** ul. Kajki 5, where the number of fish on the wall may rival the number of fish in Lake Sniardwy Mikołajki. (☎/fax 421 63 23. Entrees 5-15zł. Open daily 11am-10pm.) On the way to town, on the left-hand side of ul. 3-go Maja, you'll find **Kaskada ❶,** a clean and efficient milk bar that serves delicious homestyle eats for under 8zł. (Open daily 9am-7pm.)

SIGHTS. Mikołajki would be nothing today if it weren't for the help of **Krol Sielaw.** You too can pay your respects to this mighty whitefish by visiting the statue on al. Zeglarska. If you're lucky, you may even catch a glimpse of this finned friend tied to the bridge on ul. Kolejowa. **Zegluga Mazurska,** located on the lakeshore on al. Zeglarska, offers ferry rides on Lake Sniardwy and even shuttles passengers to various Mazurian cities several times a day for under 20zł. For details, call ☎/fax 421 66 08. For those seeking a little more lakeside adventure, **Wioska Zeglarska,** located further down the shore at ul. Kowalska 3, rents yachts. However, only those holding a Polish sailing license may rent. Wioska can provide information about sailing courses and license requirements. (☎/fax 421 60 40; www.marina-

POLAND

mikolajki.com.pl.) Further away from the town center toward the bus stop rests the **Muzeum Reformacji** (Museum of the Reformation), at the intersection of ul. Kolejowa and ul. 3-go Maja. This tiny museum offers a history of Mikołajki's Protestant church and the effects of the Reformation through recent photographs and an extensive collection of hymnals and Bibles, some dating back as far as 1680. (☎ 321 68 10. Open M-Sa 9am-4pm, Su noon-6:30pm. 4zł, students 2zł.) Just uphill is the **Kościół Sw. Trójcy** (Church of the Holy Trinity), one of few Protestant churches in Catholic Poland. Its unique wooden vaulted ceiling, pure white walls, and austere decorations are in stark contrast with the elaborate cathedrals found throughout Poland. (Services Su 10:30am.)

PODLASIE

Poland extends maximum environmental protection to this small, northeastern region, often called "the green lungs of Poland." Poland's few Russian Orthodox villages dot wide-open fields, which are interrupted only by the meandering Bug and Narew rivers. Białowieża Forest (Puszcza Białowieska), once the favorite hunting ground of Polish kings, is now a national park and the domain of the increasingly scarce European bison.

BIAŁOWIESKI PARK NARODOWY

Białowieża Primeval Forest (Puszcza Białowieska), a natural treasure of towering trees and European bison, sprawls out over oceans of flatland. Once the hunting ground of Polish kings and the former residence of Tsar Nicholas I, the park has been named a UNESCO World Cultural site and attracts visitors from all over the world. Bordering Białowieża is the park's main attraction, a large **bison preserve.** Only **guided tours** (see below) can enter this section of the park, where around 300 bison still lumber about. There would be far more, but many were wiped out by hungry soldiers during World War II. (Open daily 9am-5pm. 5zł, students 3zł.) If you don't want to pay the price of a tour, there are two much smaller preserves where bison and other animals are kept in tighter quarters. The closer of the two is 5km away from town and accessible by the yellow trail, which leads from the PTTK office (see below) into the woods. (Preserve open daily 10am-5pm. 3zł, students 2zł.) The well-marked yellow, red, green, and blue trails offer great biking and walking paths through flat, but beautiful and serene, wooded areas.

Buses run from Warsaw to Białowieski Park Narodowy via Białystok (3½hr.; M-Th and Sa 3 per day, F and Su 4 per day; 23zł), and then to Białowieża via Bialowieski Park Narodowy at 6:30am and 3pm, and return at 6am and 5:07pm (2½-3hr., 12.50-13.40zł). Leave early, as there may be a wait between buses. Do not get off at the main bus stop. Once the bus reaches Bialowieża, get off at the park gate on the left. In the gateway of the park entrance, the **PTTK** office awaits tourists. (☎/fax 681 26 24; www.pttk.sitech.pl. Open M-Sa 8am-4pm, Su 8am-3pm. English spoken. Maps 12zł. AmEx/MC/V.) The staff can point the way to accommodations, including the youth hostel (Waszkiewicza 2; ☎ 681 25 60), and arrange carriage and walking tours of the park. (All tours 3hr. Carriage tours 110-150zł, plus guide fee if going through bison preserve. Maximum 4 people. English-speaking guide 125zł.) The **park museum,** with exhibits on the park and on an observatory tower, is located on the site of the Tsar's palace, which was destroyed in 1944. (☎ 681 22 75. Open daily 9am-4pm. 5zł, students 3zł.) To **rent a bike,** head to **Zimordek,** ul. Waszkiewicza 2, opposite the bus stop. If the door is closed, head around the corner to the youth hostel to find the owner. (☎/fax 681 24 57. 3zł per hr., 20-30zł per day.)

Most travelers begin in the sleepy town of **Białowieża,** where there are plenty of inexpensive places to stay or camp. If you want to stay the night, the Białystok travel office can arrange a stay at an **eco-tourist farm ❶** in the Biełowieza area (17-45zł), which also rents **bikes** (5zł per hr; 13zł per 3hr.). After a day of long hikes, enjoy excellent Polish cuisine at **Unikat ❸,** ul. Gen. Waszkiewicza 39, with rustic indoor and pleasant outdoor dining options. (☎/fax 681 27 74. Entrees 20zł. Open daily 8am-10pm. Dinner served 1pm-9pm. Also rents newly-built and cheerful bungalow rooms. Singles with bath 50zł; doubles 100zł; triples 120zł; quads 140zł.)

ROMANIA
(ROMÂNIA)

LEI

AUS$1 = L18,233	L10,000 = AUS$0.54
CDN$1 = L21,329	L10,000 = CDN$0.47
EUR€1 = L32,655	L10,000 = EUR€0.31
NZ$1 = L15,540	L10,000 = NZ$0.64
UK£1 = L51,473	L10,000 = UK£0.20
US$1 = L33,200	L10,000 = US$0.30
ZAR1 = L3,127	L10,000 = ZAR3.20

Devastated by the lengthy reign of Nicolae Ceauşescu, Romania today suffers under the effects of a sluggish economy. Some Romanians are eager to Westernize, others are more eager just to escape the problems by moving away. The resulting state of flux, combined with a largely undeserved reputation for poverty and crime, has discouraged many foreigners from visiting. But travelers who dismiss Romania do themselves an injustice—it is a country rich in history, rustic beauty, and hospitality. The general absence of tourists is good for visitors as prices remain low, but a recent change in visa regulations has made it easier for EU citizens to enter the country and discover Romania's dark, fascinating legacy.

ROMANIA AT A GLANCE

OFFICIAL NAME: Romania

CAPITAL: Bucharest (pop. 2.1 million)

POPULATION: 22.5 million

LANGUAGES: Romanian (official), Hungarian, German

CURRENCY: 1 leu (L) = 100 bani

RELIGION: 70% Romanian Orthodox, 3% Roman Catholic, 3% Uniate Catholic, 6% Protestant

LAND AREA: 230,340km²

CLIMATE: Temperate and continental

GEOGRAPHY: Mountains and plains

BORDERS: Bulgaria, Hungary, Moldova, Serbia and Montenegro, Ukraine

ECONOMY: 41% Industry, 40% Services, 19% Agriculture

GDP: US$4353 per capita

COUNTRY CODE: 40

INTERNATIONAL DIALING PREFIX: 00

HISTORY

GROWING PAINS. The first Romanian state, **Wallachia,** was established in the early 1300s. The second, **Moldavia,** was founded east of the Carpathians in 1349. The fledgling states had it rough, though, constantly defending themselves against invasion by the **Ottoman Turks.** Moldavia's **Ştefan cel Mare** (Stephen the Great; 1457-1504) was most successful in warding off the attacks. During his 47-year rule, he built 42 monasteries and churches, one for each of his war victories (see **Bukovina Monasteries,** p. 611). Unfortunately, successful resistance died with Ştefan and Moldavia and Wallachia eventually became Turkish vassals.

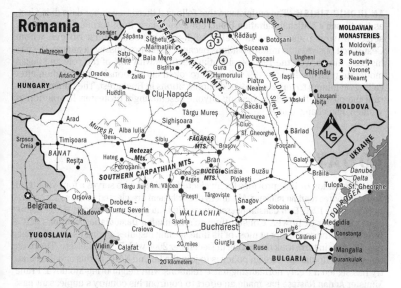

Romania

MOLDAVIAN
MONASTERIES
1 Moldoviţa
2 Putna
3 Suceviţa
4 Voroneţ
5 Neamţ

HELP YOURSELF. For the next four centuries Austria-Hungary, Russia, Turkey and the Polish-Lithuanian Commonwealth fought for control of the region. **Mihai Viteazul** (Michael the Brave) tried to create a unified Romania in 1599 when he invaded Moldavia and Transylvania, but Polish, Hungarian, and Ottoman attacks left Mihai dead and the country in tatters. Moldavia and Wallachia united in 1859 and this time the union lasted. **King Carol I** eliminated corruption, built the first railroads, and strengthened the army that finally won independence from Turkey in 1877. After Austria-Hungary's defeat in **World War I**, Romania doubled its territory, gaining Transylvania (see **Alba Iulia**, p. 602), Bukovina, and Bessarabia (modern-day Moldova). While the area doubled, increased population brought minority groups and ethnic tensions. The 1941 **Nazi-Soviet Non-Aggression Pact** caused Romania to lose its new territory to the Axis powers. Hoping the Nazis would preserve an independent Romania, the country's dictator, **General Antonescu,** chose to support Germany in World War II. In 1944 **King Mihai** orchestrated a coup and attempted to surrender to the Allies, but the bid failed when the Soviets to moved in and proclaimed the **Romanian People's Republic** on December 30, 1947.

TYRANNY AND REVOLUTION. Government opposition was violently suppressed in the postwar era. More than 200,000 Romanians died in the purges of the 1950s, and farms were forcibly collectivized. In 1965 **Nicolae Ceauşescu** ascended to the top of the Communist Party. Although his attempts to distance Romania from Moscow's influence won praise from the West, his ruthless domestic policies were hardly laudable and often deprived Romanian citizens of basic needs. By the late 1980s Ceauşescu had transformed Romania into a police state. In 1989 a **revolution** as ruthless as Ceauşescu erupted. What began as a minor event in Timişoara (see p. 606), when the dreaded **Securitate** (Secret Police) arrested a popular Hungarian priest, soon turned into a full-scale revolt. In December clashes with security forces in Bucharest brought thousands of protesters to the streets. Ceauşescu and his wife were arrested, tried, and executed—on TV—all on Christmas Day.

ROMANIA

AN IRONIC FINISH. The enthusiasm that followed these December days didn't last, as **Ion Iliescu's National Salvation Front,** composed largely of former Communists, seized power. Iliescu was himself a high-ranking communist official whom Ceauşescu pushed into minor positions because of his pro-Russian leanings. Despite his past, Iliescu won the 1990 presidential elections with 70% of the vote and began moderate reforms. In June 1990, Iliescu provoked international condemnation after calling on miners to repress student demonstrations in Bucharest. The miners terrorized the city for three days, beating anyone resembling a protester. Revolution, it seemed, had changed little.

TODAY

The constitution of 1991 provides for an elected **president** who serves a four-year term and nominates a **prime minister.** Members of **Parliament** are elected to four-year terms. In November 1996, **Emil Constantinescu** succeeded Illiescu in the country's first democratic transfer of power. Constantinescu's **Romanian Democratic Coalition** (RDC) promised reforms, but spent most of its time settling disputes among its member parties. Illiescu, in turn, took over again in December 2000 with 70% of the vote. The main objective of Romania's foreign policy is to join the **EU** and **NATO;** to this end the country has signed a treaty normalizing tense relations with neighboring Moldova. Prime Minister **Adrian Năstase** has made an effort to confront his country's unpleasant past in order to prevent fascism and preserve democracy by promoting education about Jewish history in Romania. Professor **Elie Wiesel,** winner of the Nobel Peace Prize and a native of Romania, visited his hometown of Sighet in July 2002 to aid the Cultural Society in formulating a Holocaust education program in schools and public cultural institutions. He was awarded the highest Romanian medal, *Steaua României* (Romanian Star).

PEOPLE AND CULTURE

LANGUAGE

Romanian is a Romance language; those familiar with French, Italian, Spanish, or Portuguese should be able to decipher public signs. Romanian differs from other Romance tongues, however, in its Slavic-influenced vocabulary. Romanian consists of four distinct dialects; **Daco-Romanian** is the basis for the standard language. **German** and **Hungarian** are widely spoken in Transylvania. Throughout the country, **French** is a common second language for the older generation, **English** for the younger. Avoid using **Russian,** which is often understood, but disliked. English-Romanian dictionaries are sold at book-vending kiosks everywhere. Spoken Romanian is a lot like Italian, but with three additional vowels: "ă" (pronounced like "e" in "pet") and the phonetically interchangeable "â" and "î" (like the "i" in "pill"). The other two characters peculiar to the Romanian alphabet are "ş" ("sh" in "shiver") and "ţ" ("ts" in "tsar"). At the end of a word, "i" is dropped, but softens the previous consonant. However, the "ii" and rare "iii" at the end of words is pronounced like "ee" in "cheese." "Ci" sounds like the "chea" in "cheat," and "ce" sounds like the "che" in "chess." "Chi" is pronounced like "kee" in "keen," and "che" like "ke" in "kept." "G" before "e" or "i" sounds like "j" as in judge and "gh" before those vowels is like "g" in girl. For a phrasebook and glossary, see **Glossary: Romanian,** p. 887.

FOOD AND DRINK

ROMANIA	❶	❷	❸	❹	❺
FOOD	under L60,000	L60,000-100,000	L100,000-140,000	L140,000-180,000	over L180,000

Lunch usually starts with a **soup**, called *supă* or *ciorbă* (the former has noodles or dumplings, the latter is saltier and usually has vegetables), followed by an entree (typically grilled meat), and dessert. Soups can be very tasty; try *ciorbă de perişoare* (with vegetables and ground meatballs) or *supă cu găluşte* (with fluffy dumplings). **Pork** comes in several varieties; *muşchi* and *cotlet* are of the highest quality. For **dessert**, *clătite* (crepes), *papanaşi* (doughnuts with jam and sour cream), and *torts* (creamy cakes) are all fantastic. *Inghetată* (ice cream) is cheap and good, while the delicious *mere în aluat* (doughnuts with apples) and the sugary *gogoşi* (fried doughnuts) are delectable. Some restaurants charge by weight (usually 100g) rather than by portion. It's difficult to predict how many grams you will actually receive. *Garnituri*, the extras that come standard with a meal, are usually charged separately, down to that dollop of mustard. As a rule, you're paying for everything the waiters put in front of you. Keeping **kosher** is very difficult, as pork rules in Romania, but it is possible with planning. Local **drinks** include *ţvică*, a brandy distilled from plums and apples by peasants, and *pălină*, a stronger version of *ţvică* that approaches 70% alcohol. A delicious liqueur called *vişnata* is made from *vişine* (wild cherries).

CUSTOMS AND ETIQUETTE

It is customary to give inexact change for purchases, generally rounding up to the nearest L500. Similarly, restaurants usually round up to the nearest L500 or give you candy instead of L100s. **Tip** 10% in nice restaurants and taxis; tipping too much is inappropriate. **Bargain** over private rooms and with taxis if there is no posted rate. To avoid getting ripped off, try to get 20% off in open-air markets. Romanians take pride in their **hospitality.** Most will be eager to help, offering to show you around town or inviting you into their homes. When you're visiting, bring your hostess an odd number of flowers; even-numbered bouquets are only brought to graves. Romanians, especially the women, dress well, and shorts are rare.

THE ARTS

HISTORY

LITERATURE. The first sign of literary activity in Romania came with the Roman poet **Ovid**, who wrote his last works while exiled near what is now Constanţa. The Romanian national literary tradition is rooted in 15th-century translations of Slavonic religious texts, which culminated in the first Romanian translation of the **Bible** in 1688. The literary resurgence after the end of Ottoman oppression in the late 1700s is credited in part to the **Văcărescu family:** grandfather **Ienachita** wrote the first Romanian grammar, father **Alecu** wrote love poetry, and son **Iancu's** verse was so splendid that he, not his father, is considered the master of Romanian poetry. The early 19th century saw the cultivation of new genres; **Grigore Alexandrescu's** French-inspired fables and satires are especially well-regarded. The next generation of writers—clustering around the literary magazine *Junimea*—penned the great classics of Romanian literature. Of this generation, **Ion Creangă's** (see **Iaşi**, p. 609) most important work, *Aminitiri din Copilarie* (Memories of My Boyhood), depicts life in his native village. **Mihai Eminescu** (see **Iaşi**, p. 609), considered the father of modern Romanian poetry, embodied a high literary **Romanticism**.

FINE ARTS AND MUSIC. The end of World War II brought the strictures of **Socialist Realism. Geo Bogza** and **Mihail Beniuc** were among the more prominent adherents, composing works glorifying the worker. Some native-born artists and scholars sought freedom in other lands and languages—absurdist dramatist **Eugène Ionescu** and religious scholar **Mircea Eliade** are the most prominent. More contemporary artists include folk music composer **Georges Enescu** (1881-1955), painter **Nicolae Grigorescu** (1838-1907), who combined techniques he learned in France with his experience as an icon painter to immortalize the Romanian countryside. Sculptor **Constantin Brâncuși** (1876-1957) is considered to be one of the greatest modernist sculptors of the 20th century.

CURRENT SCENE

Folk music and dancing are still extremely popular in Romania, and Romanian glassware and decorated Easter eggs are fine crafts that thrive today. Edgy, realist Romanian cinema from the post-war era is gaining international recognition, especially at the popular **Film Festival Cottbus**. Along with newfound artistic freedom, this favorable attention has allowed many more Romanian films to be produced.

FESTIVALS AND HOLIDAYS

NATIONAL HOLIDAYS IN 2003

January 1-2 New Year's Day	**May 1** International Labor Day
January 6 Epiphany	**December 1** National Unity Day (or Romania Day)
March 1 Mărțișor	
April 20-21 Easter	**December 25-26** Christmas

ROMANIA DAY. December 1 commemorates the day when Transylvania became a part of Romania in 1918 (see **Alba Iulia,** p. 602).

MARȚIȘOR. On March 1st, little *porte-boneurs* are worn and snow-drop flowers are given to friends and lovers.

ADDITIONAL RESOURCES

GENERAL HISTORY

Balkan Ghosts: A Journey Through History, by Robert Kaplan (1994). Both a deeply engaging travel narrative and an informative regional history.

Dracula, Prince of Many Faces: His Life and Times, by Radu R. Florescu (1990). Debunks cultural myths and tells the real story of Vlad Țepeș.

FICTION, NONFICTION, AND FILM

Red Rats, directed by Florin Codre (1991). Exposes Romanian disillusionment about the failed democratic revolution of 1989.

Taste of Romania: Its Cookery and Glimpses of its History, Folklore, Art and Poetry, by Nicolae Klepper (1999). The most easily digested primer on Romanian culture. Acclimate yourself to the local proclivity for larded pork and sample the illustrations, folklore, and poetry interspersed throughout.

When the Tunnels Meet, ed. by John Fairleigh (1996). An anthology of modern Romanian verse translated by Irish poets, including Nobel laureate Seamus Heaney.

ROMANIA ESSENTIALS

ENTRANCE REQUIREMENTS
Passport: Required of all travelers to Romania.
Visa: Required of citizens of Australia, New Zealand, and South Africa.
Letter of Invitation: Required of citizens of India and Pakistan.
Inoculations: Recommended up-to-date on MMR (measles, mumps, and rubella), DTaP (diphtheria), Polio booster, Hepatitis A, and Hepatitis B.
Work Permit: Required of all foreigners planning to work in Romania.
International Driving Permit: Required of all those planning to drive.

DOCUMENTS AND FORMALITIES

EMBASSIES AND CONSULATES

Embassies and consulates of other countries in Romania are all in Bucharest (see p. 584). Romanian embassies and consulates abroad include:

Australia: 4 Commonwealth of Australian Dalman Crescent, O'Malley, Canberra, ACT 2606 (☎06 286 2343; fax 286 2433; roembcbr@cyberone.com.au).

Canada: 655 Rideau St., Ottawa, ON K1N 6A3 (☎613-789-5345; fax 789-4365; romania@cyberus.ca). **Consulate:** 111 Peter St., Suite 530, Toronto, ON M5V 2H1 (☎416-585-5802 or 585-9177; fax 585-4798; cgrt@ca.inter.net).

Ireland: 47 Ailesbury Rd., Ballsbridge, Dublin 4 (☎353 269 2852; fax 269 2122).

South Africa: 117 Charles St., Brooklyn Pretoria; P.O. Box 11295, Brooklyn 0181 (☎012 466 940; fax 466 947).

UK: 4 Palace Green, Kensington, London W8 4QD (☎020 7937 9666; fax 7937 8069).

US: 1607 23rd St. NW, Washington, D.C. 20008 (☎202-332-4848; fax 232-4748; www.roembus.org). **Consulate:** 1176 Wilshire Blvd. 560, Los Angeles, CA 90025 (☎310-444-0043; fax 445-0043; consulat.la@roconla.org).

VISA AND ENTRY INFORMATION

Romanian **visa** information changes constantly; check with your embassy or consulate for the most accurate information. Citizens of Australia, New Zealand, and South Africa all need visas to enter Romania; citizens of the EU (including the UK and Ireland) do not need visas for stays up to 90 days. US citizens do not need visas for stays of up to 30 days. Americans can obtain a visa or a visa extension at police headquarters in large cities or in Bucharest at the Passport Office, Str. Luigi Cazzavillan 11 (open M and W-F 9am-2pm, Tu 3-7pm). A single-entry visa costs US$35; multiple-entry US$70. Apply early to allow the bureaucratic process to run its slow and frustrating course. There is no additional fee for crossing a Romanian **border.** The best way to leave Romania is to take a direct train from Bucharest to the capital city of the neighboring country. The next best options are planes and buses.

TRANSPORTATION

BY PLANE. Numerous airlines fly into Bucharest. **TAROM** (Romanian Airlines) is in the process of updating its aging fleet; it flies directly from Bucharest to **New York, Chicago,** and major European cities. Bucharest's **Otopeni International Airport** has improved its notoriously bad ground services, but the airport is still far from ideal.

BY TRAIN. Trains, a better choice of transport than buses for **international** travel, head daily to Western Europe via Budapest. There are also direct trains to and from Belgrade, SER; Chişinău, MOL; Moscow, RUS; Prague, CZR; Sofia, BUL; Vienna, AUS; and Warsaw, POL. To buy international tickets in Romania, go to the **CFR** (Che-Fe-Re) office in larger towns. Budapest-bound trains leave Romania through either Arad or Oradea; when you buy your ticket, you'll need to specify where you want to exit, and they'll want to see your papers. **CFR** also sells **domestic** train tickets one day before the train's departure. After that, only train stations sell tickets, which are only available one hour in advance. The English-language timetable *Mersul Trenurilor* (also available online at www.cfr.ro/IsaRR.htm; L12,000) is very useful. Schedule info is available at ☎ 221 in most cities. **Interail** is accepted; **Eurail** is not. There are four types of trains: *InterCity* (indicated by an "IC" on timetables and at train stations), *rapid* (in green), *accelerat* (red), and *personal* (black). International trains (often blue) are usually indicated with an "i" on timetables. *InterCity* trains stop only at major cities such as Bucharest, Cluj-Napoca, Iaşi, and Timişoara. *Rapid* trains are the next fastest; *accelerat* trains starting with "1" and are slower and dirtier. The sluggish and decrepit *personal* trains stop at every station. It's wise to take the fastest train you can, most often *accelerat*. There's not a big difference between **first class** (*clasa întâi;* clah-sa un-toy; wagons marked with a "1" on the side; 6 people per compartment) and **second class** (*clasa dova;* 8 people), except for on *personal* trains, where first class is markedly better. If you take an **overnight train,** shell out for first class in a *vagon de dormit* (sleeping carriage).

BY BUS. International buses connect major cities in Romania to **Athens, Istanbul, Prague,** and various cities in Western Europe. Since plane and train tickets to Romania are often expensive, buses are a good—if slow—option. It is generally cheapest to take a domestic train to a city near the border and catch an international bus from there. Inquire at tourist agencies about timetables and tickets, but buying tickets straight from the carrier saves you from paying commission. Use the **local** bus system only when trains are not available. Local buses are more expensive, but just as packed and poorly ventilated. Look for signs for the *autogară* (bus station) in each town. Another good option for short distances are **minibuses,** which can be cheaper, faster, and cleaner than the alternatives. Rates are posted inside.

BY THUMB. *Let's Go* does not recommend hitchhiking. If you do hitch, know that drivers generally expect a payment similar to the price of a train or bus ticket for the distance traveled. Hitchhikers stand on the side of the road and put out their palm, as if waving. In some places, hitchhiking is the only way to get around, but avoid hitching at night.

TOURIST SERVICES AND MONEY

Most tourist offices are intended for Romanians traveling abroad, and much of the country has poor resources for foreign travelers. **Cluj-Napoca,** however, is a welcome relief with its plethora of tourist offices. The Romanian currency is the leu, plural lei (abbreviated L). Banknotes are issued in amounts of L500, L1000, L5000, L10,000, L50,000, and L100,000. While many establishments accept US$, you should always pay in lei to avoid being ripped off and to save your hard currency for bribes and emergencies. With Romanian **inflation** running at around 34%, expect rates and prices quoted in lei to change significantly over the next year. **ATMs** generally accept MC and sometimes Visa, give lei at reasonable rates, and are the best way to get money. ATMs are found everywhere except the smallest towns, are usually 24hr., and occasionally run out of cash. Because many Romanians stave off inflation by carrying US dollars, **private exchange bureaus,** which are better than banks for exchanging currency, are everywhere. Unfortunately, very few take **credit cards** or **traveler's checks.** Most banks will cash traveler's checks in US dollar then exchange them for lei, accumulating high fees in the process. Take the 20min. to walk around and see the going rates before plunking down your money. US dollars are preferred, although Euros can usually be exchanged as well.

HEALTH AND SAFETY

 EMERGENCY: Police: ☎955 **Fire:** ☎961 **Emergency:** ☎112

HEALTH. Avoid Romanian **hospitals** as they are generally not quite up to Western standards. Be sure to pack a good first aid kit, and go to a private doctor for medical emergencies. Some American medical clinics in Bucharest have English-speaking doctors. Pay in cash. *Farmacies* (pharmacies) will probably have what you need. *Antinevralgic* is for headaches (though many pharmacists refer to this painkiller as "tylenol"), *aspirină* or *piramidon* for colds and the flu, and *saprosan* for diarrhea. *Prezervatives* (condoms) and *tampoane* (tampons) are available at all drugstores and at many kiosks. Most **public restrooms** lack soap, towels, and toilet paper, and those on trains and in stations smell rank. Attendants charge L1000-1500 for a single square of toilet paper. Pick up a roll at a newsstand or drug store and carry it with you everywhere. You can find relief at most restaurants, even if you're not a patron. Stay away from untreated **tap water;** boil it for 10 minutes before drinking, or stick to imported German or French **bottled water.** Beware of **vendor food,** especially fruits and vegetables that may have been washed in local water.

SAFETY. Petty **crimes** against tourists are a problem in Romania; be especially careful on public transportation and overnight trains. Scams are organized and well-planned; beware of con artists dressed as policemen that may ask for your passport or wallet. When in doubt, ask the officer to escort you to the nearest police station. The **drinking age** is not enforced, but if you smoke marijuana, be prepared to spend the next seven years in a Romanian prison.

WOMEN, MINORITY, AND BGLT TRAVELERS. Single **female** travelers shouldn't go out alone after dark and should say they are traveling with a male companion. Wearing tank tops, shorts, and sneakers to may attract unwanted attention. **Minorities** traveling to Romania may encounter unwanted attention or discrimination, though most is directed towards Roma (Gypsies). **Homosexuality** has been legal in Romania since 1996, but homosexual public displays of affection remain illegal and could get you arrested. Outside major cities, many Romanians hold conservative attitudes toward sexuality, which may translate into harassment of gay, lesbian, and bisexual travelers. Nonetheless, women sometimes walk arm-in-arm without anyone batting an eye.

ACCOMMODATIONS AND CAMPING

ROMANIA	❶	❷	❸	❹	❺
ACCOM.	under L350,000	L350,000-665,000	L665,000-1,000,000	L1,000,000-2,000,000	over L2,000,000

HOTELS AND HOSTELS. While some **hotels** charge foreigners 50-100% more than locals, lodging is still relatively inexpensive ($6-20). As a general rule, youth hostels are often nicer than one-star hotels, so don't let the bed bugs bite—literally. Two-star places are decent, and three-star places are luxurious but expensive. Reservations are a good idea in July and August.

HOMESTAYS, DORMS, AND CAMPING. Private rooms are a great option, but hosts rarely speak English; be aware that renting a room "together" means sharing a bed. Rooms run US$5-12 per person in the country or at least US$15 in big cities, and sometimes include breakfast and other amenities. See the room and fix a price before accepting. Many towns allow foreign students to stay in **university dorms** at remarkably low prices, although they may be hard to locate if you don't speak Romanian. **Campgrounds** are crowded and often have frightening bathrooms. Relatively cheap **bungalows** are often full in the summer; reserve far in advance.

KEEPING IN TOUCH

MAIL. At the post office, request *par avion* for **airmail,** which takes 2-3 weeks for delivery. A postcard to the US costs L22,000; a letter L27,000. **Mail** can be received general delivery through **Poste Restante.** Address envelopes as follows: Clay (first name) KAMINSKY (last name), POSTE RESTANTE, Str. Nicolae Iorga 1 (post office address), Braşov (city) 2200 (postal code), ROMANIA.

TELEPHONES. Almost all public phones are orange and accept **phone cards,** although a few archaic blue phones take L500 coins. Buy L50,000, L100,000 and L200,000 phone cards at telephone offices, major Bucharest Metro stops, and some post offices and kiosks. Never buy cards not sealed in plastic wrap. Rates run L10,000 per minute to neighboring countries, L14,000 per min. to most of Europe, and L18,000 per minute to the US. Use orange phones to call major cities (they will operate in English if you press "i"). At an analogue phone, dial ☎971 for international calls. **Local calls** cost L595 per minute and can be made from any phone. If you hear a busy signal, try again; it probably just indicates a connection problem. It may be necessary to make a phone call *prin commandă* (with the help of the operator) at the telephone office, which takes longer and costs more. At the phone office, write down the destination, duration, and phone number for your call. Pay up front, and always ask for the rate per minute. People with European cell phones can avoid roaming charges by buying a **SIM card** at **Connex, Dialog,** or **CosmoRom.** General information is ☎951, operator ☎930.

INTERNET ACCESS. Internet cafes are not difficult to find in most large cities, and cost about L10,000-L15,000 per hr.

BUCHAREST (BUCUREŞTI)   ☎(0)21

Once a fabled beauty on the Orient Express, Bucharest (pop. 2,040,000) is now infamous for its heavy-handed transformation under Communist dictator Nicolae Ceauşescu. During his 25-year reign, Ceauşescu managed to nearly undo the city's splendor, replacing Neoclassical architecture, grand boulevards, and Ottoman ruins with concrete blocks, wide highways, and Communist monuments. Although Bucharest is no longer the "Little Paris" *(Micul Paris)* it once was, life here is fast-paced, unpredictable, and anything but boring. Take a moment to look past the block architecture of the Communist era to find historic neighborhoods, secluded parks, and a club scene that means business.

■ INTERCITY TRANSPORTATION

Flights: Otopeni Airport (☎204 10 00), 18km outside the city. Bus #783 runs between the airport and Piaţa Unirii, stopping throughout the city center (45min.; every 15min., 30min. on weekends; L25,000). Airline offices located in the upper level of the departure terminal. **Bbneasa Airport** (☎231 42 57), accessible from Piaţa Romană by bus

#131, 135, or 305 and Gara de Nord by bus #205, handles domestic flights. Buy tickets at **TAROM**, Spl. Independenței 7 (☎337 20 37). Open M-F 9am-7pm, Sa 9am-1pm.

Trains: Gara de Nord (☎223 08 80, information 95 21). M3: Gara de Nord. Non-passengers must pay L4000 to enter the station. Domestic tickets available at **CFR**, Str. Domnița Anastasia 10-14 (☎313 26 43). To: **Brasov** (3-4hr.; 5 per day; L147,000); **Constanța** (3hr.; 12 per day; L170,000); **Cluj-Napoca** (8-12hr.; 4 per day; L248,000); **Iași** (6½hr.; 4 per day; L248,000); **Sighișoara** (5-7hr.; 5 per day; L186,000); **Timișoara** (8-9hr.; 8 per day; L287,000); **Budapest, HUN** (12-16hr.; 7 per day; L950,000-1,160,000); **Chișinau, MOL** (13hr.; 1 per day; L565,000); **Sofia, BUL** (10-12hr.; 3 per day; L750,000-950,000); **Warsaw, POL** (23hr.; 1 per day; L1,750,000).

Buses: Filaret, Cuțitul de Argint 2 (☎335 11 40 or 335 13 50). M2: Tineretului. Buses are the best way to reach **Athens, GRE** and **Istanbul, TUR.** To Athens, your best bet is **Fotopoulos Express** (☎335 82 49). To Istanbul, catch a **Toros** (☎223 18 98) or a **Murat** (☎224 92 93) bus from outside Gara de Nord. **Double T,** Calea Victoriei 2 (☎313 36 42), a Eurail affiliate, or **Eurolines Touring,** Str. Ankara 6 (☎230 03 70; fax 315 01 66), can get you to Western Europe.

Microbuses: Air-conditioned, comfortable microbuses leave from outside Gara de Nord for domestic destinations close to Bucharest and are generally cheaper than the train.

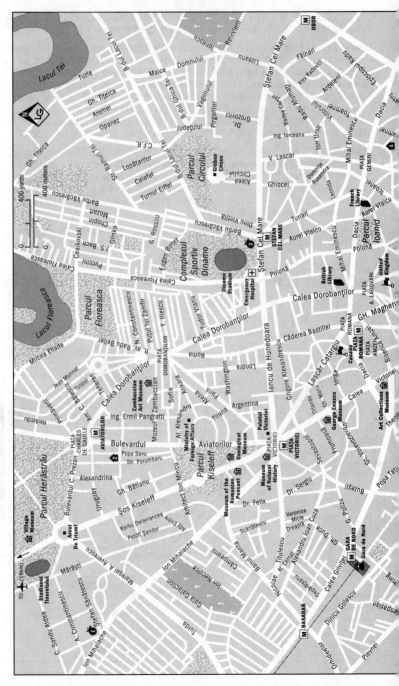

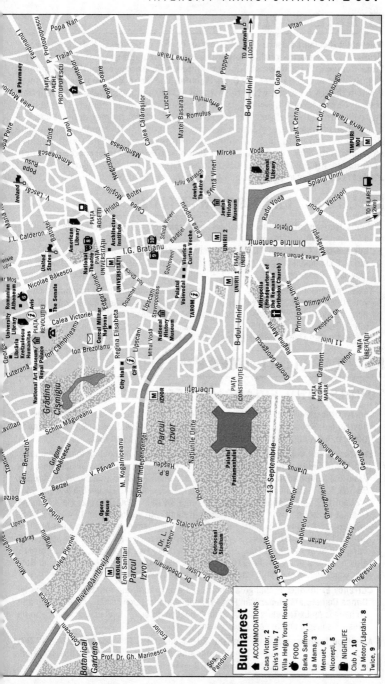

Bucharest

ACCOMMODATIONS
Casa Victor, 2
Elvis's Villa, 7
Villa Helga Youth Hostel, 4

FOOD
Barka Saffron, 1
La Mama, 3
Menuet, 6
Nicorești, 5

NIGHTLIFE
Club A, 10
La Motor/Lăptăria, 8
Twice, 9

■ ORIENTATION

Bulevardul Nicolae Bălcescu (also known as Lascăr Catargiu, GH Magheru, and IC Brătianu) runs north-south through the city's four main squares: **Piaţa Victoriei, Piaţa Romană, Piaţa Universităţii,** and **Piaţa Unirii.** Another main drag, running slightly west of Bd. Bălcescu, is **Calea Victoriei.** The **Metro** M2 line runs north-south through the town center, while the M1 and M3 lines run east-west. The main **train station,** Gara de Nord, lies along the M3 line just west of the center. To reach the city center from the station, take the M3 train toward Dristor one stop to Piaţa Victoriei, then change to the M2 train heading to Depoul IMGB. Go one stop to Piaţa Romana, two stops to Piaţa Universităţii, or three stops to Piaţa Unirii; all three stops are in the city's center and are a 15min. walk apart. **Maps,** scarce elsewhere in Romania, are sold throughout Bucharest. The ever helpful *Bucharest In Your Pocket* (L35,000) is available at many museums, bookstores, and hotels.

■ LOCAL TRANSPORTATION

Public Transportation: Buses, trolleys, and **trams** cost L6000 and run daily 5:30am-11:30pm. Validate tickets, available at kiosks, to avoid a L300,000 fine. All **express buses** except #783 take only magnetic strip cards (L15,000 for 2 trips, L70,000 for 10 trips). Pickpocketing is a problem during peak hours. The **Metro** offers reliable, less crowded service (open daily 5am-11:30pm; L12,000 for 2 trips, L40,000 for 10 trips).

Taxis: Taxi drivers in Bucharest are shameless; many will cheerfully attempt to charge you 10 times the regular fare. Only use taxis that have a company name, a phone number, and a rate-per-km posted in the window. Ask the driver to use the meter. The official rate is L6000, plus L4000-5000 per km. Reliable companies include **Prof-Taxi** (☎94 22), **H&V** (☎94 16), and **Taxi2000** (☎94 94).

■ PRACTICAL INFORMATION

TOURIST AND FINANCIAL SERVICES

Tourist Office: Private tourist offices litter the city, but they're not much help. Hotels and hostels are a good source of information. The staff of **Elvis' Villa** (See **Accommodations,** p. 589) organizes a variety of activities, including guided tours.

Embassies and Consulates: Citizens of **New Zealand** should contact the UK embassy. Citizens of **South Africa** should contact the South African embassy in Budapest (see **Practical Information,** p. 344). **Australia,** Bd. Unirii 74, Et. 5 (☎320 98 26; fax 320 98 23). M2: Piaţa Unirii, then take bus #104, 123, or 124 to Lucian Blaga. Open M-Th 9:30am-12:30pm. **Canada,** Str. Nicolae Iorga 36 (☎307 50 00). M2: Piaţa Romană. Open M-Th 8:00am-5pm, F 8:30am-2pm. **Ireland,** Str. Vasile Lascăr 42-44 (☎210 89 48; fax 211 43 84). M2: Piaţa Romană. Open M-F 10am-noon. **UK,** Str. Jules Michelet 24 (☎312 03 03; fax 312 02 29). M2: Piaţa Romană. Open M-Th 8:30am-1pm and 2-5pm, F 8:30am-1:30pm. **US,** Str. Tudor Arghezi 7-9 (☎210 40 42, ext. 403 or 318; after hours ☎210 01 49; fax 210 03 95). M2: Piaţa Universităţii. A block behind Hotel Intercontinental. Open M-Th 8am-noon and 1-5pm.

Currency Exchange: Exchange agencies are everywhere, but many won't change lei. **Banca Comercială Romană,** in Piaţa Victoriei and Piaţa Universităţii, gives a good rate. Exchanges AmEx **Travelers Cheques** for 1.5% commission. Don't change money on the street—it's illegal and almost always a scam.

American Express: Marshall Tourism, Bd. Magheru 43, 1st floor #1 (☎212 97 87). M2: Piaţa Romană. Books hotel rooms and flights, but does not cash Traveler's Cheques or replace lost cards. Open M-F 9am-5pm, Sa 9am-1pm.

LOCAL AND EMERGENCY SERVICES

Luggage Storage: Gara de Nord. L25,000-50,000; passport necessary. Open 24hr.

Bookstore: Librăria Kretzulescu Humanitas, Calea Victoriei 45 (☎313 50 35), in Piaţa Revoluţiei. M2: Piaţa Universităţii. Great Romanian bookstore with limited titles in English and French. Open M-Sa 10am-7pm.

Bi-Gay-Lesbian Organization: Accept Bucharest, Str. Lirei 10 (☎252 16 37; www.accept-romania.ro). News on gay rights in Romania, social info, and useful links.

24-Hour Pharmacies: Sensiblu pharmacies (☎203 90 09) are everywhere.

Medical Assistance: Spitalul de Urgenţă (Emergency Clinic Hospital), Calea Floreasca 8 (☎230 01 06). M3: Ştefan cel Mare. Open 24hr.

Telephones: Phone cards (L100,000 or L200,000) are good for domestic and some international calls. Place collect calls at the **telephone office,** Calea Victoriei 35 (☎313 36 35). M2: Piaţa Universităţii. Open 24hr.

Internet Access: Internet cafes abound. Try **D&D Internet Cafe,** Bd. Carol I 25 (☎313 10 48). M2: Piaţa Universităţii. With Hotel Intercontinental to your left, head down Bd. Carol I past Piaţa Rosetti. Fast connections. Printing available. 6am-midnight L25,000 per hr., midnight-6am L15,000 per hr. Minimum L10,000. Open 24hr.

Post Office: Str. Matei Millo 10 (☎315 90 30). M2: Piaţa Universităţii, then head down Bd. Regina Elisabeta, turn right on Calea Victoriei, and turn left on Str. Mille Constantin. Take a right on Str. Otetelesanu Ion. At the end, turn left on Matei Millo. Open M-F 7:30am-8pm, Sa 7:30am-2pm. **Poste Restante** is next to Hotel Carpaţi.

Postal Code: 70700

⬩ ACCOMMODATIONS

You can't go wrong with either of Bucharest's two youth hostels. Both hotel and hostel accommodations are generally more expensive here than in other Romanian cities. Renting private rooms is not common. Beware of people at Gara de Nord who claim to work for local hostels—many of these "representatives" are frauds who will try to extort a "week's rent in advance."

▨ **Elvis' Villa,** Str. Avram Iancu 5 (☎315 52 73 or 315 52 73; www.elvisvilla.ro). M2: Piaţa Universităţii. From Gara de Nord, take trolley bus #85 to the Calea Moşilor stop. From Otopeni Airport, take bus #783 to Piaţa Universităţii, then change to trolleybus #69, 70, 85, 90, or 92 and get off at the Calea Moşilor stop. Continue along Bd. Carol I and turn right on Str. Sfântul Ştefan. When you reach a playground, turn left on Str. Avram Iancu. Elvis', run by an outgoing Aussie-Kiwi couple, is a new hostel in a pleasant neighborhood. The 4 dorm-style bedrooms are clean and bright, with A/C and fat mattresses. Perks include satellite TV, laundry service, cigarettes, Internet access, beverages, and breakfast. Reservations recommended. US$12 per day, US$72 per week. ❷

▨ **Villa Helga Youth Hostel,** Str. Salcâmilor 2 (☎610 22 14). M2: Piaţa Romană. Take bus #86, 79, or 133 two stops from Piaţa Romană or 6 stops from Gara de Nord to Piaţa Gemeni (east along Bd. Dacia). Then continue 1 block along Bd. Dacia and take a right on Str. Viitorului. Romania's first hostel, Villa Helga is a pleasant and homey place with a relaxed atmosphere, an international crowd, and a friendly staff. Breakfast, kitchen access, and laundry included. Reservations recommended during summer. US$10 per day; US$60 per week. 7th night free. ❶

Casa Victor, Str. Emanoil Porumbaru 44 (☎222 57 23 or 222 96 26). M2: Piaţa Aviatorilor. Casa Victor offers lovely, air-conditioned rooms in a quiet neighborhood. A touch of casual luxury for a reasonable price. Cable TV, Internet access, sauna, and transportation to and from the airport or train station (call in advance). Singles US$40-80; doubles US$80; apartment US$90-100. ❹

🔒 FOOD

Open-air markets selling produce, meat, and cheese are all over Bucharest—try the one at **Piaţa Gemeni,** near the corner of Bd. Dacia and Str. Vasile Lascăr.

La Mama, Str. Barbu Văcărescu 3 (☎212 40 86). M3: Ştefan cel Mare. Motto: "Like at mom's house." Top-notch Romanian food served in a pleasant building with elegant decor. Unlike your mama's house, jeans or shorts are not allowed. Reservations recommended. Entrees L70,000-95,000. Open daily 10am-2am. ❷

Menuet, Str. Nicolae Golescu 14 (☎312 01 43). M2: Piaţa Universităţii. Behind the Atheneum. Excellent Romanian and pan-European cuisine served in an elegant setting below street level. Photos of 19th-century Bucharest decorate the walls. Entrees L75,000-180,000. Open daily 12:30pm-1am. ❸

Barka Saffron, Str. Sănătescu 1 (☎224 10 04). M2: Aviatorilor, or take bus #200, 205, or 282 to Piaţa Domenii. At the intersection of Str. Sănătescu and Bd. Ion Mihalache. Chef Arun Kumar whips up delicious Indian and vegetarian dishes amid nautical decor. Entrees L70,000-180,000. Open daily noon-last customer. ❸

Nicoreşti, Str. Maria Rosetti 40 (☎211 24 80). M2: Piaţa Romană, or take trolley #79, 86, or 226. Head east on Bd. Dacia and continue 2 blocks past Piaţa Gemeni, then take a right on Toamnei. Great traditional meals for very cheap prices. English menu. Entrees L30,000-100,000. Open M-Sa 11am-11pm, Su 1-11pm. ❶

👁 SIGHTS

■ **PARLIAMENTARY PALACE.** (Palatul Parlamentului.) With twelve stories, four underground levels, and 1100 rooms totaling 330,000 sq. meters, the Parliamentary Palace is the **world's second-largest building** (after the Pentagon in Washington, D.C.), and the huge centerpiece of the Civic Center. Begun in 1984, it took 20,000 forced laborers and 700 architects to complete. Its largest room, at 2200 square meters and 16m high, contains the world's largest one-piece rug, woven inside the room because it would be too big to bring in. Once called Casa Popruli (House of the People), the palace houses Romania's Parliament. *(M1 or 3: Izvor. The entrance (A3) is off Calea Izvor, on the right side of the building as seen from Bd. Unirii. Open daily 10am-4pm. Closed for special events. 45min. tours L100,000, students L30,000. Cameras L90,000.)*

CIVIC CENTER. In 1984, Ceauşescu fulfilled his long-standing plan to remodel Bucharest after Pyongyang, North Korea's capital. In order to create his idea of the perfect socialist capital, Ceauşescu destroyed 5 square kilometers of Bucharest's historic center, demolishing over 9000 19th-century houses and displacing more than 40,000 Romanians. The result is today's Civic Center (Centru Civic), conveniently completed in 1989, just in time for the dictator's overthrow. It lies at the end of the 6km Bd. Unirii, intentionally built 1m wider than the Champs-Elysées.

HISTORIC NEIGHBORHOODS. The peaceful, tree-lined side streets between Piaţa Victoriei and Piaţa Dorobanţilor are full of beautiful villas typical of pre-Ceauşescu Bucharest. During his aesthetic assault on the Romanian capital, Ceauşescu inexplicably spared **Dealul Mitropoliei,** the hill southwest of Piaţa Unirii. Atop the hill sits the **Catedralul Mitropoliei,** the headquarters of the Romanian Orthodox Church, and one of the largest cathedrals in Romania. Next to the cathedral is **Palatul Patriarhiei,** the former Communist Parliament building. This impressive Baroque structure hosts free religious concerts. *(M1, 2, or 3: Piaţa Unirii. Up Aleea Dealul Mitropoliei.)* What remains of Bucharest's **old center** lies near Str. Lipscani and Str. Gabroveni. These narrow, curving streets contain the oldest church in the city, **Biserica Curtea Veche,** and the ruins of a palace built by Vlad Ţepeş, a.k.a Vlad the Impaler, called **Palatul Voievodal.**

SIGHTS OF THE REVOLUTION. Although the protests and clashes of 1989 have begun to fade from memory, crosses and plaques throughout the city commemorate the *eroii revoluţiei Române*, the "heroes of the revolution." The first shots of the

Revolution were fired at **Piaţa Revoluţiei** on December 21, 1989. The square contains the **University Library, the National Art Museum,** and the **Senate** (formerly Communist Party Headquarters), as well as a number of houses that still display bullet holes from street fighting. Ceauşescu delivered his final speech on the Party Headquarters balcony, in front of which a white marble triangle with the inscription "Glorie martirilor nostri" (Glory to our martyrs) commemorates the rioters. Just down the street on Bd. Nicolae Bălcescu, a black cross marks the spot where the first victim of the Revolution died. *(M2: Piaţa Universităţii. With Hotel Intercontinental on your left, turn right on Bd. Regina Elisabeta and then take a right on Calea Victoriei.)* **Piata Universităţii** houses memorials to victims of both the 1989 and 1990 Revolutions. Demonstrators perished while fighting Ceauşescu's forces at Piaţa Universităţii on December 21, 1989, the day before the dictator's fall. Crosses commemorating the martyrs line the center of the square, while anti-Iliescu graffiti decorates the walls of the university and of the **Architecture Institute,** across from Hotel Intercontinental. In June of 1990, Piaţa 22 Decembrie 1989 was again gripped by student riots; Iliescu bussed in over 10,000 miners to put down the protest, killing 21 students. *(M2: Piaţa Universităţii, behind the fountain.)*

BOTANICAL GARDENS. In these gardens, located west of the center, well-labeled flora line the shaded pathways surrounding a pristine lake. During the Revolution of 1848, the park was a popular site for protests and demonstrations. *(Şos. Cotroceni 32. M1: Politehnica. Buses #62, 71, 93, 61, 306, and 336 stop at the entrance. Across from Cotroceni Palace. Open in summer daily 8am-8pm; in winter 9:30am-3:30pm. Greenhouses open Tu, Th, Su 9am-1pm. L10,000. Camera L50,000.)*

HERĂSTRĂU PARK. This immense park north of downtown has diversions ranging from row boat rentals to roller-coasters and is probably the best place in Bucharest to jog. At the southern end of the park on Şos. Kiseleff stands the **Arcul de Triumf,** built to celebrate Romania's independence from Turkey in 1877. *(Bus #131 or 331 from Piaţa Romana. M2: Aviatorilor. The Metro station sits at the southern tip of the park, which sprawls along Şos. Kiseleff. Open 24hr. Boats L40,000 per hr.)*

CIŞMIGIU GARDENS. One of Bucharest's oldest parks, the Cişmigiu Gardens are filled with pleasant walkways and a small lake where you can rent row boats. Along with Herăstrău Park, the well-groomed park is the focal point of much of the city's social life during the summer. *(M2: Piaţa Universităţii. With Hotel Intercontinental on the left, make a right on Bd. Regina Elisabeta. Open 24hr. Boats L40,000 per hr.)*

IN RECENT NEWS

GONE TO THE DOGS

In Bucharest, you can't fail to notice the droves of feral dogs in the street. They're around every corner, in every square, along every road. But these are only the survivors.

The dog problem began in the mid 1980s, when Romanian dictator Nicolae Ceauşescu ordered one of Bucharest's residential neighborhoods destroyed, thus sending hundreds of dogs to the streets. In 2001, figures were circulated that if something were not done, in a few years there would be 10 dogs for every person in the city of 2.1 million. Mayor Traian Băsescu's office has issued statistics claiming that every day over 50 people are bitten by these dogs and established a program to sterilize and exterminate the dogs in order to rid Bucharest of its canine problem.

Despite complaints of these attacks, the mayor's program has been met with heavy criticism and even with bodily resistance by local Roma (gypsies). French actress Bridget Bardot even signed a deal with Mayor Băsescu to save approximately 100,000 dogs from extermination, donating over US$140,000 to establish a 2 year program for mass sterilization and adoption of the city's stray dogs. By 2002, the number of strays in Bucharest was cut in half. Originally projected to cost 3 billion lei, the mayor's program has cost 7 billion lei and is now out of funds. And the dogs are returning in droves.

—Clay Kaminsky

🏛 MUSEUMS

■**VILLAGE MUSEUM.** (Muzeul Statuli.) This distinctive, open-air museum is a bustling village containing authentic rural houses, churches, and mills, of which all were carted to Bucharest from rural Romania. Plaques describe each structure in detail. *(Şos. Kiseleff 28-30. M2: Aviatorilor. ☎ 222 91 06 or 222 91 03. Open T-Su 9am-8pm. L40,000, students L15,000.)*

NATIONAL ART MUSEUM. (Muzeul Naţional de Artă al României.) The museum, formerly the royal residence, has recently reopened after 10 years of restoration. Paintings damaged during the 1989 revolution can be seen in their original splendor. The European exhibit (left entrance) contains works by such masters as Rembrandt, Monet, and El Greco. The Romanian section (right entrance) houses an extensive collection of medieval and modern art, such as works by Romania's most famous painter Nicolae Grigorescu, and modern sculptor Constantin Brâncuşi. *(Calea Victorei 49-53, in Piaţa Revoluţiei. M2: Piaţa Universităţii. ☎ 313 30 30. Open in summer W-Su 11am-7pm; in winter 10am-6pm. L80,000, students L40,000.)*

NATIONAL HISTORY MUSEUM. (Muzeul Naţional de Istorie al României.) A thorough look at Romanian history from its Dacian roots to the present day. English information is scarce. *(Calea Victorei 12. M2: Piaţa Universităţii. With Hotel Intercontinental on your left, turn right on Bd. Regina Elisabeta, then left on Calea Victoriei. ☎ 311 33 56 or 314 90 78. Open in summer W-Su 10am-6pm, in winter 9am-5pm. L15,000, students L6000.)*

MUSEUM OF THE ROMANIAN PEASANT. (Muzeul Ţăranului Român.) Named the best museum in Europe in 1996-97. An exhaustive presentation of Romanian rural life from the not-so-distant past. English information is incomplete: ask one of the younger curators to show you around. *(Şos. Kiseleff 3. M2 or 3: Piata Victoriei. ☎ 212 96 61. Open Tu-Su 10am-6pm; last admission 5pm. L30,000, students L5000.)*

JEWISH HISTORY MUSEUM OF ROMANIA. (Muzeul de Istorie a Evreilor din România.) A former synagogue, this museum displays remnants of synagogues from all over Romania. Be sure to also check out the other exhibits exploring Romanian-Jewish history. *(Str. Mămulari 3. M1, 2, or 3: Piaţa Universităţii. From the Metro entrance at Piaţa Unirii 2, turn right on Bd. Coposu and take the first right across a parking lot. Then turn left on Str. Mămulari. ☎ 311 08 70. English spoken. Open M, W, Su 9am-1pm, Th 9am-noon and 3-5pm. Free; donations accepted. Passport used as deposit for entrance.)*

🎭 ENTERTAINMENT

Bucharest hosts some of the biggest rock festivals this side of Berlin; guests include rising independent groups as well as established acts like Michael Jackson (who infamously responded to local screaming fans with "Hello, Budapest!"). Cinemas show a variety of foreign films (around L50,000), mostly from the US and all with Romanian subtitles. **Theater** and **opera** are inexpensive diversions (tickets L10,000-150,000.) Theaters in Bucharest are closed between June and September. Buy tickets at the theater box offices; they go on sale the Saturday two weeks before the performance. Seats go quickly, but whatever is left is available at half-price one hour before showtime.

Atheneul Român, Str. Franklin I (☎ 315 00 25). M2: Piaţa Universităţii. Excellent classical concerts in a breath-taking building. Box office open Tu-Sa noon-7pm, Su 6-7pm.

Opera Română, Bd. M.L. Kogălniceanu 70-72 (☎ 313 18 57). M1 or 3: Eroilor. Box office open daily 10am-7pm.

Teatrul Naţional, Bd. Nicolae Bălcescu 2 (☎ 314 71 17). M2: Piaţa Universităţii. Stages a wide variety of dramatic productions. Box office open daily noon-7pm.

🅝 NIGHTLIFE

Pack a map and cab fare as streets are poorly lit and public transportation stops at 11:30pm. The fun is concentrated around Str. Gabroveni and around M3: Semănătoarea in the student district, or *Regie*. For current listings, check out *Şapte Seri*, available free around the city. For current info on **gay nightlife** in Bucharest, consult the helpful staff of **Accept** (see **Local and Emergency Services**, p. 589).

La motor/Lăptăria, Bd. Băkescu 2 (☎315 85 08), on top of the National Theater. M2: Piaţa Universităţii. Enter the building through the side door facing Hotel Intercontinental; the door to the terrace is between the 3rd and 4th floors. Lăptăria means milk bar, but you won't find milk served on this lively terrace, a popular local hangout. Free open-air concerts or films during summer nightly 9:30pm. Open daily noon-2am.

Club A, Str. Blănari 14 (☎315 68 53). M2: Piaţa Universităţii. Walk down Bd. Brătianu and take the 3rd right; it's the unmarked door on the right, just after a store that says *Reparaţii Incălţăminte*.Club A is probably the most famous nightspot in Bucharest, yet it somehow remains unpretentious. Ridiculously cheap drinks: a great place for dancing and getting your game on. F-Sa men L50,000, women L20,000. Open daily 8pm-5am.

Twice, Str. Sfânta Vineri 4. M2: Piaţa Universităţii. A popular new club featuring 2 dance floors: head down to the basement for house or upstairs for disco. The ground floor is an open-air terrace. F-Sa men L50,000; women free. Open daily 9pm-5am.

🅓 DAYTRIP FROM BUCHAREST

CURTEA DE ARGEŞ ☎(0)48

Trains run to Curtea de Argeş (2½hr.; 2 per day; L85,000). Hotel Posada, Str. Basarabilor 27, provides tourist information. (☎72 14 51. Open M-F 8am-4pm.) To reach the monastery from the station, turn left and bear right up the cobblestone Str. Castenilor. Turn right at the small park, then left on the main Str. Basarabilor. Yellow and blue signs point the way to "Mănăstirea Curtea de Argeş." At the fork past the hotel, take a right.

Hidden in the foothills of the Făgăraş Mountains, Curtea de Argeş (CURT-ya DAR-jesh) is a hamlet of 14th-century buildings dating back to the town's heyday as Wallachia's capital. The **Monastery of Curtea de Argeş** (Mănăstirea Curtea de Argeş) is perhaps the most architecturally exquisite structure in the country; the chapel appears on the 10,000 lei note. Built in 1512, the monastery is distinguished by its fantastically twisted spires and golden interior. (Open daily 8am-8pm. L5,000, students L3,000.) Curtea de Argeş also serves as an excellent base for would-be slayers seeking **Count Dracula's real castle,** Cetatea Poienari (27km). Partially restored, the castle sits atop a hill, commanding an impressive view of the village below. A bus from the station in Curtea de Argeş (take a right from the train station) takes you most of the way to the castle (1hr.; 8 per day; L22,000). Continue 500m on foot along the main road until you see snack bars and the Cetatea Poienari sign; from there, head up the stairs to the left. The 1500 steps leading to the castle are appropriately tortuous, zig-zagging for 30min. up the mountain. Don't fear if you lose sight of both ends of the trail: the breathtaking climb yields a breathtaking view. You may expect applause upon reaching the top; instead, you'll find a grounds-keeper who will attempt to charge you L5,000 per photo of said breathtaking view. (Castle open daily 9am-6pm. L12,000.) A **taxi** (L150,000 round-trip) may seem like an easier way to reach the castle, but it won't spare you the stair climb.

SINAIA
☎(0)244

Wedged into the Prahova valley and flanked by the Bucegi mountains, Sinaia (sih-NIE-uh; pop. 15,000), Romania's celebrated alpine resort, made its mark in the late 1880s as a favorite getaway for Romania's royal family. The palaces that the royals left behind, Peleş and Pelişor, are spectacular inside and out. Today, the town's pleasant cobblestone streets and great hiking have made it a popular destination.

⌷ TRANSPORTATION. Trains (☎31 10 40) go to: **Braşov** (1hr.; 20 per day; L55,000); **Bucharest** (2hr.; 20 per day; L120,000); **Cluj-Napoca** (5hr.; 4 per day; L200,000). To get to the center of town, climb the stone steps across from the station. When the staircase forks, bear right and follow **Bd. Carol I** into town.

⚇ PRACTICAL INFORMATION. The **tourist office,** at the back of the lobby in Hotel Sinaia, Bd. Carol I 8, provides helpful information as well as **maps** (L10,000) of town and the hiking trails. (☎31 18 98. English spoken. Open M-F 8am-4pm, Sa-Su 8am-noon.) A pharmacy, **Farmacia Regala,** is at Bd. Carol I 22. (☎31 10 29. Open daily 8am-8pm.) **Banca Comercială Română,** Bd. Carol I 49, cashes traveler's checks. (Open M-F 8:30am-5:30pm, Sa 8:30am-12:30pm.) An **ATM** is out front. Another is at **Banc Post,** Bd. Carol I 19, which also has **Western Union** services. (Open M-F 8:30am-6pm, Sa 8:30am-1pm.) An Internet cafe creatively named **Internet** is located at Str. Octavian Goga 1, a right off Bd. Carol I as you walk from the train station toward the center. (10am-10pm L24,000 per hr., minimum L12,000; 10pm-5am L14,000 per hr. Open daily 10am-5am.) The **post office** (☎31 41 71), **telephone office** (☎31 01 11), and a train ticket **information booth** are all in the same building, at Bd. Carol I 33. (Post office open M-F 7am-8pm, Sa 8am-noon. Telephone office open M-F 8am-8pm, Sa 10am-6pm.) **Postal Code:** 2180.

⌷⌷ ACCOMMODATIONS AND FOOD. It's hard to go wrong in Sinaia, but it's usually best to avoid the big hotels and do as the Romanians do: stay in private villas. Though they vary in quality, most provide comfortable rooms with scenic views at affordable prices. In summer the train station is mobbed with locals offering **private rooms ❶**. Always look at a room and agree to a price before you accept (around US$8-12). If you want a sure thing, **Vila Retezat ❷**, Str. Kogalniceanu 64, has cozy doubles in a charming house uphill from the center. From the train station, head left on Bd. Carol I and then right on Str. Aosta. When Str. Aosta forks, bear left. Soon the road will fork again; take a hard left over the bridge. Take a right, then climb the first staircase on the right. At the top, look for the Vila's white sign. (☎31 47 47. Doubles L500,000.) Closer to the center is **Vila Camelia ❷**, Str. Mihail Cantacuzinu 5, with large, comfortable doubles in a large, friendly house. To get there, follow directions for Vila Retezat but bear right at the first fork onto Str. Aosta. (☎31 17 54. Doubles with bath L480,000.) **Liliana ❷**, Str. Mânăstirii 7, serves tasty Romanian and international dishes. Try the house specialty, *ciorbă de burtă* (cow's belly soup)—it's excellent. (Entrees L60,000-90,000. Open daily 8am-11pm.) **Cabana Furnica ❶**, Aleea Peleşului, near the palaces, whips up zesty traditional meals, including several bear dishes. (Entrees L40,000-L95,000. Open daily noon-11pm.) You can find an **open-air market** at Piaţa Unirii. (Open daily 7am-9pm.) For a traditional local treat, walk to the back of the **Piaţa Centrală ❶** store at the market and ask for *brânză de copac* (BRIN-zuh day co-PAHK). It's a sheep cheese of Dacian origin, made by shepherds in the trunks of fir trees (L110,000 per kg).

⌷⌷ SIGHTS AND ENTERTAINMENT. When not in Bucharest, the Romanian royal family lived in Sinaia. ⬛ **Peleş Castle** (Castelul Peleş) was completed in 1883 under the watchful eyes Carol I, then king of the newly-independent Romania (see **History: Help Yourself,** p. 576). Today, the palace astounds visitors with its opulence and exquisite detail: each room seems more delicately carved and more richly appointed than the last. The designers of the palace adopted a distinct decor for each room, including the German Baroque, Italian, Moorish, and Turkish styles. (Open W noon-5pm, Th-Su 9am-5pm; last entrance 4:15pm. Tours in English. L70,000, students L30,000.) Equally remarkable, but stylistically different, is ▓ **Pelişor Castle** (Little Peleş), down the road from Peleş itself. Built in 1902 for Carol's cousin Ferdinand, Pelişor was designed and decorated by Ferdinand's wife, Queen Maria. Maria, a poet and painter, decorated the palace in the Art Nouveau style, making use of bright, open spaces and simple wooden furniture. Vases and colored stones cover the bookcases and tabletops, while Maria's own art decorates the walls. (Open W noon-5pm, Th-Su 9am-5pm; last entrance 4:15pm. Tours in English. L50,000, students L20,000.) While you're in the neighborhood, wind your way down to the **Sinaia Monastery,** Str. Mănăstirii, named for Mt. Sinai. Pass through the gate in the monastery walls to visit a 17th-century chapel and the *paraclis* (prayer hall). If you're lucky, you might hear a monk perform *toaca,* the rhythmic striking of a wooden board with a mallet to call the others to prayer. To get to the monastery, follow Str. Octavian Goga from Carol I to Str. Mânăstirii. (Open dawn-dusk. Free.) At night, grab a few pints at the British-style pub, **Old Nick,** Bd. Carol I 22 (☎31 54 12; open daily 9:30am-late), and then dance the night away at the **Blue Angel** disco, across from Hotel New Montana. (☎31 26 17. Cover M-F and Su L20,000, Sa L30,000. Open M-F and Su 9pm-3am, Sa 9pm-4am.)

🗺 **HIKING.** A cable car, or *telecabina,* located behind Hotel New Montana connects Sinaia to the Bucegi mountains, which offer hiking and hang-gliding in the summer and skiing in the winter. From Sinaia, the cable car goes to Cota 1400 (L50,000, round-trip L90,000)—the number refers to the altitude. From there a second car continues to Cota 2000. (L40,000, round-trip L80,000.) It's also possible to buy a ticket at the base for Cota 2000 (round-trip L130,000). At the top, the **yellow stripe trail** leads hikers on a strenuous 4hr. climb past **Babele** (2200m), whose rocks are said to represent two *babe* (women) and a sphinx, to **Omu** (2505m), the highest peak of the Bucegi. If you're feeling adventurous, spend the night there at **Cabana Omu ❶.** (Open May-Dec. L15,000.) Simple bedding is provided, but bring a sleeping bag as even summer nights can be chilly. Meals are available 7am-9pm (L10,000-30,000), but bringing your own provisions is a good idea. Serious hikers can hike the yellow trail all the way to **Bran Castle,** which takes about 6hr.

TRANSYLVANIA (ARDEAL)

Though the name evokes images of a dark, evil land of black magic and vampires, Ardeal is actually a relatively Westernized region of green hills and mountains that gently descend from the Carpathians to the Hungarian Plain. In some areas, the wilderness remains largely untamed, which allows for good hiking from Sinaia into the Făgăraş Mountains. The vampire legends, however, do take root in the region's remarkable architecture: Transylvanian buildings are tilted, jagged, and more sternly Gothic than anywhere else in Europe.

SIGHIŞOARA ☎(0)265

Sighişoara (see-ghee-SHWAH-rah; pop. 39,000), in addition to being the birthplace of Vlad Ţepeş (the "real" Dracula), is perhaps the most pristine and enchanting medieval town in Transylvania. Crowning a green hill, its gilded steeples, old clocktower, and irregularly-tiled roofs have survived centuries of attacks, fires, and floods. Far from the image the Dracula legend conjures, the old city blends in beautifully with its colorful, tranquil surroundings.

IN RECENT NEWS

VE VANT TO SUCK YOUR VALLET

In 2004, **Dracula Amusement Park** is slated to open just outside of Sighişoara, the birthplace of Vlad Ţepeş. Today, it is the focus of much controversy in both Romanian and international circles.

Some of the park's opponents—including England's Prince Charles who visited Sighişoara in 2002 to protest—claim that the park would be a violation of Sighişoara's UNESCO world heritage site status; others, including Greenpeace, take issue with the choice of the site, which has 800-year-old trees on its grounds.

The park's defenders point out that the project will create 5000 jobs in this town of 39,000 residents and 37% unemployment. The expected admission cost will be €5, and marketing will focus on Western European families as the park's main audience. The park expects 1 million visitors per year, but few of these are apt to be Romanian, as the average monthly income here is between €100 and €150.

—Clay Kaminsky

📠 **TRANSPORTATION. Trains** run to: **Alba Iulia** (1½hr.; 3 per day; L135,000); **Bucharest** (5hr.; 8 per day; L186,000); **Cluj-Napoca** (3½hr.; 5 per day; L170,000); **Oradea** (6hr.; 3 per day; L212,000).

📑 **ORIENTATION AND PRACTICAL INFO.** To reach the center from the train station, take a right on to Str. Libertăţii, and then the first left on Str. Gării. Veer left at the Russian cemetery, turn right through the church courtyard, and cross the footbridge over the river **Târana Mare.** Proceed behind a large building called Sigma to **Str. Moni.** A right at the fork leads to **Str. O. Goga** and the **Citadel** *(cetatea)*; a left leads to the main **Str. 1 Decembrie 1918.** The statue of Romulus and Remus marks the center of town. To the right, Str. 1 Decembrie 1918 becomes **Str. H. Oberth** and then **Str. Ilarie Chendi.** If all else fails, aim for the clock tower.

Sighişoara Tour, Str. Teculescu 1, sells **maps.** From the train station, take a left on Str. 1 Decembrie 1918. (☎ 77 69 77. Open M-F 8am-3pm, Sa-Su 8-11am.) **Banca Română Pentru Dezvoltare,** Str. Oberth 20, in the center, has an **ATM** and **Western Union.** (Open M-Th 8am-1pm and 2-2:30pm, Sa 8am-1:30pm.) The train station has **luggage storage.** (Open 24hr. L25,500.) **Farmacia Genţiana** is at Str. Oberth 22. (Open M-F 7:30am-8pm, Sa 8am-7pm.) Log on at **Net Cafe,** Str. Teculescu. (Open M-F 10am-10pm, Sa 10am-midnight, Su 10am-11pm. L15,000 per hr., minimum L5000 per day.) The **post** and **telephone** offices are at Str. Oberth 20. (Post office open M-F 7am-8pm. Telephones open M-F 7am-9pm, Sa 8am-1pm and 5-8pm.) **Postal Code:** 3050.

🏠🍴 **ACCOMMODATIONS AND FOOD. Private rooms ❶** are available in the old city; you may be approached on the street or at the station (US$8-12). 📍 **Elvis' Villa Hostel ❶,** Str. Libertăţii 10, a right out of the train station, is the place to stay in Sighişoara. This brand-new hostel is *equipped:* free beer, cigarettes, and laundry. Ask the charismatic American owner to make his famous punch. (☎ 77 25 46. Bike rental US$5. US$10 per person.) **Hotel Chic ❷,** directly across from the train station, offers good rooms with a clean communal bathroom. (☎ 77 59 01. Singles L390,000; doubles L430,000, with TV L450,000.) 📍 **Restaurant Rustic ❶,** Str. 1 Decembrie 5, serves excellent food in an elegant dining room and at tables outside. (Entrees L40,000-130,000. Open daily 9:30am-1am.) In the Citadel, try restaurant 📍**Casa Vlad Dracul ❷,** Str. Cositorarilor 5, upstairs from Bar Beranie under the big metal dragon sign. It really is Vlad's house—he was born here in 1431 and lived here until 1436. The only hint of the house's history, however, is the breaded brain on the menu (L92,000). The traditional meals and medieval decor are truly worth the extra lei. (☎77 15 96. Entrees L70,000-190,000. Open daily 10am-midnight.) **Grocery stores** line Str. 1 Decembrie 1918.

🔲🔳 **SIGHTS AND FESTIVALS.** The **Citadel,** built by Saxons in 1191, is now a tiny medieval city-within-a-city. Enter through the **Clock Tower** (Turnul cu Ceas), off Str. O. Goga. Climb to the top of the museum to see the clock's mechanism and an expansive view of the area. (L20,000, students L10,000.) To the left as you leave the tower, the **Museum of Medieval Armory** offers a small exhibit on Vlad Ţepeş and weapons from all over the world. (L10,000, students L5,000.) Underneath the clock tower, the **Torture Museum** houses a small collection of pain-inflicting instruments and shackles. (L5000. All three open in summer Tu-F 10am-6:30pm, Sa-M 10am-4:30pm; in winter Tu-F 9am-3:30pm, Sa-M 10am-3:30pm. Combined ticket L35,000; buy at the Clock Tower. Cameras L50,000.) A left up Str. Şcolii reveals the 1642 **covered steps** built to help children get to school. At the top is the magnificent Gothic **Biserica din Deal** (Church on the Hill). Open daily 10am-5pm. No cameras. L10,000.) The second weekend in July brings the **Medieval Festival;** on Su it becomes a **rock festival.** The **Folk Art Festival** arrives the third week in August.

BRAŞOV ☎(0)268

A picturesque Transylvanian town, Braşov (BRAH-shohv; pop. 353,000) has much to offer: historic churches, museums, good restaurants, and a mellow main square where open-air concerts are held in the summer. The tourists seem to have noticed Braşov—today you can hear a good deal of German and English spoken in popular cafes. When the deluge of foreign tourists gets you down, see the ruins at Râsnov and the trails at Poiana Braşov.

📧 **TRANSPORTATION.** Trains go to: **Bucharest** (3-4hr.; 13 per day; L147,000); **Cluj-Napoca** (5-6hr.; 5 per day; L203,000); **Iaşi** (11hr.; 2 per day; L248,000); and **Sibiu** (4hr.; 6 per day; L133,000). Buy tickets at **CFR,** Str. Republicii 53. (Open M-F 8am-7pm, Sa 9am-1pm.) Braşov has two **bus stations;** the first is on the western edge of the city, at Autogară 2, a street commonly referred to as Gara Bartolomeu, and runs buses to **Bran** and **Râsnov.** The other, Autogară 1, next to the train station, is the main intercity depot. Buy tickets for city buses at kiosks around the center (L10,000).

🔳📱 **ORIENTATION AND PRACTICAL INFORMATION.** To get to town from the **train station,** take bus #4 in the direction of Piaţa Unirii to **Piaţa Sfatului** (L10,000), the main square; get off in front of **Biserica Neagra,** a large Gothic church. On foot, cross the street in front of the train station and head straight down **Bd. Victoriei.** Turn right on **Str. Mihai Kogălniceanu** and follow it as it makes a long arc to the left. When it ends, bear right on **Bd. 15 Noiembrie** (it becomes **Bd. Eroilor**) and turn left on **Str. Republicii** or **Str. Mureşenilor** (2km). To get to Piaţa Sfatului from the bus stop, turn right on Bd. Eroilor and then hang a right on Str. Mureşenilor; the plaza will be on your left.

Maps (L52,000) are available at kiosks and at **St. O. Iosif,** Str. Mureşenilor 14. (☎47 26 28. Open M-F 8am-9pm, Sa-Su 10am-4pm.) **Banca Comercială Romană,** Piaţa Sfatului 14, cashes AmEx **Traveler's Cheques** for 1.5% commission. There is an **ATM** in front of the bank; others line Str. Republicii. A **pharmacy,** Aurofarm, is at Str. Republicii 27, near the Bayer sign. (☎14 35 60. Open daily 7:30am-midnight.

ROMANIA

MC/V.) **Internet cafes** are everywhere. **Ce Faci,** Str. M. Weiss 18, off Str. Republicii, will hook you up 24hr. a day. (L20,000 per hr.) The **telephone office,** Bd. Eroilor 23, is between Str. Republicii and Str. Mureşenilor; enter from Str. Mihail Sadoveanu. (☎40 42 91. Open M-F 7am-9pm, Sa-Su 7am-8pm.) The **post office,** on the far side of Str. Eroilor, opposite the intersection with Str. Republicii, provides **Western Union** services. (Open M-F 7am-8pm, Sa 8am-1pm.) **Postal Code:** 2200.

☲☒ ACCOMMODATIONS AND FOOD. The market for **private rooms ❶** in Braşov is booming. Everybody and his grandmother has rooms to rent, and you will probably be approached many times between the train station and the town center. Always look at the room and agree on a price before you accept (around US$8-12). If you want a sure thing, head to ☒ **Elvis' Villa Hostel ❶,** Str. Democraţiei 2b. From Piaţa Unirii, walk up Sra. Bâlea and take the first right on Str. Democraţiei. This brand-new hostel is plush and beautiful, with fabulous views of the surrounding hills and free breakfast, beer, cigarettes, and laundry. (☎47 89 30; www.elvisvilla.com. Dorms US$8-12; singles US$25-28.) For a guaranteed private room, try **Casa Beke ❷,** Str. Cerbului 32. A kind Hungarian family offers comfortable rooms on a pleasant side street near the main square. To get there, follow Str. Republicii to Piaţa Sfatului and turn left on Str. Apollonia Hirscher; take your second right on Str. Cerbului. (A negotiable L330,000 per person.)

Bella Musica ❶, Str. G Bariţiu 2, is across Piaţa Sfatului from Str. Republicii. Make your way through the music store and down the stairs to a candle-lit wine cellar. Bella offers a creative and delicious Romanian-Mexican menu. You can't beat the free shots of *pălincă*, Romanian plum moonshine. (☎47 69 46. Entrees L65,000-145,000. Open daily noon-11pm.) Another standout is **Taverna ❷,** Str. Politehnicii 6. Walk up Str. Republicii from Pţa. Sfatului and turn right on Str. Politehnicii just before the intersection with Bd. Evoilor. Excellent Romanian, Hungarian, and Italian fare served in an elegant environment. (☎47 46 18. Entrees L60,000-200,000. Dress nicely. Open daily noon-midnight.)

◩ SIGHTS. Piaţa Sfatului and Strada Republicii are perfect for a stroll. Beyond the square along Str. Gh. Bariţiu looms Romania's most celebrated Gothic church, the 14th-century Lutheran **Black Church** (Biserica Neagră), so named after it was charred by fire in 1689. Inside there are 119 Anatolian Carpets, donated by 17th- and 18th-century German merchants. (Open M-Sa 10am-5pm; last entrance 4:45pm. No cameras. L20,000, students L10,000. Organ concerts mid-June to mid-July Tu 6pm; mid-July to Aug. Tu, Th, Sa 6pm. L20,000.) From the main square, follow Str. Apollonia Hirschner and turn right on Str. Poarta Schei to reach **Poarta Schei,** the city gate, built in 1828 to separate the old German citadel from the *schei* (the section allotted to the Romanian population). A 5min. walk through the gate and down Str. Prundului leads to Piaţa Unirii. Here stand both the 1495 **St. Nicholas Church** (Biserică Sfântu Nicolae) and **Romania's First School** (Prima Şcoală Românească), which contains the first Romanian books printed in the Latin alphabet. (Church open daily 8am-7pm. Free. School open daily 9am-5pm. L20,000.) The yellow building in the center of Piaţa Sfatului is the **Braşov History Museum** (Muzeul de Istorie), formerly the town hall. Inside, you'll learn more than you ever wanted to know about Braşov—if you read Romanian. Otherwise, check out the old torture paraphernalia. (Open Tu-Su 10am-6pm. L18,000, students L8,000.)

The best view of Braşov is from the summit of **Mt. Tâmpa.** A *telecabina* (cable car) will take you there from town. To get to the *telecabina*, walk up Str. Republicii from Piaţa Sfatului and turn right on Str. M. Weiss. Take a right on Str. Castelului and hang a left up the steep stairs; at the top, turn right and climb another set of stairs to the beige building. (Cable car runs Tu-F 9:30am-5pm, Sa-Su 9:30am-6pm. Round-trip L30,000.) From the cable-car station at the top, turn right to reach the peak, which is marked by a yellow metal pyramid. Another trip is the trails on Aleea T. Brediceanu, which leads to the **Weaver's Bastion** and other ruins.

📷🎭 **ENTERTAINMENT AND FESTIVALS. Operas** tend to be low budget but high on vocal talent. Purchase tickets at the box office on Str. Republicii 4. (Tickets ☎47 18 89. Open M-F 10am-5pm, Sa 10am-1pm.) The box office also sells tickets for the summer **International Chamber Music Festival.** In early September, Piața Sfatului holds the **Golden Stag Festival** (Cerbul de Aur), which brings together Romanian and international musicians. One hot night spot near the center is the red brick **Club Saloon,** Str. Mureșenilor 13. (☎41 77 05. Open daily 10am-2am.)

NEAR BRAȘOV

POIANA BRAȘOV   ☎(0)268

Bus #20 runs to Poiana Brașov from the station on Bd. Eroilor in Brașov, near the intersection with Str. Mureșenilor. (Every 30min. daily 6:30am-midnight; L10,000).

About 13km from Brașov, Poiana Brașov is a mountain niche that has long vied with Sinaia for the distinction of Romania's best alpine resort. The town itself is an unremarkable cluster of hotels and restaurants, but the view atop **Mt. Postăvarul** (1802m) is glorious and the lush valley that surrounds it is perfect for outdoor activities. In the winter, enthusiasts come for downhill and cross-country **skiing.** The many downhill runs are served by two cable-car lines (*telecabină*). Visitors can ice skate on the small frozen pond nearby or rent skis from local hotels. Swimming, tennis, and track facilities draw visitors to the town in summer, when one of the cable car lines brings hikers to the top of Mt. Postăvarul. (Open in summer daily 9am-4pm; off-season 9am-5pm. L60,000; round-trip L100,000.) To get to the center, turn right out of the parking lot and continue walking on Str. Poiana Soarelui in the direction the bus was headed. Signs for the hiking trails are at this intersection and at the top of Mt. Postăvarul. **Hikers** have a choice of four main trails from Poiana Brașov: the **blue stripe trail** leads to Cabana Cheia in Valea Cheișoara (2½-3hr.) and then on to Cabana Malaiești in the Bucegi mountains (8hr.); the **red circle** leads to Valea Cheișoara; the **red cross** leads to Cabana Postăvarul (2hr.); and the **red stripe** leads back to Brașov (1-2hr.). Signs for the trails are posted along Str. Poiana Soarelui and at the top of Mt. Postăvarul. For a complete **trail map** (L30,000), stop in at **Hotel Ana Sport,** on Str. Valea Dragă. They also rent **skis** (US$12 per day), **snowboards** (US$14 per day), and **ski passes.** (US$12 per day. ☎40 73 30. Open daily 8am-6pm.) To see the countryside in style, go horseback riding at **Centrul de Echitație.** (Horseback rides L300,000 per hr., carriage rides L500,000 per hr. Sleigh rides L500,000 per hr. Cabins US$60 for 3 people or US$100 for 6.) To get there, backtrack 1km along the road from the hotel. (☎26 21 61. Open 10am-7pm).

BRAN CASTLE   ☎(0)268

*To reach **Bran** from Brașov, take a taxi or city bus #5 or 9 to "Autogara 2" (or "Gara Bartolomeu"; 45min.; every 30min. daily 7am-6pm; L18,000). Get off when you see the souvenir market or the "Cabana Bran Castle–500m" sign. Backtrack along the main road; the castle will be on your right. Castle and village open Tu-Su 9am-5pm. L60,000, students L20,000. Cameras L55,000. Buses run between Brașov and Bran via **Râsnov;** pay on board (25min.; every 30min. daily 7am-6pm; L18,000). From the bus stop, follow Str. Republicii past an open-air market. Take a right and then a left through an arched entrance flanked by blue "muzeul cetate" signs. Fortress is a 10min. climb uphill. Open daily 10am-8pm. L35,000, students L20,000. Cameras L25,000. English information L25,000.*

ROMANIA

DRACULA, UNCENSORED
While Bran Castle may be less than striking, the gruesome exploits of its notorious visitor make the hack horror novel pale in comparison. Born in Sighişoara in 1431, Vlad Ţepeş' father (also Vlad) was a member of the Order of the Dragon, a society charged with defending Catholicism from infidels. Hence the name by which he ruled: Vlad Dragul ("Dragon"), and his son's moniker Dragula, "son of the dragon," which was corrupted to Dracula, "son of the devil" as word of his atrocities spread. In 1444, Vlad's father shipped his sons off to a Turkish prison to placate an Ottoman ruler, and there young Vlad learned his infamous methods of torture. Of these, his personal favorite was impalement. When the Turks invaded Wallachia in 1462, they were met by some 20,000 of their kinsmen impaled outside Dracula's territory. Horrified, they quickly retreated. Dracula also practiced such terror tactics on his own people. For example, in order to combat poverty in his realm, the benevolent ruler invited the destitute and disabled to his palace for a banquet...and then had them burned to death. By the height of his rule, his subjects were so terrified into obedience that Dracula placed a gold cup in Tirgovişte Square, which remained undisturbed for the duration of his reign.

Ever since Bram Stoker's novel identified Bran Castle with bloodthirsty Count Dracula, the castle and the legend have been linked in the popular imagination. Indeed, both the castle and its neighboring artisans do a brisk business on the strength of this connection. The history of this castle, however, is more complicated than the fables might suggest. Built in 1377 by Mircea the Old, Bran was the fortress that taxed trade along Bran Pass, a crucial route between Transylvania and Wallachia. Administered by Wallachia for almost 500 years, the castle became property of the city of Braşov when serfdom was abolished in 1848. It was later used as a summer residence for the royal family until it became a museum in 1956. Vlad Ţepeş, the historical model for Count Dracula, was a *voivode*, or local governor, of the 15th century who defended Wallachia from the Turks and acquired a reputation for impaling his victims on wooden stakes. He may have visited Bran Castle but never lived there. The restored castle now contains furnished royal rooms representing a wide range of time periods, from the Middle Ages to the 20th century. Also on the grounds is an **ethnographic village** with some English placards. To avoid the crowds, head to **Râşnov.** The fortress, constructed after the first Tartar invasion in 1241, offers a spectacular view of the surrounding countryside.

SIBIU
☎(0)269

The ancient capital of Transylvania, Sibiu (SEE-bee-oo; pop. 170,000) was founded by Germans in the 12th century and remains a town of medieval monuments and colorful, ornate houses. Sibiu's appeal is enhanced by its proximity to the Făgăraş Mountains and some of the best hiking in Romania. Whether you come to climb the peaks or just to relax, you'll be quickly charmed by majestic Sibiu.

TRANSPORTATION. Trains run to: **Avrig** (1hr.; 4 per day; L19,000); **Braşov** (3½hr.; 7 per day; L133,000); **Bucharest** (6hr.; 5 per day; L203,000); **Cluj-Napoca** (4hr.; 1 per day; L170,000); **Timişoara** (6hr.; 1 per day; L203,000); **Ucea** (1½hr.; 4 per day; L25,000). **CFR,** Str. N. Bălcescu 6, near Hotel Împăratul Romanilor, sells tickets. (Open M-F 7:30am-7:30pm.) **Buses** run to: **Albu Iulia** (1½hr.; 2 per day; L65,000); **Bucharest** (5hr.; 4 per day; L180,000); **Cluj-Napoca** (3½hr.; 2 per day;

L100,000); **Pitești** (2½hr.; 4 per day; L100,000); **Timișoara** (5½hr.; 1 per day; L180,000).

🖪🗷 ORIENTATION AND PRACTICAL INFORMATION. To reach the center, follow **Str. General Magheru**, the road outside the main door of the train and bus stations. When you reach the small square with a statue of Nicolaus Olahus, bear right on **Str. Avram Iancu.** This will lead to the main square, **Piața Mare.** To the right, through the tunnels under the Town Hall Clock Tower, is **Piața Mică.** Proceed through Piața Mare and down **Str. Nicolae Bălcescu** to reach **Piața Unirii,** which is also accessible by bus #5 from the train station (L9000 for two trips).

Libraria Friedrich Schiller, Piața Mare 7, sells city and hiking **maps** (L30,000-45,000) and provides other info. English spoken. (☎21 11 10. Open M-F 9am-noon and 1-5pm, Sa 10am-1pm.) **IDM Exchange,** Piața Mică 9, cashes **traveler's checks** for no commission and **exchanges currency.** (Open M-F 9am-5pm.) MC/V **ATMs** are at three locations: on Str. Bălcescu at Banca Comerciala Română, on Calea Dumărăvii by the Bruckenthal Art Museum, and in Piața Unirii on the corner of Hotel Bulevard. The local pharmacy, **Farmacia Farmasib,** is located at Str. Bălcescu 53. (☎21 78 97. Open 24hr.) There are English-language books at **Librăria Thausiă,** Piața Mică 2. (☎21 57 74. Open M-F 9am-5pm.) From Piața Mare, turn right after Hotel Împăratul Romanilor to reach **HIR Internet Cafe.** (L15,000 per hr.; L12,000 per hr. at night. Open 24hr.) The **telephone office** is at Str. Bălcescu 11. (Open M-F 7am-8pm, Sa-Su noon-8pm.) The **post office,** Str. Metropoliei 14, provides **Western Union** services. From Piața Mare, walk down Str. S. Brukenthall and take a left on Str. Metropoliei. (Open M-F 7am-8pm, Sa 8am-1pm.) **Postal Code:** 2400.

🖪 ACCOMMODATIONS. 🖾 Hotel Pensiune Leu ❶ (The Lion), Str. Moș Ion Roată 6, attracts backpackers. The friendly proprietors offer spotless rooms, laundry service, and hot showers. From Str. Magheru, walk to the far side of Piața Mare and turn right. Continue past the Bruckenthal museum and walk down the stairs on your right. At the bottom, turn left on Str. Moș Ion Roată. (☎21 83 92. Reception 24hr. Singles L300,000; doubles L500,000.) Another pleasant option is **Hotel la Podul Minciunilor ❷,** Str. Azilului 1, where a kind older couple rents out homey doubles with private baths. You just might get a chance to sample some homemade *vișinată* (cherry brandy). From Str. Magheru, turn right through the clock tower into Piața Mică, proceed through the square and down a long hill, before turning left on Str. Azilului. (☎21 72 59. Doubles L450,000; triples L600,000.) **Hotel Bulevard ❸,** Piața Unirii 10, offers modern rooms with TVs, fridges, and private baths. (☎21 60 60. Breakfast included. Singles L750,000-882,000; doubles L1,200,000.)

🖪🖾 FOOD AND FESTIVALS. To reach the **outdoor market,** follow the directions to Hotel Pensiune Leu (see above), but walk straight instead of turning left on Str. Moș Ion Roată. (Open dawn-dusk.) Restaurants in Sibiu are surprisingly mediocre. A good option for Romanian food is **Crama Sibiu Vechi ❶** (Wine Cellar of Old Sibiu), Str. Papiu Ilarian 3. The restaurant is below street level in an old brick wine cellar, and plays folk music while you eat. Take a left off Str. Bălcescu after the telephone office. (☎21 04 61. Entrees L50,000-70,000. Open daily noon-midnight.) The **International Theatre Festival** at the beginning of June attracts groups from around the world. There is also a **Medieval Festival** in late August, and from June 15 to Sept. 15 **Summer Fest** rages near Piața Unirii with free open-air concerts Th-F nights. Grab a few *mici*, some beer, and enjoy the show.

HIKING AROUND SIBIU

FĂGĂRAŞ MOUNTAINS

The Făgăraş Mountain range extends more than 60km from the Olt Valley to the Piatra Craiului mountains; the tallest peaks, **Moldoveanu** and **Negoiu**, are both 2500m. Wildflower-strewn meadows, cloud-shrouded summits, and superb views of Wallachian plains and Transylvanian hills have earned the Făgăraş range a special place in the hearts of Romanian hikers. Most hikers begin their trek by taking the train from Sibiu to **Ucea** (1½hr.; 4 per day; L25,000), where a bus connects to **Victoria** (25min.; 7 per day; L12,000), a great base camp. The range can also be entered at **Lacul Avrig**, a glacial lake along the red stripe and blue dot trails, or the **Puha Saddle** (Şaua Puha) on the blue cross trail. You can reach both from the sleepy town of **Avrig** (1hr.; 4 per day from Sibiu; L19,000); plan a day's hike to reach the trails. Parts of the range can be very challenging. For experienced hikers, **Custura Sărăţii** (1hr. east of the Puha Saddle) is the ridge trail's most spectacular and difficult portion; for 2hr. you'll cling to rocks on a path sometimes less than a foot wide, with drop-offs on either side (an alternate path avoids this route). Many end their hike with a descent into the **Simbăta Valley** (red triangle trail); the ridge ends at Cabana Plaiul Foii near the Piatra Craiului mountains, about 30km from Braşov. To get down to the valley you may have to backtrack to find a suitable trail. From Sîmbăta Valley, a day's hike will bring you back to Victoria.

A very helpful **map** and guidebook called *Crossing the Făgăraş Ridge from West to East* is sold in **Libraria Friedrich Schiller** in Sibiu (p. 601; L45,000). You can also pick up *Drumeţi În Carpaţi* in Bucharest or Braşov (in Romanian; L50,000). Hiking season lasts from July to mid-Sept., but the mountains are never crowded. Be prepared for very cold temperatures year-round. The range can be traversed in about seven days; going from west to east will keep the wind at your back. A series of **cabanas ❶** dot the area. Some cabanas offer sleeping sacks (L30,000-50,000 per person) while others offer doubles with bath (L125,000-300,000). Call **SC Salişte-Bâlea SA** in Sibiu (☎21 17 03) to make reservations for Cabana Bâlea Cascada. See **Essentials: Camping and the Outdoors**, p. 39, for hiking tips. In case of emergency, contact **Salvamont** (☎21 64 77).

ALBA IULIA ☎(0)258

Known as Apulum to the Romans, Alba Iulia (AL-bah YOU-lee-ah; pop. 72,000) is one of Romania's oldest cities. In 1600, it became the capital of Romania when Mihai Viteazul (Michael the Brave) united Wallachia and Transylvania. On December 1, 1918, Alba Iulia again saw their union when Transylvanian delegates voted here to join Romania—December 1 is now Romania's National Holiday.

▐ TRANSPORTATION. Trains run to: **Braşov** (3½hr.; 3 per day; L170,000); **Bucharest** (7hr.; 5 per day; L250,000); **Cluj-Napoca** (2hr.; 7 per day; L126,000); **Sighişoara** (1¾hr.; 3 per day; L135,000); **Timişoara** (5hr.; 4 per day; L170,000). The **bus station** is next to the train station, but you should stick to the trains.

▐▐ ORIENTATION AND PRACTICAL INFORMATION. From the train station, take bus #3 for the center or #4 for the Citadel (L6000). Get off in front of the **statue** of Romulus and Remus. Walking, take a right on the main road, which becomes **Str. Ardealului** and then **Str. Iuliu Maniu**. There is no tourist office in town. **Luggage storage** is available in the train station. (L25,000 per day. Open 24hr.) A pharmacy,

Farmacie Gelafarm, is at Str. Iuliu Maniu 8. (☎ 81 87 66. Open M-F 7am-8pm, Sa 8am-6pm, Su 8am-2pm.) Check email at **Pac Net Internet Cafe,** past the Romulus and Remus statue and the park. (L12,000 per hr. Open daily 8am-7pm.) The **post office,** opposite the statue, has an MC/V **ATM. Telephones** are next door. (Open M-F 7am-8pm, Sa-Su noon-8pm.) **Postal Code:** 2500.

⚐ ⚑ ACCOMMODATIONS AND FOOD. Pensiune Flamingo ❶, Str. Mihai Viteazul 6, offers simple but comfortable rooms. (☎ 81 63 54. Enter through the bar, just to the right of the Citadel gate, after 11pm. Singles with shared bath L300,000; doubles L600,000, with bath L800,000.) A step away from the Citadel but a step up in luxury is the **Hotel Transilvania ❸,** Piaţa Iuliu Maniu 22. Great, clean rooms with TV, phone, and bath. From the Romulus and Remus statue, follow Str. Ardealului past the telephone office to the square; the hotel is on the left. (☎ 81 20 52. Singles L640,000; doubles L850,000.) After sight-seeing, hit **Pizzeria Roberta ❶,** bd. Transilvaniei 23 (the road leading away from the Orthodox Cathedral), for pizza (L25,000-60,000) or pasta (L40,000-60,000). Follow dinner with delicious ice cream (L10,000-21,000) from **Paradis ❶,** across the street. (Both open daily 9am-10:30pm.)

⚐ ⚑ SIGHTS AND ENTERTAINMENT. The first gate to the **Citadel** *(cetatea)* is located up Str. Mihai Viteazul from the statue of Romulus and Remus. From there, orange-and-white signs will guide you along the Roman, medieval, and Vauban fortifications past the five other gates. On the way, you'll see an impressive equestrian statue of **Mihai Viteazul** (Michael the Brave; 1593-1601), who made his capital here in 1600. The nearby **Unification Hall** (Sala Unirii) was where delegates voted unanimously to unite the country, and the **Unification Museum** (Muzeul Naţional de Unirii) contains exhibitions on archaeology, history, ethnography, and art. (Hall and museum open daily 10am-5pm; last entrance 4:30pm. Each L20,000, students L10,000. Tours of both L100,000; with the rest of the Citadel L150,000.)

CLUJ-NAPOCA ☎(0)64

Transylvania's unofficial capital and its undisputed student center, Cluj-Napoca (CLOOZH na-PO-ka; pop. 400,000), is home to a mixed population and a vocal Hungarian minority comprises a fifth of the city's residents. The city's name reflects its rich heritage: "Cluj" (derived from Klausenburg) is rooted in its medieval German domination, while "Napoca" traces back to Roman times. The old city is vibrant, and life here is exciting.

⚐ TRANSPORTATION. CFR is at Piaţa Mihai Viteazul 11. (☎ 42 30 01 or 13 40 09. Open M-F 7am-7pm.) **Trains** run to: **Braşov** (5-7hr.; 5 per day; L205,000); **Bucharest** (8-13 hr.; 7 per day; L250,000); **Iaşi** (7hr.; 4 per day; L250,000); **Sibiu** (4 hr.; 1 per day; L170,000); **Sighetu Marmatiei** (7hr.; 2 per day; L170,000); **Timişoara** (6hr.; 4 per day; L215,000); **Budapest, HUN** (6½-7hr.; 2 per day; L835,000). **Local buses** and **trams** run from 5am to 11:15pm; purchase tickets (L13,000 for 2 trips) at **RATUC** kiosks.

⚐ ⚑ ORIENTATION AND PRACTICAL INFORMATION. From the **train station,** walk to the right and cross a bridge to reach the intercity **bus station** at Str. Giordano Bruno 3. Trolleys #3, 4, and 9 run from the front of the train station to the main square, **Piaţa Unirii.** On foot, cross the street and head down Str. Horea, which changes to **Bd. Regele Ferdinand** after crossing the river. You'll see Piaţa Unirii (1km), on your right at the end of Bd. Regele Ferdinand. The best **map** of the city is sold at RATUC Kiosks (L45,000).

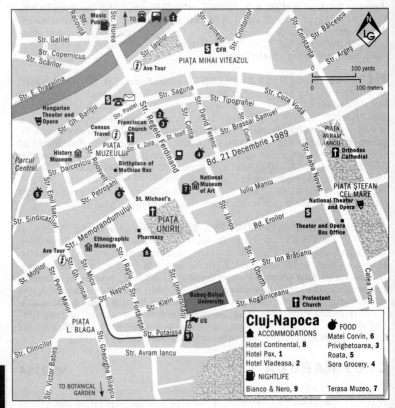

Cluj-Napoca

▲ ACCOMMODATIONS
Hotel Continental, 8
Hotel Pax, 1
Hotel Vladeasa, 2

■ NIGHTLIFE
Bianco & Nero, 9

◆ FOOD
Matei Corvin, 6
Privighetoarea, 3
Roata, 5
Sora Grocery, 4

Terasa Muzeo, 7

Tourist Offices: Oddly enough, Cluj has an overabundance of indispensable tourist offices. **Ave Tour,** Str. Motilor 1a (☎ 19 69 55; avetour@rdslink.ro), 3 blocks from Piaţa Unirii, provides information on **hiking** in the nearby **Apuseni Mountains.** Open M-F 8am-8pm, Sa 10am-2pm. **Consus Travel,** Piaţa Muzeului 6 (☎ 19 30 44; www.sonsus-travel.com), arranges tours (US$5) and books plane reservations. Open M-F 9am-6pm, Sa 10am-2pm. Both agencies hand out the free *Cluj-Napoca: What, Where, When.*

Consulate: US, Str. Universităţii 7/9 (☎ 19 38 15). Open M-F 8am-5pm.

Bank: Bancă Transilvania, Bd. Eroilor 36 (☎ 19 88 33), off Piaţa Avram Iancu, cashes **traveler's checks** for no commission and offers **Western Union** services. Open M-F 8am-2pm and 2:30-6pm, Sa 9:30am-12:30pm. MC/V **ATMs** line Bd. Ferdinand.

Pharmacy: Farmacia Clematis, Piaţa Unirii 10 (☎ 19 13 63). Open daily 8am-10pm.

Telephones: The **telephone office** (☎ 13 48 24) is behind the post office (see below).

Internet Access: Kiro Internet Cafe, Bd. Regele Ferdinand 6, 3rd fl. L9000 per hr., L5000 at night; minimum L2000. Open 24hr.

Post Office: Bd. Ferdinand 33. Open M-F 7am-8pm, Sa 7am-1pm. The **branch** (☎ 13 45 16) on Str. Aurel Vlaicu has **Poste Restante.** Open M, W, F 8am-1pm.

Postal Code: 3400.

⌐⌐ ACCOMMODATIONS AND FOOD. Hotel Vladeasa ❷, Str. Regele Ferdinand 20, has a good location and clean, simple rooms with private showers. (☎19 44 29. Breakfast included. Singles L550,000; doubles L800,000.) If you don't want to carry your bags to the center of town, try **Hotel Pax ❷**, across from the train station. (☎43 29 27. Singles L420,000; doubles L500,000, with shower L650,000.) **Hotel Continental ❹**, Str. Napaoca 1, in Piața Unirii, offers two types of rooms. One-star rooms are clean, with sinks, and share a well-kept shower, while three-star rooms are large, well-furnished, and have private showers. (☎19 14 41. Breakfast US$4. One-star singles US$27, with HI card US$9, three-star US$48; doubles US$36/$18/$62.)

Cluj loves its desserts—**pastry shops** are everywhere. Be sure to try *Doboș Cluj*, a local cake baked in layers of light, pudding-like chocolate. The **Sora grocery store**, Bd. 21 Decembrie, is open 24hr. ▨ **Matei Corvin ❸**, Str. Malei Corvin 2, just down from the king's old house, serves big portions of Transylvanian cuisine and many Hungarian options. (Entrees L100,000-140,000. Open daily noon-last customer; kitchen closes at 10pm.) **Roata ❶**, Str. Alexandru Civra 6a, off Str. Emil Isac, is a self-described "traditional Romanian restaurant." Dine in the elegant interior or outside in the tranquil courtyard. (☎19 20 22. Entrees L40,000-L200,000. Open M-Sa 11am-midnight, Su 11am-5pm.) **Privighetoarea ❷** (Nightingale), Bd. Regele Ferdinand 16, serves mushroom specialties and meat dishes. (☎19 34 80. Entrees L62,000-80,000. Open M-Sa 10am-11pm, Su noon-10pm. MC/V.)

◪ SIGHTS. Most strolls begin at **Piața Unirii**, where the 80m Gothic steeple of the Catholic **Church of St. Michael** (Biserica Sf. Mihail) pierces the skyline. Check out the Roman ruins in front of the statue of Mathia Rex. **Bánffy Palace,** Piața Unirii 30, houses the **National Museum of Art** (Muzeul Național de Artă), which specializes in Romanian works. (☎19 69 53. Open W-Su noon-7pm. L20,000, students L10,000; with temporary exhibitions L30,000/L15,000.) The nearby **Franciscan Church** (Biserica Franciscanilor), founded on a Roman temple site, has a Baroque interior. (Open M-F 8am-5pm, Sa-Su 9am-3pm; services daily 9am and noon.) Across Piața Muzeului, the **History Museum** (Muzeul de Istorie), Str. Constantin Daicoviciu 2, exhibits an impressive collection, including a flying machine built by a local professor in 1896. (☎19 56 77. Open Tu-Su 10am-4pm. Treasury open Tu-F 11am-3pm. L10,000, students L5,000.) For a dazzling view of the city, head to **Cetățuie Hill.** Walk up Str. Regele Ferdinand from Piața Unirii, turning left after the river onto Str. Dragalina, and climb the stairs on your right. **Parcul Central** (Parcul Barnutiv) is a good place to bring a picnic lunch. To get there, walk up Str. Regele Ferdinand from Piața Unirii and take a left on Str. Barițiu. Bear right when Str. Barițiu intersects Str. Emil Isac. (Open Apr.-Oct. M-F 9am-9pm, Sa-Su 9am-10pm.) The **Botanical Garden** (Grădină Botanica), on Str. Bilașcu off Str. Napoca, has a Japanese garden and an exotic greenhouse. (Open daily 9am-8pm. Lily-pad exhibit closes at 6pm. L15,000. Map L10,000.) The **University District** lies south of Piața Unirii on Str. Universității. In front of the 15th-century **Protestant Church** stands a replica of Prague's famous statue of St. George slaying a dragon. Many of the townsfolk took refuge here whenever the city was attacked; a cannonball is embedded in the left wall of the church, above the escape door opposite Kogălniceanu 23.

◪◪ ENTERTAINMENT AND NIGHTLIFE. The **National Theater and Opera** (Teatrul Național și Opera Română) in Piața Ștefan cel Mare, imitates the Garnier Opera House of Paris. The box office is across the street at Piața Ștefan cel Mare 24. (☎19 53 63. Tickets L30,000-50,000, students L20,000. Open Tu-Su

11am-7pm. Theater season mid-Sept. through June; opera season mid-Aug. through mid-July.) For the latest on Cluj's nightlife, pick up the free *a'la Cluj* from the lobby of big hotels. Located in an old wine cellar, **Music Pub** would be a good place to plot the French Revolution. As is, it's ideal for kicking back with students, cheap alcohol, and the latest sounds in rock, jazz, and techno. (☎43 25 17. Live music F-Sa starting at 9 or 10pm. Open in summer daily 6pm-3am; off-season M-Sa 9am-4am, Su noon-4am.) **Terasa Muzeu,** in the courtyard of the Museum of Art, is an elegant outdoor cafe where the artsy set hangs out. (Open May-Oct. daily 9am-midnight.) On weekends after dark, students gets down to a house beat at **Bianco & Nero,** Str. Universității 7/9. (☎19 65 01. Terrace open in summer W-Su 11am-11pm; disco open 10pm-last customer. Cover W-Th L20,000, students L10,000; F retro L30,000/L20,000; Sa house L40,000; Su latin L30,000/L20,000.)

THE BANAT

Romania's westernmost province, the Banat was heavily influenced by its Austrian and Hungarian rulers. Today, its population is more ethnically diverse than the rest of Romania, and its chicken paprikash is second to none. Timișoara, still flush with the excitement of the revolution that overthrew the Communist regime, is one of Romania's largest and liveliest cities.

TIMIȘOARA   ☎(0)256

In 1989, 105 years after becoming the first European city illuminated by electric street lamps, Timișoara (Tee-mee-SHWAH-rah; pop. 334,000) ignited a revolution that left Romanian Communism in cinders. As the nation's westernmost city, it has always been a channel for Western ideas and a hotbed of political activity.

▐ TRANSPORTATION. To reach the town by train, get off at **Timișoara Nord,** not Timișoara Est. **CFR** is at Str. Măchieșor 3 downstairs. (☎22 05 34. Open M-F 8am-7pm; domestic bookings until 8pm.) **Trains** run to: **Alba Iulia** (4½hr.; 4 per day; L170,000); **Brașov** (9hr.; 1 per day; L250,000); **Bucharest** (8hr.; 7 per day; L300,000); **Cluj-Napoca** (7hr.; 4 per day; L220,000); **Iași** (17hr.; 3 per day; L362,000); **Sibiu** (7hr.; 1 per day; L200,000); **Budapest, HUN** (5hr.; 2 per day; L300,000).

▐▌ ORIENTATION AND PRACTICAL INFORMATION. Trams #1, 8, and 11 and trollies #11 and 14 run from the station to the center of town (2 trips L14,000); get off after crossing the river, when you see **Piața Victoriei** with its multicolored cathedral. **Libraria Mihai Eminescu,** in Piața Victoriei, sells maps. (L62,000. Open M-F 9am-7pm, Sa 9am-1pm.) **Banc Post,** Bd. Mihai Eminescu, off Piața Victoriei, offers **Western Union** services. (Open M-F 8am-5pm.) **Banca Comercială Română,** Piața Sf. Gheorghe 1, near Piața Libertății, cashes AmEx **Traveler's Cheques.** (☎19 01 08. Open M-F 8:30am-2pm and 3pm-5:50pm, Sa 8:30am-12:30pm.) **ATMs** are not hard to find around Piața Victorie. **Librăria Noi,** Str. Hector 2, offers a good selection of English books. (☎22 09 49. Open M-F 10am-8pm, Sa 10am-2pm.) A **Sensiblu** pharmacy is at Str. Piatra Craiului 3, off Piața Victoriei. (☎24 16 48. Open 24hr.) The **telephone office** is at Mihai Eminescu 2. (Open M-F 8am-2pm and 2:30-8pm, Sa 8am-1pm.) For **Internet access,** try **Club 30,** in Cinema Timiș, off Piața Victoriei. (L417 per minute. Open daily 9am-3am.) **Limit Up Club,** Str. F. Mercy 9, 2nd floor, in Piața Unirii, provides 24hr. **Internet access.** (Open 24hr., L13,000 per hour.) The **post office,** Str. Piatra Craiului 1, is off Bd. Republicii and Piața Victoriei. (Open M-F 8am-4pm.) **Postal Code:** 1900.

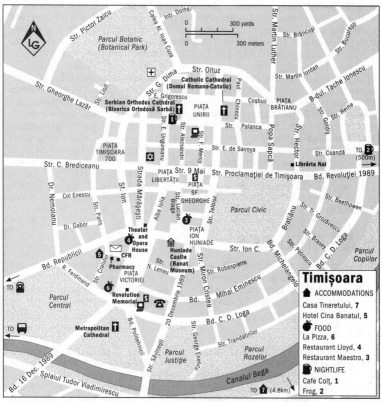

Str. Pictor Zaicu
Intr. Doinei
Calea Al. Ioan Cuza
Str. Martin Luther
Str. Brâncuși
Str. București
Parcul Botanic
(Botanical Park)
0   300 yards
0   300 meters
Str. Gheorghe Lazăr
Str. Liszt
Str. G. Dima
Str. Oituz
Catholic Cathedral
(Domul Romano-Catolic)
Paul Chinezu
Str. Martin Iordan
B-dul. Tache Ionescu
Str. Heine
E. Grigorescu
Serbian Orthodox Cathdral
(Biserica Ortodoxă Sârbă)
Coșbuc
PIAȚA
BRĂTIANU
PIAȚA
UNIRII
Str. E. Ungureanu
Str. Alecsandri
Str. Palanca
Str. Goldiș
Str. F. Mercy
Str. Coandă
TO
(500m)
PIAȚA
TIMIȘOARA
700
Str. C. Brediceanu
Str. E. de Savoya
Popa Șapcă
Str. Hector
■ Librăria Noi
Dr. Nemoianu
Col Enescu
Dr. Gabor
Strada Mărășești
Sf. Ion
Str. Paris
Alba Iulia
Str. Lucian Blaga
PIAȚA Str. 9 Mai
LIBERTĂȚII
PIAȚA
SF.
GHEORGHE
Str. Teluisz
Str. Proclamației de Timișoara
Bd. Revoluției 1989
Str. Beethowen
Bratianu
Str. Tr. Grozăvescu
Str. Brasey
Str. Petrescu
Bd. C. D. Loga
Parcul
Copiilor
Parcul Civic
Theater
and
Opera
House
PIAȚA
ION
HUNIADE
Huniade
Castle
(Banat
Museum)
Str. Ion C.
Bd. Michelangelo
Str. Miron Cristea
Str. N. Lenau
Str. Robespierre
CFR
Pharmacy
PIAȚA
VICTORIEI
Revolution
Memorial
20 Decembrie 1989
Mihai Eminescu
Bd. C. D. Loga
Bd. Republicii
R. Ferdinand
Str. Craiului
Bd.
TO
Parcul
Central
TO
Metropolitan
Cathedral
Bd. Politehnicii
Str. Sălvnesti
Str. George Enescu
Str. Trandafirilor
Parcul
Justiție
Parcul
Rozelor
Canalul Bega
Bd. 16 Dec. 1989
Splaiul Tudor Vladimirescu
TO (4.8km)

Timișoara

♠ ACCOMMODATIONS
Casa Tineretului, 7
Hotel Cina Banatul, 5
♦ FOOD
La Pizza, 6
Restaurant Lloyd, 4
Restaurant Maestro, 3
▮ NIGHTLIFE
Cafe Colț, 1
Frog, 2

ROMANIA

▮▯ ACCOMMODATIONS AND FOOD. Hotel Cina Banatul ❷, Str. Craiului 4, is centrally located. Its clean, beautiful rooms (all with TVs and private showers) are the most reasonable option in the center. (☎ 19 01 30. Breakfast included. Singles L600,000; doubles L800,000; triples L140,000.) If you're strapped for cash, try **Casa Tineretului ❶**, Str. Arieș 16, south of the center. Take train #8 from the train station. (☎ 16 24 19. L113,00-178,500 per person.) **Restaurant Maestro ❸**, Str. Iános Bolyai 3, on a pleasant side street off Str. Lucian Blaga, off Piața Victoriei, serves scrumptious Romanian cuisine in an elegant outdoor setting. (☎ 29 38 61. Entrees L70,000-300,000. Open 24hr.) There are a number of good restaurants with outdoor tables in Piața Victoriei itself: **Restaurant Lloyd ❷** serves Romanian and international dishes (L60,000-300,000; open daily 10am-11pm), while **La Pizza ❶** is a popular place to grab a slice (pizzas L31,000-50,000; open daily 9am-9pm).

◙ ♫ SIGHTS AND ENTERTAINMENT. The **National Theater** (Teatrul Național) and **Opera House** (Opera Timișoara) are on one side of **Piața Victoriei** and the **Metropolitan Cathedral** is on the other. The square was a gathering place for protesters during the anti-Ceaușescu uprising; the plaques at the entrance record the sacrifices made by the young revolutionaries of December 1989. Off the square but near the opera, the old **Huniade Castle** houses the **Banat Museum** (Muzeul Banatului), which traces Timișoara's history from ancient times through World

War II. The exhibits are fantastic, but nothing is in English. (Open Tu-Su 10am-4:30pm. L10,000; students L5000.) Outisde the musuem, you'll see original **lamp posts** from when Timişoara became the first European city illuminated by electric streetlights on November 12, 1884. The **Metropolitan Cathedral,** also located off the square, was built between 1936 and 1946 in Moldavian folk style, with a rainbow-tiled roof and 8000kg bells. (Open daily 6:30am-8pm. Services M-F 7:30am and 6pm; Su 7am, 10am, and 6pm.) An impressive **museum** downstairs displays religious artifacts. (Open W-Su 10am-3pm. L5000, students free.) The **Park of Roses** (Parcul Rozelor), to the south, has cozy white benches surrounded by roses. Free concerts often fill the park with music. Farther north is **Piaţa Unirii,** whose fountain spouts water said to remedy stomach ailments. In June, the annual **International Folk Music Festival** comes to town. The **Opera House** box office is down the street from the opera, on Str. Mărăşeşti. (Open Sept.-May daily 10am-1pm and 5-7pm.) On the corner by the Serbian Church, the smoky **Cafe Colţ,** Str. Ungureanu 10, has background music and a friendly young crowd. (Open 24hr.) **Frog,** Str. 3 August 1919 nr. 1, is a Breton pub playing jazz and blues and catering to a Francophile crowd. Follow Bd. Revoluţiei 1989 over the bridge; Frog is on the right. (Open 10am-late.)

MARAMUREŞ

The Maramureş (mah-rah-MOOR-esh) region, wedged between Hungary and Ukraine, is known for its woodcarving and folk culture. Some residents still don traditional clothing, especially for church, feasts, and holidays. Few visitors venture into the area's rolling hills, but those who do are richly rewarded.

SĂPÂNTA ☎(0)262

A remote village in the farthest reaches of Maramureş, Săpânta (suh-PUNT-sah, pop. 5000) is famous world-wide for its unique "merry" cemetery. Despite its fame, this tiny village has steadfastly maintained the traditional lifestyle. Head straight on the main road before taking a left on the only other paved road in town to reach the ◙**Merry Cemetery** (Cimitrivl Vesel). Created by sculptor **Stan Ion Pătras,** the cemetery is a monument to the power and appeal of folk art. Graves are marked by a sea of vividly colored, sculpted crosses with inscriptions about the deceased in the form of witty poems written in archaisms, slang, dialect, and (usually) the first person. In front of the entrance to the **church,** you can see the cross Pătras sculpted for himself. Inside the 1886 church are beautiful frescoes in colors almost as bright as those on the crosses. Up the road to the right of the cemetery is the **Stan Ion Pătraş Memorial House** which contains a tiny museum dedicated to the sculptor. (Open daily 8am-10pm. L5000, students L3000.) In back you'll find his **workshop,** where his student Dumitru Pop has continued to produce the famous crosses since Pătraş's death in 1977. **Pălincă** is made behind the AF Pop bar by the bus stop. They'll sell you some in an old plastic bottle for L100,000 per liter, but be careful: pălincă's alcoholic content often exceeds 60%. Under the nearby bridge, you can see the apparatus where village women still do their washing in the Săpânta River. Cross over the bridge in the direction the bus came from, and take your first left to see a traditional wooden **monastery** under construction.

To get to Săpânta, take the train north to **Sigheu Marmatiei.** To: Bucharest (12½hr.; 1 per day; L329,000); **Cluj-Napoca** (7-9hr.; 3 per day; L150,000); **Timişoara** (12hr.; 1 per day; L329,000). You have to go through **Salva** (3-5hr.; 5 per day; L83,000), to reach **Iaşi** (7hr.; 4 per day; L212,000). From Sigheu, a **bus station** opposite the train station sends buses to **Săpânta** (40min.; M-F 7-8 per day, Sa-Su 1 per day). Hitchhiking is common, but *Let's Go* does not recommend it.

MOLDAVIA

Eastern Romania, which once included neighboring Moldova, extends from the Carpathians to the Prut River. Moldavia, an area starker than Transylvania but more developed than Maramureş, saw its greatest glory 7under the rule of Ştefan cel Mare (1457-1504; see **History**, p. 576). The tranquil hills of Bukovina, world renowned for their breathtaking painted monasteries, will delight any traveler.

IAŞI   ☎(0)232

During the second half of the 19th century, Iaşi (YASH; pop. 340,000) was one of Romania's primary administrative and cultural centers. Its intellectual life revolved around the Junimea Society, a literary club founded by the same writers, nobles, and thinkers who filled Iaşi with Neoclassical homes and palaces. These buildings, remarkably well preserved after 45 years of Soviet communism, draw tourists to the city's peaceful streets.

📠 **TRANSPORTATION.** The **train station** is on Str. Silvestru. To: **Braşov** (6hr.; 1 per day; L250,000); **Bucharest** (7½hr.; 4 per day; L250,000); **Cluj-Napoca** (9hr.; 4 per day; L250,000); **Constanţa** (8hr.; 2 per day; L250,000); **Suceava** (2hr.; 4 per day; L135,000); **Timişoara** (17hr.; 3 per day; L359,000). **CFR**, Piaţa Unirii 9/11. (☎ 14 52 69. Open M-F

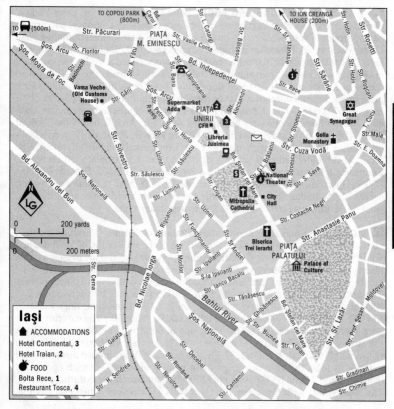

Iaşi

🏠 ACCOMMODATIONS
Hotel Continental, **3**
Hotel Traian, **2**

🍴 FOOD
Bolta Rece, **1**
Restaurant Tosca, **4**

ROMANIA

8am-8pm.) The **bus station,** Str. Moara de Foc 15 (☎14 65 87), sends buses to **Braşov** (8hr.; 1 per day; L230,000) and **Chişinău, MOL** (5hr., 4 per day, L150,000).

■ ORIENTATION AND PRACTICAL INFORMATION. Standing in the parking lot with the train station behind you, cross the street and walk up **Str. Gării** to the right of the **Vama Veche** (Old Customs Tower). Follow Str. Gării uphill until the next major intersection, where the tram tracks curve off to the right. These tracks will guide you to **Str. Arcu** (which becomes **Str. Cuza Vodă**). The center of town begins at the place where Str. Cuza Vodă opens into a square, **Piaţa Unirii,** and where **Str. Ştefan cel Mare** curves to the right. The center is also accessible by trams #3, 6, and 7 (L12,000 for 2 trips) opposite the Vama Veche. **Libraria Junimea,** Piaţa Unirii 4, sells **maps.** (L25,000. ☎31 46 64. Open M-F 9am-8pm, Sa 9am-3pm.) **Banco Commercială Română,** Str. Ştefan cel Mare 8a, cashes AmEx **Traveler's Cheques** for 1.5% commission. (☎21 17 38. Open M-F 8am-2pm and 2:30-5pm, Sa 8am-12:30pm.) **ATMs** can be found all over the city, especially on Str. Cuza Vodă and Str. Ştefan cel Mare. **Luggage storage** is available at the train station (L25,000 per day for small bags, L50,000 for large). Internet cafes are common, but for a centrally located option, check out **Non-Stop Internet Cafe** on Str. Ştefan cel Mare, off Piaţa Unirii. (L12,000 per hr. Open daily non-stop, of course.) The **post office,** Str. Cuza Vodă 10, offers **Western Union** services at window #2. Window #6 is **Poste Restante.** (☎21 22 22. Open M-F 7am-8pm, Sa 7am-1pm.) **Postal Code:** 6600.

ACCOMMODATIONS AND FOOD. Hotel Continental ❷, Str. Cuza Vodă 4, stands in a good location and offers quality rooms with TVs, phones, and private baths. From the train station, it's on the right at the next intersection after Piaţa Unirii. (☎21 18 46. Breakfast included. Singles L465,000; doubles L620,000, with bath L760,000; triples L870,000/L1,140,000.) If hotels named after Roman conquerers attract you, visit the two-star **Hotel Traian ❷,** Piaţa Unirii 1. The well-furnished rooms are large and the first two floors have been beautifully renovated; for a price break, take an unrenovated room on the third floor. (☎14 33 30; fax 21 21 87. Singles L570,000-815,000; doubles L740,000-1,150,000. Suites and apartments available. MC/V.) For groceries, try **Supermarket Adda,** Str. Arcu 5, below the TAROM office. (Open 24hr.) Established in 1786, ◪**Bolta Rece ❶,** Str. Rece 10, serves Iaşi's best dishes. Follow Str. Cuza Vodă past Hotel Continental and turn left on Str. Bră tianu. At Bd. Independenţei, make a right and then an immediate left on Str. M. Eminescu; a few streets up, turn left on Str. Rece. (☎21 22 55. Entrees L20,000-75,000. Open daily 8am-midnight.) **Restaurant Tosca ❶,** near the National Theater, serves hearty Italian dishes with a little Greek, Arab, and Romanian in the mix. (☎21 66 64. Entrees L30,000-110,000. Open daily 11am-11pm.)

SIGHTS. The massive, neo-Gothic ◪**Palace of Culture** (Palatul Culturii), marked by a clock tower that plays the anthem of the 1859 union of Moldavia and Wallachia, contains historical, ethnographic, polytechnic, and art museums. The history museum takes Moldavia from its prehistory through World War I, while the polytechnic museum has a fascinating exhibit on music boxes and player pianos. The art museum contains splendid 19th-century paintings by such masters as Nicolae Grigorescu and Theodor Aman. (Open Tu-Su 10am-5pm. Each museum L15,000; students L10,000. Combined ticket L50,000/L30,000.) The exterior of the gorgeous **Trei Ierarhi church,** on the right side of Str. Ştefan cel Mare as you walk toward the Palace of Culture, is adorned with Moldavian, Romanian, and Turkish raised reliefs that date back to 1637. Though invading Tatars melted down the gold exterior in 1650, the interior retains its original gold sheen. (Church open daily 9am-noon and 3-7pm. L3000, students L1500; free for worshippers during service). The 16th-century **Golia Monastery,** Str. Cuza Vodă 51, was once a medieval fortress.

Climb the 29m tower for a brilliant view of the city. Writer Ion Creangă, "Romania's Mark Twain" (see **The Arts,** p. 579), spent his last years in Iaşi in what is now known as the **Ion Creangă House** (Bojdeuca Ion Creangă), Str. Simion Bărutiu 4. Join the March 1 celebration of Creangă's birthday. From the town center, take a left from Bd. Independenţei onto Str. Sărăriei. Take a right when you see a sign for the house; it's down a small hill. (Open Tu-Su 10am-5pm. L10,000, students L6000.) To get to **Copou Park,** Bd. Carol I, ride tram #1 or 13 from Piaţa Unirii or take a scenic stroll from Piaţa Eminescu. Inside the park, created by Prince Mihail Sturza in 1836, is the famous **Mihai Eminescu Linden,** the tree that shaded Romania's great poet as he worked (see **The Arts,** p. 579). Statues of other artists line a nearby promenade. The adjacent **Eminescu Museum** exhibits pictures of the poet and some of his documents. (Open Tu-Su 10am-5pm. L10,000.) Take a walk along Bd. Copou to see **Alexandru Ioan Cuza University** and the **Sadoveanu House.**

BUKOVINA MONASTERIES

Hidden among green hills and rustic farming villages, Bukovina's painted monasteries are a source of pride in Moldavia. Built 500 years ago by Ştefan cel Mare and his successors—rumor has it that he built one after every victory over the Turks—the exquisite structures meld Moldavian and Byzantine architecture with Christian images. It is said that since the Moldavians of old lacked the resources to build large chapels, they built small ones and painted them both inside and out. Getting to monasteries other than Voroneţ and Humor by public transport can be a trial of faith; try one of the tours running out of Gura Humorului or Suceava. Locals often hitch during the summer, but *Let's Go* does not recommend hitchhiking.

SUCEAVA ☎(0)230

The capital of Moldavia under Ştefan cel Mare, Suceava (soo-CHAY-vah) has more than just proximity to offer the monastery-seeker. Here you'll find intriguing museums, thriving nightlife, Ştefan's citadel, and, yes, more religious sites.

▐ TRANSPORTATION. Gara Cuceava Nord sends **trains** to: **Braşov** (8hr.; 1 per day; L248,000); **Bucharest** (6hr.; 4 per day; L248,000); **Cluj-Napoca** (6hr.; 4 per day; L250,000); **Gura Humorului** (1hr.; 6 per day; L53,000); **Iaşi** (2hr.; 5 per day; L126,000); **Timişoara** (14hr.; 2 per day; L329,000). Buy tickets at **CFR,** Str. N. Bălcescu 4. (☎21 43 35. Open M-F 7am-7pm.) The **bus station** (☎52 43 40), at the intersection of Str. N. Bălcescu and Str. V. Alecsandri, sends buses to: **Bucharest** (8hr.; 2 per day; L200,000); **Cluj-Napoca** (7hr.; 2 per day; L200,000); **Constanţa** (9hr.; 3 per day; L300,000); **Gura Humorului** (1hr.; 9 per day; L24,000); **Iaşi** (3hr.; 1 per day; L90,000).

▐▞ ORIENTATION AND PRACTICAL INFORMATION. From the train station, take any of the Maxi taxis waiting outside to reach the center, **Piaţa 22 Decembrie** (10min., L5000). **Librăria Cipiran Porumbescu,** Aleea Ion Grămadă 5, sells English-language **city guides.** (L60,000. Open M-F 7am-7:30pm, Sa 9am-6pm.) Several agencies give tours of the monasteries. **Bucovina-Estur,** Str. Ştefan cel Mare 24, offers tours of varying length with a car and driver. Tours include Suceava, the monasteries, an ethnological museum, and a pottery workshop. (☎52 26 94 or 52 48 94. Tours 3-9hr., US$30-70. Open M-F 9am-5pm, Sa 10am-2pm.) **Bilco Agenţia de Turism,** Str. N. Bălcescu 2, gives private two-day car tours of the area. (☎52 24 60. US$60. Open M-F 9am-6pm, Sa 9am-2pm.) **Store luggage** at the train station. (L25,000 per day. Open 24hr.) **Banca Commercială Română,** Str. Ştefan cel Mare 31, cashes AmEx **Traveler's Cheques** for 1.5% commission and has an **ATM.** (☎21 02 23. Open M-F 8:30am-2:30pm.) **Banca Românească,** Str. N. Bălcescu 4a, offers **Western Union** services. (☎52 16 88. Open M-F 9am-4:30pm, Sa 9am-1pm.) Other services include:

ROMANIA

Farmacia Centrala, Str. N. Bălcescu 2b (☎ 21 72 85; open daily 7am-9pm); **telephones** off Piaţa 22 Decembrie (open daily 7am-11pm); **Internet access** in the tower in Piaţa 22 Decembrie (L15,000 per hr.; open daily 9am-11pm); and a **post office,** Str. Dimitrie Onciul 1 (open M-F 7am-8pm, Sa 8am-1pm). **Postal Code:** 5800.

⌂ ☐ ACCOMMODATIONS AND FOOD. Hotel Suceava ❷, Str. N. Bălcescu 4, in Piaţa 22 Decembrie, lets large, comfortable rooms with private baths and cable TV; some even have refrigerators. (☎ 52 10 72. Breakfast L85,000. Singles L570,000; doubles L730,000.) **Villa Alice ❸,** Str. Simion Florea Marian 1b, offers beautiful private rooms in a quiet neighborhood. Walk up Str. Porumbescu from Piaţa 22 Decembrie and bear right through the park. (☎ 52 22 54. Breakfast L100,000. Singles L650,000; doubles L750,000.) Check out the impressive **fresh produce market** in Piaţa Agroalimentara on Str. Petru Rareş. (Open daily dawn-dusk.) **Latino ❷,** Curtea Domnească 9, by the bus station, serves filling Italian fare. (☎ 52 36 27. Entrees L65,000-150,000. Open daily 9am-11pm.)

◙ ☐ SIGHTS AND NIGHTLIFE. The mammoth equestrian **statue** of Ştefan cel Mare is visible above the trees from Piaţa 22 Decembrie. Near the statue lies the **Citadel of the Throne** (Cetatea de Scaun). It's only about a 20min. walk through the park, but take a taxi (5min., L30,000) since the park isn't always safe. The Citadel was built in 1388 by Petru Muşat I, who moved Moldavia's capital to Suceava. It was refortified by Ştefan cel Mare and withstood the 1476 siege by Mehmet II, conqueror of Constantinople. Be sure to climb the ramparts for the fabulous view. (Open in summer daily 8am-8pm; in winter 9am-5pm. L10,000, students L5000.) The adjacent **Bukovina Village Museum** (Muzeul Satului din Bucovina) displays 18th-through 20th-century houses from the region. (Open Tu-Su 8am-6pm. L10,000, students L5000. Cameras L30,000.) The **Bukovina Ethnographic Museum,** Str. Cipiran Porumbescu 5, is an excellent exposition of the material life of Bukovina's peasants. (Open Tu-Su 10am-6pm. L10,000, students 5000.) The **Bukovina History Museum,** Str. Ştefan cel Mare 33, contains a recreation of Ştefan's throne room. (Open Tu-Su 10am-6pm. L16,000, throne room only L8000; students L8000/L40000.) What you came to Bukovina for, of course, are the religious sights. **Biserica Sf. Ioan cel Nou** (Church of St. John the New), completed in 1522 by Bogdan III, holds beneath its colorful tiled roof the body of Saint Ioan of Suceava, martyred in 1330. Original 1535 frescoes still decorate **Biserica Sf. Dumitro,** Str. Curtea Domnească.

To reach **Cinema Modern,** Str. Dragoş Vodă 1, follow Str. N. Bălcescu out of Piaţa 22 Decembrie to Str. M. Eminescu. Films in English run four times per day and change weekly. (Open daily 11am-6:30pm. L25,000.) The best **nightlife** in town is at the Citadel, where two terraces serve up food and drinks (entrees L35,000-100,000; open daily 8am-10:30pm) and the disco **Crama** beats away beneath (open F-Su 10:30pm-last customer). Another **disco** is located in the basement of Casa Culturii, in the center of Piaţa 22 Decembrie. (Open F-Su 9pm-3am. Cover L20,000.)

GURA HUMORULUI   ☎ (0)230

Within walking distance of Humor and Voroneţ, and on the way to other monasteries, the small town of Gura Humorului is an ideal place to crash after a day of exploring the area. While the center does not share the divine inspiration of its surroundings, its family-run villas are shining examples of Moldavian hospitality.

⌨ TRANSPORTATION. Trains, Bd. Castanilor, run to: **Bucharest** (6hr.; 1 per day; L248,000); **Cluj-Napoca** (5hr; 4 per day; L186,000); **Iaşi** (3hr.; 4 per day; L152,000); **Suceava** (1hr.; 9 per day; L43,000); **Timişoara** (12hr.; 3 per day; L330,000).

⊞ ⊠ ORIENTATION AND PRACTICAL INFORMATION. To reach the center, make a right on **Str. Ştefan cel Mare** in front of the train station and continue over the bridge. After crossing a small river, Ştefan cel Mare curves to the right as it intersects **Str. Mănăsteria Humorului** at **Piaţa Republicii** and becomes **Str. Bucovina.** Get tourist info at ⊠ **Dispecerat de Cazare,** at the end of Str. Câmpului on Str. Voroneţ, which offers car tours of local sights: monasteries, a pottery workshop, and a nearby underground salt mine that oddly features two chapels and a tennis court. From the train station, turn left on Str. Ştefan cel Mare and left again on Str. Câmpului. (☎23 38 63; fax 23 23 87. Tours US$30-35 per car per day. Rent **bikes** for a negotiable US$5-10 per day. Open Mar.-Nov. 11am-9pm; Dec.-Feb. ask at Vila Fabian across the street.) Buy **maps** of the monasteries at **Librăria Sedcomlibris,** Bd. Bucovina 5. (Open M-F 7:30am-7:30pm, Sa 9am-6pm.) The only **ATM** in town is at **Banca Commercială Romănă,** Piaţa Republicii 19, but agencies *(Schimb valutar)* on Str. Ştefan cel Mare and on Str. Mănăsteria Humorului will **exchange currency** for you. The **pharmacy,** Farmica Delia, is at Bd. Bucovina 4. (☎23 15 55. Open M-F 8am-9pm, Sa 8am-8pm, Su 8am-2pm.) The **telephone office** is at Bd. Bucovina 7. (Open daily 7am-10pm.) Send your epiphanies to friends from the **Internet Cafe,** Bd. Bucovina. (L20,000 per hr. Open 24hr.) The **post office** is at Str. Ştefan cel Mare 1. (Open M-F 8am-8pm.) **Postal Code:** 5900.

⊓ ⊠ ACCOMMODATIONS AND NIGHTLIFE. Gura Humorului is a portal to scores of comfortable, family-run villas in the sacred hills of Bukovina. The proprietors of ⊠ **Pensiunea Casa Ella ❶,** Str. Cetaţii 7 off Bd. Bucovina, make travelers feel at home with pleasant rooms, soft beds, and English-speaking hospitality—not to mention home-cooking. Almost everything served is produced in house, from the peas to jam to eggs. (☎23 29 61. Breakfast L60,000. Lunch or dinner L70,000-100,000. Singles L350,000; doubles L400,000.) A step up in luxury and in price is **Villa Fabian ❷,** Str. Câmpului 30, opposite Str. Voroneţ from Dispecerat de Cazare. (☎23 23 87. Breakfast included. Singles EUR€13; doubles EUR€25.) If you arrange a room through **Dispecerat de Cazare ❷** (see above), a guide will show you to your villa of choice. (July-Aug. doubles US$10-20; Sept.-June 20-30% less, except during holidays.) The staff can also arrange stays and meals at some monasteries. After a visit to the monasteries, reenter the world of sin at **VIP Dance Club,** Str. Sf. Gavril 12, left off Str. Mănăsteria Humorului. (Bar open M 5pm-midnight, Tu-Th 10am-midnight, F 10am-2am, Sa 5pm-4am, Su 5pm-2am. Disco open F 9pm-3am, Sa 9pm-4am, Su 9pm-2am. **Internet access** L20,000 per hr.)

MONASTERIES AND CONVENTS

VORONEŢ

Buses run from Gura Humorului (15min.; Sept. 15-June 15 M-F 3 per day; L10,000). On foot, take Cartierul Voroneţ; the monastery is a scenic 5km down the road. Open daily dawn-dusk. L30,000; students L25,000. Cameras L60,000.

The church was built in 1488 by Ştefan cel Mare, supposedly on the advice of St. Daniel, whose body now lies in the **camera moruintelor** (tomb chamber) of the church. The rich "Voroneţ blue" pigment, which changes shades depending on the humidity, earned Voroneţ Monastery the name "Sistine Chapel of the East," and is so distinctive that restoration of the entire building has been delayed while the paint is reproduced. As in other Moldavian monasteries, the west wall depicts the **Last Judgment,** but Voroneţ's is particularly spectacular; it is painted in five tiers and crossed by a river of fire from Hell—the damned wear the faces of Moldavia's enemies, Turks and Tatars. Animals, too, take part in the scene: they hand back pieces of human flesh ripped apart by beasts. Only the deer is empty-handed, as it represents innocence in Romanian folklore.

THE LOCAL STORY

ROMANIAN HUMOR

ust as every joke is based in truth, he humor of a nation provides an nsight into the character of its peo- ple. Romanians tell jokes in order to augh good-naturedly at their trou- bles, and, of course, to rib the guys 'rom Transylvania. The following inter- view was conducted by Let's Go Researcher Clay Kaminsky with Andrei Tanase and Irina Costache, wo university students from Walla- chia.

Q: I understand that you're an expert on Romanian jokes, Andrei.

A: I would like that to be true, yes.

Q: I've heard of Bula jokes, and I was old that Bula is supposed to repre- ent Ceauşescu. Is that right?

A: No. Bula was the character opposed to Ceauşescu. He represents the common people. Bula is some- body who is not very smart—virtually dumb—but always asks the right ques- ions. He's used in particular in jokes or younger kids.

Q: Is Bula a particular age?

A: I'd say his age ranges from 7-20. 've never heard a joke with an old Bula. It's always about Bula and his parents or Bula and the teachers...

Q: Would you like to tell a Romanian oke?

A: Sure. There is a very old joke that I still like. It's from the Ceauşescu era, when the Securitate [Secret Police] was listening to everybody, or every- body believed so. It takes place in a rain compartment, on a train from Constanţa to Bucharest. There were 6 people in the cabin, and 5 of them were telling political jokes.

(continued on next page)

PUTNA

Direct trains run a scenic route from Suceava to Putna, which lies 75km to the northwest (2½hr.; 5 per day; L31,000). The last train leaves Putna at 3:47pm. The monastery is 1km from the train station. Turn right as you exit the platform and then left at the 1st intersec- tion. Monastery open daily 6am-8pm. Free. Cameras L60,000. Museum open daily 9am-8pm. L30,000; stu- dents L5000. No cameras.

Ştefan cel Mare's first religious construction, the immaculately white 1469 Putna Monastery appears deceptively newer than its counterparts. Only one of the original towers has survived the ravages of fires, earthquakes, and attacks; not even the frescoes remain. There is something austere and beautiful about Putna's high, arching, blank white walls. The church contains the marble-canopied **tomb of Ştefan cel Mare** and his sons. He left Putna's location up to God; climbing a nearby hill to the left of the monas- tery (marked by a cross), he shot an arrow into the air. A slice of the oak that it struck is on display at the museum, as are a number of manuscripts, icons, and tapestries. On the way back, stop by the 14th-century **Dragoş Vodă** wooden church, one of the oldest reli- gious monuments in Bukovina. The church is on the main road, halfway to the railway station. Take your first right on the way back to town to climb **Dealul Crucii** (Hill of the Cross), Ştefan's shooting point, for fantastic views of the monastery, the town, and the sacred hills of Bukovina. Two hills are marked with crosses—Ştefan's is the smaller.

MOLDOVIŢA

From Gura Humorului take a train to Vama (20min.; L26,000), then to Vatra Moldoviţei (35min.; L30,000). Open daily 7am-9pm. L30,000, students L20,000. Cam- eras L60,000.

Moldoviţa is the largest of the painted monasteries and its frescoes are among the best preserved. Built by Petru Rareş in 1532 and painted in 1537, it por- trays the Last Judgment, Jesse's Tree, and the monu- mental Siege of Constantinople. As in the other monasteries, the first room, or *pronaos*, of the church is a calendar fresco. Each day of they year is represented by the corresponding saint, many in the act of being martyred. The monastery was closed from 1785 until 1945 and the north wall displays the neglect of the years. Elaborately carved grapevine columns painted with gold jut out from the iconosta- sis. The museum houses the wooden throne of Prince Petru and an 18th-century Bible in Old Church Slavonic given to the monastery by Catherine the Great of Russia. The monastery's small doors were designed to keep out mounted enemies.

NEAMȚ

Târgu Neamț is accessible by train via Pașcani from Gura Humorului (2hr.; 3 per day; L90,000) and Suceava (1hr.; 17 per day; L31,000). From the trains station, the bus station is a straight walk along Str. Cuza Vodă (15min.). Few buses go directly to the monastery (35min.; M-F 3 per day, Sa-Su 2 per day; L19,000), but any will stop at the intersection 3km from the monastery (L15,000). Monastery open daily 7:30am-9pm. L20,000, students L10,000. Aghiasmatar open daily 8am-8:30pm.

Built by Ștefan cel Mare between 1485 and 1497, Neamț is the largest monastery in Romania. The outside of the church is not painted, but actually decorative colored brick. Inside see an impressive golden iconostasis and the tomb of Ukrainian Starets Paisie, "St. Paise of Neamțu," who is credited with the renewal of Orthodox spiritual life. The monastery's museum displays spiritual and material artifacts, including old manuscripts, printing presses, and paintings by master Grigorescu. Outside the monastery walls the **Aghiasmatar** (Holy Water Tower), now a bookstore, contains beautiful frescoes in shades of orange and yellow. The ceiling depicts the Old and New Testaments; the walls tell the history of Moldavia.

SUCEVIȚA

Suceviţa lies 32km north of Moldovița (see above). Public transportation to Suceviţa is unavailable; inquire in Gura Humorului or in Suceava about alternative transportation. Open daily 8am-8pm. L30,000; students L15,000. Cameras L60,000.

Suceviţa, the newest of the monasteries at 406 years young, is fortified in the hills. Thick walls belie a time when Turkish conquerors forbade the construction of castles; during an attack the population would take refuge here. Its frescoed south wall presents a genealogy of Jesus, Moses receiving the ten commandments at Mt. Sinai, and a procession that includes the philosophers Pythagoras, Socrates, Plato, Aristotle, and Solon. Green paint predominates, mirroring the unique color of Bukovina's hills. Unlike the north faces of the other monasteries, Suceviţa's is well preserved, protected by the oversized roof. On the north wall, the spirits of the dead are depicted climbing a ladder of 30 rungs, each of which represents a virtue and a sin. The west wall remains unpainted—the artist fell from a scaffolding and his ghost supposedly prevents completion. A museum in the monastery displays religious artifacts, including a tapestry containing 10,000 pearls woven by the daughter of Ieemia Movila, the builder of the monastery.

The sixth, Bula, kept saying, "No, no! Stop it guys! Let's just get home." But the others just said, "Who's listening?" and so on. So Bula goes out into the corridor, talks with the steward, and asks him to bring six cups of coffee in five minutes. Then he comes back into the compartment and says, "Okay, guys. I'll prove it to you." he picks up the ashtray and says into it, "Six cups of coffee please." Everybody laughs, but in three minutes here comes the steward with the coffee. Everybody turns white, and there are no more political jokes the whole way to Bucharest. Finally, the train arrives in Bucharest, and the Securitate is waiting for them at the station. "You, you, you, you, and you, come with us. And you, Bula, stop playing stupid practical jokes!"

Q: Is there anything in Romanian jokes specific to the character of the Romanian people?

A: I think what is specific to us is that we mock the mishappenings of life. We laugh at trouble.

Q: Are there rivalries between the different regions of Romania?

A: Yes, definitely. Basically it's like this: the guys from Transylvania and those from near Timișoara are said to be slower...

Q: By whom?

A: By us in Wallachia! And the guys in Moldavia are said to be less fortunate, and the guys in Oltenia, from near Craiova, are considered to be moody... But also a little bit smarter than the rest. They're always getting the most out of any situation.

BLACK SEA COAST

The turbulent history of the land between the Danube and the Black Sea has made coastal Romania the country's most ethnically diverse region. Conquered by Turks in the 14th century, it remained part of the Ottoman Empire until 1877, when it was ceded to Romania (see **History,** p. 576). The stunning coastline stretches south, while the interior valleys and rocky hills hold Roman, Greek, and early Christian ruins, as well as some of Romania's best wines. Crowds packed the area in the past, but now prices are too steep for many Romanians, particularly during high season (July-Aug.). If you tire of resorts, take refuge to the north where the Danube meets the Black Sea.

DANUBE DELTA (DELTA DUNĂRII)

Here the mighty Danube, the 2850km river of nine countries and four capitals, pours itself into the Black Sea with savage beauty. The Delta, the youngest region of the European continent, is home to over 200 species of birds and 1150 species of plants, but very few humans. The region is so far off the tourist track that often it will often be only you and a great expanse where the sky blends into river and sea. To experience the Danube, visit **Sfântu Gheorghe,** a tiny fishing village on an island wedged between the Danube and the Black Sea. This is a one-church-town: there are only two public telephones, a lighthouse, about 300 houses, and a fantastic beach. The sand streets don't even have names.

Black Sea Coast of Romania

The Delta is accessible via **Tulcea,** the best base for exploring the Danube. **Trains** run from Tulcea to **Bucharest** (6hr.; 1 per day; L203,000) and **Constanţa** (4½hr.; 1 per day; L78,000). **Buses** connect to: **Bucharest** (4hr.; 14 per day; L150,000); **Constanţa** (1½hr.; 27 per day; L150,000); **Iaşi** (4¼hr.; 1 per day; L210,000). **Boats** depart from the Marina, behind the bus station, to **Sfântu Gheorghe** (5hr.; leaves Tu-F 1:30pm, returns W-F and Su 6am; L130,000). In **Sfântu Gheorghe,** the **telephone office** (open M-F 8am-noon and 5-9pm) and **post office** (open M-F 9am-1pm and 4:30-7pm) are in the same building. **Postal Code:** 8835. You may be offered **private rooms** at the dock; for a sure bet and some good home-cooking, stay with "Tanti" **Tina Cazacu ❶,** house #240, past the church. "Aunt" Tina offers comfortable, rustic rooms, and for meals serves whatever her husband catches during the day. Call ahead and she'll meet you at the dock. (☎54 68 22. Lunch and dinner included. L250,000 per person.) After a day at the beach, head to the town's only **bar**, near city hall. Drink vodka and play chess under the willow trees. (Open daily 7am-3am.)

CONSTANȚA ☎(0)241

Once the Greek port of Tomis, Constanța (con-STAN-tsa; pop. 500,000) has been the prize of various empires for over 2500 years. It is Romania's second largest city and a bustling commercial port and cultural center. Greek, Roman, and Byzantine ruins bear witness to the city's antiquity, while dozens of dormant mechanical cranes, reminders of a more recent period as a Communist-planned commercial port, still loom over the downtown. Beyond the tourist traps of Str. Ștefan cel Mare, old Tomis charms with its historical and religious monuments.

■❼ ORIENTATION AND PRACTICAL INFORMATION. Constanța, 225km east of Bucharest, lies north of most Black Sea resorts. **Trains** head to: **Bucharest** (2½-4½hr.; up to 15 per day in high season; L220,000); **Iași** (8hr.; 2 per day; L250,000); **Tulcea** (4½hr.; 2 per day; L78,000). Buy tickets in advance from June to August. Northbound buses leave from **Autogară Tomis Nord** (from the station go 5 stops on tram #100 or 9 stops on bus #43, then head left) to **Tulcea** (1½hr.; 27 per day; L70,000). To reach the center from the train station, take bus #5, 41, or 43 to the intersection of **Bd. Tomis** and **Bd. Ferdinand.** Buy tickets (L11,000, good for 2 trips) from kiosks that display *"Bileți RATC"* signs. Validate your ticket in one of the machines on the bus, or suffer a L500,000 fine. **Buses** and **microbuses** to Mangalia leave from the improvised parking lot next to the train station (20-40min.; every 5-10min.; L15,000-26,000). **Luggage storage** is available at the train station. (L25,000 per day. Open 24hr.) **Trans Danubius Tourist Office,** Bd. Ferdinand 36, provides **maps.** (☎61 58 36. Open M-Sa 9am-8pm, Su 9am-2pm.) **Banca Comercială Română,** Str. Traian 1, in Piața Ovidu, cashes AmEx **Traveler's Cheques** for 1.5% commission. (☎61 95 00. Open M-F 8am-2pm and 2:30-5:30pm, Sa 8:30am-12:30pm.) **Internet access** is available at **Sky Games,** Bd. Tomis 129. (☎61 47 65. L15,000 per hr., midnight-7am L55,000 for 7hr. Open 24hr.) **No. 2 Pharmacy,** Bd. Tomis 80, at the intersection with Bd. Ferdinand, is open 24hr. (☎61 19 83.) The **telephone office** (open daily 7am-10pm), on the corner of Bd. Tomis and Str. Ștefan cel Mare, shares a building with the **post office** (open M-F 7am-1pm and 1:30-8pm, Sa 7am-2pm). **Postal Code:** 8700.

❰❒ ACCOMMODATIONS AND FOOD. While it's difficult to find a cheap bed in Constanța, the quality of accommodations far surpasses that of other coastal towns. Locals greet you at the train station with offers for cheap **private rooms** ❶ (L150,000-300,000). It's nearly impossible to find a hotel room after July 1, so make reservations. For cheap lodging, seek out the hotels and campgrounds farther south in Neptune, Saturn, and Vama Veche. **Hotel Tinertului ❸,** Bd. Tomis 20-26, offers comfortable, if non-descript, doubles with private baths. Once in the center, follow Bd. Tomis toward Piața Ovidu to the right facing the sea. (☎61 35 90. Doubles L750,000.) The more luxurious **Hotel Sport ❸,** Str. Cuza Vodă 2, has pleasant singles and doubles with spectacular views a stone's throw from the beach. Take Bd. Ferdinand and turn left on Str. Cuza Vodă when you reach the water. (☎61 75 58. Breakfast included. Singles L750,000; doubles L930,000.)

Food kiosks, fast-food joints, and pizzerias line Str. Ştefan cel Mare. At the corner of Bd. Tomis and Bd. Ferdinand, the **Grand supermarket** has it all, all the time. (Open 24hr.) **Aspendos ❶**, Bd. Tomis 48, serves some of the best Turkish cuisine on the coast. (☎61 76 12. Entrees L45,000-120,000. Open daily 8am-last customer.) To reach the **Irish Pub ❷**, Str. Ştefan cel Mare 1, off Str. Mircea cel Batrân, follow the directions to Hotel Sport (see above) but continue past the hotel; the pub is on a terrace overlooking the beach. Many locals come here to toss back a few brews (L40,000-100,000) or to taste beef cooked in Guinness for L95,000. (☎55 04 00; www.irishpub.ro. Open daily 10am-5pm.) For the best seafood in town, head down to **On Plonge ❶**, in the Marina. With the sea to your left, follow the coast past the fountain and hang a left into the Marina. Have fish or mussels fresh from the Black Sea. (Entrees L30,000-88,000. Open daily 10:30am-midnight.)

◙ ♫ SIGHTS AND ENTERTAINMENT. With your back to the train station, turn right on Bd. Tomis to reach the center of **Old Tomis,** the Old Town. Continue along Bd. Tomis, following it until it curves left and ends in Piaţa Ovidu, to reach the **Statue of Ovid** (see **The Arts,** p. 579), who penned some of his most famous poems while in exile here. He was ostensibly exiled for writing *The Art of Love*, although the real reason was more likely his practice of that art with Emperor Augustus's daughter. The epitaph on the statue is Ovid's own verse: "Here lies Ovid. The singer of delicate loves, killed by his own talent. Oh, passerby, if you have ever loved, pray for him to rest in peace." The poet's actual resting place is not under the statue, but somewhere in the Black Sea. The nearby **Museum of National and Archaeological History** (Muzeul de Istorie Naţională şi Arheologie), Piaţa Ovidu 2, displays hundreds of ancient Greek and Roman artifacts and recounts the 19th-century War of Independence against Turkey. (See **History,** p. 576. ☎61 87 63. Open in summer daily 9am-8pm; off-season W-Su 9am-5pm. L20,000, students L10,000. English pictorial guide L6500.) An excavated Roman port with the **world's largest floor mosaic** is hidden behind the Roman columns to the right of the museum. The mosaic covers the topmost of four large terraces cut in the steep coastline. Although incomplete and somewhat faded, the 700 square meters of mosaic are still quite impressive. (English placards. Open in summer daily 9am-8pm; off-season W-Su 9am-5pm. L20,000, students L10,000.)

The **mosque** on Str. Arhiepiscopiei, is one of the few remaining vestiges of Turkish domination. Dating originally from 1823 and rebuilt in 1910 by Romanian King Carol I, this mosque combines Byzantine, Romanian, and Turkish architectural elements. On its floor lies one of the world's largest **Oriental carpets** (144 sq. meters), which was woven in the 18th century in Turkey and presented as a gift to the mosque by the Sultan himself. Don't step on the carpets—they are for kneeling during prayer. The 47m minaret provides a wonderful view of the city and coastline. Women must cover their heads before entering the mosque. (Open June-Sept. daily 9:30am-9:30pm; Oct.-May during services only. L15,000, students L7500.) The **Naval History Museum** (Muzeul Marinei Române), Str. Traian 53, dazzles with its stockpile of instruments, uniforms, and models. The museum's most precious piece is a 700-year-old trunk boat, carved from a single tree. (☎61 90 35. Open Tu-Su 10am-6pm. L20,000.) The **archaeological park** opposite Trans Danubius offers respite among Greek amphorae and Roman sarcophagi. The **Art Museum,** Bd. Tomis 82/84, near the intersection of Bd. Tomis and Bd. Fedinand, is surprisingly good. The collection includes works by scores of famous Romanian artists. (Open in summer daily 9am-8pm; off-season W-Su 9am-5pm. L20,000, students L10,000.)

BLACK SEA RESORTS

The coast to the south of Constanţa is lined with sandy beaches and 1970s revival tourist resorts. Costineşti is especially popular with young Romanians, while Neptun has the most luxurious amenities. **Eforie Nord** and **Eforie Sud** are family destinations. Resorts are open during the high season (late June through early Sept.) and on May 1, a school holiday. The peak of high season, July 1 through August 15, brings heavy crowds and high prices. Reserve rooms well in advance.

COSTINEŞTI

Costineşti, south of the Efories, is the coastal hot spot. Wonderfully crowded with young Romanians, it offers loud fun and cheap prices. Hot running water is not a given; be sure to ask when it's running at your hotel or villa. Ask in Constanţa whether the **bus** stops in Costineşti or merely passes by to avoid a 4km hike from the regular bus stop. The **train** drops you closer to town; get off at "Costineşti Tabără" and circle right around the lake. Trains go to **Bucharest** (4½hr., 14 per day, L256,000) via **Constanţa** (40min., L26,000). A **currency exchange** in the telephone office changes cash for no commission. (Open daily 9:30am-8pm.) **Albatros ❷** offers villa rooms near the sea with a fridge, a shower, and 24hr. hot water. From the bus stop, walk toward the beach and turn right at the water. Reception is on the second alley back from the beach with "Albatros" written on the wall. (June 30-July 14 and Aug. 15-Sept. 1 doubles L480,000; July 15-Aug. 14 L600,000.) **Hotel Azur ❶**, a little farther along with the beach on your left, offers comfortable, modern doubles and triples with private baths and 24hr. hot water. (☎73 40 14. L190,000-450,000 per person.) **Cheap meals ❶** abound near the train station, on the main street, and on terraces overlooking the coast. At night, follow the main street to **Disco Ring,** where Romanian youth boogie to an eclectic mix of music. (Open daily noon-6pm and 9pm-6am. Cover L20,000 after 9pm.) Renting a **boat** for a spin around the lake is a popular evening activity. (L50,000 per hr.)

MANGALIA

As the beginning and end of all resort minibus routes, Mangalia is an excellent base from which to explore the Southern coast. Beyond the reach of most tourists, Mangalia beaches are pristine, and the more adventurous beach bums can venture far away from civilization by bike or foot.

From in front of the Mangalia train station, minibuses go to 2 Mai (10min., every 15min. from 5:30am-8:10pm in summer, L10,000) and Vama Veche (15min., every 20min. from 6am-7pm in summer, L11,000). While at the beach, **store luggage** at the train station (L25,000). The **post office** (open M-F 7am-8pm, Sa 9am-5pm), to the left when facing the train station past the archaeology museum and through the traffic circle, has **telephones** (open daily 7am-8pm). An **ATM** stands on the left side of Casa Rosemarie (see below). With keys and *cazare* signs in hand, locals swarm backpackers in front of the train station in Mangalia, offering inexpensive **private rooms ❶** (L300,000 per person). Another option is to camp in a nearby town. Back in Mangalia at **Casa Rosemarie ❶**, you can choose from a surprising variety of salads (L40,000-70,000) inside an Art Deco dining area. To get there, walk 1km to the left when facing the train station past the archaeology museum. (English menu available. Open daily 10am-11pm.) At the north end of 2 Mai's beach, industrial cranes overlook a **campground ❶** (☎091 269 417; L35,000). At the beach's south end you can camp for free and rid yourself of tan lines at the nude beach. At Vama Veche, camp for free on the beach or arrange **private rooms** with **Dispecerat de Cazare ❶**. (☎0722 889 087 or 041 743 870; www.vamaveсheholidays.ro. Open June-Sept. L200,000-1,000,000.)

NEPTUN

Neptun, once home to Ceaușescu's summer villa, is the shining star of Romania—this well-known resort boasts carriage rides and the best food on the coast. The pristine beach is on the street to the left facing the minibus stop Complexul Comercial. At the beach, ride an **oversized rubber banana** (L75,000 for 15min.), or explore the area on a **two-person bike** (L30,000 for 30min.; rent from road leading to beach; open daily 10am-10pm) or **moped** (250,000 for 1hr., 300m to the right when facing Hotel Romanta).

Minibuses from Constanța (25min.; every 20min.; L40,000) travel to Neptun from the lot to the left when facing the train station. Mangalia also has a fleet of minibuses that service the resort from stops marked by blue-and-white signs that read "Statie, Mangalia-Olimp." While Neptun has several stops, get off at Complexul Comercial Neptun (with the McDonald's) for the center. Find an **ATM** and exchange **traveler's checks** at **Banka Comerciala Romana,** opposite Complexul Comercial. (☎ 73 19 34. 1.5% commission plus 2% per check, min. US$5. Open M-F 8:30am-noon and 12:30-5pm, Sa 8:30am-noon.) The Neptun **post office** (open M-Sa 7am-8pm, Su 9am-5pm) has **telephones** (open daily 7am-10pm) and is opposite Compexul Comercial. **Internet access** is available in Complexul Comercial, to the left when facing McDonald's (L30,000 per hr. Open 24hr.).

The **Dispecerat de Cazare ❸,** next to the Levent Market, helps find rooms for prices lower than those of hotels. Call ahead for reservations. (☎ 70 13 00. Hotel singles US$16.50-24. 10% commission. Open May-Sept. 24hr.) **Hotel Apollo ❹,** 300m to the left of Complexul Comercial, is a standard two-star tower hotel with clean doubles. Call ahead for reservations. (☎ 70 10 16. Breakfast included. Reception 24hr. Check-out noon. Singles L1,040,000; doubles L1,300,000.) **Campe Zodiac ❶,** between Jupiter and Neptun just before the right turn to Neptun, is one of the cleanest campgrounds in the area, with new bathroom facilities, electricity, and barbeque grills. (☎ 75 31 39 or 73 14 04. L30,000 per person. Tourist tax L50,000.) **Disco Why Not,** in the same shopping complex as Dispecerat da Cazare (see above), attracts many Romanians and tourists. (Open daily 10pm-4am. Cover L20,000.)

RUSSIA
(РОССИЯ)

RUBLES

AUS$1 = 17.21R	1R = AUS$0.58
CDN$1 = 20.15R	1R = CDN$0.50
EUR€1 = 30.86R	1R = EUR€0.32
NZ$1 = 14.69R	1R = NZ$0.68
UK£1 = 48.62R	1R = UK£0.21
US$1 = 31.36R	1R = US$0.32
ZAR1 = 2.95R	1R = ZAR3.39

Ten years after the fall of communism, vast Russia stumbles forward without clear direction. Vaguely repentant former Communists run the state, while impoverished, outspoken pensioners long for a rosy-tinted Soviet past. Heedless of the failing provinces, cosmopolitan Moscow gobbles down hyper-capitalism, while majestic St. Petersburg struggles not to become a ghost capital. Russia is in many ways the ideal destination for a budget traveler—inexpensive and well served by public transportation, with hundreds of monasteries, kremlins, and churches. It can be a bureaucratic nightmare, but it can also offer a mixture of opulent tsarist palaces, fossilized Soviet edifices, and newfound symbols of prestige found nowhere else on Earth.

RUSSIA AT A GLANCE

OFFICIAL NAME: Russian Federation

CAPITAL: Moscow (pop. 8.4 million)

POPULATION: 146 million (Russian 81.5%, Tatar 3.8%, Ukrainian 3%, Chuvash 1.2%, Bashkir 0.9%, Belorussian 0.8%, Moldovan 0.7%, other 8.1%)

LANGUAGE: Russian

CURRENCY: 1 ruble (R) = 100 kopeks

RELIGION: 74% unaffiliated, 16% Russian Orthodox, 10% Muslim

LAND AREA: 17,075,200km²

CLIMATE: Temperate to subarctic

GEOGRAPHY: Western plains, Ural Mountains, Siberian plateau

BORDERS: Belarus, China, Estonia, Latvia, Lithuania, Mongolia, Poland, Ukraine, others

ECONOMY: 59% Services, 34% Industry, 7% Agriculture

GDP: US$7000 per capita

COUNTRY CODE: 7

INTERNATIONAL DIALING PREFIX: 810

HISTORY

EARLY SETTLERS. The earliest recorded settlers of European Russia were the Scandinavian **Varangians**, or **Rus**, in the 9th century. Over the course of the 10th century one Varangian clan, led by **Prince Svyatoslav**, gained power over the others, establishing a new center of power in **Kyiv**. Svyatoslav's son **Volodymyr the Great**, however, laid the foundations of **Kyivan Rus** by converting to **Orthodox Christianity** in

Western Russia

AD 988. Following the death of Volodymyr in 1015, the Kyivan state was increasingly strained by clan wars and declining trade.

TARTAR CONTROL. European Russia was in no position to resist the march of the Mongol **Golden Horde,** which arrived in 1223. Despite numerous myths to the contrary, the Mongol conquest was not particularly violent and most of the subjected city-states were able to carry on much as before. Mongol influence on the culture of the Varangian and East Slavic tribes was minimal, but this period saw the emergence of **Muscovy** (today's Moscow) as a commercial center and increasing contact with Western and Central Europe. Eventually the Mongol Khanate fell victim to wars between competing local rulers, permitting Muscovy, **Lithuania, Novgorod,** and the **Volga Bulgar Region** (later Kazan) to become powerful states.

IVANS AND BORIS AND BOYARS, OH MY! Duke of Muscovy **Ivan III** (1462-1505) filled the void left by the departure of the Mongols and began a drive to unify all East Slavic lands—parts of present-day Belarus, Russia, and Ukraine—under his rule. His grandson **Ivan IV (the Terrible)** was the first ruler to take the title "tsar." Ivan's second son, **Fyodor I,** proved too weak to rule alone; his brother-in-law **Boris Godunov** secretly ruled in his stead. When Fyodor died childless in 1598, Boris became tsar. Conspiring against Godunov, the Russian **boyars** (nobles) brought forward a pretender named Dmitry who claimed Fyodor I had been his father. After Godunov's mysterious death, the *boyars* crowned this **"False Dmitry"** tsar. Unprecedented instability followed until **Mikhail Romanov** ascended to the throne in 1613, ushering in the dynasty that ruled until the Bolshevik Revolution of 1917.

PETER THE (DEBATABLY) GREAT. Mikhail's grandson **Peter the Great,** whose reign began in 1682, dragged Russia reluctantly westward, inciting the East-West schizophrenia that has plagued its national identity ever since. Peter created his own **Westernized** elite—even forcing Russian nobles to shave off their cherished beards—and built European-style St. Petersburg in the middle of a Finnish swamp. He killed hundreds of thousands of workers in the process, hanged the opposition, traipsed around Europe causing even more damage than the average *Let's Go* traveler, and left Russia with a statue and monument surplus when he died in 1725.

ENLIGHTENED ABSOLUTISM. The nobility gained the political upper hand until the reign of **Catherine the Great** (1762-96). The meek, homely daughter of an impoverished Prussian aristocrat, Catherine came to Russia to marry heir to the throne **Peter III,** whom she promptly overthrew. Catherine extended the empire and partook of certain modish **Enlightenment** trends, but also increased landowners' power over their serfs. This move provoked the 1773 **Pugachov rebellion,** a peasant revolt that Catherine quickly crushed.

TO NAPOLEON: FROM RUSSIA, WITH LOVE. Napoleon rose to power in France and after quickly conquering Western Europe set his eyes on Russia. Napoleon's invasion foundered as the Russians burnt their crops and villages in retreat, leaving the French to face the harsh winter without supplies and wearing summer uniforms. **Victory** over the little Corsican, who retreated in disgrace, brought prestige and new contact with the rest of Europe, but led to internal strife. Russian officers returning from the West, inspired by the Republican ideals of France, attempted a coup on December 14, 1825. Some of these **Decembrists** were hanged, others were exiled to Siberia. Russia's loss to the West in the **Crimean War** (1853-1856) spurred reforms that included the **emancipation of the serfs** in 1861. **Alexander II,** "The Great Emancipator," was assassinated shortly thereafter.

WAR AND PEACE... The famine, peasant unrest, terrorism, and strikes of the late 1800s culminated in the failed **1905 Revolution.** Coupled with the humiliating loss of the Russo-Japanese War, the uprising forced **Tsar Nicholas II** to establish a legislative body, the **Duma,** and make vague attempts to address the demands of his people. **World War I,** stalemate with the Duma, and fermenting revolution led him to abdicate the throne in March 1917. Vladimir Ilyich Ulyanov, a.k.a. **Lenin,** leader of the Bolsheviks, steered the coup of October 1917; a few well-placed words to **Aleksandr Kerensky,** leader of the provisional government, and a menacing ring around the Winter Palace turned the nation Red. A **Civil War** followed the October Revolution, but the Communists won and the **Union of Soviet Socialist Republics (USSR)** was established in 1922. Lenin died soon thereafter. Ioseb Dzhugashvili, a.k.a. **Joseph Stalin,** emerged triumphant from the infighting that followed Lenin's death and proceeded to eliminate his rivals in the **Great Purges,** killing millions of Russians and imprisoning countless others. Stalin forced **collectivization** of Soviet farms and filled Siberian **gulags** (labor camps) with "political" prisoners based on regional quotas. Priority was given to national defense and heavy industry, which led to shortages of consumer goods.

...OR NOT. Stalin was able to find an ally only in **Adolf Hitler,** with whom he concluded the **Nazi-Soviet Non-Aggression Pact**—more of a stalling tactic than an actual alliance—in August 1939. Later that year the USSR helped Germany in its attack on Poland, and the Red Army subsequently occupied the Baltics. Having executed most of his top generals in the Purges, Stalin brought the USSR into **World War II** unprepared when the Nazi-Soviet alliance finally soured. Yet Hitler, who didn't learn from Napoleon's mistakes, invaded Russia and was defeated by the long winter combined with the tactics of military commander **Georgy Zhukov.** The **Battle of Stalingrad** (today **Volgograd**), in which 1.1 million Russian troops are thought to have been killed, broke the German advance and turned the tide of the war on the Eastern Front. In 1945, the Soviets took **Berlin** and gained status as a postwar superpower. Stalin, feeling abandoned by the Allies—as Russia had been left to defend the Eastern Front on its own and suffered more casualties than all other participating nations combined—reneged on previous agreements made at the **Yalta Conference** and refused to allow free elections in the nations of Eastern Europe. The USSR left its victorious Red Army in Eastern Europe as far west as East Germany, and the **Iron Curtain** descended on the continent.

I WANT MY KGB. In 1949, the Soviet Union formed the Council for Mutual Economic Assistance, or **COMECON,** which reduced the Eastern European nations to satellites of the Party's headquarters in Moscow. After Stalin's death in 1953, **Nikita Khrushchev** emerged as the new leader of the Soviet Union. In 1955 the **Warsaw Pact** drew Eastern Europe into a military alliance with the USSR to counterbalance **NATO** in the West. In the 1956 **"Secret Speech,"** Khrushchev denounced the terrors of the Stalinist period. He also inaugurated the space race with the US, putting the 84-kilogram **Sputnik,** the first satellite, into orbit in 1957. A brief political and cultural **"thaw"** followed, lasting until 1964, when Khrushchev was ousted by **Leonid Brezhnev.** The Brezhnev regime remained in power until 1983, overseeing a period of economic stagnation and political repression. Internal dissent was quashed as well, as in the case of exiled physicist **Andrei Sakharov,** the reluctant father of the Soviet H-Bomb, who had become a staunch advocate of disarmament. The brutal regimes of **Yuri Andropov** and **Konstantin Chernenko** followed Brezhnev in quick succession. As the decline of the aging elite consumed political circles, the army became frustrated with its losses in the war against the anti-communist Muslim guerillas in **Afghanistan.** The geriatric regime finally gave way to 56-year-old firebrand **Mikhail Gorbachev** in 1985. Gorbachev's political and economic reforms were aimed at helping the country regain superpower status. Reform began slowly, with **glasnost** (openness) and **perestroika** (rebuilding). The state gradually turned into a bewildering hodgepodge of near-anarchy, economic crisis, and cynicism. Gorbachev became the architect of his own demise; despite his popularity abroad (and the 1990 **Nobel Peace Prize**), discontent with his reforms and a failed right-wing coup in August 1991 led to his resignation and the **dissolution of the Soviet Union** on Christmas Day, 1991.

THE PARTY IS OVER. With the collapse of the USSR, **Boris Yeltsin,** named President of the Russian Republic in June 1991, assumed power. Most of the former Soviet republics nominally banded together in the **Commonwealth of Independent States (CIS),** but the confederation has since become increasingly meaningless in all but the economic sense as most republics—with the exception of Belarus, which is attempting to reunify with Russia (see **Belarus: Today,** p. 625)—have drifted farther along their own trajectories.

RUSSIA

TODAY

The constitution ratified in December 1993 gave the president sweeping powers, but Yeltsin's tenure quickly exposed the shortcomings of this provision. Those economic policies he did attempt came crashing down in August 1998, when the pyramid schemes Russia had played with its natural resources and bond sales were halted abruptly. The ruble was devalued in an attempt to lessen the country's foreign debt. As a result, **inflation** skyrocketed, hitting 84% by the end of 1998. Inadequate as he frequently was, Yeltsin did have the good sense to resign on January 1, 2000, installing ex-KGB official **Vladimir Putin** as acting President. Yeltsin's peaceful departure marked the first-ever voluntary transfer of power by a Russian leader—Soviet leaders had maintained the tsarist tradition of either being forced from office or leaving in a casket. Like his predecessor, Putin has combined the ideas of a democrat with the methods of an autocrat, although with greater sobriety and broader political support than Yeltsin ever displayed. Since his victory in the 2000 election, Putin has displayed political strength, persuading the Duma to ratify the **START II** disarmament treaty and to confirm his reformist Prime Minister, **Mikhail Kasyanov,** by an overwhelming majority. While Putin's charm and reformist pledges have earned him the adulation of the media, many in the West have questioned his often-brutal prosecution of the war in **Chechnya,** a war which has caused his domestic approval ratings to skyrocket. But don't dust off your CCCP flag yet. In June 2002, Russia's economy officially achieved **open market** status.

PEOPLE AND CULTURE

LANGUAGE AND RELIGION

Take time to familiarize yourself with the **Cyrillic** alphabet. It's not as difficult as it looks and it will make getting around much easier. Once you get the hang of the alphabet, you can pronounce just about any Russian word, though you will probably sound like an idiot. Although more and more people are speaking **English** in Russia, come equipped with at least a few helpful Russian phrases. Note that улица (ulitsa; abbreviated ul./ул.) means "street," проспект (prospekt; pr./пр.) means "avenue," площадь (ploshchad; pl./пл.) means "square," and бульвар (bulvar; bul./бул.) is "boulevard." Кремль (kreml; fortress); рынок (rynok; market square); гостиница (gostinitsa; hotel); собор (sobor; cathedral); and церков (tserkov; church) are also good words to know.

The **atheist** program of the Communists discouraged the open expression of religious faith. But with the fall of the USSR, **Russian Orthodoxy,** headed by **Patriarch Aleksei II,** has emerged from hiding and is now winning an increasing number of converts. The Russian state has favored the Orthodox Church by making it difficult for other religious groups, such as **Roman Catholics,** to own property or worship in public. Adherents to Orthodoxy are predominantly Slavic. Most Turkish groups in Russia are **Muslim,** and the Mongolian-speaking groups, such as the **Buryat,** are **Buddhist.** For a phrasebook and glossary, see **Glossary: Russian,** p. 889.

FOOD AND DRINK

RUSSIA	❶	❷	❸	❹	❺
FOOD	under 50R	50-120R	121-300R	301-500R	over 500R

Russian cuisine is a medley of dishes both delectable and unpleasant; tasty *borscht* (beet soup) can come in the same meal as *salo* (pig fat). The largest meal of the day, *obed* (обед; **lunch**), is eaten at midday and includes: *salat* (салат; salad),

RUSSIA

usually cucumbers and tomatoes or beets and potatoes with mayonnaise or sour cream; *sup* (суп; soup); and *kuritsa* (курица; chicken) or *myaso* (мясо; meat), often called *kotlyety* (котлеты; cutlets) or *bifshteaks* (бифштекс; beefsteaks). Ordering a number of *zakuski* (закуски; small **appetizers**) instead of a main dish can save money. **Dessert** includes *morozhenoye* (мороженое; ice cream) or *tort* (торт; cake) with *cofe* (кофе; coffee) or *chai* (чай; tea), which Russians will drink at the slightest provocation. On the streets, you'll see a lot of *shashlyki* (шашлыки; barbecued meat on a stick) and *kvas* (квас), a slightly alcoholic dark-brown drink. Kiosks often carry **alcohol;** imported cans of beer are safe (though warm), but be wary of Russian labels—you have no way of knowing what's really in the bottle. *Zolotoye koltso, Russkaya,* and *Zubrovka* are the best **vodkas;** the much-touted *Stolichnaya* is mostly made for export. Among local **beers**, *Baltika* (Балтика; numbered 1 through 7 according to brew and alcohol content) is the most popular and arguably the best. *Baltika* 1 is the weakest (10.5%), *Baltika* 7 the strongest (14%). *Baltikas* 4 and 6 are dark; the rest are lagers. Numbers 3 and 4 are the most popular; 7 is extreme.

CUSTOMS AND ETIQUETTE

Decades of collective lifestyle forced people very close together; as a result, the notion of **personal space** is almost nonexistent in Russia. People pack tightly in lines and on buses, tolerating the discomfort with stoic patience. When boarding a bus, tram, or Metro car, forceful shoving is required. On **public transportation,** it's polite for women to give their seats to elderly or pregnant women and women with children. For men, it's gallant to yield seats to all women. In St. Petersburg and Moscow (but nowhere else) a 5-10% **tip** is becoming customary. Most establish-ments, even train ticket offices and restaurants, close for a **lunch break** sometime between noon and 3pm. Places tend to close at least 30 minutes earlier than they claim, if they choose to open at all. "24hr." stores often take a lunch or "technical" break and one day off each week. Visiting a museum in **shorts** and **sandals** is regarded as disrespectful. Many locals say that criminals spot foreigners by their sloppy appearances, so dress up and don't smile when stared at.

THE ARTS

LITERATURE. Ever since Catherine the Great exiled **Alexander Radishchev,** whose *Journey from St. Petersburg to Moscow* had documented the dehumanizing nature of serfdom, to Siberia, literature and politics in Russia have been inextrica-bly bound together. The country's most beloved literary figure, **Aleksandr Pushkin,** was sympathetic to the Decembrist revolution but ultimately chose aesthetics over politics. His novel in verse, *Eugene Onegin,* was a biting take on the poet's own earlier Romanticism. The 1840s saw a turn, under the goading of Westernizer critic **Vissarion Belinsky,** to the realism and social awareness that would produce the masterpieces of Russian literature. While the absurdist works of **Nikolai Gogol** were hardly realist, they were read as masterful social commentary in his own time; *Government Inspector* exposed the corruption of Russian society, as did his great novel *Dead Souls.* **Fyodor Dostoyevsky's** penetrating psychological novels, such as *Crime and Punishment* (see **Crime and Punishment,** below) and *The Brothers Karamazov,* remain classics in Russia and abroad. The same can be said for the sweeping epics of **Leo (Lev) Tolstoy,** including *Anna Karenina* and *War and Peace.* The 1890s saw the rise of **Maxim Gorky,** whose "tramp period" fic-tions explored the dregs of Russian society and foreshadowed his position as the literary figurehead of the Bolshevik Revolution. Realism's last great voice belonged to **Anton Chekhov,** whose dramas and short stories distilled the power of his verbose predecessors.

With the beginning of the 20th century, literature entered its **Silver Age,** with many poets emulating French symbolism. **Aleksandr Blok** tinted his verse with mystic and apocalyptic hues. Symbolism was soon challenged, however, by the **Acmeist** movement, which prized elegance and clarity over the metaphysical vagueness of the Symbolists. Among the members of the Acmeist moment, **Anna Akhmatova** became known for her haunting, melancholic love verses, and later for *Requiem,* her memorial to the victims of Stalin's purges. Competing with the Acmeists, the **Futurists** embraced industrialization and technology in their verse, with such poets as **Vladimir Mayakovsky** urging that Pushkin be "thrown from the steamship of modernity" as a superfluous relic of the past.

In the 1920s the state mandated **Socialist Realism,** a coerced glorification of international socialism. Along with political opponents, the regime targeted the intelligentsia in the Great Purges. **Boris Pasternak** was internally exiled for his Civil War epic *Doctor Zhivago.* Acmeist poet **Osip Mandelstam,** perhaps the greatest Russian poet of the 20th century, composed many of his works in exile before dying in a Siberian *gulag.* The political "thaw" of the early 1960s allowed **Joseph Brodsky's** verse and **Alexander Solzhenitsyn's** novel *One Day in the Life of Ivan Denisovich,* detailing life in a labor camp, to emerge. The rise of Leonid Brezhnev, however, plunged the arts into an ice age from which they have yet to fully recover.

MUSIC. Mikhail Glinka began the modern Russian musical tradition, fusing folk melodies with the European harmonic system. His ballets *A Life for the Tsar* (1836) and the Pushkin-inspired *Ruslan and Lyudmila* (1842) remain in the repertoire of opera companies today. **Pyotr Tchaikovsky,** closest to Belinsky's Western-minded school, tempered native melodies with European restraint. His *Piano Concerto No. 1 in B Flat Minor* (1874-5) and *Symphony No. 6 "Pathetique"* (1893) are highly regarded and widely performed, as are his ballets, including *The Nutcracker* (1892). The work of **Nikolai Rimsky-Korsakov,** best known for the symphonic suite *Scheherazade* (1888), in contrast, was bombastically Slavophilic. The early 20th century brought revolutionary ferment and artistic experimentation. This period saw the collaboration of **Igor Stravinsky** and **Sergei Diaghilev,** impresario of the Paris-based **Ballets Russes.** It was for Diaghilev's company that Stravinsky wrote his three greatest ballets: *The Firebird* (1910), *Petrushka* (1911), and *The Rite of Spring* (1913). All three are now considered masterpieces, but *The Rite of Spring* represented such a departure—it is frequently used to mark the birth of the modern era due to its radical, unresolved dissonances—that it caused a riot in the theater following its Paris premiere. The revolution of 1917 imposed ideological restrictions on such great composers as **Dmitri Shostakovich.** Despite repeated falls from official favor, Shostakovich maintained his stylistic integrity, often satirizing the unwitting Soviet authorities in his famous symphonies. His contemporary **Sergei Prokofiev** enjoyed more consistent official favor, composing a variety of excellent pieces from the children's piece *Peter and the Wolf* (1936) to symphonies, concertos, and films scores for Eisenstein's films. Virtuoso pianist and composer **Sergei Rachmaninov** fused the traditional romanticism of the Westernizer school with a unique lyricism, producing such lasting works as his four piano concerti and *Rhapsody on a Theme of Paganini* (1934).

ARCHITECTURE, FINE ARTS, AND FILM. Even if you don't know its name, **St. Basil's Cathedral** (the pretty onion domed building; see **Moscow,** p. 646) defines the splendor that is Russian architecture. This style of architecture dates back to the 11th century, when church construction began to follow a general

RUSSIA

design: a Greek cross, with all four arms equal in length, high walls with almost no openings, a sharply sloped roof, and a plethora of **domes** to top it all off. The period following the revolution saw the **fine arts** gain some of the prominence Russian music and literature had long enjoyed, with artists **Wassily Kandinsky, Marc Chagall,** and **Natalya Goncharova** gaining international acclaim. Kandinsky, of Russian and Mongolian ancestry, is acknowledged as one of the pioneers of **Abstraction;** he was convinced as a child that each color had its own "internal life." Soviet-period artists, confined by the strictures of Socialist Realism, were limited to painting canvases with such bland titles as "The Tractor Drivers' Supper." The young Soviet Union quickly produced **Sergei Eisenstein,** considered by some the greatest **filmmaker** ever to live. Eisenstein, who began his career as a theatrical costume and set designer, revolutionized film theory by juxtaposing symbolic images to increase the psychological effect of his films.

CURRENT SCENE

With the collapse of the Soviet Union, Russia has seen a rebirth of many starving, but satisfied artists. Modern architecture has been assuming a more traditional Russian folk character. Post-modern writers like **Dmitry Prigov, Victor Pelevin,** and **Lev Rubenstein** can finally publish freely, but the fabric of their world has changed little. Russian filmmakers all agree that money has been a large problem in the production of new cinematic masterpieces, and an esteemed look at nature and post-communist life continues to dominate the few plots.

HOLIDAYS AND FESTIVALS

NATIONAL HOLIDAYS IN 2003	
January 1-2 New Year's Day	**May 1-2** Labor Day
January 7 Orthodox Christmas	**May 9** Victory Day
February 23 Defenders of the Motherland Day	**June 12** Independence Day
March 8 International Women's Day	**November 7** Day of Accord and Reconciliation
May 5 Easter	**December 12** Constitution Day

WHITE NIGHTS. From June 21 to July 11, St. Petersburg and Moscow celebrate the beautiful sun-filled nights with musical performances, concerts, fireworks, and other festive goodies.

MASLYANITSA. "Butter" is a traditional carnival in the spring just before Lent, during which people cook a slew of delectable dishes as a farewell to winter.

ADDITIONAL RESOURCES

GENERAL HISTORY

The Icon and the Axe, by James Billington (1966). A classic study of Russian culture.

A People's Tragedy, by Orlando Figes (1996). An amazing overview of the late imperial period, the Russian revolution, and the Civil War.

The Russian Revolution, by Richard Pipes (1990). Remains the authoritative history of the revolutionary era by the foremost authority on Russian history.

FICTION AND NONFICTION

Casino Moscow, by Matthew Brzezinski (2002). A *Wall Street Journal* reporter's fast-paced account of his days covering the wild and wooly reality of newly-capitalist Russia.

The Gulag Archipelago, by Alexsandr Solzhenitsyn (1974). A morally forceful account of Stalinism.

Lectures on Russian Literature, by Vladimir Nabokov (1981). The best introduction to 19th-century Russian literature.

Lenin's Tomb and **Resurrection,** both by David Remnic (1993 and 1997). Chronicles the fall of the Soviet Union and post-Soviet life.

Russian Thinkers, by Isaiah Berlin (1978). The most profound Western book on 19th-century Russian thought.

RUSSIA ESSENTIALS

ENTRANCE REQUIREMENTS
Passport: Required of all travelers.
Visa: Required of all travelers.
Letter of Invitation: Required of all travelers.
Inoculations: HIV test required for stays of 3 months or more. Recommended up-to-date on MMR (measles, mumps, and rubella), DTaP (diphtheria), Polio booster, Typhoid, Tetanus, Hepatitis A, and Hepatitis B.
Work Permit: Required of all foreigners planning to work in Russia.
International Driving Permit: Required of all those planning to drive.

DOCUMENTS AND FORMALITIES

EMBASSIES AND CONSULATES

Embassies of other countries in Russia are all in Moscow (see p. 634). Russia's embassies and consulates abroad include:

Australia: 78 Canberra Ave., Griffith, ACT 2603 (☎06 295 9033; fax 295 1847). Consulate: 7-9 Fullerton Street, Woollahra, NSW 2025 (☎06 326 1866; fax 327 5065).

Canada: 285 Charlotte St., Ottawa, ON K1N 8L5 (☎613-235-4341, visa info 236-7220; fax 236-6342). **Consulate:** 3655 Ave du Musee, Montreal, Quebec, H3G 2EI (☎514-843-5901; fax 542-2012).

Ireland: 186 Orwell Rd., Rathgar, Dublin 14 (☎/fax 01 492 3525; russiane@indigo.ie). **Consulate:** 184-186 Orwell Rd., Rathgar, Dublin 14 (☎492 3492; fax 492 6938).

New Zealand: 57 Messines Rd., Karori, Wellington (☎04 476 6113, visa info 476 6742; fax 476 3843; eor@netlink.co.nz). **Consulate:** 1 Speight Rd., Kohimarama, Auckland (☎09 528 0237; fax 528 4060).

South Africa: Butano Building, 316 Brooke St., Menlo Park 0081, Pretoria; P.O. Box 6743, Pretoria 0001 (☎012 362 1337; fax 362 0116; www.icon.co.za/~rusco).

UK: 5 Kensington Palace Gardens, London W8 4QX (☎020 7229 3628, visa info 7229 8027; fax 7229 3215; harhouse1@harhouse1.demon.co.uk). **Consulate:** 58 Melville Street, Edinburgh, EH3 7HF, Scotland (☎131 225 7121; fax 225 9287).

US: 2650 Wisconsin Ave., N.W., Washington, D.C. 20007 (☎202-298-5700; fax 298-5735). **Consulate:** 2641 Tunlaw Rd, N.W., Washington D.C. 20007 (☎202-939-8907; fax 483-7579).

VISA AND ENTRY INFORMATION

Citizens of Australia, Canada, Ireland, New Zealand, South Africa, the UK, and the US all require a visa to enter Russia. Several types of visas exist; the standard tourist visa is valid for 30 days. All Russian visas require an invitation stating the traveler's itinerary and dates of travel. They are notoriously difficult to get without a Russian connection; the easiest way is to go through a travel agency.

GETTING A VISA ON YOUR OWN. If you have an invitation from an authorized travel agency and want to get the visa on your own, apply for the **visa** in person or by mail at a Russian embassy or consulate. Bring your original invitation; your passport; a completed application; three passport-sized photographs; a cover letter stating your name, dates of arrival and departure, cities you plan to visit in Russia, date of birth, and passport number; and a money order or certified check (single-entry, 60-day visas US$70 for 2-week processing, US$80 for 1-week service, US$110 for 3 business days, US$300 for same-day; double-entry visas add US$50; multiple-entry US$200 for 3 business days, US$350 for same-day processing; prices change constantly, so check with the embassy). If you have even tentative plans to visit a city, add it to your visa.

TRAVEL AGENCIES. Travel agencies that advertise discounted tickets to Russia often are also able to provide invitations and visas to Russia (starting at US$150), but they require at least three weeks notice. HOFA, Red Bear Tours, and Traveler's Guest House (see below) require that you book accommodations with them. Try the following agencies:

Host Families Association (HOFA), 5-25 Tavricheskaya ul., 193015 St. Petersburg, RUS (☎/fax 812 275 19 92; hofa@usa.net). Arranges homestays in more than 20 cities of the former Soviet Union. Visa invitations (US$30, US$50 for non-guests) available for Russia, Ukraine, and Belarus. Single rooms start at US$25, doubles at US$50. Discount of US$5 per day for non-central locations and after the first week of a stay with the same family; US$10 after the 2nd week with the same family (non-central locations only). For an additional fee HOFA can also arrange for Russian tutors, theater tickets, meals, and transport to and from the airport.

Info Travel, 387 Harvard St., Brookline, MA 02146, USA (☎617-566-2197; fax 734-8802; infostudy@aol.com). Invitations and visas to Russia starting at US$150. Also provides visas and invitations throughout the former USSR.

Red Bear Tours/Russian Passport, 401 St. Kilda Rd., Suite 11, Melbourne 3004, AUS (☎0613 9867 3888; fax 9867 1055; www.travelcentre.com.au). Provides invitations to Russia and the Central Asian Republics. Also sells rail tickets for the Trans-Siberian, Trans-Manchurian, Trans-Mongolian, and Silk routes and arranges tours.

Russia House, 1800 Connecticut Ave. NW, Washington, D.C. 20009, USA (☎202-986-6010; fax 667-4244; lozansky@aol.com). **Branch,** 44 Bolshaya Nikitskaya, Moscow 121854, RUS (☎095 290 34 59; fax 250 25 03; rushouse@clep.ru). Invitations and visas to Russia, Belarus, and Ukraine starting at US$225.

ENTERING RUSSIA. The best way to cross the **border** is to fly directly into Moscow or St. Petersburg. Another available option is to take a train or bus into one of the major cities. This option, while easy, can also be frustrating. Expect long delays and red tape. Russian law dictates that all visitors must **register** their visas within three days of arrival. Many hotels will register your visa for you, as should the organizations listed above, but can only do so if you fly into a city where they are represented. Some travel agencies in Moscow and St. Petersburg (see **Tourist and Financial Services,** p. 632 and p. 672) will also register your visa for approximately US$30. As a last resort, or if you enter the country somewhere other than the two major cities, you'll have to head to the central OVIR (ОВИР) office (in Moscow called UVIR—УВИР) to register. Many travelers skip this purgatory, but it is the law and taking care of it will leave one less thing over which bribe-seeking authorities can hassle you.

TRANSPORTATION

 BEFORE YOU GO. See **Essentials: Safety and Security,** p. 28, for info on how to find the latest travel advisories. In August 1999, the US State Department issued a travel advisory regarding bringing Global Positioning Systems (GPS), cellular phones, and other radio transmission devices into Russia. Failure to register such devices can (and does) result in search, seizure, and arrest.

BY PLANE. Most major international carriers fly into Sheremetevo-2, Moscow's international airport, or Pulkovo-2 Airport in St. Petersburg. **Aeroflot** is the most popular domestic carrier. The majority of domestic routes are served by Soviet-model planes, many of which are in disrepair and have a poor safety record.

BY TRAIN. In a perfect world, everyone would fly into St. Petersburg or Moscow, skipping customs officials who tear packs apart and demand bribes, and avoiding Belarus entirely. But it's not a perfect world, and you'll likely find yourself on a westbound **train.** If that train is passing through **Belarus** you will need a US$40 transit visa. If you wait until you reach the border, you'll likely pay more and risk a forced no-expense-paid weekend getaway in Minsk. **Domestically,** trains are generally the best option. Weekend or holiday trains between Petersburg and Moscow sometimes sell out a week in advance. If you plan far enough ahead, you'll have your choice of four **classes.** The best class is *lyuks* (люкс), with two beds, while the second-class *kupeyny* (купейний) has four bunks. The next class down is *platskartny* (плацкартный), an open car with 52 shorter, harder bunks. Aim for places 1-33. Places 34-37 are next to the unnaturally foul bathroom, while places 38-52 are on the side of the car and get horribly hot during the summer. **Women traveling alone** can try to buy out a *lyuks* compartment for security, or can travel *platskartny* with the regular folk and depend on the crowds to shame would-be harassers into silence. *Platskartny* is also a good idea on the theft-ridden St. Petersburg-Moscow line, as you are less likely to be targeted there. This logic can only be taken so far; the fourth class, *obshchy*, may be devoid of crooks, but you'll be traveling alongside livestock.

BY BUS. Buses, slightly less expensive than trains, are better for shorter distances. However, they are often crowded and overbooked; don't be shy about ejecting people who try to sit in your seat.

BY THUMB OR TAXI. Hailing a **taxi** is indistinguishable from **hitchhiking,** and should be treated with equal caution. Most drivers who stop will be private citizens trying to make a little extra cash (despite the recent restriction on this illegal activity). Those seeking a ride should stand off the curb and hold out a hand into the street, palm down; when a car stops, riders tell the driver the destination before getting in; he will either refuse altogether or ask "*Skolko?*" (How much?), leading to protracted negotiations. Non-Russian speakers will get ripped off unless they manage a firm agreement on the price—if the driver agrees without asking for a price, you must ask "*skolko?*" yourself (sign language works too). **Never get into a car that has more than one person in it.** *Let's Go* does not recommend hitchhiking.

RUSSIA

TOURIST SERVICES AND MONEY

There are two types of Russian **tourist office**—those that only arrange tours and those that offer general travel services. Offices of the former type are often unhelpful or even rude, but those of the latter are usually eager to assist, particularly with visa registration. Big hotels are often a better bet for maps and other information. For **trekking** and **adventure travel,** consult Wild Russia (see **St. Petersburg: Tourist and Financial Services,** p. 674), which plans guided excursions to wilderness destinations throughout the country.

 PAYING IN RUSSIA. Due to the fluctuating value of the Russian ruble, some establishments list their prices in US dollars. For this reason, some prices in this book may also appear in US$, but be prepared to pay in rubles.

The **ruble** was redenominated in 1998, losing three zeros, and the old currency is gradually being phased out. Government regulations require that you show your passport when you exchange money. Find an *Obmen Valyuty* (Обмен Валюты; Currency Exchange), hand over your currency—most will only exchange US dollars and Euros—and receive your rubles. With **inflation** running at around 18.6%, expect prices quoted in rubles and **exchange rates** to undergo frequent, significant changes. **Do not exchange money on the street.** Banks offer the best combination of good rates and security. You'll have no problem changing rubles back at the end of your trip (just keep exchange receipts), but it's best not to exchange large sums at once, as the rate is unstable. **ATMs** (*bankomat;* банкомат), linked to all major networks and credit cards, can be found in most cities. Banks, large restaurants, ATMs, and currency exchanges often accept major **credit cards,** especially Visa. Main branches of banks will usually accept **traveler's checks** and give cash advances on credit cards. Although you'll have to pay in rubles, it's wise to keep a small amount (US$20 or less) of dollars on hand. Be aware that most establishments do not accept crumpled, torn, or written-on bills of any denomination. Russians are also wary of old US money; bring the new bills.

HEALTH AND SAFETY

 EMERGENCY NUMBERS: Fire ☎01 **Police:** ☎02 **Emergency** ☎03

HEALTH. In a **medical emergency,** either leave the country or go to the American Medical Centers in St. Petersburg or Moscow; these clinics have American doctors who speak English (see **Emergency and Communications,** p. 640 and p. 674). Russian **bottled water** is often mineral water; you may prefer to boil or filter your own, or buy imported bottled water at a supermarket. Water is drinkable in small doses in much of Russia, but not in Moscow and St. Petersburg; boil it to be safe. Men's **toilets** are marked with an "M," women's with a "Ж." The 0.5-5R charge for public toilets generally gets you a hole in the ground and a measured piece of toilet paper; get into the habit of carrying your own. **Pharmacies** are among the few places where the positive effects of capitalism are apparent, with a range of Western medicine and hygiene products available.

SAFETY. Reports of **crime** against foreigners are on the rise, particularly in Moscow and St. Petersburg. Although it is often tough to blend in (especially with a huge pack on your back), try not to flaunt your true nationality. Reports of mafia warfare are scaring off tourists, but unless you bring a shop for them to blow up, you are unlikely to be a target. After the recent eruption of violence in the Northern Caucasus, the **Dagestan** and **Chechnya** regions of Russia should be avoided. It is extremely unwise, though not illegal, to take pictures of anything **military** or to do anything that might attract the attention of a man in uniform—doing something suspicious provides an excuse to detain you or extort money.

WOMEN, MINORITY, AND BGLT TRAVELERS. The concept of **sexual harassment** hasn't yet reached Russia. Local men will try to pick up women and will get away with offensive language and actions. The routine starts with an innocent-sounding *"Devushka..."* (young lady); just say *"Nyet"* (No) or simply walk away. Women in Russia generally wear skirts or dresses rather than pants. Travelers of non-European descent will often receive rude treatment in stores or restaurants, as Russians **discriminate** against even their own non-Slavic citizens in the south. The authorities on the Metro will frequently stop and question **dark-skinned** individuals, particularly anyone who looks Chechen or Dagestani. The laws outlawing **homosexuality** were taken off the books about seven years ago, but gay, lesbian, and bisexual travelers should not expect tolerance of public displays of affection outside of the gay clubs that have sprung up in Moscow and St. Petersburg.

ACCOMMODATIONS

RUSSIA	❶	❷	❸	❹	❺
ACCOM.	under 400R	401-700R	701-1200R	1201-2000R	over 2001R

HOTELS AND HOSTELS. Hotels offer several classes of rooms. "Lux," usually two-room doubles with TV, phone, fridge, and bath, are the most expensive. "Polu-lux" rooms are singles or doubles with TV, phone, and bath. Rooms with bath and no TV, when they exist, are cheaper. The lowest priced rooms are *bez udobstv* (без удобств), which means one room with a sink. Expect to pay 300-450R for a single in a budget hotel. As a rule, only cash is accepted as payment. In many hotels, **hot water**—sometimes all water—is only turned on for a few hours per day. Reservations are not necessary in smaller towns, but they may help you get on the good side of management, which is often inexplicably suspicious of backpackers. The only **hostels** in Russia are in St. Petersburg and Moscow, and even those average US$18 per night. Reserve well in advance.

DORMS AND HOMESTAYS. University dorms offer cheap rooms; some accept foreign students for about US$5-10 per night. The rooms are livable, but don't expect sparkling bathrooms or reliable hot water. Make arrangements through an educational institute from home. **Homestays,** often arranged through a tourist office, are often the cheapest (50-100R per night) and best option in the countryside.

FROM RUSSIA WITH LOVE

MAIL. Mail service is more reliable leaving the country than coming in. Letters to the US will arrive as soon as a week after mailing; letters to other destinations take 2-3 weeks. Domestic mail will usually reach its destination; from abroad, send letters to Russia via friends who are traveling there. Airmail is *avia* (авиа). Send your mail "заказное" (certified; 16R) to reduce the chance of it being lost. Letters to the US cost 7R; postcards 5R. **Poste Restante** is "Писмо До Востребования" (Pismo Do Vostrebovania). Address envelopes as follows: BLACK (last name), Charlie (first name). 103 009 (postal code) Москва (city), Писмо До Востребования, RUSSIA.

RUSSIA

TELEPHONES. Old **local** telephones in Moscow take special tokens, sold at Metro *kassy;* in St. Petersburg, they take Metro tokens. These old public phones are gradually becoming obsolete; the new ones take phonecards, are good for both local and intercity calls, and often have instructions in English. Phonecards are sold at central telephone offices, Metro stations, and newspaper kiosks. When you are purchasing phonecards from a telephone office or metro station, the attendant will often ask, "На улицу?" (Na ulitsu; On the street?) to find out whether you want a card for the phones in the station/office or for outdoor public phones. For five-digit numbers, insert a "2" between the dialing code and the phone number. Direct **international** calls can be made from telephone offices in St. Petersburg and Moscow: calls to Europe run US$1-1.50 per min., to the US and Australia about US$1.50-2. **Telegrams** to the US cost 10R per word. **Faxes** cost 170R per page to Australia, 90R to Europe, 18-98R within Russia, and 120R to the US. To make international calls from **Kaliningrad** or the rest of Russia, telephone offices must call through St. Petersburg or Moscow, making the prices go through the roof.

INTERNET ACCESS. Email is your best bet for keeping in touch. Internet cafes have made quite a mark through St. Petersburg and Moscow, but aren't as popular outside these cities. When all else fails, check at the post office.

MOSCOW (MOCKBA) ☎(8)095

Like few other cities on Earth, Moscow (pop. 9 million) has an audacious sense of itself as a focal point of world history. Change happens quickly here, and Western visitors may feel like they're balancing on a tightrope held tense between the cosmopolitan and the underworld. Yet in keeping to the 16th-century side streets, it's still possible to glimpse a few of the same quiet, golden domes that Napoleon saw after conquering the city in 1812. Of course, when Communism swept through like a hurricane, it leveled most of the domes and left behind dust, pain, and countless statues of Lenin. But now that residents are speaking up and building up, Moscow is recreating itself as a beautiful capital, using the same resourcefulness that helped it engineer (and then survive) the most ambitious social experiment in history.

■ INTERCITY TRANSPORTATION

Flights: International flights arrive at **Sheremetyevo-2** (Шереметьево-2; ☎578 90 05). Take the van under the "автолайн" sign in front of the airport to M2: Rechnoy Vokzal (Речной Вокзал; 20min., every 10min. 7am-10pm, 15R). Or, take bus #851 or 551 to M2: Rechnoy Vokzal or bus #517 to M8: Planyornaya (Планёрная; 10R). Buses run 24hr., but the Metro closes at 1am. Most flights originate at: **Bikovo** (Биково; ☎558 47 38); **Domodedovo** (Домодедово; ☎323 81 60); **Sheremetyevo-1** (☎578 23 72 or 578 91 01); or **Vnukovo** (Внуково; ☎436 28 13). Buy tickets at the *kassa* (касса) at the **Tsentralny Aerovokzal** (Центральный Аэровокзал; Central Airport Station), Leningradsky pr. 37 corpus 6 (☎941 99 99), 2 stops on almost any tram or trolley from M2: Aeroport (the sign on the front of the bus says Центральный Аэровокзал; Tsentralny Aerovokzal). **Taxis** to the center charge up to US$60—bargain it down to US$25. Cars lined outside departures will take you for US$15-20. Agree on a price before getting in.

Air France, ul. Korovy Val 7 (Коровый Вал; ☎937 38 39; fax 937 38 38). M5: Dobryninskaya (Добрынинская). Open M-F 9am-6pm. **Branch** at Sheremetyevo-2, 2nd fl. (☎578 52 37). Open M-F 6:15am-4:15pm.

British Airways, 1-ya Tverskaya-Yamskaya ul. 23 (1-я Тверская-Ямская; ☎363 25 25; fax 258 22 72). M2: Mayakovskaya (Маяковская). Open M-F 10am-7pm, Sa 10am-2pm. **Branch** at Sheremetyevo-2, 6th fl. (☎578 29 23; fax 578 29 36). Open daily 11am-9pm.

Delta, 11 Gogolevsky Blv., 2nd fl. (Гоголевский; ☎937 90 90; fax 937 90 91; www.delta-air.com). M1: Kropotkinskaya (Кропоткинская). Open M-F 9am-5:30pm, Sa 9am-1pm. **Branch** at Sheremetyevo-2 (☎578 29 39). Open M-F 9am-5pm.

Finnair, Kropotkinsky per. 7 (Кропоткинский; ☎933 00 56; www.finnair.com). M1 or 5: Park Kultury (Парк Культуры). Open M-F 9am-5pm. **Branch** at Sheremetyevo-2 (☎/fax 956 46 23).

Lufthansa, Olimpiysky pr. 18/1 (Олимпийский; ☎737 64 00; fax 737 64 01), in Hotel Renaissance. M5 or 6: Prospekt Mira (Проспект Мира). Open M-F 9am-6pm.

Trains: Moscow has 8 train stations arranged around the M5 line. Due to financial problems, many train routes are being cut, so prices and frequency of trains may change.

Belorussky Vokzal (Белорусский), Tverskoi Zastavy pl. 7 (☎973 81 91). M5: Belorusskaya (Белорусская). To: **Kaliningrad** (22hr., 2 per day, 1400R); **Berlin, GER** (27hr., 1 per day, 3500R); **Brest, BLR** (15hr., 3-4 per day, 1250R); **Minsk, BLR** (10hr., 3-4 per day, 750R); **Prague, CZR** (35hr., 1 per day, 2860R); **Vilnius, LIT** (16hr., 1-2 per day, 1950R); **Warsaw, POL** (21hr., 2 per day, 2520R).

Kazansky Vokzal (Казанский), Komsomolskaya pl. 2 (Комсомольская; ☎264 31 81). M5: Komsomolskaya. Opposite Leningradsky Vokzal. To: **Kazan** (12hr., 2 per day, 850R) and **Rostov-na-Donu** (20hr., 1-2 per day, 1200R).

Kievsky Vokzal (Киевский), pl. Kievskovo Vokzala 2 (Киевского Вокзала; ☎240 11 15 or 240 04 15). M3 or 5: Kievskaya (Киевская). Trains to **Bulgaria, Romania, Slovak Republic,** and **Ukraine.** To: **Kyiv, UKR** (14hr., 4 per day, 950R); **Lviv, UKR** (26hr., 2 per day, 1100R); **Odessa, UKR** (25-28hr., 1-2 per day, 1100R).

Kursky Vokzal (Курский), ul. Zemlyanoi Val 29/1 (Земляной Вал; ☎917 31 52 or 916 20 03). M3: Kurskaya (Курская). To **Sevastopol, UKR** (26hr., 1-2 per day, 1100R) and the **Caucasus.**

Leningradsky Vokzal (Ленинградский), Komsomolskaya pl. 3 (☎262 91 43 or 262 96 58). M1 or 5: Komsomolskaya. To: **St. Petersburg** (8hr., 10-15 per day, 700R); **Helsinki, FIN** (13hr., 1 per day, 2720R); **Tallinn, EST** (14hr., 1 per day, 1550R).

Paveletsky Vokzal (Павелецкий), Paveletskaya pl. 1 (Павелецкая; ☎235 05 22 or 235 68 07). M2: Paveletskaya. Trains to **Crimea, eastern Ukraine, Georgia, Azerbaijan,** and **Armenia.** To **Astrakhan** (30hr., 1-2 per day, 1450R) and **Volgograd** (20-30hr., 2-4 per day, 1100R).

Rizhsky Vokzal (Рижский), Prospekt Mira 79/3 (☎971 15 88). M6: Rizhskaya (Рижская). Trains to **Latvia** and **Estonia.** To **Riga, LAT** (16hr., 2 per day, 2050R).

Yaroslavsky Vokzal (Ярославский), Komsomolskaya pl. 5a (☎921 08 17 or 921 59 14). M1 or 5: Komsomolskaya. To **Siberia** and the **Far East.** The starting point for the legendary **Trans-Siberian Railroad** (see p. 715). To **Novosibirsk** (48hr., every other day, 1900R).

Train Tickets: Tickets for long trips within Russia can be bought at the **Tsentralnoe Zheleznodorozhnoe Agenstvo** (Центральное Железнодорожное Агенство; Central Train Agency; ☎266 93 33), to the right of Yaroslavsky Vokzal (see above). Your ticket will have your name and seat on it and tells you at which station (*vokzal*) to catch your train. A schedule of trains, destinations, departure times, and *vokzal* names is posted on both sides of the hall. (*Kassa* open M-F 7am-9pm, Sa 7am-7pm, Su 7am-5pm.) 24hr. service is available at the stations. If you plan to take the **Trans-Siberian Railroad** (see p. 715), check out G&R Hostel Asia or Traveler's Guest House (see **Russia Essentials,** p. 629). They can explain how the TSR works and arrange a special ticket that allows you to get on and off the train at all major cities along the way. For shorter lines in a more obscure location, try the other **branch** at Maly Kharitonevsky per. 6 (Малый Харитоневский; ☎262 06 04 or 262 25 66). M1 or 6: Turgenevskaya/Chistye Prudy (Тургеневская/Чистые Пруды). Take a right off ul. Myasnitskaya (Мясницкая); it's the building on the right. (Open daily 8am-1pm and 2-7pm.)

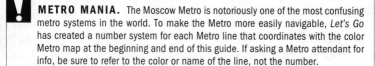

! METRO MANIA. The Moscow Metro is notoriously one of the most confusing metro systems in the world. To make the Metro more easily navigable, *Let's Go* has created a number system for each Metro line that coordinates with the color Metro map at the beginning and end of this guide. If asking a Metro attendant for info, be sure to refer to the color or name of the line, not the number.

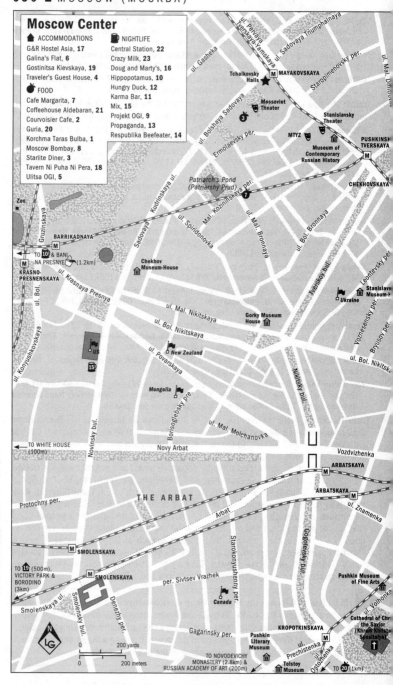

Moscow Center

🏠 ACCOMMODATIONS
G&R Hostel Asia, **17**
Galina's Flat, **6**
Gostinitsa Kievskaya, **19**
Traveler's Guest House, **4**

🍎 FOOD
Cafe Margarita, **7**
Coffeehouse Aldebaran, **21**
Courvoisier Cafe, **2**
Guria, **20**
Korchma Taras Bulba, **1**
Moscow Bombay, **8**
Starlite Diner, **3**
Tavern Ni Puha Ni Pera, **18**
Ulitsa OGI, **5**

◼ NIGHTLIFE
Central Station, **22**
Crazy Milk, **23**
Doug and Marty's, **16**
Hippopotamus, **10**
Hungry Duck, **12**
Karma Bar, **11**
Mix, **15**
Projekt OGI, **9**
Propaganda, **13**
Respublika Beefeater, **14**

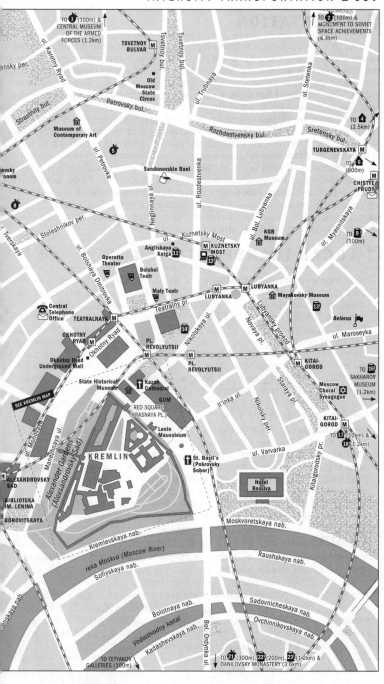

TO **1** (100m) &
CENTRAL MUSEUM
OF THE ARMED
FORCES (1.2km)

TO **2** (100m) &
MONUMENT TO SOVIET
SPACE ACHIEVEMENTS
(6.4km)

TSVETNOY
BULVAR **M**

Tsvetnoy bul.

Tsvetnoy bul.

ul. Karetny Ryad

ensky per.

Old
Moscow
State
Circus

ul. Trubnaya

ul. Sretenka

Strastnoy bul.

Petrovsky bul.

Rozhdestvensky bul.

Sretensky bul.

Museum of
Contemporary Art

TO **4**
(2.5km)

evsky
onom

5

ul. Petrovka

TURGENEVSKAYA **M**

Sandunovskie Bani

ul. Rozhdestvenka

TO **6**
(800m)

M
CHISTYE
PRUDY
✉

8

Neglinnaya ul.

Kuznetsky Most

ul. Bol. Lubyanka

KGB
Museum

ul. Myasnitskaya

TO **9**
(100m)

Tverskaya

Stoleshnikov per.

ul. Bolshaya Dmitrovka

ul.

Angliskaya
Kniga **11**

M KUZNETSKY
MOST

12

Operetta
Theater

Bolshoi
Teatr

Maly Teatr

M
LUBYANKA

M LUBYANKA

Mayakovsky Museum

13

Central
Telephone
Office
✉

TEATRALNAYA **M**

Teatralny pr.

Nikolskaya ul.

Novaya pl.

Belarus 🏳

OKHOTNY
RYAD **M**

14

ul. Maroseyka

Okhotny Ryad

Lubyansky proezd

PL.
REVOLYUTSII
M

Okhotny Ryad
Underground Mall

M
PL.
REVOLYUTSII

M KITAI-
GOROD

TO **16**
SAKHAROV
MUSEUM
(1.2km)

SEE KREMLIN MAP

State Historical
Museum 🏛

Kazan
Cathedral 🛈

Il'inka ul.

Staraya pl.

Nikolsky per.

Moscow
Choral
Synagogue ✡

GUM

RED SQUARE
(KRASNAYA PL.)

Lenin
Mausoleum

Manezhnaya ul.

Kitaigorodsky pr.

KITAI-
GOROD **M**

ul. Mokhovaya

Alexander Gardens
(Aleksandrovsky Sad)

KREMLIN

St. Basil's
(Pokrovsky
Sobor) 🛈

ul. Varvarka

TO **17** (10m) &
18 (1.2km)

1
ALEKSANDROVSKY
SAD

BIBLIOTEKA
IM. LENINA

BOROVITSKAYA

Hotel
Rossiya

Moskvoretskaya nab.

Kremlevskaya nab.

reka Moskva (Moscow River)

Sofiyskaya nab.

Raushskaya nab.

RUSSIA

skaya nab.

Bolotnaya nab.

Vodootvodny kanal

Kadashevskaya nab.

Bol. Ordynka ul.

Sadovnicheskaya nab.

Ovchinnikovskaya nab.

TO TETYAKOV
GALLERIES (100m)

TO **21** (300m) **22** (200m) **23** (1-2km) &
DANILOVSKY MONASTERY (3.6km)

◼ ORIENTATION

A series of concentric rings radiates from the **Kremlin** (Кремль; Kreml) and **Red Square** (Красная площадь; Krasnaya ploshchad). The outermost street, the **Moscow Ring** (Московское Кольцо; Moskovskoye Koltso), marks the city limits, but most sights lie within the much smaller **Garden Ring** (Садовое Кольцо; Sadovoe Koltso). The tree-lined **Boulevard Ring,** made up of ten short, wide boulevards, makes an incomplete circle within the center. **Ul. Tverskaya** (Тверская), considered Moscow's main street, begins just north of Red Square and continues northwest along the green line of the Metro. The **Arbat** (Арбат) and **Novy Arbat** (Новый Арбат), respectively Moscow's hippest and most commercialized streets, lie west of the Kremlin. **Zamoskvareche** (Замоскварече) and **Krimskiy Val** (Крымский Вал), the neighborhoods directly across the **Moscow River** to the south of Red Square, are home to numerous pubs, museums, mansions, and monasteries. To the east of Red Square is the 9th-century **Kitai-Gorod** (Китай-Город) neighborhood, packed with towering churches and bustling commercial thoroughfares. English and Cyrillic **maps** (20-50R) are at kiosks and bookstores all over the city. See this book's color insert for Cyrillic maps of the Metro and the city center.

◼ LOCAL TRANSPORTATION

Public Transportation: The **Metro** (Метро) is large, fast, clean, and efficient—a masterpiece of urban planning. A station serving more than one line may have more than one name. The M5 is known as the *koltsevaya linia* (кольцевая линия; circle line). Trains run daily 6am-1am, but catch one by 12:30am to be safe. Rush hours are 8-10am and 5-7pm. Buy token cards (5R, or 10 trips for 35R) from the *kassy* inside stations. **Bus** and **trolley** tickets are available at kiosks labeled "проездные билеты" (proyezdnye bilety) and from the driver (4R). Punch your ticket when you get on, especially during the last week of the month when ticket cops need to fill their quotas, or risk is a 10R fine. Buy monthly passes (единые билеты; edinye bilety) after the 20th of the preceding month (320R). Monthly passes (150R; 60 trips within a calendar month) and 30-day unlimited passes (200R; plus a first-time 50R fee for the card) are more cost-effective. Purchase either from the *kassa*.

Taxis and Hitchhiking: Avoid the taxis (☎722 11 69 or 927 00 00), especially if you're new in Moscow. The practice of hailing a car on the street is common and always cheaper. Hold your arm out horizontally, and when the driver stops, tell him where you need to go and haggle over the price. You should be able to get almost anywhere in town for 100R, and most of the time you'll pay around 50R. Catching a car doesn't guarantee your safety, but you should be fine as long as you follow the rule of thumb: don't get into a car with more than one person already in it, and don't get into a Mercedes with tinted windows. *Let's Go* does not recommend hitchhiking.

WE BRAKE FOR NO ONE. Moscow drivers are notorious: unbelievably fast and blissfully ignorant of the gentle art of yielding to pedestrians. Should you venture onto the blacktop, they will honk, yell, and gesticulate obscenely, but they will not touch their brakes. One day of such confrontations will suffice to convince you that the underpass beneath nearly every intersection—called a *perekhod* (переход)—is there out of dire necessity. Perhaps more disturbing is the Muscovite fondness for driving, often in reverse, on the sidewalks, which they use as parking lots, driveways, and passing lanes. On the streets of Moscow, there are pedestrians and there are drivers. And pedestrians are most decidedly not wanted.

🔒 PRACTICAL INFORMATION

TOURIST AND FINANCIAL SERVICES

Tourist Office: As of 2002, there was no tourist office in Moscow. However, the city government plans to open one up near Red Square. Check with any of the companies that organize tours (see below) for more info.

Tours: The folks with loudspeakers on the north end of Red Square offer walking tours of the area (1hr., every 30min. 10am-12:30pm, 50R) and excellent bus tours of the city's main sights (1½hr.; 90R). In Russian only, but translators are sometimes available for an extra charge. Or, try **Intourist**, Milyutinsky per. 13/1 (Милютинский, ☎924 31 01). M1 or 6: Turgenyevskaya. Tours and translation services. Open M-Sa 10am-7:30pm. **Branch** at Teatralny pl. 3/5 (Театральня; ☎923 36 37). Open M-F 10am-6:30pm. M1 or 7: Kuznetsky Most/Lubyanka (Кузнецкий мост/Лубянка).

Budget Travel: Student Travel Agency Russia (STAR), ul. Baltiyskaya 9, 3rd fl. (Балтийская; ☎797 95 55; www.startravel.ru). M2: Sokol (Сокол). Discount plane tickets, ISICs, and worldwide hostel booking. Open M-F 10am-7pm, Sa 10am-4pm. **Moskovsky Sputnik** (Московский Спутник), Maly Ivanovsky per. 6, corpus 2 (Малый Ивановский; ☎925 92 78; fax 230 27 87; mows@mowsput.ru). M6 or 7: Kitai-gorod (Китай-город). Arranges student travel, visas, and ISICs. Open M-F 9am-7pm. MC/V.

Passport Office: OVIR (ОВИР), ul. Pokrovka 42 (Покровка; ☎200 84 27). M1: Krasnye Vorota (Красные ворота). From the Metro, turn right on Sadovaya Chernogryazskaya, continue until ul. Pokrova, and turn right (10min.). OVIR is possibly the 7th circle of Russian bureaucratic hell—to avoid an unpleasant encounter, secure a visa invitation and stamp from your 1st night's accommodation whenever possible. Open M and Tu-Th 9am-12:45pm and 2-5:45pm, F 9am-12:45pm and 2-4:30pm. **Branch** at ul. Usacheva 62 (Усачева; ☎245 21 32), M1: Sportivnaya (Спортивная). Open M-Tu and Th 9am-1pm and 2-6pm, W 9am-1pm, F 9am-1pm and 2-4:45pm.

Embassies and Consulates:

Australia, Kropotkinsky per. 13 (☎956 60 70; fax 956 61 62). M3 or 5: Smolenskaya/Park Kultury (Смоленская/Парк Культуы). Open M-F 9am-12:30pm and 1:15-5pm; visas M-F 9:30am-12:30pm.

Belarus, ul. Maroseyka 17/6 (Маросейка; ☎777 66 44; fax 77 66 33). Consular section at Armyansky per. 6 (Армянский; ☎924 70 95; fax 956 78 13). M6 or 7: Kitai gorod. Open M-F 9am-1pm and 2-6pm.

Canada, Starokonyushenny per. 23 (Староконюшенный; ☎956 66 66; fax 232 99 50;). M1: Kropotkinskaya or M4: Arbatskaya (Арбатская). Open M-F 8:30am-1pm and 2-5pm.

China, ul. Druzhby 6 (Дружбы; ☎938 20 06, visa 143 15 40; fax 938 21 82;). M1: Universitet (Университет). Open M-F 8:30am-noon and 3-6pm.

Finland, Kropotkinsky per. 15/17 (☎246 40 27; fax 247 07 45). M1 or 5: Park Kultury. Open M-F 9am-1pm and 2-5pm. Consular section (☎247 31 25) open M-F 10am-noon and 2-4pm.

Ireland, Grokholsky per. 5 (Грохольский; ☎937 59 11, visa 937 59 00; fax 975 20 66). M5 or 6: Prospekt Mira. Open M-F 9:30am-1pm and 2:30-5:30pm.

Mongolia, Spasopeskovsky per. 7/1 (Спасопесковский; ☎241 15 48; fax 244 78 67). M3: Smolenskaya. Open M-F 10am-1pm.

New Zealand, ul. Povarskaya 44 (Поварская; ☎956 35 79, visa 956 26 42; fax 956 35 83). M7: Barikadnaya (Баррикадная). Open M-F 9am-5:30pm.

South Africa, Bolshoy Strochenovsky per. 22/25 (Большой Строченовский; ☎230 68 69; fax 230 68 65). Open M-F 8:30am-5pm. Consular section open M-F 8am-noon.

Ukraine, Leontyevsky per. 18 (Леонтьевский; ☎229 10 79, visa 229 34 22; fax 924 84 69), off ul. Tverskaya. M2: Tverskaya (Тверская). Open M-F 9am-1pm and 2pm-6pm.

UK, Smolenskaya nab. 10 (Смоленская; ☎956 72 00; fax 956 74 80). M3: Smolenskaya. Open M-F 9am-1pm and 2-5pm. Consular section (☎956 72 50) open M-F 8am-12:30pm.

US, Novinsky 19/23 (Новинский; ☎728 50 00; www.usia.gov/posts/moscow.html). Open M-F 9am-6pm. Consular section (☎728 55 88) open M-F 9am-noon. M5: Krasnoprenenskaya (Краснопресненская). Flash a US passport and cut the long lines. **American Citizen Services** (☎728 55 77, after-hours emergency 728 51 07; fax 728 50 84) connects citizens to various organizations and arranges annual July 4th celebrations. Open M-F 9am-12:30pm and 3-4pm.

Currency Exchange: Banks are on almost every corner; check ads in English-language newspapers. The **Moscow Express Directory,** updated biweekly and free in most luxury hotels, lists the addresses and phone numbers of many banks, as well as places to buy and cash **traveler's checks.** Except for main branches, most banks do not change traveler's checks or issue cash advances; a posted sign or even a sticker that says "We accept (company) traveler's checks" is no guarantee.

ATMs: Nearly every bank and hotel has an ATM that allows withdrawals in either US$ or rubles. Beware of ATMs on the sides of buildings; not only do they work irregularly, but making a withdrawal in the middle of a busy street invites muggers.

American Express: Ul. Usacheva 33 (☎933 84 00). M1: Sportivnaya. Exit at the front of the train, turn right, and turn right again after the Global USA shop onto Usacheva. Open M-F 9am-6pm.

LOCAL SERVICES

English-Language Bookstores: Anglia British Bookshop, Khlebny per. 2/3 (Хёаáíûё; ☎203 58 02; fax 203 06 73). M3 or 4: Arbatskaya. Decent selection, including Russian and American fiction, textbooks, and travel guides. Open M-F 10am-7pm, Sa 10am-6pm, Su 11am-5pm. ISIC discount. AmEx/MC/V. **Angliyskaya Kniga** (Английская Книга), ul. Kuznetsky most 18 (☎928 20 21). M7: Kuznetsky most. Large selection, including travel guides, phrasebooks, trashy novels, and Russian literature in translation. Open M-F 10am-2pm and 3-7pm, Sa 10am-2pm and 3-6pm. MC/V.

International Press: Several free English-language newspapers are available in English-friendly hotels and restaurants, but not in kiosks. *The Moscow Tribune* and the more widely read *Moscow Times* have foreign and national articles for travelers. Both also have weekend sections on F that list theatrical events, English-language movies, housing, and job opportunities. *Where* magazine is published monthly and has shopping, dining, and entertainment listings, as well as excellent maps (www.WhereRussia.com). *The Moscow Courier* is a monthly paper with both English and German sections. An "alternative" paper, *The eXile* (www.exile.ru), is one of the funniest and most irreverent papers on Earth. Its nightlife section is indispensably candid.

Cultural Centers: The Western countries have all their cultural centers in the **Foreign Library,** ul. Nikoloyamskaya 1, 3rd fl. (Николоямская). M5 or 7: Taganskaya (Таганская). Walk up Zemlyanoy Val and turn left on Nikoloyamskaya. The **American Cultural Center** (☎777 65 30) is open in summer M-F 10am-7:45pm, Sa 10am-5:45pm; off-season also open Su 10am-5:45pm. The **British Council Resource Centre** (☎782 02 00) is next door. Open in summer M-F noon-7pm; off-season M-F 9am-5pm, Sa 10am-5pm.

Laundromat: California Cleaners, Pokhodny Proyezd 24 (Походный; ☎493 53 11). Pickup and delivery 105R; free for loads of 8kg or more. Wash and dry 105R per kg. Open M-Sa 9am-8pm, Su 9am-6pm.

EMERGENCY AND COMMUNICATIONS

Emergencies: Fire: ☎01. **Police:** ☎02. **Ambulance:** ☎03. **Lost property:** Metro ☎222 20 85, other transport 298 32 41. **Lost documents:** ☎200 99 57. **Lost credit cards:**

☎956 35 56 or 234 18 31. **24hr. free crisis line for English speakers:** ☎244 34 49 or 931 96 82. **International Medical Clinic:** ☎280 71 71.

24-Hour Pharmacies: Look for "круглосуточно" (kruglosutochno; always open) signs. Leningradsky pr. 74 (Ленинградский; ☎151 45 70). M2: Sokol. Ul. Tverskaya 25 (☎299 24 59 or 299 79 69). M2: Tverskaya/Mayakovskaya. Ul. Zemlyanoi Val 25 (☎917 12 85). M5: Kurskaya. Kutozovsky (Кутозовский) Prospekt 24 (☎249 19 37) M4: Kutuzovskaya (Кутузовская).

Medical Assistance: American Medical Center (AMC), Prospekt Mira 26 (☎933 77 00; fax 933 77 01). M5 or 6: Prospekt Mira. From the Metro, turn left on Grokholsky per. Walk-in medical care for hard currency, US$175 per visit. Membership US$50 per year. Open 24hr. AmEx/MC/V. **American Clinic,** Grokholsky per. 31 (☎937 57 57; fax 937 57 74; www.klinik.ru). M5 or 6: Prospekt Mira. See directions for AMC. American board-certified doctors; pediatric, family, and internal medicine services. Consultations US$98-130. Open 24hr., with house calls. MC/V. **European Medical Clinic,** Spirido-nievskiy Per. 5 (☎787 70 00 or 797 67 67; www.emcmos.ru) offers psychiatric, pediatric, gynecologic, dental, laboratory, and medical evaluations. Consultations US$40-US$80; specialist consultations US$60-US$200. Open 24hr.

Telephones: Moscow Central Telegraph (see **Post Offices,** below). To call abroad, go to the 2nd hall with telephones. Collect and calling card calls not available. Prepay at the counter for the amount of time you expect to talk, or buy a prepaid phonecard, which can only be used in the telegraph office. **Local calls** require new phone cards, available at some Metro stops and kiosks. Dial ☎09 for directory assistance.

Internet Access: Timeonline (☎363 00 60), on the bottom level of the Okhotny Ryad underground mall. M1: Okhotny Ryad. At night, enter through the Metro underpass. Over 200 computers in the center of the city. 30-60R per hr. depending on time of day. Student discount. Open 24hr. **Image.ru** (Имидж.ру), ul. Novoslobodskaya 16 (Новослободская; ☎737 37 00, ext. 176). M9: Mendeleevskaya (Менделеевская). 40R per hr. Open daily 9am-5:30am. **Kukushka** (Ктҟушка), ul. Rozhdedestvenka 6/9/ 20. M7: Kuznetsky Most. Look for the "Internet Cafe" sign right by the Metro. Fast connections 60R per hour. Open daily 11am-midnight.

Post Offices: Moscow Central Telegraph, ul. Tverskaya 7, a few blocks uphill from the Kremlin. M1: Okhotny Ryad. Look for the globe and the digital clock. **International** mail at window #23. **Faxes** at #11-12. **Telegram** service. Open M-F 8am-2pm and 3pm-8pm, Sa-Su 7am-2pm and 3pm-7pm. Pick up at window #24, although they might send you to the main post office at Myasnitskaya 26 (Мясницкая) if they don't have it. Bring packages unwrapped; they will be wrapped and mailed for you.

Postal Code: 103 009.

╠ ACCOMMODATIONS

The lack of backpackers in Moscow results in slim pickings and overpriced rooms. Women standing outside major rail stations rent **private rooms** or **apartments** ❶ (as low as 200R per night; don't forget to haggle); just look for the signs advertising rooms (сдаю комнату) sdayu komnatu) or apartments (сдаю квартиру; sdayu kvartiru). If you're interested in a **homestay ❶,** book it in advance (see **Russia Essentials,** p. 621). The **Moscow Bed and Breakfast ❸** is a US-based organization that rents out apartments in the city center; contact them before you arrive in Moscow. (US ☎603-585-3347; fax 603-585-6534; jkates@top.monad.net. Singles US$35; doubles US$52.) **"Moscow Rick" Moncher ❸** rents clean, comfortable, apartments in the city center with satellite TV, phone, washing machines, and Western-style bathrooms. (☎212 25 20; www.enjoymoscow.com. US$30-40 per person.)

Galina's Flat, ul. Chaplygina 8, #35 (Чаплыгина; ☎921 60 38; galinas.flat@mtu-net.ru. M1: Chistye Prudy. From there, head down bul. Chistoprudny (Чистопрудный), take a left on Kharitonevsky per. (Харитоньевский), and then a right on Chaplygina. Go into the courtyard at #8 (under the blue sign), curve around the building to the right, and enter the building with the faint "Уникум" sign; the flat is on the 5th floor on the right. Superb location, rock-bottom price, and Russian hospitality. Affable Galina and her sidekick Sergei welcome you to their homey Russian apartment. Several cats roam the apartment. Breakfast 30R. Kitchen access. Airport pickup US$25, drop-off US$20. 5-bed dorm US$8; singles US$15; doubles US$40. Discounts for longer stays. ❶

Traveler's Guest House (TGH), ul. Bolshaya Pereyaslavskaya 50, 10th fl. (Большая Переславская; ☎971 40 59; fax 280 7686; www.infinity.ru/tgh). M5 or 6: Prospekt Mira. Exiting the Metro, turn left. Take the 2nd right onto the *pereleuk* (without a sign) across from 61 Prospekt Mira. Walk to the end of the *pereleuk* and go left on B. Pere-yaslavskaya. TGH is in a white high-rise on the right. Although a trek from the city center, its greatest virtue is the clientele: almost every budget traveler in town stays here. Friendly and helpful staff. Kitchen access, Internet (1R per min.), luggage storage, laundry service (80R for 3kg), airport pickup and drop-off (US$30), and visa invitations (US$40, US$20 if you stay here). Check-out 11am. Dorms US$18; singles US$36; doubles US$48, with bath US$54. 5% ISIC discount, 10% HI discount. MC/V. ❷

G&R Hostel Asia, ul. Zelenodolskaya 3/2 (Зеленодольская; ☎/fax 378 28 66; www.hostels.ru). M7: Ryazansky Prospekt (Рязанский Проспект). On the 15th fl. of the tall gray building with "Гостиница" on top. Clean rooms and helpful staff. TV in private singles and shared fridge. Visa invitations US$35, US$25 if you prepay for 1 night. Airport transport US$25. Reception 8am-midnight. Singles US$22, with bath US$30; doubles US$36/US$44; triples US$48. US$1 HI discount. 10th day free. MC/V. ❸

Gostinitsa Kievskaya (Гостиница Киевская), ul. Kievskaya 2 (☎240 14 44). M3, 4, or 5: Kievskaya. Outside the train station. Soviet-style rooms, soft beds, and a good location. Singles 540R, with bath 740R; doubles 570R/820R; luxury suite 1100-1400R. ❷

🗂 FOOD

> ❗ Many restaurants list prices in US dollars to avoid having to change their menus to keep up with inflation, but payment is always in rubles.

Restaurant prices in Moscow can be very expensive compared with the rest of Russia. Some higher-priced establishments have begun to offer business lunch (бизнес ланч) specials, which are typically available noon-4pm and cost US$4-8. Russians tend to eat late in the evening, so you can avoid crowds by eating earlier. The **Food Court** at the Okhotny Ryad underground mall has inexpensive fast-food establishments. The ubiquitous and varied kiosk fare offers a cheap alternative, with *sloiki* (5-15R), *bliny* (pancakes; 10-50R), and a multitude of prepackaged treats.

RUSSIAN RESTAURANTS AND CAFES

Courvoisier Cafe, Malaya Sukharevskaya 8, bldg. 1 (Малая Сухаревкая; ☎924 82 42). M6: Sukharevskaya. With its attentive service and Russo-European flavors, this delightful, inexpensive cafe feels like it belongs on a Parisian sidestreet. Soups 60-80R; *blini* 40-60R; omelets 40-100R; entrees 220-350R. Breakfast served 5-11:30am. Open 24hr. MC/V. ❸

Ulitsa OGI (Улица ОГИ), Petrovka 26/8 (Петровка; ☎200 68 73). M7: Kuznetsky Most. Pass through the arch and walk straight for 150ft. This well-kept secret serves Russian and European food. The Gallic trout is superb (230R). Salads 90-350R; entrees 230-400R; business lunch 250R. Open daily 8am-11pm. MC/V. ❸

Tavern Ni Puha Ni Pera (Трактир Ни Пуха Ни Пера), ul. Nikolayamskaya 28/60 (☎502 99 08). M5 or 7: Taganskaya. Walk down Zemlyanoi Val away and take a left on Nikolayamskaya. Modeled on a hunting lodge, this tavern serves Russian fare, like duck and rabbit, at reasonable prices. Wild game such as deer and boar are more expensive (700-800R). Although the waitresses wear cartridge belts, they are not actually packing heat, as far as we know. Entrees 170-310R. Open daily 10am-midnight. MC/V. ❸

Coffeehouse Aldebaran (Альдебарань), Bolshoy Tolmachevsky per. 4, bldg. 1 (☎953 62 68). A coffeehouse in name only, this sidewalk cafe features a sophisticated menu and a variety of fine teas (110R). A little pricey, but the romantic ambience is enjoyable. Entrees 350-470R. Open M-F 10am-midnight, Sa-Su 11am-midnight. MC/V. ❹

Cafe Margarita (Кафе Маргарита), ul. Malaya Bronaya 28 (Малая Вроная; ☎299 65 34), at the intersection of Maly Kozikhinsky per. (Малый Козихинский). M2: Mayakovskaya. Take a left on Bolshaya Sadovaya, then another left on Malaya Bronaya. A small cafe serving Russian and Georgian food, opposite Patriarch's Ponds, where Bulgakov's *The Master and Margarita* begins. Tomatoes stuffed with garlic and cheese 130R. Full meals 300-500R. Live piano after 8pm (cover 100R). Open daily 1pm-midnight. ❹

INTERNATIONAL RESTAURANTS AND CAFES

Korchma Taras Bulba (Корчма Тарас Бульва), ul. Sadovaya-Samotechnaya 13 (☎200 00 56). M9: Tsvetnoi Bulvar (Цветной бульвар). From the Metro, turn left and walk up Tsvetnoi Bulvar. An authentic Ukrainian restaurant serves generous portions at the right price in a homey setting. Excellent stuffed cabbage leaves 125R. Dumplings with choice of 11 different fillings 109-165R. Entrees 140-300R. Open 24hr. MC/V. ❸

Moscow Bombay (Москва Бомбей), Glinishchevsky per. 3 (Глинищевский; ☎292 93 75). M7: Pushkinskaya (Пушкинская) or M9: Chekhovskaya (Чеховская). Walk downhill on Tverskaya and turn left on Glinishchevsky. Dark carved wood, soothing Indian music, and gracious service create a relaxing atmosphere. English menu with veggie options. Appetizers 130-280R; naan 35-60R; entrees 250-450R. Live Indian dancing F-Sa after 9pm. Open daily noon-midnight. AmEx/MC/V. ❹

Guria (Гуриа), Komsomolsky pr. 7/3 (Комсомольский; ☎246 03 78), opposite St. Nicholas of the Weavers and behind Dom Modeley (Дом Моделей). M1 or 5: Park Kultury. Tasty Georgian fare for some of the city's lowest prices; convenient if you're going to Gorky Park or the art galleries. Don't be intimidated by the bear chained to the wall in the lobby–it's stuffed. Entrees 80-180R. Open daily noon-midnight. ❷

Starlite Diner (☎290 96 38). Aquarium Park, near Mayakovsky Square. M2: Mayakovskaya. Walk down Bolshaya Sadovaya toward the Mayakovsky staute; the park is on your left, by the Mossoviet Theater. This surprisingly authentic American diner serves a mix of staples—including pasta, pizza (US$7-9), and milkshakes—amid a tolerable level of kitsch. Entrees US$11-22. Breakfast all day. Open 24hr. AmEx/MC/V. ❸

MARKETS AND SUPERMARKETS

Vendors bring everything from a handful of cherries to an entire produce section to Moscow's **markets.** A visit is worthwhile just for the sights: sides of beef, grapes, and pots of flowers crowd together in a visual bouquet. Impromptu markets spring up around Metro stations; some of the best are at Turgenyevskaya and Kuznetsky most. Vendors arrive around 10am and leave by 8pm. Bring your own bag. **Eliseevsky Gastronom** (Елисеевский), ul. Tverskaya 14 (☎209 07 60), is Moscow's most famous supermarket. (Open M-Sa 8am-9pm, Su 10am-8pm.) There are other supermarkets all over the place; look for "продукти" (prodookty; food products) signs.

◙ SIGHTS

Moscow's sights reflect the city's strange history: since St. Petersburg was the Tsar's seat for 200 years, there are 16th-century churches and Soviet-era museums, but little in between. There are no grand palaces, but Moscow's museums contain the very best of Russian art. Tourists will notice that the political upheaval of the last decade has taken its toll on the museums dedicated to Lenin, Marx, and Engels, which are closed indefinitely while their political significance is reassessed. The "political reconstruction" of the capital has also led to physical renovation and the city seems to be constantly under construction, with new buildings going up practically overnight. Though 80% of Moscow's pre-revolutionary splendor was torn down by the Soviet regime, the capital still packs plenty of sights. For information on guided tours, see **Practical Information: Tours,** p. 639.

THE KREMLIN

The Kremlin (Кремль; Kreml) is geographically and historically in the center of Moscow, the birthplace of much of Russian history and religion. It was here that Napoleon simmered while Moscow burned and here that the Congress of People's Deputies dissolved itself in 1991, breaking up the USSR. Much of the triangular complex is still government offices; the watchful police will blow whistles if you stray into a forbidden zone. *(Open F-W 10am-5pm; last entrance 4:30pm. Buy tickets at the kassa in Alexander Gardens. Enter through Borovitskaya gate tower in the southwest corner if you're going to the Armory; otherwise, enter between the kassy if you're skipping it. Entrance to the territory and all cathedrals 200R, students 100R; after 4pm 90R/45R. Audio guides 150R. English-speaking guides offer tours, sometimes at outrageous prices; haggle away. Local hotels also offer tours. Cameras 50R, mandatory bag check 60R.)*

▓**ARMORY MUSEUM AND DIAMOND FUND.** (Оружейная и Выставка Алмазного Фонда; Oruzheynaya i Vystavka Almaznovo Fonda.) All the most beautiful treasures of the Russian state can be found in these nine rooms. Room 2, on the second floor, holds the legendary Fabergé Eggs and the royal silver. Room 6 holds pieces of the royal wardrobe (Empress Elizabeth is said to have had 15,000 gowns, only one of which is on display). The thrones of Ivan the Terrible and Elizabeth stand imposingly in Room 7, next to the hats of Peter the Great and Vladimir Monomakh. Room 9 contains royal coaches and sleds—Elizabeth (not one for understatement) had her sled pulled by 23 horses. The **Diamond Fund,** in an annex of the Armory, has still more glitter, including a 190-carat diamond given to Catherine the Great by Gregory Orlov, a "special friend." Among the emerald necklaces and ruby rings of the tsars are Soviet-era finds, including the **world's largest chunks of platinum.** *(To the left as you enter the Kremlin. ☎203 03 49. Open F-W. The armory lets in groups for 1½ hr. visits at 10am, noon, 2:30, and 4:30pm. The Diamond Fund lets in groups every 20min. 10am-1pm and 2pm-6pm. Buy tickets early in the day, as group size is limited. Armory 350R, students 175R. Camera 50R. Diamond Fund 350R. Bags, cameras, and glasscutters must be checked before entering the Diamond Fund.)*

CATHEDRAL SQUARE. (Соборная Площадь; Sobornaya Ploshchad.) From the Armory, follow the eager masses to Cathedral Square, home of the most famous gold domes in Russia. The first church to the left, **Annunciation Cathedral** (Благовещенский Собор; Blagoveshchensky Sobor), guards the loveliest iconostasis in the country, with luminous icons by Andrei Rublyov and Theophanes the Greek. Originally only three-domed, the cathedral was enlarged and gilded by Ivan the Terrible. The second entrance is also his; Ivan's seven marriages made him ineligible to enter the church, so he was forced to stand in the porch during services as penance. Across the way, the square **Archangel Cathedral**

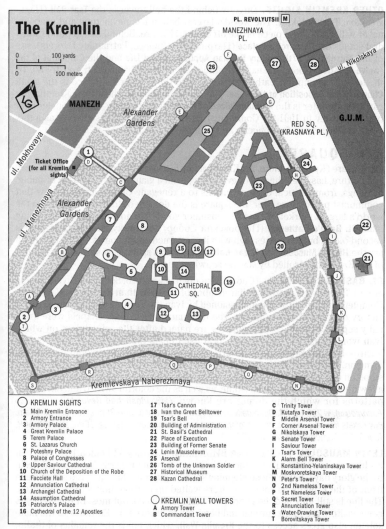

The Kremlin

0 ————— 100 yards
0 ————— 100 meters

MANEZH

Alexander Gardens

Ticket Office (for all Kremlin sights)

Alexander Gardens

ul. Mokhovaya

ul. Manezhnaya

Kremlevskaya Naberezhnaya

PL. REVOLYUTSII Ⓜ

MANEZHNAYA PL.

ul. Nikolskaya

RED SQ. (KRASNAYA PL.)

G.U.M.

○ **KREMLIN SIGHTS**
1 Main Kremlin Entrance
2 Armory Entrance
3 Armory Palace
4 Great Kremlin Palace
5 Terem Palace
6 St. Lazarus Church
7 Poteshny Palace
8 Palace of Congresses
9 Upper Saviour Cathedral
10 Church of the Deposition of the Robe
11 Facciete Hall
12 Annunciation Cathedral
13 Archangel Cathedral
14 Assumption Cathedral
15 Patriarch's Palace
16 Cathedral of the 12 Apostles

17 Tsar's Cannon
18 Ivan the Great Belltower
19 Tsar's Bell
20 Building of Administration
21 St. Basil's Cathedral
22 Place of Execution
23 Building of Former Senate
24 Lenin Mausoleum
25 Arsenal
26 Tomb of the Unknown Soldier
27 Historical Museum
28 Kazan Cathedral

○ **KREMLIN WALL TOWERS**
A Armory Tower
B Commandant Tower

C Trinity Tower
D Kutafya Tower
E Middle Arsenal Tower
F Corner Arsenal Tower
G Nikolskaya Tower
H Senate Tower
I Saviour Tower
J Tsar's Tower
K Alarm Bell Tower
L Konstantino-Yelaninskaya Tower
M Moskvoretskaya Tower
N Peter's Tower
O 2nd Nameless Tower
P 1st Nameless Tower
Q Secret Tower
R Annunciation Tower
S Water-Drawing Tower
T Borovitskaya Tower

(Архангельский Собор; Arkhangelsky Sobor), gleaming with vivid icons, colorful frescoes, and metallic coffins, is the final resting place of many tsars who ruled before Peter the Great. Ivans III (the Great) and IV (the Terrible) are on either side of the right end of the iconostasis, respectively; Mikhail Romanov is by the front right column. The center of Cathedral Square is **Assumption Cathedral** (Успенский Собор; Uspensky Sobor), one of the oldest religious buildings in the Russian state, dating from the 15th century. Napoleon used the Cathedral as a stable in 1812. To the right of Uspensky Sobor stands **Ivan the Great Belltower** (Колокольня Ивана Велнкого; Kolokolnya Ivana Velikovo), which holds rotating exhibitions. The tower is visible more than 30km away.

OTHER KREMLIN SIGHTS. Directly behind the bell tower is the **Tsar Bell** (Царь-колокол; Tsar-kolokol). The world's largest bell, it has never rung and probably never will; an 11.5-ton piece broke off after a 1737 fire. Behind Assumption Cathedral stands the **Patriarch's Palace** (Патриарший Дворец; Patriarshiy Dvorets), site of the **Museum of 17th-Century Russian Applied Art and Life** and the **Cathedral of the Twelve Apostles** (Собор Двенадцати Апостолов; Sobor Dvenadtsati Apostolov). To the left of Assumption Cathedral and next to the Patriarch's Palace is the small **Church of the Deposition of the Robe.** The only other building inside the Kremlin you can actually enter is the **Kremlin Palace of Congresses,** a square white monster built by Khrushchev in 1961 for Communist Party Congresses. It also serves as a theater, open in season for concerts and ballets.

RED SQUARE

Red Square (Красная площадь; Krasnaya Ploshchad), a 700m long lesson in history and culture, has been the site of everything from a giant farmer's market to public hangings, from political demonstrations to a renegade Cessna landing. Now that communist parades are over, the square is the domain of tourists. **GUM,** once the world's largest market of Soviet "consumer goods," is now an upscale shopping mall. **St. Basil's Cathedral** (Покровский Собор; Pokrovsky Sobor), the square's second-oldest building, rises high with its patterned onion domes. At the other end are the **History Museum** and **Kazan Cathedral. Lenin's mausoleum** still stands in front of the Kremlin, patrolled by several scowling guards.

ST. BASIL'S CATHEDRAL. (Собор Василия Блаженного; Sobor Vasiliya Blazhennovo.) There is no more familiar symbol of Moscow than St. Basil's Cathedral. Completed in 1561, it was commissioned by Ivan the Terrible to celebrate his 1552 victory over the Tatars in Kazan. The nine narrow octagonal chapels were originally separate churches. The chapels are named after the saints' days on which Ivan won his battles, but the cathedral itself bears the moniker of the holy fool Vasily—Basil in English—who correctly predicted that Ivan would murder his own son. Before the Kazan victory, Vasily died and was buried in the church that stood on this ground. The grand cathedral that replaced it has seen the addition of a few minor domes since Ivan's time, as well as the colorful swirled and checkered patterns for which the domes are known. *(M3: Ploshchad Revolutsii (Площадь Революции).* **☎** *298 33 04. Open daily 11am-7pm; kassa closes at 6:30pm. Services Su 10am. Buy tickets from the kassa to the left of the entrance, then proceed upstairs. 100R, students 50R. Tour 350R. Cameras 40R, video 100R.)*

LENIN MAUSOLEUM. (Мавзолей ВИ Ленина; Mavzoley VI Lenina.) You've seen his likeness in bronze all over the city, now see him in the eerily luminescent flesh. In the glory days, fierce goose-stepping soldiers guarded this squat red structure in front of the Kremlin as somber visitors waited up to three hours to be admitted. The line is still long and the guards are still stone-faced, but most of the gravity is gone; visitors are more curious and bemused than reverent. Entrance to the mausoleum also gives access to the **Kremlin Wall,** which holds the remains of Stalin, Brezhnev, Andropov, Gagarin, and John Reed (author of *Ten Days that Shook the World*). Note the balcony on top of the mausoleum, where Russia's leaders stood during the May 1 and November 7 parades. Rumor has it that the plushest bathroom in Moscow is hidden in the back. Unfortunately it's not open to the public. *(Open Tu-Th and Sa-Su 10am-1pm.)*

STATE DEPARTMENT STORE GUM. (Государственный Универсальный Магазин (ГУМ); Gosudarstvenny Universalny Magazin.) Built in the 19th century, GUM was designed to hold 1000 stores. Its arched wrought iron and glass roofs resemble a Victorian train station. During Soviet rule, going to GUM was quite depressing—the sight of 1000 empty stores always is. These days, it's depressing only to those (almost everyone) who can't afford the goods. The complex has been renovated and is now a high-class, if somewhat tacky, arcade of boutiques and restaurants. *(M3: Ploshchad Revolutsii. From the Metro, turn left, then left again at the gate to Red Square. ☎ 929 33 81. Open M-Sa 9am-9pm, Su 11am-9pm.)*

KAZAN CATHEDRAL. (Казанский Собор; Kazansky Sobor.) The bright pink-and-green Kazan Cathedral has been rebuilt and reopened for services after being demolished in 1936 to make way for the May 1 parades. The interior of the faithful 1990s reconstruction is plainer than that of most Russian churches, and the iconostasis is relatively free of golden Baroque madness. *(M3: Ploshchad Revolutsii. Opposite St. Basil's, just to the left of the main entrance to Red Square. Open daily 8am-7pm. Services M-Sa 9am and 5pm; Su 7, 10am, and 5pm.)*

NORTH OF RED SQUARE

AREAS FOR WALKING. Just outside the main gate to Red Square is an elaborate gold circle marking **Kilometer 0,** the spot from which all distances from Moscow are measured. But don't be fooled by this tourist attraction—the real Kilometer 0 sits underneath the Lenin Mausoleum. Just a few steps away, the **Alexander Gardens** (Александровский Сад; Aleksandrovsky Sad) are a green respite from the pollution of central Moscow. At the north end of the gardens is the **Tomb of the Unknown Soldier** (Могила Неизвестного Солдата; Mogila Neizvestnovo Soldata), where an **Eternal Flame** burns in memory of the catastrophic losses suffered in World War II, known in Russia as the Great Patriotic War. Twelve urns containing soil from the Soviet Union's "Hero Cities," which suffered heavy casualties, also stand there.

AREAS FOR SHOPPING. Bordering Red Square are two other major squares: on the west side is **Manezh Square** (Манежная площадь; Manezhnaya Ploschad), only recently converted into a pedestrian area. The famous **Moscow Hotel** overlooks the square and separates it from the older, smaller **Revolution Square** (Площадь Революции; Ploschad Revolutsii). Both squares are connected in the north by **Okhotny Ryad** (Охотный Ряд; Hunters' Row), once a market for game. Across Okhotny Ryad from the Moscow Hotel is the **Duma,** or lower house of Parliament, and across from Revolution Square is **Theatre Square** (Театральная площадь; Teatralnaya Ploschad), home of the **Bolshoi and Maly Theatres** (see **Theatres,** p. 654). More posh hotels, chic stores, and government buildings line **Tverskaya Street,** which starts at Manezh Square and runs northwest. Tverskaya, home to some of Moscow's richest residents, is the closest the city gets to having a main street. The glass domes on Manezh Square provide sunlight to the ritzy **Okhotny Ryad underground mall,** overflowing with new trends and New Russians. *(Open daily 11am-11pm. Enter directly from the square or through the underpass.)*

RELIGIOUS SIGHTS

If the grime and bedlam get to you, escape to one of Moscow's houses of worship. Before the Revolution, the city had more than 1000 churches; today, there are fewer than 100, though many are being restored and reconstructed. Shorts are not permitted in Orthodox monasteries and women should cover their heads.

CATHEDRAL OF CHRIST THE SAVIOR. (Храм Христа Спасителя; Khram Khrista Spasitelya.) No one should leave Moscow without visiting the city's most controversial landmark; the enormous, gold-domed Cathedral of Christ the Savior, visible from just about anywhere in west Moscow. Nicholas I originally built a cathedral on this spot to commemorate Russia's victory over Napoleon, but in 1934 Stalin had it demolished, claiming it interfered with the city's biannual military parades. The minute the church was leveled, however, the truth came out: Stalin wanted to erect a "Palace of the Soviets," which he intended to be the tallest building in the world, on the spot. The ground ultimately proved too soft to hold a building of such weight, and after Stalin's death Khrushchev abandoned the project, converting the site into an outdoor swimming pool. In the early 1990s it was discovered that vapor from the heated water damaged paintings at the nearby Pushkin Museum, so the pool was closed. A controversy erupted over what was to become of the site; the Orthodox Church and Moscow's mayor finally won out and raised funds to build the US$250 million cathedral in just two years. As for where they got the money—well, let's just say it was a miracle. *(Volkhonka 15, between ul. Volkhonka (Волхонка) and the Moscow River. M1: Kropotkinskaya. ☎202 47 17; www.xxc.ru. Open daily 10am-5pm. Service schedule varies, but morning services are frequently at 8am, evening services at 5 or 6pm. Donations welcome. Tours (55R per person, students 35R) provide access to the building's observation deck with a rare view of the city.)*

NOVODEVICHY MONASTERY. (Новодевичий Монастырь; Novodevichi Monastyr.) The high brick walls of one of Moscow's most famous monasteries are crumbling slightly and its golden domes require some repair, but the complex is still worth seeing. The highlight, however, is the **cemetery** (кладбище; kladbishche), a pilgrimage site that cradles the graves of famous artists, politicians, and military men. Many tombstones are decorated with stylized representations of the deceased. Gogol, Chekhov, Stanislavsky, Bulgakov, Shostakovich, Tretyakov, Mayakovsky, Eisenstein, Prokofiev, and Scriabin all lie to the right of the dividing wall. Khrushchev's grave is also open to the public. **Smolensk Cathedral** (Смоленский Собор; Smolensky Sobor), in the center of the convent, shows off Russian icons and frescoes. English/Russian keys decode the elaborate maze of scenes depicted on the walls. Other buildings of interest include the red **Assumption Church** (Успенская Церковь; Uspenskaya Tserkov), to the right of the cathedral, and a small two-room exhibit hall at the far end of the grounds. *(M1: Sportivnaya. Take the exit that does not go to the stadium. Turn right and the monastery is several blocks down on the left. ☎246 85 26. Open W-M 10am-5:30pm; kassa closes at 4:45pm. Closed 1st M of each month. Cemetery open in summer daily 9am-7pm; off-season daily 9am-6pm. Very helpful English or Russian maps of the cemetery 5R. Smolensk cathedral closed on humid days. Call in advance. Grounds 40R, students 20R. Smolensk Cathedral and special exhibits each 93R, 53R. Cemetery 30R. Cameras 60R, video 150R. English tour 300R.)*

DANILOVSKY MONASTERY. (Даниловский Монастырь; Danilovsky Monastyr.) This monastery is home to the **Patriarch**, head of the Russian Orthodox Church. The well-preserved and recently restored white exterior is complemented by stunning grounds and long-robed monks. Unfortunately, visitors can enter only the church and the small museum, both to the left of the main entrance. The Patriarch's office is hard to miss, as it is marked by an enormous mosaic of a stern-looking man. *(M9: Tulskaya (Тульская). From the square, follow the trolley tracks down Danilovsky val., away from the gray buildings. Open daily 6:30am-7pm. Services M-F 6, 7am, and 5pm; Sa-Su 6:30, 9am, and 5pm. Museum open W and Sa-Su 11am-1pm and 1:30-4pm.)*

MOSCOW CHORAL SYNAGOGUE. First constructed in the 1870s, the Moscow Choral Synagogue is a much-needed break from the city's ubiquitous onion domes. Although it functioned during Soviet rule, all but the bravest Jews were scared off by KGB agents who photographed anyone that entered. Today more than 200,000 Jews live in Moscow, and services are increasingly well attended. The graffiti occasionally sprayed on the building is a sad reminder that anti-Semitism in Russia is not dead. Regular services are held every morning and evening, and a cafe on the premises serves kosher food. The entire Kitai-Gorod area around the synagogue, especially toward Red Square, is great for exploring on foot. *(Bolshoy Spasoglinishchevsky per. 10 (Большой Спасоглинищевский). M6 or 7: Kitai-Gorod. Go north on*

Solyansky Proezd (Солянский Проезд) and take the first left. ☎924 24 24 or 923 96 97. Open daily 8am-9pm. Su-Th services 8:30am and 8pm., F services 7:30pm, Sabbath services Sa 9am and 10am. Cafe open M-F 2-9pm.)

CHURCH OF ST. NICHOLAS OF THE WEAVERS. (Церковь Николы в Хамовниках; Tserkov Nikoly v Khamovnikakh.) One of Moscow's better-known churches, St. Nicholas's reddish-brown and green trim gives it the appearance of a giant Christmas ornament. Enter off ul. Lva Tolstovo (Лва Толстого) for the best view of the low ceilings and equally vivid interior. *(At the corner of Komsomolsky pr. M1 or 5: Park Kultury. Open daily 8am-8pm. Services M-Sa 8am and 5pm; Su 7, 10am, and 5pm.)*

AREAS TO EXPLORE

MOSCOW METRO. (Московское Метро.) The Metro, one of the most beautiful in the world, is worth a tour of its own. All of the stations are unique, and those inside the Circle Line are elaborate, with mosaics, sculptures, stained glass, and chandeliers. It's only 5R and you can stay as long you as like. Stations Kievskaya (Киевская), Mayakovskaya (Маяковская), Ploshchad Revolutsii (Площадь Революций), Komsomolskaya (Комсомольская), Novoslobodskaya (Новослободская), Rimskaya (Римская), and Mendeleevskaya (Менделеевская) are particularly noteworthy. Note the molecular-model light fixtures in the Mendeleevskaya station. *(Open daily 6am-1am.)*

ARBAT. (Арбат.) A pedestrian shopping arcade, the Arbat was once a showpiece of *glasnost* and a haven for political radicals, Hare Krishnas, street poets, and *metallisty* (heavy-metal rockers). Today, the flavor of political rebellion has been replaced by the more universal taste of capitalism. Still, some of the old Arbat remains, particularly in the large numbers of street performers and guitar-playing youths. Intersecting, but nearly parallel to the Arbat runs the bigger, newer, grayer **Novy Arbat,** a thoroughfare lined with foreign businesses, massive Russian stores, campy restaurants, and flashy lights. *(M3: Arbatskaya or Smolenskaya.)*

PUSHKINSKAYA PL. (Пушкинская пл.) Pushkinskaya has inherited the Arbat's tendency to political fervor. Missionary groups evangelize while amateur politicians gather to hand out petitions, and during the Thaw, dissidents came here to protest and voice their visions of a democratic Russia. Everything here is large—from the Golden Arches to the **Kinoteatr Rossiya,** Moscow's largest movie theater. Follow ul. Bolshaya Bronnaya down the hill, turn right, and follow ul. Malaya Bronnaya to **Patriarch's Pond** (Патриарший Пруд; Patriarshy Prud), where Bulgakov's *The Master and Margarita* begins. This area is popular with artsy students and old men who play dominoes by the pond. *(M7: Pushkinskaya.)*

PAN-RUSSIAN EXPOSITION CENTER. (Все-российский Выставочный Центр—ВВЦ; Vserossiysky Vystavochny Tsentr—VVTs.) The enormous center has changed a great deal since its conception. Formerly the **Exhibition of Soviet Economic Achievements** (VDNKh for short), this World's Fair-esque park filled with pavilions has ironically become a giant shopping mecca. *(M6: VDNKh (ВДНХ). Exiting the Metro to "ВВЦ," go left down the kiosk-flanked pathway and cross the street. Most shops open 10am-7pm.)*

PARKS

VICTORY PARK. (Парк Победы; Park Pobedy.) Victory Park is a popular gathering point, and its museum (see **Historical Museums,** p. 652) was built as a lasting monument to World War II. The main square showcases stones, each inscribed with a year that the Soviet troops fought in the war (1941-45). The gold-domed **Church of St. George the Victorious** (Храм Георгия Победаносного; Khram Georgiya Pobedanosnova) commemorates the 27 million Russians who died in battle. *(M4: Kutuzovskaya. Past the Triumphal Arch.)*

KOLOMENSKOYE SUMMER RESIDENCE. The tsars' summer residence sits on a wooded rise above the Moscow River. Directly above the river stands the white cone-shaped 16th-century **Assumption Cathedral** (Успенский Собор; Uspensky Sobor), Russia's first brick church built like a traditional wooden building (St. Basil's is the more famous example). The nearby **Church of Our Lady of Kazan** (Церковь Казанской Богоматери; Tserkov Kazanskoy Bogomatyeri), with its seven blue-and-gold cupolas, commemorates the Polish-Lithuanian expulsion of 1612. Several small historical museums stand on the extensive grounds; most notable is **Peter the Great's 1702 log cabin.** *(M2: Kolomenskaya (Коломенская). Follow the exit signs to "к музею Коломенское." Exiting the Metro, walk down the shaded, merchant-lined path that starts at the tall gray building. Go through the small black gate and follow the leftmost path up the hill to the main entrance gate (10min.). Map with an English key available at the entrance. Grounds open daily Apr.-Oct. 7am-10pm; Oct.-Apr. 9am-9pm. Free. Museums open Tu-Su 10am-5:30pm; kassa closes at 5pm. Each museum 60-70R, students 30-35R. Camera 5R.)*

IZMAYLOVSKY PARK. (Измайловский Парк.) Your one-stop-shop for all of your souvenir needs is Izmaylovsky Park and its colossal art market, **Vernisazh** (Вернисаж). Arrive late Sunday afternoon, when people want to go home and are willing to make a deal. Compare prices, as the first painted box you see will not be the last, guaranteed. If souvenirs aren't your bag, head to the park itself. *(M3: Izmaylovsky Park (Измайловский Парк). For the market, go left and follow the hordes. Open W 8am-3pm, Sa-Su 9am-6pm. Entrance W 5R, Sa-Su 10R. For the park, turn right and cross the street.)*

GORKY PARK. (Парк Горкого; Park Gorkovo.) In summer, out-of-towners and young Muscovites promenade, relax, ride the roller coaster, and even bungee jump at Moscow's **amusement park.** In winter, the paths are flooded to create a park-wide **ice rink.** Those seeking an American-style amusement park will be disappointed, as attractions are far outnumbered by ice cream kiosks, and the rides are on their last legs. Nevertheless, it's a fun place to mingle with delighted children, teenage couples, and a menagerie of "pet" animals, including monkeys and alligators. *(M1 or 5: Park Kultury or M5 or 6: Oktyabrskaya. From the Park Kultury stop, cross Krimskiy Most (Кримский Мост). From Oktyabrskaya, walk downhill on Krimskiy Val. Park open 24hr. Ice rink open Nov.-Apr. Admission M-F 35R, ages 7-12 10R; Sa-Su 40R/10R. Free after 9pm and for children under 7. Most rides 80-160R.)*

KRASNAYA PRESNYA AND ZOOPARK. (Красная Пресня и Зоопарк.) One of the cleanest of the city's serene green areas, Krasnaya Presnya attracts readers and small children with its scattered wooden playgrounds and quiet benches. *(M7: Ulitsa 1905 goda (Улица 1905 года). Exit to and then cross ul. Krasnaya Presnya; the park stretches along ul. 1905 goda.)* The action is livelier a few blocks down ul. Krasnaya Presnya at the **Zoopark.** Going to the zoo used to be a bit like watching calves raised for veal, until Mayor Luzhkov directed his energy and fund-raising talents toward improving the animals' quality of life. *(Main entrance across from M7: Barikadnaya. ☎ 255 53 75. Open Tu-Su 10am-8pm; kassa closes at 7pm. 60R. Cameras free, video 25R.)*

🏛 MUSEUMS

Moscow's museum scene remains the most patriotic and least Westernized part of the city. Large government museums and small galleries alike proudly display Russian art, and dozens of historical and literary museums are devoted to the nation's past. They want you to see it thoroughly, too—*babushki* spill their wealth of knowledge on visitors and yell at those who breeze through exhibits too quickly, while entry into museums stops well before closing time. Ticket prices are much lower for natives than for foreigners; prices get up to 80% if you are a foreigner.

ART GALLERIES AND MUSEUMS

■ **STATE TRETYAKOV GALLERY.** (Государственная Третьяковская Галерея; Gosudarstvennaya Tretyakovskaya Galereya.) Founded with Tretyakov's 1892 donation of his private collection, this gallery is a veritable treasure chest of Russian national art. The 18th- and 19th-century portraits and landscapes comprise most of the collection, although it contains works by early 20th-century artists as well. The museum also displays a magnificent collection of icons, including works by Andrei Rublyov and Theophanes the Greek. The neighboring gallery, located at Lavrushinsky per. 12, holds rotating exhibits of both Russian and foreign art. *(Lavrushinsky per. 10 (Лаврушинский). M8: Tretyakovskaya* (Третьяковская). *Exiting the Metro, turn left and then left again, followed by an immediate right on Bolshoy Tolmachevsky per. Walk 2 blocks and turn right on Lavrushinsky per. ☎230 77 88 or 951 13 62; www.tretyakov.ru. Open Tu-Su 10am-7:30pm.* Kassa *closes at 6:30pm. 225R, students 130R. Audio guide 240R. For an English tour call ☎953 52 23. 430R.)*

■ **NEW TRETYAKOV GALLERY.** (Новый Третьяковская Галерея; Novii Tretyakovskaya Galereya.) Built to house newer works and exhibitions of Russian art, the New Tretyakov Gallery shares a building with the Central House of Artists and picks up chronologically where the State Tretyakov leaves off. The collection starts on the third floor with early 20th-century art and moves through the Neo-Primitivist, Futurist, Suprematist, Cubist, and Social Realist schools. The second floor holds temporary exhibits that often draw huge crowds; it's best to go on weekday mornings. Behind the gallery to the right lies a graveyard for fallen statues. Once the main dumping ground for decapitated Lenins and Stalins, it now contains plaques and neat pathways to ease your journey among sculptures of Gandhi, Einstein, and Niels Bohr. A controversial statue of Soviet secret police founder Dzerzhinsky was nearly returned to its original location before the Duma passed legislation to keep it in the graveyard. *(Ul. Krimskiy Val 10 (Крымский Вал). M5: Oktyabraskaya. From the Metro, walk towards the big intersection at Kaluzhskaya pl. (Калужская пл.); turn right on Ul. Krimskiy. ☎238 13 78 . English captions. Open Tu-Su 10am-7:30pm;* kassa *closes 6:30pm. 225R, students 130R. Camera 30R. Call ahead for an English tour, 430R.)*

PUSHKIN MUSEUM OF FINE ARTS. (Музей Изобразительных Искусств им. А.С. Пушкина; Muzey Izobrazitelnykh Iskusstv im. A.S. Pushkina.) The Pushkin, Moscow's most important non-Russian art collection, was founded in 1912 by poet Marina Tsvetaeva's father, who wanted his art students to see original pieces of Classical art. Today—no doubt to his chagrin—plaster copies of Greek statues and lifesize architectural models dominate much of the floor space. Still, the museum boasts some major Egyptian, Classical, and European Renaissance works, a superb collection of modern painting (including Van Gogh, Chagall, and Picasso), and various temporary exhibits. *(Ul. Volkhonka 12 (Волхонка). M1: Kropotkinskaya. ☎203 95 78. Open Tu-Su 10am-7pm;* kassa *closes at 6pm. 160R, students 60R. Audio guide 100R, deposit 200R. Call ahead for an English tour ☎203 74 12.)*

MUSEUM OF CONTEMPORARY ART. (Музей Современного Искусства; Muzey Sovremennovo Iskusstva.) A large collection of works in varied media by Russian artists, including Zurab Tsereteli, Miró, Alexander Calder, and N. B. Hogans. *(Petrovka 25 (Петровка). M9: Chekhovskaya. Walk down Strasnoy bul. and go right on Petrovka. ☎200 66 95. Open W-M noon-8pm.* Kassa *closes at 7pm. 90R, students 45R. Tours 350R.)*

EXHIBITION HALL OF THE RUSSIAN ACADEMY OF ART. This 60-room gallery displays both old and new Russian art, including painting, sculpture, mosaic, and costume design. Zurab Tsereteli, the builder of the monument to Peter the Great, has many works on permanent display here. *(Ul. Prechistenka 19 (Пречистенка). M1: Kropotkinskaya. From the Pushkin Literary Museum, go 2 blocks to the left. ☎201 47 71. Open Tu-Sa noon-8pm, Su noon-7pm; last entrance 1hr. before closing. 120R.)*

RUSSIA

CENTRAL HOUSE OF ARTISTS. (Центральный Дом Художника; Tsentralny Dom Khudozhnika.) One part art museum, one part gallery, and one part upscale gift shop, this central house inspires dilettantes and serious collectors alike to come check out the cutting edge exhibits. *(Ul. Krimskiy Val 10. In the same building as the State Tretyakov Gallery (see above). M1 or 5: Park Kultury. ☎238 96 34. Open Tu-Su 11am-8pm; kassa closes at 7pm. 25R, students 10R.)*

THE MONUMENT TO SOVIET SPACE ACHIEVEMENTS. Because of its enviable phallus-like semblance, locals jokingly refer to this tall, aesthetically-challenged obelisk as "the dream" (мечта, mechta). It stands atop the Cosmonaut Museum (Музей Космонавтики; Muzey Kosmonavtiki), equally garish in its displays of life in space and aboard Sputnik, complete with Russian cosmonaut food: freeze-dried borscht. *(Pr. Mira 111, among the kiosks by the Metro. ☎283 79 14. Open Tu-Su 10am-7pm; closed last F of the month. 20R, students 6R. Camera 25R, video 60R.)*

HISTORICAL MUSEUMS

■ **KGB MUSEUM.** (Музей КГБ; Muzey KGB.) The museum exhibits holdings and strategies of Russian secret intelligence from the reign of Ivan the Terrible to the present. Visitors will love the entertaining stories and the Bond-esque devices of the most feared secret police in the world. *(Ul. Bul. Lubyanka 12 (Бул. Лубянка). M1: Lubyanka. The building behind the concrete bohemoth that towers over the northeast side of the square. This museum is actually a training center for the FSB (the new KGB), so it is only open for pre-arranged tours. Patriarshy Dom Tours (see **Tourist and Financial Services,** p. 639) leads 2hr. group tours of the museum. US$15, plus extra for a private tour.)*

STATE HISTORICAL MUSEUM. (Государственный Исторический Музей; Gosu-darstvennyi Istoricheskii Muzey.) A comprehensive collection, tracing Russian history from the Neanderthals through Kyivan Rus to modern Russia. Highlights include ancient idols and jewelry, elaborate medieval icons, and paintings of various historical figures. *(Krasnaya pl. 1/2. M1: Okhotny Ryad. Entrance to the right just inside Red Square. ☎292 37 31. Open W-M daily 11am-7pm; kassa closes at 6pm. Closed the 1st M of the month. 150R, students 75R. Camera 60R, video 100R.)*

MUSEUM OF CONTEMPORARY RUSSIAN HISTORY. (Центральный Музей Современной Истории России; Tsentralny Muzey Sovremennoi Istorii Rossii.) Housed in the former mansion of the Moscow English club, the museum covers Russian history from the late 19th century to the present in exhaustive detail. Cold War propaganda posters are complemented by newly displayed statistics on the ill effects of socialism. *(Ul. Tverskaya 21. M7: Pushkinskaya. Exiting the Metro, walk 1 block uphill on Tverskaya and through the gates on the left. ☎299 67 24. Open Tu-Sa 10am-6pm, Su 10am-5pm. Last entry 30min. before closing. Closed last F of the month. 25R. Camera 75R, video 150R. Call ahead for English tour; 700R for 25 people.)*

CENTRAL MUSEUM OF THE ARMED FORCES. (Центральный Музей Вооруженных Сил; Tsentralny Muzey Vooruzhennykh Sil.) The museum exhibits a large collection of weapons, uniforms, and artwork from the time of Peter the Great to the debacle in Chechnya. Don't miss the big outdoor display of tanks and planes behind the museum. *(Ul. Sovetskoy Armii 2 (Советской Армии). M5: Novoslobod-skaya. Walk down ul. Seleznevskaya (Селезневская) to the rotary (10min.). Turn left after the theater and bear right at the fork. ☎281 63 03. Open W-Su 10am-5pm. 20R, students 10R. Camera 20R. Call ahead for an English tour 300R.)*

MUSEUM OF THE GREAT PATRIOTIC WAR. (Музей Отечественной Войны; Muzey Otechestvennoy Voyny.) This impressive museum was one of Mayor Luzh-kov's most ambitious building projects, but the grandiosity of the building itself can undermine the solemnity of its subject matter. The museum includes an art gallery, war history exposition, dioramas, and Halls of Glory, Memory, and others. *(Pl. Pobedy. M3: Kutuzovskaya. Behind the tall black WWII monument obelisk in Victory Park.* ☎ *142 38 75. Open Tu-Su 10am-5pm. Closed last Th of the month. 80R, students 40R. Camera 15R, video 20R.)* In the park behind the museum to the left (as you face it) is the **Exposition of War Technology** (Експозиция Военной Техники; Ekspozitsiya Voyennoy Tekhniki), a large outdoor display of aircraft, tanks, and weaponry. *(Open Tu-Su 10am-5pm. Closed last Th of the month.)*

BORODINO. (Бородино.) The popular blue cylindrical museum, guarded by an equestrian statue of General Kutuzov, houses a large 360° panorama of the bloody battle against Napoleon in August 1812 *(see* **History,** p. 621. *Kutuzovsky pr. 38. M3: Kutuzovskaya. Walk 10min. down Kutuzovsky pr. toward the Triumphal arch.* ☎ *148 19 67 or 148 19 27. Open M-Th and Sa-Su 10am-6pm. Kassa closes at 4:45pm and takes a break 2-2:30pm. Open to tourists after 2pm. Closed last Th of the month. Different hours for Russians—flash a passport if the guards give you trouble. 45R, students 30R. Camera 20R, video 50R.)*

ANDREI SAKHAROV MUSEUM. (Музей и Общественный Центр имени Андрея Сахарова; Muzei i Obshchestvennyi Tsentr imeni Andreya Sacharova.) This two-story complex commemorates the nuclear scientist and patron saint of anti-Soviet ideologues throughout the country and abroad. *(Ul. Zemlyanoi Val. 57, ctr. 6. M10: Chkalovskaya* (Чкаловская). *Proceed to the main street, turn left, and walk 1½ blocks.* ☎ *923 44 01; www.sakharov-center.ru. Open Tu-Su 11am-7pm. Free.)*

HOUSES OF THE LITERARY AND FAMOUS

Russians take immense pride in their literary history, to the extent of preserving authors' houses in their original state, down to half-empty teacups on the mantelpiece. Each is guarded by a team of fiercely loyal *babushki*. Plaques on buildings mark where writers, artists, and philosophers lived and worked.

▨ PUSHKIN LITERARY MUSEUM. (Литературный Музей Пушкина; Literaturny Muzey Pushkina.) If you haven't seen Pushkin-worship first-hand, this large museum will either convert or frighten you. The beautiful modern building is full of Pushkin artifacts, from art illustrating his works to costumes, portrait busts, and other memorabilia dating from the poet's time to the present. *(Ul. Prechistenka 12/2* (Пречистерка). *M1: Kropotkinskaya. Entrance on Khrushchevsky per.* (Хрущевский). ☎ *201 56 74. Open Tu-Su 11am-7pm;* kassa *closes 6pm. Closed last F of the month. 25R, students 10R. Camera 40R, video 150R.)*

TOLSTOY MUSEUM. (Музей Толстого; Muzey Tolstovo.) This yellow-and-white building in the neighborhood of Tolstoy's first Moscow residence displays original texts, paintings, and letters related to Tolstoy's masterpieces. *(Ul. Prechistenka 11* (Пречистенка). *M1: Kropotkinskaya.* ☎ *202 21 90. English captions. Open Tu-Su 11am-7pm;* kassa *closes at 6pm. Closed last F of the month. 70R, students 30R. Camera 50R.)*

MAYAKOVSKY MUSEUM. (Музей им. В. В. Маяковского; Muzey im. B.B. Mayakovskovo.) This is more of a walk-through work of Futurist art than a biographical museum, with the artist's papers and art arranged in a bizarre four-story assemblage of chairs, spilled paint, and chicken wire. Mayakovsky lived here in a communal apartment from 1919 until 1930 when he shot himself. His room is preserved at the top of the building, and the rest of the museum was built around it as a poetic reminder. *(Lubyansky pr. 3/6* (Лубянский). *M1: Lubyanka. Look for the bust of Mayakovsky surrounded by huge crimson metal shards on ul. Myasnitskaya; the museum is in the building behind it.* ☎ *928 25 69. Open F-Tu 10am-6pm, Th 1-9pm. Closed last F of the month. 60R. Call ahead for an English tour 600R.)*

GORKY MUSEUM-HOUSE. (Музей-дом Горкого; Muzey-dom Gorkovo.) This museum is a pilgrimage site as much for its architectural interest as for its collection of Maxim Gorky's possessions. Designed by F.O. Shekhtel in 1900, it's one of the best examples of Art Nouveau in Moscow. *(Ul. Malaya Nikitskaya 6/2 (Малая Никитская). M3: Arbatskaya. From the Metro, cross Novy Arbat and turn right on Merzlyakovsky per. (Мерзляковский пер.) Cross the small park to reach ul. Malaya Nikitskaya. ☎290 51 30. Open W and F noon-7pm, Th and Sa-Su 10am-5pm. Closed last Th of the month. Free, but donations requested. Camera 50R. Group tour 500R.)*

STANISLAVSKY MUSEUM-HOUSE. (Музей-дом Станиславского; Muzey-dom Stanislavskovo.) The venerated theater director held lessons and performances in his home, which now displays his collection of the costumes used for his famous theatrical productions. *(Leontyevsky per. 6. M7: Pushkinskaya. Walk down ul. Tverskaya and go right on Leontevsky per. Enter in back and ring the doorbell. ☎229 24 42 or 229 90 88. Open Th and Sa-Su 11am-6pm, W and F 2-8pm; kassa closes one hour before museum. Closed last Th of the month. Concerts Sept.-June (info ☎299 11 92). Museum 50R. Camera 20R. Tours 500R.)*

LEO TOLSTOY ESTATE. The author lived here during the winters of 1882-1901. His furniture, family photographs, and other possessions are on display in the small building next to his home, where they'll be returned after renovation is completed in 2003. *(Ul. Lva Tolstovo 21. M1 or 5: Park Kultury. Exiting the Metro, walk down Komsomolsky pr. toward the colorful Church of St. Nicholas of the Weavers; turn right at the corner on ul. Lva Tolstovo. ☎246 94 44. Open Tu-Sa 10am-5pm; in winter 10am-3:30pm; kassa closes 30min. earlier. Closed last F of the month. 100R, students 50R. Camera 30R, video 50R.)*

DOSTOYEVSKY HOUSE-MUSEUM. (Дом-Музей Достоевского; Dom-Muzey Dostoyevskovo.) This museum in the author's childhood home displays some of the family's original furniture and photographs. The tour ends with the author's fountain pen. *(Ul. Dostoyevskovo 2. M5: Novoslobodskaya. From ul. Seleznevskaya (Селезневская), take a left at the trolley tracks onto Dostoyevsky per. and follow the tracks onto ul. Dostoyevskovo; the museum is on the left. ☎281 10 85. Open May-Sept. W-F 2-8pm, Th and Sa-Su 11am-6pm; Oct.-Apr. W-F 2-6pm, Th and Sa-Su 11am-6pm. Closed the last day of the month. 50R, students 10R. Camera 50R, video 100R.)*

CHEKHOV HOUSE-MUSEUM. (Музей-дом Чехова; Muzey-dom Chekhova.) Chekhov lived here with a baffling number of relatives from 1886 to 1890, writing, receiving patients, and thinking. *(Ul. Sadovaya-Kudrinskaya 6 (Садовая-Кудринская) M7: Barikadnaya. Exiting the Metro, turn left on ul. Barikadnaya, and left again on Sadovaya-Kudrinskaya. ☎291 61 54. English captions. Open Tu, Th, and Sa-Su 11am-6pm, W and F 2-8pm; kassa closes 1hr. early. Closed the last F of the month. 10R, students 8R.)*

◨ ENTERTAINMENT

THEATER, BALLET, AND OPERA

Summer (July-Aug.) is the wrong season for theater in Moscow. Russian companies are on tour and the only folks playing in Moscow are touring productions from other cities, which, with the exception of those from St. Petersburg, tend to be of lesser quality. From September through June, however, Moscow boasts some of the world's best **theater, ballet,** and **opera,** as well as excellent **orchestras.** Most of these are in the northern part of the city center. If you buy **tickets** far enough in advance and don't demand front row center, you can attend very cheaply (US$2-5). Tickets can usually be purchased from the *kassa* located inside the theater. (Usually open from noon until curtain.) Tickets to most events are also sold at the "Театры" kiosks around the city.

Bolshoi Theater (Большой Театр), Teatralnaya pl. 1 (Театральная; ☎292 00 50; fax 292 90 32; www.bolshoi.ru). M2: Teatralnaya (Театральная). Literally, "The Big Theater." Home to both the opera and the world-renowned ballet companies. *Kassa* open M-W and F-Su 11am-3pm and 4-7pm, Th 11am-3pm and 4-9pm. Daily performances Sept.-June at noon and 7pm. Tickets 20-3500R. MC/V.

Maly Theater (Малый Театр), Teatralnaya pl. 1/6 (☎923 26 21). M2: Teatralnaya. Just right of the Bolshoy as you face it. Affiliate at Bolshaya Ordynka 69 (☎237 31 81 or 237 44 72). All performances in Russian. *Kassa* open daily noon-3pm and 4-7pm. Daily performances 7pm. Tickets 20-300R. from the *kassa* located inside the theater.

Musical Operetta Theater, ul. Bolshaya Dmitrovka 6 (Большая Дмитровка; ☎292 12 37; www.operetta.org.ru). To the left of the Bolshoy. Famous operettas staged year-round. *Kassa* open M-Th noon-3pm and 4-7pm, F-Su noon-3pm and 4-6pm. Performances M-Th 7pm, F-Su 6pm, with additional daytime performances. Tickets 30-300R.

The Young Spectators' Theater (Московский Театр Юного Зрителя; Moskovky Teatr Yunovo Zritelya), Mamonovsky per. 10 (Мамоновский; ☎299 53 60; www.theatre.ru/mtyz). M7: Pushkinskaya. Walk 2 blocks up Tverskaya toward Mayakovskaya and turn left on Mamonovsky. Though named after its occasional children's shows, this theater is known for its excellent productions of 20th-century plays. *Kassa* open daily noon-3pm and 4-7pm. Performances daily at 7pm. Tickets 50-500R.

CIRCUS

Old Moscow State Circus, Tsvetnoi Bulvar 13 (Цветной Бульвар; ☎200 10 60). M9: Tsvetnoi Bulvar. Turn right and walk half a block; it's on the right, recently renovated. Animal acts in the 1st half and glittery acrobatics in the 2nd. Buy a ticket to the popular show 2-3 days in advance. *Kassa* open M-F 11am-2pm and 3-7pm, Sa-Su 11am-12:30pm and 1:30-7pm. Performances Th-M 6 or 7pm, with an occasional 2:30pm show on weekends. Tickets 20-350R.

THE BANYA EXPERIENCE. If weeks of traveling on sweltering, crowded trains and living out of a backpack have you feeling not-so-fresh, a trip to a Russian *banya* (bath) is in order. Similar in theory to a Turkish bath, the *banya* experience is a cyclical whirlwind of hot and cold extremes that rejuvenate by shock therapy. The men's and women's sections of each *banya* are divided into four rooms. The first stop is the dressing room, staffed by attendants who rent linen, assign places, and sell drinks and snacks. Next comes the shower room, whose purpose is self-explanatory. The *parilka* (steam room) is the third and most lavishly praised room of the *banya*. With temperature upwards of 110°F (43°C) and the air thick with the fragrance of scented oils, the steam's magic will draw out your tensions along with a lot of sweat. Before you pass out, plunge into the dipping pool; at 60°F (16°C), the water is sure to cool you off quickly. The final stage is a return to the *parilka*, this time engaging in the quasi-masochistic tradition of the birch branches. While showering, soften a bundle of birch branches *(veniki)* with hot water, then beat yourself to exfoliate dead skin and improve circulation. *Banya* sessions typically last two hours; prices are listed for the standard experience, but myriad other services, including massages and manicures, can be enjoyed at additional cost. The heat can be dangerous, so don't go if you're pregnant or have a weak heart, and try to bring an experienced friend on your first trip. Save some rubles by bringing a towel, sheet, soap, and shampoo.

HUNGRY FOR MORE

The club that started the wild clubbing tradition in Moscow, and arguably the most famous—or infamous—club in the world, the Hungry Duck in Moscow has certainly made a name of itself. As much a Moscow landmark as the Kremlin, the club has become known internationally for its debauched parties and Sodomesque Ladies' Nights.

Uninhibited women are welcomed into the bar to freely consume mass quantities of alcohol and get down on top of the circular, arena-like bar. In short time they're too drunk to protest when the floodgates of testosterone are opened. Hordes of howling men, tourists and businessmen alike, egg the women onto the central platform, where men are not allowed, to entertain the crowd with some naughty behavior. Ladies who get fully naked (often together) are rewarded with a shower of golden champagne as the manager pops the cork, shakes the bottle, and slams it down on the bar, drenching half the crowd in the process.

In all fairness though, the "Duck," as it is called by locals, provides equal opportunity for male bacchanalia—in theory. Although officially men are not allowed to take off their shirts, the rules are sometimes broken when

(continued on next page)

BANYAS

Sandunovskiye Bani (Сандуновские Бани), a.k.a. Nomerny Bani (Номерные Бани), ul. Neglinnaya 14 (Неглинная; ☎925 46 31). M7: Kuznetsky Most. Enter on Zvonarsky per (Звонарский). Moscow's oldest *banya* features high ceilings, cavernous rooms, and classical statues. 2hr. sessions 500-600R, but worth it. If your wallet can handle it, ask for the "upper-class" treatment. Massages start at 500R. Open W-M 8am-10pm.

Bani Na Presnye (Бани На Пресне), Stolyarny per. 7 (Столярный; ☎255 53 06). M7: Ulitsa 1905 Goda. Stolyarny per. is the first right on ul. Presnensky (Пресненский) from the square. This Large and sparsely decorated *banya* gets crowded on weekends. 2hr. sessions 350R, weekends 450R. Open daily 8am-10pm.

📧 NIGHTLIFE

Moscow's nightlife, the most Bacchanalian experience this side of the Volga, is certainly the most varied, expensive, and dangerous in Eastern Europe. Some of the more interesting clubs enjoy flaunting their high cover charges and face-control policies, but these places invariably have a short lifespan. Restaurants often transform into dance clubs after dark, while myriad casinos stay open all hours of the night. Several more sedate venues draw bohemians and absinthe-seeking students with their cheap prices. *The Moscow Times*'s Friday pull-out section, *The Beat*, and the *The Exile*'s nightlife section (www.exile.ru) each provide excellent synopses of the week's events, as well as up-to-date reviews.

CLUBS

📧 **Propaganda** (Пропаганда), Bolshoy Zlatoustinsky per. 7 (Большой Златоустинский; ☎924 57 32). M6 or 7: Kitai-Gorod. Exiting the Metro, walk down ul. Maroseyka and take a left on Bolshoy Zlatoustinsky per.; the club is on the right. Once voted one of the best clubs in Europe, Propaganda is the best place in Moscow to dance to good house and not feel like you're in a meat market. The big night is Th: every Muscovite under 25 (and his brother) comes in hip threads, and the huge crowd inevitably spills out onto the street. Su night is reputedly one of the city's best gay parties. Beer 70R. 0.5L sangria 120R. Cover F-Sa 70R. Su cover 100R. Open daily noon-6am.

📧 **Projekt OGI** (Проэкт ОГИ), 8/12 Potapovsky per., bldg. 2 (Потаповский; ☎927 57 76; http://proekt.ogi.ru).

M1: Chistye Prudy. From the Metro, head down bul. Chistoprudny past the statue of Griboedov. Make the 1st right and then the 1st left on Potapovsky per. Hip but convivial, colorful but laid-back, this club has a lot of character and a unique atmosphere. Exceptional food and wine at low prices. Concerts start at 11pm. Cover 100-150R. Open 24hr. MC/V.

Respublika Beefeater, ul. Nikolskaya 17 (Никольская; ☎928 46 92). M3: Ploshchad Revolutsii. Follow the signs to ul. Nikolskaya away from Red Square; the bar is on the left. Great dance music and a lively student crowd, with plenty of room for eating, lounging, and good conversation. Beer 65R-125R. Live DJ Th-Sa at 11pm. Occasional live music. Cover F-Sa men 100R, women 50R; varies when there's a concert. Open daily 11am-6am. MC/V.

Karma Bar, ul. Pushechnaya 3 (☎924 56 33). M: Kuznetzky Most. With your back to the Metro, walk through the archway on your left, and turn right on ul. Pushechnaya. This club spins crowd-pleasing dance music and attracts hordes on the weekends. Hookahs, plush couches, and amazing club dancers entertain those who come without their dancing shoes, and Su's hip-hop night is the weekly favorite of Moscow's African community. 0.33L beer 100-140R, vodka 80-150R, cocktails 180R. Cover for men 150R, women 50R. Open W-Su 7pm-6am.

Mix, Novinsky Blvd. 11 (☎255 43 33). M3: Smolenskaya. Walk up Novinsky Blvd. away from Smolenskaya pl. and cross under Novy Arbat; look for the neon "X" sign. This small, hipped-out techno club appeals to the same crowd that goes to Propaganda on Th nights. Futuristic, with TVs in the walls and funky glass bars. Considered by some an after-party club; the crowds actually roll in around 5am. DJs spin "deep house." Beer from 60R, cocktails 140-200R. Cover F-Sa 150R. Open Th-Sa 24hr.

Hippopotamus (Гиппопотам), ul. Mantulinsky 5/1 (☎256 23 46). M7: Ulitsa 1905 Goda. Cross and continue down Tryokhgornyy Val (Труохгорный). After the park, go right on Shmitovskiy Per. (Шмитовский), then take the first left onto Ulitsa 1905 Goda. Take the next right on ul. Mantulinsky; the club is on the left. The entrance is around back. The consistent hip-hop, R&B, and soul music attracts local students, expats, and businessmen alike. W Arabian night, Th Latin night, with a live band and dance lessons; Su Ladies' Night, with no cover and free champagne for ladies. Beer US$2-3, cocktails US$2-5. Cover free-US$6. Open W-Su 10pm-6am.

a female stripper finds an impressionable young man who's wasted and willing to have his drawers dropped for all to see. If champagne showers and simulated sex aren't enough, bathrooms and corners can become impromptu bordellos, where the masses get not-so-discreetly busy to the sonic sex pulsing through the sound system.

By the end of Ladies' night, a hundred people will get laid, a few plastered women will have to be helped out, and occasionally someone breaks a limb from a drunken plummet off the bar. While the Duck closed with most other Moscow clubs during the financial crisis of 1998, it reopened and continues with the same infamous vigor. If you don't want to become an active part of the stripshow—i.e. be stripped—don't stand too close to the bar. Women have fun, but be warned: the concept of sexual harassment does not seem to exist in Moscow

(Ul. Pushechnaya 9 (Пушечная; ☎923 61 58, www.hungryduck.com). M7: Kuznetsky Most. Beer 70-100R. Tu, F, and Su Ladies' Night: women drink free while watching male strippers. W Oktoberfest: all-you-can-drink beer men 200R, women 50R. Cover M, Th, and Sa men 100-200R, women free-50R. Open daily 8pm-6am.)

—*Charles L. Black*

EXPAT HANGOUTS

■ **Central Station** (Центральная Станция), 16/2 Bolshaya Tartarskaya ul., bldg. 2 (☎959 46 43; www.gaycentral.ru). M6 or 8: Tretyakovskaya (Третьяковская). Turn right out of the station and left on Bolshaya Tartarskaya. Nightly live music and vigorous pole dancing presage acclaimed "Gay Broadway," a drag fantasia that might make Rupaul blush. Outdoor patio. Live shows Th-Su 1:30-3am. Cover before 1am 160R, women 500R; students 80/250R.

Crazy Milk, ul. Bolshaya Polyanka 54 (Большая Полянка; ☎230 73 33). M5: Dobryninskaya. Cross ul. Zhitnaya (Житная) to your left and make a left on Bolshaya Polyanka. Impressive decor is elegant, eclectic, and crazy all at the same time. American favorites (buffalo wings 29R Su-Th 6pm-midnight) and drink specials (Happy Hour Su-Th 5-7pm) pack the place. Cuban cigars 320-520R. Ask for the cheaper patio menu (210-570R). Beer US$3-5. Breakfast served 10am-1pm. Open daily noon-6am. AmEx/MC/V.

Doug and Marty's Boar House, Zemlyanoi Val. 26 (☎917 01 50). M3: Kurskaya. Opposite the train station. About as American as you can get in Moscow, prices included. Packed on weekends. Happy Hour 6-9pm. 50% discount on food noon-9pm. Texas Chili 235R. Beer 90-145R. Billiards 50R per game. Cover men 150R, women 75R. Open daily noon-6am. AmEx/MC/V.

⚑ DAYTRIP FROM MOSCOW

SERGIEV POSAD (СЕРГИЕВ ПОСАД)

Elektrichki run to "Sergiev Posad" from Yaroslavsky Vokzal (1½ hr., every 20-50min., round-trip 61R). Departure times are listed immediately outside the prigorodnaya kassa (пригородная касса; suburban cashier). Alternatively, purchase a one-way train ticket (31R) and return via the bus outside the Sergiev Posad station (every 20min., 30R). Buses back to Moscow go to either Yaroslavsky Vokzal or VDNKh. To get to the monastery, turn right, look up to find the gold domes, cross the street, and follow the road to the city (10-15min.). Monastery open 9am-6pm. English tours 250R. Museums open W-Su 10am-5:30pm. Entrance to the monastery is free, but there are fees to enter special sections and museums. Cameras 100R.

Russia's famous pilgrimage point, Sergiev Posad (pop. 200,000), attracts believers to the several churches clustered at its main sight, **St. Sergius's Trinity Monastery** (Свято-Троицкая Сергиева Лавра; Svyato-Troitskaya Sergieva Lavra). During Soviet times, Sergiev Posad was called Zagorsk, and many locals still use the name. After decades of state-propagated atheism, this stunning monastery, founded in the 1340s, has again become a thriving religious center. The patriarch of the Russian Orthodox Church, also known as the Metropolitan, resided here until 1988, when he moved to Moscow's Danilovsky Monastery (see **Religious Sights,** p. 647).

Each church is exquisite, but Russian Orthodoxy's opulent colors come out in the **Trinity Cathedral** (Троицкий Собор; Troitsky Sobor), filled with gilded Andrei Rublyov icons. Nearby, the magnificently frescoed ceiling of the **Refectory** (Трапезная; Trapeznaya), supported by vine-clad columns, is a delightful sight to behold. The **Chapel-at-the-Well** (Надкладезная Часовия; Nadkladeznaya Chasoviya) has a superstitious history: allegedly, it was established after a spring with magical healing powers appeared here. *Babushki* still come with empty bottles to carry the holy water home. Next door, **Assumption Cathedral** (Успенский Собор; Uspensky Sobor), modeled after the eponymous cathedral in Moscow's Kremlin (see p. 644) proves itself as splendid as any larger house of worship. Upon leaving, go left to see the **grave of Boris Godunov** (see **History,** p. 623). The fortress wall at the far end of the monastery gives access to the 55m **Pilgrim's tower** and its panoramic view of the monastery and city (20R).

THE GOLDEN RING (ЗОЛОТОЕ КОЛЬЦО)

To the north and east of Moscow lies the Golden Ring (Zolotoye Koltso), a string of towns with some of the most beautiful and best-loved churches and kremlins (fortresses) in Russia. Many of the towns reached their zenith in the 12th century, as power shifted north with the weakening of Kyiv. Since then, they have struggled to remain important to their ever-changing nation. Formerly Russian capitals, Suzdal and Rostov still maintain kremlins of extraordinary elegance. Yaroslavl, the capital of its own principality in the 13th century, is today one of the most attractive cities in Russia. The slower, more elegant pace of these towns provides a much-needed break from the chaos of Moscow.

YAROSLAVL (ЯРОСЛАВЛЬ) ☎(8)0852

Yaroslavl (yi-ra-SLAH-vl; pop. 630,000), which acquired its wealth from 16th century trade with the Middle East and the West, has always fought hard to retain its autonomy. In earlier eras, its citizens tried to get fair deals and keep foreign influence to a minimum. Fortunately for visitors and residents alike, they had some success, and the city still has wide, green boulevards, parks, and riverside walks perfect for romantic strolls. With its relative proximity to Moscow, Yaroslavl offers the best of two worlds: provincial charm and capital-city comforts.

▐ TRANSPORTATION

Trains: Glavny Vokzal (☎79 21 12 or 79 21 11) sends trains to: **Moscow** (4½hr., 19 per day, 125R); **St. Petersburg** (12hr., 4 per day, 229R); **Vologda** (4hr., 1 per day, 112R). Some trains also stop at **Moskovsky Vokzal,** including trains for **Nizhny Novgorod** (8½hr., 1-2 per day, 145R). *Kassa* #4 open 24hr.

Buses: Avtovokzal (☎44 18 37), in the same building as Moskovsky Vokzal. To: **Vladimir** (5½hr., 4 per week, 130R); **Vologda** (4½hr., 1 per day, 104R). For those trying to go from Yaroslavl to Vladimir when the buses don't run, take a bus to **Ivanovo** (3 hr., 2 per day, 76R) where you can catch one of many buses to Vladimir (2½ hr., 60R).

Public Transportation: Yaroslavl's public transportation system is excellent; trolleys and buses stop every 3min. Buy tickets (4R) at the light blue kiosks next to main stops labeled "яргортранс" or on board if there is no kiosk. Once aboard, hand your ticket or money to the person with the black waist pouch. 10R fine for getting caught ticketless.

▐ ORIENTATION

Yaroslavl lies at the confluence of the **Volga** and **Kotorosl** (Которосль) **Rivers,** 280km northeast of Moscow. Locals call the area where the Kotorosl meets the Volga *strelka* (стрелка; arrow or promontory). The city center is defined on the south and northeast by the two rivers and on the west by **ul. Pervomayskaya** (Первомайская), which runs from **Krasnaya pl.** (Красная) to **pl. Bogoyavlenskaya** (Богоявленская). Pl. Bogoyavlenskaya is the site of Yaroslavl's main monastery and the beginning of **Moskovsky pr.** (Московский), which runs south across the Kotorosl to **Moskovsky Vokzal,** the main bus station. From Moskovsky Vokzal, cross Moskovsky pr. and take trolley #5 or 9 three stops to **pl. Volkova** (Волкова). From the main train station, **Glavny Vokzal** (Главный Вокзал; Main Station), **ul. Svobody** (Свободы) hits the center at **pl. Volkova,** from which **Ul. Kirova** (Кирова) a pedes-

RUSSIA

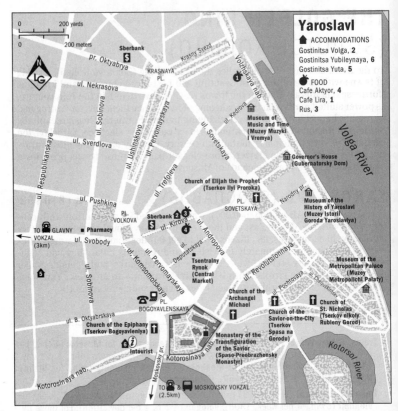

trian walkway, runs east toward the Volga. To get to the center from Glavny Vokzal, take trolley #1 and ride six stops to pl. Volkova. To avoid confusion, street signs often list a whole genealogy of names; posts often bear up to four different plates. Cyrillic **maps** (35R) of the center are sold at the House of War Books (Дом Военной Книги), Pervomayskaya 39.

✔ PRACTICAL INFORMATION

Tourist Office: Intourist, (☎/fax 30 54 13), on the 1st floor of Gostinitsa Yubileynaya (see **Accommodations,** below). English-speaking staff leads tours, provides pamphlets, and books hotel rooms for a minimal commission. Open M-F 9am-5:30pm.

Currency Exchange: Sberbank, ul. Kirova 16, cashes AmEx/V and Thomas Cook **traveler's checks** for 3% commission. Open M-Sa 8:30am-1pm and 2-6:30pm, Su 9am-1pm and 2-4pm. Closed last day of the month.

Luggage Storage: Available at Glavny Vokzal for 12R per day. Open 24hr.

24-Hour. Pharmacy: Ul. Svobody 8 (☎32 95 61 or 30 38 98), 1 block from pl. Volkova. The door is locked 8pm-8am, so ring the buzzer. MC/V.

Telephone Office: In the same building as the post office. Buy tokens for local calls (3R per min.); prepay at the counter for a booth to call long-distance. 3 tones mean the call has yet to go through. Press the "ответ" button when someone answers. Also provides **Internet** access for 0.6R per minute. Open 24hr.

Post Office: Ul. Komsomolskaya 22 (Комсомольская; ☎32 90 71), across the square from the monastery. Open M-Sa 8am-8pm, Su 8am-6pm.

Postal Code: 150 000.

▐ ACCOMMODATIONS

Yaroslavl's hotel prices reflect its popularity among both Russians and foreigners. Foreigners are often charged more than Russians, and 10-25% is usually added to the first night's bill if you reserve in advance. With some luck and some sacrifice of convenience, however, it's possible to get by on a tight budget. Rooms are scarce in summer, and it's best to avoid Yaroslavl altogether around June 20, graduation day for the town's two military academies.

Gostinitsa Volga (Волга), ul. Kirova 10 (☎30 81 31; fax 72 82 76). From pl. Volkova, walk south toward pl. Bogoyavlenskaya and take a left on ul. Kirova. Right in the middle of everything, and at the right price. Check-out noon. Singles 540R, lux 900R; doubles 1000R, lux 1500R; lux suite 2000R. ❷

Gostinitsa Yubileynaya (Юбилейная), Kotoroslnaya nab. 26 (Которосльная; ☎72 65 65; call Intourist (see **Practical Information,** p. 660) for English info. From pl. Volkova, walk down ul. Komsomolskaya to pl. Bogoyavlenskaya. Pass the church on your left and turn right at the river to reach this modern, comfortable 8-floor hotel. In the summer, ask for a room at the back if you're not paying for A/C; front ones have a nice view but get hot. Fitness center available. Breakfast included. Singles US$40; doubles US$60; lux room US$100. MC/V. ❹

Gostinitsa Yuta (Юта), ul. Respublikanskaya 79 (Республиканская; ☎21 87 93). From pl. Volkova, walk 2 blocks down ul. Svobody, take a left on Respublikanskaya, and walk 2 blocks. Old but spacious rooms, each with TV, phone, and private bath. The staff also runs a restaurant, weekend disco, casino, "DVD bar," and tourist agency. Singles 650R; doubles 850R; lux double 1000R; lux suite 1225R. ❷

▐ FOOD

Sidewalk cafes hawking beer, ice cream, and sweet rolls reign supreme in Yaroslavl; restaurants take the back-seat. Stock up on produce at the **tsentralny rynok** (центральный рынок; central market), ul. Deputatskaya 5 (Депутатская; open M-Sa 8am-6pm, Su 8am-4pm). The sometimes crowded **grocery** at Kirova 13 sells just about everything else. (Open daily 8am-10pm.)

Cafe Aktyor (Актёр; Actor), ul. Kirova 5 (☎72 75 43). Follow the cartoons up the courtyard stairs to this Russian cafe, decorated with theater posters and velvet curtains. The chocolate-banana *blini* (50R) are heavenly. Full meal 125R. Open daily 8am-2am. ❷

Rus (Русь), ul. Kirova 10 (☎72 94 08). Near the Gostinitsa Volga (see **Accommodations,** above). Russian and Georgian cuisine in the spacious elegance of a silver age ballroom. Entrees 100-270R. Open daily noon-midnight. ❸

Cafe Lira (Лира), Volzhskaya nab. 43 (Волжская; ☎72 79 38). Great view of the Volga. Plain but decent menu. Entrees 20-135R. Open daily noon-11pm. ❷

◉ SIGHTS

▐ **CHURCH OF ELIJAH THE PROPHET.** (Церковь Ильи Пророка; Tserkov Ilyi Proroka.) Yaroslavl's most beautiful sight, the white-and-green church is the centerpiece of Sovetskaya pl. (Советская), at the end of ul. Kirova. The elaborate and lovingly-restored iconostasis and frescoes flood this 17th-century church with color. *(Open Th-Tu 10am-1pm and 2-6pm. 25R, students 15R. Camera 20R, video 50R.)*

▓**MUSEUM OF MUSIC AND TIME.** (Музей Музыки н Времени; Muzey Muzyky i Vremeny.) When you step inside this little museum, you enter a magical world of ticking, ringing, chiming and music. Russia's first private museum and one of Yaroslavl's most popular, the Museum of Music and Time exhibits a collection of clocks, gramophones, and music boxes, a street organ, a harmonium, and all manner of bells. The guides can demonstrate most of the instruments. *(Volzhskaya nab. 33a. ☎32 86 37. Open Tu-Su 10am-7pm. 25R, all tours guided.).*

MONASTERY OF THE TRANSFIGURATION OF THE SAVIOR. (Спасо-Преобра-женский Монастырь; Spaso-Preobrazhensky Monastyr.) Since the 12th century, this fortified monastery has guarded the banks of the Kotorosl. The high white walls surround a number of buildings and exhibitions with separate entrance fees. Enter the grounds through the Holy Gate (Святые Ворота; Svyatye Vorota), on the side facing the Kotorosl. Climb to the top of the bell tower (звонница; zvonnitsa) for a view of the city. Behind the bell tower stands the Cathedral of the Transfiguration of the Savior (Спасо-Преображенский Собор; Spaso-Preobrazhensky Sobor), one of the only religious buildings constructed during the reign of Ivan the Terrible. The rest of the complex houses exhibitions of art and natural history, as well as a writhing collection of live snakes. Perhaps the most fascinating exhibit is the collection of Old Russian Art (Древнерусское и Народно-Прикладное Искусство; Drevnerusskoye i Narodno-Prikladnoe Iskusstvo), which contains icons, embroidery, enamel work, and wooden sculptures. Most captions in Russian only. *(Pl. Bogoyavlenskaya 25. Monastery open daily 8am-7pm. Exhibitions open Tu-Su 10am-5pm; kassa closes at 4:30pm. 9 exhibits, 15-30R each, students 5-15R. Camera 20R, video 50R. Entrance free with purchase of museum tickets.)*

ART MUSEUM. (Художественный Музей; Khudozhestvenny Muzey.) The Art Museum has two branches. The first, **Museum of the Metropolitan Palace** (Музей Метрополичьи Палаты; Muzey Metropolichi Palaty), displays the best of Yaroslavl's icons—the craftmanship in the 3rd room is particularly impressive. *(Volzhskaya nab. 1. ☎72 92 87. Open Sa-Th 10am-5pm; kassa closes 4:30pm. 30R. Camera 20R, video 50R.)* The modern branch, in the former **Governor's house**, displays 18th- to 20th-century Russian paintings and sculpture, mostly by local artists. *(Volzhskaya nab. 23. ☎30 35 04 or 32 81 85; www.artmuseum.yar.ru. Open Tu-Su 10am-5:30pm; kassa closes 5pm. 30R. Camera 20R, video 50R.)*

CHURCH OF THE EPIPHANY. (Церковь Богоявления; Tserkov Bogoyavleniya.) Opposite the monastery, the red-brick Church of the Epiphany shows off fragments of frescoes recovered from the ruins of Yaroslavl churches. The main room has an ornately carved Baroque iconostasis and several beautiful frescoes currently being restored. *(Pl. Bogoyavlenskaya. ☎30 34 29. Open W-M 10:30am-4:30pm. Knock on the door if the church seems closed. 12R, students 4R. Camera 10R.)*

SUZDAL (СУЗДАЛЬ)   ☎(8)09231

Set amid lazy streams, dirt roads, cucumber fields, and free-range chickens, Suzdal (SOOZ-dull; pop. 12,000) looks much as it always has. In the 12th century, the powerful Rostov-Suzdal principality ruled Moscow and even collected tribute from Byzantium; nine centuries later, serene Suzdal still boasts a splendid kremlin, a quiet river, and several monasteries. Cleaner than its neighbor Vladimir and largely unscathed by Soviet construction and post-Soviet tourism, this quaint medieval town still teems with old-world charm and the ghosts of the Middle Ages.

E TRANSPORTATION. The **bus station,** *avtovokzal* (автовокзал), ul. Vasilevskaya 44 (Василевская), send buses to: **Ivanovo** (1½hr., 18 per day, 40R); **Vladimir** (50min., every 40-70min., 16R); and **Yaroslavl** (4hr., 8 per week, 109R). The connection to Vladimir is the most convenient, and fast-paced travelers can view Suzdal as a long daytrip. Departure times are listed at the *kassy.* (Open 5am-8pm.) **Taxis** charge 7R per km. Phoning for a cab (☎2 06 34) will get you a ride within 5-10min. for an extra 10R. Rides within the city cost 10-20R; to the bus station 20-30R.

◪⛶ ORIENTATION AND PRACTICAL INFORMATION. Suzdal's main north-south thoroughfare is **ul. Lenina** (Ленина), and most sights and accommodations are clustered just west of it (the far side from the bus station), on the strip of land between ul. Lenina and the Kamenka River (Каменка). From the bus station, turn left on ul. Vasilevskaya for the 20-minute walk to ul. Lenina, or take the trolley (every 30-60min., 2.50R). To reach the tourist office, **Excursionny Otdel** (Экскурсионный Отдел), at ul. Lenina 22, turn left from Vasilevskaya on Lenina and walk for 10-15 minutes (☎2 09 37). They offer general information and city tours in English, French, and German. (Call in advance; from US $14. Open daily 8:30am-5:30pm.) You can exchange currency at **Sberbank,** ul. Lounskaya 1a (Лоунская; ☎2 19 18), off ul. Lenina opposite the bell tower of the Convent of the Deposition of the Robe. The bank also cashes **traveler's checks.** (Open M-F 9am-12:30pm and 1:30pm-4:30pm.) **Telephones** are in the post office building. Prepay for international and intercity calls or buy a 42R card for calls within Russia. (Open 24hr.) The **post office,** Krasnaya pl. 3, off ul. Lenina across from the Convent of the Deposition of the Robe, is guarded by a statue of Lenin. (Open M-Th 8am-6pm, F 8am-5pm, Sa 8am-3pm.) **Postal Code:** 601 293.

⛶⛶ ACCOMMODATIONS AND FOOD. **Gostinitsa Rizopolozhenskaya ❶** (Ризоположенская) takes its name from its home, the Convent of the Deposition of the Robe, but its reasonably priced rooms are not just for ascetics. From ul. Vasilevskaya, turn right on ul. Lenina and take the first left on Slobodskaya; the hotel is immediately on the right, within the convent walls. (☎2 05 53. Singles 250R; doubles 370R; lux 600R; 25% added to first night for reservation). To get to the **Merchant Likhonin House ❷** (Дом Купца Лихонина; Dom Kuptsa Likhonina), ul. Slobodskaya 34, follow the directions above, but go straight instead of turning into the monastery. Enter at the sign. In an 18th-century house, the beautiful wooden rooms of this well-reputed hotel have a homey, log cabin feel. (☎2 19 01. Breakfast included. Singles 420R; doubles 630R, lux double 700R; 10% added to first night for reservation.) Of course, if you want to relax like an exiled Tsarina within the peaceful confines of the Convent of the Intercession (see below), the Suzdal **Tourcenter ❹,** ul. Korovniki 7, can accommodate you. (☎2 09 08 or 2 05 46; www.suzdaltour.ru. Singles 1300R; doubles 1360R; lux 1770R.)

The **Harchevnya ❷** (Харчевня), ul. Lenina 73 (☎2 07 22), not far from the Kremlin, cooks up satisfying homestyle Russian meals (100-150R). For higher quality and higher prices, try the 300-year-old **Trapeznaya ❺** (Трапезная), right inside the Kremlin. (☎2 17 63. Entrees 150-350R. Open daily 11am-11pm.)

◪ SIGHTS. To reach the **Kremlin,** town's main tourist destination, start on ul. Vasilevskaya, turn left on ul. Lenina, then make an immediate right on ul. Kremlin. Although vegetation and time have softened the profile of the mighty fortress, the star-studded blue domes of the Nativity Cathedral (Рождественский Собор; Rozhdestvensky Sobor) still dazzle. Its brightly colored frescoes and ornate arches are closed to visitors until 2006, but its main relics—Suzdal's most famous icons, irregularly-shaped coins of Ivan the Terrible, and a huge, ornate ceramic oven— are on

R U S S I A

display inside the 15th-century Archbishop's Palace. (Open M and W-Su 10am-6pm. Closed last F of the month. 4 exhibits, 20-25R each.) A walk along the Kremlin's ramparts provides a great view of the river. Cross the river, turn left, and walk a short distance to reach the **Museum of Wooden Architecture** (Музей Деревянного Зодчества; Muzey Derevyannovo Zodchestva), an outdoor museum with two churches, two windmills, a well, and several houses dating from the 17th-19th centuries. Most buildings are open to visitors for an additional charge. (Open W-M 9:30am-4:30pm, closed last F of the month. 20R. Camera 10R, video 20R.)

The area north of the Kremlin is home to several large, serene **monasteries** and convents, complete with colorful domes, quiet grounds, and medieval fortifications. Walk back from the Kremlin, past the **old marketplace** on your left, and turn left on ul. Lenina. After the intersection with Vasilevskaya, the **Convent of the Deposition of the Robe** (Ризоположенский Монастырь; Rizopolozhensky Monastyr), with a Classical-style bell tower visible from almost anywhere in Suzdal, will be on your left. The cathedral and the Holy Gate—and its two teepee-shaped towers—date from the 16th and 17th centuries. (Open Tu-Su 10am-6pm, closed last Th of the month. Free.)

Ten minutes farther down ul. Lenina, also on the left, the **Spaso-Yevfimiev Monastery** (Спасо-Евфимиев Монастырь) stands surrounded by a large stone wall. Inside, the green-domed **Cathedral of the Transfiguration** displays excellent murals, while a **museum** exhibits 13th-20th century decorative arts and old books, including **Russia's first printed book** and a huge 17th-century Gospel, the largest book in Russia. (Open Tu-Su 10am-6pm, closed last Th of the month.) Behind the monastery wall and across the river stands the beautifully manicured **Convent of the Intercession.** This pure-white complex once served as a prison for women of the highest class: Peter the Great, Ivan the Terrible, his son, and Basil III each exiled at least one wife here. (Open daily 8am-8pm. Free.)

VLADIMIR (ВЛАДИМИР) ☎(8)0922

Once the capital of Russia and the headquarters of the Russian Orthodox Church, Vladimir (vlad-EE-mir; pop. 380,000) suffered at the hands of the Tatars and eventually fell to Moscow in the early 14th century. Before its fall, the city rivaled Kyiv in size and splendor. Since then, Vladimir has moved forward at a much slower pace. But the city is no pristine medieval relic. Past the 12th-century white stone monuments and cathedrals, the Soviet industrial buildings will remind you of the progress that has occurred since the construction of the city's treasures.

▐ TRANSPORTATION. Trains (☎29 23 00) run from Vokzalnaya pl. (Вокзальная) to: **Moscow's Kursky Vokzal** (3hr., 15-20 per day, 64R) and **Nizhny Novgorod** (4hr., 10-15 per day, 80R). Trips to Moscow can be made more cheaply on a *prigorodny* (пригородный; suburban) train. Opposite the train station, **buses** (☎32 37 90) go to: **Moscow** (3½hr., 18-20 per day, 57-63R); **Ivanovo** (2.5hr. , 12-14 per day, 65R); **Suzdal** (50min., every 30min, 13R); and **Yaroslavl** (5hr., 4 per week, 112R).

▐ ORIENTATION. A 5min. walk uphill from the train station will bring you to the old city, whose main street is ul. Bolshaya Moskovskaya (Большая Московская), sometimes called by its former name, ul. III-evo Internatsionala (III-его интернационала). Nearly everything is on or near this thoroughfare. Trolley #5 (2.50R) starts at the train station and runs the street's length, stopping at both of the hotels listed below.

▐ PRACTICAL INFORMATION. The tourist office, Excursionny Otdel (Экскурсионный Отдел), ul. B. Moskovskaya 43, provides general information and arranges English-language tours of Vladimir and Suzdal. (3-4hr., from US$12;

☎32 42 63. Open daily 8:30am-5:30pm.) **Sberbank,** ul. B. Moskovskaya 27, offers most financial services, including **MC/V cash advances** and an **ATM**. (Open M-F 9:30am-12:30pm and 1:30-4:45pm, Sa 9am-12:30pm and 1:30-3:45pm.) The train station houses a **24-hour telephone office** that sells prepaid international calls and 40R telephone cards. There is a **pharmacy** at ul. Gogolya 2. (☎27 22 15. Open daily 9am-9pm.) Slow **Internet** connections are available at XXI Vek (XXI Век; 21st century), ul. B. Moskovskaya 11 (☎32 64 71; enter on the side of the building; 0.80R per min; open daily 9am-8pm), or at ul. B. Moskovskaya 51 (☎32 30 64; 30R per hour; open daily 8:30am-9pm). To get to the **post office**, ul. Podbelskovo 2, head down ul. Muzeynaya near the Excursionny Otdel turn left on Podbelskovo. (☎32 44 60. Open M-F 8am-8pm, Sa-Su 8am-6pm.) **Postal Code:** 600 000.

⌂❐ ACCOMMODATIONS AND FOOD. Gostinitsa Vladimir ❶ (Гостиница Владимир), ul. B. Moskovskaya 74, rents clean, pleasant rooms. There's a restaurant and an **ATM** on the first floor and a well-stocked **grocery** next door. To get there, head uphill on the far left path from the train station. (☎32 30 47; fax 32 72 01. Singles with sinks 180-660R; doubles 260-890R, lux 1300-2480R. Expect a 25% first-night surcharge if you reserve in advance.) If there are no vacancies, try **Gostinitsa Zarya ❶** (Заря; Dawn), Studyonaya Gora 36a (Студёная), 15 minutes from the Golden Gate on the main street, just past where it curves left. (☎/fax 32 14 41. Singles 215-450R; doubles 350-700R, lux 860-1730R.)

The **Pirozhki Bar,** ul. B. Moskovskaya 22, provides cheap Russian food. (*Pirozhki* 6.8R; entrees 12-30R. Open M-Sa 8am-8pm.) **Cafe Pizza ❶,** ul. B. Moskovskaya 14, does the same, without the Russian. (Pizza 35-45R. Open daily 11am-3pm and 4-11pm.) For a bit more money and a lot more taste, **U Zolotykh Vorot ❹** (У Золотых Ворот; By the Golden Gates), on the second floor of ul. B. Moskovskaya 17, makes an elegant setting for classy Russian meals (70-860R), including lobster, tuna, and pork. (☎32 31 16. Open daily noon-midnight. MC/V.)

◙ SIGHTS. The 12th-century **St. Dmitry's Cathedral** (Дмитриевский Собор; Dmitrievsky Sobor), is the only surviving building of Prince Vsevelod III's former palace. At press time, restoration kept the cathedral's Byzantine interior closed to visitors, but the lavishly carved stories of Hercules, King David, and Alexander the Great on the outer walls are impressive. To get there, walk left on B. Moskovskaya from Gostinitsa Vladimir until a fenced wooded park appears on the left. With your back to the street, the church will be through the park on the left. To the right is the yellow-and-white **Vladimir-Suzdal Historical, Archaeological, and Artistic Museum,** ul. B. Moskovskaya 58. The museum contains a slew of exhibits; the most worthwhile are the Picture Gallery (Картинная Галерея; Kartinnaya Galereya), which displays paintings from the 15th-20th centuries, and the exhibit on the lifestyles of the nobility (Минувших Оней Очарованье; Minuvshikh Onei Ocharovanye). Each exhibit has its own admission price, but 100R will let you see everything on the first and second floors. (☎32 24 29. Open Tu-W 10am-4pm, Th-Su 10am-5pm; closed last Th of the month.)

Up the hill, to the right of the museum, is the 12th-century **Assumption Cathedral** (Успенский Собор; Uspensky Sobor) with its 19th-century bell tower. The original model for the cathedral of the Moscow Kremlin, this sacred building was guarded by one of the most famous Russian icons until it was removed to Moscow's Tretyakov Gallery (see p. 651). Fortunately, the Tretyakov couldn't take the frescoes by renowned artists Andrei Rublyov and Daniil Chiorny. (Open Tu-Su 2:30pm-4:45pm. Respectful attire required. 25R.) In front of Assumption Cathedral lies peaceful **Cathedral Square** (Соборная Площадь; Sobornaya Ploshchad).

The 12th-century **Golden Gate** (Золотые Ворота; Zolotye Vorota), just down ul. B. Moskovskaya, marks the boundary of the old city. Climb to the top for a brief

RUSSIA

military history of the city. (Open M and Th 10am-5pm, W and F-Su 10am-4pm. Closed last Th of the month. 20R.) Facing Cathedral Square, a path to the right leads to the **Exhibit of Old Vladimir** (Выставка Старого Владимира; Vystavka Starovo Vladimira), housed in an old water tower. It displays assorted items from 19th-century Vladimir and offers a view of the old city. (☎32 54 51. Open T, Th, and Sa-Su 10am-5pm; W and F 10am-4pm. Closed last Th of the month. 20R.) The red brick, early-20th-century **Trinity Church,** on the left past the gate, displays **crystal** and lacquer crafts. (☎32 48 72. Open M and W 10am-4pm; Tu, Th-F, and Su 10am-5pm, Sa 11am-6pm. Closed last F of the month. 20R.)

The **Bogolyubov Monastery** (Боголюбовь Монастырь), the city's most beautiful religious complex, is a short ride from the center. Grand Prince Andrey Bogolyubsky (literally, the God-loving) sacked Kyiv in 1169 and moved the Russian capital to Vladimir, establishing a monastery that still boasts colorful blue domes, quiet grounds, and an excellent choir. (Open daily 6:30am-10pm. Free.) Take any bus or van with a "Боголюбого" sign from Gostinitsa Vladimir or from the center and get off when you see the blue domes on the right (20-25min., every 5-15min., 3R).

THE NORTHWEST

The Northwest has won a lion's share of Russia's political power and European riches, as the glory of the Orthodox church and the tsars testifies. The kremlins and monasteries of Novgorod and Pskov, along with St. Petersburg and its nearby palaces, remind tourists of historical prominence both sacred and secular. But throughout the lush greenery and pastoral charm of the wide, open countryside between these cultural centers, life has changed little over the past century. Horse-drawn carts and *babushki* on bicycles confront the traveler with the Russia of the peasants that has puzzled intellectuals and politicians since the time of Peter the Great.

ST. PETERSBURG ☎(8)812
(САНКТ-ПЕТЕРБУРГ)

St. Petersburg is Russian...but it is not Russia.
—Tsar Nicholas II

In St. Petersburg, Russia suddenly transforms herself into an elegant European lady, steeped in ballet, opera, classical music and fine art. Her sophistication culminates in mid-June's White Nights, when the city's languorous streets and glorious palaces remain sun-lit for nearly 23 hours a day. This splendor is exactly what Peter the Great intended when he founded his "window on the West" atop a Finnish swamp in 1703. Its location was strategically chosen to turn Russia away from Byzantium and toward an "enlightened" Europe. Little did Peter know that his capital would become the center of a revolutionary movement that would oust his descendants from power and rename the city after Marxist leader V.I. Lenin. Despite the name change, Soviet authorities remained suspicious of Leningrad's continued intellectualism and favored proletarian Moscow. Even Soviet neglect could not compare to the horrors Leningrad suffered at the hands of the Nazis. Germany's siege of the city is perhaps the worst 900 days in *any* modern city's history, claiming close to one million lives. Reluctant as the Soviets were to embrace St. Petersburg, they did contribute to its reconstruction after the Nazi devastation. With Italian fashion and American fast food lining the streets, St. Petersburg stands once more as a "window on the West." Many people choose to pass the days in the city's parks, where time drifts by almost unnoticed. Moscow may be the embodiment of Mother Russia's post-apocalyptic youth, but St. Petersburg remains the majestic and mysterious symbol of Peter I's great Russian vision.

✈ INTERCITY TRANSPORTATION

Flights: The main airport, **Pulkovo** (Пулково), has 2 terminals: Pulkovo-1 (☎ 104 38 22) for domestic flights and Pulkovo-2 (☎ 104 34 44) for international flights. M2: Moskovskaya (Московская). From the Metro, take bus #39 for Pulkovo-1 (25min.) or bus #13 for Pulkovo-2 (20min.). Hostels can arrange a taxi (usually US$30-35).

Air France, Bolshaya Morskaya 35 (Большая морская; ☎ 325 82 52). M3: Gostiny Dvor. Open M-F 9:30am-5:30pm.

British Airways, ul. Malaya Konyushennaya 1/3 (Малая конюшенная; ☎ 329 25 65). M2: Gostiny. Open M-F 9am-5:30pm.

Delta Airlines, Bolshaya Morskaya 36 (☎ 311 58 19 or 311 58 20; fax 325 62 28). M2: Nevsky Prospekt. Open M-F 9am-5:30pm.

Finnair, ul. Kazanskaya 44 (Казанская; ☎ 326 18 70). M4: Sadovaya. Open M-F 9am-5pm.

Lufthansa, Nevsky pr. 32, 3rd fl. (Невский; ☎ 320 10 00). M2: Nevsky Prospekt. Open M-F 9am-5:30pm.

SAS, Nevsky pr. 57, Sheraton Nevsky Palace Hotel (☎ 325 32 55). M2: Nevsky Prospekt. Open M-F 9am-5pm.

Swissair, ul. Malaya Konyushennaya 11/3 (Малая Конюшеная; ☎ 325 25 25). M2: Nevsky Prospekt. Enter on Shvedsky per. (Шведский). Open M-F 9am-5pm.

Trains: Tsentralnye Zheleznodorozhnye Kassy (Центральные Железнодорожные Кассы; Central Ticket Offices; ☎ 168 01 11), Canal Griboedova 24 (Грибоедого). Open M-Sa 8am-8pm, Su 8am-6pm. International tickets at windows #4-6. Prices vary slightly depending on the train running, and fluctuate widely over time. Purchase tickets from **Intourist** offices at each of St. Petersburg's train stations on the day of departure. Check your ticket to see from which station your train leaves.

Finlyandsky Vokzal (Финляндский Вокзал; Finland Station; ☎ 168 76 87). M1: Pl. Lenina (Ленина). To **Helsinki, FIN** (6hr., 2 per day, 1375R).

Moskovsky Vokzal (Московский Вокзал; Moscow Station; ☎ 168 45 97). M1: Pl. Vosstaniya (Восстания). To: **Moscow** (5-8hr., 12-15 per day, 600-1200R); **Novgorod** (3-4hr., 2 per day, 66R); **Sevastopol, UKR** (35hr., 1 per day, 754-1186R).

Vitebsky Vokzal (Витебский Вокзал; Vitebsky Station; ☎ 168 58 07). M1: Pushkinskaya (Пушкинская). To: **Kaliningrad, RUS** (26 hr., 1 per day); **Kyiv, UKR** (25hr., 2 every 2 days, 506-637R); **Odessa, UKR** (36hr., 1 per day, 654R); **Rīga, LAT** (13hr., 1 per day, 887R); **Tallinn, EST** (9hr., 1 per day, 350R); **Vilnius, LIT** (14hr., every 2 days, 647R).

Buses: Nab. Obvodnovo Kanala 36 (Обводного Канала; ☎ 166 57 77). M4: Ligovsky pr. Take tram #19, 25, 44, or 49 or trolley #42 to the stop just across the canal. Facing the canal, turn right and walk 2 long blocks alongside it. The station will be on your right, behind the abandoned building. 4R surcharge for advance tickets. One-way tickets only. Open daily 6am-8pm. To: **Minsk, BLR** (15hr., 1 per day, 350R); **Riga, LAT** (13hr., 1 per day, 352R); **Tallinn, EST** (6hr., 1 per day, 300-400R). For destinations in the Baltic States, also consult **Eurolines Agency** (see **Budget Travel,** p. 674).

🏛 ORIENTATION

St. Petersburg sits at the mouth of the **Neva River** (Нева) on the **Gulf of Finland** (Finsky Zaliv; Финский Залив), occupying 44 islands among 50 canals. The heart of the city lies on mainland St. Petersburg between the south bank of the Neva and the **Fontanka River.** Many of St. Petersburg's major sights—including the Hermitage

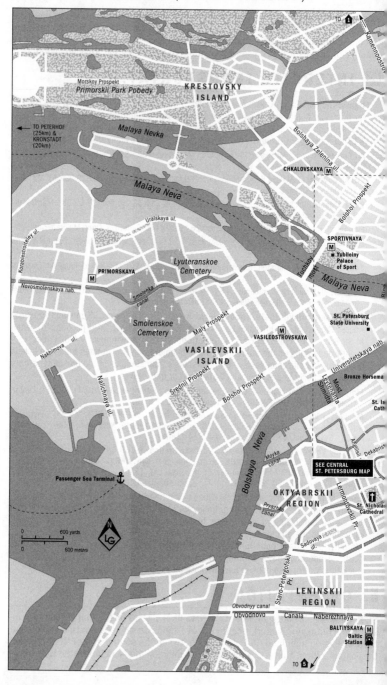

TO ①

Morskoy Prospekt
Primorskii Park Pobedy

KRESTOVSKY ISLAND

Bolshaya Zelenina ul.

← TO PETERHOF
(25km) &
KRONSTADT
(20km)

Malaya Nevka

CHKALOVSKAYA Ⓜ

Bolshoi Prospekt

Malaya Neva

SPORTIVNAYA
Ⓜ
■ Yubileiny
Palace
of Sport

Uralskaya ul.

Korablestroiteley ul.

Lyuteranskoe Cemetery

PRIMORSKAYA
Ⓜ

Malaya Neva

Novosmolenskaya nab.

Smolenka
canal

St. Petersburg
State University ■

Smolenskoe Cemetery

Maly Prospekt

Universitetskaya nab.

Nakhimova ul.

VASILEOSTROVSKAYA Ⓜ

Bronze Horsema

VASILEVSKII ISLAND

Most
Leytenanta
Shmidta

Nalichnaya ul.

Sregni Prospekt

St. Is
Cath

Bolshoi Prospekt

Aglisii

Dekabris

Bolshaya Neva

**SEE CENTRAL
ST. PETERSBURG MAP**

Passenger Sea Terminal ⚓

*Moyka
canal*

**OKTYABRSKII
REGION**

Lermontovskii Pr.

🕆
St. Nichola
Cathedral

*Pryazhka
canal*

0 ——— 600 yards
0 ——— 600 meters

N

*Sadovaya
ul.*

Staro-Petergofskii
Pr.

**LENINSKII
REGION**

Obvodnyy canal   Obvodnovo   Canala   Naberezhnaya

BALTIYSKAYA Ⓜ
🚆 Baltic
Station

TO ⑤

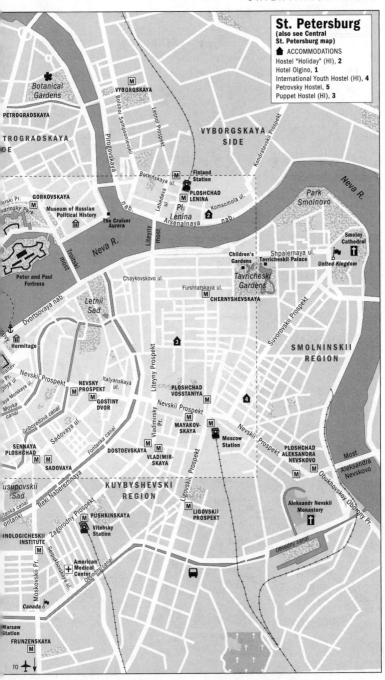

St. Petersburg
(also see Central
St. Petersburg map)

🏠 ACCOMMODATIONS
Hostel "Holiday" (HI), **2**
Hotel Olgino, **1**
International Youth Hostel (HI), **4**
Petrovsky Hostel, **5**
Puppet Hostel (HI), **3**

Botanical
Gardens

PETROGRADSKAYA

VYBORGSKAYA Ⓜ

TROGRADSKAYA
DE

VYBORGSKAYA
SIDE

Bolshoi Sampsonievskii

Lesnoi Prospekt

Pirogovskaya

Kondratievskii Prospekt

Botkinskaya ul.

Ⓜ Finland
Station

Ⓜ PLOSHCHAD
LENINA

Park
Smolnovo

Neva R.

GORKOVSKAYA

Ⓜ

Museum of Russian
Political History 🏛

Lebedeva ul.

The Cruiser
Aurora

Pl.
Lenina
Arsenalnaya

Komsomola ul.

2

nab.

nab.

Smolny
Cathedral

Children's
Gardens

Shpalernaya ul.
Tavricheskii Palace

🏳 🏳

United Kingdom

Neva R.

Liteyny most

Chaykovskovo ul.

Tavricheski
Gardens

Suvorovski Prospekt

Troitski most

Letnii
Sad

Furshtatskaya ul.

Ⓜ CHERNYSHEVSKAYA

SMOLNINSKII
REGION

Dvortsovaya nab.

🏛 Hermitage

3

Liteyny Prospekt

Nevskii Prospekt

NEVSKY
PROSPEKT Ⓜ

Italyanskaya
ul.

Ⓜ GOSTINY
DVOR

Nevskii Prospekt

PLOSHCHAD
VOSSTANIYA
Ⓜ

4

Nevskii Prospekt

ya Morskaya ul.
olya ul.

Moyka
canal

Griboyedova canal

Vladimirsky
Pr. Ⓜ

Ⓜ MAYAKOV-
SKAYA

Ⓜ
Moscow
Station

Nevskii Prospekt

PLOSHCHAD
ALEKSANDRA
NEVSKOVO

Most
Aleksandra
Nevskovo

SENNAYA
PLOSHCHAD

Sadovaya ul.

Fontanka canal

DOSTOEVSKAYA Ⓜ

VLADIMIR-
SKAYA Ⓜ

Obukhovskoy Oborony Pr.

Ⓜ Ⓜ
SADOVAYA

Reki Naberezhnaya

KUYBYSHEVSKI
REGION

Ligovskii Prospekt

Ⓜ

usupovskii
Sad

Zagorodny Prospekt

Ⓜ PUSHKINSKAYA

LIGOVSKII
PROSPEKT

Aleksandr Nevskii
Monastery

🏳

nka canal
ontanki

🚊 Vitebsky
Station

INOLOGICHESKII
INSTITUTE

Ⓜ

American
✚ Medical
Center

Obovodny canal

Obvodny canal

Moskovski Pr.

Serpukhovskaya ul.

Canada 🏳

Warsaw
Station

FRUNZENSKAYA
Ⓜ

TO ⬇

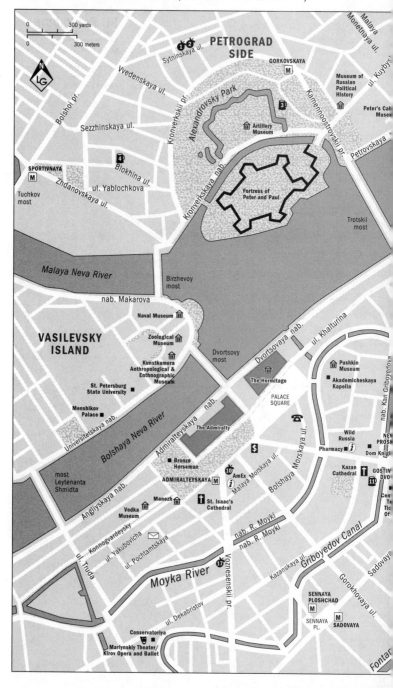

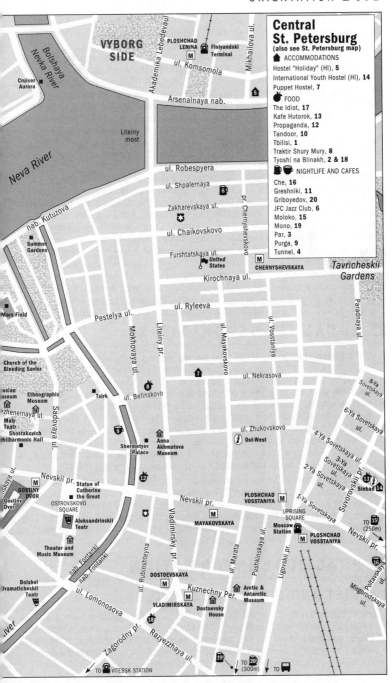

Central St. Petersburg
(also see St. Petersburg map)

🏠 ACCOMMODATIONS

Hostel "Holiday" (HI), **5**
International Youth Hostel (HI), **14**
Puppet Hostel, **7**

🍴 FOOD

The Idiot, **17**
Kafe Hutorok, **13**
Propaganda, **12**
Tandoor, **10**
Tbilisi, **1**
Traktir Shury Mury, **8**
Tyoshi na Blinakh, **2 & 18**

☕ NIGHTLIFE AND CAFES

Che, **16**
Greshniki, **11**
Griboyedov, **20**
JFC Jazz Club, **6**
Moloko, **15**
Mono, **19**
Par, **3**
Purga, **9**
Tunnel, **4**

VYBORG SIDE

Bolshaya Nevka River

Cruiser Aurora

PLOSHCHAD LENINA Ⓜ 🚂 Finlyandski Terminal

ul. Komsomola

Mikhailova ul.

Akademika Lebedeva l.

Arsenalnaya nab.

Neva River

Liteiny most

Liteiny most

nab. Kutuzova

Summer Gardens

ul. Robespyera

ul. Shpalernaya

Zakharevskaya ul.

ul. Chaikovskovo

Furshtatskaya ul. 🏛 United States

pr. Chernyshevskovo

Ⓜ CHERNYSHEVSKAYA

Tavricheskii Gardens

Kirochnaya ul.

Mars Field

Church of the Bleeding Savior

ul. Ryleeva

Pestelya ul.

ul. Mayakovskovo

ul. Vosstaniya

Paradnaya ul.

ssian useum

Ethnographic Museum

zhenenaya ul.

Maly Teatr

Shostakovich hilharmonic Hall

Tsirk

Mokhovaya ul.

Liteiny pr.

ul. Belinskovo

ul. Nekrasova

8-Ya Sovetskaya ul.

6-Ya Sovetskaya ul.

4-Ya Sovetskaya ul.

3-Ya Sovetskaya ul.

2-Ya Sovetskaya ul.

Sadovaya ul.

Shermetyev Palace

🏛 Anna Akhmatova Museum

ul. Zhukovskovo

ⓘ Ost-West

Suvorovskii pr.

🏛 Sinbad ⓘ

Nevskii pr.

Gostiny Dvor

Ⓜ GOSTINY DVOR

Statue of Catherine the Great

OSTROVSKOVO SQUARE

🎭 Aleksandrinskii Teatr

Theater and Music Museum

Nevskii pr.

PLOSHCHAD VOSSTANIYA Ⓜ

Ⓜ MAYAKOVSKAYA

UPRISING SQUARE

🚂 Moscow Station

1-Ya Sovetskaya ul.

Ligovskii pr.

PLOSHCHAD VOSSTANIYA Ⓜ

TO Ⓜ (250m)

Nevskii pr.

Poltavskaya ul.

Vladimirsky. pr.

ul. Marata

Pushkinskaya ul.

Mirgorodskaya ul.

Bolshoi Dramaticheski Teatr

nab. Fontanki

ul. Rubinshteyna

ul. Lomonosova

DOSTOEVSKAYA Ⓜ

Kuznechny Per.

VLADIMIRSKAYA Ⓜ

🏛 Arctic & Antarctic Museum

🏛 Dostoevsky House

River

ul. Razyezzhaya

Zagorodny pr.

TO 🚂 VITEBSK STATION

TO 🚌 (300m)

TO 🚌

and the three main cathedrals—are on or near **Nevsky Prospekt** (Невский Проспект), the city's main street. South and east of the Fontanka on the mainland are central St. Petersburg's newest neighborhoods, developed primarily in the late 19th century; they house the **Smolny Institute,** the **Aleksander Nevsky Monastery,** and most of the **train** and **bus stations: Moskovsky Vokzal** (Московский Вокзал; Moscow Train Station) is near the midway point of Nevsky pr., while **Vitebsky Vokzal** (Витебский Вокзал) is near the Fontanka on Zagorodny pr. (Загородный).

North of the center and across the Neva sprawls **Vasilevsky Island,** the city's largest island and the original, intended site of Peter's dream city. Most of the island's sights, which are among St. Petersburg's oldest, sit on its eastern edge in the **Strelka** neighborhood. The western portion of the island is a wasteland of grid-patterned streets and apartment complexes; the city's **Sea Terminal,** the ferry port, is at the island's southwestern edge on the Gulf coast. On the north side of the Neva, across from the **Winter Palace,** is the small **Petrograd Side** archipelago, which houses the Peter and Paul Fortress, quiet residential neighborhoods, and the wealthy **Kirov Island** trio. Outside the city center on the mainland are the southern suburbs and the northern **Vyborg Side** neighborhoods; both are vast expanses of tenements and factories and hold little interest to most tourists. **Finlyandsky Vokzal** (Finland Train Station; Финляндский) is just north of the Neva.

> **!** The pipes and drainage system in St. Petersburg have not changed since the city was founded. There is no effective water purification system, so exposure to giardia is very likely. Always boil tap water for at least 10 minutes, dry your washed veggies, and drink bottled water. See **Essentials: Health,** p. 30.

⊑ LOCAL TRANSPORTATION

Public Transportation: The **Metro** (Метро), the deepest in the world, is a comprehensive, cheap, and efficient way to explore the city. It runs daily 6am-midnight and is always busy; avoid peak hours from 8-9am and 5-6pm. A Metro **token** (zheton; жетон) costs 6R; stock up, as lines are often long and cutting is common. **Buses, trams, and trolleys** run fairly frequently, depending on the time of day. Read the destination of each numbered line on the signs at the bus stop or check the list of stops posted on the outside of the bus. Trolleys #1, 5, and 22 go from Uprising Square to the bottom of Nevsky pr., near the Hermitage. Buses, trams, and trolleys run 6am-midnight; tickets (5R) should be purchased from the driver. A **monthly transportation card** (365R) is good for unlimited public transportation; purchase one at any Metro station.

Taxis: Both marked and private cabs operate in St. Petersburg. Marked cabs have a metered rate of 9R per km; add 20R if you call ahead. Many locals get around by "catching a car": they flag down a car on the street, determine where it's going, agree on a price, and hop a ride. This practice is usually cheaper than marked cabs, but quite unsafe. Never get into a car with more than one person already in it. And, for your own sake, don't get into the black Mercedes SUV with tinted windows.

◪ PRACTICAL INFORMATION

TOURIST AND FINANCIAL SERVICES

Tourist Office: Ost-West Contact Service, ul. Mayakovskovo 7 (Маяковского; ☎327 34 16; fax 327 34 17; www.ostwest.com). M3: Mayakovskaya. Resourceful staff offers brochures and maps of the city and arranges homestays (US$20 in center, US$15 elsewhere), hotel rooms, tours, and theater tickets. Provides visa invitations and registration (US$35-50). English spoken. Open M-F 10am-6pm, Sa noon-6pm.

St. Petersburg Metro

❷ Prospekt Prosveshcheniya/
Проспект Просвещения

❶ Devyatkino/
Девяткино

Ozerki/
Озерки

Grazhdansky Pr./
Гражданский Проспект

Udelnaya/
Удельная

Akademicheskaya/
Академическая

Pionerskaya/
Пионерская

Politekhnicheskaya/
Политехническая

Staraya
Derevnya/
Старая
Деревня ❹

Chernaya Rechka/
Черная Речка

Ploshchad Muzhestva/
Площадь Мужества

Bus 80

Krestovsky Ostrov/
Крестовский Остров

Petrogradskaya/
Петроградская

Lesnaya/
Лесная

Chkalovskaya/
Чкаловская

Gorkovskaya/
Горьковская

Vyborgskaya/
Выборгская

Finland Station/ Финляндский Вокзал

Primorskaya ❸
Приморская

Sportivnaya/
Спортивная

Ploshchad Lenina/
Площадь Ленина

Neva River

Chernyshevskaya/
Чернышевская

Vasileostrovskaya/
Василеостровская

Passenger
Sea Terminal

Ladozhskaya/
Ладожская

SEE INSET
BELOW

Prospekt
Bolshevikov/
Проспект
Большевиков

Gulf of
Finland

Novocherkasskaya/
Новочеркасская

Baltiyskaya/
Балтийская

Moscow
Station/
Московский
Вокзал

Narvskaya/
Нарвская

Vitebskii
Station/
Витебский Вокзал

Ulitsa Dybenko/
Улица Дыбенко ❹

Baltic Warsaw
Station/ Station/
Балтийский Варшавский
Вокзал Вокзал

Frunzenskaya/
Фрунзенская

Elizarovskaya/
Елизаровская

Kirovskii Zavod/
Кировский Завод

Moskovskiye Vorota/
Московские Ворота

Lomonosovskaya/
Ломоносовская

Elektrosila/
Электросила

Avtovo/
Автово

Park Pobedy/
Парк Победы

Proletarskaya/
Пролетарская

Leninskii Prospekt/
Ленинский Проспект

Moskovskaya/
Московска

Obukhovo/
Обухово

❶
Prospekt Veteranov/
Проспект Ветеранов

Zvyozdnaya/
Звёздная

Kupchino/
❷ Купчино

Rybatskoe/ ❸
Рыбацкое

Gostiny
Dvor/
Гостиный
Двор

Nevsky Pr./
Невский Пр.

Pl. Vosstaniya/
Пл. Восстания

Mayakovskaya/
Маяковская

Sennaya Pl./
Сенная Пл.

Dostoyevskaya/
Достоевская

Sadovaya
Садовая

Vladimirskaya/
Владимирская

Pushkinskaya/
Пушкинская

Pl. Al. Nevskovo/
Пл. Ал. Невского

Ligovsky Pr./
Лиговский Пр.

Tekhnologicheskiy Institute/
Технологтической Институт

❶ Kirovsko-Vyborgskaya line
❷ Moskovsko-Petrogradskaya line
❸ Nevsko-Vasileostrovskaya line
❹ Pravoberezhnaya line
Rail lines
Waterways
Transfer stations
End stops

RUSSIA

Tours: Russian **bus tours** leave from the corner of Nevsky pr. and the Griboyedov Canal (Грибоедов), in front of the Kazan Cathedral and cover the main sights (80 min.; 100R, students 80R). The "intercity service" offers guided tours in English of St. Petersburg, Peter and Paul Fortress, Pushkin, the Cathedrals, the Hermitage, Pavlovsk, and Peterhof daily at 10am and 2pm. Prices range from US$18-US$45; call ahead to see what tour is offered that day. (Nevsky Prospekt 30, at the corner with Griboyedov Canal. M2: Nevsky Prospekt. ☎318 92 89.) **Boat cruises** (1 hr.) leave from the Neva, in front of the Bronze Horseman. (Daily noon-10pm, every hour or so, and June-Aug. 1:20am to see the raising of the bridges. 150R.) Cruises also leave from the Fontanka, at the corner of Nevsky pr., (every 30-40min. 11am-8pm; 160R, children under 12 80R), as well as from the Griboedov Canal, at the corner of Nevsky pr. (every hour; 300R, foreign children 150R, Russians 150R).

Budget Travel: Sindbad Travel (FIYTO), ul. 3-ya Sovetskaya 28 (3-я Советская; ☎324 08 80; fax 329 80 19; www.sindbad.ru), in the International Hostel. Arranges tickets, as well as adventure trips. Student discounts on airplane tickets 10-80%. English spoken. Open M-F 9:30am-8pm, Sa-Su 10am-5pm. Also at Universitetskaya nab. 11 (Университетская наб.; ☎/fax 324 08 80). Open M-F 10am-6pm.

Adventure Travel: Wild Russia, Nevsky pr. 22/24 (☎325 93 30; fax 273 65 14; www.wildrussia.spb.ru). In addition to arranging expensive expeditions to the outermost regions of Russia, Wild Russia provides guides, gear, and accommodations for outdoor excursions near St. Petersburg and Moscow. One weekend expedition US$40-100.

Consulates: Citizens of **Australia** and **New Zealand** should contact their embassies in Moscow but can use the UK consulate in an emergency. **Canada:** Malodetskoselsky pr. 32 (Малодетскосельский; ☎325 84 48; fax 325 83 93). M2: Frunzenskaya. Open M-F 9am-5pm. **UK:** Pl. Proletarskoi Diktatury 5 (Пролетарской Диктатуры; ☎320 32 00; fax 320 32 11; www.britain.spb.ru). M1: Chernyshevskaya. Open M-F 9am-5pm. **US:** Ul. Furshtatskaya 15 (Фурштатская; ☎275 17 01; 24hr. emergency 274 86 92; fax 110 70 22; acs_stpete@state.gov). M1: Chernyshevskaya. Open M-F 9am-5:30pm. Services for US citizens (fax 274 82 35) open 9:30am-1:30pm.

Currency Exchange: Look for "Обмен валюты" (obmen valyuty) signs everywhere. **Menatep Bank** (Менатеп; ☎312 26 92), Nevsky pr. 1, at the corner of Admiralteysky pr. M2: Nevsky Prospekt. Cashes AmEx/MC/Thomas Cook/V **traveler's checks** and offers **Western Union** services. Open daily 10:30am-1:30pm and 2:30-9pm.

American Express: Ul. Malaya Morskaya 23 (☎326 45 00). Open M-F 9am-5pm.

English-Language Bookstore: Anglia British Bookshop (Англия), nab. Reki Fontanki 40 (Реки Фонтанки; ☎279 8284; www.anglophile.ru). Just off Nevsky pr., Petersburg's only exclusively English bookstore stocks a wide variety of titles. Open daily 10am-9pm.

EMERGENCY AND COMMUNICATIONS

Pharmacy: Near the city center pharmacies (аптеки; apteki) are common, with one every few blocks. A particularly useful one at Nevsky pr. 22 stocks Western medicines and toiletries. Open 24hr. Pharmacist on duty daily 8am-10pm. MC/V.

Medical Assistance: American Medical Center, ul. Serpukhovskaya 10 (Серпуховская; ☎326 17 30; fax 326 17 31). M1: Tekhnologichesky Institut. Turn right on Moskovsky pr., take an immediate right on Zagorodny pr. (Загородный), and take the second right on Serpukhovskaya. English-speaking doctors provide comprehensive services, including house calls and emergency medical and dental services. Consultation US$165, students US$135. Open daily 24hr. AmEx/MC/V. **British-American Family Clinic,** Grafsky Pereulok 7 (☎327 60 30; fax 327 60 40), on the corner of Vladmirsky pr. Expat staff offers primary care services and evaluations. Open 24hr. **Euromed Clinic,** Suvorovsky pr. 60 (☎327 03 01; www.euromed.ru) provides 24hr. emergency and evaluation services, dental, billing services for major European and Asian insurance policies, and reduced fees for students.

Telephones: Central Telephone and Telegraph (Междугородный Междуяродный Телефон; Mezhdugorodny Mezhduyarodny Telefon). While the central office at ul. Bolshay Morskay 3/5 is closed for repairs, several other branch offices remain open: Nevsky pr. 27, Nevsky pr. 88, Nevsky pr. 107, Kronversky pr. 21, Moskovsky Vokzal b.o. 3-ya Linya 8. Open daily 8am-10pm.

Internet Access: 5.3 GHz Internet Club, Nevsky pr. 63 (☎314 60 06). M4: Pl. Vosstaniya. On the left side of Nevsky pr. as you walk towards the Hermitage from pl. Vosstaniya. 65R per hour, or 190R for all night. Open daily 9am-11pm. **Tetris Internet Cafe** (Тетрис), Chernyakhovskovo 33 (Черняховского; ☎164 48 77). M4: Ligovsky Prospekt. Turn left on Ligovsky pr., take the first left, and then the first right on Chernyakhovskovo. 30-60R per hr. Open 24hr., except 9-10am.

Post Office: Ul. Pochtamtskaya 9 (Почтамтская). From Nevsky pr., go west on ul. Malaya Morskaya, which becomes ul. Pochtamtskaya. It's about 2 blocks past St. Isaac's Cathedral on the right, before an overhanging arch. **Currency exchange** and **telephone** service. International mail at windows #24-30. **Poste Restante** held up to 1 month at windows #1 and 2. Open M-Sa 9am-8pm, Su 10am-6pm.

Postal Code: 190 000.

ACCOMMODATIONS

Travelers can choose among deluxe new joint ventures, old Intourist dinosaurs, **hostels,** and **private apartments.** *The St. Petersburg Times* lists apartments for rent, both long- and short-term; pick up a free copy in the Grand Hotel Europe. Budget accommodations, however, are rare and not very "budget." Russian speakers may want to consider a **homestay.** The **Host Families Association** (**HOFA;** ☎/fax 275 19 92), based at the St. Petersburg Technical University, arranges bed and breakfast in apartments within 5km of the center.

International Youth Hostel (HI), ul. 3-ya Sovetskaya 28 (☎329 80 18; fax 329 80 19; www.ryh.ru). M1: Pl. Vosstaniya. Walk along Suvorovsky pr. (Суворовский) for 3 blocks, then turn right on ul. 3-ya Sovetskaya. Tight security, a variety of amenities (TV, English films, common room), and a choice location near Nevsky pr. make this hostel an excellent choice. Internet 1R per min. Breakfast included. Communal showers 8-11am and 4-11:30pm. Laundry US$4 for 5kg. Reception 8am-1am. Check-out 11am. No curfew. 2- to 5-bed dorms US$19, US$2 off with HI, US$1 with ISIC. ❷

Puppet Hostel (HI), ul. Nekrasova 12, 4th fl. (Некрасова; ☎272 54 01; fax 272 83 61; www.hostelling-russia.ru). M3: Mayakovskaya. Walk up ul. Mayakovskaya (Маяковская) and take the 2nd left on Nekrasova. The hostel is on your right, next to the Bolshoy Puppet Theater. Friendly, English-speaking staff and clean, simple rooms. Breakfast included. Reception 8am-midnight. Check-out noon. May-Sept.: Dorms US$16; doubles US$19 per person. Oct.-Apr.: US$18/$21. US$1 off with HI or ISIC. ❷

Hostel "Holiday" (HI), nab. Arsenalnaya 9 (Арсенальная; ☎/fax 327 10 70; www.hostel.spb.ru). M1: Pl. Lenina. Exit at Finlyandsky Vokzal (Финляандский Вокзал), turn left on ul. Komsomola (Комсомола), then right on ul. Mikhailova (Михаилова). At the end of the street turn left on nab. Arsenalnaya. Visitors enjoy a great view of the glittering Neva, but must deal with noisy traffic. Not as clean as others, but boasts a welcoming staff, ping-pong, satellite TV, and a piano. Internet (150R per hour), kitchen, laundry, visa support. Breakfast included. Reception 24hr. Check-out noon. Call ahead. May-Oct.: 15 3- to 5-bed dorms US$14; singles US$37; doubles US$19 per person. Oct. 16-Apr.: US$12/US$15/US$27. US$1 off with HI or ISIC or if under age 16; US$2 off after 5 days. MC/V. ❷

Petrovsky Hostel, ul. Baltiiskaya 26 (Балтийская; ☎252 75 63 or 252 53 81; fax 252 65 12). M1: Narvskaya. Facing the triumphal arch from the Metro station, turn left on Stachek pr.; when you reach the square, go left on Baltiskaya. The hostel is a few blocks ahead in the Petrovsky College building. Though a trek from the center, this hostel's clean, comfortable rooms and low prices attract many guests. Kitchen, common room with TV, and a few private *luks* (luxury) rooms with bath, TV, and phone. Reception 9am-5pm. Check-in 24hr. 2- to 5-bed dorms 200R; *luks* rooms 400-800R. ●

Hotel Olgino (Отель Ольгино), Primorskoye Shosse 18 (Приморское Шоссе; ☎238 36 71; fax 238 37 63). M4: Staraya Derevnya. From the Metro, take bus #110 (20-25min.). The bus will make a U-turn and then stop in front of the hotel. Also accessible by *marshrutka* #25 or 417 from M2: Chyornaya Rechka (20min.; tell the driver where you're going). Located outside the city, this hotel offers peace and quiet. Horseback riding (200R per hr.), sauna (500R per hr.), and *banya* (700R per hr.) available. Restaurant and disco. Check-in 24hr. Check-out noon. Call ahead. Parking 116R. Singles US$41; doubles US$49; *luks* rooms US$58-70; camping US$8 per night. ●

🍴 FOOD

Markets stock fresh produce, meat, bread, pastries, and honey. Beware of vendors who try to cheat foreigners; watch for fingers on the scales and count your change. Don't forget to bring bags and jars, although some vendors provide them for a couple of rubles. The **covered market,** Kuznechny per. 3 (Кузнечный; open M-Sa 8am-7pm, Su 8am-6pm), just around the corner from M1: Vladimirskaya, and the **Maltsevsky Rynok** (Мальцевский Рынок), ul. Nekrasova 52 (M1: Pl. Vosstaniya; open daily 9am-8pm), at the top of Ligovsky pr. (Лиговский), are the biggest markets.

RUSSIAN RESTAURANTS

🏛 **The Idiot** (Идиоть), nab. Reki Moyki 82 (Реки Мойки; ☎315 16 75). M2: Sennaya pl. Turn right on Grivtsova per. and walk toward the Moyka and Admiralty, then left on nab. Reki Moiki. The Idiot is on the left just past the bridge to Isaakyevskaya pl., identifiable by a single globular lamp. Named for the Dostoyevsky novel, this laid-back cafe captures the decadent feel of a Silver Age salon. Vegetarian Russian cuisine. Fun drinks: try "Crime (theirs) and Punishment (yours)." Entrees 150-300R. Happy Hour 6:30-7:30pm offers 2-for-1 beer or wine. Open daily 11am-1am. ●

Propaganda, nab. Reki Fontanka 40 (Реки Фонтанка; ☎275 35 58). M2: Gostiny Dvor. Walk toward pl. Vosstaniya on Nevsky pr. until you cross the Fontanka. Turn left on nab. Reki Fontaka. With its military-bunker decor, this meat and seafood restaurant finds the balance between hip and corny. Entrees 225-400R. 20% discount 1am-5am. Open daily noon-5am. ●

Traktir Shury Mury, ul. Belinskovo 8 (Белинсково; ☎279 85 50). M2: Gostiny Dvor or M1: Vladimirskaya. From Vladimirskaya, walk toward Admiralty on Nevsky pr. and take a right on nab. Reki Fontanka. At next bridge, go right on Belinskovo. This delightfully inexpensive country bistro serves up a hint of romance with a lot of bang for your buck. Menu features Russian and European dishes. Entrees 100-250R. MC/V. ●

Kafe Hutorok (Хуторок), ul. 3-ya Sovetskaya 24 (☎277 15 23). M1: Pl. Vosstaniya. Next to the International Youth Hostel. Don't be put off by the low profile; this basement cafe whips up homestyle Russian food. The sizeable menu revolves around meat and seafood. Entrees 75-140R. Drinks 10-90R. Open daily 10am-11pm. ●

Tyoshi na Blinakh (Тёщи на Блинах; Mother in Law's Blini), Zagorodny pr. 18 (Загородый; ☎315 63 41). M1: Vladimirskaya. At the corner of ul. Razyezhskaya (Разьежская), 1 block from the Metro. **Branch** at ul Sytninskaya 16 (Сытнинская;

☎232 76 69). Great for a lunch on the run. Salads, meat dishes, and *blini* (pancakes) stuffed with fillers ranging from proletarian cabbage (15R) to bourgeois caviar (32R). Zagorodny location open daily 24hr. Sytninskaya location open daily 10am-9pm. ❶

INTERNATIONAL RESTAURANTS

Tbilisi (Тбилиси), ul. Sytninskaya 10 (☎232 93 91). M2: Gorkovskaya. Follow the fence that wraps around Park Lenina away from the fortress toward the Sytny (Сытный) market; Tbilisi is just behind it. For those who believe anything tastes better when cooked on a stick, Georgian restaurants offer some of the best food in Russia. Try the *mazoni*, a sour, milky drink with mint and garlic; 20R) or the *kharcho* (spicy beef soup; 45R). Salads available. Entrees 40-260R. Live music. Open daily noon-11pm. ❸

Tandoor (Тандур), Voznesensky pr. 2 (Вознесенский; ☎312 38 86). M2: Nevsky Prospekt. On the corner of Admiralteysky pr. (Адмиралтейский), at the end of Nevsky pr. Between the refined Indian decor and the English conversation, Tandoor makes it easy to forget that Russia is just outside. Vegetarian dishes available. Lunch special M-F noon-4pm US$10. Dinner US$5-8. Open daily noon-11pm. AmEx/DC/MC/V. ❸

SUPERMARKETS

24 Super Market, at ul. Zhukovskovo (Жуковсково) and ul. Vosstaniya. M3: Pl. Vosstaniya (☎279 14 27). Open 24hr. MC/V.

Eliseevsky (Елисеевский), Nevsky pr. 56. M2: Nevsky Prospekt. Across from pl. Ostrovskovo. Fancy stained glass and elaborate chandeliers frame Russian delicacies and expensive everyday goods. Open M-F 9am-9pm, Sa-Su 11am-9pm. MC/V.

◉ SIGHTS

St. Petersburg is a city steeped in the past. Citizens speak of the time "before the Revolution" as though it were only a few years ago, and of dear old Peter and Catherine as if they were good friends. Signs such as the one at Nevsky pr. 14 recall the harder times of WWII: "Citizens! During artillery bombardments this side of the street is more dangerous." The effects of those bombardments were reversed by Soviet-era reconstruction, and a second wave of projects has carefully restored the best sights in preparation for the city's 300th anniversary in 2003.

▨ THE HERMITAGE

Dvortsovaya nab. 34 (Дворцовая). *M2: Nevsky Prospekt. Exiting the Metro, turn left and walk down Nevsky pr. to its end at the Admiralty. Head right across Palace Square. ☎311 34 20; www.hermitage.ru. The kassa is located on the river side of the building. Lines can be long, so come early. Allow at least 3-4hr. to see the museum. Open Tu-Su 10:30am-6pm, cashier and upper floors close 1hr. earlier. 300R, students free. Camera 100R, video 250R. Four different 90min. English audio tours 120R each.*

Originally a collection of 225 paintings bought by **Catherine the Great** in 1764, the State Hermitage Museum (Эрмитаж), the world's largest art collection, rivals both the Louvre and the Prado in architectural, historical, and artistic significance. After commissioning its construction in 1769 and filling it with works of art, Catherine II wrote of the treasures: "The only ones to admire all this are the mice and me." Fortunately, since 1852, the five buildings have been open to all.

Ask for an indispensable English floor guide at the information desk near the *kassa*. The rooms are numbered, and the museum is organized chronologically by floor, starting with **Egyptian, Greek,** and **Roman** art on the ground floor of the Small and Great Hermitages and **prehistoric artifacts** in the Winter Palace. On the second floors of the Hermitages are collections of **15th- to 19th-century European art.** It is impossible to absorb the museum's entire collection in a day or even a week—indeed, only 5% of the three-million-piece collection is on display at any one time. If you're running late, visit the upper floors first—the museum closes top-down.

THE WINTER PALACE. Commissioned in 1762, the Winter Palace (Зимний Дворец; Zimny Dvorets) reflects the extravagant tastes of Empress Elizabeth, Peter the Great's daughter, and the architect Rastrelli. Rooms 190-198 on the second floor are the palace **state rooms.** The rest of the second floor is dominated by 15th- to 18th-century **French art** (Rooms 273-297) and by 10th- to 20th-century Russian art (Rooms 151-187). The third floor exhibits **Impressionist, Post-Impressionist,** and **20th-century European art.** The famous **Malachite Hall** (Room 189), contains six tons of malachite columns, boxes, and urns, each painstakingly constructed from thousands of matched stones to give the illusion of having been carved from one massive rock. If you wondered why the revolution occurred, decadence like this might clear up your confusion. The Provisional Government of Russia was arrested in the adjacent dining room in October 1917.

OTHER BUILDINGS. By the end of the 1760s, the collection amassed by the Empress had become too large for the Winter Palace, and Catherine appointed Vallin de la Mothe to build the **Small Hermitage** (Малый Эрмитаж; Maly Ermitazh), a retreat for herself and her lovers. The **Large Hermitage** (Большой Эрмитаж; Bolshoy Ermitazh) and the **Hermitage Theater** (Эрмитажный Театр; Ermitazhny Teatr) were completed in the 1780s. The Hermitage Theater is closed to visitors, but the Large Hermitage displays excellent **Italian** (Rooms 207-238) and **Dutch art** (Rooms 248-254). In Rooms 226-27, an exact copy of Raphael's *Loggia*, commissioned by Catherine the Great, covers the walls just as in the Vatican. In 1851, Stasov, a famous imperial Russian architect, built the fifth building, the **New Hermitage** (Новый Эрмитаж; Novy Ermitazh). The tsars lived with their collection in the Winter Palace and Hermitage until 1917, when the museum was nationalized.

NEAR THE HERMITAGE

PALACE SQUARE. The huge windswept expanse in front of the Winter Palace, Palace Square (Дворцовая Площадь; Dvortsovaya Ploshchad) has witnessed many milestones in Russia's history. It was here that Catherine took the crown after overthrowing her husband, Tsar Peter III, and years later Nicholas II's guards fired into a crowd of peaceful demonstrators on "Bloody Sunday," which precipitated the 1905 revolution. In October 1917, **Lenin's Bolsheviks** seized power from Kerensky's provisional government during the storming of the Winter Palace. Today, vendors peddle ice cream and souvenirs while the angel at the top of the **Aleksander Column** (Александрийская Колонна; Aleksandreeskaya Colonna) commemorates Russia's 1812 victory over Napoleon. The column weighs 700 tons, took two years to cut from a cliff in Karelia, and required another year to bring to St. Petersburg. It was raised in just 40 minutes by 2000 war veterans and a complex pulley system, and is held in place by its massive weight alone.

ADMIRALTY. (Адмиралтейство; Admiralteystvo.) Nevsky Prospekt begins at the Admiralty, whose golden spire soars over the Admiralty gardens and Palace Square. The spire was painted black during WWII to disguise it from German artillery bombers. The **tower**—one of the first buildings in St. Petersburg—supposedly allowed Peter to supervise the construction of his city. He also directed Russia's new shipyard and navy from its offices. The **gardens,** initially designed to allow for a wider firing range, now hold statues of important Russian literary figures. *(M2: Nevsky Prospekt. Exit the Metro, turn toward the golden spire, and walk to the end of Nevsky pr.)*

BRONZE HORSEMAN. This hulking statue of Peter the Great astride a rearing horse terrorized the protagonists in novels by Pushkin and Andrei Bely by coming to life and chasing them through the streets. In real life, the statue hasn't moved from the site on which Catherine the Great had it set in 1782. Standing on the same rock from which he first surveyed the city, Peter gazes across the Neva while crushing a snake beneath his horse's hooves. The menacing effect of Etienne Falconet's bronze sculpture is tempered by nearby ice cream vendors and a playground. The likeness of the city's founder, however, remains a powerful symbol of the city. *(M2: Nevsky Prospekt. On the river, in the park left of the Admiralty.)*

VASILEVSKY ISLAND. (Василевский Остров; Vasilevsky Ostrov.) Just across the bridge from the Hermitage, the **Strelka** (Стрелка; arrow or promontory) section of the city's biggest island juts into the river, dividing it in two and providing a spectacular view of both sides. The former **Stock Exchange** (now the Naval Museum) dominates the square on the island's east end, and the ships' prows and anchors sticking out of the two red **rostral columns** proclaim the glory of Peter's modern navy. Some of the city's best and strangest museums (see **Museums,** p. 684) are housed by the embankment facing the Admiralty. *(Take bus #10 from Nevsky pr.)*

⬛ ST. ISAAC'S CATHEDRAL

Between Admiralteysky pr. and ul. Malaya Morskaya. M2: Nevsky Prospekt. Exiting the Metro, turn left and walk almost to the end of Nevsky pr. Turn left on Malaya Morskaya. ☎315 97 32. Cathedral open daily 11am-7pm, kassa closes at 6pm. Colonnade open 11am-6pm. Last entry 1hr. before closing. Enter on the south side (from Malaya Morskaya). The kassa is to the right of the entrance, but foreigners buy tickets inside. Cathedral 250R, students 125R; colonnade 100R, students 50R.

Glittering, intricately carved masterpieces of iconography await beneath the dome of the 101.5m **St. Isaac's Cathedral** (Исаакиевский Собор; Isaakievsky Sobor), a massive example of 19th-century architecture. On a sunny day, the 100kg of pure gold that coats the dome shines for miles. The cost of this opulent cathedral was well over five times that of the Winter Palace and 60 laborers died from inhaling mercury fumes during the gilding process. Due in part to architect Auguste de Montferrand's lack of experience, construction took 40 years. The superstition that the Romanov dynasty would fall with the cathedral's completion didn't speed things up either. The cathedral was completed in 1858, but alas, the Romanovs endured until 1917. While the exterior was chipped by German artillery fire during the siege of the city and is still partially covered in scaffolding, the interior is overwhelming. Some of Russia's greatest artists worked on the murals and mosaics inside. Although officially designated a museum in 1931, the cathedral still holds religious services on major holidays. The breathtaking 360-degree view of St. Petersburg is worth the 260-step climb to the top of the **colonnade.**

FORTRESS OF PETER AND PAUL

M2: Gorkovskaya. Exiting the Metro, bear right on Kamennoostrovsky pr. (Каменноостровский), the unmarked street in front of you. Follow it to the river and cross the wooden bridge to the island fortress. ☎238 07 61. Open Th-M 10am-5pm, Tu 10am-4pm; closed last Tu of the month. Purchase a single ticket for most sights (120R, students 60R) at the kassa in the "boathouse" in the middle of the fortress or in the smaller kassa to the right just inside the main entrance. English tours approx. 300R (call ahead). Fortress wall 30R, children under 10 15R. Beach 10R. On the north side of the fortress Baltic Airlines (☎812 238 4520) offers 10-15min. helicopter rides over the city (1000R) and skydiving (tandem US$200).

Across the river from the Hermitage, the walls and golden spire of the Fortress of Peter and Paul (Петропавловская Крепость; Petropavlovskaya Krepost) beckon.

Construction of the fortress, supervised by Peter the Great himself, began on May 27, 1703, a date now considered the birthday of St. Petersburg. Originally intended as defense against the Swedes, it never saw battle; Peter I defeated the invaders before the bulwarks were finished. With the Swedish threat gone, Peter converted the fortress into a prison for political dissidents. Sardonic graffiti by inmates still covers the citadel's stone walls. The **Military History Museum** (see **Museums, p. 684**) can be found in the old arsenal.

■ **CRUISER AURORA.** (Аврора; Avrora.) Initially deployed in the 1905 Russo-Japanese war, the ship later played a critical role in the 1917 Revolution when it fired a blank by the Winter Palace, scaring the pants off Kerensky and his Provisional Government. Cannons, boats, and exhibits await on board. *(5min. down the river past Peter's Cabin, on the Bolshaya Nevka River. Open Tu-Th and Sa-Su 10:30am-4pm. Free.)*

PETER AND PAUL CATHEDRAL. (Петропавловский Собор; Petropavlovsky Sobor.) The main attraction within the fortress, the cathedral glows with walls of rose and aquamarine marble and a breathtaking Baroque iconostasis. At 122.5m, it's the tallest building in the city. From the ceiling, cherubs keep watch over the ornate coffins of Peter the Great and his successors. Before the main vault sits the recently restored **Chapel of St. Catherine the Martyr.** The bodies of the Romanovs—Nicholas II and his family—were entombed here on July 17, 1998, the 80th anniversary of their murder at the hands of the Bolsheviks. Outside the church, Mikhail Shemyakin's controversial bronze statue of Peter the Great at once fascinates and offends Russian visitors with its tiny head and elongated body.

NEVSKY GATE AND TRUBETSKOI BASTION. The site of numerous executions, the Nevsky gate (Невские Ворота; Nevskiye Vorota) stands to the right of the statue. The condemned awaited their fate in the fortress's southwest corner at the **Trubetskoi Bastion** (Трубецкой Бастион), where Peter the Great held and tortured his first son, Aleksei. Dostoyevsky, Gorky, Trotsky, and Lenin's brother spent time here as well. Plaques in Russian next to each cell identify notable inmates.

PETER'S CABIN. (Домик Петра Первого; Domik Petra Pervovo.) The first building constructed in St. Petersburg, the Cabin served as home to Peter the Great while he supervised the construction of the city. Now it's a shrine, with exhibits on the founding of the city and the Tsar's victory over Sweden. *(In a small brick house along the river outside the Petrograd (east) side of the fortress. Open W-M 10am-6pm; kassa closes at 5pm. Closed last M of the month. 40R, students 20R.)*

ALONG NEVSKY PROSPEKT

The easternmost boulevard of central St. Petersburg, Nevsky pr., is the city's equivalent of Paris's Champs-Elysées. In accordance with Peter's vision for the city, the avenue is of epic scale, running 4.5km from the Neva in the west to the Alexander Nevsky Monastery in the east; the golden dome of the Admiralty is visible all the way from Uprising Square, two-thirds of the way down the avenue.

■ **CHURCH OF THE BLEEDING SAVIOR.** (Спас На Крови; Spas Na Krovi.) The colorful forest of elaborate "Russian-style" domes known as the Church of the Bleeding Savior (or the Savior on the Blood) was built from 1883 to 1907 over the site of Tsar Aleksander II's 1881 assassination. The church, partially modeled on St. Basil's Cathedral in Moscow, has been reopened and beautifully renovated after 20 years of Soviet condemnation. The walls are covered with 650 square meters of mosaics, restored according to the designs of the original Russian artists. The southern wall displays the events from the Nativity up to the baptism of Christ; the northern wall shows Christ's miracles and healings in the last three years of his life; the western wall illustrates his death as a martyr. The adjacent chapel houses an exhibit paying homage to the life and death of the reformer Aleksander II. *(M2: Nevsky Prospekt. 3 blocks off Nevsky pr. up Canal Griboedova from Dom Knigi (see p. 672).* ☎*315 16 36. Open Th-Tu 11am-7pm; kassa closes at 6pm. Church 250R for foreigners, foreign students with ID 150R, Russians 30R, Russian students with ID 15R, children under 10 free. Aleksandr II exhibit 20R, students with ID 10R.)*

KAZAN CATHEDRAL. (Казанский Собор; Kazansky Sobor.) This colossal edifice, on the corner of Nevsky pr. and the Griboyedov Canal, was modeled after St. Peter's in Rome, but was designed and built by Russian architects. Completed in 1811, the cathedral was originally created to house Our Lady of Kazan, a now-lost sacred icon of the Romanovs. *(M2: Nevsky Prospekt.* ☎*318 45 28. Open daily 8:30am-7:30pm. Services daily 10am and 6pm. Tours daily 11:30am-5:30pm. Free.)*

GOSTINY DVOR. (Гостиный Двор; Merchants' Yard.) Completed under Catherine the Great in the 18th century, this large yellow complex next to the metro is one of the oldest indoor shopping malls in the world. Though it lacks a central artery, this two-floored ring of stores is in essence a street market taken inside and dramatically upscaled. Come for your vodka, electronics, pipes, and just about anything else you may need. *(M3: Gostiny Dvor. Open daily 10am-9pm.)*

OSTROVSKOVO SQUARE. (Островского; Ostrovskovo.) Ostrovskovo Square is home to a monument of Catherine the Great surrounded by the principal political and cultural figures of her reign: Potemkin, Marshall Suvorov, Princess Dashkova, poet Derzhavin, and others. To the right (with the Alexandrinsky at your back) is St. Petersburg's main public library, decorated with sculptures of ancient philosophers. The oldest Russian theater, **Alexsandrinsky** (Александринский), built by the architect Rossi in 1828, is behind Catherine's monument. The first production of Gogol's *The Inspector General* was staged here in 1836. On ul. Zodchevo Rossi (Зодчево России), behind the theater, is the **Vaganova School of Choreography,** which graduated such greats as Vaslav Nizhinsky, Anna Pavlova, Rudolf Nureyev, and Mikhail Baryshnikov. *(M3: Gostiny Dvor. Exit the Metro and head toward pl. Vosstaniya on Nevsky pr. The square is on the right.)*

SHEREMETYEV PALACE. (Дворец Шереметьевых; Dvorets Sheremetevykh.) Constructed in the early 1700s as a residence for Peter the Great's marshal, Boris Sheremetyev, this restored palace houses a music museum. Music lovers won't be able to resist the 300 piece collection of antique instruments, especially the pianos of Rubenstein and Shostakovich and the violin of Antonio Stradivarius. The palace's mirrored hall hosts concerts on weekends. *(Nab. Reki Fontanki 34. M3: Gostiny Dvor. From the Metro, cross the Fontanka and turn left. The palace is about 2 blocks down on your right.* ☎*272 44 41. Open W-Su noon-5pm; closed last W of the month. 80R, students 25R; camera 25R, video 50R. Concerts Oct.-May F 6:30pm, Sa-Su 4pm. Admission to concert 5R.)*

UPRISING SQUARE. (Пл. Восстания; Pl. Vosstaniya.) Some of the bloodiest confrontations of the February Revolution took place in Uprising Square, including the Cossack attack on police during a demonstration. The obelisk, erected in 1985, replaced a statue of Tsar Aleksandr III that was removed in 1937. Across from the train station, the green Oktyabrskaya Hotel bears the words "Город-герой Ленинград" (Leningrad, the Hero-City) in remembrance of the crippling losses suffered during the German siege. *(M1: Ploshchad Vosstaniya. Near Moskovsky Vokzal; Nevsky pr. runs through the square.)*

ALEXANDER NEVSKY MONASTERY

Pl. Alexander Nevskovo 1. M3 or 4: Pl. Aleksandra Nevskovo. The 18th-century Necropolis lies behind and to the left of the entrance archway, while the Artists' Necropolis lies behind and to the right. ☎*277 35 07. Grounds open daily 6am-10pm, cathedral open daily 6am-*

8pm, cemeteries open F-SW 9:30am-5:30pm. Annunciation Church open T-W and F-Su 11am-5pm (kassa closes 4:30pm). Services daily 5:45, 6, 6:20, 7, 10am, and 5pm. Admission to both cemeteries 40R, students 20R; cameras 20R, video 50R. Annunciation Church 50R, students 25R; camera 30R, video 60R. Donations requested.

A major pilgrimage spot and a peaceful place to stroll, Alexander Nevsky Monastery (Александро-невская Лавра; Aleksandro-Nevskaya Lavra) derives its name and fame from Prince Aleksandr of Novgorod, whose body was moved here by Peter the Great in 1724. In 1797, it received the highest monastic title of *lavra*, bestowed on only four Orthodox monasteries. Many of the tombs in the two cemeteries are extremely elaborate, depicting the deceased and their art. A cobblestone path connects the cathedral and the two cemeteries. Maps in both cemeteries indicate the graves of famous people.

18TH-CENTURY NECROPOLIS. The 18th-century Necropolis, known as the Lazarus Cemetery (Лазаревское Кладбище; Lazarevskoye Kladbishche), is the city's oldest burial ground. Walk around the edge of the cemetery to the left to find the plain black tomb of **Natalya Goncharova**, the wife of Aleksandr Pushkin. The tomb is marked N. N. Lanskaya (Н. Н. Ланская). The cemetery also holds the tombs of several famous St. Petersburg architects, including **Andrei Voronikhin,** who designed the Kazan Cathedral (see p. 681), **Adrian Zakharov,** architect of the Admiralty (see p. 678), and **Rossi,** the brains behind Ostrovskovo Square (see p. 681).

ARTISTS' NECROPOLIS. The Artists' Necropolis (Некраполь Мастеров Искусств; Nekropol Masterov Uskusstv), also known as the Tikhvin Cemetery (Тихвинское Кладбище; Tikhvinskoye Kladbishche), is newer and larger and larger than its next-door neighbor, the Lazarus Cemetery, and is the permanent home of a still more distinguished group. **Fyodor Dostoyevsky** could only afford to be buried here thanks to the Russian Orthodox Church; his grave is along the wall to the right, near the entrance and always strewn with flowers. Continuing along the cemetery's right edge, you arrive at the graves of famous musicians. The resting place of **Mikhail Glinka,** composer of the first Russian opera and a contemporary of Pushkin's, lies facing that of **Mikhail Balakirev,** who taught **Nikolai Rimsky-Korsakov.** Rimsky-Korsakov's white marble grave is recognizable by its hovering angels and Orthodox cross. Many are drawn to **Aleksandr Borodin**'s grave by the gold mosaic of a composition sheet from his famous String Quartet #1. **Modest Mussorgsky, Anton Rubinstein,** and **Pyotr Tchaikovsky** are in magnificent tombs next to Borodin.

OTHER SIGHTS. The **Church of the Annunciation** (Благовещенская Церковь; Blagoveshchenskaya Tserkov), farther along the central stone path on the left, was the original burial place of the Romanovs, who were moved to Peter and Paul Cathedral in 1998 (see p. 679). The church now houses the graves of military heroes, including **Suvorov** and minor members of the royal family. The **Holy Trinity Cathedral** (Свято-Троицкий Собор; Svyato-Troitsky Sobor), at the end of the path, is a functioning church, teeming with priests and devout *babushki.*

SUMMER GARDENS AND PALACE

*M2: Nevsky Prospekt. Turn right on nab. Kanala Griboyedova (Канала Грибоедова), pass the Church of the Bleeding Savior, cross the Moyka, and turn right on ul. Pestelya (Пестеля). The palace and gardens will be on your left, just after the next small canal. ☎ 314 04 56. **Garden** open May-Oct. daily 10am-9:30pm. 10R, students 7R, children 5R. Open Nov.-Apr. daily 10am-8pm. Free. **Palace** open May-Oct. W-M 11am-6pm; closed last M of the month. Palace signs in English. 75R, students 45R, free the 3rd Th of the month. Camera 30R, video 70R. Call ahead for tours of 15-20 people; 50R per person.*

The Summer Gardens and Palace (Летний Сад и Дворец; Letny Sad i Dvorets) are a lovely place to rest and cool off, and one of the city's more romantic spots. Both the northern entrance and the southern entrance lead to long, shady paths lined with replicas of Classical Roman sculptures. In the northeast corner of the Garden sits Peter's **Summer Palace,** which seems like more of a *dacha* (summer home) than a palace. The decor reflects Peter's diverse tastes: Spanish and Portuguese chairs, German clocks, and Japanese paintings fill the rooms. The **Coffee House** (Кофейный Домик; Kofeyny Domik) and the **Tea House** (Чайный Домик; Chayny Domik) in the garden near the palace have small exhibits and gift shops, respectively, but neither sells coffee or tea. **Mars Field** (Марсово Поле; Marsovo Pole), named after military parades held here in the 19th century, extends next to the Summer Gardens. The broad, open park is now a memorial to the victims of the Revolution and the Civil War (1917-19). A round monument in the center holds an eternal flame. Don't walk on the grass, lest you tread on a massive common grave.

SMOLNY INSTITUTE AND CATHEDRAL

From M2: Nevsky Prospekt, take bus #22 away from the Admiralty. Or, from the stop across Kirochnaya ul. from M1: Chernyshevskaya, take bus #46, or 136 . Get off at the blue towers with gray domes (10-15min.) ☎271 91 82. Open F-W 11am-6pm; kassa closes 5:15pm; tower closes 4pm. 150R, students 75R; camera 20R, video 50R.

Once a prestigious school for aristocratic girls, the **Smolny Institute** (Смольный Институт) earned its place in history when Trotsky and Lenin set up the headquarters of the **Bolshevik Central Committee** here in 1917 and planned the Revolution from behind its yellow walls. The gate to the buildings at the end of the drive reads "First Soviet of the dictatorship of the proletariat" and "Proletariats of all nations, unite!" Farther down are busts of Engels and Marx. Next door the blue-and-white **Smolny Cathedral** (Смольный Собор; Smolny Sobor) is notable for combining Baroque and Orthodox Russian architectural styles. The church now functions as an exhibition and concert hall. Climb to the top of the 68m high bell tower and survey Lenin's—er, Peter's—city.

OCTOBER REGION

In St. Petersburg's most romantic quarter, the October Region (Октябрьский Район; Oktyabrsky Rayon), Canal Griboyedova meanders through quiet neighborhoods along with the summer breeze.

ST. NICHOLAS CATHEDRAL. (Никольский Собор; Nikolsky Sobor.) A striking blue-and-gold structure, St. Nicholas Cathedral was constructed in 18th-century Baroque style. Inside, candles lit by the faithful illuminate gold-plated icons. *(M4: Sadovaya. Cross the square, head down ul. Sadovaya (Садовая), and go right on ul. Rimskovo-Korsakovo (Римского-Корсакого). The cathedral is on the left, across the canal. Enter through the gate on the right side. Open daily 6:30am-7:30pm. Services daily at 7, 10am, and 6pm.)*

YUSUPOVSKY GARDENS. (Юсуповский Сад; Yusupovsky Sad.) On the borders of the October Region, the Yusupovsky Gardens—named after the prince who succeeded in killing Rasputin only after poisoning, shooting, and ultimately drowning him—provide a patch of green in the middle of the urban expanse. Locals come here to relax, smooch, and knit along the edges of the pond. *(M4: Sadovaya. At the intersection of ul. Sadovaya and ul. Rimskovo-Korsakovo.)*

THEATER SQUARE. (Театралная Площадь; Teatralnaya Ploschad.) Theater Square, between the Griboyedov and Krukov (Круков) Canals, is dominated by two imposing aquamarine buildings. The larger is the **Mariinsky Theater** (formerly the Kirov), home of the world-famous **Kirov Ballet.** Across the street stands the **Conservatory,** flanked by statues of composers Glinka and Rimsky-Korsakov. See **Entertainment,** p. 687. *(M2: Sennaya Ploshchad. From the Western corner of Sennaya pl., follow the Griboyedov Canal left for 5-7min. until you reach the square.)*

RUSSIA

GREAT CHORAL SYNAGOGUE. (Большая Хоралная Синагога; Bolshaya Horalnaya Sinagoga.) Hidden between buildings two blocks west of Theater Square, this Orthodox synagogue is not only a spiritual center of St. Petersburg but also Europe's second-largest, and perhaps most beautiful, synagogue. Built in 1893 by decree of Alexander II, its main dome covers a grand, two-tiered worship space. By orthodox law, women worship on the top tier, men on the bottom, and at least 10 men must be present for services. The large synagogue holds services only on Shabbat (Sa) and holidays; a smaller, connected synagogue holds daily services at 9am. *(Lermontovsky (Лермонтовский) pr. 2. M4: Sadovaya. Turn right off ul. Sadovaya and cross the canal onto ul. Rimskovo-Korsakovo. Continue to Lermontovsky pr. and turn right. ☎ 113 62 09. Open daily 9am-9pm.)*

OTHER SIGHTS

MENSHIKOV PALACE. (Меншиковский Дворец; Menshikovsky Dvorets.) In the middle of the Strelka district on Vasilevsky Island, Menshikov Palace is an unassuming yellow building with a small courtyard. Peter entertained guests here before he built the Summer Palace, and then gave it to Alexandr Menshikov, his good friend and governor of St. Petersburg. The museum displays an exhibition on "Russian Culture of Peter's Time." Call ahead for the English tour, without which the museum is lovely but rather incomprehensible, or ask for printed information in English. *(Universitetskaya nab. 15 (Университетская). M3: Vasileostrovskaya or bus #10. On foot, cross the bridge north of the Admiralteystvo and walk left. ☎ 323 11 12. Open Tu-Su 10:15am-4:30pm. 200R, students 100R. Camera 50R, video 125R. English tour 200R.)*

PISKARYOV MEMORIAL CEMETERY. (Пискарёвское Мемориальное Кладбище; Piskaryovskoye Memorialnoye Kladbishche.) To understand St. Petersburg's obsession with WWII, come to the remote and hauntingly tranquil Piskaryov Memorial Cemetery. Close to a million people died during the 900 days that the German army laid siege to the city; 490,000 of them are buried here. An eternal flame and a statue of Mother Russia mark the dead. The place is nearly empty, yet the emotion is palpable—this is the grave of a "Hero City" (Город-Герой). The monument reads: "No one is forgotten; nothing is forgotten." *(M2: Ozerki. Exit the Metro and go right out of the exit, without crossing the street, to catch bus #123. Ride 20 stops (35min.) until you reach the cemetery on the left, marked by a low granite wall and two square stone gate buildings, each with four columns. Open 24hr. Free.)*

🏛 MUSEUMS

There are three main kinds of museums in St. Petersburg: the giant, famous ones, the Soviet shrines, and recreated homes of cultural figures. If you only have one day for museums, spend it in the Hermitage (see p. 677) and the Russian Museum. If time allows, pay homage to the homes of your authorial idols, and don't neglect the fun and often well-executed smaller museums like the Vodka Museum (how could anyone!), the Kunstkamera, and the Museum of Russian Political History.

ART AND LITERATURE

▩ **RUSSIAN MUSEUM.** (Русский Музей; Russky Muzey.) This museum boasts the world's second-largest collection of Russian art after Moscow's Tretyakov Gallery. If you're trying to understand the many-chambered heart of St. Petersburg, this museum is a necessary stop, and a sure crowd-pleaser to boot. 12th- to 17th-century icons, 18th- to 19th-century paintings and sculpture, and Russian folk art are arranged chronologically. The Benois Wing shows avant-garde art of the early 20th century, including internationally famous artists like Kandinsky and Chagall.

(M3: Gostiny Dvor. In the yellow 1825 Mikhailov Palace (Михаиловский Дворец; Mikhailovsky Dvorets), behind the Pushkin monument. From the Metro, go down ul. Mikhailovskaya past the Grand Hotel Europe. Enter through the basement in the right corner of the courtyard; go downstairs and turn left. Or, enter through the Benois Wing on canal Griboyedova. ☎318 16 08; fax 314 41 53; www.rusmuseum.ru. English signs. Open M 10am-5pm, W-Su 10am-6pm; kassa closes 1hr. earlier. 240R, students 120R. Wheelchair accessible.)

PUSHKIN MUSEUM. (Музей Пушкина; Muzey Pushkina.) For anyone who likes poetry, visiting this museum represents a sort of pilgrimage. The former residence of Russia's greatest poet displays his personal effects and tells the tragic story of his last days. In the library where he died, the furniture is original and the clock is stopped at the time of death. Paying for the audio tour may be irksome, but it will greatly enrich your experience. *(Nab. Reki Moyki 12. M2: Nevsky Prospekt. Walk toward the Admiralty, then turn right on nab. Reki Moyki and follow the canal; it's the yellow building on the right. Enter through the courtyard; the kassa is on the left. ☎314 00 07. Open W-M 10:30am-5pm; closed last F of the month. 80R, students 16R. English-language audio tour 80R. Camera 25R, video 50R.)*

DOSTOYEVSKY HOUSE. (Дом Достоевского; Dom Dostoevskovo.) This is the house where the great Dostoevsky wrote *The Brothers Karamazov*, surrounded—unlike most of his troubled characters—by a supportive wife and loving children. Don't be afraid to gaze at the artist's top hat, hopelessly wishing you could try it on. *Crime and Punishment* junkies should check out Sennaya pl. (Сенная; M2: Sennaya Ploshchad), the setting of the book's grisly murder. *(Kuznechny per. 5/2 (Кузнечный). M1: Vladimirskaya. On the corner of ul. Dostoevskovo (Достоевского), just past the market. ☎311 40 31. Open Tu-Su 11am-6pm; closed last W of each month. Kassa closes 5:30pm. 60R, students 30R. Film versions of Dostoyevsky's novels shown Sept.-May Su at noon. 10R, students 5R. Expensive (250R) neighborhood tours available.)*

ANNA AKHMATOVA MUSEUM. (Музей Анны Ахматовой; Muzey Anny Akhmatovoi.) This modest museum exhibits the apartment and possessions of the poet whose courageous Soviet-era writings made her an icon. Free English films on various writers, including Akhmatova. *(Liteiny pr. 53 (Литейный). In the Sheremetev Palace (see p. 681). Enter through an archway off Liteiny pr.; keep left and follow the signs. ☎272 22 11; www.artexpo.spb.ru/akhmatova). Open Tu-Su 10:30am-6:30pm; closed last W of each month; kassa closes 5:30pm. Museum 60R, students 40R. Camera 25R, video 50R. English tours 120R, recorded tour in English 60R.)*

HISTORICAL AND SCIENTIFIC

KUNSTKAMERA ANTHROPOLOGICAL AND ETHNOGRAPHIC MUSEUM. (Музей Антропологии и Этнографии—Кунсткамера; Muzey Antropologyi i Etnografii—Kunstkamera.) Russia's oldest and probably most bizarre museum. After you've been enthralled by the "Lives and Habits" of the world's indigenous peoples, gawk at the real reason why you came: Peter the Great's grisly anatomical collection, featuring a severed head and deformed babies bathed in formaldehyde. Don't miss the two-headed calf. Entry grants access to the small, neighboring Lomonosov Museum. *(Universitetskaya nab. 3 (Университетская). The museum faces the Admiralty from across the river; enter on the left, on Tamozhenny per. (Таможенный). ☎328 14 12. Open Tu-Su 11am-6pm; kassa closes at 4:45pm; closed last Tu of the month. 50R. Camera 20R, video 50R. English tour 520R; call ahead.)*

ETHNOGRAPHIC MUSEUM. (Музей Этнографии; Muzey Etnografii.) This museum exhibits the arts, traditions, and cultures of the 159 ethnic groups of the former Russian empire. *(Inzhenernaya ul. 4, bldg. 1 (Инженерная). ☎313 43 20. Signs in Russian only. Open Tu-Su 11am-6pm; kassa closes at 5pm. 40R, students 20R.)*

RUSSIA

THE LOCAL STORY

LOVE THAT VODKA

Victoria Petrova, curator of the Vodka Museum in St. Petersburg, tells Let's Go Researcher Charles L. Black how to spot a drunk, in what circumstances vodka is good for you, and why Russians love the stuff so much.

Q: What is your favorite aspect of working here at the Vodka Museum?
A: Well, there are a few. We have a special gesture here. We touch the side of the neck to show that someone is drunk or someone is an alcohol addict. We have a legend in St. Petersburg about the man who once climbed the peak of St. Paul and Peter Cathedral and put an angel on top of it. In order to reward him, they let him choose the reward he wanted. He asked for a paper with a stamp and a sign from the tsar authorizing him to come to the tavern and have vodka free anywhere in Russia. They granted this request, but then he lost it, so he pleaded for another one. They said, "Because you're such a drunk, you would lose it again." So they gave him the stamp on his neck. That's where the gesture comes from.
Q: What do you think the significance of vodka is to Russian culture?
A: I always thought vodka was something dangerous, like any other alcohol. But vodka can be safe and even healthy if you drink it in reasonable proportions. It's especially good for Russian cuisine, which has lots of fatty meals; vodka's good for dissolving fat, for helping metabolize it better. Vodka is essential to the traditional Russian table.

(continued on next page)

ZOOLOGICAL MUSEUM. (Зоологический Музей; Zoologichesky Muzey.) Contains 40,000 specimens of animals, fish, and insects, including a fully preserved mammoth and an enormous blue whale skeleton. *(Universitetskaya nab. 1. Take bus #10. Next to the Kunstkamera Museum (see p. 685), across the bridge from the Admiralty (see p. 678). ☎318 01 12. Open Sa-Th 11am-6pm; kassa closes at 5pm. Museum and live insect zoo each 30R, students 10R. Th free.)*

MUSEUM OF RUSSIAN POLITICAL HISTORY. (Музей Политической Истории России; Muzey Politicheskoi Istorii Rossii.) You don't need to be an academic to appreciate this museum's vast collection of historical artifacts and propaganda posters. The museum has housed Matilda Kshesinskaya, prima ballerina of the Mariinsky Theater and a lover of Nicholas II, and the Bolsheviks after the revolution. Today the museum contains an exhibit about Kresinskaya and a memorial to Lenin. The east wing displays a range of Soviet propaganda, as well as artifacts from WWII. Many signs in Russian, some in English. *(Ul. Kuybysheva 2 (Куйбышева). M2: Gorkovskaya. Go down Kamennoostrosky toward the mosque and turn left on Kuybysheva. ☎233 70 52; www.museum.ru/museum/polit_hist. Open F-W 10am-6pm. 60R, students 10R, children 8R. Camera 40R, video 250R. English tour (5-25 people) 3600R, up to 4 people 500R each.)*

CENTRAL NAVAL MUSEUM. (Центральный Военно-Морской Музей; Tsentralny Voyenno-Morskoy Muzey.) The old Stock Exchange building displays the boat that inspired Peter I to create the Russian navy, as well as model ships, submarines, weapons, paintings, and sculptures that chronicle the development of the modern navy. *(Birzhevaya pl. 4 (Биржевая; Stock Exchange Square). Take bus #10 across the bridge to Vasilevsky island and get off at the first stop. Walk toward Peter and Paul fortress; the museum will be past the Kunstkamera and Zoological museums, on your left. ☎328 25 02. Open W-Su 11am-6pm; last entry 5:15pm. 90R, students 30R. Camera 20R, video 60R. Tours in English 90R per person.)*

MILITARY HISTORY MUSEUM. (Военно-Исторический Музей; Voenno-Istorichesky Muzey.) This museum showcases military hardware from 15th-century armor to the 20th-century tanks. Here's your chance to see real AK-47s and medium range missiles up close. Exhibits on all of the Russian wars of the 19th and 20th centuries. *(Aleksandrovsky Park 7 (Александровский Парк). M2: Gorkovskaya. Exit the metro and walk toward the river, then bear right on Kronverskaya nab; the museum is on your right. ☎232 02 96. Open W-Su 11am-5pm. 100R, students 50R.)*

RUSSIAN VODKA MUSEUM. (Музей Водки; Muzey Vodki.) Opened in 2001, the world's first vodka museum features exhibits that chronicle the colorful history of Russia's favorite pastime. The entertaining and knowledgeable staff (see p. 686) takes vodka seriously, and the quaint cafe in the back offers hands-on learning. Indulge yourself with the delectable 3-shot tasting meal (US $12). You'll leave this museum happier—and with more neat facts to whip out at cocktail parties—than when you entered. *(Konnogvardeysky bul. 5 (Конногвардейский). Walk one block toward the river from the Manezh and take a left on Konnogvardeysky bul. The museum is one block down on the right. ☎ 312 34 16; russian-vodkamuseum@hotmail.com). Call ahead for an English tour. Open daily 11am-11pm. 50R. Vodka shots 30-40R. MC/V.)*

ARCTIC AND ANTARCTIC MUSEUM. (Музей Арктики и Антарктики; Muzey Arktiki i Antarktiki.) Everyone who likes stuffed arctic animals or has a penguin fetish should check out this peculiar little museum of Russia's dalliances in the polar regions. The museum features nifty ship models, nautical accoutrements, a lifesize arctic seaplane, an explorer's hut, and a cuddly stuffed polar bear. *(M1: Vladimirskaya. From the metro, walk down Kuznechny per. two blocks from Vladimirskaya Metro. On the corner of Kuznechny per. and ul. Marata (Марата). ☎ 311 25 49. Open W-Su 10am-6pm; kassa closes 5pm. 45min. tour 100R, 90min. 200R. 50R, students 15R.)*

🎭 ENTERTAINMENT

Throughout the month of June, when the evening sun barely touches the horizon, the city holds a series of outdoor concerts as part of the famed **White Nights Festival.** Watch the bridges over the Neva go up at 1:30am, but remember to walk on the side of the river where your hotel is located—the bridges don't go back down until 4-5am, though some are down briefly from 3 to 3:20am.

The city of Tchaikovsky, Prokofiev, and Stravinsky continues to live up to its reputation as a mecca for the performing arts. It is fairly easy to get tickets to world-class performances for as little as 100R. *Yarus* (ярус) are the cheapest seats. Many renowned theaters are known to grossly overcharge foreigners; so buying Russian tickets from scalpers will save you money; be *very* sure that they aren't for last night's show. If you get Russian tickets, dress up and do not speak English, or the ushers may ask to see your passport and refuse you entrance. The theater season ends in June and begins again in early September, but check for summer performances at the **ticket office** (Nevsky pr. 42, opposite Gostiny Dvor; ☎ 310 42 40; schedule 20R) or at kiosks and tables near Isaakievsky Sobor and along Nevsky pr.

Q: What do you think of foreign vodkas, such as Gray Goose or Belvedere? Do you think they're any good?

A: It's funny, but I don't drink vodka at all. I prefer wine.

Q: You're the tour guide of the Vodka museum and you don't drink any vodka?

A: I'm a very unbiased expert. That's why I can't judge the taste of those vodkas. I can only tell you that Russian vodkas are only distilled from grain alcohol, which isn't true of most foreign vodkas. I call them pseudo-vodkas because they're usually made from potato alcohol, rice alcohol, or grapes. Even when it's made from grain alcohol, the grain is of a different quality. In Russia the grain is rough and different, so it depends on the soil and the water that is used in the vodka. So I think only Russian vodka can be original.

Q: Cheap vodka can sometimes make people ill. Good vodka should not make you feel sick the next day, right?

A: Well, usually they have some special ingredients that prevent this hangover effect.

Q: Nutrients?

A: Yes, maybe. So if you want safe vodka, just look at the label on the bottle and check if it's the "lux" quality alcohol. It can be of several qualities, depending on the level of alcohol purification. The purer it is, the better the effect.

JUBILEE. All of St. Petersburg is gearing up for the city's year-long 300th anniversary celebration in 2003. Billions of roubles have gone into restoring major sights and planning glorious displays. In an effort to outshine Moscow's 850th anniversary in 1997, annual city festivals will be bigger than ever. If you plan on visiting in 2003, book accommodations well in advance. Check the *St. Petersburg Times* or the jubilee's website (www.300.spb.ru) to get the scoop on the latest shows and exhibits.

BALLET AND OPERA

Mariinsky Teatr (Мариинский), a.k.a. the "Kirov," Teatralnaya pl. 1 (Театральная; ☎ 114 52 64 or 114 43 44). M4: Sadovaya. Walk along Canal Griboyedova, then turn right into the square. Bus #3, 22, or 27. This large aqua building, formerly known as the Kirov, premiered Tchaikovsky's *Nutcracker* and *Sleeping Beauty* and launched the careers of Pavlova, Nureyev, and Baryshnikov. For 4 weeks in June, it hosts the **White Nights Festival.** Evening performances 7pm; matinees Sept.-June 11:30am. *Kassa* open Tu-Su 11am-3pm and 4-7pm. Foreigners 1450-2320R, Russians 500-700R. Tickets go on sale 20 days in advance. MC/V. Look for people trying to sell their tickets in the entrance hall of the theater 15-30 minutes before a show.

Maly Teatr (Малый Театр; Small Theater), a.k.a. "Mussorgsky" or "Theater of Opera and Ballet," pl. Iskusstv 1 (Искусств; ☎ 595 43 05), near the Russian Museum. Impressive concert hall hosting excellent performances of Russian ballet and opera. Bring your passport; documents are checked at the door. Open July-Aug. when the Mariinsky is closed. Evening performances 7pm; matinees noon. *Kassa* open W-M 11am-7pm, Tu 11am-6pm. Foreigners 120-1800R, Russians 100-300R.

Conservatoriya (Консерватория), Teatralnaya pl. 3 (☎ 312 25 19 or 311 85 74), across from Mariinsky Teatr. M4: Sadovaya. Bus #3, 22, or 27. Excellent student ballets and operas. Performances 6:30pm, matinees noon. *Kassa* open daily noon-8pm. Foreigners 450R, students 100-250R.

CIRCUS

Tsirk (Цирк; Circus), nab. Fontanki 3 (☎ 313 44 11; www.uraldrama.ru). M3: Gostiny Dvor. From the metro turn away from the Admiralty on Nevsky pr. Go left on Sadovaya and bear right on ul. Inzhernaya, continuing until you reach the Fontanka. Wax nostalgic for your lost childhood at Russia's oldest traditional circus, featuring a live orchestra. Open Nov.-June. Shows 11:30am, 3, and 7pm. *Kassa* open daily 11am-7pm. 30-200R.

CLASSICAL MUSIC

Shostakovich Philharmonic Hall, ul. Mikhailovskaya 2 (Михайловская; ☎ 164 38 83), across the square from the Russian Museum. M3: Gostiny Dvor. Large concert hall with both classical and modern performances. The Philharmonic is on tour for most of the summer; other groups perform daily 4 and 7pm. *Kassa* open daily 11am-3pm and 4-7:30pm. Tickets 150-750R.

Akademicheskaya Kapella (Академическая Капелла), nab. Reki Moyki 20 (☎ 314 10 58). M2: Nevsky Prospekt. Small hall for choirs, soloists, and orchestras. Concerts at 7pm. *Kassa* open daily noon-3pm and 4-7pm. 50-150R, Russians free-100R.

THEATER

Aleksandrinsky Teatr (Александринский Театр), pl. Ostrovskovo 2 (Островсково; ☎ 311 15 33). M3: Gostiny Dvor. Turn right on Nevsky pr., then right at the park with Catherine's statue and head straight back. Ballet and theater of mostly Western classics like *Hamlet* and *Cyrano de Bergerac*. Performances throughout the summer. *Kassa* open daily 11am-3pm, and 4-7:15pm. Tickets 80-800R.

Bolshoy Dramatichesky Teatr (Большой Драматический Театр), nab. Reki Fontanki 65 (☎310 92 42). M3: Gostiny Dvor. Conservative productions of Russian classics. Season ends mid-June. *Kassa* open daily 11am-7pm. Tickets 20-120R.

Marionette Theater, Nevsky pr. 52 (☎311 21 51; http://art.internord.ru/alt/theater). M3: Gostiny Dvor. Across from the metro stop, 1 block toward pl. Vosstaniya. Russia's first professional puppet theater, established in 1918, puts on various fairy tales daily. *Kassa* open 10:30am-2:15pm and 3:15-6pm. Tickets 20R.

▉ NIGHTLIFE

St. Petersburg is home to plenty of expensive clubs for Russian businessmen, but you'll find better times hidden away off the main drag. Be careful going home late at night, especially if you've been drinking—loud, drunk foreigners might as well be carrying neon signs saying, "Rob me!" Taking taxis home is common and fairly safe, but in summer check to see when your bridge rises or you may be stuck on the wrong side of the river. Check the Friday issues of the *St. Petersburg Times* and *Pulse* for current events and special promotions.

▓ **Tunnel,** ul. Blokhina 16 (Блохина; ☎233 40 15; www.tunnelclub.ru). M2: Gorkovskaya. Exit the metro and bear left, walking along the circular Kronversky pr. (Кронверский) in Alexandrinsky Park toward Vasilevsky Island. Turn right on ul. Blokhina, bearing right at the fork, until you come to an open area on your right. Tunnel is in the unmistakable camouflage bomb shelter. Russia's pioneering techno club, Tunnel offers live DJs spinning cutting-edge jungle and house over what must be the best sound system in the city. The club has spared no expense on the nuclear-chic style of its dance floors and bars. Beer and vodka 40R. Cover 100-200R. Open Th-Sa midnight-9pm.

▓ **Par,** 5B Alexandrovsky Park (☎233 33 74; www.icc.sp.ru). M2: Gorkovskaya. Finding Par is a little tricky: exit the metro and bear right, walking through the park in the direction of Peter and Paul Fortress; look for the red brick building inside the park. Popular among the cosmopolitan set, this club spins underground music from the European house scene, with jazzy and funky flavors. Beer and vodka from 30R. Cover 100-200R. Open Th-Su 11pm-late.

Moloko (Молоко; Milk), Perekupnoy per. 12 (Перекупной; ☎274 94 67; www.moloko-club.ru). Off Nevsky pr., halfway between M1: Pl. Vosstania and M3, 4: Pl. Aleksandra Nevskovo. One room of this glitz-free rock club invites drinking and conversation among its loyal contingent of friendly local students. Another holds a stage where local rock bands perform. When Moloko closes, many clubbers migrate to Griboyedov (see below). Beer 25R. Cover 50-100R. Open W-Su 7pm-midnight; music starts at 8pm.

Griboyedov (Грибоедов), ul. Voronezhskaya 2A (Воронежская; ☎164 43 55; www.mfiles.spb.ru/griboyedov). M4: Ligovsky Prospekt. Exit the Metro and take the underpass. Exit to the left; with your back to the station, you'll face an intersection; bear left on Konstantina Zaslonova (Константина Заслонова) and walk 2 blocks; bear left on Voronezhskaya and look for the big, grassy mound. This popular old bomb shelter has become a pillar of the club scene in St. Petersburg. Beer and wine 30R, vodka 20-50R. M house night, Tu reggae, W disco, Th trance, F techno, Sa garage/house, Su acid jazz/funk. 21+. Cover 60-130R. Live DJ's daily 11pm-1am. Open daily 6pm-6am.

JFC Jazz Club, ul. Shpalernaya 33 (Шпалерная; ☎272 98 50 or 327 38 65). M1: Chernyshevskaya. Go right on pr. Chernyshevskovo (Чернышевского), continue 4 blocks, and take a left on Shpalernaya; there will be a sign on the left, inside the courtyard. Exciting local jazz (as well as blues, latin, and salsa) music in an intimate setting. Beer 50R, hard liquor 40-150R. Live music 8-10pm. Cover 50-100R. Arrive early or call ahead for a table. Open daily 7-11pm.

CAFES

If the smoky basements and throbbing music of the club scene aren't your thing, the city offers cafes where the hip can find good drinks and better conversation.

Che, ul. Poltavskaya 3 (Полтавская; ☎277 76 00). M1: Vosstaniya. Walk down Nevsky pr. towards pl. Alexander Nevskovo 2-3 blocks, then make a right on Poltavskaya. Che is on the right. Even though it's named for a fiery revolutionary, the vibe of this cafe is one of calm and composure. Sit back on the comfortable couches with coffee or tea and practice your Russian with the hip clientele. Drinks 50-250R. Live music every night. AmEx/MC/V.

Purga, Reki Fontanka 11 (☎313 41 23). M3: Gostiny Dvor. Walk toward pl. Vosstaniya on Nevsky pr., and make a left on Reki Fontanki (don't cross the Fontanka). The demonic, skeletal snow rabbits hanging upside down on the ceiling demonstrate that this cafe is decidedly upbeat and funky. Enjoy the silent slapstick films, the Santa Claus, and the waiters' rabbit ears, all of which give this club its unique character. Beer 40R, food 40-150R. Open daily noon-6am.

BI-GAY-LESBIAN NIGHTLIFE

Greshniki (Грешники; Sinners), nab. Canala Griboyedova 28/1 (☎318 42 91; www.greshniki.gay.ru), 2 blocks off Nevsky pr., past the Kazan Cathedral. M2: Nevsky Prospekt. Unpretentious gay club with 4 floors of dancing, talking, and drinking. Music ranges from Euro pop to techno to disco. Drinks 40-200R. Drag shows W-Su 1am and 2am. Male stripshows daily midnight-4am. 18+. Cover 70R. Open daily 10pm-6am.

Mono, Kolomenskaya ul. 4 (☎164 36 78). M4: Ligovsky pr. With your back to the Metro turn right and walk down Ligovsky pr. Go left on Kuznechny, then left on Kolomenskaya; the club is on your left. What this club lacks in size it makes up for in friendliness. An outgoing staff and reasonable prices have allowed it to stay alive, while bigger gay clubs have gone belly up. Eurodance, pop and cabaret. Beer 30R, vodka 50R. M-W men 20R, women 50R; Th lesbian night 200R/20R; F-Su 50R/100R. Bar open daily 5pm-9pm, dance club 10pm-6am.

⚄ DAYTRIPS FROM ST. PETERSBURG

Many residents of the city go to *dachas* (summer cottages) outside the city every weekend; families crowd outgoing trains loaded with groceries and pets. Not to be outdone, the tsars built country houses of their own—if "house" is the proper word for these imperial monoliths. The palaces at Peterhof, Pushkin, and Pavlovsk were all burned to the ground during the Nazi retreat, but Soviet authorities provided staggering sums of money to rebuild these symbols of a rich cultural heritage. Today, diligent maintenance has restored the palaces to their original opulence, and they make worthwhile daytrips from St. Petersburg.

PETERHOF (ПЕТЕРГОФ)

In summer, the Meteor hydrofoil (Метеор; ☎325 6120) leaves from the quay on Dvortsovaya nab. (Дворцовая) in front of the Hermitage (30min.; every 20-40min. 9:30am-6pm; 150-350R, students 120-200R). The less picturesque train runs year-round from Baltiysky Vokzal (Балтийский; M1: Baltiyskaya; 35min., every 10-50min., 24R). Buy round-trip tickets from the suburban ticket office (Пригородная касса; prigorodnaya kassa)—ask for "NO-viy Peter-GOFF, too-DAH ee oh-BRAHT-nah" (Новый Петергоф, туда и обратно; New Peterhof, round-trip). Any train to Oranienbaum (Ораниенбаум), Kalishye (Калище), or Lebazhe (Лебаже) will get you there. Get off at Novy Peterhof. Sit at the front or you might not see the sign for the station. From the station, take any bus (10min., 6R) or van (5min, 10-15R) bound for the fontany (Фонтаны; fountains); get off when you see the palace.

LOWER GARDENS. Formerly known as Petrodvorets (Петродворец), 300-year-old Peterhof is the largest and best-restored of the palaces. To get through the gates you must pay a fee that includes access to the well-pruned **Lower Gardens,** a perfect place for a picnic. Most of the fountains are reconstructions, as post-war Germany misplaced the stolen originals. *(Gardens open daily May-Sept. 10:30am-6pm, last entrance 5pm; Oct.-Apr. 9am-5pm. 160R, students 80R. Fountains operate 10:30am-5pm).*

GRAND PALACE. (Большой Дворец; Bolshoy Dvorets.) Wanting to create his own Versailles, Peter started building a residence here in 1714. His daughter Empress Elizabeth, and later Catherine the Great, greatly expanded and remodeled it. The rooms reflect the conflicting tastes of the various tsars and interior fashions from early Baroque to Neoclassical. Ascend the exquisite main staircase to the 2nd-floor rooms, including the **Chesme Gallery**—a room larger than most single-family homes—whose artwork depicts the 1770 Russian victory over the Turks. Catherine arranged for a frigate to explode in front of the painter to ensure authenticity. Farther along, two Chinese-themed lobbies flank a gallery that contains 368 portraits by Italian Pietro Rotari; his widow, strapped for cash, sold the whole lot to Catherine the Great. Through the silk-lined opulence of the women's quarters lies the last room on the tour—**Peter's study,** which is lined with elegantly carved wood panels. *(☎ 420 00 73. Open Tu-Su 10:30am-6pm; kassa closes 5pm. Closed last Th of the month. Buy tickets inside. Palace 300R, students 150R. Cameras 100R, video 200R. Russian tour 150R. Obligatory bag check 2R.)*

GRAND CASCADE. The 64 elegant, gravity-powered fountains of the Grand Cascade send their waters into the Grand Canal. The largest of the shining gold statues, *Samson Tearing Open the Jaws of a Lion*, is a vivid symbol of Peter's victory over Sweden. To enter the impressive stone grotto underneath the fountains, buy tickets just outside the palace. Carefully placed stones cover the walls and ceiling of this quiet, cave-like royal hangout spot, which contains sculptures, a small historical exhibit, and a view of the fountains' plumbing. *(Grotto open Tu-Su 11am-4:30pm. 100R, students 50R.)*

HERMITAGE PAVILION. Russia's first Hermitage initially served as a setting for the amusements of the palace residents. Fans of 17th- and 18th-century European art might enjoy the 2nd-floor room filled floor-to-ceiling with paintings. *(Open Tu-Su 10:30am-6pm; kassa closes at 5pm. 100R, students 50R. Cameras 60R, video 150R.)*

MONPLAISIR. On the right side of the path facing the quay stands Monplaisir, where Peter actually lived (the large palace was only used for special occasions). Smaller and less ostentatious than its neighbors—he was the tsar with good taste—it is built in a modest Dutch style. *(Open Th-Tu 10:30am-6pm; kassa closes at 5pm. Closed 3rd Tu of the month. 190R, students 95R. Camera 60R, video 150R.)*

OTHER BUILDINGS. Next door to Monplaisir are the **Bath House** (Банный Корпус; Banny Korpus), which served Empress Maria Alexandrovna as a private health center, and the **Catherine Building** (Екатерининский Корпус; Ekaterininsky Korpus), where Catherine the Great laid low while her orders to overthrow her husband were being carried out. In the courtyard between the three buildings, follow the sound of children's happy shrieks to the **"joke fountains,"** which splash their giggling victims. *(Bath House open Th-Tu 0:30am-6pm; kassa closes at 5pm. Closed 3rd Th of the month and when it's raining. 125R, students 62R. Camera 60R, video 150R. Catherine Building open F-W 10:30am-6pm. 100R, students 50R. Camera 60R, video 150R.)* Near the end of the central path, a **wax museum** contains likenesses of historical figures, most of which look rather evil. *(Open daily 11am-6:30pm. 70R. Camera 45R, video 100R.)*

RUSSIA

TSARSKOYE SELO (ЦАРСКОЕ СЕЛО)

The elektrichka runs from Vitebsky vokzal (M1: Pushkinskaya). Buy tickets and board at the rightmost platforms. Ask for "Pushkin" (tickets 9R) and say "too-DAH ee oh-BRAHT-nah" (туда и обратно) to get a round-trip ticket. Don't worry that none of the signs say Pushkin; all trains leaving from platforms 1-3 stop there. It's the first stop outside Petersburg that actually looks like a station, recognizable by the large number of people (30min.). From the station, take bus #371 or 382 to the last stop (4R, 10min.). Knowing where to get off is tricky; ask the conductor or get off after spotting the blue-and-white palace through the trees to the right.

About 25km south of St. Petersburg, Tsarskoye Selo (Tsar's Village) surrounds Catherine the Great's summer residence, a gorgeous azure, white, and gold Baroque palace overlooking sprawling, English-style parks. The area was renamed "Pushkin" during the Soviet era, although the train station, Detskoye Selo (Детское Село; Children's Village) retained part of the old name.

CATHERINE'S PALACE. (Екатерининский Дворец; Ekaterininsky Dvorets.) Built in 1756 by the architect Rastrelli before he began work on the Winter Palace, this Baroque palace was remodeled by Charles Cameron on the orders of Catherine the Great. She had the good taste to remove the gilding from the facade, desiring a modest "cottage" where she could relax. This opulent residence was largely destroyed by the Nazis. The **Amber Room** suffered the most; its walls were stripped and lost forever (one rumor places the stolen furnishings somewhere in Paraguay). Even the exorbitant entrance fees haven't sufficed to repair these mansions completely, but many of the salons, especially the glittering **Grand Hall** ballroom, have been returned to their former glory. The **"golden" suites**—so named for their lavish Baroque ornamentation—hold the original furnishings that survived World War II. Latch onto one of the many English-speaking tours. *(☎ 465 53 08. Open W-M 10am-6pm. Museum open 10am-4pm for tourist groups, noon-6pm for private individuals. Closed last M of the month. 300R, students 150R. Camera 150R, video 350R. English tour free.)*

PARKS. The landscaping, designed by Rastrelli, mixes the wild with the well-manicured. Here Catherine would ramble with her dogs—some believe she loved them more than her children. The dogs now rest in peace beneath the **Pyramid**. In summer it is possible to take a ferry across the **Great Pond** to the **Island Pavilion**. The **Cold Bath Pavilion** stands in front of the palace to the left. Designed by Charles Cameron, it contains the exotic Agate Rooms. Across the street from Catherine's Palace, just outside the park, the **lycée** schooled a 12-year-old Pushkin. His spartan dorm room, along with the classrooms, laboratory, and music rooms, can still be seen through hordes of awestruck Russians. *(A ferry goes to the island on Great Pond (every 40min., in summer daily noon-6pm, weather permitting; round-trip 100R, students 50R; includes 30min. Russian tour of island). Parks open May-Sept. daily 9am-11pm; Oct.-Apr. 10am-11pm. 60R, students 30R; free after 6pm. All buildings open May-Sept. Bath Pavilion open W-Su 10am-5pm. Closed last W of the month. 160R, students 80R. Lycée ☎476 64 11. Open W-M 10:30am-5:30pm; kassa closes 4:30pm. 80R, students 16R. Camera 50R, video 150R.)*

PAVLOVSK (ПАВЛОВСК)

Get off the train at the stop after Pushkin. To get to the palace from the train station, take bus #370, 383, 383A, or 493. If you have time, cross the street in front of the station and walk the 2km through the serene park. To get to Pushkin from Pavlovsk, take bus #370 or 383 from the Great Palace or bus #473 from Pavlovsk Station (6R). Small garden open daily 11am-5pm. Park open daily 10am-6pm. 40R, students 20R. Palace ☎420 61 55. Open Sa-Th 10am-6pm, last entrance 5pm. Closed 1st M of the month. 240R, students 120R. Camera 120R, video 240R. English tour 200R.

Catherine the Great gave the park and gardens at Pavlovsk to her son Paul in 1777. The grounds include the largest park of all the outlying palaces, where shady paths wind among wild foliage, classical statuaries, bridges, and pavilions. The **Three Graces Pavilion,** in the small garden behind the palace, is renowned for the beauty of its central sculpture, carved by Paolo Triscorni in 1802 from a single piece of white marble. To the east stands the **Monument to Maria Fyodorovna,** widow of Paul I. Paul's **Great Palace** is not as spectacular (or garish, depending on your architectural taste) as his mother's at Tsarskoye Selo, but is nonetheless worth a visit. The marble columns and sculpted ceilings of the **Greek Hall** are particularly noteworthy, as is the **Gala Bedroom.** Marie Fyodorovna's apartments are among the few examples of modest royal taste.

NOVGOROD (НОВГОРОД)   ☎(8)81622

Founded in the ninth century by Prince Rurik, Novgorod (pop. 250,000) blossomed during the Middle Ages. In its medieval heyday, it housed twice its current population, triumphed over the Mongols, and challenged Moscow for Slavic supremacy. Moscow ultimately won out and tried to punish Novgorod (see **History,** p. 621), but the upstart river city survived unscathed. Close to St. Petersburg, larger and better restored than Pskov, Novgorod offers visitors a picturesque introduction to early Russia.

> Novgorod uses both 5- and 6-digit phone numbers. When dialing 6-digit numbers from out of town, drop the last 2 from the city code.

■ TRANSPORTATION

Trains: ☎753 72 or 13 93 80. To: **Moscow** (8½hr., 1 per day, 235R) and **St. Petersburg** (3-4hr., 3 per day, 108R). Watch your belongings closely on the Novgorod-Moscow train. *Kassa* open 24hr., but closed for random breaks.

Buses: To the right as you face the train station, in a building labeled "Автостанция." (Avtostantsia; ☎7 73 00 or 7 61 86.) Open 5am-10pm. To: **Moscow** (10hr., 1 per day, 221R); **Pskov** (4½hr., 2 per day, 130R); **St. Petersburg** (3hr., 7 per day, 116R).

■ ORIENTATION

Novgorod's heart is its **kremlin,** from which a web of streets spins outward from the **west side** of the river. The **train** and **bus station** lie on **ul. Oktyabrskaya** (Октябрьская). **Pr. Karla Marksa** (Карла Маркса) runs from the train station to what remains of the earthen walls that surrounded old Novgorod. Follow **ul. Lyudogoshchaya** (Людогощая) from the walls, through **Sofiyskaya pl.** (Софийская) to the kremlin. The **east side** of the river is home to most of the churches as well as Yaroslav's court, and the streets form a rectangular grid. Purchase à **map** (30R) from a kiosk in the train station, at any major hotel, or at the tourist office. Names on the map may not always match older street signs.

▉ PRACTICAL INFORMATION

Tourist Office: **Krasnaya Izba** (Красная Изба; The Red Wooden Hut), Sennaya Pl. 5 (Сенная; ☎7 30 74), 1 block down ul. Meretskovo (Мерецкого) from Sophiyskaya pl. Probably the only truly Western tourist office in Russia. **Free English maps** and info on

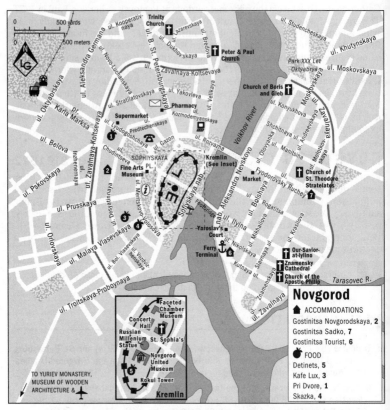

Novgorod

▲ ACCOMMODATIONS

Gostinitsa Novgorodskaya, **2**

Gostinitsa Sadko, **7**

Gostinitsa Tourist, **6**

● FOOD

Detinets, **5**

Kafe Lux, **3**

Pri Dvore, **1**

Skazka, **4**

everything from clubs to hospitals. English spoken, wheelchair accessible. Open daily 10am-5pm. **Excursion Office** (Экскурсионный отдел; ekskursionny otdel), ul. Meretskovo 2 (☎7 37 70), across the square from Krasnaya Izba on the 2nd floor of the red brick building. Open M-F 10am-6pm, Sa-Su 10am-4pm. For English tours of the kremlin, see the advertisement by the Russian Millennium statue (see below, 20-50R).

Currency Exchange: At any "Обмен Валюты" sign and in all the major banks; there's one on ul. Bolshaya Moskovskaya, opposite Yaroslav's court (see **Sights**, p. 695).

ATMs: In the train station, the telephone office, and in major banks.

Luggage Storage: In the train station (26R per day). Open 24hr.; talk to the station manager if the door is locked.

Pharmacy: Panacea N, B. St. Peterburgskaya 7/2 (Санкт Петербургская; ☎13 82 66). Open daily 8am-10pm.

Telephones: Novgorod Telecom, at the corner ul. Lyudogoshchaya and ul. Gazon (Газон), on Sophiyskaya pl. Pre-pay for intercity or international calls. Alternatively, the train station has a pay phone next to the baggage *kassa,* where you can buy phone cards to place intercity and international calls (128R for 100 units).

Internet: Technotron, ul. Velikaya 3 (Великая; ☎7 63 62 or 7 82 31). Image and text scanning services. Internet 40R per hour. Open M-F 9am-8pm, Sa 9am-4pm.

RUSSIA

Post Office: B. Sankt Peterburgskaya 9 (☎ 7 42 74). Open M-F 9am-2pm and 3-7pm, Sa 10am-4pm.

Postal Code: 173 001.

ACCOMMODATIONS

Gostinitsa Sadko (Гостиница Садко), ul. Fyodorovsky Ruchei 16 (Фёдоровский Ручей, formerly Gagarina; ☎ 66 30 04; fax 66 30 17; root@sadko.vnov.ru). From the stop opposite and to the right of the train station, buses #4 and 20 cross the river and stop at the corner of Bolshaya Moskovskaya (4R). Quiet, but somewhat remote location. Breakfast included. Singles with bath 470-660R; doubles 700-1100R. MC/V. ❷

Gostinitsa Novgorodskaya (Новгородская), ul. Desyatinnaya 6a (Десятинная; ☎/fax 7 22 60). From the train station, go down pr. Karla Marksa past the rotary and turn right on Desyatinnaya. Good location and simple, comfortable rooms with TV, phone, and private bath. Singles 480R; doubles 520R. MC/V. ❷

Gostinitsa Tourist (Турист), nab. Aleksandra Nevskovo 19/1 (Александра Невского; ☎ 3 41 85; fax 3 60 86), sometimes called Hotel Russia. From the kremlin, cross the foot bridge and walk right past the walls of Yaroslav's court. Large rooms, some of which look out on the kremlin. Breakfast included. Singles with bath 230R; doubles 420R. ❶

FOOD

The few restaurants in Novgorod with any sort of ambiance cater to tourists—and have prices to match. The well-stocked **grocery store** Vavilon (Вавилон), ul. Lyudogoshchaya 10 (Людогощая), is an alternative to fancy dining. (Open daily 8am-11pm.) Be sure to stop by the **market** on ul. Fyodorovsky Ruchei; you'll find everything from fresh fruit to shoes. (Open daily 8am-8pm.)

Detinets (Детинец; ☎ 7 46 24), in the west wall of the kremlin. Rough brick walls, wooden spoons, and authentic Russian food take diners back to the Middle Ages. Call ahead. Entrees 70-170R. Open M noon-9pm, Tu-Su 11am-11pm. ❷

Pri Dvore (При Дворе), in the park outside the kremlin. *Shashlyky* are grilled outside (35-42R) while sandwiches (8-10R) are served inside. Open daily noon-midnight. For heartier, classier fare go to their **restaurant** at ul. Lyudogoshchaya 3 (☎ 7 43 43), a block past Sophiyskaya pl. Entrees 60-200R. Open M-Sa 1pm-6pm and 7pm-midnight, Su noon-6pm and 7pm-midnight. MC/V. ❸

Skazka (Сказка; Fairy Tale), ul. Meritskovo 13 (☎ 7 71 60), outside the kremlin's park on the corner with Vlasyevskaya (Власьевская). Entrees 50-200R; salads 35-80R. In the less formal dessert hall, snack on pastries (4-6R), pizza (30R), or ice cream (16R). Open daily noon-midnight; dessert hall open daily noon-10pm. ❶

Kafe Lux (Люкс), Vlasevskaya 6 (☎ 7 24 15). Just up Vlasyevskaya from Skazka (see above). This intimate cafe near the kremlin offers the traditionals as cheap as you'll find them. Sandwiches 6-15R, salads 9-28R, entrees 12-45R. Open daily 7am-6am. ❶

SIGHTS

THE KREMLIN

Sometimes known as *detinets* (small kremlin), Novgorod's pride and joy is impressive nonetheless. Its walls, 3m thick and 11m high, and nine spiraling towers protect most of the city's sights, which are clustered inside around a grassy park. Bells are at the base of the **belfry** by the riverside entrance; at the west gate stands the **clock tower** (часовня; chasovnya). The tower's bell used to call citizens to meetings of the city council. *(Belfry open daily 6am-midnight. Free.)*

ST. SOPHIA'S CATHEDRAL. (Софийский Собор; Sofiysky Sobor.) This golden-spired Byzantine Cathedral—the oldest stone structure in Russia, built in the 11th century—dominates the complex. The intricately carved Western doors depict scenes from the Bible. *(Entering from the river side it's the first building on the right. Open daily 8am-1pm and 2-8pm; services 10am and 6pm. Free.)*

NOVGOROD UNITED MUSEUM. Exhibits in the Novgorod United Museum lead visitors through the city's history. Architectural finds and birch-bark inscriptions dominate the first few rooms but give way to medals and uniforms of the tsarist era. *(Open W-M 10am-6pm. Kassa closes 5:20pm. Closed last Th of the month. 48R, students 24R. Camera 20R, video 100R.)*

OTHER KREMLIN SIGHTS. Between the cathedral and the clock tower sits the **Faceted Chamber** (Грановитая Палата; Granovitaya Palata), a monument to religious devotion with an elaborate collection of golden artifacts and textiles. *(Enter between the small lion statues. Open Th-Tu 10am-6pm. Closed last F of the month. 70R, students 30R. Camera 20R, video 100R.)* In the center of the kremlin, directly in front of the museum, stands the **Russian Millennium** (Тысячелетие России; Tysyacheletie Rossii). It was built in 1852 as one of three identical bell-shaped monuments; its sisters stand in St. Petersburg and Kyiv. Just inside the west entrance, the **Philharmonic Concert Hall** showcases a variety of theatrical and musical performances *(☎ 7 27 77 or 7 44 45, kassa open M-F noon-7pm, Sa-Su noon-5pm. 20-500R).* In the Kremlin's west wall past the restaurant, the 17th-century **Kokui Tower** (Кокуй) affords a spectacular panoramic view of the Kremlin and the old city. *(Open Tu-W and F-Su 11am-2pm and 3-7pm. 35R, students 17R).* Outside the Kremlin walls, at the southern edge of the park, the **Novgorod Horseman** commemorates the city's longevity, but only by default: designed for Moscow after World War II, the statue was sent to Novgorod after the capital rejected it. In front of it stretches a clean **beach** where you can lounge with the locals after you've seen enough history for one day.

OTHER NOVGOROD SIGHTS

YAROSLAV'S COURT. (Ярославого Дворище; Yaroslavovo Dvorishche.) Across the footbridge from the Kremlin lies Yaroslav's Court, the old market center and the original site of the Novgorod princes' palace. It contains what's left of the 17th-century waterfront arcade, several 12th- to 16th-century churches, and the market gate house, now a **fresco museum.** *(Grounds open 24hr. Free. Museum open W-Su 10am-4:30pm; closed last F of the month. 35R, students 17R. Camera 20R, video 50R.)*

FINE ARTS MUSEUM. (Музей Искусства; Muzey Iskysstva.) This new museum displays the city's most important artwork of the 18th-20th centuries. *(Sophiyskaya pl. 2, in the white-columned building next to ul. Meretskovo. Open Tu-Su 10am-6pm. Kassa closes at 5:20pm. Closed first Th of the month. 48R, students 24R. Camera 20R, video 100R.)*

YURIEV MONASTERY. (Юрьев Монастырь; Yuriev Monastyr.) Dating from 1030, Yuriev is one of three monasteries around the city. From here you can see Lake Ilmen, the site of Rurik's 9th-century court, where the state of Russia first took shape. On the way in, note the blue cupolas of **Khristovozdvizhensky Sobor** (Христогоздвиженский Собор) and the golden stars that symbolize the monastery's high status. The twin-domed **St. George's Cathedral** (Георгиевский Собор; Georgievsky Sobor), founded in 1119, houses icons from the 12th century, as well as a kafedra (кафедра), a unique round pulpit. *(Take bus #7 (5min., every 20-30min., 4R) from the stop on Meritskovo (Меритского) between Chudintseva (Чудинцева) and*

Prusskaya, on the side opposite the park. Go well past the airport and get off when you see the gold dome of the monastery on your right. Open daily 7am-7pm. Free. Services at 6:30, 9am, and 6pm. Camera 10R, video 30R.)

VITOSLAVITSY MUSEUM OF WOODEN ARCHITECTURE. (Музей Деревянного Зодчества "Витославици;" Muzey Derevyannovo Zodchestva "Vitoslavitsi.") This interactive outdoor museum preserves a late 19th-century town, including its houses, its church, its art, and its residents—or at least their period-costumed descendents. The tree-shaded grounds overlook a lake. *(☎ 7 81 60. The bus stop after the Yuriev Monastery. To return to Novgorod, get on at the same stop. Open daily 10am-6pm. 48R, students 24R. Camera 20R, video 100R.)*

PSKOV (ПСКОВ) ☎(8)8112

Pskov (pop. 230,000) made its first foray into the history books in 903 as a flourishing regional trading post. As such, it was a popular target for invaders, including Swedes, Poles, Lithuanians, and Germans. While the invaders never actually took the city, the damage they wrought drove the Pskovians into the protective arms of the Russian Empire in 1510. However, trade routes began to shift and Pskov soon lost its stature as an economic center. Today, with more churches than restaurants and hotels combined, Pskov has found its niche as a spiritual center. The absence of tourists helps preserve the relaxed atmosphere of the city's wide avenues, quiet side streets, lazy rivers, and green parks. Many sights are in disrepair, but those that remain open dazzle the eye and recall Pskov's spiritual history.

⌷ TRANSPORTATION

Trains: ☎ 2 37 37. *Kassa* open 24hr. To: **Kaliningrad** (13hr., 1 per day, 625R); **Moscow** (12hr., 1-2 per day, 275R); **St. Petersburg** (6hr., 2-3 per day, 165R); **Minsk, BLR** (15hr., 2 per week, 370R); **Riga, LAT** (7hr., 1 per day, 787R); **Vilnius, LIT** (7hr., every 2 days, 500R).

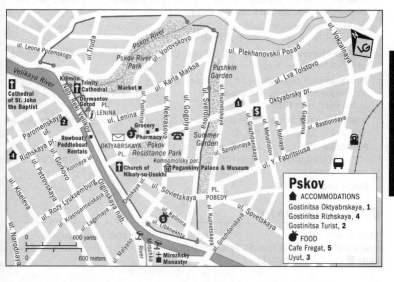

Pskov

▲ ACCOMMODATIONS
Gostinitsa Oktyabrskaya, **1**
Gostinitsa Rizhskaya, **4**
Gostinitsa Turist, **2**

● FOOD
Cafe Fregat, **5**
Uyut, **3**

RUSSIA

Buses: ☎ 2 40 02. To: **Novgorod** (4hr., 2 per day, 129R) and **St. Petersburg** (7hr., 5 per day, 177R). Each *kassa* sells tickets for different destinations, as indicated to the right of the window. Advance sales *kassa* #5. Open daily 5am-8pm.

Public Transportation: Bus #17 departs from the front of the train station and stops in front of Gostinitsa Oktyabrskaya, between Gostinitsa Turist and Gostinitsa Rizhskaya (see **Accommodations,** below), and at the kremlin. Buy tickets (4R) on board.

ORIENTATION

The **bus** and **train stations** are next to each other on ul. Vokzalnaya (Вокзальная). This street intersects with the end of **Oktyabrsky pr.** (Октябрьский пр.), Pskov's main axis, a couple of blocks to the right as you exit either station. In the main square, **Oktyabrskaya pl.** (Октябрьская пл.) intersects **ul. Sovetskaya** (Советская), which runs north to the kremlin. The **Velikaya** (Великая) and **Pskova** (Пскова) **Rivers** meet at the northernmost corner of the kremlin. On pleasant afternoons, sunbathers gather on the west (non-kremlin) bank of the Velikaya near the **Mirozhsky Monastery.** The outer **town walls** surround the old city and run 9km along **ul. Sverdlova** (Свердлова), the river, and past Pskov's two large parks. City maps available at Gostinitsa Oktyabrskaya (see **Accommodations,** p. 698).

PRACTICAL INFORMATION

Tourist Offices: Oktyabrskaya Tourist Bureau (☎ 16 42 27). In Gostinitsa Oktysbrskaya (see **Accommodations,** below). Provides maps and brochures, and arranges English tours (call ahead). Open daily 9am-6pm. The **tourist bureau** (☎ 2 19 06 or 2 39 88; fax 72 32 57), on the right after the entrance to the kremlin, arranges English tours of the city (250R) and the kremlin (150R). Open M-F 9am-1pm and 2-6pm, Sa-Su 9am-2pm.

Currency Exchange: The office at Oktyabrsky pr. 23/25 (☎ 16 19 83), next to Sberbank (Сбербанк), cashes **traveler's checks** for 3% commission. Open M-F 9am-2pm and 3-8pm, Sa 9am-3pm. Better exchange rates at most "Обмен Валюты" signs.

ATM: MC/V ATMs in the train station, at the currency exchange, the phone office, Gostinitsa Oktyabrskaya, and Gostinitsa Rizhskaya.

Luggage Storage: At the train station 23.10R for a large locker. Open 24hr. At the bus station. 10R per bag. Open daily 7am-6:40pm.

24-Hour Pharmacy: Oktyabrsky pr. 16, near Oktyabrskaya pl. (☎ 72 32 51). Ring the doorbell for service 9pm-8am.

Telephones: Ul. Nekrasova 17 (Некрасова), in a large gray building facing Oktyabrsky pr. Prepay for intercity and international calls. Open 24hr. **Faxes** at *kassy* 4 and 5. Open daily 8am-10pm.

Internet Access: Inside the Telephone Office. 30R per hr. Fill out a form and prepay at *kassa* 4 or 5 in the main hall. Open M-F 8am-10pm, Sa 11am-9pm.

Post Office: Ul. Sovetskaya 20 (Советская; ☎ 2 27 19). Obscured by trees on the north side of Oktyabrskaya pl. Open M-F 9am-2pm and 3-7pm, Sa-Su 9am-2pm, last Tu of month 2pm-7pm.

Postal Code: 180 000.

ACCOMMODATIONS

Most hotels offer reasonably priced rooms, but there aren't any incredible bargains in Pskov. HOFA (see **St. Petersburg: Accommodations,** p. 675) provides **homestays ❶** (US$25 per night).

Gostinitsa Oktyabrskaya (Октябрьская), Oktyabrsky pr. 36 (☎16 42 46; fax 16 42 54). Take bus #11, 14, or 17 from the train station. The hotel is on your right, just before the park with the Pushkin monument. Weary travelers will find the shiny, marble lobby a sight for sore eyes, but consider paying for your own bathroom–the common ones are less than desirable. Nevertheless, reasonably comfortable rooms in a convenient location. Dorms 70R; singles 120R, with bath 300-400R; doubles 240R/540-600R. ❶

Gostinitsa Rizhskaya (Рижская), Rizhskaya pr. 25 (☎46 22 23; fax 46 23 01; hotelr@com.psc.ru). Take bus #17 from the train station (4R) to the first stop across the bridge. Walk down Rizhskaya pr. away from the bridge; the hotel is on the right. This 3-star hotel aims for Western chic, with luxuries like a posh lobby and soft foam mattresses. Every room has private bath, cable TV, phone, and fridge. Laundry, beauty center, and solarium also available. Singles 420R-540R; doubles 760R-960R. ❷

Gostinitsa Turist (Турист), ul. Paromenskaya 4 (Пароменская; ☎44 51 51). Bus #17 stops just past the bridge. Tucked between Upeniya Paromenya and Velikaya. Evidently capitalism hasn't fully penetrated Russia yet: this hotel claims to be for Russians only, and other tourists should go to Gostinitsa Rizhskaya. In any case, an unspectacular but decent budget hotel close to the kremlin. Single 110R, with amenities 265R; doubles 220R/265R, with bath 310R. ❶

◖ FOOD

Restaurants sell salty, fatty, and potato-based foods. Fortunately, the numerous kiosks situated throughout the city's streets sell fresh bread, fruits, and vegetables. Vendors congregate at the **Central Market** (Центральный Рынок; Tsentralny Rynok) on ul. Karla Marksa (Карла Маркса) at the top of ul. Pushkina (Пушкина). Look for the entrance gate, labeled "РЫНОК" in huge letters. (Open daily 8am-4pm.) There is a **grocery** store at Oktyabrsky pr. 22. (Open daily 8am-9pm. MC/V.)

Cafe Fregat, (☎17 13 17), on ul. Libknekhta (Либкнехта). Walk away from the Kremlin on Sovyetskaya until you reach its intersection with ul. Nekrasova. Take a right on ul. Ouritskovo, toward the river. At the end of Ouritskovo, go left on Libknekhta; the cafe is on the right on the 2nd floor of the boathouse. The terrace of this nautically-themed cafe offers a great view overlooking the Velikaya and the nearby beach. Serves salads (25-60R), cheap *blini* (from 9R), and traditional entrees (50-130R). Open 24hr. ❷

Uyut (Уют; Comfort), Oktyabrsky pr. 10B (☎2 31 53), behind the cheaper, greasier Cafe Cheburechnaya (Кафе Чебуречная). A backstreet Russian cafe with a dark but tidy wooden interior and a pool table. Disco/bar on upper floor. Salads 13-14R, entrees 30-75R. Cafe open daily noon-midnight. Bar open Su-Th 10pm-2am, F-Sa 10pm-5am. ❶

◉ SIGHTS

If you aren't passionate about medieval Russian art and architecture, spend the afternoon gazing at the Kremlin walls from the beach near the Mirozhshky Monastery. Paddleboats and rowboats are available for rent at the stand by the river on the opposite side of the Rizhsky pr. bridge from the kremlin (20R per 30min.).

KREMLIN. With its thick stone walls topped by authentic wooden roofs and spires, this 9th century kremlin keeps modernity outside its arched portals. In the courtyard inside the main gate stand the ruins of **Dovmont's City** (Довмонтов Город; Dovmontov Gorod), named for Prince Dovmont, who ruled here from 1266 to 1299. A small museum displays icons and other relics. In contrast to the numerous attractions within Novgorod's kremlin, the interior courtyard here has only one major building: the tall, golden-domed **Trinity Cathedral** (Троицкий Собор;

Troitsky Sobor). The 17th-century structure boasts an elaborate, seven-tier iconostasis and frescoes that exemplify the Pskovian school of icon painting. An archway at the far end of the grounds grants access to the **Kremlin wall** between the courtyard and the Pskov River. *(From the train station, take bus #17 or any bus going to pl. Lenina; get off when you spot the kremlin walls. Kremlin open 6am-10pm. Museum open Tu-Su 11am-6pm. 15R, students 10R. Camera 40R, video 80R. Church open daily 8am-9pm. Services daily 9-11am and 6-8pm. Donations appreciated.)*

MIROZHSKY MONASTERY. (Мирожский Монастырь; Mirozhshky Monastyr.) Up-river from the kremlin, monastery walls enclose the **Cathedral of the Transfiguration** (Спасо-Преображенский Собор; Spaso-Preobrazhensky Sobor), which dates from 1156 and features frescoes typical of the Pskov region. *(Take bus #2 down ul. M. Gorkovo (5 min.); get off at ul. Krasnoarmeiskaya (Красноармейская) and walk down ul. Gorkovo until you reach a fork; make a hard left on ul. Malyaso (Мялясо), following it to the beach. Cross the bridge to your right; enter on the far side of the monastery. ☎46 73 02. Open Tu-Su 11am-6pm. Liturgy Su 9am. 100R, students 80R.)*

CATHEDRAL OF ST. JOHN THE BAPTIST. (Собор Иоанна Предтечи; Sobor Ioanna Predtechi.) The white, 12th-century cathedral, Pskov's oldest building, stands calmly at the north end of ul. Gorkovo, overlooking the west bank of the Velikaya River. First a convent and later a KGB garage, the cathedral has been partially restored to its earlier Byzantine splendor and now houses a respected school of icon painting. As a religious site, the church remains an important spiritual center of Pskov. All the students use ancient icon-painting techniques, and since 1993 the superior and his students have been painting the cathedral's white walls with frescoes in an effort to restore the ancient iconographical scheme. Choral services are also held in the old style, with the majority of the liturgical chants sung in the ancient, oriental analogue of the Gregorian chant "Znamenniy Raspev." *(Ring the doorbell of the peach-colored house across the path. Call ahead ☎44 50 01. Open daily 10am-8pm. Services Sa 6pm, Su 9:30am. Free tours available, some in English.)*

POGANKIN PALACE AND MUSEUM. (Поганкины Палать и Музей; Pogankiny Palaty i Muzey.) The wealth and heritage of Pskov rest in Pogankin Palace and Museum, originally the home of a 17th-century merchant. Start by climbing to the 2nd floor of the old building, which is often populated by students meticulously copying the icons on display. Vaulted ceilings and well-lit cases of coins and jewelry await visitors on the first floor. The newer wing houses a picture gallery and an exhibit on Pskov's role in World War II. *(Nekrasova 7, facing Komsomolsky pr. (Комсомольский). Enter through the new wing, buy your ticket, and go down the stairs and out through the courtyard to the main house. ☎16 33 11. Open Tu-Su 11am-6pm; closed last Tu of the month. 100R, students 80R. Tours in English 280R. Camera 40R, video 80R.)*

▶ DAYTRIPS FROM PSKOV

PECHORY MONASTERY (ПЕЧОРЫ МОНАСТЫРЬ)

Take a bus to Pechory that goes through Old Izborsk (Старый Изборск; Starii Izborsk; 1½hr., 6 per day, 32R), as other routes take much longer. You may want to get in line for a ticket up to an hour ahead of time. Since tickets often sell out, buy a return ticket as soon as you arrive, unless you want to camp with the monks. Schedules vary and don't always give accurate information, but the last bus back to Pskov usually leaves M-Th 5:50pm, F-Su 7:40pm. Exit the station, go across the square and down the very short Yurevskaya ul. (Юревская). Follow it past the tower in the middle of the square until it ends. Take a right; the monastery is on the left (5-10min.). ☎2 21 45. Open daily 6am-

10pm. Pay the gatekeeper for permission to bring a camera. Women must cover their heads and wear skirts (available at the entrance). Russian tours from 100R.

Founded in 1473, **Pechory Monastery** (Pechory Monastyr) sheltered more than 200 monks in the 16th century, when it doubled as a fortress. Today the complex is home to 60 monks. The golden-domed 1827 **St. Michael Church** (Михайловская Церковь; Mikhaylovskaya Tserkov), straight ahead from the main gate, stands beyond the "no entrance" (Нет Входа) sign. Through the archway to the left and down the hill is the yellow-and-white **Assumption Cathedral** (Успенский Собор; Uspensky Sobor), crowned with gold-starred blue domes. (Services daily 6am and 6pm.) The door on the left leads to the sacred caves, where monks and hermits are buried in the walls. (The caves are generally closed to visitors, but you can try negotiating with the guard.) A whitewashed **belfry** stands near the Cathedral, and a beautiful **flower garden** surrounds the **sacred water fountain,** the destination of many pilgrims. The water is holy, pure, and potable.

IZBORSK (ИЗБОРСК)

Buses arrive from Pskov (1hr., 6 per day, 13R) and go to Pechory (30min., 6 per day, 13R). Last bus to Pskov M-Th 5:25pm, F-Su 7:40pm. On the way back, wait at the side of the road, as not all buses pull into the station. If the kassa is closed, pay on board. From the bus station, cross the street and walk down the small road past a small museum on the left. Take the first right to get to the fortress (10-15min.). Open 24hr. Free.

Old Izborsk (Старый Изборск), not to be confused with New Izborsk, makes a great stop on the way to or from Pechory. The 8th-century town is older, smaller, and much less modernized than Pskov. Its secluded fortress stands proudly on its own hill, surrounded by trees, a pond, and the occasional free-roaming horse. The fortress walls are not as fully restored as those of Pskov's kremlin, but the cool, quiet 14th-century Cathedral of St. Nicholas is in excellent condition. Past the cathedral and outside the fortress, a path leads down to the left on an easy 10-minute hike to a pond where locals relax and gather water.

BLACK SEA (ЧЛРНОЕ МОРЕ)

Like all Eastern European countries that touch the warm waters of the Black Sea, Russia treasures its strip of palm-lined coast. In the 19th century and later Soviet period, the Crimea drew Russia's aristocracy and literati. These days, however, Sochi and the other Black Sea resorts call to Russia's elite, promising sunshine, palm trees, and respite from the bitter cold of the north.

SOCHI (СОЧИ)   ☎ 8622

In an earlier era, admirers dubbed Russia's Black Sea coast the "Caucasian Riviera," but it now seems that Sochi aspires to be the next Miami. Its beachfront—gaudy, raucous, and packed with scantily-clad Russians—reflects a concerted effort to squeeze a year's income from three months of tourism. Nevertheless, Sochi's subtropical climate, hilly streets, warm waters, and pebble beaches are intoxicating enough to forgive the crowds, if not forget them. Sochi is not the place to experience traditional Russian culture—but this may be precisely why so many Russians are here.

RUSSIA

▐ TRANSPORTATION

Flights: The **airport** in Adler (☎92 03 75) handles flights to Moscow (2½hr., 2000-3000R one-way).

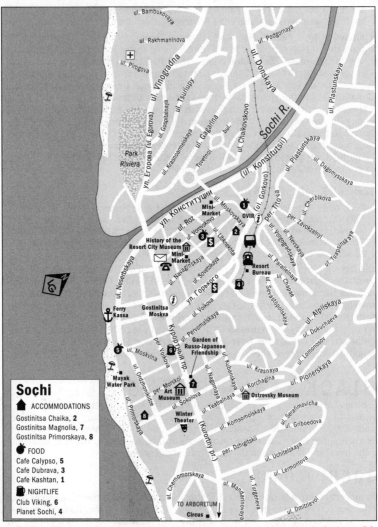

Sochi

⌂ ACCOMMODATIONS

Gostinitsa Chaika, **2**
Gostinitsa Magnolia, **7**
Gostinitsa Primorskaya, **8**

🍎 FOOD

Cafe Calypso, **5**
Cafe Dubrava, **3**
Cafe Kashtan, **1**

🍸 NIGHTLIFE

Club Viking, **6**
Planet Sochi, **4**

Trains: Zheleznodorozhny vokzal (железнодорожный вокзал), ul. Gorkovo 56 (Горьково). Sochi still clings to a 2-tier pricing system—foreigners must buy tickets at the *kassa* (#8), which charges 3 or 4 times the Russian rate. (☎92 30 44. Open daily 8:30am-1pm and 2-6:30pm.) To: **Kyiv** (34hr., every other day, 700-1100R); **Moscow** (34-41hr., 5-7 per day, 650-1100R)—choose a train via Aiksi (Аикси), RUS, *not* Kharkiv (Харьков), UKR, where you run the risk of meeting dollar-hungry border officials; **Rostov-na-Donu** (16hr., 2 per day, 270R-450R). The *elektrichka* train runs north along the coast to **Tuapse** (Туапсе; 2hr., 6 per day, 13.50R) via **Dagomis** (Дагомис).

Buses: Avtovokzal (автовокзал), next to the train station on ul. Gorkovo (☎62 03 30). *Kassa* open daily 6:40am-10pm. Shuttles and minibuses head to **Adler** (1hr., every 20-30min., 7-10R) and **Dagomis** (30min., every 30-45min., 7.40R). Long-distance buses run to **Port Kavkaz** (Порт Кавказ) at the Ukrainian border (12hr., 1 per day, 170R) and **Rostov-na-Donu** (14hr., 1 per day, 265R).

Ferries: ☎ 60 96 55 or 60 97 38. Hydrofoils to **İstanbul, TUR** (45hr., 1 per week, 3470R) and **Trabzon, TUR** (5hr., 2-3 per week, 2170R). Temporary *kassa* #7 to the far right.

Public Transportation: Buses make life easier (4-7R). Stops are marked on side of bus; pay on board. Bus #2 goes to the base of **Gora Akhun** and on to **Adler** (7R). Bus #122 goes to the base of the **National Park** and the Agura waterfalls (20min., 7R). **Marshrutniye** (маршрутные; minibuses; 7R) stop less and are faster than regular buses. *Marshrutka* #125 goes from the station to the Adler market. Tell the driver where you want to get off. Both buses and *marshrutniye* are scarce after dark.

Taxis: ☎ 62 35 62. Haggling may bring the price down, though it's unlikely to get you a bargain. Verbally agree on a price before embarking, even if the driver resists.

⭐ ORIENTATION

Greater Sochi extends 145km along the Caucasian coast of the Black Sea, from Tuapse to the border of Abkhazia. To the north lie the resort towns of Lazarevskoye and Dagomis; to the south are Khosta and Adler. The city center is roughly 1400km south of Moscow, at the same latitude as Marseilles. Central Sochi has two focal points: the **train station** and the **seashore.** As you exit the train station, hang a left on **ul. Gorkovo** (Горького) and follow it on foot, or take any bus to Gostinitsa Moskva (Москва) on **Kurortny pr.** (Курортный), which runs along the shore. Going straight across Kurortny pr. leads to the **port** and the beaches; turning right on Kurortny takes you to the **Park Riviera. Ul. Roz** (Роз) and **ul. Moskovskaya** (Московская) both run perpendicular to ul. Gorkovo (ul. Roz is farther to your right), while a block past the station, **ul. Vorovskovo** (Воровского) runs parallel to ul. Gorkovo. **Maps** (20R) are available at newsstands.

> The nearby mountains provide potential for a scenic adventure, but they also mark the border with Georgia's breakaway republic, Abkhazia. The crowds have returned to Sochi, but border guards with machine guns still keep many of the most beautiful mountain hikes and coastal cruises off-limits. If you do decide to savor the natural surroundings, take a guide.

⭐ PRACTICAL INFORMATION

Tourist Offices: Ekka-Sochi Travel (Экка-Сочи Трэвел; ☎ 62 41 74 or 62 25 96; ekka@sochi.ru), in the lobby of Gostinitsa Moskva. Offers inexpensive daytrips to the attractions around Sochi, including Krasnaya Polyana (160-250R), the dolphinarium (100R), and the Dolmeny Ruins (150R). Make reservations a day in advance. Open daily 9am-7pm. Many booths along the beach offer similar tours for 60-90R.

Passport Office: OVIR (ОВИР), ul. Gorkovo 60 (☎ 92 25 71). Registration is desirable but not compulsory if you've registered elsewhere in Russia. Most hotels will register you automatically, but be sure to check. Open for registration M 9am-1pm, Tu-W and F 9am-1pm and 2-6pm, Sa 9am-1pm.

Bank: Sberbank, ul. Gorkovo 36 (☎ 92 29 73). Offers **currency exchange** (open M-F 9am-1pm and 2-6pm), an **ATM,** and cashes AmEx/MC/Thomas Cook **traveler's checks.** Open M-F 8am-8pm, Sa-Su 9am-7pm.

Luggage Storage: At the **train station,** through the door as you enter the circular courtyard from the parking lot. 26R per day. Open daily 3:30-12:30am.

Medical Service: The **hospital** is at ul. Pirogova 10 (Пирогова; ☎ 93 72 69).

24-Hour Pharmacy: The *apteka* (☎ 92 52 51) at ul. Vorovskovo 60 is well-stocked.

Telephones: The **telephone office,** at ul. Vorovskovo 6 (☎ 66 00 41; fax 66 01 66), opposite the post office, sells **phone cards** (50-1050R). Open 24hr.

Internet Access: Comstar, ul. Moskovskaya 5 (☎ 62 26 95; www.comstar.ru), 2 blocks from the train station. 20-40R per hr. Open M-F 8:30am-10pm, Sa-Su 9am-10pm. **Internet Club Palermo,** ul. Vorovskovo 22 (☎ 62 60 13), in a cellar just off the street. 30R per hr.

Post Office: Ul. Vorovskovo 1 (☎ 92 20 15), on the corner of Kurortny pr. **Poste Restante** (до востребования; do vostrebovanya) available. For **express mail,** enter to the right of the main entrance. Open M-Sa 8am-8pm, Su 8am-7pm.

Postal Code: 354000.

ACCOMMODATIONS

The moment you arrive in Sochi, you will be accosted by *babushki* offering you a room. Be aware, however, that the nice old lady you meet at the train station may not be the one who owns the room she's advertising, but rather a field agent for higher-ups in the *babushka* chain of command. Your best bet is to get a phone number and an address and check the place out for yourself. Expect to pay 200-300R per night in the summer months; most rooms require a minimum two-night stay. The 24hr. **Resort Bureau** ❶ (Курортное Бюро), just right of the *Prigorodniye kassy* (Пригородные кассы) as you face the train station, can help locate accommodation. (☎ 62 28 22; propan@sochi.ru. Singles 300-400R; apartments 600R.)

Gostinitsa Primorskaya (Приморская), Sokolova 1 (Соколова; ☎ 92 26 56; fax 92 59 81; primor@mail.sochi.ru.), between Kurortny pr. and Leningrad Beach. A palatial yellow-and-white building with an ocean view. Cheerful, basic rooms. Hall toilets of the hole-in-the-ground variety. Call ahead. Singles with sink and TV 451R, with shower 964R; doubles 609R/1607R. ❷

Gostinitsa Magnolia (Магнолия), Kurortny pr. 50 (☎ 62 01 66 or 62 19 87). The rooms are expensive, but spacious. All rooms include fridge, phone, TV, breakfast, and admission to the water park at the beach. Singles with bathroom 700R, with A/C 1541R; doubles 1200R/2033R. MC/V. ❸

Gostinitsa Chaika (Чайка), ul. Moskovskaya 3 (☎ 92 14 36; fax 92 35 32), facing the train station across ul. Gorkovo. Large but aging rooms with balconies overlooking the station. Breakfast included. Singles with bath and TV 370R; doubles 535R. ❶

FOOD

A **market** in front of Gostinitsa Chaika sells food. At night, a battalion of cafes serve the hordes that descend upon Park Riviera. There are **24-hour mini-markets** at 7 Navaginskaya (Навагинская) and on ul. Roz near ul. Moskovskaya.

Cafe Calypso (Калипсо; ☎ 62 40 33), between the water park and the ferry terminal. A step up from the unremarkable cafes that line the streets of Sochi. Italian fare and a large array of desserts are served with simplicity and style. Entrees 140-475R, soups 65-90R, salads 80-180R, ice cream 145-180R. Open daily noon-2am. MC/V. ❸

Cafe Dubrava (Кафе Дубрава), ul. Ostrovskovo 47 (Островсково; ☎ 92 57 03). Walk down Ostrovskovo towards the ocean; the cafe is past ul. Karla Libnekhta (Карла Либнехта) on the right. Enjoy traditional favorites among the charming plants and paintings of this tranquil cafe. Entrees 32-90R. Open daily 10am-11pm. ❶

Cafe Kashtan (Каштан), ul. Roz 113, one block from the train station. A simple, family-run operation whose authentic Caucasian fare is largely bypassed by the tourist hordes. Entrees 20-70R. Open daily 9am-8pm. ❶

🅖 SIGHTS

Sochi is home to a remarkable **arboretum** (дендрарий; dendrary) that straddles Kurortny pr. 74. Its international trees and plants offer blessed shade on hot afternoons. (Open daily 8:30am-7pm. 50R, with tour 70R.) Take bus #11 or any bus labeled "Dendry" (Дендри) to Svetlana (Светлана). Continue walking in the same direction, or take the cable car from Kurortny pr. to the observation post at the top of the park. (Open M 1-8pm, Tu-Su 9am-8pm. 80R, with park admittance 130R.) For cheaper if less charming shade, try **Park Riviera**, ul. Yegorova 1 (Егорова), on the north side of the ferry terminal across the Sochi river. The sprawling park teems with evergreens, outdoor cafes, marble statues, and the occasional war monument. The **Garden of Russo-Japanese Friendship,** on Kurortny pr. just right of Gostinitsa Magnolia (see above) with your back to the lobby, is a pleasant oddity as well. On a rainy day, visit the **History of the Resort-City Museum** (Музей истории города-курорта; Muzey istorii goroda-kurorta), ul. Vorovskovo 54/11 (☎92 23 49), past the post office, with its motley collection of archaeological finds, butterflies, and astronaut gear. (Open daily 10am-8pm. Main hall 10R, special exhibition 30R.)

🅒 BEACHES

Follow the throngs to the **beach,** Sochi's main draw. The city beaches tend to be crowded—if you're not in the mood to mingle, there are long stretches of quieter beach to the north or south, many of which are accessible by *elektrichka.* Hotel beaches (30-70R) also offer more space. If you get tired of soaking up the sun, rent a **banana boat** (10min. ride 60R per person) or a **jetski** (10min. ride 600R). Near the ferry terminal, the **Mayak Water Park** (Аква Парк Маяк; Akva Park Mayak) provides a break from the beach. (Open daily 10am-7pm. 500R, children 250R.)

To avoid dozens of screaming Russian children, visit the beaches at **Dagomis,** 12km north of Sochi, which offers emptier, cooler, and pricier beaches for those willing to make the trip. From the Sochi bus station, take bus #153 or 154 to Dagomis (30min., every 30min., 4R), or one of the *marshrutniye* labeled "Дагомыское пассажирское" (Dagomyskoe passazhirskoe; 20min., every 40min., 10R). The **Dagomis Complex** is on a hill above the beach. To reach the complex, exit the bus at the Dagomyskoe Passazhirskoe stop, cross the street, and, if you have the time and energy, walk 30min. up the winding ul. Leningradskaya (Ленинградская). The *marshrutniye* will take you to the top for an additional 25R, as will a taxi (60R if you haggle). Follow the "Пляж" signs along ul. Leningradskaya past the mountainous Gosinitsa Dagomis on your right, then continue along the path until you reach the vertical lift (15min.); this will drop you at the pristine beach (50R per day).

🅙 ENTERTAINMENT

The city currently hosts a major annual **independent film festival** during the first ten days of June and an **art festival** each September. During the peak tourist season in July and August, theater troupes, orchestras, and rock bands come to play for the vacationing elite. Despite its name, the **Winter Theater** (Зимний Театр; Zimny Teatr), ul. Teatralnaya 2 (Театральная), by Kurortny pr., puts on more shows and ballets in the summer months. (☎99 77 06. *Kassa* open daily 10am-7pm. 100-600R.) The **Cir-**

cus (Цирк), ul. Pushkina 5 (Пушкина), just off Kurortny pr. before the arboretum, features regular shows. (☎92 03 75. *Kassa* open daily 10am-1pm and 2-7pm. Shows, W and F-Su 7:30pm, Sa-Su 3 and 7:30pm. 40R.)

Many of the small **bars** lining the beach offer live music after dark, but those who need an entire club to contain their dance moves might try **Club Viking** (Викинг), Kurortny pr. 31, which includes a neon-lit nightclub and a booming outdoor disco. With your back to Gostinitsa Moskva, walk to your left along Kurortny pr. (5-10min.). (☎92 58 71. Beer 75-180R, cocktails 90-250R. Cover for men 200R, women 100R. Tu and F women free. Open 24hr.) That garish circular complex to the right of the train station is, as its beaming red letters suggest, **Planet Sochi.** Though subdued early in the week, this disco heats up over the weekend. (Cocktails 80-250R. Cover 100R. Open Tu-Su 10pm-4am.)

DAYTRIP FROM SOCHI

MOUNT AKHUN (ГОРА АКУН)

*Take bus #2 (7R) to Sputnik and either hike 12km up the paved road (3-4hr.) or backtrack across the bridge, where eager taxi drivers await (one-way 150R, round-trip 300R, 10R for the taxi to park at the top). If the driver drops you off on the main highway, you'll have to cross it and go down the ramp to reach Sputnik. If you're hiking the mountain, start early and don't expect a ride down. To get to the Agura Waterfalls, take bus #2 or 122 (7R) to Sputnik and head up the road to the left until you reach a kassa at the start of the trail (20min.). The tourist office (see **Practical Information**, p. 703) in Sochi offers tours that hit both Agura and Akhun in one fell swoop. (6hr., 2 per week, 90R plus entrance fees.)*

A rewarding trip from Sochi, the ▧**observation tower** at the summit of **Mt. Akhun** (Gora Akhun; 700m) commands magnificent views of the sea and mountains. (Open daily 9am-7pm. 20R.) Along the way to Mt. Akhun is the splendid **Sochi National Park** (25R), a lush, mountainous preserve where visitors can hike to the **Agura Waterfalls** past mountain springs that twist their way through fruit trees and wildlife. ▧**Shashlychnaya Akhun Cafe ❶**, at the base of the observation tower, serves a huge selection of vegetables, breads, and charbroiled kebabs (30-50R) in a charming setting. (Open M and W-Su 9am-7pm.)

THE KALININGRAD REGION (КАЛИНИНГРАДСКАЯ ОБЛАСТЬ)

History and fate have conspired to leave the Kaliningrad region (Kaliningradskaya Oblast) part of Russia. The capture of the region, once East Prussia, by the Soviets at the end of World War II marked the end of a 700-year period during which the city was a focal point of German culture. In the decades that followed, Kaliningrad underwent intense Sovietization, as thousands of ethnic Germans were exiled to Germany and Siberia. With the unraveling of the Soviet Union, the region found itself an island of armed, bewildered Russians severed from the Motherland by independent Latvia, Lithuania, and Belarus.

KALININGRAD (КАЛИНИНГРАД) ☎(8)0112

The birthplace of philosopher Immanuel Kant, the former Königsberg (King's Mountain) was completely razed during World War II. For security reasons, the city, renamed after Stalin's henchman Mikhail Ivanovich Kalinin (who never set foot here) was only opened to tourists in 1991. Granted special trade status in

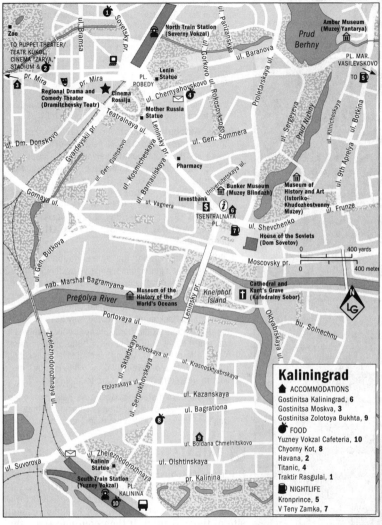

Kaliningrad

🛏 ACCOMMODATIONS
Gostinitsa Kaliningrad, **6**
Gostinitsa Moskva, **3**
Gostinitsa Zolotoya Bukhta, **9**

🍖 FOOD
Yuzney Vokzal Cafeteria, **10**
Chyorny Kot, **8**
Havana, **2**
Titanic, **4**
Traktir Rasgulai, **1**

🎵 NIGHTLIFE
Kronprince, **5**
V Teny Zamka, **7**

sia. The city is in the process of repair, restoration, and renewal—offering a glimpse of rapidly changing Russia without leaving Europe.

TRANSPORTATION

Trains: Kaliningrad has two stations:

Yuzhny Vokzal (Южный Вокзал; South Station; ☎58 46 06), ul. Zheleznodorozhnaya 15-23 (ул. Жепезнодожная), next to the bus station and behind the statue of Kalinin, mainly handles inter-

IN RECENT NEWS

RUSSIAN VISAS FOR RUSSIANS?

Citizens of Kaliningrad may have something to fear as Lithuania and Poland make preparations to join the European Union (EU)—they might find themselves even more isolated from the rest of the Russian Federation.

Generally, citizens of non-EU member nations need visas to enter any of the EU states. When Lithuania joins the EU—as it is projected to do in 2004—Kaliningraders will be required to obtain a visa to pass through either border country in order to travel to or from Russia proper.

What does this mean for the average citizen of the Kaliningrad region? He will need permission from a foreign government whenever he wants to visit friends or relatives in his *own* country. Not to mention the EU will dictate harsher guidelines for visa distribution than restrictions already in place in countries hoping to join the club. It also could mean economic stagnation for the region of Russia that has, up to now, advanced in leaps and bounds economically, leading the country along the rocky path from Communism to capitalism.

(continued on next page)

national connections (long ticket lines can keep you waiting up to 2hr.). Open daily 5am-10pm. Information booths open daily 8am-noon and 1-5pm. To: **Moscow** (23-24hr., 1 per day, 680-880R); **St. Petersburg** (25½hr., 1 every other day, 700R); **Gdynia, POL** (3hr., 1 per day, 400R) via **Gdańsk, POL** and **Malbork, POL; Odessa, UKR** (18hr., 1 every other day, 900-1320R).

Severny Vokzal (Северный Вокзал; North Station; ☎58 64 02), near pl. Pobedy (Победы); with the Lenin statue behind you, turn right. Sends trains to cities within Kaliningrad. Electric trains run to **Svetlogorsk** (1hr., 1 per hr., 20R).

Buses: Autobusny Vokzal (Автобусный Вокзал), ul. Zheleznodorozhnaya 15-23, next to Yuzhny Vokzal (☎44 36 35, international reservations 44 65 00; fax 44 65 00). Open daily 5am-11pm. To: **Gdansk, POL** (3½hr., 2 per day, 184R); **Hrodna, BLR** (10½hr., 1 per day, 218R); **Kaunas, LIT** (4½hr., 1 per day, 183R); **Klaipfda, LIT** (3-4hr., 4 per day, 89-99R); **Riga, LAT** (9½hr., 3 per day, 272R); **Warsaw, POL** (6½hr., 1 per day M-F, 263R); **Vilnius, LIT** (7hr., 1 per day, 264R).

Public Transportation: The transportation system in Kaliningrad has undergone a massive overhaul. **Buses**, which are now privatized, are speedy. Prices (5R) are posted in the bus window; pay the conductor if there is one. If there isn't, pay the driver when you get off. Some buses lack numbers, so you may have to check the destination on the front. Slower public **trams** still traverse the city (3.50R); trams #2 and 3 run from pl. Kalinina to pl. Pobedy via pl. Tsentralnaya, connecting Yuzhny Vokzal and Severny Vokzal, while tram #1 runs east to west from the zoo toward the market.

Taxis: At the train stations, Gostinitsa Kaliningrad, the zoo, and pl. Pobedy. Agree on a price before setting off. Don't get into a car with more than 1 person in it.

✈ ORIENTATION

Both the **Autobusny** and **Yuzhny Vokzal** are by **pl. Kalinina** (Калинина). **Leninsky pr.** (Ленинский), the main artery, runs perpendicular to pl. Kalinina opposite **Pregolya** (Преголя) and **Kneiphof Island**, site of the cathedral. It then continues past the dark, crumbling House of Soviets to **pl. Tsentralnaya** (пл. Центральная), home to **Gostinitsa Kaliningrad** (Гостиница Калининград; Hotel Kaliningrad). Finally, it heads toward a park dedicated to Mother Russia—see the wind-swept lady holding the hammer-and-sickle—before veering left to its end, **pl. Pobedy** (Победы; Victory Square), presided over by a statue of Lenin. Forking off just before the square, **Teatralnaya pr.** (Театральная) splits off from Leninsky to the left before the park, becoming **Mira pr.** (Мира), and heading toward the zoo. **Ul. Chernyakhovskovo** (Черняховского) lies to the right perpendicular to Leninsky as you enter pl. Pobedy coming from the stations, and travels east to the market.

🔂 PRACTICAL INFORMATION

Currency Exchange: Official currency exchange **kiosks,** "Обмен Валюты" (obmen valyuty), dot major downtown intersections. **Investbank** (Инвестбанк), Leninsky pr. 28 (☎/fax 35 14 40). Facing away from Gostinitsa Kaliningrad, it's across the street to the right. Accepts AmEx **Traveler's Cheques** and gives MC/V **cash advances,** both for 2% commission. There's a 24hr. MC **ATM** outside and a MC/V one outside Gostinitsa Kaliningrad (see **Accommodations,** p. 710). Open M-Sa 9:30am-1pm and 2-4pm. **Alfabank** (Алфабанк), pl. Pobedy, also has a **currency exchange** and a MC/V **ATM** inside. Most banks are around pl. Pobedy.

Luggage storage: Lockers are at the bus station and the south train station (26.25R for 24hr., large bags 41R). Open daily 7am-noon, 1-5pm, and 6-9:30pm.

24-Hour Pharmacy: Gippocrat (Аптека Гиппократ), Leninsky pr. 43 (☎54 11 11).

Telephones: Ul. Leonova 20 (☎21 94 10), next to the post office. **Faxes** and **Internet access** (30R per hr.) available. Open daily 8am-9pm. **International Telephone Center** (☎45 15 15; fax 46 95 90), inside Gostinitsa Kaliningrad (see **Accommodations,** p. 710), on the left. Open 24hr.

Internet Access: Internet Hall Etype (Етайп), ul. Morehodnaya 3 (ул. Мореходная). Central location in the pink building off pl. Pobedy. 20 speedy connections (20R per hr.). Open M-F 9am-9pm, Sa 9am-7pm. **Kiberda Internet Club** (☎51 18 30), ul. Komsomolskaya 87 (ул. Комсомольская), near the post office. Lightening-fast connections (32R per hr.). Open daily noon-11pm.

Post Office: Ul. Leonova 22 (Леонова; ☎21 98 68). A right off pr. Mira, past Gostinitsa Moskva. **Poste Restante** at window #8 (☎21 16 10), around the corner from the main entrance. Open M-F 9am-8pm, Sa 10am-6pm.

Postal Code: 236 000.

The new visa requirements have not yet been finalized. In fact, Lithuanian Prime Minister Algirdas Brazauskas has stated that Lithuania would have nothing against creating a visa-free corridor for Russian citizens traveling between Kaliningrad and the rest of Russia, a system which has already been in place for twelve years. But the final decision may not be up to Lithuania, and it may very well be the EU itself which will have to come to some sort of agreement with Russia over the visa issue.

The signs are not good for Kaliningrad. In May 2002, the EU declined Russia's request to create such a visa-free corridor, claiming that the system would not be beneficial for either the EU or its candidate countries. Unless Russia and the EU reach some sort of compromise, Kaliningraders will undoubtedly find themselves in a sticky situation. They may very well lose their ability to leave the region, thereby losing the right to travel freely around their own country.

—*Dunia Dickey*

ACCOMMODATIONS

Looking to attract German tourists and the growing number of international businessmen, hotels in Kaliningrad have undergone renovations in hope of reaching Western standards. Still, many hotels are cheap enough to please the budget traveler. Most places charge a 20R visa registration fee, unless otherwise noted.

Gostinitsa Moskva (Гостиница Москва), Mira pr. 19 (☎27 20 89 or 35 23 00; fax 35 23 33), a few blocks past pl. Pobedy and the Baltika Stadium on the left. Take any tram in the direction of "Парк Калинина" (Park Kalinina). Marvel at the sparkling marble lobby. Renovated rooms include bath, phone, and TV. Unrenovated rooms share a bath. Reception 24hr. Reservations recommended. Singles 450R, renovated 1100-1200R; doubles 600R/1300-1700R. ❷

Gostinitsa Kaliningrad (Гостиница Калининград), Leninsky pr. 81 (Ленинский пр.; ☎46 94 40 or 35 05 00; ☎/fax 53 60 21; www.hotel.kaliningrad.ru), at pl. Tsentralnaya (пл. Центральная). The largest and most convenient hotel in the city. Rooms have bath, TV, and international phone; lux suites are larger and have fridges. English-speaking reception 24hr. Singles 800-1340R; doubles 1040-1940R; lux suites 1480-1900R; apartment 3000R. MC/V. ❸

Gostinitsa Zolotoya Bukhta (Гостиница Золотоя Бухта; Golden Cake Hotel), ul. Khmelnitskovo 53 (ул. Хмельницкого; ☎44 57 77; fax 44 62 21). From the bus station, turn left on Leninsky and take the 3rd right on Khmelnitskovo. High-style hotel run by the Baltic Fleet, with comfortable rooms stocked with phones, fridges, and TV. Singles 250-336R, with bath 735-840R; doubles 576R/1207R. ❶

FOOD

For fresh fruits and vegetables, head to the indoor **central market** (центральный рынок; tsentralny rynok), originally built for a 1930s trade exhibition, at the intersection of ul. Chernyakhovskovo and ul. Gorkovo. (Open daily 8am-6pm.) The excellent **Vester** (Вестер) supermarkets all around town stock both food and supplies. Try the one at Leninsky pr. 16. Open daily 9am-11pm. **Yuzhny Vokzal** ❶ has an incredibly cheap Soviet-style cafeteria. (Entrees 20-40R. Open 8am-9pm.)

Traktir Rasgulai (Трактир Разгуляй), Sovetsky pr. 13 (Советский пр.; ☎/fax 21 48 97), off pl. Pobedy. Large portions of excellent Russian cuisine and a festive, country-style decor. For a true Russian meal, order borsht (40R) and the traditional *kvas Rasgulai* (fermented bread; 18R). Live music Tu-Su 9pm-1am. English menu. Entrees 40-240R. Open daily 10am-1am. MC/V. ❶

Titanic (Титаник), Chernyakhovskovo pr. 74 (☎53 67 68), between pl. Pobedy and the central market. Possibly the most unexpected dining experience in the city, this restaurant aims to recreate the blockbuster that recreated the ship that...never mind. Two-story replica features lifeboats that double as booths. Full selection of "bourgeois" dishes mapped out on an English menu. Excellent fish specialties 80-300R. Open daily 11am-midnight. MC/V. ❷

Havana (Хавана), pr. Mira 10/12 (☎55 55 22), directly opposite the stadium. Nothing particularly Cuban about the menu, other than the photo of Ché Guevara and the bamboo-hut bar. Dress up for dinner or stop by after a night at the theater (see **Entertainment,** p. 712). Lunch special noon-4pm. Entrees 54-248R. Happy Hour 2-3pm. Open daily noon-midnight. ❷

Chyorny Kot (Чёрный Кот; Black Cat), Leninsky pr. 111 (☎47 15 86), on the same side of the bridge as the bus station. Follow the stream of ravenous Russians downstairs to

RUSSIA

sample fast and delicious Russian dishes. The staff is happy to oblige foreigners and the menu has pictures. Entrees 55-90R. Open daily noon-midnight. ❷

⚙ SIGHTS

CATHEDRAL. The city's pride and joy during its 700-year stint as Königsberg, the Cathedral ages away on the large Kneiphof Island in the middle of the Pregolya River. It was damaged by fire in 1944, but funds are being raised to build a new roof and renovate its towers. Restoration experts have already made headway on the interior. Upon completion (expected in 2004 or 2005), the main space will be turned into a concert hall. You can now see the vandalized and eroding tombs lining the Cathedral's walls where once Prussian kings were crowned; climb the steps made famous by German Romantic writer E.T.A. Hoffmann. The cathedral houses an excellent **museum** on Königsberg, with four floors of historic items. Two floors are dedicated to the philosopher Kant; don't miss the macabre copy of his death mask. Although the Cathedral is out of use, music still permeates its stone and mortar: the **Kaliningrad Symphony** occasionally holds concerts here on the last Sa of the month. The shady park surrounding the cathedral was a residential neighborhood until British bombing during World War II leveled the area. (☎44 68 68 or 27 25 83. Open daily 9am-4:30pm. 60R, students 15R.)

KANT'S GRAVE. Walk outside to the back of the Cathedral to find the immaculate grave of Immanuel Kant (1724-1804). The German philosopher spent his entire life in Königsberg and taught at the local university. His grave is enclosed by pink marble colonnades, there to protect him from the German tourists who visit daily. The museum upstairs in the cathedral (see above) has more on the brain-man, if you just Kant get enough. (You knew it was coming...)

JULIUS RUPP MEMORIAL. Behind the Cathedral stands a monument erected in 1991 to Julius Rupp (1809-1884), one of Königsberg's most famous pastors, whose house once stood on this spot. Rupp founded a new, unofficial religious order called *Druzya Sveta* (Друзья Света; Friends of the World), which stood for harmony among all peoples and religions. Though Rupp was frequently chastised for his views, he remained one of Königsberg's most influential thinkers and passed on many of his beliefs to his niece, famed artist Käthe Kollwitz.

MONUMENTS TO SOVIET GLORY. Since 1255, when Teutonic knights first arrived in this area, a castle has guarded the hill east of what is now Tsentralnaya pl. As part of the effort to turn Königsberg into a truly Soviet city, the original castle was blown up in 1962 and replaced by the **House of Soviets** (Дом Советов; Dom Sovetov), an H-shaped monstrosity that, after 35 years, stands incomplete even as it begins to crumble. In the middle of **pl. Pobedy** (Victory Square), a 7m **statue of Lenin** is now a popular meeting place for university students. A glorious pink-and-white building that once housed the Kaliningrad **KGB** stands two blocks to the left of Lenin, at Sovetsky pr. 3-5. Across the park that Lenin faces, rows of red flowerbeds lead up to a statue of **Mother Russia**, which looks out at bustling Leninsky pr. Don't miss the genial figure of **Mikhail Ivanovich Kalinin**, the city's namesake, who waves to travelers from outside of the south train station.

RUSSIA

🏛 MUSEUMS

MUSEUM OF THE HISTORY OF THE WORLD'S OCEANS. (Музей Истории Мирого Океана; Muzei Istorii Mirovo Okeana.) Wander through exhibits on the submarine *Vityaz*—visible from the Leninsky bridge—which once belonged to Germany and helped thousand of Germans flee the invading Red Army. Other exhibits include a garden of submersibles, an expeditional ship, and a showcase of carvings on the heads of pins. *(Bagramyana 1 (Баграмяна), on the Pregolya River near the Hotel Ademi.* ☎ *34 02 44; fax 34 02 11. Open Apr. 1-Oct. 31 W-Su 11am-6pm; Nov. 1-Mar. 31 W-Su 10am-5pm. 30R.)*

AMBER MUSEUM. (Музей Янтарья; Muzey Yantarya.) Nearly 90% of the world's amber comes from nearby Yantar—much of it smuggled out illegally every year—and this museum showcases the best specimens. Glimpse the world's largest single piece of amber, which weighs in at 4.28kg. The museum also contains reconstructed fragments from the legendary Amber Room of St. Petersburg, which was stolen by the Germans in World War II and brought back to Königsberg. When the Russians invaded the city in 1945, the Germans destroyed the room and dumped the fragments into the sea; Russians still hope that the original may one day be fully recovered. *(Pl. Vasilevskovo 1 (Василевский).* ☎ *46 12 40. Open Tu-Su 10am-6pm; kassa closes at 5:30pm. 30R, students 20R.)*

BUNKER MUSEUM. (Музей Блиндаж; Muzey Blindazh.) The Nazis directed their fruitless defense of Königsberg from this underground complex. The museum details the capture of the city battle-by-battle, with plenty of photos and models recreating key moments; unlucky Room 13 has been left exactly as it was when the commander signed the city over to the Red Army. *(Ul. Universitetskaya 2 (Университетская), off Leninsky pr., opposite the garden of the University of Kaliningrad.* ☎ *53 65 93. English captions. Open daily 10am-5pm. 30R, students 20R.)*

MUSEUM OF HISTORY AND ART. (Историко-Художественный Музей; Istoriko-Khudozhestvenny Muzey.) The first floor contains archaeological and ethnographic exhibits about Kaliningrad's natural past; the second floor is devoted to the heroic Soviet army and its 1945 conquest of the German city of Königsberg. Another room displays propaganda promoting various Communist ideals. A small sideroom honors Kaliningraders who have recently died in Chechnya. *(Klinicheskaya 21 (Клиническая). From Tsentralnaya pl., walk up the north side of the House of Soviets along ul. Shevchenko, which becomes ul. Klinicheskaya and snakes around Nizhny Lake. The museum is halfway around the lake.* ☎ *45 38 44. English captions. Open Tu-Su 10am-6pm; kassa closes at 5pm. 30R, students 20R.)*

🎭🎬 ENTERTAINMENT AND NIGHTLIFE

A Weimar-era residence houses the beautiful **Dramatichesky Teatr** (Драматический Театр), pr. Mira 4. Ask the friendly director Anatoly Kravtsov for a tour of the building. (☎ 21 24 22. *Kassa* open daily 10am-7pm; shows start at 7pm. Tickets 30-100R.) The **stadium** opposite the zoo, on pr. Mira; near Gostinitsa Moskva, is home to Kaliningrad's beloved **soccer** team, Baltika. It's worth seeing the team play if you're a soccer fan, but beware the crowd of drunk men. The newly-renovated **Cinema Zarya** (Эаря; Dawn), pr. Mira 41, has comfortable, steeply-graded seats and state-of-the-art surround sound, as well as a cafe and bar. Movies are dubbed in Russian, but some late-night showings are in the original language. The Zarya is where the city's chic come to be seen; those who show up in sweats will be turned away. (☎21 45 88. Tickets 100R.) **Cinema Rossiya** (Россия), ul. Baranova 40, opposite the Lenin statue in pl. Pobedy, is also newly renovated, but is still not as classy as the Zarya. Hollywood films dubbed in Russian (and the occasional concert) are shown in the 1200-seat theater. (☎43 62 35. Tickets 90R, F-Su 100R.)

If you go out at night, it is advisable not to walk alone, especially if you don't know the neighborhood—catch a cab home. **V Teny Zamka** (В Тени Эамка; In the Shade of the Castle), Staraya Bashnya 63, is perfect for an after-dinner coffee and dessert. Sip flavored coffee (28.50R), espresso, cappucino, or various alcoholic coffee cocktails (53-85R), and sink into a plush, wicker loveseat. (Open daily 11am-9:30pm.) Beer and vodka gardens dot the city. For a genuine bar, try **Kronprince** (Кронпринц), Litovsky Val 38 (Литовский Вал), near the Amber Museum. Cozy sofas, low tables, and stained glass decorate the establishment. Live sax or guitar nightly at 9pm, and dancing between vodka shots. Russian entrees also served (27-200R) to dilute the alcohol. (☎46 43 70. Open daily noon-3am.)

DAYTRIP FROM KALININGRAD

SVETLOGORSK (СВЕТЛОГОРСК)

Svetlogorsk is best reached by train, as buses are usually packed. Trains from Kaliningrad (1hr., 12 per day, 20R) stop at both Svetlogorsk 1 and Svetlogorsk 2, which is closer to the center of town. From Svetlogorsk 2, ul. Lenina (Ленина) runs parallel to the sea. The impatient can take the chairlift from behind the station directly to the beach. (Daily 10am-8pm. 6R.) Otherwise, a left down ul. Lenina leads to the center of town (5min.). ATMs are difficult to find; bring rubles. The last train back to Kaliningrad leaves at 9:40pm.

Formerly the German town of Rauschen, this seaside resort was used by Soviet officials as a spot for rest and relaxation. Today, Germans have returned to Svetlogorsk, this time as tourists. Those old enough to remember can tell you that much of the old charm is still here; not much has changed in the quiet streets, lined with pines and lovely old villas. The main attraction is the **beach,** which is long and pleasant. Stroll along the promenade and enjoy the tranquil vistas, at least until you reach the area full of vendors hawking amber. At the east end of the promenade sits a **sundial,** purportedly the largest in Europe, with a beautiful multicolored mosaic on its face. At ul. Lenina 5, on the outskirts of town, a small **chapel** stands in memory of the 34 people who died—among them 23 children—when a Soviet military aircraft crashed into a kindergarten on the site on May 16, 1972. The incident was covered up until 1991, when the Russian Orthodox Church built the chapel. The **House-Museum of Hermann Brachert** (Дом-Музей Германа Брахерта; Dom-Muzey Germana Brakherta), ul. Tokareva 7, lies just outside Svetlogorsk proper. From the train station, turn right on ul. Lenina. Turn right after the "Отрадное" sign. The German Brachert lived in the house surrounded by the sculpture garden between 1933 and 1944. The museum contains some of the artist's reliefs and small statues of women; Brachert is also responsible for the nymph statue at the beach in Svetlogorsk. Ask the curator to show you around. (☎211 66. Open in summer daily 10am-5pm; off season Tu-Su 10am-4pm. 45R.)

KURSHSKAYA KOSA (КУРШСКАЯ КОСА)

Nearly 80km long and never more than 4km wide, the Kurshskaya Kosa (Curonian Spit) is essentially a giant sandbar. Beautiful pine forests cover all but the western side, which has been molded by Baltic winds into a series of famous sand dunes.

The eastern side faces the calmer waters of the Kurshisky Zaliv (Кушиский Залив; Curonian Lagoon), and is home to a few villages, including tiny Rybachy (Рыбачий), the best base for exploring the Spit.

⚏🔁 TRANSPORTATION AND PRACTICAL INFORMATION. The best way to get to the Spit is to take a **bus** from **Kaliningrad** to **Klaipėda, LIT** (4 per day, 53R) via **Lesnoe** and **Rybachy**. Once you're there, public transportation links the three major settlements along the Russian part of the Spit: **Lesnoe** (Лесное), the forest village; **Rybachy** (Рибачий), the fishing village; and **Morskoe** (Морское), the sea village. From Rybachy's bus-station, take a right on **ul.** Pobedy (Победы), which ends at the main highway; down the road toward Zelenogradsk stands a large **map**. Rybachy's **post** and **telephone office** is at ul. Pobedy 29. (Open M-Sa 9am-5pm.)

⚏🔁 ACCOMMODATIONS AND FOOD. Since the Spit is a national park, there are restrictions on hotel development. The most obvious place to stay in Rybachy is **Traktir Forosh ❹** (Трактирб Форош), which has small but nice rooms with hardwood floors, TV, phone, and bath. Make reservations up to two weeks in advance in summer. (☎412 90 or 412 96. Singles US$45; doubles US$55.) The cost includes dinner and breakfast in the adjoining **restaurant ❷**, famous for its fish dishes (96-410R). Otherwise, seek out a **private room ❶** in Rybachy; call ahead for availability and rates. First try **Usadba Tronnikovoi** (Усадьба Тронниковой), ul. Pogranichnaya 4 (ул. Пограничная; ☎504 12 04). Turn left after Traktir Forosh and look for the yellow house on the left. The friendly lady of the house is happy to show visitors around. Otherwise, try one of the following houses: **Gostevoy Dom Rossiten** (Гостевой Дом Росситен), ul. Gagarina 7 (ул. Гагарина; ☎502 13 91); **Gostevoye Pokoi Darye** (Гостевые Покои Дарий), ul. Stroitelei 6-1 (ул. Строителей; ☎502 13 13); or **Usadba Timohinoi** (Усадьба Тимохиной), ul. Zarechnaya 15 (ул. Заречная; ☎502 12 54). **Cafe Chaika ❶** (Кафе Чайка), on ul. Pobedy, is known for inexpensive but good Russian food. The owner, Tatiana, who also runs Usadba Tronnikovi (see above), loves to help tourists curious about the town. (Open daily 9am-midnight.)

◪ SIGHTS. Tourist infrastructure on the Spit ranges from minimal to nonexistent, so don't expect visitor centers or many hiking trails. There are a few access points to the sea and a lagoon between towns; these usually have a bus stop. Otherwise, scores of unpaved roads and unmarked footpaths crisscross the forest. Most of these, the product of grazing cattle, lead to private homes or nowhere at all. Before you hit the trails, visit Rybachy's **Ornothological Station,** ul. Pobedy 32. Having recently celebrated its 100th anniversary, the station is the only institution in Kaliningrad that has continued its pre-war scientific research. The station contains a small museum that explains its bird-catching, banding, and research activities. Students can direct visitors to the bird-catching site, 12km south of Rybachy in the direction of Zelenogradsk. (☎250 41 25; www.zin.ru/rybachy. Museum open Apr.-Oct. daily 10am-4pm.)

The one **hiking trail** in the area, about 15min. from Rybachy down the road toward Zelenogradsk, should not be missed. Look for English signs along the road for Excursion Route "Island" (Остров). The trailhead is on the right just after the lake on the left. The gentle 3.5km loop was built in 1998 by a group of environmentalists. Follow the wooden arrows (some of which are missing, in which case follow the bigger path) to the top of **Müller's Hill,** the highest point on the Spit. Müller was the German naturalist who discovered how to grow vegetation on the sands of the Spit, which used to blow wildly and bury entire villages. The view from the taller observation tower will make even the most jaded hiker gape in awe. From here, the trail descends into a pleasant pine forest whose trees slant to one side from the force of the wind. This part of the trail is poorly maintained; you may find yourself forced back the other way to return to town. Once there, take a walk down the **beach**. Head down the road toward Nida. Just after a bend (10min.), a power line crosses the road; turn left here onto the path beneath it. This path continues straight until you reach the sand.

THE TRANS-SIBERIAN RAILROAD

The Trans-Siberian railroad is the lifeline that connects the gilded domes and tinted windshields of Moscow with the rest of her proud but crumbling empire. Over the course of six and a half days, the train rolls across 9289km, two continents, and seven time zones. Begun in 1891, construction of the railway took over 25 years and US$320 million. While the view from the window is often unvarying—imagine birch trees and concrete stations stretching from the Urals to Mongolia—travelers are unlikely to forget what goes on inside the train. Whether you find yourself riding with a nightgowned *babushka* and her bucket of berries or with middle-aged men who drink vodka before bed and beer for breakfast, a Trans-Siberian journey is the ultimate crash course in Russian culture.

LOGISTICS. The term "Trans-Siberian" generally doesn't refer to a single train, but to three sets of tracks and the numerous trains that run along them. The **Trans-Siberian** line links Moscow and Vladivostok, the **Trans-Mongolian** connects Moscow with Beijing by way of Ulaanbaatar, Mongolia, and the **Trans-Manchurian** loops through Manchuria en route to Beijing. *Let's Go* covers the Trans-Siberian and Trans-Mongolian routes in detail. Unfortunately, Russian Railways has yet to develop a flexible ticket that allows multiple stops; if you plan to stop at any point along the way, you'll need to purchase individual tickets for each leg of the trip. If you're making short hops, getting a ticket is rarely a problem. When purchasing a ticket for a multi-day journey, plan at least 3 days in advance. Service centers in train stations and hotel lobbies can help you bypass the maddening ticket booths at the train station for a 50-200R fee. You'll need **visas** to enter China, Russia, and Mongolia; both the Chinese visa and Mongolian visa are best obtained in Moscow (see p. 639); a Mongolian visa can also be picked up either in Irkutsk (see p. 722) or Ulan Ude (see p. 727). Mongolian consular representatives will need a passport-sized photo to process visas. US citizens do not need Mongolian visas for visits less than 30 days. (No invitation needed for a one-month tourist visa. One-month tourist visa with one-week processing US$45, 48hr. transit visa US$35, multiple-entry visa US$85; double these prices for overnight processing.)

COSTS. The cost of a Trans-Siberian ticket depends on myriad variables, including where and when you buy it, how far you're going, what class you want, whether you're Russian or foreign, and whether the salesperson likes you. The most popular class among foreigners is *coupé* (купе), a four-bed berth with adequate facilities and a modicum of cleanliness. *Lux* (люкс) cabins are roughly twice as expensive and sleep two. Almost all budget travelers take *coupé* tickets, and all *Let's Go* prices are for *coupé* berths. Tickets purchased in Moscow are most expensive, but are still cheaper than buying a string of tickets from town to town. Prices are always higher in summer than in winter. If you're only making a few stops, **G&R Hostel Asia** in Moscow (see p. 642) offers several Trans-Siberian packages and can help arrange tickets for 200R commission. More importantly, their staff can explain in excellent English how the railroad works and can help you choose the ticket best suited to your itinerary. Allow at

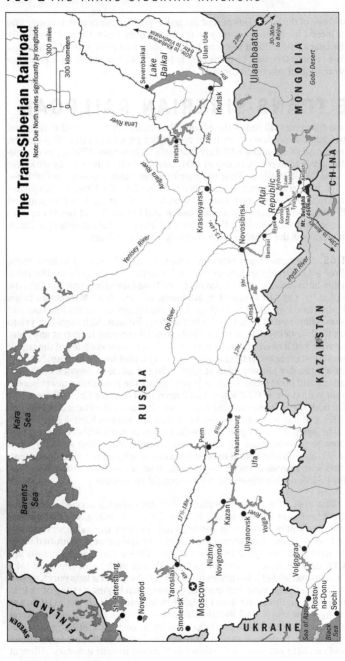

The Trans-Siberian Railroad

Note: Due North varies significantly by longitude.

0 — 300 miles
0 — 300 kilometers

RUSSIA

least five days for processing during high season. Their website (www.hostels-trains.ru) is a helpful resource, consolidating information on pricing and schedules. They offer prearranged tickets for the following routes: Beijing via **Mongolia** (US$212); **Beijing** via **Manchuria** (US$223); **Vladivostok** (US$225); and **Ulaanbaatar** (US$145). (All prices are for *coupé* class tickets during the high season.) If you speak Russian or can fake it with a written itinerary, you can save nearly 30% by buying directly from the **Tsentralnoe Zheleznodorozhnoe Agenstvo** (Центральное Железнодорожное Агенство; Central Train Agency) in Moscow (see **Intercity Transportation,** p. 634).

 TRAIN TIME. The Trans-Siberian traverses 7 time zones, but all train arrivals and departures are listed in **Moscow time** at stations as well as in *Let's Go.*

TRAINS TO BEIJING (DEPARTURES IN MOSCOW TIME)

TRAIN	MOSCOW	NOVOSI-BIRSK	KRASNO-YARSK	IRKUTSK	ULAN UDE	ULAAN-BAATAR	BEIJING
4	Tu 11:42pm	Th 10:10pm	F 10:10am	Sa 3:46am	Sa 11:16am	Su 8:50am	M 3:53pm
6	W and Th 11:42pm	F and Sa 10:10pm	Su and M 10:10am	Su and M 3:46am	Su and M 11:16am	arrives M and Tu 8:15am	
10*	odd days 9:29pm	odd days 9:16pm	even days 9:29am	odd days 3:04am			
20*	F 10:56pm	Su 9:42pm	M 9:39am	Tu 3:36am	Tu 11:06am		F 5:30am
*Firmeny trains							

TRAINS TO VLADIVOSTOK (DEPARTURES IN MOSCOW TIME)

TRAIN	MOSCOW	NOVOSI-BIRSK	KRASNO-YARSK	IRKUTSK	ULAN UDE	VLADIVO-STOK
2*	odd days 3:26pm	odd days 3:10pm	even days 3:48am	even days 9:45pm	odd days 5:18am	even days 11:53pm
10*	odd days 9:29pm	odd days 9:16pm	even days 9:29am	odd days 3:04am		
*Firmeny trains						

DEPARTING. All outbound Trans-Siberian trains depart from Moscow's **Yaroslavsky Vokzal** (see p. 635). The better long-distance trains, called *firmeny* (фирменный; quality), offer cleaner facilities but can also cost twice as much as the regular *skory* (скорый; rapid) trains. Local color aboard *skory* makes for an entertaining short trip, but drunks and offensive odors make the *firmeny* worth the money for trips longer than 24hr. Usually, you will automatically be on *firmeny*. From Moscow, the *firmeny* trains are: **train #2** (Россия; Rossia; Russia) to **Vladivostok; train #10** (Байкал; Baikal) to **Irkutsk** and **Lake Baikal;** and **train #20** (Русский Поезд; Russky Poezd; the Russian Train) to **Beijing** via **Manchuria.** Other trains include **train #4** (Китайский Поезд; Kitaisky Poezd; the Chinese Train) to **Beijing** via **Ulaanbaatar** and **train #6** to **Ulaanbaatar.** Check out the train schedule above for more info. Smaller and more frequent trains serve these cities with varying availability. *Firmeny* trains usually have a plaque on the side of each car stating the train's name. In all cases, "odd" (нечетный) and "even" (четный) refers to calendar days.

FROM THE ROAD

THE ALTAI REPUBLIC

The fundamental backpacker paradox is this: everyone wants to find a place that's heartbreakingly beautiful, yet free from the circus atmosphere of the standard tourist circuit. These locations are becoming increasingly hard to find as, one by one, they are "discovered" and rapidly converted into the latest extension of the frantic cultural going-out-of-business sale that pursues backpackers across the developing world. There are solutions to this paradox, but most of them involve either fantastic strokes of luck or the willingness to accept not-quite-as-wonderful destinations in exchange for smaller crowds.

A third solution presents itself to Trans-Siberian backpackers in the Altai Republic. This semi-autonomous region lies in the middle of Siberia, bordering China, Mongolia, and Kazakhstan, so it's not likely to become over-crowded anytime soon. And it's quite simply one of the most beautiful places on earth. The muscular geography gives rise to a diverse range of ecosystems: arid semi-desert, dense forest, churning river canyons, open steppe, mountain glaciers, and high-altitude tundra are just a sampling of what the Altai has to offer.

The Altai's strange and immense beauty has long been an inspiration to mystics and dreamers of all sorts. The indigenous Altai people revere the region as Shambhala, the paradise from which a new civilization will spring once our present one destroys itself.

(continued on next page)

LIFE ABOARD THE TRAIN. Two attendants—*provodnik* (male) or *provodnitsa* (female)—sit in each train wagon to make sure all goes smoothly; they offer tea (2R) and tend the *samovar* at the end of the wagon, which is your source of boiled water. Try to avoid the first or last *coupé* in the wagon; these neighbor the toilets and, especially on non-*firmeny* trains, the stench can become unbearable (on *firmeny* trains they're cleaned often). Always carry your own toilet paper. Toilets close approximately 5min. before each stop and will only reopen once civilization is but a speck on the horizon. Be forewarned, as no amount of pleading with the *provodnik* will do you any good. Cabin-mates tend to be gregarious and willing to engage in a game of cards, chess, or backgammon. You'll likely find the opportunity to share family photos or a meal with curious companions. Your compartment-mates will probably come aboard with lots of sausage and veggies to share; you will make friends if you do the same. A posted schedule in each wagon lists arrival times for each *stoyanka* (стоянка; stop). When the train stops for longer than 15min., locals come out to sell food to passengers. Although harassment is uncommon, **female travelers** should be prepared to wade through droves of drunks and field unprovoked niceties. If you have problems with men in your compartment, ask to be transferred elsewhere. In serious cases the *provodnitsa* will summon the military official on every train.

NOVOSIBIRSK (НОВОСИБИРСК) ☎(8)3832

Novosibirk's nondescript face hides its bizarre past. While most other Siberian cities were churning out heavy machinery during the Cold War, Novosibirsk was splitting atoms and genetically engineering superior flora and fauna. When funding dried up in the late 1980s, the city inherited a league of ghost towns and disgruntled mad scientists. Today, neighboring Akademgorodok—the Soviet Union's Los Alamos—isn't producing much academically, and you won't encounter much mad science unless you venture out of the city center. As a result of the construction of the Trans-Siberian and Stalin's industrial build-up during World War II, Novosibirsk's population soared from virtually zero to 1.6 million in under a century, making it Siberia's most populous city.

TIME CHANGE. Novosibirsk is 3hr. ahead of Moscow (GMT+6).

▐ **TRANSPORTATION.** The **train station**, on ul. Shamshurina (Шамшурина), sends trains to: **Krasnoyarsk** (13hr., 5-6 per day, 450R); **Moscow** (48-52hr., 5-6 per day, 1800R); and **Yekaterinburg** (22hr., 7-8 per day, 759R). Novosibirsk is a gateway to Central Asia. The main route, the Turkistan-Siberian railway, goes to **Almaty, Kazakstan** (35-40hr., daily 2pm, 1100R); less frequent trains run to **Tashkent** and **Samargand, Uzbekistan.** For a schedule of Trans-Siberian trains see p. 717.

▐▐ **ORIENTATION AND PRACTICAL INFORMATION.** The **Metro** (4R) connects the city center, **pl. Lenina** (Ленина), to the **train station** at Garina-Mikhailovskovo (Гарина-Михайловского).Walk out of the train station and then underground at the "M." Take the Metro one stop to **Sibirskaya** (Сибирская), then walk upstairs to change stations; one more stop takes you to pl. Lenina. The Sibirskaya Metro is close to the circus, the Ascension Church, the market, and the stadium, but most other sights are near pl. Lenina. **Krasny pr.** (Красный), Novosibirsk's main drag, runs north-south through pl. Lenina. Directly opposite the statue of Lenin, ul. Lenina (Ленина) runs out of the square. Next to ul. Lenina, at the corner of the square, **Vokzalnaya Magistral** (Вокзальная Магистраль) runs down a couple blocks to **pr. Dmitrova** (Димитрова). Buy a **map** of the city at **Art-Salon Book-Salon**, Krasny pr. 23, on the street level of the Lenina Metro. (35R. Open M-Sa 10am-7:30pm.) **Alfa Bank** (Альфа Банк), Dimitrova 1, opposite New York Pizza, **exchanges currency** and **traveler's checks** for no commission. (Open M-Sa 8:30-7:30pm, Su 9am-3pm.) Besides offering **cash advances** and **Western Union** services, it also has an MC/V **ATM**. There are several other exchange bureaus on Krasny pr. **Store luggage** in the basement of the train station; look for "Камера Хранения" (7-20R). There is a **pharmacy** at Krasny pr. 15, at the intersection with ul. Chaplygina (Чаплыгина), opposite St. Nicholas's Church. (☎22 55 35. Open daily 8am-8pm.) **City Hospital #1** (Поликлиника), in the gray building with green awnings at ul. Serebrennikovskaya 42 (Серебренниковская), one block south of the Opera and Ballet House behind the Lenin statue, will see foreigners at window #13. (☎23 59 22. Doctor's visit 100R. Open M-F 8am-8pm, Sa 9am-3pm, Su 9am-3pm.) The **telephone office**, ul. Lenina 5, a block west of Ploshchad Lenina (Площадь Ленина, Lenin Square) offers **international calls** to North America (27R per min.) and Europe (22R per min.). You can access the **Internet** in the post office. (21R per hr. Open daily 9am-9pm.) There are also 24hr. Internet terminals inside the Dimitrova branch of **New York**

The Altai has vistas that rival the world's top trekking routes, yet because of its remoteness you'll find it relatively uncrowded. The placid banks of Lake Teletskoye often fill up with vacationers from Novosibirsk and other nearby cities, but the more serious (and more thrilling) mountain treks—such as the week-long trek from the village of Tyungur to the high-altitude lakes near the foot of Mount Belukha and back—are populated only by the occasional Russian youth group or adventurous European. Trekking is only one of a range of possible outdoor activities. More serious mountaineers and whitewater rafting enthusiasts will also find plenty to delight in.

It's best to arrange a visit to the Altai through a trekking agency. They provide transportation—which frees you from dependency on the unreliable bus network—equipment, and, most importantly, guides who can lead you safely along the often unmarked trails. Reputable agencies include **Plot** (☎3852 36 73 49; www.plot-altai.ru/engl/eindex.htm), an agency based in Barnaul that draws on a pool of experienced guides with companionable dispositions, and **Wild Russia** (☎8122 73 65 14; www.wildrussia.spb.ru), a highly professional St. Petersburg-based outfit that caters well to Western visitors. For more information on Altai, visit the Republic's official visitor's site, www.altai-republic.com.

David Egan was a Researcher for Let's Go: Eastern Europe 2001 and India & Nepal 2002. He now works for Shakespeare & Company.

Pizza (see below), but you'll have to contend with swarms of teenagers struggling to destroy alien civilizations. (10-15R per hr. 8am-midnight, 70R midnight-8am.) The **post office** sits at ul. Lenina 5 at the corner of Sovetskaya. (Советская; ☎ 10 07 22. Open M-F 8am-7pm, Sa-Su 8am-6pm; 8am-1pm on 4th M of the month.) **Postal Code:** 630 099.

▮▯ ACCOMMODATIONS AND FOOD. The city's most convenient accommodation for short-term visitors is the surprisingly posh **Gostinitsa ❶** (Гостиница), located on the second floor of the train station. These comfy, renovated rooms overlook the main waiting hall. The PA system is audible at night, but it isn't loud enough to keep up most sleepers. (☎ 29 23 76. Singles 400R; doubles 700-900R. Incoming or outgoing train ticket required.) **Hotel Tsentralnaya ❶** (Центральная), ul. Lenina 3, has adequate rooms in the center. Take the Metro to pl. Lenina, then head down ul. Lenina one block towards the post office. (☎ 22 36 38; fax 22 76 60. Singles 500-1200R; doubles 700-2400R.)

The ▮**Sickle and Hammer ❷** (Серп и Молот), in the basement of St. Patrick's Corner (see below), is an eatery that makes you hanker for the old days of U-2 spy planes, *samizdat* pamphlets, and mutually assured destruction. Covered in Soviet memorabilia, Khrushchev kitsch, and Cold War collectibles, the restaurant also features live music, pool, and karaoke. (☎ 22 44 77. Appetizers 40-195R. Entrees 110-280R. Open daily 4pm-2am.) **Derby Club ❷** (Дерби Клуб), pr. Krasny 31, serves a heaping, well-prepared, 3-course business lunch for as low as 110R. (☎ 22 43 70. Open daily noon-midnight.) **St. Patrick's Corner ❸**, ul. Lenina 8, serves typical Irish fare in an atypically pleasant setting. (☎ 22 44 77. Appetizers 70-210R. Entrees 130-410R. Guinness 165R. English menu. Open daily noon-2am.) For pizza as good as any you'll find in Manhattan, head to **New York Pizza ❶**, ul. Lenina 12 or Dimitrova 4. The Lenina location is much better. (Slices 30-40R; burritos 40-45R; quesadillas 34-39R. Open 24hr.) A large outdoor **food market** on ul. Krylova (Крылова) covers nearly as much area as the stadium next door. From Metro station Krasny Pr., go left along ul. Krylova for two blocks. (Open daily 8am-9pm.) **Gastronom,** Krasny pr. 30, is a standard Russian grocery store. (Open daily 8am-9pm.)

◉▯ SIGHTS AND ENTERTAINMENT. The **Novosibirsk Art Gallery** (Новосибирская Картинная Галерея; Novosibirskaya Kartinnaya Galereya), Krasny pr. 5, features a varied collection with works by Surikov and Roerich. (☎ 22 20 42. Open Tu-Su 10am-6pm. 30R, students 20R.) In the middle of Krasny pr., 500m south of pl. Lenina, the gold-domed **St. Nicholas's Chapel** (Часовня во имя Святитиля Николая; Chasovnya vo imya Svyatitilya Nikolaya) supposedly sits in the exact center of Russia. (Services daily 2pm. Open daily noon-5pm.) The larger **Ascension Church** (Храм Вознесения Господня; Khram Vozneseniya Gospodnya), at the intersection of ul. Gogolya (Гоголя) and ul. Sovetskaya (ул. Советская), flaunts a heavenly blue ceiling and a dazzling white and gold iconostasis. The largest **Opera House** in Russia stands at Krasny pr. 36 behind the Lenin Statue. Built largely by women and the elderly during World War II, the building is modeled after the Bolshoy in Moscow (see **Moscow Entertainment,** p. 654; ☎ 22 59 90; season runs Sept.-May. Tickets start at 40R.). The **Novosibirsk Museum,** Krasny pr. 23, south of the Lenina Metro station, traces regional history from Neolithic to modern times. An unimpressive art exhibit awaits upstairs. (☎ 18 17 33. Open Tu-Su 10am-5:30pm. 12R.) Swing by the **Wedding Palace,** Krasny pr. 68, to witness a Vegas-style public wedding ceremony. The nuptials take around 20min., as one couple after another piles through, smiles, and smooches. (Metro Krasny. Services daily.) If you have time, swim in **Obskoe More** (Обское Море), a huge lake created by a dam in the Ob River. From the train station, catch a suburban train to "Обское Море."

KRASNOYARSK (КРАСНОЯРСК) ☎(8)3912

Founded as a Cossack fort in 1628, Krasnoyarsk attracted a rough crowd: by the end of the 19th century, one-fourth of the city's citizenry were ex-cons. Straddling the 2km wide Yenisey River, this city of 930,000 is Siberia's third-largest. During World War II, Stalin pushed much of Russia's defense industry to Krasnoyarsk on the backs of Japanese POWs. When Krasnoyarsk opened to foreigners in 1991, the world discovered an industrial quagmire and a Yenisey too polluted to freeze. The city retains military affinities: former general Aleksandr Lebed was the region's governor until his death in 2002. Krasnoyarsk still may not be the prettiest city, but the work of artist V.I. Surikov and the Stolby Reserve attract a few visitors.

 TIME CHANGE. Krasnoyarsk is 4hr. ahead of Moscow (GMT+7).

TRANSPORTATION. The **train station**, on ul. Tridsatovo Iyulia (30-го Июля; ☎29 34 34), on the north bank of the Yenisey, 2km west of the city center, sends trains to: **Irkutsk** (19hr., 1-5 per day, 580R); **Novosibirsk** (14hr., 2-6 per day, 440R); and **Vladivostok** (3 days, 1-3 per day, 1200R). **International tickets** must be purchased at the downtown ticket office, between pr. Mira and ul. Karla Marxa at ul. Robespiera 29. (Робеспиера. ☎23 04 94. Open M-F 8am-8pm, Sa 9am-6pm, Su 9am-3pm.) For a schedule of Trans-Siberian trains see p. 717.

ORIENTATION AND PRACTICAL INFORMATION. Everything of interest, with the exception of the Stolby Nature Reserve, lies on the north bank. From the train station, take bus #6 or 55 from the parking lot on the right to the centrally located Hotel Krasnoyarsk (4 stops; 4R). To return, catch #36, 50a, or 81 opposite the hotel. Krasnoyarsk's three main streets, **ul. Lenina** (Ленина), **pr. Mira** (Мира), and **ul. Karla Marksa** (Карла Маркса), all run west-east from the **train station**, parallel to the river. There's **no tourist office,** but the **Service-Center Trans-Sib** (Сервис-Центр Транс-Сиб), in the far left corner on the train station's main floor, reserves domestic train tickets and provides international **telephone** and **fax** service. (☎29 26 92; fax 21 65 71. Open M-F 9am-8pm.) Snag a **map** (30R) in the lobby of **Hotel Krasnoyarsk.** Outside is a 24hr. MC/V **ATM. Exchange currency** at the hotel, or at any of dozens of bureaus on ul. Lenina, pr. Mira, and ul. Karla Marksa. **Luggage storage** is in the train station basement—look for "Камера Хранения." (Kamera Khraneniya; 23R per bag. Open 24hr.) For **ambulance** service, call ☎45 39 04 or 45 39 75. The **24hr. pharmacy** at pr. Mira 37 is well stocked. An international **telephone office** is at ul. Lenina 49, slightly east of Hotel Krasnoyarsk. (☎22 18 01. Open M-F 7am-10pm, Sa-Su 8am-1pm.) **Internet Cafe MaxSoft,** behind the government building across the bridge from Hotel Krasnoyarsk at ul. Uritskovo 61, 4th fl., is all Internet and no cafe. (☎65 13 85. Open M-F 9am-8pm. 30R per hr.) The **post office** is at ul. Lenina 62. (☎27 07 48. Open M-Sa 8am-2pm and 3-7pm). **Postal Code:** 660 049.

ACCOMMODATIONS AND FOOD. Hotel Krasnoyarsk ❷, ul. Uritskovo 94, (Урицкого), on the corner of ul. Venbauma and ul. Karla Marksa, is a convenient option. Take bus #6 or 55 from the train station. (☎27 37 69 or 27 37 54; fax 27 02 36; hotelkrs@online.ru. 435-540R per person. Breakfast buffet 100R.) **Hotel Ogni Enseiya ❶** (Гостиница Огни Енсейя), ul. Dubrovinskovo 80 (Добровинского),

RUSSIA

faces the water one block west of Mayak. Its adequate rooms are buoyed by a friendly staff. (☎27 52 62. Singles 260-1100R; doubles 320-1200R.)

Restaurant Volna ❷ has a typical Russian menu with an emphasis on seafood. (☎29 04 81. Salmon *pelmeny* 60R. Sturgeon *shashlik* 100R. Open daily noon-4pm and 6pm-2am.) **Rosso Pizza ❷**, pr. Mira 111 and ul. Lenina 121, is an American-style pizza joint. The salmon (сёмга; syomga) pizza stands out. (Slices 20-40R. Salmon *shashlik* 60R. Open daily 11am-midnight.) Serve yourself at the 24hr. **Gastronom Krasny Yar** (Красный Яр), pr. Mira 50a.

◙ ⚑ SIGHTS AND OUTDOORS. Although he studied in St. Petersburg, 19th-century Russian painter Vasily Ivanovich Surikov (1848-1916) was born and raised in Krasnoyarsk. His estate has now been turned into the **V. I. Surikov Museum-Estate** (Музей-усадьба В. И. Сурикова; Muzey-usadba V. I. Surikova), ul. Lenina 98. Inside the elegant house, ten rooms on two floors showcase his life and work. (☎27 08 15. Open Tu-Su 11am-7pm. 20R.) The gold-domed **Russian Orthodox Church** (Покровский Кафедральный Собор; Pokrovsky Kafedralny Sobor), at ul. Surik-ova and pr. Mira, was built in the late 18th century. (Open daily 8am-7pm.) Farther east, the **Krasnoyarsk Art Museum**, ul. Parizhskoy Kommuny 20 (Парижской Коммуны), at ul. Karla Marksa, displays works by Surikov, Shishkin, and others. (☎27 55 81. Open Tu-Su 11am-7pm. 20R.) The **Museum-Ship St. Nicholas** (Музей-Пароход Св. Николай; Muzey-Parokhod Sv. Nikolai) sits at the east end of ul. Dubrovinskovo, near the Philharmonic Hall. In 1897, the ship carried Lenin up the Yenisey to his exile in Shushensk; it later transported Tsar Nicholas II to a similar fate. Now the museum features wax figures of both men. The museum guide gives only Russian tours. (☎23 94 03. Open Tu-Su 11am-6pm. 5R, students 2R.) To reach the nearby **Stolby Nature Reserve**—a mecca for hiking and rock-climbing—catch bus #50 (4R; 30min.) to Bazaika (Базайка) or hop a regional train to Turbaza (Турбаза). It's a 90min. walk to the tick-infested nature reserve.

IRKUTSK (ИРКУТСК)　　　☎(8)3952

A grand lot of libraries, museums, theaters, and cafes has led this one-time Cossack fur-trading post to call itself the "Paris of Siberia." After all, it does have a vibrant riverfront, lovely old houses, and the world's northeasternmost Benetton. When the Trans-Siberian arrived in 1898, however, it found a lawless bazaar of fur-traders, ex-cons, gamblers, and prospectors. In this bastion of propriety, nearly one in every hundred citizens died of unnatural causes, such as a pick-axe in the skull. Like the rest of Siberia, the city's pre-Soviet infrastructure and culture took a hit under socialism. Nonetheless, Irkutsk's cultural heritage and proximity to Lake Baikal have made it the most popular stop on the Trans-Siberian.

 TIME CHANGE. Irkutsk is 5hr. ahead of Moscow (GMT+8).

▐ TRANSPORTATION

Trains: on ul. Vokzalnaya (Вокзальная; ☎43 17 17 or 28 28 20). To: **Krasnoyarsk** (19hr., 3-4 per day, 640R); **Moscow** (3½ days, 1-3 per day, 2078R); **Ulan Ude** (8hr., 3 per day, 305R); **Yekaterinburg** (53hr., 1-3 per day, 1393R). Foreigners purchase tickets from the *mezhdunarodnaya kassa* (Международная касса; international ticket booth) in the waiting room left of the restaurant. (Open 24hr. except 5-6am, 7:30-9am, 1-2pm, and 8-9pm. French spoken.) For a **Trans-Siberian schedule** see p. 717.

Irkutsk

🏠 ACCOMMODATIONS
Americansky Dom, **3**
Hotel Arena, **2**
Hotel Gornyak, **4**

🍴 FOOD
Cafe Sport Express, **6**
Club 1952, **5**
Restoran Hunan, **1**

Buses: Ul. Oktyabrskoy Revolutsiye 11 (Октябрьской Революции; ☎27 24 11), near the Decembrists' houses (see **Sights and Entertainment,** p. 725). To **Listvyanka** (90 min., 3 per day, 49R).

⚹ 🛈 ORIENTATION AND PRACTICAL INFORMATION

The **Angara River** (Ангара Река) bisects the town. The old city center and all the sights lie on the right bank, while the train station is on the residential left bank. From the station, buses #16 and 20, as well as trams #1 and 2, run to ul. Lenina (Ленина) in the city center (4R).

Tourist Services: Lida Sclocchini at **Amerikansky Dom** (see **Accommodations,** below, p. 724) arranges tours (2hr. car tour US$20) and buys train tickets (US$3 commission).

Consulates: Mongolian consulate, ul. Lapina 11 (☎/fax 34 21 43). Arranges visas (passport photos required). Tourist visa: 3-4 day processing US$15, 48hr. US$30. Transit visa: US$15/US$30. Open M-Tu and Th-F 9:30am-noon and 2:30-5pm.

Currency Exchange: Vneshtorg-bank (Внешторг-Банк), ul. Sverdlova 40 #201 (Свердлова; ☎24 39 16). Cashes **traveler's checks** (2% commission, US$0.50 per check). MC/V **cash advances** for 2% commission. Open M-F 9:30am-1pm and 2-4pm.

ATM: A MC/V machine is at **Alfabank,** bul. Gagarina 34.

Luggage Storage: Exit the train station and go left past the post office to the door marked "Камера Хранения" (Kamera Khraneniya). 20-45R.

24-Hour Pharmacy: Apteka Doverie (Аптека Доверие), ul. Lenina 21. Open 24hr.

Medical Service: English-speaking Dr. George Bilikh (☎34 36 10) will perform basic medical services or get you someone who can help.

Telephones: Ul. Proletarskaya 12 (Пролетарская), opposite the circus, at ul. Sverdlova. Offers international telephone and fax service. Open 24hr.

Internet Access: Internet Klub 38 Net, ul. Marata 38 (Марата; ☎24 23 52), at ul. Sverdlova. 36R per hr. Open 24hr.

Post Office, ul. Stepana Razina 23 (Степана Разина), at the corner of ul. Sverdlova. **Poste Restante** at window #6. **EMS** available. Open M-F 8am-8pm, Sa-Su 9am-6pm.

Postal Code: 664 000.

ACCOMMODATIONS

Finding a place to stay in Irkutsk can be a problem. Most places are generally overpriced and fill up quickly, especially in summer. Phone ahead if possible.

Amerikansky Dom (Американский Дом), ul. Ostrovskovo 19 (Островского; ☎43 26 89; slida@irk.ru or molga@irk.ru). With the train station behind you, follow the tram tracks to the left and veer right when the tracks fork. From there, walk up 1 block and continue past the right of the water pump. Take a right after the kiosks, and then take the 2nd full left on ul. Kaiskaya (Кайская). Ul. Ostrovskovo is up the hill, past the fire station (15-20min.). Owner Lida Sclocchini is the Russian widow of the man from Philadelphia whose early-80s love affair broke Cold War barriers and attracted attention from *People* magazine. Her Western-style house tends to fill quickly with Trans-Siberian backpackers; call at least 4 days ahead. Laundry US$3. US$20; US$15 without breakfast. ❷

Hotel Arena (Арена; ☎34 46 42), behind the circus at ul. Sverdlova (Свердлова). Central and modern, clean private bathrooms. Singles 192-300R; doubles 340-1200R. ❶

Hotel Gornyak ul. Lenina 21 (Горняк; ☎24 37 54), at ul. Dzerzhinskovo (Дзержинского). Convenient, but the rooms are small and the bathrooms are shared. Singles 650R; doubles 700R. ❷

FOOD

What it lacks in fair accommodations, Irkutsk supplements with outstanding dining options. **Magazin Okean** (Магазин Океан), at the corner of ul. Sverdlova and ul. Stepana Razina, which sells everything from fruit to film. (Open M-F 9am-9pm, Sa 9am-8pm.) The **central market** hawks fresh fruit, veggies, cheese, and meat. From the station, walk about 10min. along ul. Dzerzhinskovo and take a right on ul. Chekhova (Чехова). Any form of transport that reads "рынок" (rynok) will also do. (Open daily 8am-8pm.)

Club 1952, ul. Lenina 15 (☎33 62 82). Provides superior German and Russian dishes in a nostalgic setting at refreshingly nostalgic prices. Entrees 33-180R. Open M-Sa noon-3am. MC/V. ❶

Restoran Hunan (Ресторан Хун-ян), ul. Sukhe Batora 16 (Сухэ Батора), at the end of the bridge over the Angara River, on the right bank. Russian and Chinese food, minus the spices. Large noodle bowl 80R. Open daily 11am-2am. ❷

Cafe Sport Express, in the stadium off ul. Karla Marksa (Карла Маркса). Serves killer *pelmeny* (45R) and other dishes. The take-out cafe in the same building serves similar food that is even cheaper. Salads 45-198R. Open daily 10am-10pm. ❷

🔊 🎵 SIGHTS AND ENTERTAINMENT

Irkutsk's most illustrious residents, the **Decembrists** (see **History,** p. 621), arrived as exiles in the 19th century. Two of their houses are now museums. **Muzey-Dekabrista Volkonskovo** (Музей-Декабриста Волконского), ul. Volkonskovo 10, is a pleasant old house on a dusty side street off ul. Timiryazeva (Тимирязева). To get there, take trams #1-4 to Dekabersky Sabitiye (Декарберский Собитие) and walk to the right of the big domed church. If you had the stamina to read *War and Peace,* this one should be a real treat. (☎27 57 73. Open Tu-Su 10am-6pm; last entry at 5:30pm. 45R, students 30R.) A block away, the **Prince Sergey Trubetskoy House-Museum** (Музей Трубецкого), ul. Dzerzhinskovo 64, exhibits the books, lavish furniture, tapestried icons, and photos of this prominent Decembrist's jail cell. (Open M and Th-Su 10am-6pm; last entry 5:30pm. 45R, students 30R.) Near the river, the **Regional Museum** (Краеведческий Музей; Kraevedchesky Muzey), in a Victorian building at ul. Karla Marxa 2, exhibits furs, Buddhist masks, and pipes of local Siberian tribes. It also documents the city's Slavic history and years as a frontier town in the Wild East. (☎33 34 49. Open Tu-Su 10am-6pm. 50R, students 30R.) The **Sukachev Art Museum** (Художественный Музей Имени Сукачева; Khudozhestvenny Muzey Imeni Sukacheva), ul. Lenina 5, houses Chinese vases, Buddhist *thanka,* and paintings from the 16th to 20th centuries. (☎34 42 30. Open M and W-Su 10am-5:30pm. 30R.) Chandeliers brighten the gold-columned iconostasis in **Znamensky Monastery** (Знаменский Монастырь), north of the town center on ul. Angarskaya (Ангарская). Several Decembrists are buried in the gardens. Take trolley #3 or buses #8, 13, or 31 to the first stop past the northern bridge or walk along ul. Frank Kamenetskovo (Франк Каменецкого), bear right at the fork, and cross the street to the blue-green domes. (Open daily 8:30am-5pm; services 8:30 and 11am. Free.)

On sunny days and warm nights, locals head to the end of ul. Karla Marksa to drink and display gratuitous amounts of affection in public. When it gets dark, the crowd heads across the cove to **Youth Island** (Остров Юности; Ostrov Yunosty) to drink more and rock until dawn. **Club Stratosphere,** ul. Karla Marksa 15, at the corner of ul. Gryaznova (Грязнова), is Irkutsk's premier disco/bowling alley. Its teen crowd dolls up to meet the strict dress code and consequently doesn't show up until at least midnight. (☎24 30 33. Bowling 300R per hr. Open Th and Su 6pm-4am, 40R; F-Sa 6pm-6am, 150R. MC/V.) The **Russian Winter Festival** (Русский Зимской фестиваль, Russkii Zimskoy Festival), where troika-rides, *Khorovod* performances (traditional round dancing), and *blini* with salmon roe abound, takes place annually from Dec. 25 to Jan. 5.

LAKE BAIKAL (ОЗЕРО БАЙКАЛ)

Lake Baikal—**the deepest body of fresh water in the world** at 1637m—contains one-fifth of the earth's fresh water. Its surface (23,000km²) is twice as large as North America's Lake Superior, and it is far older than any other lake in the world (25 million years). Surrounded by snow-capped peaks, its waters teem with 450 species found nowhere else, including **translucent shrimp, oversized sturgeon,** and **deepwater fish** that explode when brought to the surface. One such fish has evolved into a gelatinous blob of fat—so fatty, in fact, that locals stick wicks in its lipidinous lumps and use them as candles. Meanwhile, the local *nerpa* freshwater seal lives

RUSSIA

3000km from its closest relative, the Arctic seal. If you know how it got here, then give yourself a pat on the back, because no one else seems to.

Baikal's shores are no less fascinating than its waters. **Reindeer, polar foxes, wild horses, brown bears, wild boars,** and nefarious **Siberian weasels** hide in the surrounding mountains. Small glacial lakes melt into ice-cold waterfalls. Buryat *ger* (traditional Buryat tent-homes, also known as yurts) border the edges. Painted rocks and "wishing" trees strung with colored rags recall the area's shamanistic heritage, while the Buryat region to the northeast holds 45 Buddhist monasteries. Deserted gulags near Severobaikal, where many Buddhist lamas and shamans spent their last days under the atheist Soviet regime, pepper the outskirts. Your best bet is to visit in March, when the picturesque ice retains its splendor.

LISTVYANKA (ЛИСТВЯНКА)   ☎(8)3952

The most popular destination for daytrippers and Baikal over-nighters is this lakeside hamlet of 2500. Meandering cows battle visitors for control over the one and only real street, ul. Gorkovo (Горького), which runs from the boat dock to Hotel Baikal, five kilometers away (45min.). The wooden **St. Nicholas Church,** ul. Kylekova 88 (Кайлкова), built out of gratitude for a miraculous sea rescue, sits in a small valley away from the lake. The walk is a charming stroll through local neighborhoods and houses. Facing away from the docks, go left, and turn right when you see the green spire on the right. Detailed, golden-framed icons adorn the fragrant interior of the church. (Open M-F 9am-7pm. Services M-F 1-3pm.)

A **hydrofoil** runs between Irkutsk and Listvyanka from June to September. (70 min. Departs Tu-Th 8:30am, F-Sa 8:30am and 2pm, Su 8:30am, noon, 2pm; returns Tu-Th noon, F-Sa noon and 4:30pm, Su 8:30am, noon, 4, 4:30pm; 50R.) It departs from Irkutsk's **ferry terminal** (☎35 88 60) on ul. Solnichnaya (Сольничная), south of town. From ul. Lenina in Irkutsk, take bus #16 or trolleybus #5; ask for the "raketa" stop (ракета; rocket) and walk along the river against the current to the terminal (20min., 2R). **Buses** run daily from Irkutsk to Listvyanka; buy return tickets at the bus stop in the blue shack at the boat dock or on the bus. (90min.; to Listvyanka 9am, 2:30, 4:30, 7pm; to Irkutsk 7, 11am, 4:45, 6pm; 50R.)

Hotel Baikal in Listvyanka houses an **exchange office** that gives MC/V **cash advances** for 1.5% commission. The bus from Irkutsk stops at the hotel 5min. before reaching the docks. (☎25 03 91. Open daily 8am-2pm and 6pm-midnight.) Take a left out of the boat dock to get to the **post office,** ul. Gorkovo 49, just past the white WWII obelisk on the right. (Open M-F 8:30am-1pm and 3-5:30pm, Sa 8:30am-noon; closed last Th of each month.)

Past the white obelisk on the first road that heads away from the water, going left and facing away from the dock, the **Art Gallery** ❶(Картиная Галерея) was built by an architect extremely enthusiastic about Siberian art. He can arrange comfortable housing for US$10 per night, US$15 with breakfast. **Green Express** ❸, ul. Chelnokova 46, offers resort-style service on a hill overlooking the lake. To get there, walk back 1km from the bus stand to the hill overlooking St. Nicholas Church. (☎11 25 99, in Irkutsk 56 49 64; info@greenexpress.ru. Breakfast included. Singles 900R; doubles 1950R.) A short distance back up the road from the bus stop is a fine seafood restaurant, **Preshlyi Vek** ❷ (Прешлыи Век). The cooking is far better than the English translations in the menu. (Lake fish 110R. Open daily noon-11pm.)

OLKHON ISLAND

Khuzhir, the main town on Olkhon Island, has as many telephones as paved roads and as many toilets as restaurants (pick a number and multiply it by zero). On the shores north of Khuzhir, rocky cliffs give way to sandy beaches. You can pretend you're in Hawaii, but don't try jumping into the frigid waters. It's also possible to **camp** for free in the hills near the beach. **Shaman Rock,** behind Nikita's (see below), was a ritual site until local Russians co-opted it for **recreational climbing.**

Olkhon is accessible by **bus** from Irkutsk, but only starting in early June, when the ferry service starts. Bus tickets sell like hotcakes, especially on weekends; try to purchase one in advance. (June Tu and F 8am, return W and Sa 9am; 196R; July-Aug daily 8am, return daily 9am; 182R.) If you don't mind going without a seat, track down the bus labeled Khuzhir (Хужир), look obliging and pitiable, or try to slip the bus driver a few extra US dollars. If your travel dates are definite, it may be worth the effort to contact one of the **tour operators** in Irkutsk. **Green Express,** ul. Chelnokova 46, makes private runs to Olkhon and can arrange accommodations on the island. (☎38 01 11; info@greenexpress.ru. Leaves Irkutsk Tu and Th-F 9am; returns from Olkhon M, W, F 8am. Round-trip US$20. Bed in a shared *Yurt* US$6, with 3 meals US$10.) Lida Scloc-chini at **Amerikansky Dom** (see **Accommodations,** p. 724) can assist with bus tickets and homestays starting at US$10 per day with meals. A **post office** sits on ul. Lenina, a couple of blocks toward the water from the gastronom (see below) and to the left.

Khuzhir's tourist industry is monopolized by the affable Nikita Bercharov. ⓈNikita's "place where you can stay" ❷ (he doesn't want to call it a hotel), ul. Kirpichnaya 8 (Кирпичный), is full of friendly faces and blessed with a nightly campfire. Warm, cozy beds and three meals per day will cost you US$15-20. Nikita can organize a variety of excursions, from boat tours to horse treks (US$3-20). Enjoy his *banya* (sauna) for US$5. With your back to the *gastronom* in the center of town, walk left for half a block, then take the first right. Ul. Kirpichnaya is the last left before the edge of town. Nikita's place is an unmarked complex surrounded by a wooden fence. (☎46 67 76; nikita@olkhon.irkutsk.ru.) The **gastronom** in the center of town makes a convenient stop for grub. (Open daily 8am-midnight.) To get to the better-stocked **Khoroshy Magazin** (Хороший Магазин; Good Store), head from the gastronom toward the WWII memorial.

ULAN UDE (УЛАН УДЭ) ☎(8)3012

When Stalin suppressed Russia's ethnic minorities, he made exceptions for Ulan Ude. The result is an odd, modern city that feels much less Russian than any other major stop on the Trans-Siberian. Long a haven for political and religious dissidents, Ulan Ude also served as Russia's customs port for the tea trade with China. But rather than develop closer ties to Asia, the capital of the Buryat Republic saw itself cemented to the Russian Empire when the Trans-Siberian appeared in 1900. Today, the Buryat comprise less than a quarter of the region's population. Reopened to tourists in 1990, the city's main landmark is its bust of Lenin. It overlooks the city center, where its ominous stare might still set the tone were the whir of cafes, kiosks, and Buddhist *datsans* not so insistently strong.

 TIME CHANGE. Ulan Ude is 5hr. ahead of Moscow and is in the same time zone as Mongolia (GMT+8).

▐▀ TRANSPORTATION. Ulan Ude is the last Russian city on the Trans-Mongolian line. To: **Irkutsk** (8hr., 4-5 per day, 400-600R); **Moscow** (4-8 per day, 2575R); **Vladivostok** (63hr., 5:15am and 11:55pm, 1900R); **Beijing, CHI** (47hr., Tu 11:06am and Sa 11:16am, 3000-3600R); and **Ulaanbaatar, MON** (24hr., 12:52am, 720-1050R). For a schedule of Trans-Siberian trains see p. 717. Foreigners may purchase tickets from the *kassa* in the front corner of the station's first floor; look for the

THE TRANS-SIBERIAN OPERA

Ulan Ude may be half way to Mongolia, but there are curious reminders of its Russian heritage. The rotting but grand **Buryat Opera House**, in the southwest corner of pl. Sovetov, feebly mimics the large opera houses of European Russia. Its music, however, is no mere imitation; the Buryats are producing European sounds with much talent and gusto. Pick up a ticket to one of the spirited performances of nineteenth-century European favorites such as *Carmen* and *The Barber of Seville*. Although there are no Pavarottis among local stars, it is hard not to appreciate the irony of hearing a French opera, set in Spain, and sung in Russian by a Mongolian cast. For something more indigenous, watch one of the opera house's many productions of recent works by Buryat authors or a performance of *Enkhe Bulat Baatar*—"The Iron Warrior." Celebrating traditional myths and legends, this opera was the first to be performed in the Buryat language. *(Tickets 40R).*

—*Graeme Wood*

"Международные Кассы" sign. (Open daily 9am-noon, 1-7pm, and 2-7am.) See **Practical Information** below for less harried ticket-purchasing options.

🔋📋 ORIENTATION AND PRACTICAL INFORMATION.

Ulan Ude's main square, **pl. Sovetov** (Советов), lies 500m south of the **train station** (☎34 25 31), off Revolutsiye 1905-a goda (Революцие 1905-го года). To get there on foot, cross the tracks on the pedestrian bridge. Then, with your back to the station, walk left for one block along ul. Borsoyeva (Борсоева), take the first full right, and then the first full left on ul. Sukhe-Batora (Сухэ-Батора).

Baikal Naran Tour, in room 105 of Hotel Buryatiya (Бурятия), 47a ul. Kommunisticheskaya (Коммунистическая), off ul. Lenina, offers tour packages and arranges train tickets for 105R. (☎/fax 21 50 97 or 21 91 48; baikalnarantour@mail.ru. Buryat visits US$60. City tours US$10. Open M-F 9am-8pm.) The **Mongolian Consulate** is in a bright building 100m west of ul. Lenina, south of the Opera House and pl. Sovetov. (☎21 05 07. Open M,W, F 10am-1pm. One-week visa processing US$25, 1-day US$50.) **Exchange currency** in the lobby of Hotel Buryatiya. (see above; Open M-F 9am-5pm.) It also has an **ATM. Luggage storage** is in the center hall of the train station (10-30R). The **hospital** at the corner of bul. Karla Marksa (Карла Маркса) and ul. Navsova (Навсова) will see foreigners. Take the tram from the east side of Hotel Buryatiya and ask for the "Sayany" stop. Ascend the slope to your right, make a left at the arcade, and walk to the complex of pink buildings on your right. (☎33 15 05, emergency 03.) A **24hr. pharmacy** sits at ul. Lenina 29, three blocks south of pl. Sovetov. (☎21 24 37. Ring bell midnight-6am.) The **post office** provides **Internet access** (30R per hr.) and international **phone service.** (Open M-Sa 8am-7pm. Internet open M-F 9am-9pm, Sa-Su 9am-7pm.) **Postal Code:** 670 000.

🏠🍴 ACCOMMODATIONS AND FOOD.

Hotels fill up fast in the summer, so call ahead. **Hotel Odon** ❶ (Гостиница Одон, ul. Gagarina 43 (Гагарина), two blocks north of the train station, is good for short stays. (☎34 34 80. 150R per person.) **Hotel Barguzina** ❶ (Баргузина), ul. Sovetskaya 28, is a little cozier, and is close to the bus station. Take bus #36 from the train station and ask the driver for the hotel. Or, from pl. Sovetov, walk two blocks down ul. Lenina, and go right (25min.) on ul. Sovetskaya. (☎21 57 46. Singles 230-250R; doubles 340-630R; triples 390R.)

In the forest suburbs of Ulan Ude sits the inimitable **Baatari Urgoo** ❷ (Баатари Ургоо), which serves meaty specialities in a *ger* (traditional Buryat tent-dwelling also known as a 'yurt'). From the Ethnographic Museum (see below), walk away from the city center; the colorful *ger* is 1km down the road on your right. (Sheep and horse stomach salad 75R. Lamb heart salad 75R. Cover 15R. Open daily noon-11pm.) In the city center, **U Druzei ❶** (У Друзей; At Friends) is a tasty Armenian bistro. It is located two storefronts north of the corner of ul. Kommunisticheskaya (Коммунистическая) and ul. Profsoyuznaya (Профсоюзная), across the tracks from Hotel Buryatiya. (Kebab 43R. Open daily 11am-midnight.)

◪ **SIGHTS.** A freakishly large **Lenin head** dominates Ulan Ude's main square, **pl. Sovetov.** Forty-two tons and 18m high, this bronze bohemoth was designed by the Neroda brothers in 1972. At the southwest corner of the square on the corner of ul. Lenina stands the majestic **Buryat State Academic Theater of Opera and Ballet** (Бурятский Государственный Академический Театр Оперы и Балета; Buryatsky Gosudarstvenny Akademichesky Teatr Opery i Baleta), a classical building with two enthusiastic horsemen guarding the entrance. (Open daily.)

The **Museum of Buryat History** (Музей истории Бурятии; Muzey Istorii Buryatii), ul. Profsoyuznaya 29 (Профсоюзная), off ul. Kommunisticheskaya opposite Hotel Buryatia, details the history of the city and the БАМ (BAM), the costly second Trans-Siberian railway. There's also a collection of Buddhist medical texts on the 2nd floor. (☎21 65 87. Open Tu-Su 10am-6pm. Each floor 20R.) Follow the tram tracks down ul. Kommunisticheskaya away from pl. Sovetova and take a right at the bottom of the hill, past some kiosks and umbrellas, to reach the local **Buddhist shrine** (ламрим; lamrim), 100m down on the left. Walk past the black gate and ask to take a peek inside. Visit in the morning or early afternoon.

The most interesting sights lie outside the city limits. The **Ethnographic Museum** (Этнографический Музей; Etnografichesky Muzey), north of the city, can be reached via bus #8 (every 30min., 6R) from the south end of pl. Sovetov; if you're looking into Lenin's left ear, you're in the right place. Get off at the first stop after the stadium. Walk 1km down the road that veers left from the bus stop. The museum is on the right, sprawled over a quiet patch of Siberian countryside. It features traditional Buryat *gers*, a shamanist compound, and an unfortunately unkept zoo. (☎33 57 54. Open M-F 9am-5pm, Sa-Su 10am-6pm. 40R, students 20R.)

Perhaps the most fascinating spot in the region is the hamlet of **Ivolga** (Иволга), west of Ulan Ude. Amidst the hills stands **Datsan-Ivolga,** a Buddhist monastery complete with a yellow curved roof and Mongolian-trained lamas. Built in 1942, the shrine serves as the Buddhist center of the Soviet Union. In the main building next to the temple are Buddhist scriptures handwritten in Tibetan, Pali, and Sanskrit. Around the complex sit 120 prayer drums, and in the greenhouse is a relative of India's *bodhi* tree, under which Buddha attained enlightenment. The **lamas' houses** are behind the complex. Arrive before 9am to hear the monks chanting. To reach the *datsan*, take bus #130 from the station on ul. Sovetskaya (7:10am, noon, and 5pm; 15R).

ULAANBAATAR, MONGOLIA ☎1

The view from the train window changes as you enter Mongolia. The Russian birches disappear, leaving a vast expanse dotted with occasional *gers* (yurts). The only break in the emptiness is Ulaanbaatar, a city so hip that it needed a nickname ("UB"). It's a big, noisy mess that throws together folk in traditional garb, young up-and-comers, expats, and enough alcoholics to make a Moscow vodka bar look like a Mormon picnic. UB has some of the best sights and nightlife between Moscow and Beijing, but a proper visit includes the surrounding countryside—from

RUSSIA

TUGHRIK

AUS$1 = 614.43MNT	1000MNT = AUS$1.63
CDN$1 = 712.74MNT	1000MNT = CDN$1.40
EUR€1 = 1092.93MNT	1000MNT = EUR€0.91
NZ$1 = 522.26MNT	1000MNT = NZ$1.91
UK£1 = 1719.78MNT	1000MNT = UK£0.58
US$1 = 1110.42MNT	1000MNT = US$0.90
ZAR1 = 10.60MNT	1000MNT =ZAR9.50

Lake Khousgol in the north to the Gobi desert in the south—where much of the population still lives, unaffected by the cosmopolitan fever of the capital.

 TIME CHANGE. Mongolia is 5hr. ahead of Moscow (GMT+8).

 VISAS. Mongolian tourist visas can be arranged at the Mongolian embassies in **Moscow** (see **Embassies and Consulates, P. 629**) and **Beijing** (see **P. 869**), or at the consulates in **Irkutsk** (**P. 722**) and **Ulan Ude** (**P. 727**). As of June 2002, US citizens do not require visas, but are advised to inquire before traveling in case the situation has changed.

■◆ **ORIENTATION AND PRACTICAL INFORMATION.** Map labels and street names are in Mongolian, which usually uses a Cyrillic script. The center of town is **Sukhbaatar Square**, named for the patron saint of Mongolian Communism. **Enkh Tayvan Av.**, UB's main east-west artery, borders the square to the south; **Baga Toyruu St.** and **Ikh Toyruu St.** form half-circles enclosing the square, intersecting Enkh Tayvan at both ends. To reach the square from the train station, take bus #4 (200T; taxi 900T). The **train station** is on Teeverchid St., southwest of Sukhbaatar Sq. (☎94 194). **International tickets** must be bought in room 212, on the second floor of the **International Railway Ticketing Office.** (Open M-F 9am-1pm and 2-5pm, Sa-Su 9am-2pm.) Exit the train station, turn left, and walk 2min. to the yellow building set back from the road on the right. Schedules are in UB time, not Moscow time.

The **Chinese Embassy,** Zaluuchuudyn Ave. 5, is one block from the northeast corner of the square. (30-day tourist visa US$30 for 7-day processing, US$50 for 2-3-day processing, US$60 for same-day processing. ☎32 09 55. Open M, W, F 9:30am-noon.) The **Russian Embassy** is located at 6A Enkh Tayvan Ave. From the south side of Sukhbaatar Square facing the statue, walk left along Enkh Tayvan Av. for 3 blocks; it's on the left. (☎32 70 71. Open daily 2-3pm.) The **US Embassy** is at 59/1 Ikh Toyruu St., northeast of the square. (☎32 90 95 or emergency 99 11 4 168; fax 32 07 76; www.us-mongolia.com.) **Currency exchange** is available at any of the banks near Sukhbaatar Sq., most of which are open weekdays only. For **maps** of the city (5000T), head to **Hotel Ulaanbaatar,** one block past Sukhbaatar Sq. coming from the train station. Located at Sukhbaatar Sq. 14, it's the only place that exchanges currency and cashes traveler's checks after hours and on weekends. (☎32 02 37 or 32 06 20.) There are **no ATMs** in town, so bring cash and checks. **Mongol Bank** can wire cash via **Western Union** for 10% commission. Facing the grayish government building with your back to the statue in Sukhbaatar Square, make a left at the yellow building on the corner to your left and proceed for two blocks. (☎31 15 30. Open M-F 9am-4pm.) **Scrolls English Bookstore,** Khudaldaany St. 22, next to the Wrangler Jeans store, has a limited selection. (Open M-Sa 11am-6pm, Su 11am-4pm.) The

Yongsei Hospital (☎31 09 45) in the Medical Academy will provide care for foreigners. From the square, walk east along Enkh Tayran Ave. for one block; make the first right into the Academy. **Tavin-Us Anmeka 24,** a **24hr. pharmacy** (☎31 77 59 or 91 75 357), is on Enkh Tayvan Ave., opposite the Centerpoint shopping complex. From the south edge of the square facing the statue, walk left along Enkh Tayvan 5-6 blocks. **Internet** access is available in Internet clubs all over the city for 1000T per hour. The **post office** is on the corner of Enkh Tayvan Ave. and Sukhbaatar St., around the corner from the clock tower in the square. It holds **Poste Restante** inside the main entrance to the left. (Open M-F 7:30am-9pm, Sa 8am-8pm.) and has **telephones** (Open 24hr.). **Postal Code:** 210 613.

⌐⌐ ACCOMMODATIONS AND FOOD. ▨ **Nassan's Guest House ❷,** one block west of Sukhbaatar Square, is a longtime backpacker favorite run by a savvy Mongolian woman and her English-speaking lieutenants. Call or email ahead for free pick-up from the train station. (☎32 10 78; nassan2037@yahoo.com. Dorms US$4; doubles US$12.) For a truly Mongolian experience, head to **Gana's Guest House ❶** (☎/fax 36 73 43; ganasger@magicnet.mn.) near the Gandan Khiid monastery. To get there from Sukhbaatar Sq., follow Khudaldaany St. west until it ends at a small canal. Walk over the pedestrian bridge; the guesthouse is 50m ahead, in a less than pleasant neighborhood. The guest house consists of five *gers* (yurts) with four to five beds each, a dormitory with 20 beds, and private doubles. The hot shower and outhouses are in back, but the comfy beds and panoramic views compensate for the inconvenience. (Dorms US$3; *ger* US$5; doubles US$10.)

The distinctive smell of mutton fat wafts from every authentic Mongolian eatery. Virtually all Mongolian dishes, such as the popular *buza* (буза; meat dumplings), contain this staple ingredient. Many street cafes offer Mongolian fare for less than US$2. However, if it's not to your liking, other options are readily available. A lavish buffet of local and Korean fare awaits at **Chinggis Restaurant ❹,** 15-20min. northwest of the square on Boga Toyruu St. on the right-hand side. (Buffet 7000T before 6pm, 8500T after 6pm. Music nightly 7-10pm. Open daily noon-10pm.) For decent pizza (2800T), head to the **Khan Brau Restaurant and Pub ❷,** a block south of the square on the left side of Chinggis Ave. The place jumps with live music and is an excellent place to try Mongolian beer and Chinggis vodka. (Open Tu-Sa 10am-midnight.) At **Taj Mahal ❺,** on Boga Toyruu St. behind the white radar towers, Mongolian women in Indian dress serve a variety of south Indian dishes. (Kebabs 2600-6650T; vegetarian meals 2600-3500T. Open daily noon-2:30pm and 6-10pm. MC/V.) **Sapphire ❷,** a Thai restaurant opposite the southern edge of Sukhbaatar Square, has an excellent lunch special for 2300T. (Open M-Sa 11am-11pm, Su 1pm-9pm.)

◙ **SIGHTS.** South of Sukhbaatar Sq., between Chinghis Khaan Ave. and Marx St., stands the fantastic ▨ **Monastery-Museum of Choijin Lama,** a complex of five temples converted into a museum. It is crammed with colorful treasures, including 108 masks used in ceremonial Tsam dancing, and a handful of Tantric sculptures worthy of careful study. (Open May-Sept. daily 9am-8pm; Oct.-Apr. W-Su 10am-6pm. US$2.) The **Gandan Khiid Monastery** is the center of Mongolian Buddhism. Built in 1785, the monastery was partially destroyed by the Communists in the 1930s and restored in 1990. The main temple houses a colossal statue of Janraisig, the Buddha of compassion and mercy. Follow the directions to Gana's Guest House (see **Accommodations**, p. 731), but continue through the residential neighborhood and turn right at the main road; the monastery is on the top of the hill. Visit on Sunday around noon to see the complex at full throttle. (Monastery open 24hr. Main temple open daily 9am-4pm.) The elegant, overgrown home of Mongolia's last king, the **Bogd Khaan Winter Palace Museum,** exhibits religious and cultural artifacts from the 17th to 20th centuries, as well as a collection of preserved animals. From the

RUSSIA

Bayangol Hotel on Chinggis Ave., take bus #7 (200T) or any bus marked "зайсан" (zaisan) two stops. (Open Su-Tu and F-Sa 10am-5pm. US$2.) The **National Museum of Mongolian History** displays remnants from the Hunnu Empire, Halh marriage headdresses, and an exhibit detailing the domination of Asia by Chinggis Khan. The three-floored museum also catalogues Mongolia's socialist and aerospace histories. The museum is located to the left of the government building, at the north edge of the square. Ask for the free English brochure. (☎32 56 56; nmmh@mongol.net. Open daily in summer 10am-6pm, last admittance 5:15pm; in winter daily 10am-5pm. 2000T, students 500T. Photos 10,000T.) The **Zanabazar Museum of Fine Arts,** on Khudaldaany St., two blocks west of the square, is named for the king, painter, linguist, and architect. It exhibits his works and a collection of prehistoric and folk-art masterpieces. (☎326 060. Open in summer daily 9am-6pm; in winter daily 10am-5pm. 2400T, students 1000T.) To see **modern Mongolian art,** check out the gallery next to Sapphire (see **Accommodations and Food**), which displays the work of local artists. The popular **Naadam Festival,** held annually July 11-13, features national competitions in wrestling, archery, and horsemanship. Book accommodations well in advance if you plan to be in town during the festival.

🔲 NIGHTLIFE. Raid your rucksack for those hotpants, iron them out, and ask any cab driver to take you to "the disco"—he'll bring you to whichever one is currently hip among UB's night crowd. Or try **UB Palace,** a huge disco on the outskirts of the city. (Open Th-Su 8pm-3am. 1000T.) A quieter crowd ponders in Dali-esque decor at **Apollon Art Cafe,** 7 Enkh Tayvan, opposite the Russian Embassy, two and a half blocks east of the square. (☎32 98 53. Open M-Sa noon-midnight.)

KHABAROVSK (ХАБАРОВСК) ☎(8)4212

If you're ever exiled to Siberia, hope that you're sent to Khabarovsk (pop. 700,000). During the summer, the last major Trans-Siberian city before Vladivostok blooms; wide boulevards sprout cafes, the banks of the Amur River fill up with sunbathers, and ice-cream vendors make out like bandits. The city's rough past—as a garrison and fur-trading post—seems like a myth during the months when Khabarovsk's youth lounge in the sun for hours on end in Lenin Square. Today Khabarovsk remains a vital trade center for Russian and Chinese goods, and if you can spare a moment to lift your head from your beach blanket, you'll see an extremely pleasant city bustling with both commerce and leisure.

 TIME CHANGE. Khabarovsk is 7hr. ahead of Moscow (GMT+10).

E TRANSPORTATION. Few people start or end a Trans-Siberian journey in Khabarovsk, but it's certainly possible. Trains run to **Ulan Ude** (50hr., 1-2 per day, 1496R) and **Vladivostok** (14hr., 2 per day, 750R). **Aeroflot** and other airlines sell tickets on the ground floor of Hotel Intourist. (Open daily 9am-9pm. ☎38 71 54. MC/V.) They go to **Moscow** (1-2 per day, 6000-8000R); **Novosibirsk** (daily, 4000R); **Harbin, CHI** (M, W, F; US$150). It's also possible to take a **boat** up the Amur into China. Agencies around the boat terminal (rechnoy vokzal; речной вокзал) sell tickets for boats to **Fuyuan, CHI** (9am, about 900R); from there you can catch a bus to Harbin.

🔳🔂 ORIENTATION AND PRACTICAL INFORMATION. Khabarovsk's **train station** is on the eastern edge of the city; the **Amur River** forms the western edge. **Ul. Leningradskaya** (Ленинградская) follows the train tracks north-south. From the train station, **Amursky bulvar** (Амурский булвар) heads east-west to the river; **ul.**

Lenina (Ленина) runs parallel to Amursky farther south. Between these streets are **ul. Karla Marksa** (Карла Маркса) and **ul. Muravyova Amurskovo** (Муравьова Амурского), which meet at **Lenin Square** (ploshchad Lenina; Площад ленина).

In the corner of the stadium by the waterfront, there is a **Chinese consulate** that will issue visas in five days. (Open M, W, F 10am-1pm.) The most convenient **ATM** and **currency exchange** facilities are near Gostinitsa Sapporo, close to the river at the end of ul. Muravyova Amurskovo. A **telephone office** in Lenin Square allows for calls to Europe or North America. (Open daily 8am-10pm.) The **Internet Center** on ul. Muravyova Amurskovo, one block from Lenin Square, charges more during peak hours. (Open daily 8am-10pm. 31-42R per hr.) The **post office,** 28 ul. Muravyova Amurskovo, is several blocks from Lenin Square. (Open M-F 8am-8pm, Sa-Su 9am-6pm.)

ⁿⁿ ACCOMMODATIONS AND FOOD. Khabarovsk is lovely in many ways, but accommodation and food are not among them. **Gostinitsa Turist ❷** (Гостиница Турист), on ul. Leningradskaya, 1km south of the train station, is as cheap as you'll get. It's a drab but harmless Soviet throwback. (☎31 04 17. Singles 400R; doubles 700R; triples 850R.) A more luxurious option is **Gostinitsa Amur ❸** (Гостиница Амур), ul. Lenina 29, at the corner of ul. Dzerzhinskovo (ул. Дзержинского), which has a friendly staff and big rooms. (☎22 12 23. Singles 630-730R; doubles 640-840R.)

A few tourist-oriented restaurants on ul. Muravyova Amurskovo serve good food, but in general the city has slim pickings. **Restoran Sapporo ❺** (Песторан Саппоро), at the river end of ul. Muravyova Amurskovo, is probably one of the best sushi bars in the Russian Far East. Its prices are not as high as those in Tokyo, but then neither is the quality of the sushi. (Open daily noon-midnight. Sushi platter 410R. MC/V.) **Kafe Fregat ❸** (Кафе Фрегат), on the south side of Amursky bul., 500m from the train station, is an excellent seafood joint hidden underground. (Open daily 11am-11pm.) Khabarovsk's other options include an array of street food served on the riverfront, including *morozhenoe* (мороженое; ice cream).

◙ SIGHTS. Khabarovsk's main attraction is its riverfront, which varies from sandy beach near ul. Muravyova Amurskovo to rocky gravel at points farther south. For rainy days, consider a trip to the trio of museums set 50m back from the river, a short walk north of ul. Muravyova Amurskovo. The **Khabarovsk Lore Museum,** in a red brick building, combines exhibits on history, prehistory, and natural history. The taxidermy leaves something to be desired, but the ethnographic department has Siberia's best showcase of aboriginal artifacts. (Open Tu noon-6pm, W-Su 10am-6pm. 90R; W free.) The adjacent **Art Museum** displays Russian and indigenous art. (Open Tu-Su 10am-5pm.) The **Military Museum** across the street commemorates Khabarovsk's beginnings as a garrison and is surrounded by a graveyard of decommissioned tanks. (Open Tu-Su 10am-7pm. 90R.) A few hundred meters south of the train station on ul. Leningradskaya sits the **Church of Christ's Birth** (Христорождесвенская церков), a small orthodox establishment packed with icons and idols. There is a regular evening service at 5pm. Finally, the **Trader's Market** outside of town provides a diversion if you don't mind wading through stalls of cheap clothes and gadgets from across the border. Take minibus #42 (5R) to get there. (Open daily 9am-early afternoon. 1R.)

VLADIVOSTOK (ВЛАДИВОСТОК)   ☎(8)4232

The Trans-Siberian's eastern terminus lies on a small crook of land at the far lower-right side of the Russian landmass. Land borders with China and North Korea provide trade routes for East Asian goods, and a ferry crosses the Sea of

RUSSIA

Japan regularly. Nevertheless, Vladivostok is a distinctly Russian city, and a short-term visitor might easily mistake it for a metropolis much closer to Moscow. European faces vastly outnumber those with Asiatic features, and few speak languages other than Russian. This Slavic domination would please Vladivostok's founders, who were proud that their hilly city represented the farthest reach of Russia's cultural tentacles. During the Soviet period, Vladivostok was sealed from foreigners, and even today it has the air of a city not quite used to showing its public face.

 TIME CHANGE. Vladivostok is 7hr. ahead of Moscow (GMT+10).

TRANSPORTATION. Flights leave at least once a day for Moscow, but the train is much cheaper and more popular. Trains go to **Khabarovsk** (14hr., 2-3 per day, 740R), **Moscow** (7 days, every other day, 4700R), and **Harbin, CHI** (20hr., 3-4 per week, 1150R). Buy tickets on the ground floor of the **train station**. (Ul. Aleutskaya. Open 24hr.) **Ferries** leave for the Japanese port of Niigata 2-3 times per week. Prices vary by port, class, and time of year, but expect to pay at least US$300 for a one-way trip.

ORIENTATION AND PRACTICAL INFORMATION. Vladivostok's curving coastline and rolling landscape make it tough to navigate beyond the city center. The **airport** is several kilometers north of the city; taxi drivers should settle for less than 300R for a trip to town. Bus #205 (22R) runs every hour toward the city; at the end of the line just hop into any of the minibuses marked "tsenter" (центр) or "vokzal" (вокзал) to continue into the city center (5R). The center itself is easily walkable. The main drags are **ul. Aleutskaya** (Алейтская), which runs north-south, and **ul. Svetlanskaya** (Светланская), which runs east-west. West of the city center is **Amursky Gulf** (Амурский Залив), and southeast of it is **Golden Horn Bay** (Бухта Золотой Рог). The **train station** and **ferry station** are on ul. Aleutskaya.

A **24hr. ATM** (MC/V) sits across ul. Aleutskaya from the station in a square with (surprise!) a statue of Lenin. At the south end of the train station is **24hr. luggage storage** (15-40R). The square has a well-stocked **pharmacy** (☎51 57 54. Open daily 8am-8pm.), as well as a **phone** and **Internet** center (45R per hour; open daily 8am-9pm). The **post office** is also in the square. (Open daily 8am-8pm.)

ACCOMMODATIONS AND FOOD. Vladivostok's hotels are not kind to the budget traveler. The better ones cater to Chinese and Japanese visitors willing to shell out more than the average backpacker, while the cheaper ones might not meet your desired comfort level. The best of the latter category is the centrally-located **Na Domu ❶** (На Дому). To get there, go north from the train station on ul. Aleutskaya and take the third left onto ul. Semyenovskaya (Семеновская). Na Domu is on the right, set back from the street, above a Korean restaurant. It is relatively cozy, although passing trains may give you some headaches. (☎26 51 38. Singles 200R; doubles 500-600R.) **Gostinitsa Vladivostok ❺** (Гостиница Владивосток) boasts the best views over Amursky Gulf. To get there, walk toward Amursky Gulf on ul. Morskaya (ул. Морская) from the ferry terminal. As you walk uphill, follow the road as it bends right over the gulf. The hotel has become a favorite among Chinese tourists and North Korean delegations. Call ahead, as the cheap rooms fill up fast. (☎41 28 08; vladhotel@fastmail.vladivostok.ru. Singles 1000R; doubles 1500-3600R. MC/V.) **Gostinitsa Primorye ❹** (Гостиница Приморье), uphill from the business center across from the train station, is lower-key and a little cheaper, but offers a similar level of comfort. (☎41 14 22. Doubles 1000-4000R.)

Vladivostok's high-quality Asian restaurants mark it as a cultural crossroads. Near the Lenin statue, **Phoenix ❹** (Феникс) cooks fried rice and noodles alongside

Russian standards. (Entrees 100-300R. Open daily noon-2am.) Hidden underground is a fine sushi bar, **Edem ❸** (Эдем). Walk east on ul. Svetlanskaya from ul. Aleutskaya until you reach Oleansky Prospekt, opposite the statues. Go one block uphill and turn right; Edem is 20m away on the right side. The chefs are Russian, the wasabi is Japanese, and the atmosphere is a cross between Tokyo-business-lunch and medieval dungeon. (Sushi with red caviar 120R. Open M-Th and Su 11am-midnight, F-Sa 11am-2am.) For Russian cuisine, try **Nostalgia ❺** (Ностalgия), on ul. Morskaya, 50m north of the Lenin statue. (Delicious salmon with white sauce 210R. Open daily 10am-10pm.)

◙ **SIGHTS.** Three huge statues overlooking Golden Horn Bay comprise the **Memorial to the Fighters for Soviet Power in the Far East,** south of ul. Svetrlanskaya. The figures' rough attire and scruffy appearance reflect the frontiersmanship inherent in the conquest of the East. The square surrounding the memorial is Vladivostok's premier site for public gatherings, street performances, and weekend vendors. Facing the central statue, turn left on ul. Svetlanskaya and walk 500m to get to the **Arsenev Regional Museum** (Muzey Arseneva; Музей Арсенева). The museum showcases the history and ethnography of the Russian Far East. On the ground floor is an exhibit of wild Siberian beasts stuffed with sawdust and labeled with helpful English signs that say things like "valuable furry animal." (Open Tu-Su 10:30am-5:30pm. 70R.) Pieces were donated from Moscow's Tretyakov Museum (p. 651) and the Hermitage (p. 677) to start the collection of Vladivostok's excellent **Primorsky Art Gallery** (Primorskaya Kartinnaya Galereya; Приморская Картинная Галерея), 200m south of the Arsenev Museum on ul. Aleutskaya. The Titian in the first gallery is a fake, but nearly all the other canvases are genuine—and impressive. The children's exhibition on the ground floor indicates astonishing talent among Siberian youth. (Open W-Sa 10am-1pm and 2pm-6:30pm, Su 11am-5pm. 70R.) On the waterfront east of the monument is a **Soviet submarine** that has been gutted and converted to a museum. Claustrophobics beware. (Open Tu-Su. 15R.) Vladivostok's coastline teems with aquatic life, some of which has been trapped in glass boxes for your amusement at the local **aquarium.** Species are named in Latin and Russian only, but their diversity makes for a worthwhile visit. To get there, follow the coast of Amursky Gulf north for 20 minutes from Hotel Vladivostok. (Open daily 10am-8pm. 70R.) Slightly farther up the coast is a **dolphinarium** with a handful of beautiful and well-behaved dolphins and sea lions. (Open Tu-Su 10am-6pm. 70R.)

RUSSIA

SLOVAK REPUBLIC
(SLOVENSKA REPUBLIKA)

KORUNA

AUS$1 = 24.22SK	10SK = AUS$0.41
CDN$1 = 28.32SK	10SK = CDN$0.35
EUR€1 = 43.39SK	10SK = EUR€0.23
NZ$1 = 20.64SK	10SK = NZ$0.48
UK£1 = 68.36SK	10SK = UK£0.15
US$1 = 44.08SK	10SK = US$0.23
ZAR1 = 4.15SK	10SK = ZAR2.41

After a history scarred by nomadic invasions, Hungarian domination, and Soviet industrialization, the Slovak Republic has finally emerged as an independent nation. However, freedom has introduced new challenges and the nation remains in a state of flux between industry and agriculture, unable to muster the resources necessary for a complete modernization and unwilling to return to its past. What remains is an unusual mixture of fairy-tale traditionalism and easy-going youthfulness that combine with low prices to create a haven for budget travelers. From its tiny villages to the busy capital, the Slovak Republic is coming to grips with the modern world, as the good old days retreat to castle ruins, pastures, and the stunning Tatras above.

SLOVAK REPUBLIC AT A GLANCE

OFFICIAL NAME: Slovak Republic

CAPITAL: Bratislava (pop. 452,000)

POPULATION: 5.4 million (86% Slovak, 11% Hungarian, 3% other)

LANGUAGES: Slovak, Hungarian

CURRENCY: 1 koruna (Sk) = 100 halierov

RELIGION: 60% Roman Catholic, 10% Atheist, 8% Protestant, 22% other

LAND AREA: 48,845km²

GEOGRAPHY: Mountainous, with lowlands in the southwest and east

CLIMATE: Temperate

BORDERS: Austria, Czech Republic, Hungary, Poland, Ukraine

ECONOMY: 65% Services, 30% Industry, 5% Agriculture

GDP: US$10,200 per capita

COUNTRY CODE: 421

INTERNATIONAL DIALING PREFIX: 00

HISTORY

CAN'T WE ALL JUST GET ALONG? After **Roman occupation** from AD 6 until the fall of the Roman Empire, the area of the Slovak Republic was brutally contested. The **Slavs** established dominance by the 6th century, defeating the Franks in 631. An initial Slav empire fell in 665, but the Slavs remained strong enough to contain invasions from Asian tribes. A new Slav state was formed in 833 after **Prince Mojmír** of Moravia came to power. Despite this unification, the Slavs were unable to fend off the Franks and Germans, and, with the triumph of the Magyars in 907, the independent Slav state was incorporated into the Hungarian Kingdom.

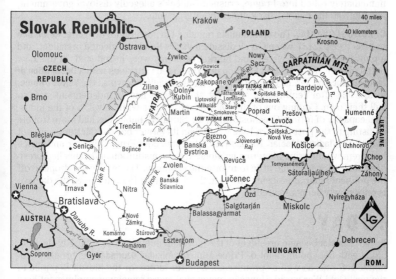

THOSE HAPPENIN' HABSBURGS. The Tatar invasions of 1241-43 devastated the already weakened Hungarians, who were finally defeated by the Ottomans in 1526. The Empire was subsequently divided and the Slovak region fell to the Habsburgs, who, from their Bratislava headquarters, managed to wrench all of Hungary free from Turkish hands.

POWER HUNGARY. A Slovak nationalist movement emerged in the 18th century, but despite the movement's momentum, Hungarian power continued to grow thanks to the establishment of the **Austro-Hungarian Dual Monarchy** in 1867. Ignoring the advice of intellectuals, the Hungarian government intensified a policy of Magyarization. This only further inspired the Slovakian nationalist movement, which blossomed through the turn of the century. On October 28, 1918, Slovakia, Bohemia, Moravia, and Ruthenia combined to form **Czechoslovakia.** The country quickly became a liberal democracy, repelling a 1919 Communist attack.

WORLD WAR II. Czechoslovakia was one of Hitler's first targets. Abandoned by Britain and France in the **Munich Agreement** of September 1938, the Slovaks clamored for their autonomy and soon got their wish, as Slovakia was proclaimed an autonomous unit within Czechoslovakia. When Hitler occupied Prague, Slovakia withdrew from the federation and established the first independent Slovak Republic, with **Father Jozef Tiso** as head of state. Tiso's decision to ally the new state with Nazi Germany dealt a devastating blow to the Slovaks, and over 70,000 Slovak Jews were sent to concentration camps. A partisan resistance emerged, culminating in August 1944 with the two-month **Slovak National Uprising.**

THE AFTERMATH. After World War II, the Slovaks again became a part of democratic Czechoslovakia. The **Communist Party** won 36% of the vote in 1946 and soon dominated the government. In February 1948, as the Popular Front government fell apart, the Communists mounted a coup, subjecting the state to Soviet domination. It took a Slovak, **Alexander Dubček,** to shake the regime from the grips of Moscow. In the 1968 **Prague Spring,** Dubček focused on expanding intellectual discussion and debate throughout the heavily censored society. Soviet tanks immediately rolled into Prague, crushed Dubček's allegedly disloyal government, and plunged the country back under totalitarian rule.

CZECHOSLOVAKIA. The communists remained in power until the **Velvet Revolution** of 1989 (see p. 218), when Czech dissident **Václav Havel** was elected president, and a pluralistic political system and market economy were introduced. In this new political environment, Slovak nationalism emerged victorious with a **Declaration of Independence** on January 1, 1993. This bloodless split, known as the **Velvet Divorce,** meant that after centuries of conquest, the Slovaks had an independent state to call their own. Coming out of the 1993 Velvet Divorce with only 25% of the industrial capacity of former Czechoslovakia, the Slovak Republic has had more trouble adjusting to the post-Eastern Bloc world than its former partner. Matters were not helped by **Vladímir Mečiar.** He has thrice been elected Prime Minister and thrice been removed. During his terms he violated the constitution and cancelled presidential elections, but did little to reform the economy. Though Mečiar dropped off the political radar after losing power in the September 1998 elections, the damage is only slowly being repaired.

TODAY

Rudolf Schuster became president of the Slovak Republic in May 1999. His election, along with the appointment of Prime Minister **Mikuláš Dzurinda,** has brought economic reforms, as well as promises of a better future for the Slovak Republic in the post-Cold War world. However, many challenges remain; unemployment hovers around 20%, one of the highest rates in Europe. As a result, many young Slovakians have opted to leave the country for its more prosperous neighbor, the Czech Republic. Racially-motivated violence is also a serious problem in the Slovak Republic, and minorities, especially the Roma (Gypsies), face substantial discrimination. In April 2002 the country was rocked by the desecration of over one hundred Jewish graves in Košice, the worst attack of its kind since the Holocaust.

PEOPLE AND CULTURE

LANGUAGE

Slovak, closely related to **Czech,** is a complex Slavic language, but any attempt to speak it will be appreciated. **English** is not uncommon among Bratislava's youth, but people outside the capital are more likely to speak **German. Russian** is occasionally understood but use it carefully, as it is sometimes unwelcome. When speaking Slovak, the two golden rules are to pronounce every letter—nothing is silent—and to emphasize the first syllable. Accents on vowels affect length, not stress. See the guidelines for pronouncing Czech (p. 220) for further guidance. For a phrasebook and glossary, see **Glossary: Slovak,** p. 891.

FOOD AND DRINK

SLOVAK	❶	❷	❸	❹	❺
FOOD	under 70Sk	70-200Sk	201-400Sk	401-700Sk	over 700Sk

The good news for vegetarians in the Slovak Republic is that the national dish, *bryndžové halušky,* is a plate of dumpling-esque pasta smothered in a thick sauce of sheep or goat cheese; the bad news is that, like many other Slovak dishes, it often comes flecked with bacon. Pork products are, in fact, central to the majority of traditional meals. *Knedliky* (dumplings) frequently accompany entrees, but it is possible to opt for *zemiaky* (potatoes) or *hranolky* (fries) instead. Dessert is *kolačky* (pastry), baked with cheese, jam or poppy seeds, and honey. White **wines** are produced northeast of Bratislava, especially around the town of Pezinok. *Tokaj* wines (distinct from Hungarian *Tokaj Aszú*) are produced around Košice. Enjoy any of these at a *vináreň* (wine hall). *Pivo* (beer) is served at a *pivnica* or *piváreň* (tavern). The favorite Slovak beer is the slightly bitter *Zlatý Bažant*.

CUSTOMS AND ETIQUETTE

Tipping is common in restaurants, although the exact rules are rather ambiguous. Most people round up to a convenient number by refusing change when they pay. **Bargaining** is not acceptable in the Slovak Republic—special offence is taken when foreigners attempt the practice. Most bus and train stations and some restaurants are **non-smoking,** though most Slovaks do smoke. Social mores tend to be fairly conservative; dressing neatly and being polite will help you to blend in. Most **museums** close Mondays, and **theaters** take a break during July and August. And be warned: **grocery store attendants** will not hesitate to accost patrons who fail to utilize the shopping baskets found by the entrance of stores.

THE ARTS

HISTORY

The Slovak arts have struggled long and hard to escape the orbit of neighboring traditions. Since the Slovak tongue only emerged as a distinct language in the 18th century, the earliest Slovak novels, such as **Ignác Bajza's** *René* (1785), were written in a Slovak dialect of Czech. A literary tradition really got started after 19th-century linguist **L'udovít Štúr**'s "new" language based on the Central Slovak dialects inspired a string of national poets. Foremost among these was **Andrej Sládkovič**, author of the national epic *Marína* (1846). Visual artists of the early 1800s looked abroad for inspiration, but toward the end of the century, painters such as **Mikoláš Aleš** turned their attention back to Slovak soil.

In the wake of World War I, Slovak nationalism and literature matured concurrently. Cosmopolitan influences began to appear alongside Romanticism: **E. B. Lukáč** introduced **Symbolism** to the Slovak tradition while **Rudolf Fábry** championed **Surrealism.** The well-established primacy of the lyric began to give way to novels and short stories. **Janko Jesenský** savaged the linchpins of the post-war government in his novel *The Democrats (Demokrati)*. Meanwhile, **Andrej Ocenasa** led a generation of composers who blended classical and folk strands in their works. After World War II, the Slovak literati reacted strongly to communist rule. In fact, **Ladislav Mnacko** was one of the first writers to speak out against Stalin, which he did through his 1967 novel *The Taste of Power*. Around the same time, **Ján Kadar** directed *The Shop on Main Street*, an Academy Award-winning film.

CURRENT SCENE

A strong artistic tradition continues in the contemporary Slovak Republic. Independence has brought a renewed interest in **folk arts,** and festivals featuring traditional crafts, dance, and music proliferate throughout the country. Classical music also remains popular, and both the **Bratislava Philharmonic Orchestra** and **Slovak Chamber Orchestra** have an international reputation. Slovak directors **Martin Sulík** and **Štefan Semjan** have become players in the international film world, despite the current lack of both funding and facilities for filmmaking in the Slovak Republic.

HOLIDAYS AND FESTIVALS

NATIONAL HOLIDAYS IN 2003	
January 1 Origin of the Slovak Republic	**August 29** Anniversary of Slovak National Uprising
January 6 Epiphany	
April 18 Good Friday	**September 1** Constitution Day
April 20 Easter	**September 15** Our Lady of the 7 Sorrows
May 1 Labor Day	**November 1** All Saint's Day
July 5 Sts. Cyril and Methodius Day	**December 24-26** Christmas

The Slovak Republic is not a festival hotbed like many of its neighbors. It is, however, home to many of Eastern Europe's more unique and unusual celebrations.

FESTIVAL OF GHOSTS AND SPIRITS. An annual celebration for those beyond the grave, held in Banská Bystrica in late April or early May.

VYCHONDNA FOLK FESTIVAL. Folk dancers from across the country gather near Poprad for this traditional celebration in June and July.

ADDITIONAL RESOURCES

GENERAL HISTORY

A History of Slovakia: The Struggle for Survival, by Stanislav Kirschbaum (1996). This comprehensive history of the Slovak Republic is well-researched, but should be read with caution; the author's views on the Holocaust are highly controversial.

Czechoslovakia: The Short Goodbye, by Abby Innes (2001). An analysis of the causes and consequences of Czechoslovakia's division into the Czech and Slovak Republics.

NONFICTION AND FILM

A History of Slovak Literature, by Peter Petro (1997). An exploration of the Slovak literary tradition with a keen eye to its political and cultural interactions.

The Shop on Main Street, directed by Jan Kadar (1965). An Academy Award-winner about a Slovak man who befriends a Jewish woman during the Holocaust.

SLOVAK REPUBLIC ESSENTIALS

ENTRANCE REQUIREMENTS
Passport: Required of all travelers.
Visa: Not required of citizens of Australia, Canada, Ireland, New Zealand, South Africa, the UK, and the US.
Letter of Invitation: Not required.
Inoculations: None required. Recommended MMR (measles, mumps, rubella), DTaP (diptheria), Polio booster, Hepatitis A, and Hepatitis B.
Work Permit: Required of all foreigners planning to work.
International Driving Permit: Required of all those planning to drive.

DOCUMENTS AND FORMALITIES

EMBASSIES AND CONSULATES

Embassies of other countries in the Slovak Republic are all in Bratislava (see p. 746). The Slovak Republic's embassies and consulates abroad include:

Australia: 47 Culgoa Circuit, O'Malley, Canberra, ACT 2606 (☎06 290 1516; fax 290 1755).

Canada: 50 Rideau Terrace, Ottawa, ON K1M 2A1 (☎613-749-4442; fax 749-4989; slovakemb@sprint.ca)

Ireland: 20 Clyde Rd., Ballsbridge, Dublin 4 (☎01 660 0012 or 660 0008)

South Africa: 930 Arcadia St., Arcadia, Pretoria; P.O. Box 12736, Hatfield, 0028 (☎012 342 2051; fax 342 3688).

UK: 25 Kensington Palace Gardens, London W8 4QY (☎020 7243 0803; fax 7313 6481; www.slovakembassy.co.uk).

US: 2201 Wisconsin Ave. NW, Suite 250, Washington, D.C. 20007 (☎202-237-1054; fax 965-5166; www.slovakemb.com).

VISA AND ENTRY INFORMATION

Citizens of South Africa and the US can visit the Slovak Republic without a visa for up to 30 days; Australia, Canada, Ireland, New Zealand for 90 days; and the UK 180 days (30-day single-entry US$28; 90-day multiple-entry US$58; 180-day multiple-entry US$79; 30-day transit US$28). Visa prices vary with the exchange rate. To apply for a visa, contact an embassy or consulate; processing may take up to 30 days. Submit your passport (which must be valid for eight months from the date of application), one visa application per planned entry, two passport photos, and a check or money order for the fee. Visas are not available at the Slovak border and there is no fee for entering or exiting the country. Travelers must **register** their visas within three days of entering the Slovak Republic; most hotels do this automatically. If you plan to stay longer or obtain a visa extension, you must notify the Office of Border and Alien Police in the town where you are staying within three business days of arrival.

TRANSPORTATION

BY PLANE. Bratislava does have an international airport, but entering the country via air is often inconvenient and expensive, as few international carriers fly here directly. Flying to nearby **Vienna,** Austria, and taking a bus or train from there is much cheaper and takes about the same amount of time.

BY TRAIN. Large train stations operate **BIJ-Wasteels** offices, which offer discounted tickets to European cities (except Prague) for those under 26. **EastRail** is valid in the Slovak Republic, but **Eurail** is not. *InterCity* or *EuroCity* fast trains cost more, and if there's a boxed R on the timetable, a *miestenka* (reservation; 7Sk) is required. If you board an international train without a reservation, expect to pay a fine. **ŽSR** is the national rail company; every information desk has a copy of **Cestovný poriadok** (58Sk), the master schedule, which is also printed on a large boards in most stations. Reservations are often required and generally recommended for *expresný* (express) trains and first-class seats, but are not necessary for *rychlík* (fast), *spešný* (semi-fast), or *osobný* (local) trains. Both first and second class are safe and relatively comfortable. Buy tickets before boarding the train, except in the tiniest towns.

BY BUS. In hilly regions, **ČSAD** or **SAD buses** are the best and sometimes the only option. Except for very long trips, buy the ticket once you have boarded the bus. You can probably ignore most of the footnotes on the bus schedules, but the following are important: **X** (two crossed hammers) means weekdays only; **a** means Saturdays and Sundays only; and **r** and **k** mean excluding holidays. **Numbers** refer to the days of the week on which the bus runs—1 is Monday, 2 is Tuesday, and so forth. *"Premava"* means including; *"nepremava"* is except; following those words are often lists of dates (the day is listed first, followed by the month).

BY BIKE. The rambling wilds and ruined castles of the Slovak Republic inspire great bike tours. The Slovaks love to ride bicycles, especially in the Tatras, the foothills of West Slovakia, and Šariš. **VKÚ** publishes color bike maps (70-80Sk).

BY THUMB. *Let's Go* does not recommend hitchhiking. Hitchhiking is neither convenient nor common in the Slovak Republic. If you decide to try it, use a sign.

TOURIST SERVICES AND MONEY

The main tourist information offices form a loose conglomeration called **Asociácia Informačných Centier Slovenska (AICS);** look for the green logo. The offices are often on or near the town's main square; the nearest one can often be found by dialing ☎ 186. English is often—but not always—spoken, and accommodation bookings can usually—but not always—be made. **Slovakotourist,** a travel agency, can be of assistance in arranging transport and accommodations. MasterCard and Visa are the most useful **credit cards** in the Slovak Republic, although credit cards are not accepted in most places. After the 1993 Czech-Slovak split, the Slovak Republic hastily designed its own currency, which is now its only legal tender. One hundred **halér** make up one Slovak **koruna (Sk).** Inflation is currently around 7%. **Banks** are usually the best, and often the only, place to exchange currency. **Všeobecná Úverová Banka (VÚB)** has offices in most town and cashes AmEx Travelers Cheques for 1% commission; most offices also give MC **cash advances.** Many **Slovenská Sporiteľňa** offices handle **Visa** cash advances. **ATMs** can be found in all but the smallest towns.

HEALTH AND SAFETY

 EMERGENCY NUMBERS: Police: ☎ 123 **Fire:** ☎ 23 **Ambulance:** ☎ 233

HEALTH AND SAFETY. Tap water varies in quality and appearance but is generally safe. If it comes out of the faucet cloudy, let it sit for five minutes—it's just air bubbles. A reciprocal agreement between the Slovak Republic and the UK entitles Brits to free medical care here. *Drogeries* (drugstores) stock Western brand names; obtaining supplies shouldn't be hard. Bandages are *obväz*, aspirin *aspirena*, tampons *tampony*, and condoms *kondómy*. Petty **crime** is common; be vigilant in crowded areas and ensure that passports and other valuables are secure.

WOMEN, MINORITY, AND BGLT TRAVELERS. Women traveling alone should have few problems in the Slovak Republic, though they may encounter stares. Cautionary measures, such as dressing modestly and avoiding walking or riding public transportation at night are recommended. **Minority** travelers with darker skin may be mistaken for Roma (Gypsies), who suffer discrimination in the Slovak Republic, and are thus advised to exercise caution at all times. **Homosexuality** is legal, though a gay couple walking down the street may experience stares or insults.

ACCOMMODATIONS AND CAMPING

SLOVAK	❶	❷	❸	❹	❺
ACCOM.	under 400Sk	400-800Sk	801-1100Sk	1101-1800Sk	over 1800Sk

Foreigners are often charged up to twice as much as Slovaks for the same room. Finding cheap accommodations in Bratislava before the student dorms open in July is very difficult and without reservations the outlook in Slovenský Raj and the Tatras can be bleak. In other regions, it's relatively easy to find a bed provided you call ahead. The tourist office, **SATUR**, or **Slovakotourist** can usually help.

HOSTELS AND HOTELS. There are a limited number of hostels in the Slovak Republic. Most hostels provide guests with a towel and a bar of soap. **Juniorhotels (HI),** though uncommon, are a step above the usual hostel. **Hotel** prices fall dramatically outside Bratislava and the Tatras, and accommodations outside these areas are rarely full. **Pensions** *(penzióny)* are smaller and less expensive than hotels.

CAMPING. Campgrounds lurk on the outskirts of most towns and many offer bungalows for travelers without tents. Camping in national parks is illegal. In the mountains, **chaty** (mountain huts/cottages) range from plush quarters for 400Sk per night to a friendly bunk and outhouse for 200Sk.

KEEPING IN TOUCH

MAIL. The Slovak Republic has an efficient mail service. Letters abroad take two to three weeks depending on the destination. Mail can be received general delivery through **Poste Restante.** Address envelopes as follows: Vik (first name) VAZ (last name), POSTE RESTANTE, Horná 1 (post office address), Banská Bystrica (city) 97400 (postal code), SLOVAKIA. Almost every post office *(pošta)* provides **express mail** services. To send a package abroad, head to a *colnice* (customs office).

TELEPHONES. Card phones are common and are usually much better than the coin-operated variety. Purchase cards (200Sk) at kiosks. Be sure to buy the "Global Phone" card if you plan on making international calls.

INTERNET. Internet access is common in the Slovak Republic, even in smaller towns. Internet cafes usually offer the cheapest and fastest access.

BRATISLAVA
☎ (0)2

One of only two regions in Eastern Europe with living standards above the European Union average, the Slovak capital will surprise those who take the time to discover it. Ambient cafes and elegant edifices line its cobblestoned Old Town, while vineyards and castles lace the outskirts of the city. The city has undergone major renovations since the collapse of communist rule after the Velvet Revolution of 1989, and the peaceful division of Czechoslovakia in 1993. The past ten years have seen vast improvements in the city's outlook, and progress now shows no sign of stopping. Forging ahead in both industry and the arts, Bratislava is reveling in its new independence.

✈ INTERCITY TRANSPORTATION

Flights: M.R. Štefánik International Airport (☎48 57 11 11), 15km northeast of the center. To reach the center, take bus #61 to the train station and then take tram #1 to "Poštová" on Nám. SNP. More airlines frequent the airport in nearby Vienna. The follow-

IN RECENT NEWS

THE WAITING GAME

Anyone who has had the pleasure of riding a bus or tram during Bratislava's rush hour would agree that the city's public transport system leaves something to be desired. For decades, there has been talk about building a subway to ease the pressure on the city's buses, and at one point construction on a subway system even began. Unfortunately, before the idea could be realized, the then-Communist government found itself unemployed, and with the new government came reluctance to finance public projects which would increase the already substantial public debt.

In recent years, however, as Bratislava's prosperity has led to an increasing number of cars crossing the city's four bridges and a growing population that overcrowds public transportation, the dream of a subway has resurfaced. In 1997, the city magistrate created a company called "Metro" to design and construct a subway system beneath the city. Public support for the once-popular project began to decline as it became increasingly evident that progress was not occurring at a rapid pace. In fact, the city recently took steps to address discontent by increasing the subway company's workload: plans for a subway system have once again been put on hold while "Metro" takes charge of the construction of a new bridge over the Danube in a more immediate attempt to ease traffic while people "wait" for the subway.

—Matej Sapak

ing carriers have local offices: **Austrian Airlines** (☎ 54 41 16 10; www.ava.com), **ČSA** (☎ 52 96 10 42; www.czech-airlines.com), **Delta** (☎ 52 92 09 40; www.delta-air.com), **LOT** (☎ 52 96 40 07; www.lot.com), **Lufthansa** (☎ 52 96 78 15; www.lufthansa.com).

Trains: Bratislava Hlavná Stanica (☎ 52 49 82 75). From the center, head up Štefánikova, turn right on Šancová, then left on the road lined with buses. International tickets at counters #5-13. The **Wasteels** office (☎ 52 49 93 57; www.wasteels.host.sk) sells discounted international tickets to those under 26. Open M-F 8:30am-4:30pm. To: **Banská Bystrica** (5½hr., every 2-3hr., 230Sk); **Košice** (6hr., every 2hr., 414Sk); **Poprad-Tatry** (4¾hr.; every 2hr.; 336Sk); **Berlin, GER** (10hr., 2 per day, 3136Sk); **Budapest, HUN** (2½-3hr., 7 per day, 499Sk); **Kraków, POL** (8hr., 1 per day, 1460Sk); **Prague, CZR** (5hr., 7 per day, 415Sk); **Vienna, AUS** (1½hr., 3 per day, 561Sk); **Warsaw, POL** (8hr., 1 per day, 1707Sk).

Buses: Mlynské nivy 31 (☎ 55 42 16 67). From Nám. SNP, turn left on Suché Mýto and left again on Dunajska. Mlynské nivy is 2km up on the right. More frequent and more consistent than trains. Check your ticket for the bus number (*č. aut.*), as several buses may depart from the same stand. To: **Banská Bystrica** (3-4hr., 12 per day, 100Sk); **Košice** (7-8hr., every 2hr., 300-500Sk); **Poprad-Tatry** (5½-6½hr., 5 per day, 350Sk); **Berlin, GER** (12hr., F 9pm, 1800Sk); **Budapest, HUN** (4hr., 1 per day, 480Sk); **Prague, CZR** (5hr., 7 per day, 320Sk); **Vienna, AUS** (1½hr., 7 per day, 350Sk); **Warsaw, POL** (13hr., F 9:20pm, 670Sk).

Hydrofoils: Lodná osobná doprava, Fajnorovo nábr. 2 (☎ 52 93 22 or 52 93 35 18; fax 52 93 22 31; www.spap.sk), along the river. A scenic alternative for Danube destinations. Book tickets at least 48hr. in advance and show up at least 30min. early. May-Oct. 1. To: **Devín Castle** (20min., T-Su 2 per day, 70Sk); **Budapest, HUN** (4hr., 1-2 per day, 750Sk); **Vienna, AUS** (1½hr., 1 per day, 240Sk). AmEx/MC/V.

◼ ORIENTATION

The **Dunaj** (Danube) runs west-east across Bratislava. The city's southern half consists mainly of a convention center, an amusement park, the shopping mall **AuPark,** and **Petrzalka,** miles of high-rises usually referred to as the "concrete jungle." Four bridges span the Danube; **Nový Most** (New Bridge) connects **Staromestská** and the commercial and entertainment area on the river's southern bank. **Bratislavský Hrad** (Bratislava Castle) towers on a hill to the west, while the city center sits between the river and **Námestie Slovenského Národného Povstania** (**Nám. SNP;** Slovak National Uprising Square). When entering Bratislava by train, make sure to get off at **Hlavná Stanica,** the central train station. From the station, take tram #1 to "Poštová" near Nám. SNP. From the **bus station,** take trolley #202 to the center, or turn right on Mlynské nivy and walk to Dunajská, which leads to **Kamenné nám.** (Stone Square) and the center of town.

⊟ LOCAL TRANSPORTATION

Local Transportation: Tram and **bus** tickets are sold at kiosks or at the orange *automaty* in bus stations. (10min. 12Sk; 30min. 14Sk; 60min. 20Sk) Be sure the light is on before dropping coins into an *automat*. Trams and buses run 4am-11pm. **Night buses,** marked with black and orange numbers in the 500s, run between midnight and 4am; these require 2 tickets. Stamp your ticket when you get on board; joyriding will cost you 1200Sk. Some kiosks and ticket machines sell **tourist passes.** (1 day 75Sk, 2 days 140Sk, 3 days 170Sk, 7 days 255Sk for a ticket valid on all lines; 65Sk/120Sk/145Sk/215Sk for tickets valid in the center only.)

Taxis: BP (☎16 999); **FunTaxi** (☎16 777); **Profi Taxi** (☎16 222).

Hitchhiking: Those hitching to **Vienna, AUS** cross Most SNP and walk down Viedenská cesta. This road also heads to **Hungary** via Győr, though fewer cars head in that direction. Hitchers to **Prague, CZR** take bus #21 from the center to the Patronka stop. For destinations within the Slovak Republic, take tram #2 or 4 to "Zlaté Piesky." Hitching is legal (except on major highways), but *Let's Go* does not recommend it.

Bratislava

⌂ ▲ ACCOMMODATIONS

Autocamping Zlaté Piesky, **1**
Družba, **12**
Hotel Astra, **5**
Pension Gremium, **10**
Ubytovacie Zariadenie Zvárat, **2**

🍴 FOOD

1. Slovak Pub, **4**
Black Rose, **8**
Prašná Bašta, **7**
Prešporská Kúria, **6**

🍸 NIGHTLIFE

Club 39, **13**
Dubliner Irish Pub, **9**
Duna, **3**
Kelt Bar and Grill, **11**

SLOVAK REPUBLIC

🛈 PRACTICAL INFORMATION

TOURIST AND FINANCIAL SERVICES

Tourist Office: Bratislavská Informačná Služba (BIS), Klobúčnicka 2 (☎16 186 or 54 43 37 15; fax 54 43 27 08; www.bratislava.sk/bis). Books **private rooms** and hotel rooms for a 50Sk fee, sells **maps** (60Sk), and gives **city tours** (1000Sk for a group of 1-19). Open M-F 8am-7pm, Sa 9am-2pm. Also sells a **museum pass** (75Sk) that allows free entrance to four of the city's major museums and the zoo. **Branch** in the train station annex open M-F 9am-6pm, Sa-Su 9am-2pm.

Budget Travel: CKM 2000 Travel, Vysoká 32 (☎52 73 10 24; www.ckm.sk).

Embassies: For a list of all local consulates and embassies, check www.foreign.gov.sk. **Australians** and **New Zealanders** should contact the British Embassy in an emergency. **Canada,** Mišíkova 28D (☎52 41 21 75; fax 52 41 21 76). Open M-F 8:30am-noon and 1:30-4pm. **Ireland,** Mostová 2 (☎54 43 57 15; fax 54 43 06 90). Open M-F 9am-noon. **South Africa,** Jančova 8 (☎53 11 582; fax 53 12 581; embassy@sae.sk). Open M-F 8:30am-5pm. **UK,** Panská 16 (☎54 41 96 32 or 54 41 96 33; fax 54 41 00 02; bebra@internet.sk). Open M-F 8:30am-12:30pm and 1:30-5pm. Visa office open M-F 9-11am. **US,** Hviezdoslavovo nám. 4 (☎54 43 08 61, emergency 0903 70 36 66; fax 54 41 51 48; front@usis.sk). Open M-F 8am-4:30pm. Visa office open M-F 8-11:30am.

Currency Exchange: VÚB, Gorkého 7 (☎59 55 11 11; fax 59 92 18 80). Cashes **traveler's checks** for 1% commission and handles MC/V **cash advances.** Open M-W and F 8am-5pm, Th 8am-noon. There's a 24hr. **currency exchange machine** outside Československá Obchodná Banka on the corner of Michalská and Zámočnícka. There are 24hr. MC/V **ATMs** at the train station and throughout the center.

LOCAL SERVICES

Luggage Storage: At the bus station. 10Sk, 20Sk for bags over 15kg. Open M-F 6am-noon, 12:30-7:30pm, and 8-10pm, Sa-Su 6am-noon and 12:30-6pm. Also at the train station 10Sk, 20Sk for bags over 10kg. Open daily 6:30am-10pm.

English-Language Bookstores: Eurobooks, Jesenského 5/9 (☎/fax 54 41 79 59; www.eurobooks.sk). Extensive selection of English-language literature. Open M-F 8:30am-6:30pm, Sa 9am-1pm. **Interpress Slovakia** (☎44 87 15 01; interpress@interpress.sk), on the corner of Sedlárska and Michalská, carries foreign press. Open M-F 7am-11pm, Sa 9am-11pm, Su 10am-10pm.

Laundromat: INPROKOM, Laurinská 18 (☎54 13 11 42). 2-day dry cleaning 10-85Sk per garment; 1-week laundry 12-49Sk per garment. Open M-F 10:30am-6pm.

EMERGENCY AND COMMUNICATION

Police: ☎ 158 **Fire:** ☎ 150 **Medical Emergencies:** ☎ 155

24-Hour Pharmacy: Lekáreň Pod Manderlom, Nám. SNP 20 (☎54 43 29 52), on the corner of Štúrova and Laurinská. Open M-F 7:30am-7pm, Sa 8am-5pm, Su 9am-5pm. Ring the bell after hours for emergency service.

Internet Access: On-Line Internet Cafe, Obchodná 2. A large Internet cafe and bar, often open longer than the official hours. 1Sk per min., 42Sk per hr. with 30Sk registration fee. Open M-F 9:30am-midnight, Sa 10am-midnight, Su 10am-11pm. **Internet Centrum,** Michalská 2. 4 computers and a kind staff that brings you tea as you type (1Sk per min.). Open M-Su 9am-midnight.

Telephones: All over town. Purchase cards (150Sk) at the post office and at kiosks.

Post Office: Nám. SNP 34 (☎49 22 24 13). **Poste Restante** at counter #5. Offers **fax** service. Open M-F 7am-8pm, Sa 7am-6pm, Su 9am-2pm. Poste Restante M-F 7am-8pm, Sa 7am-2pm.

Postal Code: 81000 Bratislava 1.

ACCOMMODATIONS

During July and August, several university dorms open up as hostels. Contact **BIS** ❶ (see **Tourist Office**, p. 746) for further information. Although the beds are cheap (starting below 150Sk), their age tends to show. Pensions or **private rooms** (600-2500Sk; see **Tourist Office**, above) are a cheap and comfortable alternative.

Ubytovacie Zariadenie Zvárat, Pionierska 17 (☎49 24 66 00; fax 49 24 62 76; www.vuz.sk). Take tram #3 from the train station or #5 or 11 from the city center toward "Raca-Komisárky" to "Pionierska." Walk back to the intersection, then turn right. This lively university dorm houses modest but clean rooms with shared baths. Check-in noon. Check-out 10am. Ring the bell after midnight. Singles 700Sk, F-Su 560Sk, with TV 750Sk/600Sk; doubles 800-1000Sk/640-800Sk. ❷

Hotel Astra, Prievozská 14/A (☎58 23 81 11, reservations 58 23 82 22; fax 53 41 35 26; www.hotelastra.sk). Take bus #201 from the train station or 202 from the bus station toward "Cilizská" to "Mileticova." Communist in appearance, though the recently renovated rooms are comfortable and equipped with satellite TV, phone, radio, and balcony. One bathroom and refrigerator for every two rooms. Breakfast 70Sk. Doubles 1000Sk; triples 1200Sk; apartments 2000-2500Sk. ❸

Pension Gremium, Gorkého 11 (☎54 13 10 26; fax 54 43 06 53; cherry-tour@mail.pvt.sk). Just off Hviezdoslavovo nám. Sparkling private showers, a cafe, and English-speaking receptionists make this pension truly agreeable. Breakfast 67-157Sk. Check-out noon. Only 5 rooms, so call several weeks in advance. Singles 890Sk; doubles 1290Sk-1590Sk. AmEx/MC/V. ❸

Družba, Botanická 25 (☎65 42 98 08). Take tram #1 from the train station toward "Pri Kríži" to "Botanická Záhrada." Known among university students as the "interhotel," Družba is the most luxurious of Bratislava's student dorms. Although not quite what its nickname promises, the rooms here are clean and comfortable. Singles 650Sk; doubles 900Sk. ❷

Autocamping Zlaté Piesky, Senecká Cesta 2 (☎44 45 05 92; fax 44 25 73 73; www.intercamp.sk), at the suburban Zlaté Pieksy lake. Take tram #2 from the train station or #4 from the city center to the last stop and cross the footbridge. Campground and bungalows by the lake, 25min. from town. Clean bathroom facilities. Laundry 60Sk. 60-70Sk per adult, 30-40Sk per child. Tent 30-60Sk. Car 40Sk. Caravan 80-90Sk. Cottage doubles (no bath) 250-310Sk; triples 370-470Sk; quads 490-620Sk; bungalow triples (with bath) 660-830Sk; quads 1000-1400Sk. ❶

FOOD

Although most restaurants now serve mainly Austrian and international cuisine, you can usually find a few local specialities on the menu. A particular Slovak favorite is *bryndžové halušky*, potato dumplings with sheep's cheese. Vegetarians, beware; although they are often listed as "meatless" the dumplings usually come with fried bacon. **Tesco Potraviny**, Kamenné nám. 1, is a huge grocery store. (Open M-F 8am-9pm, Sa 8am-7pm, Su 9am-7pm.) For a late-night snack, head to **Potraviny Nonstop**, Nám. 1. Mája 15. (Open 24hr.)

1. Slovak Pub, Obchodná 62 (☎52 63 19 51; www.slovakpub.sk). A gigantic restaurant with an outdoor terrace offering Slovak soups (28Sk) and entrees (50-120Sk) at an unbeatable price. Open M-Th 10am-midnight, F-Sa 10-2am, Su noon-midnight. ❷

Prešporská Kúria, Dunajská 21 (☎52 96 79 81; fax 52 96 47 72). A bistro, cafeteria, and restaurant, all in a small park near Kamenné nám. The bistro sells tasty pizzas (60-100Sk), while the cafeteria has a more traditional menu. Entrees 50-100Sk. Bistro open M-F 8am-5pm, cafeteria and restaurant noon-9pm. ❶

SLOVAK REPUBLIC

Prašná Bašta, Zámočnícka 11 (☎ 54 43 49 57; www.prasnabasta.sk). Sit with the sculptures in the alcoves inside, or on the leafy terrace outside. The largely 20-something crowd comes here for the most affordable cuisine in Old Town (100-185Sk). *Bryndzove halusky* 85Sk. Open daily 11am-11pm. MC/V. ❷

Black Rose, Michalská 7 (☎ 54 41 14 94). The boisterous crowd sits in the sidewalk cafe or amid fake street lanterns in the basement pub. Tasty pizza (80-140Sk) and entrees (100-200Sk). Open M-F 10-1am, Sa 11-1am, Su 11am-midnight. ❷

◙ SIGHTS

Most of the sights in Bratislava are roughly bordered by Nám. SNP, Štúrova, the Danube, and Staromestská. Bratislava Castle overlooks the Old Town from a hill just outside the city center, across Staromestská.

PRIMATE'S PALACE. (Primaciálny Palác.) The pink Baroque palace on Primaciálne nám. houses the city magistrate and a small art gallery with extravagant furniture and intricate 17th-century tapestries. Watch the dog's head follow you around the room at the "Polovnícke zátišie" painting, or stare at yourself reflecting away to infinity in the paired mirrors in the side corridor. The Peace of Pressburg between Austrian Emperor Franz I and Napoleon was signed here in the **Hall of Mirrors** (Zrkadlová Sieň) in 1805. *(Primaciálne nám. 1. Buy tickets on the 2nd floor. Open Tu-Su 10am-5pm. 30Sk, students under 15 free. Self-guided tour 40Sk.)*

HVIEZDOSLAVOVO NÁMESTIE. The recently restored promenade surrounded by 19th-century edifices at Hviezdoslavovo nám. offers a great place to relax. In the evenings, the square fills with Austrian tourists coming to watch ballets and operas at the gorgeous 1886 **Slovak National Theater** (Slovenské Národné Divadlo) by the square. *(From Hlavé nám., follow Rybárska Brana until the road ends at Hviezdoslavovo nám.)*

NEW BRIDGE. (Nový Most.) Built by the communist government in 1972, Nový Most's space-age design was intended to balance the antiquated presence of Bratislava Castle (see below). Suspended from a giant flying saucer, the bridge offers spectacular panoramic views and a restaurant to boot. *(10Sk for the lift to the top. Open daily 10am-10pm.)*

ST. MARTIN'S CATHEDRAL. (Dóm. Sv. Martina.) When war with the Ottoman empire forced the Hungarian kings to flee Budapest, this Gothic church became Hungary's coronation cathedral. Positioned precariously atop the cathedral's steeple, a golden replica of St. Stephan's crown remind church-goers of its glorious past. *(Open daily dawn-dusk. Masses daily at 6:45am, noon, and 5pm, Su also 3:45pm.)*

ST. MICHAEL'S TOWER. (Michalská Brána.) The emerald green St. Michael's Tower is the only preserved gateway from the town's medieval fortifications. Although the billing here is the **Museum of Arms and Fortifications,** the real attraction is the view from the 13th-century tower above. *(On Michalská, near Hurbanovo nám. ☎ 54 43 30 44. Open Oct-Apr. Tu-Su 9:30am-4:30pm; May-Sept. Tu-F 10am-5pm, Sa-Su 11am-6pm. Last entry 30min. before closing. 30Sk, students 10Sk.)*

GRASALKOVICOV PALACE. (Grasalkovicov Palác.) Guarded by two unyielding soldiers in traditional uniform, the former Hungarian aristocratic residence now houses the offices of the Slovak president, but the public park in the gardens behind it is open to public. Enter through the second gate to avoid irking the presidential security staff. *(Hodžovo nám. Gardens open daily dawn-dusk.)*

BRATISLAVA CASTLE. (Bratislavský Hrad.) Visible from the Danube's banks, the four-towered Bratislava Castle is the city's defining landmark. Ruined by a fire in 1811 and finished off by WWII bombings, the castle's current form is largely a communist-era restoration that *almost* captures its 18th-century glory. The **Historical Museum** (Historické Muzeum) inside displays temporary exhibits from the National Museum; the tourist office has updated info on current exhibits. The **Crown Tower** (Korunná Veža) offers a spectacular view of the Danube; *(From underneath Nový Most climb the stairs to Židovská, then turn right on Zámocké schody and follow it to the Castle. Open Tu-Su 9am-6pm; last entry 5pm. 100Sk, students 40Sk.)*

DEVÍN CASTLE. (Hrad Devín.) These castle ruins perch on a promontory 9km west of downtown Bratislava. A stone's throw from neighboring Austria, the fortress overlooks the confluence of the mighty Morava and Danube rivers. Originally a Celtic fortress, the castle was held by Romans, Slavs, and Hungarians before it was completely decimated by Napoleon's armies in 1809. As Communism took hold of the country, Devin Castle grew to symbolize totalitarianism, sheltering sharpshooters who were ordered to fire at anyone trying to cross the "Iron Curtain"—the barbed-wire fence alongside the Morava. These days, visitors can walk unhindered along the paths winding through the rocks and ruins, and visit the **museum** that highlights the castle's history. *(Take bus #29 from Nový Most to the last stop. ☎65 73 01 05. Open May-Oct. Tu-Su 10am-5pm; July-Aug. Tu-F 10am-5pm, Sa-Su 10am-6pm. Last entrance 30min. before closing. 40Sk, students 10Sk.)*

🏛 MUSEUMS

OLD TOWN HALL. (Stará Radnica.) The Old Town Hall houses the **Town History Museum** (Muzeum Histórie Mesta). An impressive 1:500 scale brass model of 1945-55 Bratislava awaits at the entrance. The rest of the collection includes a battery of untranslated Slovak notices describing the medieval town, a series of galleries illustrating Bratislava's development, and the symbolic town key. For the more morbidly minded, the dungeon downstairs now offers a thorough display of some grisly medieval torture techniques in the **Museum of Feudal Justice.** *(Hlavé Nám. 1. From Primaciálne nám., head down Kostolná away from the tourist office. ☎59 20 51 30. Open Tu-F 10am-5pm, Sa-Su 11am-6pm. 30Sk, students 10Sk. English info available.)*

SLOVAK NATIONAL GALLERY. (Slovenská Národná Galéria.) Well-preserved sculptures, frescoes, and paintings from the Gothic and Baroque periods are on display in this museum on the Danube. The outside courtyard offers beautiful modern sculptures and benches for respite. *(Rázusovo nábr. 2. ☎54 43 20 81; www.sng.sk. Open Tu-Su 10am-6pm. 25Sk, students 20Sk.)*

THE HIDDEN DEAL

BEERS WITH THE KGB

A picture of a beer mug on a small circular sign along one of the city's side streets is all that hints at the location of one of the most popular establishments in Bratislava, **Krcma Gurmanov Bratislavy (KGB).** The name translates as "Bratislava's Gourmet Pub," and the food inside, though simple, should satisfy most epicureans.

It's no accident that the pub's name can be abbreviated "KGB": a life-sized statue of Karl Marx welcomes guests, while the decorations, including a medal to the workers who built a nearby nuclear power plant, harken back to the city's years under Communist rule. Creatively-named entrees, such as "Stalin's Diet" and "Light Lunch in the Gulag," complete the atmosphere.

If you prefer drinking to eating, visit KGB in the evening, when it becomes one of the most popular pubs in town. *(Obchodna 52. ☎52 73 12 79; www.angelfire.com/sk/kgb. Entrees 25-125Sk; beer 15-50SK; cocktails 20-100Sk. Open M-Th 11am-1:30am, F 11am-3:30am, Sa 3:30pm-1:30am, Su 3:30-11pm. Kitchen closes at midnight.)* ❶

—Matej Sapak

SLOVAK NATIONAL MUSEUM. (Slovenské Národné Múzeum.) This museum features local archaeological finds, including Neanderthal skeletons, as well as natural history and geology exhibits. *(Vajanského nábr. 2. ☎59 34 91 11; www.snm.sk. Open Tu-Su 9am-5pm. 20Sk, students 10Sk.)*

MUSEUM OF JEWISH CULTURE. (Múzeum Zidovskej Kultúry.) This museum preserves valuable fragments of a vanished population: **Schlossberg,** the old Jewish quarter, was bulldozed in the 1970s in the name of "progress." *(Židovská 17. ☎54 41 85 07. Open Su-F 11am-5pm. Last entry 4:30pm. 60Sk, students 40Sk.)*

DANUBIANA-MEULENSTEEN ART MUSEUM. (Múzeum Danubiana-Meulensteen.) A modern art gallery just outside Bratislava, near the Hungarian and Austrian borders. If the visibility is good, then just looking at the gallery, with the Danube and Bratislava castle in the background, makes the visit worthwhile. *(Take bus #91 to the last stop "Cunovo," then continue in the direction of the Gabčíkovo Dam. www.danubiana.sk. 60Sk, students 30Sk. Open Tu-Su 10am-6pm.)*

🎭🎨 ENTERTAINMENT AND FESTIVALS

The monthly *Kam v Bratislave*, available at BIS (see **Tourist Office,** p. 746), provides current film, concert, and theater schedules. **Slovenské Národné Divadlo** (Slovak National Theatre), Hviezdoslavovo nám. 1, puts on ballets and operas that attract crowds from across the country as well as neighboring Austria. (☎54 43 30 83; www.snd.sk. Box office open M-F 8am-5:30pm, Sa 9am-1pm. Closed July-Aug. 100-200Sk.) The **Slovenská Filharmónia** (Slovak Philharmonic) plays regularly at Medená 3. The box office is around the corner at Palackého 2. (☎54 43 33 51; fax 45 43 59 56; www.filharm.sk. Open M-Tu and Th-F 1-7pm, W 8am-2pm. 100-200Sk.) **Cinemas** are scattered across the city; most show British and American films with Slovak subtitles (80-85Sk). A convenient multiplex cinema is in the **AuPark** shopping mall on the southern bank of the Danube (139Sk, students 119Sk). In late September and early October, the **Bratislava Music Festival** brings dozens of acts to the city, and is almost immediately followed by the **Bratislava Jazz Days.**

🌙 NIGHTLIFE

By day, Hlavné nám. is a popular spot for shopping and free outdoor performances, but by night it's filled with strolling couples and local teens warming up for a night on the town.

Kelt Bar and Grill, Hviezdoslavovo nám. 26 (☎54 41 15 89). A popular international restaurant and bar that serves a lively mix of tourists and locals late into the night. Drinks 50-100Sk; entrees 50-150Sk. Open daily 11am-1am.

Dubliner, Sedlárska 6 (☎54 41 07 06; www.irishpub.sk). Bratislava's original Irish pub is hugely popular after dinner, when its mix of patrons spills out into the street. Guinness 85Sk; local brews 45Sk; cocktails 120Sk. Occasional live music. Open M-Sa 9am-1am, Su 11am-midnight.

Duna, Radlinského 11 (www.duna.sk). Located in a former civil defense bunker beneath the Slovak Technical University, Duna attracts a crowd of teens and 20-somethings. Drinks 40-100Sk. Open Su-Th 5pm-2am, F-Sa 5pm-4am.

Club 39, Staré Grunty 51/A (☎65 42 39 89). Near the largest university dorms in Bratislava, this 2-floor dance club takes its name from the bus route that runs by it, #39. Beer 25Sk; cocktails 70Sk. Cover 30Sk. Open M 8pm-4am, Tu-Sa 8pm-5am.

CENTRAL SLOVAKIA

It might be tempting to speed through Central Slovakia on the way to the snow-capped Tatras, but it's well worth stopping here to explore the region's history. Rarely visited by tourists, the area has preserved Slovak folk traditions better than anywhere else in the country and has endless opportunities for hiking and biking.

BANSKÁ BYSTRICA ☎(0)88

Banská Bystrica (BAN-skaah bis-TREE-tsah; pop. 84, 280) has a perfect mix of cosmopolitan flare and rural scenery that makes it an ideal stop en route to the Tatras. The lively Old Town is filled with some of the best folk-art boutiques in the Slovak Republic and dozens of outdoor cafes. Just outside town, forested hills serve as an ideal playground for bikers, hikers, and hang-gliders.

⚒ 🛈 ORIENTATION AND PRACTICAL INFORMATION

You may spend a fair stretch of time in Banská Bystrica's hills and valleys, as transport connections in the area are poor. The **train** and **bus stations** are next to each other on Cesta K. Smrečine. (☎436 14 73. Open daily 6am-10pm.) Trains go directly to **Bratislava** (4hr., 1 per day, 230Sk) and **Košice** (4hr., 1 per day, 230Sk), but it's easier to get there via **Zvolen** (30min., every 30min., 20Sk), a regional transportation hub. **Buses** go to: **Bratislava** (4hr., 17 per day, 230Sk); **Košice** (4-5hr., 6 per day, 200Sk); and **Liptovský Mikuláš** (2hr., 8 per day, 92Sk). To get to the town center, head out behind the bus station and cross Cesta K. Smrečine into the gardens. Take the pedestrian underpass under the highway and continue along Cesta K. Smrečine. A left on Horná at the bookstore brings you to **Námestí SNP,** the town center (15min.). Alternatively, the city bus runs from the stations to the city center. Get off at the "Nám. Š. Moyzesa" stop (10Sk).

Kultúrne a Informačné Stredisko (KIS), Nám. Š. Moyzesa 26, between Horná and Nám. SNP, has **maps** (18Sk) and accommodations info. The staff organizes city tours and books **private rooms.** (☎/fax 415 22 72; www.banskabystrica.sk. Open May 15-Sept. 15 M-F 8am-7pm, Sa 9am-7pm; Sept. 16-May 14 M-F 9am-5pm.) **VÚB,** Námestí Slobody 1 and Dolná 17, **exchanges currency** and cashes **traveler's checks** for 1% commission. (Open M-W and F 7:30am-4:30pm, Th 7:30am-noon.) There's a 24hr. MC/V **ATM** outside the tourist office. There's **luggage storage** at the train station (10Sk per day, heavy bags 20Sk). **Interpress Slovakia,** Dolná 19, sells English-language newspapers. (☎412 30 75. Open M-F 7am-7pm, Sa 8am-2pm.) Several **pharmacies** operate around Námestí SNP. **Internet Club,** Horná Strieborná 8, has **Internet access,** as its name might imply. (☎415 50 40. 25Sk per 15min. Open M-F 9am-8pm, Sa 10am-1pm.) Card **phones** stand outside the **post office,** Horná 1, off Nám. SNP, next to the tourist office. (☎415 26 37. Open M-F 8am-8pm, Sa 8am-noon.) **Postal Code:** 97401.

🏠 🍴 ACCOMMODATIONS AND FOOD

KIS ❶ (see **Orientation and Practical Information,** above) can help arrange **hostel** accommodations and affordable, comfortable **private rooms** (250-350Sk). **Hotel Milvar ❶,** Školská 9, rents out basic singles and doubles with shared baths and lots of natural light. From Nám. SNP, turn right through the arch across from the clock tower to Horná Strieborná and follow the road as it angles left to become Strieborná. Once over the river, take a right on J.G. Tajovského and follow it under the highway. Take your first right and then the first left on Školská. Alternatively, hop on bus #3 or 34, which both run to J. G. Tajovského. (☎413 87 73. Check-out 9am. 300Sk per person.) **Hotel Národný dom ❷**, Národná 11, off Nám. SNP, is conveniently central. Its common rooms are more elegant than the bedrooms, which are simple and clean. The cafe downstairs and opera house next door keep the place lively well into the evening. (☎412 37 37; fax 412 50 12. Singles 700Sk; doubles 1080Sk; triples 1380Sk.)

🍴 **Slovenská Pivnica ❶**, on Lazovná 18 off Nám. SNP, in a cozy underground bunker, serves an astonishing variety of traditional Slovak food. (☎415 50 36. Entrees 40-132Sk. Open M-Sa 11am-10pm. MC/V.) **Copaline Baguette ❶**, Dolná 1, stuffs its subs with ham, cheese, eggs, shrimp, salmon, and anything else they can think up—just point at what you want (45-95Sk). Look for groceries at **Prior,** on the corner of Horná and Cesta K. Smrečine. (Open M-F 8am-7pm, Sa 8am-3pm. MC/V.) An **outdoor market** is in the courtyard of the Prior building.

🄖 SIGHTS

The 🏛 **Museum of the Slovak National Uprising** (Múzeum Slovenského národného povstania) looks like an old spaceship that crashed in the gardens of Kapitulská. Banská Bystrica was the rebels' headquarters during the conflict that ensued after the Nazis entered Slovak territory on August 29, 1944 (see **History,** p. 736). The museum chronicles the failed insurrection and the grim Nazi reprisals that followed. Turn right from the tourist office into Nám. SNP and then take an immediate left on Kapitulská to reach the museum. (☎412 32 58; www.muzeumsnp.sk. English tours by request. Open May-Sept. Tu-Su 9am-6pm; Oct.-Apr. Tu-Su 9am-4pm. 50Sk, students 10Sk.)

A cluster of the town's oldest buildings stands on Nám. Š. Moyzesa. The restored **Pretórium,** once the town hall, now the **Štátna Galéria,** displays three floors of local avant-garde art. (☎412 48 64. Open Tu-F 9am-5pm, Sa-Su 10am-4pm. 40Sk, students 7Sk.) Behind the Galéria is the Romanesque **Church of the Virgin Mary** (Kostol Panny Márie), with gorgeous frescoes adorning the Baroque ceiling and an even finer Gothic altarpiece by Majstr Pavel of Levoča (see **Levoča,** p. 759).

The restored 18th-century villa of local artist Dominik Skutecký (1848-1921), **Skuteckého Dom,** Horná 55, now displays his work. To get there head left from the tourist office on Horná. A dogged realist in the age of Impressionism, Skutecký focused on social and folk scenes. (☎412 54 50. Open Tu-Su 10am-4pm. 15Sk, students 8Sk.) You can view miles of countryside, as well as the rest of Banská Bystrica, from the city's enormous yellow **clock tower,** Nám. SNP 29. (Open daily 10am-8pm. 20Sk, students 10Sk.) Just down the street, the **Museum of Central Slovakia** (Stredoslovenské Múzeum), Nám. SNP 4, presents a historical collection in a Renaissance house. (Open M-F and Su 8am-noon and 1-4pm. 15Sk, students 8Sk.)

🄖 OUTDOORS

For more active entertainment, Banská Bystrica offers ample outdoor adventures, including bike rental, hiking, horseback riding, and rock climbing. Consult the tourist office for information on the various companies that offer services. **Mr. Spedik-Jahn,** a travel agent in the village Tajov, arranges six-day **whitewater rafting** trips on the Hron River. (☎/fax 419 76 03; www.spedik.host.sk. 2600Sk, including accommodations.) To visit him, take the city **bus** from the bus station to **Tajov** (7km, 12Sk). Popular hiking trails run from **Donovaly,** the ski area accessible by bus from Banská Bystrica (22km, 40Sk). **Pegas Škola Paragliding,** Mistriky 230 (☎419 98 89), will teach you to fly for around 3500Sk. Call a week in advance. **Pony Farma-Suchý Urch,** Jazdiareň Uhlisko (☎410 48 58), offers horseback riding for all levels.

◨ DAYTRIP FROM BANSKÁ BYSTRICA

BOJNICE

To get to Bojnice, take the bus to Prievidza from Banská Bystrica (1-2hr., 12 per day, 92Sk) or Bratislava (2½hr., 12 per day, 133Sk). Facing ul. A. Hlinku from the Prievidza bus station, take bus #3 from the "Bojnice-ajka" stop on the right side of the street (8Sk). Castle ☎ 543 06 24; fax 543 13 01; www.bojnicecastle.sk. Open May-Sept. daily 9am-5pm; Oct.-Apr.Tu-Su 10am-3pm. 130Sk. Mandatory tour; English tours available. Cameras 50Sk.

Although many Slovak castles live on only as ruins or as reconstructions, the ▨ **castle** at Bojnice remains a real-life fairy tale (*sans* dragon) and easily outdoes any other in the Slovak Republic in both opulence and splendor. Originally a 12th-century wooden fortress for a Benedictine monastery, its deed was passed on to a noble family soon after its construction. The deed passed through various hands over the years. Its last noble occupant, Jan Pálffy, spent his life (1829-1908) renovating the palace in the Romantic style of a Loire Valley chateau. You can see the indelible imprint of his efforts through the guided tour, which covers galleries, gardens, hunting rooms, bedrooms, a citadel, a crypt, a cave, medieval washrooms, and the magnificent Oriental and Golden Halls. In some rooms, fully clothed statues of former owners rest in everyday positions. If you prefer real ghosts to spirited mannequins, come in early May for the **International Festival of Ghosts and Spirits,** when the castle hosts evening festivities to celebrate haunting spirits; check out the candlelit ceremony of the Rising of the Dead. The **Festival of Knights,** in late September, reenacts dozens of sword fights and battles.

MALÁ FATRA MOUNTAINS

The Malá Fatra mountain range is an exhilarating medley of alpine meadows, steep ravines, and limestone peaks. Whether you're out for a day or staying overnight in *chaty* (huts) along the way, the Malá Fatras offer hikes for all ability levels. The nearby town of Žilina makes an ideal base.

ŽILINA   ☎(0)89

Žilina's (ZHI-li-na) the Slovak Republic's third-largest town, is a convenient headquarters from which to explore the nearby Malá Fatra mountains. The picturesque mountain setting, along with a fountain-rich town square and friendly locals, make Žilina ideal for an extended stay.

☷ TRANSPORTATION. The **train station** is on ul. Hviezdoslava. Trains run to **Bratislava** (3hr., 17 per day, 212Sk) and **Košice** (3¼hr., 16 per day, 250Sk). The **bus station,** on the corner of ul. Hviezdoslava and ul. 1. Maja, is opposite the train station. Buses head to: **Banská Bystrica** (1¾hr., 17 per day, 93Sk); **Bratislava** (4hr., 4 per day, 217Sk); and **Liptovský Mikuláš** (1¾hr., 14 per day, 84Sk).

▨◨ ORIENTATION AND PRACTICAL INFORMATION. To get to the center from the train station, take the underpass to **ul. Narodná,** which leads to **Nám. A. Hlinku.,** the new town square. Go through the square and take the stairs to **Farská ul.** to reach **Marlánske nám.,** the old town square. Pick up a **hiking map** (89Sk) of the mountains at the tourist office **Selinan,** Burianova Medzierka 4, on the small street to the left of Farská ul. (☎ 562 14 78; fax 562 31 71. Open May 15-July M-F 8am-6pm; Aug. 8am-5pm; Sept.-May 14 8am-4:30pm.) **VÚB,** on the corner of Nám. A. Hlinku and ul. Narodná, **exchanges currency** and cashes **traveler's checks** for 1% commission. (Open M-W and F 8am-noon and 1-4pm, Th 8am-noon, Su 9am-1pm.) 24hr. MC/V **ATMs** are all over town. **Polnobanka,** on the corner of Jána Milca and ul. Narodná, provides AmEx/V **cash advances.** (Open M 8am-3pm, Tu-F 8am-5pm.)

⌂ ACCOMMODATIONS. Due to a shortage of private rooms, budget options in Žilina are few. Set in a grim skyscraper, **Hotel Garni ❷,** Vysokoskolakov 4, two tram stops from Žilina's center, offers moderately priced singles, doubles, and triples. (☎724 61 53. Curfew midnight . Check-out 10am. 500-850Sk.) Alternatively, the dorms at **Domov Mládeže ❶,** Hlinská Ulica 1, offer clean beds in tiny doubles. Take tram #4 or 7 from the train station to "Billa." Reservations recommended as most rooms are booked by June. (☎723 89 10. 150Sk per person. AmEx/MC/V.)

⌂ FOOD. Zábavné Centrum ❷, Sládkovičova ul. 164, serves a wide range of entrees (80-210Sk), including a selection of vegetarian meals. (Open daily 9am-11pm.) For trail food, **Tesco,** on Nám. A. Hlinku, has groceries on the ground floor. (☎562 22 61. Open M-F 8am-6pm, Sa 7am-6pm, Su 8am-2pm.) Across the street from Domov Mládeže (see **Accommodations,** above), there's a huge grocery store, **Billa,** at Tomašikova 26. (Open M-Sa 7am-8pm, Su 8am-8pm.) In the summer, an outdoor **fruit market** opens daily in the square.

HIKING IN MALÁ FATRA

Dress warmly for hikes, as the wind above tree level is cold and gusty. **Emergency rescue** is available (☎569 52 32). While the trail marking system in the Slovak Republic is generally accurate, it is not always perfectly maintained; a **map** (VKU map #110, available from any tourist agency) is vital.

MOUNT VEL'KÝ ROZSUTEC. Although it's not the highest mountain in the range, the steep **Vel'ký Rozsutec** (1609m) boasts some of the most exciting slopes in Malá Fatra. The ■ **Štefanová** hike is possibly the best hike in the region. However, it is challenging and should be undertaken only by experienced hikers. Take the Terchova-Vrátna bus from platform #10 in Žilina to Štefanová (39Sk) and follow the yellow trail to **Sedlo Vrchpodžiar** (30min.). A right onto the blue trail takes you past a mass of tumbling waterfalls and rapids known as **Horne Diery** (Upper Hole). Ladders and chains make several nearly vertical ascents possible, but these sections are not for the fainthearted. Continue along the blue trail to **Sedlo Medzirozsutce** (1½hr.); a right onto the red trail leads to the **summit** (1¼hr.). To descend, follow the red trail to its intersection with the green trail near **Sedlo Medziholie** (1hr.). Turn right onto the green trail to reach Štefanova (1¼hr.; total trip 5½hr.). For a less vigorous hike, follow the blue trail from Sedlo Medzirozsutce around the summit to its intersection with the green trail near Sedlo Medziholie (1hr.). A right here leads across a field of wildflowers and back to Štefanova.

MOUNT VEL'KÝ KRIVÁN. At 1709m, **Vemký Kriván** is the highest peak in the range. Take the bus from platform #10 in Žilina to **Terchová, Vrátna** (37Sk), and get off at Chata Vrátna at the end of the road. The green trail heads straight up to **Snilovské Sedlo** (1¾hr.); from there, turn right on the red trail to reach the **summit** (3hr. total). It's more pleasant, however, to take the chairlift from Chata Vrátna to Snilovské Sedlo to connect with the red trail. (Open daily June-Sept., every 30min. 8:30am-4:00pm., 90Sk.) The red trail runs along 4km of beautiful vistas on the ridge to **Poludňový Grúň** (1460m). From Poludňový Grúň, turn left onto the yellow trail to return to Chata Vrátna (round-trip 6½hr.).

LOW TATRAS (NÍZKE TATRY)

The Nízke Tatry (Low Tatras) are deceptively named; many peaks tower above the tree-line. Endowed with an extensive trail system and valleys that teem with caves and mountain streams, the relatively unexplored Nízke Tatry are the perfect spot for adventurous hikes.

LIPTOVSKÝ MIKULÁŠ   ☎(0)44

Despite its gory fame as the place where Juraj Jánošík, Slovak outlaw and champion of the poor, was captured and impaled for stealing from the rich in 1713, Liptovský Mikuláš (LIP-tov-skee Mee-koo-LASH; pop. 33,000) is a quiet town surrounded by mountains. Buses run to many Nízke Tatry trailheads, making Liptovský Mikuláš a charming and convenient base for outdoor activities.

The **train station** (☎551 24 84) lies on Štefánikova, and the **bus station** (☎552 36 38) is located outside it. Schedules and information are available in the white building; purchase bus tickets on board. **Trains** run to: **Bratislava** (4hr., 9 per day, 280Sk); **Košice** (2hr., 13 per day, 174Sk); and **Poprad** (1hr., 13 per day, 74Sk). **Buses** run to **Poprad** (1-2hr., 5 per day, 110Sk). The **town center** is an easy walk from the bus and train terminals. Follow Štefánikova toward the gas station at the far end of the lot, then turn right on Hodžu and follow it to the town center. **VÚB**, Štúrova 19, **exchanges currency**, cashes **traveler's checks** for 2% commission, and has a 24hr. Visa **ATM**. (☎552 23 57. Open M-W and F 7:30am-4:30pm, Th 7:30am-noon.) There's also an **exchange office** (*zmenárén;* ☎52 67 59) in the Prior building just across the street. **Z@vinác Internet Bar,** Nám. Osloboditel'ov 21, offers **Internet** access for 1Sk per min. (Open daily 10am-midnight.) **Postal Code:** 03101.

The tourist office, **Informačné Centrum,** Nám. Mieru 1, in the Dom Služieb complex, books **private rooms ❶** (180-400Sk) and sells local hiking **maps,** including the indispensable VKÚ maps. Ask for the *Orava Litpov Horehronie,* a hiking and cycling **map** (125Sk; ☎551 61 86; fax 551 44 48; www.lmikulas.sk. Open June 15-Sept. 15 and Dec. 15-Mar. 31 M-F 8am-7pm, Sa 8am-2pm, Su noon-6pm; Sept. 16-

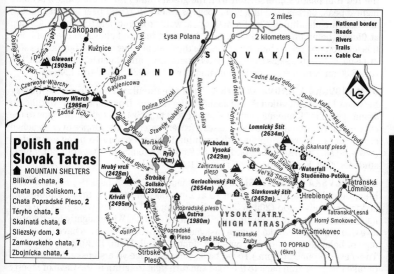

Polish and Slovak Tatras

▲ MOUNTAIN SHELTERS

Bilíková chata, **8**
Chata pod Soliskom, **1**
Chata Popradské Pleso, **2**
Téryho chata, **5**
Skalnatá chata, **6**
Sliezsky dom, **3**
Zamkovskeho chata, **7**
Zbojnícka chata, **4**

National border
Roads
Rivers
Trails
Cable Car

Dec. 14 and Apr.-June 14 M-F 9am-6pm, Sa 8am-noon). **Rent bikes** from Cycloturistika (60Sk per hr., 220Sk per 4hr., 300Sk per day).

The central **Hotel Kriváň ❷**, Štúrova 5, directly opposite the tourist office, offers small, peaceful rooms. (☎552 24 14; fax 551 47 48. Check-out 10:30am. Singles 400Sk; doubles 750Sk; triples with bath and TV 800Sk.) Comfortable rooms are also available at **Hotel SI ❷**, ul. 1 Maja 117. To get there, head left from the tourist office on Štúrova, and then turn right on Tranovskeho, which intersects ul. 1 Maja. (☎552 29 11; fax 552 29 67. Check-out 11am. Doubles 500Sk; apartments 1300Sk.) Boating, canoeing, and swimming are available at **Autocamping Liptovský Trnovec ❶**, 6km from Liptovský Mikuláš on Liptovský Mara dam. To reach the campsite, take bus #14 to Liptovský Trnovec. (☎/fax 559 84 58. May 1-June 15 tents 60Sk per person; 3-bed bungalow 550Sk; 4-bed bungalow 700Sk. June 16-Oct. 31 60Sk/700Sk/900Sk.) Restaurants are surprisingly scarce, though some options are clustered along Nám. Osloboditel'ov. The staff at **Liptovská Izba Reštaurácia ❶**, Nám. Osloboditel'ov 22, serves up delicious local dishes amid highland decor. (Entrees 60-100Sk. Open M-Sa 10am-10pm, Su 3-10pm.) Locals flock to **Alcatraz ❷**, Garbiarska 14, to enjoy Slovak cuisine with a French twist. (Entrees 80-175Sk. Open daily 10am-11pm.) Stock up on hiking provisions at **Supermarket Delvita** in the Prior building on Nám. Mieru. (Open M-F 8am-7pm, Sa 8am-7pm, Su 8am-5pm.)

HIKING IN NÍZKE TATRY

MOUNT ĎUMBIER AND CHOPOK. To get to the top of Mt. Ďumbier (2043m), catch an early bus from platform #11 at the Liptovský Mikuláš bus station to Liptovský Ján (25min., every hr., 13Sk). The gentle blue trail winds along the Štiavnica river until it reaches the Svidovské Sedlo by Chata generála M.R. Štefanika (5hr.). Bear left onto the red trail to reach Ďumbier's summit (45min.; 2043m). For a more strenuous hike, turn right on the red trail to reach Sedlo Javorie (1½hr.), then head left on the yellow trail (1½hr.). As you follow this rigorous trail, you'll pass two peaks, **Tanečnica** (1680m) and **Prašivá** (1667m). Head along the ridge and continue on the red trail past its intersection with the green trail to reach the range's second-highest peak, **Chopok** (2024m), and a **lodge ❶** where *Martiner* beer is on tap (35Sk) and beds are plentiful (80Sk). From Chopok, walk down the blue trail to the bus stop at **Otupné**, behind Hotel Grand (1¾hr.). A **chairlift** runs to Lukova on the half-hour; this lets you hop on the blue trail to tackle the peak in a mere hour. (Lift tickets sold in Jasná. Follow the signs from the Hotel Grand. Box office open 8:20am-3:40pm. Lift runs 8:30am-5pm in summer, 8:30am-4pm in winter. 80Sk, round-trip 120Sk.)

DEMÄNOVSKÁ L'ADOVÁ JASKYŇA. This spectacular ice cave rests midway between Liptovský Mikuláš and Jasná. Take the bus from Liptovský Mikuláš to Jasná, get off at "Kamenná chata" (15min., every hr., 9Sk) and follow the signs to the cave entrance (10min.). The tour passes a frozen waterfall that drapes over bleached stone and a cavern dripping with stunning icicles. Be sure to bring a sweater. (www.ssj.sk. Open May 15-Sept. 15 Tu-Su 9am-4pm. 45min. tours every 1-2hr. 110Sk, students 90Sk. English tour upon request 130Sk/110Sk.)

DEMÄNOVSKÁ JASKYŇA SLOBODY. (Demänov Cave of Liberty.) For a shorter hike, take the bus from platform #3 at Liptovský Mikuláš to the "Demänovská jaskyňa slobody" stop (20min., every hr. 9am-5pm, 11Sk) and walk past the cave itself on the blue trail to Pusté Sedlo Machnate (1½hr.). While slightly less impressive than the Demänovská l'Adová Jaskyňa (see above), these caves have the advantage of being less crowded. (Tours Oct.-June Tu-Su 9, 11am, 12:30, 2pm; July-Sept. Tu-Su every hour 9am-4pm.) To get back, simply retrace your steps on the blue trail or take the green trail back to the road and turn right to return to the Cave of Liberty (round-trip 3½hr.).

SPIŠ

Although most tourists know Spiš (SPISH) only as a neighbor of the Tatras, the region should be appreciated for its distinctive cities and towns, and for its national parks, the most beautiful in the Slovak Republic. For centuries, Spiš was an autonomous province of Hungary with a large Saxon population. It was later absorbed into Czechoslovakia and, after the Velvet Revolution in 1993, into the Slovak Republic. On its eastern flatlands lie tiny towns where villagers walk their cows and scythes are still in style. Meanwhile, Levoča and the sprawling ruins of Spišský Castle recall the region's rich past.

KEŽMAROK
☎ (0)52

Prosperous Kežmarok (KEZH-ma-rok; pop. 18,000) was named a free city in 1380 and granted many rights of which its neighbors in the Spiš region could only dream. With its doors open to trade, Kežmarok rapidly became one of the wealthiest and most beautiful Slovak towns. With cheap accommodations and easy transport to Poprad, it is a great base for visitors to the nearby High Tatra mountains.

▐ TRANSPORTATION. Trains run to **Poprad** (20-30min., 14 per day, 15Sk) from the yellow station at the junction of Toporcerova and Michalská (☎452 32 98). **Buses** leave from under the canopies opposite the trains to: **Levoča** (1hr., 8 per day, 40Sk); **Poprad** (20-30min., 3 per hr., 17Sk); **Starý Smokovec** (40-55min., 14 per day, 24Sk); and **Tatranská Lomnica** (30min., 14 per day, 20Sk). Buy tickets on board.

▐▟ ORIENTATION AND PRACTICAL INFORMATION. To reach the center from the train station, cross the footbridge on the left (*not* the main transport bridge) and follow **Alexandra** to **Hlavné nám.**, where the Baroque tower of the town hall (*radnica*) rises above two-story dwellings. Hidden in an alcove at Hlavné nám. 46, the tourist office, **Kežmarská Informačná Agentura**, sells **maps**. (12Sk; ☎/fax 452 40 47; www.kezmarok.tripod.com. Open June-Sept. M-F 8:30am-noon and 1-5pm, Sa-Su 9am-2pm; Oct.-May closed Su.) **Slovenská Sporteľňa**, Alexandra 41, **exchanges currency** for no commission and cashes AmEx/MC/V **traveler's checks** for 2% commission. (☎452 30 41. Open M and F 7:30am-4pm, Tu 7:30am-1pm, W 7:30am-5pm, Th 7:30am-2pm.) The town's only MC/V **ATM** stands outside. The **pharmacy, Lekáreň Na Námestí,** is at Hlavné nám. 58. (☎452 25 51. Open M-F 7:30am-5pm, Sa 8am-noon.) The **post office,** Mučeníkov 2, sits where Hviezdoslavova becomes Mučeníkov. (☎452 28 22. Open M-F 8am-noon and 1-7pm, Sa 8-10am.) **Postal Code:** 06001.

▐▛ ACCOMMODATIONS AND FOOD. You shouldn't have a problem finding cheap accommodations unless you arrive during the 2nd weekend in July, when Kežmarok hosts a European folk arts festival. The tourist office (see above) books **private rooms ❶** (200Sk). **◪ Pension Hubert ❷**, Hradská cest č. 8, behind the castle, is so comfortable that you'll wonder why you aren't paying more. (☎/fax 452 30 05; www.slovakholiday.com. Sauna 100Sk per 30min. Check-out 10am. Doubles with bath 500Sk 1st night, 400Sk subsequent nights; triples with bath 750Sk/600Sk.) **Penzión No. 1 ❷**, Michalská 1, is run by a congenial couple who encourage you to relax and play golf on their two-hole backyard green. Turn left out of the train station; it's the first building you come to. Ring the bell upon arrival. (☎452 46 00. Continental breakfast 120Sk. Check-out 10am. Reserve two weeks in advance July-Aug. Doubles 450Sk 1st night, 400Sk subsequent nights; triples 650Sk/600Sk.)

For a good, cheap Slovak meal, try **Restaurant Tiffany ❶**, Hlavné nám. 40, which features a beer garden and a rare non-smoking area in back. (Entrees 46-84Sk; beer 15Sk. Open M-Sa 8am-10pm, Su 9am-9pm.) **Barónka Restaurant ❶**, Hlavné nám. 46, behind the tourist office, is a little more upscale, but attracts far more tourists than

GOT CURDS?

Slovaks have been making the brine-cured sheep cheese *bryndza* for more than 200 years, and it is certainly an acquired taste. Visitors often wonder whether the *bryndza* they're sampling dates back to the original batch. Those who haven't acquired the taste swear it could be cottage cheese that's been left in a gym locker over summer vacation.

Don't be quick to laugh, though; Slovaks take their *bryndza* seriously, and they churn out about 3500 tons each year. A national soft spot for these creamy curds has even led to newspaper editorials such as "Bryndza is a Part of our Identity," a reflection the country's rural heritage of mountain-bound shepherds. Even the EU accession question is seen through cream-colored glasses—*bryndza* will soon have to be produced under hygienic conditions that are being negotiated with Brussels.

Bryndza is never found far from *halusky,* the small potato dumplings that fall somewhere between *spaetzel* and gnocchi on the pasta spectrum. Together, the two foods form Slovakia's unofficial national dish—*bryndzove halusky.* Although *bryndzove halusky* is usually included in the vegetarian section of menus, they are almost always served with Orava bacon. If you don't eat meat, order yours *"bez slaniny"* (without bacon). To cut the taste of the *bryndza,* you can also order your dish *"s oprazenymi cibulami"* (with fried onions).

(continued on next page)

locals. (☎452 45 01. Entrees 58-120Sk. Open M-F 10am-11pm, Sa-Su noon-10pm.) The friendly staff at **Staria Reštaurácia/Bageteria ❶,** Alexandra 30, opposite Sporteľňa Bank, prepares subs and burgers to your specifications. (Subs 33-50Sk; burgers 24-34Sk. Open M-F 7am-10pm, Sa 9am-10pm, Su 1-10pm.) There's a **grocery store** at Alexandra 35. (Open M-Sa 7am-10pm, Su 8am-10pm.)

◑ ◮ SIGHTS AND ENTERTAINMENT. From Hlavné nám., walk down Hviezdoslavova to reach Kežmarok's highlight, the ▨ **Wooden Articulated Church** (Drevený Atikulárny Kostol). Three anti-Protestant regulations governed its construction in 1717: the church had to be built outside the town walls, hence the location; it could not have a foundation, hence the sinking sensation; and it had to be financed with parish funds alone, hence the decision to build it entirely out of wood. Constructed in the shape of a Greek cross, the church bursts with imagination; the porthole-shaped windows bear the mark of the Swedish sailors who helped build it, while the fairy tale clouds on the ceiling are the mark of daydreaming painters. Although the church is still used for services, some locals felt more secure with a solid foundation and thus built the colossal **New Evangelical Church** (Nový Evanjelický Kostol), which blends Romanesque, Byzantine, Renaissance, and Middle Eastern styles. The Kežmarok-born **Imre Thököly,** exiled to Turkey for fighting the Habsburgs, rests here. (Both churches open June-Sept. daily 9am-noon and 2-5pm; Oct.-May Tu and F 10am-noon. 25Sk.) The last of the town's three churches, the **Basilica of the Holy Cross** (Kostol sv. Križa) stands in the middle of Staré Mesto. From Hlavné nám. walk down Dr. Alexandra and turn right on Nám. Požiarnikov. The church's prized possession is a statue of Jesus carved by Slovak artist Vit Słwosz. (Masses daily 6am, 6:30pm; Su also 8, 10am. Open June-Sept. daily 9am-5pm. 10Sk.) Hlavné nám. and Nová meet at the impressive **Kežmarok Castle,** Hradné nám. 42. Owned by the powerful Habsburgs, Thurzos, and Thökölys, the castle rarely stayed in one family's possession for longer than a generation. Renaissance decor hangs from its stocky Gothic frame and the courtyard contains the foundations of a 13th-century Saxon church. The **Kežmarok Museum** runs a mandatory tour in Slovak; stop at the ticket office to pick up the English guidebook (6Sk). (☎452 26 18. Open Tu-Su 9am-5pm. Tours every 30-60min. 50Sk, students 25Sk.)

The **Castellan Club,** underneath the castle on Starý trh, carries on the noble tradition of raucous revelry. Hit the dance floor or relax at the bar under the trees. (☎452 27 80. Beer 30Sk. Open Su-Th 3pm-3am, F-Sa 8pm-3am.) **Kino Iskra,** Hlavné nám. 3 (☎452 25 41), in the Unibanka building, shows Hollywood flicks (50-55Sk).

LEVOČA ☎(0)53

Levoča (LEH-vo-cha; pop. 13,500), the former capital of Spiš, gained fame and fortune through an odd little 16th-century imperial concession: the "Law of Storage" forced merchants passing through to remain in town until they sold all their goods. Quick to cash in on the rule, the town grew wealthy and fostered a burgeoning network of craft guilds, many of which were led by the renowned Master Pavol. Pavol brought artistic distinction to the town with his expressive wood-carving style; he also built the world's tallest Gothic altar. Today people stay in Levoča willingly, especially during the **Festival of Marian Devotion** (see below) in July.

▐ TRANSPORTATION. Levoča can only be reached by bus. The **bus station** (☎451 22 30) lists departure times on a large billboard. **Buses** run to: **Košice** (2hr., 3-5 per day, 100Sk); **Poprad** (45min., 12 per day, 27Sk); **Prešov** (1½hr., 12 per day, 95Sk). While there is a **train station** in Levoča, you must make several connecting trains before you can make it to the first major town. Buses are a better option.

▐▐ ORIENTATION & PRACTICAL INFO. To get to the center, take a right out of the station and walk to the intersection with the main road, **Probstnerová Cesta.** Walk straight through and continue on the footpath to the right, which heads uphill to **Nová.** Turn right on Nová, which leads into the main square, **Nám. Majstra Pavla** (15min.). Alternatively, a **local bus** (6Sk) runs to the post office in the square, but it comes infrequently and its route is circuitous. To catch it, turn left from the station and follow the road to the red-and-white bus stop sign.

The **tourist office,** Nám. Majstra Pavla 58, recommends *penzióny* and **private rooms** that cost 250-300Sk per person. (☎161 88; fax 451 37 63; www.levoca.sk. Open May-Sept. M-F 9am-5pm, Sa-Su 9:30am-2pm; Oct.-Apr. M-F 9:30am-4:30pm.) **Slovenská Sporiteľňa,** Nám. Majstra Pavla 56, gives MC/V **cash advances** and cashes AmEx **Traveler's Cheques** for 1% commission. (Open M, Th, F

In Bratislava, **Vinaren Bakchus,** Hlboka 5 (☎52 49 41 78), is a traditional cellar near the train station with classic *brynzdove halusky* for 69Sk. (Open M-Th 11am-11pm, F 11-midnight, Sa noon-11pm, Su noon-10pm.) You can even sample a *bryndza* pizza, complete with bacon, for 79Sk at **La Pizzeria Sole Mio,** Grosslingova 31. (Open M-F 9am-10pm, Sa 10am-10pm.) Outside of Bratislava, look for signs in restaurants featuring "Slovak specialties."

If you aren't up for the full *bryndzove halusky* experience, many restaurants also offer *bryndza* as a starter. In the Tatras, try a *bryndza* spread at **Zbojnicka Koliba** (Robber's Cottage; ☎524 46 76 30), in Tatranska Lomnica, a short walk from the Grandhotel Praha. (Open daily 4pm-midnight.) Do-it-yourselfers can head to the nearest grocery store for a carton of **Liptov Bryndza** (20-40Sk), a log of **Pol'ana Bryndza** (about 50Sk), or fresh *brynzda* from the deli counter (10-15Sk per 100g). Finally, there's always the legendary **bryndza stand** off Highway 66 just north of Zvolen in the direction of Banska Bystrica—look for the shack with the cars parked out front.

Susan Legro was a Researcher for Let's Go: Europe 1990 *in the former Soviet Union and an editor for* Let's Go: California and Hawaii 1989. *She now covers energy and environmental projects for the UN Development Program in 28 countries.*

7:35am-3pm, Tu 7:35am-1pm, W 7:35am-4pm.) A MC/V **ATM** stands outside. The **pharmacy** at Nám. Majstra Pavla 13 posts the hours of other pharmacies as well. (☎451 24 56. Open M-F 7:30am-5pm, Sa 8am-noon.) **Internet Cafe,** Nová 79 charges 1Sk per minute. (Open M-F 9am-4pm.) The **post office** is at Nám. Majstra Pavla 42. (☎451 24 89. Open M-F 8am-noon and 1-4:30pm, Sa 8-10:30am.) **Postal Code:** 05401.

[icon] ACCOMMODATIONS AND FOOD. Finding accommodations is not difficult except during the festival in the first weekend of July, when your best bet is to stay in Poprad and daytrip to Levoča. The tourist office (see **Practical Information,** above) can point you to **pensions** and nearby **campsites.** While cheaper accommodations generally lie outside the center, the family-run 🖺 **Penzión Šuňavský ❶,** Nová 59, offers clean, comfortable, and affordable rooms in the center of town. Follow the directions above to the town center; the pension is on the left side of Nová. (☎451 45 26. Breakfast 50Sk. Call 2 days ahead in Aug. June-Sept. 350Sk per person; Oct.-May 300Sk.)

There's a **grocery store** at Nám. Majstra Pavla 45. (Open M-Th 6:15am-6pm, F 6:15am-6:30pm, Sa 6:45am-noon, Su 8:30-11:30am.) The upscale, yet casual **U 3 Apoštolov ❷,** Nám. Majstra Pavla 11, serves Apostle "specials" for the daring diner, vegetarian dishes, and traditional Slovak food. (☎451 23 52. Entrees 20-145Sk. Open daily 9am-10pm. AmEx/V.) **Restaurant Janusa ❷,** 22 Kláštorská, dishes up hearty fare, including the house specialty: *pierogi* with a side of spicy homemade sausage. (☎/fax 451 45 92. Entrees 55-106 Sk. Open M-F 10am-10pm, Sa-Su with reservations only.) **Vegetarián ❶,** Uhoľná 3, serves five dishes each day (39-47Sk), as well as soups (8-10Sk) and salads (8-10Sk), in a cafeteria-style setting. (☎451 45 76. Open M-F 10am-3:15pm.)

[icon] SIGHTS. Levoča's star attraction is the 14th-century **St. Jacob's Church** (Chrám sv. Jakuba), home to the world's tallest Gothic altar (a staggering 18.62m) carved by Majster Pavol from 1507 to 1517. Pavol's extremely detailed relief carvings, murals, altars, and beautifully preserved frescoes depict stories from the Old and New Testaments. Putting 5Sk into the automatic info box yields commentary on the sculptures in English or Hungarian. (No sleeveless shirts. Buy entrance tickets at the booth across the street. Entrance to the church available on the half hour in the mornings, and on the hour in the afternoons. Open summer M 11am-5pm, Tu-F 9am-5pm, Sa 9am-noon, Su 1-2:30pm; off-season M 11am-4pm, Tu-Sa 9am-4pm, Su 1-4pm. 40Sk, students 20Sk.)

Three branches of the **Spišské Museum** dot Nám. Majstra Pavla. Each museum features an English-language video about Levoča's history (20min.); it just might persuade you that the town is more than a one-master show. It even details the wedding rules specific to Lavoča's St. Jacob's Church. By far the best museum is **Dom Majstra Pavla** at #20, with an exhibition of Master Pavol's work that contains high-quality facsimiles of many of his greatest works and allows you to get much closer to the *Last Supper* than you can in St. Jacob's Church. The beautiful **town hall** *(radnica)* in the middle of the square is adorned by fading frescoes. The main entrance leads to an assortment of wineries and small stores. Take the stairs on the right of the main entrance to get to the **2nd branch,** which houses relics of Levoča's past. According to legend, the white lady in the painting on one of the doors betrayed the town by giving the city's keys to her lover, an officer in the invading Hungarian army. In the **Cage of Shame** (Klietka Hanby), next to the town hall, women of supposedly loose morals were pilloried in the 16th century. The **3rd branch,** at #40, has a small collection of masterful portraits and statues. (All open May-Oct. Tu-Su 9am-5pm; Nov.-Apr. Tu-Su 8am-4pm. Each 20Sk, students 10Sk.) The neo-Gothic **Basilica of the Virgin Mary** (Bazilika Panny Marie), separated from Levoča by 3km of wheat fields but visible from town, stands on top of Mariánská hora. It attracts 600,000 pilgrims during the first weekend in July for the **Festival of Marian Devotion.** The festival, which began in the 13th century, culminates in a Sunday mass (10am), which the Pope himself led in 1995. (Open year-round M-Sa 9am-6pm. Entry is free, but it is customary to make an offering. The **Handicraft Museum,** Kukucinova 1, showcases jewelry, lace, wood carvings, and other Levoča crafts. Many items are for sale at the museum. (☎ 0905 691 253; zurcşpost.sk. Open M and Th-Sa 11am-5pm, Su 1pm-6pm.)

🛐 DAYTRIP FROM LEVOČA

SPIŠSKÉ PODHRADIE AND ŽEHRA

Buses come from Levoča (20min., every 30min. until 9:30pm, 17Sk); Poprad (1hr., 9 per day, 47Sk); Prešov (1½hr., every hr. until 6pm, 57Sk). Many uphill paths lead to the cas-tle (check the info map at the castle end of the main square), but the most satisfying is the grassy 2km trek from the left side of the town's cemetery. With your back to the departure board at the bus stop, head right to the main square. Turn left on to the bridge leading out of town. When you reach the castle walls, climb uphill for 10-15min. To reach the church, take a right on the main road, with your back to the church. It's about 6km back to Spišské Podhradie.

If you are going to visit only one castle during your stay in the Slovak Republic, make it ▨ **Spišské Castle** (Spišský hrad). Central Europe's largest, the ruins of the castle lie on the mountain at the opposite end of Spišské Podhradie. There's been a fortified settlement here for two millennia, but the present ruins are the remains of the 13th- to 17th-century Hungarian castle that dominated the Spiš region until it burned down in 1780. ☎ 454 13 36. Entrance with English-speaking guides every 30min. 9am-4:30pm. Open daily 8:30am-6pm; last admission 5:15pm. 50Sk, students and children 30Sk. Camera 10Sk, video 50Sk.)

There's not much to see in Spišské Podhradie (SPISH-skay POD-hra-dyeh) itself, but two of the Slovak Republic's finest monuments lie in hills above the valley. West of town, walled **Spišské Kapitula,** the region's religious capital, contains **St. Martin's Cathedral** (Katedrála sv. Martina). Although more impressive for its historical and cultural significance than for its visual appeal, it does feature some magnificently constructed stained-glass windows and artistically-inspired frescoes and altars. Science-loving socialists drove out the clergy in 1950, but they have since regrouped. From the side of the bus stop with the awnings, walk left through the gardens and over the river. The main road winds up and around to the cathedral (15min.). Get tickets from the info building 10m from the church. (No sleeveless shirts or leg showing above the knee. Open May-Oct. 10am-5pm. Entrance every hour, on the hour. 30Sk, students 20Sk.) The castle also houses a **museum,** which displays artifacts from the different eras and reigns. Much of the better-preserved section is roped off, but the grounds, walls, and four-storey central turret provide terrific views.

A beautiful but long walk from the castle brings you to the tiny ancient village of **Žehra,** home of the **Church of the Holy Spirit** (Kostol Svätého Ducha). Built in a late Romanesque to early Gothic style, it is not to be missed if you have the energy to trek the 4km to its doors. The interior is decorated with remarkable 14th-century frescoes uncovered in the 1950s. Though faded and in need of restoration, these UNESCO-protected decorations have made the church famous. From the castle entrance, descend to the closer parking lot and hike the yellow trail from the bar/cafe in the back of the lot. This trail will only be recognizable by its closely cut grass. Continue past the limestone crags and bear left into the valley below. The church's brown onion-domed tower is easy to spot. (Open M-Sa 9:30am-4pm, Su 2-4pm. 20Sk, students 10Sk.)

SLOVAK REPUBLIC

SLOVENSKÝ RAJ NATIONAL PARK ☎ (0)53

Slovenský Raj (Slovak Paradise) National Park, southeast of the Nízke Tatry, has an entirely different feel from the Slovak Republic's more mountainous parks. Instead of heavily touristed peaks, it encompasses forested hills and deep limestone ravines carved by fast-flowing streams. Life moves at a slow pace in the tiny villages and grassy meadows, even as hikers and skiers speed by on the nearby trails.

🗲 TRANSPORTATION. Nestled by the shores of Lake Palčmanská Maša, **Dedinky** (pop. 400) is the largest town on Slovenský Raj's southern border. Despite its tourist-friendly services, Dedinky has yet to lose its old-fashioned spirit. The road to paradise is rocky; negotiate it by catching the **bus** from **Poprad** toward Rožňava (1hr., 6 per day, 37Sk). The bus stops first at the Dobšinská ľadová jaskyňa, then at the village Stratená, and finally at a junction 2km south of Dedinky. A cluster of blue signs marks the intersection. Two routes lead to Dedinky, but you're in for a hike either way. From the intersection, take the road not taken by the bus, which curves down into the basin. Turn right at the next intersection and follow the road as it veers right and begins to head in the opposite direction. After 5min., you will find the Dedinky railway station and a big dam on your left. Cross the dam, turn left, and walk to Dedinky (30min.). To get there a bit faster, take the yellow trail that branches off to the right 200m from the first intersection. When you reach the road at the bottom, turn left. The dam will be on your right.

🛈 PRACTICAL INFORMATION. Pick up a copy of **VKÚ sheet #4,** an excellent hiking map (85-140Sk) at Hotel Priehrada (see below). Behind Hotel Priehrada, a **chairlift** runs to Chata Geravy. (See below. Open July-Aug. M 9am-3pm, Tu-Su 9am-4:30pm; May-June M 9am-4pm, Tu-Su 9am-5pm. 60Sk, round-trip 100Sk.) **Tókóly Tours,** 200m from Hotel Priehrada by the lake, rents **boats** and **bikes.** (☎905 592 30 11. Bikes 20Sk per hr.; rowboats 50Sk per hr.; paddle boats 60Sk per hr. Open June-Aug. daily 9am-7pm.) Dedinky's **post office** is behind the wooden tower, near the bus stop. (Open M-F 8-10am, 12:30-1:30pm, and 2-3pm.) **Postal Code:** 04973.

🛏🍴 ACCOMMODATIONS AND FOOD. It's wise to book rooms at least two weeks ahead in January, July, and August, though the ubiquitous **private rooms** ❶ (150-300Sk) rarely fill up: look for *"privat," "ubytowanie,"* or *"zimmer"* signs. **Penzión Pastierňa ❶,** Dedinky 42, offers tasteful rooms with shared baths. Facing Hotel Priehrada, turn left and take the second right. Follow the signs to the end of the street. (☎798 11 75. Reception 8am-10pm. Singles 250Sk; doubles 500Sk.) **Hotel Priehrada ❶** rents tidy rooms with private baths. It also runs a wonderfully cheap **campsite** by the lake. (☎798 12 12; fax 798 16 82. Reception 24hr. Check-out 10am. Rooms 250Sk per person, with bath 300Sk. Camping 30Sk per person. Tents 30-40Sk. MC/V.) At the trailhead, **Chata Geravy ❶** offers small rooms with comfy beds. (Reception until 11pm. 150Sk per person.)

You can get groceries at **Delika,** near the bus stop (open M-F 7:30am-9pm, Sa 7am-7pm, Su 9am-5pm), or at the base of the ice-cave trail (open M and Th 7-10am and 1-2pm, Tu 10am-3pm, F 8am-3pm, Sa 7am-noon). The restaurant in **Penzión Pastierňa ❷** serves Slovak standards and a few vegetarian options. (Entrees 82-172Sk. Open daily 8am-10:30pm.) Quality fare is also offered at the restaurant in **Hotel Priehrada ❶.** (Entrees 40-150Sk. Open daily 7:30am-9pm.) Plan to eat in Dedinky if you're heading to the caves, where the only restaurant is overpriced.

◩ **SIGHTS.** Some 110,000 cubic meters of water are still frozen from the last Ice Age in the **Dobšinská Ice Caves** (Dobšinská ľadová jaskyňa), which comprise a 23km stretch of ice. The 30min. tour covers only 475m of the cave, but even that's awe-inspiring, with hall after hall of frozen columns, gigantic ice walls, and hardened waterfalls. Bring a sweater—the cave temperature hovers between -3.8° and +0.5°C year-round. To get here from Dedinky, take the 12:37pm or 2:37pm **train** for two stops (11Sk, 15min.). The one road from the cave train station leads 100m out to the main road. Turn left; the cave parking lot is 250m ahead. From there, the blue trail leads up a steep incline to the cave (20min.). Alternatively, a **bus** (14Sk) leaves from outside Hotel Priehrada at 10am and drops you off at the parking lot. (Caves ☎798 11 59; www.ssj.sk. Open May 15-June and Sept. Tu-Su 9am-2pm; July-Aug. Tu-Su 9am-4pm. English tours 110Sk, students 90Sk. 20-person minimum. Cameras 150Sk, video 300Sk.)

◪ **HIKING.** As this is a national park, camping and fires are prohibited. Cascade trails, which involve climbs up the park's rapids, are one-way—you can go up, but not down. All cascade trails are closed from November to June to those without certified guides. Guides can be hired in one of the nearby resorts (3000-4000Sk).

Biele vody (White Waters; 1¾hr.): A moderately difficult cascade hike up a series of rapids. Watch your footing on slippery rocks, wooden ladders, and bridges. From the parking lot to the right of Hotel Priehrada in Dedinky, take the red trail to Biele vody (788m). The blue cascade trail is on the left. Chata Geravy (see **Accommodations and Food,** p. 762) and a chairlift wait at the top, and the green trail leads back down.

Veľký sokol (Big Falcon; 6½hr.): This is a far more demanding hike into the heart of Slovenský Raj and up its deepest gorge. Follow the road west from Stratená or east from the ice caves (with your back to the caves, take a right). At the big U-bend, follow the green trail along the stream and then over Sedlo Kopanec (987m). Continue on the green trail past Štvrtocká pila until it meets the red path. The yellow trail to the right leads up to the ravine, crisscrossing the mountain stream. From the top (971m), a right on the red path returns to Chata Geravy and the chairlift descent to Dedinky. Those who don't like wet feet can take the red trail from Sokol at the bottom of the gorge to the top, following the northern edge (30min. longer).

Havrania skala (Crow's Cliff; 3hr.): This moderately difficult hike offers remarkable views from the top and 2 cliffside caves to explore. From the Stratená bus stop, the green trail leads up the hill to the Občasný prameň spring (1hr.); from Chata Geravy, it's 1¾hr. along the yellow trail, which follows the Vrábľovsky potok stream. From the spring, climb up the steep yellow trail to the top of Havrania skala (1153.5m; 30min.) for a gorgeous view. The trail descends steeply for 1hr. to meet the road west of Stratená—turn left to reach the bus stop.

HIGH TATRAS (VYSOKÉ TATRY)

Spanning the border between Slovakia and Poland, the Vysoké Tatry are home to the highest peaks in the Carpathian range (2650m) and the mesmerizing valleys beneath them. While millions of visitors pack the slopes and trails each year, budget accommodations remain easy to find, as cheap beds abound in mountain *chaty* (huts). After reaching the Tatras via Poprad, most hikers sleep near the transportation hub Starý Smokovec or the peaceful Tatranská Lomnica.

The Tatras are a wonderful place for a hike, but in winter a guide is a necessity. Snowfall in the Tatras is very high and avalanches are common. Each year, dozens of winter hikers die here, often on "easy" trails. Even in summer many of these hikes are extremely demanding and require experience. Be sure you have a map and information about the trail before beginning. Updated trail conditions and weather information are available at www.tanap.sk, but at the highest elevations, the weather is prone to frequent and abrupt changes. Check with a mountain rescue team, a local outdoors store, or a tourist office before going anywhere without an escort. Always inform the receptionist at your hostel or hotel of your hiking route and the estimated time of your return.

POPRAD   ☎(0)92

Poprad (pop. 56,000), while a convenient base for Tatras travel, is more than just a bus and train station, as those who take the time to discover it will soon realize. Well-maintained and pleasant, this town is home to a charming center and some of the friendliest locals in the country, making it an attraction in its own right.

▤ TRANSPORTATION. Trains run to: **Banská Bystrica** (3½hr., 10 per day, 221Sk); **Bratislava** (5hr., 10 per day, 336Sk); and **Košice** (1¼ hr., 15 per day, 146Sk). The *Tatranská elektrická železnica* (TEŽ; electric train) takes longer than the bus, but runs more frequently between Poprad and the **Tatran resorts** (every 20min., up to 30Sk). **Buses** (☎772 35 65; info open M-F 7am-3pm) stop at the corner of Wolkerova and Alžbetina on the way to: **Banská Bystrica** (2½hr., 11 per day, 150Sk); **Košice** (2hr., 9 per day, 220Sk) the **Tatran resorts** (20-30Sk); and **Zakopane, POL** (2hr., 2 per day July-Aug. and Dec.-Mar., 130Sk).

▉▐ ORIENTATION AND PRACTICAL INFORMATION. To reach the center, take a left from the **train station** and follow **Alžbetina** away from the **bus station**. Turn left on **Hviezdoslavova** and then right on **Mnoheľova**, which leads to **Nám. sv. Egídia**. To reach the old square from the train station, walk up Alžbetina, then turn left on **Štefánikova**. When it intersects **Továrenska,** turn left and stay straight until you enter **Sobotské nám.** At **Popradská Informačná Agentúra (PIA),** Nám. sv. Egídia 114, the English-speaking staff sells **maps** and offers accommodations and recreation info. (☎772 17 00; infopp@pp.psg.sk. Open Sept.-June M-F 8:30am-5pm, Sa 9am-1pm; July-Aug. M-F 8am-6pm, Sa 9am-1pm. Private rooms 200Sk.) **VÚB**, Mnoheľova 9, cashes AmEx/V **traveler's checks** and provides **cash advances** for 1% commission. (☎713 11 11. Open M-W and F 8am-5pm, Th 8am-noon.) 24hr. MC/V **ATMs** are all over town. **Store luggage** at the train station. (10-20Sk per day. Open 24hr.) For **Internet access,** try **Allegro,** Štefánikova 14. Be forewarned—students pack the place when school isn't in session and the wait becomes unbearably long. (☎772 33 39. Open daily noon-midnight. 0.8Sk per min.) **Postal Code:** 05801.

▛▟ ACCOMMODATIONS AND FOOD. The PIA (see above) books **private rooms ❶** (200Sk). **Hotel Garni ❷,** Karpatská 11, can be easily spotted from the bus station. Walk down Alžbetina away from the train station toward the bus station, then go right on Karpatská. Garni has spotless rooms and a central location. (☎776 38 77; fax 630 77. Breakfast 70Sk. Check-out 10am. Doubles 510Sk, with bath 640Sk; triples 690Sk. MC/V.) **Domov Mladeze ❶,** in the same complex as Hotel Garni, is somewhat less luxurious than its neighbor, but offers the same convenient location at a lower price. (☎776 34 14; fax 776 25 15. Doubles 200Sk per person.) Another option is to take the local TEŽ train to **Nová Lesna ❶**, a small village of private accommodations only 10min. from the town center. Just look for the *pokoj* or *zimmer* signs. (200Sk. Tourist tax 10Sk.) There's a **supermarket** on the top floor of Prior at Mnoheľova and Nám. sv. Egídia. (Open M-F 8am-7pm, Sa 8am-2pm, Su 9am-3pm.) **Egídius ❷**, Mnoheľova 18, has a beer garden, a Slovak restaurant, and a candlelit cafe. (☎772 28 98. Entrees 90-270Sk. Open daily 11am-11:30pm.) Another excellent option is **Slovenska Restauracia ❶**, ul. 1 Maja 216, which serves both Slovak and international dishes amid traditional decor. (☎772 28 70. Entrees 30-210Sk. Open daily 10am-11pm.) At night, head to the old square and **Vináreň sv. Juraj,** Sobotské nám. 29, a popular bar and dance club. (☎776 95 58. *Tatran* 30Sk. Open daily 4-11pm; disco open 9pm-2am.)

STARÝ SMOKOVEC ☎(0)52

Starý Smokovec (STAH-ree SMO-ko-vets), founded in the 17th century, is the High Tatras' oldest and most central resort. While signposts with a dozen arrows may seem daunting, it's difficult to get lost in the town's nameless streets; Starý Smokovec's was developed with tourism in mind, making it easy to navigate.

E TRANSPORTATION. TEŽ **trains** go to: **Poprad** (30min., every hr., 16Sk); **Štrbské Pleso** (45min., every 30min., 20Sk); and **Tatranská Lomnica** (15min., every 30min., 13Sk). **Buses** to many Tatran resorts stop in a parking lot to the right of the train station. A **funicular** runs to **Hrebienok** (see below; every 30-40min 6:35am-7:45pm; one-way 80Sk, round-trip 100Sk).

⁊ PRACTICAL INFORMATION. There are no street names, but signs point to hotels, restaurants, and services. To get to the center from the train station, go uphill on the road that runs just left of the station and cross the main road, veering left. The friendly staff of **Tatranská Informačná Kancelária (TIK),** in Dom Služieb, provides weather info and sells both town and hiking **maps,** including the crucial **VKÚ sheet #113** (89Sk) of the High Tatras. (Open July-Aug. M-F 8am-5:30pm, Sa-Su 8am-1pm; Sept.-June M-F 9am-4:30pm, Sa 8am-1pm.) **Slovenská Sporiteľňa,** also in Dom Služieb, cashes **traveler's checks** and gives MC/V **cash advances** for 1% commission. A 24hr. MC/V **ATM** is just outside. (☎442 24 70; fax 442 32 53. Open M 7:30am-3:30pm, Tu 7:30am-1pm, W 7:30am-5pm, Th-F 7:30am-3pm.) A pharmacy, **Lekáreň U Zlatej Sovy,** is on the 2nd fl. of Dom Služieb. (☎442 21 65. Open M-F 8am-noon and 12:30-4:30pm, Sa 9am-noon.) **Internet access** is available in **Rogalr.** (☎442 50 43. 60Sk per 30min. Open daily 9am-10pm.) The **post office** is uphill from the train station. (☎442 24 71. Open M-F 7:30am-noon and 1-4pm, Sa 8-10am.) **Telephones** are located outside. **Postal Code:** 06201.

⌂◨ ACCOMMODATIONS AND FOOD. Up the road from the train station on the way to Dom Služieb, an electronic **InfoPanel** lists current vacancies in hotels, pensions, and hostels in the greater Smokovec area. The TIK (see above) lists **private rooms ❶** (350-450Sk) available to tourists. Most budget options are in the hamlet of **Horný Smokovec.** Turn right on the main road from the train or bus stations and walk 5min. to **Hotel Šport ❷**. It shares facilities with the nearby Hotel Bellevue, including a restaurant, cafe, sauna, swimming pool, and massage parlor. (☎442 23 61; fax 442 27 19. Breakfast 80Sk. English-speaking reception 24hr. Check-out 10am. Book one month in advance in peak months of July and Aug. July-Aug. singles 420Sk; doubles 705Sk; triples 975Sk. Sept.-June 295Sk/515Sk/695Sk.) Another 15min. along the road (or two stops from Starý Smokovec on the TEŽ toward Tatranská Lomnica) and across the train tracks, down a short path through the

SLOVAK REPUBLIC

trees, is **Hotel Junior ❷**, featuring compact rooms, shared baths, and a disco. The facilities resemble camping bungalows and are popular with child-toting families. (☎442 26 61; fax 442 24 93. Check-out 10am. Book one month in advance July-Aug. Doubles 440Sk; triples 580Sk; quads 720Sk. With ISIC, 250Sk per person including breakfast.) If you're intent on staying in Starý Smokovec itself, **Hotel Smokovec ❸**, directly uphill from the train station, offers beautiful rooms, a swimming pool, a weight room, and a restaurant. (☎442 51 91; www.slovakia.net/smokovec. Reception 24hr. Check-out 10am. July-Aug. singles 990Sk; doubles 1980Sk; triples 2820Sk; Sept.-June 890Sk/1780Sk/2370Sk. MC. Restaurant open daily 7am-10pm.)

Grocers clutter Starý Smokovec; the largest is the *potraviny* in the shopping block above the bus station. (Open M-F 7:45am-6pm, Sa 8am-12:30pm, Su 9am-12:30pm.) Decent restaurants, however, are few and far between. **Restaurant Koliba ❷** (☎442 22 04) is an exception. Facing downhill, head through the parking lot to the right of the train station and across the tracks. Try the *Tatranský čaj* (Tatran tea, 40Sk), which is spiked with pure grain alcohol. (Entrees 90-280Sk. Open daily 6pm-midnight.) **Bistro Tatra ❶**, up the steps from the bus station, is a popular choice for Slovak families and for those who like quick service. (☎442 53 04. Entrees 52-105Sk. Open daily 10am-7pm.)

𝕂 OUTDOOR ACTIVITIES AND HIKING. T-ski, in the funicular station, offers everything from ski classes to river-rafting trips, and rents sleds and skis. (☎442 32 65. Sleds 90Sk per day; skis 350-400Sk per day; guides from 490Sk per day. Open daily 8am-6pm.) **Tatrasport,** uphill from the bus lot, rents **mountain bikes** for 299Sk per day. (☎442 52 41; www.tatry.net/tatrasport. Open daily 8am-6pm. MC/V.)

The funicular to **Hrebienok** (1285m) carries people daily to the crossroads of numerous trails. To reach Hrebienok by foot, hike the **green trail** behind Hotel Gran (35min.). More a hotel than a mountain shelter, the deluxe **Bilikova Chata ❷**, just beyond the funicular station on the green trail, has food, warm beds, and a terrific view from its terrace. (☎442 24 39; fax 442 22 67. 750Sk per person.) Another 20min. from Hrebienok, the green trail leads north to the **Volopády studeného potoka** (Cold Stream Waterfalls). The incline is small and the hike through trees and past the waterfall is well worth the effort. Follow the **red trail** past Rainerova Chata, then head right on the eastward **blue trail,** which descends gradually through the towering pines to Tatranská Lomnica (1¾hr.). The **yellow trail** meanders along the river to Tatranská Lesná (1¾hr.). A local TEŽ train can whisk you from Tatranská Lomnica and Tatranská Lesná back to Starý Smokovec. The long, red Tatranská magistrála trail travels west from Hrebienok along the side of mountains and hits **Horský Hotel ❶** (300Sk per person) at **Sliezsky dom** (2¼hr.; 1670m), then zig-zags down to **Chata Popradské Pleso ❶** (☎449 21 77; 210-300Sk per person) on the shore of the lake Popradské Pleso (1500m; 5½hr.). From here, the red trail continues to **Štrbské Pleso** (7hr. from Hrebienok; see below). From Sliezksy dom there are two trails back toward civilization: the green trail leads back to **Tatranská Polianka** and a left on the **yellow trail** opposite Batizovske Pleso goes to **Vyšné Hágy** (2hr. each). A more daunting blue trail branches north from the Tatranská magistrála 20min. west of Hrebienok to climb one of the highest peaks, **Slavkovský Štít** (2452m; 8hr. round-trip from Hrebienok; for advanced hikers in good weather only).

The magistrála trail also heads north from Hrebienok to the lake **Skalnaté Pleso** and its nearby *chata* (2¼hr.; ☎446 70 75; 300Sk per person). The hike to **Malá studená dolina** (Little Cold Valley) is fairly relaxed; take the red trail from Hrebienok to **Zamkovského Chata ❶** (1475m; 40min.; ☎442 26 36; 290Sk per person) and then take the green trail to **Téryho Chata ❶** (2015m; 2hr.; ☎442 52 45; 280Sk per person, with breakfast 390Sk) for a spectacular view of nearby Lomnický Štít.

An extremely difficult but rewarding hike traverses the immense **Veľká studená dolina** (Big Cold Valley) to **Zbojnícka Chata**. From Sliezsky Dom (see above), take a left on the green trail to **Zamrznuté Pleso** (Frigid Lake; 2047m) and then head right on the blue trail at the lake. This trail passes the Zbojnicka Chata and crosses over the crashing **Veľký studený potok** (Big Cold Stream). Continuing along the blue trail past the intersection with the red trail brings you to the **Studeného vodopády** (waterfalls). From here, the quick 15min. descent along the green trail brings you to Hrebienok. (8hr. total from Sliezsky dom to Hrebienok; for advanced hikers only. All trails open July-Sept.; many closed Nov.1-June 15.)

NEAR STARÝ SMOKOVEC

ŠTRBSKÉ PLESO

The hotels and ski jump towers that clutter placid **Štrbské Pleso** (Štrbské Lake; SHTERB-skay PLEH-soh) recapture the cosmopolitan spirit of the "Interski" Championship held in 1975. While the tourist presence is heavy , Štrbské Pleso's natural beauty and hiking opportunities have yet to be diminished by the tides of visitors that crowd its streets.

🖥🔢 TRANSPORTATION AND PRACTICAL INFORMATION. TEŽ **trains** go to: **Poprad** (1¼hr., every hr., 30Sk); **Starý Smokovec** (30min., every 30min., 20Sk); and **Tatranská Lomnica** (55min., every 30min., 30Sk). Budget travelers should leave the town before dusk, since hotel prices are higher than the elevation and cheap beds are available in nearby Starý Smokovec and Tatranská Lomnica. Before starting a hike, purchase supplies at the mini-market uphill from the train station. (Open daily 7am-6pm.) Opposite the train station is the **Internet Cafe**. (☎449 26 90. Noon-7pm 60Sk per 30min., 7pm-midnight 30Sk per 30min. Open daily noon-midnight.)

🗺 HIKING. Several beautiful hikes lead out from the town. In the summer, a lift carries visitors to **Chata pod Soliskom** (1840m), which overlooks the lake and the expansive valleys that spread behind Štrbské Pleso. The lift is 10min. up the road from the trains; follow the signs or the **yellow trail**. (June 25-Sept. 9 8:30am-4pm. July-Aug. one-way 115Sk, round-trip 180Sk; June and Sept. 80Sk/100Sk.) Once at the top, hike the **red trail** to the peak of **Predné Solisko** (2093m) and commence your descent via the steep **blue trail**, which leads back to Štrbské Pleso (1½hr.). If you prefer a more scenic trip down, turn right on the blue trail from the chata and head left when you reach the yellow trail. Follow the yellow trail until it meets the red trail. Hang a left here to get back to town (2¾hr.).

Two magnificent day hikes loop outwards from Štrbské Pleso. For both, dress warmly and bring plenty of food and water. The **yellow route** heads from the east side of the lake (follow the signs to Hotel Patria) along **Mlynická dolina** past several enchanting mountain lakes and the **Vodopády Skok** waterfalls. It then crosses **Bystré Sedlo** (2314m), winds by **Veľke Solisko** (2412.5m), and circles **Štrbské Solisko** (2302m) before returning to Štrbské Pleso (7-8hr.). This route involves some strenuous ascents that take you well above the tree line, but the stunning scenery is well worth the effort.

The second hike takes you to the top of **Rysy** (2499m) on the Polish-Slovak border, Poland's highest peak and the highest Tatra scalable without a guide. From Štrbské Pleso, follow the *magistrála* to **Chata Popradské Pleso ❶**. (1500m; 1¼hr. ☎449 21 77. 210-300Sk per person. Tourist tax 50Sk.) The awe-inspiring views of the valley along this part of the trail draw thousands each year. A green trail branches off the *magistrála* after 30min. and rolls by the **Hincov potok** (stream) to the *chata* and its lake. From the *chata*, take the blue trail that runs alongside the valley (30min.) and then turn right on the red trail to tackle Rysy. Walk past the lake **Žabie Plesá** to the remains of Chata pod Rysmi (2250m), which stands as a solemn reminder of the power of winter storms in the mountains. Rysy is 40min. from the *chata*; allow 8-9 hours for the round-trip. This hike is for advanced hikers and should be attempted in good weather only.

From the *chata*, 15min. on the yellow trail (open July-Oct.) will take you south to the **Symbolic Cemetery** (Symbolický cintorín; 1525m). Built between 1936 and 1940 by painter Otakar Štafl, the field of wooden crosses, metal plaques, and broken propeller blades serves as a memorial to the dead hikers who have attempted the great Tatras. The trail ends at a paved blue path that the weary can descend to reach the Popradské Pleso TEŽ stop (45min.). Those hardy souls looking to hike back to Štrbské Pleso will be rewarded with striking views from the rigorous course. The *magistrála* continues from the *chata* for over 5hr. along scenic ridges to **Hrebienok** (see **Starý Smokovec: Hiking,** p. 766).

TATRANSKÁ LOMNICA ☎(0)52

Of all the Tatran resorts, peaceful Tatranská Lomnica (TA-tran-ska LOM-nee-tsa) is by far the best place to stay. It's only a short distance from Štrbské Pleso, but the difference is astonishing. The snow is deep and the sleeps are cheap, though the town itself is little more than a scattering of buildings that dot the perimeter of a lush park. Few trails lead directly from town, but thanks to frequent TEŽ trains, all of hiking country is relatively close.

📟 TRANSPORTATION. TEŽ **trains** run to **Starý Smokovec** (13Sk) and **Štrbské Pleso** (30Sk). **Buses,** however, are the best way to get to **Poprad** (30min., every hr., 20Sk). If there's no one at the counter, buy your tickets at the station's machines. The fees for riding ticketless run upwards of 600Sk.

🖫 PRACTICAL INFORMATION. There is no real plan to this cloistered community. Even the helpful signs that point toward local restaurants, hotels, and services end about 100m from the train station, and it's easy to get lost when the streets have no names and most buildings hide behind overgrown pine trees. The attentive and well-informed staff at **Tatranská Informačná Kancelária,** uphill from the train station, behind Uni banka, can help clear up confusion. (☎ 446 81 18; tik.tatry@sinet.sk. Open July-Aug. M-F 8am-6pm, Sa-Su 9am-2pm; Sept.-June M-F 8am-5pm.) The electronic **InfoPanel** halfway between the train stop and Hotel Lomnica, away from the tracks, displays the locations of hotels, pensions, sights, and restaurants, as well as current vacancies. Collect a hard-to-find town map here. **Slovenská Sporitel'ňa,** in the woods behind the train station, cashes **traveler's checks** for 1% commission and has a 24-hour MC/V **ATM.** (Turn right at the first intersection heading away from the tracks. ☎ 46 72 59; fax 46 76 67. Open M 7:30am-3pm, Tu 7:30am-1pm, W 7:30-11:30am and noon-5pm, Th-F 7:30-11:30am and noon-3pm.) **Poľnobank,** along the track opposite the railroad station, has a MC/V **ATM. Sport & Moda,** between the main road and the train station, sells **skis.** (☎ 446 70 27. Open M-F 9am-6pm.) There's a **pharmacy** in the white building opposite Kino Tatry. (Open M-F 7:30am-noon and 1-3:30pm.) Follow the signs to Reštaurácia Júlia (see below) to reach the **post office,** behind the train station. (☎ 44 68 25 34. Open M-F 8:30-noon and 1-3:30pm, Sa 8-10am.) **Postal Code:** 05960.

⚑🛏 ACCOMMODATIONS AND FOOD. Virtually all of the hotels and pensions in Tatranská Lomnica are remarkably cheap. **Penzión Bělín ❶,** in the center of town, is one of the best, renting out warm rooms for bargain prices. The shared bathrooms are impeccably clean. Kitchens and satellite TVs are located in the common room on each floor. Follow the sign from the InfoPanel to the gardens. At the second junction (50m), head up the left path. Turn right to find Bělín. (☎446 77 78; belin@tatry.sk. Check-out 9am. July-Aug. 2- and 4-person rooms 240Sk; Sept.-June 192Sk. 30Sk discount after first night.) For **camping,** follow the main road away from town. Turn right at the first intersection to reach the campsites along the perimeter of the national park. The second facility, the colossal **Eurocamp FICC ❶,** 4km from town, has its own **train stop** (every hr., 7Sk). It lets spacious bungalows with spotless showers. On-site offerings include a sports store (open daily 8am-8pm) that rents **bikes** (250Sk per day) and **in-line skates** (200Sk per day), as well as a grocery store, disco, restaurant, and bar. (☎446 77 41; fax 446 73 46. Tents 90Sk, plus 120Sk per person. 2-person bungalows with bath 1000Sk; quads 1500Sk. V.) From Eurocamp, take a right on the road and head away from the mountains to reach **Športcamp ❶** and its tiny 14- to 20-bed dorms and tent sites. (☎/fax 446 72 88. Reception 7am-10pm. Showers 15Sk. Tents 80Sk per person. Dorms 200Sk.)

The **supermarket** is behind the main train station. (Open M-F 7:45am-9pm, Sa 7:45am-3pm, Su 8am-3pm.) Restaurants line both the train tracks and the main road, but the majority are touristy. One of the few that offers authentic Slovak cuisine, **⬛ Reštaurácia Júlia ❷,** 200m below the station, transcends the town's ubiquitous kitsch with its specialty dishes. Try their delicious ice cream topped with fruit salad (55Sk) to top off a delightful dinner. (☎446 79 47. Entrees 60-180Sk. Open daily 11:30am-9:30pm.)

◧🔥 SIGHTS AND HIKING. Buy tickets a few hours in advance for the remarkable lift ride to **Lomnický Štít** (2634m), the Tatras' second-highest peak. Follow the signs around town to the *lanová draha* **lifts** that ride up to the glacial lake of **Skalnaté Pleso** (1751m). The 4-person lift runs every hour from behind Hotel Sasanka. (Open 8am-7pm; last ascent 6:30pm. One-way 200Sk, round-trip 340Sk.) From the lake, a larger mini-cabin ascends to the summit of **Lomnický Štít** while a chairlift plows on to **Lomnické Sedlo.** (Mini-cabin 400Sk round-trip; chairlift 180Sk round-trip.) Purchase a 550Sk day ticket to **ski** the excellent trails from Skalnatá Chata to Tatranská Lomnica. On a clear day, the peak offers a staggering view. It also has some fabulous picnic spots. At the lake, **Skalnatá Chata** is a relaxing refreshment stop. Be sure to dress warmly as snow falls even in July.

Hiking is generally better from Starý Smokovec or Štrbské Pleso, but a few full-day hikes are accessible from Tatranská Lomnica's lift. The red *magistrála* trail heading southwest from **Skalnaté Pleso** toward **Lomnická vyhliadka** (1524m; 50min.) and then to **Zamkovského Chata** (1¼hr.) is challenging to say the least, but your efforts are rewarded with remarkable views (see **Hiking: Starý Smokovec,** p. 766). The blue trail leads to a gentler hike; follow it from the InfoPanel to **Vodopády studeného potoka** (Cold Stream Waterfalls) and back to Tatranská Lesná (4½hr.). The terrain here is flat enough to make this trip by bike.

🎭 ENTERTAINMENT. The long days of skiing and hiking put most people to bed by 8pm, but some life sparkles through the night. **Kino Tatry,** in the Tatranské Kulturne Centrum, probably requires the least energy, with the usual Hollywood films. From the bus or train station, turn right on the main road, and then right at the Muzeum Tanaf signs. (☎446 72 19. Centrum open M-F 8am-noon and 1-5pm, Sa 8am-3pm. Cover 50-56Sk. Shows daily at 7pm; Su matinees 4:45pm.) **Oaza Bar,** in the same building, entertains a small crowd with billiard tables. (Happy Hour M-Sa 4-5pm. Beer 0.51-9.90Sk. Open Su-Th 3pm-midnight, F-Sa 9pm-3am.)

ŠARIŠ

Hidden away in the green hills of eastern Slovakia, Šariš has spent the last century keeping to itself. Before that, however, the region was forced to be more politically oriented and to act as a buffer against Turkish invasions. These days, the towns of Prešov and Bardejov are gaining more popularity among tourists. Each offers a feel for what the Slovak Republic was like before Westernization, with all of the amenities that one longs for when far from home.

KOŠICE   ☎(0)55

Košice (KO-shih-tseh; pop. 300,000), is the Slovak Republic's second largest city. Lying only 20km north of Hungary, its cultural and architectural development date back to the 19th century, when it was an important industrial center. Hungarian nobles settled here and pumped money into the city and its artistic institutions, setting the stage for a strikingly innovative and attractive city center. The medieval craftsmen who founded the town would likely wince at Košice's steel foundries and suburban highrises, but would take comfort in the wrought-iron fountains and Glockenspiel bells. The favorite city of most Slovaks, Košice is gaining fame among foreigners; visit now before the crowds arrive.

▎ TRANSPORTATION

Trains: On Predstaničné nám. (☎613 21 75). To: **Bratislava** (6hr., 11per day, 414Sk); **Budapest, HUN** (5hr., 3 per day, 640Sk); **Kraków, POL** (6-7hr., 3 per day, 879Sk); **Kyiv, UKR** (12hr., 1 per day, 1855Sk); **Lviv, UKR** (6hr., 1 per day, 960Sk); **Prague, CZR** (9½hr., 7 per day, 977Sk).

Buses: ☎680 73 06. Next to the train station. More expensive than trains, but sometimes faster for local trips. Buses go to many domestic destinations, and prices, which fluctuate annually, are based on the number of km traveled.

Public Transportation: Trams and **buses** traverse the city and its suburbs. Tickets 12Sk from kiosks and orange boxes at bus stops, 14Sk from the driver.

Taxis: Taxis await on almost every corner. **Radio Taxi** (☎163 33), **Classic Taxi** (☎622 22 44), and **CTC** (☎43 34 33).

ORIENTATION AND PRACTICAL INFORMATION

Košice's **Staré Mesto** (Old Town) lies close to the **train station.** To get to the central **Nam. Hlavná** and the tourist office, exit the station and follow the "Centrum" signs across the park to **Mlynská,** which intersects Hlavná at the cathedral. Turn right on Hlavná to reach the tourist office.

Tourist Office: Mestské Informačna Centrum, Hlavná 8 (☎625 88 88). Dispenses info on hotels and cultural happenings. Internet access (10Sk per 10min). Open M-F 9am-6pm, Sa 9am-1pm.

Currency Exchange: VÚB branches are everywhere; the one at Hlavná 8 (☎622 62 50) **exchanges currency** for no commission, cashes **traveler's checks** for 1% commission, and gives MC **cash advances.** Open M-Tu and F 7:30am-5pm, W 8am-7pm, Th 8am-noon, Sa 9am-1pm. 24hr. MC/V **ATMs** are in front of many VÚB branches.

Luggage Storage: At the train station. 10Sk per bag under 15kg; heavier bags 20Sk. Small lockers 5Sk. Open 24hr.

International Bookstore: SFA, Hlavná 97 (☎623 36 76), upstairs and through the arch. Small selection of English language classics (79-99Sk) and popular literature (320-480Sk). Open M-F 10am-6pm.

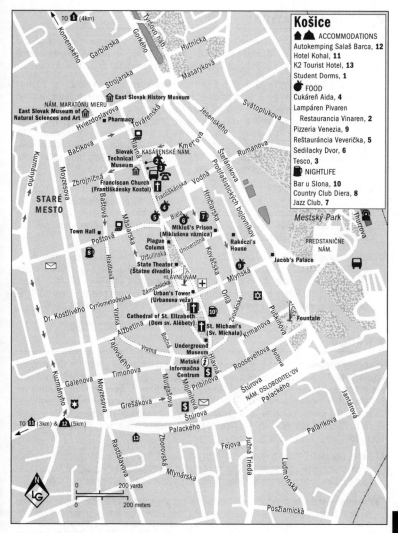

Košice

🏠🏔 ACCOMMODATIONS
Autokemping Salaš Barca, **12**
Hotel Kohal, **11**
K2 Tourist Hotel, **13**
Student Dorms, **1**

🍎 FOOD
Cukáreň Aida, **4**
Lampáren Pivaren
  Restaurancia Vinaren, **2**
Pizzeria Venezia, **9**
Reštauráncia Veverička, **5**
Sedilacky Dvor, **6**
Tesco, **3**

🍸 NIGHTLIFE
Bar u Slona, **10**
Country Club Diera, **8**
Jazz Club, **7**

Pharmacy: Lekáreň Pri Dóme, Mlynská 1. Open M-F 7:30am-6:30pm, Sa 8am-noon.

Telephones: Around Hlavná and outside the post office (see below).

Internet Access: At the central **tourist office** (see above), 40Sk per hr. **Internet café 115,** Hlavná 115. M-F 50Sk per hr., Sa-Su 29Sk per hr. Open M-Th 9am-10pm, F 9am-midnight, Sa 10am-midnight, Su 10am-10pm. **Net Internet Cafe,** Poštová 3. Ring the bell to get in. 25-39Sk per hr. Open daily 7am-4pm.

Post Office: Poštová 20. Open M-F 7am-7pm, Sa 7am-2pm.

Postal Code: 04001.

ACCOMMODATIONS

Keep in mind that some larger hotels can be cheaper, nicer, and closer to the center than *penzióny*. **Student dorms ❶** (☎796 11 35; about 200Sk per night) are the cheapest option in July and August, but are very far from the center.

K2 Tourist Hotel, Štúrova 32 (☎625 59 48). Take tram #6 or bus #16, 21, or 30 from the train/bus station to the "Dom Umenia" stop. Or, for a 20min. walk, follow directions to Hlavná (see **Orientation,** p. 770) and turn left, then right on Štúrova. You'll see a red and yellow sign for K2 on your left; walk through the gate into a yard with a fountain. Turn left and head up the stairs. Small, basic rooms and a friendly staff. Massages 5Sk per min. Tanning 5.20Sk per min. Sauna 100Sk per 2hr. Hot tub 6.50 Sk per min. Breakfast 70Sk. Restaurant open M-Sa 10am-10pm, Su noon-10pm. Reception 24hr. Check-out 10am. Triples and quads 290Sk per person. ❶

Hotel Kohal, Trieda SNP 61 (☎642 55 72). Take tram #6 in front of the train/bus station to a roundabout at Toryská and Trieda SNP. Get off at the "Ferrocentrum" stop; Kohal will be on your right. Almost every room has a balcony. Shared baths in some rooms. Breakfast 90Sk. Laundry 4-50Sk per item. Reception 24hr. Check-out 2pm. Singles 230-460Sk; doubles 420-980Sk. AmEx/MC/V. ❷

Autokemping Salaš Barca (☎623 33 97). From the train/bus station, take tram #6 to the "Ferrocentrum" stop and switch to tram #9. Get off at "Autokemping" and backtrack 100m; turn left at sign. Simple, clean bungalows and tent sites on a beautiful green. Reception 24hr. Reserve 3 days in advance. Camping 70Sk per person. Tents 80Sk. 2-bed bungalows 480Sk per person; 3-bed 720Sk; 5-bed 870Sk. AmEx/MC/V. ❷

FOOD

With restaurants on roof-top terraces, hidden under arches, and on the central square itself, Košice is a gastronomic paradise. Although most cheap food seems to go by the name "pizza," there *is* good Slovak fare here at reasonable prices. Even connoisseurs of Slovak cuisine will find enough *knedle* (dumplings) to fill their cravings. For **groceries,** try the **Tesco** at Hlavná 109 right next door to Pizza Hut. (☎670 48 10. Open M-W 8am-8pm, Th-F 8am-9pm, Sa-Su 8am-6pm. MC/V.)

Sedliacky Dvor, Biela 2 (☎622 04 02), off Hlavná. Look no farther for those Slovak dishes you've been longing for, but don't expect any English menus, as this place is frequented by Košice residents. Entrees 50-120Sk. Open daily 10am-midnight. ❷

Pizzeria Venezia, Mlynská 20 (☎622 33 35). People-watch on the patio or join the more sedate crowd inside. Expertly prepared pizza 88-110Sk. Open daily 10am-midnight. ❷

Reštaurácia Veverička (Squirrel Restaurant), Hlavná 97 (☎622 33 60). Look for the pair of rodents carved out of dark wood. Luckily, the name has nothing to do with the food. A good Slovak restaurant. Entrees 59-198Sk. Open daily 9am-11pm. ❷

Cukráreň Aida, Hlavná 80. The crowds come for gourmet sweets (15-65Sk) and fabulous ice cream (5Sk per scoop). Open daily 8am-10pm. ❶

Lampáren Pivaren Restaurancia Vinaren, Hlavná 115 (☎622 49 95), through the archway and on the right. Upscale Slovakian fare and a great "beer garden" atmosphere. Vegetarian menu available. A pool table awaits in the back, and this area becomes a disco F and Sa. Entrees 95Sk. Open M-Su 11am-midnight. Disco open F-Sa until 2am. ❶

🜨 SIGHTS

▓**CATHEDRAL OF ST. ELIZABETH.** (Dom sv. Alžbety.) This gigantic cathedral practically spans the width of **Hlavná.** Begun in 1378 as a high-Gothic monument, the cathedral has undergone repeated renovations; it now stands as a conglomeration of almost every style known to Western architecture, from its Baroque tiling to its vibrant and varied stained-glass windows, to its Rococo Pillars. In 1900, restorers built a crypt under the cathedral's north nave. Košice's revolutionary hero **Ferenc Rakóczi II,** transported from Turkey in 1906, is chilling here in his sarcophagus. The cathedral's little brother next door, the **Chapel of St. Michael** (Kaplnka sv. Michala), currently under renovation, serves as a mortuary. Outside, a relief depicts St. Michael weighing the souls of the dead. On the other side of the cathedral, the barren facade of **Urban's Tower** (Urbanova veža) seems almost two-dimensional next to the ornaments of St. Elizabeth's. A closer look, however, reveals 36 tombstones lining the exterior, one of which dates from the 4th century. Next to the tower sits a fountain, which on weekend afternoons performs a water "dance." Across the park from St. Michael's, stairs lead down to the **ruins** of the town's fortifications.

AROUND JACOB'S PALACE. (Jakubov Palác.) Walking down Mlynská from the cathedral toward the train station leads to the 19th-century **Jacob's Palace,** built of stones discarded from the cathedral in a style described by the staff as "Pseudo-Gothic." Before you scoff and start hunting for the genuine Gothic you know is out there, take a look—it's worth it. Currently occupied by the British Council, the palace served as a temporary home to Czechoslovakia's president in the spring of 1945. Behind the cathedral on Hlavná, on the far side of the dancing fountain, stands the neo-Baroque **State Theater** (Štátne divadlo), built at the end of the 19th century. The theater doesn't host performances during July and August, but its beautiful interior remains open for viewing M-F 10am-2pm. Past the theater on Hlavná, the **Marian Plague Column** (Morový Sloup), decorated with statues of angels, commemorates the devastating plague of 1711.

EAST SLOVAK MUSEUM. (Východoslovenské Múzeum.) Univerzitná runs from Hlavná to the right (between the column and the theater) to two branches of the East Slovak Museum: **Mikluš's Prison** (Miklušova väznica) and **Rakóczi's House.** Housed in the former city jail, Mikluš's prison details life behind bars from the 17th to the 19th century, exhibiting prisoner graffiti and torture instruments. The tour covers reconstructed prison chambers and photo collections. Rakóczi's House is a shrine to Ferenc Rakóczi II, Hungary's anti-Habsburg national hero. A guidebook is available in English and each display case has a broken English translation. (Hrnčiarska 7. Ticket office behind the gate at Hrnčiarska. Open Tu-Sa 9am-5pm, Su 9am-1pm. Mandatory tours every hr. 20Sk, students 10Sk. Guidebook 30Sk.)

At Nám Mieru Maratónu, in the ornate building closest to the runner's statue, stands the archaeological branch of the **East Slovak Museum,** which exhibits finds from near Košice and details the region's history. The museum's best exhibit awaits downstairs in the vault: a copper bowl filled with 2920 gold *tholars* and a gold Renaissance chain over 2m long. Workers discovered both in 1935 while laying foundations for new finance headquarters at Hlavná 68. (Hviezdoslavova 2. ☎622 05 71. Open Tu-Sa 9am-5pm, Su 9am-1pm. 20Sk, students 10Sk.)

Across the street, the **Art and Natural Science Museum** is housed in a Baroque-inspired building. The collections change regularly, but a permanent exhibit exists as well. (Hlavná 27. ☎622 11 87. Open Tu-Sa 9am-5pm, Su 9am-1pm. 20Sk, students 10Sk.)

🎵 ENTERTAINMENT

Fans of high and low culture alike will not be disappointed by Košice. Information about Košice's **philharmonic orchestra** and four **theaters** is available at the tourist office (see **Practical Information,** p. 770). Seasons run Sept.-June. On the first Sunday of October, the annual **Košice Peace Marathon** keeps runners on their toes from Turňa nad Bodvov to the statue of the bronze runner on Hlavná. The event, which first took place in 1924, is the second-oldest marathon in the world (after Boston's). The winners' names are inscribed on the statue's pedestal. Bars, discos, and live music venues hide under archways and on the side streets off Hlavná; the hassle of reaching these hot spots will certainly be rewarded.

Jazz Club, Kovača 39 (☎622 42 37). Jazz only comes around a few times a week, but disco, oldies, salsa, and swing fill in the gaps. Beer 25Sk-35Sk. Mixed drinks 80Sk-200Sk. Cover Tu, W, Sa 50Sk; F 30Sk. Free M, Th, Su. Open M-Th 11am-midnight, F 11am-2am, Sa 4pm-2am, Su 4pm-midnight.

Country Club Diera (The Hole), through the arch at Poštová 14 (☎622 05 51). Quenches the Slovak thirst for bluegrass. Tequila shots and 7 types of whiskey await in this spirited bastion of wild west culture. Tex-Mex inspired pub grub with many veggie options available until closing. Beer 20Sk-40Sk. W and F disco, Th live rock. Whiskey 50Sk-60Sk. Open M-Tu and Th 11am-1am, W 11am-2am, F 11am-3am, Sa noon-2am, Su noon-midnight.

Bar u Slona (At the Elephant), Hlavná 37 (☎622 62 31). In a quiet courtyard concealed by a short passageway. Frequented by a more sedate crowd. Pizza 48-58Sk. Heineken 60Sk, Pilsner 26Sk. Open M-Sa 10am-11pm, Su 2-11pm.

PREŠOV   ☎51

More than a millennium ago, the first Slavic farms were already in place where Prešov (preh-SHOV; pop. 92,600), the capital of Šariš, now stands. The current atmosphere in Slovakia's third-largest city is decidedly cosmopolitan, but the colorful town square and historic buildings attest to its rural roots.

🚆 TRANSPORTATION. Trains (☎773 10 43) travel to: **Bardejov** (1¼hr., 5 per day, 44Sk); **Bratislava** via **Kysak** (4½hr., 9 per day, 414Sk);; **Košice** (50min., 15 per day, 34Sk); **Budapest, HUN** (5hr., 1 per day, 896Sk); **Kraków, POL** (5½hr., 3 per day, 710Sk). **Buses** (☎773 13 47), across the street from the train station, travel to: **Bardejov** (50min., 12 per day, 46Sk); **Košice** (30-45min., 3 per hr., 37Sk); **Poprad** (1½hr., 10 per day, 101Sk).

🔷🔶 ORIENTATION AND PRACTICAL INFORMATION. Prešov's   stem, **Košická,** sprouts straight from the train station, becoming **Masarykova,** then **Hlavná,** home of the Church of St. Nicholas. To get to the town center, take the walkway under Masarykova, purchase an 8Sk (exact change required) ticket from the kiosk, and hop on any **tram** or **bus** (except #19 or 31) heading in the Centrum direction from the train station. Otherwise, walk left from the train station along Košická (20min.) or take a taxi (70Sk). The **tourist office, Mestské Informačné Centrum,** Hlavná 67, provides info on the town and hotels, as well as a great pocket map (15Sk) of the city. (☎/fax 73 11 13; www.pis.sk. Internet 50Sk per hr. Open May-Oct. M-F 10am-6pm, Sa 9am-1pm; Nov.-Apr. M-F 8am-4:30pm.) **Exchange currency** at **Istrobanka**, Hlavná 75, which has good rates and a 24hr. MC/V **ATM** outside. The bank also cashes **traveler's checks** for no commission. (☎758 04 18; fax 772 31 65. Open M-F 8am-5pm.) Lockers are available at the train or bus station for 5Sk. A **24hr. pharmacy** is at Sabinovská 15 (☎771 94 05). Walk up Hlavná away from the train station toward the center; Sabinovská is to the left past the intersection. The tourist office has **Internet access** (see above), as does **Arcadia Internet Club**, Slovenská 46. (☎771 26 34. June-Aug. M-F 25Sk per 30min., Sa-Su 20Sk; Sept.-May M-F 15Sk per 30min., Sa-Su 10Sk. Open daily 10am-10pm.) Card **telephones** are outside the **post office**, Masarykova 2, sits just south of the city center. (☎773 45 24. Open M-F 8am-7pm, Sa 8am-1pm.) **Postal Code:** 08001.

▐▌◩ ACCOMMODATIONS AND FOOD. To get to **Turistická Ubytovňa Sen ❶**, Vajanského 65, take a bus toward the center. Get off at "Na Hlanéj," at the entrance to the main square. Follow the departing bus and take the first right on Metodova. The unmarked Vajanského is the second-to-last street off Metodova (5min.). Turn left; the hostel is on the right (look for the blue sign). It rents 27 beds, has three showers, and is close to the center. (☎773 31 70. Reception 24hr., staff takes break 11am-2pm some days. Check-out noon. Singles 350Sk; doubles 280Sk per person; quads 250Sk per person.) **Penzión Lineas ❷**, Budovatelská 14, is closer to the train station than to the center. From the station, walk toward the town center, take the first left on Škultétyho and then your second left on Budovatelská. You'll come upon nine floors of comfortable doubles with baths and balconies. Snacks are available at reception and a small coffee shop opens daily 7:30am-10am and 6pm-8pm. (☎772 33 25, ext. 28; fax 772 32 06. Reception 24hr. Check-out 11am. Doubles 500Sk, 650Sk with TV.) **Penzión Antonio ❸**, on Jarková, lets comfortable, clean, and well-ventilated rooms in the center of town. Follow the bus directions for Turistická Ubytovňa Sen, then take a left on Florianova (directly across the square from Metodova). Hang another left on Jarková; the pension is on the left. This inn also has a pizza restaurant, which you can enter on Hlavná, to the left of the tourist office. (☎772 32 25. Reception M-F 10am-10pm, Sa-Su 3-10pm. Check-out noon. Call 3 days ahead. Doubles 800-1100Sk.)

What it lacks in accommodations, Prešov makes up for in dining. For do-it-yourselfers, there's a **Tesco** supermarket, Legionarova 1, where Hlavná becomes Masarykova. (Open M-F 8am-8pm, Sa 8am-5pm, Su 8am-3pm.) **Florianka ❷**, Baštová 23, sits through the archway to your right next to Slovakia's best hotel and restaurant management school. This former firehouse is now the training ground of culinary students. Dine outside if the blazing red interior is too much for you; just don't try to ride the pushcart fire truck. (☎77 40 83. Entrees 34-119Sk. Open M-Sa 10am-9:30pm.) **Senator ❷**, Hlavná 67, overlooking Staré Mesto, caters to all appetites with vegetarian dishes and meatier Slovak fare. A beer hall is attached. (☎773 11 86. Entrees 44-245Sk. 0.5L Šariš 19Sk. Open M-F 8am-10pm, Sa-Su 11am-10pm. Beer hall open daily 3pm-midnight.) **Slovenská Bageta ❶**, Hlavná 36, serves baguette sandwiches (17-56Sk) with and without meat. (☎773 26 02. Open M-F 6am-10pm, Sa 7:30am-10pm, Su 8am-10pm.) Down the street from Bageta, **Veliovič Cukráreň ❶**, Hlavná 28, is heavenly. Indulge in its sweets (6-17Sk), hefty desserts (banana splits 50Sk), homemade ice cream (55Sk per scoop), and cappuccino (20Sk). (Open M-F 8am-9pm, Sa-Su 9am-9pm.)

SLOVAK REPUBLIC

◘ SIGHTS. Hlavná's Renaissance houses stand back in deference to the town's older **Church of St. Nicholas** (Kostol sv. Mikuláša; built 1347). The Gothic church's distinctive turrets attest to Saxon influence in Prešov during the late Middle Ages. The gold-laden altar crafted by Majster Pavol (see **Levoča,** p. 759) lies under a 66m late Gothic tower. The church opens for services, but rarely for visits. (Wear long-sleeved shirts for services). Near the church is the **Wine Museum,** Floriánova ul., which showcases more than 3000 varieties of wines, many of which you can sample for 100Sk. If you're looking to indulge in more than a sample, pick up a bottle. Common local vintages cost 60Sk, but a few rare bottles are more expensive: a 1942 Argentine wine, the pride of their international collection, is 35,000Sk. (☎773 31 08. Open M-F 8am-7pm, Sa 8am-noon. 40Sk.)

Also near the church, the 16th-century **Rákoczi Palace,** Hlavná 86, with its attic gable of plants and saints, houses the **Regional Museum** (Krajské múzeum). The exhibition on fire moves from making it in the Stone Age to fighting it in more recent eras, concluding with old fire trucks parked out back. A particularly well-designed section of the museum features regional folk costumes, local craftsmanship, and everyday utensils. (☎773 47 08. Open Tu-F 8am-noon and 12:30-5pm, Sa 9am-1pm, Su 1-5pm. 30Sk, students 15Sk.) Amble down to the Greek Orthodox **St. John's Cathedral** (Katedrálny chrám sv. Jána Krstiteľa), at the base of Hlavná, to peek at the breathtaking altar. On the west side of Hlavná, the restored Gothic **Šarišská Gallery,** Hlavná 51, features local art. (☎772 54 23. Open Tu-W and F 9am-5pm, Th 9am-6pm, Sa 9am-1pm, Su 2-6pm. 20Sk, students 10Sk; Su free.)

Heading left from the town hall on Hlavná, the narrow, medieval Floriánova leads to **St. Florian's Gate** (Brána sv. Floriána), a remnant of Prešov's early Renaissance fortifications and a tribute to the town's patron saint. Walking up Hlavná away from St. Nicholas Church, take a left on Ku Kumštu which will lead to Švermova and a courtyard at #56. Inside is a **synagogue,** with an ornate interior and a monument to Prešov's 6000 victims of the Holocaust and the Tiso regime. If the doors are closed, you can still see the interior via the **Judaica Museum,** on the upper balcony, which uses artifacts from the Jews of Presov to detail the Jewish holidays and rites of passage. (☎773 16 38. Open Tu-W 11am-4pm, Th 3-6pm, F 10am-1pm, Su 1-5pm. 60Sk, students 10Sk.)

⬛ NIGHTLIFE. There's a surprising amount of nightlife in this placid town. The most popular spots are the six beer gardens along the west side of Hlavná. Little differentiates these canopied bars; just plop down where there's room. **Vináreň Neptun,** Hlavná 64, provides a refreshing break from ABBA and friends. Sprawling across seven rooms, this winery and pub has space for all. Head through the arch; the entrance is on the right. (☎773 25 38. Open M-Th 10am-10pm, F 10pm-2am, Sa 6pm-3am.) If it's ABBA you want, **Alfa,** Kováčska 3, is the place to be. For those too tired to shake it Slovak style, there's plenty of comfy seating. (☎772 52 52. Cover on live music nights. Open F-Sa 8:30pm-4:30am, W-Th and Su 8pm-4am.)

BARDEJOV ☎(0)54

The scenic countryside of Bardejov (bar-day-YOV; pop. 38,000) has a history of both great prosperity and terrible disaster. Settled 800 years ago, the town was situated on a trade route to Poland and Kyivan Rus, profiting from caravans that would pass through town. The wealth, however, couldn't stop the earthquakes, Turkish armies, and fires that have rolled through in the last 500 years. Bardejov's last reconstruction effort won it a 1986 UNESCO Heritage Gold Medal, proving that neither plague nor natural disaster could keep the town in ruins. The town's laid-back pace, cobblestone walkways, pleasant views, and serene springwater make it a favorite honeymoon spot for Slovak couples and an undeniably worthwhile stop for tourists.

F TRANSPORTATION. Trains (☎472 36 05) go to: **Košice** (1¾-2¼hr., 3 per day, 76Sk); **Prešov** (1¼hr., 5 per day, 44Sk); **Kraków, POL** (7hr., 4 per day, 850Sk). The quickest way to and from Bardejov is by **bus** (☎472 31 21). To: **Košice** (1¾hr., 12 per day, 79Sk); **Poprad** (2½ hr., 12 per day, 119Sk); **Prešov** (50min., 12 per day, 46Sk).

■ ⊡ ORIENTATION AND PRACTICAL INFORMATION. From the train station, turn left, walk through the parking lot, cross the road, and turn right. Take the stone path to the right through the ruined, lower gate of **Staré Mesto** (Old Town) onto the unmarked Stöcklova. Follow **Stöcklova** around to the left and turn right on Paštová to reach **Radničné nám.**, the main square. **Globtour Bratislava, the tourist office** at Radničné nám. 21, sells maps (10Sk) of Bardejov and Bardejovské Kúpele, and also provides useful accommodation, restaurant, and attraction information. (☎/fax 472 62 73. Open June 15-Sept. 15 M-F 9am-6pm, Sa-Su 10am-noon and 1:30-4pm; Sept. 16-June 14 M-F 9am-4:30pm.) Get MC/V **cash advances,** or cash AmEx/V **traveler's checks** for 1% commission at **VÚB,** Kellerova 1. A 24hr. MC/V **ATM** stands outside. (☎472 26 71. Open M-W and F 8am-5pm, Th 8am-noon.) A **pharmacy** lies at Radničné nám. 43. (☎472 75 62. Open M-F 7:30am-5pm, Sa 7:30-9:30am.) **Internet access** is available at: **Dot.Com Internet Club,** opposite the train station (☎488 21 31; 0.4-0.8Sk per min; open daily 8am-midnight); and **Internetovy Klub,** Radničné nám. 12, through the arch at #12 and up two flights of stairs (☎485 28 03. 35Sk per hour; open daily 10am-10pm). The **post office** is at Dlný rad 14. (☎472 40 62. Open M-F 7:30am-6pm, Sa 8-11:30am.) The outer foyer sells phone cards; **telephones** are outside. (Open M-F 7:30am-6pm, Sa 7:30-11:30am.) **Postal Code:** 08501.

⌐⊡ ACCOMMODATIONS AND FOOD. More accommodations are available outside of town, but are generally accessible only by car. The tourist office keeps the most updated accommodations list and will book rooms at no charge. Vladimír Kaminsky and his wife at **Penzión Semafór ❸**, (Kellerova 13) welcome visitors with unmatched hospitality. Follow directions to Športhotel (below), but turn left on Kellerova and look for the green fence on the right. The three plush doubles have TV and bath. (☎583 09 84. Breakfast 805Sk. Doubles 1000Sk.) **Športhotel ❷**, Katuzovovo 31, 15min. from the train station, is a basic hotel popular with the younger crowd. With your back to the train tracks, take a right on Slovenská and then the first left on Jilemnického. After 200m, hang a right on Kellerova (not well-marked, but you'll see a bridge when you turn). Turn left after the bridge; the hotel is on the right. (☎472 49 49; fax 472 82 08. Reception until 10pm. Check-out 10am. Call ahead. Doubles with bath 500Sk; triples 700Sk; quads 800Sk.)

Most restaurants in Bardejov are inexpensive, but a few rise above the ranks of snack bars and drab beer halls. The new **Cafe Restaurant Hubert ❷,** Radničné nam. 6 serves delicious grilled fare, from beef to the local catch of the day. (☎474 26 03. Entrees 89-139Sk. Open M-Th 10am-11pm, F-Sa 10am-1am, Su 11am-11pm.) The classy and romantic **Roland ❷,** Radičné nám. 12, serves delicious Italian meals, several vegetarian dishes, and some Slovak favorites. In the summer, dining is available on the outdoor patio. Go through the arch and to the back to reach the patio. (☎472 92 20. Entrees 75-110Sk. Open daily 11am-11pm. MC/V.) **Reštaurácia Na Bráne ❷,** Jiráskova 3, at the end of Hziezdoslavova, whips up Slovak delicacies. (☎472 23 48. Entrees 35-106Sk. Open M-F 8am-8pm, Sa-Su 8am-7:30pm.) Next to the Bardejov Museum, **Bagetária U Paliho ❶,** Rhodýho 4, serves tasty salads, hamburgers, and subs. (Entrees 14-80Sk. Open Su-Th 10am-11pm, F-Sa 10am-midnight). Get groceries at **Bumerang Potraviny,** Dlný Rad 21. (☎472 87 53. Open M-F 7am-6pm, Sa 7am-noon.)

◙ SIGHTS AND FESTIVALS. Take some time to wander through the square and its surrounding streets to get a sense of Bardejov's history. When the urge to visit a church strikes, stop at the **Church of St. Egidius** (Kostol sv. Egídia), Radničné nám., which contains 11 Gothic wing altars crafted between 1450 and 1510. The largest of these, the scrupulously detailed 15th-century **Nativity Altar,** was consecrated by St. Gilles, the patron saint of the town and the church. (Open M-F 10am-4pm, Sa 10am-2:30pm, Su open for services. 25Sk, students 15Sk; tower 40Sk/20Sk.) Follow Veterna over the main road and turn left up Pod lipken to reach the **Church of the Holy Cross** (Kostol sv. Kríža). A forest path winds through 14 stark **Stations of the Cross** before opening onto a weed-filled graveyard. Veterna ends at one of Bardejov's 12 remaining **bastions,** which served as a crossroads beacon and, later, as the local beheading stock. Bardejov's **Jewish quarter** lies on ul. Mlynská, west of the city center, where there is a closed **synagogue** and a memorial plaque to the more than 7000 Jews who perished during the Holocaust.

The **town hall** (*radnica*), Radničné nám. 48 (☎474 60 38), now serves as a **museum,** displaying historic trinkets. Among them is the key to the city, which the mayor's wife lent to her treacherous Turkish lover in 1697; she was later executed for her deceit. The most interesting item in the collection is the enormous **statue of the Last Supper,** with its unflattering portraits of the dinner guests. The **icon exhibition,** Radničné nám. 27 (☎472 20 09), houses a huge collection of Orthodox icons. The aptly named "Nature of Northeastern Slovakia" display in the **Prírodopisné Múzeum,** on Rhodýho 4, will tickle the taxidermist in you. (☎472 26 30. Museums open May-Sept. 15 daily 8:30am-noon and 12:30-5pm; Oct.-Apr. Tu-Su 8am-noon and 12:30-4pm. 25Sk, students 10Sk. Camera 50Sk. Video 100Sk.) Take note of the **maple tree** at the uphill end, a gift from the US, brought in 1991 by former Vice President Dan Quayle.

During the last weekend of Aug., the town square comes alive for an annual market in celebration of **St. Egidus.** Bardejov hosts an annual festival to celebrate their UNESCO honor—and to give thanks to the town's patron saint, Roland. The festival, known as **Deň Mesta** (Day of the Town), takes place in the first week of June.

◪ NIGHTLIFE. Although Bardejov is a gentle and sedate city, it has its fair share of evening entertainment. The fashionable winery **Viecha,** Hziezdoslavova 6, is frequented day and night by 20-somethings. (Slovak wines 10Sk per 0.10L. Open M-Th 10am-10pm, F 10am-midnight, Sa 5pm-midnight, Su 4-10pm.) Party harder (but watch out for offers of straight Becherovka) at **Pub u Smádného Mnícha,** Radničné nám. 27. At night, the bar teems with the regulars. (☎474 45 24. Beer 0.5L 19-21Sk. Open daily noon-midnight.) The **Irish Pub** at Radničné nám. 32 is touted by the local "beer connoisseurs" as a hip place to enjoy a Guinness. (☎377 18 30. Guinness 35-65Sk. Open M-Th 11am-11pm, F-Sa 11am-2am, Su 11am-11pm.)

NEAR BARDEJOV

BARDEJOV BATHS (BARDEJOVSKÉ KÚPELE)

6km from Bardejov. Take bus #1, 6, or 12 to the end of the line from the front entrance of the train station in Bardejov (20min., 7Sk). ☎472 20 72. Skanzen museums open daily May-Sept. 8:30am-noon and 12:30-5pm; Oct.-Apr. 8:30am-noon and 12:30-3pm. Buy tickets for the outdoor museum from the kassa behind the fence, and for the ethnographic museum just inside its doors. 25Sk, students 10Sk. Camera 50Sk. Video 100Sk.)

The Bardejovské Kúpele (Bardejov Baths) provide a fabulous change of scenery from the city. Enjoy the country air, natural springs, and buildings scattered around a giant central park. The pace of life here is slow and sedate, broken only by locals quibbling over who is next in line to fill up his bottle with the public fountain's curative water. Be prepared for the less-than-pleasant acidic taste. Although distasteful 1970s style hotels line the periphery of the park, well-maintained 18th- and 19th-century buildings are located within the boundaries of the park at the **Skanzen outdoor museum.** The **museum** next door, holding the Slovak Republic's oldest folklore exhibition, regularly displays ethnographic objects, religious icons, and relics from casino days. It also occasionally hosts folk festivals and craft days. Catch a glimpse of the drinking glasses of the spa's most famous past clients, including Tsar Alexander I of Russia, Joseph II of Austria-Hungary, Napoleon, and the wives of Austrian Emperor Franz Joseph. For a dip, head to the **swimming pool,** formed from natural springs. (☎47 44 21. Open M-F noon-7pm, Sa-Su 8am-7pm. 25Sk, students 15Sk; weekends 40Sk/30Sk).

If you're looking for a treat, drop into any of the hotels for various spa treatments. Massages, manicures, pedicures, and more can be enjoyed for relatively inexpensive fees. Ask the receptionists at each hotel for prices and availablity.

SLOVENIA (SLOVENIJA)

TOLAR

AUS$1 = 127.41 SIT	100 SIT = AUS$0.78
CDN$1 = 149.13 SIT	100 SIT = CDN$0.67
EUR€1 = 228.38 SIT	100 SIT = EUR€0.44
NZ$1 = 108.63 SIT	100 SIT = NZ$0.92
UK£1 = 359.83 SIT	100 SIT = UK£0.28
US$1 = 232.07 SIT	100 SIT = US$0.43
ZAR1 = 21.86 SIT	100 SIT = ZAR4.57

Slovenia, the most prosperous of Yugoslavia's breakaway republics, revels in its newfound independence. Having quickly separated itself from its neighbors, Slovenia now looks to the West, using liberal politics and a high GDP to gain entrance into highly sought-after trade and security alliances like the EU and NATO. Modernization has not, however, had adverse effects on the country's natural beauty and diversity; in tiny Slovenia, you can breakfast on an Alpine peak, lunch under the Mediterranean sun, and dine in a vineyard on the Pannonian plains, all in one day.

SLOVENIA AT A GLANCE

OFFICIAL NAME: Republic of Slovenia

CAPITAL: Ljubljana (pop. 276,000)

POPULATION: 2 million (88% Slovenian, 3% Croat, 9% other)

LANGUAGE: Slovenian

CURRENCY: 1 tolar (SIT) = 100 stotins

RELIGION: 69% Roman Catholic, 4% atheist, 27% other

LAND AREA: 20,253km²

GEOGRAPHY: Mountains and plateaus

CLIMATE: Mediterranean, Alpine

BORDERS: Austria, Croatia, Hungary, Italy

ECONOMY: 61% Services, 35% Industry, 4% Agriculture

GDP: US$12,000 per capita

COUNTRY CODE: 386

INTERNATIONAL DIALING PREFIX: 00

HISTORY

THE EARLY YEARS. The **Alpine Slavs,** predecessors of the Slovenes, migrated to the eastern Alps in the 6th century, absorbing the existing cultures. In the 10th and 11th centuries, when Christianity was accepted by the Slavs, the Slovenes converted to **Catholicism** and firmly lodged on the Western side of the European fence.

AGE OF EMPIRES. Following the fall of the Frankish Empire in the 10th century, Slovene lands were given to the Germans and the Slovenes were enserfed. Between 1278 and 1335 all but Istria (nabbed by Venice) fell to the **Austrian Habsburgs.** The dynasty lasted for several centuries, although in the early 1800s

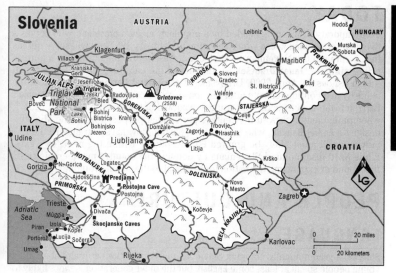

some of the Slovene lands were overrun by **Napoleon.** Inadvertently the French triggered the development of Slovene **nationalism** in the 19th century by working to make Slovene the official language of the territory, leading to the formation of Slovene political parties and codification of the Slovene language.

FIGHTING FOR FREEDOM. After the collapse of Austria-Hungary (see **Hungary: History,** p. 330) following **World War I,** Slovenia agreed to join the newly formed Kingdom of Serbs, Croats, and Slovenes (renamed **Yugoslavia** in 1929). The new state was too weak, however, to withstand Hitler's forces during **World War II.** When Yugoslavia fell in 1941, Slovenia was partitioned among Germany, Italy, and Hungary. Slovene resistance groups formed and united under the **Slovene National Liberation Front,** which soon joined the Yugoslav Partisan Army of **Josip Brož Tito**.

GAINING A VOICE. By the end of World War II, Communist-dominated partisans had spread throughout the Yugoslav territories. After "liberation" by the Red Army, a unified state once again emerged, this time as the **communist** nation of Yugoslavia, with Slovenia as a republic. Tito liquidated Slovene politicians and leaders who failed to cooperate; tens of thousands of Slovene patriots were murdered at **Kočevje.** The anniversary of this massacre was commemorated for the first time in 1995, ending 50 years of silence about the event. Slovenia's economy and politics adhered to the Stalinist model, but after a rift between Tito and Stalin in 1948, Yugoslavia began to introduce a market economy. Slovenia was soon acknowledged as the wealthiest and most Westernized of the Yugoslav republics.

BREAKING FREE. Political dissent emerged after Tito's death in the 1980s, as long-stifled ethnic conflicts increasingly came to the foreground. In April 1990, Slovenia held the first contested elections in Yugoslavia since before the war, empowering a rightist coalition that called for **independence.** On June 25, 1991, Slovenia seceded from the federation and in 1992 was recognized by the European Community.

TODAY

Contemporary Slovenia is headed by a popularly elected **president,** who serves a five-year term; **Milan Kučan** won re-election in February 1997 and will serve out his final term until the November 2002 election. Despite trouble during his tenure as prime minister, **Janez Drnovšek** is considered the candidate most likely to fill Kučan's shoes. In April 2000, Drnovšek, of the **Liberal Democratic Party,** lost the majority in a confidence vote after his conservative coalition partner, the **People's Party,** left the government. The country was without a government until June 7, when parliament approved the center-right cabinet proposed by Prime Minister-designate **Andrej Bajukin,** who promised to hasten Slovenia's entrance to the EU. Slovenia will most likely be granted **EU** acceptance within the next few years. While **NATO** disappointed Slovenians by denying the country membership in its first round of expansion, the nation looks ahead to the second round.

PEOPLE AND CULTURE

LANGUAGE

Slovene, a grammatically complex Slavic language, uses the Latin alphabet. Most young people speak at least some **English,** but the older generation is more likely to understand **German** or **Italian.** The tourist industry is generally geared toward Germans, though most tourist office employees speak English. When speaking Slovene, "*č*" is pronounced "ch," "*š*" is "sh," and "*ž*" is "zh." "*R*" is at times a vowel (pronounced "er"), while "*v*" and "*l*" turn silent at the strangest times.

FOOD AND DRINK

SLOVENIA	❶	❷	❸	❹	❺
FOOD	under 400Sit	400-800Sit	800-1200Sit	1200-1600Sit	over 1600Sit

For home-style cooking, try a *gostilna* or *gostišče* (country-style inn or restaurant). Traditional meals begin with *jota*, a soup with potatoes, beans and sauerkraut. Pork is the basis for many dishes, such as *Svinjska pečenka* (roast pork) or *kanst* ham. **Vegetarians** should look for *štruklji*—slightly sweet dumplings eaten as a main dish. Slovenes savor their desserts; a favorite is *potica*, pastry with a rich filling. Popular fillings include walnuts, poppy seeds, raisins, cottage cheese, and honey. The country's **winemaking** tradition dates from antiquity. *Renski*, *Rizling*, and *Šipon* are popular whites and *Cviček* and *Teran* are favorite reds. Brewing is centuries old as well; good beers include *Laško* and *Union*. For something stronger, try *žganje*, a fruit brandy or *Viljamovka*, distilled by monks who know the secret of getting a whole pear inside the bottle.

CUSTOMS AND ETIQUETTE

When eating out it is rude to split the bill. **Tipping** is not expected, although rounding up will be appreciated; 10% is sufficient for good service. **Bargaining** is not done in Slovenia, and attempts at it may give offense. **Smoking** is accepted. **Hiking** trails throughout Slovenia are marked with a white circle inside a red one. Hikers greet each other on the path. The person ascending the path should speak first; respect belongs to those who have already seen the summit.

THE ARTS

LITERATURE. Before the modern era, Slovenia's artistic works were purely religious. In the 19th century, however, Slovene literature emerged as an important secular art form with the codification of the language by **Jernej Kopitar** in 1843 and the writings of the Romantic poet **France Prešeren** (see **Ljubljana: Sights,** p. 792). Prešeren was instrumental in revitalizing Slovene literature through his use of Western European literary models. Throughout the later **Realist** period (1848-1899), writers such as **Fran Eriaveć** focused on folkloric themes with a patriotic flavor; the first Slovene novel, *The Tenth Brother (Deseti brat)*, by **Josip Jurčič**, was published in 1866. In the first half of the 20th century, **Modernist** prose flowered in **Ivan Čankar's** 1904 *The Ward of Our Lady of Mercy (Hisa Marije pomocnice)*, while **Expressionism** showed the social and spiritual tensions brought on by World War I in the poetry of **Tone Seliskar, Miran Jarc,** and **Anton Vodnik.** Soviet **Socialist Realism** crushed many of the avant-garde impulses of the Slovene literature.

ARCHITECTURE, MUSIC, AND FINE ARTS. Coincident with the Modernist and Expressionist movements in Slovene literature, architect **Jože Plečnik** was a major figure in the development of **Art Deco.** While he designed buildings in both Vienna and Prague, his masterpiece was the transformation of his hometown, Ljubljana, from a provincial city to a cosmopolitan capital (see **Ljubljana: Sights,** p. 790). Musically, Slovenia experienced a **folk** revival after World War II, which was followed by an explosion of punk and industrial sounds led by the group **Laibach,** which maintains an international following.

CURRENT SCENE

Slovenia has slowly but surely become a player in the contemporary art scene thanks to the artistic cooperative **IRWIN.** Founded in the 1980s, this group continues to exhibit eclectic paintings and sculpture. Postmodern literary trends emerged in the **Young Slovene Prose"** movement, which has its strongest representation in short prose pieces. Two current authors with international reputations include poet **Tomaž Šalamun** and cultural critic and essayist **Slavoj Žižek.**

HOLIDAYS AND FESTIVALS

NATIONAL HOLIDAYS IN 2003	
January 1-2 New Year's Day	**June 25** National Day
February 8 Culture Day (Prešeren Day)	**August 15** Assumption
April 20-21 Easter	**October 31** Reformation Day
April 27 National Resistance Day (WWII)	**November 1** Remembrance Day
May 1-2 Labor Day	**December 25** Christmas
June 8 Pentecost	**December 26** Independence Day

INTERNATIONAL SUMMER FESTIVAL. Hitting Ljubljana July through September, the Summer Festival is the largest and longest of national festivals, featuring ballet, theater, and classical music.

PEASANT'S WEDDING DAY. Held each year at the end of July in the Lake Bohinj region, this presentation of ancient wedding customs involves a real ceremony in which local couples tie the knot.

ADDITIONAL RESOURCES

GENERAL HISTORY

Independent Slovenia: Origins, Movements, Prospects, by Jill Benderly (1996). A volume of essays exploring the transition to independence with writings from economic theorists, Slovenia's foreign minister, punk sociologists, and radical feminists.

Slovenia and the Slovenes: A Small State and the New Europe, by James Gow and Cathie Carmichael (2001). A critical assessment of the modern Slovene experience through examinations of Slovenian language, literature, culture, and geography.

FICTION, NONFICTION, AND TRAVEL

Betwitching Istria: A Never-Ending Story, by Roman Latkovic (out of print, but available through used book stores and public libraries). A fantastic travelogue through Slovenia, written by one of its native sons.

Feast: Poems, by Tomaž Šalamun (2000). The most recent volume produced by Slovenia's internationally acclaimed poet.

The Žižek Reader, by Slavoj Žižek (1999). A foray into the wacky yet brilliant world of a cultural critic who deals with everything from Hegel to Hitchcock.

SLOVENIA ESSENTIALS

ENTRANCE REQUIREMENTS
Passport: Required of all travelers.
Visa: Required of citizens of South Africa.
Letter of Invitation: Not required.
Inoculations: None required. Recommended up-to-date MMR (measles, mumps, rubella), DTaP (diptheria), Polio booster, Hepatitis A, and Hepatitis B.
Work Permit: Required of all foreigners planning to work in Slovenia.
International Driving Permit: Required of all those planning to drive.

DOCUMENTS AND FORMALITIES

EMBASSIES AND CONSULATES

Embassies of other countries in Slovenia are all in Ljubljana (see p. 787). Slovenia's embassies and consulates abroad include:

Australia: Level 6, Advance Bank Center, 60 Marcus Clarke St. 2608, Canberra, ACT 2601 (☎06 243 4830; fax 243 4827).

Canada: 150 Metcalfe St. #2101, Ottawa, ON K2P 1P1 (☎613-565-5781; fax 565-5783).

New Zealand: Eastern Hutt Rd., Pomare, Lower Hutt, Wellington (☎04 567 0027; fax 567 0024).

UK: Cavendish Ct. 11-15, Wigmore St., London W1U 1AN (☎020 7495 7775; fax 7495 7776).

US: 1525 New Hampshire Ave. NW, Washington, D.C. 20036 (☎202-667-5363; fax 667-4563; www.embassy.org/slovenia).

VISA AND ENTRY INFORMATION

Australian, Canadian, Irish, New Zealand, UK, and US citizens can visit visa-free for up to 90 days. South Africans need visas (3-month single-entry or 5-day transit US$26; 3-month multiple-entry US$52). Apply in person in your home country. Processing takes 4-7 business days and requires your passport; a money order for the fee; two passport-size photos; and a self-addressed, stamped (certified mail) envelope. Visas cannot be purchased at the border. For more information, consult the website of the Slovene Ministry of the Interior at www.sigov.si/mzz/ang. There is no entry fee at the border.

TRANSPORTATION

BY PLANE. There are three international airports, but commercial flights all arrive at **Ljubljana Airport. British Airways** offers direct flights to Slovenia while other major carriers offer connections to the national carrier **Adria Airways.** To enter the country cheaply, consider flying to **Vienna** and taking a train to Ljubljana.

BY TRAIN. Trains are cheap, clean, and reliable. First and second class do not differ much; save your money and opt for the latter. Travelers under 26 can get a 20% discount on most fares to international destinations. ISIC holders get 30% off domestic tickets; ask for a *"popust"* (discount). *"Vlak"* means train, *"prihodi vlakov"* means arrivals, and *"odhodi vlakov"* means departures. Schedules usually list trains by direction; look for trains that run *dnevno* (daily).

BY BUS. Slovenia has an extensive bus network. Though usually more expensive than trains, they're often the only option in mountainous regions. Tickets are sold at the station or on board; put your luggage in the passenger compartment if it's not too crowded. All large backpacks cost 220Sit extra.

BY CAR, BOAT, BIKE, AND THUMB. For those traveling by car, the **Automobile Association of Slovenia's** emergency telephone number is ☎987. Car rental agencies in Ljubljana offer reasonable rates. A regular **hydrofoil** service runs between **Venice** and **Portorož** during the summer. If not traveling by bus or train, most Slovenes transport themselves by bike. Nearly every town has a bike rental office. *Let's Go* does not recommend **hitchhiking,** which is extremely uncommon in Slovenia.

TOURIST SERVICES AND MONEY

Tourist offices are located in most major cities and tourist spots. Staffs generally speak **English** or **German** and, on the coast, perfect **Italian.** They can usually find accommodations. The main tourist organization in Slovenia is **Kompas.** The national currency is the Slovenian **tolar** (Sit). Slovenian **inflation** is around 6%, so expect some change in prices over the next year. **Ljubljanska Banka** and **Gorenjska Banka** are common banks. AmEx **Travelers Cheques** and **Eurocheques** are accepted in most towns and cities. Most **exchange offices** offer fair rates. Major **credit cards** are not consistently accepted, but MC/V **ATMs** are everywhere.

HEALTH AND SAFETY

 EMERGENCY NUMBERS: Police and Fire: ☎112 **Ambulance:** ☎113

HEALTH AND SAFETY. Medical facilities are of high quality, and most have English-speaking doctors. UK citizens receive free medical care with a valid passport; other foreigners must pay cash. **Pharmacies** are also stocked to Western standards; ask for *obliž* (band-aids), *tamponi* (tampons), and *vložki* (sanitary pads). **Tap water** is safe to drink everywhere. **Crime** is rare Slovenia. Even in the largest cities, overly friendly drunks and bad drivers are the greatest public menace.

WOMEN, MINORITY, AND BGLT TRAVELERS. Women do experience occasional unwanted looks and pick-up lines. Female travelers should, as always, exercise caution and avoid walking or riding public transportation alone after dark. There are few **minorities** in Slovenia, and minority travelers may thus encounter curious stares, especially in rural areas. Few incidents of discrimination are reported, but it is always advisable to exercise caution. **Homosexuality** is legal, but is still not common and may elicit unfriendly reactions outside of urban areas.

ACCOMMODATIONS AND CAMPING

SLOVENIA	❶	❷	❸	❹	❺
ACCOM.	under 1000Sit	1000-3500Sit	3500-5000Sit	5000-6000Sit	over 6000Sit

HOTELS, HOSTELS, AND HOMESTAYS. Hotels fall into five categories (L (deluxe), A, B, C, and D) and are expensive. Youth **hostels** and student dormitories are cheap, but generally open only in summer (June 25-Aug. 30). **Pensions** are the most common form of accommodation; usually they have private singles as well as inexpensive triples and dorms. While hostels are often the cheapest (2500-3000Sit) and most fun option, **private rooms** are the only cheap option on the coast and at Lake Bohinj. Prices vary according to location, but rarely exceed US$30, and most rooms are very comfortable. Inquire at the tourist office or look for *Zimmer frei* or *Sobe* signs on the street.

CAMPING. Campgrounds can be crowded, but are in excellent condition. Camp only in designated areas in order to avoid fines.

KEEPING IN TOUCH

MAIL. To send letters by airmail, ask for *letalsko*. Airmail takes 1-2 weeks to reach North America, Australia, New Zealand, and South Africa. Letters to the US cost 105Sit and postcards cost 95Sit; to the UK 100Sit/90Sit; to Australia and New Zealand 110Sit/100Sit. Mail can be received through **Poste Restante.** Address envelopes as follows: Jessica (first name) HAGUE (last name), Poste Restante, Ljubljanska 4 (post office address), Bled (city) 4260 (postal code), SLOVENIA.

 PHONE CHANGES. Slovenia is in the process of changing all of its phone numbers. Although we've accounted for as many as possible, many will continue to change through 2002, and therefore some of the numbers we list will be wrong. When you call a changed number, a voice will tell you in both English and Slovenian what the new number is.

TELEPHONES AND INTERNET ACCESS. All phones now take **phone cards,** which are sold at post offices, kiosks, and gas stations (750Sit per 50 impulses, which yields 1½min. to the US). Most international telecommunications companies **do not have international direct dialing** numbers in Slovenia. Dial ☎ 115 for English-speaking operator-assisted collect calls. For countries to which direct dialing is unavailable, dial ☎ 8, wait for the second tone, and dial ☎ 194 or 195 for English-speaking operators. Calling abroad is expensive (over US$6 per min. to the US). If you must, try the phones at the post office and pay when you're finished. **Internet** access is very common throughout Slovenia.

LJUBLJANA

A city of contrasts, Ljubljana (pop. 330,000) is small yet cosmopolitan, easy to reach yet still isolated from swarms of tourists, and charming yet frustratingly kitschy. While its Baroque monuments, Art Nouveau façades, and modern high rises are best viewed from graceful Ljubljana Castle, the city is best felt in its colorful, curving streets.

■ INTERCITY TRANSPORTATION

Flights: A **"Super Shuttle"** (☎877 77 66; fax 541 66 34; supershuttleşsiol.net) runs from major hotels to the **airport** (☎04 202 27 00; fax ☎202 12 20). Reservations are required. **Bus #28** runs from the city center (1hr.; M-F 10 per day, Sa-Su 6 per day; 600Sit). **Adria Airways,** Gosposvetska 6 (☎231 33 12; fax 232 16 68); **Aeroflot,** Dunajska 21 (☎236 85 66; fax 236 85 93); **Austrian Airlines,** Dunajska 58 (☎436 12 83; fax 436 12 82); **British Airways,** Slovenska 56 (☎300 10 00; fax 300 10 39); **Lufthansa,** Gosposvetska 6 (☎234 72 45; fax 232 66 72); **Swissair,** Dunajska 156 WTC (☎569 10 10; fax 569 10 00).

Trains: Trg OF 6 (☎291 33 32). To: **Budapest, HUN** (9hr., 2 per day, 10,000Sit); **Munich, GER** (6-7hr., 2 per day, 12,800Sit); **Trieste, ITA** (3hr., 2-3 per day, 4400Sit); **Venice, ITA** (6hr., 3 per day, 7027Sit); **Vienna, AUS** (5-6hr., 2 per day, 11,600Sit); **Zagreb, CRO** (2hr., 5 per day, 2452Sit).

Buses: Trg OF 4 (☎090 42 30), in front of the train station. To **Rijeka, CRO** (3hr., 1 per day, 2880Sit) and **Zagreb, CRO** (3hr., 2 per day, 2970Sit).

■ ORIENTATION

The curvy **Ljubljanica River** divides Central Ljubljana, with the picturesque **Stare Miasto** (Old Town) on one bank and 19th- and 20th-century buildings on the other. About a half-mile from either bank the historic area turns into a concrete business district. The **train** and **bus** stations are on **Trg Osvobodilne Fronte (Trg OF).** To get from the train station to the center, turn right and then left on **Miklošiceva cesta** and follow it to **Trg Prešernova,** the main square. After crossing the **Tromostovje** (Triple Bridge), you'll see Stare Miasto at the base of the castle hill. The **tourist office** is on the left at the corner of Stritarjeva and Adamič-Lundrovo nabr. To reach **Slovenska** (Ljubljana's main artery), walk up **Čopova** from Prešernov Trg.

■ LOCAL TRANSPORTATION

Buses: Run daily until midnight. Drop 230Sit in the box beside the driver or buy 170Sit tokens *(žetoni)* at post offices and kiosks. Daily **passes** (660Sit) sold at **Ljubljanski Potniški Promet,** Trdinova 3, or online at www.hddingmestorljubljane.si/lpp.

Taxis: ☎97 00 through 97 09. 150Sit plus 100Sit per km. Taxis are generally much more expensive than other options.

Car Rental: Avis Rent-a-Car, Cufarjeva 2 (☎430 80 10; fax 430 80 14); **Kompas Hertz,** Miklosiceva 11 (☎231 12 41; fax 507 20 88).

Bike Rental: Propil (☎04 169 65 15) rents bikes via the **Cutty Sark Pub,** Knafljiev Prehod 1 (☎251 47 74), through the arch on Wolfova, and **Maček Pub,** Krojaška 5 (☎425 37 91). 600Sit per hr., 3100Sit per day. Both open daily 9am-8pm.

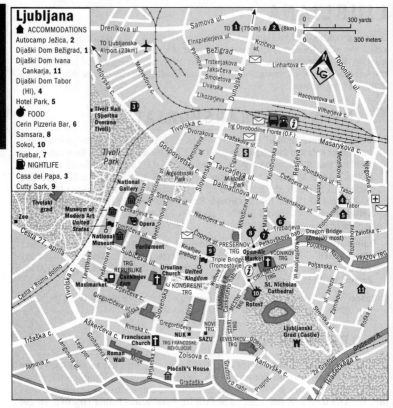

Ljubljana

▲ **ACCOMMODATIONS**
Autocamp Ježica, **2**
Dijaški Dom Bežigrad, **1**
Dijaški Dom Ivana
  Cankarja, **11**
Dijaški Dom Tabor
  (HI), **4**
Hotel Park, **5**
🍴 **FOOD**
Cerin Pizzeria Bar, **6**
Samsara, **8**
Sokol, **10**
Truebar, **7**
🌙 **NIGHTLIFE**
Casa del Papa, **3**
Cutty Sark, **9**

🔢 PRACTICAL INFORMATION

TOURIST AND FINANCIAL SERVICES

Tourist Office: Tourist Information Center (TIC), Stritarjeva 1 (☎306 12 15; 24hr. information in English from within Slovenia 090 93 98 81; fax 306 12 04; tic@ljubljana-tourism.si). Distributes free **maps,** sells the useful guide *Ljubljana from A to Z,* and arranges accommodations. Open June-Sept. M-F 8am-8pm, Sa-Su 10am-6pm; Oct.-May M-F 8am-6pm, Sa-Su 10am-6pm. **Branch** at the train station (☎/fax 433 94 75) open June-Sept. daily 8am-9pm; Oct.-May M-F 10am-5:30pm.

Budget Travel: Erazem, Trubarjeva cesta 7 (☎433 10 76; fax 430 35 90). Student-oriented with a helpful staff. Open June-Sept. M-F 10am-5pm; Oct.-May M-F noon-5pm.

Embassies: Australia, Trg Republike 3 (☎425 42 52; fax 426 47 21). Open M-F 9am-1pm. **Canada,** Miklošičeva 19 (☎430 35 70; fax 430 35 77). Open M-F 9am-1pm. **UK,** Trg Republike 3 (☎200 39 10; fax 425 01 74). Open M-F 9am-noon. **US,** Prešernova cesta 31 (☎200 55 00; fax 200 55 55). Open M-F 8am-5pm.

Currency Exchange: *Menjalnice* booths abound. **Ljubljanska banka** has branches all over that **exchange currency** and cash **traveler's checks** for decent rates and no commission.

ATMs: 24hr. MC/V ATMs are all over the city.

American Express: Trubarjeva 50 (☎433 20 24; amex@siol.net). Open M-F 8am-8pm.

Work Opportunities: Ljubljanski Studentski Servis, Borstnikov Trg 2 (☎01 200 88 00). Open M-F 10am-6pm, Sa 10am-1pm. **MB Studentski Servisvlj,** Slovenska 27 (☎01 421 45 50). Open M-Sa 11am-4pm.

LOCAL SERVICES AND COMMUNICATIONS

Luggage Storage: At the train station. Look for the *"garderoba"* sign. 400Sit per day. Open 24hr.

International Bookstore: MK-Knjigarna Konzorcij, Slovenska 29 (☎252 40 57). English-language books and international press. Open M-F 9am-7:30pm, Sa 9am-1pm.

Laundromat: Tic, Student Campus, cesta 27, Aprila 31 Building 9 (☎257 43 97). Self-service. Open M-F 8am-2pm and 4-7pm, Sa 8am-2pm.

Emergency: ☎112. **Police:** ☎113. **Road Assistance:** ☎1987.

Medical Services: Bohoričeva Medical Center, Bohoričeva 4 (☎232 30 60). Open daily 5am-8pm. **Klinični Center,** Zaloška 27 (☎433 62 36). Open 24hr.

24-Hour Pharmacy: Lekarna Miklosič, Miklošičeva 24 (☎231 45 58).

Telephones: 24hr. phones situated around the post office and all over town. Buy magnetic phone cards at the post office and newsstands (1700Sit).

Internet Access: Free access upstairs at **Cerin Pizzeria Bar** (see **Food,** p. 790). **Maximarket,** (see **Food,** p. 790) charges 190Sit per 15min.

Post Office: Trg OF 5 (☎433 06 05). Open 24hr. Various branches throughout the city. **Poste Restante,** Slovenska 32 (☎426 46 68), at the counter labeled *"poštno ležeťe pošiljke."* Open M-F 7am-8pm, Sa 7am-1pm.

Postal Code: 1000.

▐ ACCOMMODATIONS

Finding cheap accommodations in Ljubljana is easier in July and August, when school dorms open their doors to tourists. The **TIC ❷** can help you find **private rooms.** (Singles 3000-4500Sit; doubles 5000-7500Sit.) The **Slovene National Hostel Association** (**PZS;** ☎231 21 56) provides information about youth hostels throughout Slovenia. There is a nightly **tourist tax** (160Sit) at all establishments.

▨ **Dijaški Dom Tabor (HI),** Vidovdanska 7 (☎234 88 40; fax 234 88 55). Clean rooms, a friendly staff, and proximity to nightlife make this hostel popular with backpackers. Free Internet access. Breakfast included. Laundry 1200Sit. Reception 24hr. Check-out 11am. Open June 25-Aug. 28. 3200-3850Sit per person with student ID. ❷

Dijaški Dom Bežigrad, Kardeljeva pl. 28 (☎534 28 67; fax 534 28 64). From the train station, cross the street and turn right. Walk to the intersection with Slovenska and take bus #6 (Črnuče) or #8 (Ježica) to "Stadion" (5min.). Walk 1 block to the crossroads and look for the sign. Rooms are clean and comfortable. Reception 24hr. Flexible check-out 8am. Open June 20-Aug. 25. Singles 3300Sit, with shower 3800Sit; doubles 2200Sit/3300Sit; triples 2200Sit/2600Sit. ❷

Hotel Park, Tabor 6 (☎433 1306; fax 433 0546). Clean, with knowledgeable staff. The best centrally-located option in the off-season. Luggage storage. Check-out noon. Singles 5254-9354Sit; doubles 7908-11708Sit. Students 10% off with ID. MC/V. ❹

Autocamp Ježica, Dunajska 270 (☎568 39 13; fax 568 39 12; acjezica@siol.net). Follow directions to Dijaški dom Bežigrad (see above); get off at "Ježica," where you'll see a roundabout on the left. Large rooms, some with TVs and private showers. Reception 24hr. Flexible check-out 1pm. Reservations recommended. 1320Sit per adult. 143Sit

ꓑUTTING THE "LOVE" BACK IN
S"LOVE"NIA

Most foreigners couldn't tell you if
ꓢlovenia even *has* a national airline,
ᴠet many Europeans know at least
ᴛhree Slovenian air hostesses: Mar-
ena, Daphne, and Emperatrizz. This
ᴛransvestite trio, known as *Sestre* (Sis-
ᴛers), made their name across Europe
ᴡhen they appeared in the Eurovision
ꜛ002 Song Competition, the annual
ꝑop-telethon in which European coun-
ꞇries vie for the dubious honor of Euro-
ᴠision Song of the Year. The gals—who
ꝑerformed in sparkly air hostess uni-
ᶠorms—caused quite a stir in their tran-
ꝗuil homeland, where 70% of the
ꝑopulation is Catholic.

The controversy began during the
ꜱelection of the Slovenian representa-
ᴛive in a televised sing-off, where the
ᴡinner was to be picked by two juries
ꜱnd a public tele-vote. The juries gave
ᴛhe Sisters the win by a single vote,
ꝺespite overwhelming public support
ꜰor Karmen Stavec—runner up for the
ꜱecond year in a row—who proved her-
ꜱelf the real diva of the evening by flee-
ꜱng the stage in tears.

Allegations of voting improprieties
ꜱompounded the nation's shock, and it
ᴡas revealed that the tele-vote had
ꜱtarted three minutes early, and had
ꜱsted eight—rather than five—minutes.
ꜱonspiratorial questions were raised
ꜱs to who had let the phone lines open
ꜱarly, and eventually the TV station
ꜱad to declare the public vote invalid.
ꜰollowing *Sestre*'s win, viewers
ꜱammed the TV station's switchboards
ꜱn protest. Both pro-gay activists and
ꜱnti-gay religious and conservative
ꜱroups hit the streets of Ljubljana with
ꝑlacards, banners, and flags.

(continued on next page)

tourist tax, 330Sit car tax , 440Sit electricity tax. Bungalow singles 5720Sit; doubles 9240Sit; triples
11,600Sit. MC/V. ❶

Dijaški Dom Ivana Cankarja, Poljanska 26 (☎474 86
00; fax 432 03 69). Turn right and go into the courtyard; reception is on the other side of the complex.
Convenient location and decent dorm accommodations. Breakfast included. Reception 24hr. Flexible
check-out 11am. Open June 25-Aug. 30. Singles
3200Sit; doubles 3200Sit; triples 2400Sit. Students
10% off. ❷

🗋 FOOD

The largest **grocery store** is located in the basement of
the **Maximarket** on Trg Republike. (Open M-Th 9am-
8pm, F 9am-10pm, Sa 8am-3pm.) At Trg Vodnikov,
next to the cathedral, there's a huge outdoor **market**
stocked with all kinds of fresh fruit. (Open June-Aug.
M-Sa 9am-6pm; Sept.-May M-Sa 9am-4pm.) Fast-food
stands feature such favorites as the *burek*—fried
dough filled with meat *(mesni)* or cheese *(sirov)*.

Sokol, Ciril Metodov Trg 18 (☎530 95 40). Off Trg
Prešernova, or take bus #2, 11, or 20 to Metodov.
Tastefully decorated, specializing in Slovenian delicacies. Try the *Svinjski naravni* (pork chops in a cream
sauce; 1390Sit). Open M-Sa 9am-midnight. ❸

Samsara, Petkovško Nabrezje, next to the triple bridge.
The city's largest selection of ice cream concoctions
(570-1450Sit) and mixed fruit drinks (600-850Sit).
Also serves sandwiches in generous portions. Open
Apr. 15-Oct. 10 daily 9am-midnight. ❶

Cerin Pizzeria Bar, Trubarjeva 52 (☎133 11 05).
Watch your pizza cooked Italian-style in the open
kitchen. Pastas (1130-1290Sit) and fabulous desserts
(550Sit). Free Internet access upstairs. Open M-Sa
10am-11pm, Su noon-10pm. AmEx/MC/V. ❷

Truebar, Trubarjeva 23 (☎433 20 06). Truebar is the
epitome of Eastern European cool. Dine outdoors or in
several eclectic dining rooms, or swing by for take-out
sandwiches (from 480Sit) and cake (starting at
400Sit). Open M-Sa 7:30am-10pm. ❶

👁 SIGHTS

One way to see the city is to meet in front of the city
hall *(rotovž)*, at Mestni Trg 1, for a 2hr. walking tour
given in English and Slovene. (June-Sept. daily 5pm;
July-Aug. also Su 11am. 1200Sit, students 600Sit. Buy
tickets at the tour or at the TIC.) Otherwise, explore
Ljubljana's historic neighborhoods on your own.

LJUBLJANA CASTLE. (Ljubljanski Grad.) The castle was built around 1144, but most of the present buildings date from the 16th and 17th centuries. It has served as a prison for important captives, such as Slovenia's most famous author, nationalist Ivan Cankar. The view of the city from the tower is breathtaking, and the castle is rapidly becoming a new cultural center, hosting various exhibitions and performances. *(Tower: ☎ 232 99 94; www.festival-lj.si/virtualnimuzej. Open June-Sept. daily 10am until dark; Oct.-May 10am-5pm. 700Sit, students 400Sit. Castle: Open Nov.-Apr. daily 10am-7pm; May-Oct. 10am-9pm. 400-700Sit. Guided tours available in English. 750-1200Sit depending on group size, 3 person minimum.)*

ST. NICHOLAS CATHEDRAL. (Stolnica.) The cathedral occupies the site of an old Romanesque church. Fishermen and townsfolk once threw garbage into the Ljubljanica from this site. When the litterers were forced by law to live on the very banks they had defiled, they built a small chapel dedicated to their patron, St. Nicholas. Today's cathedral dates from the early 18th century; little original artwork remains, but visitors can still admire the 15th-century Gothic *Pietà* and the impressive triple organ. *(On the Stari Miasto side of the river, walk left along the water in order to walk by the gorgeous arcades, also designed by Plečnik, that form part of the nearby market. The Cathedral is to the right. Open daily 7am-noon and 3-5pm.)*

DRAGON BRIDGE. (Zmajski Most.) The Dragon Bridge crosses over the Ljubljanica and offers a pleasant view of the flowered banks and the Triple Bridge. Built in 1901 to replace the old "Butcher's Bridge," it was originally named after Emperor Franz Jozef, but has taken its name from the dragon on Ljubljana's coat of arms that adorns the bridge. *(From the river, turn left on Ciril Metodov cesta and continue until you hit Vodnikov Trg, where you take a left.)*

PREŠEREN SQUARE. The main square of Ljubljana, Prešernov Trg was named for celebrated Slovene poet **France Prešeren** (see **The Arts,** p. 783), whose statue watches over the crowds. The square is dominated by an enormous, pink 17th-century **Franciscan Church** (Frančiškanska cerkev). Local master Francesco Robba crafted the impressive altar inside. *(A short walk from the city hall down Stritarjeva and across the Triple Bridge. Open daily 3-8pm.)*

TRIPLE BRIDGE. (Tromostovje.) This bridge is an attraction in itself. It dates from the 1930s, when revered architect Josip Plečnik (see **The Arts,** p. 783) modernized the old Špitalski by supplementing the stone construction with two footbridges. They now provide a majestic entrance to Old Ljubljana.

Local NGOs worried about the levels of homophobia and intolerance. As a survey published in Slovenia's newspaper *Nedelo* reported that 51% of Slovenes felt that a group of transvestites should not represent their nation, Slovenia's Parliament hotly debated who had the right to represent Slovenian culture abroad. Others in Parliament asked whether the contest had been rigged. The head of Slovenia's biggest opposition party noted at a press conferences that although he felt the song was not *that* bad, it should be clear that the female impersonators represented his foes in the government coalition.

The story reached the international newswires, piquing the interest of the European Parliament in Brussels, which voiced its concerns that the rights of sexual minorities might be violated in Slovenia. "That the issue of gay rights is coming up, confirms to us that, perhaps, Slovenia is not yet ready for EU membership," remarked one member of the European Parliament, much to the dismay of Slovenia's keenly pro-EU citizenry.

Through it all, the Sisters kept themselves above the fray. In the European finals they achieved a respectable 14th place, but more importantly they made inroads into their country's heart. As their winning love song "*Samo Ljubezen*" (Only Love) declares: "Love is the only thing that I can give you / Love is the only hope for everyone."

Bede Sheppard was an Editor of Let's Go: Australia 2000, *a Managing Editor for the 2001 series, and worked for a humanitarian agency in Croatia.*

SLOVENIA

OTHER SIGHTS. French Revolution Square (Trg Francoske Revolucije) and its environs were once occupied by the Teutonic Knights; the neighborhood **Križanke,** the Slovene translation of their name, still commemorates them. *The ruins of a Roman wall are also nearby; to see them, take a right on Zoisova Cesta and then a left on Barjanska cesta from the Square. If, instead of taking a left on Barjanska cesta at the intersection, you took a right, you hit Ljubljana's main artery, Slovenska cesta.* Behind the Ursuline Church on the left is **Trg Republike,** home to the **Parliament** and **Cankarjev dom,** the city's cultural center. In front of the city hall sits a **fountain** embellished with allegorical representations of three rivers—the Ljubljanica, Sava, and Krka. *(☎ 425 8121. Open Tu-Sa 10am-7pm, Su 10am-2pm. 500Sit, students 300Sit.)*

🏛 MUSEUMS

THE PLEČNIK COLLECTION. (Plečnikova Zbrika.) This museum chronicles the marvelous work of Plečnik, Slovenia's premier architect, in a house built by the master himself. *(Karunova 4. Walk toward the center on Slovenska, turn left on Zoisova, then right on Emonska. Cross the bridge and head behind the church. ☎ 280 16 00; fax 283 50 66. Open Tu and Th 10am-2pm. Guided tours required; available in English. 600Sit, students 300Sit.)*

NATIONAL MUSEUM. (Narodni Muzej.) Detailed exhibits on archaeology, culture, and Slovene history. The Museum of Natural History upstairs showcases of bird and geology exhibits. *(Muzejska 1. ☎ 241 44 00. Open Tu-Su 10am-6pm. Prices for temporary exhibits vary. 700Sit, students 500Sit.)*

NATIONAL GALLERY. (Narodna Galerija.) Hangs 17th- and 18th-century portraits, Impressionist paintings, and religious icons from as far back as 1270. *(Cankarjeva 20. ☎ 241 54 34. Open Tu-Su 10am-6pm. 500Sit, students 400Sit; Sa afternoons free.)*

TIVOLI CASTLE. (Tivolski Grad.) Home to the International Center of Graphic Art, the castle features about 7 temporary exhibits a year. Also hosts the International Biennial of Graphic Art from June to September every odd year. *(Pod turnom 3. From Cankarjeva, follow Jakopičevo sprehajališče in Tivoli Park. ☎ 241 38 00. Open Tu-Sa 11am-7pm, Su noon-6pm. 500Sit, students 150Sit.)*

🎵 🎭 ENTERTAINMENT AND FESTIVALS

Ljubljana's calendar is packed with festivals, including the **International Jazz Festival** in late June. The vaguely titled **International Summer Festival,** which takes place in 2003 from June 14-Sept. 13, is a conglomeration of musical, operatic, and theatrical performances. In November, check out the **Ljubljana International Film Festival. Cankarjev dom,** Trg Prešernova 10 (☎ 425 81 21), hosts the **Slovenian Symphony Orchestra.** (Oct.-June. Box office in the Maximarket. Tickets 2000-7000Sit.) The **opera house,** Župančičeva 1, hosts performances from Sept. to June. (☎ 425 48 40. Tickets 1500-4500Sit.) **Tivoli Hall,** a sports arena in Tivoli Park, hosts basketball, hockey, and rock concerts. Inquire about these and all other events at the TIC (see **Tourist Office,** p. 788). A new cinema, **Kolosej** (www.kolosej.si), shows English-language movies. Free buses run from the town center to the multiplex.

☕ NIGHTLIFE

Innumerable cafes and bars line **Trubarjeva, Stari Trg,** and **Mestni Trg.**

🍸 **Casa del Papa,** Celovška 54a (☎ 434 31 58). The decor pays homage to Hemingway and Key West alike, while the downstairs club pulsates with Cuban beats, serves up exotic Cuban cocktails, and sells Cuban cigars. Popular with 20- and 30-something crowds; all 3 floors lively until late. Serves beer (0.25L 280-550Sit), mixed drinks (800Sit), and sandwiches (600-1200Sit). Open Th-Sa 9pm-5am.

Oz, Smartinska 152 (☎ 520 55 56), near the Kolosej. Take bus #17, 2, or 7 to reach this trendy disco and bar, one of Ljubljana's most popular dance destinations. Cocktails 700-1300Sit. Open M-Tu 6pm-1am, W-Su 6pm-5am.

Cutty Sark, Knafljev prehod 1 (☎ 425 14 77). Walk down Wolfova and turn right into an arched entrance about 150m from Trg Prešernova. This lively, foreigner-friendly bar is near several other busy nightspots. Try a *Union* for 250Sit. Open daily 9am-midnight.

⚡ DAYTRIPS FROM LJUBLJANA

▓ ŠKOCJANSKE CAVES ☎ (0)57

Trains run from Ljubljana to Divača en route to the coast (1½hr., 10 per day, 1370Sit). Signs from the station lead to the ticket booth (40min.). Ask the ticket office for a trail map. ☎ 63 28 40; fax 632 844. Children 6-12 800Sit, children under 6 free. Tours June-Sept. daily 10am-5pm; Oct.-May 10am, 1, and 3pm. 1500Sit, students 700Sit.

UNESCO-protected Škocjanske (one of only two protected caves in the world) is an amazing system of caverns said to have inspired literary great Dante Allighieri. The Silent Cave features enormous limestone formations including stalactites, stalagmites, and rock curtains. This impressive hall pales in comparison to the Reca River underground gorge, the largest of its type in Europe. This spelunking trip, much more physically demanding than Postojna Caves, is for the truly adventurous.

POSTOJNA CAVES

From Ljubljana, trains (1¼hr., 10 per day, 1530Sit) and buses (1hr., every 30min., 1360Sit) go to Postojna on the way to Koper. Turn right on Kolodvorska cesta and follow its curves to the intersection with Ljubljanska cesta. Turn left and follow it to the center of town, then follow signs to the cave (35min.). ☎ 700 01 00; www.postojna-cave.com. Open May-Sept. daily 9am-6pm; Oct.-Apr. 10am-4pm. English and German tours available. Tours leave May-Sept. every hr.; Oct.-Apr. every even hr. 2200Sit, students 1100Sit.

If you visit only a single chamber of the two million-year-old Postojna Cave (Postojnska Jama), it would still be worth the trip. The constant and abundant flow of tourists, however, has turned the caverns into more of an amusement park than anything else. If you can forget the crowds, you'll be blown away by the astonishing array of plant-like stalagmites, alabaster curtains, and multi-colored stalactites. The obligatory tour covers only 20% of the cave's 27km and lasts an hour and a half; part is on foot and part on a train. Bring a jacket or rent a cloak for 400Sit; the temperature in the cave is a constant 8°C.

PREDJAMA CASTLE

Taxis run from Postojna (5000Sit). During the school year, 2 school buses go to Bukovje, 2km from the castle (15min., M-F 2 per day, 300Sit). ☎ 756 82 60. Open June-Aug. daily 9am-7pm; May and Sept. 9am-6pm; Mar.-Apr. and Oct. 10am-5pm; Jan.-Feb. and Nov.-Dec. Tu-F 10am-4pm, Sa-Su 10am-5pm. 700Sit, students 350Sit. Arranged visits of the cave below Predjama Castle are possible—call ahead.

Predjama Castle (Predjamski Grad), 9km from Postojna, is expensive and difficult to reach, since you must take a cab. It is, however, definitely worth the effort. Carved into the face of a huge cliff, the former home of the robber baron Erazem is, as a tour guide calls it, "almost arrogant in its simplicity." In 1483 German knight Erazem Lueger stepped across the border between what were then the Hungarian and German empires, thereby disrespecting Friedrich III, the German emperor. For his crime, he was outlawed, arrested, and sentenced to death. Miraculously, he managed to escape and hole himself away in Predjama Castle. Friedrich III sent his entire army after the errant knight, but Erazem had a secret tunnel by which he received supplies, and the siege lasted more than a year. It looked like the besieged might even outlast the besiegers, who were running low on supplies, when one of Erazem's servants turned the tides by agreeing to betray his employer. The servant promised to light a candle when his lord went to the outhouse to answer nature's call. With a single catapult round, Friedrich won his revenge on the rebel knight, who died in the least honorable of positions. On the last Su in August, a colorful **knights' tournament** takes place outside the castle.

THE JULIAN ALPS (JULIJSKE ALPE)

Slovenians say, "water is good, air is better, and light is the best." Covering northwest Slovenia, the Julian Alps fuse all three elements perfectly. Although not as high as their Austrian or Swiss cousins, these mountains are no less stunning. With pristine wilderness near Lake Bohinj, cultural festivities in Kranjska Gora, and refreshing spas in Bled, the Julian Alps can satisfy all those who love the outdoors.

BLED
☎(0)4

Bled (pop. 6000) has the beauty and stillness of a postcard: green Alpine hills, snow-covered peaks, a turquoise lake, and a stately castle rising above the panorama. For centuries, people have come to this internationally-renowned paradise to recuperate in spas. The resort experience in Bled is unparalleled, but vacationers here are not sequestered in isolated communities: visitors can easily get a glimpse of the real life that takes place in these manicured surroundings.

TRANSPORTATION. **Trains** leave for **Ljubljana** (1hr., 11 per day, 900Sit), from the Lesce-Bled train station, about 4km from Bled itself (☎574 11 13). To reach Bled from the station, take one of the frequent commuter buses (10min., 280Sit). These stop on Ljubljanska and at the bus station at cesta Svobode 4 (☎74 11 14). **Buses** roll in from **Ljubljana** (1½hr., every hr., 1200Sit). Camping Bled (see **Accommodations and Food,** below) rents **bikes** (1100Sit per 4hr., 1700Sit per day).

ORIENTATION AND PRACTICAL INFORMATION. The town spreads around Bled Lake, and most buildings cluster along the eastern shore. **Ljubljanska,** the main street, leads straight to the water. The **tourist office,** cesta Svobode 15, sells **maps** (1400Sit) of Bled and the local walking trails. (☎574 11 22; fax 574 15 55. Open in winter M-Sa 8am-7pm, Su 11am-5pm; in summer daily 8am-8pm.) **Gorenjska Banka,** cesta Svobode 15, **exchanges currency,** cashes **traveler's checks,** gives MC **cash advances,** and has a MC/V **ATM** outside. (☎574 13 00. Open July-Aug. M-F 8am-6pm, Sa 8am-noon; Sept.-June M-F 9-11:30am and 2-5pm, Sa 8-11am.) There's a **pharmacy** at Prešernova 36. (☎578 07 70. Open M-F 7am-7:30pm, Sa 7am-1pm.) **Internet access** is available at the library, Ljubljanska 10. (☎575 16 00. 1000Sit per hr. Open M 8am-7pm, Tu-F 2-7pm, Sa 8am-noon.) The **post office** is at Ljubljanska 4. (☎575 02 00. Open July-Aug. M-F 7am-8pm, Sa 7am-1pm; Sept.-June M-F 7am-7pm, Sa 7am-noon.) **Postal Code:** 4260.

ACCOMMODATIONS. **Globtour ❸,** Ljubljanska 7, can arrange **private rooms.** (☎574 18 21; fax 574 41 85; www.bled.mona-globtour.si. July-Aug. and Dec. 21-Jan.4: singles 3300-4800Sit; doubles 3000-3900Sit. Sept. 1-Dec. 20 and Jan. 5-Apr. 15: 2550-3500Sit/3500-4400Sit. Apr. 16-June 20 2300-3200Sit/3200-4150Sit. Tourist tax 154Sit. Stays under 3 nights 30% more.) You can also find a private room on your own; look for *Sobe* signs. The newly renovated ■ **Bledec Youth Hostel (HI) ❸**, Grajska cesta 17, is a supernova in the backpacker's dark sky. Everything, from the stylish furniture to the private bathrooms, is squeaky clean. Facing away from the bus station, turn left and walk along the steep street all the way to the top, bearing left at the fork. (☎574 52 50; fax 574 52 51. Breakfast and tourist tax included. Laundry 800Sit. Reception 24hr. Check-out 10am. Reserve one month in advance June-Aug. HI members 3750Sit, non-members 4750Sit. Sept.-May 3500Sit/ 4250Sit.) **Hotel Krim ❺**, Ljubljanska cesta, clean and conveniently located, offers 115 bedrooms with balconies (☎579 70 00; fax 574 37 29; hotelkrim@hotel-krim.si. 6600Sit per person in double.) **Camping Bled ❷**, Kidričeva 10c, sits in a beautiful valley on the opposite side of the lake. Walk around the bus station, follow cesta Svobode downhill, turn left at the lake and walk 25min. A store, a restaurant, and a beach are available at the campground. (☎575 20 00; fax 575 20 02; camping-bled@s5.net. Reception 24hr. Check-out 3pm. Open Apr.-Oct. 1100-1725Sit per person. 10% off with student ID. Tourist tax 115Sit.)

❏ FOOD. Gostilna pri Planincu ❸, Grajska cesta 8, near the bus station, has great pizza (790Sit-850Sit) and crepes (400Sit). (☎574 16 13. Open daily 9am-11pm.) **P'hram ❹**, cesta Svobode 19a, serves Slovene entrees—including delicious sausage—for 750-1700Sit. (☎579 12 80. Open daily 9am-11pm.) **Franci Šmon ❶**, Grajska cesta 3, offers sweets and coffee. Their famous tortes (350Sit) include the *gramada*, a chocolate biscuit with vanilla cream, nuts, raisins, and rum, and the *gibanica*, a turnover with cottage cheese, apple, pumpkin, and nuts. (☎574 22 80. Open daily 7:30am-9:30pm.) For **groceries,** head to **Mercator,** in the shopping complex on Ljubljanska cesta 13. (Open M-Sa 7am-7pm, Su 8am-noon.)

◙ SIGHTS. The **Church of the Assumption** (Cerkev Marijinega Vnebovzetja) stands on the **island** in the center of the lake. There are a number of ways to reach the island. The managed swimming area below the castle **rents boats,** as does **Janez Palak,** Koritenska 27, (☎574 33 22; 3-seater 1700Sit per hr., 5-seater 2000Sit). You can also cross the lake on one of the *plentas*, the gondola-style boats stationed at the Rowing Center and in Mllino under Hotel Park. (Round-trip 1½hr., 1800Sit.) In the summer, **swimming** to the island is permitted; dive in from the well-kept Castle Swimming Grounds under Bled Castle. The becomes an ice-skating rink in winter. (Lake open daily 7am-7pm. Swimming 600Sit per day, students 500Sit. Lockers 400Sit.) Slovenia's oldest citadel, **Bled Castle** (Blejski grad), rises 100m above the water. The official path to the castle is on Grajska cesta, but there are several more pleasant hikes through the forest. One runs uphill from St. Martin's Church (Cerkev sv. Martin), on Kidričeva cesta near the lake. Another route begins behind the swimming area; follow blazes marked with a number "1" up the hill. A ticket to the castle also lets you into the **History Museum,** which is stocked with furniture, weapons, and the skeleton of an Alpine Slav woman from a nearby excavation site. (Castle open daily 8am-8pm. Museum open Mar.-Nov. daily 8am-7pm; Dec.-Feb. 9am-4pm. 700Sit, students 600Sit.)

◗◖ ENTERTAINMENT AND NIGHTLIFE. The tourist office carries a free monthly brochure that lists local events. **Bled Days,** the town's most famous annual festival, takes place the fourth weekend of July each year and features concerts and fireworks on the lake. The folk music extravaganza **No Borders Music Festival** (☎574 14 58) is each August. Bled's nightlife centers around gambling and hotel lounges. Locals gather at the ingeniously named **Pub,** cesta Svobode 8a, under Hotel Jelovica. (☎574 22 17. 0.3L *Union* 400Sit. Open M-Su 7am-1am.)

SLOVENIA

◪ OUTDOOR ACTIVITIES. Freedom of Slovenia, in the shopping center on Ljubljanska, dispenses info on **trekking, tobogganing, skiing,** and **hiking.** (☎418 68 423; fax 594 91 50; www.humanfish.com.) The **Kompas agency,** also in the shopping center, rents **bikes** and offers **white-water rafting trips.** (Bikes 700Sit per hr., 1500Sit per half-day, 2200Sit per full day. Rafting 4000Sit per person. Open daily 8am-7pm.) Numerous **hiking paths** snake from the lake into the neighboring hills. • **Blejski Vintgar,** a 1.6km gorge traced by the waterfalls and rapids, carves through the rocks of the nearby Triglav National Park (Triglavski Narodni; admission 600Sit, students 500Sit). A series of bridges winds through the gorge, leading to the **Šum Waterfall.** To get there from Bled, go over the hill on Grajska cesta and turn right at the bottom. After 100m, turn left and follow the signs for Vintgar. You can also hop on one of the frequent buses to Podhom (260Sit) and follow the 1.5km route. From mid-June to September, **Alpetour** (☎532 04 40) runs a **bus** to the trail. (9:30am, 350Sit.)

LAKE BOHINJ (BOHINJSKO JEZERO) ☎(0)4

Bohinjsko Jezero (BOH-heen-sko YEH-zeh-roh), 30km southwest of Bled, is surrounded by three farming villages that retain a traditional Slovene atmosphere. Protected by the borders of Triglav National Park, this glacial lake—with its surrounding wildflowers, waterfalls, and blustery peaks—is arguably the best place in Slovenia for alpine fun. Some travel here for the water sports, but most come to scale the local summits and experience mountain hospitality.

◪ TRANSPORTATION. Trains do not run to or from Bohinjsko Jezero, but you can always catch a bus to Bohinjska Bistrica and take a train from there to **Ljubljana** (2½hr., 8 per day, 1360Sit) via **Jesenice** (you may need to change trains). **Buses** run to: **Bled** (35min., 14 per day, 680Sit); **Bohinjska Bistrica** (10min., 300Sit); and **Ljubljana** (2hr., every hr., 1620Sit). Buses arriving in Bohinjsko Jezero stop at Hotel Jezero in Ribčev Laz or at Hotel Zlatorog, on the other side of the lake in Ukranc.

◪◪ ORIENTATION AND PRACTICAL INFORMATION. The nearest town is **Bohinjska Bistrica,** 6km to the east. The lake itself is surrounded by three villages: Ribčev Laz, Stara Fužina, and Ukranc. You should find everything you need in **Ribčev Laz,** where the bus arrives. The **Tourist Information Office (TIC),** Ribčev Laz 48, provides maps, issues fishing permits, and arranges guided excursions. (☎572 33 70; fax 572 33 30; tdbohinj@bohinj.si. Open July-Aug. daily 8am-8pm; Sept.-June M-Sa 8am-6pm, Su 9am-3pm.) **Alpinsport,** Ribčev Laz 53, near the bridge, rents **mountain bikes, kayaks, canoes,** and organizes **canyoning** trips in nearby gorges. (☎/fax 572 34 86. Bikes 800Sit per hr., 2000Sit per 3hr., 3100Sit per day. Kayaks 800Sit/2000Sit/3100Sit. Canoes 800Sit/2200Sit/3900Sit. Canyoning 7900Sit per 2-3hr., 9900Sit per 4hr. Open July-Aug. daily 9am-7pm; Sept.-June daily 10am-5pm.) The closest **pharmacy** is in Bohinjska Bistrica at Triglavska 15. (☎572 16 30. Open M-F 8am-7:30pm, Sa 8am-1pm.) The nearest bank, **Gorenjska Banka,** Trg Svobode 26, also in Bohinjska Bistrica, **exchanges currency** and cashes **traveler's checks** for no commission. (☎572 16 10. Open July-Aug. M-F 8am-6pm, Sa 8am-noon; Sept.-June daily 9-11:30am and 2-5pm.) The **post office,** Ribčev Laz 47, has a MC/V **ATM** outside. (Open July-Aug. M-F 8am-7pm, Sa 8am-noon; Sept.-June M-F 8am-6pm, Sa 8am-noon.) **Postal Code:** 4265.

◪◪ ACCOMMODATIONS AND FOOD. Find a **private room ❷** by looking for the *Sobe* signs around town or contacting the **TIC,** which arranges accommodations for all three villages. (Breakfast 1000Sit. July 8-Aug. 24 1900Sit per person; May 1-July 7 and Aug. 26-Dec. 22 2050Sit per person. Tourist tax 154Sit. 30% more for stays under 3 nights. 20% more for a single.) **AvtoCamp Zlatorog ❷,** Ukanc 2, is on the west side of the lake close to the Savica Waterfall and many trailheads. The complex, run by Alpinum Tourist Agency (see **Orientation and Practical Information,** above), usually has spaces available. Take a bus from the bus stop in Ribčev Laz to the Hotel Zlatorog (see **Transportation,** above) and backtrack for a few minutes. (☎572 34 82; fax 572 34 46. Reception July-Aug. 24hr.; Sept.-May 8am-noon and 4-8pm. Check-out noon. Open May-Sept. July-Aug. 1900Sit per person; May-June and Sept. 1300Sit. Tourist tax 154Sit.) **Camping Danica ❶,** Bohinjska Bistrica 4264, is just outside of town. Get off the bus in Bohinjska Bistrica and continue in the direction of the bus; the site is on the right. (☎572 10 55; fax 572 33 30. Open May-Sept. only. May 1-June 16 and Sept. 1100Sit per person; June 17-July 21 and August 19-August 31 1300Sit; July 22-August 18 1500Sit. 10% off stays longer than 7 days. Tourist tax 100Sit, children 50Sit. AmEx/MC/V.)

To reach ▨ **Gostišče Kramar ❸,** Stara Fužina 3, walk just past the stone bridge and follow the dirt path that heads left to Sara Fužina for 10min. Patio seating and wall-to-wall windows ensure that you'll be able to enjoy an astounding view of the lake wherever you sit. (☎572 36 97. 0.5L *Laško* or *Union* 400Sit. Entrees 900-1500Sit. Open M-F noon-8pm, Sa-Su 11am-9pm.) **Restavracija Center ❹,** Ribčev Laz 50, has a great "tourist menu" (1300-1500Sit) that includes soup, salad, and a main dish. The menu always features a vegetarian option. (☎572 31 70. Open daily 8am-11pm.) **Mercator Supermarket,** Ribčev Laz 49, near the tourist office, sells **groceries.** (Open M-F 7am-8pm, Sa 7am-5pm.)

▧ **OUTDOOR ACTIVITIES.** The shores of Bohinj serve as a gateway to all kinds of outdoor excursions, from the casual to the nearly impossible. Good **hiking maps** are available at the tourist office (1500Sit). The most popular destination is **Savica Waterfall** (Slap Savica), on the Bohinj River. Take a bus from Ribčev Laz toward "Bohinj-Zlatorog," get off at Hotel Zlatorog, and follow the signs uphill to Savica Waterfall. (1hr. to the trailhead, then 20min. to the waterfall.) In July and August a bus runs to the trailhead from Ribčev Laz (4 per day 9am-6pm). If you forego the bus, turn left at the lake in Ribčev Laz and follow the road along the lake past Ukanc (3hr.). Along the way, you can wander into the 1743 **Church of the Holy Ghost** and stop by the sobering **Austro-Hungarian World War I Cemetery.** Visitors must pay a fee (300Sit) at the entrance to the waterfall. If the hiking spirit compels you to continue on after the waterfall, follow the signs toward **Black Lake** (Črno Jezero) to hit the base of the gigantic **Julian Peaks** (1½hr.). The hiking is steep; be extremely cautious. After the ridge line, a trail to the right (Dol Pod Stadorjem) leads to **Mt. Viš0evnik.** Turn south from this peak to reach **Pršivec** (1761m; 2½hr.) and a breathtaking view of the lake. Return the way you came or follow the trail east to return along the ridge via **Stara Fužina** and **Ribčev Laz** (2½hr.). In the winter, Bohinj becomes an enormous **ski** resort with three ski centers: **Soriška Planina, Kobla,** and **Vogel.** Contact Vogel, Ukanc 6 (☎574 60 60; vogel@bohinj.si), or Kobla, cesta na Ravne 7 (☎574 71 00; kobla@bohinj.si).

▣▩ **SIGHTS AND FESTIVALS.** While resting between hikes, you can take in a bit of Alpine culture. The 15th-century **Church of John the Baptist,** across the stone bridge on Ribčev Laz, is adorned with colorful frescoes and an ornate altar. (Open daily June-Sept. 15 9am-noon and 4-7pm. 100Sit). The **Alpine Highlander Museum** (Planšarska Muzej), 1.5km north in Stara Fužina, exhibits artifacts from the life of a 19th-century mountain man. (Open July-Aug. Tu-Su 11am-7pm; Sept.-Oct. and Dec. 25-June Tu-Su 10am-noon and 4-6pm. 400Sit, students 300Sit.) Fireworks galore make **Kresna Noč** (Midsummer Night) in mid-August the most spectacular of the summer festivals. **Peasant's Wedding Day** occurs at the end of each July. It's an elaborate (and real) wedding ceremony that's more for locals than tourists. The **International Folk Festival** hits town in mid-August. The mid-September **Kravji Bal** (Cow Ball) in Ukanc is a dance held on the day the cows come in for the winter.

KRANJSKA GORA ☎ 0(4)

The mountain village of Kranjska Gora (pop. 1500) is an enclave of traditional Julian Alpine culture. For serious mountaineering, this portion of the Alps is superb. Less-experienced climbers can also enjoy the area, as the Karavanke ridge to the north—where Italy, Austria, and Slovenia meet—provides gentler inclines. Equally appealing to both hikers in summer and skiers in winter, Kranjska Gora is an ideal getaway for the outdoor adventurer.

TRANSPORTATION. Buses run to **Bled** (40min., every hr., 1050Sit) and **Ljubljana** (2¼hr., every hr., 1720Sit). Rent **mountain bikes** and **skis** at **Sport Bernik**, Borovška 88a. (☎588 14 70; fax 588 16 82; sport@S5.net. Bikes 700Sit per hr., 1400Sit per half-day, 2000Sit per day. Skis and poles 1600Sit per day, boots 700Sit, Snowboards 2000Sit, Sleds 800Sit. Open daily 8am-6pm.)

ORIENTATION AND PRACTICAL INFORMATION. The village is spread along **Borovška cesta.** To get there from the **bus stop** on Koroška cesta, walk in the same direction as the bus and take the first left on **Kolodvorska cesta.** Turn right at the end of the street on Borovška and follow it past the church. **Turistično društvo Kranjska Gora,** Tičarjeva 2, in the center of town on the corner of Tičarjeva and Borovška, arranges private rooms and sells maps. (☎588 17 68; fax 588 11 25; turisticno.drustvo.kg@siol.net. Open July-Sept. daily 8am-8pm; Oct.-June daily 8am-3pm.) **Globtour,** 90 Borovška cesta, arranges mountain excursions. (☎582 02 00; globtour-kr.gora@g-kabel.si.) **SKB Banka,** Borovška cesta 99a, cashes AmEx **Traveler's Cheques** for 500Sit commission, **exchanges currency** for no commission, and has a 24hr. MC/V **ATM.** (☎588 20 06. Open M-F 8:30am-noon and 2-5pm.) The **pharmacy, Lekarna Kranjska Gora,** is at Naselje Slavka Černeta 34. (☎588 17 85. Open M-W and F 7:30am-3pm, Th noon-7pm, Sa 8am-1pm.) **Internet access** is available in **Gostilna Frida,** Koroška 4a. (20Sit per min. Open daily 10am-11pm.) **Telephones** are in the **post office,** Borovška 92. (☎588 17 70. Open Mar. 16-Dec. 14 M-F 8am-7pm, Sa 8am-noon; Dec.15-Mar. 15 M-Sa 8am-8pm.) **Postal Code:** 4280.

ACCOMMODATIONS AND FOOD. There are plenty of **private rooms ❷** in town; look for the *Sobe* signs. The **tourist office** can also arrange rooms. (Breakfast 800Sit. Sept.-June 2100-3000Sit; July-August 2500-4000Sit per person in double. Singles 1000Sit extra.) **Mercator ❶,** Borovška 92, is a sure bet for **groceries.** (Market open M-F 7am-8pm, Sa 7am-6pm; in Dec. also Su 8am-noon.) The traditionally clad waiters at **Gostilna pri Martinu ❹,** Borovška 61, deliver huge portions of Slovene fare (1100-1700Sit). For dessert, try the *kranjska-štruklji* (kranjska walnut pie; 450Sit). (☎582 03 00. Open daily 10am-11pm.) **Papa Joe Razor ❺,** Borovška 83, serves hot meals (1500Sit for 4 courses) until 4am. With live music every night, it's also the best alternative to the pricey casinos. (☎588 15 26. Open daily 8am-5am.)

HIKING AND ENTERTAINMENT. **Agencija Julijana,** near the parking lot on Borovška cesta, arranges **hiking** and **skiing** excursions near town. (☎/fax 588 13 25; julijana@siol.net. Open daily 8am-noon and 3-8pm.) Hiking and walking **maps** of the area are available from the tourist information center (1300Sit), as is a listing of guides for hire. Look for the village of **Podkoren,** 3km from Kranjska Gora toward the Austrian border, known for its well-preserved folk architecture. It harbors the natural reserve **Zelenci,** which is the source of the Sava Dolinka River. **Rateče,** a small village with Alpine houses 7km from Kranjska Gora, sits below **Pec** (1510m) and near the border with Austria and Italy. One of the best hikes in the area runs through the **Planica Valley** to the mountain of **Tamar.** From town, follow the abandoned railroad westward. After passing the ski lifts that loom on the left, you'll reach the old railroad station in Rateče. Turn left into the Planica valley to enjoy an amazing view of the **Mojstrovka, Travnik,** and **Šit Mountains.** Continue past the ski ramps for 30min. to reach the mountain home **Tamar,** from which **Jalovec,** one of the most beautiful peaks, can be seen. During summer the village enjoys three months of festivities that include concerts, farm markets, and sports events. **Hotel Prišank,** Borovška 93, has billiards (200Sit) and a bar. (Open daily 7:30am-11pm.) You can also wet your whistle across the street in the tiny **Caffe Pinki,** Borovška 91. (☎88 17 66. 0.3L *Union* 400Sit. Open daily 9am-11pm.)

ISTRIA

Slovenia claims only 40km of the Adriatic coast, but it's a remarkable stretch of green bays, vineyards, and small towns that has a palpable Italian flavor. Reminiscent of the French Riviera or the nearby Dalmatian coast of Croatia, Slovenian Istria is both a picturesque resort and the site of active, bustling coastal villages. Quaint Piran and vivacious Portoroz ("port of roses") are particularly striking examples of the Slovenian coast at its finest.

KOPER   ☎(0)66

With plenty of train and bus connections, Koper (pop. 20,000) serves as Istria's transportation hub. Though it offers little in terms of sightseeing, Koper is a often a necessary stop for those making their way to the beach.

The **bus** (☎639 52 69) and **train** (☎639 52 63) station is at Kolodvorska 11. Direct buses run to: **Ljubljana** (2½hr., 13 per day, 2450Sit); **Piran** (40min., every 20min. until 11pm, 580Sit) via **Portorož** (25min., 530Sit); and **Trieste, ITA** (45min., 16 per day, 690Sit). Trains run to **Ljubljana** (2¼hr., 5 per day, 1730Sit). There is a **Tourist Information Office (TIC)** on Kolodvorska (☎663 20 10). **ATMs** are abundant in the city center. The hostel **Dijaški Dom Koper ❸,** Cankarjeva 5, is convenient and clean. From the station, turn right and follow Kolodvorska toward the city center. (☎627 32 50; fax 627 31 82. Breakfast included. Check-in after noon. Check-out 10am. Open June 15-Aug. 21. 3400Sit, 3150Sit with ISIC or IH. Tourist tax 77Sit.) **Gostišče Istrska Klet ❸,** Župančičeva 39, in the center, serves Slovene dishes (950Sit) and specialties from the sea. (Open M-Sa 6:30am-9pm.)

PORTOROŽ   ☎(0)5

If Slovenian Istria were condensed into one town, with Koper as the bus station and Piran the museum, Portorož (port-oh-ROZH; pop. 9000) would provide the entertainment. Streams of visitors have washed away the distinctly Slovene flavor that neighboring coastal towns retain, but the grassy beach, seaside restaurants, and deep blue tide of Portorož remain undiminished.

⌗ TRANSPORTATION. A **bus** connects Portorož to **Koper** (25min., every 20min. until 11pm, 530Sit) and **Ljubljana** (2¾hr., 9 per day, 2610Sit), while a **minibus** runs the full length of Obala, from Lucija through Portorož (every 15min. until 11pm, 240Sit). A **catamaran** connects Portorož to **Venice, ITA.** (2½hr; Apr.-Nov. 2-4 per week; 9000-13,800Sit, depending on departure date.) **Atlas Express,** Obala 55, **rents bikes** and **scooters.** (☎674 50 77; fax 674 55 97; atlas.portoroz@siol.net. Bikes 1300Sit per 2hr., 2000Sit per 6hr., 3300Sit per day. Scooters 4400Sit/7700Sit/8800Sit. Open July-Sept. daily 8am-8pm; Oct.-June M-Sa 8am-7pm.)

SLOVENIA

▄▎ 🔁 ORIENTATION AND PRACTICAL INFORMATION. Most streets start at **Obala,** the waterfront boulevard. The main bus stop is a little way up the road across from the **tourist office,** Obala 16. (☎674 82 60; fax 674 82 61. Open July-Aug. daily 9am-1:30pm and 3-9:30pm; Sept.-June Th-Tu 10am-5pm, W 10am-3pm.) Another **branch** of the tourist office books private rooms at Obala 52. Numerous **exchange offices** are on Obala, and there is a 24hr. MC/V **ATM** at Obala 32. A **pharmacy, Lekarna Portorož,** is at Obala 41. Walk down Obala in the direction of Piran, turn right into the Hotel Palace Courtyard, and follow the sign. (☎674 86 70. Open M-F 8am-7pm, Sa 8am-1pm.) **Internet access** is available about 1km away in the direction of Piran at Obala 11. (1000Sit per hr. Open M-F 1-9pm, Sa-Su 3-9pm.) **Telephones** line Obala. The **post office,** Stari cesti 1, cashes **traveler's checks** for 2% commission. (☎671 32 20. Open M-F 8am-9pm, Sa 8am-noon.) **Postal Code:** 6320.

🔂 🗂 ACCOMMODATIONS AND FOOD. Accommodations are often difficult to obtain in Potorož. **Maona Potorož,** Obala 53, arranges **private rooms ❸.** (☎674 03 63; fax 674 64 23; www.maona.si. July-Aug. singles 3800Sit; doubles 5700-6600Sit; triples 7200-7700Sit. Sept.-June 3100Sit/4600-5400Sit/5800-6600Sit.) To get to **Lucija ❷,** Seča 204, a **campground,** hop on a minibus from any point along Obala and ride it away from Piran to the stop "Lucija." Continue in the direction of the bus and turn right at the sign. (☎690 60 00; fax 690 69 00. Reception 7am-10pm. Guarded 24hr. July-Aug. 2000Sit per person; May-June and Sept. 1500Sit. Tourist tax 77Sit.) The best bet for food is the **supermarket Mercator Degro,** on Obala next to the bus station. (Open M-Sa 7am-8pm, Su 8-11am.)

NIGHTLIFE AND ENTERTAINMENT. The Club, at the Hotel Belvedere in nearby Izola, is probably the region's most popular nightclub. (☎153 93 11. Beer 400Sit. Open daily 11pm-6am). **News Cafe,** Obala 4f, is a trendy bar that attracts both the young and the not-so-young. (☎674 10 04, 0.3L beer 360Sit. Open daily 8am-1am.) If the opportunity arises, visit the nightclub **Ambaceda Gavioli,** which is internationally famous for its wild parties. The club is not open regularly, so look for flyers advertising an event. Potorož is also home to the **Pust,** a carnival in February that attracts visitors from all along the coast.

PIRAN ☎(0)5

The central buildings of Piran (pop. 5000) form an oval around a statue of native-born violinist and composer Giuseppe Tartini, whose serene composure reflects the town's atmosphere. Medieval Venice, under whose rule the town flourished, is still alive in well-preserved Piran.

🚍 TRANSPORTATION. Buses connect Piran to **Ljubljana** via **Koper** (40min., every 20min., 580Sit) and **Trieste, ITA** (1¼hr., 6 per day, 1050Sit). At the station, you can also catch the **minibus** (240Sit) to Portorož and Lucija.

🔁 PRACTICAL INFORMATION. From the bus stop along the quay, face the sea and take a right to the marina. From there, head to the central **Tartinijev Trg.** The **tourist office** is at Tartinijev Trg 2. (☎673 02 20; fax 673 02 21; ticpi@portoroz.si. Open July-Aug. M-F and Su 9am-1:30pm and 3-9:30pm, Sa 9am-10pm; Sept.-June W 9am-noon and 2-5pm, Sa 10am-2pm.) There is a **pharmacy** at Tartinijev Trg 4. (☎673 01 50. Open M-F 8am-7pm, Sa 8am-1pm.) **Banka Koper,** Tartinijev Trg 12, **exchanges currency,** cashes **traveler's checks** for no commission, and has a 24hr. MC/V **ATM.**

(☎673 32 00. Open M-F 8:30am-noon and 3-5pm, Sa 8:30-noon.) **Cyber Point,** Župančičeva 14, has **Internet access**. (1000Sit per hr. Open M-F 1-9pm and Sa-Su 3-9pm.) **Telephones** are in the **post office** at Leninova 1. (☎673 16 45; open M-F 8am-8pm, Sa 8am-noon.) **Postal Code:** 6330.

⌂⌂ ACCOMMODATIONS AND FOOD. To book a **private room**, visit **Maona ❷,** Cankarjeva nabrežie 7. Walk toward the marina from the bus station; the office is on the right. (☎673 45 90; fax 673 45 19; maona@siol.net. Open M-Sa 9am-1pm and 5-7pm, Su 9am-noon and 5-7pm. July-Aug. singles 3500Sit; doubles 5200Sit; triples 6800Sit. 50% more for stays under 3 nights. Tourist tax 154Sit. MC.) Mr. and Mrs. Humar of ▨ **Val Piran (HI) ❸,** Gregorčičeva 38a, run a hostel near the lighthouse that has clean doubles, triples, and quads. From the bus station, walk toward the tip of the peninsula and look for the sign on the right. (☎673 25 55; fax 673 25 56. Reception 24hr. Check-out 11am. June 15-Sept. 15 4500Sit per person, 5800Sit with half-board, 6800Sit with full board; Sept. 16-June 14 3500Sit/4800Sit/5800Sit. Stays under 3 nights 10% more June 15-Sept. 15. 500Sit ISIC discount.) **Tri Vdove ❺,** opposite Hotel Piran, serves delicious steak and seafood. (☎673 22 32. Entrees 1500-2000Sit.) **Restaurant Neptun ❸,** Cankarjeva Nab. 7, is a less expensive seafood option. (Entrees 1100-1500Sit. Open 8am-11pm.) **Supermarket Kras,** Zelenjavni Trg 1, has an **outdoor market**. (Open M-F 7am-7pm, Sa 7am-2pm, Su 8am-noon.)

◉⚑ SIGHTS AND ENTERTAINMENT. The sea is Piran's central sight, but a stroll along its streets is also worthwhile. The Gothic **Church of St. George** (Crkva sv. Jurja), built in the 12th century, is a short walk uphill from Tartinijev Trg. Next door is the **St. George Tower,** built in 1608. Climb all 146 stairs and you'll be rewarded with impressive views of Piran and the Adriatic. (Church and tower open daily 10am-10pm. Tower entrance 200Sit.) The **aquarium,** Tomažičeva 4, on the water opposite the marina, has an enormous variety of marine life in 25 tanks. (Open daily 10am-noon and 2pm-7pm. 500Sit.) The summer is graced with endless theater performances during the **Primorska Summer Festival.** The **Melodies of the Sea and Sun Festival,** a national song contest, resonates during the last weekend of July.

UKRAINE
(УКРАЇНА)

HRYVNA

AUS$1 = 2.93HV	1HV = AUS$0.34
CDN$1 = 3.42HV	1HV = CDN$0.29
EUR€1 = 5.24HV	1HV = EUR€0.19
NZ$1 = 2.49HV	1HV = NZ$0.40
UK£1 = 8.26HV	1HV = UK£0.12
US$1 = 5.33HV	1HV = US$0.19
ZAR1 = 0.50HV	1HV = ZAR1.99

Translated literally, the word "Ukraina" means "borderland," and it is this precarious position that the country has occupied for most of its history. Newly independent Ukraine still oscillates between nostalgic, overbearing Russia on one side, and a bloc of *nouveau riche* countries on the other. Historic Kyiv, the cradle of Slavic Orthodox culture, now finds itself besieged by Western Ukraine with its Uniate congregations in lavish cathedrals, its bold rhetoric of Ukrainian nationalism, and its traditional affinity for Europe. On the other side lies the Crimea, whose predominantly Russian population longs for the days of Soviet stability and tourist industry. Traveling through Ukraine's landscape is an absolutely unique experience; with no beaten path from which to stray, the challenges of exploration reward travelers with a genuine and intriguing look into Ukrainian life.

UKRAINE AT A GLANCE

OFFICIAL NAME: Ukraine

CAPITAL: Kyiv (pop. 2.6 million)

POPULATION: 48.8 million (73% Ukrainian, 22% Russian, 1% Jewish, 4% other)

LANGUAGES: Ukrainian, Russian, Crimean Tatar

CURRENCY: 1 hryvna = 100 kopiykas

RELIGION: 29% Ukrainian Orthodox, 7% Uniate, 4% Protestant

LAND AREA: 603,700km²

GEOGRAPHY: Mountains; plains near the Hungarian border

CLIMATE: Temperate continental

BORDERS: Belarus, Hungary, Moldova, Poland, Romania, Russia, Slovak Republic

ECONOMY: 62% Services, 26% Industry, 12% Agriculture

GDP: US$3850 per capita

COUNTRY CODE: 380

INTERNATIONAL DIALING PREFIX: 810

HISTORY

KYIVAN RUS. Recorded Ukrainian history dates from the **Kyivan Rus** dynasty that sprang from the infiltrations of Viking (Varangian) warrior-traders into the Dnieper River region in AD 882. These warriors grew wealthy from the new north-south fur trade. The Kyivan aristocracy quickly became Slavicized, adopting Christianity and the Cyrillic alphabet. **Prince Volodymyr the Great** welcomed missionaries from Constantinople and was baptized in 988. With Christianity came a flow of Byzantine thought and culture; Kyivan Rus grew so enamored that it tried to con-

quer its southern neighbors three times. Volodymyr's son **Yaroslav** promoted architecture, music, and the development of Old Church Slavonic (see p. 820). Unfortunately, Yaroslav's rule marked the high before the crash, as changes in trade routes and internal squabbling left the empire a target for invaders.

HOW TO SURVIVE FOUR CONQUERING EMPIRES. Invasion is exactly what **Genghis Khan** had in mind when he moved into Ukraine in the 1230s; his grandson Batu sacked Kyiv in 1240. Batu's death halted the **Golden Horde**'s march into Europe but not Mongol rule in Ukraine, which persisted as late as 1783 in the Crimea. By the mid-14th century, Ukraine proper was ruled by the Horde and the Grand Duchy of Lithuania (including present-day Poland). Eastern Ukrainian **Cossack** bands came under the employ of the Polish-Lithuanian government as soldiers against Constantinople and Muscovy. A rebellion led by Cossack (commander) **Bohdan Khmelnitsky** in 1648 led to a war with Poland, but a tenuous treaty with Russia eventually led to what is know as **"the Ruin."** By 1667, the nation was forced to divide Ukraine along the Dnieper River. Russia won the east (Left Bank), including Kyiv and Odessa, and the west went to Poland. On the Russian side, most of Ukraine was reorganized into provinces. Jews were restricted to the Polish-controlled Right Bank, which became known as the **Pale of Settlement.** Local culture was given a freer reign in Western Ukraine and its capital city, Lviv, which fell into Austro-Hungarian hands after the **First Partition of Poland** in 1772.

MODERN UKRAINE. In the 19th century Ukraine become a more vital part of the Russian empire. Ukrainian nationalism also resurfaced, led by the poet and painter **Taras Shevchenko,** who sought to revitalize the Ukrainian language and establish a democratic state. For his efforts, Shevchenko was arrested and exiled to Central Asia. Ukraine declared its independence in 1918, but the **Bolsheviks** set up a rival government in Kharkiv and seized complete power during the Civil War (1918-20); meanwhile the Poles retook Lviv and Western Ukraine only to lose them again in 1940. The next 70 years saw one tragedy after another, as this "bread basket of Russia" bore the brunt of Stalin's murderous collectivization of agriculture, Nazi invasion, a long-standing ban against the Ukrainian language, and the 1986 meltdown at the **Chernobyl** nuclear power plant.

FROM THEM TO US. Ukraine pulled out of the Soviet Union on December 1, 1991, following a vote by 93% of its population for complete **independence.** The Soviet legacy, however, was not easily shed: the **Black Sea Fleet** at Sevastopol was in dispute, as was the status of the Crimea. On May 28, 1997, after nearly five years of conflict, Prime Ministers Lazarenko and Chernomyrdin agreed to divide the fleet and to lease key port facilities to the Russian Navy.

TODAY

President Leonid Kuchma won a second five-year term in October 1999, despite his dismal record of economic stagnation and political repression. Kuchma has used tax and libel laws to shut down media critical of his regime. Huge public outcry erupted recently after evidence surfaced suggesting that Kuchma had ordered the September 2001 murder of journalist Grigory Gongadze, representing the possibility of ruthless media control by government. Thirty-eight Ukrainian journalists have been murdered since 1991. Russia and Ukraine reached a diplomatic breakthrough in August 2002, when ownership disputes concerning 10 former Soviet properties were resolved after nearly seven years of negotiations. They also remain strategic partners in the formation of an international gas consortium that would use Ukraine's main gas lines to service Eastern Europe, and leaders from both countries met on August 16, 2002 to finalize the agreement. In addition to maintaining its ties with Moscow, Ukraine has also begun to look west. Plans are in progress to replace the broad-gauge Soviet railroad leading west from Lviv with standard tracks in an effort to strengthen relations with the **EU.** Pre-Soviet denizens of the region such as the **Crimean Tartars**, deported to Uzbekistan in 1944, have finally begun to return home. The GDP initially shrunk 72% after the nation declared independence. A strong export-based growth in GDP of 6% in 2002 gave hope to the once-falling nation. Still, this growth is expected to decline to 3% by 2003. The new hryvna has gone sour as creditors, notably the IMF, are sick of the lack of financial reform. Corruption is endemic, with an estimated four of five Ukrainian banks controlled by organized crime and 6.5% of all business income spent in bribes to government officials. Currently, 50% of Ukrainians live below the poverty line.

PEOPLE AND CULTURE
LANGUAGE

It is much easier to travel in Ukraine if you know some **Ukrainian** or **Russian.** In Kyiv, Odessa, and Crimea, Russian is more common than Ukrainian (although all official signs are in Ukrainian). In Transcarpathia, Ukrainian is preferred—people will speak Russian with you only if they know you are not Russian. *Let's Go* uses Ukrainian names in Kyiv and Western Ukraine, and Russian in Crimea and Odeshchina. The Ukrainian alphabet resembles Russian (see **The Cyrillic Alphabet,** p. 14), but with a few character and pronunciation differences. The most notable additions are the "*ï*" (ee sound) and the "*ï*" (yee sound)—the "*u*" is closest to "s*i*t." The rarely used "*є*" sounds like "ye" in "yep!" The "*ґ*" (hard "g") has been reintroduced since independence but is not yet widely used, and the "*г*," pronounced "*g*" in Russian, comes out like an "h." Roll your "*r*"s, but not too flamboyantly. For a phrasebook and glossary, see **Glossary: Russian,** p. 889.

RELIGION

In Western Ukraine, centuries of Polish influence have led **Uniate Catholicism** to be the dominant religion. The eastern portion of the country is dominated by the **Ukrainian Orthodox Church.** The Pope's recent visit to Orthodox Kyiv created some tension between the churches, as some religious leaders accused the Pope of trying to proselytize the locals.

FOOD AND DRINK

UKRAINE	❶	❷	❸	❹	❺
FOOD	under 11hv	11-27hv	28-54hv	55-105hv	over 105hv

New, fancy restaurants are popping up to accommodate tourists and the few Ukrainians who can afford them. There are few choices between these and the *stolovayas* (cafeterias), dying bastions of the Soviet Union, which serve cheap, hot food. *Stolovayas* usually serve similar meals: a choice of two soups, two entrees, and some *kompot* (a homemade fruit drink), but quality varies greatly. Less-than-fresh *stolovaya* food can knock you out for hours, while a good *stolovaya* meal is a triumph of the human spirit. Ravioli-like noodles with various fillings (including fish, meat, and potato) called *vaveiniki* are quite good. **Vegetarians** will have to create their own meals from potatoes, mushrooms, and cabbage. Fruits and veggies are sold at **markets;** bring your own bag. Markets are open daily. **State food stores** are classified by content: *hastronom* (гастроном) packaged goods; *moloko* (молоко) milk products; *ovochi-frukty* (овочі-фрукты) fruits and vegetables; *myaso* (мясо) meat; *hlib* (хліб) bread; *kolbasy* (колбаси) sausage; and *ryba* (риба) fish. In the suburbs, there is one grocery per designated region, simply labeled *mahazyn* (магазин; store). **Tea** is a popular national drink, as is *kvas,* a beer-like drink served from cisterns in the street.

CUSTOMS AND ETIQUETTE

When buying flowers for hosts, purchase an even number, as an odd number is only bought for funerals. Unless you know the political situation in Ukraine well, confine your comments to the beauty of the countryside and the hospitality of the people. At the Ukrainian dinner table, hands are usually kept on the table. Dinners can last long into the evening; leaving early may offend your hosts. Not eating your food is equally insulting. Conversely, asking for and eating seconds is considered a compliment. Although locals don't usually leave tips, most expats leave 10%. It is unheard of for women to pay in restaurants. Several gestures that are considered positive in other cultures have a different significance in Ukraine. The 'OK' sign, with the thumb and forefinger touching each other and forming a circle, can be considered crude. The same goes to a shaken fist, chewing gum while speaking, and pointing your index finger. When in a theater or any other seated public arena, always face seated patrons when entering or exiting a row; passing with your back to them is considered offensive. When entering a church, men should wear long pants and women should cover their heads.

THE ARTS

HISTORY

LITERATURE. Ukraine's written tradition shares roots with Russia and Belarus in the histories and sermons of Kyivan Rus. Religious works in Old Church Slavonic gave way to original works, characterized by stylized writing and exuberant praise of the empire. Perhaps the most important literary endeavor of this era was the 12th-century *Song of Igor's Campaign (Slavo o polku Ihorevi)*, a largely symbolic epic unsurpassed in the courtly tradition. (Vladimir Nabokov rendered the epic in English in 1960.) Ukrainian literature re-emerged in the 17th and 18th centuries. The most accomplished author of the period, **Ivan Kotliarevsky,** established the Ukrainian vernacular with his comic travesty of Virgil's *Aeneid,* the *Eneïda.* In 1830s Kyiv, **Mykola Kostomarov, Panteleymon Kulish,** and **Taras Shevchenko** (see **Kyiv: Sights,** p. 818) joined the **Brotherhood of St. Cyril and Methodius,** devoted to increasing Ukrainian national consciousness. The early 20th century saw a dramatic outburst of artistic activity. Major literary movements overtook one another rapidly: the Modernism of **Lesya Ukrainka** (the country's foremost female poet) gave way to decadent Realism in prose and Symbolism in verse. Another newly developed movement, **Futurism,** created one of Ukraine's greatest poets, **Mykola Bazhan.** Communist-imposed Socialist Realism rained on the artistic parade, with mass censorship and Stalinist purges of dissenting writers. The so-called **Writers of the Sixties,** Vasyl Stus, Lina Kostenko, and others, wrote just enough to warrant even tougher repression in the coming decades. The result was a coma that the arts—at least among non-exiles—are just beginning to awaken from.

FINE ARTS. Iconic art lies at the heart of Ukrainian painting, as many of the early paintings feature Christ, the Virgin Mary, and other religious paragons. Later centuries of art saw the portrayal of historical scenes and portraits. As books began to be printed, the art of engraving quickly ensued. In the visual arts, **Monumentalism** dominated painting while a **Neo-Baroque** style dominated in the graphic arts. Under Communism, however, creativity lay dormant until the thaw of the early 1960s allowed it burst forth in expressionistic paintings of communist horrors.

CURRENT SCENE

Over 40 concert organizations and 140 artistic collectives currently flourish in Ukraine. Several **outdoor museums,** featuring an array of crafts and buildings of current and past centuries, have opened amidst bustling pavilions. In the **theater** scene, the Kyiv Opera House, among others, continues to feature Ukrainian and Russian theater and ballet companies.

HOLIDAYS AND FESTIVALS

NATIONAL HOLIDAYS IN 2003	
January 1 New Year's Day	**May 1-2** Labor Day
January 7 Orthodox Christmas	**May 9** Victory Day
March 8 International Women's Day	**June 15** Holy Trinity
April 18 Good Friday	**June 28** Constitution Day
April 20-21 Easter	**August 24** Independence Day

MUSIC FESTIVALS. One of the most widely celebrated festivals among music lovers is the **Donetsk Jazz Festival,** usually held in March. The conclusion of the 20th century brought the **Chervona Ruta Festival,** an interesting affair that aims to commemorate both modern Ukrainian pop and more traditional music.

FILM AND THEATER FESTIVALS. The **Molodist Kyiv International Film Festival,** held in the last week of October, sets the stage for student films and film debuts. Many other annual festivals have sprouted in recent years, including the **S. Krushelny-tska Festivals of Opera Art,** a Lviv celebration which begins when the fat lady sings.

ADDITIONAL RESOURCES

GENERAL HISTORY

Borderland: A Journey Through the History of Ukraine, by Anna Reid (2000). Provides a general overview of Ukrainian history.

A History of Ukraine, by Paul Robert Magocsi (1996). A comprehensive text that navigates all the turns of Ukraine's complex history.

FICTION AND NONFICTION

Execution by Hunger: The Hidden Holocaust, by Miron Dolot (1987). A riveting memoir of Stalin's forced collectivization of agriculture.

The Ukrainians: Unexpected Nation, by Andrew Wilson (2000). An up-to-date report of life in Ukraine today.

Journey to Chernobyl: Encounters in a Radioactive Zone, by Glenn Cheney (1995). A depiction of Ukraine's most recent national tragedy.

From Three Worlds: New Ukrainian Writing, edited by Ed Hogan (1996). If chasing radiation isn't your game, cozy up with the country's best young poets and prose writers.

UKRAINE ESSENTIALS

ENTRANCE REQUIREMENTS

Passport: Required of all travelers to Ukraine.
Visa: Required of all travelers.
Letter of Invitation: Required of citizens of Australia, New Zealand, and South Africa.
Inoculations: None required. Recommended up-to-date on MMR (measles, mumps, and rubella), DTaP (diphtheria), Polio booster, Typhoid, Tetanus, Hepatitis A, and Hepatitis B.
Work Permit: Required for all foreigners planning to work in Ukraine.
International Driving Permit: Required for all those planning to drive.

DOCUMENTS AND FORMALITIES

EMBASSIES AND CONSULATES

Embassies of other countries in Ukraine are all located in Kyiv (see p. 811). Ukraine's embassies and consulates abroad include:

Australia: Honorary Consulate: 902-912 Mt. Alexander Road, Ground fl. #3, Essendon, VIC 3040 (☎03 326 0135; fax 326 0139).

Canada: 331 Metcalfe St. Ottawa., ON K2P 0J9 (☎613-230-2961; fax 230-2400; ukremb@cyberus.ca).

South Africa: 398 Marais Brooklyn, Pretoria (☎012 461 946; fax 461 944).

UK: 78 Kensington Park Rd. London W11 2PL (☎020 7727 6312; fax 7792 1708).

US: Embassy: 3350 M St. NW, Washington, D.C. 20007 (☎202-333-0606; fax 333-0817; www.ukremb.com). **Consulate:** 240 East 90th Street, New York, NY 10017 (☎212-371-5691; fax 371-5547).

VISA AND ENTRY INFORMATION

Travelers from Australia, Canada, Ireland, New Zealand, South Africa, the UK, and the US arriving in Ukraine must have a visa. Citizens of Canada, the EU, and the US do not require an invitation, while citizens of Australia, New Zealand, and South Africa require an invitation. Single-entry visas cost US$30, double-entry US$60, multiple-entry US$120. Transit visas cost US$15, not including the US$45 processing fee. Three-day rush service costs US$60, double-entry US$120; same or next-day service costs US$100, not including the US$45 processing fee. The visa fee is waived for children under 16 years of age and American students with proper documents. Submit a completed visa application, your passport, two passport-size photos, and payment by money order or cashier's check. If you need an invitation, there are organizations that arrange visas and invitations. **Diane Sadovnikov,** a former missionary living and working in Ukraine, arranges invitations (US$40). Fax Diane a month in advance (US ☎757-573-8362; fax 622-4693; UKR ☎/ fax 044 516 2433; www.travel-ims.com). **Janna Belovsova,** of Eugenia Travel in Odessa, can also help with invitations. (☎482 21 85 83; ☎/fax 482 22 05 54; janna@eugen.intes.odessa.ua.)

When proceeding through **customs** you will be required to declare all valuables and foreign currency above US$1000 (including traveler's checks). It's illegal to bring Ukrainian currency into Ukraine. Foreigners arriving at Kyiv's Borispol airport must purchase a US$23-per-week **health-insurance** policy for their stay; bring exact change. The policy is really an entry tax; it doesn't provide access to any health care services. **Do not lose the paper given to you when entering the country to supplement your visas.** The **Office of Visas and Registration** (OVIR; ОВИР)—in Kyiv at blv. Tarasa Shevchenka 34 (Тараса Шевченка), or at police stations in smaller cities—extends visas.

TRANSPORTATION

BY PLANE. Air Ukraine flies to Kyiv, Lviv, and Odessa from a number of European capitals. **Air France, ČSA, Lufthansa, LOT, Malév, SAS,** and **Swissair** also fly to Kyiv, generally once or twice a week.

BY TRAIN. Trains run frequently from all of Ukraine's neighbors, and are the best way to travel. They usually run overnight and are timed to arrive in the morning. When coming from a non-ex-Soviet country, expect a two-hour stop at the border while the wagons get their wheels changed. When purchasing a train ticket, you must present a positive ID in the form of a passport, driver's license, or student ID. Once on board, you must present both your ticket and identification to the *konduktor*. On most trains within Ukraine there are three **classes:** *platzkart*, where you'll be crammed in with *babushki* and their baskets of strawberries; *coupé*, a clean, more private 4-person compartment; and first class, simply referred to as *SV*, which is twice as roomy and expensive as *coupé*. Unless you are determined to live like a local, pay the extra two dollars for *coupé*; it can make a huge difference. The *kassa* will sell you a *coupé* seat unless you say otherwise. Except in larger cities, where **platform** numbers are posted on the electronic board, the only way to figure out which platform your train leaves from is by listening to the distorted announcement. In large cities, trains arrive well before they are scheduled to depart, so you'll have a few minutes to show your ticket to cashiers or fellow passengers, look helpless, and ask "plaht-FORM-ah?"

BY BUS. Buses cost about the same as trains, but are often much shabbier. For long distances, the train is usually more comfortable. One exception is **AutoLux** (АвтоЛюкс), which runs buses with A/C, snacks, and movies, and is located at bus stations. Bus schedules are generally reliable, but low demand sometimes causes cancellations. Buy tickets at the *kassa* (ticket office); if they're sold out, try going directly to the driver, who might just magically find a seat and pocket the money.

BY FERRY. Ferries across the Black Sea are limited to a few routes from Odessa, Sevastopol, and Yalta to **Istanbul.**

BY TAXI. Taxi drivers love to rip off foreigners, so negotiate the price beforehand. Get better rates by grabbing a cab a few blocks from any major tourist locations.

BY THUMB. Hitchhiking is uncommon in Ukraine, but if you must, hold a sign with your desired destination. *Let's Go* does not recommend hitchhiking.

TOURIST SERVICES AND MONEY

The tourist office in Lviv is extremely helpful, but is the only official one in Ukraine. There is no state-run tourist office. The remains of the Soviet giant **Intourist** have offices in hotels and provide tourist-related information, though usually not in English. They're used to dealing with groups, to whom they sell "excursion" packages to nearby sights, exclusively. Local travel agencies can be helpful, and often have English-speaking staff. The Ukrainian unit of currency is the **hryvna,** and **inflation** is around 6.1%. If you're looking to **exchange currency,** *Obmin Valyut* (Обмін Валют) kiosks in the center of most cities offer the best rates. **Traveler's checks** can be changed into dollars for small commissions in many cities. **Western Union** and **ATMs** are everywhere. Most banks will give MC/V cash advances for a high commission. The lobbies of fancier hotels usually exchange US dollars at lousy rates. **Private money changers** lurk near kiosks, ready with brilliant schemes for ripping you off. **Do not exchange money with them;** it's illegal.

HEALTH AND SAFETY

 EMERGENCY NUMBERS: Police: ☎01 **Fire:** ☎02 **Emergency:** ☎03

MEDICAL EMERGENCIES. Foreigners are required to have medical insurance to receive health care, but be prepared to front the bill yourself. When in doubt, get to your embassy, and they will find you adequate care or fly you out of the country.

HEALTH. Boil all **water** or learn to love brushing your teeth with soda water. **Fruits and vegetables** from open markets are generally safe, although storage conditions and pesticides make thorough washing imperative. Meat purchased at public markets should be checked very carefully and cooked thoroughly; refrigeration is a foreign concept and insects run rampant. Don't trust the tasty-looking hunks of meat for sale out of buckets on the Kyiv subway—they are not safe. Embassy officials declare that Chernobyl-related **radiation** poses minimal risk to short-term travelers, but the region should be given a wide berth. Public restrooms range from disgusting to frightening. Pay **toilets** (платний; platnyi) are cleaner and (gasp!) might provide toilet paper, but bring your own anyway. **Pharmacies** are quite common and carry basic Western products. Aspirin is the only painkiller on hand, but plenty of cold remedies and bandages are available. Anything more complicated should be brought from home. **Sanitary napkins** (гігієнічні пакети; hihienchni paketi), **condoms** (презервативи; prezervativy), and **tampons** (прокладки; prokladki) are intermittently sold at kiosks.

SAFETY. While Ukraine is neither violent nor politically volatile, it is poor. Keep a low profile and watch your belongings. The risk of **crime** isn't greater than in the rest of Eastern Europe. It's wise to **register** with your embassy once you get to Ukraine. For more information, see **Safety and Security**, p. 39.

WOMEN, MINORITY, AND BGLT TRAVELERS. Women traveling alone *will* be addressed by men on the street, in restaurants, and pretty much anywhere they go, but are usually fairly safe. Ukrainian women rarely go to restaurants alone, so expect to feel conspicuous if you do. Women may request to ride in female-only compartments during long train rides, though most do not. Although non-Caucasians may experience **discrimination,** the biggest problems are from the militia, which frequently stops people whom it suspects to be non-Slavic. **Homosexuality** is not very accepted in Ukraine; discretion is advised.

ACCOMMODATIONS AND CAMPING

UKRAINE	❶	❷	❸	❹	❺
ACCOM.	under 55hv	55-105hv	106-266hv	267-480hv	over 480hv

HOTELS. Not all hotels accept foreigners, and those that do often charge them many times more than what a Ukrainian would pay. Though room prices in Kyiv are astronomical, singles run anywhere from 5 to 90hv in the rest of the country. There are no youth hostels, and budget accommodations are usually in unrenovated Soviet-era buildings. The phrase "самое дешёвое место" (samoe deshovoe miesto) means "the cheapest place." More expensive hotels aren't necessarily nicer and in some hotels women lodging alone may be mistaken for prostitutes. Standard hotel rooms include a TV, a phone, and a refrigerator. You will be given a *vizitka* (визитка; hotel card) to show to the hall monitor (дежурная; dezhurnaya) to get a key; surrender it upon leaving. **Hot water** is rare—ask before checking in.

PRIVATE ROOMS AND CAMPING. Private rooms can be arranged through overseas agencies or bargained for at the train station. Most cities have a camp-ground, which is a remote hotel with trailers for buildings. The old Soviet complexes can be expensive, and sometimes include saunas and restaurants. Camping outside designated areas is illegal, and enforcement is merciless.

KEEPING IN TOUCH

MAIL. Mail is cheap and quite reliable, taking about 10 days to reach North America. The easiest way to mail letters is to buy pre-stamped envelopes at the post office. Mail can be received general delivery through **Poste Restante** (До Запитание). Address envelopes as follows: Werner (first name), SCHAFER (last name), До Запитание, Хрещатик 22 (post office address), 01001 (postal code) Київ (city), Україна.

TELEPHONES. Telephones are stumbling toward modernity. The easiest way to make international call is with **Utel.** Buy a Utel phonecard (sold at most Utel phone locations) and dial the number of your international operator (counted as a local call; see the back cover). Alternatively, call at the central telephone office—estimate how long your call will take, pay at the counter, and they'll direct you to a booth. Calling is expensive: to Eastern Europe US$0.06 per min., Western Europe US$1.50, North America US$2.50. Local calls from gray payphones generally cost 10-30hv. For an English-speaking operator, dial ☎ 8 192.

INTERNET. Email is the easiest and cheapest way of communicating with the outside world. Internet cafes are just beginning to make their presence known throughout Ukraine. You'll be able to find at least one in each major city. Otherwise, several post offices offer Internet service at decent prices.

KYIV (КИЇВ) ☎ (8)044

Straddling the wide Dniper River, Kyiv (pop. 2,600,000) is a becoming place, even though it still hasn't quite figured out how to become a thriving metropolis. The sprawling city (once the third-largest in the USSR) has struggled to adjust to its new role as the capital of an independent and nationalist Ukraine. Slow development has left the city with a provincial air and a relative dearth of tourists. Yet, while many of its sights and museums often stand empty, extensive construction and remodeling projects promise great changes to come.

■ INTERCITY TRANSPORTATION

Flights: Boryspil International Airport (Бориспіль; ☎ 296 72 43), 30km southeast of the capital by car. **Polit** (Політ; ☎ 296 73 67) sends buses from Boryspil to Ploscha Peremohi. (Buy tickets on the bus; every 30min.-1hr.; 8-10hv.) A taxi to the center costs 70-100hv. **Kyiv-Zhulyani Airport** (Київ-Жуляни; ☎ 242 23 08 or 242 23 09), a smaller hub located on pr. Povitroflotskiy (пр. Повітрофлотський), handles domestic flights to Lviv, Odessa, and Simferopol.

Aeroflot, vul. Saksahanskoho 112a (☎ 245 43 59). Open M-Th 9am-1pm and 2-5:30pm; F 9am-1pm and 2-4:30pm.

Austrian Airlines, vul. Velyka Vasylkivska 9/2 (☎ 244 35 40 or 244 35 41; fax 490 34 94). Open M-F 9am-5:30pm.

British Airways, vul. Yaroslaviv Val. 5 (☎ 490 60 60; fax 235 59 61). Open M-F 9am-5:30pm, Sa 10am-2pm.

ČSA, vul. Ivana Franka 36 (☎ 246 56 27). Open M-F 10am-5pm.

Delta Airlines, blv. Tarasa Shevchenka 10 (☎ 246 56 56 or 246 38 48). Open M-F 9:30am-6pm.

KLM, vul. Ivana Franka 34/33. (☎ 490 24 90; fax 495 24 06). Open M-F 9:30am-5pm.

LOT, vul. Ivana Franka 36 (☎ 246 56 20), next to ČSA. Open M-F 9am-5pm.

Lufthansa, vul. Khmelnytskoho 52 (☎ 490 38 00; fax 490 38 01). Open M-Sa 9am-8pm.

Malév, vul. Hospitalna 12G (☎ 247 86 72; fax 247 86 72). Open M-F 9am-6pm.

Ukraine International Airlines, Peremohi Prospect 14 (☎ 461 50 50).

Trains: Kyiv-Pasazhrysky (Київ-Пасажирський), Vokzalna pl. (☎ 005). MR: Vokzalna (Вокзальна). Trains are better than buses for long-distance travel. Purchase tickets in the main hall. A passport is required to purchase tickets. An info kiosk (Довидка;

UKRAINE

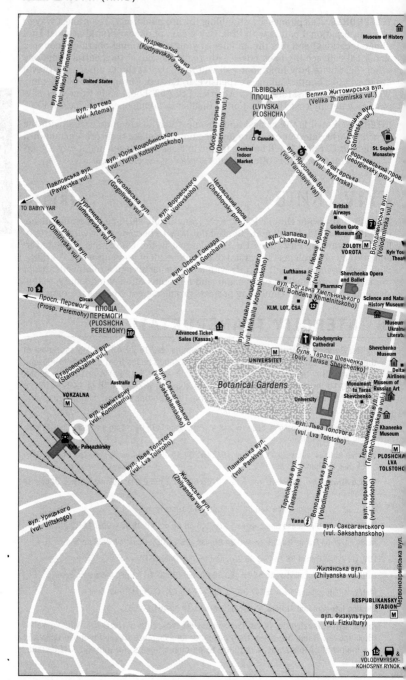

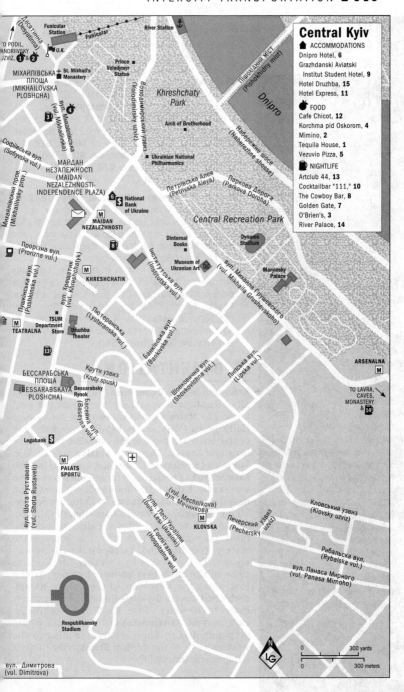

Central Kyiv

🏠 ACCOMMODATIONS
Dnipro Hotel, **6**
Grazhdanski Aviatski
Institut Student Hotel, **9**
Hotel Druzhba, **15**
Hotel Express, **11**

🍴 FOOD
Cafe Chicot, **12**
Korchma pid Oskorom, **4**
Mimino, **2**
Tequila House, **1**
Vezuvio Pizza, **5**

🎵 NIGHTLIFE
Artclub 44, **13**
Cocktailbar "111," **10**
The Cowboy Bar, **8**
Golden Gate, **7**
O'Brien's, **3**
River Palace, **14**

TOURIST SCAMS

Expats will tell you that Kyiv is an exceptionally safe city with little violent crime, so you really shouldn't worry too much about your safety. But a growing tourism industry has been accompanied by the emergence of scams to get a share of the traveler's wealth.

The local favorite is a theme with variations. A local who speaks some English walks next to the victim and suddenly "finds" a wallet on the ground. It contains a lot of cash and—surprisingly—no cards that would identify the owner. Overjoyed, the scamster shows this treasure to the victim and offers them a piece of pie, either in cash, or by inviting them to a bar or restaurant.

The scamster, of course, has a companion in crime—the man who "lost" the wallet. This is where the variations come in, which are completely dependent on the victim. The smart victim doesn't accept any money, and the scamsters pretend to be fighting over wallet. Yet in a different situation, involving any victim who even slightly looks at the lost wallet, the true scam evolves. His new-found friend, scamster no. 1, deserts him and pretends to not have any of the money, or simply disappears. Now the victim has the lost wallet and scamster no. 2 demands "his" money back, usually everything the victim has.

How to avoid all of this? Be the smart victim. Or do as your mother told you back in kindergarten: don't talk to strangers.

—Werner Schäfer

dovidka) is in the center of the main hall. (Open daily 6:30am-11pm.) There is an **Advance-Ticket Office** next to Hotel Express, blv. Shevchenka 38, straight up vul. Kominternu from the train station. Many travel agencies also book train tickets. Trains go to: **Ivano-Frankivsk** (16hr., 2 per day, 43hv); **Kharkiv** (9hr., 2 per day, 49hv); **Lviv** (12hr., 4 per day, 52hv); **Odessa** (11hr., 3 per day, 57hv); **Sevastopol** (19hr., 2 per day, 51hv); **Uzhhorod** (19½hr., 3 per day, 52hv); **Bratislava, SLK** (18hr., 1 per day, 329hv); **Budapest, HUN** (25hr., 1 per day, 419hv); **Minsk, BLR** (12-13hr., 1 per day, 84hv); **Moscow, RUS** (15-17hr., 4 per day, 156hv); **Prague, CZR** (34hr., 1 per day, 446hv); **Warsaw, POL** (15hr., 1 per day, 222hv).

Buses: Tsentralny Avtovokzal (Центральний Автовокзал), Moskovska pl. 3 (Московська; ☎250 99 86), 10min. from Libidska, the last stop on the MG line. Take a right and then a left out of the Metro, and look for trolleybus #4. If it isn't there, walk 100m to the highway, take a right and follow it for 500m. The bus station is right next to McDonald's. **Avtoljuks** (Автолюкс), to the left of the main entrance provides more comfortable buses at a slightly higher price. To: **Kharkiv** (7½hr., 6 per day, 50hv); **Lviv** (8hr., 2 per day, 52hv); **Odessa** (10hr., 4 per day, 57hv). Window #12 sells international tickets to: **Minsk, BLR** (47hv) and **Moscow, RUS** (21hr., 75hv).

◼ ORIENTATION

Kyiv straddles the **Dniper River** (Дніпро), but almost all of its attractions and services lie on the west bank. The **Metro's** three intersecting lines—blue (MB), green (MG), and red (MR)—cover the city center but leave most of the outskirts to the trolleys and trams. The **train station** lies at MR: Vokzalna (Вокзальна). Three stops away is the **MR: Khreshchatyk** (Хрещатик) stop and the street of the same name, Kyiv's main thoroughfare. Khreshchatyk runs from **Bessarabska Square** to European Square. Within the square is **Maydan Nezalezhnosti** (Майдан Незалежності; Independence Plaza), a fountain-filled spot next to the post office that becomes the stately, tree-lined **vul. Volodymyrska** (Володимирська) To the west is Kyiv's **Upper City,** home to some of the city's best-known churches. To the east, along the west bank of the Dniper, **Khreshchatyk Park** covers the slope that runs from the city center to the water's edge. **Blv. Shevchenka** (Шевченка) and **vul. Khmelnytskoho** (Хмельніцького) run perpendicular to Khreshchatyk, leading to the western edge of the central **Starokyivsky** District (Старокиевский; Old Kyiv).

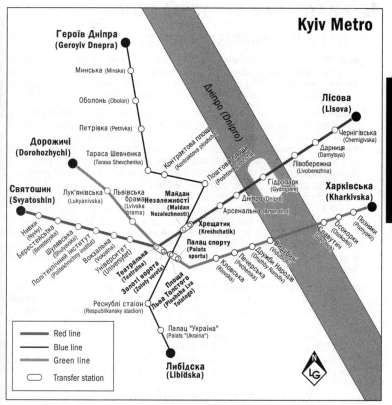

Kyiv Metro

Героїв Дніпра (Geroyiv Dnepra)
Минська (Minska)
Оболонь (Obolon)
Петрівка (Petrivka)
Дорожичі (Dorohozhychi)
Тараса Шевченка (Tarasa Shevchenka)
Контрактова площа (Kontraktova ploshcha)
Поштова площа (Poshtova ploshcha)
Лісова (Lisova)
Чернігівська (Chernigivska)
Дарниця (Darnytsya)
Лівобережна (Livoberezhna)
Гідропарк (Gydropark)
Дніпро (Dnipro)
Арсенальна (Arsenalna)
Харківська (Kharkivska)
Позняки (Poznyaki)
Осокорки (Osokorki)
Славутич (Slavutych)
Видубичі (Vidubichi)
Дружби народів (Druzhny Narodiv)
Печерська (Pecherska)
Кловська (Klovska)
Святошин (Svyatoshin)
Лук'янівська (Lukyanivska)
Львівська брама (Lvivska brama)
Майдан Незалежності (Maidan Nezalezhnosti)
Хрещатик (Kreshchatik)
Палац спорту (Palats sportu)
Ниви (Nyvy)
Берестейська (Beresteyska)
Шулявська (Shulyavska)
Політехнічний інститут (Politekhnichny Institut)
Вокзальна (Vokzalna)
Університет (Universytet)
Театральна (Teatralna)
Золоті ворота (Zoloty vorota)
Площа Льва Толстого (Ploshcha Lva Tolstogo)
Республіканський стадіон (Respublikansky stadion)
Палац "Україна" (Palats "Ukraina")
Либідська (Libidska)

Red line
Blue line
Green line
Transfer station

U K R A I N E

LOCAL TRANSPORTATION

Public Transportation: Kyiv's **Metro** covers the city center, but its 3 intersecting lines (MB, blue; MG, green; MR, red) leave large areas between stops and do not reach most residential areas. Buy your token (жетон; zhiton) at the *kasa* (каса) for 0.50hv. If you're in Kyiv for a while, buy a Metro pass, good on all public transportation. Show your card or punch your tickets to avoid the 10hv fine for riding without a ticket. "Перехід" (perekhid) indicates a walkway to another station, "вихід у місто" (vykhid u misto) an exit onto the street, "вхід" (vkhid) an entrance to the Metro, and "нема входу" (nema vkhidu) no entrance. **Buses** stop at each station, but request stops from *marshrutki* drivers. Buy *marshrutki* tickets (1hv) on board and bus tickets at kiosks or from badge-wearing conductors. **Trolleys** and buses with identical numbers may have very different routes; buy a route map. Public transport runs 6am-midnight, but some buses go later.

Taxis: Call ☎058. Taxis are everywhere. Negotiate the price before traveling to avoid rip-offs. A ride within the city center should be 10hv or less. Owners of **private cars** often act as taxi drivers. Hold your arm down at a 45°angle to hail a ride, and set the price before getting in. It is not advisable to get in a private car with more than one person already in it. Write down your destination in case the driver doesn't understand English.

⚡ PRACTICAL INFORMATION

TOURIST AND FINANCIAL SERVICES

Tourist Offices: Kyiv still lacks official tourist services. Representatives of various agencies at the airport offer vouchers, excursion packages, hotel arrangements, and other services. Travel agencies also provide tours. Try **Yana Travel Group,** vul. Saksaganskoho 42 (Саксаганського; ☎246 62 13; www.travel.kiev.ua/yana). Open M-F 9am-5pm.

Embassies: Australia, vul. Kominternu 18/137 (Комінтерну; ☎235 75 86). Open M-Th 10am-1pm. **Belarus,** vul. Sichnevoho Povstannya 6 (Січневого Повстання; ☎293 22 48). MR: Arsenalna. **Canada,** vul. Yaroslaviv Val 31 (Ярославів Вал; ☎464 11 44). Open M-Th 8:30am-noon. **Moldova,** vul. Sichnevoho Povstannya 6 (☎/fax; 290 06 10.) MR: Arsenalna. Open M-F 10am-1pm. **Russia,** Povitroflotsky pr. 27 (Повітрофлотський; ☎244 09 63; fax 246 34 69). Open M-Th 9am-6pm, F 9am-5pm. Visa section at vul. Kotuzova 8v (Котузова; ☎296 45 04). Open M-Th 9am-1pm, and 3-6pm, F 9am-1pm and 3-5pm. **UK,** vul. Desyatynna 6 (Десятинна; ☎462 00 11; fax 462 79 47). Visa section at vul. Sichnevoho Povstannya 6 (☎290 73 17 or 290 29 17). Open M-F 9am-1pm and 2-5pm. **US,** vul. Kotsyubinskoho 10 (Коцюбинського; ☎490 44 22; fax 244 73 50; www.usinfo.usemb.kiev.ua). From the corner of Maydan Nezalezhnosti and Sofievska (Софиевска), take trolley #16 or 18 for 4 stops. Continue on vul. Artema (Артема) until it curves to the right, then take the first right, vul. Pimonenka. Call ahead for an appointment.

Currency Exchange: *Obmin-Valyut* (Обмін-Валют) windows are everywhere, but often only take US$ and Euros. Most new booths have unfavorable rates, but try **Legbank** (Легбанк), vul. Shota Rustaveli 12 (Шота Руставелі). From MB/G: Palats sportu (Палац спорту), go northwest on vul. Rohnydinska (Рогнидінська) and turn right on Rustaveli. Cashes **traveler's checks** for a US$5 fee; 2% commission if over US$250. Gives MC/V **cash advances** for 3% commission. Open M-F 10am-4pm, Sa 10am-3pm. The **National Bank of Ukraine,** on the corner of Institutska and Khreshchatyk, charges 3.5% commission for all services. It also offers **Western Union** services. Open daily 9am-1pm and 2-8pm.

ATMs: MC/V machines are all along Khreshchatyk, at the post office, and at various banks and fancy hotels. Look for Банкомат (bankomat) signs.

LOCAL SERVICES, EMERGENCY AND COMMUNICATIONS

Luggage Storage: At the train station. Look for *kamery skhovu* (Камери с хову; luggage storage), down the stairs outside the main entrance (4.4hv). Open daily 8am-noon, 1-7:30pm, 8pm-midnight, and 1-7:30am. Most major hotels have lockers that might be more secure; usually, you do not need to be a guest to use them. Try **Hotel Rus,** Hospitalna 4.30hv per bag per night. Open 24hr.

English-Language Bookstores: Dinternal English Books, vul. Museyny Provulok 2b, 2nd fl. (Музейный Провулок; ☎228 63 14; dinter@public.ua.net), opposite Dynamo Stadium, through the courtyard, has a large selection. Open M-Sa 10am-7pm. The Kyiv business directory, available in major hotels, has useful information about dining, shopping, and travel. Golden Gate (see **Nightlife,** p. 824) and several hotels sell foreign language newspapers.

24-Hour Pharmacy: Apteka, vul. Ivana Franka 25/40 (☎224 29 88), on the corner with vul. Khmelnytskoho, carries high-quality products. Ring the bell 8pm-8am.

Medical Assistance: Ambulance: ☎03. The **American Medical Center,** vul. Berdicherska 1 (Бердичерска; ☎/fax 490 76 00; patientservices@amc.com.ua), staffs English-speaking doctors. AmEx/MC/V.

Telephones: Myzhmisky Perehovorny Punkt (Мижміський Переговорний Пункт), at the post office (see below), or **Telefon-Telefaks** (Телефон-Телефакс), around the corner (entry on Khreshchatyk). Both offices open 24hr. **Public telephones** (Таксофон; Taksofon) work only with a phone card, which can be purchased at any post office. English operator ☎81 92. Not as widespread as Taksofon, Utel **phone cards** are available in denominations of 10hv, 20hv, and 40hv at the post office and upscale hotels. Utel phones can be found in the post office, the train station, hotels, and nice restaurants.

Internet Access: Cyber Cafe (Кібер Кафе), Prorizna 21 (Прорізна; ☎228 05 48; www.cybercafe.com). Centrally located and in the evening. 10hv per hr. Open daily 9am-11pm. The main **post office** also houses an Internet cafe. Walk through the doors to the right of the entrance and up the stairs. 10hv per hr. Pay in advance. Open daily 8am-9pm.

Post Office: Vul. Khreshchatyk 22 (☎228 17 93; fax 228 72 72), next to Maydan Nezalezhnosti. **Poste Restante** at counters #29-30. Pre-stamped airmail envelopes (3.67hv at counter #1) are the easiest way to send international mail. To pick up packages, enter on the Maydan Nezalezhnosti side. Also houses a full-service copy/fax/photo center. Open M-Sa 8am-9pm, Su 9am-7pm.

Postal Code: 01 001.

▐ ACCOMMODATIONS

Hotels are geared toward high-paying customers, and foreigners often pay twice as much as Ukrainians. Unless you have money to spare, be prepared to stay in a Soviet subdivision. People at the train station, and occasionally outside of hotels, offer **private rooms**. There are also private room listings in the *Kyiv Post*.

Hotel Express (Експрес), blv. Shevchenka 38/40 (☎239 89 95; fax 239 89 47), straight up vul. Kominternu from the train station. Inexpensive, clean, and renovated rooms in a convenient location. Internet 4hv per 30min. Breakfast included. Shower 5hv. Singles with telephone, TV, fridge, and toilet US$24; doubles US$42. ❷

Hotel Druzhba, Druzhby Narodiu blv. 5 (Дружбый Народю). ☎268 34 06). From MB: Libidska (Либідска), take a left on Druzhby Narodiu blv. and walk 200m; hotel is to your left. Clean rooms with recently renovated bathrooms. Singles 136hv; doubles 202hv. ❷

Grazhdanski Aviatski Institut Student Hotel (Гражданский Авіатский), vul. Nizhinska 29E (Ніжінська; ☎484 90 59). From behind MR: Vokzalna, turn right into the passageway leading to the trams. Ride 6 or 7 stops on tram #1K or 1 to Гарматна (Harmatna); get off at Індустріальна (Industrialna). Backtrack 1½ blocks, turn right on vul. Nizhinska, cross at the 1st intersection, and follow the stairs into the complex. Keep the first building on your right as you walk diagonally to block "Д." After passing Д on the right, look for the "Готел НАУ" (Hotel NAU) sign above. Their clean rooms are the best deal around if you don't mind the trek. Check-out noon. Singles 35hv, lux (with private bath, TV, fridge) singles 98hv; doubles 160hv. ❶

Dnipro Hotel, vul. Kreshchatyk. 1/2 (☎291 84 50; fax 229 82 13; www.dniprohotel.kiev.ua), right in the center on European Square. Julio Iglesias, Sting, Joe Cocker, and David Copperfield all stayed in the executive suite (US$295) of this upscale hotel, which offers clean but unrenovated rooms on its first 7 floors. The "superior" rooms on floors 8-12 offer a view of the Dniper, renovated bathrooms, and other amenities. Singles US$110; doubles US$130. "Superior" singles US$186; doubles US$205. Prices are lower on weekends and select times during the year. ❺

🗂 FOOD

Good restaurants tend to be expensive in Kyiv, but there is a large selection.

RESTAURANTS

Korchma pid Osokorom (Корчма під осокором), vul. Mikhaylivsky 20b (Михайловский, across the street from O'Brien's (see **Bars,** p. 824). MB: Maydan Nezalezhnosti (Майдан Незалежності). An intimate cafe serving traditional food. A sign on the wall instructs patrons how to drink *pervak* (первак), a vodka for the serious drinker (40-50% proof, 0.50L 1.90hv). English menu. Entrees 5-8hv. Open daily 10am-10pm. ❶

Cafe Chicot (Кафе Шикот), vul. Ivana Franka 27 (☎246 52 83) MR:Universitet (Університет). Inexpensive Ukrainian and European fare. Entrees 30-50hv. MC/V. ❷

Tequila House, Spasskaya ul. 8, (Спасская; ☎417 03 58, www.tequilahouse.com.ua). MB: Kontraktova ploshcha (Контрактова площа). This popular Tex-Mex restaurant in the Podil District is worth the high prices. Entrees 50-80hv. Cocktails 29hv. Everything except alcohol 20% off 11am-3pm. Open daily 11am-1am. ❸

Mimino (Мимино), ul. Spasskaya 10a (☎417 35 45). M: pl. Koutraktkova. Walk to the back of the train coming from the center and continue underground to the last exit, where you take a left. Cross ul. Mezhigorskaya (Межигорская) and walk down Spasskaya. Big portions of Georgian specialties in a traditionally decorated venue. 20% discount before 3pm on weekdays. Entrees 50-120hv. Open daily 11am-1am. ❹

Vezuvio Pizza (Везувіо), vul Reytarska 25 (Рейтарська; ☎228 30 28, delivery 234 52 68). MG: Zoloty vorota (Золоті ворота). Indoor and outdoor dining. Pizza 18-33hv; pasta 18-25hv. Tea 2hv. Open daily 10am-10pm. ❷

MARKETS

Bessarabsky Rynok (Бессарабський Ринок), at the intersection of vul. Khreshchatyk and blv. Shevchenka. Enter in back. No mere gaggle of *babushki* selling berries. On the edge of Kyiv's most chic neighborhood, Bessarabsky offers the best meat, fruit, and vegetables of the countryside, all in a classical yellow structure.

Volodymyrsky-Kolhospny Rynok (Володимирський-Колгоспний Ринок), on vul. Telmana (Тельмана), between vul. Velika Vasylkivska (Велика Василкивска) and blv. Horkoho (Блв. Горкого). MB: Palats Ukraina (Палац Україна). Larger than the Bessarabsky. Plenty of food, flowers, clothes, and caged animals. Open daily 6:30am-8pm.

👁 SIGHTS

Kyiv boasts almost as many sights as green parks. Many of the older monuments are being renovated, but a glance out of an upper-story window will quickly remind you of Shevchenko's favorite green-and-gold city.

CENTRAL KYIV

TARAS SHEVCHENKO BOULEVARD. The boulevard (Блв. Тараса Шевченка; Blv. Tarasa Shevchenka) is dedicated to Taras Shevchenko, whose poetry reinvented the Ukrainian language in the mid-19th century (see The Arts, p. 806). Banished in 1847, he never returned to Kyiv. The Taras Shevchenko University, which still promotes independent thought in Ukraine, is on the boulevard. The many-domed Volodymyrsky Cathedral, at #20, was built to mark 900 years of Christianity in Kyiv. Its interior features examples of Byzantine and Art Nouveau art. *(Perpendicular to vul. Khreshchatyk at the Lenin statue. MR: Universitet. Cathedral open daily 9am-9pm.)*

KHRESHCHATYK STREET. Kyiv centers around this broad commercial avenue, built after World War II. Khreshchatyk begins at the intersection with blv. Shevchenka, where a statue of **Lenin**, surrounded by inspirational phrases, still gazes off into the future. **TSUM** (ЦУМ), Kreshchatyk 2, the central department store, sells everything from guitars to lawn chairs. *(Open M-Sa 9am-8pm. MC/V.)* An archway leads to the *passazh*, Kyiv's most cosmopolitan area, and its fashionable, high-priced cafes and bars. *(MB/R: Khreshchatyk; Хрещатик.)*

INDEPENDENCE PLAZA. (Майдан Незалежності; Maydan Nezalezhnosti; formerly October Revolution Square.) Recently overhauled, this square now features the glass rooftops of an underground shopping mall next to a statue of Archangel Michael, a giant TV screen, and lots of Ukrainian flags. On Sundays and holidays, a public stereo system blares heroic Ukrainian songs. *(MR: Khreshchatyk.)*

OTHER SIGHTS. Past Independence Plaza to the right is **vul. Institutska** (Інститутська), another facade-filled promenade. Uphill to the left glows the yellow **Palace of Culture** (Палац Культурни; Palats Kulturny), one of Kyiv's largest concert halls and a Neoclassical rival to the Rococo **National Bank of Ukraine** (Національний Банк України; Natsionalny Bank Ukrainy), also on the right.

KHRESHCHATYK PARK

Vul. Khreshchatyk continues up into Європейська пл. *(Evropeyska Ploshchad; European Sq.), where it meets the stately vul. Volodymyrsky that runs through Kyiv's Khreshchatyk Park. The park is enormous, and each monument is tucked away in its own corner; you'll do best to just wander.*

ARCH OF BROTHERHOOD. Referred to by locals as the "Yoke," this silver croquet wicket towers over the park as it commemorates the 1654 Russian-Ukrainian Pereyaslav Union (see **History,** p. 802). It now serves as a meeting spot for couples, who come for a romantic view of the Dniper. To visit the **monument to Kyiv's brave soccer players** (see **"Kyiv 3, Nazis 0,"** below), go right at the arch and into the park.

PRINCE VOLODYMYR STATUE. Brandishing a cross, the statue of Prince Volodymyr overlooks the river in which he had the city baptized in 988, making Orthodox Christianity the official religion of Kyivan Rus. *(Statue is to the left of vul. Volodymyrsky.)*

MARIYINSKY PALACE. Built by Francesco Rastrelli, who also designed Kyiv's St. Andrew's Church and much of St. Petersburg, the palace was ordered for Tsaritsa Elizabeth's visit in the 1750s. It began to be called Mariyinsky in honor of Maria Alexandrovna, consort of Russian Tsar Alexander II. Today the palace is used for formal state receptions. *(From European Square, walk down vul. Grushevskoho. The Palace is on your left, about 500m after the entrance to Dynamo Stadium.)*

KYIV 3, NAZIS 0 After the Nazis invaded Kyiv and took thousands of Ukrainians as prisoners in September 1941, a German soldier supposedly discovered that one of his prisoners was a member of the city's *Dynamo Kyiv* soccer team. Apparently, his discovery was enough to prompt soccer frenzy: the Nazi officers quickly rounded up the other players and arranged a "death match" between them and the German army team. Despite the Dynamo's players weakened condition and a referee dressed in a Gestapo uniform, Ukraine won, 3-0. Shortly thereafter the entire team was thrown into a concentration camp, where most of them perished in front of a firing squad. Their memory—and Kyiv's pride—lives on in a monument overlooking Khreshchatyk Park. Recent scholarship suggests, however, that such a match never took place and was fiction created by Soviet propagandists.

UKRAINE

ST. SOFIA AND ENVIRONS

MG: Zoloty Vorota or trolley #16 from Maydan Nezalezhnasti.

GOLDEN GATE. (Золоти Ворота; Zoloty Vorota.) Made of wood and stone, the gate has marked the entrance to the city since 1037. As legend has it, the gate's strength saved Kyiv from the Tatars during the reign of **Yaroslav the Wise,** whose statue stands nearby (see **History,** p. 802). A **museum** devoted to the gate is located inside. As of September 2002, the museum was closed due to major construction and restoration work. *(300m down vul. Volodymyrska from St. Sofia. Open F-Tu 10am-5:30pm, W 10am-4:30pm. 2hv, students 1hv.)*

ST. SOFIA MONASTERY COMPLEX. Enormous and elaborate, St. Sofia Monastery is the reason many tourists visit Kyiv: golden onion domes, decorated facades, and exquisite Byzantine icons from the 11th century. The monastery was the cultural center of Kyivan Rus and is still the focal point of Ukrainian nationalism. In July 1995, the government denied the Uniate Church's wish to bury its patriarch here. When the funeral procession, led by the Ukrainian nationalist militia, attempted to enter the complex, it was violently rerouted by the police. A statue of Bohdan Khmelnytsky (see **History,** p. 802) stands over pl. Khmelnytskoho, by the entrance to St. Sofia. (*Volodymyrska vul. 24. ☎ 228 61 52. Monastery open daily 10am-7:30pm. 1hv. Museums open F-Tu 10am-6pm, W 10am-5pm. 10hv, 3hv for other exhibits. English tours available. 40hv for 45min., 80hv for 90min. Cameras 20hv, video 80hv.)*

MIKHAILIVSKYI ZOLOTOVERKHY MONASTERY. (Михайлівский Золотоверхий Монастир.) This 11th-century monastery was destroyed in 1934 to make way for a government square. Plans never materialized, however, and a sports center and tennis courts came to occupy the sacred territory—and remained there for over 60 years. Before the monastery was destroyed, some of the original mosaics and frescoes were moved to St. Sofia, where many are on display today. The church was reconstructed in the 1990s and this blue-and-gold-domed monastery now draws tourists from around the world. *(At the top of Mikhaylivska pl. Open daily 9am-9pm. Free.)*

A **museum** in the bell tower leads to the chamber of the bells, which houses the city's only **carillon.** The bells ring every 15min. *(☎ 228 66 46. Open Tu-Su 10am-5pm. 6hv.)* To the right of the monastery, vul. Tryokhsvyatytelska passes a series of smaller churches as it winds its way down to the park Volodymyrska Hirka (Володимирска Гірка), full of tiny pavilions and sculptures by folk artists.

MIKHAILIVSKA SQUARE. (Михайлівська пл.) With the recent renovations of this square came the installation of a new statue of **Princess Olga,** grandmother of Volodymyr I. She is surrounded by St. Cyril, St. Methodius, and St. Andrew the Apostle. Behind the princess and to her left stands the monumental **Ministry of Foreign Affairs,** which is 90% pillar and 10% building. *(Vul. Volodomyrska.)*

ANDRIYIVSKY PATH AND THE PODIL DISTRICT

A funicular goes up Andriyivsky from MB: Poshtova (Поштова; every 5min.; 6:30am-11pm, 0.50hv). Alternatively, walk from Mikhailivska Square.

The cobblestone **Andriyivsky path** (Андріївскі узвіз; Andriyivsky uzviz), is Kyiv's most touristy area, featuring cafes, souvenir vendors, and galleries, all eager to sell you whatever kitsch your heart desires. As you start down the path, immediately to your right is **St. Andrews,** a recently renovated 18th-century baroque church, designed by Italian B. Rastrelli, who also designed the Winter Palace in St. Petersburg. *(☎ 228 58 61. Open daily 10am-6pm. 10hv. Call in advance to arrange an English tour. 15hv. Camera 20hv, video 50hv.)* Walking down Andriyivsky for about 100m, you'll see steep wooden stairs to your right. Climb up for a great view of Podil, Kyiv's oldest district and the city center in the 10th and 11th centuries. Still farther down are **Bulgakov's house** and the **One Street Museum** (see **Museums**, p. 831). Andriyivsky path ends at **Kontraktova Sq.** (Контрактова пл.), the center of **Podil**.

TITHE CHURCH. (Десятинна Церква; Desyatinna Tserkva.) Ruins are the only remnant of the oldest stone church of Kyivan Rus (989-96), which converted pagan Kyivans to Christianity in the 10th century. It endured for centuries, only to be destroyed by the Soviet "Socialist Reconstruction" program in 1937. *(Walk up the gray steps at the corner of Andriyivsky uzviz, Desyatinna, and Volodymyrska. Next to the National Museum of Ukrainian History.)*

BABYN YAR. (Бабин Яр.) The monument at Babyn Yar marks the graves of the first Holocaust victims in Ukraine, buried in September 1941. Although plaques state that 100,000 Kyivans died here, current estimates double that figure. Many of the victims—most of them Jews—were buried alive. On an incline above the grass-covered pit, a statue shows the victims falling to their deaths. In June 2001, Pope John Paul II made a visit to the site and prayed for its Jewish victims. *(MG: Dorotozhiychy (Доротожичи). The monument—a large group of interlocking figures—stands in the park near the TV tower, at the intersection of vul. Oleny Telihy and vul. Melnykova.)*

KYIV-PECHERY MONASTERY

MR: Arsenalna (Арсенальна). Turn left as you exit and walk 10min. down vul. Sichnevoho Povstaniya. Trolleybus #20 can also take you here. The tourist office is on the left past the main entrance. Open daily 9am-7pm. Monastery 16hv, students 8hv. Each museum 3hv, students 1hv. Prices vary for English tours (☎ 290 30 71). Private guides are willing to negotiate prices.

Kyiv's oldest and holiest religious site, the mysterious Kyiv-Pechery Monastery (Києво-Печерська Лавра) deserves a full day of exploration. The monastery is first mentioned in chronicles dating back to 1051, and the spot has been named a UNESCO World Heritage Site. The 12th-century **Holy Trinity Gate Church** (Троїцка надбрамна церква; Troitska Nadbramna Tserkva) serves as the entrance to the monastery. The church's interior contains some beautiful frescoes, a 600kg censer, and the ruins of an ancient church. Be sure to step into the functioning **Refectory Church,** home to one of the largest and most decorated domes in the complex. The 18th-century **Great Cave Bell Tower** (Велика лаврська дзвіниця; Velyka lavrska dzvinytsya) offers fantastic views of the river and the golden domes. *(Open daily 10am-8pm. 3hv, students 1hv.)*

MONASTERY MUSEUMS. The monastery is surrounded by patriotic museums dedicated to Ukrainian history. The **Museum of Books and Bookmaking** (Музей книги и друкарства; Muzey Knigi i Drukarstva) details the development of print in Ukraine, while the **Museum of Historical Treasures of Ukraine** (Музей Історичних коштовностей Україна; Muzey Istorichnykh Koshtovnostey Ukraina) displays precious stones and metals. The **Micro-Miniature Museum** displays the world's smallest book (0.6sq. mm) among other amazingly tiny things. An English map (3hv) is available at the entrance. *(Museums open daily 10am-5pm. Museum of Books and Bookmaking closed Tu. Museum of Historical Treasures closed M.)*

■ **CAVES.** After their death, the monastery's monks were mummified and entombed in these caves, the most interesting part of the complex. Buy a candle as you enter. Women are required to cover their heads (head scarves are available for 5hv); men must wear pants. *(Open daily 8am-2pm.)*

THE LOCAL STORY

FREEDOM AND CULTURE

Let's Go Researcher Werner Schäfer interviewed Vladislava Osmak, a research assistant at the privately-owned Museum of One Street.

Q: What are the main difficulties you—and independent cultural institutions in general—face today?
A: There are a lot of remnants of the past in this country, which hold up change. One example is that our museum falls under two different legal categories, which aren't always compatible. Legally, what is a prviate museum in the rest of the world doesn't exist here. And what is private in this country is still often seen as the enemy, or at least with suspicion. We get no money from the state and have to raise all funds ourselves. This gives us no opportunity to buy our own rooms for the exhibits. As a result, we've had to move four times since the museum was founded, which is always a lot of work. Other museums usually rent their spaces as well and local officials often try to push them out if the building becomes attractive for other purposes. Then there is a kind of "black archaeology" in Ukraine. A lot of ancient artifacts can still be found in the Black Sea region. Some half-scientific, half-criminal people, often government officials, make millions selling these artifacts to Western Europe and North America.

Q: Has there been an upsurge of cultural activity, be it theater, art, music, or literature, since the end of the Soviet Union?

(continued on next page)

🏛 MUSEUMS

◼ MUSEUM OF ONE STREET. This tiny, privately run museum creatively covers the history of Kyiv's most famous street. The collection is quite eclectic, but beautifully arranged and a refreshing change from the ideology-laden exhibitions run by the Ukrainian government. *(Andriyivsky uzviz 2B. ☎ 416 03 98; mus1str@ua.fm. Open Tu-Su noon-6pm. 3hv.)*

CHERNOBYL MUSEUM. An excellent multimedia tour details the explosion, clean-up, and ensuing evacuation of the area (5hv), but not in English. *(Provulok Khorevii 1 (Провулок Хореві). MB: Kontraktova Ploscha. At the lower end of Andriyivsky uzviz: walk diagonally through Kontraktova Sq., turn left at Kyiv Mohyla Academy, pass the Musical Theater, take a right, then an immediate left. ☎ 417 54 22. Open M-F 10am-6pm, Sa 10am-5pm. Closed last M of the month. 5hv.)*

MUSEUM OF FOLK ARCHITECTURE AND RURAL LIFE.
(Музей Народний та Побуту України; Muzey Narodnii ta Pobutu Ukrani.) Over 70 Ukrainian huts are spread out over the grounds of this open-air museum. Ideal for children. *(Just outside of Kyiv in the Pirohiv village. MB: Libidska. Take trolleybus #11 just outside the Metro station to the park's entrance (10min. walk to museum entrance). Marshrutka #15 will drop you off at the museum entrance for US$1 extra. ☎ 266 24 16. Open daily 10am-5pm. 3hv. 1½hr English-language tour. 60hv; 2½hr. 80hv. Map 1hv. Camera 5hv, video 10hv.).*

MUSEUM IN HONOR OF BOHDAN AND VAVRAVA KHANENKO. (Музей Мистецтва им. Богдана та Варвара Ханенко; Muzei Mistetstva im. Bohdana ta Varvara Khanenko). The museum's dark wooden interior houses an impressive collection of Renaissance art. *(Vul. Tereschenkivska 15. MR: Universitet. ☎ 235 32 90. Open W-Su 10:30am-5pm. Call ahead to arrange an English tour for 120hv. 5hv, students 2hv.)*

NATIONAL MUSEUM OF UKRAINIAN HISTORY.
(Національний Музей Історії України; Natsionalny Muzey Istorii Ukrainy.) Glorifies Ukraine's ancient past and its most recent achievements. *(Vul. Volodymyrska 2, up the stairway at the crossroad with Andriyivsky uzviz. ☎ 228 48 64. Open Th-Tu 10am-5pm. 4.20hv, additional exhibits 1.20hv each.)*

TARAS SHEVCHENKO MUSEUM. This museum dedicated to the artist contains a huge collection of sketches, paintings, prints, and this 19th-century mansion, straight out of a Russian novel. *(Blv. Tarasa Shevchenka 12. MR: Universitet. ☎ 224 25 56. Open Tu-Su 10am-5pm; closed last F of the month. 2hv, students 1hv. English tours 40hv.)*

MUSEUM OF UKRAINIAN LITERATURE. (Музей Літератури України; Muzey Literatury Ukrainy.) The nationalistic museum traces Ukrainian literature from its inception to the present. A wax museum on the second floor features full-size figures of Lenin, Kuchma, and other leaders. (*Vul. Khmelnytskoho 11, 3rd fl. MG: Zoloty Vorotu. Open M-Sa 9am-5pm. 1.20hv, students 0.60hv; W free. Wax museum 6hv.*)

🎵 ENTERTAINMENT AND

📷 FESTIVALS

Shopping in the weekend **bazaars** in the summer at Respublikansky Stadion and Vokzalny is an experience in itself. In May, a two-week theater festival leads to **Kyiv Days,** when stages for drama, folklore, jazz, and rock music performances are set up all over town. The famed **Kyiv International Film Festival** comes to town in July.

During the soccer season from late spring to fall, don't miss **Dynamo Kyiv,** one of the top teams in Europe. The ticket office is in front of the stadium (tickets 5-20hv). On hot summer days, locals display their flesh on the beaches of 🏖 **Hydropark** (Гідропарк), an **amusement park** and **beach** on an island on the Dniper (MR: Hidropark). The beach has showers, toilets, and changing booths. Pin-topplers meet at **Strike Bowling Club,** pr. Peremohy 84 (☎ 442 64 64). The **National Philharmonic,** Volodymyrsky uzviz 2, grooves the old-fashioned way. (☎ 228 16 97. *Kassa* open Tu-Su noon-3pm and 4-7pm.) **Shevchenko Opera and Ballet Theater,** vul. Volodymyrska, puts on several shows each week at noon and 7pm. (MR: Teatralna. ☎ 224 71 65. Ticket office open M 11am-3pm, Tu-Su 11am-3pm and 4:30-7pm.)

💷 NIGHTLIFE

Clubs and bars open so frequently that even locals can't keep up. *What's On* (www.whatson-kiev.com) and the *Kyiv Post* (www.kyivpost.com) for the latest hotspots in town.

CLUBS

River Palace (☎ 495 25 25). MR: Dnipro (Дніпро). Features a nightclub, casino, and music bar (live music every night), all located on a boat anchored on the right bank of the Dniper. Catering to Ukrainians and expat 20-somethings alike, River Palace is a bit pricey, but draws a fun crowd every night. Cocktails 30-50hv. Entrees 70-200hv. Tu is ladies' night. Dress nicely. Cover 30-50hv. Open daily noon-6am.

A: In terms of quality, yes. Let's not talk about quantity. There were tons of activities in the Soviet Union, but it was all one big pyramid with the Communist Party at the top. There was an underground culture, however, and that became free and open. The variety is much greater now and nobody is ruling over artists anymore. A lot of work is part of the very serious endeavor of recreating national traditions. It's a very endearing thing to see how people work to improve their culture, to help it revive. We are much freer now. In the museum, nobody tells us to change exhibits for idealogical reasons anymore. But for the older generations it is more difficult to be free than for us who were students at the end of the Soviet Union. They were so accustomed to Soviet rules and ways.

Q: What do you see as Ukraine's greatest problems today and what needs to happen to address them?
A: We've had a very damaging history. Being serfs, being slaves for centuries has ruined our mentality. We were spoiled by being slaves. Now we need to find a way to recover, be more active in presenting ourselves abroad, in recreating—or rather creating—a feeling of national self-respect. That is missing from our current lives. I don't even want to speak of our economy, of corruption, of bribes. There are a lot of things that make our lives difficult, but the most depressing thing is that we don't know how to do something patiently, step by step, day by day.

Cocktailbar "111", Peremohy pl. 1 (☎238 02 86), in Hotel Lybid. Named for the "III classic cocktails" served at the revolving bar. Disco and house music every night. Cocktails 10-40hv. Open daily 7am-2am. Cover 20hv (except M and Tu).

BARS

Golden Gate, vul. Zolotovoritskaya (Золотоворитская; ☎235 51 88), directly opposite the entrance to the Golden Gate. MG: Zoloty vorota. Live rock music Tu and Th-Sa 8:30-11pm. Beer 8-12hv; mixed drinks 27-39hv. Tea 8-12hv. Billiards 8hv per game; darts 10hv. Open daily 11am-late. AmEx/MC/V.

Artclub 44, Khreshchatyk pr. 44 (☎229 41 37), in the basement. Walk into the courtyard; it's through an unmarked door on the left. Kyiv's jazz mecca boasts more than 150 kinds of whiskey. Live music daily 10pm-midnight. Open daily 10am-2am.

O'Brien's Pub, vul. Mykhailivska 17a (Михайлівська; ☎229 15 84), off Maydan Nezalezhnosti. The only Irish cellar in town, full of expats, and perhaps the most relaxed drinking atmosphere outside Khreshchatyk Park. Satellite TV and billiards (7hv per game). Beer 8-29hv; tea 4hv. Live music Th-Sa 9-11pm: Th Irish, F-Sa blues and rock. Open daily 8am-2am. AmEx.

The Cowboy Bar, vul. Khreshchatyk 15 (☎228 17 17), at the far end of the *passazh.* A piece of America in Kyiv. Unpainted wood, cigarette smoke, and live music nightly after 10:30pm. Beer starts at 8hv. Cover F-Sa 20hv. Open daily 24hr. MC/V.

GAY AND LESBIAN ENTERTAINMENT

Discrimination and homophobia are widespread, and thus the gay scene in Kyiv has failed to take off as it has in Moscow. Homosexuality is slowly gaining acceptance in Kyiv, however, and gay nightlife is beginning to develop. In summer, the scene revives substantially, thanks to **Hydropark;** follow the mob to **Youth Beach** (Molodizhny Plyazh). There, buy a 1hv boat ride to the opposite beach, where the crowd is mixed and clothes are optional. There's also an **all-gay beach** nearby, but it's muddy. **Big Boy Club,** vul. Harmatna 26/2 (☎441 44 32; MR: Shulyavska), is one of the few gay clubs in town. **Matrosskaya Tishina** (Sailor's Silence; ☎254 48 82), vul. Kiovsky Uzviv 10, is another popular gay hangouts.

CRIMEA (КРЫМ)

Thanks to its position on the Black Sea Coast, the Crimea has been a political hotbed and trading thoroughfare since antiquity. After centuries of Greek, Turkish, and Mongol rule, the Crimea was annexed by Russia and then bequeathed to Ukraine. Russian-speaking and proud-spirited, Crimea has reacted rebelliously to the collapse of the USSR: streets retain their Soviet name and locals still call their currency "rubles." Despite the staggering economy, the rocky shores to which Mongols, Tsars, and Soviets have flocked for over 2500 years retain their appeal. From Simferopol, redeemed only by its rail connections and the splendor of nearby Bakhchisarai, travelers can reach the sandy shores of Feodosia or the maritime history of Sevastopol. Then there's Yalta, where *literati* once vacationed, but only the ghost of Chekhov remains. Livadia, where Roosevelt, Churchill, and Stalin divided up the post-World War II world, and Alupka, a testament to the decadence of empire, await exploration just off the coast.

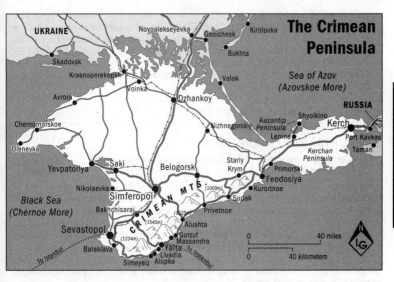

The Crimean Peninsula

SIMFEROPOL (СІМФЕРОПОЛЬ) ☎(8)0652

God made Crimea, and all Simferopol (sim-fer-ROH-pul) got was a train station, a larger than average bust of Lenin, the peninsula's only airport, and proximity to Bakhchisarai (see p. 826). Most travelers visit the city only as a stopping point on en route to Bakhchisarai.

▐ TRANSPORTATION. The **train station** (вокзал; vokzal) at ul. Gagarina (Гагарина; ☎005), sends trains to: **Kyiv** (19hr., 6 per day, 78hv); **Lviv** (32hr., 2 per day, 72hv); **Odessa** (14hr., 1 per day, 38hv); **Minsk, BLR** (35hr., 3 per day, 170hv); and **Moscow, RUS** (28hr., 10 per day, 153hv). Most trains run overnight. Tickets for the *elektrichka* (commuter rail) are sold behind the main station building at the window marked *prigorodny kassy* (пригородный кассы). These head to **Sevastopol** (2-2½hr., 8 per day, 3.23hv) via **Bakhchisarai** (1hr., 2.44hv). **Buses** leave from the station at ul. Kyivskaya 4; to get there, take trolleybus# 6 (0.40hv). Be sure to buy tickets in advance. To: **Bakhchisarai** (1hr., 5 per day, 2.97hv); **Feodosia** (2hr., every hr. 6am-8pm, 10hv); **Kyiv** (4 per day, 100hv); and **Sevastopol** (2hr., 7 per day, 7.23hv). **Buses, trolleys,** and *marshrutki* to **Yalta** leave from the train station, next to the McDonald's (2hr.; every 20min.; buses 4hv, trolleys 6hv). **Taxis** to **Yalta** are 15hv+.

▐▌▐ PRACTICAL INFORMATION AND ACCOMMODATIONS. Avalbank, vul. Naperezhnaya 32 (Набережная) has **Western Union** services, cashes **traveler's checks** for 2% commission, and gives MC/V **cash advances** for 3% commission. (Open daily 9am-1pm, M-Th 2-4:30pm). Take a right coming out of Gostinitsa Ukraina (see below) and turn right into the pedestrian area; Avalbank is in the last building on the left. 24hr. **ATMs** are located at the post office, the train station, and along vul. Pushkina. At the train station, **store luggage** at the door marked *kamera chraneniya* (камера хранения) There's a **24hr. medical center** (медпункт) to the left of the luggage storage on the first track. A **pharmacy** (аптека) is in the same building as Hotel Ukraina (☎54 56 82. Open daily 8am-8pm). An **Internet cafe** and a **telephone office** are both housed in the post office (Internet 4.32hv from 8am to

9pm, 2.16 hv otherwise.) The **post office** is next to Gastinitsa Ukraina. (Open M-F 7am-7pm, Sa-Su 8am-6pm.) **Postal Code:** 65 000. If you're staying overnight before catching the next train, take trolleybus# 5 three stops to **Hotel Ukraine** (Гостиница Украина; Gostinitsa Ukraina), ul. Rozy Lyuksemburg 7-9 (Люксембург; ☎51 01 65; fax 27 84 95. Singles 50hv, with bath 110-240hv; doubles 70hv/116-240hv). Not much goes on at night, but there are a few cafes and bars along vul. Pushkina and environs, close to Gostinitsa Ukraina.

⚡ DAYTRIP FROM SIMFEROPOL

BAKHCHISARAI (БАХЧИСАРАЙ)

The elektrichka is the cheapest and fastest transport from Simferopol (1hr., 8 per day, 2.40hv). Several buses (1hr., 5 per day, 2.80hv) leave from the Simferopol bus station.

An outpost of the Byzantine Empire at the end of the 6th century and the seat of Tatar power, Bakhchisarai now lives the rural life around three of Crimea's most evocative monuments: the rose-speckled Khan's Palace, the Saint Assumption Monastery, and the excavated Jews' Fortress. All three lie along the same main road, but a round-trip hike means over two hours in the summer sun (or winter cold). Bring good hiking shoes, a hat, and water. The local specialty here, *moloko*, consists of cannabis boiled in goat's milk; however, it is illegal and not to be found in local restaurants. *Let's Go* does not recommend cannabis boiled in goat's milk.

KHAN'S PALACE. (Ханський Палац; Khansky Palats.) Built in the early 16th century by the second Crimean Khan, the Palace that stands today was largely added piecemeal over the centuries. Its fountains and the courtyards (where the Khan used to confine his black-market harem) are delightful. In the Fountain Courtyard the 1733 **Golden Fountain** and the famous 1764 **Fountain of Tears,** supposedly built by a disconsolate khan who had fallen in love with a dying slave, still flow today. The fountain was later immortalized in *Bakchisarai Fountain* (Бахчисарайский Фонтан; Bakhchisaraisky Fontan), one of Pushkin's great poems. *(From the train station, take a marshrutka (0.50hv) or a cab (5hv). Open daily 9am-5pm. 14hv, students 7hv. English brochures 6hv.)*

SAINT ASSUMPTION MONASTERY. (Свято-Успенский Печерний Монастир; Svyato-Uspensky Pecherny Monastir.) Carved out of a cliff in the 15th century, the monastery commands one of the best views in all of the central steppes. The monastery was central to religious life in the times when Orthodox Christianity competed with the Tatars' Islam. Empty for most of the last 200 years, it reopened only a decade ago, hence the rather modern-looking buildings. *(Walk up the road from the Khan's palace until it ends (20min). At the parking area, take the pathway up the hill on your right, which will take you to the monastery. Alternatively, take a marshrutka or taxi from the palace.)*

JEWS' FORTRESS AND BEYOND. (Чуфут-кале; Chufut-kale.) The settlement received its current name when the capital of the Crimean Khanka moved away from what is now Bakhchisarai some time in the 16th century, leaving only Jews and Armenians to occupy the old fort. As you enter the complex, climb up through the caves to reach the main road of the settlement. Inside the fortress on your right, there are the two *kenassi* (кенасси; prayer houses). The one to the left was built in the 14th century from the cliff stones, while the red-pillared *kenassa* on the right dates back to the 18th century and includes a Hebrew inscription commending Bakchisarai. Up the road lie the ruins of a 1346 **mosque** and, farther along, the domes of a 1437 **mausoleum** built for Dzhanike Khan. Look behind the mausoleum for a fascinating view of the landscape. Nearby is a small **wishing-tree,** where you can add your piece of cloth to the others hanging in the wind. Beyond the Byzantine wall stands a 15th-century **cave complex** with two stories, a central pillar, and hollows for wine production and storage. *(Continue on the pathway that led you to the monastery for about 25min. and you will see the fortress up on your left. 8hv, students 4hv.)*

FEODOSIYA (ФЕОДОСИЯ)   ☎(8)06562

Founded as a slave-trading town over two and a half millennia ago, the 16km stretch of bronze sand known as Feodosiya has attracted vacationers ever since. From the **bus station,** head past the little church, turn right on ul. Fedko (Федко), and cross the bridge over the tracks to reach the **beach.** Beaches with toilets and shower cost 1-2hv but there are also free beaches (without amenities) farther to your left. City **buses** #2 and 4 run along ul. Fedko and ul. Karla Marksa (Карла Маркса), and connect the bus station with the city center (0.60hv). Get off after the bus makes a left turn on pr. Lenina, the main thoroughfare along the waterfront. Ul. Galereyna and ul. Nazukina (Назукина) run inland from pr. Lenina, and ul. K. Libknekhta (К. Либнехта) connects the two. As you head away from the station, the beachfront pr. Lenina becomes ul. Gorkovo; follow it uphill and turn left into a residential area to see a 1348 **Genoese fortress** and two **Armenian churches.**

Buses connect Feodosiya with: **Kazantip** (5 per day, 6.38hv); **Kirch** (every hr., 10.10hv); **Kyiv** (1 per day, 110.80hv); **Simferopol** (3hr., every 40min., 10-14hv); and **Yalta** (3hr., 12 per day, 15hv). Many buses on the Simferopol-Kirch route (11 per day, 11hv) pass through Feodosiya. The **telephone office** at the corner of ul. K. Libknekhta and ul. Nazukina also has a **24hr. ATM** on its premises. For financial needs, **Oshadbank** (Ошадбанк), at ul. K. Libknekhta and ul. Kirova (Кірова), gives MC/V **cash advances** for 2.5% commission, cashes AmEx/MC/V **traveler's checks** for 2% commission, and offers **Western Union services.** (Open daily 8am-1pm and 2-6pm, Sa-Su 8am-1pm and 2-5pm.) A **pharmacy** (аптека) is at ul. K. Libknekhta 16 (open daily 8am-11pm). Check email at **Internet Center,** ul. Galereyna 9. (5.42hv per hr. Open daily 9am-midnight.) The **train station,** opposite Hotel Astoriya, also offers **Internet access.** (5.76hv per hr. Open 24hr.) The **post office** (open M-F 8am-8pm, Sa-Su 8am-6pm) and **telephone office** (open 24hr.) are at ul. Galereyna 9.

On the beachfront, the **Gostinitsa Astoriya** (Гостиница Астория), pr. Lenina 9, provides clean and relatively affordable rooms. (☎323 16, reservations 323 43. Hall shower 3hv. Call ahead in summer. Singles 25-67hv; doubles 18hv-99hv.) **Grinvikh** (Гринвих), ul. Galereyna 7, offers great food and an English menu. (☎309 52. Pizza 6-17hv. Open daily 9am-4am.) At night, the cafes, bars, and discos that line pr. Lenina offer live music and dancing well into the morning. The **fountain of light and music** enlivens the walk up pr. Lenina.

YALTA (ЯЛТА)   ☎(8)0654

Yalta is the crown jewel of the Crimea, as its crowded streets will attest. A former respite for the Russian elite, Yalta's beautiful beaches and palatial sanatoria now crawl with the throngs they came here to evade. Ubiquitous blaring Russian folk-pop attests that the proletariat does indeed rule supreme these days. On a bright summer day, however, the narrow, tree-lined streets, cloud-topped mountains, and sparkling sea give visitors a momentary hint of the city that inspired Chekhov, Rachmaninov, and Tolstoy. Only a short jaunt from the center of town, the idyllic palaces of Alupka and Livadia and the spectacular Swallow's Nest evince the city's rich historical legacy, while its streets display colorful monuments to the artists who came here to find their muse.

UKRAINE

⌐ TRANSPORTATION

Trains: Yalta is not accessible by train, but the city does have an Advance Booking office where you can get tickets from Simferopol to any destination. Purchase your tickets well in advance (at least one week during the summer). From pl. Lenina, walk up ul. Igantencko and look for the "Железнодорожные кассы" sign. Open 8am-8pm.

Buses: ul. Moskovskaya 57 (☎34 20 92). To: **Feodosiya** (5hr., 3 per day, 18hv); **Kyiv** (18hr., 2 per day, 110hv); **Sevastopol** (2½hr., 4-7 per day, 9.62hv); **Simferopol** (2hr., every 10-30min., 8.70hv). Advance tickets available above and behind the *kassa*. *Marshrutki*, which run the same routes as buses, depart from the square at the corner of ul. Moskovskaya and ul. Karla Marksa. These minibuses are faster and make fewer stops, but cost 3-5hv more.

Ferries: Shuttles go to **Alupka** (1hr., 16 per day, 8hv) via **Swallow's Nest** (45min., 6hv) and **Livadia** (15min., 2.50hv). Buy tickets on the waterfront past the Gastronom store with the "Orbit" window shades, coming from pl. Lenina. Ferry tickets to **İstanbul, TUR** (36hr; Tu 7pm; US$90 one-way, US$160 round-trip) are available at the Omega window in the front right-hand corner of the Sea Terminal (Морской Вокзал; Morskoy Vokzal; ☎34 64 02), ul. Roosevelta 5 (Рузевелта). Open daily 9am-2pm.

Public Transportation: Run throughout the city (0.40hv). #1 covers most of the central area; it travels from the bus station to pl. Sovetskaya. From there, bus #8 goes to Poliana Skazok and Chekhov's house. 3hv fine for riding ticketless.

◼ ORIENTATION

Sprawled along the Black Sea, Yalta centers around the pedestrian **nab. Lenina** (Ленина), which runs a good length of the waterfront *(naberezhnaya)* from **Lenina Square** (Ленинская площадь; Leninskaya Ploshchad), where a statue of Vladimir Ilyich still rules over the palms. From the **bus** and **trolley stations,** take trolley #1 toward the center. The trolley runs down **ul. Moskovskaya** (Московська) past the circus and the market to **pl. Sovetskaya** (Советськая), where ul. Moskovskaya converges with **ul. Kyivskaya** (Киевськая). You can get off here and walk two blocks to nab. Lenina, with its seaside restaurants and street performers. A left turn leads to the **old quarter,** where you'll find most of Yalta's cheaper hotels. Both the pedestrian **ul. Pushkinskaya** (Пушкинськая) and the parallel **ul. Gogolya** (Гоголя) go inland from nab. Lenina to **Kinoteatr Spartak;** trolley #1 also stops here.

⑦ PRACTICAL INFORMATION

Tourist Office: Eugenia Travel, ul. Roosevelta 5 (☎32 81 40; fax 22 05 54; http://co.net/travel), at the sea terminal. A great resource for info on Ukraine, this English-speaking office also offers tours and assists with accommodations. Open daily 9am-6pm. **Intourist,** ul. Drazhinskovo 50 (☎35 01 32), in Hotel Yalta, uphill from Massandra (see **Accommodations,** p. 830), books flights and organizes excursions with English-speaking guides. A tour of Alupka and Livadia palaces, including transportation, admission, and guide, costs US$100. Open daily 9am-5pm.

Currency exchange: Exchanges are virtually everywhere, but offer uniformly bad rates. **Avalbank,** in the central post office, offers **Western Union** services and gives MC/V **cash advances** for 2.5% commission. (Open daily 9am-1pm and 2-7pm.) **Ukreksimbank,** ul. Moskovskaya 31a, to the left of the circus at the Tsirk (Цирк; circus) stop, cashes **traveler's checks** for 2% commission. Open daily 9am-5:45pm.

ATM: Bankomats (Банкоматы) are at the bus station, the post office, Hotel Oreanda, and along nab. Lenina.

Central Yalta

🔺▲ **ACCOMMODATIONS**

Gostinitsa Krym, **3**
Massandra, **1**
Motel-Camping Polyana
Skazok, **5**
Oreanda Hotel, **8**

🍴 **FOOD**
Cafe Voshad, **4**
Mountain Stream, **6**
Oreanda Cafe, **9**

🍸 **NIGHTLIFE**
Beach Club, **2**
Kaktus, **7**

Luggage Storage: At the bus station. Look for "Камера-хранения" (Kamera-Khraneniya) at the bottom of the stairs in the back of the building. 0.90hv for 24hr. Open daily 7am-noon and 1-8pm.

Pharmacy: Ul. Botkinskaya 1 (Боткинская). From nab. Lenina, walk up Pushkinskaya and turn right. Open 8am-9pm.

Telephones: Ul. Moskovskaya 9 (☎32 43 02), down the alley across from a flower market. If you're persistent, they'll let you make a collect call. Call to North America 15.37hv per min., to Western Europe 8.78hv per min. Open 24hr. **Fax** and **copy services** available 9am-5pm.

Internet Access: Internet Centre, ul. Yekaterinskaya 3, 1st fl. (☎32 30 72), between nab. Lenina and the Museum of Lesya Ukraina (see **Museums,** p. 831). Decent connection, though often crowded. 4.5hv per hr. Open 24hr. Slightly cheaper but even more crowded are the computers at the phone office (see above). 9am-8pm 4hv per hr., 8pm-9am 2hv per hr. Open 24hr.

Post Office: Pl. Lenina. **Poste Restante** at window #4. Packages held for 30 days. Fax and copy center. Open daily 9am-1pm and 2pm-5pm. Post office open daily 8am-8pm.

Postal Code: 98 600.

IN RECENT NEWS

A DYING INDUSTRY

Ukraine's coal mines are among the deadliest in the world. Each year, more than 300 miners lose their lives in subterranean fires and other accidents. Despite much talk from the government, conditions have not improved over the past decade.

One reason for the high fatality rate is a lack of investment, both in the mines and in safety equipment. Many are unprofitable and the government has continuously cut subsidies. Also, most of Ukraine's coal reserves are deep underground where coal bed methane, a colorless, odorless, easily ignitable gas, is abundant. Moreover, miners often don't take proper precautions. Since wages are usually paid months late or not at all, experienced miners have left the industry, leaving behind unskilled workers. Irresponsible management worsens the situation.

The World Bank estimates that 75% of Ukraine's 200 mines are in the highest accident risk category. It has even offered the country's government a US$100 million "mitigation loan" for closing the 100 least efficient mines. Fearing the social consequences in regions where alternative employment opportunities are few and far between, the government refused the money and kept the mines open, as the industry employs 400,000 Ukrainians.

There is some hope on the horizon, however. Research suggests that pumping the coal bed methane to the surface might turn what was once known as the "miners' curse" into an efficient, profitable source of energy.

—*Werner Schäfer*

▐ ACCOMMODATIONS

Bus station *babushki* often offer unbeatable deals on **private rooms ❶**. A good rate during high season is 30-60hv, but expect to pay more for rooms closer to the water. A *kvartirnoe byuro* (квартирное бюро; housing office) to the right of the trolley-bus *kassa*, across the street from the main bus station building, can help you find a room as well. (☎34 26 79, open M-Sa 8am-6pm, Sa 8am-5pm.)

Gostinitsa Krym (Крым), ul. Moskovskaya 1/6 (☎27 17 10 or 27 17 03). Clean rooms in a convenient, central location. 3 stops on trolley #1 from the bus station. Hot water usually 7-11pm. Hall shower 3.25hv. Call ahead. Singles without bath from 35hv; doubles 50hv; triples 75hv. ❶

Massandra (Массандра), ul. Drazhinskovo 46 (Дражинского; ☎27 24 01), 20min. from the town center but just minutes from the beach. Walk up Drazhinskovo and turn left at Avalon Cafe (Авалон), or take *marshrutka* #34 up the hill. No singles, but all suites have renovated bathrooms. Prices start at US$28; 3-room suite US$128. ❸

Motel-Camping Polyana Skazok (Поляна Сказок; Fairy Tale Meadow), ul. Kirova 167 (☎39 52 19; www.pskaz.crimea.com). Take bus #26, 27, or 28 from the bus station or bus #8 from the center to "Polyana Skazok," then head uphill (20min.) along the busy country road. No tents allowed, but offers bungalows with shared bathrooms (100hv). Singles start at 130hv; doubles start at 195hv. ❸

Oreanda Hotel, nab. Lenina 35/2 (☎32 82 86; fax 32 83 36). Perhaps the most luxurious hotel on the Crimea, Oreanda's prices range from expensive to ridiculous. Yet the price is justified by 2 indoor pools, a Turkish bath, a fitness center, a private beach, and a central location. Singles start at 952hv; "apartment superior" with balcony, sea view, 3 TVs, and your own private treadmill 5600hv. ❺

◖ FOOD

Most of the restaurants that populate nab. Lenina and the passage toward ul. Sadovaya dish out good food, strong beverages, and very high prices. A well-stocked **Gastronom** (Гастроном), nab. Lenina 15, sells delicious bread for pennies. (Open daily 8am-midnight.) The open-air **market** opposite the circus, accessible by foot or trolley #1, has a big selection of fresh fruits and vegetables. (Open daily 8am-8pm.)

▩ **Mountain Stream** (Горный Ручей), 100m up the road past the Motel-Camping Polyana Skazok (see **Accommodations**, above), feeds you traditional Ukrainian and Russian dishes in your own little log-hut, decorated with folkloristic embroidery. The only noise comes from the nearby stream and twitching birds. Entrees 20-50hv. English menu. Open daily 11am-midnight. ❸

Cafe Voshad (Вошад), between ul. Karla Marksa and ul. Ignatenko (Игнатенко; ☎32 75 46), serves reasonably priced Turkish cuisine, as well as some Russian and European dishes. Entrees 10-20hv. Open June-Sept. 24hr.; Nov.-May 8am-midnight. ❷

Oreanda Cafe, in the Oreanda Hotel, on nab. Lenina. Head to this elegant cafe for a delicious pancake breakfast (12hv). Open 24hr. ❹

⊙ SIGHTS

ON THE WATERFRONT. Yalta's shady **parks,** which border nab. Lenina, provide an intermediate level of cool between the bracing sea and the scorching sun. For a great view of the city, take the chairlift (канатная дорога; kanatnaya doroga) to the right of the Gastronom Store on nab. Lenina to the **mock Greek temple,** properly named Olymp, which houses a disco at night. *(Open June-Oct. daily 10am-3am. 6hv.)*

ANTON CHEKHOV LEGACY. The author (see **Russia: The Arts,** p. 626) lived here for the last five years of his life, fighting off tuberculosis, and you can very nearly retrace his every step in monuments and plaques. Through the archway at nab. Lenina 7, you can see where he once slept; on ul. Litkensa (Литкенса), you'll find the **school** where he taught. At ul. Kirova 112, explore the ▨ **white dacha** he built in 1899, the garden he planted, the desk at which he wrote *Three Sisters* and *The Cherry Orchard,* and the **museum** his sister dedicated to him, all remarkably well-preserved. The museum displays manuscripts, old editions, and the room where the author entertained such luminaries as Sergei Rachmaninov and Lev Tolstoy. Members of the Moscow Art Theater still come to Yalta every spring for performances at the "Days of Chekhov." *(Take bus #8 from Kinoteatr Spartak on ul. Pushkinskaya (every 40min.). Alternatively, take the much more frequent trolleybus #1 to Pionerskaya (Пионерская), cross the street, turn left, then right into the walkway, and left at the top of the stairs. ☎39 49 47. Open Tu-Su 10am-5:15pm. English video upon request. English brochure 10hv. Admission 10hv, students 5hv.)*

OTHER SIGHTS. The kitschy ▨ **Fairy-Tale Meadow** (Поляна Сказок; Polyana Skazok) is dotted with wooden sculptures of Snow White (Belaya Snegichka) and characters from Russian and Ukrainian fairy tales. *(Take bus #8 from pl. Sovetskaya or #26, 27, or 28 from Kinotheatr Spartak a few stops past the Chekhov Museum. Open June-Sept. daily 9am-8pm; Oct.-May 9am-5pm. 6hv.)* To get to the **Uchan Su Waterfall,** keep going up the road to Polyana Skazok past the campground to the end of the paved road. Turn right up the hill on one of the footpaths. Eventually, you will get to a road that leads you to the waterfall if you take a right. Despite the many unmarked trails, it's hard to get lost: down leads to civilization, up to the cliffs. *(Waterfall entrance 3hv.)* The **Nikitsky Botanical Gardens** (Никитский Сад; Nikitsky Sad), founded in 1812, boast over 15,000 species of native and foreign flora, including 2000 varieties of roses. *(Take bus #34 past Massandra to the "arboretum" stop on your left (15min.). Open daily 8am-8pm. 5hv.)*

🏛 MUSEUMS

The **Museum of Lesya Ukraina,** on ul. Yekaterinskaya 8, two blocks from nab. Lenina, pays tribute to the famous Ukrainian writer who lived here briefly in 1897 (see **The Arts,** p. 806). Established in 1991, the museum pays tribute to the Ukrainian cultural heritage of Crimea, which was part of Russia until the 1950s. *(☎32 55 25. Open Tu-Su 9am-6pm. 2hv. English tour 10hv.)* The **Yalta Cultural Museum,** in the same building, highlights aspects of local life from the 19th and 20th centuries.

(Knock on the door to your left as you enter the house. Open Tu-Su 9am-6pm. 2hv.) Fifty meters up from ul. Lenina to the right, the **Yalta Historical-Literary Museum,** ul. Pushkinskaya 5a, commits more space to its **wax collection,** which emphasizes strange and scary figures. (Museum open daily 11am-7pm. 2hv. Wax collection open daily 11am-11pm. 6hv.)

♫ 📷 ENTERTAINMENT AND NIGHTLIFE

Follow the seashore either way from the harbor to reach one of Yalta's many **beaches**. (Entrance to most city beaches 1.50hv, commercial beaches 2-5hv; some free after 6pm.) Most are crowded and all lack sand. If boredom strikes, try renting a **jet ski** or **hydroplane.** The nightly **amusement park** (*lunapark*) on nab. Lenina has a roller coaster and bumper cars (12hv and 7hv respectively). If you feel the urge to make a fool of yourself, try one of the many karaoke places on nab. Lenina

Nightlife in Yalta tends to be sedate. Bars along the beach stay open as long as there are customers, and at **Tuborg,** ul. Sverdlova 7, you can get 0.5L of beer for 4hv. If the beat of the nostalgic Russian songs along the waterfront doesn't do it for you, **Beach Club** (Пляж Клуб; Plash Club) on pl. Sovetskaya, spins fresh house in a concrete Soviet building. (Cover 10-20hv. Open daily 10pm-last customer.) Or, try the more exclusive **Kaktus** (Кактус; Cactus), upstairs at the Morskoy Vokzal, which offers Tex-Mex food, disco music, and a great view of the sea. (Cover 30hv.)

📷 DAYTRIPS FROM YALTA

LIVADIA (ЛІВАДИЯ)

The easiest way to get to Livadia is by water shuttle (15min., every 30min., 2.50hv). Marshrutka #45 and several others marked Livadia will also go there (1hv). From the dock go straight up the stairs and head back down to your left to reach the lift (лифт; leeft), which takes you almost up to the palace (open daily 7am-2pm and 4-7pm, 0.50hv). Alternatively, hike up all the way; as long as you going uphill, you should be on the right track.

Only an hour's hike or a 15min. boat ride away from the city, Livadia hosted the imprecisely named **Yalta Conference** of 1945. Winston Churchill, Franklin Delano Roosevelt, and Joseph Stalin met for a week in February at Tsar Nicholas II's summer palace to hash out postwar territorial claims. Stalin would join the war against Japan after the German defeat, while in return, Roosevelt and Churchill promised the return of all Soviet prisoners of war. Many felt that the Anglo-American side had conceded too much, as Soviet influence subsequently blossomed over Eastern Europe. Tour guides present a second school of thought, which claims that the conference guaranteed "50 years of peace." The **Great Palace** (Великий Дворец; Veliky Dvorets), an Italian-style villa with an exquisite marble-and-wood interior and a tiled Arab Courtyard, was built in 1911 and is worth the visit. The view from Nicholas's windows reminds us that it's good to be tsar—until the masses figure out that they got the short end of the stick. The lower level commemorates the conference, while the upper level houses the sentimentally royalist **Nicholas II Museum.** The guides will make you don felt slippers inside, which will stay on your feet about as well as Roosevelt, Churchill, and Stalin stuck to their agreement.

ALUPKA (АЛУПКА)

Take a water shuttle (1hr., every ½hr., 8hv) or marshrutka #27 (every 40min.-1hr., 2hv) to Alupka from Yalta. On your way back, head past the cable car to Miskhor (Мисхор), and return to Yalta from there (every every 30min. from 9:30am, 7hv). Palace open July-Aug. daily 8am-7:30pm; Mar.-June daily 9am-5pm; Nov.-Feb. Tu-Su 9am-4pm. 15hv, students 7.50hv. Cable car runs M-W and F-Su 9am-6:30pm. 20hv.

The fishing village of Alupka is home to the most extravagant *dacha* (summer home) in Greater Yalta. **Vorontsov Palace** (Дворец Воронцова; Dvorets Vorontsova) is a still-active compound built by Odessa's wealthiest governor-general, Count Mikhail Vorontsov (see **History,** p. 802). The palace, which took over 30 years to construct, was finished in 1841. The interior is full of Romantic English landscapes and portraits of renowned figures, including Catherine the Great and her advisor Grigori Potemkin. Every summer hordes of half-naked Russians are guided through the hallowed halls. The British delegations lodged here during the Yalta Conference. From the museum exit, walk through the park 1km back up the coast toward Yalta to a **cable car** (канантная дорога; kanatnaya doroga), which ascends 1200m to the Ay-Petra Plateau, a breathtaking spot for an afternoon picnic. Dress warmly and be prepared to wait in line. And by line, we mean a mob that periodically erupts into a stampede whenever a cable car arrives.

En route to Alupka, **Swallow's Nest** (Ласточкино Гнездо; Lastochkino Gnezdo) is Crimea's most photogenic, or at least most photographed, site. The castle, perched on a cliff, has starred in postcards since its construction in 1912. You can use the short ferry stopover to take in the view and take a picture of your own. If you do bother to get off, the entrance fee is 2hv. The castle now houses a restaurant.

SEVASTOPOL (СЕВАСТОПОЛЬ) ☎(8)0692

Sevastopol (pop. 400,000) is positioned so ideally it couldn't help but become a focal point in world history. It first gained international attention in the Crimean War (1854-55) and returned to the limelight in World War II, when its tragic losses placed it among the ranks of Soviet "Hero Cities." Rebuilt before ornament became taboo in Soviet circles, central Sevastopol, unlike its Crimean counterparts, is elegant and formal; monuments and memorials dot its landscape. Russia and Ukraine have recently resolved their long-standing quarrel over the ownership of the Black Sea Fleet moored at Sevastopol's docks, and today sailors dressed in the uniforms of both countries fill the streets. With a story to tell on every corner, Sevastopol maintains an independence of spirit that's proud even for Crimea.

◨ TRANSPORTATION

Trains: Vokzal, ul. Vokzalnaya 10 (Вокзальная; ☎54 30 77). To: **Kyiv** (19hr., 2 per day, 59hv); **Moscow, RUS** (28hr., 1 per day, 190hv); **St. Petersburg, RUS** (37hr., 1 per day, 250hv). The *elektrichka* (commuter rail) runs to **Simferopol** (3hr., 8 per day, 2.44hv), where you can connect to other destinations. *Elektrichka* tickets are sold next to the train station. Purchase advance tickets in the white concrete building behind the bus station. (Open daily 7am-6pm.) Trolley bus #7 runs between the station and the city center (0.40hv). Take the overpass across the tracks to reach the bus stop.

Buses: Pl. Revyakina 3 (☎46 16 32). Across a few tracks behind the train station or 1 stop on trolleybus #7. To: **Feodosiya** (7hr., 4 per day, 17.90hv); **Rostov-na-Donu** (14hr., 1 per day, 71.30hv); **Simferopol** (2hr., every hr., 7.23-11.13hv); **Yalta** (2hr., every hr., 8.72-12.50hv). Station open daily 6am-8:30pm.

Public Transportation: The slightly more expensive and less crowded *marshrutki* run the same routes as the bus (0.70-1hv). **Trolleybuses** (0.40hv; pay on board) are efficient and convenient. #12 runs up ul. Bolshaya Morskaya. #7 and 9 circle the center, stopping at the train station. #5 goes up ul. Admirala Oktyabrskova to the west of the peninsula. **Ferries** leave from Artilleriyskaya Bay behind Gostinitsa Sevastopol for the north shore (Северная Сторона; Severnaya Storona), landing near pl. Zakharova (20min., every hr., 0.60hv). A passenger boat leaves from a nearby dock for **Uchkuyuvka Beach** (Учкуевская Пляж), on the sea north of town (30-40min., every 2hr., 1.50hv). Purchase tickets on board. Ferries for **İstanbul, TUR** (28hr.) leave W 8am from the Moskoy Vokzal (Морской Вокзал; ☎55 93 41 or 54 40 82) at the corner of ul. Lenina and pr. Nakhimova. (Bed in 4-bed cabin 405hv, round-trip 756hv; with shower 540hv/972hv.)

◪ ORIENTATION

Greater Sevastopol is impossibly complicated; its poorly marked streets meander through several peninsulas that jut into the harbor. The town center is on a single peninsula along the southwestern tip of the Crimea, below the Sevastopol harbor. **Pl. Lazaryova** (Лазариова), up the street from **Gostinitsa Sevastopol**, is a good starting point for exploring the city center. From here, **ul. Bolshaya Morskaya** (Болшая Морская) runs up the hill to converge with **ul. Lenina** (Ленина) at its intersection with **pr. Nakhimova** (Нахимова), which runs from there to **pl. Lazaryova** (Лазарёва), where it turns into **ul. Generala Petrova** (Генерала Петрова). Down **pl. Ushakova** (Ушакова), **ul. Admirala Oktyabrskova** (Адмирала Октябрьского) is the first intersecting road on the left. The promenades **Primorskaya blv.** (Приморская) and **nab. Kornilova** (Корнилова), by Artilleriyskaya Bay, run parallel to pr. Nakhimova.

▨ PRACTICAL INFORMATION

Tourist Offices: Excursion offices abound on Primorsky blv., offering convenient, if pricey, guided tours of the city and its sites, as well as boat tours of the harbor (20-30hv). **Submarine** (Санмарин; ☎ 16 55 00 81; tur@stel.sevastopol.ua), in Gostinitsa Sevastopol, provides individual walking tours of the city (US$15), and can arrange accommodations at local sanatoria (US$5-25 per day). Open M-Sa 9am-7pm.

Currency Exchanges: Exchanges are everywhere, but most only offer dollars, Euros, and Rubles. **Ashadbank** (Ашадбанк; ☎ 54 12 16), at ul. Bolshaya Morskaya 41, cashes AmEx/Thomas Cooke **traveler's checks**, and gives MC/V **cash advances**, all for 2.5% commission. **Western Union** is available here and at the **post office.** Open M-F 8am-6pm, Sa 8am-4pm.

Luggage Storage: Lockers in bus station lobby 0.90hv for 24hr. Open daily 6am-6pm.

Pharmacy: Apteka #4 (Аптека), ul. Bolshaya Morskaya 43. Open M-F 8am-8pm, Sa-Su 10am-6pm.

Telephones: To the left of the post office. Open 24hr.

Internet Access: Internet Cafe Jam, ul. Bolshaya Morskaya 13a (☎ 55 77 56), up the stairs to the left of Magic Burger. 6hv per hr. Open 24hr.

Post Office: ul. Bolshaya Morskaya 21. **Photocopy services. Western Union** available. Open M-F 8am-7pm, Sa-Su 8am-6pm. **Postal Code:** 99 011.

▮ ACCOMMODATIONS

For extended summertime stays, it's hard to beat the **private rooms** aggressively advertised by *babushki* in the train station (15-30hv). Travel agencies can help you find private accommodations. Hotels charge foreigners outrageous prices.

Gostinitsa Sevastopol, pl. Nakhimova 8 (☎ 54 36 82; fax 54 34 48). 5 stops from the bus station on trolleybus #1, 3, 7, or 9. Combines the elegance of pre-Soviet architecture with the blandness of Soviet interior design. Centrally located. Hot showers 2.50hv. Singles with toilet and sink 60hv, with bath 180hv; doubles 90hv/165hv. Reservations recommended during the summer. MC/V.

Gostinitsa Krym (Крым), ul. 6 Bastionnaya 46 (Бастионная; ☎ 55 71 54), up ul. Admirala Oktyabrskova from ul. Bolshaya Morskaya. On trolleybus line #5, 6, or 10. A 14-story monument to Soviet design with wide beds and funky carpets. Hot water 6-8am and 8-10pm. Singles with bath 148hv; doubles 162hv; triples 204hv.

◖ FOOD

The well-stocked, outdoor **central market** lies downhill from pl. Lazaryova at the intersection of ul. Partizanskaya (Партизанская) and ul. Odesskaya (Одесская). (Open Tu-Su 6am-8pm.) An elegant **Gastronom** grocery store, at pr. Nakhimova 3, has a take-out counter that serves fresh-baked pastries (0.45-0.90hv) and pizzas (1hv). Open M-Sa 8am-2pm and 3-8pm, Su 8am-3pm. MC/V.

▩ **Tavern 1854,** (Трактир), ul. Bolshaya Morskaya (☎54 47 60). Surrounded by Crimean War memorabilia, waiters dressed up as sailors serve authentic Crimean fare at insanely low prices. Very popular among locals. Free *kvas* and traditional bread. *Kulebyaka* pie with meat, fish, or cabbage 14hv. *Golubzy* 6.25hv. Vodka infused with honey or ashberry 1.60hv. Open daily 9am-midnight. ❶

Kafe-Bistro Dialog (Диалог), ul. Bolshaya Morskaya 23 (☎54 54 96), 2nd fl. An old-school *stolovaya* (cafeteria) repackaged as a slick new cafe. Dine on the outdoor patio, or sit indoors where a stucco ceiling and Soviet wood-panelling makes for an interesting atmosphere. Entrees 7-26hv. Open daily 10am-midnight. ❷

◉ ♬ SIGHTS AND ENTERTAINMENT

The 2500-year-old ▩ **Ruins at Chersonesus** (Херсонес) boast an ancient amphitheater, coin mint, and acres of fundament that look out over the sea. From June 20-Aug. 31 each year, local thespians take to the stage here, performing everything from Euripedes to Shakespeare. (Call ☎54 33 96 for tickets or purchase them there.) To reach the site, take the trolleybus or *marshrutka* #10 from the central market to Dmitry Ulyanova (Дмитри Улянова; 7 stops; 0.40/0.75hv). Walk back a few meters, take the first left, and follow the road for about 800m. (Open daily 8am-9pm. 10hv.) Also located at Chersonesus is the pseudo-Byzantine **St. Vladimir's Cathedral** (Владимирский Собор; Vladimirsky Sobor), a reconstruction of its medieval predecessor, which was built to commemorate the site of the Duke's alleged christening in AD 88.

The rotunda of the **Panorama Museum of the Defense of Sevastopol** (Панорама Оборона Севастополь; Panorama Oborona Sevastopola), at the end of Istorichesky blv. (Исторический), was built in 1905 to commemorate the 50th anniversary of the siege on the city; it's an impressive 3-D image that thrusts you into the midst of battle. To get there, enter the part at pl Ushakova, pass the large monument and continue to go straight past the small amusement part until you see the museum on your left. (Open daily 9:30am-5:30pm. English tour for up to five people, 70hv.) A smaller museum around the right side of the building displays war relics of the invading armies of the Crimean War. (Open daily 9am-4pm, 0.50hv.) The **Museum of the Black Sea Fleet** (Музей Чёрноморского Флота; Muzey Chornomorskovo Flota), ul. Lenina 11, founded in 1869, displays model ships, naval paintings, and personal effects of notable sea dogs. (☎54 22 89 or 52 03 92. Open W-Su 10am-6pm. 10hv, students 5hv.) **Private skiffs** leave several times daily from the Morskoy Vokzal on 30min. **harbor tours** (10-15hv).

Like every other beach in Crimea, **Plyazh Omega** (Пляж Омега) is a madhouse by day; at night, however, things get even wilder along its strip of cafes, discos, and pubs—all of which rock until dawn. Take trolleybus #10 to "Pleeyash Omega." Artilleryskaya Bay has its own share of bars and clubs right by the city center.

ODESSA (ОДЕССА)   ☎ (8)0482

Since its 1794 founding by Catherine the Great, Odessa (pop. 1,100,000) has been blessed by prosperity and cursed with corruption. With French, British, Turkish, Greek, Italian, and Russian influences, life in the port town has always been exciting. Attractive to intellectuals as well as thieves and *mafiosi*, Odessa has served as a background for writers from Pushkin to Isaac Babel. Since the collapse of the Soviet Union, many tourist establishments and the city's ancient beauty have kept the visitors, both Russian and Western, coming to the "evil empire's party town."

▐▀ TRANSPORTATION

Flights: Ovidiopolskaya Doroga (Овидиопольская дорога; ☎006 21 35 49), southwest of the center. Flights to: **Kyiv; İstanbul, TUR; Moscow, RUS; St. Petersburg, RUS; Vienna, AUS; Warsaw, POL.** *Marshrutka* #129 goes from the airport to the train station, #101 goes to the city center (Grechetskaya). Book tickets at Seasons Travel, Zhukova vul. 3/7, off Deribasovskaya (☎728 60 60). Open M-F 10am-7pm, Sa 10am-3pm.

Trains: Zheleznodorozhny Vokzal (Железнодорожный Вокзал), pl. Privokzalnaya 2 (Привокзальная; ☎005 or 22 42 42), at the south end of ul. Pushkinskaya. Purchase international and advance tickets (a good idea in summer) in the hall to your left as you enter the building. The information booth to the right of the main entrance charges 0.50hv per question. To: **Dniepropetrovsk** (17hr., 1 per day, 47hv); **Kharkiv** (15½hr., 1 per day, 56hv); **Kyiv** (12hr., 2 per day, 58hv); **Simferopol** (13hr., 1 per day, 43hv); **Minsk, BLR** (19hr., 1 per day, 148hv); **Moscow, RUS** (26hr., 2-3 per day, 78hv); **St. Petersburg, RUS** (35hr., 1 per day, 170hv).

Buses: Avtovokzal (Автовокзал), ul. Kolontayevskaya 58 (Колонтаевская; ☎004). From the train station, cross the road behind McDonald's and take tram #5 to the last stop. From there, walk down one block, continuing straight where the tram turns right. To: **Kyiv** (12hr., 2 per day, 36hv); **Simferopol** (8hr., 1 per day, 43hv); **Chişinău, MOL** (5hr., 2 per day, 19hv).

Ferries: Morskoy Vokzal (Морской Вокзал; Sea Terminal), ul. Primorskaya 6 (Приморская; ☎22 32 11). Buy tickets at Eugenia Travel or other agencies. To **İstanbul, TUR** (1-2 days, 2 per week, US$80-90). Open daily 9am-6pm. **Eugenia Travel** (see **Tourist Office**, below) arranges occasional cruises to **Yalta** (2 days, US$115-190).

Public Transportation: Trams and **trolleybuses** run almost everywhere 7am-midnight. Buy your tickets (0.50hv) from the badge-wearing *konduktor*. It is hard to tell the difference between **buses** and *marshrutkas* (0.60-1hv), but locals can point you to the one you need. On buses, pay as you exit.

Taxis: ☎070. The new yellow taxis are on the expensive side—haggle away. Always set the price before the ride and have the driver write it down. Don't pay more than 10hv from pl. Grechetskaya to the train station.

▐▄ ORIENTATION

Odessa's center is bounded by the **train station** to the south and the **port** to the north. All streets have been recently renamed and labeled in both Ukrainian and Russian; *Let's Go* lists Russian names. Numbering of streets begins at the sea and increases as you head inland. **Vul. Deribasovskaya** (Дерибасовская) is the main pedestrian thoroughfare. The main transport hub is right off of **pl. Grechetskaya** (Гречетская). From the McDonald's opposite the train station, take trolley #1, or any number of *marshrutki* to get there. The tree-lined promenade of **Primorsky blv.** (Приморский) is separated from the sea terminal by the famous **Potemkin Stairs.** Odessa's **beaches** stretch for miles east of the center and can be reached by trolleybus #5 or 9 from pl. Grechetskaya.

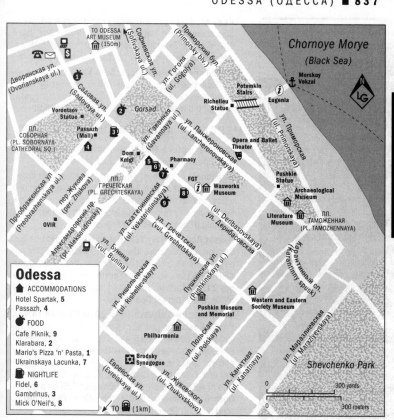

Odessa

🏠 **ACCOMMODATIONS**
Hotel Spartak, **5**
Passazh, **4**

🍴 **FOOD**
Cafe Piknik, **9**
Klarabara, **2**
Mario's Pizza 'n' Pasta, **1**
Ukrainskaya Lacunka, **7**

🍸 **NIGHTLIFE**
Fidel, **6**
Gambrinus, **3**
Mick O'Neil's, **8**

🛈 PRACTICAL INFORMATION

TOURIST, FINANCIAL, AND LOCAL SERVICES

Tourist Offices: FGT Travel (also known as Fagot; Фагот) ul. Rishelievskaya 4 (☎37 52 01; www.odessapassage.com), in the wax museum. Provides info about accommodations and over 20 city **tours**. (75-150hv per person. 2 person minimum.) Availability of tours may vary. Open daily 8:30am-10pm. **Eugenia Travel,** ul. Primorskaya 6 (☎21 85 81; fax 22 40 47), located in the sea terminal, sells plane and ferry tickets. Call the English-speaking director Janna Belovsova (☎22 05 54) to arrange special tours. Open daily 9am-6pm. AmEx/MC/V.

Visa Registration: OVIR (ОВИР), ul. Bunina 37, 2nd fl. (Бунина; ☎28 28 22). Foreigners no longer have to register in Ukraine, but the office continues to assist travelers with visa issues. Open M-F 9am-1pm and 2-6pm.

Tourist Police: Kantselyariya dlya inostrantsev (Канцелярия для иностранцев; Office for Foreigners), ul. Bunina 37, 2nd fl (☎28 28 46), next to OVIR.

Currency Exchange: Obmen Valyut (Обмен Валют) are on every corner. Rates may vary, so check several. **Bank Aval,** ul. Sadovaya 9 (Садовая) cashes AmEx/TC/V **traveler's checks** for 2% commission and gives **cash advances** for 3% commission. Open M-F 9am-1pm and 2-3pm.

THE BIG SPLURGE

GRAND HOTEL LVIV

Are you tired of staying in Soviet-era hotels with rotary phones, cold showers, and crumbling furniture that was ugly even when it was new? Tired of black-and-white televisions with two channels, one of which doesn't even work? Tired of fearing your bed will suddenly fall into pieces right underneath you? Well, are you ready to spend some dough?

If you've answered yes to any of these questions, treat yourself to a few nights at Lviv's Grand Hotel. Located on pr. Svobody, right in the city center, it offers first-rate amenities: an indoor pool, gym and sauna, restaurants, a bar, and even a casino. The palatial building was designed in the late 19th century and its spacious, authentic halls add to its grandeur. Classically furnished singles with renovated modern bathrooms are US$85 per night, including breakfast.

For the really big splurge, rent the presidential suite (US$255). Help yourself to the complimentary champagne, sprawl out in the elegant living room, mix your favorite drink at the bar, and walk around in a fresh white bathrobe after cleaning yourself of the pain, sweat, and dirt accumulated on the road.

Though expensive by Eastern European standards, a night at this hotel is well worth the dent in the wallet. *13 Pr. Svobody. ☎72 76 65; fax 76 96 00; www.ghgroup.com.ua.)* ❺

—Werner Schäfer

Luggage Storage: *Kamera Zberigannya* (Камера Зберіганния), in train station. Small bag 3hv, large 4hv. *Kamera Skhodu* (Камера сходу; storage), downstairs in sea terminal. 1hv per bag per day. Open 24hr.

English-Language bookstore: **Dom Knigi** (Дом Книги), ul. Deribasovskaya 27. Sells *The Economist* (4.70hv) about a week late, a small selection of English books, and good city **maps** (4hv). Open M-Sa 10am-6pm.

EMERGENCY AND COMMUNICATIONS

Pharmacy: Apteka #32, Deribasovskaya 16 (☎22 49 06). Open M-F 8am-8pm, Sa-Su 10am-6pm.

Telephones: At the post office, to the left as you enter. Pay in advance. Open 24hr. Local calls require phone cards, sold at the post office and used in blue or yellow booths around town. **Utel** cards for international calls are sold at post offices and hotels.

Internet Access: Novy Vek (Новый Век), ul. Bunina 33. Comfortable couches. 4hv per hr. **Printing** 0.50hv per page. Cafe in back. Coffee 1.50hv, beer 2hv. Open daily 9am-1am, or until last customer leaves. **Technology 21,** ul. Sadovaya (☎22 44 80), opposite the post office. 2-3hv per hr. Open 24hr.

Post Office: Ul. Sadovaya 10 (☎26 64 67 or 26 74 93). **Poste Restante** (до востребования; do vostrebovaniya) at counters #15 and 16; pre-stamped airmail envelopes (конверт с марками; konvert s markami) and packages in the small room to the left of the central hall. Open M-Sa 8am-8pm, Su 8am-6pm. **Fax** service at #21 (☎26 64 17) 0.50hv plus 1.50hv per min. Open daily 8am-1pm and 1:45pm-5pm. **Photocopy** at window #33. Open M-Sa 8am-8pm, Su 8am-6pm.

Postal Code: 65 000.

🏠 ACCOMMODATIONS

Private rooms ❶, starting at US$5 per person, are the cheapest option, but you'll be lucky to get anything near the city center. Train station hawkers hold signs—some variation on "Сдаю комнату" (Sdayu komnatu; room to rent). Ask *"Skolko?"* (Сколько?; how much?). The *babushki* invariably start at US$10, so haggle down and don't pay until you see the room. Truly budget-minded travelers request *samoye deshovoye mesto* (самое дешёвое место; the cheapest place), which lands you in a triple or a quad. The city turns its water off from midnight to 6am, and there is no hot water in the summer. Take tram #3 or 12 from the train station to the downtown hotels. Most of these accommodations are near noisy pl. Grechetskaya and vul. Deribasovskaya, so try to get a room away from the street. A key deposit is often required in summer.

Passazh (Пассаж), ul. Preobrazhenskaya 34 (☎22 48 49; fax 22 41 50). From Pl. Grecheskaya, take ul. Grecheskaya toward pl. Sobonaya (Собоная) and turn right on Preobrazhenskaya. Pleasant rooms. Luggage storage 2hv. Reservations recommended. Singles 67hv, with bath 130hv; doubles 112hv/157hv; triples with bath 220hv. ❷

Odessa State University Dormitory #8, ul. Dovzhenko 9B (Довженко; ☎21 87 60, reservations 63 04 67). From the left side of the train station, take trolley #7 or, from pl. Grecheskaya, take trolley #5 or 9 to the Dovzhenko stop. Cross the street and walk through the alley to the left of the cafe. The dorms are in a tall 9-story building to the left at end. Check in at room #207, 208, 214, or 215. Non-Russian speakers should call the dean, Irina Kdegaeva, for information (☎23 84 77). Very spartan, but the price can't be beat. Open July-Aug. All rooms 10hv. ❶

Hotel Spartak (Спартак), vul. Deribasovskaya 25 (☎26 89 24). The building has seen better days, but rooms are clean and cheap, and the location couldn't be better. Single with bath 110hv; double with sink 103hv, with bath 146hv; triple with sink 132hv. ❷

🍴 FOOD

Odessa has more good restaurants, markets, and cafes than any other city in Ukraine. Ul. Deribasovskaya is packed with classy and interchangeable cafes that all serve great food, but open and close at will. The Privoz (Привоз) **mega-market**, Privoznaya ul. (Привозная), to the right of the train station, sells fruit, vegetables, dairy products, clothing, and hardware. (Open daily 8am-6pm.)

🍴 **Klarabara** (Кларабара), ul. Preobrazhenskaya 28 (☎20 03 31; www.klarabara.od.ua), in the Gorsad. This pleasant restaurant offers its entrees (26-39hv) against the background of a fireplace in winter and the lively outdoors in summer. English menu. Breakfast 12-18hv. Beer 6-17hv. Live jazz and blues F-Su 8-11pm. Open Su-Th 10am-midnight, F-Sa 10am-1am. MC/V. ❸

Mario's Pizza 'n' Pasta, ul. Sadovaya 15 (☎26 67 95, delivery 777 00 00), near the post office. Nice Italian restaurant with outdoor seating and satellite TV. Pizza 14-28hv. Breakfast 7-13hv. Open daily 9am-11pm. ❷

Ukrainskaya Lacunka (Українська Ласунка), ul. Deribasovskaya 17 (☎/fax 25 75 12). A bit touristy, but serves tasty authentic Ukrainian food. Waiters and waitresses dress in national costume and the interior is decorated with traditional handicrafts. Live folk music 8-10pm. *Vareniki* 8-17hv. Entrees 20-40hv. Open daily 10am-midnight. V. ❷

Café Piknik (Пикник) ul. Yekaterininskaya 23 (☎24 13 18). Italian and Caucasian specialties minutes away from Odessa's cosmopolitan center. Eat off glass tables while watching the fashion channel. Entrees 40-60hv. Open daily 11am-1pm. V. ❹

👁 SIGHTS

🏛 **CATACOMBS.** When Catherine the Great decided to build Odessa, the limestone used for construction was mined from below, leaving the longest series of dark and intertwining catacombs in the world. During World War II, Odessa's resistance fighters hid in these tunnels for almost three years, surfacing only for raids against the Nazis. The accessible portion of the catacombs lies under the village of Neribaiskoye, where the city has set up an outstanding subterranean **museum**. The catacombs are only accessible through one entrance, and with a guide. Lantern in hand, your guide will explain the recreated resistance camp, including the well, the bathrooms, the sitting room, the makeshift weapons factory, and the shooting range. At Guard Point #1, soldiers had to sit for two-hour shifts in complete darkness waiting for German attackers. Rocks with graffiti have been transported from the original site; one declares "Blood for blood; death for death." *(30min. by car from Odessa. Eugenia Travel (see **Tourist Office,** p. 837) provides rides and guided tours. 3hr. English tour US$50 per person, 3 person minimum. Excursion times and prices vary depending on demand. FGT offers English tours for 75hv per person, including transportation. Dress warmly.)*

411TH BATTALION MONUMENT. Far from the busy commercial center lies the Memorial Complex of the 411th Battalion, one of Odessa's more entertaining monuments. The typical armaments of the Soviet forces are here in all their glory, spread over a large park. You'll think the guns and torpedoes are impressive until you get to the other end of the park and see the tanks (the turrets even move), a bomber, and a submarine. There is a small museum by the battleship. The cliffs along the rocky coast are a short walk from behind the bus stop to the left. At high tide, the sea provides its own violent spectacle. *(From the train station, take* marshrutka #127 *to the last stop (30-40min.). Walk straight and take a right at the concrete "411." Museum open Sa-Th 10am-6pm. 2hv.)*

UL. DERIBASOVSKAYA. The center of Odessa's street culture, ul. Deribasovskaya attracts performers of all kinds, including clowns and New Age monks. On the east end of the street is the captivating **Gorsad** (Горсад), where artists sell jewelry, landscape painting, and *matrioshka* dolls. Beyond the Gorsad, ul. Deribasovskaya ends at the intersection with ul. Preobrazhenskaya, on the corner of which is the dazzling ornate 19th-century **Passazh courtyard.** Cross the street to see the **statue of Mikhail Vorontsov,** Odessa's powerful governor during the 1820s. The square is called **Cathedral Square** (Пл. Соборная; pl. Sobornaya). A block to the left on ul. Preobrazhenskaya is the aromatic **flower market,** where old women advise suitors about the best flowers to buy.

UL. PUSHKINSKAYA. With cobblestones and charming street lamps, this avenue is quite possibly Odessa's most beautiful street. Ul. Pushkinskaya's namesake poet lived at #13 during his exile; the house is now a museum (see **Museums,** p. 822). At #17, the **Filarmoniya** (Филармония), built from 1894 to 1899, looks out sternly from the corner with ul. Bunina (Бунина). It's one of only two surviving opera houses constructed with special 19th-century acoustics—the other is Milan's La Scala. A block farther down on the right, the large, gray **Brodsky Synagogue** used to be the center of Odessa's Jewish community. A left at the Filarmoniya, another right, then left, leads toward **Park Shevchenko,** a vast stretch of greenery that separates the city from the sea. At the entrance stands a **monument** to the poet Taras Shevchenko (see **The Arts,** p. 806). Within are the ruins of the **Khadjibei Fortress,** a sports stadium, monuments to the dead of the Great Patriotic War and the Afghanistan War, and, overlooking the sea, an obelisk memorial and eternal flame dedicated to the **Unknown Seaman.** *(From Deribasovskaya, turn right on ul. Pushkinskaya.)*

PRIMORSKY BLV. AND THE POTEMKIN STAIRS. (Потёмкинская Лестница; Potomkinskaya Lestnitsa.) Primorsky Blv. is a shaded promenade right above the harbor, with some of the finest facades in Odessa. The **statue of Aleksandr Pushkin** turns its back unceremoniously to the City Hall, which refused to help fund its construction. On either side of the City Hall are Odessa's two symbols: **Fortuna,** goddess of fate, and **Mercury,** the god of trade. From Primorsky Blv. the 192 steps of the **Potemkin Stairs,** which are featured in Sergei Eisenstein's 1925 silent epic *Battleship Potemkin,* climb to ul. Suvorova and the Sea Terminal. A concrete statue of the **Duc de Richelieu,** the city's first governor, stares down the steps toward the port. Past the bridge to the left is the long, white **Mother-in-Law Bridge.** The bridge was supposedly built so that an elderly lady could more easily visit her son-in-law, a high-ranking Communist official.

MUSEUMS

ODESSA ART MUSEUM. (Одеський художественный музей; Odesskii Khudozhetsvenii Muzey.) A great collection of 19th-century art, including works by Kandinsky and Ayvazovskiy, in the former palace of Polish magnate Felix Potoski's daughter Olga. It is rumored that Olga used the underground passageways of the catacombs to conduct secret trysts with Count Vorontsov. Entrance is permitted only with a guide to prevent curious tourists getting lost in the catacomb labyrinth. The grotto is a bit chilly, so dress warmly. *(Ul. Sofiyevskaya 5a (Софиевская). ☎ 23 82 72. Call in advance for an English guide (☎ 23 84 62) or arrange a tour with a travel agency. Open W-M 10:30am-5pm; ticket office closes at 4pm. Closed last F of every month. Museum 2hv; grotto 2 hv, plus negotiable guide fee.)*

LITERATURE MUSEUM. (Литературный Музей; Literaturny Muzey.) Located in the beautiful, 19th-century summer residence of Prince Gagarin, this museum provides a fascinating look at the city's intellectual and cultural heritage, with an emphasis on Pushkin and Gogol. The collection includes the famous letter from Vorontsov to the Tsar asking that Pushkin be sent out of Odessa "for his own development," because he "is getting the notion into his head that he's a great writer." *(Lanzheronovskaya 2. ☎ 22 33 70. Difficult for non-Russian speakers. Open Tu-Su 10am-5pm. 9hv. English tour 54hv.)*

WAXWORKS MUSEUM. (Музей восковых скульптур; Muzey voskovikh skulptur.) The small museum features wax figures of the city's most famous inhabitants, starting with city governor, Spaniard De Ribas, and continuing on through city governor and benefactor Duke Vononsov, writer Bulgarin, and, of course, Pushkin. *(Ul. Rishelievskaya 4, in same building as the FGT travel agency. ☎ 22 34 36. English placards. Open daily 8:30am-10pm. 11hv, students 5hv. Free photo with adult admission.)*

PUSHKIN MUSEUM AND MEMORIAL. (Литературно-мемориальный музей Пушкина; Literaturno-memorialny Muzey Pushkina). This 1821 building was Pushkin's residence during his exile from St. Petersburg from 1823 to 1824 (see **The Arts,** p. 806). The museum devotes much space to the "novel in verse" *Eugene Onegin,* much of which he wrote in Odessa. *(Ul. Pushkinskaya 13. Enter through the courtyard. ☎ 24 92 55. Open Tu-Su 10am-5pm; last entrance 4:30pm. 9hv, students 6hv.)*

ARCHAEOLOGICAL MUSEUM. (Археологический музей; Arkheologichesky muzey). Displays ancient Greek and Roman artifacts found in the Black Sea region, including a collection of gold coins stored in a basement vault. Its Egyptian collection is the only one in Ukraine. Museum is closed until autumn 2003. *(Lanzheronovskaya 4. ☎ 22 63 02. Open Tu-Su 10am-5pm. 6hv. Call ahead to arrange English tour.)*

⚓🎵 BEACHES AND ENTERTAINMENT

Most of Odessa's beaches can be reached either by public transportation or on foot. **Arkadiya** (Аркадия), the city's most popular beach on summer nights, is the last stop on trolley or tram #5. *Marshrutka* #195 stops here as well. The shoreline from Park Shevchenko up to Arkadiya makes a good path for an early-morning jog. **Zolotoy Bereg** (Золотой Берег; Golden Shore) is farther away, but boasts the most impressive sea and surf. Trams #17 and 18 stop here and at the **Chayka** (Чайка) and **Kurortny** (Курортный) beaches. **Chornomorska** (Чёрноморска), the beach of the proletariat, lies just outside a high-rise monstrosity of a neighborhood. Take tram #29 to the last stop and keep going. Tram #5 stops at **Lanzheron** (Ланжерон), the beach closest to central Odessa, and at **Otrada** (Отрада). Some beaches are free, but others charge up to 10hv admission. The pricier beaches provide waiter service, beach chairs, and umbrellas.

The **Theater of Opera and Ballet** (Театр Оперы и Балета; Teatr Opery i Baleta), pr. Chaikovskovo 1 (Чайковского; ☎29 13 29), at the end of ul. Rishelevskaya, has nightly performances. Sunday matinees begin at noon and evening performances (Tu-Su) start at 6 or 7pm. Buy tickets a day in advance from the ticket office to the right of the theater. Russian theater tours are available before most performances. (2hv, for ticket holders only). Meet outside the theater 30min. before curtain. *(Central ticket office on the corner of Deribosovskaya and Rishelivskaya, but is under renovation in 2002. ☎25 69 03. Open Tu-Su 10am-6pm. 15-30hv, major acts 100-600hv.)*

◨ NIGHTLIFE

The restaurants, cafes, and bars on **ul. Deribasovskaya** hop all night with beer, vodka, and music ranging from Euro-techno to Slavic folk. Odessa's trendiest evening hot spots have recently sprouted in Arkadiya, along the beach. **Ibiza** offers live music on Sunday and attracts dancing 20-somethings on other nights. (Cover 15-35hv.) From Ibiza, take a right to get to **Club Assol,** located in a wooden boat and open all year. (Cover 15-25hv.) Taking a left at Ibiza leads you to **Itaka,** where you can dance between pseudo-Greek columns, and enjoy the occasional (male and female) striptease show. (Cover 20-50hv.)

▧ **Gambrinus** (Гамбринус), Deribasovskaya 31 (☎22 51 51), at the intersection with ul. Zhukova (Жукова). This historical landmark, which was the center of Odessa's cultural scene before the Revolution, can still sustain hours of drunken literary talk. The dark, spacious interior resembles a beer hall and is always refreshingly cool. Live folklore music Th-M 6-11pm. Open daily 10am-11pm.

Mick O'Neil's (a.k.a. Irish Pub), Deribasovskaya 13. Odessa's elite gather here to get noticed talking on cell phones and drinking beer (0.33L 9-23hv) and fancy fruit shakes (12hv). Live music daily 7:20-11:20pm. Breakfast 20-45hv. Open daily 24hr.

Fidel (Фидел), Deribasovskaya 23 (☎22 71 16). This Cuban-themed bar draws a devoted group of regulars who come to hear groups of Latin guitarists perform in the palm-lined interior (daily 8:45-11pm). Special events on weekends, starting at 11pm. Beer 7-16hv. 75g Georgian wine 14-60hv. Cuban entrees 17-45hv. Open 24hr. MC/V.

LVIV (ЛЬВІВ) ☎(8)0322

Divorced from Poland in 1945, Lviv has been tied to Kyiv for the last half-century, even though the two cities don't even speak the same language. While its Polish half-sister, Kraków, sees thousands of tourists each year, Lviv and its steeple-filled center greet few visitors. Nonetheless, the city teems with energy that can't be found anywhere else in Ukraine.

◨ TRANSPORTATION

Flights: Vul. Lyubinska (Любінська; ☎69 21 12). The travel agency **Traident** (Траидент), vul. Kopernika 18 (☎97 14 93), books tickets for most major airlines.

Trains: Pl. Vokzalna (Вокзальна; ☎748 20 68, info 005). **Tickets** at window #20-25 on the top floor. Tickets can also be bought at the railway ticket office at Hnatyuka 20 (Гнатюка). Tickets to non-CIS destinations must be bought at the railway station. Open M-Sa 8am-2pm and 3-8pm, Su 8am-2pm and 3-6pm. To: **Kyiv** (11hr., 3 per day, 51hv); **Odessa** (14hr.; 1 per day, 50hv); **Bratislava, SLK** (18hr., 1 per day, 215hv); **Budapest, HUN** (14hr., 1 per day, 250hv); **Kraków, POL** (8hr., 1 per day, 136hv); **Moscow, RUS** (29hr., 1 per day, 161hv); **Prague, CZR** (21hr., 1 per day, 336hv); **Przemyśl, POL** (3½hr., 1 per day, 36hv); **Warsaw, POL** (13hr., 1 per day, 130hv).

Buses: Main station at vul. Stryska 189 (Стрийська; ☎63 24 73). From town, take trolley #5 or *marshrutka* #80. The ticket offices are on the 2nd fl. To: **Kraków, POL** (8hr.,

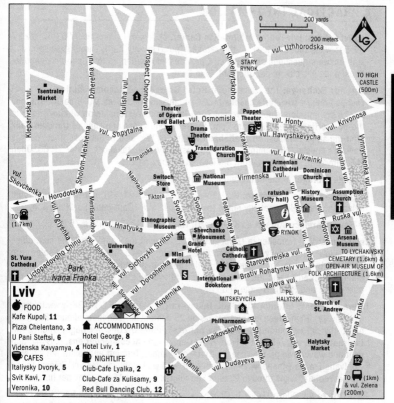

Lviv

🍎 FOOD
Kafe Kupol, 11
Pizza Chelentano, 3
U Pani Steftsi, 6
Videnska Kavyarnya, 4

☕ CAFES
Italiysky Dvoryk, 5
Svit Kavi, 7
Veronika, 10

🏠 ACCOMMODATIONS
Hotel George, 8
Hotel Lviv, 1

🎵 NIGHTLIFE
Club-Cafe Lyalka, 2
Club-Cafe za Kulisamy, 9
Red Bull Dancing Club, 12

UKRAINE

1 per day, 73hv); **Przemyśl, POL** (4hr., 11 per day, 29hv); **Warsaw, POL** (10hr., 3 per day, 82hv). Lviv also has a series of smaller **regional stations.** The one at vul. Khmelnytskoho 225 (Хмельницького; ☎52 04 89), can be reached by bus #4 from vul. Shevchenka (Шевченка). Buses to **Brest, BLR,** leave from here on odd-numbered days, and from the **train station** on even-numbered days (8hr., 2 per day, 30hv).

Public Transportation: Maps, available at the English-language bookstore (see below), include public transit lines for **trams, trolleys,** and **buses.** Buy tickets (0.45hv for trams and trolleys, 0.60hv for buses) on board from the badge-wearing conductor. 9hv fine for riding ticketless; don't forget to buy tickets for your baggage as well. *Marshrutki* 0.80hv. In Old Town, pl. Halitska (Галицька) is a hub for buses. A lot of road construction is being done in Lviv, which may lead to delays or temporary cancellations of trams.

✈ ORIENTATION

The center of town is **pl. Rynok** (Ринок), the old market square. Around it, a grid of streets forms **Old Town,** which holds most of the sights. A few blocks back toward the train station, the broad and stately **pr. Svobody** (Свободи) runs from the **Opera House** to **pl. Mitskevycha** (Міцкевича), Old Town's center of commerce. **Prospekt Shevchenko** (Шевченка) extends to the right of pl. Mitskevycha. Trams #1 and 9 run from the main train station to Old Town's center, tram #6 to the north end of pr. Svobody. Tram #9 goes from Old Town to the station.

⚡ PRACTICAL INFORMATION

Tourist Offices: Lviv Tourist Information Center, pl. Rynek 1 (Рінок; ☎97 57 67; fax 97 57 51; www.about.lviv.ua), in the *ratusha* (ратуша; city hall). The English-speaking staff answers questions about the city, provides information on tours and accommodations, and sells city maps. Open M-F 9am-6pm.

Currency Exchange: The exchange in **Hotel George** (see **Accommodations,** p. 844) cashes AmEx/V **traveler's checks** at 2% commission and gives MC/V **cash advances** for 3% commission. Open daily 9am-7pm. There is a **Western Union** window (#10) in the **post office.** Open M-F 9am-7pm, Sa 9am-2pm. Other branches of **UkrExim** bank offer the same services. An **Availabank** window (#12), also at the post office, cashes traveler's checks (2% commission) and gives MC/V cash advances. (☎97 29 66. Open M-F 9am-1pm, 2pm-4pm). Both are located on the 2nd fl.

Luggage Storage: At the train station. 1.50hv. Open 24hr.

English-Language Bookstore: Pl. Mitskevycha 8 (☎72 27 29). A small international selection. Also sells great city **maps** (5-7hv). Open M-F 10am-6pm, Sa 10am-3pm.

24-Hour Pharmacy: Apteka #28 (Аптека), vul. Zelena 33 (Зелена; ☎75 37 63).

Telephones: Vul. Doroshenka (Дорошенка) 39, around the corner from the post office (see below). Open daily 7am-11pm. Blue phones marked "Таксофон" (Taksofon) are operated by phone cards available at the post office and some kiosks. **Utel** cards, mainly for intercity and international calls, are available at the telephone center, the post office, and Hotels George and Lviv.

Internet Access: Internet Klub, vul. Dudayeva (Дудаева; ☎72 27 38; www.internet-club.lviv.ua). High-speed Internet access on 23 computers. 15min. minimum. 8am-midnight 4hv per hr., midnight-8am 2hv per hr. Printing 0.20hv per page. Open 24hr. **Internet Cafe,** vul. Zelena 14. From Hotel George (see **Accommodations,** p. 844), turn right and walk down pr. Shevchenka to the monument. Turn left and follow the street to vul. Ivana Franka (Ивана Франка), turn right, and walk until you see vul. Zelena; follow the "интернет" signs through Pizzeria San Piemo. 1hv per 15min., 3hv per hr.

Post Office: Vul. Slovatskoho 1 (Словатского; ☎72 39 43), 1 block from Park Ivana Franka, to the right as you face the university. **Poste Restante** on the 2nd fl., window #3. Take claim slip downstairs to window #3 to collect package. ID required. Open M-F 8am-8pm, Sa 8am-6pm, Su 8am-4pm.

Postal Code: 79 000.

🏠 ACCOMMODATIONS

Hotel Lviv, vul. Chornovola 7 (Чорновола; ☎79 22 70; fax 79 25 47), at the northern tip of pr. Svobody. Take tram #6 from the train station to the 1st stop after you see the Opera House on your right. Walk back to the Opera House and turn right on pr. Chornovola; it's the concrete building. A bit noisy, but central. Spartan singles with TV 35hv, with bath 70hv; doubles 25hv/50hv; triples or quads 20hv. ❶

Hotel George (Готель Жорж), pl. Mitskevycha 1 (☎74 21 82; fax 97 11 44). Take tram #1 from the train station to "Дорошенка" (Doroshenka). Walk another block and head right at the park—the hotel is the big pink building at the end. The George is located in a neo-Renaissance building constructed by Viennese architects at the turn of the century. Known for its luxury suites, the George can also accommodate budget travelers, who are willing to go without their own bath. Breakfast included. Singles 111hv, with bath 361hv; doubles 157hv/381hv. ❷

◘ FOOD

Pl. Rynok is the restaurant and cafe center. The most convenient **market** is **Halytsky Rynok** (Галицький Ринок), behind the flower stands across from St. Andrew's Church and one block from Hotel George. (Open in summer daily 7am-6pm.) A little farther out is the cheaper and bigger **Tsentralny Rynok** (Центральний), called **Krakivsky Rynok** (Краківський) by the locals. (Open M-Sa 6am-9pm.) There are several 24hr. grocery stores; **Mini Market,** vul. Doroshenka 6, is a block from the Grand Hotel. (Closed 9:30-10am.) Lviv is also famous for its *Svitoch* confectionery, now a subsidiary of Kraft foods. The company's main store is at the intersection of pr. Svobody and vul. Tiktora (Open M-F 9am-9pm, Sa 9am-8pm, Su 11am-6pm. MC/V.)

Videnska Kavyarnya (Віденська Кавярня), pl. Svobody 12 (☎72 20 21), across from the Shevchenko statue. A Viennese coffeehouse through and through. This is Lviv's trendiest place to have dessert, but it serves great dinner and breakfast as well. English menu. Breakfast 3-13hv. Entrees 10-25hv. Desserts 3-10hv. **ATM** inside. Open daily 9am-11pm. MC/V. ❷

Kafe Kupol (Кафе Купол), vul. Tchaikovskovo 37 (Чайковского; ; ☎74 42 54). From Hotel George walk down pr. Shevchenka, turn right on the second street, and continue to a hill; Kafe Kupol is the 2nd house. Have dinner under ancient trees on the patio's wooden tables or in the more elegant 1920s-style dining room. Entrees 15-30hv. Salads 2hv. Open daily 11am-11pm. MC/V. ❷

U Pani Steftsi (У Пані Стефци), pr. Svobody 8. Traditional Ukrainian food and music, carved wooden tables, and waitresses in colorful, traditional garb. Entrees 10-15hv. Open daily 10am-10pm. ❶

Pizza Chelentano (Челентано), pr. Svobody 24, behind the Opera to the right. Popular with the after-theater and student crowds. Pizza made to order—choose from a number of meat and vegetable toppings. Basic cheese pizza 4.50hv. Toppings 1.50-3hv. Salads 1.50-2hv. Crepes 1-3.40hv. Open daily 10am-11pm. ❶

◪ CAFES

Lviv's cafe culture is so renowned that there are even songs about it. Maybe it's the Viennese atmosphere, but the elegant little cafes always attract a crowd of locals happy to have a cup of joe with friends.

Italiysky Dvoryk (Італійський Дворик), pl. Rynok 6. Lviv's unpretentious crowd of intellectuals and art-lovers sip coffee (1.20hv) among Renaissance statues in the courtyard of a 16th-century Italian merchant's house. A museum upstairs displays his most fashionable belongings. Walk through the museum entrance to reach the cafe. Open daily 10am-8pm.

Veronika (Вероніка), pr. Shevchenko 21 (☎97 81 28). Pick your dessert of choice from the beautiful display behind the counter in this elegant cafe. The cakes and truffles are absolutely sinful—you won't be able to resist ordering more than one. Piece of cake 4.50hv, truffle 0.90hv. Open daily 10am-11pm.

Svit Kavi (Світ Кави; Coffee World), pl. Katedralna 6 (Катедральна), behind the cathedral. The exotic blends (2-7hv) at this tiny coffee shop have become famous. 100g of coffee beans 5.20-110hv. Open daily 9am-10pm.

UKRAINE

◉ SIGHTS

Lviv's churches, squares, and ancient tenements create a city as splendid as Prague or St. Petersburg. With a heavy Polish and Austrian influence, the city has a Western air. If you are specifically interested in seeing churches, the best time to visit is between 5 and 7pm, when doors open for the faithful.

PROSPEKT SVOBODY (FREEDOM BOULEVARD). From the dazzling Theater of Opera and Ballet (Театр Опери а Балету; Teatr Opery a Baletu; see **Entertainment,** p. 848) walk down the boulevard past shops and hotels, lodged behind the facades of old Polish apartments. The promenade that runs through the center is popular for early-evening ice cream, strolling, and intense chess matches. In the middle of pr. Svobody, a monument to the celebrated national poet Taras Shevchenko overlooks patriotic parades and other high-energy gatherings. At the end of pr. Svobody, the Mickiewicz statue honors the Polish poet and patriot and serves as a site for concerts, heated political discussions, and the occasional Hare Krishna sing-along.

OLD TOWN

PLOSCHAD RYNOK. This historic market square lies in the heart of the city and is surrounded by richly decorated merchant homes dating from the 16th to 18th centuries. The **town hall** (ратуша; ratusha) is a 19th-century addition. Climb up the tower's 366 steps for a view of the old city. *(Enter to the left of the main entrance, downstairs. ☎97 57 73. Open M-F 11am-5pm, Sa-Su 11am-8pm. 10hv, children 2hv.)*

BOYM'S CHAPEL. (Каплиця Боїмів; Kaplytsya Boimiv.) The Renaissance Boym's Chapel is the only example of religious architecture in Lviv that serves more as a tourist attraction than as a house of worship. It was commissioned in the early 17th century by a rich Hungarian merchant, Gregory Boym, and contains the remains of 14 members of his family. *(Open May-Oct. daily 11am-5pm; Nov.-Apr. F-Su 11am-5pm. 1hv, students 0.50hv.)*

GOLDEN ROSE SYNAGOGUE. For centuries, Lviv was an important center of Jewish culture. Today, little remains of the Golden Rose Synagogue, which was built in the late 16th century and destroyed by the Nazis in 1942. Walk up vul. Staroyevrejska (Old Jewish Road) and it will be on your left before the Arsenal Museum. The Lviv Tourist Information Center (see **Tourist Office,** p. 844) offers guided tours of the city's Jewish heritage.

OTHER SIGHTS. The massive **Assumption Church** (Успенська Церква; Uspenska Tserkva) lies just up vul. Pidvalna (Підвальна); enter through the archway. Next to the church, **Kornyakt's Tower** (Башта Корнякта; Bashta Kornyakta) hoists a bell 60m above ground. A stroll up vul. Federova, then a left on vul. Virmenska, lands you at the barricaded **Armenian Cathedral** (Вірменський Собор; Virmensky Sobor).

OUTSIDE THE OLD TOWN

HIGH CASTLE HILL. (Высокий Замок; Vysoky Zamok.) For a great workout and an ever better view of the city, climb up High Castle Hill, the former site of the Galician king's palace. A Ukrainian flag and a cross—the two most potent symbols of Lviv in the age of Ukrainian independence—sit high atop the hill. *(Follow vul. Krivonoca (Кривоноса) from its intersection with Hotny and Halytskono. Go until you pass #39, then take a left down the dirt road and wind your way up around the hill counter-clockwise.)*

LICHAKIVSKY CEMETERY. (Личаківський Цвинтар; Lychakivsky Tsvyntar.) Combine a trip to the nearby open-air museum (see below) with the cemetery. The paths of Lviv's famous necropolis provide a pleasant strolling ground. For the most instructive visit, follow Mechnykova down past the empty space to the main gate. Upon entering through the main gate, follow the path to the right to visit the graves of famous Ukrainian artists. On the left, a hammer-armed Stakhanovite decorates the eternal bed of **Ivan Franko** (Іван Франко), poet, socialist activist, and celebrated national hero. *(Take tram #4 or 7 from the beginning of vul. Lichakivska (Личаківська), and get off at the first stop after the sharp right turn. ☎ 75 54 15. Open daily 9am-9pm. 3hv, students 1hv. Tours in English 25hv for up 10 people. Call ahead.)*

IVAN FRANKO PARK

From pr. Svobody, head down Hnatyuka, then take a left on Sichovka Stritsiv to **Ivan Franko Park** (Парк ім. Ивана Франка; Park im. Ivana Franka), which faces the columned facade of **Lviv University.** Walk uphill through the park to **St. Yura's Cathedral** (Собор св. Юра; Sobor sv. Yura). The interior of this 18th-century wonder houses an elaborate altar. Outside, the equestrian dragon-slayer Yura (George) guards the entrance. *(Open daily 7am-1pm and 3-8pm.)* Toward the train off vul. Horodetska is **St. Elizabeth's Cathedral.** Constructed by Poles when they first settled in Lviv, its spires purposefully reach higher than St. Yura's domes to assert the dominance of Polish Catholicism over Ukrainian Orthodoxy. Now, both churches have become Uniate, the predominant religion of the region.

🏛 MUSEUMS

▨ OPEN-AIR MUSEUM OF FOLK ARCHITECTURE AND RURAL LIFE. (Музей Народної Архітектури та Побуту у Львові; Muzey Narodnoi Architektury ta Pobutu u Lvovi), at Shevchenkivsky Hay (Шевченківський Гай). This open-air ethnographic museum features a collection of wooden houses (скансен; skansen) from all around Western Ukraine. *(From vul. Doroshenka, take tram #2 or 7 to Mechnikova, cross the street, and head all the way up the hill, bearing right at the top to reach the outdoor museum. Call ☎ 71 23 60 to arrange a tour. Open Apr.-Oct. Tu-Su 11am-7pm; Nov.-Mar. 10am-6pm. 1.50hv, children 0.75hv. Tours in English 10hv.)*

HISTORY MUSEUM. (Історичний Музей; Istorychny Muzey.) A complex of museums, each with separate admission price (0.50-1hv). The museum at #4 was revamped was declared and recounts episodes of the city's history that were ignored by the Soviets. Caught between Nazi Germany and Soviet Russia in World War II, Lviv's Ukrainian citizens first fought on the side of the former and later faced repression from both. Other rooms show the birth of the Ukrainian nationalist movement in the 19th and early 20th centuries and the horrors of Soviet occupation. The King's Hall (Королівських Зал), at #6, presents military clothing, paintings, and other household treasures of the Italian *mascalzone* (rascals) who lived here in the 16th century. In the 17th century, the building was home to Polish King Jan III Sobielski, and it was here that the famous "eternal peace" of 1686 was signed. The agreement split Ukraine in two—the Western half went to the Polish empire, and the Eastern to the Russian empire. Check out the 18th-century music box (1hv). The museum at #24 traces the history of the region from Kyivan Rus to the Galician Kingdom in the 13th century, and finally to its incorporation into the Polish empire in 1686. *(Pl. Rynok #4, 6, and 24. ☎ 72 06 71. Open Th-Tu 10am-5pm. English tours depending on availability of guides, 5-10hv.)*

ENTERTAINMENT

Pr. Svobody fills up after lunch with colorful characters singing wartime and harvest tunes with accordion accompaniment. By 8pm, the sounds of light jazz from sidewalk cafes fill the avenue, coffeehouses cloud up with smoke and reverberate with political discussion, and auditoria echo with arias or tragic monologues. Purchase tickets at the *teatralny kasy* (театральни каси; box office), pr. Svobody 37. (Open M-Sa 10am-1pm and 2-5pm.) Indoor and outdoor concerts, theatre performances, and competitions are held at various venues around the city during the **Lviv City Days** (☎97 59 13) on the third weekend of September. Easter is celebrated annually in the **Museum for Folk Architecture** (☎97 59 13) with folk and religious traditions, and games for children.

■ **Teatr Opery Ta Baletu** (Театр Опери Та Балету), pr. Svobody 1 (☎72 88 60). You don't have to love opera and you don't even need a tux. Great space, great voices, great set. Hear Verdi, Puccini, or Mozart (10-400hv). Ticket office open daily 11am-7pm.

Philharmoniya (Філармонія), vul. Tchaikovskoho 7 (☎72 10 42), around the corner from Hotel George. Less frequent performances than the Opera, but many renowned guest performers. Ticket office open Sept.-May 11am-2pm and 4-6pm. 5-20hv.

Organ and Chamber Music (Будинок органної і камерної музики), S. Bandery 8 (Бандери; ☎39 88 42). Tickets at the door. To reach the concert hall, take tram #9 or 2 down S. Bandery and get off at the Lviv Polytechnic stop. Concerts at 5pm. 4hv.

NIGHTLIFE

■ **Club-Cafe Lyalka** (Клуб-Кафе Лялька), vul. Halytskoho 1 (Галицького; ☎98 08 09; www.city.lviv.ua/lyalka), below the Teatr Lyalok (Театр Лялок; Puppet Theater). The management guarantees that "everything you see here is real, even dreams, feelings, and hallucinations." The program varies between disco, live performances, and art installations; consult the website beforehand. Wine 3hv. Cover 7-10hv, depending on program. Open M-Th 11am-midnight, F-Su 11am-2am, or when last guest leaves.

Red Bull Dancing Club, vul. Ivan Franka 15 (☎75 32 72). This downstairs "discotheque" combines techno music with run-down brick walls. A bit slow on weeknights. Cover US$5. Dancing daily 10pm-3pm.

Club-Cafe za Kulisamy (Клуб-Кафе за Кулісами), vul. Tchaikovskoho 7, on the 2nd fl. of the Philharmonic. Enter through the left door. Enthusiastic students frequent this small, hidden bar. Try *Bamburyk* (1hv), a shot of Vodka mixed with tomato juice, pepper, onions, garlic, and salt. Bite the lemon for the right finish. Open daily noon-midnight.

GATEWAY CITIES

VIENNA, AUSTRIA   ☎(0)222

EUROS

AUS$1 = EUR€0.55	1EUR€ = AUS$1.82
CDN$1 = EUR€0.65	1EUR€ = CDN$1.55
NZ$1 = EUR€0.47	1EUR€ = NZ$2.13
UK£1 = EUR€1.57	1EUR€ = UK£0.64
US$1 = EUR€1.01	1EUR€ = US$0.99
ZAR1 = EUR€0.09	1EUR€ = ZAR10.69

PHONE CODES   Country code: **43**. International dialing prefix: **43**.

Vienna (Wien) is a cultural monument, a living memorial to the geniuses of music, art, and academia who once walked its streets. This is where Freud struggled with the human psyche, Mozart found inspiration for symphonies, and Kafka crafted his masterpieces. At the height of its artistic foment at the turn of the century, during the smoky days of the great cafe culture, the Viennese were already self-mockingly referring to their city as the "merry apocalypse." Vienna has a reputation for living absent-mindedly in this grand past, but as the last fringes of the Iron Curtain have been drawn back, Vienna has tried to re-establish itself as the gateway to Eastern Europe and a place where creativity and experimentalism still thrive.

VISAS. EU citizens do not require visas to visit, study, or work in Austria. Citizens of Australia, Canada, New Zealand, South Africa, and the US can visit for up to 90 days without a visa.

✈ INTERCITY TRANSPORTATION

Flights: The **airport** is 18km from the city center; the cheapest way to reach the city is S7 "Flughafen/Wolfsthal," which stops at **Wien Mitte** (30min., every 30min. 5am-9:30pm, €3). The heart of the city, **Stephanspl.**, is a short metro ride from Wien Mitte on the U3 line. It's more convenient (but also more expensive) to take the **Vienna Airport Lines Shuttle Bus,** which runs between the airport and the City Air Terminal, at the Hilton opposite Wien Mitte (every 20min. 6:30am-11:10pm, every 30min. midnight-6am; €5). **Buses** connect the airport to the **Südbahnhof** and **Westbahnhof** (see below; every 30min. 8:55am-7:25pm, every hr. 8:20pm-8:25am).

Trains: Vienna has two main international train stations. For general train information, dial ☎17 17 or check www.bahn.at. **Westbahnhof**, XV, Mariahilfer str. 132. To: **Budapest, HUN** (3-4hr., 6 per day, €32). For other destinations, visit the **info counter** (open daily 7:30am-8:40pm). **Südbahnhof**, X, Wiedner Gürtel 1a. To get to the city take tram D to "Opera/Karlspl." The **info counter** is open daily 6:30am-9:20pm. To **Krakow, POL** (7-8hr., 3 per day, €36) and **Prague, CZR.**

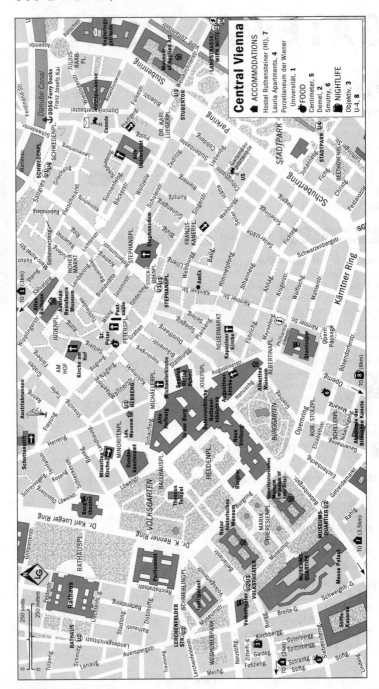

Central Vienna

🛏 ACCOMMODATIONS
Hostel Ruthensteiner (HI), 7
Lauria Apartments, 4
Porzellaneum der Wiener
Universität, 1

🍴 FOOD
Centimeter, 5
Demel, 2
Smutny, 6

🎷 NIGHTLIFE
Objektiv, 3
U-4, 8

ORIENTATION

Vienna is divided into 23 **districts** *(bezirke)*. The first is the *Innenstadt* (city center), defined by the **Ringstraße** on three sides and the Danube Canal on the fourth. The Ringstraße (or "Ring") consists of many different segments, each with its own name: **Opernring, Kärntner Ring, Burgring, Dr. K. Renner Ring, Schubertring, Stubenring,** and **Dr. Karl Lueger Ring.** Many of Vienna's major attractions are in District I and immediately around the Ringstraße. Districts II-IX spread out from the city center following the clockwise, one-way traffic of the Ring. The remaining districts expand from another ring, the **Gürtel** ("belt"). Like the Ring, this major two-way thoroughfare has numerous segments, including **Margaretengürtel, Währinger Gürtel,** and **Neubaugürtel.** Street signs indicate the district number *before* the street and number. *Let's Go* includes district numbers for establishments in Roman numerals before the street address.

LOCAL TRANSPORTATION

Public Transportation: Transportation in Vienna is extensive and dependable; call ☎580 00 for general info. The **public transportation information line** has live operators that give public transportation directions to any point in the city. (☎790 91 05. Open M-W and F 8am-3pm, Th 8am-5:30pm.)

Local Transportation: The **subway** (U-Bahn), **tram** (Straßenbahn), **elevated train** (S-Bahn), and **bus** systems operate under one ticket system. A single fare (€1.60 if purchased on a bus, €1.40 if purchased in advance), lets you travel to any single destination in the city and switch from bus to U-Bahn to tram to S-Bahn, as long as your travel is uninterrupted. To validate a ticket, punch it in the machine immediately upon entering the first vehicle, but don't stamp it again when you switch trains. A ticket stamped twice or not stamped at all is invalid, and plainclothed inspectors may fine you €40 plus the ticket price. Other options are a 24hr. pass (€5), a 3-day "rover" ticket (€11), a 7-day pass (€12; valid M 9am to the following M 9am), or an 8-day pass (€22; valid any 8 days, not necessarily consecutive; valid also for several people traveling together). The **Vienna Card** (€16) offers free travel for 72hr. as well as discounts at museums, sights, and events. **Night buses** run every 30min. along most tram, subway, and major bus routes. "N" signs with yellow cat eyes designate night bus stops. (€1.10 or 4 for €3.30; day transport passes not valid.) A complete night bus schedule is available at bus info counters in U-Bahn stations.

Taxis: ☎313 00, 401 00, or 601 60. Stands at Westbahnhof, Südbahnhof, Karlsplatz in the city center, and by the Bermuda Dreiecke. Accredited taxis have yellow-and-black signs on the roof. €2, plus €1 per km. €2 extra Su, holidays, and from 11pm-6am.

PRACTICAL INFORMATION

Tourist Office: I, Albertinapl. (www.info.wien.at). Follow Operng. up 1 block from the Opera House. Dispenses a free map of the city and the pamphlet *Youth Scene,* and books rooms for a €3 fee plus 1-night deposit. Open daily 9am-7pm.

Embassies: Generally, each country's embassy and consulate are located in the same building, listed under *"Botschaften"* or *"Konsulate"* in the phone book. **Australia:** IV, Mattiellistr. 2 (☎50 674; www.australian-embassy.at). **Canada:** I, Laurenzerberg 2 (☎531 38 30 00; fax 38 33 21; www.dfait-maeci.gc.ca). **Ireland:** I, Rotenturmstr. 16-18, 5th fl. (☎71 54 24 60; vienna@iveath.irlgov.ie). **New Zealand: Consulate** only, XIX, Karl-Tornay-g. 34 (☎318 85 05; p.sunley@demmer.at). **South Africa:** XIX, Sandg. 33 (☎320 64 93; fax 64 93 51; www.southafrican-embassy.at). **UK:** III, Jauresg. 12 (☎716 13 51 51; fax 13 59 00; www.britishembassy.at). **US:** IX, Boltzmanng. 16 (☎313 39; fax 310 06 82; www.usembassy-vienna.at).

Currency Exchange: ATMs are your best bet. The 24hr. exchange at the **main post office** has excellent rates.

Bi-Gay-Lesbian Organizations: The BGLT community in Vienna is more integrated than in other Austrian cities. Pick up either the monthly magazine (in German) called *Extra Connect* or the free monthly publication *Bussi* at any gay bar, cafe, or club. **Rosa Lila Villa,** VI, Linke Wienzeile 102 (gay men: ☎586 43 43; lesbians: ☎586 81 50), is a favored resource and social center for homosexual Viennese and visitors alike. Friendly staff speaks English and provides info, a library, and nightclub listings. Open M-F 5-8pm.

Laundromat: Schnell und Sauber, VII, Westbahnhofstr. 60 (☎524 64 60). From Westbahnhof, take tram #18 to "Urban-Loritzpl." 6kg wash €4.50, dry €1 per 20min.

Emergency: Police ☎133. **Ambulance** ☎144. **Fire** ☎122.

Crisis Lines: All hotlines locate English speakers. **Rape Crisis Hotline:** ☎523 22 22. M 10am-6pm, Tu 2-6pm, W 10am-2pm, Th 5-9pm. **24hr. immediate help:** ☎717 19.

Medical Assistance: Allgemeines Krankenhaus, IX, Währinger Gürtel 18-20 (☎404 00 19 64). **Emergency care** ☎141. **24hr. pharmacy** ☎15 50. Consulates offer lists of English-speaking physicians, or call **Fachärzte Zugeck** (☎512 18 18; open 24hr.).

Internet Access: bigNET.internet.cafe, I, Karntnerstr. 61 (☎503 98 44); I, Hoher markt 8-9 (☎533 29 39); and new largest Internet cafe in Austria, Mariahilferstr. €3.50 per 30min. Hip English-speaking "crew." **Cafe Stein,** IX, Wahringerstr. 6-8 (☎31 97 24 19). €4 per 30min. **Cafe Einstein,** VIII, Rathauspl. 4 (☎405 26 26). Open M-F 7am-2am, Sa 10am-2am, Su 10am-midnight.

Post Office: Hauptpostamt, I, Fleischmarkt 19. Vast structure contains exchange, phone, fax, and mail services. Open 24hr. Address **Poste Restante** to "LASTNAME, Firstname; *Postlagernde Briefe;* Hauptpostamt; Fleischmarkt 19; A-1010 Wien."

Postal Codes: 1st district A-1010, 2nd A-1020, 3rd A-1030, etc., to the 23rd A-1230.

VIENNA	❶	❷	❸	❹	❺
ACCOM.	under €9	€9-15	€16-30	€31-70	over €70
FOOD	under €5	€5-10	€11-16	€17-25	over €25

■ ACCOMMODATIONS

In high season (June-September), reserve a room at least five days ahead, or come before 9am for a shot at a same-day spot. If your choice is full, ask to be put on a waiting list. University dorms convert into hostels in high season. *Pensionen* ❹ in districts VII, VIII, and IX offer singles from €30 and doubles from €40.

▨ **Hostel Ruthensteiner (HI),** XV, Robert-Hamerlingg. 24 (☎893 42 02; www.hostelruthensteiner.com). Turn right on Mariahilferstr. and continue until Haidmannsg. Turn left, then take the first right on Robert-Hammerlingg; continue to the middle of the block. This hostel is an exceptional value with knowledgeable, English-speaking staff, spotless rooms, snack bar, and rose-filled courtyard. Kitchen available. Breakfast €2.50. Internet €2. 4-night max. stay. Reception 24hr. Reservations recommended, but owners often hold beds for spontaneous travelers. "The Outback" summer dorm €10.50; 3- to 10-bed dorms €12-13.50; singles and doubles from €20-22. AmEx/MC/V. ❷

Lauria Apartments, VII, Kaiserstr. 77, apt. #8 (☎522 25 55). From Westbahnhof, take tram #5 to "Burgg." Find solace among backpackers of all sorts. Fully equipped kitchens. Sheets and TV included. 2-night min. Reception 8am-noon. Dorms €12.50; singles and student-bunk twins €35; doubles €40, with shower €60; student-bunk triples €45; triples €75-120. AmEx/MC/V, except for dorm beds. ❷

Porzellaneum der Wiener Universität, IX, Porzellang. 30 (☎317 72 82; fax 317 72 82; www.neuhotels.com). From Südbahnhof, take tram D (dir.: Nußdorf) to "Fürsteng." From Westbahnhof, take tram #5 to "Franz-Josefs Bahnhof," then tram D (dir.: Südbahnhof) to "Fürsteng." Great location in the student district. No lockers. Reception 24hr. Call ahead. Singles €16-18; doubles €30-35; quads €56-64. ❸

🍴 FOOD

Restaurants near **Kärntnerstr.** tend to be pricey—try north of the university near the Votivkirche (U-2: Schottentor), where **Universitätsstr.** and **Währingerstr.** meet, or the area around the **Rechte** and **Linke Wienzeile** near Naschmarkt (U-4: Kettenbrückeg.). The **Naschmarkt** is full of vendors selling delicacies to snack on while shopping at the city's best flea market (Sa-Su only). For the basics, try the Supermarkets **Billa, Hofer,** and **Spar** (most closed Su). Kosher groceries are available at the **Kosher Supermarket,** II, Hollandstr. 10 (☎216 96 75).

🍴 **Smutny,** I, Elisabethstr. 8 (☎587 13 56; www.smutny.com). Exit Karlspl. on Elizabethstr. and it is directly on the right. A green-tiled, modern restaurant offering delicious traditional Austrian schnitzel and gulasch. Try the *Menü* (€7; veggie €6.50). ❷

🍴 **Demel,** I, Kohlmarkt 14 (☎535 17 17; ademel@demel.at), 5min. from the Stephansdom down Graben. The most luxurious Viennese *Konditorei* (bakery), Demel was confectioner to the imperial court until the empire dissolved. All of the chocolate is made fresh every morning. A fantasy of mirrored rooms, cream walls, and a display case of legendary desserts. Waitresses in convent-black serve divine confections (€5). Don't miss the *crème-du-jour.* Open daily 10am-7pm. AmEx/MC/V. ❷

Centimeter, IX, Liechtensteinstr. 42 (☎319 84 04). Take tram D to "Bauernfeldpl." This chain offers huge portions of greasy Austrian fare and an large beer selection. Pay by the centimeter. Schnitzel with salad and fries €5.80. *Maß* (1L) €6. Meter (8.33L beers) €17.60. Other **branches** at VIII, Lenaug. 11 (☎405 78 08), and VII, Stiftg. 4 (☎524 33 29). Open M-F 10am-2am, Sa 11am-2am, Su 11am-midnight. AmEx/MC/V. ❷

👁 SIGHTS

Viennese streets are by turns startling, scuzzy, and grandiose; the best way to see the city is simply to get lost. To wander in a more organized manner, get the brochure *Vienna from A to Z* (€4) or *Walks in Vienna* at the tourist office. **Vienna Bike,** IX, Wasag. (☎319 12 58), runs 2-3hr. **cycling tours** (€20). Another great way to see the city is to ride around the Ring on trams #1 or 2.

INSIDE THE RING

District I is Vienna's social and geographical epicenter as well as a gallery of the history of aesthetics, from Romanesque to *Jugendstil* (Art Nouveau).

STEPHANSPLATZ, GRABEN, AND PETERSPLATZ. Right at the heart of Vienna, this square is home to the massive **Stephansdom** (St. Stephen's Cathedral), Vienna's most treasured symbol. The elevator in the North Tower leads to a view of the city; the 343 steps of the South Tower climb to a 360° view. Downstairs in the **catacombs,** the skeletons of thousands of plague victims line the walls. The **Gruft** (vault) stores all of the Habsburg innards. From Stephanspl., follow **Graben** for a landscape of Art Nouveau architecture, including the **Ankerhaus** (#10), the red-marble **Grabenhof** by Otto Wagner, and the underground public toilet complex, designed by Adolf Loos. Graben leads to **Peterspl.** and the 1663 **Pestsaüle** (Plague Column), built to commemorate the passing of the Black Death. *(Take U1 or U3 to*

"Stephansplatz." North Tower open Apr.-June and Sept.-Oct. 8:30am-4pm. €3.50. South Tower open 9am-5:30pm. €2.50. Gruft tours M-Sa 10-11:30am and 1-4:30pm every 30 min.; Su and holidays 1:30-4:30pm every 30 min. €3.)

ALTES RATHAUS, AM HOF, AND FREYUNG. The **Altes Rathaus** (Old Town Hall) served as the city center from 1316 to 1885. It's also home to the **Austrian Resistance Museum,** chronicling anti-Nazi activity during World War II and temporary exhibits. *(Wipplingerstr. 8. Backtrack to Hoher Markt and follow Wipplingerstr. Open M and W-Th 9am-5pm. Free.)* Follow Drahtg. to Am Hof, a grand courtyard which was once a medieval jousting square and now houses the **Kirche am Hof** (Church of the Nine Choirs of Angels). Just west of Am Hof, **Freyung** is an uneven square with the **Austriabrunnen** (Austria fountain) in the center. Freyung ("sanctuary") got its name from the **Schottenstift** (Monastery of the Scots) just behind the fountain, where fugitives could claim asylum in medieval times. It was once used for public executions, but the annual **Christkindl markt** held here blots out such unpleasant memories.

HOFBURG. The sprawling **Hofburg** was the winter residence of the Habsburg emperors. Construction began in 1279, and hodgepodge additions and renovations continued until the end of the family's reign in 1918. When you come through the **Michaelertor,** you'll first enter the courtyard called **In der Burg** ("within the fortress"). On your left is the red-and-black-striped **Schweizertor** (Swiss Gate), erected in 1552. On your right is the entrance to the **Kaiserappartements** (Imperial Apartments), which were once the private quarters of Emperor Franz Josef and Empress Elisabeth. Beneath the stairs is the entrance to the **Weltliche und Geistliche Schatzkammer** ("Worldy and Spiritual Treasury"), containing Habsburg jewels, the "horn of a unicorn" (really a narwahl's horn), and a tooth from the mouth of John the Baptist. *(From Freyung, follow Herreng. to Michaelerpl. and head through the half-moon-shaped Michaelertor. Open W-M 10am-6pm. €7, students €5. Free English audio guide.)* Attached to the northeast side of the Alte Burg is the **Stallburg,** the home of the **Royal Lipizzaner stallions**. The cheapest way to get a glimpse of the famous steeds is to watch them train. *(From mid-Feb. to June and late Aug. to early Nov. Tu-F 10am-noon, except when the horses tour. Tickets sold at Josefspl., Gate 2. €11.60, children €5.)* The **Neue Burg** houses the fantastic **Völkerkunde Museum** and the **Österreichische Nationalbibliothek** (Austrian National Library), whose buff statues are said to have inspired the 11-year-old Arnold Schwarzenegger. *(☎ 53 41 03 97. Open Oct.-June M-F 9am-7pm, Sa 9am-12:45pm; July-Aug. and Sept. 23-30 M-F 9am-3:45pm, Sa 9am-12:45pm; closed Sept. 1-22. Museum €7.30, students €5.)* High masses are still held in the 14th-century **Augustinerkirche** (St. Augustine's Church), and the **Herzgrüftel** (Little Heart Crypt) contains the Hapsburgs' hearts. *(Open M-Sa 10am-6pm, Su 11am-6pm. Mass 11am. Free.)*

OUTSIDE THE RING

As the city expands beyond the Ring in all directions, the distance between notable sights also expands. But what the area outside the Ring gives up in accessibility, it makes up for in its varied attractions.

KARLSPLATZ AND NASCHMARKT. Karlspl. is home to Vienna's most beautiful Baroque church, the **Karlskirche,** an eclectic masterpiece with a Neoclassical portico, a Baroque dome and towers on either side. *(Take U1, U2, or U4 to "Karlspl." Or, from the Hofburg, walk down Tegetthoffstr. to Neuer Markt and follow Kärntnerstr. to Karlspl. Open M-F 7:30am-7pm, Sa 8:30am-7pm, Su 9am-7pm. Free.)* West of Karlspl., along Linke Wienzeile, is the **Naschmarkt,** a colorful, multi-ethnic food bazaar. On Saturdays, the Naschmarkt becomes a massive flea market. *(Open M-F 7am-6pm, Sa 7am-1pm.)*

ZENTRALFRIEDHOF. The **Zentralfriedhof** (Central Cemetery) is the place to pay respects to your favorite (de)composer. Behind **Tor II** (2nd gate) are Beethoven, Strauss, and an honorary monument to Mozart, whose true resting place is an unmarked paupers' grave in the **Cemetery of St. Mark,** III, Leberstr. 6-8. **Tor I** leads to the **Jewish Cemetery**, which mirrors the fate of Vienna's Jewish population—many of the headstones are cracked, broken, or neglected because the families of most of the dead have left Austria. **Tor III** leads to the Protestant section and the new Jewish cemetery. *(Main entrance at XI, Simmeringer Hauptstr. 234. Take tram #71 from Schwarzenbergpl., tram #72 from Schlachthaus, or S7 to "Zentralfriedhof."*

🏛 MUSEUMS

Vienna owes its selection of masterpieces to the acquisitive Habsburgs, as well as to the city's crop of art schools and world-class artists. All city-run museums are free Friday mornings; check out the tourist office's free *Museums* brochure.

▓ ÖSTERREICHISCHE GALERIE. (Austrian Gallery.) The **Upper Belvedere** houses European art of the 19th and 20th centuries, including Klimt's *The Kiss*. The **Lower Belvedere** contains an extensive collection of sculptures, David's portrait of Napoleon on horseback, and the **Museum of Medieval Austrian Art.** *(III, Prinz-Eugen-Str. 27, in the Belvedere Palace behind Schwarzenbergpl. Walk up from the Südbahnhof, take tram D to "Schloß Belvedere," or tram #71 to "Unteres Belvedere." Both open Tu-Su 10am-6pm; upper open Tu-W and F-Su 10am-6pm, Th 10am-9pm. €7.50, students €5.)*

▓ MESSEPALAST, Museumspl. 1/5, originally the imperial barracks, contains the **MuseumsQuartier.** *(☎523 58 81; www.mqw.at).* The modern complex houses the **Leopold Museum** (which holds one of Austria's most significant collections, including a number of valuable Schieles), a **Museum of Modern Art,** and a new **Kunsthalle**.

KUNSTHISTORISCHES MUSEUM. (Museum of Fine Arts). The KHM houses the world's 4th-largest art collection, including Venetian and Flemish paintings, classical art, and an Egyptian burial chamber. *(Take U2 to "Museumsquartier," U2/U3 to "Volkstheater," or tram 1, 2, D, J. Across from the Burgring and Heldenpl. on Maria Theresia's right. Open Tu-Su 10am-6pm. €9, students €6.50. Audioguides €2.)*

HAUS DER MUSIK. Near the Opera House, this new, interactive science-meets-music museum easily captures the fancy of both adults and children. On four different floors, experience the physics of sound, learn about famous Viennese composers (each has his own room) and play with a neat invention called the Brain Opera. *(I, Seilerstatte 30. ☎516 48; fax 512 03 15; www.hdm.at. Open daily 10am-10pm. €8.50, students €6.50. Combined admission including Philharmonic exhibit €10.50/€8.50.)*

HISTORISCHES MUSEUM DER STADT WIEN. (Historical Museum of the City of Vienna.) This amazing collection of historical artifacts and paintings documents Vienna's evolution from a Roman encampment through the Turkish siege of Vienna to the subsequent 640 years of Habsburg rule. Don't miss the memorial rooms to Loos and Grillparzer, the *fin-de-siècle* art, or the 19th-century Biedermeier collection. *(IV, Karlspl, to the left of the Karlskirche. ☎50 58 74 70; www.museum.vienna.at. Open Tu-Su 9am-6pm. €3.50, students €1.50.)*

SIGMUND FREUD HAUS. The famed couch is not here, Freud's former home now holds lots of interesting documents, including the young psychoanalyst's report cards and circumcision certificate. *(IX, Bergg. 19. Take U2 to Schottentor, then walk up Währingerstr. to Bergg or take tram D to Schlickg. ☎319 15 96; www.freud-museum.at. Open July-Sept. 9am-6pm; Oct.-June daily 9am-4pm. €5, students €3.)*

🎭 ENTERTAINMENT

While Vienna offers all the standard entertainments in the way of theater, film, and festivals, the heart of the city beats to music. All but a few of classical music's great composers lived, composed, and performed in Vienna. Mozart, Beethoven, and Haydn wrote their greatest masterpieces in Vienna, creating the **First Viennese**

School; a century later, Schönberg, Weber, and Berg teamed up to form the **Second Viennese School.** All year, Vienna has performances ranging from the above-average to the sublime, with many accessible to the budget traveler. Note that the venues below have **no performances in July and August.**

Staatsoper, Opernring 2 (☎514 44 78 80; fax 514 44 29 69; www.wiener-staatsoper.at). The box office (Bundestheaterkasse), Hanuschg. 3, is around the corner from the opera. Vienna's premier opera, performing nearly every night May.-June. Buy tickets in advance at the box office or online (20% commission). Standing-room tickets are available right before the performance (1 per person; balcony €2, orchestra €3.50). Open M-F 8am-6pm, Sa-Su 9am-noon; first Sa of each month 9am-5pm.

Wiener Philharmoniker (Vienna Philharmonic Orchestra; www.wienerphilharmoniker.at) plays in the Musikverein, Austria's—and perhaps the world's—premier concert hall. Write or visit the box office of the Musikverein for tickets, including standing room (Gesellschaft der Musikfreunde, Bösendorferstr. 12, A-1010 Wien) or stop by the Bundestheaterkasse (see **Staatsoper,** above). Tickets are available online for a hefty commission.

Wiener Sängerknaben (Vienna Boys' Choir; Contact hofmusikkapelle@asn-wien.ac.at for info; for info on the boys' daily lives, www.wsk.at. The main showcase is mass every Su 9:15am (mid-Sept. to late June) in the **Hofburgkapelle** (U3 "Herreng."). To get tickets (€6-30) to these masses, write to Hofmusikkapelle, Hofburg, A-1010 Wien, 2 months in advance, but do not enclose money. You will be sent a slip and can pick up tickets at the Burgkapelle on the Friday before mass 11am-1pm or 3-5pm, or before Su mass 8:15-9am. **Unreserved seats** are sold in small quantity the Friday before mass 11am-1pm and 3-5pm (get in line 30min.-1hr. early), max. 2 per person. Some tickets sold early Sunday morning. Standing room is free, despite rumors to the contrary, but arrive before Su 8am to have a chance. The lads also perform every Friday at 3:30pm at the **Konzerthaus** (see **Wiener Symphoniker**) May-June and Sept.-Oct. For tickets (€28.50-32), contact *Reisebüro Mondial,* Faulmanng. 4, A-1040 Wien (☎58 80 41 41; fax 587 12 68; ticket@mondial.at).

▣ NIGHTLIFE

Vienna is a great place to party, whether you're looking for a quiet evening with a glass of wine or a wild night in a disco full of black-clad Euro musclemen and drag queens. Take U1 or U4 to "Schwedenplatz," which will drop you within blocks of the **Bermuda Dreiecke** (Triangle), an area packed with lively, crowded clubs. If your vision isn't foggy yet, head down **Rotenturmstr.** toward Stephansdom or walk around the areas bounded by the Jewish synagogue and Ruprechtskirche. Slightly outside the Ring, the streets off **Burgg.** and **Stiftg.** in the 7th district and the **university quarter** (Districts XIII and IX) have tables in outdoor courtyards and hip bars. Viennese nightlife starts late, often after 11pm. Pick up a copy of the indispensable **Falter,** which prints listings of everything from opera and theater to punk concerts and updates on the gay/lesbian scene.

▨ **Objektiv,** VII, Kirchbergg. 26 (☎522 70 42). Take U2 or U3 to "Volkstheater," walk down Burgg. 2 blocks, and turn right on Kirchbergg. With old stoves and sewing machines as tables and cowboy boots as decorations, this small bar offers funky local flavor. A mellow atmosphere and cheap drinks. Daily discounted drink special €2.50. Happy Hour daily 11pm-1am. Open 6pm-2am; closed Sun.

▨ **U-4,** XII, Schönbrunnerstr. 222 (☎815 83 07). Take U4 to "Meidling Hauptstr." In the late 80s, U-4 hosted Nirvana, Mudhoney, and Hole before they were huge. These days the joint is hit-or-miss—check in advance to find out the theme night. 2 dance areas, multiple bars. Th Heaven Gay Night. Cover €8. Open daily 10pm-5am.

HELSINKI, FINLAND   ☎ 09

EUROS

AUS$1 = EUR€0.55	1EUR€ = AUS$1.82
CDN$1 = EUR€0.65	1EUR€ = CDN$1.55
NZ$1 = EUR€0.47	1EUR€ = NZ$2.13
UK£1 = EUR€1.57	1EUR€ = UK£0.64
US$1 = EUR€1.01	1EUR€ = US$0.99
ZAR1 = EUR€0.09	1EUR€ = ZAR10.69

PHONE CODES   Country code: **358**. International dialing prefix: **00**.

With all the appeal of a big city but none of the grime, Helsinki's broad avenues, grand architecture, and green parks make it a model of 19th-century city planning. The city also distinguishes itself with a decidedly multicultural flair: Lutheran and Russian Orthodox cathedrals stand almost face-to-face, and youthful energy mingles with old-world charm. Baltic Sea produce fills the marketplaces and restaurants, while St. Petersburg and Tallinn are only a short cruise away.

VISAS. EU citizens do not require visas to visit, study, or work in Finland. Citizens of Australia, Canada, New Zealand, and the US can visit for up to 90 days without a visa. South Africans need a visa to enter the country.

⊏ TRANSPORTATION

Flights: Helsinki-Vantaa Airport (☎020 046 36). **Buses** #615 and 616 (less direct) run frequently between the airport and the train station square (€3). A **Finnair bus** shuttles between the airport and the train station (35min., every 15min. 5am-midnight, €5).

Trains: ☎030 072 09 00. Reserve tickets in advance. To **Moscow** (15hr., 5:40pm, €83) and **St. Petersburg** (7hr., 2 per day, €50).

Buses: ☎020 040 00, for Espoo and Vantaa buses 010 01 11. From the Mannerheimintie side of the train station, take Postikatu past the statue of Mannerheim. Cross Mannerheimintie to Salomonkatu; the station will be to your left.

Ferries: For route options, see **Estonia: Ferries,** p. 304. **Silja Line,** Mannerheimintie 2 (☎980 07 45 52 or 091 80 41). Take tram #3B or 3T from the city center to the Olympic terminal. **Viking Line,** Mannerheimintie 14 (☎12 35 77). **Tallink,** Erottajankatu 19 (☎22 82 12 77).

Public Transportation: ☎010 01 11. **Metro, trams,** and **buses** run roughly 5:30am-11pm; major tram and bus lines, including tram #3T, run until 1:30am. There is one Metro line (running approximately east to west), 10 tram lines, and many more bus lines. **Night buses,** marked with an N, run after 1:30am. Single-fare tickets are €2; cheaper advance tickets (€1.40) and 10-trip tickets (€12.80) are available at R-kiosks and at the **City Transport** office in the Rautatientori Metro station (open in summer M-Th 7:30am-6pm, F 7:30am-4pm; off-season M-Th 7:30am-7pm, F 7:30am-5pm, Sa 10am-3pm). Tickets are valid for 1hr. (transfers free); punch your ticket on board. The **Tourist Ticket,** a convenient bargain for a 5-day stay, is available at City Transport and tourist offices and provides unlimited bus, tram, Metro, and local train transit (1-day €4.20, 3-day €8.40, 5-day €12.60; children 50% discount).

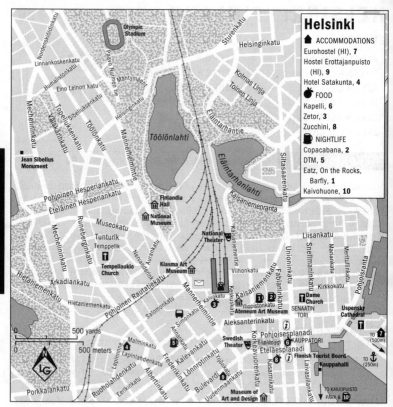

Helsinki

🏠 ACCOMMODATIONS
Eurohostel (HI), **7**
Hostel Erottajanpuisto
(HI), **9**
Hotel Satakunta, **4**
🍎 FOOD
Kapelli, **6**
Zetor, **3**
Zucchini, **8**
🌙 NIGHTLIFE
Copacabana, **2**
DTM, **5**
Eatz, On the Rocks,
Barfly, **1**
Kaivohuone, **10**

GATEWAY CITIES

✴ 🔢 ORIENTATION AND PRACTICAL INFORMATION

Sea surrounds Helsinki on the east and west, and the city center is bisected by two lakes. Water shapes everything in the Finnish capital, from relaxing city beaches to gorgeous parks around the lakes. Helsinki's main street, **Mannerheimintie**, passes between the bus and train stations on its way to the city center, eventually crossing **Esplanadi**. This tree-lined promenade leads east to **Kauppatori** (Market Square) and the beautiful South Harbor. Both Finnish and Swedish are used on all street signs and maps; *Let's Go* uses the Finnish names in all listings and maps.

Tourist Offices: City Tourist Office, Pohjoisesplanadi 19 (☎ 169 37 57; www.hel.fi). From the train station, walk two blocks down Keskuskatu and turn left on Pohjoisesplanadi. Open May-Sept. M-F 9am-8pm, Sa-Su 9am-6pm; Oct.-Apr. M-F 9am-6pm, Sa-Su 10am-4pm. The **Finnish Tourist Board,** Eteläesplanadi 4 (☎ 41 76 93 00; www.mek.fi), has information on all of Finland. Open May-Sept. M-F 9am-5pm, Sa-Su 11am-3pm; Oct.-Apr. M-F 9am-5pm. The **Helsinki Card,** sold at the tourist office, Hotel-likeskus, central R-kiosks, and most hotels, provides unlimited local transportation and free or discounted admission to most museums (24hr. €24; 48hr. €32; 72hr. €38).

Embassies: Canada, Pohjoisesplanadi 25B (☎17 11 41; www.canada.fi). Open M-F 8:30am-noon and 1-4:30pm. **Ireland,** Erottajankatu 7A (☎64 60 06). **South Africa** Rahapajankatu 1A 5 (☎68 60 31 00). **UK,** Itäinen Puistotie 17 (☎22 86 51 00; www.ukembassy.fi). Also handles diplomatic matters for **Australians** and **New Zealanders.** Open M-F 8:30am-5pm. **US,** Itäinen Puistotie 14A (☎17 19 31; www.usembassy.fi). Open M-F 8:30am-5pm.

Currency Exchange: Forex, with 5 locations in Helsinki. Best rates in the city. The **branch** in the train station is open 8am-9pm. **Exchange,** Kaivokatu 6, opposite the train station. €3.50 fee to convert to euros; €6 fee per traveler's check.

Laundromat: ◙**Cafe Tin Tin Tango** (☎27 09 09 72), Töölöntorinkatu 7, a combination bar, cafe, laundromat, and sauna. Laundry €3.40. Sandwiches €4.50-5.30. Sauna €17. Open M-F 7am-2am, Sa-Su 10am-2am. More typical is **Easywash,** Runeberginkatu 47 (☎40 69 82). Open M-Th 10am-9pm, F 10am-6pm, Sa 10am-4pm.

Emergency: ☎112. **Police:** ☎100 22.

24-Hour Pharmacy: Yliopiston Apteekki, Mannerheimintie 96 (☎41 78 03 00).

Medical Assistance: 24hr. medical advice **hotline** (☎100 23). 24hr. medical clinic **Mehilainen,** Runeberginkatu 47A (☎431 44 44).

Internet Access: Cable Library, Mannerheimintie 22-24, in the Lasipalatsi mall opposite the bus station. Free; 30min. limit. Open M-Th 10am-8pm, Sa-Su noon-6pm. **Academic Bookstore,** Keskuskatu 2. Free; 15min. limit. Open M-F 9am-9pm, Sa 9am-6pm.

Post Office: Mannerheiminaukio 1A (☎98 00 71 00). Open M-F 9am-6pm. Address **Poste Restante** to: "Firstname SURNAME, Poste Restante, Mannerheiminaukio 1A, 00100 Helsinki, Finland. Open M-F 9am-6pm.

Postal Code: 00100.

HELSINKI	❶	❷	❸	❹	❺
ACCOM.	under €12	€12-25	€25-50	€50-75	over €75
FOOD	under €8	€8-15	€15-20	€20-30	over €30

ACCOMMODATIONS

Helsinki hotels tend to be expensive, but budget hostels are often quite nice. In June and July, it's wise to make reservations a few weeks in advance.

◙ **Hostel Erottanjanpuisto (HI),** Uudenmaankatu 9 (☎64 21 69). Head right from the train station, turn left on Mannerheimintie, bear right on Erottajankatu, and turn right on Uudenmaankatu. Well-kept rooms, friendly staff, and an unbeatable location. Kitchen. Breakfast €5. Reception 24hr. Reserve in advance. In summer, dorms €19.50; singles €43.50; doubles €55. Off-season €1.70-6 less. Nonmembers add €2.50. ❷

Eurohostel (HI), Linnankatu 9, Katajanokka (☎622 04 70; www.eurohostel.fi). 200m from the Viking Line/Finnjet ferry terminal. The largest hostel in Finland, with bright rooms, non-smoking floors, and a sauna. Kitchen and cafe. Breakfast €5. Lockers. Sheets included. Internet €1 per 10min. Reception 24hr. Dorms €19.50; singles €34; doubles €19.50. Non-members add €2.50. ❷

Hotel Satakunta (HI), Lapinrinne 1A (☎69 58 52 31; ravintola.satakunta@sodexho.fi). Take the Metro to "Kampi" and walk downhill. Spacious, well-equipped rooms, most with balconies. Breakfast and linen €5 each. Laundry €5.50. Reception 24hr. Check-in 2pm. Check-out noon. Open June-Aug. Dorms €11; singles €32.50; doubles €47.50; triples €57.50; quads €67.50. Non-members add €2.50. ❶

✂ FOOD

Restaurants and cafes are easy to find on **Esplanadi** and the streets branching off from **Mannerheimintie** and **Uudenmaankatu.** An **Alepa supermarket** is under the train station. (Open M-F 7:30am-10pm, Sa 9am-10pm, Su 10am-10pm.)

> **Kapelli,** Eteläesplanadi 1, at the Unionkatu end of Esplanadi park. Frequented by well-heeled bohemians since 1837. Outdoor cafe is perfect for the Esplanadi jazz concerts (see **Entertainment,** below). In the cafe, salads and sandwiches €5-8. In the restaurant; entrees €12-18. Open daily 9am-2am; kitchen closes at 1am. ●

> **Zetor,** Kaivokatu 10, in Kaivopiha, the mall directly opposite the train station. The name translates to tractor, explaining the farm decor. Homemade beer €4. Entrees €7-21. 22+ after 9pm. Open Su-M 3pm-1am, Tu-Th 3pm-3am, F 3pm-4am, Sa 1pm-4am. ❷

> **Zucchini,** Fabianinkatu 4, near the tourist office. A casual *kasvisravintola* (vegetarian restaurant). Daily lunch special €7.20. Open Aug.-June M-F 11am-4pm. ●

◉ SIGHTS

Home to bold designs and polished Neoclassical works, Helsinki exemplifies famed Finnish architect Alvar Aalto's statement, "Architecture is our form of expression because our language is so impossible." **Tram #3T** circles past the major attractions in an hour, offering the cheapest city tour. Better yet, pick up a copy of *See Helsinki on Foot* and walk—most sights are within 2km of the train station.

SENAATIN TORI. (Senate Square.) The square and its gleaming white Tuomi-okirkko (Dome Church) showcase Carl Ludvig Engel's work and exemplify the splendor of Finland's Russian period. *(At Aleksanterinkatu and Unioninkatu. Open June-Aug. M-Sa 9am-midnight, Su noon-midnight; Sept.-May M-Sa 9am-6pm, Su noon-6pm.)*

USPENSKINKATEDRAADI. ((Uspensky Orthodox Cathedral.) Mainly known for its red-and-gold cupolas and great spires, which jut prominently out of the city skyline, the Cathedral also has an ornate interior. *(Follow Esplanadi down to Kauppatori. Open M and W-Sa 9:30am-4pm, Tu 9:30am-6pm, Su 9:30am-3pm.)*

SUOMEN KANSALLISMUSEO. T (National Museum of Finland.) The museum displays intriguing bits of Finnish culture, from Gypsy and Sami costumes to *ryijyt* (rugs), as well as a magnificent roof mural by Akseli Gallen-Kallela. *(Up the street from the Finnish Parliament House. Open Tu-W 11am-8pm, Th-Su 11am-6pm. €4.)*

ART MUSEUMS. Ateneum Taidemuseo, Finland's largest art museum, features a comprehensive look at Finnish art from the 1700s to the 1960s. *(Kaivokatu 2, opposite the train station. Open Tu and F 9am-6pm, W-Th 9am-8pm, Sa-Su 11am-5pm. €5.50; special exhibits €7.50.)* **Kiasma** picks up where Ateneum leaves off, showcasing great modern art in a funky silver building. *(Mannerheiminaukio 2. Open Tu 9am-5pm, W-Su 10am-10:30pm. €5.50; special exhibits €7.50.)*

TEMPPELIAUKIO KIRKKO. Designed in 1969 by Tuomo and Timo Suomalainen, this inspiring church is built into a hill of rock, with only the roof visible from the outside. Inside, its huge domed ceiling appears to be supported by rays of sunshine. *(Lutherinkatu 3. Walk away from the main post office on Paasikivenaudio, which becomes Arkadiagatan, then turn right on Fredrikinatu and follow it to the end. Open M-F 10am-8pm, Sa 10am-6pm, Su noon-1:45pm and 3:15-5:45pm. Services in English Su 2pm.)*

SUOMENLINNA. This 18th-century Swedish military fortification consists of five beautiful interconnected islands used by the Swedes to repel attacks on Helsinki. The old fortress's dark passageways are great to explore, and a number of the islands' six museums are worth a visit. *(www.suomenlinna.fi. Most museums open May-Aug. daily 11am-5pm; Sept.-Apr. hours vary. €5.50, students €2.50; some museums have additional admission. Ferries depart from Market Square every 20min. 8am-11pm; round-trip €4.)*

SEURASAARI. A quick walk across the beautiful white bridge from the mainland brings you to the many paths of the island of Seurasaari, repository of old churches and farmsteads transplanted from all over the country. An open-air museum allows entrance into many of the island's historical buildings. Visit during midsummer to witness the *kokko* (bonfires) and Finnish revelry in its full splendor. *(Take bus #24 from Erottaja, outside the Swedish Theater, to the last stop. The island is always open for hiking. Museum open M-F 9am-3pm, Sa-Su 11am-5pm. €3.40, children free.)*

 ## ENTERTAINMENT AND NIGHTLIFE

Helsinki's beautiful parks are always animated. There is afternoon jazz all July in the **Esplanadi park** near the Kauppatori (www.kultturi.hel.fi/espanlava) and occasional pop/rock events at **Kaivopuisto park** (on the corner of Puistokatu and Ehrenstromintie, in the southern part of town) and **Hietaniemi beach** (down Hesperiankatu on the western shore). The free English-language papers *Helsinki This Week, Helsinki Happens,* and *City* list popular cafes, bars, nightclubs, and events; pick up copies at the tourist office. You must be at least 22 years old to enter many clubs. Bars and clubs, ranging from laid-back neighborhood pubs to sleek discos, line **Mannerheiminkatu, Uudenmaankatu,** and nearby streets. East of the train station, the scene flourishes around **Yliopistonkatu** and **Kaisaniemenkatu.** The current hot spot is on Mikonkatu, where three popular bar/clubs share a terrace: international **Eatz** (no cover), edgy **On the Rocks** (cover €6-7), and chic **Barfly** (F-Sa cover €7). **Copacabana,** Yliopistonkatu 5, has salsa each Sunday night (F-Sa cover €7-8.50). A student crowd gathers at **Vanha,** Mannerheimintie 3, in the Old Students' House (F-Sa cover €2). **DTM** (Don't Tell Mama), Annankatu 32, is a popular gay club with a mixed following (F-Sa cover €4.50-5.50). Wednesday night turns **Kaivohuone,** in Kaivopuisto park, into a swimming pool (cover €4-10). Finland's best DJs play six-hour sets at the roving **Club Unity** (www.clubunity.org).

İSTANBUL, TURKEY ☎ 212/6

! İstanbul, Turkey was not updated for the 2003 edition. The following information was last updated in summer 2002.

TURKISH LIRA

AUS$1 = TL907,712 ()	100,000TL = AUS$0.114	
CDN$1 = TL1,067,057	100,000TL = CDN$0.097	
EUR€1 = TL1,652,077	100,000TL = EUR€0.063	
NZ$1 = TL775,524	100,000TL = NZ$0.134	
UK£1 = TL2,592,422	100,000TL = UK£0.04	
US$1 = TL1,656,500	100,000TL = US$0.063	
ZAR1 = TL153,950	100,000TL = ZAR0.677	

PHONE CODES — Country code: **90.** International dialing prefix: **00.**

Straddling two continents and almost three millennia of history, İstanbul exists on an incomprehensible scale. The city unfolds against a landscape of Ottoman mosques, Byzantine mosaics, and Roman masonry. In its current incarnation, İstanbul is the most crowded and cosmopolitan city in the Turkish Republic. This urban supernova explodes out into the surrounding countryside behind an ever-expanding front of new construction sites, but no crane or cement truck could possibly hope to keep up with the pace of life in İstanbul.

VISAS New Zealanders can stay for up to three months without a visa; South Africans are permitted to stay visa-free for one month. Citizens of Australia, Canada, Ireland, the UK, and the US require visas; it's most convenient to get them upon arrival in Turkey. A 3-month visa costs US$45.

TRANSPORTATION

Flights: Atatürk Havaalanı, 30km from the city. The domestic and international terminals are connected by **bus** (every 20min. 6am-11pm). To reach **Sultanahmet,** take a Havaş **shuttle bus** from either terminal to Aksaray (every 30min., US$7), then walk 1 block south to Millet Cad. and take an Eminönü-bound **tram** to the Sultanahmet stop. Or take a **taxi** (US$4) to the Yeşilköy train station and take the commuter rail (*tren*) to the end of the line in Sirkeci. A direct taxi to Sultanahmet costs US$9. To reach **Taksim,** take the Havaş shuttle to the end of the line (every 30min., 6am-9pm, US$5). To reach the airport, have **Karasu** (☎638 66 01) or **Zorlu** (☎638 04 35) pick you up (US$5.50) or take the Havaş shuttle from Taksim (45min., every 30min., US$6.75).

Trains: It's almost always faster and cheaper to take intercity buses. All trains to Anatolia leave from **Haydarpaşa Garı** (☎216 336 04 75), on the Asian side. Take the ferry (every 20min., US$0.65) from Karaköy pier #7, halfway between Galata Bridge and the Karaköy tourist office. Rail tickets for Anatolia can be bought in advance at the **TCDD** office upstairs. To **Ankara** (6½-9½hr., 6 per day, US$6-12). Europe-bound trains via **Athens** or **Bucharest** leave from **Sirkeci Garı** (☎212 527 00 50) in Eminönü, downhill from Sultanahmet. To **Bucharest** (17hr., 1 per day, US$30) and **Budapest** (40hr., 1 per day, US$90).

Buses: Esenler Otobüs Terminal (☎658 00 36), in Esenler, 3km from central İstanbul. Serves intercity buses. Take the tram to Yusufpaşa (1 stop past Aksaray; US$0.50), walk 1min. to the Aksaray Metro station on broad Adnan Menderes bul., and take the Metro to the *otogar* (15min., US$0.40). Most companies have **courtesy buses** (*servis*) that run to the *otogar* from Eminönü, Taksim, and elsewhere (free with bus ticket).

Public Transportation: Buses serve most stops every 10min. 5am-10:30pm, less frequently 10:30pm-midnight. Signs on the front indicate destination; on the right side, major stops. **Dolmuş** run during daylight hours and early evening and are found near most major bus hubs, including Aksaray and Eminönü. In neighborhoods far from the bustle of Taksim and Sultanahmet, they serve as local group taxis; it's best to hail them on their way back into the center of İstanbul. A **tramvay** (tram) runs from Eminönü to Zeytinburnu (US$0.50); follow the tracks back to Sultanahmet even if you don't actually take it. **AKBİL** is an **electronic ticket system** that works on municipal ferries, buses, trams, seabuses, and the subway (but not *dolmuş*). A deposit of US$5 will get you a plastic tab to which you can add money in 1,000,000TL increments and which will save you 15-50% on fares. Add credit at any white IETT public bus booth with the "*AKBİL satılır*" sign (at bigger bus and tram stops); press your tab into the reader, remove it, insert a 1,000,000TL note, and press again. **Regular tickets** are not interchangeable. Tickets for trams and buses without ticket sellers are available from little white booths, while ferries and seabuses take *jeton* (tokens), available at ferry stops.

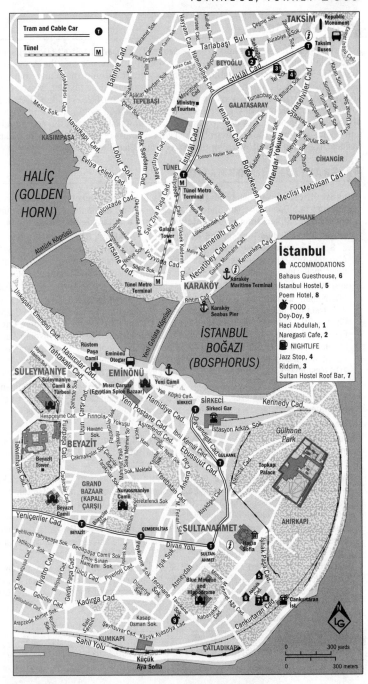

⚿ ORIENTATION

Waterways divide İstanbul into three sections. The **Bosphorus Strait** (Boğaz) separates Asia from Europe. Turks call the European side Avrupa and the Asian side Asya. The **Golden Horn**, a sizeable inlet, splits Avrupa into northern and southern parts. Directions in İstanbul are usually further specified by district. Most of the sights and tourist facilities are in **Sultanahmet,** south of the Golden Horn and toward the eastern end of the peninsula, which is framed by the Horn and the **Sea of Marmara.** The other half of Avrupa is focused on **Taksim Square,** the commercial and social center of the northern bank. Two main arteries radiate from it: **İstiklâl Caddesi,** the main downtown shopping street, and **Cumhuriyet Caddesi.**

⁊ PRACTICAL INFORMATION

Tourist Office: 3 Divan Yolu (☎/fax 518 87 54), at the north end of the Hippodrome in Sultanahmet. Open daily 9am-5pm. Branches in Taksim's **Hilton Hotel Arcade** on Cumhuriyet Cad., **Sirkeci train station, Atatürk Airport,** and **Karaköy Maritime Station.**

Budget Travel: Indigo Tourism and Travel Agency, 24 Akbıyık Cad. (☎517 72 66; fax 518 53 33; www.indigo-tour.com), in Sultanahmet's hotel cluster. IYTC cards US$10. Also sells bus, plane, and ferry tickets, arranges airport shuttle service, and tours, and holds mail. Open in summer daily 8:30am-7:30pm; off-season M-Sa 9:30am-6pm.

Consulates: Australia, 58 Tepecik Yolu, Etiler (☎257 70 52; fax 257 70 54). Visas 10am-noon. **Canada,** 107/3 Büyükdere Cad., Gayrettepe (☎272 51 74; fax 272 34 27). **Ireland** (honorary), 25/A Cumhuriyet Cad., Mobil Altı, Elmadağ (☎246 60 25). Visas 9:30-11:30am. **New Zealand,** 100-102 Maya Akar Center, Büyükdere Cad., Esentepe (☎211 11 14; fax 211 04 73). **South Africa,** 106/15 Büyükdere Cad., Esentepe (☎275 47 93; fax 288 76 42). Open M-F 9am-noon. **UK,** 34 Meşrutiyet Cad., Beyoğlu/Tepebaşı (☎293 75 40; fax 245 49 89). Open M-F 8:30am-noon. **US,** 104-108 Meşrutiyet Cad., Tepebaşı (☎251 36 02; fax 251 32 18). Open M-F 8:30-11am.

Currency Exchange: *Bureaux de change* around the city are open M-F 8:30am-noon and 1:30-5pm. Most banks exchange **traveler's checks.** Exchanges in Sultanahmet have poor rates and charge 2% commission, but are open late and on the weekends.

Emergencies: Police ☎155. **Ambulance** ☎112.

Tourist Police: 24hr. hotline ☎527 45 03 or 528 53 69; fax 512 76 76, in Sultanahmet, at the beginning of Yerebatan Cad. Officers speak English, and their mere presence causes hawkers and postcard-selling kids to scatter.

Hospitals: American Hospital, Admiral Bristol Hastanesi, 20 Güzelbahçe Sok., Nişantaşı (☎231 40 50) has many English-speaking doctors. **German Hospital,** 119 Sıraselviler Cad., Taksim (☎251 71 00), also has a multilingual staff and is conveniently located for Sultanahmet hostelers.

Internet Access: The Antique Internet Cafe, 51 Kutlugün Sok., offers a fast connections and big plush chairs in a relaxing spot. Antique also serves tea, cold sodas, and tasty meals (omelettes and salads from US$1.50). US$1.50 per hr. Open 24hr.

Post Office: 25 Büyük Postane Sok, in Sirkeci train station. Stamp and currency exchange services open 8:30am-7pm. 24hr. **telephones.** A **branch** off Taksim Sq. at the mouth of Cumhuriyet Cad. mails packages. No collect calls. Phonecards for 30, 60, or 100 *kontür* (credits). Open M-F 8am-8pm, Sa 8am-6pm.

Sirkeci Postal Code: 5270050 and 5270051.

İSTANBUL	❶	❷	❸	❹	❺
ACCOM.	under US$10	US$10-25	US$26-50	US$51-100	over US$100
FOOD	under US$5	US$5-10	US$11-20	US$21-50	over US$50

ACCOMMODATIONS

Budget accommodations are concentrated in **Sultanahmet** (a.k.a. Türist Şeğntral), bounded by Aya Sofia, the Blue Mosque, and the walls of the Topkapı Palace. The side streets around **Sirkeci** railway station and **Aksaray** have dozens of dirt-cheap and pretty dirty hotels. Hotels in **Lâleli** are the center of prostitution in İstanbul and should be avoided. Some rates rise by 20% in July and August. The accommodations listed below are in Sultanahmet.

İstanbul Hostel, 35 Kutlugün Sok. (☎516 93 80). From the path between the Hagia Sophia and the Blue Mosque, walk down Tevkifane Sok. to Kutlugün Sok; it's on the right. Breezy, sunny bedrooms; the marble-floored bathrooms are the cleanest in town. Internet access. Happy Hour 6:30-9:30pm. Dorms US$7; doubles US$16. ❶

Poem Hotel, Akbıyık Cad., 12 Terbıyık Sok. (☎/fax 517 68 36; hotelpoem@superon-line.com). Quet, luxurious rooms are marked with titles of Turkish poems instead of numbers; all have Bosphorus views. 12 rooms with bath, TV, A/C. Free Internet. Singles US$45; doubles US$65; triples from US$80. 25% discount in winter. ❸

Bahaus Guesthouse, Akbıyık Cad., 11 Bayram Fırını Sok. (☎517 66 97; fax 517 66 97). From the Blue Mosque, walk down Mimar Mehmet Ağa Cad. and turn left on Akbıyık Cad. This bright yellow hotel has spare, classy rooms and a terrace view of the Sea of Marmara. Breakfast included. Singles US$20; doubles US$25; triples US$40. ❷

FOOD

Sultanahmet's heavily advertised "Turkish" restaurants are easy to find, but much better meals can be found on **İstiklâl Caddesi** and around **Taksim**. Bosphorus towns such as **Arnavutköy, Sarıyer** (on the European side), and **Çengelköy** (on the Asian side) are the best places for fish. **Kanlıca,** on the Asian side, reputedly has the best **yogurt.** Boats in **Eminönü** and **Karaköy** fry up **fish sandwiches** on board (US$1.50).

Doy-Doy, 13 Şifa Hamamı Sok. From the south end of the Hippodrome, walk down the hill around the Blue Mosque and look for the blue-and-yellow signs. Easily the best and cheapest of Sultanahmet's cheap eats. Tasty *kebap* and salads (US$3.50 and under). Open daily 8:30am-late. ❶

Hacı Abdullah, 17 Sakizağacı Cad., down the street from Ag'a Camii. This family-style restaurant has been serving real Turkish food (hint: it's not *kebap*) since 1888. Entrees US$3-6, delicious soups US$1. Open daily noon-11pm. ❷

Naregatsi Cafe, upstairs at the mouth of Sakizağacı Cad., across from the Ağa Camii. Gourmet cafe fare in a kitschy setting. Inflatable superheroes, live accordion, and cappuccino (US$3.50). A must see. Open daily noon-11:30pm. ❶

SIGHTS

HAGIA SOPHIA. (Aya Sofia.) Built in AD 537 under Justinian the Great (flush from reconquering Italy) as the main cathedral of a resurgent Byzantine Empire, the Aya Sofia was for 900 years the largest church in the world. When Constantinople fell to the Ottomans in 1453, it was converted into a mosque—indeed, its domed shape became the template for mosques all over the Ottoman Empire. Its religious life came to a close in 1932, when Atatürk declared it a museum. The **nave** is overshadowed by a gold-leaf mosaic **dome** lined with hundreds of circular windows. The **mihrab,** the calligraphy-adorned portal pointing towards Mecca, stands in the **apse,** which housed the altar of the Christian cathedral. The marble square on the floor marks the spot where Byzantine emperors were crowned. The **gallery**

contains Byzantine mosaics as well as the famed **sweating pillar,** sheathed in bronze. *(Museum open Tu-Su 9:30am-4:30pm. Gallery open Tu-Su 9:30am-4pm. US$6.50.)*

BLUE MOSQUE. (Sultanahmet Camii.) Located between the Hippodrome and Hagia Sofia; the six-minareted, multi-domed structure is the Blue Mosque. Completed in 1617, it was Sultan Ahmet's response to the architectural challenge of Hagia Sofia. *(Open Tu-Sa 8:30am-12:30pm, 1:45-3:45pm, and 5:30-6:30pm. Dress modestly and remove your shoes. Women should cover their heads.)*

THE HIPPODROME. (At Meydanı.) Built by the Roman Emperor Septimus Severus in AD 200, the Hippodrome served as a place for chariot races and public executions. The politically opposed **Hippodrome Factions** arose out of the Hippodrome's seating plan, which was determined by social standing. In AD 532, a tax protest turned into the full-out Nika Revolt. The city was ravaged in the ensuing melée. The tall, northernmost column with hieroglyphics is the **Dikili Taş,** an Egyptian obelisk erected by the Pharaoh Thutmosis III in 1500 BC and brought to Constantinople in the 4th century by Emperor Theodosius I. Farther south, the subterranean bronze stump is all that remains of the **Serpentine Column,** originally placed at the Oracle of Delphi. The southernmost column is the **Column of Constantine.** On the east side along Atmeydan Sok. is İbrahim Paşa Sarayı, the **Museum of Turkish and Islamic Art.** *(Behind the Blue Mosque. Open Tu-Su 9:30am-4:30pm. US$2.)*

UNDERGROUND CISTERN. (Yerebatan Sarayi.) Sultanahmet's most mysterious attraction is the oft-overlooked Underground Cistern. This palace is actually an underground cavern whose shallow water eerily reflects the images of its 336 supporting columns, all illuminated by colored lighting. Underground walkways originally linked the cistern to **Topkapı Palace,** but were blocked to curb the rampant trafficking of stolen goods and abducted women. *(As you stand with your back to Aya Sofia, the entrance lies 175m from the mosque in the small stone kiosk on the left side of Yerebatan Cad. Open daily 9:30am-5:30pm. US$4, students US$3.25.)*

TOPKAPI PALACE. (Topkapı Sarayi.) Towering from the high ground at the tip of the old city and hidden behind walls up to 12m high, the palace was the nerve center of the Ottoman Empire. Built by Mehmet the Conqueror between 1458 and 1465, it became an imperial residence during the reign of Süleyman the Magnificent. The palace is divided into a series of courts, all surrounded by the palace walls. The general public was permitted entrance to the **first courtyard** through the **Imperial Gate** to watch executions, trade, and view the nexus of the Empire's glory. At the end of the first courtyard, the **Gate of Greeting** (Bab üs-Selam) marks the entrance to the **second court.** To the right, the **imperial kitchens** house collections of porcelain and silver. The last set of doors of the narrow alley lead to the palace's Chinese and Japanese **porcelain collections.** The **Inner Treasury,** next door, is where various instruments of cutting, bludgeoning, and hacking are kept. The third court, officially known as **Enderun** (inside), is accessible through the inappropriately named **Gate of Felicity** (Eunuch's gate). Moving along down the colonnade brings you to the **Palace Treasury.** One of the highlights is the legendary **Topkapı dagger,** a gift Sultan Mahmut I presented to Nadir Shah of Iran in return for the solid gold throne displayed elsewhere in the treasury. Wrestle your way to the front of the line leading up to all 86 karats of the Pigot Diamond, better known as the **Spoonmaker's Diamond** because it was traded to a spoonmaker in exchange for three spoons. The **Pavilion of Holy Relics,** just on the other side of the courtyard, is leagues ahead in beauty and elegance. It holds the booty taken from Egypt by Selim the Grim as well as relics from Mecca, including the **staff of Moses** and hairs from **Mohammad's beard.** The highlight of the **fourth courtyard** is the **Circumcision Room.** The **Harem's** 400-plus rooms housed the sultan, his immediate family, and an entourage of servants, eunuchs and general assistants. The mandatory tour begins at the **Black Eunuchs' Dormitory.** Next is the women's section of the harem, including the lavish chambers of the **Valide Sultan,** the sultan's mother and the most powerful woman in the Harem. Surrounding the room of the queen mum are the chambers of the **concubines.** *(Open Tu-Su 9am-4:30pm. Each day's open galleries are posted next to the ticket window. Palace US$6.50. Harem closes 4pm. Mandatory tours of the Harem leave every 30min. 9:30am-3:30pm. Harem US$4.)*

GRAND BAZAAR. Consisting of over 4000 shops, several banks, mosques, police stations, and restaurants, the enormous Grand Bazaar could be a city unto itself. It forms the entrance to the massive mercantile sprawl that starts at **Çemberlitaş** and covers the hill down to Eminönü, ending at the **Egyptian Spice Bazaar** (Mısır Çarşısı) and the Golden Horn waterfront. *(From Sultanahmet, follow the tram tracks toward Aksaray for 5min. until you see the mosque on your right. Enter the mosque's side gate, and walk with the park on your left to the entrance. Open M-Sa 9am-7pm.)*

TURKISH BATHS

Most İstanbul baths *(hamams)* have separate women's sections or women's hours, but not all have designated female attendants.

Çemberlitaş Hamamı, 8 Verzirhan Cad. Near Çemberlitaş tram stop. Built by Sinan in 1584, this place has beautiful, clean marble interiors and good service. Vigorous "towel service" afterward requires a tip (US$1-3). Bathe with your own towel and soap (US$9), or get a rubdown, massage, and wash (US$15; tip included, but the washers wait around after you've changed, expecting another US$1-3). Open daily 6am-midnight.

Mihrimah Hamamı, next to Mihrimah Mosque on Fevzi Paşa Cad., about 50m from Edirnekapı. One of the better local baths: large, quiet, clean, cheap, and hot. Women's facilities are good, though smaller. Bath US$3; massage US$2.50. Men's section open daily 7am-midnight; women's section 8am-7pm.

NIGHTLIFE

Nightlife is centered around **Taksim** and **İstiklâl Cad.** In **Sultanahmet,** all pubs are within 100m of another and have standardized beer prices (US$1-1.25). The Beşiktaş end of **Ortaköy** is a maze of upscale hangouts; along the coastal road toward Arnavutköy there is a string of open-air clubs. Cover charges are high (US$18-45), and bouncers highly selective, but wander between **Ortaköy** and **Bebek** and try your luck.

Jazz Stop, at the end of Büyük Parmakkapı Sok in Taksim. Live bands lay the blues on thick to a mixed crowd. Live music nightly 11pm. Beer US$3. Liquor from US$6. June-Aug. no cover; Sept.-May F-Sa US$10. Open daily 11am-4am.

Riddim, 6 Büyük Parmakkapı Sok., in Taksim, spins reggae, island, and African music all night long. Unaccompanied men are turned away on weekends. Beer US$2.50. Open F-Sa 8pm-4am, Su-Th 9pm-1:30am.

Sultan Hostel Roof Bar, Terbıyık Sok., off Akbıyık Sok. A different party every night: belly dancing Tu and Sa; water pipes M and Th; "punch" W. Beautiful evening view of the Golden Horn and the Sea of Marmara. Sizeable, well-stocked bar. Open daily 8am-2am.

BEIJING, CHINA ☎ 010

Beijing, China was not updated for the 2003 edition. The following information was last updated in summer 2002.

YUAN

AUS$1 = 4.54CNY	1CNY = AUS$0.22	
CDN$1 = 5.34CNY	1CNY = CDN$0.19	
EUR€1 = 8.26CNY	1CNY = EUR€0.12	
NZ$1 = 3.88CNY	1CNY = NZ$0.26	
UK£1 = 12.97CNY	1CNY = UK£0.08	
US$1 = 8.29CNY	1CNY = US$0.12	
ZAR1 = 0.77CNY	1CNY = ZAR1.30	

PHONE CODE   Country code: **86**. International: **00**.

China's forefathers have cultivated the nation's dreams of grandeur for as long as the Chinese have grown rice. Born of these visions of greatness, Beijing's Forbidden City, its Summer Palace, and the nearby Great Wall testify to a long history of imperial ostentation. Today, modern skyscrapers tell of capitalism's encroachment, the latest grand-scale revolution in Beijing's tumultuous history, and life for most Beijing residents is quickly changing. Whether the national capital is your first or last stop on a Trans-Siberian itinerary, take a moment to enjoy Beijing, the enigmatic gateway to the People's Republic of China.

VISAS Visas are required of all travelers to China. Those arriving on the Trans-Siberian railroad should get a visa from the Chinese Embassy in **Moscow** (p. 639) before their departure.

⌐ TRANSPORTATION

Flights: Capital Airport (☎6456 2580), 1hr. outside the city by taxi (at least Y80; more to book in advance). **Civil Aviation Administration of China** (**CAAC;** zhōngguó mínháng) in the Aviation Bldg., 15 Xi Changan Jie, 1st fl. (☎6601 7755, domestic inquiry 6256 7811, international inquiry 6601 6667).

Trains: Foreigners enter and exit through the **Beijing Main Station** (běijīng huǒchē zhàn; ☎6512 9525 or 6512 9525) or **Beijing West Station** (běijīng xī zhàn; ☎6321 6253), on Lianhuachi Dong Lu near Lianhuachi Park (bus #52). Beijing is the endpoint of the Trans-Manchurian and Trans-Mongolian branches of the Russian Trans-Siberian Railroad. For ticket and route info, see p. 715. Beijing is 7hr. ahead of Moscow (GMT+8).

◢◤ ORIENTATION

Beijing is vast. Sprawling. Immense. Really, really big. Everything in Beijing is far away from everything else, and most of the budget accommodations are littered around the city's perimeters. The **Forbidden City** and **Tiananmen Square** form the city center on either side of **Changan Jie,** the main downtown east-west thoroughfare. **Dazhalan** and **Wangfujing,** southwest and northeast of Tiananmen Square, respectively, are full of shopping options. To the northeast is **Gongren Tiyuchang Bei Lu,** commonly known as Gongti Bei Lu, which leads to **Sanlitun,** one of the city's embassy compounds. Many older neighborhoods and *hutongs*

(Beijing alleyways) are preserved in the **Drum Tower** and **Lama Temple** sectors to the north. To the far northwest is the zoo, the silicon district, and Beijing and Qinghua Universities. The **Summer Palace** and **Old Summer Palace** are outside the center, farther northwest.

◱ PRACTICAL INFORMATION

Travel Agencies: There is a **tourist information service** in Beijing (☎ 6513 0828), but no actual tourist bureau. **China International Travel Service** (CITS; zhōngguó guójì lǚxíng shè), in the west lobby of the Beijing International Hotel, 9 Jianguomennei Dajie (☎ 6512 1368; fax 6528 2017). Open M-F 9am-noon and 1-5pm, Sa 9am-noon. **Branch** in the World Trade Tower #2, 1 Jianguomenwai Dajie, Rm. 301 (☎ 6505 3775 or 6505 3776; fax 6505 0503). Open M-F 9am-noon and 1-5pm, Sa 9am-noon. **Tianhua International Travel Service** (tiānhuá guójì lǚxíng shè; ☎ 8727 5387; fax 8727 5389) sits to the left of the business center and lobby of Jinghua Hotel. Arranges Mongolian, Russian, and Kazak **visas,** as well as railway tickets. Open daily 8:30am-8pm.

Embassies: Beijing has two huge embassy compounds. One is at **Jianguomenwai,** near the Friendship Store, and the other is at **Sanlitun,** home to dozens of expat bars. **Australia,** 20 Dongzhimenwai Dajie, Sanlitun (☎ 6532 2331; fax 6532 4605). **Canada,** 19 Dongzhimenwai Dajie, Sanlitun (☎ 6532 3536; fax 6532 4311). **Ireland,** 3 Ritan Dong Lu, Jianguomenwai (☎ 6532 2914; fax 6532 6857). **Mongolia,** 2 Xiushui Bei Jie, Jianguomenwai (☎ 6532 1203; fax 6532 5045). **New Zealand,** 1 Donger Jie, Ritan Lu (☎ 6532 2731; fax 6532 3424). **Russia,** 4 Dongzhimennei, Beizhong Jie (☎ 6532 2051; fax 6532 4853), near, but not in, Sanlitun. **South Africa,** 5 Dongzhimenwai Dajie (☎ 6532 0171). **UK,** 11 Guanghua Lu, Jianguomenwai (☎ 6532 1961; fax 6532 1939). **US,** 3 Xiushui Dong Jie, Jianguomenwai (☎ 6532 3431; fax 6532 6057).

Currency Exchange: The **Bank of China** and almost every other every hotel and hostel can exchange **traveler's checks** and US dollars. To cash traveler's checks into US dollars, head to **CITS** or the **Bank of China Head Office** (☎ 6601 6688), 410 Fuchengmennei Dajie, 2nd fl., Counter #1 or 2.

Emergency: Police ☎ 110. **Fire** ☎ 119. **Ambulance** ☎ 120.

Police: Public Security Bureau (gōngān jú), 9 Quinmen Dajie (☎ 6524 2063, foreigners section 8401 5292, visa extensions 6532 3861).

Telephones: Almost all accommodations have telephones for international (IDD) calls. **Directory Assistance:** ☎ 114. **International Directory Assistance:** ☎ 115.

Internet Access: Qianyi Internet Cafe (qiányì wǎngluò kāfeī wū; ☎ 6705 1722), Station Shopping Mall, 3rd fl., opposite the southeast corner of Tiananmen Square. Y10 per 30min. Drinks and snacks Y15-25. Open daily 9:30am-11pm.

Post Office: International Post Office (guójì yóujú; ☎ 6512 8120), on the west side of Jianguomen Bei Dajie. **Poste Restante.** Open daily 8am-6:30pm.

BEIJING	❶	❷	❸	❹	❺
ACCOM.	under Y40	Y40-80	Y81-150	Y151-250	over Y250
FOOD	under Y20	Y20-30	Y31-50	Y51-70	over Y70

◪ ACCOMMODATIONS

In Beijing, "budget" typically means a poor location around the city's southern periphery. The hostels and hotels along the mid-stretch of **Nansanhuan Lu,** between the **Yangqiao** and **Muxiyuan** exits, teem with backpackers.

GATEWAY CITIES

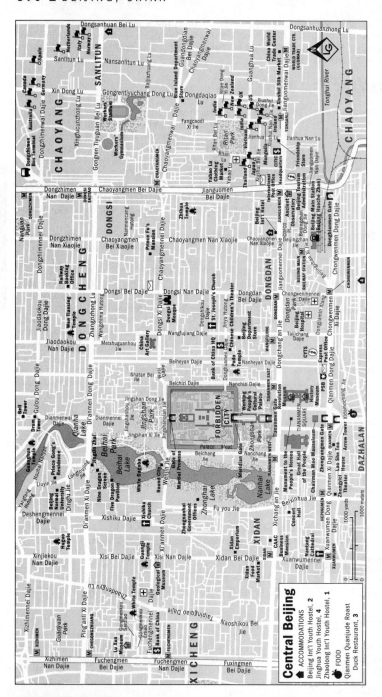

Central Beijing

▲ ACCOMMODATIONS
Beijing Int'l Youth Hostel, **2**
Jinghua Youth Hostel, **4**
Zhaolong Int'l Youth Hostel, **1**

● FOOD
Qianmen Quanjude Roast
Duck Restaurant, **3**

📧 **Beijing International Youth Hostel** (HI; bêijīng guójì qīngnián læshè), 9 Jianguomennei Dajie, bldg. 2, 10th fl. (☎6512 6688, ext. 6145 or 6146; fax 6522 9494), behind the Beijing International Hotel. Accessible by bus to Beijing Zhan, the subway, and airport buses. Clean rooms, cute wooden bunk beds, and convenience for unbeatable prices. Packed with chatty foreigners. Bike rental Y5 per hr., deposit Y300. Internet Y10 per 30min. Laundry Y10. 6- to 8-bed dorms with A/C Y50, non-members Y60. ❷

📧 **Jinghua Youth Hostel** (jīnghuá fàndiàn), Xiluoyuan Nanli, Yongdingmenwai Dajie, Fengtai (☎6722 2211 ext. 3359; fax 6721 1455). Take bus #66 from Qianmen to Yangqiao. Offers co-ed dorms, a pool, and an endless flow of travelers. Bike rental Y10 per day (deposit Y100). Internet Y10 per hr. (deposit Y50). 20-bed dorm Y25; 4-bed dorms Y30-35; 3-bed dorms with bath and A/C Y50; doubles with bath Y140-230. ❶

Zhaolong International Youth Hostel (HI; zhàolóng qīngnián lüshè), 2 Gongren Tiyuguan Bei Lu (☎6597 2299 ext. 6111; fax 6597 2288), at Dongsanhuan Lu. Take bus #3, 43, or 300 to Baijiazhuang; it's a 5min. walk north. This cozy multi-level hostel boasts sparkling rooms with A/C, bunk beds, tile floors, kitchen, and reading room. 3- to 6-bed dorms Y50; 2-bed dorms Y60. Non-members: Y60/Y70. ❷

🍴 FOOD

The streets of Beijing burst with food options. The *hutongs* (alleyways) overflow with stalls that vary in quality but are consistently low in price; special attention should be paid to the areas around **Qianmen** and **Wangfujing**, and **Tiantan, Ritan,** and **Beihai Parks.** Some great restaurants can be found around **Liangmaqiao.** An absolute must-see, the night food market at **Donganmen,** off Wangfujing Dajie, serves treats like fried ice cream and more exotic fare like whole-sparrows-on-a-stick nightly from dusk to 9:30pm. For an easy sit-down meal, just head into any restaurant that advertises *jiachangcai* (everyday family food). Tasty, filling meals are about Y10-20 per person, but foreigners are sometimes ripped off, so be careful. **Beijing duck** is as intrinsic to the capital's history as *jingiu* (proposing toasts) and the Forbidden City. Food fit for kings is available at **Qianmen Quanjude Roast Duck Restaurant ❺** (qiánmén quánjùdé kǎoyā diàn), 32 Qianmen Dajie. Founded in 1864, the Qianmen location is the oldest of the 15 branches. A pictorial menu helps walk tourists through a first-time Beijing duck experience. (☎6511 2418 or 6701 1379. Meals Y75-100, carving extra. "Fancier" part open daily 11am-1:30pm and 4:30-8:30pm; "less fancy" part 10am-9pm.)

🌐 SIGHTS

TIANANMEN SQUARE. (tiānānmén guǎngchǎng.) China's equivalent of Red Square, Tiananmen Square, one of the world's largest public meeting spaces, has created enough historical and political fodder to last a lifetime. The political epicenter of popular protest in modern China, the square has witnessed May 4th anti-imperialist demonstrations, anti-Japanese protests, Mao Zedong's proclamation of the People's Republic of China, the Red Guard rallies of the Cultural Revolution, politically charged outpourings of grief for Zhou Enlai, and pro-democracy protests. For most Chinese, Tiananmen Square remains an ideological mecca, a field of cement where they pay tribute to the heroes and victims of China's tumultuous history. Vivid images of the bloody events of 1989 may at times surface, but for now, the square seems rooted in a celebratory atmosphere, a prime kite-flying and picture-taking site. On the north side of the square, the **Monument to the People's Heroes,** an angular slab of granite erected in 1958, depicts heroic, revolutionary events from recent Chinese history. Mao rests peacefully in the stately **Chairman Mao Mausoleum** (máo zhǔxí jìniàn táng), at the city's southern end. (*Between Changan*

Dajie and Qianmen Dajie. Subway: Qianmen. Buses #1, 4, 10, and 20 stop along Changan Jie to the north, while #5, 9, 17, 22, 47, 53, 54, 59, and 307 reach Qianmen to the south. Bus #116 runs along the side of the square. Mausoleum open M-Sa 8:30-11:30am.)

FORBIDDEN CITY. (zǐjìn chéng.) During the palace's 500-year history, only 24 emperors and their most intimate attendants could have known every part of its 800 buildings and 9000 chambers. The Forbidden City, so named because commonfolk were barred from entry, was opened to the public in 1949. Now referred to as the **Imperial Palace** (gù gōng), the complex is the most impressive example of ancient architecture in China. Construction of the Forbidden City was completed in 1406, the 4th year of Ming Emperor Yongle's reign. It was based on a principle of work before play; the administrative offices and temples are in the front, while the markets are in the back. The Son of Heaven conducted his stately affairs in the **ceremonial halls** of Taihedian, Zhonghedian, and Baohedian. The first hall contains the imperial throne. Past the **imperial living quarters**, Qianqinggong, Jiaotaidian, and Kunninggong (now voyeur-friendly peering halls), is the **Imperial Garden** and an impressive artificial **Mountain of Piled Excellence** topped with a pagoda. *(Take any bus to Tiananmen Square. Open daily 8:30am-5pm, winter 8:30am-4:30pm; last admission 1hr. before closing. English translations. Audio tours (narrated by Roger Moore) Y30, Y200 deposit. Palace Museum Y40. Students half-price, children under 1.2m free.)*

SUMMER PALACE. (yìhé yuán.) Constructed in 1750, the Summer Palace is the largest imperial palace and garden complex in China. Scattered across the emperors' enormous summertime playground are over 3000 halls, pavilions, towers, courtyards, and even a re-creation of the southern Chinese city of Suzhou where empresses could go "shopping" for fine silk. **Suzhou Jie** is the one area so far off the beaten path that it doesn't make the mapped walking tour; it is a must-see all the same. Cool green water laps the sidewalks, stylized gondolas idle beside dumpling restaurants, and stone walkways wind between water on one side, and shops, snack stands, and street artists on the other. Other sights include Empress Dowager Ci Xi's infamous **Marble Boat** (built in 1888 courtesy of embezzled funds), the **Seventeen Arch Bridge** topped with 544 stone lions, the **Pavilion for Listening to Orioles,** and the **Porcelain Pagoda.** A stroll along the stunning 728m **Long Corridor** (cháng láng) winds past 8000 paintings and most of the sights. *(The quickest way to the Summer Palace is to take minibus #375 from Xizhimen station. From Qianmen, the Palace is 2hr. away by bicycle. Open daily in summer 6:30am-6pm, in winter 7am-5pm. April 31-Oct. 31 Y30, students Y15, through ticket Y50; Sept. 1-March 3 Y20/Y10/Y40. Map Y5.)*

BADALING GREAT WALL. (bādálíng cháng chéng.) Badaling is the part of the wall to visit if you want to take pictures and have admirers back home recognize them as the Great Wall. The government has taken great pains to restore this part to its "original" condition. Every tower and turret stands just as it did when the Mongols overran the country 700 years ago, give or take a few souvenir shops. Guard rails and a cable car (Y40, round-trip Y50) make Badaling the best, almost easy, way to see the Great Wall. You'll get to rub elbows with tourists from all around the world. *(Take bus #5 or 44 from Qianmen to Deshengmen, then walk over the nearby overpass, and hop on bus #919 from in front of a monstrous circular building. Badaling is the next stop (1½hr., Y5.5). Official tour buses #1, 2, and 4 leave for Badaling Great Wall and the Ming Tombs from the northeast corner of Qianmen (5:30-10:30am), Beijing Train Station (6-10am), and the zoo (6-11am). Hotel services and tour guides are the most expensive means. Open in summer daily 6am-10pm; in winter 7am-6pm. Y45, students and elderly Y25.)*

OTHER GREAT WALL SIGHTS. Badaling isn't the only stop along the Great Wall. More difficult to access, but slightly more satisfying experiences await visitors at **Mutianyu, Simatai,** and **Huanghua.** Jinghua Youth Hostel (see **Accommodations,** p. 871) runs tours and arranges other means of transportation to these sections.

GLOSSARY

BULGARIAN (БЪЛГАРСКИ)

PHRASEBOOK

ENGLISH	BULGARIAN	PRONUNCIATION
Yes/no	Да/Не	dah/neh
Please	Извинете	eez-vi-NEH-teh
Thank you	Благодаря	blahg-oh-dahr-YAH
Hello	Добър ден	DOH-bur den
Good-bye	Добиждане	doh-VIZH-dan-eh
Good morning	Добро утро	doh-BROH U-troh
Good evening	Добър Вечер	DOH-bur VEH-cher
Good night	Лека Нощ	LEH-ka nosht
Sorry/Excuse me	Извинете	iz-vi-NEE-tye
Help!	Помощ!	PO-mosht
When?	Кога?	ko-GA
Where is...?	Къде е?	kuh-DEH eh
How do I get to...?	Как да стигна...?	kak dah STEEG-na
How much does this cost?	Колко Струва?	KOHL-ko STROO-va
Do you have...?	Имате Ли...?	EEH-mah-teh lee
Do you speak English?	Говорите ли Английски?	go-VO-rih-te li an-GLIS-keeh
I don't understand	Не разбирам.	neh rahz-BIH-rahm
I don't speak Bulgarian	Не говоря по-български	ne gah-var-YA po-bul-GAR-ski
Please write it down.	Може лида ми го запишете	MAW-zhe LEE-dah mee gah za-pi-SHEE-tye
Speak a little slower, please.	Малко по-бавно, ако обичате.	MAHL-ka pah-BAHV-na, AH-ka ahb-i-CHAT-ye
I'd like to order...	Искам да порьчам...	EES-kahm da pah-ROO-cham
I'd like to pay/We'd like to pay.	Бих искал(а/и) да платя(им)	Bikh is-KAHL-(a/ee) da plat-YA-(yim)
I think you made a mistake in the bill.	Мисля че има трешка в сметката.	mis-LYA che EE-mah TRESH-ka v smyet-KAH-ta
Do you have a vacancy?	Имате ли свободна стая?	ee-MAH-tye lee svah-BOHD-na-ya sta-YA
I'd like a room.	Искам стая.	EES-kahm STAH-yah
May I see the room?	Може ли да видя стаята?	MOH-zhe lee da vid-YA sta-YA-ta
No, I don't like it.	Не, не ми харесва.	nee, nee mee kha-RYES-va
Yes, I'll take it.	Да, ще я взема	dah, shi-YE ya b-ZYE-mah
Will you tell me when to get off?	Извинете, кода тряба да сляза?	eez-vee-NEH-teh ko-GAH TRYAHB-vah dah SLYAH-zah?
Is this the right train/bus to...?	Това ли е верният влак/рейс да...?	TOH-va lee ver-NYAT vlak/rehs dah
I want a ticket to...	Искам билет да...	is-KAHM beel-YET da
How long does the trip take?	Колка?	KOHL-ka?
Where is the bathroom/nearest telephone booth/center of town?	Къде е тоалетната/най-близкия телефон/центърът на града?	koo-DYE ye toh-ah-LYET-na-ta/nai-bliz-kee-ya te-ke-FOHN/TSENT-ur-ut na GRAD-ah

ENGLISH	BULGARIAN	PRONUNCIATION
I've lost my...	Загубил(а) съм си...	zah-goo-BEEL-(a) soom see
Would you like to dance?	Искате ли да танцуваме	ees-KAH-tye lee dah tan-tsoo-VAHM-ye
Go away.	Махнете се	makh-NEE-tye seh

GLOSSARY

ENGLISH	BULGARIAN	PRONOUNCE

ENGLISH	BULGARIAN	PRONOUNCE	ENGLISH	BULGARIAN	PRONOUNCE
one	едно	ehd-NO	post office	поща	POH-sha
two	две	dveh	stamp	марка	MAR-ka
three	три	tree	airmail	въздушна поща	vooz-DOOSH-na POH-sha
four	четири	CHEH-tee-ree	departure	заминаващи	zaminavashti
five	пет	peht	arrival	пристигащи	pristigashti
six	шест	shesht	one-way	отиване	o-TEE-vahn-eh
seven	седем	SEH-dehm	round-trip	отиване и Връщане	o-TEE-van-e ee VRI-shtah-neh
eight	осем	O-sehm	luggage	багаж	ba-GAZH
nine	девет	DEH-veht	reservation	резевация	re-zer-VAH-tsee-yah
ten	десет	DEH-seht	train	влак	vlahk
twenty	двадесет	DVAH-DEH-seht	bus	автобус	ahv-to-BOOS
thirty	тридесет	TREE-deh-set	airport	летище	LYET-i-shye
forty	четиридесет	TCHE-TEE-REE-deh-set	station	гара	gara
fifty	петдесет	peht-deh-SEHT	ticket	билет	bi-LYET
sixty	шестдесет	shest-deh-SEHT	grocery	бакалия	bah-kah-LIH-ya
seventy	седемдесет	se-dem-deh-SEHT	breakfast	закуска	za-KOO-ska
eighty	осем	OH-sem	lunch	обяд	ah-BYAD
ninety	деветдесет	de-vet-deh-SEHT	dinner	вечеря	veh-cher-YA
one hundred	сто	stoh	menu	меню	men-YOO
one thousand	хиляда	hi-LYA-da	bread	хляб	hlyab
Monday	понеделник	pa-ne-DYEL-nik	vegetables	зеленчуци	zelenchutzee
Tuesday	вторник	FTOR-nik	beef	телешко	teleshka
Wednesday	сряда	s-RYA-da	chicken	пиле	PEE-lye
Thursday	четвъртък	chet-VUR-tuk	pork	свинско	SVIN-ska
Friday	петък	pe-TUK	fish	риба	REE-ba
Saturday	събота	su-BOH-ta	coffee	кафе	kah-FEH
Sunday	неделя	ni-DYEL-ya	milk	мляко	MLYAH-ko
a day	ден	dyen	beer	бира	BEE-rah
a few days	няколко дни	ni-KOL-ka dnee	sugar	захар	ZAH-khar
a week	семица	syed-MEE-tsa	eggs	яйца	yai-TSAH
morning	сутрин	SOO-trin	holiday	ваканция	vah-KAHN-tsee-ya
afternoon	следобед	SLYE-dob-yed	open	отварят	ot-VAR-yaht
evening	вечер	VEH-cher	closed	затварят	zaht-VAR-yaht
today	днес	d-NYES	bank	банка	BAHN-ka
tomorrow	утре	OO-trye	police	полиция	pohl-EE-tsee-ya
spring	пролет	pro-LYET	exchange	обменно бюро	OB-myen-na byu-ROH

ENGLISH	BULGARIAN	PRONOUNCE
summer	лято	LYA-ta
fall	есен	YE-sen
winter	зима	zee-MAH
hot	топло	tah-PLOH
cold	студено	stoo-DYEN-a
single room	единична	ye-din-EECH-nah
double room	двойна	dvoy-NAH
reservation	резевация	re-zer-VAH-tsee-yah

ENGLISH	BULGARIAN	PRONOUNCE
toilet	тоалетна	to-ah-LYET-na
square	площад	PLO-shad
monastery	манастир	mah-nah-STEER
church	църква	TSURK-ba
passport	паспорт	pahs-PORT
market	пазар	pah-ZAR
right	дясно	DYAHS-no
left	ляво	LYAH-vo

CROATIAN (HRVATSKI)

PHRASEBOOK

ENGLISH	CROATIAN	PRONUNCIATION
Yes/no	Da/Ne	Da/Neh
Please/You're welcome	Molim	MO-leem
Thank you	Hvala lijepa	HVAH-la leepa
Hello/Hi	Dobardan/Bog	Do-bar-DAHN/bog
Good-bye	Bog	Bog
Good morning	Dobro jutro	DO-bro YOO-tro
Good evening	Dobra večer	DO-bra VE-Cher
Good night	Laku noć	LA-koo noch
Sorry/Excuse me	Oprostite	o-PRO-sti-teh
Help!	U pomoć!	OO pomoch
When?	Kada?	KA-da
Where is...?	Gdje je...?	GDYE je
How do I get to...?	Kako mogu doći do...?	KAH-ko MO-goo DO-chee do...
How much does this cost?	Koliko to košta?	KO-li-koh toh KOH-shta
Do you have...?	Imate li...?	EEM-a-teh lee
Do you speak English?	Govorite li engleski?	GO-vor-i-teh lee eng-LEH-ski
I don't understand.	Ne razumijem.	neh ra-ZOO-mi-yem
I don't speak Croatian.	Ne govorim hrvatski.	Nye GOH-voh-rim KHR-va-tskee
Speak a little slower, please.	Govorite polako, molim.	go-VOR-iteh PO-la-koh MOH-leem
I'd like to order...	Želio bih naručiti...	Jelim na-ROO-chiti
Check, please.	Račun, molim.	RACH-un mo-leem
Do you have a vacancy?	Imate li slobodne sobe?	IMA-te li SLO-bo-dneh SOH-beh?
I'd like a room.	Želio bih sobu.	ZHEL-i-o bih SO-bu
Will you tell me when to get off?	Hoćete li mi reći kada tebam sići?	ho-CHEH-teh lee mee REH-cheh KAH-dah TREH-bahm SEE-chee
I want a ticket to...	Htio bih kartu za...	HTEE-o beeh KAHR-too zah...
Where is the bathroom/nearest public phone/center of town?	Gdje je kadom/nalazi najbliža telefonska govornica/centar grada?	gdyeh yeh KAH-dom/NAH-lahzee nahy-BLEE-zhah tehleh-FON-skah govor-NEE-tsah/TSEN-tahr GRAH-dah
I've lost my...	Jaz sam izgubil(a)...	YA SAM eez-GU-bee-lah
Go away.	Bježi	BYEH-zhee

GLOSSARY

ENGLISH	CROATIAN	PRONOUNCE
one	jedan	yehd-an/NO
two	dva	dvah/DVEE-jeh
three	tri	tree
four	četiri	CHEH-tee-ree
five	pet	peht
six	šest	shesht
seven	sedam	SEH-dahm
eight	osam	O-sahm
nine	devet	DEH-veht
ten	deset	DEH-seht
twenty	dvadeset	DVAH-deseht
thirty	trideset	TRI-deseht
forty	četrdeset	CHETR-deseht
fifty	pedeset	peh-DEH-seht
sixty	šestdeset	shest-DEH-seht
seventy	sedamdeset	sedam-DEH-seht
eighty	osamdeset	osam-DEH-seht
ninety	devedeset	de-vet-DEH-seht
one hundred	sto	sto
one thousand	tisuća	TEE-soo-chah
Monday	ponedeljak	POH-ne-djel-yak
Tuesday	utorak	UH-to-rak
Wednesday	srijeda	SREE-yeda
Thursday	četvrtak	CHET-ver-tak
Friday	petak	PE-tak
Saturday	subota	SUH-bo-tah
Sunday	nedjelja	NE-djel-yah
a day	dan	dan
a week	sedmica	SED-mi-tsah
morning	ujutro	oo-YU-troh
afternoon	popodne	poh-POH-dne
evening	večer	VE-cher
today	danas	DAH-nas
tomorrow	sutra	SUH-tra
spring	proljeće	proh-LYE-cheh
summer	ljeto	LYE-toh
fall	jesen	YE-sen
winter	zima	ZI-ma
hot	vruće	vRUH-che
cold	zima	ZI-ma
passport	putovnica	PU-to-vnee-tsa

ENGLISH	CROATIAN	PRONOUNCE
pharmacy	ljekarna	lye-KHA-rna
post office	pošta	POSH-ta
stamp	markica	MAR-ki-tsa
airmail	zrakoplovom	ZRA-ko-plo-vom
departure	odlažak	OD-lazh-ak
arrival	polazak	PO-lazh-ak
one-way	u jednom smjeru	oo YEH-dnom smee-YEH-roo
round-trip	povratna karta	POV-rat-na KAR-ta
reservation	rezervacija	re-ze-VAH-tsee-yah
bus	autobus	au-TOH-bus
airport	zračna luka	ZRA-chna lu-kah
station	kolodvor	KO-lo-dvor
grocery	trgovina	TER-goh-vee-na
breakfast	doručak	doh-RUH-chak
lunch	ručak	RUH-chak
dinner	večera	VE-che-ra
menu	karta	KA-rta
bread	kruh	krooh
vegetables	povrće	POH-ver-chay
beef	kravji	kra-vlyi
chicken	koka	ko-kah
pork	svinja	SVI-nya
fish	riba	REE-bah
coffee	kava	KAH-vah
milk	mlijeko	mli-YE-koh
beer	pivo	PEE-voh
eggs	jaje	YA-yeeh
holiday	praznik	PRAZ-nik
open	otvoreno	OT-vo-re-noh
closed	zatvoreno	ZAT-vor-re-noh
police	policija	po-LEE-tsee-ya
bank	banka	BAN-kah
exchange	mjenjačnica	myen-YACH-ni-tsa
toilet	WC	vay-tsay
square	trg	terg
castle	grad	grad
church	crkva	TSR-kvah
sugar	šećer	SHE-cher
market	trgovina	TER-goh-vee-na
left	lijevo	lee-YEH-vo
right	desno	DES-no

CZECH (ČESKY)

PHRASEBOOK

ENGLISH	CZECH	PRONOUNCE
Yes/no	Ano/ne	AH-no/neh
Please/You're welcome	Prosím	PROH-seem
Thank you	Děkuji	DYEH-koo-yih
Hello	Dobrý den (formal)	DO-bree den
Good-bye	Nashedanou	NAH sleh-dah-noh-oo
Good morning	Dobré ráno	DO-breh RAH-no
Good evening	Dobrý večer	DO-breh VE-tcher
Good night	Dobrou noc	DO-broh NOTS
Sorry/excuse me	Promiňte	PROH-mihn-teh
Help!	Pomoc!	POH-mots
When?	Kdy?	k-DEE
Where is...?	Kde je...?	k-DEH
How do I get to...?	Jak se dostanu do...?	YAK seh dohs-TAH-noo doh
How much does this cost?	Kolik to stojí?	KOH-lihk STOH-yee
Do you have...?	Máte...?	MAH-teh
Do you speak English?	Mluvíte anglicky?	MLOO-vit-eh ahng-GLIT-ski
I don't understand.	Nerozumím.	NEH-rohz-oo-meem
I don't speak Czech.	Nemluvím Česky.	NEH-mloo-veem CHESS-kee
Write it down, please.	Napište to, prosím.	PRO-seem nah-PEESH-tye
Speak a little slower, please.	Mluvte pomaleji, prosím.	MLUV-te PO-ma-le-yi PRO-seem
I'd like to order...	Prosím...	khtyel bikh
I'd like to pay/We'd like to pay.	Zaplatím/Zaplatíme.	ZAH-plah-teem/ZAH-plah-tee-meh
I think you made a mistake in the bill.	Myslím, že máte chybu v účtu.	MYS-leem zhe MAH-te khybuh v UHCH-tuh
Do you have a vacancy?	Máte volný pokoj?	MAA-teh VOL-nee PO-koy
I'd like a room.	Prosím pokoj.	pro-SEEM PO-koy
May I see the room?	Mohl(a) bych se podívat na ten pokoj?	MO-hul (MO-hla) bikh se PO-dyeh-vat na ten PO-koy
No, I don't like it.	Promiňte, nelíbí se mi.	RZHEK-nete mi gdy mahm VI-stohpit
Yes, I'll take it.	Ano, vezmu si ho.	yeh TOH-leh vlahk DO
Will you tell me when to get off?	Řekněte mi, kde mám vys-toupit?	RE-kne-te MI PRO-seem khde MAAM VYS-tou-pit
Is this the right train/bus to...?	Je tohle vlak/autobus do...?	Ye TOH-le AUTO-bus do
I want a ticket to...	Prosím jízdenku do...	khytel a bikh YEEZ-denkoo DO
How long does the trip take?	Jak dlouho trvá ta cesta?	YAK DLOU-ho TRH-vaa TSE-stah
Where is the bathroom/nearest telephone booth/center of town?	Kde je koupelna/nejbližší telefonní budka/centrum města?	gde ye TO-aleti/TA-di NE-yblish-nee TE-le-fo-nee BOOT-ka/MNE-HST-skeh TSEN-troom
I've lost my...	Ztratil(a) jsem...	ZTRA-til(a) YSEM
Would you like to dance?	Chtěl(a) byste si zatancovat?	khtyehl(a) BI-ste si ZA-tan-chit
Go away.	Prosím odejděte.	pro-SEEM ODEY-dhe-te

GLOSSARY

ENGLISH	CZECH	PRONOUNCE
one	jeden	YEH-den
two	dva	dv-YEH
three	tři	tr-ZHIH
four	čtyři	SHTEER-zhee
five	pět	p-YEHT
six	šest	shest
seven	sedm	SEH-duhm
eight	osm	OSS-uhm
nine	devět	dehv-YEHT
ten	deset	des-SEHT
twenty	dvacet	dvah-TSEHT
thirty	třicet	tr-zhih-TSEHT
forty	čtyřicet	SHTEEh-ri-TSETH
fifty	padesát	PA-des-aath
sixty	šedesát	shest-des-aath
seventy	sedmdesát	SEH-duhm-des-aath
eighty	osmdesát	OSS-uhm-des-aath
ninety	devadesát	DE-va-des-aath
one hundred	sto	STO
one thousand	tisíc	TI-seets
Monday	pondělí	PO-ndeh-lee
Tuesday	úterý	UH-te-reeh
Wednesday	středa	STRHE-dah
Thursday	čtvrtek	CZ-tvr-tekh
Friday	pátek	PAA-tekh
Saturday	sobota	SO-bo-tah
Sunday	neděle	NEH-dyeh-leh
a day	den	DEN
a few days	několik dní	NYE-ko-lik DNEEH
a week	týden	TYH-den
morning	ráno	RAH-no
afternoon	odpoledne	OT-pol-ed-ne
evening	večer	VE-cher
today	dnes	d-NEHS
tomorrow	zítra	ZEE-trah
spring	jaro	YA-ro
summer	léto	LEE-to
fall	podzim	POD-zim
winter	zima	ZI-ma
hot	teplý	TEP-leeh
cold	studený	STU-de-neeh
single room	jednolůžkový pokoj	YED-noh-luu-zhko-veeh PO-koy

ENGLISH	CZECH	PRONOUNCE
post office	pošta	POSH-ta
stamps	známka	ZNAHM-ka
airmail	letecky	LE-tets-ky
departure	odjezd	OD-yezd
arrival	příjezd	PREE-yezd
one-way	jen tam	yen tam
round-trip	zpáteční	SPAH-tech-nyee
bathroom	kúpelňa	KOO-pail-na
reservation	místenka	mis-TEN-kah
train	vlak	vlahk
bus	autobus	OUT-oh-boos
airport	letiště	LEH-tish-tyeh
station	nádraží	NA-drah-zhee
ticket	lístek	LIS-tek
grocery	potraviny	PO-tra-vee-nee
breakfast	snídaně	SNEE-dan-ye
lunch	oběd	OB-yed
dinner	večeře	VE-cher-zhe
menu	listek	LIS-tek
bread	chléb	khleb
vegetables	zelenina	ZE-le-nee-na
beef	hovězí	HO-vye-zee
chicken	kuře	KOO-rzheh
pork	vep	VEPRZH
fish	ryba	RY-bah
coffee	káva	KAH-va
milk	mléko	MLEH-koh
beer	pivo	PEE-voh
sugar	cukr	TSOO-kur
eggs	vejce	VEY-tse
holiday	prázdniny	PRAHZ-dni-nee
open	otevřeno	O-te-zheno
closed	zavřeno	ZAV-rzhen-o
bank	banka	BAN-ka
police	policie	PO-lits-iye
exchange	směnárna	smyeh-NAR-na
toilet	WC	VEE-TSEE
square	náměstí	NAH-mye-stee
castle	hrad	KHRAD
church	kostel	KO-stel
tower	vě	VYEZH
market	trh	TH-rh

ENGLISH	CZECH	PRONOUNCE
double room	dvoulůžkový pokoj	DVOU-luu-zhko-veeh PO-koy
reservation	rezervace	RE-zer-va-tse
with shower	se sprchou	SE SPR-khou
pharmacy	lékárna	LEE-khaar-nah

ENGLISH	CZECH	PRONOUNCE
passport	cestovní pas	TSE-stov-neeh
bakery	pekařství	PE-karzh-stvee
left	vlevo	VLE-voh
right	vpravo	VPRA-voh

ESTONIAN (ESTI KEEL)

PHRASEBOOK

ENGLISH	ESTONIAN	PRONUNCIATION
Yes/no	Jaa/Ei	jah/ay
Please/You're welcome	Palun	PAH-loon
Thank you	Tänan	TA-nahn
Hello	Tere	TEH-reh
Good-bye	Head aega	heh-ahd EYE-gah
Good morning	Tere hommikust	TEH-re hõm-mee-KOOST
Good evening	Head õhtut	heh-ahd EUW-toot
Good night	Head ööd	heh-ahd euwd
Sorry/Excuse me	Vabandage	vah-bahn-DAHG-eh
Help!	Appi!	AHP-pee
When?	Millal?	meel-LAL
Where is...?	Kus on...?	koos õn
I'd like to go to...	Soovin minna...	sõõ-veen MEEN-nah
How much does this cost?	Kui palju?	kwee PAHL-yoo
Do you have...?	Kas teil on...?	kahs tayl õn
Do you speak English?	Kas te räägite inglise keelt?	kahs teh raa-GEE-teh een-GLEE-seh kehlt
I don't understand.	Ma ei saa aru.	mah ay sah AH-roo
I don't speak Estonian	Ma ei räägi Eesti keelt.	mah ay RAA-gee ehs-tee kehlt
Please write it down.	Palun kirjutage maha.	PAH-loon KEER-yoo-TAH-geh MAH-hah
Speak a little slower, please.	Palun rääkige natuge aeglasemalt.	PAH-loon RAA-kee-geh nah-too-geh EYE-glah-seh-mahlt
I'd like to order...	Ma sooviksin...	mah SOO-veek-seen
I'd like to pay/We'd like to pay.	Ma sooviksin maksta.	ma SOO-veek-seen MAHKS-tah
I think you made a mistake...	Arvan et eksisite...	AHR-vahn eht EHK-see-see-teh
I'd like to make a reservation.	Sooviksin broneerida tuba.	SÕÕ-veek-seen BRÕ-neh-ree-dah too-bah
Do you have a vacancy?	Kas teil on vaba tuba?	kahs TAYL õn vah-bah TOO-bah
I'd like a room.	Ma sooviksin tuba.	mah SOO-vik-sin TUH-bah
May I see the room?	Kas võiksin tuba näha?	kahs VEUWK-seen too-bah NA-hah
No, I don't like it.	Ei meeldi/Ei sobi.	ay mehl-dee/ay sõ-bee
Yes, I'll take it.	Jaa, võtan.	Yah, VEUW-tahn.
Will you tell me when to get off?	Palun öelge kus ma pean väljuma?	PAH-loon EULL-geh koos mah peh-ahn VAL-yoo-mah
Does this train/bus go to...?	Kas see rong/buss läheb...?	kahs seh rõng/boos LA-hehb
I want a ticket to...	Ma sooviksin ühte piletit...	mah SOO-veek-seen EWKH-teh PEE-leh-teet

ENGLISH	ESTONIAN	PRONUNCIATION
How long is the trip?	Kui pikk on reis?	koo-wee peek ōn rays
When is the first/next/last train to...	Millal lahkub esimine/järgmine/viimane et minna...	meel-lahl lah-koob EHS-ee-mee-neh/JARG-mee-neh/VEE-mah-neh eht meen-nah
Where is the bathroom/nearest telephone booth/center of town?	Kus on tualett/kõige lähedam telefon/kesklinn?	koos ōn twa-LEHT/keuw-geh LA-heh-dahm teh-leh-fōn/kehs-kleen
I've lost my...	Olen kaotanud...	ō-lehn KAŌ-tah-nood
Would you like to dance?	Soovite tansida?	soo-vee-teh tahn-SEE-dah
Go away.	Minge ära.	MEEN-geh A-ra

GLOSSARY

ENGLISH	ESTONIAN	PRONOUNCE	ENGLISH	ESTONIAN	PRONOUNCE
one	üks	euwks	post office	post kontor	pōst KŌN-tör
two	kaks	kahks	stamp	mark	mahrk
three	kolm	kōlm	airmail	lennu post	LEHN-noo pōst
four	neli	NEH-lee	departs	väljub	VAL-yoob
five	viis	veese	arrives	saabub	SAH-boob
six	kuus	koose	one-way ticket	üheotsa piletit	EUW-heh-OHT-sah PEE-leh-teet
seven	seitse	SAYT-seh	round-trip	edasi-tagasi piletit	Eh-dah-see-TAH-gah-see PEE-leh-teet
eight	kaheksa	KAH-heks-ah	luggage	bagaaž	BAH-gahzh
nine	üheksa	EUW-eks-ah	train	rong	rōng
ten	kümme	KEUW-meh	bus	buss	boos
twenty	kakskümmend	KAHKS-keuwm-mehnd	airport	lennujaam	LEHN-noo-yahm
thirty	kolmkümmend	KŌLM-keuwm-mend	station	jaam	yahm
forty	nelikümmend	NEH-lee-keuwm-mend	ticket	pilet	PEE-leht
fifty	viiskümmend	VEES-keuwm-mend	grocery	toidupood	TŌY-doo-PŌŌD
sixty	kuuskümmend	KOOS-keuwm-mend	breakfast	hommiku söök	HŌM-mee-koo seuhk
seventy	seitsekümmend	SAYTS-seh-keuwm-mend	lunch	lõunasöök	LEUH-nah-seuhk
eighty	kaheksaküm-mend	KAH-hek-sah-keuwm-mend	dinner	õhtusöök	EUH-too-seuhk
ninety	üheksaküm-mend	EUW-hek-sah-keuwm-mend	menu	menüü	MEH-neuh
one hundred	sada	SA-da	bread	leib	LAY-eeb
one thousand	tuhat	TU-hat	vegetables	juurvili	YOOR-vee-lee
Monday	esmaspäev	EHS-mahs-pav	beef	loomaliha	LŌŌ-mah-lee-hah
Tuesday	teisipäev	TAYS-ee-pav	chicken	kana	kah-nah
Wednesday	kolmapäev	KOHL-mah-pav	pork	sealiha	seh-ah-LEE-hah
Thursday	neljapäev	NEHL-yah-pav	fish	kala	kah-lah
Friday	reede	REE-eed	coffee	kohv	kohv
Saturday	laupäev	LAH-oo-pav	milk	piim	peem
Sunday	pühapäev	PEUW-hah-pav	beer	õlu	elu

ENGLISH	ESTONIAN	PRONOUNCE	ENGLISH	ESTONIAN	PRONOUNCE
a day	üks päev	EUWKS pav	sugar	suhkur	SOOH-koor
a few days	mõni päev	MEUH-nee pav	eggs	munad	MOO-nahd
a week	üks nädal	euwks na-DAHL	holiday	püha	PEUW-hah
morning	hommik	HÕM-meek	open	avatud/lahti	AH-vah-tood/ LAH-tee
afternoon	õhtupool	EUH-too-põõl	closed	suletud/kinni	SOO-leh-tood/ KEEN-nee
evening	õhtu	EUH-too	bank	pank	pahnk
today	täna	TA-nah	police	politsei	POH-leet-say
tomorrow	homme	HÕM-me	exchange	valuutavahetus	vah-loo-TAH-vah-heh-toos
spring	kevad	keh-VAHD	toilet	tualett	twa-LET
summer	suvi	SOO-vee	square	plats/väljak	plahts/val-yahk
fall	sügis	SEUW-gees	castle	loss	lõs
winter	talv	tahlv	church	kirik	kee-reek
hot	kuum	koom	tower	torn	tõrn
cold	külm	keuwlm	market	turg	toorg
single room	üheline	EUW-heh-LEE-neh	passport	pass	pahs
double room	kaheline	KAH-heh-LEE-ne	bakery	pagar	PAH-gahr
with shower	duššiga	DOOSH-ee-gah	on the left	vasakul	VAH-sah-keul
pharmacy	apteek	ahp-TEEK	on the right	paremal	PAH-reh-mahl

HUNGARIAN (MAGYAR)

PHRASEBOOK

ENGLISH	HUNGARIAN	PRONUNCIATION
Yes/no	Igen/nem	EE-ghen/nem
Please	Kérem	KAY-rem
Thank you	Köszönöm	KUH-suh-num
Hello	Szervusz/Szia/Hello	SAIR-voose/See-ya/Hello
Good-bye	Viszontlátásra	Vi-sont-lah-tah-shraw
Good morning	Jó reggelt	YOH raig-gailt
Good night	Jó éjszakát	YOH ay-sokat
Excuse me	Elnézést	EL-nay-zaysht
When?	Mikor?	MI-kor
Where is...?	Hol van...?	hawl von
How do you get to...?	Hogy jutok...?	hawdj YOO-tawk
How much does this cost?	Mennyibe kerül?	MEN-yee-beh KEH-rewl
Do you have...?	Van...?	von
Do you speak English?	Beszél angolul?	BESS-ayl ON-goal-ool
I don't understand.	Nem értem.	nem AYR-tem
I don't speak Hungarian.	Nem tudok magyarul.	Nehm TOO-dawk MAH-dyah-rool
Please write it down?	Kérem, írja fel.	KAY-rem, EER-yuh fell.
Speak a little slower, please.	Kérem, beszéljen lassan.	KAY-rem, BESS-ayl-yen LUSH-shun
I'd like to order...	...kérek.	KAY-rek
Do you have a vacancy?	Volna valami?	VAWL-na VO-lom-mee
I'd like a room.	Szeretnék egy szobát.	seret-naik edj SOW-baat.

ENGLISH	HUNGARIAN	PRONUNCIATION
May I see the room?	Megnézhetném a szobát?	MEg-naiz-HETnaim aw SOW-baat?
No thanks, I won't take it.	Kősőnőm, nem vészem.	KUH-suh-num, nem vess-em
That's fine. I'll take it.	Ez jó, Kiveszem.	ez-yo key-vess-em
Is this the right train/bus to...?	Ez a jó vonat/busz...ba?	ez a yo vaw-not/boos...bah
I want a ticket to...	Szeretnék jegyet.	serr-et-nake yedge-at
Will you tell me when to get off?	Megtudja Mondani, mikor kell leszállni?	MEG-tood-ya Mondanee me-kor kell less-all-knee
Where is the *bathroom*/nearest *telephone booth*/(public phone)/*center of town*?	Hol van a WC/a legkőzelebbi telefanfülke/a városkőzpont...?	Hole vun a WC/a leg-koz-ELL-EBEE telephone-foolkey/a varosh-koz-pont
I've lost my...	Elvesztettem a...	elle-vest-tet-tem ah
Go away.	Távozzék.	TAH-vawz-zayk
My name is...	A nevem...	A nev-em
What is your name?	Hogy hívják?	hawdj HEE-vyahk
Check, please.	A számlát, kérem.	uh SAHM-lot KAY-rem
I'm lost.	Eltèvedtem	elle-taav-e-te

GLOSSARY

ENGLISH	HUNGARIAN	PRONOUNCE
one	egy	edge
two	kettő	ket-tuuh
three	három	hah-rom
four	négy	naydj
five	öt	uh-t
six	hat	hut
seven	hét	hayte
eight	nyolc	nyoltz
nine	kilenc	kih-lentz
ten	tíz	tease
twenty	húsz	hoose
thirty	harminc	har-mintz
forty	negyven	nedj-ven
fifty	ötven	ut-ven
sixty	hatvan	hut-von
seventy	hetven	het-ven
eighty	nyolcvan	nyoltz-van
ninety	kilencven	kih-lentz-ven
hundred	száz	saaz
thousand	ezer	eh-zehr
Monday	hétfő	hayte-phuuh
Tuesday	kedd	ked
Wednesday	szerda	sayr-dah
Thursday	csütörtök	chew-ter-tek
Friday	péntek	paine-tek

ENGLISH	HUNGARIAN	PRONOUNCE
post office	posta	pawsh-tuh
stamp	bélyeg	BAY-yeg
airmail	légipostán	LAY-ghee-pawsh-tahn
departure	indulás	IN-dool-ahsh
arrival	érkezés	ayr-keh-zaysh
one-way	csak oda	chok AW-do
round-trip	oda-vissza	AW-do-VEES-so
train	vonat	VAW-not
bus	autobussz	auto-boos
airport	repülőtér	rep-ewlu-TAYR
station	pályaudvar	pa-yo-OOT-var
ticket	jegyet	YED-et
grocery	élelmiszerbolt	Ay-lel-meser-balt
breakfast	reggeli	REG-gell-ee
lunch	ebéd	EB-ayhd
dinner	vacsora	VOTCH-oh-rah
menu	étlap	ATE-lop
bread	kenyér	KEN-yair
vegetables	zöldségek	ZULD-segek
beef	marhahús	MOR-ho-hoosh
pork	disznóhús	disnow-hoosh
fish	hal	hull
water	víz	veez
juice	gyümölcslé	DYEW-murl-chlay
coffee	kávé	KAA-vay

ENGLISH	HUNGARIAN	PRONOUNCE
Saturday	szombat	SAWM-baht
Sunday	vasárnap	VAHSH-ahr-nahp
evening	este	ES-te
today	ma	mah
tomorrow	holnap	HAWL-nahp
spring	tavasz	TO-vos
summer	nyár	njaar
fall	ősz	öss
winter	tél	tail
holiday	ünnepnap	ewn-nap-nop
single/double	egyagyas/ kétágyas szoba	edge-agas/ket-agas so-ba

ENGLISH	HUNGARIAN	PRONOUNCE
milk	tej	tay
beer	sör	shurr
wine	bor	bawr
market	piac	PEE-ots
bakery	pék	paik
pharmacy	patika	PA-teek-ha
bank	bank	bonk
city center	Belváros	Bell-VA-rosh
exchange	valutabeváltó	VO-loo-tob-be-vaal-taw
left	bal	bol
right	jobb	yowb

LATVIAN (LATIVSKA)

PHRASEBOOK

ENGLISH	LATVIAN	PRONUNCIATION
Yes/no	Jā/nē	yah/ney
Please/You're welcome	Lūdzu	LOOD-zuh
Thank you	Paldies	PAHL-dee-yes
Hello	Labdien	LAHB-dyen
Good-bye	Uz redzēšanos	ooz RE-dzeh-shan-was
Good morning	Labrīt	LAHB-reet
Good night	Ar labu nakti	ar LA-boo NA-kti
Help!	Palīgā!	PAH-lee-gah
When?	Kad?	KAHD
Where is...?	Kur ir...?	kuhr ihr
How do I get to...?	Kā es varu nokļūt uz...?	kah ess VA-roo NOkly-oot ooz
How much does this cost?	Cik maksā?	sikh MAHK-sah
Do you have...?	Vai jums ir...?	vai yoomss ir
Do you speak English?	Vai jūs runājat angliski?	vai yoos ROO-nah-yat AN-glee-ski
I don't understand.	Es nesaprotu.	ehs NEH-sah-proh-too
I'd like to order...	Es vēlos...	ess VE-lwass
I'd like to pay/We'd like to pay.	Lūdzu rēķinu.	LOOD-zu RAY-tyi-noo
Do you have a vacancy?	Vai jums ir brīvas istabas?	vai yums ir BREE-vas IS-tab-as
May I see the room?	Vai es varu redzēt istabu?	vay ehs VAH-roo REHD-zeht IHS-tah-boo
Will you tell me when to get off?	Lūdzu pasakiet, kad jāizkāpj?	LOOD-zoo pah-sah-kee-aht, kahd YAH-IHS-kah-pye
I want a ticket to...	Es vēlos biļeti uz...	ehss VAAL-wass BIHL-yet-ih ooz

GLOSSARY

GLOSSARY

ENGLISH	LATVIAN	PRONOUNCE
one	viens	vee-yenz
two	divi	DIH-vih
three	trīs	treese
four	četri	CHEH-trih
five	pieci	PYET-sih
six	seši	SEH-shih
seven	septini	SEHP-tih-nyih
eight	astoņi	AHS-toh-nyih
nine	devini	DEH-vih-nyih
ten	desmit	DEZ-miht
twenty	divdesmit	DIHV-dehs-miht
fifty	piecdesmit	PEE-AHTS-dehs-miht

ENGLISH	LATVIAN	PRONOUNCE
one hundred	simts	sihmts
one thousand	tūkstots	TOOKS-twats
one-way	vienā virzienā	VEEA-nah VIR-zee-an-ah
round-trip	turp un atpakaļ	toorp oon AT-pakal
station	stacija	STAH-tsee-uh
grocery	pārtikas veikals	PAHR-tih-kas VEY-kalss
bread	maizi	MAI-zi
vegetables	dārzeņi	DAR-ze-nyih
coffee	kafija	KAH-fee-yah
beer	alus	AH-lus
left	pa kreisi	PAH kreh-ih-sih
right	pa labi	PAH lah-bih

LITHUANIAN (LIETUVIŠKAI)

PHRASEBOOK

ENGLISH	LITHUANIAN	PRONUNCIATION
Yes/no	Taip/ne	TAYE-p/NEH
Please/You're welcome	Prašau	prah-SHAU
Thank you	Ačiū	AH-chyoo
Hello	Labas	LAH-bahss
Good-bye	Viso gero	VEE-soh GEh-roh
Good morning	Labas rytas	LAH-bahss REE-tahss
Good night	Labanaktis	lah-BAH-nahk-tiss
Sorry/Excuse me	Atsiprašau	aHT-sih-prh-SHAU
Help!	Gelbėkite!	GYEL-behk-ite
When?	Kada?	KAH-da
Where is...?	Kur yra...?	Koor ee-RAH
How do I get to...?	Kaip nueti į...?	KYE-p nuh-EH-tih ee
How much does this cost?	Kiek kainuoja?	KEE-yek KYE-new-oh-yah
Do you have...?	Ar turite..?	ahr TU-ryite
Do you speak English?	Ar kalbate angliškai?	AHR KULL-buh-teh AHN-gleesh-kye
I don't understand.	Aš nesuprantu.	AHSH neh-soo-PRAHN-too
I'd like to order...	Norėčiau...	nor-RAY-chyow
I'd like to pay/We'd like to pay.	Sąskaitą, prašau.	SAHS-kai-ta, prah-SHAU
Do you have a vacancy?	Ar turite laisvų kambarių?	ahr TU-ryite lai-SVOO KAHM-bah-ryoo
May I see the room?	Ar galiu pamatyti kambarį?	ahr gah-LEE-OO pah-mah-TEE-tih KAHM-bah-ree
I want a ticket to...	Aš norėčiau bilieto į...	ahsh nohr-YEH-chee-ah-oo BYEE-lee-eh-toh ee...

GLOSSARY

ENGLISH	LITHUANIAN	PRONOUNCE
one	vienas	VYEH-nahss
two	du	doo
three	trys	treese
four	keturi	keh-TUH-rih
five	penki	PEHN-kih
six	šeši	SHEH-shih
seven	septyni	sehp-TEE-nih
eight	aštuoni	ahsh-too-OH-ni
nine	devyni	deh-VEE-nih
ten	dešimt	deh-SHIMT
one hundred	šimtas	SHIM-tahs
one thousand	tukstantis	TOOK-stan-tis
today	šiandien	SHYEHN-dih-ehn
tomorrow	rytoj	ree-TOY

ENGLISH	LITHUANIAN	PRONOUNCE
departure	išvyksta	ish-VEEK-stah
arrival	atvyksta	at-VEEK-stah
one-way	i vieną galą	ee VIE-naa GAH-laa
round-trip	grįžtamasio bilieto	GREEZH-tah-mah-sio BI-lieto
train	traukinys	trow-kih-NEES
bus	autobusas	ow-TOH-boo-suhs
station	stotis	stow-TISS
grocery	maisto prekės	MYE-stoh PREH-kays
bread	duona	DWOH-na
vegetables	daržovė	dar-ZHO-ve
coffee	kava	KAH-vah
beer	alus	AH-lus
left	kairę	KAH-ihr-aa
right	dešinę	DEHSH-ihn-aa

POLISH (POLSKI)

PHRASEBOOK

ENGLISH	POLISH	PRONUNCIATION
Yes/no	Tak/nie	tahk/nyeh
Please/You're welcome	Proszę	PROH-sheh
Thank you	Dziękuję	jen-KOO-yeh
Hi	Cześć	cheshch
Good-bye	Do widzenia	doh veedz-EN-yah
Sorry/Excuse me	Przepraszam	psheh-PRAH-shahm
Help!	Na pomoc!	nah POH-mots
When?	Kiedy?	KYEH-dih
Where is...?	Gdzie jest...?	g-JEH yest
How do I get to...?	Którędy do...?	ktoo-REN-dih doh
How much does this cost?	Ile to kosztuje?	EE-leh toh kohsh-TOO-yeh
Do you have...?	Czy są...?	chih sawn
Do you (male/female) speak English?	Czy pan(i) mówi po angielsku?	chih PAHN(-ee) MOO-vee poh ahn-GYEL-skoo
I don't understand.	Nie rozumiem.	nyeh roh-ZOOM-yem
I don't speak Polish.	Nie mowię po polsku.	nyeh MOO-vyeh poh POHL-skoo
Please write it down.	Proszę napisać.	PROH-sheh nah-PEE-sahch
I'd like to order...	Chciałbym zamówić...	kh-CHOW-bihm za-MOOV-eech
I'd like to pay.	Chciałbym zapłacić	kh-CHOW-bihm zap-WACH-eech
I think there is a mistake in the bill.	Myślę, ze jest błęd w rachunku.	MIHSH-leh zheh yest bwend v ra-KHOON-koo
Do you have a vacancy?	Czy są jakieś wolne pokoje?	chih sawn YAH-kyesh VOHL-neh poh-KOY-eh

ENGLISH	POLISH	PRONUNCIATION
I (male/female) would like a room.	Chciał(a)bym pokój.	kh-CHOW-(ah)-bihm POH-kooy
May I see the room?	Czy mogę zobaczyć pokój?	chi MOH-geh zoh-BAH-chihch POH-kooy
No, I don't like it.	Nie, nie podoba mi się.	nyeh, nyeh poh-DOH-bah mee shyeh.
Yes, I'll take it.	Tak, go wezmę.	tahk, goh VEH-zmeh.
Will you tell me when to get off?	Proszę mi powiedzieć kiedy wysiąść?	PROH-sheh mee pohv-YEDGE-ehch KYEH-dih VIH-shonshch?
Is this the right train/bus to...?	Czy to pociąg/autobus do...?	chih toh yehst POH-chawng/ow-TOH-booss doh
I want a ticket to...	Poproszę bilet do...	poh-PROH-sheh BEE-leht do...
How long does the trip take?	Jak długo trwa podróż?	yahk DWOO-goh tr-fah POHD-roosh
When is the first/next/last train to...	Kiedy jest pierwszy/następny/ostatni pociąg do...?	KYEH-dih yehst PYEHR-fshih/nah-STEH-pnih/oh-STAHT-nyee POHT-shawng do...
Where is the bathroom/nearest telephone booth/center of town?	Gdzie jest łazienka/najbliżej budka telefoniczna/centrum miasta?	g-JYEH yest wahzh-YEHN-ka/neye-BLEEZH-ay BOOT-kah teh-leh-foh-NEE-chnah/TSEHN-troom MYAH-stah
I've lost my...	Zgubiłem...	zgoo-BEE-wehm
Go away!	Spadaj!	SPAHD-eye!

GLOSSARY

ENGLISH	POLISH	PRONOUNCE		ENGLISH	POLISH	PRONOUNCE
one	jeden	YEH-den		post office	poczta	POH-chtah
two	dwa	dvah		stamp	znaczki	ZNATCH-kee
three	trzy	tshih		airmail	lotniczą	loht-NYEE-chawng
four	cztery	ch-TEH-rih		departure	odjazd	OHD-yazd
five	pięć	pyench		arrival	przyjazd	PSHEE-yazd
six	sześć	sheshch		one-way	w jedną stronę	VYEHD-nong STROH-neh
seven	siedem	SHEH-dem		round-trip	tam i z powrotem	tahm ee spoh-VROH-tehm
eight	osiem	OH-shem		luggage	bagaż	BAH-gahsh
nine	dziewięć	JYEH-vyench		seat reservation	miejscówka	myeh-TSOOF-ka
ten	dziesięć	JYEH-shench		train	pociąg	POH-chawnk
twenty	dwadzieścia	dva-JESH-cha		bus	autobus	ow-TOH-booss
thirty	trzydzieści	tshi-JESH-chee		airport	lotnisko	laht-NEE-skoh
forty	czterdzieści	chter-JESH-chee		station	dworzec	DVOH-zhets
fifty	pięćdziesiąt	pyench-JESH-ont		ticket	bilet	BEE-leht
sixty	sześćdziesiąt	sheshch-JESH-ont		grocery store	sklep spożywczy	sklehp spoh-ZHIV-chih
seventy	siedemdziesiąt	shed-em-JESH-ont		breakfast	śniadanie	sh-nyah-DAHN-yeh
eighty	osiemdziesiąt	ohsh-em-JESH-nt		lunch	obiad	OH-byaht
ninety	dziewięćdziesiąt	JYEH-vyench-JESH-ont		dinner	kolacja	koh-LAH-tsyah

ENGLISH	POLISH	PRONOUNCE	ENGLISH	POLISH	PRONOUNCE
one hundred	sto	stoh	menu	menu	MEH-noo
one thousand	tysiąc	TIH-shonts	bread	chleb	khlehp
Monday	poniedziałek	poh-nyeh-JAH-wehk	vegetables	jarzyny	YAH-zhny
Tuesday	wtorek	FTOH-rehk	beef	wołowina	vo-wo-VIN-ah
Wednesday	środa	SHROH-dah	smoked sausage	kabanosy	kah-ba-NOH-sy
Thursday	czwartek	CHVAHR-tehk	chicken	kurczak	KOOR-chak
Friday	piątek	PYAWN-tehk	pork	wieprzowina	vye-psho-VEE-nah
Saturday	sobota	soh-BOH-tah	fish	ryba	RIH-bah
Sunday	niedziela	nyeh-JEH-lah	coffee	kawa	KAH-vah
a day	dzien	j-EHN	milk	mleko	MLEH-koh
a week	tydzien	TI-jehn	cheese	ser	sehr
morning	rano	RAH-no	beer	piwo	PEE-voh
afternoon	popołudnie	poh-poh-WOOD-nyeh	sugar	cukier	TSOOK-yehr
evening	wieczor	v-YEH-chohr	eggs	jajka	y-EYE-kah
today	dzisiaj	JEESH-eye	open	otwarty	ot-FAR-tih
tomorrow	jutro	YOO-troh	closed	zamknięty	zahmk-NYENT-ih
spring	wiosna	v-YOH-snah	bank	bank	bahnk
summer	lato	LAH-toh	police	policja	poh-LEETS-yah
fall	jesień	YEH-shen	pharmacy	apteka	ahp-TEH-ka
winter	zima	ZHEE-mah	church	kościół	kosh-CHOOW
right	prawo	PRAH-vo	market	rynek	RIH-nehk
left	lewo	LEH-voh	nun	zakonnica	za-KON-it-sa

ROMANIAN (ROMÂN)

PHRASEBOOK

ENGLISH	ROMANIAN	PRONUNCIATION
Yes/no	Da/nu	dah/noo
Please/You're welcome	Vă rog/Cu plăcere	vuh rohg/coo pluh-CHEH-reh
Thank you	Mulţumesc	mool-tsoo-MESK
Hello	Bună ziua	BOO-nuh zee wah
Good-bye	La revedere	lah reh-veh-DEH-reh
Good morning	Bună dimineaţa	BOO-nuh dee-mee-NYAH-tsa
Good night	Noapte bună	NWAP-teh BOO-ner
Sorry/Excuse me	Îmi pare rău/Scuzaţi-mă	im PA-reh rau/skoo-ZAH-tz muh
Help!	Ajutor!	AH-zhoot-or
I'm lost.	M-am rătăcit.	mahm rehr-tehr-CHEET
When?	Cind?	kihnd
Where is...?	Unde...?	OON-deh
How do I get to...?	Cum se ajunge la...?	koom seh-ZHOON-jeh-la
How much does this cost?	Cît costă?	kiht KOH-stuh
Do you have...?	Aveţi...?	a-VETS
Do you speak English?	Vorbiţi englezeşte?	vor-BEETS ehng-leh-ZESH-te
I don't understand.	Nu înţeleg.	noo-ihn-TZEH-lehg

ENGLISH	ROMANIAN	PRONUNCIATION
Please write it down.	Vă rog scrieţi aceasta.	vuh rog SCREE-ets a-CHAS-ta
A little slower, please.	Vorbiţi mai vă rog.	vor-BEETS my vuh rohg
I'd like to order...	Aş vrea nişte...	ash vreh-A NEESH-teh
Check, please.	Plata, vă rog.	PLAH-tah, VUH rohg
Do you have a vacancy?	Aveţi camere libere?	a-VETS KUH-mer-eh LEE-ber-e
I'd like a room.	Aş vreao cameră.	ash vreh-UH KUH-mehr-ahr
With private shower?	Cu duş?	koo doosh
May I see the room?	Pot să văd camera, vă rog?	poht sehr vehrd KUH-mehr-uh vehr rohg
No, I don't like it.	Nu-mi place.	noomy PLAH-cheh
It's fine, I'll take it.	E bine, o iau.	yeh BEE-neh oh yah-oo
Will you tell me when to get off?	Puteţi să-mi spuneţi cînd să cobor?	poo-TEHT-sy sermy SPOO-nehtsy kihnd sehr koh-BOHR
I want a ticket to...	Vreau un bilet pentru...	vrah-oo oon bee-LEHT PEHN-troo
When is the first/next/last train to...?	La ce ora pleacă primul/urma-torul/ultimul tren spre...?	lah cheh OH-rehr pleh-UH-kehr PREE-mool/oor-mehr-TOH-rool/ OOL-tee-mool trehn spreh...
Where is the bathroom/near-est public phone/center of town?	Unde este cameră de baie/un telefon prin apropiere/centrul oraşului?	OON-deh YEHS-teh KUH-mehr-ahr deh BAH-yeh/oon teh-leh-FOHN preen ah-proh-PYEH-reh oh-rah-SHOO-looy
My name is...	Mă cheamă...	muh-KYAH-muh
What is your name?	Cum vă numiţi?	koom vuh noo-MEETS

GLOSSARY

ENGLISH	ROMANIAN	PRONOUNCE		ENGLISH	ROMANIAN	PRONOUNCE
one	unu	OO-noo		post office	poşta	POH-shta
two	doi	doy		stamps	timbru	TEEM-broo
three	trei	tray		airmail	avion	ahv-ee-OHN
four	patru	PAH-tru		departures	plecări	play-CUHR
five	cinci	CHEEN-ch		arrivals	soşiri	so-SHEER
six	şase	SHAH-seh		one-way	dus	doos
seven	şapte	SHAHP-teh		round-trip	dus-întors	doos-in-TORS
eight	opt	ohpt		luggage	bagajul	bah-GAHZH-ool
nine	nouă	NO-uh		reservation	rezervarea	re-zer-VAR-eh-a
ten	zece	ZEH-cheh		train	trenul	TRAY-null
twenty	douăzeci	doh-wah-ZECH		bus	autobuz	AHU-toh-booz
thirty	treizeci	tray-ZECH		airport	aeroportul	air-oh-POR-tull
forty	patruzeci	pa-TROO-zech		station	gară	GAH-ruh
fifty	cincizeci	chin-ZECH		ticket	bilet	bee-LET
sixty	şaizeci	shay-ZECH		grocery	o alimentară	a-lee-men-TA-ra
seventy	şaptezeci	shap-teh-ZECH		breakfast	micul dejun	MIK-ul DAY-zhun
eighty	optzeci	ohpt-ZECH		lunch	prinz	preunz
ninety	nouăzeci	noah-ZECH		dinner	cină	CHEE-nuh
one hundred	o sută	o SOO-tuh		bread	pîine	PUH-yih-nay
one thousand	o mie	oh MIH-ay		beef	carne de vacă	CAR-ne de VA-cuh
Monday	luni	loon		pork	carne de porc	CAR-neh deh pork
Tuesday	marţi	marts		fish	peşte	PESH-teh

ENGLISH	ROMANIAN	PRONOUNCE
Wednesday	miercuri	MEER-kur
Thursday	joi	zhoy
Friday	vineri	VEE-ner
Saturday	sîmbătă	SIM-buh-tuh
Sunday	duminică	duh-MIH-ni-kuh
today	azi	az
tomorrow	mîine	MUH-yih-neh
spring	primăvară	PREE-mehr-vahr-ehr
summer	vară	VAH-rehr
fall	toamnă	TWAM-nehr
winter	iarnă	YAHR-nehr
hot	cald	kahld
cold	rece	REH-cheh
single room	cu un pat	koo oon paht
with shower	cu duş	koo doosh

ENGLISH	ROMANIAN	PRONOUNCE
chicken	pui	poo-EE
vegetables	legume	LEH-goom-eh
salad	salate	sah-LAH-teh
salt	sare	SAH-ray
milk	lapte	LAHP-tay
beer	bere	BE-reh
open	deschis	DESS-kees
closed	închis	un-KEES
bank	bancă	BAN-cuh
exchange	un birou de de schimb	oon bee-RO deh skeemb
toilets	toaleta	toh-AHL-eh-tah
passport	paşaportul	pah-shah-POHR-tool
bakery	o brutărie	o bru-ter-REE-e
left	stînga	STUHN-guh
right	dreapta	draap-TUH

RUSSIAN (РУССКИЙ)

PHRASEBOOK

ENGLISH	RUSSIAN	PRONUNCIATION
Yes/no	Да/нет	Dah/Nyet
Please/You're welcome	Пожалуйста	pa-ZHAL-u-sta
Thank you	Спасибо	spa-SEE-bah
Hello	Добрый день	DOH-bri DEN'
Good-bye	До свидания	da svee-DAHN-ya
Good morning	Доброе утро	DOH-breh OO-tra
Good evening	Добрый вечер	DOH-briy VEH-cher
Good night	Спокойный ночи	spa-KOI-niy NOCH-ee
Sorry/Excuse me	Извините	iz-vi-NEET-yeh
Help!	Помогите!	pah-mah-GI-tye
When?	Когда?	kahg-DAH
Where is...?	Где...?	gdyeh
How do I get to...?	Как пройти...?	kak prai-TEE
How much does this cost?	Сколько это стоит?	SKOHL'-ka E-ta STO-it
Do you have...?	У вас есть...?	oo vas YEST'
Do you speak English?	Вы говорите по-английски?	vy ga-va-REE-tye pa an-GLEE-ski
I don't understand.	Я не понимаю.	ya ni pa-nee-MAH-yoo
I don't speak Russian	Я не говорю по-русски.	yah ni gah-vah-RYOO pah ROO-skee
Please write it down.	Напишите пожалуйста	nah-pi-SHEET'-yeh pah-ZHAHL-u-stah
Speak a little slower, please.	Медленее, пожалуйста	MED-li-ne-eh, pah-ZHAHL-u-stah
I'd like to order...	Я хотел(а) бы...	ya khah-TYEL(a) byi
I'd like to pay/We'd like to pay.	Счёт, пожалуйста.	shchyot, pah-ZHAHL-u-stah
Are you not mistaken?	Вы не ошиблись?	vih ni ah-SHIH-blis

GLOSSARY

ENGLISH	RUSSIAN	PRONUNCIATION
Do you have a vacancy?	У вас есть свободный номер?	oo vahss yehst' svah-BOD-niy NO-mehr
I'd like a room.	Я бы хотел(а) номер.	yah byi khah-TYEL(a) NO-mehr
May I see the room?	Можно посмотреть номер?	MOZH-nah pah-smah-TREHT' NO-mehr
No, I (don't) like it.	Нет, это мне (не) нравится.	nyeht, E-ta mnyeh (ni) NRAH-vit-sah
Yes, I'll take it.	Да, это подходит.	dah, EH-tah pahd-KHO-dit
Will you tell me when to get off?	Вы мне скажите, когда надо выйдти?	vui mnyeh skah-ZHIH-tyeh, kahg-DAH NAH-dah VYI-ti
Is this the right train/bus to...?	Это поезд на...?	EH-tah PO-ist nah
I want a ticket to...,please.	Один билет до...., пожалуйста.	ah-DEEN bi-LYET dah...., pah-ZHAHL-u-stah
How long does the trip take?	Долго ли надо ехать?	DOHL-gah li NAH-dah YEH-khaht'
When is the first/next/last train to...?	Когда первый/следующий/последний поезд на...?	kahg-DAH PYEHR-vyi/slyeh-DOO-yu-shyi/pa-SLEEHD-nyi PO-ist nah
Where is the bathroom/nearest telephone booth/center of town?	Где находится туалет/ближайший телефон-автомат/центр города?	gdyeh nah-KHOH-di-tsah TOO-ah-lyet/blee-ZHAI-shii te-le-FOHN-af-tah-MAHT/TSEN-ter GOR-rah-dah
I've lost my...	Я потерял(а)...	ya po-tir-YAL-(a)
Would you like to dance?	Вы хотите танцевать?	vyi kha-TE-tyeh tan-se-VAT'
Go away!	Уходите!	oo-khah-DEE-tye

GLOSSARY

ENGLISH	RUSSIAN	PRONOUNCE		ENGLISH	RUSSIAN	PRONOUNCE
one	один	ah-DEEN		post office	почта	POCH-ta
two	два	dvah		stamp	марка	MAR-ka
three	три	tree		airmail	авиа	AH-via
four	четыре	chi-TIH-rih		departure	отъезд	at-YEZD
five	пять	pyat'		arrival	приезд	pree-YEZD
six	шесть	shest'		one-way	в один конец	v ah-DEEN kah-NYETS
seven	семь	syem'		round-trip	туда и обратно	too-DAH ee ah-BRAHT-nah
eight	восемь	VOH-sim'		luggage	багаж	ba-GAZH
nine	девять	DYEV-it'		reservation	предваритель-ный заказ	pred-va-RI-tyel-nui za-KAZ
ten	десять	DYES-it'		train	поезд	PO-ezd
twenty	двадцать	DVAH-dtsat'		bus	автобус	av-toh-BOOS
thirty	тридцать	TREE-dtsat'		airport	аэропорт	a-ero-PORT
forty	сорок	SOR-ak		station	вокзал	VOK-zal
fifty	пятьдесят	pi-de-SYAHT		ticket	билет	bil-YET
sixty	шестьдесят	shis-de-SYAHT		grocery	гастроном	gah-stra-NOM
seventy	семьдесят	Sim-de-SYAHT		breakfast	завтрак	ZAF-trak
eighty	восемьдесят	Vasim-de-SYAHT		lunch	обед	a-BYED
ninety	девяносто	de-vi-NO-sta		dinner	ужин	OO-zhin
one hundred	сто	sto		menu	меню	min-YOO
one thousand	тысяча	TI-si-cha		bread	хлеб	khlyep
Monday	понедельник	pa-ne-DYEL-nik		vegetables	овощи	OH-va-shi

G L O S S A R Y

ENGLISH	RUSSIAN	PRONOUNCE
Tuesday	вторник	FTOR-nik
Wednesday	среда	srih-DAH
Thursday	четверг	chit-VERK
Friday	пятница	PYAHT-nit-sah
Saturday	суббота	soo-BOT-tah
Sunday	воскресенье	vahs-kre-SEH-nye
a day	день	dyen
a few days	немногие дней	nim-NOG-iye dnei
a week	неделя	ni-DEL-ya
morning	утром	OO-tram
afternoon	днём	dnyom
evening	вечером	VE-cher-um
today	сегодня	see-VOHD-nya
tomorrow	завтра	ZAHV-trah
spring	весна	vehs-NAH
summer	лето	LYEH-ta
fall	осень	OHS-syen'
winter	зима	zee-MAH
hot	жаркий	ZHAR-ki
cold	холодный	kha-LOD-nyi
single room	на одного	nah AHD-nah-voh
double room	двойная комната	dvai-NA-ya KOM-na-ta
reservation	предваритель-ный заказ	pred-va-RI-tel-niy za-KAZ
with shower	с душом	s DOO-sham
pharmacy	аптека	ahp-TYE-kah

ENGLISH	RUSSIAN	PRONOUNCE
beef	говядина	ga-VYAH-dee-na
chicken	курица	KOO-ri-tsa
pork	свинина	svi-NEE-na
fish	рыба	REE-ba
coffee	кофе	KO-feh
milk	молоко	mah-lah-KOH
beer	пиво	PEE-vah
sugar	сахар	SA-khar
eggs	яйца	yai-TSAH
holiday	день отдыха	dyen OT-dui-kha
open	открыт	ot-KRIHT
closed	закрыт	za-KRIHT
bank	банк	bahnk
police	милиция	mee-LEE-tsi-ya
exchange	обмен валюты	ab-MYEN val-YU-tyi
toilet	туалет	tu-a-LYET
square	площадь	PLOH-shad'
castle	замок	ZAH-mak
church	церковь	TSER-kaf
tower	башня	BASH-nya
market	рынок	RYHN-nak
passport	паспорт	PAS-pahrt
bakery	булочная	BOO-lahch-na-yah
left	налево	nah-LYEH-va
right	направо	nah-PRAH-va

SLOVAK (SLOVENSKY)

PHRASEBOOK

ENGLISH	SLOVAK	PRONUNCIATION
Yes/no	áno/nie	ah-NOH/NEH
Please	prosím	PROH-seem
Thank you	d'akujem	DAK-oo-yem
Hello	Dobrý deň	doh-BREE den
Good-bye	Dovidenia	doh-vee-DEN-eea
Good morning	Dobré ráno	doh-BREH RAH-no
Good evening	Dobrý večer	doh-BREE VE-tcher
Good night	Dobrú noc	doh-BROO NOTS
Sorry/Excuse me	Prepáčte/Prepáčte mi	PREH-pach-te/PREH-pach-te mee
Help!	Pomoc!	pah-MOTS
When?	Kedy?	keh-DEE
Where is...?	Kde je?	k-DEH yeh

ENGLISH	SLOVAK	PRONUNCIATION
How do I get to...?	Ako sa dostanem...?	AH-koh sa doh-STAN-em
How much does this cost?	Koľko to stojí...?	KOHL-ko toh STOH-yee
Do you have...?	Máte...?	MAH-teh
Do you speak English?	Hovoríte po anglicky?	ho-vo-REE-te poh ahng-GLIT-ski
I don't understand.	Nerozumiem.	neh-rohz-OOM-ee-em
I don't speak (language)	Nehovorím po.	NE-kho-vo-reem po...
Please write it down.	Prosím napište to.	PRO-seem nah-PEESH-tye toh
Speak a little slower, please.	Prosím pomaly.	PRO-seem poh-MAH-le
I'd like to order...	Poprosil by som...	khtyel bikh...
I'd like to pay/We'd like to pay.	Rád by som zaplatil/Radi by sme saplatili.	RAAD bih som ZA-plah-tyil
I think you made a mistake in the bill.	Myslím, že ste sa pomýlili v úcte.	MEE-sleem zhe steh sa PO-mee-lili v UH-tste
Do you have a vacancy?	Máte voľnú izbu?	MAH-te VOL-noo iz-BOO
I'd like a room.	Poprosil by som izbu.	PO-pro-sil bih som IZ-buh
May I see the room?	Môžem izbu vidieť?	MO-zhem IZ-buh VI-dy-et
No, I don't like it.	Nie, nepáči sa mi.	NEH, ne-pah-chi sa mi.
Yes, I'll take it.	Áno, vezmem ju.	ANOH, VEZ-mem yu
Will you tell me when to get off?	Poviete mi kedy vystúpit?	PO-vye-teh mi KE-dy VY-stoo-pith
Is this the right train/bus to...?	Je toto správny vlak/autobus do...?	Ye toto SPRAA-vnee vlak/auto-bus doh...
I want a ticket to...	Chcern listok do...	KH-cem lee-stok doh...
How long does the trip take?	Ako dlho trvá cesta?	AKOH dl-HO TR-vah tse-stah
When is the first/next/last train to...	Kedy ide prvý/ďalší/posledný vlak do...	KE-dy ye PR-vee/DYA-lshee/PO-sled-neeh vlak doh...
I've lost my...	Stratil som môj...	STRA-til som muoy...
Would you like to dance?	Smiem prosiť?	SMYEM PRO-sit?
Go away.	Choď preč.	KHOD PRECH

GLOSSARY

ENGLISH	SLOVAK	PRONOUNCE
one	jeden	YED-en
two	dva	dvah
three	tri	tree
four	štyri	sh-TEE-ree
five	pät	peht
six	šesť	shest
seven	sedem	SE-dem
eight	osem	O-sem
nine	devät'	DEH-veht
ten	desat	DEH-saht
twenty	dvadsat'	DVAHD-saht
thirty	tridsat'	TREED-saht
forty	štyridsat'	SHTIH-rihd-saht
fifty	pät'desiat	PEHTY-dehs-ee-aht
sixty	šesťdesiat	SHEST-dehs-yat

ENGLISH	SLOVAK	PRONOUNCE
post office	pošta	PO-shtah
stamp	známka	ZNAA-mka
airmail	letecká pošta	LE-te-tskaa po-shta
departure	odchod	OD-khod
arrival	príchod	PREE-khod
one-way	jedno smerný	YED-nyo SMER-nye
round-trip	spiatočný	SPYAH-toch-nee
station	stanica	STAH-nee-tsa
ticket	lístok	LEE-stok
train	vlak	vlak
bus	autobus	AUH-to-bus
airport	letisko	LE-ti-skoh
grocery	potraviny	PO-tra-vi-nee
breakfast	raňajky	RA-nya-ky
lunch	obed	O-bet

ENGLISH	SLOVAK	PRONOUNCE
seventy	sedmdesiat	SEHDM-dehs-yat
eighty	osemdesiat	OH-sehm-dehs-ee-aht
ninety	deväťdesiat	DEH-vehty-dehs-ee-aht
one hundred	sto	stoh
Monday	pondelok	PO-nde-lok
Tuesday	utorok	UH-to-rok
Wednesday	streda	SRE-dah
Thursday	štvrok	SCHTVR-tok
Friday	piatok	PYA-tok
Saturday	sobota	SO-bo-tah
Sunday	nedeľa	NE-dye-jya
a day	deň	dyenh
a week	týždeň	TEE-zhde-nh
morning	ráno	RAH-no
afternoon	poobede	PO-O-beh-de
evening	večer	VE-cher
today	dnes	dnes
tomorrow	zajtra	ZAY-trah
spring	jar	yar
summer	leto	leh-to
fall	jeseň	YE-senh
winter	zima	ZI-ma
hot	horúco	KHO-ruh-tso
cold	chladno	KHLA-dnoh
pharmacy	lekáreň	LE-kaa-renh
water	voda	VO-da
with shower	so sprchou	so spr-kho

ENGLISH	SLOVAK	PRONOUNCE
dinner	večera	VE-che-ra
menu	menu	me-nuh
sugar	cukor	CU-kor
bread	chlieb	chleep
vegetables	zelenina	ze-LEH-nee-na
beef	hovädzie	KHO-veh-dzye
chicken	kura	KUH-rah
pork	bravčové	braucove
fish	ryba	RI-bah
coffee	káva	KAH-va
milk	mlieko	m-LYE-ko
beer	pivo	PEE-vo
eggs	vajcia	VAY-tsi-ya
holiday	sviatok	SVEE-a-tokh
open	otvorené	O-tvoh-re-nee
closed	zatvorené	ZA-tvoh-re-nee
bank	banka	BAN-kah
police	policia	PO-lee-tsi-ya
exchange	zmenáreň	ZME-naa-renh
toilet	toaleta/WC	VEH-TSEH
square	námestie	NAH-mes-tye
castle	zámok	ZAA-mok
church	kostol	KO-stol
tower	veža	VE-zha
market	trh	trch
right	vpravo	fpravo
left	vľavo	flyavo

INDEX

A

Book your air, hotel, and transportation all in one place.

Hotel or hostel? Cruise or canoe? Car? Plane? Camel? Wherever you're going, visit Yahoo! Travel and get total control over your arrangements. Even choose your seat assignment. So. One hump or two? travel.yahoo.com

powered by *hp*

YAHOO!
Travel

MAP INDEX

MAP LEGEND

✚ Hospital	✈ Airport	🏛 Museum	✠ Monastery
Police	Bus Station	Hotel/Hostel	Ruin
✉ Post Office	Train Station	Camping	Fountain
ⓘ Tourist Office	M METRO STATION	Food	Bath
$ Bank	⚓ Ferry Landing	Internet Café	Beach
Embassy/Consulate	Church	Entertainment	P Parking Lot
▪ Point of Interest	Synagogue	Nightlife	Garden
☎ Telephone Office	Mosque	Cafe	Monument
Theater	Castle	Steps	
Library	Mountain	Pedestrian Zone	The Let's Go compass always points NORTH.